WRITING ANALYTICALLY

WITH READINGS

THIRD EDITION

DAVID ROSENWASSER
Muhlenberg College

JILL STEPHEN
Muhlenberg College

CENGAGE
Learning·

Australia • Brazil • Mexico • Singapore • United Kingdom • United States

CENGAGE
Learning·

Writing Analytically with Readings, Third Edition
David Rosenwasser and Jill Stephen

Product Director: Monica Eckman

Product Team Manager: Christopher Bennem

Associate Product Manager: Laura Ross

Senior Content Developer: Leslie Taggart

Content Developer: Stephanie Carpenter

Associate Content Developer: Rachel L. Smith

Product Assistant: Kerry DeVito

Media Developer: Janine Tangney

Marketing Manager: Erin Parkins

Senior Content Project Manager: Rosemary Winfield

Art Director: Marissa Falco

Manufacturing Planner: Betsy Donaghey

Intellectual Property Analyst: Ann Hoffman

Production Service: MPS Limited

Compositor: MPS Limited

Text Designer: Carol Miglitta

Cover Designer: Carol Miglitta

Cover Image: Palimpsest (old gods), 2006 Ink and Acrylic on Canvas 60 × 84 inches (152.4 × 213.4 cm) Private Collection; Photo Credit: Erma Estwick © Julie Mehretu. Courtesy White Cube

© 2015, 2012, 2008 Cengage Learning

WCN: 01-100-101

ALL RIGHTS RESERVED. No part of this work covered by the copyright herein may be reproduced, transmitted, stored, or used in any form or by any means graphic, electronic, or mechanical, including but not limited to photocopying, recording, scanning, digitizing, taping, web distribution, information networks, or information storage and retrieval systems, except as permitted under Section 107 or 108 of the 1976 United States Copyright Act, without the prior written permission of the publisher.

For product information and technology assistance, contact us at **Cengage Learning Customer & Sales Support, 1-800-354-9706**

For permission to use material from this text or product, submit all requests online at **www.cengage.com/permissions** Further permissions questions can be emailed to **permissionrequest@cengage.com**

Library of Congress Control Number: 2014952808

Student edition ISBN: 978-1-285-43647-0

Looseleaf edition ISBN: 978-1-305-08141-3

Cengage Learning
20 Channel Center Street
Boston, MA 02210
USA

Cengage Learning is a leading provider of customized learning solutions with office locations around the globe, including Singapore, the United Kingdom, Australia, Mexico, Brazil, and Japan. Locate your local office at **www.cengage.com/global**

Cengage Learning products are represented in Canada by Nelson Education, Ltd.

To learn more about Cengage Learning Solutions, visit **www.cengage.com**

Purchase any of our products at your local college store or at our preferred online store **www.cengagebrain.com**

Printed in the United States of America
Print number: 01   Print year: 2014

BRIEF CONTENTS

CONTENTS

CHAPTER 2   39
Reading Analytically

CHAPTER 3   71
Responding to Traditional Writing Assignments More Analytically

CHAPTER 4   89
Reasoning from Evidence to Claims

CHAPTER 5   119

Interpretation

CHAPTER 6   147

Finding and Evolving a Thesis

CHAPTER 8   207
Finding, Evaluating, and Citing Sources

CHAPTER 11 305
Nine Basic Writing Errors (BWEs) and How to Fix Them

APPENDIX 333

PART 2   The Readings 341

CHAPTER 12 343

Manners, Communication, and Technology

CHAPTER 13 415

Places and Spaces: Cities and Suburbs

CHAPTER 14 491

Race, Ethnicity, and the "Melting Pot"

PREFACE

Writing Analytically with Readings is two books in one. Part One (Chapters 1–11) is the latest version of our stand-alone writing text, *Writing Analytically*, now in its seventh edition. Part Two (Chapters 12–16), which contains exercises and writing assignments keyed to Part One, is a revised collection (third edition) of readings and images for students to analyze and to use as models and lenses for analyzing other material.

Our original book, *Writing Analytically*, grew out of our experience as directors of a Writing Across the Curriculum program and Writing Center at a small liberal arts college and out of our writing pedagogy workshops for faculty at our own and other colleges and universities. Since the beginning of our work on *Writing Analytically* in the early 1990s, we have studied what faculty say about their goals for student writing and used this information to develop a book that would allow faculty to talk to each other across disciplinary lines. Two decades later, we are still working on that goal and learning about what college students need in order to succeed at academic writing both in first-year composition courses and in the various discourse communities they migrate among during their undergraduate careers and beyond.

We learned from faculty across the curriculum that what they want from student writing is not passive summary, not "mere" opinions and personal reactions, and not debate-style argument, but analysis, with its patient and methodical inquiry into the meaning of information. They want writing aimed at understanding rather than at promoting a particular point of view. They want students to think on the page about what things mean—which is our primary definition of analysis.

Most books of writing instruction devote only a chapter, if that, to analysis. This book is organized entirely around analytical writing. We acknowledge that analytical essays inevitably make arguments, but we think there is value in distinguishing between argument and analysis, and we think that students learn to write better arguments when they are taught first to analyze and to dwell more comfortably with uncertainty. *Writing Analytically* offers alternatives to oversimplified thinking of the like/dislike, agree/disagree variety. It argues that an idea is not the same thing as an opinion and teaches students how to respect the complexity of subjects where there is no single right answer.

This edition of *Writing Analytically with Readings* remains committed to the goal of giving students the tools they need in order to engage in the analytical habits of mind that will be expected of them in their courses and in the world they encounter after graduation. Students who learn to analyze information and who know how to use writing in order to discover and develop ideas will continue to be in demand in the workplace, regardless of the forms they find themselves writing in or the medium in which their writing appears.

As the book seeks to demonstrate, the analytical process is surprisingly formulaic: it consists of a fairly limited set of moves. People who think well have these moves at their disposal, whether they are aware of using them or not. Analysis, the book argues, is a frame of mind, a set of habits for observing and making sense of the world.

Entering this analytical frame of mind requires specific tasks that will reduce students' anxiety for instant answers, impede the reflex move to judgments, and encourage a more hands-on engagement with materials. *Writing Analytically with Readings* supplies these tasks for each phase of the writing and idea-generating process: making observations, inferring implications, and making the leap to possible conclusions. The root issue here is the writer's attitude toward evidence. The book argues that the ability of writers to discover ideas and improve on them in revision depends largely on their ability to use evidence as a means of testing and revising ideas rather than just supporting them.

This book's employment of verbal prompts like "so WHAT?" and its recommendation of step-by-step procedures, such as the procedure for making a thesis evolve, should not be confused with prescriptive slot-filler formulae for writing. Our book does not prescribe a fill-in-the-blank grid for producing papers. Instead it offers schematic descriptions of what good thinkers do—as acts of mind—when they are confronted with data.

We continue to have faith in the book's heuristics for their ability to spur more thoughtful writing, and also for the role they can play in making the classroom a more collaborative space. When students and teachers can share the means of idea production, reading and writing and class discussion become better connected, and students can more easily learn to see that good ideas don't just happen—they're made.

New to *Writing Analytically with Readings*

The new edition retains *Writing Analytically with Readings'* emphasis on observation skills, but it now integrates key heuristics, such as NOTICE AND FOCUS and THE METHOD, under broader organizing rubrics such as the Five Analytical Moves. Our primary task has been to better integrate, contextualize, and condense materials in the book. The book's main topics, such as thesis, evidence, and writing with sources, now appear in single rather than multiple chapters. For example, the discussions of how to word thesis statements and how to revise weak ones have now been combined. Similarly, the chapters on Forms & Formats and Introductions and Conclusions have been condensed into a single chapter on organization, Chapter 9, "From Paragraphs to Papers: Forms and Formats Across the Curriculum." Such changes enable readers to pick and choose what they need.

The anthology of readings contains some new pieces as well as revised introductions and assignments. As in past editions, the assignments provide links among the readings to suggest coherent sequences for a semester-long or year-long writing course. The "for further research" sections have been revised and updated by reference librarian Kelly Cannon. These sections also contain additional opportunities for writing.

- **New Chapter 1, "The Analytical Frame of Mind."** The new first chapter now integrates counterproductive habits of mind, the five analytical moves, and the first set of tools.

- **More help for reading analytically.** The second set of analytical tools is now integrated into "Reading Analytically" (Chapter 2), where they are given a clearer context for use. The early placement of the reading chapter allows students to begin immediately to use writing to better understand the kinds of complex reading they are asked to do in college.

- **New chapter overviews.** Each chapter begins with a brief overview that orients readers to the chapter's contents. These overviews make the book more browseable and easier to navigate.

- **New student essay with an evolving thesis.** Chapter 6, "Finding and Evolving a Thesis," includes an essay with an evolving thesis, annotated to help students track the evolution.

- **A more linear progression.** Chapters have been rearranged and in some cases combined to allow for a clearer progression from using analytical tools to discovering evidence, writing theses, working with sources, and revising for style.

- **Four-color design and new illustrations.** The four-color design helps students identify key information on each page more quickly, while graphic illustrations of the main analytical tools divide these into steps in order to make them more accessible to students.

- **Even more help for writing across the curriculum.** Chapter 4, "Reasoning from Evidence to Claims," and Chapter 6, "Finding and Evolving a Thesis," evenhandedly address differences between deductively and inductively organized papers.

- **New, more comprehensive style chapter.** In place of what were separate chapters on sentence structure and diction, there is now Chapter 10, "Style: Choosing Words, Shaping Sentences."

- **New anthology readings.** This edition contains six new readings: a pivotal one by Zadie Smith in Chapter 14, Race, Ethnicity, and the "Melting Pot," and five rhetorically focused selections in Chapter 15, The Language of Politics and the Politics of Language, including one by Harvard historian Jill Lepore on the history of political consulting. Smith's "Speaking in Tongues" is interestingly positioned between the two competing metaphors taken up by other authors in the chapter and in our national discourse on diversity: rainbow vs. melting pot. Lepore's "The Lie Factory: How Politics Became a Business," adds depth and resonance to contemporary framing wars via an account of the influential careers of two of the founders of political consulting.

Features of *Writing Analytically with Readings*

- Every chapter of the book is aimed at helping students to develop an **analytical frame of mind**. Chapters 1–2 offer a set of habits for entering this frame of mind so students can learn to do what strong thinkers do when they are confronted with data. The chapters also discuss counterproductive habits of mind to help students identify and work through common problems such as the premature leap, the judgment reflex, and so on.

- Because we have heard from instructors that **breaking the mold of the five-paragraph essay** is particularly challenging, we present organizational strategies that can act as alternatives to the familiar five paragraphs; and we offer a full chapter, Chapter 3, on making common assignments (such as summary, personal response, agree/disagree, compare/contrast, and definition) more analytical.

- Because it is designed to be used in writing-intensive courses in a variety of subject areas, as well as in first-year composition courses, *Writing Analytically with Readings* features **Voices from Across the Curriculum** commentaries, which speak directly to students on stylistic, rhetorical, and epistemological differences across the curriculum. Each is written for the book by professors from disciplines other than English, Rhetoric, and Composition.

- **Sample readings** (both brief and extended) represent a wide range of disciplines, including biology, chemistry, sociology, literary studies, political science, film studies, and art history.

- Chapter 7 offers six strategies for **analyzing sources,** along with discussions of plagiarism, integrating quotations, and writing an abstract. In Chapter 8, a college reference librarian presents methods for finding quality sources in print and on the Web and for citing sources. Documentation styles included are **MLA, APA, Chicago, and CSE**.

- The **writing exercises** in *Writing Analytically with Readings* take two forms: end-of-chapter assignments that could produce papers, and informal writing exercises called "Try This" that are embedded inside the chapters near the particular skills being discussed. Many of the "Try This" exercises can generate papers, but usually they are more limited in scope, asking readers to experiment with various kinds of data-gathering and analysis.

- Each of the **readings** in the anthology features an introduction as well as a series of concluding thinking and writing tasks designed to encourage analysis that are contained in **Things to Do with the Reading**.

- **For Further Research** sections that close each anthology chapter provide a series of print and online leads for readers (and instructors) to pursue if they wish to extend the path of inquiry begun by the chapter's reading selections.

Principles of Selection for the Readings

At the heart of *Writing Analytically with Readings* is the notion that readings function in three ways in a writing course:

- **As objects for analysis:** The readings offer interesting and relatively sophisticated primary material for students to analyze. Writing tasks attached to the readings teach readers to use writing in order to read more deeply and reflectively.

- **As lenses for viewing other material:** The readings contain theories and analytical methods that students can extract and use for viewing other materials, both verbal and nonverbal. The ability to apply theories and information in other settings is a critical skill in college writing.

- **As models for imitating:** The readings demonstrate ways of approaching a topic. Tasks linked to specific readings show writers how to emulate the ways that effective analytical writing operates.

We think we have put together a collection of readings and images that are informative and interesting but—most important—thought-provoking and imitable. Each of the book's five topic categories contains essays of sufficient depth and complexity to comprise an interpretive context to guide readers' own analyses as they move from writing about the reading to applying the reading to other readings, and to their observations about the world.

Typically, each chapter of the anthology of readings begins with an essay that establishes a theoretical framework or framing issue for the chapter as a whole. Subsequent readings approach the chapter's topic from different analytical perspectives. The final essay in each chapter usually offers a different and re-orienting twist on the chapter as a whole.

Two essays that appear among the readings were written especially for our book. One, which takes the form of a series of conversations between us and a photography professor at our college, offers an historical and theoretical framework for looking at and thinking about photographs and other kinds of visual images. This essay appears as the lead piece in the anthology's final chapter, "Seeing," which invites students to revisit topics discussed in the Reader's earlier chapters from the perspective of visual rhetoric.

The other essay written for this book offers a political science professor's history and analysis of the political labels "liberal" and "conservative," including discussion of how the meaning of these labels has changed over time. These essays exemplify what we most want to offer in the readings: theoretical frameworks that model careful analytical thinking and that invite students to apply them in their own analyses of a range of different kinds of materials.

Acknowledgments

First and foremost, thanks to our students who test-drive and troubleshoot the book's writing advice. Thanks especially to our wonderful cadre of writing tutors who have developed workshops for students and faculty based on our book. Special thanks to former students Sarah Kersh, James Patefield, and Anna Whiston for allowing us to use essays of theirs in the book. Sarah Kersh, now a professor herself, has also kindly agreed to work with us on upcoming instructors' guides for the book.

We are very grateful to our faculty colleagues at Muhlenberg who created workshops for our writing tutors on writing in their disciplines and then contributed expanded versions of these materials for the book: Christopher Borick, Keri Colabroy, Thomas Craigin, Paul McEwan, Marcia Morgan, and Mark Sciutto. Much thanks as well to Troy Dwyer for his feedback on organization and tone, and to Kelly Cannon, reference librarian extraordinaire, for his contribution to the book of an excellent and student-friendly guide to print and online research and the For Further Research sections that end each chapter of the Reader.

The cross-curricular dimension of this book would be sadly impoverished without the interest and support of our faculty colleagues who participate in the writing cohort at our college, many of whom are included in the Voices from Across the Curriculum boxes in the book. Our colleagues have shared with us examples of good student and professional writing in their fields, writing assignments from their writing-intensive classes, examples of their own writing, and responses to our question on what constitutes an analytical question: Linda Bips, James Bloom, Christopher Borick, Susan Clemens-Bruder, Keri Colabroy, Ted Conner, Amy Corbin, Karen Dearborn, Daniel Doviak, Laura Edelman, Kim Gallon, Jack Gambino, Barri Gold, William Gruen, Kathleen Harring, John Malsberger, Eileen McEwan, Brian Mello, Holmes Miller, Marcia Morgan, Richard Niesenbaum, Jefferson Pooley, Tad Robinson, Pearl Rosenberg, Susan Schwartz, Jordanna Sprayberry, Jeremy Teissere, Alan Tjeltveit, and Bruce Wightman. We are also grateful to Katherine Kibblinger Gottschalk of Cornell University for permission to quote her paper on the correspondence of E.B. White.

Thanks to Emily Stockton-Brown, Assistant Director of the Writing Center, for her sensitivity and her outstanding managerial skills. She tirelessly negotiated the day-to-day needs of faculty and tutors at the Writing Center and in the first-year seminar program while we were busy writing. And thanks to our colleague Linda Bips, with whom we co-direct the Writing Program. We and it would be much less sane without her.

The person we would have been least able to do without in our work on this edition is Stephanie Pelkowski Carpenter, who has worked closely with us as our developmental editor through a long revision process. Thanks to her discerning and experienced eye, her tenacity, her attention to detail, her tact, and her ever-present goodwill, we accomplished more than we initially could have hoped for. We also benefitted from the guidance of our editors at Cengage, Christopher Bennem and Leslie Taggart, and from the patience and professionalism of Teresa Christie and Rosemary Winfield, who took the book from manuscript to print. Thanks as well to Mavanee Anderson, who copy edited the manuscript, noticing a lot more than just our errors. To editors and publishers associated with past editions of the book, we offer our continued gratitude: Mary Beth Walden, Karl Yambert, Michael Rosenberg, Dickson Musslewhite, Aron Keesbury, John Meyers, Michell Phifer, Karen R. Smith, Julie McBurney, Mandee Eckersley, Margaret Leslie, and Michael Lepera.

Finally, our deep thanks are due to Eddie Singleton, Scott DeWitt, Wendy Hesford, and their graduate students at The Ohio State University: our annual visits there have nourished our thinking about writing in countless ways. Christine Farris at Indiana University has been a friend of the book from its earliest days, and we cannot imagine sitting down to revise without the trenchant advice she offers us. Thanks, too, to her colleague, the unsinkable John Schilb, and to Ted Leahey, teacher of teachers. And for the many conversations about teaching and writing that have sustained us over the years, we thank Richard Louth, Dean Ward, Kenny Marotta, Alec Marsh, Miles McCrimmon, Noreen Lape. Thanks finally to our families: Elizabeth Rosenwasser, and Mark, Lesley, and Sarah Stephen.

Diann Ainsworth, *Weatherford College*
Jeanette Adkins, *Tarrant County College*
Stevens Amidon, *Indiana University–Purdue University Fort Wayne*
Derede Arthur, *University of California, Santa Cruz*
Joan Anderson, *California State University, San Marcos*
Lisa Bailey, *University of South Carolina Moore School of Business*
Todd Barnes, *Ramapo College of New Jersey*
Candace Barrington, *Central Connecticut State University*
Maria Bates, *Pierce College*
Karin Becker, *Fort Lewis College*
Laura Behling, *Gustavus Adolphus College*
Stephanie Bennett, *Monmouth University*
Tom Bowie, *Regis University*
Roland Eric Boys, *Oxnard College*
David Brantley, *College of Southern Maryland*
Jessica Brown, *City College of San Francisco*
Christine Bryant Cohen, *University of Illinois at Urbana-Champaign*
Alexandria Casey, *Graceland University*
Anthony Cavaluzzi, *SUNY Adirondack Community College*

Johnson Cheu, *Michigan State University*
Jeff Cofer, *Bellevue College*
Helen Connell, *Barry University*
Sally Cooperman, *California State University, East Bay*
Kristi Costello, *Binghampton University – SUNY*
Cara Crandall, *Emerson College*
Rose Day, *Central New Mexico Community College*
Christopher Diller, *Berry College*
Susan de Ghize, *University of Denver*
Virginia Dumont-Poston, *Lander University*
David Eggebrecht, *Concordia University*
Anthony Edgington, *University of Toledo*
Karen Feldman, *University of California, Berkeley*
Dan Ferguson, *Amarillo College*
Gina Franco, *Knox College*
Sue Frankson, *College of DuPage*
Anne Friedman, *Borough of Manhattan Community College*
Tessa Garcia, *University of Texas–Pan American*
Susan Garrett, *Goucher College*
Edward Geisweidt, *The University of Alabama*
Nate Gordon, *Kishwaukee College*
Katherine Hagopian, *North Carolina State University*
Laura Headley, *Monterey Peninsula College*
Devon Holmes, *University of San Francisco*
Sally Hornback, *Indiana University-Purdue University Indianapolis*
Glenn Hutchinson, *University of North Carolina at Charlotte*
Habiba Ibrahim, *University of Washington*
Joseph Janangelo, *Loyola University Chicago*
Esther Jones, *Clark University*
Charlene Keeler, *California State University, Fullerton*
Douglas King, *Gannon University*
Constance Koepfinger, *Duquesne University*
Anne Langendorfer, *The Ohio State University*
Dawn Lattin, *Idaho State University*
Kim Long, *Shippensburg University of Pennsylvania*
Laine Lubar, *SUNY Broome Community College*
Phoenix Lundstrom, *Kapi`olani Community College*
Cynthia Martin, *James Madison University*
Lisa Maruca, *Wayne State University*
Andrea Mason, *Pacific Lutheran University*
Darin Merrill, *Brigham Young University–Idaho*
Sarah Newlands, *Portland State University*
Emmanuel Ngwang, *Mississippi Valley State University*
Leslie Norris, *Rappahannock Community College*

Ludwig Otto, *Tarrant County College*
Adrienne Peek, *Modesto Junior College*
Adrienne Redding, *Andrews University*
Julie Rivera, *California State University, Long Beach*
Jenica Roberts, *University of Illinois at Urbana-Champaign*
John Robinson, *Diablo Valley College*
Pam Rooney, *Western Michigan University*
Linda Rosekrans, *The State University of New York–SUNY Cortland*
Becky Rudd, *Citrus College*
Arthur Saltzman, *Missouri Southern State University*
Deborah Scaggs, *Texas A&M University*
Vicki Schwab, *State College of Florida, Manatee-Sarasota*
Edgar Singleton, *The Ohio State University*
John Sullivan, *Muhlenberg College*
Michael Suwak, *College of Southern Maryland*
Eleanor Swanson, *Regis University*
Kimberly Thompson, *Wittenberg University*
Tammy Trucks-Bordeaux, *Peru State College*
Kathleen Walton, *Southwestern Oregon Community College*
James Ray Watkins, *The Art Institute of Pittsburgh, Online; Colorado Technical University, Online; and The Johns Hopkins Center for Talented Youth*
Lisa Weihman, *West Virginia University*
Robert Williams, *Radford University*
Sally Woelfel, *Arizona State University*
Nancy Wright, *Syracuse University*
Meredith Zaring, *Georgia State University*
Robbin Zeff, *The George Washington University*

Ancillaries

MindTap

Writing Analytically is also available on MindTap. MindTap® English is a personalized teaching experience with relevant assignments that guide students to analyze, apply, and improve thinking and writing, allowing you to measure skills and outcomes with ease. Easily integrate your own content into the learning path and eBook and select readings to include from a vast database, providing a single place for students to access all their course materials. Encourage students to get individualized feedback on their writing from a professional tutor, manage electronic paper submission, grading and peer review, assign multimodal activities that help students apply writing skills to real life, and track student progress and engagement with powerful, visual analytics. MindTap® English helps you teach your course, your way.

Online Instructor's Manual

This manual is available for downloading or printing on the instructor website. It includes an overview of the book's pedagogy, chapter-by-chapter teaching suggestions, and guidelines for evaluating students' writing. Whether you are just starting out or have been teaching for years, the authors have designed this manual to accommodate you.

CHAPTER 1

The Analytical Frame of Mind

Overview In this chapter we define analysis and explain why it is the kind of writing you will most often be asked to do in college and beyond. We explain the characteristics that college teachers look for in student writing and the changes in orientation this kind of writing requires: the analytical frame of mind. The chapter identifies the counterproductive habits of mind most likely to block good writing and offers in their place the book's first set of strategies for becoming a more observant and more confident writer: NOTICE & FOCUS, Free-writing, ASKING "SO WHAT?" and THE METHOD. These strategies are embedded in a discussion of what we call The Five Analytical Moves.

Writing as a Tool of Thought

Learning to write well means more than learning to organize information in appropriate forms and to construct clear and correct sentences. Learning to write well means learning ways of using writing in order to think well.

Good writing does, of course, require attention to form, but writing is not just a container for displaying already completed acts of thinking; it is also a mental activity. Through writing we figure out what things mean.

This book will make you more aware of your own acts of thinking and will show you how to experiment more deliberately with ways of having ideas—for example, by sampling various kinds of informal, exploratory writing that will enhance your ability to learn.

As this chapter will show, the analytical process consists of a fairly limited set of basic moves—strategies—that people who think well have at their disposal. *Writing Analytically* describes and gives names to these strategies, which are activities you can practice and use systematically in order to arrive at better ideas.

Our attempt to formulate these moves is not without precedent. Long before there were courses on writing, people studied a subject called rhetoric—as they still do. Rhetoric is a way of thinking about thinking. It offers ways of generating and evaluating arguments as well as ways of arranging them for maximum effect in particular situations. This book is a rhetoric in the sense that it offers methods for observing all manner of data and arriving at ideas. The division of rhetoric devoted to the generation of ideas is called "invention." *Writing Analytically* is an invention-oriented rhetoric.

In classical rhetoric, procedures and forms that served as aids to discovery were called *heuristics*. The term comes from the Greek word *heuriskein*, which means "to find out" or "to discover." This book's analytical methods, such as the ones you will find in this chapter, are heuristics.

You know how in the cartoons when a character gets an idea, we see a light bulb go on over his or her head? That's the point of view this book opposes, because that scenario dooms you to waiting for the light bulb to go on. Heuristics are more reliable ways of turning on that light bulb than lying around waiting for inspiration.

Why Faculty Want Analysis

For over two decades we've co-directed a Writing Across the Curriculum program in which writing is taught by our colleagues from all of the other disciplines. They have helped us to see why analysis is what they expect from student writing. They want analysis because of the attitudes toward learning that come along with it—the way it teaches learners to cultivate curiosity, to tolerate uncertainty, to respect complexity, and to seek to understand a subject before they attempt to make arguments about it.

Overall, what faculty want is for students to learn to do things with course material beyond merely reporting it on the one hand, and just reacting to it (often through like-dislike, agree-disagree responses) on the other (see Figure 1.1). This is the issue that *Writing Analytically* addresses: how to locate a middle ground between passive summary and personal response. That middle ground is occupied by analysis.

Analysis Defined

To analyze something is to ask what that something means. It is to ask how something does what it does or why it is as it is. Analysis is, then, a form of detective work that typically pursues something puzzling, something you are seeking to understand rather than something you believe you already have

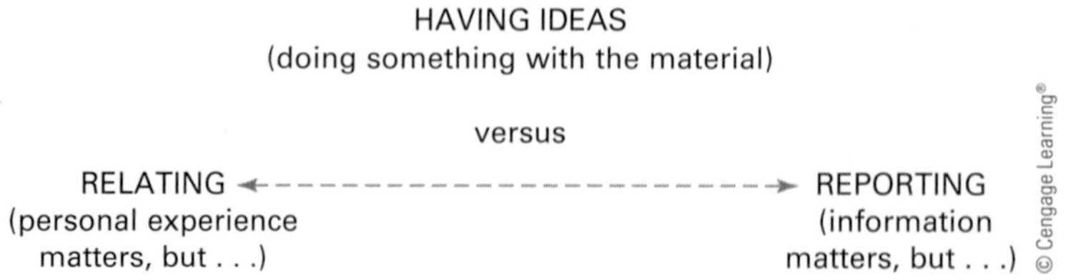

HAVING IDEAS
(doing something with the material)

versus

RELATING ← – – – – – – – – – – – – – – – – – – – → REPORTING
(personal experience   (information
matters, but . . .)   matters, but . . .) © Cengage Learning®

FIGURE 1.1

What Faculty Want from Student Writing

the answers to. Analysis finds questions where there seemed not to be any, and it makes connections that might not have been evident at first. Analysis is, then, more than just a set of skills: it is a frame of mind, an attitude toward experience.

Analysis is the kind of thinking you'll most often be asked to do in college, the mainstay of serious thought. Yet, it's also among the most common of our mental activities. The fact is that most people already analyze all of the time, but they often don't realize that this is what they're doing.

If, for example, you find yourself being followed by a large dog, your first response—other than breaking into a cold sweat—will be to analyze the situation. What does being followed by a large dog mean for me, here, now? Does it mean the dog is vicious and about to attack? Does it mean the dog is curious and wants to play? Similarly, if you are losing at a game of tennis or you've just left a job interview or you are looking at a large painting of a woman with three noses, you will begin to analyze. How can I play differently to increase my chances of winning? Am I likely to get the job, and why (or why not)? Why did the artist give the woman three noses?

Analysis Does More than Break a Subject into Its Parts

Whether you are analyzing an awkward social situation, an economic problem, a painting, a substance in a chemistry lab, or your chances of succeeding in a job interview, the process of analysis is the same:

- divide the subject into its defining parts, its main elements or ingredients
- consider how these parts are related, both to each other and to the subject as a whole.

In the case of the large dog, for example, you might notice that he's dragging a leash, has a ball in his mouth, and is wearing a bright red scarf around his neck. Having broken your larger subject into these defining parts, you would try to see the connection among them and determine what they mean, what they allow you to decide about the nature of the dog: possibly somebody's lost pet, playful, probably not hostile, unlikely to bite me.

Analysis of the painting of the woman with three noses, a subject more like the kind you might be asked to write about in a college course, would proceed in the same way. Your end result—ideas about the nature of the painting—would be determined—as with the dog—not only by noticing its various parts, but by your familiarity with the subject. If you knew little about painting, scrutiny of its parts would not tell you, for instance, that it is an example of the movement called cubism. You would, however, still be able to draw some analytical conclusions—ideas about the meaning and nature of the subject. You might conclude, for example, that the artist is interested in perspective or in the way we see, as opposed to being interested in realistic depictions of the world.

One common denominator of all effective analytical writing is that it pays close attention to detail. We analyze because our global responses, say, to a play or a speech or a social problem, are too general. If you try, for example, to comment on an entire football game, you'll find yourself saying things like "great game," which is a generic response, something you could say about almost anything. This "one-size-fits-all" kind of comment doesn't tell us very much except that you probably liked the game.

In order to say more, you would necessarily become more analytical—shifting your attention to the significance of some important piece of the game as a whole—such as "they won because the offensive line was giving the quarterback all day to find his receivers" or "they lost because they couldn't defend against the safety blitz." This move from generalization to analysis, from the larger subject to its key components, is a characteristic of the way we think. In order to understand a subject, we need to discover what it is "made of," the particulars that contribute most strongly to the character of the whole.

If all analysis did was take subjects apart, leaving them broken and scattered, the activity would not be worth very much. The student who presents a draft to his or her professor with the encouraging words, "Go ahead, rip it apart," reveals a disabling misconception about analysis—that, like dissecting a frog in a biology lab, analysis takes the life out of its subjects.

Analysis means more than breaking a subject into its parts. When you analyze a subject you ask not just "What is it made of?" but also "How do these parts help me to understand the meaning of the subject as a whole?" A good analysis seeks to locate the life of its subject, the aims and ideas that energize it.

Distinguishing Analysis from Summary, Expressive Writing, and Argument

How does analysis differ from other kinds of thinking and writing? A common way of answering this question is to think of communication as having three possible centers of emphasis: the writer, the subject, and the audience. Communication, of course, involves all three of these components, but some kinds of writing concentrate more on one than on the others (see Figure 1.2). Autobiographical writing, for example, such as diaries or memoirs or stories about personal experience, centers on the writer and his or her desire for self-expression. Argument, in which the writer takes a stand on an issue, advocating or arguing against a policy or attitude, is reader-centered; its goal is to bring about a change in its readers' actions and beliefs. Analytical writing is more concerned with arriving at an understanding of a subject than it is with either self-expression or changing readers' views.

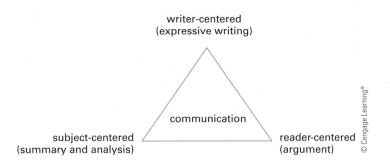

FIGURE 1.2
The Communication Triangle

These three categories of writing are not mutually exclusive. So, for example, expressive (writer-centered) writing is also analytical in its attempts to define and explain a writer's feelings, reactions, and experiences. And analysis is a form of self-expression since it inevitably reflects the ways a writer's experiences have taught him or her to think about the world. Similarly, analysis is a close cousin of argument in its emphasis on logic and the dispassionate scrutiny of ideas ("What do I think about what I think?"). But as we shall see, analysis and argument are not the same.

Analysis and Summary

One of the most common kinds of writing you'll be asked to do in college, in addition to analysis, is summary. Summary differs from analysis, because the aim of summary is to recount in reduced form someone else's ideas. But summary and analysis are also clearly related and usually operate together. Summary is important to analysis, because you can't analyze a subject without laying out its significant parts for your reader. Similarly, analysis is important to summary, because summarizing is more than just shortening someone else's writing. To write an accurate summary you have to ask analytical questions, such as:

- Which of the ideas in the reading are most significant? Why?
- How do these ideas fit together? What do the key passages in the reading mean?

Like an analysis, an effective summary doesn't assume that the subject matter can speak for itself: the writer needs to play an active role. A good summary provides perspective on the subject as a whole by explaining, as an analysis does, the meaning and function of each of that subject's parts. So, summary, like analysis, is a tool of understanding and not just a mechanical task. But a summary stops short of analysis because summary typically makes much smaller interpretive leaps.

Laying out the data is key to any kind of analysis, not simply because it keeps the analysis accurate, but also because, crucially, it is *in the act of carefully* describing a subject that analytical writers often have their best ideas. The writer who can offer a careful description of a subject's key features is likely to arrive at conclusions about possible meanings that others would share.

Here are two guidelines to be drawn from this discussion of analysis and summary:

1. Describe with care. The words you choose to summarize your data will contain the germs of your ideas about what the subject means.

2. In moving from summary to analysis, scrutinize the language you have chosen, asking, "Why did I choose this word?" and "What ideas are implicit in the language I have used?"

Analysis and Expressive Writing

At their extremes, analysis and expressive writing differ significantly in method and aim. The extreme version of expressive writing focuses on the self, with other subjects serving only to evoke greater self-understanding. The extreme version of analytical writing banishes the "I" and, although its insights may derive from personal experience, it foregrounds the writer's reasoning, not his experiences.

In practice, though, the best versions of analysis and expressive writing can overlap a lot. Although most analytical writing done in the academic disciplines is about some subject other than the self, all writing is, in a sense, personal, because there is an "I" doing the thinking and selecting the details to consider. Writing about the self, about one's own memories and defining experiences, is a useful way to stimulate our thinking about words and about the role of detail in shaping our ideas about things.

Virtually all forms of description are implicitly analytical. When you choose what you take to be the three most telling details about your subject, you have selected significant parts and used them as a means of getting at what you take to be the character of the whole. This is what analysis does: it goes after an understanding of what something means, its nature, by zeroing in on the function of significant detail.

Two Examples of Description as a Form of Analysis   In the two passages below, think about what it is that each writer is analyzing through the use of description. Which sentences and which details reveal the implicit analysis contained in the description?

First student description

22 Green Hill Road was the most beautiful house I had ever seen. The bricks a light brown, and the ivy growing along the sides reflected the sun with such perfection every afternoon. Everything about it was magnificent, but the best part about it was how it never changed—even from the moment I moved in when I was three, the house itself had always been there for me to come back to.

It was junior year in high school and I was visiting 22 Green Hill Road to pick up a few things, when I noticed something different under the clock that wasn't there when I moved out with my mom months earlier. It was a frame filled with pictures of a woman in the process of rolling down a luscious light green hill. I couldn't stop staring at her: her hair was dark brown and her jeans were a size too big. I had never met her before, and she certainly did not belong in my kitchen—the kitchen that was once so familiar I could recall every detail on every wall. My father walked in.

I turned to him. "Who . . . is this?" I asked him. It took him a while to figure out what to say. He sighed and answered, "That's my friend Beth." He had an ultimate innocence in his voice that never went away; I could never stay mad at him for long.

"Oh," I replied. Then I asked what I wished I had not for a long time afterward. "Did you take this?" He backed away from me.

Whenever I stopped by, from that moment on, he turned the frame around so I could not see the images of a strange yet now so familiar woman in what used to be my kitchen.

Second student description

I wish I could tell you more about that night, but it's kind of blurry. What do I remember? My father's voice, "Mommy passed away." I know I cried, but for how long I don't remember. My boyfriend was there; he only heard my end of the conversation. He drove me home from college. I guess that took a couple of hours. There was a box of tissues on my lap, but I didn't use any. He smoked a cigarette at one point, and opened up a window. The black air rushed in and settled on me like a heavy cloak.

The following assignment treats the writer's self as the subject of an analysis and calls for the writer to conduct that analysis through the careful selection and arrangement of telling detail.

TRY THIS 1.1: Writing the Self

Write a brief (two-page) descriptive piece about yourself that you would be willing to read out loud to others engaged in the same exercise. Do this by offering a narrative of some revealing and representative "moment"—perhaps a kind of moment that tended to recur—in your life. Sometimes the most telling moments, those that play a significant role in how we come to be who we are, are subtle, small moments, rather than "big" life-changing experiences. Some of these small but significant moments are barely remembered until we start looking for them with writing. Thus, they engage readers in the writer's process of discovery, which is what good writing should do. Your piece will necessarily be a blend of showing and telling, of description and more explicit analysis, but make sure not to substitute telling readers how you felt for re-creating the experience that made you feel as you did.

Analysis and Argument

Analysis and argument proceed in the same way. They offer evidence, make claims about it, and supply reasons that explain and justify the claims. In other words, in both analysis and argument you respond to the questions "What have you got to go on?" (evidence) and "How did you get there?" (the principles and reasons that caused you to conclude what you did about the evidence).

Although analysis and argument proceed in essentially the same way, they differ in the kinds of questions they try to answer. Argument, at its most dispassionate, asks, "What can be said with truth about x or y?" In common practice, though, the kinds of questions that argument more often answers are more committed and directive, such as "Which is better, x or y?"; "How can we best achieve x or y?"; and "Why should we stop doing x or y?"

Analysis, by contrast, asks, "What does x or y mean?" In analysis, the evidence (your data) is something you wish to understand, and the claims are assertions about what that evidence means. The claim that an analysis makes is usually a tentative answer to a *what*, *how*, or *why* question; it seeks to explain why people watch professional wrestling or what a rising number of sexual harassment cases might mean or how certain features of government health care policy are designed to allay the fears of the middle class.

The claim that an argument makes is often an answer to a *should* question: for example, readers should or shouldn't vote for bans on smoking in public buildings or they should or shouldn't believe that gays can function effectively in the military. The writer of an analysis is more concerned with discovering how each of these complex subjects might be defined and explained than with convincing readers to approve or disapprove of them.

Analysis versus Debate-Style Argument Many of you may have been introduced to writing arguments through the debate model—arguing for or against a given position, with the aim of defeating an imagined opponent and convincing your audience of the rightness of your position. The agree/disagree mode of writing and thinking that you often see in editorials, hear on radio or television, and even practice sometimes in school may incline you to focus all of your energy on the bottom line—aggressively advancing a claim for or against some view—without first engaging in the exploratory interpretation of evidence that is so necessary to arriving at thoughtful arguments. But as the American College Dictionary says, "to argue implies reasoning or trying to understand; it does not necessarily imply opposition." It is this more exploratory, tentative, and dispassionate mode of argument that this book encourages you to practice.

Adhering to the more restrictive, debate-style definition of *argument* can create a number of problems for careful analytical writers:

1. By requiring writers to be oppositional, it inclines them to discount or dismiss problems on the side or position they have chosen; they cling to the same static position rather than testing it as a way of allowing it to evolve.

2. It inclines writers toward either/or thinking rather than encouraging them to formulate more qualified (carefully limited, acknowledging exceptions, etc.) positions that integrate apparently opposing viewpoints.
3. It overvalues convincing someone else at the expense of developing understanding.

As should now be clear, the aims of analysis and argument can sometimes be in conflict. Nevertheless, it's important to remember that, in practice, analysis and argument are inevitably linked. Even the most tentative and cautiously evolving analysis is ultimately an argument; it asks readers to accept a particular interpretation of a set of data.

Similarly, even the most passionately committed argument is an analysis. If you approach an argument with the primary goals of convincing others that you are right and defeating your opponents, you may neglect the more important goal of arriving at a fair and accurate assessment of your subject. In fact, you will be able to argue much more effectively from evidence if you first take the time to really consider what that evidence means and, thereby, to find valid positions to argue about it.

Ethos and Analysis Analysis, as we have been arguing, is interested in how we come to know things, how we make meaning. This focus privileges not just conclusions about a subject, but also sharing with readers the thought process that led to those conclusions. Rather than telling other people what to think, the best analytical writers encourage readers to think collaboratively with them. This is true of the best writers in the civic forum as well as in colleges and universities.

It follows that the character of the speaker (*ethos*) in an analysis will serve to create a more collaborative and collegial relationship with readers than might be the case in other kinds of writing.

Classical rhetoric thought of the impact that writers/speakers had on audiences in terms of three categories: *logos*, *pathos*, and *ethos*. They are very useful, especially as you go about trying to construct a written version of yourself that will allow you to succeed and grow as a college writer. The word *logos* (from Greek) refers to the logical component of a piece of writing or speaking. *Pathos* refers to the emotional component in writing, the ways that it appeals to feelings in an audience. *Ethos* will be familiar to you as a term because of its relation to the word ethics. In classical rhetoric, *ethos* is the character of the speaker, which is important in determining an audience's acceptance or rejection of his or her arguments.

Much of this book is concerned with the *logos* of academic writing, with ways of deriving and arguing ideas in colleges, universities, and the world of educated discourse. *Ethos* matters too. The thinking you do is difficult to separate from the sense the audience has of the person doing the thinking. In fact, the personae (versions of ourselves) we assume when we write have a formative impact on what we think and say. *Ethos* is not just a mask we assume in order to appeal to a particular audience. The stylistic and thinking moves prescribed by the *ethos* of particular groups become, with practice, part of who we are and thus of how we think and interact with others.

Eventually, college writers need to learn how to adopt different self-representations for different academic disciplines. So the acceptable *ethos* of a chemistry lab report differs in significant ways from the one you might adopt in a political science or English paper. Nevertheless, in most academic disciplines *ethos* is characterized by the following traits:

- nonadversarial tone—not looking for a fight
- collaborative and collegial—treats readers as colleagues worthy of respect who share your interest
- carefully qualified—not making overstated claims
- relative impersonality in self-presentation—keeps focus primarily on the subject, not the writer.

Counterproductive Habits of Mind

Analysis, we have been suggesting, is a frame of mind, a set of habits for observing and making sense of the world. There is also, it is fair to say, an anti-analytical frame of mind with its own set of habits. These habits shut down perception and arrest potential ideas at the cliché stage. Having ideas depends on noticing things in a subject that we wish to better understand rather than glossing things over with a quick and too-easy understanding.

The nineteenth-century poet, Emily Dickinson, writes that "Perception of an object/Costs precise the object's loss." When we leap prematurely to our perceptions about a thing, we place a filter between ourselves and the "object," shrinking the amount and kinds of information that can get through to our minds and our senses. The point of the Dickinson poem is a paradox—that the ideas we arrive at actually deprive us of material with which to have more ideas. So we have to

THE PROBLEM

        leaps to

data ⎯⎯⎯→ evaluative claims (like/dislike; agree/disagree)

              leaps to

data (words, images, other detail) ⎯⎯⎯→ broad generalization

© Cengage Learning®

be careful about leaping to conclusions because if we are not careful, this move will lead to a form of mental blindness—loss of the object.

Habit: The Judgment Reflex

In its most primitive form—most automatic and least thoughtful—judging is like an on/off switch. When the switch gets thrown in one direction or the other, the resulting judgment predetermines and over-directs any subsequent thinking we might do. Rather than thinking about what X is or how X operates, we lock ourselves prematurely into proving that we were right to think that X should be banned or supported.

The psychologist Carl Rogers has written at length on this problem of the judgment reflex. He claims that our habitual tendency as humans—virtually a programmed response—is to evaluate everything and to do so very quickly.

When people leap to judgment, they usually land in the mental pathways they've grown accustomed to traveling, guided by family or friends or popular opinion. The fact that you liked or didn't like a movie probably says more about you—your tastes, interests, biases, and experiences—than it does about the movie. What makes a movie boring: that it doesn't have enough car chases? that its plot resembles half the plots on cable channels? that the leading man was miscast or the dialogue was too long-winded? At the very least, in such cases, you'd need to share with readers your *criteria* for judgment—your reasons and your standards of evaluation.

This is not to say that all judging should be avoided—only delayed. A writer needs to take into account how his or her judgment has been affected by the details of a particular situation (context) and to acknowledge how thinking about these details has led to restricting (qualifying) the range of the judgment: X is sometimes true in these particular circumstances. Z is probably the right thing to do but only when A and B occur.

As a general rule, try to figure out what your subject means before deciding how you feel about it. If you can break the judgment reflex and press yourself to analyze before judging a subject, you will often be surprised at how much your initial responses change.

Cures for the Judgment Reflex

- Become conscious of the like/dislike switch in your own thinking and try to avoid it altogether.
- Neither agree nor disagree with another person's position until you can repeat that position in a way the other person would accept as fair and accurate. Carl Rogers recommends this strategy to negotiators in industry and government.
- Try eliminating the word "should" from your vocabulary for a while. Judgments often take the form of *should* statements.
- Try eliminating evaluative adjectives—those that offer judgments with no data.

"Jagged" is a descriptive, concrete adjective. It offers something we can experience. "Beautiful" is an evaluative adjective. It offers only judgment. Sometimes the concrete-abstract divide is complicated. Consider for example the word "green," a literal color with figurative associations (envious, innocent, ecological, etc.).

TRY THIS 1.2: Experiment with Adjectives and Adverbs

Write a paragraph of description—on anything that comes to mind—without using any evaluative adjectives or adverbs. Alternatively, analyze and categorize the adjectives and adverbs in a piece of your own recent writing, a book review, or an editorial.

Habit: Naturalizing Our Assumptions (Overpersonalizing)

The word *naturalize* in this context means we are representing—and seeing— our own assumptions as natural, as simply the way things are *and ought to be*. Writers who naturalize their own assumptions—a version of the judgment reflex—tend to make personal experiences and prejudices an *unquestioned* standard of value.

It is surprisingly difficult to break the habit of treating our points of view as self-evidently true—not just for us, but for everyone. The overpersonalizer assumes that because he or she experienced or believes X, everyone else does too. But what is "common sense" for one person and so not even in need of explaining can be quite uncommon and not so obviously sensible to someone else. More often than not, "common sense" is a phrase that really means "what seems obvious to me and therefore should be obvious to you."

VOICES FROM ACROSS THE CURRICULUM

Arguments vs. Opinions: A Political Scientist Speaks

Writers need to be aware of the distinction between an argument which seeks support from evidence, and mere opinions and assertions. People too often assume that in politics one opinion is as good as another. (Tocqueville thought this was a peculiarly democratic disease.) From this perspective any position a person might take on controversial issues is simply his or her opinion to be accepted or rejected by another person's beliefs/prejudices. The key task, therefore, is not so much the substitution of knowledge for opinions, but substituting well-constructed arguments for unexamined opinions. An argument presupposes a willingness to engage with others. To the extent that a writer operates on the assumption that everything is in the end an opinion, they have no reason to construct arguments; they are locked into an opinion.

— JACK GAMBINO, PROFESSOR OF POLITICAL SCIENCE

Habit: Generalizing

What it all boils down to is . . . What this adds up to is . . . The gist of her speech was . . . We generalize from our experience because this is one way of arriving at ideas. The problem with generalizing as a habit of mind is that it removes the mind—usually much too quickly—from the data that produced the generalization in the first place.

Most of us tend to remember our global impressions and reactions. The dinner was dull. The house was beautiful. The music was exciting. But we forget the specific, concrete causes of these impressions (if we ever fully noticed them). As a result, we deprive ourselves of material to think with—the data that might allow us to reconsider our initial impressions or to share them with others.

The problem comes when generalizations omit any supporting details. Consider for a moment what you are actually asking others to do when you offer them a generalization such as "The proposed changes in immigration policy are a disaster." Unless the recipient of this observation asks a question—such as "Why do you think so?"—he or she is being required to take your word for it: the changes are a disaster because you say so.

What happens instead if you offer a few details that caused you to think as you do? Clearly, you are on riskier ground. Your listener might think that the details you cite lead to different conclusions and a different reading of the data, but at least conversation has become possible.

Cures for the Problem of Generalizing

- The simplest antidote to the problem of generalizing is to train yourself to be more conscious of where your generalizations come from. *Press yourself to trace your general impressions back to the particulars that caused them.* Deciding to become more aware of your own responses to the world and their causes counteracts the inevitable numbing that takes place as habit takes control of our daily lives.

- Here's another strategy for bringing your thinking down from high levels of generality. Think of the words you use as steps on an abstraction ladder, and consciously climb down the ladder from abstract generalization to concrete detail.

"Mammal," for example, is higher on the abstraction ladder than "cow." A concrete word appeals to the senses. Abstract words are not available to our senses of touch, sight, hearing, taste, and smell. "Peacekeeping force" is an abstract phrase; it conjures up a concept. "Submarine" is concrete. We know what people are talking about when they say there is a plan to send submarines to a troubled area. We can't be so sure what is up when people start talking about peacekeeping forces.

TRY THIS 1.3: Distinguishing Abstract from Concrete Words
Make a list of the first ten words that come to mind and then arrange them from most concrete to most abstract. Then repeat the exercise by choosing key words from a page of something you have written recently.

Habits of Mind in Psychology: A Psychologist Speaks

Psychologists who study the way we process information have established important links between the way we think and the way we feel. Some psychologists, such as Aaron Beck, have identified common "errors in thinking" that parallel the habits of mind discussed in this chapter. Beck and others have shown that falling prey to these counterproductive habits of mind is associated with a variety of negative outcomes. For instance, a tendency to engage in either/or thinking, overgeneralization, and personalization has been linked to higher levels of anger, anxiety, and depression. Failure to attend to these errors in thinking chokes off reflection and analysis. As a result, the person becomes more likely to "react" rather than think, which may prolong and exacerbate the negative emotions.

— MARK SCIUTTO, PROFESSOR OF PSYCHOLOGY

Get Comfortable with Uncertainty

Most of us learn early in life to pretend that we understand things even when we don't. Rather than ask questions and risk looking foolish, we nod our heads. Soon, we even come to believe that we understand things when really we don't, or not nearly as well as we think we do. This understandable but problematic human trait means that to become better thinkers, most of us have to cultivate a more positive attitude toward not knowing. Prepare to be surprised at how difficult this can be. Start by trying to accept that uncertainty—even its more extreme version, confusion—is a productive state of mind, a precondition to having ideas. The poet John Keats coined a memorable phrase for this willed tolerance of uncertainty. He called it *negative capability*.

> I had not had a dispute but a disquisition with Dilke, on various subjects; several things dovetailed in my mind, & at once it struck me, what quality went to form a Man of Achievement especially in Literature & which Shakespeare possessed so enormously—I mean *Negative Capability*, that is when man is capable of being in uncertainties, Mysteries, doubts, without any irritable reaching after fact & reason.

— LETTER TO GEORGE AND THOMAS KEATS, DECEMBER 1817

The key phrases here are "capable of being in uncertainties" and "without any irritable reaching." Keats is not saying that facts and reason are unnecessary and therefore can be safely ignored. But he does praise the kind of person who can remain calm (rather than becoming irritable) in a state of uncertainty. He is endorsing a way of being that can stay open to possibilities longer than most of us are comfortable with. Negative capability is an essential habit of mind for productive analytical thinking.

Tell yourself that you don't understand, even if you think that you do. You'll know that you are surmounting the fear of uncertainty when the meaning of your evidence starts to seem less rather than more clear to you, and perhaps even strange. You will begin to see details that you hadn't seen before and a range of competing meanings where you had thought there was only one.

Habit: The Slot-Filler Mentality (Five-Paragraph Form)

Can a format qualify as a counterproductive habit of mind? Yes, if you consider how many high school students have naturalized five-paragraph form as the structure for organizing the writing they do in school.

The shift from high school to college writing is not just a difference in degree but a difference in kind. The changes it requires in matters of form and style are inevitably also changes in thinking. The primary change in thinking for many students demands saying good-bye to five-paragraph form.

Of course it can be anxiety-producing to bid farewell to this one-size-fits-all writing format and replace it with a set of different forms for different situations. But it's essential to let go of this particular security blanket.

So, what's wrong with five-paragraph form? Its rigid, arbitrary, and mechanical organizational scheme values structure over just about everything else, especially in-depth thinking in depth.

The formula's defenders say that essays need to be organized and that the simple three-part thesis and three body paragraphs (one reason and/or example for each) and repetitive conclusion meet that need. They also say that five-paragraph form is useful for helping writers to get started.

But the problem with treating five-paragraph form as a relatively benign aid to clarity is that—like any habit—it is very hard to break. The form actually discourages thinking by conditioning writers to be afraid of looking closely at evidence. If they look too closely, they might find something that doesn't fit, at which point the prefabricated organizational scheme falls apart. And it is precisely the something-that-doesn't-seem-to-fit, the thing writers call a "complication," that triggers good ideas.

We will return in Chapter 4 to the problems created by five-paragraph form and how to remedy them. For now, keep in mind that if you can't break the slot-filler habit, you'll remain handicapped because five-paragraph form runs counter to virtually all of the values and attitudes that you need in order to grow as a writer and a thinker.

Learn to Notice

Some people, especially the very young, are good at noticing things. They see things that the rest of us don't see or have ceased to notice. Growing up, we all become increasingly desensitized to the world around us; we tend to forget the specific things that get us to feel and think in particular ways.

But why is this? Is it just that people become duller as they get older? The poet William Wordsworth thought so: he argued that we aren't the victims of declining intelligence, but of habit. That is, as we organize our lives so that we can function more efficiently, we condition ourselves to see in more predictable ways and to tune out things that are not immediately relevant to our daily needs.

You can test this theory by considering what you did and did not notice this morning on the way to work or class or wherever you regularly go. Following a routine for moving through the day can be done with minimal engagement of either the brain or the senses. Moving along the roadway in cars, we periodically realize that miles have gone by while we were driving on automatic pilot, attending barely at all to the road or the car or the landscape. Arguably, even when we try to focus on something that we want to consider, the habit of not really attending to things stays with us.

The deadening effect of habit on seeing and thinking has long been a preoccupation of artists as well as philosophers and psychologists. Some people have even defined the aim of art as "defamiliarization." "The essential purpose of art," writes the novelist David Lodge, "is to overcome the deadening effects of habit by representing familiar things in unfamiliar ways." The man who coined the term *defamiliarization*, Victor Shklovsky, wrote, "Habitualization devours works, clothes, furniture, one's wife, and the fear of war. . . . And art exists that one may recover the sensation of life" (David Lodge, *The Art of Fiction*. New York: Penguin, 1992, p.53).

We all know the buzz phrase "thinking outside the box," which appears to mean getting beyond outworn ways of thinking about things. The phrase assumes that most of the time most of us are trapped inside the box—inside a set of prefabricated answers (clichés) and like/dislike responses.

In this context, we come to the Five Analytical Moves that thinkers regularly make when they analyze things. To become a more confident and observant writer, you will need to become more aware of these moves in your thinking and practice them systematically.

The Five Analytical Moves

The act of analyzing can be broken down into five essential moves:

> Move 1: Suspend judgment.
> Move 2: Define significant parts and how they are related.
> Move 3: Make the implicit explicit. Push observations to implications by ASKING "SO WHAT?"
> Move 4: Look for patterns of repetition and contrast and for anomalies (THE METHOD).
> Move 5: Keep reformulating questions and explanations.

Move 1: Suspend Judgment

A lot of what passes for thinking is merely reacting: right/wrong, good/bad, loved it/hated it, couldn't relate to it, boring. As we noted in our discussion of Counterproductive Habits of Mind, responses like these are habits, reflexes of the mind. And they are surprisingly tough habits to break. Experiment:

eavesdrop on people walking out of a movie. Most of them will immediately voice their approval or disapproval, usually in either/or terms: "I think it was a good movie and you are wrong to think it was bad." And so on.

A first move in conducting analysis—in fact, a precondition—is to delay judgment, especially of the agree-disagree, like-dislike kind. In the opening pages of *The Great Gatsby*, Nick Carraway cites as the one piece of wisdom he learned from his father the following statement: "Reserving judgments is a matter of infinite hope." In analysis the goal is always to understand before you judge.

Move 2: Define Significant Parts and How They Are Related

In order to define significant parts and figure out how they are related, writers need to train themselves to attend closely to details. Becoming observant is not natural; it's learned. Toward that end, this book offers a series of observation and interpretation strategies to equip you to see more and to make more of what you see.

The first of these is a strategy we call NOTICE & FOCUS, which will help you to stay open longer to what you can notice in your subject matter. Do this by starting not with "What do I think?" or, worse, with "What do I like/dislike?" but with "What do I *notice?*" This small shift in words will engineer the major conceptual shift this chapter asks you to make: to locate more of your time and attention in the observation stage, which necessarily precedes formulating a thesis.

NOTICE & FOCUS **(Ranking)**

NOTICE & Focus: SLOW DOWN

Not "What do you think?" &

Not "What do you like or dislike?"

but

"What do you notice?"

A few prompts:

What do you find most INTERESTING?

What do you find most STRANGE?

What do you find most REVEALING?

© Cengage Learning®

This exercise is governed by repeated return to the question, "What do you notice?". Most people's tendency is to generalize and thus rapidly move away from whatever it is they are looking at. The question "What do you notice?" redirects attention to the subject matter, itself, and delays the pressure to come up with answers (see Figure 1.3).

© 2015 Cengage Learning®

1	**Repeatedly answer the question, "What do you notice?,"** being sure to cite actual details of the thing being observed rather than moving to more general observations about it. (This is more difficult than it sounds.) This phase of the exercise should produce an extended and unordered list of details—features of the thing being observed—that call attention to themselves for one reason or another.
2	**Rank (create an order of importance) for the various features you have noticed.** Answer the question "What three details (specific features of the subject matter) are most interesting (or significant or revealing or strange)?" The purpose of relying on "interesting" or one of the other suggested words is that these will help to deactivate the like/dislike switch, which is so much a reflex in all of us, and replace it with a more analytical perspective.
3	**Say why the three things you selected struck you as the most interesting.** Remember to start by noticing as much as you can about what you are looking at. Dwell with the data. Record what you see. Don't move to generalization or judgment. What this procedure will begin to demonstrate is how useful description is as a tool for arriving at ideas. Stay at the description stage longer (in that attitude of uncertainty we've recommended) and have better ideas. Training yourself to notice is fun. It will improve your memory as well as your ability to think.

FIGURE 1.3
Notice & Focus + Ranking

Remember to start by noticing as much as you can about what you are looking at. Dwell with the data. Record what you see. It will improve your memory as well as your ability to think.

"Interesting," "Revealing," "Strange"

These three words are triggers for analysis. Often we are interested by things that have captured our attention without our clearly knowing why. To say that something is interesting is not the end but the beginning of analysis. If you press yourself to explain why something is interesting, revealing, or strange, you will be prompted to make an analytical move.

Revealing (or *significant*) requires you to make choices that can lead to interpretive leaps. If something strikes you as revealing or significant, even if you're not yet sure why, you will eventually begin producing some explanation. The word *strange* gives us permission to notice oddities and things that initially seem not to fit. *Strange*, in this context, is not a judgmental term, but one denoting features of a subject that aren't readily explainable. Where you locate something strange, you have isolated something to figure out—what makes it strange and why.

TRY THIS 1.4: Notice and Focus Fieldwork

Try this exercise with a range of subjects: an editorial, the front page of a newspaper, a website, a key paragraph from something you are reading, the style of a favorite writer, conversations overheard around campus, looking at people's shoes, political speeches, a photograph, a cartoon, and so forth. (The speech bank at americanrhetoric.com is an excellent source.) Remember to include all three steps: notice, rank, and say why.

Noticing and Rhetorical Analysis

When you become attuned to noticing words and details rather than register-ing general impressions, you inevitably focus not only on the message—what gets said—but on how things get said. To notice how information is deliv-ered is to focus on its rhetoric. To analyze the rhetoric of something is to assess how that something persuades or positions us as readers or viewers or listeners.

Rhetorical analysis is an essential skill because it reveals how voices in the world are perennially seeking to enlist our support and shape our behavior.

Everything has a rhetoric, not just political speeches and not even just words: classrooms, churches, supermarkets, department store windows, Starbucks, photographs, magazine covers, your bedroom, this book. Intention, by the way, is not the issue. It doesn't matter whether the effect of a place or a piece of writ-ing on its viewers (or readers) is deliberate and planned or not. What matters is that you can notice how the details of the thing itself encourage or discourage certain kinds of responses in the "consumers" of whatever it is you are studying.

What, for example, does the high ceiling of a Gothic cathedral invite in the way of response from people who enter it? How might the high ceilings make people feel about their places in the world? What do the raised plat-form at the front of a classroom and the tidy rows of desks secured to the floor say to the students who enter there?

To get you started on rhetorical analysis, here is a brief example on the layout of our college campus.

> The campus is laid out in several rows and quadrangles. It is interesting to observe where the different academic buildings are, relative to the academic departments they house. It is also interesting to see how the campus positions student housing. In a way, the campus is set up as a series of quadrangles— areas of space with four sides. One of the dormitories, for example, forms a quadrangle. Quadrangles invite people to look in—rather than out. They are enclosed spaces, the center of which is a kind of blank. The center serves as a shared space, a safely walled-off area for the development of a separate community. The academic buildings also form a quadrangle of sorts, with an open green space in the center. On one side of the quadrangle are the buildings that house the natural and social sciences. Opposite these—on the other side of a street that runs through the center of campus—are the modern brick and glass structures that house the arts and the humanities....

What might these details lead us to conclude about the rhetoric of the campus layout?

- that the campus is inward-looking and self-enclosed
- that it invites its members to feel separate and safe
- that it announces the division of the sciences and the social sciences from the arts and humanities, so the campus layout arguably creates the sense of a divided community.

TRY THIS 1.5: Doing NOTICE & FOCUS with a Room
List a number of details about it, then rank the three most important ones. Use as a focusing question any of the three "trigger" words: interesting, revealing, or strange. Or come up with your own focus for the ranking, such as the three aspects of the room that seem most to affect the way you feel and behave in the space.

Doing Exploratory Writing in the Observation Stage: Freewriting

What is especially useful about so-called "prewriting" strategies such as NOTICE & FOCUS is freedom—freedom to experiment without worrying about readers saying that you are wrong, freedom to just pay attention to what you notice and to see where these observations might lead you. But NOTICE & FOCUS and other forms of listing can also arrest you in the list stage: you have your column of ranked observations, but now what?

The answer to that last question is to start writing consecutive sentences explaining why you found particular details especially interesting and revealing. Your goal at this stage is not to produce a finished paper, but to start some trains of thought on features of your subject that seem worth writing about.

The name that is most often attached to this kind of exploratory writing—which can, by the way, happen at various points in the writing process, not just at the beginning—is "freewriting."

"How Do I Know What I Think Until I See What I Say?" Freewriting is a method of arriving at ideas by writing continuously about a subject for a limited period of time without pausing to edit or revise. The rationale behind this activity can be understood through a well-known remark by the novelist E.M. Forster (in regard to the "tyranny" of prearranging everything): "How do I know what I think until I see what I say?" Freewriting gives you the chance to see what you'll say.

The writer Anne Lamott writes eloquently (in *Bird by Bird*) about the censors we all hear as nasty voices in our heads that keep us from writing. These are the internalized voices of past critics whose comments have become magnified to suggest that we will never get it right. Freewriting allows us to tune out these voices long enough to discover what we might think.

Freewriting opens up space for thinking by enabling us to catch different thoughts as they occur to us, without worrying prematurely about how to communicate these to a reader. The order in which ideas occur to us is not linear. Things rarely line up in a straight, forward-moving sequence. As we try to pursue one thought, others press on our attention. The act of writing allows us to follow our mental trails and to experiment with alternate routes without losing track of where we've been. Without writing, in all but the most carefully trained memories, the trails keep vanishing, sometimes leaving us stranded.

In paper-writing, you are required to develop ideas sequentially. In freewriting you have the freedom to make sudden, often unanticipated leaps. These frequently take you from a bland, predictable statement to an insight. You learn what you think by seeing what you say.

Freewriting seeks to remove what the rhetorician Peter Elbow saw as the primary cause of much poor writing: the writer's attempt to conduct two essentially opposed activities—drafting and editing, inventing and arranging—at the same time. Freewriting helps you to separate these activities until you've generated enough material to actually be worth arranging for an audience.

In general, only the most practiced analytical thinkers can arrive at their best ideas before they begin to write. The common observation, "I know what I want to say, I'm just having trouble getting it down on paper," is a half-truth at best. Getting words on paper almost always alters your ideas, and leads you to discover thoughts you didn't know you had. If you expect to have all the answers before you begin to write, you are more likely to settle for relatively superficial ideas. And, when you try to conduct all of your thinking in your head, you may arrive at an idea, but not be able to explain to your readers how you got there.

When you make the shift from freewriting to writing a first draft, you may not—and most likely will not—have all of the answers, but you will waste significantly less time chasing ill-focused and inadequately considered ideas than might otherwise have been the case.

The Rules for Freewriting There aren't many rules to freewriting.

The first is: pick a concrete starting point. Find *something specific* to be interested in. Notice & Focus works well for locating that focus as do "interesting" and "strange."

Write your focus at the top of the page—a few lines or a short list of details or a short passage. Then launch the freewrite from there.

Commit to an allotted time in which you will write continuously. Ten minutes is a minimum. You may be surprised at how much you can find to say in this amount of time. The more you do freewriting, the better you will get at it, and the longer you will be able to go.

Most importantly, keep your pen (or fingers on the keyboard) moving. Don't reread as you go. Don't pause to correct things. Don't cross things out. Don't quit when you think you have run out of things to say. Just keep writing.

Move 3: Make the Implicit Explicit. Push Observations to Implications by Asking "So What?"

NOTICE & FOCUS, "interesting" and "strange," as well as freewriting—these moves aim to keep writers dwelling longer in the observation phase of analysis, to spend more time exploring and amassing data before they leap to making some kind of claim. It's time now to shift our focus to the leap, itself.

One of the central activities and goals of analysis is to make explicit (overtly stated) what is implicit (suggested). When we do so, we are addressing such questions as "What follows from this?" and "If this is true, what else is true?" The pursuit of such questions—drawing out implications—moves our thinking and our writing *forward*.

MOVING FORWARD

Observation $\longrightarrow$ So what? $\longrightarrow$ Implications

Implications $\longrightarrow$ So what? $\longrightarrow$ Conclusions

© Cengage Learning®

This process of converting suggestions into direct statements is essential to analysis, but it is also the feature of analyzing that, among beginning writers, is least well understood. The fear is that, like the emperor's new clothes, implications aren't really "there," but are instead the phantasms of an overactive imagination. "Reading between the lines" is the common and telling phrase that expresses this anxiety. Throughout this book we will have more to say about the charge that analysis makes something out of nothing—the spaces between the lines rather than what is there in black and white. But for now, let's look at a hypothetical example of this process of drawing out implications, to suggest not only how it's done, but how often we do it in our everyday lives.

Imagine that you are driving down the highway and find yourself analyzing a billboard advertisement for a particular brand of beer. Such an analysis might begin with your noticing what the billboard photo contains, its various "parts"—six young, athletic-looking and scantily clad men and women drinking beer while pushing kayaks into a fast-running river. If you were to stop at this point, you would have produced not an analysis but a summary—a description of what the photo contains. If, however, you went on to consider what the particulars of the photo imply, your summary would become more analytical.

You might say, for example, that the photo implies that beer is the beverage of fashionable, healthy, active people, not just of older men with large stomachs dozing in armchairs in front of the television. Thus, the advertisement's meaning goes beyond its explicit contents; your analysis would lead you to convert to direct statement meanings that are suggested but not overtly stated, such as the advertisement's goal of attacking a common, negative stereotype about its product (that only fat, lazy, male people drink beer). The naming of parts that you do in analysis is not an end unto itself, is not an exercise in making something out of nothing; it serves the purpose of allowing you to better understand the nature of your subject. The implications of the "parts" you name are an important part of that understanding.

The word *implication* comes from the Latin *implicare*, which means "to fold in." The word *explicit* is in opposition to the idea of implication. It means "folded out." An act of mind is required to take what is folded in and to fold it out for all to see. This process of drawing out implications is also known as making inferences. *Inference* and *implication* are related but not synonymous terms. The term *implication* describes something suggested by the material

PUSHING OBSERVATIONS TO CONCLUSIONS: ASKING SO WHAT?

(shorthand for)

What does the observation imply?

Why does this observation matter?

Where does this observation get us?

How can we begin to theorize the significance of the observation?

© Cengage Learning®

itself; implications reside in the matter you are studying. The term *inference* describes your thinking process. In short, you infer what the subject implies.

ASKING "SO WHAT?"

ASKING "SO WHAT?" is a universal prompt for spurring the move from observation to implication and ultimately to interpretation. ASKING "SO WHAT?"—or its milder cousin, "And so?"—is a calling to account, a way of pressing yourself to confront that essential question, "Why does this matter?" The tone of "So what?" can sound rude or at least brusque, but that directness can be liberating. Often writers will go to great lengths to avoid stating what they take something to mean. After all, that leaves them open to attack, they fear, if they get it wrong. But ASKING "SO WHAT?" is a way of forcing yourself to take the plunge without too much hoopla. And when you are tempted to stop thinking too soon, ASKING "SO WHAT?" will press you onward.

ASKING "SO WHAT?" in a Chain

Experienced analytical writers develop the habit of "ASKING SO WHAT?" repeatedly. That is, they ask "So what?," answer, and then ask "So what?" of that answer, and often keep going (see Figure 1.4). The repeated asking of this question causes writers to move beyond their first attempt to arrive at a claim.

By sustaining their pursuit of implications, seasoned writers habitually reason in a chain rather than settling prematurely for a single link, as the next example illustrates.

The following is the opening paragraph of a talk given by a professor of Political Science at our college, Dr. Jack Gambino, on the occasion of a gallery

1. Describe significant evidence

2. Begin to query your own observations by making what is implicit explicit

3. Push your observations and statements of implications to interpretive conclusions by *again* asking So What?

© 2015 Cengage Learning®

FIGURE 1.4
ASKING "SO WHAT?"

opening featuring the work of two contemporary photographers of urban and industrial landscapes. We have located in brackets our annotations of his turns of thought, as these pivot on "strange" and "So what?" (Note: images referred to in the example are available from Google Images—type in Camilo Vergara fern street 1988, also Edward Burtynsky.)

If you look closely at Camilo Vergara's photo of Fern Street, Camden, 1988, you'll notice a sign on the side of a dilapidated building:

Danger: Men Working

W. Hargrove Demolition

Perhaps that warning captures the ominous atmosphere of these very different kinds of photographic documents by Camilo Vergara and Edward Burtynsky: "Danger: Men Working." Watch out—human beings are at work! But the work that is presented is not so much a building-up as it is a tearing-down—the work of demolition. **[strange: tearing down is unexpected; writer asks "So what?" and answers]**

Of course, demolition is often necessary in order to construct anew: old buildings are leveled for new projects, whether you are building a highway or bridge in an American city or a dam in the Chinese countryside. You might call modernity itself, as so many have, a process of creative destruction, a term used variously to describe modern art, capitalism, and technological innovation. The photographs in this exhibit, however, force us to pay attention to the "destructive" side of this modern equation. **[strange: photos emphasize destruction and not creation; writer asks "So what?" and answers]**

What both Burtynsky and Vergara do in their respective ways is to put up a warning sign—they question whether the reworking of our natural and social environment leads to a sustainable human future. And they wonder whether the process of creative destruction may not have spun recklessly out of control, producing places that are neither habitable nor sustainable. In fact, a common element connecting the two photographic versions is the near absence of people in the landscape. **[writer points to supporting feature of evidence, about which he will further theorize]**

While we see the evidence of the transforming power of human production on the physical and social environment, neither Vergara's urban ruins nor Burtynsky's industrial sites actually show us "men working." **[writer continues to move by noticing strange absence of people in photographs of sites where men work]** Isolated figures peer suspiciously out back doors or pick through the rubble, but they appear out of place. **[writer asks a final "So what?" and arrives at a conclusion:]** It is this sense of displacement— of human beings alienated from the environments they themselves have created—that provides the most haunting aspect of the work of these two photographers.

The Gambino opening is a good example of how ASKING "SO WHAT?" generates forward momentum for the analysis. Notice the pattern by which the paragraph moves: the observation of something strange, about which the writer asks and answers "So what?" several times until arriving at a final "So what?"—the point at which he decides what his observations ultimately mean. We call the final "So what?" in this chain of thinking the ultimate "So what?" because it moves from implications to the writer's culminating point.

TRY THIS 1.6: Track the "So What?" Question
The aim of this exercise is to sensitize you to the various moves a writer makes when he or she presents and analyzes information. Locate any piece of analytical prose—perhaps an article from *Arts & Letters Daily* online (aldaily.com)—and identify in the margins the writer's moves as we have done for the Gambino example.

TRY THIS 1.7: Inferring Implications from Observations
Each of the statements below is rich in implication. Write a list of as many plausible implications as you can think of for each of the statements. After you have made your list of implications for each item, consider how you arrived at them. You might find it useful to do this exercise along with other people, because part of its aim is to reveal the extent to which different people infer the same implications.

1. The sidewalk is disappearing as a feature of the American residential landscape. [Here are a couple of implications to prime the pump: people don't walk anywhere anymore; builders lack much sense of social responsibility.]

2. New house designs are tending increasingly toward open plans in which the kitchen is not separated from the rest of the house.

3. "Good fences make good neighbors." — Robert Frost

4. An increasing number of juveniles—people under the age of eighteen—are being tried and convicted as adults, rather than as minors, in America, with the result that more minors are serving adult sentences for crimes they committed while still in their teens.

5. Neuroscientists tell us that the frontal cortex of the brain, the part that is responsible for judgment and especially for impulse control, is not fully developed in humans until roughly the age of twenty-one. What are the implications of this observation relative to observation four?

6. Shopping malls and grocery stores rarely have clocks.

7. List as many plausible implications as you can for this statement (which has been contested by other researchers).

"In the eye-tracking test, only one in six subjects read Web pages linearly, sentence by sentence. In this study, Nielsen found that people took in hundreds of pages 'in a pattern that's very different from what you learned in school.' It looks like a capital letter F. At the top, users read all the way across, but as they proceed their descent quickens and horizontal sight contracts, with a slowdown around the middle of the page. Near the bottom, eyes move almost vertically, the lower-right corner of the page largely ignored."

— MARK BAUERLEIN, "ONLINE LITERACY IS A LESSER KIND," *THE CHRONICLE REVIEW*

Move 4: Look for Patterns of Repetition and Contrast and for Anomalies (THE METHOD)

We have been defining analysis as the understanding of parts in relation to each other and to a whole. But how do you know which parts to attend to? What makes some details in the material you are studying more worthy of your attention than others?

The procedure we call THE METHOD offers a tool for uncovering significant patterns. Like NOTICE AND FOCUS, THE METHOD orients you toward significant detail; but whereas NOTICE AND FOCUS is a deliberately unstructured activity, THE METHOD applies a matrix or grid of observational moves to a subject. In its most reduced form, THE METHOD organizes observation and then prompts interpretation by asking the following sequence of questions.

In virtually all subjects, repetition and close resemblance (strands) are signs of emphasis. In a symphony, for example, certain patterns of notes repeat throughout, announcing themselves as major themes. In Shakespeare's play *King Lear*, references to seeing and eyes call attention to themselves through repetition, causing us to recognize that the play is <u>about</u> seeing. Binary oppositions, which often consist of two strands or repetitions that are in tension with each other, suggest what is at stake in a subject. We can understand *King Lear* by the way it opposes kinds of blindness to ways of seeing.

Along with looking for pattern, it is also fruitful to attend to anomalous details—those that seem not to fit the pattern. Anomalies help us to revise our assumptions. Picture, for example, a TV ad featuring a baseball player reading Dostoyevsky in the dugout. In this case, the anomaly, a baseball

QUESTIONS FROM THE METHOD

What repeats?

What goes with what? (strands)

What is opposed to what? (binaries)

(for all of these) → *SO WHAT?*

What doesn't fit? (anomalies) So what?

Copyright © Cengage Learning®

player who reads serious literature, subverts the stereotypical assumption that sports and intellectualism don't belong together.

People tend to avoid information that challenges (by not conforming to) views they already hold. Screening out anything that would ruffle the pattern they've begun to see, they ignore the evidence that might lead them to a better theory. Most advances in thought have arisen when someone has observed some phenomenon that does not fit within a prevailing theory.

The Steps of THE METHOD

THE METHOD of looking for patterns works through a series of steps. Hold yourself initially to doing the steps one at a time and in order. Later, you will be able to record your answers under each of the five steps simultaneously. Although the steps of THE METHOD are discrete and modular, they are also consecutive. They proceed by a kind of narrative logic. Each step leads logically to the next, and then to various kinds of regrouping, which is actually rethinking (see Figure 1.5).

1	**List exact repetitions and the number of each (words, details).** For example, if forms of the word *seems* repeat three times, write "seems × 3." With images, the repeated appearance of high foreheads would constitute an exact repetition. Concentrate on substantive (meaning-carrying) words. Only in rare cases will words like "and" or "the" merit attention as a significant repetition. At the most literal level, whatever repeats is what the thing is about.
2	**List repetitions of the same or similar kind of detail or word—which we call strands** (for example, *polite, courteous, decorous*). Be able to explain the strand's connecting logic with a label: *manners.*
3	**List details or words that form or suggest binary oppositions**—pairs of words or details that are opposites—and select from these the most important ones, which function as **organizing contrasts** (for example, *open/closed, ugly/beautiful, global/local*). Your goal here is not to engage in either/or thinking but to locate what is at stake in the subject, the tensions and issues that it is trying to resolve.
4	**Choose ONE repetition, strand, or binary as a starting point for a healthy paragraph** (or two) in which you discuss its significance in relation to the whole. (This ranking, as in Notice and Focus, prompts an interpretive leap.)
5	**Locate anomalies: exceptions to the pattern, things that seem not to fit**. Once you see an anomaly, you will often find that it is part of a strand you had not detected (and perhaps one side of a previously unseen binary).

© 2015 Cengage Learning®

FIGURE 1.5

THE METHOD

Expect ideas to suggest themselves to you as you move through the steps of THE METHOD. Strands often begin to suggest other strands that are in opposition to them. Words you first took to be parts of one strand may migrate to different strands. This process of noticing and then relocating words and details into different patterns is one aspect of doing THE METHOD that can push your analysis to interpretation.

It may be helpful to think of this method of analysis as a form of mental doodling. Rather than worrying about what you are going to say, or about whether or not you understand, you instead get out a pencil and start tallying up what you see. Engaged in this process, you'll soon find yourself gaining entry to the logic of your subject matter.

Two Examples of THE METHOD Generating Ideas

In the paragraph below you can see how the writer's noticing strands and binaries directs his thinking.

> The most striking aspect of the spots is how different they are from typical fashion advertising. If you look at men's fashion magazines, for example, at the advertisements for the suits of Ralph Lauren or Valentino or Hugo Boss, they almost always consist of a beautiful man, with something interesting done to his hair, wearing a gorgeous outfit. At the most, the man may be gesturing discreetly, or smiling in the demure way that a man like that might smile after, say, telling the supermodel at the next table no thanks he has to catch an early-morning flight to Milan. But that's all. The beautiful face and the clothes tell the whole story. The Dockers ads, though, are almost exactly the opposite. There's no face. The camera is jumping around so much that it's tough to concentrate on the clothes. And instead of stark simplicity, the fashion image is overlaid with a constant, confusing pattern. It's almost as if the Dockers ads weren't primarily concerned with clothes at all—and in fact that's exactly what Levi's intended. What the company had discovered, in its research, was that baby-boomer men felt that the chief thing missing from their lives was male friendship. Caught between the demands of the families that many of them had started in the eighties and career considerations that had grown more onerous, they felt they had lost touch with other men. The purpose of the ads—the chatter, the lounging around, the quick cuts—was simply to conjure up a place where men could put on one-hundred-percent-cotton khakis and reconnect with one another. In the original advertising brief, that imaginary place was dubbed Dockers World.
>
> — MALCOLM GLADWELL, "LISTENING TO KHAKIS"

First Gladwell notes the differences in two kinds of fashion ads aimed at men. There are the high fashion ads and the Dockers ads. In the first of these, the word "beautiful" repeats twice as part of a strand (including "gorgeous," "interesting," "supermodel," "demure"). The writer then poses traits of the Dockers ads as an opposing strand. Instead of a beautiful face there is no face; instead of "gorgeous outfit," "it's tough to concentrate on the clothes." These oppositions cause the writer to make his interpretive leap, that the Dockers ads "weren't primarily concerned with clothes at all" and that this was intentional.

In the student essay, below, Lesley Stephen develops a key contrast between two thinkers, Sigmund Freud and Michel Foucault, by noticing the different meanings that each attaches to some of the same key words. THE METHOD helps to locate the key terms and to define them by seeing what other words they suggest (strands).

Freud defines civilization as serving two main purposes. The first is to protect men against nature, and the second is to adjust their mutual relations. Freud seems to offer returning to nature as a possible solution for men's sexual freedom. I think Freud might believe that returning to nature by rejecting civilization could bring about sexual freedom, but that sexual freedom does not necessarily equal happiness.

Foucault completely defies Freud's idea that sexuality is natural and that repression exists as anti-sexuality. He believes that everything is created from discourse; nothing is natural. And because nothing is natural, nothing is repressed. There is no such thing as a natural desire; if the desire exists, it is because it is already part of the discourse.

By focusing on repetitions of the words "nature" and "natural" and then seeing what goes with what, the writer creates a succinct and revealing comparison.

Doing THE METHOD on a Poem

Here is an example of how one might do THE METHOD on a piece of text—in this case—a student poem. We use a poem because it is compact and so allows us to illustrate efficiently how THE METHOD works.

Brooklyn Heights, 4:00 A.M.
Dana Ferrelli

sipping a warm forty oz.

Coors Light on a stoop in

Brooklyn Heights. I look

across the street, in the open window;

Blonde bobbing heads, the

smack of a jump rope, laughter

of my friends breaking

beer bottles. Putting out their

burning filters on the #5 of

a hopscotch court.

We reminisce of days when we were

Fat, pimple faced—

look how far we've come. But tomorrow

a little blonde girl will

pick up a Marlboro Light filter, just to play.

And I'll buy another forty, because

that's how I play now.

Reminiscing about how far I've come

Here are the steps of THE METHOD, applied to the preceding poem.

1. *Words that repeat exactly:* forty × 2, blonde × 2, how far we've (I've) come × 2, light × 2, reminisce, reminiscing × 2, filter, filters × 2, Brooklyn Heights × 2

2. *Strands:* jump rope, laughter, play, hopscotch (connecting logic: childhood games, the carefree worldview of childhood), Coors Light, Marlboro Light filters, beer bottles (connecting logic: drugs, adult "games," escapism?),

   Smack, burning, breaking (connecting logic: violent actions and powerful emotion: burning)

3. *Binary oppositions:* how far we've come/how far I've come (a move from plural to singular, from a sense of group identity to isolation, from group values to a more individual consideration)

   Burning/putting out

   Coors Light, Marlboro Lights/jump rope, hopscotch

   How far I've come (two meanings of *far?*, one positive, one not)

   Heights/stoop

   Present/past

4. *Ranked repetitions, strands and binaries plus paragraph explaining the choice of one of these as central to understanding.*

   Most important repetitions: forty, how far we've/I've come

   Most important strands: childhood games and adulthood games

   Most important binaries: Burning versus putting out, open and laughter versus putting out

5. *Anomaly:* Fat, pimple faced—

   This detail does not fit with the otherwise halcyon treatment of childhood.

ANALYSIS (HEALTHY PARAGRAPHS) The repetition of *forty* (forty ounce beer) is interesting. It signals a certain weariness—perhaps with a kind of pun on forty to suggest middle age and thus the speaker's concern about moving toward being older in a way that seems stale and flat. The beer, after all, is warm—which is not the best state for a beer to be in, once opened, if it is to retain its taste and character. Forty ounces of beer might also suggest excess—"supersizing."

The most important (or at least most interesting) binary opposition is *burning versus putting out.* This binary seems to be part of a more intense strand in the poem, one that runs counter to the weary prospect of moving on toward a perhaps lonely ("how far *I've* come") middle-aged feeling. Burning goes with breaking and the smack of the jump rope, and even putting out (a strand), if we visualize putting out not just as fire extinguished but in terms of putting a cigarette out by pushing the burning end of it into something (the number 5 on the Hopscotch court). The poem's language has a violent and passionate edge to it, even though the violent words are not always in a violent context (for example, the smack of the jump rope).

This is a rather melancholy poem in which, perhaps, the speaker is mourning the passing, the "putting out" of the passion of youth ("burning"). In the poem's more obvious binary—the opposition of childhood games to more "adult" ones— the same melancholy plays itself out, making the poem's refrain-like repetition of "how far I've come" ring with unhappy irony. The little blonde girl is an image of the speaker's own past self (since the poem talks about reminiscing), and the speaker mourns that little girl's (her own) passing into a more uncertain and less carefree state. It is 4:00 A.M. in Brooklyn Heights—just about the end of night, the darkest point perhaps before the beginning of morning. But windows are open, suggesting possibility, so things are not all bad. The friends make noise together, break bottles together, revisit hopscotch square 5 together, and contemplate moving on.

Note: the reference to "Fat, pimple faced—" in the poem is an anomaly in the otherwise idealized representation of childhood in terms of games and laughter. The young women in the poem are sad that they can re-enact childhood games but they can't recover childhood's innocent happiness. The anomaly usefully reminds us of adults' desire to idealize the past by forgetting that the past has pimples as well as hopscotch. "Fat, pimple faced—" goes with what we might also be able to see as an anomaly—the open windows in what the poem otherwise describes as a steady closing down of hope.

Notice how this discussion moves from analysis of a key repetition and a key binary to a series of claims about the meaning of the poem as a whole. Writing about the data that THE METHOD has gathered leads us to see how the significant parts are related (Move 2 of the Five Analytical Moves).

TRY THIS 1.8: Doing THE METHOD on a Poem

Go online and locate "The Crowd at the Ballgame" by William Carlos Williams (a famous American poet). A useful site for finding poems is poetryfoundation .org. Do THE METHOD on the poem individually or in groups, using our treatment of "Brooklyn Heights, 4:00 A.M." as a model. Be sure to do the steps, including the healthy paragraph, in writing.

Troubleshooting THE METHOD

THE METHOD is a means to an end, not an end in itself. Deciding what goes with what is an analytical move. It's not just listing. One aim of THE METHOD is to induce you to pay more attention, and a different kind of attention, to what you are studying.

Don't let the procedure turn into tedious or superficial data-gathering. Look for the *interesting* repetitions, strands and binaries, not just the most prevalent ones. Let this activity generate ideas.

In applying THE METHOD to longer texts, don't try to cover everything, and don't start making your lists until you have done a chunk of the reading. After all, you can't be expected to recognize a repetition in an extended essay until it has reappeared several times. Keep informal lists in the margins as you read, or in the inside cover of a book. When you become aware of an opposition, you can mark it with a +/− next to the paragraph where you were struck.

THE METHOD is designed to prompt thinking. You should be able to offer your reasons for why you think a given repetition or strand is most important. You should be able to express what issue you think is at stake in the organizing contrast you choose as most important.

As you look over your binaries, choose the binary that you think organizes the thinking in the subject as a whole—the *organizing* contrast. Which binary contains, implicitly or explicitly, the central issue or question or problem that is being addressed?

To make THE METHOD spark ideas, remember to ask So what? as a way of moving from observation to implication.

TRY THIS 1.9: Do THE METHOD on a Visual Image

We recommend using an image by Adrian Tomine, a frequent contributor to *The New Yorker* magazine and a graphic novelist. Use Google Images for "New Yorker covers + Tomine" to obtain a range of possibilities. We suggest his August 24, 2009 cover, "Double Feature"—an image of a crowd at dusk beneath the Brooklyn Bridge. Then, for homework repeat the exercise alone, using a second Tomine cover—we suggest the November 8, 2004 cover, "Missed Connection," featuring a man and a woman looking at each other from passing subway cars.

TRY THIS 1.10: Do THE METHOD on a Reading

Select any article from *Arts & Letters Daily* (aldaily.com), and do THE METHOD on it. Or use THE METHOD on the front page of the newspaper, a speech from the American Rhetoric website, or perhaps a series of editorials on the same subject. You can work with as little as a few paragraphs or as much as an entire article or chapter or book.

Move 5: Keep Reformulating Questions and Explanations

The preceding four analytical moves can be thought of in question form. The process of posing and answering such questions—the analytical process—is one of trial and error. Learning to write well is largely a matter of learning how to frame questions. Whatever questions you ask, the answers you propose won't always turn out to be answers, but may, instead, produce more questions. It follows that you need to keep the process of understanding open, often longer than feels comfortable. You do so by repeatedly reformulating your questions and explanations and going back to the original data for nourishment.

The following three groups of questions (organized according to the analytical moves they're derived from) are typical of what goes on in an analytical writer's head as he or she attempts to understand a subject. These questions will work with almost anything that you want to think about. As you will see, the questions are geared toward helping you locate and try on explanations for the meaning of various patterns of details.

> Which details seem significant? Why?
> What does the detail mean?
> What else might it mean?
>> (Moves: Define Significant Parts; Make the Implicit Explicit)
> How do the details fit together? What do they have in common?
> What does this pattern of details mean?
> What else might this same pattern of details mean? How else could
>> it be explained?
>> (Move: Look for Patterns)
> What details don't seem to fit? How might they be connected with other
>> details to form a different pattern?
> What does this new pattern mean? How might it cause me to read the
>> meaning of individual details differently?
>> (Moves: Look for Anomalies and Keep Asking Questions)

We conclude this chapter with an analysis of a famous painting that has come to be known as *Whistler's Mother*.

Summing Up: Analyzing *Whistler's Mother*

Throughout the chapter we have emphasized the importance of slowing down leaps to conclusions in order to spend more time dwelling with the data, carefully describing what you notice. We have stressed the importance of focusing on the details, looking for questions rather than answers, and telling yourself you don't understand even when you think you might. We've also said that summary and description are close cousins of and necessary to analysis, but that analysis provides more interpretive thinking—making the implicit explicit.

Key to any kind of analysis is laying out the data, not simply because it keeps the analysis accurate, but also because, crucially, it is in the act of carefully describing a subject that analytical writers often have their best ideas. What might an analysis of Whistler's painting include and why? (see Figure 1.6).

The first step is to describe with care. Look for the painting's significant parts and how they're related (Move 2) and for patterns of repetition and contrast (Move 4). The words you choose to describe your data will contain the germs of your ideas about what the subject means. In moving from description to analysis, scrutinize the language you have chosen, asking, "Why did I choose this word?" and "What ideas are implicit in the language I have used?" This attention to your own language will help you to make the implicit explicit (Move 3).

RMN-Grand Palais/Art Resource, NY

FIGURE 1.6

Arrangement In Grey and Black: The Artist's Mother by James Abbott
McNeill Whistler, 1871

Figure 1.7 is a depiction of this analytical process in outline form.

What does this analysis tell us? It might tell us that the painter's choice
to portray his subject in profile contributes to our sense of her separateness
from us and of her nonconfrontational passivity. We look at her, but she does
not look back at us. Her black dress and the fitted lace cap that obscures
her hair are not only emblems of her self-effacement, shrouds disguising her
identity like her expressionless face, but also the tools of her self-containment and thus of her power to remain aloof from prying eyes.

What is the attraction of this painting (this being one of the questions
that an analysis might ask)? What might draw a viewer to the sight of this
austere, drably attired woman, sitting alone in the center of a mostly blank
space? Perhaps it is the very starkness of the painting, and the mystery of
self-sufficiency at its center, that attracts us.

You may not agree with the terms by which we have summarized the
painting, and thus you may not agree with such conclusions as "the mystery
of self-sufficiency." Nor is it necessary that you agree, because there is no

Data	Analytical Moves	Interpretive Leaps (So What?)
subject in profile, not looking at us	→ make implicit explicit (speculate about what the detail might suggest)	→ figure strikes us as separate, nonconfrontational, passive
folded hands, fitted lace cap, contained hair, expressionless face	→ locate pattern of same or similar detail; make what is implicit in pattern of details explicit	→ figure strikes us as self-contained, powerful in her separateness and self-enclosure— self-sufficient?
patterned curtain and picture versus still figure and blank wall; slightly frilled lace cuffs and ties on cap versus plain black dress	→ locate organizing contrast; make what is implicit in the contrast explicit	→ austerity and containment of the figure made more pronounced by slight contrast with busier, more lively, and more ornate elements and with little picture showing world outside
slightly slouched body position and presence of support for feet	→ anomalies; make what is implicit in the anomalies explicit	→ these details destabilize the serenity of the figure, adding some tension to the picture in the form of slightly uneasy posture and figure's need for support: she looks too long, drooped in on her own spine

© Cengage Learning®

FIGURE 1.7

Summary and Analysis of Whistler's Mother Diagram

single, right answer to what the painting means. But the process of careful observation and description and repeated tries at interpretation by ASKING SO WHAT? has produced claims about what and how the painting communicates that others would at least find reasonable and fair.

Analysis and Personal Associations

Although observations like those offered in the "Interpretive Leaps" column in Figure 1.7 go beyond simple description, they stay with the task of explaining the painting, rather than moving to private associations that the painting might prompt, such as effusions about old age or rocking chairs or the character and situation of the writer's own mother. Such associations could well be valuable unto themselves as a means of prompting a searching piece of expressive writing. They might also help a writer to interpret some feature of the painting that he or she was working to understand. But the writer would not be free to use pieces of his or her personal history as conclusions about what the painting communicates, unless these conclusions could also be reasonably inferred from the painting itself.

Analysis is a creative activity, a fairly open form of inquiry, but its imaginative scope is governed by logic. The hypothetical analysis we have offered is not the only reading of the painting that a viewer might make, because the same pattern of details might lead to different conclusions. But a viewer would not be free to conclude anything he or she wished, such as that the woman is mourning the death of a son or is patiently waiting to die. Such conclusions would be unfounded speculations, since the black dress is not sufficient to support them. Analysis often operates in areas where there is no one right answer, but like summary and argument, it requires the writer to reason from evidence.

Becoming a Detective

As we began this chapter by saying, analysis is a form of detective work. It can surprise us with ideas that our experiences produce once we take the time to listen to ourselves thinking. But analysis is also a discipline; it has rules that govern how we proceed and that enable others to judge the validity of our ideas.

A few rules are worth highlighting here:

1. The range of associations for explaining a given detail or word must be governed by context.

2. It's fine to use your personal reactions as a way into exploring what a subject means, but take care not to make an interpretive leap stretch further than the actual details will support.

3. Because the tendency to transfer meanings from your own life onto a subject can lead you to ignore the details of the subject itself, you need always to be asking yourself: "What other explanations might plausibly account for this same pattern of detail?"

A good analytical thinker needs to be the attentive Dr. Watson to his or her own Sherlock Holmes. That is what the remainder of this book will teach you to do. (See Chapter 5 for more on the rules governing interpretation, again using *Whistler's Mother* as a primary example.)

Assignments: The Analytical Frame of Mind

1. **Do THE METHOD on a Reading.** Look for repetitions, strands, and binaries in the paragraphs below, the opening of an article entitled "The End of Solitude" by William Deresiewicz, which appeared in *The Chronicle of Higher Education* on January 30, 2009 and at http://chronicle.com/article/The-End-of-Solitude/3708. After selecting the repetition, strand, or organizing contrast that you find most important, try writing several paragraphs about it.

What does the contemporary self want? The camera has created a culture of celebrity; the computer is creating a culture of connectivity. As the two technologies converge — *broadband* tipping the Web from text to image, social-networking sites spreading the mesh of interconnection ever wider—the two cultures betray a common impulse. Celebrity and connectivity are both ways of becoming known. This is what the contemporary self wants. It wants to be recognized, wants to be connected: It wants to be visible. If not to the millions, on Survivor or Oprah, then to the hundreds, on Twitter or Facebook. This is the quality that validates us, this is how we become real to ourselves—by being seen by others. The great contemporary terror is anonymity. If Lionel Trilling was right, if the property that grounded the self, in Romanticism, was sincerity, and in modernism it was authenticity, then in *postmodernism* it is visibility.

If you can, visit this article online and include the paragraph that follows as well in your analysis.

2. **Analyze an Image in Relation to Text.** The Adrian Tomine *New Yorker* covers that we referred to in TRY THIS 1.8 could produce a good short paper. You could either do THE METHOD on the two covers in order to write a comparative paper. Or you could do THE METHOD on the Tomine cover called "Double Feature" and the paragraph from "The End of Solitude" above, and write about them comparatively. (Note: the entire article is available online.)

   What do you think Tomine's cover says about the issues raised in "The End of Solitude" by William Deresiewicz? How might Tomine see the issues differently? And how might Deresiewicz interpret Tomine's cover, and So what?

3. **Analyze a Portrait or Other Visual Image.** Locate any portrait, preferably a good reproduction from an art book or magazine, one that shows detail clearly. Then do a version of what we've done with *Whistler's Mother*. Your goal is to produce an analysis of the portrait with the steps we included in analyzing *Whistler's Mother*. First, summarize the portrait, describing accurately its significant details. Do not go beyond a recounting of what the portrait includes; avoid interpreting what these details suggest.

   Then use the various methods offered in this chapter to analyze the data. What repetitions (patterns of same or similar detail) do you see? What organizing contrasts suggest themselves? In light of these patterns of similarity and difference, what anomalies do you then begin to detect? Move from the data to interpretive conclusions.

   This process will produce a set of interpretive leaps, which you may then try to assemble into a more coherent claim of some sort—a short essay about what the portrait "says."

CHAPTER 2

Reading Analytically

Overview Virtually all college-level writing assignments call for students to write about reading and to use writing in order to better understand reading. The chapter suggests skills that will help writers become more active and more confident readers.

The chapter's strategies include a sequence for writing and talking about reading, including POINTING, PARAPHRASE × 3, and PASSAGE-BASED FOCUSED FREEWRITING. The chapter demonstrates how to unearth the logical structure of a reading by UNCOVERING ASSUMPTIONS and TRACKING BINARIES, and it explains how to apply a reading as a lens for understanding other material. For more extended discussion of summary and other traditional reading-based writing assignments, see Chapter 3. On using secondary sources in research-based writing, see Chapter 7.

Becoming Conversant Instead of Reading for the Gist

This chapter will teach you how to do things with readings:

- how to find the questions rather than just the answers,

- how to put key passages from readings into conversation with each other,

- how to use an idea or methodology in a reading in order to generate thinking about something else, and

- how to gain control of complex ideas on your own rather than needing others (such as teachers) to do this work for you.

These tasks require you to change your orientation to reading. How, you might ask, do I make this change, given that I am reading difficult material produced by experts?

The challenge of reading well is to become conversant rather than reading for the gist. Many readers operate under the mistaken impression that they are to read for the gist—for the main point, to be gleaned through a glancing speed-reading. Reading for the gist causes readers to leap to global (and usually unsubstantiated) impressions, attending only superficially to what they are reading. Although there are virtues to skimming, the vast majority of writing tasks that you will encounter in college and in the workplace require your *conversancy* with material that you have read.

To become conversant means that you should be able to:

- talk about the reading conversationally with other people and answer questions about it without having to look everything up, and

- converse with the material—to be in some kind of dialogue with it, to see the questions the material asks, and to pose your own questions about it.

Few people are able to really understand things they read or see without making the language of that material in some way their own. We become conversant, in other words, by finding ways to actively engage material rather than moving passively through it.

If you are to play this more active role in writing about reading, you must accept that you need to:

1. *Learn to speak the language of the text.* Every course is in some sense a foreign language course: if a writer wishes to be heard, he or she needs to acquire the vocabulary of the experts. That's why it's so important to pay attention to the actual words in a reading and to use them when you write.

2. *Treat reading as a physical as well as a mental activity.* Passing your eyes or highlighter over the text or generalizing about it or copying notes from someone else's power point will not teach you the *skills* to become an independent thinker. These activities are too passive; they don't trigger your brain into engaging the material. To get physical with the reading, focus on particular words and sentences, copy them out, restate them, and clarify for yourself what you do and do not understand.

Beyond the Banking Model of Education

The educational theorist Paolo Friere famously criticized a model of education that he compared to banking. In the banking model of education, students are like banks, accepting deposits of information from their teachers and then withdrawing them to give back on exams. Friere argued that an education consisting entirely of "banking"—information in/information out—does not teach thinking. Being able to recite the ideas other people have had does not automatically render a person capable of thinking about these ideas or producing them. So how can a reader accomplish the goal of acquiring new information from a reading while also learning to think about it—to be more than a passive conduit through which ideas pass? In a word, you multitask. The rest of this chapter will offer strategies to help you assimilate the information in a reading as you begin to formulate ways of responding to it. To start, let's look at how the way the information is presented contributes to what it means.

Rejecting the Transparent Theory of Language

Any child psychology textbook will tell you that as we acquire language, we acquire categories that shape our understanding of the world. Words allow us to ask for things, to say what's on our mind. To an enormous extent, we understand the world and our relation to it by working through language.

Considering how central language is in our lives, it's amazing how little we think about words themselves. We tend to assume that things mean simply or singly, but virtually all words have multiple meanings, and words mean differently depending on context. Consider the following examples of memorably silly headlines: "Teacher Strikes Idle Kids," "New Vaccines May Contain Rabies," "Local High School Drop-outs Cut in Half," and "Include Your Children When Baking Cookies" (or if you prefer, "Kids Make Nutritious Snacks"). Language is always getting away from us—in such sentences as "The bandage was wound around the wound," or in the classic, "Time flies like an arrow; fruit flies like a banana." The meanings of words and the kinds of sense a sentence makes are rarely stable.

The transparent theory of language assumes the opposite, that words are more like clear windows opening to a meaning that can be separated from language. It also assumes that the meanings of words are obvious and self-evident. This theory is roundly rejected by linguists and other language specialists. They know that to change a word is inevitably to change meaning. This view, which is known as the constitutive theory of language, holds that what we see as reality is shaped by the words we use. What we say is inescapably a product of how we say it. And so failure to arrest attention on the words themselves causes readers to miss all but the vaguest impression of the ideas that the words constitute.

Seek to Understand the Reading Fairly on Its Own Terms

Most good reading starts by giving the reading the benefit of the doubt: this is known as producing a sympathetic reading, or reading with the grain. This advice applies whether or not you are inclined to agree with the claims in the reading. When you are seeking to entertain the reading on its own terms, first you have to decide to suspend judgment as an act of mind, trying instead to think *with* the piece.

Reading with the grain does not mean passive restatement—just ventriloquizing what the author has to say. A sympathetic reading can and should also be *an active reading*, one in which you as the writer help your reader gain some perspective on the piece. Chapter 1 has already given you some tools for accomplishing this task: NOTICE AND FOCUS (ranking), and THE METHOD to find patterns and uncover tensions (what is opposed to what). These tools allow you to answer the crucial question, "what is at stake in the piece, and why?" And as we will discuss later in this chapter, you also ask the standard rhetorical question, "what is this piece inviting us to think, and by what means?"

This chapter will add several new strategies, beginning with ways of focusing more closely on key words and sentences. But first let us take up briefly what writers are being asked to do when instructed to write a critique of a reading.

How to Write a Critique

We have just said that good reading starts by seeking to understand a piece on its own terms, regardless of your point of view on the subject. Does understanding a piece on its own terms mean that your role as a writer is limited to supportive restatement of what another writer has said?

In a critique, you still are expected to help readers to understand a reading as an author might wish it to be understood, but you are also expected to provide some thinking of your own on the reading. Note that this does not mean your thinking about the subject of the reading, but instead your thinking about the writer's thinking about the subject.

Because people take critique to mean "criticize," they usually assume that they should find ways of being oppositional. An effective critique usually does not sit in judgment. You are not being asked on the model of talk-show, big-opinion culture, to go in and demolish the piece. Critique does not mean to attack. Instead, you are trying to put the piece into some kind of perspective, often more than one possible perspective, for your readers.

It helps to remember that a reading's ways of presenting its ideas (the "how") is part of its content (the "what"). So a good critique includes attention to both what the reading says and how it says it. Here is a list of *some* of the things that you might choose to do in a critique (you can't do them all). These include strategies from Chapter 1 as well as moves you will encounter later in this or subsequent chapters.

- Explain what is at stake in the piece. What, in other words, is opposed to what, and why, according to the writer (implicitly, explicitly, or both) and why does the writer think it matters?

- Determine what the reading seems to wish to accomplish, which is not always the same thing as that which it explicitly argues. Do this in the context of what this chapter will later define as THE PITCH, THE COMPLAINT, AND THE MOMENT.

- Make the implicit explicit. What might the piece be saying that goes beyond what it overtly argues? This is Move #3 of the Five Analytical Moves.

- Try to figure out what the consequences of the piece might be. That is, if we think in the way that the reading suggests, what might follow? What might we gain? What might we lose?

- Locate the reading in the context of other similar readings as part of an ongoing conversation.

- Consider how well the evidence in the piece seems to support its claims and how well the writer explains her reasons for saying the evidence means what she says it does. See Chapter 4.

- Consider the logical structure of the piece by UNCOVERING ASSUMPTIONS and TRACKING BINARIES, which you will find discussed later in this chapter. In this way you might locate arguments the piece is having with itself, and potentially conflicting or contradictory assumptions upon which the piece is built. Revealing such tensions need not launch an attack on the piece. Rather, it establishes perspective on the way that the reading goes about making its case.

Consider the following rhetorical analysis of a commencement address delivered by novelist David Foster Wallace at Kenyon College in 2005 (later published as "This Is Water"). Notice how the writer uses description in order to arrive at ideas about the speech. Description is essential in a critique, just as it is in any analytical writing. You need to start by offering your reader some significant detail in order to ground your thinking. When you select particular details and call attention to them by describing them, you are likely to begin noticing what these details suggest. Description presents details so that analysis can make them speak.

Consider how the writer of this analysis makes implicit tensions in the speech explicit. As a result, we get some perspective on the character of the speech as a whole and on the character of its writer (*ethos*), which goes beyond simple restatement. We are given some critical distance on the piece, which is what critique does, without inviting us to approve or disapprove.

"I am not the wise old fish" (1).

"Please don't worry that I am getting ready to lecture you about compassion"(2).

"Please don't think that I am giving you moral advice" (5).

"Please don't dismiss it as just some finger-wagging Dr. Laura sermon"(7).

A recurrent feature of the address is the author's imploring his audience ("Please") not to assume that he is offering moral instruction. The sheer repetition of this pattern suggests that he is worried about sounding like a sermonizer, that the writer is anxious about the didacticism of his speech.

But obviously the piece does advance a moral position; it does want us to think about something serious, which is part of its function as a commencement address. What's most interesting is the final apology, offered just as the piece ends (7). Here Wallace appears to shift ground. Rather than denying that he's "the wise old fish" (1), he denies that he is Dr. Laura, or rather, he pleads not to be dismissed as a Dr. Laura. So he's saying, in effect, that we should not see him as a TV personality who scolds ("finger wagging") and offers moral lessons for daily life ("sermon").

Why is he so worried about the didactic function? Obviously, he is thinking of his audience, fearful of appearing to be superior, and fearful that his audience does not want to be preached at. But he cannot resist the didactic impulse the occasion bestows. In these terms, what is interesting is the divided nature of the address: on the one hand, full of parables—little stories with moral intent—and on the other hand, full of repeated denials of the very moral impulse his narratives and the occasion itself generically decree.

VOICES FROM ACROSS THE CURRICULUM

What Do We Mean by Critical Reading? A Music Professor Speaks

As a first step, we consider what we mean by a "critical reading." Because the term itself has become so ingrained in our consciousness, we rarely think critically about what it means. So, we discuss moving beyond a summary of the content and cursory judgment. I ask students to take notes on each reading (content and commentary) and conclude with three points. These points may include a main idea of the article or a part of the author's argument they found particularly interesting. We try to locate insights into the author's reason for writing the essay and rhetorical gestures or techniques used by the author to influence the reader.

Does the author make his or her objectives and biases explicit? If not, we examine the rhetorical strategies authors employ to convince us of their objectivity. We observe the ways that language colors the presentation of facts—how "a bitter civil war that pitted the slaveholding Southern states against the rest of the country" was probably not written by an author sympathetic to the Confederacy.

Much of our time is spent investigating how authors construct their narratives: the way the argument is formed and its ideological position. These ways of viewing the reading help us to move beyond restatement, delay judgment, and evaluate readings on a more sophisticated level.

—TED CONNER, PROFESSOR OF MUSIC

Focus on Individual Sentences

Analyzing needs to be anchored. Anchoring to a general impression—a global sense of what the reading is about—is like putting a hook in a cloud. There is nothing specific to think about, to rephrase, to nudge toward implications or back to assumptions. The best way to remember what you read and to have ideas about it is to start with the local: focus on individual sentences and short passages, and build up a knowledge base from there.

It does not matter which sentences you start with. What matters is to choose sentences that strike you as especially interesting, revealing, or strange (See NOTICE AND FOCUS, Chapter 1.) Good reading is slow reading: it stops your forward momentum long enough to allow you to dwell on individual sentences and make the effort necessary to understand them.

A second and related way that people neglect the actual words is that they approach the reading *looking to react*. They are so busy looking to respond to other people's statements that they don't listen to what the other person is saying. A recent article on reading by the literary and educational theorist Robert Scholes suggests that people read badly because they substitute for the words on the page some association or predetermined idea that the words accidentally trigger in them. As a result, they replay their own perceptions rather than taking in what the writer is actually saying. (See Robert Scholes, "The Transition to College Reading," *Pedagogy*, volume 2, number 2, Duke UP, 2002, pp. 165–172.)

We will now survey a few techniques for focusing on individual sentences.

Pointing

Pointing is a practice (associated with two writing theorists and master teachers, Peter Elbow and Sheridan Blau) in which members of a group take turns reading sentences aloud. Pointing provides a way of summarizing without generalizing, and it is one of the best ways to build community and to stimulate discussion (see Figure 2.1).

1	**Select sentences from a reading that you are willing to voice.**
2	**Take turns reading individual sentences aloud.** No one raises hands or comments on the sentences during the pointing. Read only one of your chosen sentences at a time. Later in the session, you may read again.
3	**Let the recitation build.** Some sentences repeat as refrains; others segue or answer previous sentences. Pointing usually lasts about five minutes and ends more or less naturally, when people no longer have sentences they wish to read.

© 2015 Cengage Learning

FIGURE 2.1
Pointing

Pointing stirs our memories about the particular language of a piece. In reading aloud and hearing others do it, you hear key words and discover questions you'd not seen before; and the range of possible starting points for getting at what is central in the reading inevitably multiplies. Pointing is an antidote for the limiting assumption that a reading has only one main idea. It also remedies the tendency of group discussion to veer into general impressions and loose associations.

Using Quotation

Quoting key words and sentences from a reading keeps you focused on specific words and ideas rather than general impressions. It is not enough, however, to quote key sentences from a reading without discussing what you take them to mean, for what a sentence means is never self-evident. A mantra of this book is that analytical writers quote *in order to* analyze. That is, they follow up quotation by voicing what specifically they understand that quote to mean. The best way to arrive at that meaning is to paraphrase. (Some disciplines, it must be acknowledged, refrain from quoting and include only the paraphrase.) In any case, a quote cannot serve as your "answer" by itself; you can't use a quote in place of your own active explanation of what a reading is saying. Quotes only help you to focus and launch that explanation. (For more on this subject, see Chapter 7.)

Paraphrase × 3

Paraphrasing is one of the simplest and most overlooked ways of discovering ideas and stimulating interpretation. Like POINTING, PARAPHRASE × 3 seeks to locate you in the local, the particular, and the concrete rather than the global, the overly general and the abstract. Rather than make a broad claim about what a sentence or passage says, a paraphrase stays much closer to the actual words.

The word *paraphrase* means to put one phrase next to ("para") another phrase. When you recast a sentence or two—finding the best synonyms you can think of for the original language, translating it into a parallel statement— you are thinking about what the original words mean. The use of "× 3" (times 3) in our label is a reminder to paraphrase key words more than once, not settling too soon for a best synonym (see Figure 2.2).

1	**Select a short passage** (as little as a single sentence or even a phrase) from whatever you are studying that you think is interesting, perhaps puzzling, and especially useful for understanding the material. Assume you *don't* understand it completely, even if you think you do.
2	**Find synonyms for all of the key terms.** Don't just go for the gist, a loose approximation of what was said. Substitute language virtually word-for-word to produce a parallel version of the original statement.
3	**Repeat this rephrasing several times** (we suggest three). This will produce a range of possible implications that the original passage may possess.
4	**Contemplate the various versions you have produced.** Which seem most plausible as restatements of what the original piece intends to communicate?
5	**Decide what you now recognize about the meaning of the original passage.** What do you now recognize about the passage on the basis of your repeated restatements? What now does the passage appear to mean? What implications have the paraphrasings revealed?

© 2015 Cengage Learning

FIGURE 2.2
Paraphrase × 3

When you paraphrase language, whether your own or language you encounter in your reading, you are not just defining terms but opening out the wide range of implications those words inevitably possess. When we read, it is easy to skip quickly over the words, assuming we know what they mean. Yet when people start talking about what particular words mean—the difference, for example, between *assertive* and *aggressive* or the meaning of ordinary words such as *polite* or *realistic* or *gentlemanly*—they usually find less agreement than expected.

Note: Different academic disciplines treat paraphrase somewhat differently. In the humanities, it is essential first to quote an important passage and then to paraphrase it. In the social sciences, however, especially in Psychology, you paraphrase but rarely if ever quote. In more advanced writing in the social sciences, paraphrase serves the purpose of producing the literature review— survey of relevant research—that forms the introduction to reports.

How Paraphrase × 3 Unlocks Implications: An Example Like the "So what?" question, paraphrasing is an effective way of bringing out implications, meanings that are there in the original but not overt. And especially if you paraphrase the same passage repeatedly, you will discover which of the words are most "slippery"—elusive, hard to define simply and unambiguously.

Let's look at a brief example of Paraphrase × 3. The sentence comes from a book entitled *The Literature Workshop* by Sheridan Blau. We have paraphrased it three times.

> "A conviction of certainty is one of the most certain signs of ignorance and may be the best operational definition of stupidity" (213).

1. Absence of doubt is a clear indication of cluelessness and is perhaps the top way of understanding the lack of intelligence.
2. A feeling of being right is one of the most reliable indexes of lack of knowledge and may show in action the meaning of mental incapacity.
3. Being confident that you are correct is a foolproof warning that you don't know what's going on, and this kind of confidence may be an embodiment of foolishness.

Having arrived at these three paraphrases, we can use them to explore what they suggest—i.e., their implications. Here is a short list. Once you start paraphrasing, you discover that there's a lot going on in this sentence.

- One implication of the sentence is that as people come to know more and more, they feel less confident about what they know.

- Another is that ignorance and stupidity are probably not the same thing, though they are often equated.

- Another is that there's a difference between feeling certain about something and being aware of this certainty as a conviction.

- Another implication is that stupidity is hard to define—perhaps it can only be defined in practice, "operationally," and not as an abstract concept.

As we paraphrased, we were struck by the repetition of "certainty" in "certain," which led us to wonder about the tone of the sentence. Tone may be understood as the implicit point of view, the unspoken attitude of the statement towards itself and its readers. The piece overtly attacks "a conviction of certainty" as "a sign of ignorance" and perhaps ("may be") "a definition of stupidity." So by implication, being less sure you are right would be a sign of wisdom. But the statement itself seems extremely sure of itself, brimming with confidence: it asserts "a certain sign."

One implication of this apparent contradiction is that we are meant to take the statement with a grain of salt—that is, read it as poking fun at itself (ironically), demonstrating the very attitude it advises us to avoid.

TRY THIS 2.1: Experiment with Paraphrase × 3

Recast the substantive language of the following statements using PARAPHRASE × 3:

- "I am entitled to my opinion."

- "We hold these truths to be self-evident."

- "That's just common sense."

What do you come to understand about these remarks as a result of paraphrasing? Which words, for example, are most slippery (that is, difficult to define and thus rephrase) and why?

It is interesting to note, by the way, that Thomas Jefferson originally wrote the words "sacred and undeniable" in his draft of the Declaration of Independence, instead of "self-evident." So what?

TRY THIS 2.2: Paraphrase and Implication

Consider for a moment an assignment a former student of ours, Sean Heron, gave to a class of high school students he was student-teaching during a unit on the Civil War. He asked students to paraphrase three times the following sentence: "The South left the country." His goal, he reported, was to get them to see that "because language is open to interpretation, and history is conveyed through language, history must also be open to interpretation." Use PARAPHRASE ×3 to figure out how Sean's sentence slants history.

Passage-Based Focused Freewriting

PASSAGE-BASED FOCUSED FREEWRITING increases your ability to learn from what you read. It is probably the single best way to arrive at ideas about what you are reading. The passage-based version differs from regular freewriting (see Chapter 1) by limiting the focus to a piece of text. It prompts in-depth analysis of a representative example, on the assumption that you'll attain a better appreciation of the whole after you've explored how a piece of it works.

The more you practice PASSAGE-BASED FOCUSED FREEWRITING, the better you will get—the easier you will find things to say about your chosen passage. Ask yourself:

- "What one passage in the reading do you think most needs to be discussed—is most useful and interesting for understanding the material?"

- "What one passage seems puzzling, difficult to pin down, anomalous, or even just unclear—and how might this be explained?"

The impromptu nature of PASSAGE-BASED FOCUSED FREEWRITING encourages you to take chances, to think out loud on the page. It invites you to notice what you notice in the moment and take some stabs at what the passage might mean without having to worry about formulating a weighty thesis statement or maintaining consistency. It allows you to worry less about what you don't understand and instead start to work things out as you write.

A lot of great papers start not as outlines but as freewrites, written in class or out (see Figure 2.3).

1	**Choose a short passage to focus on and write about it without stopping for 10 to 20 minutes.** Pick a passage you find interesting and that you probably don't quite understand. Copy out the passage at the beginning of your freewrite. This act will encourage attention to the words and induce you to notice more about the particular features of your chosen passage.
2	**Contextualize the passage.** Where does the passage come from in the text? Of what larger discussion is it a part? Briefly answering these questions will prevent you from taking things out of context.
3	**Focus on what the passage is inviting readers to think**—its point of view—not your point of view of that subject.
4	**Make observations about the passage.** Stay close to the language you've quoted, paraphrasing key phrases and teasing out the possible meanings of these words. Then reflect on what you've come to better understand through paraphrasing. Remember to share your reasoning about what the evidence means.
5	**Address how the passage is representative, how it connects to broader issues in the reading.** Move from your analysis of local details to consider what the work as a whole may plausibly be "saying" about this or that issue or question. It's okay to work with the details for almost the entire time and then press yourself to an interpretive leap with the prompt, "I'm almost out of time but my big point is. . . ."

© 2015 Cengage Learning

FIGURE 2.3

PASSAGE-BASED FOCUSED FREEWRITING

Note: It's okay to work with the details for almost the entire time and then press yourself to an interpretive leap with the prompt, but my big point is. . .

Some Moves to Make in PASSAGE-BASED FOCUSED FREEWRITES PASSAGE-BASED FOCUSED FREEWRITING incorporates a number of the methods we have been discussing in these first two chapters. So, for example:

- it often starts with observations discovered by doing NOTICE AND FOCUS

- it grows out of doing THE METHOD, further developing the paragraph that explains why you chose one repetition, strand or binary as most important

- in analyzing the chosen passage, writers normally paraphrase key words

- and they keep the writing going by insistently ASKING "SO WHAT?" at the ends of paragraphs.

The best PASSAGE-BASED FOCUSED FREEWRITES usually arrive at one or more of the following:

- **Interpretation**, which uses restatement to figure out what the sentence from the text means.

- **Implication**. A useful (and logical) next step is to go after implication. If X or Y is true, then what might follow from it? (Or "So what?")

- **Application**. A passage that is resonant in some way for the reader might lead him or her to write about some practical way of applying the reading—for example, as a lens for understanding other material.

- **Assumptions**. We lay out implications by moving forward (so to speak). We unearth assumptions by moving backwards. If a text asks us to believe X, what else must it already believe? From what unstated assumptions, in other words, would X follow?

- **Queries**. What questions, what interpretive difficulties and struggles are raised by the reading?

Notice how the writers use these moves in the examples that follow.

From PASSAGE-BASED FOCUSED FREEWRITE to Formal Essay It is often productive to take a focused freewrite and type it, revising and further freewriting until you have filled the inevitable gaps in your thinking that the time limit has created. (One colleague of ours has students revise and expand in a different font, so both can see how the thinking is evolving.) Eventually, you can build up, through a process of accretion, the thinking for an entire paper in this way.

An especially useful way of making PASSAGE-BASED FOCUSED FREEWRITING productive academically is to freewrite for fifteen minutes every day on a different passage as you move through a book. If, for example, you are discussing a book over four class periods, prepare for each class by giving fifteen minutes to a passage before you attend. You will not only discover things to say, but also you will begin to write your way to an essay.

A way to get from a freewrite to an essay is to keep starting new freewrites from the best ideas in your earlier ones. Try putting an asterisk in the margin next to your best idea or question, and start another PASSAGE-BASED FOCUSED FREEWRITE from there.

PASSAGE-BASED FOCUSED FREEWRITING: An Example Below is an example of a student's exploratory writing on an essay by the twentieth-century African-American writer Langston Hughes. The piece is a twenty-minute reflection on two excerpts. Most notable about this piece, perhaps, is the sheer number of interesting ideas. That may be because the writer continually returns to the language of the original quotes for inspiration. She is not restricted by maintaining a single and consistent thread. Notice, however, that as the freewrite progresses, a primary focus (on the second of her two quotes) seems to emerge.

Passages from "The Negro Artist and the Racial Mountain" by Langston Hughes

"But jazz to me is one of the inherent expressions of negro life in America; the eternal tom-tom beating in the Negro soul—the tom-tom of revolt against weariness in a white world, a world of subway trains, and work, work, work; the tom-tom of joy and laughter, and pain swallowed in a smile. Yet the Philadelphia clubwoman is ashamed to say that her race created it and she does not like me to write about it. The old subconscious "white is best" runs through her mind. . . . And now she turns up her nose at jazz and all its manifestations—likewise almost everything else distinctly racial."

"We build our temples for tomorrow, strong as we know how, and we stand on top of the mountain, free within ourselves."

Langston Hughes's 1926 essay on the situation of the Negro artist in America sets up some interesting issues that are as relevant today as they were in Hughes's time. Interestingly, the final sentence of the essay ("We build our temples. . .") will be echoed some four decades later by the Civil Rights leader, Martin Luther King, but with a different spin on the idea of freedom. Hughes writes, "we stand on top of the mountain, free within ourselves." King says, "Free at last, free at last, my God almighty, we're free at last." King asserts an opening out into the world—a freeing of black people, finally, from slavery and then another century of oppression.

Hughes speaks of blacks in a more isolated position—"on top of the mountain" and "within ourselves." Although the mountain may stand for a height from which the artist can speak, it is hard to be heard from the top of mountains. It is one thing to be free. It is another to be free within oneself. What does this phrase mean? If I am free within myself I am at least less vulnerable to those who would restrict me from without. I can live with their restrictions. Mine is an inner freedom. Does inner freedom empower artists? Perhaps it does. It may allow them to say what they want and not worry about what others say or think. This is one thing that Hughes seems to be calling for. But he is also worried about lack of recognition of Negro artists, not only by whites but by blacks. His use of the repeated phrase, tom-tom, is interesting in this respect. It, like the word "mountain," becomes a kind of refrain in the essay—announcing both a desire to rise above the world and its difficulties (mountain) and a desire to be heard (tom-tom and mountain as pulpit).

The idea of revolt, outright rebellion, is present but subdued in the essay. The tom-tom is a "revolt against weariness" and also an instrument for expressing "joy and laughter." The tom-tom also suggests a link with a past African and probably Native American culture—communicating by drum and music and dance. White culture in the essay stands for a joyless world of "work work work." This is something I would like to think about more, as the essay seems to link the loss of soul with the middle and upper classes, both black and white.

And so the essay seeks to claim another space among those he calls "the low down folks, the so-called common element." Of these he says ". . .they do not particularly care whether they are like white folks or anybody else. Their joy runs, bang! into ecstasy. Their religion soars to a shout. Work maybe a little today, rest a little tomorrow. Play awhile. Sing awhile. O, let's dance!" In these lines Hughes the poet clearly appears. Does he say then that the Negro artist needs to draw from those of his own people who are the most removed from middle class American life? If I had more time, I would start thinking here about Hughes's use of the words "race" and "racial". . . . (Reprinted with permission from the June 23, 1926 issue of The Nation. For subscription information, call 1-800-333-8536. Portions of each week's Nation magazine can be accessed at http://www.thenation.com.)

PASSAGE-BASED FOCUSED FREEWRITING: Another Example PASSAGE-BASED FOCUSED FREEWRITING is especially well-suited to doing rhetorical analysis, as in the following example. As we explained in Chapter 1, rhetorical analysis seeks to understand how a writer's word choice reveals his or her way of appealing to a target audience. Sometimes in-class writings are done in response to a prompt. The prompt for this freewrite was, "How does Obama's first inaugural address compare with his election night victory speech?"

> What was most interesting to me about Obama's inaugural speech was his use of the collective first person—"we," "our," "us," etc.—as opposed to the singular "I." This is especially different from his victory speech, which did make use of the singular "I" and addressed the audience as "you." These pronoun choices are actually very conducive to the tone of each speech. Obama's victory speech was a *victory* speech—it was meant to be joyful, hopeful, optimistic, and, of course, thankful… so every use of "you" is not accusatory. but rather congratulatory and proud—e.g. "this is because of you," "you have done this," "this is your victory."

> On the other hand, Obama's inaugural speech was by and large a more somber piece of writing—as the President said to George Stephanopolous, he wanted to capture that moment in history as exactly as possible. "You" here is not the American public as in the victory speech; rather, "you" is any "enemy" of America. And "I," it seems, has become "we." This choice automatically makes Obama the voice of society, as though speaking for every American. This is a really subtle but smart choice to make, because the listener or reader is hearing everything he says as his or her own position. Using that collective first person also puts Obama on the same level as everyone else, and when he does blame America for its own problems, the "our's" and "we's" soften the blow. The "you's" here are harsh and accusatory but meant for that great, terrible, unnamed enemy to "our" freedom and happiness.

> I found a lot more obvious echoes to Lincoln in this speech as compared to the victory speech, coupled with earth imagery—for example, "we cannot hallow this ground" (Lincoln) vs. "what the cynics fail to understand is that the ground has shifted" (Obama). This ties America to the actual physical land. It romanticizes and makes permanent the ideas of our country – a nice setting behind all of the nation's troubles—while simultaneously adding to the so-desired degree of "timelessness" of Obama's first inaugural address.

You can sense the writer, Molly Harper, gathering steam here as she begins to make connections in her evidence, yet her rhetorical analysis got started from simple observation of Obama's pronouns and then the significance of the contrast between them in the two speeches she is comparing.

TRY THIS 2.3: Do a Passage-Based Focused Freewrite

Select a passage from any of the material that you are reading and copy it at the top of the page. Remember to choose the passage in response to the question, "What is the single sentence that I think it is most important for us to discuss and why?" Then do a twenty-minute focused freewrite, applying the steps offered above. Discover what you think by seeing what you say.

TRY THIS 2.4: Writing & Reading with Others: A Sequence of Activities

1. Spend 5–10 minutes pointing on some piece of reading. Remember that no one should comment on his or her choice of sentences during the pointing exercise.

2. Without pausing for discussion, spend 10 minutes doing a PASSAGE-BASED FOCUSED FREEWRITE on a sentence or several similar sentences from the reading. It is important to write nonstop and to keep writing throughout the appointed time.

3. Volunteers should then take turns reading all or part of their freewrites aloud to the group without comment. It is useful for people to read, rather than describe or summarize, what they wrote. As each person reads, listeners should jot down words and phrases that catch their attention.

4. After each freewrite is read, listeners call out what they heard in the freewrite by responding to the question, "What did you hear?"

Keep a Commonplace Book

Professional writers have long kept commonplace books—essentially, records of their reading. Most such books consist primarily of quotations that the writers have found striking and memorable. This practice is closely related to POINTING, PARAPHRASE × 3, and PASSAGE-BASED FOCUSED FREEWRITING.

The word "place" comes from the Latin *locus* in classical rhetoric and is related to places that rhetoricians thought of as reliable starting points from which a writer could launch arguments. A commonplace book is a collection of ideas, a storehouse for thinking that a writer might later draw on to stimulate his or her own writing.

The goal of keeping a commonplace book in a course is to bring you closer to the language you find most interesting, which you inscribe in your memory as you copy it onto the page. (Aim for two quotations with citation from each reading.) It's remarkable what you will notice about a sentence if you copy it out, rather than just underlining or highlighting it. Moreover, you will find yourself remembering the original language that has struck you most forcefully in the reading. That way you can continue to ponder key words and phrases and to stay engaged, almost physically, with what the writers have said.

In addition to being a record of your reading, the commonplace book is also a record of your thinking about the reading. Try to write a sentence or two after most of your quotes, noting what you find of interest there, perhaps paraphrasing key terms. Alternatively, you might append a paragraph after all of your quotes from the reading, responding to them as a group. Remember not to judge the passages you select in like-dislike terms.

Situate the Reading Rhetorically

There is no such thing as "just information." Virtually all readings possess what speech-act theorists call "illocutionary force," by which is meant the goal of an utterance. Everything you read, to varying degrees, is aware of you, the audience, and is dealing with you in some way.

One of the most productive ways of analyzing a reading is to consider the frame within which a piece is presented: who its intended audience is, what it seeks to persuade that audience about, and how the writer presents himself or herself to appeal to that audience. Readings virtually never treat these questions explicitly, and thus, it is a valuable analytical move to infer a reading's assumptions about audience.

Find the Pitch, the Complaint, and the Moment

An element of situating a reading rhetorically is to locate what it seeks to accomplish and what it is set against at a given moment in time. We address these concerns as a quest to find what we call THE PITCH, THE COMPLAINT, AND THE MOMENT:

- THE PITCH, what the piece wishes you to believe.

- THE COMPLAINT, what the piece is reacting to or worried about.

- THE MOMENT, the historical and cultural context within which the piece is operating.

Here's a bit more on each.

THE PITCH: *A reading is an argument*, a presentation of information that makes a case of some sort, even if the argument is not explicitly stated. Look for language that reveals the position or positions the piece seems interested in having you adopt.

THE COMPLAINT: *A reading is a reaction to some situation,* some set of circumstances that the piece has set out to address, even though the writer may not say so openly. An indispensable means of understanding someone else's writing is to figure out what seems to have caused the person to write the piece in the first place. Writers write, presumably, because they think *something* needs to be addressed. What is that something? Look for language in the piece that reveals the writer's starting point. If you can find the position or situation he or she is worried about and possibly trying to correct, you will more easily locate the pitch, the position the piece asks you to accept.

THE MOMENT: *A reading is a response to the world conditioned by the writer's particular moment in time.* In your attempt to figure out not only what a piece says but also where it is coming from (the causes of its having been written in the first place and the positions it works to establish), history is significant. When was the piece written? Where? What else was going on at the time that might have shaped the writer's ideas and attitudes?

Rhetoricians sometimes use a term from classical rhetoric, *kairos*, for what this book calls the moment. This Greek word has been translated roughly as "the right time." Another useful term for the concept of the moment is exigence, which refers to a writer's reasons for writing, such as a problem that requires immediate attention.

The Pitch, the Complaint, and the Moment: **Two Brief Examples** Here are two examples of student writing in response to the request that they locate THE PITCH, THE COMPLAINT, AND THE MOMENT for a famous essay in the field of Composition and Rhetoric, "Inventing the University" by David Bartholomae.

> Bartholomae's complaint seems to center around the idea that writing is typically taught at a grammatical, not intellectual, level. "Basic" writers are identified by their sentence level compositional errors, not by the content of their ideas or ability to present a complex argument. Bartholomae argues that students must be drawn into the language and mindset of academia before they have the authority to confidently expand upon more complicated ideas. Students are expected to fluently participate in academic discourse long before they have the authority to pull it off with ease. Therefore, students should be familiarized with the world of academia and led through the preliminary steps towards becoming proficient in its language. This is the only way to make them more authoritative writers.

And here is another example that treats the moment in particular:

> The moment, or the specific time in which the essay was written, offers some valuable insight into what might have shaped Bartholomae's perspective. First, it is important to note the other writers and thinkers Bartholomae cites throughout the essay. Take the author's frequent mention of writer Pat Bizzell whom Bartholomae deems "one of the most important scholars now writing on 'basic writers'" and whom he recognizes as "owing a great debt to." He credits Bizzell with seeing how difficult it is for young writers to learn the complex vocabularies and conventions of academic discourse.

> There are most likely other, more broadly cultural, influences at work as well, such as the American political scene in 1985. In 1984 Ronald Reagan was re-elected president. His presidency and the conservative climate it fostered sparked change in Americans' attitude toward education. Reagan's policies mandated spending cuts and, it can reasonably be assumed, invited certain anti-academic and more pre-professional attitudes. In this moment, then, Bartholomae's concerns about higher education and the need for students to gain access into the privileged world of the educated begins to make more sense.

Audience Analysis: A Brief Example Consider the following paragraph of student writing on the same essay, this time focused on how the essay's author establishes his relationship with his target audience. Here is the assignment the writer was responding to: Write a brief analysis of the essay's rhetoric—the various methods it employs to gain acceptance with its target audience. a) Who is the target audience? How can you tell? Cite and analyze evidence. b) What decisions has the author made on how best to "sell" his argument to this audience? How do you know?

> Bartholomae often uses the inclusive "us" to describe academia, putting the reader (presumably, academics) above the level of those being discussed. Students must be taught "to speak our language, to speak as we do, to try on the peculiar ways of knowing, selecting, evaluating, reporting, concluding and arguing that define the discourse of our community" (3). He effectively builds up the reader, perhaps making him or her more open to absorbing the argument that follows. He refrains from

criticizing, including his audience in his idea and putting them on the same level as he is. He refers to the students as "our students" and writes almost as though the reader is separate from any flaws in the current system. He writes to colleagues, with the tone of one sharing something new and interesting.

TRY THIS 2.5: Locating THE PITCH AND THE COMPLAINT

Go to aldaily.com (Arts & Letters Daily, the website sponsored by the Chronicle of Higher Education). Locate an article on a topic you find interesting. It should be a substantive piece of thinking, as opposed to an editorial or a piece of popular commentary. Find language that you think reveals THE PITCH and THE COMPLAINT in your chosen article. Type out these sentences and be ready to explain your choices.

Focus on the Structure of Thinking in a Reading

One reason readers get lost is because they lack perspective: they're trying so hard to understand what a text is saying word by word and sentence by sentence that, as the old saying goes, they can't see the forest for the trees. It can often be immensely useful to read for the larger cognitive structure of a piece, and two of the best ways to see this structure are to focus on its underlying assumptions or to track its use of binary oppositions. The first uncovers its premises; the second reveals its preoccupations. (For more on logical analysis, see Chapter 4, Reasoning from Evidence to Claims.)

UNCOVERING ASSUMPTIONS

To read well requires you to see the writer's reasoning process, especially the assumptions (the premises) upon which the writer's thinking rests. An assumption is an underlying belief from which other statements spring. Assumptions are often left unstated, which is why they need to be uncovered.

UNCOVERING ASSUMPTIONS is a version of Move 3 of the Five Analytical Moves from Chapter 1: it renders the implicit explicit. But in this case, what is revealed is not what follows from a given statement, but rather, what precedes it.

The ability to UNCOVER ASSUMPTIONS is a powerful analytical procedure to learn. It gives you insight into the root, the basic givens that a piece of writing has assumed are true. When you locate assumptions in a text, you understand the text better—where it's coming from, what else it believes that is more fundamental than what it is overtly declaring. The essential move is to ask, *"Given its overt claim, what must this reading also already believe?"* To answer this question you need to make inferences from the primary claims to the ideas that underlie them. In effect, you are reasoning backwards, reinventing the chain of thinking that led the writer to the position you are now analyzing (see Figure 2.4).

The practice of UNCOVERING ASSUMPTIONS will also help you to develop and revise your own work. When you work back to your own premises, you will often find what else you believe, at a more basic level, that you did not realize you believed.

1	**Determine the key terms in a statement and paraphrase them.**
2	**Ask what assumptions the statement rests on**, the implicit ideas underlying it that the writer seems to assume to be true.
3	**Consider how these underlying assumptions contribute to your understanding of the reading as a whole.**

© 2015 Cengage Learning

FIGURE 2.4

UNCOVERING ASSUMPTIONS

UNCOVERING ASSUMPTIONS: An Example Consider the claim, "Tax laws benefit the wealthy."

We might paraphrase the claim as "The rules for paying income tax give rich people monetary advantages" or "The rules for paying income tax help the rich get richer."

Now let's look at the implicit ideas that the claim assumes to be true:

Tax laws don't treat people equally.

Tax laws may have unintended consequences.

If we assume that the speaker is worried about tax laws possibly benefitting the wealthy, then a few more assumptions can be inferred:

Tax laws shouldn't benefit anybody.

Tax laws shouldn't benefit those who are already advantaged.

This process of definition will help you see the key concepts upon which the claim depends. Regardless of the position you might adopt—attacking tax laws, defending them, showing how they actually benefit everyone, or whatever—you would risk arguing blindly if you failed to question what the purpose of tax law is in the first place.

The wording of this claim seems to conceal an egalitarian premise: the assumption that tax laws should not benefit anyone, or, at least, that they should benefit everyone equally. But what is the purpose of tax laws? Should they redress economic inequities? Should they spur the economy by rewarding those who generate capital? Our point here is that you would need to move your thesis back to this point and test the validity of the assumptions upon which it rests.

TRY THIS 2.6: UNCOVER ASSUMPTIONS Implied by a Statement

In the reference application sent to professors at our college for students who are seeking to enter the student-teaching program, the professor is asked to rank the student from one to four (unacceptable to acceptable) on the following criterion: *"The student uses his/her sense of humor appropriately."* Use the three-step procedure for UNCOVERING ASSUMPTIONS to explore what the authors of this criterion must also already believe—about education, about humor, and about anything else the evidence suggests—if they think this category of evaluation is important.

TRY THIS 2.7: Uncover Assumptions: Fieldwork

You can practice UNCOVERING ASSUMPTIONS with all kinds of material—newspaper editorials, statements you see on billboards, ideas you are studying in your courses, jokes, and so forth. Try a little fieldwork: spend a week jotting down in your notebook interesting statements you overhear. Choose the best of these from the standpoint of the implied (but unstated) premises upon which each statement seems to rest. Then make a list of the UNCOVERED ASSUMPTIONS.

Reading Against the Grain Earlier in the chapter we counseled that you should start by reading with the grain. When you begin to UNCOVER ASSUMPTIONS, however, you may discover interesting ways in which a reading seems to say things it may not have intended to communicate.

When we ask ourselves what a work (and, by implication, an author) might not be aware of communicating, we are doing what is called *reading against the grain*. When we ask ourselves what a work seems aware of, what its (and, by implication, its author's) conscious intentions are, we are *reading with the grain*.

Writers can never be fully in control of what they communicate, that words always, inescapably, communicate more (and less) than we intend. Any of us who has had what we thought to be a perfectly clear and well-intentioned e-mail misinterpreted (or so we thought) by its recipient can understand this idea. When we look at the letter again we usually see what it said that we hadn't realized (at least not consciously) we were saying.

Communication of all kinds takes place both directly and indirectly. Reading against the grain—looking for what a work is saying that it might not know it is saying, that it might not mean to say—requires us to notice and emphasize implicit patterns and make their significance explicit. So, for example, in the classic novel *Jane Eyre*, the narrator Jane repeatedly remarks on her own plain appearance, with the implication that physical beauty is transient and relatively insignificant. Reading against the grain, we'd see the novel's very obsession with plainness as a symptom of how worried it is about the subject, how much it actually believes (but won't admit) that looks matter.

Tracking Binaries in a Reading

Once you begin looking at chains of thought—UNCOVERING ASSUMPTIONS—you will often discover that key binaries rise to the surface. We have encountered binaries before—pairs of words or details that are opposites (for example, *open/ closed, ugly/beautiful, global/local*). In Chapter 1, locating binaries was introduced as a key component of looking for pattern using THE METHOD.

The assumption that underlies binaries is that we understand that which is in terms of that which is not. In other words, fundamental contrasts and oppositions are sites of uncertainty, places where there is a struggle among various points of view.

Thus, the swiftest way to apprehend what's at stake in a reading is to discern its organizing contrasts. To track the thinking in a piece is to track how it moves among its various binary formulations.

Writers think through binaries, consciously or unconsciously reformulating them, as we can see when we TRACK THE BINARIES through a reading. Notice how James Howard Kunstler develops his thinking in the following excerpt:

> Civic life is what goes on in the public realm. Civic life refers to our relations with our fellow human beings—in short, our roles as citizens. Sometime in the past forty years we ceased to speak of ourselves as citizens and labeled ourselves consumers. That's what we are today in the language of the evening news—*consumers*—in the language of the Sunday panel discussion shows—*consumers*—in the blizzard of statistics that blows out of the U.S. Department of Commerce every month. Consumers, unlike citizens, have no responsibilities, obligations, or duties to anything larger than their own needs and desires, certainly not to anything like the common good. How can this be construed as anything other than an infantile state of existence? In degrading the language of our public discussion this way—Labeling ourselves consumers—have we not degraded our sense of who we are? And is it any wonder that we cannot solve any of our social problems, which are problems of the public realm and the common good? [From James Howard Kunstler, *Home From Nowhere: Remaking Our Everyday World for the Twenty-First Century, (Simon & Schuster, 1996)]*

The implicit binary that organizes the thinking in this paragraph is public versus private. Here is a rough approximation of how this binary generates a range of opposing terms as the paragraph progresses:

PUBLIC	PRIVATE
civic life	
our relations with/ fellow humans	labeled ourselves consumers
our roles as citizens	panel discussion tv shows and govt statistics
responsibilities to others	no responsibilities beyond own needs and desires
the common good	
implicitly, adult	infantile state of existence
the public realm	implicitly, the private realm

Kunstler doesn't just settle for a simple binary, he develops and expands and clarifies it by renaming it. In this way, the thinking grows and develops to arrive, at the end, in an explanation of why "we cannot solve any of our social problems."

If you leap too quickly to a binary, however, one that is too general or inaccurate, you can get stuck in oversimplification, in rigidly dichotomized points of view. At that point, you are in the grasp of a reductive habit of mind called either/or thinking. The solution is to keep in mind that the binaries you discover in a reading are sites at which the piece is arguing with itself, figuring out in some qualified way what ultimately it believes.

Reformulating Binaries

We wish now to focus on a related use of binaries, one that takes place in higher order analysis. This move we call REFORMULATING BINARIES.

Thinking is not simply linear and progressive, moving from point A to point B to point C like stops on a train. Careful thinkers are always retracing their steps, questioning their first—and second—impressions, assuming that they've missed something. All good thinking is *recursive*—that is, it repeatedly goes over the same ground, rethinking connections. And that's why REFORMU-LATING BINARIES is an essential analytical move.

You know that a writer is REFORMULATING BINARIES when a reading does one or more of the following:

- Discovers that the binary has not been named adequately and that another formulation of the opposition would be more accurate.

- Values both sides of the binary (rather than seeing the issue as all or nothing), but weights one side of the binary more heavily than the other.

- Discovers that the two terms of the binary are not really so separate and opposed after all but are actually parts of one complex phenomenon or issue. (This is a key analytical move known as "collapsing the binary.")

When you formulate a binary opposition in your own analytical prose—the place where something is at issue—your next step is to immediately begin to ask questions about and complicate the binary. To "complicate" a binary is to discover evidence that unsettles it and to formulate alternatively worded binaries that more accurately describe what is at issue in the evidence (see Figure 2.5).

1 **Locate a range of opposing categories (binaries).** Finding binaries will help you find the questions around which almost anything is organized. Use THE METHOD to help you uncover the binary oppositions in your subject matter that might function as organizing contrasts.

2 **Define and analyze the key terms.** By analyzing the terms of most binaries, you should come to question them and ultimately arrive at a more complex and qualified position.

3 **Question the accuracy of the binary and rephrase the terms.** Think of the binary as a starting point—a kind of deliberate overgeneralization—that allows you to set up positions you can then test in order to refine.

4 **Substitute "to what extent?" for "either/or."** The best strategy in using binaries productively is usually to locate arguments **on both sides** of the either/or choice that the binary poses and then choose a position somewhere between the two extremes. Once you have arrived at what you consider the most accurate phrasing of the binary, you can rephrase the original either/or question in the more qualified terms that asking "To what extent?" allows.

© 2015 Cengage Learning

FIGURE 2.5

REFORMULATING BINARIES

REFORMULATING BINARIES: An Example Suppose you are analyzing the following topic in a management course: *Would the model of management known as Total Quality Management (TQM) that is widely used in Japan function effectively in the American automotive industry?*

Step 1: There are a range of opposing categories suggested by the language of the topic, the most obvious being function versus not function. But there are also other binaries here: Japanese versus American, and TQM versus more traditional and more traditionally American models of management. These binaries imply further binaries. The question requires a writer to consider the accuracy and relative suitability of particular traits commonly ascribed to Japanese versus American workers, such as communal and cooperative versus individualistic and competitive.

Step 2: Questions of definition might concentrate on what it means to ask whether TQM *functions effectively* in the American automotive industry? Does that mean "make a substantial profit"? "Produce more cars more quickly"? "Improve employee morale"? You would drown in vagueness unless you carefully argued for the appropriateness of your definition of this key term.

Step 3: How accurate is the binary? To what extent do American and Japanese management styles actually differ? Can you locate significant differences between these management styles that correspond to supposed differences between Japanese and American culture that might help you formulate your binary more precisely?

Step 4: To complicate the either/or formulation, you might suggest the danger of assuming that all American workers are rugged individualists and all Japanese workers are communal bees. Insofar as you are going to arrive at a qualified claim, it would be best stated in terms of the extent to which TQM might be adaptable to the auto industry.

COLLAPSING THE BINARY: A Brief Example In an essay called "In Defense of Distraction" writer Sam Anderson argues that contemporary American culture is suffering from what he terms "a crisis of attention." He initially proposes a binary between attention (focus) and distraction. But as the essay progresses, he comes to argue that the two are not so opposed but in fact comprise one complex phenomenon: focused distraction. He finds value in both, he finds limitation in both, and he discovers that they rely on each other.

Tracking the Thinking Through Complication and Qualification: An Example In the following excerpt from "On Political Labels," political scientist Christopher Borick complicates the definition of liberalism by tracking it historically. Look in the first paragraph for the historical roots of liberalism as favoring public control over government actions. Then in the second paragraph see how this emphasis moves almost to its opposite—the belief that "government intervention in society is necessary." You'll learn a lot from the excerpt by seeing how it pivots around more than one sense of the word "freedom."

> Let's look at liberalism for a start. The term liberal can be traced at least back to 17th-Century England, where it evolved from debates dealing with the voting franchise among English citizens. Proponents of including greater numbers of Englishmen in elections came to be known as liberals, thanks in part to the writings of John Locke, whose ideas about the social contract helped to build the philosophical underpinnings of this political ideology. Over time, liberalism has maintained its focus on public control over government actions, but there have been splits that have led to its current manifestation. In the 18th and 19th Centuries, liberalism began to stress the importance of individual freedom and broader rights of the citizenry in terms of limits on government. In essence, this type of liberalism focused on "negative rights" or the restrictions on what government could do to its citizens. The First Amendment of the Constitution includes numerous examples of negative rights. The granting of the right to freedom of speech or the press is achieved through the prohibition of government from creating laws that abridge such freedoms. Thus negating an action of government creates rights for the people.
>
> In the 20th Century, however, liberalism became synonymous with the view that government had to be much more active in helping citizens get to the point where they would be able to truly live a free life. In this expanding view of liberalism, government intervention in society is necessary to create a more level playing field on which individuals can then use their freedom to achieve desired goals. Such beliefs have been at the roots of government expansion into social welfare policies such as public housing, food stamps, and affirmative action, and have formed the core of government agendas such as Franklin Roosevelt's New Deal and Lyndon Johnson's Great Society.

As this piece progresses, you can expect that it will either resolve the significant gap between the two historical definitions of liberalism or that it will in various ways show us how the gap has continued to produce tensions or misunderstandings.

In the case of most academic writing, it is usually a mistake to assume that the piece is making a single argument. A smarter assumption is that the piece is interested in exploring an issue or a problem from multiple points of view.

TRY THIS 2.8: REFORMULATING BINARIES: Fieldwork
Locate some organizing contrasts in anything—something you are studying, something you've just written, something you saw on television last night, something on the front page of the newspaper, something going on at your campus or workplace, and so forth. Consider, for example, the binaries suggested by current trends in contemporary music or by the representation of women in birthday cards. Having selected the binaries you want to work with,

pick one and transform the either/or thinking into more qualified thinking using the "to-what-extent" formula (step 4).

TRY THIS 2.9: Practice Tracking Reformulated Binaries in a Reading

In the following paragraph, writer Jonathan Franzen explores a problem by locating, defining, analyzing, and REFORMULATING BINARIES. Track the thinking in the Franzen paragraph. How does it engage readers' expectations? What happens to the binary *public* versus *private*?

> Walking up Third Avenue on a Saturday night, I feel bereft. All around me, attractive young people are hunched over their StarTacs and Nokias with preoccupied expressions, as if probing a sore tooth, or adjusting a hearing aid, or squeezing a pulled muscle; personal technology has begun to look like a personal handicap. All I really want from a sidewalk is that people see me and let themselves be seen, but even this modest ideal is thwarted by cell-phone users and their unwelcome privacy. They say things like "Should we have couscous with that?" and "I'm on my way to Blockbuster." They aren't breaking any laws by broadcasting these breakfast-nook conversations. There's no PublicityGuard that I can buy, no expensive preserve of public life to which I can flee. Seclusion, whether in a suite at the Plaza or in a cabin in the Catskills, is comparatively effortless to achieve. Privacy is protected as both commodity and right; public forums are protected as neither. Like old-growth forests, they're few and irreplaceable and should be held in trust by everyone. The work of maintaining them gets only harder as the private sector grows ever more demanding, distracting, and disheartening. Who has the time and energy to stand up for the public sphere? What rhetoric can possibly compete with the American love of "privacy"? [From Jonathan Franzen, "Imperial Bedroom" in *How to Be Alone* (Farrar, Straus, and Giroux, 2003)]

Apply a Reading as a Lens

This final section of the chapter discusses how to apply a reading to other material you are studying. Using a reading as a lens means literally looking at things as the reading does, trying to think in its terms.

In college, students are expected to be able to take readings, often complex theoretical readings, and use them in order to understand other material. This is one of the biggest differences between writing about reading in high school versus college. As lens, the reading shapes how we come to understand whatever it is being applied to.

Your first goal when working with a reading as a lens is to explore its usefulness for explaining features of your subject. Because the match between lens and new material will never be perfect, you need to remember that whenever you apply the lens A to a new subject B, you are taking lens A from its original context and using its ideas in somewhat different circumstances for at least somewhat different purposes. Using the lens in a different context upon a different kind of information will often require you to adjust the lens—to refocus it a bit to bring this new content into clear focus.

Let's say, for example, that you have read a smart review essay on the representation of black/white race relations in contemporary films in the 1970s, and you decide to use the review as a lens for exploring the spate of black/white buddy films that emerged in the 1990s.

"Yes, but. . . ," you find yourself responding: there are places where the 1990s films appear to fit within the pattern that the article claims, but there are also exceptions to the pattern. What do you do? What <u>not</u> to do is either choose different films that "fit better" or decide that the article is wrong-headed. Instead, start with the "yes": talk about how the film accords with the general pattern. Then focus on the "but," the claims in the reading (the lens) that seem not to fit, or material in your subject not adequately accounted for by the lens.

Because cultural climates and trends are constantly shifting and reconfiguring themselves, particularly in popular culture, you will learn from examining the films how the original review might be usefully extended to account for phenomena that were not present when it was originally written.

Using a Reading as a Lens: An Extended Example   In the following example of applying a reading as a lens, one of our students, Anna Whiston, applies her lens (the theories of linguist Deborah Tannen on gender and conversation styles) to her subject: the conversational tactics of male celebrities on late night talk shows. The assignment was to use concepts from two books by socio-linguist Deborah Tannen—*You Just Don't Understand: Women and Men in Conversation* and *That's Not What I Meant: How Conversational Style Makes or Breaks Relationships*— to explore a conversational topic of the student's choice.

In her essay, excerpted here from a longer draft, Whiston shows how to do more with a theoretical reading than use it in a matching exercise. More than simply demonstrating the match between her evidence and Tannen's theories, she extends their range. She also shows how seemingly contradictory evidence actually can be seen to support Tannen's primary claims.

"I think my cooking, uh, sucks:" Self-Deprecation on Late Night Television by Anna Whiston

In *You Just Don't Understand*, linguist Deborah Tannen explores conversation as a process affected largely by the gender of the speaker. For men, according to Tannen, "…life is a contest in which they are constantly tested and must perform, in order to avoid the risk of failure" (178). This sense of competition often manifests itself in "one-upsmanship," a strategy in which men attempt to outdo each other in order to achieve a superior position within a conversation (Tannen 26). There are, however, certain situations in which being on top of the hierarchy is not necessarily desirable. The interactions between men on late night talk shows provide examples of such situations.

Low confidence is not exactly typical in Hollywood. Celebrities are known just as much for their egos as they are for the movies that they headline and the scandals that they induce. And yet, late night talk shows, such as *The Tonight Show with Jay Leno, Late*

Night with Conan O'Brien, The Late Show with David Letterman, and *Jimmy Kimmel Live,* include endless examples of self-deprecation on the parts of both the male hosts and the male celebrity guests.

Self-deprecation is, on the surface, a way of belittling oneself. However, examination of the conversations that take place on these television programs helps show that this strand of apparent humility is actually a much more nuanced conversational technique. Conversations on late night talk shows reveal that self-deprecation does not necessarily pit one man as inferior to another. Instead, it actually serves to maintain rather than diminish a speaker's higher status in the conversation.

In another one of her works on conversation, *That's Not What I Meant,* Tannen discusses framing, the idea that "everything about the way we say something contributes to establishing the footing that frames our relationships to each other"(75). The guests on talk shows are entering a frame, or conversational alignment, that is inherently asymmetrical. Though both guest and host are technically celebrities, the guest is presented as the centerpiece of the program, the one who answers the questions, while the host is simply the asker.

This frame is not always one that is appealing for the guest, who may want to create a persona that is not that of an elite star, but of a likable and approachable everyman. In order to cultivate this persona, the guest can use conversation to downplay his star status and success in order to establish a more symmetrical alignment to the host, thereby changing the frame of the conversation. As we will see, however, this reframing is complicated, since it essentially shifts the asymmetry to a different ground. An example of this technique can be found in actor Paul Rudd's interview with former NBC late night talk show host Conan O'Brien:

Rudd: I'm great, how are you?
O'Brien: I'm very good. You know things are going very well for you. You've been in so many successful movies. You have this new film *Role Models*. People love this movie, very funny, big hit for you, you've gotta be excited. I mean you you're a big, big star.
Rudd: It...I don't know about that, but it's very exciting. Oh God, I'm still out of breath! I swear to God.

By negating O'Brien's compliment, Rudd downplays his fame and thus reframes the conversation. By saying, "Oh God, I'm still out of breath," Rudd draws attention away from his stardom to some goofy dancing that O'Brien and Rudd did at the beginning of the interview. When O'Brien again tries to draw attention to Rudd's star power, Rudd again dodges the compliment.

O'Brien: But I would have to think by now that it's reaching critical mass, so many successful movies you must be getting the star treatment now. I bet you're treated like—
Rudd: I met Bruce Springsteen. I met him but it wasn't a...I snuck backstage at a Police concert and he was there.

Rudd's move, which allows him to segue into a self-deprecating anecdote about his encounter with Bruce Springsteen, represents an effort to resist the frame that O'Brien attempts to establish. Instead of accepting the frame that situates Rudd as a star and O'Brien as an average fan, Rudd strategically reframes the conversation by invoking a third party, a star whom both O'Brien and Rudd admire. Now, the conversation is not taking place between a "big star" and his fan, but rather between two fans.

To help understand Rudd's move, we can use Tannen's conversational categories of "report-talk" and "rapport-talk," the former being a way of "exhibiting knowledge and skill" and the latter being a way of "establishing connections" by "displaying similarities and matching experiences" (*Understand 77*). While men are generally associated with report talk rather than rapport talk, the two categories are not necessarily gender exclusive. Humility, which often takes the form of self-deprecation, can help to remove asymmetry from a conversation. Such a move allows the men to capitalize on their similarities rather than emphasize their differences. We see Rudd do just that by transforming his conversational role from that of the star to that of the fan, a fan that must sneak backstage to meet his musical idols, just like the proverbial rest of us.

[. . .]

One possible explanation for the desire to dismiss and minimize praise is that compliment-giving is not the selfless act it may appear to be, but is, in fact, pure one-upmanship. According to Tannen, "Giving praise, like giving information, is also inherently asymmetrical. It too frames the speaker as one-up, in a position to judge someone else's performance" *(Understand 69)*. Thus, accepting praise may force the man on the receiving end of the praise to surrender supremacy to the praise-giver. By negating or avoiding praise, hierarchy can be reserved.

[. . .]

If this is so, then perhaps self-deprecating humor functions as a sort of preemptive move in which one man points out his own flaws before the other man has the chance to do so. If a man makes fun of himself, he still has control. He refuses to surrender this power to another man and thus surrender a hierarchical position in the conversation. Take, for example, this excerpt from Senator John McCain's conversation with NBC host Jay Leno:

Leno: And you went up to the mountains too?
McCain: We went up to our place near Sedona and had a very nice time and—
Leno: Now which house is that, number twel—
McCain: You know that's uh let's see it's a very...let's see...twenty-seven.

Leno was on the verge of making a dig about the senator's many homes, but McCain, seeing this coming, beat Leno to the punch, cutting him off before he even finished the word "twelve." McCain then goes on to exaggerate the number of homes that he owns. This shows that McCain not only understands the public's perception of him, he also is aware that his surplus of homes is a funny, and perhaps even embarrassing, subject. Thus, McCain uses self-deprecation to control the conversation, taking away Leno's opportunity to laugh at him before he laughs at himself.

Perhaps the most frequent and telling place in which self-deprecation pops up is in stories. Late night television is an excellent medium through which to study storytelling; in addition to the release dates of the projects they are promoting, celebrities always come equipped with an anecdote or two. Tannen includes a study of the differences found in stories told by men from those told by women. Her findings indicated that "the stories the men told made them look good" while the women were more likely to tell stories "in which they [women] violate social norms and are scared or embarrassed as a result" *(Understand 177)*.

The behavior of men on late night talk shows would seem to contradict these findings: the men's stories usually involve them telling of an incident in which, they were, indeed, "embarrassed as a result." When we look at the content of these stories, however, it becomes apparent that these stories function on a more sophisticated level than simple self-effacement.

Whether it is Paul Rudd's story about showing an embarrassing movie at a friend's wedding or Steve Carrell's anecdote about his parents flying on a plane with a Thanksgiving turkey because his cooking "sucks," the men doing the self-deprecating do not ultimately portray themselves in an embarrassing or pathetic light. The stories that they tell at their own expense draw laughs—and the storyteller is laughing with them.

In this regard, the stories told are actually more flattering than they are embarrassing. The stories send the message, or metamessage, that the storyteller is able not only to laugh at himself, but also to draw laughs from his audience, all the while coming across as likable and humble. What appears to be humility or lack of self-confidence actually serves a purpose more akin to a joke. And when a joke is told, conversational asymmetry is unavoidable as one man is doing the joke telling while the other functions as the audience *(Understand 90)*. Thus, what seems like a way to put one's self down is, in fact, one-upmanship.

Self-deprecation is a complex conversational tool. On the surface, it seems to be simply a way for the speaker to disparage himself. It also, however, can function as a tool for humility and compromise, a way to create conversational symmetry from a situation of asymmetry. The most subtle and fascinating way in which self-deprecation functions, however, is a bit of a paradox: by putting himself down, a man can actually build himself up. Conversation is not merely a straightforward exchange of words; it is a skill, that when used strategically and with great awareness, can help a speaker to get ahead—often without anyone else realizing that he is doing it.

Assignments: Reading Analytically

1. **Analyze a Piece of Writing Using One or More of the Chapter's Methods:**
   a. PARAPHRASE × 3
   b. Finding the underlying structure by UNCOVERING ASSUMPTIONS and TRACKING BINARIES
   c. Attending to THE PITCH, THE COMPLAINT, AND THE MOMENT
   d. PASSAGE-BASED FOCUSED FREEWRITING

2. **Paraphrase a Complicated Passage.** Paraphrasing can help you to understand sophisticated material by uncovering the implications of the language. As a case in point, consider this passage from an article about *Life* magazine by Wendy Kozol entitled "The Kind of People Who Make Good Americans: Nationalism and *Life's* Family Ideal." Try PARAPHRASE × 3 with this passage. Paraphrase each sentence at least twice. Then rewrite the paragraph based on the understanding you have arrived at through paraphrasing.

   > Traditional depictions of the family present it as a voluntary site of intimacy and warmth, but it also functions as a site of consumption. At the same time capitalism lauds the work ethic and the family as spheres of morality safe from the materialism of the outside world. These contradictions produce a "legitimation crisis" by which capitalist societies become ever more dependent for legitimacy on the very sociocultural motivations that capitalism undermines. (186; rpt in *Rhetorical Visions* by Wendy Hesford, pp 177–200).

3. **UNCOVER ASSUMPTIONS and Read Against the Grain.** Take a paragraph from an analytical essay you are reading in one of your courses or from a feature article from a newspaper or website such as Slate or aldaily.com—and do the following:

   - First, UNCOVER ASSUMPTIONS by reasoning back to premises. Ask yourself, if the piece believes this, what must it also already believe? Answer that question and be sure to share your reasoning (why you think so).

   - Try reading against the grain. What if anything is the piece saying that it might not know it is saying?

   Or you could also UNCOVER THE ASSUMPTIONS of a policy decision at your school or place of work. This will work best if you have not just the policy but some kind of written manifesto on it.

4. **Use a Reading as a Lens for Examining a Subject.** For example, look at a piece of music or a film through the lens of a review that does not discuss the particular piece or film you are writing about. Or you might read about a particular theory of humor and use that as a lens for examining a comic play, film, story, television show, or stand-up routine.

5. **Put the Tools to work: Compose an Analytical Portfolio.** Select a subject—which could be a film, an advertising campaign, a political campaign, a television series, something that you are currently reading for a course or on your own, etc.—and do a series of PASSAGE-BASED FOCUSED FREEWRITINGS as a way of generating ideas.

CHAPTER 3

Responding to Traditional Writing Assignments More Analytically

Overview This brief chapter is a companion to the two previous chapters, applying strategies from them in the service of making your response to traditional kinds of writing assignments more analytical. These frequently assigned types of writing include:

- Summary

- Personal Response (reaction paper)

- Agree/disagree

- Comparison/contrast (DIFFERENCE WITHIN SIMILARITY, similarity despite difference)

- Definition

The chapter argues that as a general rule, you should seek out *live questions over inert answers*. Rather than leading you to a single or obvious answer, an analytical topic aims to define a space in which you can have ideas about (explore the questions in) what you've been learning.

Interpreting Writing Assignments

One fact of college writing is that someone is usually telling you not only what to write about, but also what form to write it in. This situation is not, however, as straightforward as it sounds. Consider, for example, an assignment to "discuss how a supply-side economist might respond to the idea of eliminating most tariffs on imported goods." How do you interpret the word *discuss*? Should you confine your response to summarizing (restating) the reading you've done on the subject? Should you analyze the reading, by, for example, drawing out its unstated assumptions or pointing to inconsistencies in its position? Should you write an argument about the reading, revealing the extent to which you agree or disagree with the supply-side view? And what do you do about the other most common writing situation, the open topic, wherein the assignment is essentially to go write your own assignment?

By the time you reach college, you will have learned to recognize certain kinds of instructions that writing assignments characteristically contain: compare and contrast, define, agree or disagree. The key words of a topic trigger different kinds of writing. Some topics call for *argument*—for taking a firm stand on one side of an issue and making a case for that stand. Some call for *summary*—for restating ideas and information in a focused and concise way. Some call for *personal response*—for testing an idea or attitude or question against your own life experience.

All of these kinds of writing assignments have a significant analytical component, though this fact is often overlooked. This chapter will show you how to make your responses to common kinds of topics more analytical.

Find the Analytical Potential: Locate an Area of Uncertainty

The best way to become more analytical in your response to topics is to actively search out an area of your subject where there are no clear and obvious answers—to look for something that needs explaining, rather than reiterating the obvious. The analytical component in a topic is often not apparent. You have to actively look for it.

Although disciplines vary in the kinds of questions they characteristically ask, every discipline is concerned with asking questions, exploring areas of uncertainty, and attempting to solve—or at least clarify—problems. An analytical response to a topic calls on you, in other words, to *deliberately situate yourself among sites of potential ambiguity or conflict,* so that your writing can explore the complexity of your subject. In order to learn how to enter this uncertain space, you will first have to get over the fear that you are doing something wrong if you cannot arrive quickly at a clear and obvious answer.

We now turn to six rules of thumb that can help you to discover and respond to the complexities that are there but not always immediately apparent in your subject matter nor explicitly asked for in the writing assignments you encounter. What all of our suggestions have in common is the single requirement that you train yourself to look for questions rather than leaping too quickly to answers. It is this orientation toward topics that will move you beyond merely reporting information and will lead you to think with and about it.

Six Rules of Thumb for Responding to Assignments More Analytically

The following rules of thumb can help you to discover and respond to the complexities of the topics that you encounter, rather than oversimplifying or evading them.

Rule 1: Reduce Scope

Whenever possible, reduce drastically the scope of your inquiry. Resist the temptation to include too much information. Even when an assignment calls for broad coverage of a subject, an effective and usually acceptable strategy is for you to begin with an overview and then analyze one or two key points in greater depth.

For example, if you were asked to write on President Franklin Roosevelt's New Deal, you would obviously have to open with some general observations, such as what it was and why it arose. But if you tried to stay on this general level throughout, your paper would have little direction or focus. You could achieve a focus, though, by moving quickly from the general to some much smaller and more specific part of the subject, such as attacks on the New Deal. You would then be able to limit the enormous range of possible evidence to a few representative figures, such as Huey Long, Father Coughlin, and Alf Landon. Once you began to compare the terms and legitimacy of their opposition to the New Deal, you would be much more likely to manage a complex analysis of the subject than if you had remained at the level of broad generalization. Typically you will find that some mixture of wide-angle coverage with more narrowly focused discussion is the best way to cover the ground without sacrificing depth.

Rule 2: Study the Wording of Topics for Unstated Questions

Nearly all formulations of an assigned topic contain one or more overt questions, and also other questions that are implied by the topic's wording. Taking the time to ponder the wording and to articulate the questions that wording implies is often the first step to having an idea—to finding an angle of approach.

Consider, for instance, a topic question such as "Is feminism good for Judaism?" The question, itself, seems to invite you simply to argue yes or no, but the wording implies preliminary questions that you would need to articulate and answer before you could address the larger issue. What, for example, does "good for Judaism" mean? That which allows the religion to evolve? That which conserves its tradition? The same kinds of questions, defining and contextualizing and laying out implications, might be asked of the term "feminism." And what of the possibility that feminism has no significant affect whatsoever?

As this example illustrates, even an apparently limited and straightforward question presses writers to make choices about how to engage it. So don't leap from the topic question to your plan of attack too quickly. One of the best strategies lies in smoking out and addressing the unstated assumptions implied by the wording of the topic.

Rule 3: Suspect Your First Responses

If you settle for your first response, the result is likely to be superficial, obvious, and overly general. A better strategy is to examine your first responses for ways in which they are inaccurate and then to develop the implications of these overstatements (or errors) into a new formulation. In many cases, writers go through this process of proposing and rejecting ideas ten times or more before they arrive at an angle or approach that will sustain an essay.

A first response is okay for a start, as long as you don't stop there. For example, many people might agree, at first glance, that no one should be denied health care, or that a given film or novel that concludes with a marriage is a happy ending, or that the American government should not pass trade laws that might cause Americans to lose their jobs. On closer inspection, however, each of these responses begins to reveal its limitations. Given that there is a limited amount of money available, should everyone, regardless of age or physical condition, be accorded every medical treatment that might prolong life? And might not a novel or film that concludes in marriage signal that the society offers too few options, or more cynically, that the author is feeding the audience an implausible fantasy to blanket over problems raised earlier in the work? And couldn't trade laws resulting in short-term loss of jobs ultimately produce more jobs and a healthier economy?

As these examples suggest, first responses—usually pieces of conventional wisdom—can blind you to rival explanations. Try not to decide on an answer to questions too quickly.

Rule 4: Begin with Questions, Not Answers

Whether you are focusing an assigned topic or devising one of your own, you are usually better off to begin with something that you don't understand very well and want to understand better. Begin by asking what kinds of questions the material poses. So, for example, if you are already convinced that Robinson Crusoe changes throughout Defoe's novel and you write a paper cataloguing those changes, you will essentially be composing a selective plot summary. If, by contrast, you wonder why Crusoe walls himself within a fortress after he discovers a footprint in the sand, you will be more likely to interpret the significance of events rather than just to report them.

Rule 5: Expect to Become Interested

Writing gives you the opportunity to cultivate your curiosity by thinking exploratively. Rather than approaching topics in a mechanical way or putting them off to the last possible moment and doing the assignment grudgingly, try giving yourself and the topic the benefit of the doubt. If you can suspend judgment and start writing, you will often find yourself uncovering interests where you had not seen them before. In other words, accept the idea that interest is a product of writing—not a prerequisite.

Rule 6: Write All of the Time about What You Are Studying

Because interest is so often a product and not a prerequisite of writing, it follows that writing informally about what you are studying while you are studying it is probably the single best preparation for developing interesting topics. By writing spontaneously about what you read, you will accustom yourself to being a less passive consumer of ideas and information, and you will have more ideas and information available to think actively with and about. In effect, you will be formulating possible topics long before an actual topic is assigned. In any case, you should not wait to start writing until you think you have an idea you can organize a paper around. Instead, use writing to get you to the idea.

Using Freewriting to Find and Interpret Topics As we have argued in both of the previous chapters, freewriting offers one of the best antidotes to both superficial writing and writer's block. It also enables you to develop and organize your ideas when you begin drafting more formally because you already will have explored some of the possible paths you might travel and will have rejected others as dead ends.

PASSAGE-BASED FOCUSED FREEWRITES (see Chapter 2) are an especially useful way to move from a broad topic to one that is more carefully directed and narrowed. Start by choosing passages in response to the question, "What in the reading needs to be discussed; poses a question or a problem; or seems in some way difficult to pin down, anomalous, or even just unclear?" You can vary this question infinitely, selecting the passage that you find most puzzling or most important or most dissonant or most whatever. Then write without stopping for fifteen minutes or so.

One advantage of PASSAGE-BASED FOCUSED FREEWRITING is that it forces you to articulate what you notice as you notice it, not delaying—or, as is more common, simply avoiding—thinking in a persistent and relatively disciplined way about what you are reading. There is no set procedure for such writing, but it usually involves the following:

- It selects key phrases or terms in the passage and paraphrases them, trying to tease out the possible meanings of these words.

- It addresses how the passage is representative of broader issues in the reading; perhaps it will refer to another, similar passage.

- It attends, at least briefly, to the context surrounding the passage, identifying the larger section of which the passage is a part.

If you assign yourself several PASSAGE-BASED FOCUSED FREEWRITES on a given topic, you can build up, through a process of accretion, the thinking for an entire paper.

The remainder of the chapter offers strategies for upping the analytical quotient in your response to traditional writing assignments.

Summary

All analytical topics require a blend of two components: a thinking component and an information component. Summary provides the information component. Summarizing is basically a translation process, and as such, it is an essential part of learning. It is the way that not just facts and figures but also other people's theories and observations enter your writing.

Summary performs the essential function of contextualizing a subject accurately. It creates a fair picture of what's there. Summarizing isn't simply the unanalytical reporting of information; it's more than just condensing someone else's words. To write an accurate summary, you have to ask analytical questions, such as the following:

- Which of the ideas in the reading are most significant? Why?
- How do these ideas fit together?
- What do the key passages in the reading mean?

Summarizing is, then, like paraphrasing, a tool of understanding and not just a mechanical task.

When summaries go wrong, they are just lists, a simple "this and then this" sequence. Often lists are random, as in a shopping list compiled from the first thing you thought of to the last. Sometimes they are organized in broad categories: fruit and vegetables here, canned goods there. Lists do very little logical connecting among the parts beyond "next." Summaries that are just lists tend to dollop out the information monotonously. They omit the thinking that the piece is doing—the ways it is connecting the information, the contexts it establishes, and the implicit slant or point of view.

Writing analytical summaries can teach you how to read for the connections, the lines that connect the dots. And when you're operating at that level, you are much more likely to have ideas about what you are summarizing.

Strategies for Making Summaries More Analytical

Strategy 1: Look for the underlying structure. Use THE METHOD to find patterns of repetition and contrast (see Chapter 1). If you apply it to a few key paragraphs, you will find the terms that get repeated, and these will suggest strands, which in turn make up organizing contrasts. This process works to categorize and then further organize information and, in so doing, to bring out its underlying structure. See also UNCOVERING ASSUMPTIONS and TRACKING BINARIES in Chapter 2.

Strategy 2: Select the information that you wish to discuss on some principle other than general coverage. Use NOTICE & FOCUS to rank items of information in some order of importance (see Chapter 1). Let's say that you are writing a paper on major changes in the tax law or on recent developments in U.S. policy toward the Middle East. Rather than simply collecting the information, try to arrange it into hierarchies. What are the least or most significant changes or developments, and why? Which changes or developments are most overlooked or most overrated or most controversial or most practical, and why? All of these terms—significant, overlooked, and so forth—have the effect of focusing the summary, guiding your decisions about what to include and exclude.

Strategy 3: Reduce scope to say more about less. Reducing scope is an especially efficient and productive strategy when you are trying to understand a reading you find difficult or perplexing. It will move you beyond passive summarizing and toward having ideas about the reading. You can still begin with a brief survey of major points to provide context before narrowing the focus.

If, for example, you are reading Chaucer's *Canterbury Tales* and start cataloguing what makes it funny, you are likely to end up with unanalyzed plot summary—a list that arranges its elements in no particular order. But narrowing the question to "How does Chaucer's use of religious commentary contribute to the humor of 'The Wife of Bath's Tale'?" reduces the scope to a single tale and the humor to a single aspect of humor. Describe those as accurately as you can, and you will begin to notice things.

Strategy 4: Get some detachment: shift your focus from *what?* **to** *how?* **and** *why?* Most readers tend to get too single-minded about absorbing the information. That is, they attend only to the *what*: what the reading is saying or is about. They take it all in passively. But you can deliberately shift your focus to *how* it says what it says and *why*.

If, for example, you were asked to discuss the major discoveries that Darwin made on *The Beagle*, you could avoid simply listing his conclusions by redirecting your attention to *how* he proceeded. You could choose to focus, for example, on Darwin's use of the scientific method, examining how he built and, in some cases, discarded hypotheses. Or you might select several passages that illustrate how Darwin proceeded from evidence to conclusion and then *rank* them in order of importance to the overall theory. Notice that in shifting the emphasis to Darwin's thinking—the how and why—you would not be excluding the what (the information component) from your discussion.

One way to focus on the how and the why—whether it be a sign on a subway or the language of a presidential speech—is to situate the reading rhetorically. Like analysis in general, rhetorical analysis asks what things mean, why they are as they are, and how they do what they do. But rhetorical analysis asks these questions with one primary question always foregrounded: how does the thing achieve its effects on an audience? Rhetorical analysis asks not just "What do I think?", but "What am I being invited to think (and feel) and by what means?" See Noticing and Rhetorical Analysis in Chapter 1 and Situate the Reading Rhetorically: THE PITCH, THE COMPLAINT, AND THE MOMENT in Chapter 2.

Personal Response: The Reaction Paper

How do you know when you are being asked for a personal response? And what does it mean to respond personally? When asked for your reactions to a particular subject, or for what you think is most important or interesting or revealing in it, you are being asked to select your own starting point for discussion, for the initial impressions that you will later analyze more systematically. You will often discover in such reactions the germ of an idea about the subject.

The biggest advantage of personal response topics is that they give you the freedom to explore where and how to engage your subject. Such topics often bring to the surface your emotional or intuitive response, allowing you to experiment with placing the subject in various contexts. You might, for example, offer your personal response to an article on the abuses of hazing in fraternity and sorority life in the context of your own experience. Or you might think about it in connection to some idea about in-groups and out-groups that you read about in a sociology course, or as it relates to what you read about cultural rituals in an anthropology course.

Another advantage of personal response questions is that they often allow you to get some distance from your first impressions, which can be deceiving. If, as you reexamine your first reactions, you look for ways they might not be accurate, you will often find places where you now disagree with yourself, in effect, stimulating you to think in new ways about the subject. In such cases, the first reaction has helped to clear the way to a second, and better, response.

Personal response becomes a problem, however, when it distracts you from analyzing the subject. In most cases, you will be misinterpreting the intent of a personal response topic if you view it as an invitation either to:

1. Assert your personal opinions unreflectively or

2. Substitute narratives of your own experience for careful consideration of the subject.

In a sense, all analysis involves your opinions, insofar as you are choosing what particular evidence and arguments to focus upon. But, at least in an academic setting, an opinion is more than simply an expression of your beliefs—it's a conclusion that you earn the rights to through a careful examination of evidence.

When you are invited to respond personally, you are being asked for more than your endorsement or critique of the subject. If you find yourself constructing a virtual list—"I agree with this point", or "I disagree with that point"—you are probably doing little more than matching your opinions with the points of view encountered in a reading. At the very least, you should look for places in the reaction paper where you find yourself disagreeing with yourself.

Strategies for Making Personal Responses More Analytical

Strategy 1: Trace your responses back to their causes. As the preceding discussion of problems with personal response topics suggests, *you need to bring your reactions back to the subject so you can identify and analyze exactly what in the reading has produced your reaction, how, and why*. If you find an aspect of your subject irritating or interesting, disappointing or funny, you will be able to use—rather than simply indulge—such responses if you then examine a particular piece of evidence that has provoked them.

Tracing your impressions back to their causes is the key to making personal response analytical—because you focus on the details that gave you the response rather than on the response alone. In the planning stage, you may find it useful to brainstorm some of your reactions/responses—the things you might say about the material if asked to talk about it with a sympathetic friend. You would then take this brainstorm and use it to choose the key sentences, passages, etc. in the reading that you want to focus on in your analysis.

Let's say that you are responding to an article on ways of increasing the numbers of registered voters in urban precincts. You find the article irritating; your personal experience working with political campaigns has taught you that getting out the vote is not as easy as this writer makes it seem. From that starting point, you might analyze one (to you) overly enthusiastic passage, concentrating on how the writer has not only overestimated what campaign workers can actually do, but also condescends to those who don't register—assuming, perhaps, that they are ignorant, rather than indifferent or disillusioned. Tracing your response back to its cause may help to defuse your emotional response and open the door to further investigation of the other writer's rationale. You might, for example, discover that the writer has in mind a much more long-term effect or that urban models differ significantly from the suburban ones of your experience.

Strategy 2: Assume that you may have missed the point. It's difficult to see the logic of someone else's position if you are too preoccupied with your own. Similarly, it is difficult to see the logic, or illogic, of your own position if you already assume it to be true.

Although an evaluative response (approve/disapprove) can sometimes spur analysis, it can also lead you to prejudge the case. If, however, you habitually question the validity of your own point of view, you will sometimes recognize the possibility of an alternative point of view, as was the case in the voter registration example (see Figure 3.1). Assuming that you have missed the point is a good strategy in all kinds of analytical writing. It causes you to notice details of your subject that you might not otherwise have registered.

Strategy 3: Locate your response within a limiting context. Suppose you are asked in a religion course to write your religious beliefs. Although this topic would naturally lead you to think about your own experiences and beliefs, you would probably do best to approach it in some more limiting context. The reading in the course could provide this limit. Let's say that thus far you have read two modern religious thinkers, Martin Buber and Paul Tillich. Using these as your context, "What do I believe?" would become "How does my response to Buber and Tillich illuminate my own assumptions about the nature of religious faith?" An advantage of this move, beyond making your analysis less general, is that it would help you to get perspective on your own position.

Another way of limiting your context is to consider how one author or recognizable point of view that you have encountered in the course might respond to a single statement from another author or point of view. If you used this strategy to respond to the topic "Does God exist?," you might arrive at a formulation such as "How would Martin Buber critique Paul Tillich's definition of God?" Although this topic appears to exclude personal response entirely, it in fact does not. Your opinion would necessarily enter because you would be actively formulating something that is not already evident in the reading (how Buber might respond to Tillich).

Evaluative Personal Response: *"The article was irritating."* This response is too broad and dismissively judgmental. Make it more analytical by tracing the response back to the evidence that triggered it.

A More Analytical Evaluative Response: *"The author of the article oversimplifies the problem by assuming the cause of low voter registration to be voters' ignorance rather than voters' indifference."* Although still primarily an evaluative response, this observation is more analytical. It takes the writer's initial response ("irritating") to a specific cause.

A Non-evaluative Analytical Response: *"The author's emphasis on increased coverage of city politics in local/neighborhood forums such as the churches suggests that the author is interested in long-term effects of voter registration drives and not just in immediate increases."* Rather than simply reacting ("irritating") or leaping to evaluation ("oversimplifies the problem"), the writer here formulates a possible explanation for the difference between his or her point of view on voter registration drives and the article's.

© Cengage Learning

FIGURE 3.1
Making Personal Response More Analytical

Agree/Disagree

We offer here only a brief recap of this kind of topic, because it is discussed in both Chapter 1 (under Habit: The Judgment Reflex) and 2 (under REFORMULATING BINARIES). Assignments are frequently worded as agree or disagree, but the wording is potentially misleading because you are rarely being asked for as unqualified an opinion as agree or disagree.

Creating opposing categories (binary oppositions) is fundamental to defining things. But binaries are also dangerous because they can invite *reductive thinking*—oversimplifying a subject by eliminating alternatives between the two extremes. And so, in most cases, your best strategy in dealing with agree/disagree questions is to choose *neither* side. Instead, question the terms of the binary so as to arrive at a more complex and qualified position to write about. In place of choosing one side or the other, decide to what extent you agree and to what extent you disagree. You are still responsible for coming down more on one side than the other, but this need not mean that you have to locate yourself in a starkly either/or position. The code phrase for accomplishing this shift is "the extent to which": "To what extent do you agree (or disagree)?"

We offer here a brief review of these strategies:

Strategy 1: Locate a range of opposing categories.
Strategy 2: Analyze and define the opposing terms.

Strategy 3: Question the accuracy of the binary.

Strategy 4: Change "either/or" to "the extent to which" ("to what extent?").

Applying these strategies will usually cause you to do one or more of the following:

1. Weight one side of your binary more heavily than the other, rather than seeing the issue as all or nothing (all of one and none of the other).

2. Discover that you have not adequately named the binary: another opposition would be more accurate.

3. Discover that the two terms of your binary are not really so separate and opposed after all, but actually part of one complex phenomenon or issue.

Comparison/Contrast

Although comparison/contrast is meant to invite analysis, it is too often treated as an end in itself. The fundamental reason for comparing and contrasting is that you can usually discover ideas about a subject much more easily when you are not viewing it in isolation. When executed mechanically, however, without the writer pressing to understand the significance of a similarity or difference, comparison/contrast can suffer from pointlessness. The telltale sign of this problem is the formulaic sentence beginning "Thus we see there are many similarities and differences between X and Y"—as "chaos" and "cream cheese" might fit that formula (both begin with the letter "c").

Comparison/contrast topics produce pointless essays if you allow them to turn into matching exercises—that is, if you match common features of two subjects but don't get beyond the equation stage (a, b, c = x, y, z). Writers fall into this trap when they have no larger question or issue to explore and perhaps resolve this by making the comparison. If, for example, you were to pursue the comparison of the representations of the Boston Tea Party in British and American history textbooks, you would begin by identifying similarities and differences. But simply presenting these and concluding that the two versions resemble and differ from each other in some ways would be pointless. You would need to press your comparisons with the so what? question (see Chapter 1) in order to give them some interpretive weight.

Comparison/contrast leads to the more sophisticated task of synthesis. Synthesis involves more than two sources, often for the purpose of composing the opening frame of a researched paper or what is known as the "literature review" that typically opens papers in the social sciences. For more on synthesis, see Chapter 8, Conversing with Sources: Writing the Researched Paper. For advice on organizing comparison/contrast papers, see Chapter 9.

Strategies for Making Comparison/Contrast More Analytical, Including Difference within Similarity

Strategy 1: Argue for the significance of a key comparison. Rather than simply covering a range of comparisons, focus on a key comparison. Although narrowing the focus might seem to eliminate other important areas of consideration, in fact it usually allows you to incorporate at least some of these other areas in a more tightly connected, less list-like fashion. So, for example, a comparison of the burial rites of two cultures will probably reveal more about them than a much broader but more superficial list of cultural similarities and differences. In the majority of cases, covering less is covering more.

You can determine which comparison is key by ranking. You are ranking whenever you designate one part of your topic as especially important or revealing. Suppose you are asked to compare General David Petraeus's strategy in the Afghanistan conflict with General Douglas MacArthur's strategy in World War II. As a first move, you could limit the comparison to some revealing parallel, such as the way each man dealt with the media, and then argue for its significance above other similarities or differences. You might, for instance, claim that in their treatment of the media we get an especially clear or telling vantage point on the two generals' strategies. Now you are on your way to an analytical point—for example, that because MacArthur was more effectively shielded from the media at a time when the media was a virtual instrument of propaganda, he could make choices that Petraeus might have wanted to make, but could not.

Strategy 2: Use one side of the comparison to illuminate the other. Usually it is not necessary to treat each part of the comparison equally. It's a common misconception that each side must be given equal space. In fact, the purpose of your comparison governs the amount of space you'll need to give to each part. Often, you will be using one side of the comparison primarily to illuminate the other. For example, in a course on contemporary military policy, the ratio between the two parts would probably be roughly seventy percent on Petraeus to thirty percent on MacArthur, rather than fifty percent on each.

Strategy 3: Imagine how one side of your comparison might respond to the other. This strategy, a variant of the preceding one, is a particularly useful way of helping you to respond to comparison/contrast topics more purposefully. This strategy can be adapted to a wide variety of subjects. If you were asked to compare Sigmund Freud with one of his most important followers, Jacques Lacan, you would probably be better off focusing the broad question of how Lacan revises Freud by considering how and why he might critique Freud's interpretation of a particular dream in *The Interpretation of Dreams*. Similarly, in the case of the Afghanistan example, you could ask yourself how MacArthur might have handled some key decision in dealing with Kabul and why. Or you might consider how he would have critiqued Petraeus's decisions and why.

Strategy 4: Focus on DIFFERENCE WITHIN SIMILARITY (or similarity despite difference). Too often writers notice a fundamental similarity and stop there. Asked to compare two subjects, they typically collect a number of parallel examples and merely show how they are parallel. This practice leads to bland tallying of similarities without much analytical edge—a matching exercise. Ideas tend to arise when a writer moves beyond this basic demonstration and complicates (or qualifies) the similarity by also noting areas of difference and accounting for their significance.

The solution is to practice what we call "looking for DIFFERENCE WITHIN SIMILARITY":

Step 1: Decide whether the similarities or differences are most obvious and easily explained.

Step 2: Briefly explain the relatively obvious similarity or difference by ASKING "SO WHAT?" Why is this similarity or difference significant?

Step 3: Then focus your attention on the less obvious but revealing DIFFERENCE WITHIN THE SIMILARITY or similarity despite the difference.

The phrase "DIFFERENCE WITHIN SIMILARITY" is to remind you that once you have started your thinking by locating apparent similarities, you can usually refine that thinking by pursuing significant, though often less obvious, distinctions among the similar things.

In Irish studies, for example, scholars characteristically acknowledge the extent to which contemporary Irish culture is the product of colonization. To this extent, Irish culture shares certain traits with other former colonies in Africa, Asia, Latin America, and elsewhere. But instead of simply demonstrating how Irish culture fits the general pattern of colonialism, these scholars also isolate the ways that Ireland *does not fit* the model. They focus, for example, on how its close geographical proximity and racial similarity to England, its colonizer, have distinguished the kinds of problems it encounters today from those characteristic of the more generalized model of colonialism. In effect, looking for DIFFERENCE WITHIN SIMILARITY has led them to locate and analyze the anomalies.

A corollary of the DIFFERENCE WITHIN SIMILARITY formula is similarity despite difference—that is, focusing on unexpected similarity rather than obvious difference. Consider, for example, two popular twenty-something TV sitcoms from different generations, *Friends* and *The Big Bang Theory*. At first inspection, these would appear to differ profoundly—one presents a heterosexual group living together in which everyone is straight; the other centers on an all-male group living together in which sexual orientation is—in at least one case—ambiguous.

But how are the two shows similar despite these differences? Both offer the consoling prospect of a comfortable space between the teen years and the specter of adulthood, before the kind of separation that coupling off and having kids incurs. In other words, both suggest that adulthood can be comfortably forestalled by offering a group of friends who become family, regardless of male/female or gay/straight binaries.

Regardless of whether you begin by deciding that the similarities or the differences are most obvious, choosing to focus on less immediately noticeable differences or similarities will cause you to notice things that you otherwise might not have noticed. This is what comparison and contrast is designed to reveal. **To sum up:**

> When A & B are obviously similar,
> > look for unexpected difference.
> When A & B are obviously different,
> > look for unexpected similarity.

Definition

Definition becomes meaningful when it serves some larger purpose. You define "rhythm and blues" because it is essential to any further discussion of the evolution of rock and roll music, or because you need that definition in order to discuss the British Invasion spearheaded by groups such as the Beatles, the Rolling Stones, and the Yardbirds in the late 1960s, or because you cannot classify John Lennon or Mick Jagger or Eric Clapton without it.

Like comparison/contrast, definition can produce pointless essays if the writer gets no further than assembling information. Moreover, when you construct a summary of existing definitions with no clear sense of purpose, you tend to list definitions indiscriminately. As a result, you are likely to overlook conflicts among the various definitions and overemphasize their surface similarities. Definition is, in fact, a site at which there is some contesting of authorities—different voices that seek to make their individual definitions triumph.

Strategies for Making Definition More Analytical

Strategy 1: Test the definition against evidence. One common form of definition asks you to apply a definition to a body of information. It is rare to find a perfect fit. Therefore, you should, as a general rule, use the data to assess the accuracy and the limitations of the definition, rather than simply imposing it on your data and ignoring or playing down the ways in which it does not fit. Testing the definition against evidence will evolve your definition. The definition, in turn, will serve as a lens to better focus your thinking about the evidence.

Suppose you were asked to define capitalism in the context of third world economies. You might profitably begin by matching some standard definition of capitalism with specific examples from one or two third world economies, with the express purpose of detecting where the definition does *and* *does not* apply. In other words, you would respond to the definition topic by assaying the extent to which the definition provides a tool for making sense of the subject.

Strategy 2: Use a definition from one source to illuminate another. As a general rule, you should attempt to identify the points of view of the sources from which you take your definitions, rather than accepting them as uncontextualized answers. It is essential to identify the particular slant because otherwise you will tend to overlook the conflicting elements among various definitions of a key term.

A paper on alcoholism, for example, will lose focus if you use all of the definitions available. If, instead, you convert the definition into a comparison and contrast of competing definitions, you can more easily generate a point and purpose for your definition. By querying, for example, whether a given source's definition of alcoholism is moral or physiological or psychological, you can more easily problematize the issue of definition.

Strategy 3: Problematize as well as synthesize the definition. To explore competing definitions of the same term requires you to attend to the difficulties of definition. In general, analysis achieves direction and purpose by locating and then exploring a problem. You can productively make a problem out of defining. This strategy is known as *problematizing*, which locates and then explores the significance of the uncertainties and conflicts. It is always a smart move to problematize definitions, as this tactic reveals complexity that less careful thinkers might miss.

The definition of capitalism that you might take from Karl Marx, for example, will differ in its emphases from Adam Smith's. In this case, you would not only isolate the most important of these differences, but also try to account for the fact that Marx's villain is Smith's hero. Such an accounting would probably lead you to consider how the definition has been shaped by each of these writers' political philosophies or by the culture in which each theory was composed.

Strategy 4: Shift from "what?" to "how?" and "why?" questions. It is no accident that we earlier offered the same strategy for making summary more analytical: analytical topics that require definition also depend on "why?" or "how?" questions, not "what?" questions (which tend simply to call for information).

If, for example, you sought to define the meaning of darkness in Joseph Conrad's *Heart of Darkness* and any two other modern British novels, you would do better to ask why the writers find "darkness" such a fertile term, rather than simply to accumulate various examples of the term in the three novels. You might start by isolating the single best example from each of the works, preferably ones that reveal important differences as well as similarities. Then, in analyzing how each writer uses the term, you could work toward some larger point that would unify the essay. You might show how the conflicts of definition within Conrad's metaphor evolve historically, get reshaped by woman novelists, change after World War I, and so forth.

Assignments: Responding to Traditional Writing Assignments More Analytically

1. **Analyzing the Wording of an Assignment.** Analyze the following topic for unstated questions.

   > In a well-written essay, evaluate the truth of the assertion that follows. Use evidence and examples from your reading or experience to make your argument convincing. "It is human nature to want patterns, standards, and a structure of behavior. A pattern to conform to is a kind of shelter."

   As we began to do with "Is feminism good for Judaism?" earlier, make a list of all of the questions implicit in this topic. Which words, both in the directions given to students and in the quotation, itself, require attention? When you have compiled your list, write a paragraph or two in which you explain, as specifically as possible, what the question is asking writers to do and how a writer might go about fulfilling these tasks.

2. **Write Two Summaries of the Same Article or Book Chapter.** Make the first one consecutive (the so-called "coverage" model)—that is, try to cover the piece by essentially listing the key points as they appear. Limit yourself to a typed page. Then rewrite the summary, doing the following:

   - rank the items in order of importance according to some principle that you designate, explaining your rationale;

   - eliminate the last few items on the list or, at most, give each a single sentence; and

   - use the space you have saved to include more detail about the most important item or two.

   The second half of this assignment will probably require closer to two pages.

3. **Look for Significant Difference or Unexpected Similarity.** Choose any item from the list below. After you've done the research necessary to locate material to read and analyze, list as many similarities and differences as you can: go for coverage. Then, review your list, and select the two or three most revealing similarities and the two or three most revealing differences. At this point, you are ready to write a few paragraphs in which you argue for the significance of a key difference or similarity. In so doing, try to focus on an *unexpected* similarity or difference—one that others might not initially notice.

1. accounts of the same event from two different newspapers or magazines or textbooks
2. two CDs (or even songs) by the same artist or group
3. two ads for the same kind of product, perhaps aimed at different target audiences
4. the political campaigns of two opponents running for the same or similar office
5. courtship behavior as practiced by men and by women
6. two clothing styles as emblematic of class or sub-group in your school, town, or workplace

4. **Write a Comparative Definition.** Seek out different and potentially competing definitions of the same term or terms. Begin with a dictionary such as the *Oxford English Dictionary* (popularly known as the *OED*, available in most library reference rooms or online) that contains both historically based definitions tracking the term's evolution over time and etymological definitions that identify the linguistic origins of the term (its sources in older languages). Be sure to locate both the historical evolution and the etymology of the term or terms.

Then look up the term in one—or preferably several—specialized dictionaries. You can also ask your reference librarian for pertinent titles. Generally speaking, different disciplines generate their own specialized dictionaries.

Summarize key differences and similarities among the ways the dictionaries have defined your term or terms. Then write a comparative essay in which you argue for the significance of a key similarity or difference, or an unexpected one.

Here is the list of words: hysteria, ecstasy, enthusiasm, witchcraft, leisure, gossip, bachelor, spinster, romantic, instinct, punk, thug, pundit, dream, alcoholism, aristocracy, atom, ego, pornography, conservative, liberal, entropy, election, tariff. Some of these words are interesting to look at together, such as ecstasy/enthusiasm or liberal/conservative or bachelor/spinster. Feel free to write on a pair, instead of on a single word.

CHAPTER 4

Reasoning from Evidence to Claims

Overview The chapter begins by addressing two common problems: claims without evidence (unsubstantiated claims) and evidence without claims (pointless evidence). The chapter then offers a brief summary of rules of argument and of the two most basic forms of arranging evidence and claims: deduction (moving from a general claim to specific evidence) and induction (moving from specific evidence to a more general claim).

Ultimately, we argue for the importance of saying more about less. The phrase we use for this idea is DOING 10 ON 1—making ten points and observations about a single example. The chapter ends with several templates—step by step procedures—for organizing papers.

In all disciplines, and in virtually any writing situation, it is important to support claims with evidence, to make your evidence lead to claims, and especially to be explicit about how you've arrived at the connection between your evidence and your claims.

Linking Evidence and Claims

The relationship between evidence and claims is rarely self-evident. The word *evident* comes from a Latin verb meaning "to see." To say that the truth of a statement is "self-evident" means that it does not need proving because its truth can be plainly seen by all. The thought connections that have occurred to you about what the evidence means will not automatically occur to others. Persuasive writing always makes the connections between evidence and claim overt (see Figure 4.1).

The first step in learning to explain the connection between your evidence and your claims is to remember that evidence rarely, if ever, can be

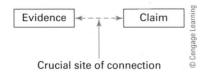

FIGURE 4.1
Linking Evidence and Claims

left to speak for itself. When you leave evidence to speak for itself, you are assuming that it can be interpreted in only one way and that others will necessarily think as you do.

Writers who think that evidence speaks for itself generally do very little with it. Sometimes they will present it without making any overt claims, stating, for example, "There was no alcohol at the party," and expecting the reader to understand this statement as a sign of approval or disapproval. Alternatively, they may simply place the evidence next to a claim: "The party was terrible—there was no alcohol," or "The party was great—there was no alcohol." Juxtaposing the evidence with the claim (just putting them next to each other) leaves out the thinking that connects them, thereby implying that the logic of the connection is obvious. But even for readers prone to agreeing with a given claim, simply pointing to the evidence is rarely enough.

The Functions of Evidence

A common assumption about evidence is that it is "the stuff that proves I'm right." Although this way of thinking about evidence is not wrong, it is much too limited. Corroboration (proving the validity of a claim) is one of the functions of evidence, but not the only one.

It helps to remember that the word *prove* actually comes from a Latin verb meaning "to test." The noun form of prove, proof, has two meanings: (1) evidence sufficient to establish a thing as true or believable, and (2) the act of testing for truth or believability. When you operate on the basis of the first definition of proof alone, you are far more likely to seek out evidence that supports only your point of view, ignoring or dismissing other evidence that could lead to a different and possibly better idea.

The advantage to following the second definition of the word proof—in the sense of testing—is that you will be better able to negotiate among competing points of view. Doing so will predispose your readers to consider what you have to say, because you are offering them not only the thoughts a person has had, but also a person in the act of thinking. Writing well means sharing your thought process with your readers, telling them why you believe the evidence means what you say it does.

"Because I Say So": Unsubstantiated Claims

Problem: Making claims that lack supporting evidence.
Solution: Using concrete details to support and sharpen the claim.

Unsubstantiated claims occur when a writer concentrates only on conclusions, omitting the evidence that led to them. At the opposite extreme, pointless evidence results when a writer offers a mass of detail attached to an overly general claim. Both of these problems can be solved by offering readers the evidence that led to the claim and explaining how the evidence led there.

The word *unsubstantiated* means "without substance." An unsubstantiated claim is not necessarily false, it just offers none of the concrete "stuff" upon which the claim is based. When a writer makes an unsubstantiated claim, he or she has assumed that readers will believe it just because the writer put it out there. Perhaps more important, unsubstantiated claims deprive a writer of details. If you lack actual "stuff" to analyze, you tend to overstate your position and leave your readers wondering exactly what you mean.

You can see the problem of unsubstantiated assertions not only in papers but also in everyday conversation. It occurs when people get in the habit of leaping to conclusions—forming impressions so quickly and automatically that they have difficulty even recalling what triggered a particular response. Ask such people why they thought a new acquaintance is pretentious, and they will rephrase the generalization rather than offer the evidence that led to it: the person is pretentious because he puts on airs.

Simply rephrasing your generalizations rather than offering evidence starves your thinking; it also shuts out readers. If, for example, you defend your judgment that a person is pretentious by saying that he puts on airs, you have ruled on the matter and dismissed it. (You have also committed a logical flaw known as a circular argument; because "pretentious" and "putting on airs" mean virtually the same thing, using one in support of the other is arguing in a circle.) If, by contrast, you include the grounds upon which your judgment is based—that he uses words without regard to whether his listeners will understand or that he always wears a bow tie—you have at least given readers a glimpse of your evaluative criteria. Readers are far more likely to accept your views if you give them the chance to think with you about the evidence. The alternative—offering groundless assertions—is to expect them to take your word for it.

There is, of course, an element of risk in providing the details that have informed your judgment. You leave yourself open to attack if, for example, your readers wear bow ties. But this is an essential risk to take, for otherwise, you leave your readers wondering why you think as you do, or worse, unlikely to credit your point of view.

Most importantly, taking care to substantiate your claims will make you more inclined to think openly and carefully about your judgments. And precisely because what people have taken to be common knowledge ("women can't do math," for example, or "men don't talk about their feelings") so often turns out to be wrong, you should take care to avoid unsubstantiated claims.

Distinguishing Evidence from Claims

To check your drafts for unsubstantiated assertions, you first have to know how to recognize them. It is sometimes difficult to separate facts from judgments, data from interpretations of the data. Writers who aren't practiced in this skill can believe that they are offering evidence when they are really offering only unsubstantiated claims. In your own reading and writing, pause once in a while to label the sentences of a paragraph as either evidence (E) or claims (C). What happens if we try to categorize the sentences of the following paragraph in this way?

The owners are ruining baseball in America. Although they claim they are losing money, they are really just being greedy. Some years ago, they even fired the commissioner, Fay Vincent, because he took the players' side. Baseball is a sport, not a business, and it is a sad fact that it is being threatened by greedy businessmen.

The first and last sentences of the paragraph are claims. They draw conclusions about as yet unstated evidence that the writer will need to provide. The middle two sentences are harder to classify. If particular owners have said publicly that they are losing money, the existence of the owners' statements is a fact. But the writer moves from evidence to unsubstantiated claims when he suggests that the owners are lying about their financial situation and are doing so because of their greed. Similarly, it is a fact that Commissioner Fay Vincent was fired, but it is only an assertion that he was fired "because he took the players' side," an unsubstantiated claim. Although many of us might be inclined to accept some version of this claim as true, we should not be asked to accept the writer's opinion as self-evident truth. What is the evidence in support of the claim? What are the reasons for believing that the evidence means what the writer says it does?

The writer of the baseball paragraph, for example, offers as fact that the owners claim they are losing money. If he were to search harder, however, he would find that his statement of the owners' claim is not entirely accurate. The owners have not unanimously claimed that they are losing money; they have acknowledged that the problem has to do with poorer "small-market" teams competing against richer "large-market" teams. This more complicated version of the facts might at first be discouraging to the writer, since it reveals his original thesis ("greed") to be oversimplified. But then, as we have been saying, the function of evidence is not just to corroborate your claims, it should also help you to test and refine your ideas and to define your key terms more precisely.

TRY THIS 4.1: Distinguishing Evidence from Claims
Take an excerpt from your own writing, at least two paragraphs in length—perhaps from a paper you have already written, or a draft you are working on—and label every sentence that seems to function as either evidence (E) or claim (C). For sentences that appear to offer both, determine which parts of the sentence are evidence and which are claim, and then decide which one, E or C, predominates. What is the ratio of evidence to claim? This is also an instructive way of working with other writers.

Giving Evidence a Point: Making Details Speak

Problem: Presenting a mass of evidence without explaining how it relates to the claims.

Solution: Make details speak. Explain how evidence confirms and qualifies the claim.

To make your thinking visible to your readers, follow through on the implications of your evidence. You have to make the details speak, conveying to your readers why they mean what you say they mean.

The following example illustrates what happens when a writer leaves the evidence to speak for itself.

> Baseball is a sport, not a business, and it is a sad fact that it is being threatened by greedy businessmen. For example, Eli Jacobs, the previous owner of the Baltimore Orioles, sold the team to Peter Angelos for one hundred million dollars more than he had spent ten years earlier when he purchased it. Also, a new generation of baseball stadiums has been built in the last few decades—in Baltimore, Chicago, Arlington (Texas), Cleveland, San Francisco, Milwaukee, Houston, Philadelphia, Washington, and, most recently, in Miami. These parks are enormously expensive and include elaborate scoreboards and luxury boxes. The average baseball players, meanwhile, now earn more than a million dollars a year, and they all have agents to represent them. Alex Rodriguez, the third baseman for the New York Yankees, is paid more than twenty million dollars a season. Sure, he continues to set records for homers by a player at his age, but is any ballplayer worth that much money?

Unlike the previous example, which was virtually all claims, this paragraph, except for the opening claim and the closing question, is all evidence. The paragraph presents what we might call an "evidence sandwich": it encloses a series of facts between two claims. (The opening statement blames "greedy businessmen," presumably owners, and the closing statement appears to indict greedy, or at least overpaid, players.) Readers are left with two problems. First, the mismatch between the opening and concluding claims leaves it not altogether clear what the writer is saying that the evidence suggests. And second, he has not told readers why they should believe that the evidence means what he says it does. Instead, he leaves it to speak for itself.

If readers are to accept the writer's implicit claims—that the spending is too much and that it is ruining baseball—he will have to show how and why the evidence supports these conclusions. The rule that applies here is that evidence can almost always be interpreted in more than one way.

We might, for instance, formulate at least three conclusions from the evidence offered in the baseball paragraph. We might decide that the writer believes baseball will be ruined by going broke or that its spirit will be ruined by becoming too commercial. Worst of all, we might disagree with his claim and conclude that baseball is not really being ruined, because the evidence could be read as signs of health rather than decay. The profitable resale of the Orioles, the expensive new ballparks (which, the writer neglects to mention, have drawn record crowds), and the skyrocketing salaries all could testify to the growing popularity, rather than the decline, of the sport.

How to Make Details Speak: A Brief Example The best way to begin making the details speak is to take the time to look at them, asking questions about what they imply.

1. Say explicitly what you take the details to mean.

2. State exactly how the evidence supports your claims.

3. Consider how the evidence complicates (qualifies) your claims.

The writer of the baseball paragraph leaves some of his claims and virtually all of his reasoning about the evidence implicit. What, for example, bothers him about the special luxury seating areas? Attempting to uncover his assumptions, we might speculate that he intends it to demonstrate how economic interests are taking baseball away from its traditional fans because these new seats cost more than the average person can afford. This interpretation could be used to support the writer's governing claim, but he would need to spell out the connection, to reason back to his own premises. He might say, for example, that baseball's time-honored role as the all-American sport—democratic and grass-roots—is being displaced by the tendency of baseball as a business to attract higher box office receipts and wealthier fans.

The writer could then make explicit what his whole paragraph implies: that baseball's image as a popular pastime in which all Americans can participate is being tarnished by players and owners alike, whose primary concerns appear to be making money. In making his evidence speak in this way, the writer would be practicing step 3 above—using the evidence to complicate and refine his ideas. He would discover which specific aspect of baseball he thinks is being ruined, clarifying that the "greedy businessmen" to whom he refers include both owners and players.

Let's emphasize the final lesson gleaned from this example. When you focus on tightening the links between evidence and claim, the result is almost always a "smaller" claim than the one you set out to prove. This is what evidence characteristically does to a claim: it shrinks and restricts its scope. This process is known as qualifying a claim.

Sometimes it is hard to give up on the large, general assertions that were your first responses to your subject. But your sacrifices in scope are exchanged for greater accuracy and validity. The sweeping claims you lose ("Greedy businessmen are ruining baseball") give way to less resounding—but also more informed, more incisive, and less judgmental—ideas ("Market pressures may not bring the end of baseball, but they are certainly changing the image and nature of the game").

More than Just "the Facts": What Counts as Evidence?

Thus far this chapter has concentrated on how to use evidence after you've assembled it. In many cases, though, a writer has to consider a more basic and often hidden question before collecting data: what counts as evidence?

This question raises two related concerns:

Relevance: in what ways does the evidence bear on the claim or problem that you are addressing? Do the facts really apply in this particular case, and if so, how?

Framing assumptions: in what ways is the evidence colored by the point of view that designated it as evidence? At what point does this coloring undercut the authority or reliability of the evidence?

To raise the issue of framing assumptions is not to imply that all evidence is merely subjective, somebody's impressionistic opinion. We are implying, however, that even the most apparently neutral evidence is the product of some way of seeing that qualifies the evidence as evidence in the first place. In some cases, this way of seeing is embedded in the established procedure of particular disciplines. In the natural sciences, for example, the actual data that go into the results section of a lab report or formal paper are the product of a highly controlled experimental procedure. As its name suggests, the section presents the results of seeing in a particular way.

The same kind of control is present in various quantitative operations in the social sciences, in which the evidence is usually framed in the language of statistics. And in somewhat less systematic—but nonetheless similar—ways, evidence in the humanities and in some projects in the social sciences is conditioned by methodological assumptions. A literature student cannot assume, for example, that a particular fate befalls a character in a story because of events in the author's life (it is a given of literary study that biography may inform, but does not explain, a work of art). Evidence is never just some free-floating, absolutely reliable, objective entity for the casual observer to sample at random. It is always a product of certain starting assumptions and procedures that readers must take into account.

In the following Voices from Across the Curriculum, Political Science Professor Jack Gambino suggests that it is always useful to try to figure out the methodological *how* behind the *what*, especially since methodology is always based in certain assumptions as opposed to others.

VOICES FROM ACROSS THE CURRICULUM

Questions of Relevance and Methodology: A Political Science Professor Speaks

What counts as evidence? I try to impress upon students that they need to substantiate their claims with evidence. Most have little trouble with this. However, when I tell them that evidence itself is dependent upon methodology—that it's not just a question of gathering "information," but also a question of how it was gathered—their eyes glaze over. Can we trust the source of information? What biases may exist in the way questions are posed in an opinion poll? Who counts as an authority on a subject? (No, Rush Limbaugh cannot be considered an authority on women's issues, or the environment, or, for that matter, anything else!) Is your evidence out-of-date? (In politics, books on electoral behavior have a shelf life only up to the next election. After two years, they may have severe limitations.)

Methodological concerns also determine the relevance of evidence. Some models of, say, democratic participation define as irrelevant certain kinds of evidence that other models might view as crucial. For instance, a pluralist view of democracy, which emphasizes the dominant role of competitive elites, views the evidence of low voter turnout and citizen apathy as a minor concern. More participatory models, in contrast, interpret the same evidence as an indication of the crisis afflicting contemporary democratic practices.

In addition to this question of relevance, methodology makes explicit the game plan of research: How did the student conduct his or her research? Why did he or she consider some information more relevant than others? Are there any gaps in the information? Does the writer distinguish cases in which evidence strongly supports a claim from evidence that is suggestive or speculative?

Finally, students need to be aware of the possible ideological nature of evidence. For instance, Americans typically seek to explain such problems as poverty in individualistic terms, a view consistent with our liberal heritage, rather than in terms of class structure, as a Marxist would. Seeking the roots of poverty in individual behavior simply produces a particular kind of evidence different from that which would be produced if we began with the assumption that class structure plays a decisive influence in shaping individual behavior.

—JACK GAMBINO, PROFESSOR OF POLITICAL SCIENCE

The preferences of different disciplines for certain kinds of evidence notwithstanding, most professors share the conviction that the evidence you choose to present should not be one-sided. They also understand that the observation of and use of evidence is never completely neutral. Whatever kind of evidence you're using, the emphasis rests on how you use what you have: how you articulate what it means and how carefully you link the evidence to your claims.

The Rules of Argument

Attempts to codify rules of argument—the reasoning process that connects evidence and claims—is part of a tradition of logic reaching back into antiquity. We will now take a brief excursion there to provide theoretical background about ways of reasoning with evidence and claims.

Philosophers have long quested for forms that might lend to human argument some greater clarity and certainty, like what is possible with formulas in math. As you will see and as most philosophers will readily admit, the reality of evaluating arguments in day-to-day life is necessarily a less tidy process than the rules of argument might make it seem.

The kinds of certainty that are sometimes possible with formulas in math are not so easily available when using words to make claims about human experience. Nevertheless, the rules of argument offer a set of specific guidelines for discovering things that go right—and wrong—in the construction of an argument.

Probably the most common way of talking about logical argumentation goes back to Aristotle. This approach doesn't always have direct applications to generating the kinds of analytical writing described in this book, but knowing the ways that philosophers have devised for evaluating arguments can expand your ability to assess your own and others' reasoning about claims and evidence.

Syllogism and Enthymeme

At the heart of the Aristotelian model is the syllogism. There are a number of rules for evaluating the validity of a syllogism's conclusion. In this short section, we cannot offer enough of the details about argument analysis to equip you with the necessary skills. But we will give you enough detail so that you can understand the basic principles and methods of this way of thinking about argument.

The syllogism is divided into three parts or steps:

1. Major premise: a general proposition presumed to be true

2. Minor premise: a subordinate proposition also presumed to be true

3. Conclusion: a claim that follows logically from the two premises, if the argument has been properly framed

Here is a frequently cited example of a syllogism:

> All men are mortal (major premise).
> Socrates is a man (minor premise).
> Therefore, Socrates is mortal (conclusion).

A premise is a proposition (assumption) upon which an argument is based and from which a conclusion is drawn. The two premises in a syllogism offer reasons for believing the conclusion of the syllogism to be valid. If both of the premises have been stated in the proper form (both containing a shared term), then the conclusion must be valid.

An important thing to know about syllogisms is that they are only as true as the premises they are made of. It is not, however, the business of the syllogism to test the truth of the premises. Syllogisms can only demonstrate that the form of the argument is valid. As you will see, this word "valid" is a key term in argument evaluation, a term that does not mean the same thing as right or true.

If a writer follows the prescribed steps of the syllogism without violating any of the rules on proper wording and on the way the steps may be put together, then the conclusion arrived at in step 3 is valid. An argument evaluated in this way can be valid and still be false. For example:

> All politicians are corrupt.
> The mayor of Chicago is a politician.
> Therefore, the mayor of Chicago is corrupt.

The problem here is not with the form of the syllogism, but with the fact that the major premise is untrue.

To make good use of syllogistic reasoning, you need to get into the habit of recasting arguments that you write or read or hear into the proper syllogistic form. The way that most people articulate claims—often without even recognizing that they are making claims—is rarely, if ever, syllogistic. Claims, for example, if they are to be most easily assessed for validity, need to be recast so that they use forms of "to be" rather than other kinds of verbs (as in the Chicago example above).

Arguments as we encounter them in daily life are considerably less easy to evaluate. These real-life arguments typically appear in a form that philosophers call the "enthymeme." An enthymeme is an incomplete syllogism. One of its premises has been left unstated, usually because the person offering the argument takes the unstated assumption to be a given, something so obviously true that it doesn't even need to be made explicit.

> Sample Enthymeme #1: Cats make better pets than dogs because cats are more independent.
> Unstated Assumption: Independent animals make better pets.
> Sample Enthymeme #2: Charter schools will improve the quality of education because they encourage competition.
> Unstated Assumption: Competition improves the quality of education.

Recognizing and testing the accuracy of the unstated assumption is critical to evaluating any claim. This one skill—uncovering unstated assumptions—is extremely useful in analyzing the claims you encounter in life and in your own writing.

Toulmin's Alternative Model of the Syllogism

The British philosopher Steven Toulmin offered a competing model of argument in his influential book, *The Uses of Argument* (1958). Toulmin's model was motivated by his belief that the philosophical tradition of formal logic, with its many rules for describing and evaluating the conduct of arguments, conflicts with the practice and idiom (ways of phrasing) of arguers. To radically simplify Toulmin's case, it is that the syllogism does not adequately account for what thinkers do when they try to frame and defend various claims. Toulmin describes the structure of argument in a way that he thought came closer to what actually happens in practice when we try to take a position.

The Toulmin model of argument re-names and reorders the process of reasoning described in the Aristotelian syllogism as follows:

1. Data: the evidence appealed to in support of a claim; data respond to the question "What have you got to go on?"

2. Warrant: a general principle or reason used to connect the data with the claim; the warrant responds to the question "How did you get there?" (from the data to the claim)

3. Claim: a conclusion about the data (see Figure 4.2)

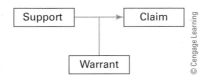

FIGURE 4.2
The Toulmin Model

Consider Figure 4.2 in terms of the chapter's opening discussion of linking evidence and claims. In the Toulmin model, the warrant is the link. It supplies the reasoning that explains why the evidence (support) leads to the conclusion (claim).

Let's look briefly at how this reasoning structure works in practice by looking at one of Toulmin's examples.

Data: Harry was born in Bermuda.
Warrant: The relevant statutes provide that people born in the colonies of British parents are entitled to British citizenship (reason for connecting data to claim);
Claim: So, presumably, Harry is a British citizen. (conclusion)

We can now follow Toulmin a little further in his critique and revision of syllogistic ways of describing thinking. A syllogism, as you saw above in the Socrates example, is designed to reveal its soundness through the careful framing and arrangement of its terms:

All men are mortal. (All x's are y.)
Socrates is a man. (Socrates is an x.)
Therefore, Socrates is mortal. (Socrates is y.)

At what price, asks Toulmin, do we simplify our phrasing of complex situations in the world in order to gain this appearance of truth? In how many situations, he asks, can we say that "all x's are y"?

The strictness of the rules necessary for guaranteeing formal validity, Toulmin argues, leaves out the greater amount of uncertainty that is a part of reasoning about most questions, issues, and problems. Toulmin observes, using his own argument structure as a case in point, that as soon as an argument begins to add information in support of its premises, the complexity and inevitable tentativeness of the argument become apparent, rather than its evident truth.

Here is Toulmin's explanation of what must happen to the form of an argument when a person begins to add more supporting information, which Toulmin calls *backing*. The backing for the warrant in the example above about the British citizenship of people born in Bermuda would inevitably involve mentioning "the relevant statutes"—acts of Parliament, statistical reports, and so forth—to prove its accuracy. The addition of such information, says Toulmin, would "prevent us from writing the argument so that its validity shall be manifest from its formal properties alone" (*The Uses of Argument* 123).

To use an analogy, if the Aristotelian syllogism appears to offer us the promise of never mistaking the forest for the trees, Toulmin's revision of that model is to never let us forget that the forest is in fact made up of trees.

As a writer, you will naturally want some guidelines and workable methods for selecting evidence and linking it to claims. But what you can't expect to find is a set of predetermined slots into which you can drop any piece of evidence and find the truth. Rather, analyses and arguments operate within the complex set of details and circumstances that are part of life as we live it. An argument depends not only on whether or not its premises follow logically, but also on the quality of the thinking that produces those premises in the first place and painstakingly tests their accuracy. This is the job of analysis.

Rogerian Argument and Practical Reasoning

Contemporary rhetoricians are less concerned about testing the adequacy of arguments than they are with making argument better serve the needs of people in everyday life and in the larger arena of public discourse. The view of argument offered throughout this book—for example, in the discussion of counterproductive habits of mind in Chapter 1—is aligned with the thinking of two such rhetoricians, Carl Rogers and Wayne Booth.

For these and other like-minded rhetoricians, the language of argument, which is often drawn from warfare, reflects its goal of gaining strategic advantage over others, who are considered as opponents. Booth and Rogers propose that the aim of argument should not be primarily to ensure certainty in order to defeat opponents, but to locate common ground.

Both Rogers and Booth emphasize the need to understand and accurately represent the positions of "opponents" in an argument rather than search for the best and quickest way to defeat them. "For Booth," as one scholar notes, "reasoning equates not just with rational thought but instead with inquiry, a term that more expansively describes the process all of us are daily engaged in to shape and make sense of the world—a process the ends of which are seldom certain or empirically measurable" (Zachary Dobbins, "Wayne Booth, Narrative, and the Rhetoric of Empathy"—a talk delivered at the 2010 Conference on College Composition and Communication). As Dobbins quotes from Booth's *Modern Dogma and the Rhetoric of Dissent*, "The supreme purpose of persuasion [. . .] should not be to talk someone else into a preconceived view; rather it must be to engage in mutual inquiry or exploration [. . .]." This goal is very much the norm in academic writing, where people try to put different points of view into conversation rather than set out to have one view defeat another.

Deduction and Induction: Two Ways of Linking Evidence and Claims

Next we will address how thinking moves in a piece of writing. The way evidence and claims are located creates different organizational shapes and sequences.

Anyone who looks seriously at the relationship between evidence and claim needs two key terms:

—induction: reasoning from particulars to the general, and
—deduction: reasoning from the general to the particular.

Take a moment to study Figure 4.3 on page 102.

As a thought process, deduction reasons from a general principle to a particular case, in order to draw a conclusion about that case. It introduces this principle up front and then uses it to select and interpret evidence. For example, a deductive paper might state in its first paragraph that attitudes toward and rules governing sexuality in a given culture can be seen, at least in part, to have economic causes. The paper might then apply this principle, already assumed to be true, to the codes governing sexual behavior in several cultures or several kinds of sexual behavior in a single culture. The writer's aim would be to use his or her general principle as a means of explaining selected features of particular cases.

A good deductive argument is, however, more than a mechanical application or matching exercise of general claim and specific details that are explained by it. Deductive reasoning uses the evidence to draw out the implications—what logicians term *inferring the consequences*—of the claim. Particularly in the sciences, the deductive process aims at predicting one phenomenon from another. A scientist asks in effect, "If x happens in a particular case, will it also happen in another similar case?"

The inductive thought process typically begins, not with a general principle, but with particular data for which it seeks to generate some explanatory principle. Whereas deduction moves by applying a generalization to particular cases, induction moves from the observation of individual cases to the formation of a general principle. Because all possible cases can obviously never be examined—every left-handed person, for example, if one wishes to theorize that left-handed people are better at spatial thinking than right-handers—the principle (or thesis) arrived at through inductive reasoning always remains open to doubt.

(A) Deduction

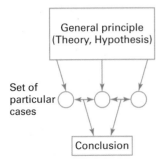

General principle
(Theory, Hypothesis)

Set of particular cases

Conclusion

(B) Induction

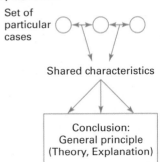

Set of particular cases

Shared characteristics

Conclusion:
General principle
(Theory, Explanation)

(C) Blend: Induction to Deduction

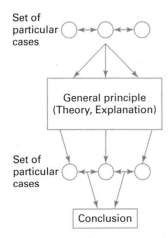

Set of particular cases

General principle
(Theory, Explanation)

Set of particular cases

Conclusion

(D) Blend: Deduction to Induction

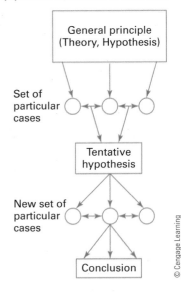

General principle
(Theory, Hypothesis)

Set of particular cases

Tentative hypothesis

New set of particular cases

Conclusion

© Cengage Learning

FIGURE 4.3

Deduction and Induction. Deduction (A) uses particular cases to exemplify general principles and analyze their implications. Induction (B) constructs general principles from the analysis of particular cases. In practice, analytical thinking and writing blend deduction and induction and start either with particular cases (C) or a general principle (D)

Nevertheless, the primary claim of an inductive paper is generally deemed credible if a writer can demonstrate that the theory is based on a reasonably sized sampling of representative instances. Obviously, a child who arrives at the claim that all orange food tastes bad on the basis of squash and carrots has not based that theory on an adequate sampling of available evidence.

Induction is a process aimed at forming theories about the meaning of things. The scientific method, for example, uses induction to evolve explanations for observed phenomenon such as the higher incidence of heart attacks among men than women. The proposed explanation (general principle) is then tested deductively according to the pattern: if theory X is true, then such-and-such should follow. If the particular results predicted by the theory do not occur when the theory is put to the test, the scientist knows that something is wrong with his or her induction. A deductive premise is only as good as the inductive reasoning that produced it in the first place. (See, in Chapter 6, our discussion of a student essay on the meaning of Velázquez's painting, *Las Meninas*, for an example of how inductive reasoning works in the writing process.)

As these examples show, in most cases induction and deduction operate in tandem (see Figure 4.3, C and D). The aim of analysis is usually to test (deductively) the validity of a hypothetical conclusion or to generate (inductively) a theory that might plausibly explain a given set of data. Analysis moves between the particular and the general, regardless of which comes first.

"1 on 10" and "10 on 1"

We use the terms 1 on 10 and 10 on 1 for deduction and induction, because these terms make it easy to visualize what in practice writers actually do when they use these thought processes. In 1 on 10, our term for deduction, a writer attaches the same claim (1) to a number of pieces of evidence. (The "10" stands for a series of examples, as shown in Figure 4.4). In 10 on 1, our term for induction, the writer makes a series of observations (arbitrarily, "10") about a single example (the "1"; see Figure 4.5). We now will talk about each of these in turn.

DOING 1 ON 10

To get started on 1 on 10, you need, of course, a 1—a claim that you think usefully illuminates the pieces of evidence you are looking at. You can arrive at this claim by searching for patterns of repetition in the evidence (see THE

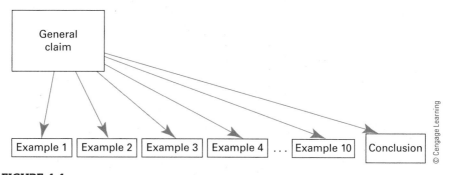

FIGURE 4.4

DOING 1 ON 10: 1 Claim, 10 Pieces of Evidence (in which 10 stands arbitrarily for any number of examples)

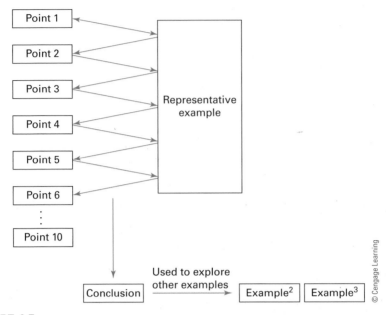

FIGURE 4.5

DOING 10 ON 1. The pattern of 10 on 1 (in which "10" stands arbitrarily for any number of points) successively develops a series of points about a single representative example. Its analysis of evidence is in depth

METHOD in Chapter 1). The primary reason you are looking at a number of examples is to determine if there is sufficient evidence to make the claim. The pieces of evidence will in effect be united by the claim. If, for example, you discover that revolutionary movements at different historical moments and geographical locales produce similar kinds of violence, you would be able to demonstrate that there is a generalizable model for organizing and understanding the evidence—a model that provides a way of seeing a vast amount of information.

The search for a claim that enables the deductive way of seeing necessarily involves focusing on similarity rather than difference. If a writer in reading the biblical book of Exodus focuses broadly on the difficulties of faith, she could formulate a principle that might be used deductively to reveal the unity in the book: that again and again the Israelites get into trouble whenever their faith in God falters.

Similarly, when scientists test a theory by seeing how well it explains certain phenomena, they are operating deductively. They use the theory—the "1"—to call attention to and explain what otherwise might have seemed entirely disconnected pieces of evidence. This is what is exciting about deduction at its best—it's revealing. It highlights a pattern in a body of evidence that, before the revelation of pattern, just seemed a collection of data.

1. Either start with a preexisting claim or generate a claim by using THE METHOD or NOTICE & FOCUS to find a revealing pattern or tendency in your evidence. (See Chapter 1.)

2. As you move through the evidence, look for data that corroborate your claim.

3. Formulate your reasons for saying that each piece of evidence supports the overarching claim.

4. Work out how the separate parts of your data connect.

5. Revise and enrich the implications of your claim (the 1) on the basis of the series of examples (the 10) you've presented.

A Potential Problem with 1 on 10: Mere Demonstration

The single biggest potential problem in 1 on 10 papers is that the form lends itself so easily to superficial thinking. This is true in part because when the time comes to compose a formal paper, it is very common for writers to panic, and abandon the wealth of data and ideas they have accumulated in the exploratory writing stage, telling themselves, "Now I better have my one idea and be able to prove to everybody that I'm right." Out goes careful attention to detail. Out goes any evidence that doesn't fit. Instead of analysis, they substitute the kind of paper we call a *demonstration*. That is, they cite evidence to prove that a generalization is generally true. The problem with the demonstration lies with its too limited notions of what a thesis and evidence can do in a piece of analytical thinking.

The 1 on 10 demonstration, as opposed to a more productive deductive analysis, results from a mistaken assumption about the function of evidence: that it exists only to demonstrate the validity of (corroborate) a claim. Beyond corroborating claims, evidence should serve to test and develop them. A writer who makes a single and usually very general claim ("History repeats itself," "Exercise is good for you," and so forth) and then proceeds to affix it to ten examples is likely to produce a list, not a piece of developed thinking.

DOING 10 ON 1: Saying More About Less

The phrase "10 on 1" is the term the book uses to describe inductive ways of proceeding in a piece of writing. Rather than looking at the whole, you are looking in depth at a part that you think is representative of the whole. Note that 10 on 1 is a deliberate inversion of 1 on 10, so that the "1" now stands for a single, rich, and representative example, and the "10" stands for the various observations that you are able to make about it. To return to the Exodus example, a writer who wished to explore the dynamics of failed faith might make his "1" the episode of the golden calf in chapter 32: 1–35. He might isolate key repetitions and strands, and actively raise questions. Why, for example, does Moses burn the idol, grind it to powder, scatter it on water, and make the Israelites drink it?

DOING 10 ON 1 will lead you to draw out as much meaning as possible from your best example—a case of narrowing the focus and then analyzing in depth. Eventually you will move from this key example to others that usefully extend and qualify your point, but first you need to let analysis of your representative example produce more thinking. In Exodus 35, for example, failed faith provokes anger (arguably, the key repetition in the chapter) and eventual bloodshed. Before a writer could see these three terms as a pattern in the text, he'd need to study other instances of failed faith in this book of the Bible.

The practice of DOING 10 ON 1 remedies the major problem writers have when they do 1 on 10: simply attaching a host of examples to an obvious and overly general claim, with little or no analysis. DOING 10 ON 1 requires writers to explore the evidence, not just generalize about it.

You can use 10 on 1 to accomplish various ends: (1) to locate the range of possible meanings your evidence suggests, (2) to make you less inclined to cling to your first claim, (3) to open the way for you to discover the complexity of your subject, and (4) to slow down the rush to generalization and thus help to ensure that when you arrive at a working thesis, it will be more specific and better able to account for your evidence.

Organizing Papers Using 10 on 1

1. Use THE METHOD or NOTICE & FOCUS to find a revealing pattern or tendency in your evidence. (See Chapter 1.)

2. Select a representative example.

3. Do 10 on 1 to produce an in-depth analysis of your example.

4. Test your results in similar cases.

A Potential Problem with 10 on 1: Not Demonstrating the Representativeness of Your Example

Focusing on your single best example has the advantage of economy, cutting to the heart of the subject, but it runs the risk that the example you select might not in fact be representative. You need to demonstrate its representativeness overtly. This means showing that your example is part of a larger pattern of similar evidence and not just an isolated instance. To establish that pattern it is useful to do 1 on 10—locating ten examples that share a trait— as a preliminary step and then select one of these for in-depth analysis.

In terms of logic, the problem of generalizing from too little and unrepresentative evidence is known as an unwarranted inductive leap. The writer leaps from one or two instances to a broad claim about an entire class or category. Just because you see an economics professor and a biology professor wearing corduroy jackets, for example, you would not want to leap to the conclusion that all professors wear corduroy jackets. Most of the time, unwarranted leaps result from making too large a claim and avoiding examples that might contradict it.

FIGURE 4.6
Tiananmen Square, Beijing, 1989

Doing 10 on 1: A Brief Example (Tiananmen Square) Note how the writer of the following discussion of the people's revolt in China in 1989 sets up his analysis. He first explains how his chosen example—a classic photograph (shown in Figure 4.6) from the media coverage of the event—illuminates his larger subject. The image is of a Chinese man in a white shirt who temporarily halted a line of tanks on their way to quell a demonstration in Tiananmen Square in Beijing.

> The tank image provided a miniature, simplified version of a larger, more complex revolution. The conflict between man and tank embodied the same tension found in the conflict between student demonstrators and the Peoples' Army. The man in the white shirt, like the students, displayed courage, defiance, and rebellious individuality in the face of power. Initially, the peaceful revolution succeeded: the state allowed the students to protest; likewise, the tank spared the man's life. Empowered, the students' demands for democracy grew louder. Likewise, the man boldly jumped onto the tank and addressed the soldiers. The state's formerly unshakable dominance appeared weak next to the strength of the individual. However, the state asserted its power: the Peoples' Army marched into the square, and the tanks roared past the man into Beijing.
>
> The image appeals to American ideology. The man in the white shirt personifies the strength of the American individual. His rugged courage draws on contemporary heroes such as Rambo. His defiant gestures resemble the demonstrations of Martin Luther King Jr. and his followers. American history predisposes us to identify strongly

with the Chinese demonstrators: we have rebelled against the establishment, we have fought for freedom and democracy, and we have defended the rights of the individual. For example, The New York Times reported that President George [H. W.] Bush watched the tank incident on television and said, "I'm convinced that the forces of democracy are going to overcome these unfortunate events in Tiananmen Square." Bush represents the popular American perspective of the Chinese rebellion; we support the student demonstrators.

This analysis is a striking example of DOING 10 ON 1. In the first paragraph, the writer constructs a detailed analogy between the particular image and the larger subject of which it was a part. The analogy allows the writer not just to describe but also to interpret the event. In the second paragraph, he develops his focus on the image as an image, a photographic representation tailor-made to appeal to American viewing audiences. Rather than generalizing about why Americans might find the image appealing, he establishes a number of explicit connections (does 10 on 1) between the details of the image and typical American heroes. By drawing out the implications of particular details, he manages to say more about the significance of the American response to the demonstrations in China than a broader survey of those events would have allowed.

TRY THIS 4.2: DOING 10 ON 1 with Newspaper Visuals

Search out photographs in the newspaper and do 10 on 1. Or alternatively, spend some time DOING 10 ON 1 on a comic strip. What perspectives emerge once you have restricted the focus? List details, and also list multiple implications. Remember to ask not just What do I notice? but What else do I notice? And not just What does it imply? but What else might it imply?

TRY THIS 4.3: DOING 10 ON 1 with a Reading

Take a piece of reading—a representative example—from something you are studying and do 10 on 1. Allow yourself to notice more and more about the evidence and make the details speak. A single, well-developed paragraph from something you are reading can be enough to practice on, especially because you are working on saying more about less, rather than less about more.

10 on 1 and Disciplinary Conventions

In some cases, the conventions of a discipline appear to discourage DOING 10 ON 1. The social sciences, in particular, tend to require a larger set of analogous examples to prove a hypothesis. Especially in certain kinds of research, the focus of inquiry rests on discerning broad statistical trends over a wide range of evidence. But some trends deserve more attention than others, and some statistics similarly merit more interpretation than others. The best writers learn to choose examples carefully— each one for a reason—and to concentrate on developing the most revealing ones in depth.

For instance, proving that tax laws are prejudiced in particularly subtle ways against unmarried people might require a number of analogous cases along with a statistical summary of the evidence. But even with a subject such as this, you could still concentrate on some examples more than others. Rather than moving through each example as a separate case, you could use your analyses of these primary examples as lenses for investigating other evidence.

Larger Organizational Schemes: Writing Papers Based on 1 on 10 & 10 on 1

The goal of this chapter has been to get you to think about all the choices you can make in arranging evidence and claims, and in clarifying the relation between the two. It's not surprising that the logical processes we've been discussing for moving between evidence and claims can be adapted into frameworks for organizing papers.

We're going to start with a negative example, a form with which many of you will be familiar, to show what can go wrong when a writer connects evidence and claims in too mechanical a fashion. We will then offer some templates (step-by- step roadmaps) that will show you how to arrange evidence and claims in a coherent fashion without sacrificing the necessary attention to detail and to careful qualification of ideas.

The Problem of 5-Paragraph Form: A Reductive Version of 1 on 10

As you've seen, some organizational schemes have the potential to resist careful thinking, as does 1 on 10, for example, when it is allowed to become a superficial demonstration. One version of this format is 5-paragraph form, an organizational scheme that we criticized in Chapter 1 as an example of the slot-filler mentality.

Many of you will find the basic five-paragraph form familiar, as it is commonly taught in schools:

1. An introduction that ends with a thesis listing three points (the so-called tripartite or three-part thesis)

2. Three body paragraphs, each supporting one of the three points

3. A conclusion beginning "Thus, we see" or "In conclusion" that essentially repeats the thesis statement as it was in paragraph one

Here is an example in outline form:

Introduction: The food in the school cafeteria is bad. It lacks variety, it's unhealthy, and it is always overcooked. In this essay I will discuss these three characteristics.

Paragraph 2: The first reason cafeteria food is bad is that there is no variety. (Plus one or two examples—no salad bar, mostly fried food, and so forth)

Paragraph 3: Another reason cafeteria food is bad is that it is not healthy. (Plus a few reasons—high cholesterol, too many hot dogs, too much sugar, and so forth)

Paragraph 4: In addition, the food is always overcooked. (Plus some examples—the vegetables are mushy, the "mystery" meat is tough to recognize, and so forth)

Conclusion: Thus, we see . . . (Plus a restatement of the introductory paragraph)

Most high school students write dozens of themes using this basic formula. They are taught to use five-paragraph form because it seems to provide the greatest good—a certain minimal clarity—for the greatest number of students. But the form does not promote logically tight and thoughtful writing. It is a meat grinder that can turn any content into sausages.

The two major problems it typically creates are easy to see.

1. *The introduction reduces the remainder of the essay to redundancy.* The first paragraph gives readers a list of what they're going to hear; the succeeding three paragraphs tell them the same thing again in more detail; and the conclusion repeats what they have just been told repeatedly. What is the primary cause of all this redundancy? As in the example above, an overly general thesis (cafeteria food is "bad") substitutes a list of predictable points for a complex statement of idea.

2. *The form arbitrarily divides content:* The format invites writers to list rather than analyze, plugging supporting examples into categories without examining them or how they are related. Isn't overcooked food unhealthy? Isn't a lack of variety also conceivably unhealthy? Why are there three points (or examples or reasons) instead of five or one? As is evident in the transitions ("first," "second," "in addition"), the form prompts the writer simply to append evidence to generalizations without saying anything about it.

The subject of the sample essay, on the other hand, is not as unpromising as the format makes it appear. It could easily be redirected along a more productive pathway. (If the food is bad, what are the underlying causes of the problem? Are students getting what they ask for? Is the problem one of cost? Why or why not?)

Now let's look briefly at the introductory paragraph from a student's essay on a more academic subject. Here we can see a remarkable feature of five-paragraph form—its capacity to produce the same kind of say-nothing prose on almost any subject.

> Throughout the film *The Tempest*, a version of Shakespeare's play *The Tempest*, there were a total of seven characters. These characters were Calibano, Alonso, Antonio, Aretha, Freddy, the doctor, and Dolores. Each character in the film represented a person in Shakespeare's play, but there were four people who were greatly similar to those in Shakespeare, and who played a role in symbolizing aspects of forgiveness, love, and power.

The final sentence of the paragraph reveals the writer's addiction to five-paragraph form. It signals that the writer will proceed in a purely mechanical and superficial way, producing a paragraph on forgiveness, a paragraph on love, a paragraph on power, and a conclusion stating again that the film's characters resemble Shakespeare's in these three aspects. The writer is so busy demonstrating that the characters are concerned with forgiveness, love, and power that she misses the opportunity to analyze the significance of her own observations.

Instead, readers are drawn wearily to a conclusion; they get no place except back where they began. Further, the demonstration mode prevents her from analyzing connections among the categories. The writer might consider, for example, how the play and the film differ in resolving the conflict between power and forgiveness (focusing on difference within similarity). Or she might complicate the relationship among her three points—for example, that the play only appears to be about love and forgiveness but is really about power.

These more analytical approaches lie concealed in the writer's introduction, but they never get discovered because the five-paragraph form militates against sustained analytical thinking. Its division of the subject into parts, which is only one part of analysis, has become an end unto itself.

Greek mythology offers a memorable way to think about the problem with five-paragraph form. On his way to Athens, the hero Theseus encounters a particularly surly host, Procrustes, who offers wayfarers a bed for the night but with a catch. If they do not fit his bed exactly, he either stretches them or lops off their extremities until they do. This story has given us the word "procrustean," which the dictionary defines as "tending to produce conformity by violent or arbitrary means." Five-paragraph form is a procrustean formula that most students learn in high school. Although it has the advantage of providing a mechanical format that will give virtually any subject the appearance of order, it usually lops off a writer's ideas before they have the chance to form, or it stretches a single idea to the breaking point.

A complex idea is one that has many sides. To treat such ideas intelligently, writers need a form that will not require them to cut off all of those sides except the one that most easily fits the bed.

Rehabilitating Five-Paragraph Form

Here are two quick checks for whether five-paragraph form has closed down the thinking in a paper of yours, in which case it needs rehabilitation:

1. Look at the paragraph openings. Do these read like a list, each beginning with an additive transition like "another" followed by a more or less exact repetition of your central point ("another example is . . . ," "yet another example is . . .")?

2. Compare the wording in the last statement of the paper's thesis (in the conclusion) with the first statement of it in the introduction. Is the wording at these two locations virtually the same?

If the answer is yes to these two questions, chances are great that you are listing, rather than analyzing, the evidence.

What can you do to remedy the situation? As we hope you can see, the problems that beset 5-paragraph form have less to do with the form, itself, than with the underdeveloped thinking habits it allows and, perhaps, encourages. There is nothing inherently wrong with partitioning, dividing a paper into three or more parts or phases and connecting each deductively to some governing claim. There is also nothing wrong with a claim that becomes, in effect, a road map for the paper.

But to rehabilitate the form, you probably need to revamp the claim and restructure the way it connects with the evidence. The claim needs to do something: to lead readers to discover a meaning or see a pattern beyond the obvious in the data.

As for the evidence, don't just say repeatedly that each point or example or reason supports your thesis. Ask yourself, what has my thesis caused me to see in my evidence that might otherwise not be evident to readers? And what are the logical connections among the three parts or phases?

Outline for a Viable Version of Five-Paragraph Form

1. Write a short paragraph, half-page, typed, double spaced in which you say what you think is the most interesting or revealing or strange thing you've noticed about your subject. Conclude the paragraph by asking and answering an initial "so what?"—as in, where might this observation get us? How might we best understand it? Make sure this is not just a three-point list. This answer is your initial shot at a thesis.

2. Spend three body paragraphs, the three phases or parts of the middle of your paper, explaining what that claim has allowed you to notice in your data.

3. Make sure to explain the links among the three phases or parts. How does one lead to another? How do they differ despite their similarity, and So what?

4. End with an ultimate "So what?" How might the things you've noticed lead to a better understanding of the subject than would otherwise have been possible? What are the implications of your conclusion for further thinking on this or related subjects?

Pan, Track, & Zoom: "Directing" Your Paper

The language of filmmaking offers a useful way for understanding the different ways that a writer can focus evidence. The writer, like the director of a film, controls the focus through different kinds of shots—pan, track, and zoom. This analogy is particularly useful for locating 10 on 1 in the context of a larger paper. The zoom (a close-up shot) is equivalent to a writer DOING 10 on 1. The zoom is then located in the context of two other kinds of shots—pans and tracks.

The pan—The camera pivots around a stable axis, giving the viewer the big picture. Using a pan, we see everything from a distance. Pans provide a context, some larger pattern, the "forest" within which the writer can also examine particular "trees." Pans establish the representativeness of the example the writer later examines in more detail, showing that it is not an isolated instance.

The track—The camera no longer stays in one place, but follows some sequence of action. For example, whereas a pan might survey a room full of guests at a cocktail party, a track would pick up a particular guest and follow along as she walks across the room, picks up a photograph, proceeds through the door, and throws the photo in a trash can. Analogously, a writer tracks by moving in on selected pieces of the larger picture and following them to make telling connections among them.

The zoom—The camera moves in even closer on a selected piece of the scene, allowing us to notice more of its details. For example, a zoom might focus in on the woman's hand as she crumples the photograph she's about to throw away or on her face as she slams the lid on the trash can. A writer zooms in by giving us more detail on a particular part of his or her evidence and making the details say more. The zoom is the shot that enables you to do 10 on 1.

Ultimately, pan, track, and zoom express a writer's authority—known in academic lingo as *agency*, the power to shape events. Many writers are not aware of their choices in how to present what they have to say; they don't realize that they can see things from different distances—close up, middle distance, far away—and that they can cover a lot of ground swiftly, or they can pause to linger over one small spot.

Pan, track, and zoom also have a lot to do with a writer's awareness of audience, and what that audience needs to know. Often in the midst of a piece of writing, you are tracking from one tree (or point) to the next in the forest, but you and your reader both can forget how you got there, where you've come from, and where you're bound.

At that point, suddenly panning on the forest, giving the reader the larger picture in one shot, can help reorient everyone. This need to reinforce the place of a particular part in terms of the larger whole (in film lingo, an establishing shot) is even more pronounced when a writer has been focused in close. After being asked to focus closely on a single issue or example, the reader needs to be brought back to the ongoing logical or narrative sequence (the what-comes-next) in order to stay on track. Just as in a film, the pan gives us a sense of the whole, the track gives us a sense of coherence and continuity, and the zoom gives us a privileged look at moments of greatest important and interest, enabling us to consider the subject in more detail.

In a short paper (three to five pages), you might devote as much as 90 percent of your writing to exploring what one example (the "1"—your zoom) reveals about the larger subject. Even in a paper that uses several examples, however, as much as 50 percent might still be devoted to analysis of and generalization from a single case. The remaining portion of the paper would make connections with other examples, testing and applying the ideas you arrived at from your single case. In-depth analysis of your best example thus creates a center from which you can move in two directions: (1) toward generalizations about the larger subject and (2) toward other examples, using your primary example as a tool of exploration.

A Template for Organizing Papers Using 10 on 1

Here is a template for writing papers using 10 on 1. It brings together much of the key terminology introduced in this chapter. Think of it—not as a rigid format—but as an outline for moving from one phase of your paper to the next. Unlike five-paragraph form, the template will give you room to think and to establish connections among your ideas.

1. In your introduction, start by noting (panning on) an interesting pattern or tendency you have found in your evidence. (As explained earlier in the chapter, you may find it useful to do 1 on 10 in order to discover the pattern.) Explain what attracted you to it—why you find it potentially significant and worth looking at. This paragraph would end with a tentative theory (working thesis) about what this pattern or tendency might reveal or accomplish.

2. Zoom in on your representative example, some smaller part of the larger pattern and argue for its representativeness and usefulness in coming to a better understanding of your subject.

3. Do 10 on 1. Analyze your representative example, sharing with your readers your observations (what you notice) and your tentative conclusions (answers to the So what? question). Then use complicating evidence to refine your claims.

4a. In a short paper, you might at this point move to your conclusion, with its qualified, refined version of your thesis and brief commentary on what you've accomplished—that is, the ways in which your analysis has illuminated the larger subject.

4b. In a longer paper, you would begin "constellating"—organizing the essay by exploring and elaborating the connections among your representative examples analyzed via 10 on 1.

When you constellate evidence, you connect the dots, so to speak, as do the imaginary lines we draw between stars when creating a constellation in the night sky. We see the evidence coming together in a meaningful pattern.

In the language of the film analogy, you would move from your initial zoom to another zoom on a similar case, to see the extent to which the thesis you evolved with your representative example needed further adjusting to better reflect the nature of your subject as a whole. This last move is a primary topic of Chapter 6, Finding and Evolving a Thesis.

DOING 10 ON 1 to Find an Organizing Claim: A Student Paper

The essay below is an exploratory draft on a film, using a single scene to generate its thinking. As you read the essay, watch how the writer uses 10 on 1. Notice how the writer repeatedly tests her tentative conclusions against the evidence until she arrives at a plausible *working thesis* that might organize the next draft.

On the Edge: A Scene from *Good-bye Lenin*!

1. The movie shows us Alex and Lara's first date, which is to a sort of underground music club where the performers wear costumes made of plastic tubing and leather, and play loud hard-core rock music. At first, the musicians look surreal, as though they are part of a strange dream from which, at any moment, Alex will awake. The Western rock is real, though, as are the sci-fi costumes, and the scene moves forward to show Alex and Lara climbing a stairway out onto what looks like a fire escape and then through a window and into an apartment.

2. Here, Alex and Lara settle down into conversation. The young couple sits, hand in hand, and gazes together into the night sky; yet, as the camera pans away, we see that the apartment where the two have retreated is missing its façade. Inside, three walls are still decorated, complete with furniture, wallpaper, and even working lamps; yet, the two sit on the ledge of the fourth wall, which has crumbled away completely.

3. [**So what?:**] On the surface, I think the movie invites us to read this as a visual representation of the new lives Alex, Lara, and the other characters face now that the wall has fallen. As a Westerner, at first I read this scene as a representation of the new relationship between Lara and Alex. In other words, I imagined the movie's placement of the couple on the ledge of a domestic space as a representation of where their lives were going together—toward some shared domestic life, toward living together, toward becoming a family. I also thought this was a clever representation of the collapse of communism—this wall has also fallen down.

4. [**complicating evidence:**] I don't think, however, that the movie lets us entertain this one romanticized reading of the scene for long—the image is too frightening. As the camera pans away, we see that this isn't a new Westernized apartment; this is an East German flat decorated in much the same way as Alex's home was only months before. The image is alarming; the wall here has been ripped down, [So what?:] and we are forced to ask, did the fall of communism violently blow apart domestic and daily living of East German people?

5. The movie allows us this dichotomy and, I think, fights to sustain it. On one hand, Alex and Lara would not be on this date if the wall hadn't come down, and yet the scene is more than just another representation of East Germany torn between Communism and the new Westernization. [**working thesis:**] <u>The movie tries</u>

hard to remind us that the rapid Westernization of East Germany devastated while it liberated in other ways. This scene uses space to represent Alex and Lara's (and East Germany's) dilemma: Alex and Lara gaze out at the night sky but only because the wall has been blown apart. The exposed apartment is uninhabitable and yet the lights still work, the pictures are still hung, and a young couple leans against one another inside.

Notice how the writer's DOING 10 ON 1 causes a main idea, a claim, to take shape. The writer would now evaluate this claim by asking herself how well it accounts for the things she has noticed. Take a look again at the Five Analytical Moves in Chapter 1 and the observational strategies included there. 10 on 1 uses these strategies repeatedly:

What do you notice? + Rank. Which observations seem the most significant, and why?

What repeats, what goes with what, what is opposed to what, and So what? (THE METHOD)

Rank by explaining which repetition, strand, or contrast (binary) you think is most significant and why. The answer to this question could become "the 1" (a tentative theory) for organizing a paper.

TRY THIS 4.4: Marking Claims, Evidence, and Complications in a Draft
As a check on the range of concepts that this and the previous chapter have introduced, mark the student draft ("On the Edge: A Scene from *Good-bye Lenin!*") as follows:

- *Mark claims—assertions made about the evidence—with the letter C.* Claims are ideas that the evidence seems to support. An example of a claim is in paragraph 4: "I don't think, however, that the movie lets us entertain this one romanticized reading of the scene for long."

- *Underline evidence.* The evidence is the pool of primary material (data)—details from the film, rather than the writer's ideas about it. An example of evidence is in paragraph 2: "The young couple sits, hand in hand, and gazes together into the night sky; yet, as the camera pans away, we see that the apartment where the two have retreated is missing its façade." This piece of evidence is the 1 of the 10 on 1. In effect, the whole draft goes after the range of possible implications that may be inferred from the image of the young couple sitting at the edge of an apartment that is missing one of its walls, presumably a result of war damage.

- *Circle complications.* Complications can be found both in the evidence a writer cites and in the claims a writer makes about it. Complicating evidence is evidence that does not fit the claims the writer has been making. For example, in paragraph 4: "As the camera pans away, we see that this isn't a new Westernized apartment; this is an East German flat decorated in much the same way as Alex's home was only months

before. The image is alarming; the wall here has been ripped down."
This evidence causes the writer to reconsider an earlier claim from
paragraph 3 that the scene is about the couple moving "toward some
shared domestic life, toward living together, toward becoming a family."

Assignments: Reasoning from Evidence to Claims

1. **Locate and Analyze Enthymemes.** Gather a list of statements—claims
   that you either overhear, find yourself saying, or read. Treat these as
   enthymemes: reason back to and articulate the unstated assumption
   already assumed to be true upon which each claim depends. Here's an
   example: Standardized testing is a problem because it tends to control
   what teachers can teach.

2. **Do 10 on 1 on a Scene from a Film.** Write a 10 on 1 analysis on a single
   scene or kind of scene from a film, using the student paper on *Good-bye
   Lenin!* as a model. On the basis of this analysis, write a single-sentence
   claim that could become a thesis for a longer paper on this film.

3. **Revise a 1 on 10 Paper Using 10 on 1.** Locate a deductively organized
   paper you have written or have in draft. Choose the single example
   that you find most interesting in the paper, and now do 10 on 1 on it to
   explore further its implications. This analysis should teach you more
   about your subject, leading you to a revised thesis. Use this revised
   thesis as a lens to revise the entire essay.

4. **Study a Feature Piece from a Magazine.** Write an analysis of an essay
   from a magazine that specializes in analytical journalism, such as *The
   New Yorker* or *The Atlantic Monthly*. Figure out the essay's organizational
   scheme by marking its claims and evidence and examining how the
   piece progresses among the various claims it makes. Describe this
   organizational pattern, noting for example how and when it moves
   inductively or deductively, and where it pauses to dwell in some detail
   (zoom) on a particular piece of its evidence.

5. **Write a Paper Following the Template for Organizing Papers Using 10
   on 1.** Choose a topic for your paper from something you are studying
   that you are trying to think more carefully about: economic stimulus
   packages, government bailouts, intelligence tests, failed revolutions,
   successful fascist dictatorships, etc. You might select a representative passage from a story or a representative story from a volume of
   stories by a single author. You might choose a representative passage
   of several pages or perhaps a chapter from a book in one of your other
   courses. Then write a short essay, following the template.

CHAPTER 5

Interpretation

Overview In this chapter we focus on the move from description to interpretation and address some of the issues that interpretation typically raises. What makes some interpretations better than others? What makes interpretations more than a matter of personal opinion? The chapter's strategies include specifying an interpretive context, interpreting figurative language, and "SEEMS TO BE ABOUT X." The chapter concludes with a brief glossary of logical fallacies.

Making Interpretations Plausible

The book has so far offered two kinds of prompts for making interpretive leaps: ranking (what is most important, or interesting, or revealing and why?) and asking "So What?" We've also demonstrated that the writer who can offer careful description of a subject's key features is likely to arrive at conclusions about possible meanings that others would share. We will now add another necessary move: specifying and arguing for a context in which the evidence might be best understood—the **interpretive context.**

Here are two key principles:

- *Everything means,* which is to say that everything in life calls on us to interpret, even when we are unaware of doing so.
- *Meaning is contextual,* which is to say that meaning-making always occurs inside of some social or cultural or other frame of reference.

HOW TO INTERPRET

Organize the data (do THE METHOD)
Move from observation to implication (ASK SO WHAT?)
Select an appropriate interpretive context
Determine a range of plausible interpretations
Assess the extent to which one interpretation explains the most

Your readers' willingness to accept an interpretation is powerfully connected to their ability to see its *plausibility*—that is, how it follows from both the supporting details that you have selected and the language you have used in characterizing those details. *An interpretive conclusion is not a fact, but a theory.* Interpretive conclusions stand or fall not so much on whether they can be proved right or wrong, but on whether they are demonstrably plausible. Often the best that you can hope for with interpretive conclusions is not that others will say, "Yes, that is obviously right," but "Yes, I can see where it might be possible and reasonable to think as you do."

Meanings must be reasoned from sufficient evidence if they are to be judged plausible. Meanings can always be refuted by people who find fault with your reasoning or can cite conflicting evidence. Let's refer back briefly to a hypothetical interpretation raised in Chapter 1's discussion of *Whistler's Mother*: that the woman in the painting who is clad in black is mourning the death of a loved one, perhaps a person who lived in the house represented in the painting on the wall. It is true that black clothes often indicate mourning. This is a culturally accepted sign. But with only the black dress and perhaps the sad facial expression (if it is sad) to go on, this "mourning theory" gets sidetracked from what is actually in the painting and moves into storytelling. Insufficient evidence would make this theory implausible.

Now, what if another person asserted that Whistler's mother is an alien astronaut, for example, her long black dress concealing a third leg? Obviously, this interpretation would not win wide support, and for a reason that points up another of the primary limits on the meaning-making process: meanings, to have value outside one's own private realm of experience, have to make sense to other people. This is to say that the relative value of interpretive meanings is to some extent socially (culturally) determined. The assertion that Whistler's mother is an alien astronaut is unlikely to be deemed acceptable by enough people to give it currency.

Although people are free to say that things mean whatever they want them to mean, saying doesn't make it so. The mourning theory has more evidence than the alien astronaut theory, but it still relies too heavily on what is not there, on a narrative for which there is insufficient evidence in the painting itself.

In experimental science, it is especially important that a writer/researcher be able to locate his or her work in the context of other scientists who have achieved similar results. Isolated results and interpretations, those that are not corroborated by others' research, have much less credibility. In this respect, the making of meaning is collaborative and communal. The collaborative nature of scientific and scholarly work is one of the reasons that writing about reading is so important in college-level writing. In order to interpret evidence in a way that others will find plausible, you first have to have some idea of what others in the field are talking about.

Context and the Making of Meaning

Most interpretations that people are willing to accept as plausible occur inside some social or cultural context. They are valid according to a given point of view—what the social commentator Stanley Fish has called an "interpretive community." We'll now try to answer questions posed at the chapter's opening—what makes some interpretations better than others? And what makes interpretations more than a matter of personal opinion?

Regardless of how the context is arrived at, an important part of getting an interpretation accepted as plausible is to argue for the appropriateness of the interpretive context you use, not just the interpretation it takes you to. *An interpretive context is a lens.* Depending on the context you choose—preferably a context suggested by the evidence itself—you will see different things.

Different interpretations will account better for some details than others—which is why it enriches our view of the world to try on different interpretations. Ultimately, you will have to decide which possible interpretation, as seen through which plausible interpretive context, best accounts for what you think is most important and interesting to notice about your subject.

Consider, for example, a reading of *Whistler's Mother* that a person might produce if he or she began with noticing the actual title, *Arrangement in Grey and Black: The Artist's Mother*. From this starting point, a person might focus exclusively on the disposition of color and arrive at an interpretation that the painting is about painting (which might then explain why there is also a painting on the wall).

The figure of the mother then would have meaning only insofar as it contained the two colors mentioned in the painting's title, black and gray, and the painting's representational content (the aspects of life that it shows us) would be assigned less importance. This is a promising and plausible idea for an interpretation. It makes use of different details from previous interpretations that we've suggested, but it would also address some of the details already targeted (the dress, the curtain) from an entirely different context.

To generalize: two equally plausible interpretations can be made of the same thing. It is not the case that our first reading (in Chapter 1), focusing on the profile view of the mother and suggesting the painting's concern with mysterious separateness, is right, whereas the painting-about-painting (or aesthetic) view, building from the clue in the title, is wrong. They operate within different contexts.

Specifying an Interpretive Context: A Brief Example

Notice how in the following analysis the student writer's interpretation relies on his choice of a particular interpretive context, post-World War II Japan. Had he selected another context, he might have arrived at different conclusions about the same details. Notice also how the writer perceives a pattern in the details and queries his own observations ("So what?") to arrive at an interpretation.

> The series entitled "Kamaitachi" is a journal of the photographer Hosoe's desolate childhood and wartime evacuation in the Tokyo countryside. He returns years later to the areas where he grew up, a stranger to his native land, perhaps likening himself to the legendary Kamaitachi, an invisible sickle-toothed weasel, intertwined with the soil and its unrealized fertility. "Kamaitachi #8" (1956), a platinum palladium print, stands alone to best capture Hosoe's alienation from and troubled expectation of the future of Japan. [Here the writer chooses the photographer's life as his interpretive context.]

The image is that of a tall fence of stark horizontal and vertical rough wood lashed together, looming above the barren rice fields. Straddling the fence, half-crouched and half-clinging, is a solitary male figure, gazing in profile to the horizon. Oblivious to the sky above of dark and churning thunderclouds, the figure instead focuses his attentions and concentrations elsewhere. [**The writer selects and describes significant detail.**]

It is exactly this *elsewhere* that makes the image successful, for in studying the man we are to turn our attention in the direction of the figure's gaze and away from the photograph itself. He hangs curiously between heaven and earth, suspended on a makeshift man-made structure, in a purgatorial limbo awaiting the future. He waits with anticipation—perhaps dread?—for a time that has not yet come; he is directed away from the present, and it is this sensitivity to time which sets this print apart from the others in the series. One could argue that in effect this man, clothed in common garb, has become Japan itself, indicative of the post-war uncertainty of a country once-dominant and now destroyed. What will the future (dark storm clouds) hold for this newly humbled nation? [**Here the writer notices a pattern of in-between-ness and locates it in an historical context in order to make his interpretive leap.**]

Remember that regardless of the subject you select for your analysis, you should directly address not just "What does this say?" but also, as this writer has done, "*What are we invited to make of it, and in what context?*"

Intention as an Interpretive Context

An interpretive context that frequently creates problems in analysis is intention. People relying on authorial intention as their interpretive context typically assert that the author—not the work itself—is the ultimate and correct source of interpretations.

Look at the drawing titled *The Dancers* in Figure 5.1. What follows is the artist's statement about how the drawing came about and what it came to mean to her.

© The Dancers, by Sarah Kersh. Pen and ink drawing, 6″ × 13.75″. Used by Permission of Sarah Kersh.

FIGURE 5.1
The Dancers by Sarah Kersh

> This piece was created completely unintentionally. I poured some ink onto paper and blew on it through a straw. The ink took the form of what looked like little people in movement. I recopied the figures I liked, touched up the rough edges, and ended with this gathering of fairy-like creatures. I love how in art something abstract can so suddenly become recognizable.

In this case, interestingly, the artist initially had no intentions beyond experimenting with materials. As the work evolved, she began to arrive at her own interpretation of what the drawing might suggest. Most viewers would probably find the artist's interpretation plausible, but this is not to say that the artist must have the last word and that it is somehow an infraction for others to produce alternative interpretations.

Suppose the artist had stopped with her first two sentences. Even this explicit statement of her lack of intention would not prohibit people from interpreting the drawing in some of the ways that she later goes on to suggest. The artist's initial absence of a plan doesn't require viewers to interpret *The Dancers* as only ink on paper.

Whenever an intention is ascribed to a person or an act or a product, this intention contributes significantly to meaning; but the intention, whatever its source, does not outrank or exclude other interpretations. It is simply another context for understanding.

Here is another example. In the early 1960s, a popular domestic sitcom entitled *Leave It to Beaver* portrayed the mother, June Cleaver, usually impeccably dressed in heels, dress, and pearls, doing little other than dusting the mantelpiece and making tuna fish sandwiches for her sons. Is the show then intentionally implying that the proper role for women is that of domestic helper? Well, in the context of post-women's movement thinking, the show's representation of Mrs. Cleaver might plausibly be read this way, but not as a matter of intention. To conclude that *Leave It to Beaver* promoted a particular stereotype about women does not mean that the writers got together every week and thought out ways to do so.

It is interesting and useful to try to determine from something you are analyzing what its makers might have intended. But, by and large, you are best off concentrating on what the thing itself communicates as opposed to what someone might have wanted it to communicate.

What Is and Isn't "Meant" to Be Analyzed

What about analyzing things that were not intended to "mean" anything, like entertainment films and everyday things like blue jeans and shopping malls? Some people believe that it is wrong to bring out unintended implications. Let's take another example: Barbie dolls. These are just toys intended for young girls, people might say. Clearly, the intention of Mattel, the makers of Barbie, is to make money by entertaining children. Does that mean Barbie must remain outside of interpretive scrutiny for such things as her built-in earrings and high-heeled feet? What the makers of a particular product or idea intend is only a part of what that product or idea communicates.

The urge to cordon off certain subjects from analysis on the grounds that they weren't meant to be analyzed unnecessarily excludes a wealth of information—and meaning—from your range of vision. It is right to be careful about the interpretive contexts we bring to our experience. It is less right—less useful—to confine our choice of context in a too literal-minded way to a single category. To some people, baseball is only a game and clothing is only there to protect us from the elements.

What such people don't want to admit is that things communicate meaning to others whether we wish them to or not, which is to say that the meanings of most things are socially determined. What, for example, does the choice of wearing a baseball cap to a staff meeting or to a class "say"? Note, by the way, that a communicative gesture such as the wearing of a hat need not be premeditated to communicate something to other people. The hat is still "there" and available to be "read" by others as a sign of certain attitudes and a culturally defined sense of identity—with or without intention.

Baseball caps, for example, carry different associations from berets or wool caps because they come from different social contexts. Baseball caps convey a set of attitudes associated with the piece of American culture they come from. They suggest, for example, popular rather than high culture, casual rather than formal, young—perhaps defiantly so, especially if worn backward—rather than old, and so on.

We can, of course, protest that the "real" reason for turning our baseball cap backward is to allow more light in, making it easier to see than when the bill of the cap shields our faces. This practical rationale makes sense, but it does not explain away the social statement that the hat and a particular way of wearing it might make, whether or not this statement is intentional. Because meaning is, to a significant extent, socially determined, we can't entirely control what our clothing, our manners, our language, or even our way of walking communicates to others.

The social contexts that make gestures like our choice of hats carry particular meanings are always shifting, but some such context is always present. As we asserted at the beginning of this chapter, everything means, and meaning is always contextual.

Avoiding the Extremes: Neither "Fortune Cookie" nor "Anything Goes"

Two of the most common missteps in producing an interpretation are the desire for a single, right answer and, at the opposite extreme, the conviction that all explanations are equally acceptable (or equally lame!). The first of these we call the Fortune Cookie School of Interpretation, and the latter we label the Anything Goes School.

The Fortune Cookie School of Interpretation

Proponents of the Fortune Cookie School believe that if a person can only "crack" the thing correctly—the subject, the problem—it will yield an extractable and self-contained "message." There are several problems with this conception of the interpretive process.

First, the assumption that things have single hidden meanings interferes with open-minded and dispassionate observation. Adherents of the Fortune Cookie School look solely for clues pointing to *the* hidden message and, having found these clues, discard the rest, like the cookie in a Chinese restaurant once the fortune has been extracted. The fortune cookie approach forecloses on the possibility of multiple plausible meanings, each within its own context. When you assume that there is only one right answer, you are also assuming that there is only one proper context for understanding and, by extension, that anybody who happens to select a different starting point or context and who thus arrives at a different answer is necessarily wrong.

Most of the time, practitioners of the fortune cookie approach aren't even aware that they are assuming the correctness of a single context, because they don't realize a fundamental truth about interpretations: they are always limited by contexts. In other words, we are suggesting that claims to universal truths are problematic. Things don't just mean in some simple and clear way for all people in all situations; they always mean within a network of beliefs, from a particular point of view. The person who claims to have access to some universal truth, beyond context and point of view, is either naïve (unaware) or, worse, a bully—insisting that his or her view of the world is obviously correct and must be accepted by everyone.

The "Anything Goes" School of Interpretation

At the opposite extreme from the Fortune Cookie School lies the completely relativist Anything Goes School. The problem with the anything goes approach is that it tends to assume that *all* interpretations are equally viable, and that meanings are simply a matter of individual choice, regardless of evidence or plausibility. Put another way, it overextends the creative aspect of interpretation to absurdity, arriving at the position that you can see in a subject whatever you want to see. But such unqualified relativism is not logical. It is simply not the case that meaning is entirely up to the individual; some readings are clearly better than others. The better interpretations have more evidence and rational explanation of how the evidence supports the interpretive claims—qualities that make these meanings more public and negotiable.

Implications Versus Hidden Meanings

While some people search for a single right answer and dismiss the rest, others dismiss the interpretive project altogether. Those who adopt this latter stance are excessively literal minded; they see any venture into interpretation as a benighted quest to impose "hidden meanings" on the reader.

The phrase itself, "hidden meaning," carries implications. It suggests that meanings exist in places other than the literal words on the page: they are to be found either "under" or "between" the lines of text.

Another phrase with which they disparage the interpretive process is "reading between the lines," suggesting that we have to look for meanings elsewhere than in the lines of text themselves. At its most skeptical, the phrase "reading between the lines" means that an interpretation has come from nothing at all, from the white space between the lines, and therefore has been imposed on the material by the interpreter.

Neither of these positions is a wholly unreasonable response because each recognizes that meanings are not always overt. But responding with these phrases misrepresents the process of interpretation. To understand why, let's spell out some of the assumptions that underlie these phrases.

The charge that the meaning is hidden can imply for some people an act of conspiracy on the part of either an author, who chooses to deliberately obscure his or her meaning, or on the part of readers, who conspire to "find" things lurking below the surface that other readers don't know about and are unable to see. A further assumption is that people probably know what they mean most of the time but, for some perverse reason, are unwilling to come out and say so.

Proponents of these views of analysis are, in effect, committing themselves to the position that everything in life means what it says and says what it means. It is probably safe to assume that most writers try to write what they mean and mean what they say. That is, they try to control the range of possible interpretations that their words could give rise to, but there is always more going on in a piece of writing (as in our everyday conversation) than can easily be pinned down and controlled. It is, in fact, an inherent property of language that it always means more than, and thus other than, it says.

It is also true that a large part of human communication takes place indirectly. A good example of this is metaphor, to which we now turn.

Figurative Logic: Reasoning with Metaphors

Metaphor, it has been said, is one of the few uses of language in which it is okay to say one thing and mean another. It is, in other words, a way of communicating things via association and implication rather than direct statement. If metaphors were to be found only in poems, as some people assume, then interpreting them would be a specialized skill with narrow application. But, in fact, metaphors are deeply engrained in the language we use every day, which becomes evident as soon as we take the time to notice them.

George Lakoff, Professor of Linguistics and Cognitive Science, and English Professor, Mark Turner, among others, have demonstrated that metaphors are built into the way we think. (See Lakoff and Turner's book, *More than Cool Reason, a Field Guide to Poetic Metaphor*, University of Chicago Press, 1989.) As such, metaphors routinely constitute our assumptions about the world and our place in it. Life, for example, is a journey. To become successful you climb a ladder. Being up is a good thing. To be down is to be unhappy (or blue). These are all metaphors.

If we accept their implicit arguments in an unexamined way, metaphors can call the shots in our lives more than we should allow them to. For example, if you believe that success involves climbing a ladder, you will be more likely to feel compelled to constantly climb higher than others in an organization rather than take a chance on a horizontal move that might lead you to something more personally rewarding (and in that respect, more successful). And if you have absorbed from the culture the idea that life is a race, then you will be worried about not moving fast enough and not competing effectively with others, as opposed to collaborating or doing something different that most others are not doing, perhaps something with no obvious prize attached.

THE LOGIC OF METAPHOR

- Metaphors pervade our ways of thinking
- Metaphor is a way of thinking by analogy
- The logic of metaphors is implicit
- The implicit logic of metaphors can be made explicit by scrutinizing the language
- We can recast figurative language to see and evaluate its arguments

The fact that metaphors require interpretation—as do most uses of language—does not take away from the fact that metaphors are a way of thinking. Being able to articulate the implicit arguments embodied in metaphors—making their meanings explicit so that they can be opened to discussion with others—is an important skill to acquire.

Although figurative logic does not operate in the same way as claims-based (propositional) logic, it nevertheless produces arguments, the reasoning of which can be analyzed and evaluated *systematically*. Let's start with a definition. Metaphors and similes work by **analogy**—a type of comparison that often finds similarities between things that are otherwise unlike.

Consider the simile "My love is like a red red rose." A simile, identifiable by its use of the words "like" or "as," operates like a metaphor except that both sides of the analogy are explicitly stated. The subject of the simile, love, is called the *tenor*; the comparative term brought in to think about love, rose, is called the *vehicle*.

In metaphors, the thought connection between the vehicle (rose) and the tenor (my love) is left unstated. But for our purposes, the clearer and more explicit simile will do. It is the nature of the resemblance between the speaker's love and roses that we are invited to infer.

Here is where the process of interpreting figurative language becomes systematic. The first step in interpreting this simile is to list the characteristics of the vehicle, red roses—especially red red (very red) roses—that might be relevant in this piece of thinking by analogy. Most people find roses to be beautiful. Most people associate red with passion. In fact, science can now measure the body's response to different colors. Red produces excitement. Red can even make the pulse rate go up. Roses are also complicated flowers. Their shape is convoluted. Roses are thought of as female. Rose petals are fragile. Many roses have thorns. So, the simile is actually a piece of thinking about love and about women.

It is not a very deep piece of thinking, and probably many women would prefer that the thorn part not be made too prominent. In fact, a reader would have to decide in the context of other language in the poem whether thorniness, as a characteristic of some roses, is significant and ought to be considered. The point is that the simile does make an argument about women that could be stated overtly, analyzed and evaluated. The implication that women, like roses, might have thorns—and thus be hard to "pick," defending them from male intruders, etc.—is part of the argument.

Figure 5.2 represents the procedure for exploring the logic of metaphor.

1 **Isolate the vehicle**—the language in the metaphor that states one side of the analogy.

2 **Articulate the characteristics of the vehicle, its defining traits.**

3 **Select the characteristics of the vehicle that seem most significant in context.**

4 **Make interpretive leaps to what the metaphor communicates.** Use significant characteristics of the vehicle to prompt these leaps.

© 2015 Cengage Learning

FIGURE 5.2
Interpreting Figurative Language

Notice how, in the rose example, our recasting of the original simile has made explicit the implicit meanings suggested by the figurative language. This recasting is a useful act of thinking, one that makes evident the thought process that a metaphor sets in motion.

What such recasting reveals is not only that metaphors do, in fact, make claims, but that they are remarkably efficient at doing so. A metaphor can say a lot in a little by compressing a complex amalgam of thought and feeling into a single image.

TRY THIS 5.1: Uncovering the Logic of Figurative Language
Uncover the figurative logic in the following statements by making what is implicit explicit in each. Follow the Steps for Interpreting Figurative Language.

- Conscience is a man's compass. *Vincent Van Gogh*

- All religions, arts and sciences are branches of the same tree. *Albert Einstein*

- All the world's a stage, and all the men and women merely players. They have their exits and their entrances. *William Shakespeare*

- America has tossed its cap over the wall of space. *John F. Kennedy*

- I am the good shepherd, … and I lay down my life for the sheep. *The Bible, John 10:14–15*

TRY THIS 5.2: Analyzing the Figurative Language of Politics
Figurative language is especially pervasive in politics. Go online and find some examples of arguments between Democrats and Republicans being carried out through metaphors and similes. You can find, for example, short articles on Obama's favorite metaphors and Republican attempts to reconfigure these for their own ends. Here is an example of Obama speaking about the midterm elections in September 2010:

> They drove our economy into a ditch. And we got in there and put on our boots and we pushed and we shoved, and we were sweatin'. And these guys were standing, watching us, and sipping on a Slurpee…. And then when we finally got the car up— and it's got a few dings and a few dents, it's got some mud on it, we're going to have to do some work on it … they got the nerve to ask for the keys back!

Unpack the logic of your examples, and write a paragraph or two on why you think a particular strand of figurative language has become prominent at this time.

Seems to Be About X, But Could Also Be (Or Is "Really") About Y

When people begin to interpret something, they usually find that less obvious meanings are cloaked by more obvious ones, and so they are distracted from seeing them. In most cases, the less obvious and possibly unintended meanings are more telling and more interesting than the obvious ones they have been conditioned to see.

The person who is doing the interpreting too often stops with the first "answer" that springs to mind as he or she moves from observation to implication, often landing upon a cliché. If this first response becomes the X, then the writer is prompted to come up with other, probably less commonplace interpretations, as the Y. (See Figure 5.3.)

This prompt is based on the conviction that understandings are rarely simple and overt. Completing the formula by supplying key terms for X and Y, writers get practice in making the implicit explicit and accepting the existence of multiple plausible meanings for something. SEEMS TO BE ABOUT X is especially useful when considering the rhetoric of a piece: its complex and various ways of targeting and appealing to an audience. It's also useful for "reading against the grain"—seeking out what something is about that it probably does not know it's about.

© 2015 Cengage Learning

1	Start the interpretive process by filling in the blank (the X) in the statement "This subject seems to be about X." X should be an interpretive leap, not just a summary or description.
2	Pose another interpretive possibility by finishing the sentence, "but it could also be (or is really) about Y."
3	Repeat this process a number of times to provoke new interpretive leaps. In effect, you are brainstorming alternative explanations for the same phenomenon.
4	Choose what you think is the best formulation for Y and write a paragraph or more explaining your choice.

FIGURE 5.3

Doing "Seems to Be About X, But Could Also Be (Or Is "Really") About Y"

Note: Don't be misled by our use of the word *really* in this heuristic into thinking that there should be some single, hidden, right answer. The aim is to prompt you to think recursively—to come up with a range of possible landing sites for your interpretive leap rather than just one.

Seems to Be About X . . .: An Example

A classic and highly successful television ad campaign for Nike Freestyle shoes contains sixty seconds of famous basketball players dribbling and passing and otherwise handling the ball in dexterous ways to the accompaniment of court noises and hip-hop music. The ad seems to be about X (basketball or shoes) but could also be about Y. Once you've made this assertion, a rapid-fire (brainstormed) list might follow in which you keep filling in the blanks (X and Y) with different possibilities. Alternatively, you might find that filling in the blanks (X and Y) leads to a more sustained exploration of a single point. This is your eventual goal, but doing a little brainstorming first would keep you from shutting down the interpretive process too soon.

Here is one version of a rapid-fire list, any item of which might be expanded:

> Seems to be about basketball but is "really" about dance.
> Seems to be about selling shoes but is "really" about artistry.
> Seems to be about artistry but is "really" about selling shoes.
> Seems to be about basketball but is "really" about race.
> Seems to be about basketball but is "really" about the greater acceptance of black culture in American media and society.
> Seems to be about individual expertise but is "really" about working as a group.

Here is one version of a more sustained exploration of a single seems to be about x statement.

> The Nike Freestyle commercial seems to be about basketball but is really about the greater acceptance of black culture in American media. Of course it is a shoe commercial and so aims to sell a product, but the same could be said about any commercial.

What makes the Nike commercial distinctive is its seeming embrace of African-American culture. The hip-hop sound track, for example, which coincides with the rhythmic dribbling of the basketball, places music and sport on a par, and the dexterity with which the players (actual NBA stars) move with the ball—moonwalking, doing 360s on it, balancing it on their fingers, heads, and backs—is nothing short of dance.

The intrinsic cool of the commercial suggests that Nike is targeting an audience of basketball lovers, not just African-Americans. If I am right, then it is selling blackness to white as well as black audiences. Of course, the idea that blacks are cooler than whites goes back at least as far as the early days of jazz and might be seen as its own strange form of prejudice.

TRY THIS 5.3: Apply the Formula SEEMS TO BE ABOUT X, BUT COULD ALSO BE (OR IS "REALLY") ABOUT Y

Try it as the first sentence of an in-class writing or as a way of drafting an essay or to lead off a paragraph of writing to prepare for class discussion. The formula is helpful for revision as well.

Making an Interpretation: The Example of a *New Yorker* Cover

A major point of this section is that interpretive contexts are suggested by the material you are studying; they aren't simply imposed. Explaining why you think a subject should be seen through a particular interpretive "lens" is an important part of making interpretations reasonable and plausible. Our discussion illustrates a writer's decision-making process in choosing an interpretive context, and how, once that context has been selected, the writer goes about analyzing evidence to test as well as support the usefulness of that context.

The example upon which we are focusing is a visual image, a cover from *The New Yorker* magazine (See Figure 5.4). The cover is by Ian Falconer and is entitled "The Competition"; it appeared on the October 9, 2000 issue.

Producing a close description of anything you are analyzing is one of the best ways to begin because the act of describing causes you to notice more and triggers analytical thinking. Here is our description of the *New Yorker* cover.

Description of a *New Yorker* Cover, dated October 9, 2000

The picture contains four women, visible from the waist up, standing in a row in semi-profile, staring out at some audience other than us, since their eyes look off to the side. All four gaze in the same direction. Each woman is dressed in a bathing suit and wears a banner draped over one shoulder in the manner of those worn in the swimsuit competition at beauty pageants. Three of the women are virtually identical. The banners worn by these three women show the letters *gia*, *rnia*, and *rida*, the remainder of the letters being cut off by the other women's shoulders, so that we have to fill in the missing letters to see which state each woman represents.

FIGURE 5.4
"The Competition" by Ian Falconer

Artwork by Ian Falconer/The New Yorker © 2000 Conde Naste Publications Inc.

The fourth woman, who stands third from the left in line, tucked in among the others who look very much alike, wears a banner reading YORK. This woman's appearance is different in just about every respect from the other three. Whereas they are blonde with long flowing hair, she is dark with her hair up in a tight bun. Whereas their mouths are wide open, revealing a wall of very white teeth, her mouth is closed, lips drawn together. Whereas their eyes are wide open and staring, hers, like her mouth, are nearly closed, under deeply arched eyebrows.

The dark woman's lips and eyes and hair are dark. She wears dark eye makeup and has a pronounced dark beauty mark on her cheek. Whereas the other three women's cheeks are high and round, hers are sharply angular. The three blonde women wear one-piece bathing suits in a nondescript gray color. The dark-haired woman, whose skin stands out in stark contrast to her hair, wears a two-piece bathing suit, exposing her midriff. Like her face, the dark-haired woman's breast, sticking out in half profile in her bathing suit, is pointed and angular. The other three women's breasts are round and quietly contained in their high-necked gray bathing suits.

Using THE METHOD to Identify Patterns of Repetition and Contrast

As we discussed in Chapter 1, looking for patterns of repetition and contrast (aka THE METHOD) is one of your best means of getting at the essential character of a subject. It will prevent you from generalizing, instead involving you in hands-on engagement with the details of your evidence. Step 1, looking for things that repeat exactly, tends to suggest items for step 2, repetition of the same or similar kinds of words or details (strands), and step 2 leads naturally to step 3, looking for binary oppositions and organizing contrasts.

Here are our partial lists of exact repetitions and strands and binary oppositions in *The New Yorker* cover:

Some Details that Repeat Exactly

Large, wide open, round eyes (3 pairs)
Long, blonde, face-framing hair (3)
Small, straight eyebrows (3 pairs)
Wide-open (smiling?) mouths with expanses of white teeth (3)
(but individual teeth not indicated)
banners (4) but each with different lettering
round breasts (3)
states that end in *a* (3)

Some Strands (groups of the same or similar kinds of details)

Lots of loose and flowing blonde hair/large, fully open, round eyes/large, open, rather round (curved) mouths:
Connecting logic = open, round
Skin uniformly shaded on three of the figures/minimal color and shading contrasts/mouths full of teeth, but just a mass of white without individual teeth showing:
Connecting logic = homogenous, undifferentiated, indistinct

Binary Oppositions

Blonde hair/black hair
Open mouths/closed mouth
Straight eyebrows/slanted (arched) eyebrows
Round breasts/pointed breasts
Covered midriff/uncovered midriff

Notice that we have tried hard to stick with "the facts" here—concrete details in the picture. If we were to try, for example, to name the expression on the three blonde women's faces and the one on the black-haired woman (expression-less versus knowing? vapid versus shrewd? trusting versus suspicious? and so on), we would move from data gathering—direct observation of detail—into interpretation. The longer you delay interpretation in favor of noticing patterns of like and unlike detail, the more thoughtful and better grounded your eventual interpretation will be.

Anomalies

Miss New York

Pushing Observations to Conclusions: Selecting an Interpretive Context

As we have argued throughout this chapter, the move from observations to conclusions depends on context. You would, for example, come up with different ideas about the significance of particular patterns of detail in The New Yorker cover if you were analyzing them in the context of the history of New Yorker cover art than you might if your interpretive context was other art done by Ian Falconer, the cover's artist. Both of these possibilities suggest themselves, the first by the fact that the title of the magazine, The New Yorker, stands above the women's heads, and the second by the fact that the artist's last name, Falconer, runs across two of the women.

What other interpretive contexts might one plausibly and fairly choose, based on what the cover itself offers us? Consider the cover's date—October 9, 2000. Some quick research into what was going on in the country in the early fall of 2000 might provide some clues about how to read the cover in a historical context. November 2000 was the month of a presidential election. At the time the cover was published, the long round of presidential primaries, with presidential hopefuls courting various key states for their votes, had ended, but the last month of campaigning by the presidential nominees—Al Gore and George W. Bush—was in full swing.

You might wish to consider whether and how the cover speaks to the country's political climate during the Gore/Bush competition for the presidency. The banners and the bathing suits and the fact that the women stand in a line staring out at some implied audience of viewers, perhaps judges, reminds us that the picture's narrative context is a beauty pageant, a competition in which women representing each of the states compete to be chosen the most beautiful of them all. Choosing to consider the cover in the context of the presidential campaign would be reasonable; you would not have to think you were imposing a context on the picture in an arbitrary and ungrounded way. Additionally, the Table of Contents identifies the title of Falconer's drawing as "The Competition."

Clearly, there is other information on the cover that might allow you to interpret the picture in some kind of political and/or more broadly cultural context. A significant binary opposition is New York versus Georgia, California, and Florida. The three states having names ending in the same letter are represented by look-alike, virtually identical blondes. The anomalous state, New York, is represented by a woman, who, despite standing in line with the others, is about as different from them as a figure could be. *So what* that the woman representing New York looks so unlike the women from the other states? And why those states?

If you continued to pursue this interpretive context, you might want more information. Which presidential candidate won the primary in each of the states pictured? How were each of these states expected to vote in the election in November? Since timing would matter in the case of a topical interpretive context, it would also be interesting to know when the cover art was actually produced and when the magazine accepted it. If possible, you could also try to discover whether other of the cover artist's work was in a similar vein. (He has a website.)

Arriving at an Interpretive Conclusion: Making Choices

As we have been arguing, the picture will "mean" differently, depending on whether we understand it in terms of American presidential politics in the year 2000 or in terms of American identity politics at the same point—specifically attitudes of and about New Yorkers.

Let's try on one final interpretive context, and then see which of the various contexts (lenses) through which we have viewed the cover produces the most credible interpretation, the one that seems to best account for the patterns of detail in the evidence. We will try to push our own interpretive process to a choice by selecting one interpretive context as the most revealing: *The New Yorker* magazine itself.

In this context, the dark-haired figure wearing the New York banner stands, in a sense, for the magazine or, at least, for a potential reader—a representative New Yorker. What, then, does the cover "say" to and about New Yorkers and to and about the magazine and its readers?

So what that the woman representing New York is dark when the other women are light, is closed (narrowed eyes, closed mouth, hair tightly pulled up and back) when the others are open (wide-open eyes and mouths, loosely flowing hair), is pointed and angular when the others are round, sports a bared midriff when the others are covered?

As with our earlier attempt to interpret the cover in the context of the 2000 presidential campaign, interpreting it in the context of other *New Yorker* covers would require a little research. How do *New Yorker* covers character-istically represent New Yorkers? What might you discover by looking for patterns of repetition and contrast in a set of *New Yorker* covers rather than just this one?

The covers are all online. A cursory review of them would make evident the magazine's fondness for simultaneously sending up and embracing the stereotype of New Yorkers as sophisticated, cultured, and cosmopolitan. How does the cover read in the context, for example, of various jokes about how New Yorkers think of themselves relative to the rest of the country, such as the cover depicting the United States as two large coastlines, east and west, connected by an almost nonexistent middle?

Armed with the knowledge that the covers are not only characteristically laughing at the rest of the country but also at New Yorkers themselves, you might begin to make explicit what is implicit in the cover.

Here are some attempts at making the details of the cover speak. Is the cover in some way a "dumb blonde" joke in which the dark woman with the pronounced beauty mark and calculating gaze participates in but also sets herself apart from some kind of national beauty contest? Are we being invited (intentionally or not) to invert the conventional value hierarchy of dark and light so that the dark woman—the sort that gets represented as the evil step-mother in fairy tales such as "Snow White"—becomes "the fairest of them all," and nobody's fool?

Let's end this sample analysis and interpretation with two possibilities—somewhat opposed to each other, but both plausible, at least to certain audiences (East and West Coast Americans, and readers of *The New Yorker*). At its most seri-ous, *The New Yorker* cover may speak to American history in which New York has been the point of entry for generations of immigrants, the "dark" (literally and figuratively) in the face of America's blonde northern European legacy.

Within the context of other *New Yorker* covers, however, we might find ourselves wishing to leaven this dark reading with comic overtones—that the magazine is also admitting, yes America, we do think that we're cooler and more individual and less plastic than the rest of you, but we also know that we shouldn't be so smug about it.

Making the Interpretation Plausible

What makes an interpretation plausible? Your audience might choose not to accept your interpretation for a number of reasons. They might, for example, be New Yorkers and, further, inclined to think that New Yorkers are cool and that this is what the picture "says." They might be from one of the states depicted on the cover in terms of look-alike blondes and, further, inclined to think that New Yorkers are full of themselves and forever portraying the rest of the country as shallowly conformist and uncultured.

But none of these personal influences ultimately matters. What mat-ters is that you share your data, show your reasons for believing that it means what you say it means, and do this well enough for a reader to find your interpretation reasonable (whether he or she actually believes it or not).

Making Interpretations Plausible Across the Curriculum

As we note at various points in this book, the practices governing data-gathering, analysis, and interpretation differ as you move from one academic division to another. In the humanities, the data to be analyzed are usually textual—visual or verbal details. In the social sciences, data are sometimes textual, as would be the case, for example, if you were analyzing the history of a particular political theory or practice, such as free speech. But much analytical thinking in the social sciences and the natural sciences involves arriving at plausible conclusions about the significance of quantitative (numerical) and experimental data. This book's primary interpretive prompt, "So what?" (where do these research data get me, and why does this data set mean what I say it means?), still applies in the sciences, though the interpretive leaps are typically worded differently.

Interpretation in the natural and social sciences considers the extent to which data either confirm or fail to confirm the expectations defined in a hypothesis, which is a theory the writer proposes in response to a research question. In the remainder of this section, we will look briefly at procedures for interpreting evidence in the sciences. As you will see, the guidelines that direct interpretation across the curriculum are similar. The emphases on careful description of evidence and on arguing for the appropriateness of a particular interpretive context are common to all three academic divisions.

Interpreting Statistical Data

Statistics are a primary tool—a virtual language—for those writing in the natural, and especially the social, sciences. Depending on how they are used, they can have the advantage of greater objectivity, and, in the social sciences, of offering a broad view of a subject. Remember, though, that like other forms of evidence, statistics do not speak for themselves; their significance must be overtly interpreted. It should never simply be assumed that statistics are valid representations of the reality they purport to measure.

When writers seek to interpret numerical data, they must decide the extent to which the data confirm or fail to confirm an expectation defined in the study's hypothesis. In order to make a case for their interpretation, writers need to demonstrate the appropriateness and relevance of their chosen context, including their reasons for choosing one possible interpretive context over another.

Here is a brief example of statistical analysis from a political science course on Public Opinion Research. The study uses a data set generated to test the hypothesis that "Republican defectors who have been members of the party for over 11 years are less likely to change party affiliation to Democrat because of the Republican Party's policies than Republican defectors registered with the party for under 10 years." Note how the writer integrates quantitative data into her discussion of the findings, a move characteristic of interpretation in the social sciences, and how she establishes the context in which this data might be best understood.

> The data suggest that long-standing Republican party members are less likely to switch party affiliation than party members registered for under 10 years. However, the data also reveal something else: that the longer a Republican defector was a member of the Republican Party, the more likely that person was to switch party affiliation to Democrat because of the Republican Party's policies as opposed to changes in his or her own belief system. For example, 35% of Republican defectors who had been members of the party for 1–5 years agreed with the statement "the Republican Party's policies led me to leave the party," while 35% said it was due to changes in their personal beliefs. Thus, it appears as though both reasons have equal influence on an individual's decision to switch parties.

> However, when you look at the defectors who were members of the party for over 6 years, roughly 20% more of them left because of the party's policies than because of a change in their personal beliefs. This suggests that long-time party members are more likely to change their party affiliation because of party policy than because of changes in their own beliefs.

In the case of statistical data, an interpretive problem arises when writers attempt to determine whether a statistical correlation between two things—blood cholesterol level and the likelihood of dying of a heart attack, for example—can be interpreted as causal. Does a statistical correlation between high cholesterol levels and heart attack suggest that higher levels of cholesterol cause heart attacks, or might it only suggest that some other factor associated with cholesterol is responsible? Similarly, if a significantly higher percentage of poor people treated in hospital emergency rooms die than their more affluent counterparts, do we conclude that emergency room treatment of the poor is at fault? What factors, such as inability of poor people to afford regular preventive health care, might need to be considered in interpretation of the data? (See "Mistaking Correlation for Cause" in the next section, the Brief Glossary of Common Logical Fallacies.)

In interpretation, as in other kinds of analytical thinking, it is always important to qualify (limit) claims. Notice how the authors in the following example speculate about, but are careful not to endorse any single cause for, the statistically significant phenomenon they analyze. Rather, they use it to ask new questions.

> Since the 1980s, there has been a growing body of data that examines the perceptions of Americans regarding the issue of global warming. This data paints a picture of generally increasing recognition, acceptance, and concern in the United States

regarding atmospheric heating of the earth (Nisbet and Myers, 2007). In the past two decades, the number of Americans who have heard of the "greenhouse effect" has steadily increased. In 1986, less than one in four respondents said they had heard of global warming. By 2006, over nine out of ten recognized the issue (Nisbet and Myers, 2007). A growing number of Americans believe that the Earth is already experiencing increased heating as Table One shows. [. . .]

Public opinion research shows Americans are increasingly acknowledging global warming (Nisbet and Myers, 2007); however, what isn't seen are the underlying causes of these beliefs. In particular, what type of evidence do Americans cite as having an important effect on their perceptions of global warming? Recent Pew Research Center polls have shown fairly significant short-term shifts in the number of Americans who believe there is evidence of global warming. Between June 2006 and January 2007, there was a 7% increase (70% to 77%) among U.S. residents who indicated there was "solid evidence" that the Earth is warming. However, between January 2007 and April 2008, the percentage decreased by 6% (77% to 71%). This decline in public acceptance of the evidence of global warming may be an aberration in a long-term trend of increasing belief. However, the shift does raise questions regarding the underlying factors affecting public acknowledgement of global warming. What types of evidence are individuals reacting to?

(Christopher Borick and Barry Rabe "A Reason to Believe: Examining the Factors That Determine Americans' Views on Global Warming" in *Issues in Governance Studies*, No.18, July, 2008).

In the following Voice from Across the Curriculum, Psychology Professor Laura Edelman offers advice on how to read statistically. She expresses respect for the value of numbers as evidence, as opposed to relying on one's own experience or merely speculating. But she also advises students to be aware of the various problems of interpretation that statistical evidence can invite.

VOICES FROM ACROSS THE CURRICULUM

Interpreting the Numbers: A Psychology Professor Speaks

The most important advice we offer our psychology students about statistical evidence is to look at it critically. We teach them that it is easy to misrepresent statistics and that you really need to evaluate the evidence provided. Students need to learn to think about what the numbers actually mean. Where did the numbers come from? What are the implications of the numbers?

In my statistics course, I emphasize that it is not enough just to get the "correct" answer mathematically. Students need to be able to interpret the numbers and the implications of the numbers. For example, if students are rating satisfaction with the textbook on a scale of one (not at all satisfied) to seven (highly satisfied) and we get a class average of 2.38, it is not enough to report that number. You must interpret the number (the class was generally not satisfied) and again explain the implications (time to choose a new text).

Students need to look at the actual numbers. Let's say I do an experiment using two different stat texts. Text A costs $67 and text B costs $32. I give one class text A and one class text B, and at the end of the semester I find that the class using text A did statistically significantly better than the class using text B. Most students at this point would want to switch to the more expensive text A. However, I can show them an example where the class using text A had an average test grade of 87 and the class with text B had an average test grade of 85 (which can be a statistically significant difference): students see the point that even though it is a statistical difference, practically speaking it is not worth double the money to improve the class average by only two points.

There is so much written about the advantages and limitations of empirical information that I hardly know where to begin. Briefly, if it is empirical, there is no guesswork or opinion (Skinner said "the organism is always right"—that is, the data are always right). The limitations are that the collection and/or interpretation can be fraught with biases and error. For example, if I want to know if women still feel that there is gender discrimination in the workplace, I do not have to guess or intuit this (my own experiences are highly likely to bias my guesses): I can do a survey. The survey should tell me what women think (whether I like the answer or not). The limitations occur in how I conduct the survey and how I interpret the results. You might remember the controversy over the Hite Report on sexual activities (whom did she sample, and what kind of people answer those kinds of questions, and do they do so honestly?).

Despite the controversy over the problems of relying on empirical data in psychology, I think that it is the only way to find answers to many fascinating questions about humans. The patterns of data can tell us things that we have no other access to without empirical research. It is critically important for people to be aware of the limitations and problems, but then to go on and collect the data.

—LAURA EDELMAN, PROFESSOR OF PSYCHOLOGY

A Brief Glossary of Common Logical Fallacies

What follows is a brief discussion of common fallacies—false moves—that can subvert argument and interpretation. The logical fallacies share certain characteristics. They offer cheap and unethical ways of "winning" an argument—usually at the cost of shutting down the possibility of negotiation among competing views and discovery of common ground.

The most noticeable feature of arguments based on the logical fallacies is sloganizing. In sloganizing, each side tries to lay claim to various of a culture's honorific words, which then are repeated so often and so much out of context that they evoke little more than a warm glow that each side hopes to attach to its cause. Words and phrases often used in this way are "liberty," "freedom," "the individual," and "the American people," to name a few.

Words like these are sometimes referred to as "weasel" words, along with words like "natural" and "real." The analogy with weasels goes to the notion that weasels suck out the contents of eggs, leaving empty shells behind. The words have become, in effect, empty shells.

The sloganizing move gets made when each side tries to attach to the other side various labels that evoke fear, even though the words have been repeated so often, in reference to so many different things, that they have become virtually meaningless. This type of sloganizing almost always takes complex circumstances and reduces them to clear-cut goods and evils. Prominent examples in the current contentious political environment are "socialist," "big government," and "capitalist."

As you will see, many of these errors involve the root problem of oversimplification.

1. **Ad hominem.** Literally, the Latin phrase means "to the person." When an argument is aimed at the character of another person rather than at the quality of his or her reasoning or performance, we are engaging in an *ad hominem* argument. If a political candidate is attacked because he or she is rich, rather than on the basis of his or her political platform, he or she is the victim of an *ad hominem* attack. In some cases an *ad hominem* argument is somewhat pertinent—e.g., if a political candidate is discovered to have mob connections.

2. **Bandwagon (*ad populum*).** Bandwagon arguments appeal to the emotions of a crowd, as in "everyone's doing it." A bandwagon argument is a bad argument from authority, because no reasons are offered to demonstrate that "everybody" is an informed and reliable source.

3. **Begging the question (circular reasoning).** When you beg the question, you attempt to prove a claim by offering an alternative wording of the claim itself. To beg the question is to argue in a circle by asking readers to accept without argument a point that is actually at stake. This kind of fallacious argument hides its conclusion among its assumptions. For example, "*Huckleberry Finn* should be banned from school libraries as obscene because it uses dirty language" begs the question by presenting as obviously true issues that are actually in question: the definition of obscenity and the assumption that the obscene should be banned because it is obscene.

4. **Equivocation.** Equivocation confuses an argument by using a single word or phrase in more than one sense. For example: "Only man is capable of religious faith. No woman is a man. Therefore, no woman is capable of religious faith." Here the first use of "man" is generic, intended to be gender neutral, while the second use is decidedly masculine.

5. **False analogy.** A false analogy misrepresents matters by making a comparison between two things that are more unlike than alike. The

danger that arguing analogically can pose is that an inaccurate comparison, usually one that oversimplifies, prevents you from looking at the evidence. Flying to the moon is like flying a kite? Well, it's a little bit like that, but . . . in most ways that matter, sending a rocket to the moon does not resemble sending a kite into the air.

An analogy can also become false when it becomes overextended: there is a point of resemblance at one juncture, but the writer then goes on to assume that the two items compared will necessarily resemble each other in most other respects. To what extent is balancing your checkbook really like juggling? On the other hand, an analogy that first appears overextended may not be: how far, for example, could you reasonably go in comparing a presidential election to a sales campaign, or an enclosed shopping mall to a village main street?

When you find yourself reasoning by analogy, ask yourself two questions: (1) are the basic similarities greater and more significant than the obvious differences? and (2) am I over-relying on surface similarities and ignoring more essential differences?

6. **False cause**. This is a generic term for questionable conclusions about causes and effects. Here are three versions of this fallacy:

   a. **Simple cause/complex effect**. This fallacy occurs when you assign a single cause to a complex phenomenon that cannot be so easily explained. A widespread version of this fallacy is seen in arguments that blame individual figures for broad historical events, for example, "Eisenhower caused America to be involved in the Vietnam War." Such a claim ignores the cold war ethos, the long history of colonialism in Southeast Asia, and a multitude of other factors. When you reduce a complex sequence of events to a simple and single cause—or assign a simple effect to a complex cause—you will virtually always be wrong.

   b. *Post hoc, ergo propter hoc*. This term is the Latin for **after this, therefore because of this.** The fallacy rests in assuming that because A precedes B in time, A causes B. For example, it was once thought that the sun shining on a pile of garbage caused the garbage to conceive flies.

      This error is the stuff that superstition is made of. "I walked under a ladder, and then I got hit by a car" becomes "Because I walked under a ladder I got hit by a car." A more dangerous form of this error goes like this:

      Evidence: A new neighbor moved in downstairs on Saturday. My television disappeared on Sunday.
      Conclusion: The new neighbor stole my TV.

As this example also illustrates, typically in false cause some significant alternative has not been considered, such as the presence of flies' eggs in the garbage. Similarly, it does not follow that if a person watches television and then commits a crime, television watching necessarily causes crime; there are other causes to be considered.

   c. **Mistaking correlation for cause.** This fallacy occurs when a person assumes that a correlation between two things—some kind of connection—is necessarily causal. The philosopher David Hume called this problem "the constant conjunction of observed events." If you speed in a car and then have a minor accident, it does not follow that speeding caused the accident. If an exit poll reveals that a large number of voters under the age of 25 voted for candidate X, and X loses, it does not follow that X lost because he failed to appeal to younger voters. There is a correlation, but the candidate may have lost for a number of reasons.

7. **Hasty generalization.** A conclusion derived from only one or two examples produces the fallacy known as hasty generalization. It is also known as an unwarranted inductive leap because the conclusion lacks sufficient evidence. When a child concludes that all purple food tastes bad because she dislikes eggplant, she has run afoul of this fallacy. Give her a grape popsicle.

8. **Non sequitur.** Latin for "it does not follow," *non sequiturs* skip logical steps in arriving at a conclusion. For example: If we mandate a new tax on people who work downtown but do not live there, businesses will all leave the city. Really?

9. **Oversimplification/overgeneralization.** An inadequately qualified claim is to blame for the fallacy of oversimplification or overgeneralization. It may be true that some heavy drinkers are alcoholics, but it would not be fair to claim that all heavy drinking is or leads to alcoholism. As a rule, be wary of "totalizing" or global pronouncements; the bigger the generalization, the more likely it will admit of exceptions.

10. **Poisoning the well.** This fallacy occurs when a person uses loaded language to trivialize or dismiss an argument before even mentioning it. For example: No reasonable person would swallow that left-wing, tax-and-spend position.

11. **Red herring.** The name comes from the practice of using herring, a smelly fish, to distract dogs from the scent they are supposed to be tracking. A red herring diverts the attention of the audience, often by provoking them with some loaded or controversial topic not really related to the matter at hand. For example, if you are talking about the quality of different kinds of computers, the issue of whether or not they were made in America would be a red herring.

12. **Slippery slope.** This error is based on the fear that once a move is made in one direction, we will necessarily continue to "slide" in that direction. So, for example, if the U.S. approves medicinal uses of marijuana, soon there will be no control of illicit drug use across the nation. A classic case of slippery slope is offered by the Vietnam War: if a single country was allowed to fall under communist rule, soon all the other countries in the region would follow.

13. **Straw man.** This move involves oversimplifying and even caricaturing another person's argument or position in order to make it easier to refute. For example, opponents of health care reform treat it as a straw man when they claim that such reform would deny benefits to the elderly and perhaps even result in so-called "death panels"—groups who would choose which people will live and which will die.

14. **Weasel word.** As we noted in our earlier discussion of sloganizing, a specialized form of equivocation results in what are sometimes called weasel words. A weasel word is one that has been used so much and so loosely that it ceases to have much meaning. The word "natural," for example, can mean good, pure, and unsullied, but it can also refer to the ways of nature (flora and fauna). Such terms ("love," "reality," and "experience" are others) invite equivocation because they mean so many different things to different people.

Assignments: Interpretation

1. **Build a Paper from Implications.** Begin this assignment by making observations and drawing out implications for one of the topics below. Then use your list as the starting point for a longer paper.

   Make some observations, for example, about the following, and then suggest the possible implications of your observations.

   - changing trends in automobiles today
   - what your local newspaper chooses to put on its front page (or editorial page) over the course of a week
   - shows (or advertisements) that appear on network television (as opposed to cable) during one hour of evening prime time
   - advertisements for scotch whiskey in highbrow magazines

2. **Analyze a Magazine Cover by Researching an Interpretive Context.** Choose a magazine that, like *The New Yorker*, has interesting covers. Write an analysis of one such cover by studying other covers from the same magazine. Follow the model offered at the end of this chapter:

   a. Apply THE METHOD—looking for patterns of repetition and contrast—to the cover itself, so that you arrive at key repetitions, strands, and organizing contrasts and begin to ponder a range of possible interpretive leaps to what they signify.

b. Use these data to suggest plausible interpretive contexts for the cover. Remember that interpretive contexts are not simply imposed from without; they're suggested by the evidence.

c. Then move to the other covers. Perform similar operations on them to arrive at an awareness of common denominators among the covers, and to analyze what those shared traits might reveal or make more evident in the particular cover you are studying. You will be trying to figure out how the magazine conceives of itself and its audience by the way that it characteristically represents its "face."

It might be illuminating to survey a range of covers by a single artist, such as Ian Falconer, who created the cover we analyze in the chapter.

CHAPTER 6

Finding and Evolving a Thesis

Overview This chapter contains one primary heuristic: Six Steps for Making a Thesis Evolve. The chapter also offers advice on how to word thesis statements and how to locate them in a piece of writing, including how to set up a thesis in an introductory paragraph and how to treat the thesis in a conclusion. Although the forms of final products in the various academic disciplines differ, the thinking process that allows a writer to arrive at and substantiate a supportable idea (thesis) about the meaning of evidence is markedly similar from discipline to discipline. The governing principle is that the thesis evolves through a series of careful reformulations in light of complicating evidence.

What a Thesis Is and Does

We've deliberately delayed the subject of thesis statements. As the earlier chapters of this book argue, writers should postpone their concern about the thesis in order to first give themselves the chance to dwell more openly and longer with evidence. At its worst, a thesis statement is a premature "answer" that shuts down a writer's ability to think about the evidence. Thinking should not stop once a writer has arrived at a thesis, as it too often does in the model of thesis-driven writing wherein a writer simply accumulates evidence in support of a single claim. In a good piece of writing, the thesis operates as a powerful tool of discovery.

A thesis is an idea that you formulate about your subject. It should offer a theory about the meaning of evidence that would not have been immediately obvious to your readers. A weak thesis either makes no claim or makes a claim that does not need proving, such as a statement of fact or an opinion with which virtually all of your readers would agree before reading your paper (for example, "exercise is good for you").

> **WHAT A PRODUCTIVE THESIS DOES**
> Promotes thinking: leads you to arrive at ideas.
> Reduces scope: separates useful evidence from the welter of details.
> Provides direction: helps you decide what to talk about and what to talk about next.

WHAT A WEAK THESIS DOES

Addicts you too early to a too-large idea, so that you stop actually seeing the evidence in its real-life complexity or thinking about the idea itself.

Produces a demonstration rather than discovery of new ideas by making the same overly general point again and again about a range of evidence.

Includes too much possible data without helping you see what's most important to talk about.

Thesis-Driven Writing: Some Pros and Cons

The term "thesis" has a long history, going back to classical rhetoric wherein a thesis involved taking a position on some subject. This idea of "taking a position" is not a good fit with the methods and goals of inquiry-based writing, the orientation that most academic writing requires. In an essay entitled "Let's End Thesis Tyranny," author and professor Bruce Ballenger argues that thesis-driven writing, especially when thought of as supporting a single idea that the writer sets out to prove, is especially ill-suited to treating "complicated problems that might raise questions with multiple answers, none of them necessarily correct" (*The Chronicle of Higher Education*, July 17, 2013).

One of the most disabling misunderstandings about thesis statements is that a writer needs to have a thesis before he or she begins writing. Arriving at claims too early in the writing process blinds writers to complicating evidence (evidence that runs counter to the thesis) and so deprives them of opportunities to arrive at better ideas.

And yet, it's also true that a writer has not really "graduated" from the exploratory writing phase to the writing of an actual paper until he or she has discovered an idea around which his or her thinking can cohere. A thesis statement gives a paper a sense of purpose and provides readers with something to follow. Without a governing idea to hold onto, readers can't be expected to understand why you are telling them what you are telling them.

Here are two ways to arrive at and use thesis statements that will foster inquiry and court rather than avoid complexity:

- Focus on an area of your subject that is open to opposing viewpoints or multiple interpretations, and

- Treat the thesis at which you arrive as a hypothesis to be tested, rather than an obvious truth.

In sum, the thesis needs to be a stimulus to the exploration of ideas—not a tyrant that reduces complex matters to oversimplified formulations.

Coming Up with a Thesis: What It Means to Have an Idea

Thesis statements are the result of having an idea about your subject. Thus, it makes sense to pause and consider what it means to have an idea. You can probably best understand what it means by considering what ideas do and where they can be found. Here is a partial list:

- An idea usually starts with an observation that is puzzling, with something that you want to figure out rather than something that you think you already understand.

- An idea often accounts for some dissonance, something that seems not to fit together.

- An idea may be the discovery of a question where there seemed not to be one.

- An idea may make explicit and explore the meaning of something implicit—an unstated assumption upon which an argument rests or a logical consequence of a given position.

- An idea may connect elements of a subject and explain the significance of that connection.

As this list demonstrates, ideas are likely to arise when there is something to negotiate—when you require yourself not just to list answers, but to ask questions, make choices, and engage in reasoning about the meaning and significance of your evidence.

Introductions, Conclusions, and the Thesis

Until you understand the expectations that introductions typically raise, it's difficult to know what kind of statement the thesis needs to be. Similarly, until you understand what a concluding paragraph does, you will have difficulty knowing what to do with your thesis in that final paragraph besides merely restating it.

Setting Up the Thesis: Two Tasks

Let's now get more specific about the thesis as a response to reader expectations created by the paper's introductory paragraph. These expectations are surprisingly uniform across the curriculum and in many kinds of writing—not just academic writing.

In setting up the thesis, the introduction accomplishes two tasks:

- It lays out something at stake—an issue, question, or problem to which the writer's thesis is a tentative answer or solution, and

- It provides an interpretive context (see Chapter 5) that locates the thesis in relation to existing thinking.

In sum, the introduction tells readers why the idea that the paper is about to explore matters—why, in other words, a paper needs to be written about it. What typically goes wrong in introductions is that the writer offers a bunch of information, usually too much information, without focusing it in a way that would help a reader understand why the thesis is worth considering.

Here are the kinds of questions an introductory paragraph should answer in order to set up a thesis:

> What is potentially interesting about what I have noticed, and why?
>
> What am I seeing that other people perhaps have not seen or have not sufficiently acknowledged?
>
> Why might what I have noticed matter in relation to the usual ways of thinking about my subject?
>
> How might what I have noticed require a new way of thinking about my subject, or at least a revision, however slight, of the usual ways of thinking?

Making the Thesis Matter: Providing an Interpretive Context

In most courses there are a limited number of acceptable ways of broadly theorizing the material. For an interpretation to be acceptable, you usually need to locate it inside one of these contexts. In the case of Irish literature, for example, an interpretive context might be postcolonial theory on how writers negotiate the formation of new national identities to replace their colonial inheritance. In a film history course, an interpretive context might be particular movements, such as neorealism, or the methods and concerns of a particular filmmaker (known as *auteur* theory).

This does not mean you won't be allowed to say what you think or to nominate new contexts in which to understand things. It means that in order to be heard and to make a contribution, you need to connect whatever you have to say with what people are talking about. In other words, thesis statements don't occur in a vacuum. For people to see why your idea might matter, they need to see it in some relation to the debates and questions that are currently energizing readers' interest in the topic.

Papers often begin by foregrounding something the writer has noticed that seems not to fit with what prevailing theories or discussion has led her to expect. The thesis is, then, not only a tentative explanation about how something you've observed fits, but also to some extent which does not fit, a particular theory. In the sciences, for example, introductions begin by showing how some phenomenon or pattern of detail has not been accounted for in existing studies. And so the writer asks the question, how might this divergence from what was expected be explained?

Two especially useful strategies for setting up a thesis are "SEEMS TO BE ABOUT X" and "DIFFERENCE WITHIN SIMILARITY," both of which can be found earlier in this book (in Chapters 5 and 3, respectively). These strategies effectively set up tension in the thesis between competing ways of viewing your subject. (For more on this, see the upcoming section on establishing tension in the thesis statement.)

How Much of the Thesis Belongs in the Introduction?

Once you have created the opening frame that leads to your thesis, you have choices about how much of your thesis to state at the outset and in what form. These choices are determined in some cases by the standard practices of the various academic disciplines. In some disciplines, for example, the introduction must offer a complete statement of the guiding claim. In many cases, this is done overtly with a procedural statement such as: "In this essay I will argue that . . ." This way of beginning is common not only in the natural and social sciences, but also in philosophy, art history, and in some other humanities disciplines. The procedural statement is sometimes followed by a roadmap that specifies the organization of the paper: "First A will be discussed, then B, etc." Such a detailed overview of a paper is not the norm, however, and is usually not necessary, especially in short essays.

To make your introduction sufficiently engaging and concrete, you should offer readers a brief preview of the particular details that led you to arrive at your thesis, or at least to the question that your thesis seeks to answer. Use these details to generate a theory, a *working hypothesis* about whatever you think is at stake in the material. As a general rule, assume that readers of your essay would need to know on page one, preferably by the end of your first paragraph or the beginning of the second, what your paper is attempting to resolve or negotiate. If you find yourself writing a page-long introductory paragraph to get to your initial statement of thesis, try settling for a simpler articulation of your central idea in its first appearance. Keep in mind that an introduction is not a conclusion. The opening claim is a hypothesis that the body of your paper will test. Your final assessment of the claim will appear in your paper's closing paragraphs.

In large and more complex pieces of thinking, though sometimes even in short ones, the introductory paragraph may be used to set up the first phase of the paper's discussion without having to frame and forecast the whole paper. Especially in inductively organized (specific to general) essays, where a full and complexly qualified articulation of the thesis becomes evident in stages, what you need is an opening claim sufficient to get the paper started. Begin with the best version of your thesis that you can come up with that will be understandable to your readers without a lengthy preamble. Set up this working thesis as quickly and concretely as you can, avoiding generic (fits anything) comments, throat clearing, and overblown historical claims ("Since the beginning of time, humans have been fascinated by technology . . ."). Once established, the working thesis will supply a relatively stable point to which you can return periodically for updating and to keep your readers (and yourself) on track.

The Conclusion: Returning the Thesis to the Larger Conversation
The conclusion is in some ways the introduction in reverse. It begins with the more carefully qualified and evolved version of your thinking that the body of your paper has produced. It then locates the thesis in some kind of larger perspective. The conclusion answers questions like this: What changes in people's ways of thinking might be needed? Where might we need to go next—i.e., what further work needs to be done? In the end, the conclusion returns the thesis to the ongoing conversation that people have been having about your subject and suggests why and how what you've said matters and where it might take us next.

Recognizing Your Thesis: A History Professor Speaks

The thesis usually is that point of departure from the surfaces of evidence to the underlying significance, or problems, a given set of sources reveal to the reader and writer. In most cases, the thesis is best positioned up front, so that the writer's audience has a sense of what lies ahead and why it is worth reading on. I say "usually" and "in most cases" because the hard and fast rule should not take precedence over the inspirational manner in which a thesis can be presented. But the inspiration is not to be sought after at the price of the thesis itself. It is my experience, in fact, that if inspiration strikes, one only realizes it after the fact.

Recognizing a thesis can be extremely difficult. It can often be a lot easier to talk "about" what one is writing, than to say succinctly what the thrust of one's discussion is. I sometimes ask students to draw a line at the end of a paper after they have finished it off, and then write one, at most two sentences, stating what they most want to tell their readers. My comment on that postscript frequently is: "Great statement of your thesis. Just move it up to your first paragraph."

—ELLEN POTEET, PROFESSOR OF HISTORY

How to Word Thesis Statements

The wording and syntax (sentence structure) of thesis statements have shaping force in the way a paper develops. Some thesis shapes are more effective than others. Here in condensed form is the advice offered in the upcoming discussion of thesis shapes:

- A productive thesis usually contains *tension*, the balance of this against that.

- Effective thesis statements often begin with a grammatically subordinate idea that will get outweighed by a more pressing claim: "Although X appears to account for Z, Y accounts for it better."

- A less effective thesis shape is the *list*.

- Active verbs and specific nouns produce strong thesis statements.

Put X in Tension with Y

One of the best and most common ways of bringing the thesis into focus is by pitting one possible point of view against another. Good ideas usually take place with the aid of some kind of back pressure, by which we mean that the idea takes shape by pushing against another way of seeing things. This is not the same as setting out to overturn and completely refute one idea in favor of another. In good thesis statements both ideas have some validity, but the forward momentum of the thesis comes from playing the preferred idea off the other one.

Look at the following two thesis statements. Notice that there is tension in each, which results from the defining pressure of one idea against another potentially viable idea.

- It may not seem like it, but "Nice Pants" is as radical a campaign as the original Dockers series.

- If opponents of cosmetic surgery are too quick to dismiss those who claim great psychological benefits, proponents are far too willing to dismiss those who raise concerns. Cosmetic surgery might make individual people happier, but in the aggregate it makes life worse for everyone.

In the first thesis sentence, the primary idea is that the new advertising campaign for Dockers trousers is radical. The back pressure against which this idea takes shape is that this new campaign may not seem radical. The writer will demonstrate the truth of both of these claims, rather than overturning one and then championing the other.

The same can be said of the parts of the second thesis statement. One part of the thesis makes claims for the benefits of cosmetic surgery. The forward momentum of the thesis statement comes from the back pressure of this idea against the idea that cosmetic surgery will also make life worse for everyone. Notice that the thesis statement does not simply say, "Cosmetic surgery is bad." The writer's job will be to demonstrate that the potential harm of cosmetic surgery outweighs the benefits, but the benefits won't just be dismissed. Both ideas are to some extent true. Neither idea, in other words, is "a straw man"—the somewhat deceptive argumentative practice of setting up a dummy position solely because it is easy to knock down. A straw man does not strengthen a thesis statement because it fails to provide genuine back pressure.

TRY THIS 6.1: Spotting the Tension in Good Thesis Statements

Find the tension in each of the following thesis statements. Decide which of the ideas is primary—the one you think the writer plans to support. Then locate the claim or claims in the thesis against which this primary claim will take shape.

1. Emphasis on the self in the history of modern thought may be an exaggeration, but the consequences of this vision of a self set apart have surely been felt in every field of inquiry.

2. We may join with the modern builders in justifying the violence of means—the sculptor's hammer and chisel—by appealing to ends that serve the greater good. Yet too often modern planners and engineers would justify the creative destruction of habitat as necessary for doubtful utopias.

3. The derogation of middlebrow, in short, has gone much too far. It's time to bring middlebrow out of its cultural closet, to hail its emollient properties, to trumpet its mending virtues. For middlebrow not only entertains, but also educates—pleasurably training us to appreciate high art.

Thesis Shapes: Subordination Versus Listing

The tension between ideas in a thesis statement is often reflected in the statement's grammatical structure. Thesis statements often combine two possible claims into one formulation, with the primary claim in the main clause and the qualifying or limiting or opposing claim in a subordinate clause: "Although X appears to account for Z, Y accounts for it better." You can more or less guarantee your thesis will possess the necessary tension by starting your thesis statement with the word "Although" or with the phrase "While it seems that . . ." or with the "yes, but" or "if x, nonetheless y" formulation. (See Chapter 10 on subordination.)

The advantage of this subordinate construction (and the reason that so many theses are set up this way) is that the subordinated idea helps you to define your own position by giving you something to define it against. The subordinate clause of a thesis helps you to demonstrate that there is, in fact, an issue involved—that is, more than one possible explanation for the evidence you are considering.

The order of clauses in a thesis statement often predicts the shape of the paper, guiding both the writer and the reader. A thesis that begins with a subordinate clause ("Although X . . .") usually leads to a paper in which the first part deals with the claims for X and then moves to fuller embrace of Y.

A less effective thesis shape that can also predict the shape of a paper is the list. This is the shape of five-paragraph form: the writer lists three points and then devotes a paragraph to each. But the list does not specify the connections among its various components, and, as a result, the writer is less inclined to explore the relationship among ideas.

How to Revise Weak Thesis Statements: Make the Verbs Active and the Nouns Specific

Weak thesis statements can be quickly identified by their word choice and syntax (sentence structure). Take, for example, the thesis statement "There are many similarities and differences between the Carolingian and Burgundian Renaissances." This thesis relies mostly on nouns rather than verbs; the nouns announce a broad heading, but the verb doesn't do anything with or to the nouns. In grammatical terms, such thesis statements don't predicate (affirm or assert something about the subject of a proposition). Instead, they rely on anemic verbs like *is* or *are*, which function as equal signs that link general nouns with general adjectives rather than specify more complex relationships.

Replacing *is* or *are* with stronger verbs usually causes you to rank ideas in some order of importance, to assert some conceptual relation among them, and to advance some sort of claim. Thus, we could revise the weak thesis above as "The differences between the Carolingian and Burgundian Renaissances outweigh the similarities." While this reformulation remains quite general, it at least begins to direct the writer along a more particular line of argument.

In sum, the best way to remedy the problem of the overly broad thesis is to move toward specificity in word choice, in sentence structure, and in idea. If you find yourself writing "The economic situation is bad," consider revising it to "The tax policies of the current administration threaten to reduce the tax burden on the middle class by sacrificing education and health care programs for everyone."

Here's the problem/solution in schematic form:

Broad Noun	**+ Weak Verb**	**+ Vague, Evaluative Modifier**
The economic situation	is	bad

Specific Noun	**+ Active Verb**	**+ Specific Modifier**
(The) tax policies (of the current administration)	threaten to reduce (the tax burden on the middle class)	by sacrificing education and health care programs for everyone

By eliminating the weak thesis formula—broad noun plus is plus vague evaluative adjective—a writer is compelled to qualify, or define carefully, each of the terms in the original proposition, arriving at a more particular and conceptually rich assertion.

Is It Okay to Phrase a Thesis as a Question?

The answer is yes and no. Phrasing a thesis as a question makes it more difficult for both the writer and the reader to be sure of the direction the paper will take, because a question doesn't make an overt claim. Questions, however, can clearly imply claims. And many writers, especially in the early, exploratory stages of drafting, will begin with a question.

As a general rule, use thesis questions cautiously, particularly in final drafts. While a thesis question often functions well to spark your thinking, it can allow you to evade the responsibility of making some kind of claim. Especially in the drafting stage, a question posed overtly can provide focus, but only if you then answer it with what could become a first statement of thesis—a working thesis.

VOICES FROM ACROSS THE CURRICULUM

Getting Beyond the All-Purpose Thesis: A Dance Professor Speaks

Not so good thesis/question: "What were Humphrey's and Weidman's reasons behind the setting of *With My Red Fires,* and of what importance were the set and costume design to the piece as a whole?"

Good thesis: "While Graham and Wigman seem different, their ideas on inner expression (specifically subjectivism versus objectivism) and the incorporation of their respective countries' surge of nationalism bring them much closer than they appear."

What I like about the good thesis is that it moves beyond the standard "they are different, but alike" (which can be said about anything) to actually tell the reader what specific areas the paper will explore. I can also tell that the subject is narrow enough for a fairly thorough examination of one small slice of these two major choreographers' work rather than some overgeneralized treatment of these two historic figures.

—KAREN DEARBORN, PROFESSOR OF DANCE

Making a Thesis Evolve

Another common misunderstanding about the thesis is that it must appear throughout the paper in essentially the same form—fixed and unchanging. In fact, it is only a weakly developed thesis that, like an inert (unreactive) material, neither makes anything happen nor undergoes any change itself. Think of the thesis as an agent of change. The thesis itself changes in an inductive essay. In a deductive essay, the thesis changes the way readers understand the range and implications of that claim.

Developing a Thesis Is More than Repeating an Idea

Weak thesis statements (poorly formulated and inadequately developed) are most easily detected by their repetitiveness and predictability. The writer says the same thing again and again, drawing the same overgeneralized conclusion from each piece of evidence ("and so, once again we see that . . .").

Weak thesis statements tend to produce demonstrations. Demonstrations point at something—"See?"—and then they're done with it. Demonstrations are not really interested in seeing into things—only at looking at them from a distance to confirm a point. The staple of the demonstration is five-paragraph form, which we critiqued at some length in Chapter 4. The form predisposes the writer to begin with a big claim, such as "Environmentalism prevents economic growth," and then offer a paragraph on each of three examples (say, statutes that protect endangered wildlife, inhibit drilling for oil, and levy excessive fines on violators). Then the big claim simply gets repeated again in the conclusion.

At the least, such a thesis is inaccurate. It's too easy to find exceptions to the claim and also to question what its key words actually mean. Mightn't environmentalism also promote economic growth by, say, promoting tourism? And is the meaning of economic growth self-evident? Couldn't a short-term economic boon be a long-term disaster, as might be the case for oil exploration in the polar regions?

In contrast, in nearly all good writing the thesis gains in complexity as well as precision and accuracy as the paper progresses. Developing a thesis, in other words, means making the paper's thinking evolve, pruning and shaping it in response to evidence.

In cases where the thesis itself cannot evolve, as, for example, in the report format of the natural and social sciences where the initial hypothesis must be either confirmed or denied, there is still movement (conceptual development) between the beginning of the paper and the end, rather than repeated assertion of one idea.

The Thesis as Lens: The Reciprocal Relationship Between Thesis and Evidence

One function of the thesis is to provide the connective tissue, so to speak, that holds together a paper's three main parts—beginning, middle, and end. Periodic reminders of your paper's thesis, its central unifying idea, are essential for keeping both you and your readers on track. But there is a big difference between developing and just repeating an idea.

It is in establishing this key difference between development and repetition that the analogy of thesis as connective tissue breaks down. A better way of envisioning how a thesis operates is to think of it as a camera lens. The advantage of this analogy is that it more accurately describes the relationship between the thesis and the subject it seeks to explain: while the lens affects how we see the subject (what evidence we select, what questions we ask about that evidence), the subject we are looking at affects how we adjust the lens.

The relationship between thesis and subject is, in other words, reciprocal. In good analytical writing, especially in the earlier, investigatory stages of writing and thinking, the thesis not only directs the writer's way of looking at evidence, the analysis of evidence should also direct and redirect (bring about revision of) the thesis. Even in a final draft, writers are usually adjusting—fine-tuning—their governing idea in response to their analysis of evidence.

The enemy of good analytical writing is the fuzzy lens—imprecisely worded thesis statements. Very broad thesis statements, those that are made up of imprecise (fuzzy) terms, make bad camera lenses. They blur everything together, muddying important distinctions. If your lens is insufficiently sharp, you are not likely to see much in your evidence. If you say, for example, that education is costly, you will at least have some sense of direction, a means of moving forward in your paper, but the imprecise terms "education" and "costly" don't provide you with a focus clear enough to distinguish significant detail in your evidence. Without significant detail for you to analyze, you can't develop your thesis, either by showing readers what the thesis is good for (what it allows us to understand and explain) or by refining and clarifying its terms.

Induction and Deduction: Two Paths a Thesis May Take

In Chapter 4, Reasoning from Evidence to Claims, we defined two ways that a piece of thinking can progress: inductively—from particular details to a general principle to which the details point, and deductively—from a general principle to details that it serves to explain. Chapter 4 presented as the mainstay of inductive thinking—in fact, of all good thinking—the practice we call 10 ON 1, making as many observations as possible (10) about a single representative example (1). We used the term 1 ON 10 for the deductive mode of progression wherein a writer attaches a single claim (1) to a number of examples (10). You will need to keep these terms—inductive and deductive, 10 ON 1 and 1 ON 10—in mind as we take you through this chapter's strategies for making a thesis evolve.

In inductively organized papers and in exploratory writing, the thesis changes as the paper progresses in order to more fully and accurately respond to evidence. Thus, the initial appearance of the thesis is usually fuzzier, less clearly worked out, than it is in the conclusion. This is because inductive writing repeatedly uses potentially conflicting evidence to bring the opening version of the thesis into better focus. In this kind of paper you should suspect that a claim worded in the conclusion almost exactly as it was in the beginning has not adequately responded to evidence.

In deductively organized papers, the wording of the thesis statement does not change, or at least not very much, but what the thesis serves to reveal in the evidence becomes progressively more complex. In social science writing, for example, which typically follows the IMRAD format common to all the sciences—Introduction, Methods, Results, Discussion—the evolution of the paper's thinking occurs in the concluding discussion section, where the writer theorizes his or her results. Here the writer does not just repeat the paper's opening claim (hypothesis). Even when the writer finds evidence to confirm the hypothesis, he or she uses the discussion section to develop a fuller understanding of what these results might mean. (For more on common formats in the sciences, see Chapter 9.)

In practice, good thinking is always a blend of induction and deduction. Claims lead to selection and analysis of evidence. Evidence leads to the reconsideration of the claims. Whether a paper is primarily inductive and the wording of its thesis actually changes as it encounters evidence, or is primarily deductive and the wording of the thesis does not change, the thesis functions as a lens that responds to evidence as the writing proceeds.

Making a Thesis Evolve: A Brief Inductive Example

First let's consider an inductive example. More often than not, when inexperienced writers face a situation in which evidence seems to be unclear or contradictory, they tend to make one of two unproductive moves: they either ignore the conflicting evidence, or they abandon the problem altogether and look for something more clear-cut to write about. Faced with evidence that complicates your thesis, the one thing not to do is run away.

The savvy writer will actively seek out complicating evidence, taking advantage of chances to bring out complications in order to make the thesis more fully responsive to evidence. Let's revisit a sample thesis from the discussion of uncovering assumptions in Chapter 2, "tax laws benefit the wealthy." If you were to seek out data that would complicate this overstated claim, you would soon encounter evidence that would press you to make some distinctions that the initial formulation of this claim leaves obscure. You would need, for example, to distinguish different sources of wealth and then to determine whether all or just some wealthy taxpayers are benefited by tax laws.

FIGURE 6.1

A strong thesis evolves as it confronts and assimilates evidence; the evolved thesis may expand or restrict the original claim. The process may need to be repeated a number of times.

Do people whose wealth comes primarily from investments benefit less (or more) than those whose wealth comes from high wages? Evidence might also lead you to consider whether tax laws, by benefiting the wealthy, also benefit other people indirectly. Both of these considerations would necessitate some reformulation of the thesis. By the end of the paper, the claim that tax laws benefit the wealthy would have evolved into a more carefully defined and qualified statement that would reflect the thinking you have done in your analysis of evidence. This, by and large, is what good concluding paragraphs do—they reflect back on and reformulate your paper's initial position in light of the thinking you have done about it (see Figure 6.1).

But, you might ask, isn't this reformulating of the thesis something a writer does before he or she writes the essay? Certainly some of it is accomplished in the early exploratory writing and note-taking stage. But your finished paper will necessarily do more than list conclusions. Your revision process will have weeded out various false starts and dead ends that you may have wandered into on the way to your finished ideas, but the main routes of your movement from a tentative idea to a refined and substantiated theory should remain visible for readers to follow. To an extent, all good writing reenacts the chains of thought that led you to your conclusions.

Making a Thesis Evolve: A Brief Deductive Example

Now let's turn to a deductive example. A good deductive paper is best thought of as an experiment. In the experiment, the writer proposes a theory and then sees how far it is possible to go in getting the theory to satisfactorily explain whatever it is the writer has been observing. Evolution of the paper's thinking takes place when the writer tries to explain what happened when the theory met the evidence.

Let's take as an example a political science paper about people's responses to global warming. In political science papers, and more generally in social science writing, papers tend to begin with a broader theory from which the writer derives an hypothesis, a conjecture about what might happen, which the paper would then test.

We might speculate, for example, that people with more education would be more likely to use evidence to change, rather than to confirm, their views on global warming. This hypothesis might flow from the broader theory that educated people are less prone to dogmatism and thus are more capable of learning. The paper would then apply this hypothesis to evidence, usually statistical evidence, to see if it holds.

The aim of the paper would not be just to support or not support the hypothesis. A good deductive paper would also analyze results that only partially supported the hypothesis or complicated it. The paper might even conclude by analyzing why the evidence did not confirm the hypothesis.

Let's suppose the results of our study revealed the opposite of what our hypothesis predicted: educated people are less likely to change their views when confronted with evidence. To explain this result, our thinking would have to evolve. Was the result a measurement issue? Were we measuring "educated" wrong? Was the result a sampling issue (a methodological explanation)? Or what if our assumptions about the effects of education were too narrow? Might the educated be less likely to believe evidence because their education has trained them to be skeptical?

In virtually any good deductive study, the thinking will evolve somehow. Perhaps some secondary feature, something new, may emerge in the discussion as the primary feature. Perhaps the results will help us understand more fully why we obtained the results that we expected. Perhaps the study will suggest possibilities for future research.

For now it is enough to emphasize that too many of us fail to recognize that a hypothesis is a speculation—a guess. The goal is not to have the answer before you begin, but to see where the results of testing the hypothesis might lead. This is where the hypothesis in a deductive paper causes new thinking to happen.

As these two examples illustrate, whether the thesis in a paper develops inductively, thus appearing in its fullest and most accurate form only at the end, or deductively, stated in full at the outset, the writer would not simply restate in the conclusion what he or she had proposed in the introduction. In both cases, the thinking would evolve.

The Evolving Thesis as Hypothesis and Conclusion in the Natural and Social Sciences

The natural and social sciences generally use a pair of terms, *hypothesis* and *conclusion,* for the single term *thesis.* Because writing in the sciences is patterned according to the scientific method, writers in disciplines such as biology and psychology must report how the original thesis (hypothesis) was tested against empirical evidence and then conclude on this basis whether or not the hypothesis was confirmed.

The scientific method is in sync with one of the chapter's main points, that something must happen to the thesis between the introduction and the conclusion. And as we have just demonstrated, although the hypothesis does not change (or evolve), the testing of it and subsequent interpretation of those results produce commentary on and, often, qualifications of the paper's central claim.

The best papers are clear and up front about what their point is, then use evidence and argument to support and evaluate the thesis. I encourage students to have a sentence immediately following their discussion of the background on the subject that can be as explicit as: "In this paper I will argue that while research on toxic effects of methyl bromide provides troubling evidence for severe physiological effects, conclusive proof of a significant environmental hazard is lacking at this time."

I try to avoid the use of the term "hypothesis." I think it gives the false sense that scientists always start with an idea about how something works. Frequently, that is not the case. Some of the best science has actually come from observation. Darwin's work on finches is a classic example. His ideas about adaptation probably derived *from* the observation.

—BRUCE WIGHTMAN, PROFESSOR OF BIOLOGY

If the empirical evidence doesn't confirm your hypothesis, you rethink your hypothesis, but it's a complex issue. Researchers whose hypotheses are not confirmed in fact often question their *method* ("if I had more subjects" or "a better manipulation of the experimental group" or "a better test of intelligence," etc.) as much as their hypothesis. And that's often legitimate. Part of the challenge of psychological research is its reliance on a long array of assumptions. Failure to confirm a hypothesis could mean a problem in any of that long array of assumptions. So failure to confirm your hypothesis is often difficult to interpret.

—ALAN TJELTVEIT, PROFESSOR OF PSYCHOLOGY

Economists do make pretense to follow scientific methodology. Thus we are careful not to mix hypothesis and conclusion. I think it's important to distinguish between what is conjectured, the working hypothesis, and what ultimately emerges as a result of an examination of the evidence. Conclusions come only after some test has been passed.

—JAMES MARSHALL, PROFESSOR OF ECONOMICS

Evolving a Thesis in an Exploratory Draft: The Example of *Las Meninas*

Because the writing process is a way not just of recording but of discovering ideas, writers, especially in the early stages of drafting, often set out with one idea or direction in mind and then, in the process of writing, happen upon another, potentially better idea that only begins to emerge in the draft. Once you've recognized them, these emerging thoughts may lead to your evolving a markedly different thesis, or they may provide you with the means of extending your paper's original thesis well beyond the point you'd settled for initially.

Writers undertake this kind of conceptual revision—locating and defining the thesis—in different ways. Some writers rely on repeatedly revising while they work their way through a first draft (which, when finished, will be close to a final draft). Others move through the first draft without much revision and then comprehensively rethink and restructure it (sometimes two, three, or more times). Whatever mode of revision works best for you, the thinking processes we demonstrate here are central. They are the common denominators of the various stages of the drafting process.

Our means of demonstrating how writers use exploratory writing to locate and develop a workable thesis is to take you through the steps a student writer would follow in revising her initial draft on a painting, *Las Meninas* (Spanish for "the ladies in waiting") by the seventeenth-century painter, Diego Velázquez. We are using a paper on a painting because all of the writer's data (the details of the painting) are on one page, allowing you to think with the writer as she develops her ideas.

As you read the draft, watch how the writer goes about developing the claim made at the end of her first paragraph—that, despite its complexity, the painting clearly reveals at least some of the painter's intentions (referred to elsewhere in the paper as what the painting is saying, what it suggests, or what the painter wants). We have underlined each appearance of potential thesis statements in the text of the paper. Using square brackets at the ends of paragraphs, we have described the writer's methods for arriving at ideas: NOTICE AND FOCUS, THE METHOD, ASKING "SO WHAT?," and 10 ON 1 (see Chapters 1 and 4).

There are a number of good things about this student paper when considered as an exploratory draft. Studying it will help you train yourself to turn a more discriminating eye on your own works in progress, especially in that all-important early stage in which you are writing in order to discover ideas.

Velázquez's Intentions in *Las Meninas*

[1] Velázquez has been noted as being one of the best Spanish artists of all time. It seems that as Velázquez got older, his paintings became better. Toward the end of his life, he painted his masterpiece, *Las Meninas*. Out of all his works, *Las Meninas* is the only known self-portrait of Velázquez. There is much to be said about *Las Meninas*. The painting is very complex, but some of the intentions that Velázquez had in painting *Las Meninas* are very clear. **[The writer opens with background information and a broad working thesis (underlined).]**

[2] First, we must look at the painting as a whole. The question that must be answered is: who is in the painting? The people are all members of the Royal Court of the Spanish monarch Philip IV. In the center is the king's daughter, who eventually became Empress of Spain. Around her are her *meninas* or ladies-in-waiting. These *meninas* are all daughters of influential men. To the right of the *meninas* is a dwarf who is a servant, and the family dog who looks fierce but is easily tamed by the foot of a child. The more unique people in the painting are Velázquez, himself, who stands to the left in front of a large canvas; the king and queen,

FIGURE 6.2
Las Meninas by Diego Velázquez, 1656. Approximately 10'5" × 9'. Museo del Prado, Madrid.

Scala/Art Resource, NY

whose faces are captured in the obscure mirror; the man in the doorway; and the nun and man behind the *meninas*. To analyze this painting further, the relationship between characters must be understood. **[The writer describes the evidence and arrives at an operating assumption—focusing on the relationship among characters.]**

[3] Where is this scene occurring? Most likely it is in the palace. But why is there no visible furniture? Is it because Velázquez didn't want the viewers to become distracted from his true intentions? I believe it is to show that this is not just a painting of an actual event. This is an event out of his imagination. **[The writer begins pushing observations to tentative conclusions by ASKING SO WHAT?]**

[4] Now, let us become better acquainted with the characters. The child in the center is the most visible. All the light is shining on her. <u>Maybe Velázquez is suggesting that she is the next light for Spain</u> and that even God has approved her by shining all

the available light on her. Back in those days there was a belief in the divine right of kings, so this just might be what Velázquez is saying. [**The writer starts ranking evidence for importance and continues to ask, SO WHAT?; she arrives at a possible interpretation of the painter's intention.**]

[5] The next people of interest are the ones behind the *meninas*. The woman in the habit might be a nun and the man a priest.

[6] The king and queen are the next group of interesting people. They are in the mirror, which is to suggest they are present, but they are not as visible as they might be. Velázquez suggests that they are not always at the center where everyone would expect them to be. [**The writer continues using NOTICE AND FOCUS plus asking SO WHAT?; in addition to looking for pattern in the painting's details, the writer has begun to notice evidence—the minimal presence of the king and queen in the painting—that could complicate her initial interpretation about the divine right of kings.**]

[7] The last person and the most interesting is Velázquez. He dominates the painting along with the little girl. He takes up the whole left side along with his gigantic easel. But what is he painting? As I previously said, he might be painting the king and queen. But I also think he could be pretending to paint us, the viewers. The easel really gives this portrait an air of mystery because Velázquez knows that we, the viewers, want to know what he is painting. [**The writer starts doing 10 ON 1 with her selection of what she has selected as the most significant detail—the size and prominence of the painter.**]

[8] The appearance of Velázquez is also interesting. His eyes are focused outward here. They are not focused on what is going on around him. It is a steady stare. Also interesting is his confident stance. He was confident enough to place himself in the painting of the royal court. I think that Velázquez wants the king to give him the recognition he deserves by including him in the "family." And the symbol on his vest is the symbol given to a painter by the king to show that his status and brilliance have been appreciated by the monarch. It is unknown how it got there. It is unlikely that Velázquez put it there himself. That would be too outright, and Velázquez was the type to give his messages subtly. Some say that after Velázquez's death, King Philip IV himself painted it to finally give Velázquez the credit he deserved for being a loyal friend and servant. [**The writer continues DOING 10 ON 1 and asking SO WHAT? about the painter's appearance; this takes her to three tentative theses (underlined above).**]

[9] I believe that Velázquez was very ingenious by putting his thoughts and feelings into a painting. He didn't want to offend the king, who had done so much for him. It paid off for Velázquez because he did finally get what he wanted, even if it was after he died. [**The writer concludes and is now ready to redraft to tighten links between evidence and claims, formulate a better working thesis, and make this thesis evolve.**]

From Details to Ideas: Arriving at a Working Thesis in an Exploratory Draft

An exploratory draft uses writing as a means of arriving at a working thesis that the next draft can more fully evolve. Most writers find that their best ideas emerge near the end of the exploratory draft, which is the case in this student draft (see the three claims underlined in paragraph 8).

The *Las Meninas* paper is a good exploratory draft. The writer has begun to interpret details and draw plausible conclusions from what she sees, rather than just describing the scene depicted on the canvas or responding loosely to it with her unanalyzed impressions. The move from description to analysis and interpretation begins when you select certain details in your evidence as more important than others and explain what they seem to you to suggest. The writer has done both of these things, and so has gotten to the point where she can begin methodically evolving her initial ideas into a perceptive analysis.

What is especially good about the draft is that it reveals the writer's willingness to push on from her first idea (reading the painting as an endorsement of the divine right of kings, expressed by the light shining on the princess) by seeking out complicating evidence. The process of revising for ideas begins in earnest when you start checking to make sure that the thesis you have formulated accounts for as much of the available evidence as possible and does not avoid evidence that might complicate or contradict it.

The writer's first idea (about divine right), for example, does not account for enough of the evidence and is undermined by evidence that clearly doesn't fit, such as the small size and decentering of the king and queen, and the large size and foregrounding of the painter himself. Rather than ignoring these troublesome details, the writer instead zooms in on them. She focuses on the painter's representation of himself and of his employers, the king and queen, as the 1 for DOING 10 ON 1 (making a number of observations about a single representative piece of evidence and analyzing it in depth).

Six Steps for Finding and Evolving a Thesis in an Exploratory Draft

Getting the thesis to respond more fully to evidence, either by formulating a mostly new thesis and beginning again, or by modifying the existing thesis, is the primary activity of conceptual revision (as opposed to correcting and editing). Your aim here is not to go round and round forever, but to go back and forth between thesis and evidence, evidence and thesis, allowing each, in turn, to adjust how you see the other, until you find the best possible fit between the two. As we say in the section of this chapter on the thesis as camera lens, the thesis not only directs a writer's way of looking at evidence; the analysis of evidence should also direct and redirect—bring about revision of—the thesis.

What follows is a six-step guide for formulating and reformulating (evolving) a thesis. As an overarching guideline, allow your thesis to run up against potentially conflicting evidence ("but what about this?") in order to build upon and revise your initial idea, extending the range of evidence it can accurately account for by clarifying and qualifying its key terms.

Here is a list of the six steps:

1. Formulate a working thesis or, in revision, locate multiple and possibly competing thesis statements in your draft.

2. Explain how the details you have focused on in the evidence lead to your working thesis.

3. Locate evidence that is not adequately accounted for by the working thesis and pursue the implications of that evidence by repeatedly ASKING "SO WHAT?" Explain how and why these pieces of evidence complicate the working thesis.

4. Use your analysis of the complicating evidence to reformulate the thesis. Share with readers your reasons for moving from your initial claim to this reformulation.

5. Test the adequacy of the evolved thesis by repeating steps two, three, and four until you are satisfied that the thesis statement accounts for your evidence as fully and accurately as possible. The best test of a thesis is to see how much of the relevant evidence it can reasonably account for.

6. Rewrite the draft into a more coherent and fuller analysis of evidence, while retaining for readers the "thesis trail"—the various steps that you went through along the way to formulating the thesis you ultimately chose.

Step 1: Formulate a working thesis or, in revision, locate multiple and possibly competing thesis statements in your draft.

Go through your draft and underline potential thesis statements (as we have done in the student's draft). View the presence of multiple, perhaps even competing, theses as an opportunity rather than a problem. In an exploratory draft, a range of interpretations of evidence constitutes raw material, the records of your thinking that might be developed in a more finished draft.

In the *Las Meninas* paper no single idea emerges clearly as the thesis. Instead, the writer has arrived (in paragraph 8) at three related but not entirely compatible ideas:

"I think that Velázquez wants the king to . . ."

Thesis 1: give Velázquez "the recognition he deserves by including him in the 'family.'"

Thesis 2: "show that his [Velázquez's] status and brilliance [as an artist] have been appreciated."

Thesis 3: give Velázquez "the credit he deserved for being a loyal friend and servant."

These three ideas about the painter's intentions could be made to work together, but at present the writer is left with an uneasy fit among them. In order to resolve the tension among her possible thesis statements, the writer appears to have settled on *"I think that Velazquez wants the king to give him the recognition he deserves by including him in the family."* This idea follows logically from a number of the details the writer has focused on, so it is viable as a working thesis—the one that she will, in revision, test against potentially complicating evidence and evolve.

It helps that the writer has specified her *interpretive context*—the painter's intentions—because a writer's awareness of her interpretive context makes it much easier for her to decide which details to prioritize and what kind of questions to ask about them. A different interpretive context for the *Las Meninas* paper, such as the history of painting techniques or the social structure of seventeenth-century royal households, would have caused the writer to emphasize different details and arrive at different conclusions about their possible significance.

The success of analytical arguments often depends on a writer's ability to persuade readers of the appropriateness of her choice of interpretive context. And so it is important for writers to ask and answer the question "In what context might my subject best be understood and why?"

It is okay, by the way, that the writer has not concerned herself prematurely with organization, introductions, or transitions. She has instead allowed her draft to move freely from idea to idea as these occurred to her. She might not have come up with the useful ideas in paragraph 8 had she pressed herself to commit to any one idea (the divine right of kings idea, for example) too soon.

Notice that this writer has prompted a sequence of thought by using the word *"interesting."* Repeated use of this word as a transition would not be adequate in a final draft because it encourages listing without explicit connections among claims or explanations of how each claim evolved into the next. In an exploratory draft, however, the word "interesting" keeps the writer's mind open to possibilities and allows her to try on various claims without worrying prematurely about whether her tentative claims are right or wrong.

Step 2: Explain how the details you have focused on in the evidence lead to your working thesis.

The writer of the *Las Meninas* paper has offered at least some evidence in support of her working thesis, "Velázquez wants the king to give him the recognition he deserves by including him in the family." She notes the symbol on the painter's vest, for example, which she says might have been added later by the king to show that the painter's "status and brilliance have been appreciated." She implies that the painter's "confident stance" and "steady stare" also support her thesis. Notice, however, that she has not spelled out her reasons for making this connection between her evidence and her claim.

Nor has she corroborated her claim about this evidence with other evidence that could lend more support to her idea. Interestingly, the potential thesis statements advanced in paragraph 8 are not connected with the rather provocative details she has noted in paragraphs 6 and 7: that "Velázquez dominates the painting along with the little girl," that he "takes up the whole left side along with his gigantic easel," and that "the king and queen are not as visible as they might be" suggesting that "they are not always at the center where everyone would expect them to be."

In revision, the writer would need to find more evidence in support of her claim and make the links between evidence and claims more explicit. She would also need to tackle the complicating evidence that she leaves dangling in paragraphs 6 and 7, which takes us to Step 3.

Step 3: Locate evidence that is not adequately accounted for by the working thesis and pursue the implications of that evidence by repeatedly asking "SO WHAT?" Explain how and why these pieces of evidence complicate the working thesis.

This is a key step in evolving a thesis—pursuing the piece or pieces of evidence that do not clearly fit with the working thesis, explaining why they don't fit, and determining what their significance might actually be. For this purpose, the writer would need to zoom in on the details of her evidence that she describes in paragraphs 6 and 7 and ASK "SO WHAT?" about them.

- **So what** that there are size differences in the painting? What might large or small size mean?

- **So what** that the king and queen are small, but the painter, princess, and dwarf (another servant) are all large and fairly equal in size and/or prominence?

Proposed answer: Perhaps the king and queen have been reduced so that Velázquez can showcase their daughter, the princess.

Test of this answer: The size and location of the princess (center foreground) seem to support this answer, as does the princess being catered to by the ladies in waiting. But, if the painting is meant to showcase the princess, what is the point of the painter's having made himself so large?

Another possible answer: Perhaps the small size and lack of physical prominence of the king and queen are relatively unimportant, in which case, what matters is that they are a presence, always overseeing events (an idea implied but not developed by the writer in paragraph 6).

Test of this answer: Further support for this answer comes from the possibility that we are meant to see the king and queen as reflected in a mirror on the back wall of the painter's studio (an idea the writer mentions), in which case they would be standing in front of the scene depicted in the painting, literally overseeing events. There isn't much evidence against this answer, except, again, for the large size of the painter, and the trivializing implications of the king and queen's diminution, but these are significant exceptions.

Another possible answer: Perhaps the painter is demonstrating his own ability to make the king and queen any size—any level of importance—he chooses. The king and queen are among the smallest as well as the least visible figures in the painting. Whether they are being exhibited as an actual painting on the back wall of the painter's studio (a possibility the writer has not mentioned) or whether they appear as reflections in a small mirror on that back wall, they certainly lack stature in the painting in comparison with the painter, who is not only larger and more prominent than they are but also who, as the writer notes, "dominates the painting along with the little girl." The little girl is the princess, herself, and the supposed subject of the painting within the painting that Velázquez is working on.

Test: This answer about the painter demonstrating his control of the representation of the king and queen seems credible. It has the most evidence in its favor and the least evidence to contradict it. The writer would probably want to choose this idea and would need to reformulate her thesis to better accommodate it, which takes us to Step 4.

Step 4: Use your analysis of the complicating evidence to reformulate the thesis. Share with readers your reasons for moving from your initial claim to this reformulation.

On the basis of the writer's answers in Step 3, it would appear that rather than showcasing royal power, the painting showcases the painter's own power. This idea is not a clear fit with the writer's working thesis about the painter's intentions, that "Velazquez wants the king to give him the recognition he deserves by including him in the family." So, what should the writer do?

What she should not do is beat a hasty retreat from her working thesis. She should use the complicating evidence to qualify, rather than abandon, her initial idea, which did, after all, have some evidence in its favor. Good writing shares with readers the thinking process that carried the writer forward from one idea to the next.

The writer's evolved thesis would need to qualify the idea of the painter wishing to be recognized as a loyal servant and accepted as a member of the family (which are, themselves, not entirely compatible ideas), since there is evidence in the painting suggesting a more assertive stance on the part of Velázquez about the importance of painters and their art.

The writer is now ready to pursue the next step in the revision process: looking actively for other features of the painting that might corroborate her theory. This takes us to step 5, the last step the writer would need to go through before composing a more polished draft.

Step 5: Test the adequacy of the evolved thesis by repeating steps two, three, and four until you are satisfied that the thesis statement accounts for your evidence as fully and accurately as possible. The best test of a thesis is to see how much of the relevant evidence it can reasonably account for.

The need to find additional corroboration is especially pressing for this writer because her new thesis formulation that the painting demonstrates the artist's power—not just his brilliance and desire for recognition—suggests an interpretation of the painting that would be unusual for an era in which most other court paintings flattered royal figures by portraying them as larger than life, powerful, and heroic.

It is unlikely that any thesis will explain all of the details in a subject, but a reasonable test of the value of one possible thesis over another is how much of the relevant evidence it can explain. So the writer would try to apply her new thesis formulation to details in the painting that have not yet received much attention, such as the painter's paralleling himself with the large dwarf on the other side of the painting.

This pairing of dwarf and painter might initially seem to spell trouble for the new thesis about the painter demonstrating his power to frame the way the monarchs are represented. If it was, in fact, the painter's intention to have his power recognized, why would he want to parallel himself—in size, placement, and facial expression—with a dwarf who is, presumably, a fairly low-level servant of the royal household, unlike the *meninas*, who are the daughters of aristocrats? So WHAT that the dwarf is paralleled with the painter?

The writer might argue that the dwarf suggests a visual pun or riddle, demonstrating that in the painter's world the small can be made large (and vice versa, in the case of the king and queen). No longer "dwarfed" by his subordinate role as court painter, Velázquez stands tall. If this reading is correct, and if it is true, as the writer suggests, that Prince Philip himself later had the honorary cross added to Velázquez's vest, we might assume that the king either entirely missed or was able to appreciate the painter's wit.

Similarly, another of the writer's key observations—that the painter "plays" with viewers' expectations—fits with the thesis that the painting asks for recognition of the artist's power, not just his loyal service. In subverting viewers' expectations both by decentering the monarchs and concealing what is on the easel, the painter again emphasizes his power, in this case, over the viewers (among whom might be the king and queen if their images on the back wall are mirror reflections of them standing, like us, in front of the painting). He is not bound by their expectations, and in fact appears to use those expectations to manipulate the viewers: he can make them wish to see something he has the power to withhold.

Step 6: Rewrite the draft into a more coherent and fuller analysis of evidence, while retaining for readers the "thesis trail"—the various steps that you went through along the way to formulating the thesis you ultimately choose.

It is tempting at the end of the exploratory writing process for the writer to simply eliminate all the ideas and analysis that did not support her final choice of thesis. Why should you include all six steps when you now know what the best version of your thesis is going to be?

Good analytical writing is collaborative. To a significant extent, good writing recreates for readers the thinking process that produced its conclusions. It shares with readers how a writer arrives at ideas, not just what the writer ultimately thinks. It takes readers along on a cognitive journey through the process of formulating and reformulating that results in a carefully qualified statement of ideas. Having made the trip, readers are more likely to appreciate the explanatory power of the most fully articulated statement of the thesis.

In a final draft, a writer can capture for readers the phases of thinking she went through by, for example, wording the thesis as a SEEMS TO BE ABOUT x claim (SEEMS TO BE ABOUT X, BUT IS REALLY—OR ALSO—ABOUT Y; see Chapter 5). This wording would allow the writer of the Las Meninas paper to share with readers the interesting shift she makes from the idea that the painting promotes the divine right of kings to the idea that it also endorses the power of the painter to cause people to see royalty in this light (a visual pun, as the light on the princess is actually produced by the painter's brush).

The writer could also set up a thesis that puts X in tension with Y, while granting some validity to both. In this case, X (the painter wanting to be recognized as a member of the family) would serve as back pressure to drive Y (the painter wanting to demonstrate, tongue-in-cheek, the power of painters).

In an inductively organized paper, you would begin with a working thesis somewhat closer to the final version of the thesis than was the case in the exploratory draft, but you would still take the readers along on your step-by-step journey to your conclusions. In a deductively organized paper, wherein the thesis must appear from the outset in something close to its full version, you would still be able to show your readers how your thinking evolved. The writer of the Las Meninas paper could do this by beginning with details that seem to obviously support the thesis (large size and prominence of the painter and his easel relative to the king and queen) and then move to details (such as the large dwarf) that readers would be less likely to connect with the thesis without her help.

Knowing When to Stop: How Much Revising Is Enough?

We emphasize before leaving this example that the version of the thesis we have just proposed is not necessarily the "right" answer. Looked at in a different context, the painting might have been explained primarily as a demonstration of the painter's mastery of the tools of his trade—light, for example, and perspective. But our proposed revision of the thesis for the Las Meninas paper meets two important criteria for evaluating thesis statements:

1. It unifies the observations the writer has made.

2. It is capable of accounting for a wide range of evidence.

The writer has followed through on her original desire to infer Velázquez's intentions in the painting. Whether or not Velázquez consciously intended to make his painting a tongue-in-cheek self-advertisement, there is clearly enough evidence to claim plausibly that the painting can be understood in this way.

How do you know when you've done enough reformulating of your thesis and arrived at the best possible idea about your evidence? Getting the thesis to account for as much of the relevant evidence as possible doesn't mean you need to discuss every detail of the subject. Writers must take care not to ignore important evidence, especially if it would alter their "case," but no analysis can address everything—nor should it. Your job as a writer is to select those features of your subject that seem most significant and to argue for their significance. An analysis says to readers, in effect, "These are the details that best reveal the nature and meaning of my subject, or at least the part of the subject that I am trying to address."

Practice Tracking Thesis Statements in Finished Drafts

Learning to write and think in the way that the six steps recommend will take time, practice, and patience—especially patience with yourself. As we hope our example of evolving a thesis in the student draft on *Las Meninas* has shown, good ideas don't come easily or naturally or magically, though sometimes it may feel that they do. Good ideas can be methodically courted, which is what the six steps teach you to do.

In addition to time and practice and patience, what you need are models of how good writers operate, how they move from evidence to idea and from initial formulations of ideas to better ones. Start looking for models on your own. When you find a smart piece of writing that you admire, look for the thesis in it and for the ways that the thesis evolves. Underline each occurrence of the thesis, taking care to note the places where the writer makes interesting shifts. Figure out what it was in the writer's evidence that caused these shifts to happen. We call this exercise "tracking the thesis." Once you train yourself to become aware of thesis statements and how they develop, you will become more comfortable with writing thesis statements yourself.

Tracking the Thesis in a Final Draft: The Example of *In Bruges*

We offer the following student paper as an example of how you might go about tracking the evolution of a thesis. As you will see, the writer repeatedly tests the paper's working hypothesis against evidence and arrives at an interestingly qualified version of his original claim. We have offered in square brackets brief comments on the development of the writer's thinking.

In Bruges: Finding Hope in the Presence of the Past

—BY JAMES PATEFIELD

In Bruges, a film by Academy-Award winning director, playwright, and Irishman Martin McDonagh, is obsessed with a sense of place. The city of Bruges, with its many old churches and old art (including a Bosch painting of the Last Judgment), seems to stand in the film for two starkly opposed ideas. One is that we can never escape our own histories—sequences of events that, once set in motion, can't and should not be stopped, and can't be changed. The other idea is that we can and must hold out for the possibility of change, for a future that past actions and rigid systems of value haven't already set in stone. Given the film's violence, dark comedy, and apocalyptic ending, it seems to offer only faint hope for change in the face of relentless cycles of determinism and fate. **[The writer puts two conflicting interpretations in tension with each other and posits a working thesis that there is only faint hope for change.]**

In the film, hitmen Ray and Ken have been sent by their boss Harry to hide out in the Belgian city of Bruges after a job has gone horribly wrong because Ray has accidentally killed a child. While in Bruges, Ray falls in love with Chloe, a Belgian drug dealer, on a film set. At the same time, Ken and Ray develop a strong bond while discussing Ray's suicidal feelings of guilt.

The story on some level is all about the fact that it takes place "in Bruges," a medieval city that embodies the presence of the past. The presence of the past is the idea that history is living and shaping the present—that it is not dead or absent but very much present and alive, actively controlling what people do. **[The writer begins to demonstrate that one side of the opposition gets considerable weight in the film.]** We can see that the past is alive in the many examples of tourists visiting the city's architecture and in the repeated discussions that Ken and Ray have about the tourist sites. As we also learn, Bruges is the crucial fairy-tale site of Harry's happy childhood. This is why it is the setting for the story in the first place: because Harry, who romanticizes the past, wants to give Ray one fairy-tale experience before ordering his death.

When we think about the film's point of view on Bruges, we find that Ken (and the cinematographer for the film) loves it while Ray hates it. This conflict defines the relationship between Ray and Ken that develops throughout the film, with Ray holding onto the present and Ken holding onto the past. The city and the relationship between the characters are intimately intertwined. **[Here the writer makes overt the two main characters' positions in the tension between closed past and future possibility.]**

It is crucial to know that Harry is set on killing Ray because Harry operates on a system of ethics and justice that operates on "honor." In this system, Ray can only pay for his sin of killing a child by dying himself. This comes into conflict with Ken and his system of justice/ethics when Ken refuses to kill Ray because he believes that Ray "has the capacity to change [and] do something decent with his life." Ken's system of ethics operates on an idea of choice, hope for personal change, and a future that is not already set in stone. In this way, it comes head to head with Harry's "honor" principles in the film. If we can read Ken as the most overtly religious character in the film, given his affinity for sightseeing Catholic churches and medieval Catholic art, we can then see Ken and Harry's conflict as one of a religious "spirit of the law" versus an honor-driven "letter of the law." (See 2 Corinthians 3:6.) **[Here the writer offers another version of the binary that is central to his interpretation.]**

Ray's guilt and the discussions it brings about in turn connect us back to Bruges as a symbolic location. Given that these churches are specifically identified as Catholic, we can link them back to a consistent theme of guilt, death, sin, and judgment. Churches are, after all, not tourist sites in the same way that something like the Empire State Building or the Statue of Liberty are. Churches imply a sense of pilgrimage for the characters—that they are going on a religious journey ending in enlightenment. The churches are refuges for Ken. They offer alternatives to a present that for Ken seems out of control and immoral.

When Ken receives orders from Harry to kill Ray, he is unwilling to obey, choosing instead to confront Harry. Harry in turn comes to Bruges to kill Ken for not killing Ray. The resulting showdown leads to Ken sacrificing his life to save Ray, Harry killing himself because of his own unyielding code of honor-driven ethics, and Ray being severely wounded as he is put onto oxygen in an ambulance, left with the hope of a new life and potential change.

In this conclusion, the film is fairly clear that Ken wins the ethics battle I've just laid out. Even though Ken dies, he does so by staying true to his code of ethics, in which preserving the potential for life and change is more important than rigid codes of honor. Harry's code of ethics also leads to his death but in a much more ironic way. When he is pursuing Ray in the final moments of the film, Harry accidentally kills Jimmy, a dwarf on the film set. When this happens, Harry thinks that he has killed a child in much the same way that Ray had in the opening scene, and he immediately kills himself, explaining "You've got to stick to your principles" before he blows his own head completely off.

This brings us to a way to interpret the ending of the film, which I think is actually quite hopeful in a situation without much hope. At the end of the film most of the main characters are dead, and Ray is being carried into an ambulance with three or four bullet wounds in his torso. One school of thought could say that the fact that the film ends with Ray's voiceover saying "I really hoped I wouldn't die" points to an interpretation that he dies and his ghost is narrating the story to us via voiceover. This interpretation seems a little bleak, however. After all, what good is Ken's sacrifice of his life if Ray dies almost immediately afterwards? **[Here the writer finds some evidence for his initial point that there is only faint hope in the film.]**

On this note, I would like to instead point to Ken's victory over Harry as a signpost for hope at the end of the film. If the film endorses Ken's viewpoint that Ray's undetermined future and possibility for change are worth dying for, the film must be holding out Ray's survival as a hopeful way of escaping the presence of the past.

In the last few moments of Ray's voiceover, as he's wheeled on a gurney towards the ambulance, he talks about how Bruges must be Hell. In this version of Hell, the past creates a vicious cycle in which we become trapped in our own histories, our own primal sins that we can never escape or gain forgiveness from. In *In Bruges*, however, Ray's primal sin of killing the child is ironically and finally reenacted by Harry, the person who is rendering justice for that very sin. **[The writer sees that Harry's choice to die by his own relentless code for what we see as a mistake starts to erode the film's support for the position that Harry represents.]**

Finally, it is significant that the last scene of *In Bruges* takes place on a film set—the film set of a Belgian dream sequence that describes and alludes to the Last Judgment, the end of time at which all humanity will be judged by God. This makes sense, given the references to the medieval painter Bosch and his painting, "The Last Judgment," which is showcased and discussed earlier in the film in relation to Ray's guilt and anxiety. The last judgment or final say of the film happens when the painting of "The Last Judgment" comes to life in the form of the film actors, who are dressed in costumes taken from Bosch's painting. **[Here the writer sees that the idea of final judgments is being presented quasi-comically as a fiction, something that takes place on a fantasy film set.]**

With all of this in mind, we come back to Ray's last line, "I really hoped I wouldn't die." This line remains unresolved by the film, in the sense that we almost expect Ray to say "And I didn't," or "But I did." The fact that this line remains unresolved makes its meaning open for interpretation and not predetermined, and thus a match for Ken's code of ethics. Lastly, even though Ray's line, "I really hoped I wouldn't die," ends on the word "die," it is more important that we look at the main verb of this sentence: "hope." This breakdown of the sentence is modeling on a smaller scale what the film is trying to say: that in the end, "hope" in the face of "dying" is all we can cling to and count on. In this way, we can view the ending of the film as offering hope for change and belief in potential—a breaking of old irreconcilable cycles of sin and punishment. This hope the film posits as necessary because without it we are held inescapably hostage to a cyclical repetition of our own histories and past deeds. **[The writer has arrived at an evolved version of his opening claim about hope, which he now sees as less faint than it had initially appeared.]** (Reprinted by permission of the author.)

Recognizing and Fixing Weak Thesis Statements

This closing section of the chapter provides a revision-oriented treatment of the five most common kinds of weak thesis statements. Typically, a weak thesis is an unproductive claim because it doesn't actually require further thinking or proof, as, for example, "An important part of one's college education is learning to better understand others' points of view" (a piece of conventional wisdom that most people would already accept as true, and thus not in need of arguing).

FIVE KINDS OF WEAK THESIS STATEMENTS

1. A thesis that makes no claim ("This paper examines the pros and cons of")

2. A thesis that is obviously true or a statement of fact ("Exercise is good for you")

3. A thesis that restates conventional wisdom ("Love conquers all")

4. A thesis that offers personal conviction as the basis for the claim ("Shopping malls are wonderful places")

5. A thesis that makes an overly broad claim ("Individualism is good")

Weak Thesis Type 1: The Thesis Makes No Claim

Problem Examples

> I'm going to write about Darwin's concerns with evolution in *The Origin of Species.*
> This paper addresses the characteristics of a good corporate manager.

Both problem examples name a subject and link it to the intention to write about it, but they don't make any claim about the subject. As a result, they direct neither the writer nor the reader toward some position or organizational plan. Even if the second example were rephrased as "This paper addresses why a good corporate manager needs to learn to delegate responsibility," the thesis would not adequately suggest why such a claim would need to be argued or defended. There is, in short, nothing at stake, no issue to be resolved.

Solution: Raise specific issues for the essay to explore.

Solution Examples

> Darwin's concern with survival of the fittest in *The Origin of Species* initially leads him to neglect a potentially conflicting aspect of his theory of evolution—survival as a matter of interdependence.
> The very trait that makes for an effective corporate manager—the drive to succeed—can also make the leader domineering and, therefore, ineffective.

Some disciplines expect writers to offer statements of method and/or intention in their papers' openings. Generally, however, these openings also make a claim: for example, "In this paper, I examine how Congressional Republicans undermined the attempts of the Democratic administration to legislate a fiscally responsible health care policy for the elderly," not "In this paper, I discuss America's treatment of the elderly."

Weak Thesis Type 2: The Thesis Is Obviously True or Is a Statement of Fact

Problem Examples

> The jean industry targets its advertisements to appeal to young adults.
> The flight from teaching to research and publishing in higher education is a controversial issue in the academic world. I will show different views and aspects concerning this problem.

A thesis needs to be an assertion with which it would be possible for readers to disagree.

In the second example, few readers would disagree with the fact that the issue is "controversial." In the second sentence of that example, the writer has begun to identify a point of view—that the flight from teaching is a problem—but her declaration that she will "show different views and aspects" is a broad statement of fact, not an idea. The phrasing of the claim is noncommittal and so broad that it prevents the writer from formulating a workable thesis.

> **Solution:** Find some avenue of inquiry—a question about the facts or an issue raised by them. Make an assertion with which it would be possible for readers to disagree.

Solution Examples

> By inventing new terms, such as "loose fit" and "relaxed fit," the jean industry has attempted to normalize, even glorify, its product for an older and fatter generation.

> The "flight from teaching" to research and publishing in higher education is a controversial issue in the academic world. As I will attempt to show, the controversy is based to a significant degree on a false assumption, that doing research necessarily leads teachers away from the classroom.

Weak Thesis Type 3: The Thesis Restates Conventional Wisdom

Problem Example

> "I was supposed to bring the coolers; you were supposed to bring the chips!" exclaimed ex-Beatle Ringo Starr, who appeared on TV commercials for Sun County Wine Coolers a few years ago. By using rock music to sell a wide range of products, the advertising agencies, in league with corporate giants such as Pepsi, Michelob, and Ford, have corrupted the spirit of rock and roll.

"Conventional wisdom" is a polite term for cultural cliché. Most clichés were fresh ideas once, but over time they have become trite, prefabricated forms of nonthinking. Faced with a phenomenon that requires a response, inexperienced writers sometimes resort to a small set of culturally approved "answers." Because conventional wisdom is so general and so commonly accepted, however, it doesn't teach anybody—including the writer—anything. Worse, because the cliché looks like an idea, it prevents the writer from engaging in a fresh exploration of his or her subject.

There is some truth in both of the preceding problem examples, but neither complicates its position. A thoughtful reader could, for example, respond to the advertising example by suggesting that rock and roll was highly commercial long before it colonized the airwaves. The conventional wisdom that rock and roll is somehow pure and honest while advertising is phony and exploitative invites the savvy writer to formulate a thesis that overturns these clichés. It could be argued that rock has actually improved advertising, not that ads have ruined rock—or, alternatively, that rock has shrewdly marketed idealism to gullible consumers. At the least, a writer committed to the original thesis would do better to examine what Ringo was selling—what he/wine coolers stand for in this particular case—than to discuss rock and advertising in such predictable terms.

Solution: Seek to complicate—see more than one point of view on—your subject. Avoid conventional wisdom unless you can qualify it or introduce a fresh perspective on it.

Solution Example

> While some might argue that the presence of rock and roll soundtracks in TV commercials has corrupted rock's spirit, this point of view not only misrepresents the history of rock but also ignores the improvements that the music has brought to the quality of television advertising.

Weak Thesis Type 4: The Thesis Bases Its Claim on Personal Conviction

Problem Examples

> Sir Thomas More's *Utopia* proposes an unworkable set of solutions to society's problems because, like communist Russia, it suppresses individualism.
>
> Although I agree with Jeane Kirkpatrick's argument that environmentalists and business should work together to ensure the ecological future of the world, and that this cooperation is beneficial for both sides, the indisputable fact is that environmental considerations should always be a part of any decision that is made. Any individual, if he looks deeply enough into his soul, knows what is right and what is wrong. The environment should be protected because it is the right thing to do, not because someone is forcing you to do it.

Like conventional wisdom, personal likes and dislikes can lead inexperienced writers into knee-jerk reactions of approval or disapproval, often expressed in a moralistic tone. The writers of the preceding problem examples assume that their primary job is to judge their subjects, or testify to their worth, not to evaluate them analytically. They have taken personal opinions for self-evident truths. (See Naturalizing Our Assumptions in Chapter 1.)

The most blatant version of this tendency occurs in the second problem example, which asserts, "Any individual, if he looks deeply enough into his soul, knows what is right and what is wrong. The environment should be protected because it is the right thing to do." Translation (only slightly exaggerated): "Any individual who thinks about the subject will obviously agree with me because my feelings and convictions feel right to me and therefore they must be universally and self-evidently true." Testing an idea against your own feelings and experience is not an adequate means of establishing whether something is accurate or true.

Solution: Try on other points of view honestly and dispassionately; treat your ideas as hypotheses to be tested rather than obvious truths. In the following solution examples, we have replaced opinions (in the form of self-evident truths) with ideas—theories about the meaning and significance of the subjects that are capable of being supported and qualified by evidence.

Solution Examples

Sir Thomas More's *Utopia* treats individualism as a serious but remediable social problem. His radical treatment of what we might now call "socialization" attempts to redefine the meaning and origin of individual identity.

Although I agree with Jeane Kirkpatrick's argument that environmentalists and business should work together to ensure the ecological future of the world, her argument undervalues the necessity of pressuring businesses to attend to environmental concerns that may not benefit them in the short run.

Weak Thesis Type 5: The Thesis Makes an Overly Broad Claim

Problem Examples

Violent revolutions have had both positive and negative results for man.
Othello is a play about love and jealousy.

Overly generalized theses avoid complexity. Such statements usually lead either to say-nothing theses or to reductive either/or thinking. Similar to a thesis that makes no claim, theses with overly broad claims say nothing in particular about the subject at hand and so are not likely to guide a writer's thinking beyond the listing stage. One of the best ways to avoid drafting overly broad thesis statements is to sensitize yourself to the characteristic phrasing of such theses: "both positive and negative," "many similarities and differences," "both pros and cons." Virtually everything from meatloaf to taxes can be both positive and negative.

Solution: Convert broad categories and generic claims to more specific, more qualified assertions; find ways to bring out the complexity of your subject.

Solution Examples

Although violent revolutions begin to redress long-standing inequities, they often do so at the cost of long-term economic dysfunction and the suffering that attends it.
Although *Othello* appears to attack jealousy, it also supports the skepticism of the jealous characters over the naïveté of the lovers.

Assignment: Finding and Evolving a Thesis

Formulate and Evolve a Thesis on a Film, Painting, or Other Visual Image.

Using the model of *Las Meninas*, produce an interpretation of a film, painting, or other visual image of your choice.

First, begin by formulating a variety of possible statements about the film or painting from which you would choose one to serve as a working thesis. These potential working theses might be in answer to the question "What is the film/painting about?" or "What does it 'say'?" Or you might begin by doing

THE METHOD to uncover pattern of repetition or contrast you have observed and can then explain.

Obviously, this assignment could be adapted to other subjects—an essay, the coverage of a current event, etc. Here are some specific suggestions:

- The contemporary appeal of a cartoon or other popular television character

- Differences in political rhetoric between Democrats and Republicans on the same issue

- The rhetoric of a popular print or television ad campaign for a familiar product, such as an insurance company or a soft drink or an automobile

Next, follow the procedure for making the thesis evolve, using the six steps.

CHAPTER 7

Conversing with Sources: Writing the Researched Paper

Overview This chapter's primary heuristic offers six strategies for analyzing sources. The idea of the chapter is that you should learn to put your sources in conversation with each other and with your own ideas, rather than just pointing to them as answers.

The chapter also offers specific advice on how to integrate quotation and paraphrase into your writing and how to do in-text citation. The last section of the chapter shows you how to write an abstract and how to manage citation in the literature review that is the common opening section in formal papers in the sciences. The book's next chapter—on finding and citing sources—provides a reference librarian's advice on finding and evaluating sources plus specifics on the citation styles used by the different academic disciplines.

Using Sources Analytically

Integrating secondary sources into your writing is often a daunting task, because it requires you to negotiate with authorities who generally know more than you do about the subject at hand. Simply ignoring sources is a head-in-the-sand attitude, and besides you miss out on learning what people interested in your subject are talking about. But what role can you invent for yourself when the experts are talking? Just agreeing with a source is an abdication of your responsibility to present your thinking on the subject. But taking the opposite tack by disagreeing with an expert who has studied your subject and written books about it would also appear to be a fool's game. So what are you to do?

This chapter attempts to answer that question. It lays out the primary trouble spots that arise when writers use secondary materials, and it suggests remedies—ways of using sources as points of departure for your own thinking rather than using them as either "The Answer" or a straw man. We call this approach conversing with sources, which will teach you how to avoid the temptation to plug in sources as answers, seeing them instead as voices inviting you into a community of interpretation, discussion, and debate.

The kind of writing you are doing will affect the way you use sources. Analytical writing uses sources to expand understanding—often to allow readers to view a subject from a range of plausible points of view. This approach differs from the kind of research-based writing wherein the goal is to locate a single position that beats out the others in a combative mode. One way that sources are often used in an academic setting is as lenses for examining other sources and primary materials.

We use the terms *source* and *secondary source* interchangeably to designate ideas and information about your subject that you find in the work of other writers. Secondary sources allow you to gain a richer, more informed, and complex vantage point on your *primary sources*. Here's how primary and secondary sources can be distinguished: if you were writing a paper on the philosopher Nietzsche, his writing would be your primary source, and critical commentaries on his work would be your secondary sources. If, however, you were writing on the poet Yeats, who read and was influenced by Nietzsche, a work of Nietzsche's philosophy would become a secondary source of yours on your primary source, Yeats's poetry.

Here are a few guidelines for using sources in analytical writing:

- Locate and highlight what is at stake in your source. Which of its points does the source find most important? What positions does it want to modify or refute, and why? (See THE PITCH, THE COMPLAINT, AND THE MOMENT in Chapter 2.)

- Look for ways to develop, modify, or apply what a source has said, rather than simply agreeing or disagreeing with it.

- If you challenge a position found in a source, be sure to represent it fairly. First, give the source some credit by identifying assumptions you share with it. Then, isolate the part that you intend to complicate or dispute.

- Look for sources that address your subject from different perspectives. Avoid relying too heavily on any one source. Aim to synthesize these perspectives: what is the common ground?

- When your sources disagree, consider playing mediator. Instead of immediately agreeing with one or the other, clarify areas of agreement and disagreement among them.

"Source Anxiety" and What to Do About It

Typically, inexperienced writers either use sources as "answers"—they let the sources do too much of their thinking—or ignore them altogether as a way of avoiding losing their own ideas. Both of these approaches are understandable but inadequate.

Confronted with the seasoned views of experts in a discipline, you may well feel that there is nothing left for you to say because it has all been said before or, at least, it has been said by people who greatly outweigh you in reputation and experience. This anxiety explains why so many writers surrender to the role of conduit for the voices of the experts, providing little more than conjunctions between quotations. So why not avoid what other people have said? Won't this avoidance ensure that your ideas will be original and that, at the same time, you will be free from the danger of getting brainwashed by some expert?

The answer is no. If you don't consult what others have said, you run at least two risks: you will waste your time reinventing the wheel, and you will undermine your analysis (or at least leave it incomplete) by not considering information and ideas commonly discussed in the field. By remaining unaware of existing thinking, you choose, in effect, to stand outside of the conversation that others interested in the subject are having.

It is possible to find a *middle ground* between developing an idea that is entirely independent of what experts have written on a subject and producing a paper that does nothing but repeat other people's ideas. A little research—even if it's only an hour's browse in the relevant databases on your library's website—will virtually always raise the level of what you have to say above what it would have been if you had consulted only the information and opinions that you carry around in your head.

A good rule of thumb for coping with source anxiety is to formulate a tentative position on your topic before you consult secondary sources. In other words, give yourself time to do some preliminary thinking. Try writing informally about your topic, analyzing some piece of pertinent information already at your disposal. That way you will have your initial responses written down to weigh in relation to what others have said.

The Conversation Analogy

Now, let's turn to the major problem in using sources—a writer leaving the experts he or she cites to speak for themselves. In this situation, the writer characteristically makes a generalization in his or her own words, juxtaposes it to a quotation or other reference from a secondary source, and assumes that the meaning of the reference will be self-evident. This practice not only leaves the connection between the writer's thinking and his or her source material unstated, but also substitutes mere repetition of someone else's viewpoint for a more active interpretation. The source has been allowed to have the final word, with the effect that it stops the discussion and the writer's thinking.

First and foremost, then, you need to *do something* with the reading. Clarify the meaning of the material you have quoted, paraphrased, or summarized and explain its significance in light of your evolving thesis.

It follows that the first step in using sources effectively is to reject the assumption that sources provide final and complete answers. If they did, there would be no reason for others to continue writing on the subject. As in conversation, we raise ideas for others to respond to. Accepting that no source has the final word does not mean, however, that you should shift from unquestioning approval to the opposite pole and necessarily assume an antagonistic position toward all sources. Indeed, a habitually antagonistic response to others' ideas is just as likely to bring your conversation with your sources to a halt as is the habit of always assuming that the source must have the final word.

Most people would probably agree on the attributes of a really good conversation. There is room for agreement and disagreement, for give and take, among a variety of viewpoints. Generally, people don't deliberately misunderstand each other, but a significant amount of the discussion may go into clarifying one's own as well as others' positions. Such conversations construct a genuinely collaborative chain of thinking: Karl builds on what David has said, which induces Jill to respond to Karl's comment, and so forth.

There are, of course, obvious differences between conversing aloud with friends and conversing on paper with sources. As a writer, you need to construct the chain of thinking, orchestrate the exchange of views with and among your sources, and give the conversation direction. A good place to begin in using sources is to recognize that you need not respond to everything another writer says, nor do you need to come up with an entirely original point of view—one that completely revises or refutes the source. You are using sources analytically, for example, when you note that two experiments (or historical accounts, or whatever) are similar but have different priorities or that they ask similar questions in different ways. Building from this kind of observation, you can then analyze what these differences imply.

TWO METHODS FOR CONVERSING WITH SOURCES

- Choose one sentence from a secondary source and one from a primary source, and put these into conversation. What does each reveal about the other?

- Pick one sentence from one source (A) and one from another (B): how does A speak to B? How does B speak to A?

Remember: go local, not global. You will be better off if you bring together two representative moves or ideas from the sources rather than trying to compare a summary of one source with a summary of another. A useful phrase here is "points of contact": look for ways that an idea or observation in source A appears to intersect with one in source B. Then stage the conversation you can imagine taking place between them.

Conversing with a Source: A Brief Example

Consider, for example, the following quotation, the opening sentences of an essay entitled "Clichés" by Christopher Ricks, which is ostensibly a review of a reissued book on the subject:

> The only way to speak of a cliché is with a cliché. So even the best writers against clichés are awkwardly placed. When Eric Partridge amassed his *Dictionary of Cliches* in

1940 (1978 saw its fifth edition), his introduction had no choice but to use the usual clichés for clichés. Yet what, as a metaphor, could be more hackneyed than *hackneyed*, more outworn than *outworn*, more tattered than *tattered*? Is there any point left to—or in or on—saying of a cliché that its "original point has been blunted"? Hasn't this too become blunted? (Christopher Ricks, "Clichés" in *The State of the Language*, ed. Leonard Michaels and Christopher Ricks (Berkeley: University of California Press, 1980), p54)

A writer would not want to cite this passage simply to illustrate that clichés are "bad"—language uses to be avoided—or to suggest, as a dictionary might, that a cliché is a form of expression one might call "hackneyed" or "outworn" or "tattered," even though this information is clearly included in Ricks' sentences. Nor would a writer simply want to reiterate Ricks' leading claim, that "The only way to speak of a cliché is with a cliché," because Ricks already said that.

Instead, you'd need to talk about how Ricks treats the topic—that he has uncovered a paradox, for example, in that first sentence. You might go on to say that his point of view provides a useful warning for those who wish to talk about clichés. And then you might make some inferences you could build on: that simply dismissing clichés on vaguely moral grounds as unoriginal (hackneyed) does not add anything to our knowledge, and so perhaps, it's time to rethink our usual response to clichés and to see them afresh. In any case, as a rule of thumb, only include a quotation if you plan to say something about it.

Ways to Use a Source as a Point of Departure

There are many ways of approaching secondary sources, but these ways generally share a common goal: to use the source as a point of departure. In the next section of this chapter we offer six new strategies for analyzing sources. Here we offer a quick summary of strategies you've already encountered in this book that can help you make better use of sources.

- Make as many points as you can about a single representative passage from your source, and then branch out from this center to analyze other passages that "speak" to it in some way. (See 10 on 1 and Pan, Track, and Zoom in Chapter 4.)

- Use NOTICE AND FOCUS to identify what you find most strange in the source (See Chapter 1.); this will help you cultivate your curiosity about the source and find the critical distance necessary to thinking about it.

- Use THE METHOD to identify the most significant organizing contrast in the source (See Chapter 1.); this will help you see what the source itself is wrestling with, what is at stake in it.

- Apply an idea in the source to another subject. (See Applying a Reading as a Lens in Chapter 2.)

- Uncover the assumptions in the source, and then build upon the source's point of view, extending its implications. (See UNCOVERING ASSUMPTIONS in Chapter 2.)

- Agree with most of what the source says, but take issue with one small part that you want to modify.

- Identify a contradiction in the source, and explore its implications, without necessarily arriving at a solution.

In using a source as a point of departure you are in effect using it as a stimulus for having an idea. If you quote or paraphrase a source with the aim of conversing rather than allowing it to do your thinking for you, you will discover that sources can promote rather than stifle your ability to have ideas. Try to think of sources not as answers but as voices inviting you into a community of interpretation, discussion, and debate.

Six Strategies for Analyzing Sources

Many people never get beyond like/dislike responses with secondary materials. If they agree with what a source says, they say it's "good," and they cut and paste the part they can use as an answer. If the source somehow disagrees with what they already believe, they say it's "bad," and they attack it or—along with readings they find "hard" or "boring"—discard it. As readers they have been conditioned to develop a point of view on a subject without first figuring out the conversation (the various points of view) that their subject attracts. They assume, in other words, that their subject probably has a single meaning—a gist—disclosed by experts, who mostly agree. The six strategies that follow offer ways to avoid this trap.

Six Strategies for Analyzing Sources

Strategy 1: Make Your Sources Speak
Strategy 2: Attend Carefully to the Language of Your Sources by
    Quoting or Paraphrasing
Strategy 3: Supply Ongoing Analysis of Sources (Don't Wait until the End)
Strategy 4: Use Your Sources to Ask Questions, Not Just to
    Provide Answers
Strategy 5: Put Your Sources into Conversation with One Another
Strategy 6: Find Your Own Role in the Conversation

Strategy 1: Make Your Sources Speak

Quote, paraphrase, or summarize *in order to* analyze—not in place of analyzing. Don't assume that either the meaning of the source material or your reason for including it is self-evident. Stop yourself from the habit of just stringing together citations for which you provide little more than conjunctions. Instead, explain to your readers what the quotation or paraphrase or summary of the source means. What elements of it do you find interesting or revealing or strange? Emphasize how those affect your evolving thesis.

In making a source speak, focus on articulating how the source has led to the conclusion you draw from it. Beware of simply putting a generalization and a quotation next to each other (juxtaposing them) without explaining the connection. Instead fill the crucial site between claim and evidence with your thinking. Consider this problem in the following paragraph from a student's paper on political conservatism.

> Edmund Burke's philosophy evolved into contemporary American conservative ideology. There is an important distinction between philosophy and political ideology: philosophy is "the knowledge of general principles that explain facts and existences." Political ideology, on the other hand, is "an overarching conception of society, a stance that is reflected in numerous sectors of social life" (Edwards 22). Therefore, conservatism should be regarded as an ideology rather than a philosophy.

The final sentence offers the writer's conclusion—what the source information has led him to—but how did it get him there? The writer's choice of the word "therefore" indicates to the reader that the idea following it is the result of a process of logical reasoning, but this reasoning has been omitted. Instead, the writer assumes that the reader will be able to connect the quotations with his conclusion. The writer needs to make the quotation speak by analyzing its key terms more closely. What is "an overarching conception of society," and how does it differ from "knowledge of general principles"? More important, what is the rationale for categorizing conservatism as either an ideology or a philosophy?

Here, by contrast, is a writer who makes her sources speak. Focus on how she integrates analysis with quotation.

> Stephen Greenblatt uses the phrase "self-fashioning" to refer to an idea he believes developed during the Renaissance—the idea that one's identity is not created or born but rather shaped, both by one's self and by others. The idea of self-fashioning is incorporated into an attitude toward literature that has as its ideal what Greenblatt calls "poetics of culture." A text is examined with three elements in mind: the author's own self, the cultural self-fashioning process that created that self, and the author's reaction to that process. Because our selves, like texts, are "fashioned," an author's life is just as open to interpretation as that of a literary character.
>
> If this is so, then biography does not provide a repository of unshakeable facts from which to interpret an author's work. Greenblatt criticizes the fact that the methods of literary interpretation are applied just to art and not to life. As he observes, "We wall off literary symbolism from the symbolic structures operative elsewhere, as if art alone were a human creation" (Begley 37). If the line between art and life is indeed blurred, then we need a more complex model for understanding the relationship between the life and work of an author.

In this example, the writer shows us how her thinking has been stimulated by the source. At the end of the first paragraph and the beginning of the second, for example, she not only specifies what she takes to be the meaning of the quotation but also draws a conclusion about its implications (that the facts of an author's life, like his or her art, require interpretation). And this manner of proceeding is habitual: the writer repeats the pattern in the second paragraph, moving beyond what the quotation says to explore what its logic suggests.

Strategy 2: Attend Carefully to the Language of Your Sources by Quoting or Paraphrasing

Rather than generalizing broadly about ideas in your sources, you should spell out what you think is significant about their key words. In those disciplines in which it is permissible, *quote sources if the actual language that they use is important to your point.*

Generally, disciplines in the humanities expect you to quote as well as paraphrase, while in the social sciences, students are encouraged to paraphrase, not quote.

Quoting and paraphrasing have the benefit of helping writers to represent the views of their sources fairly and accurately. In situations in which quoting is not allowed—such as in the report format in psychology—you still need to attend carefully to the meaning of key words in order to arrive at a summary or paraphrase that is not overly general. As we have suggested repeatedly, paraphrasing provides an ideal way to begin interpreting, because the act of careful rephrasing usually illuminates attitudes and assumptions implicit in a text. It is almost impossible not to have ideas and not to see the questions when you start paraphrasing.

Another reason that quoting and paraphrasing are important is that your analysis of a source will nearly always benefit from attention to the way the source represents its position. Although focusing on the manner of presentation matters more with some sources than with others—more with a poem or scholarly article in political science than with a paper in the natural sciences—the information is never wholly separable from how it is expressed. If you are going to quote *Newsweek* on Pakistan, for example, you will be encountering not "the truth" about American involvement in this Asian nation but rather one particular representation of the situation—in this case, one crafted to meet or shape the expectations of mainstream popular culture. Similarly, if you quote President Obama on terrorism, what probably matters most is that the president chose particular words to represent—and promote—the government's position. It is not neutral information. The person speaking and the kind of source in which his or her words appear usually acquire added significance when you make note of these words rather than just summarizing them.

In sum, you should aim to:

- Quote, paraphrase, or summarize *in order to* analyze. Explain what you take the source to mean, showing the reasoning that has led to the conclusion you draw from it.

- Quote sparingly. You are usually better off centering your analysis on a few quotations, analyzing their key terms, and branching out to aspects of your subject that the quotations illuminate. (Remember that not all disciplines allow direct quotation.)

- Recognize the value of close paraphrasing. You will almost invariably begin to interpret a source once you start paraphrasing its key language.

Strategy 3: Supply Ongoing Analysis of Sources (Don't Wait Until the End)

Unless disciplinary conventions dictate otherwise, analyze *as* you quote or paraphrase a source, rather than summarizing everything first and leaving your analysis for the end. A good conversation does not consist of long monologues alternating among the speakers. Participants exchange views, query, and modify what other speakers have said. Similarly, when you orchestrate conversations with and among your sources, you need to integrate your analysis into your presentation of them.

In supplying ongoing analysis, you are much more likely to explain how the information in the sources fits into your unfolding presentation, and your readers will be more likely to follow your train of thought and grasp the logic of your organization. You will also prevent yourself from using the sources simply as an answer. A good rule of thumb in this regard is to force yourself to ask and answer "so what?" at the ends of paragraphs. In laying out your analysis, however, take special care to distinguish your voice from the sources. (For discussion of integrating your own language with language from your sources, see Integrating Quotations Into Your Paper later in this chapter.)

In the following Voice from Across the Curriculum, psychology professor Alan Tjeltveit offers a tip about how members of his discipline orchestrate a number of sources on more than one topic.

VOICES FROM ACROSS THE CURRICULUM

Bringing Sources Together: A Psychology Professor Speaks

Avoid serial citation summaries; that is, rather than discussing what Author A found, then what Author B found, then what Author C found, and so forth, *integrate* material from all of your sources. For instance, if writing about the cause and treatment of a disorder, discuss what all authors say about cause, then what all authors say about treatment, and so forth, addressing any contradictions or tensions among authors.

—ALAN TJELTVEIT, PROFESSOR OF PSYCHOLOGY

Strategy 4: Use Your Sources to Ask Questions, Not Just to Provide Answers

Use your selections from sources as a means of raising issues and questions. Avoid the temptation to plug in such selections as answers that require no further commentary or elaboration. You will no doubt find viewpoints you believe to be valid, but it is not enough to drop these answers from the source into your own writing at the appropriate spots. You need to *do* something with the reading, even with those sources that seem to have said what you want to say.

As long as you consider only the source in isolation, you may not discover much to say about it. Once you begin considering it in other contexts and with other sources, you may begin to see aspects of your subject that your source does not adequately address. Having recognized that the source does not answer all questions, you should not conclude that the source is "wrong"—only that it is limited in some ways. Discovering such limitations is in fact advantageous, because it can lead you to identify a place from which to launch your own analysis.

It does not necessarily follow that your analysis will culminate in an answer to replace those offered by your sources. Often—in fact, far more often than many writers suspect—it is enough to discover issues or problems and raise them clearly. Phrasing explicitly the issues and questions that remain implicit in a source is an important part of what analytical writers do, especially with cases in which there is no solution, or at least none that can be presented in a relatively short paper. Here, for example, is how the writer on Stephen Greenblatt's concept of self-fashioning concludes her essay:

> It is not only the author whose role is complicated by New Historicism; the critic also is subject to some of the same qualifications and restrictions. According to Adam Begley, "it is the essence of the new-historicist project to uncover the moments at which works of art absorb and refashion social energy, an endless process of circulation and exchange" (39). In other words, the work is both affected by and affects the culture. But if this is so, how then can we decide which elements of culture (and text) are causes and which are effects? If we add the critic to this picture, the process does indeed appear endless. The New Historicists' relationship with their culture infuses itself into their assessment of the Renaissance, and this assessment may in turn become part of their own self-fashioning process, which will affect their interpretations, and so forth....

Notice that this writer incorporates the quotation into her own chain of thinking. By paraphrasing the quotation ("In other words"), she arrives at a question ("how then") that follows as a logical consequence of accepting its position ("but if this is so"). Note, however, that she does not then label the quotation right or wrong. Instead, she tries to figure out to what position it might lead and to what possible problems.

By contrast, the writer of the following excerpt, from a paper comparing two films aimed at teenagers, settles for plugging in sources as answers and consequently does not pursue the questions implicit in her quotations.

> In both films, the adults are one-dimensional caricatures, evil beings whose only goal in life is to make the kids' lives a living hell. In *Risky Business*, director Paul Brickman's solution to all of Joel's problems is to have him hire a prostitute and then turn his house into a whorehouse. Of course, as one critic observes, "the prostitutes who

make themselves available to his pimply faced buddies are all centerfold beauties: elegant, svelte, benign and unquestionably healthy (after all, what does V.D. have to do with prostitutes?)" (Gould 41)—not exactly a realistic or legal solution. Allan Moyle, the director of *Pump Up the Volume*, provides an equally unrealistic solution to Mark's problem. According to David Denby, Moyle "offers self-expression as the cure to adolescent funk. Everyone should start his own radio station and talk about his feelings" (59). Like Brickman, Moyle offers solutions that are neither realistic nor legal.

This writer is having a hard time figuring out what to do with sources that offer well-phrased and seemingly accurate answers (such as "self-expression is the cure to adolescent funk"). She settles for the bland conclusion that films aimed at teenagers are not "realistic"—an observation that most readers would already recognize as true. But unlike the writer of the previous example, she does not ask herself, "If this is true, then what follows?" Some version of the SO WHAT? question might have led her to inquire how the illegality of the solutions is related to their unrealistic quality. So what, for example, that the main characters in both films are not marginalized as criminals and made to suffer for their illegal actions, but rather are celebrated as heroes? What different kinds of illegality do the two films apparently condone, and how might these be related to the different decades in which each film was produced? Rather than use her sources to think with, in order to clarify or complicate the issues, the writer has used them to confirm a fairly obvious generalization.

Strategy 5: Put Your Sources Into Conversation with One Another

Rather than limiting yourself to agreeing or disagreeing with your sources, aim for conversation with and among them. Although it is not wrong to agree or disagree with your sources, it is wrong to see these as your only possible moves. It is okay to summarize a position that you intend to challenge in a carefully qualified way. It is not okay to construct a "dummy" position specifically in order to knock it down (a practice sometimes known as a straw man).

As this analogy suggests, setting up a straw man can be dangerous. If you do not fairly represent and put into context the straw man's argument, you risk encouraging readers to dismiss your counterargument as a cheap shot and to dismiss you for being reductive. On the other hand, if you spend a great deal of time detailing the straw man's position, you risk losing momentum in developing your own point of view.

In any case, if you are citing a source in order to frame the discussion, the more reasonable move is both to agree *and* disagree with it. First, identify shared premises; give the source some credit. Then distinguish the part of what you have cited that you intend to develop or complicate or dispute. This method of proceeding is obviously less combative than the typically blunt straw man approach; it verges on conversation.

In the following passage from a student's paper on Darwin's theory of evolution, the student clearly recognizes that he needs to do more than summarize what Darwin says, but he seems not to know any way of conversing with his source other than indicating his agreement and disagreement with it.

> The struggle for existence also includes the dependence of one being on another being to survive. Darwin also believes that all organic beings tend to increase. I do not fully agree with Darwin's belief here. I cannot conceive of the fact of all beings increasing in number. Darwin goes on to explain that food, competition, climate, and the location of a certain species contribute to its survival and existence in nature. I believe that this statement is very valid and that it could be very easily understood through experimentation in nature.

This writer's use of the word "here" in his third sentence is revealing. He is tagging summaries of Darwin with what he seems to feel is an obligatory response—a polite shake or nod of the head: "I can't fully agree with you there, Darwin, but here I think you might have a point." The writer's tentative language lets us see how uncomfortable, even embarrassed, he feels about venturing these judgments on a subject that is too complex for this kind of response. It's as though the writer moves along, talking about Darwin's theory for a while, and then says to himself, "Time for a response," and lets a particular summary sentence trigger a yes/no switch. Having pressed that switch, which he does periodically, the writer resumes his summary, having registered— but not having analyzed—his own interjections. There is no reasoning in a chain from his own observations, just random insertions of unanalyzed agree/ disagree responses.

Here, by contrast, is the introduction of an essay that uses summary to frame the conversation that the writer is preparing to have with her source.

> In *Renaissance Thought: The Classic, Scholastic and Humanist Strains,* Paul Kristeller responds to two problems that he perceives in Renaissance scholarship. The first is the haze of cultural meaning surrounding the word "humanism": he seeks to clarify the word and its origins, as well as to explain the apparent lack of religious concern in humanism. Kristeller also reacts to the notion of humanism as an improvement upon medieval Aristotelian scholasticism.

Rather than leading with her own beliefs about the source, the writer emphasizes the issues and problems she believes are central in it. Although the writer's position on her source is apparently neutral, she is not summarizing passively. In addition to making choices about what is especially significant in the source, she has also located it within the conversation that its author, Kristeller, was having with his own sources—the works of other scholars whose view of humanism he wants to revise ("Kristeller responds to two problems").

As an alternative to formulating your opinion of the sources, try constructing the conversation that you think the author of one of your sources might have with the author of another. How might they recast each other's ideas, as opposed to merely agreeing or disagreeing with those ideas? Notice how, later in the paper, the writer uses this strategy to achieve a clearer picture of Kristeller's point of view:

> Unlike Kristeller, Tillyard [in *The Elizabethan World Picture*] also tries to place the seeds of individualism in the minds of the medievals. "Those who know most about the Middle Ages," he claims, "now assure us that humanism and a belief in the present life were powerful by the 12th century" (30). Kristeller would undoubtedly reply that it was scholasticism, lacking the humanist emphasis on individualism, that was powerful in the Middle Ages. True humanism was not evident in the Middle Ages.
>
> In Kristeller's view, Tillyard's attempts to assign humanism to medievals are not only unwarranted, but also counterproductive. Kristeller ends his chapter on "Humanism and Scholasticism" with an exhortation to "develop a kind of historical pluralism. It is easy to praise everything in the past that appears to resemble certain favorable ideas of our own time, or to ridicule and minimize everything that disagrees with them. This method is neither fair nor helpful" (174). Tillyard, in trying to locate humanism within the medieval world, allows the value of humanism to supersede the worth of medieval scholarship. Kristeller argues that there is inherent worth in every intellectual movement, not simply in the ones that we find most agreeable.
>
> Kristeller's work is valuable to us primarily for its forthright definition of humanism. Tillyard has cleverly avoided this undertaking: he provides many textual references, usually with the companion comment that "this is an example of Renaissance humanism," but he never overtly and fully formulates the definition in the way that Kristeller does.

As this excerpt makes evident, the writer has found something to say about her source by putting it into conversation with another source with which she believes her source, Kristeller, would disagree ("Kristeller would undoubtedly reply"). Although it seems obvious that the writer prefers Kristeller to Tillyard, her agreement with him is not the main point of her analysis. She focuses instead on foregrounding the problem that Kristeller is trying to solve and on relating that problem to different attitudes toward history. In so doing, she is deftly orchestrating the conversation between her sources. Her next step would be to distinguish her position from Kristeller's. Having used Kristeller to get perspective on Tillyard, she now needs somehow to get perspective on Kristeller. The next strategy addresses this issue.

Strategy 6: Find Your Own Role in the Conversation

Even in cases in which you find a source's position entirely congenial, it is not enough simply to agree with it. This does not mean that you should feel compelled to attack the source but rather that you need to find something of your own to say about it.

In general, you have two options when you find yourself strongly in agreement with a source. You can (1) apply it in another context to qualify or expand its implications. Or you can (2) seek out other perspectives on the source in order to break the spell it has cast upon you. To break the spell means that you will necessarily become somewhat disillusioned but not that you will then need to dismiss everything you previously believed.

How, in the first option, do you take a source somewhere else? Rather than focusing solely on what you believe your source finds most important, locate a lesser point, not emphasized by the reading, that you find especially interesting and develop it further. This strategy will lead you to uncover new implications that depend upon your source but lie outside its own governing preoccupations. In the preceding humanism example, the writer might apply Kristeller's principles to new geographic (rather than theoretical) areas, such as Germany instead of Italy.

The second option, researching new perspectives on the source, can also lead to uncovering new implications. Your aim need not be simply to find a source that disagrees with the one that has convinced you and then switch your allegiance, because this move would perpetuate the problem from which you are trying to escape. Instead, you would use additional perspectives to gain some critical distance from your source. An ideal way of sampling possible critical approaches to a source is to consult book reviews on it found in scholarly journals. Once the original source is taken down from the pedestal through additional reading, there is a greater likelihood that you will see how to distinguish your views from those it offers.

You may think, for example, that another source's critique of your original source is partly valid and that both sources miss things that you could point out; in effect, you *referee* the conversation between them. The writer on Kristeller might play this role by asking herself: "so WHAT that subsequent historians have viewed his objective—a disinterested historical pluralism—as not necessarily desirable and in any case impossible? How might Kristeller respond to this charge, and how has he responded already in ways that his critics have failed to notice?" Using additional research in this way can lead you to situate your source more fully and fairly, acknowledging its limits as well as its strengths.

In other words, this writer, in using Kristeller to critique Tillyard, has arrived less at a conclusion than at her next point of departure. A good rule to follow, especially when you find a source entirely persuasive, is that if you can't find a perspective on your source, you haven't done enough research.

In the following Voice from Across the Curriculum, molecular biologist Bruce Wightman suggests the range of tasks he expects students to do when they engage a source—not only to supply ongoing analysis of it and to consider its contributions in light of other research—but also to locate themselves in relation to the questions their analysis of the source has led them to discover.

VOICES FROM ACROSS THE CURRICULUM

Engaging Sources in the Sciences: A Biology Professor Speaks
One of the problems with trying to read critical analyses of scientific work is that few scientists want to be in print criticizing their colleagues. That is, for political reasons

scientists who write reviews are likely to soften their criticism or even avoid it entirely by reporting the findings of others simply and directly.

What I want from students in molecular biology is a critical analysis of the work they have researched. This can take several forms.

First, *analyze* what was done. What were the assumptions (hypotheses) going into the experiment? What was the logic of the experimental design? What were the results?

Second, *evaluate* the results and conclusions. How well do the results support the conclusions? What alternative interpretations are there? What additional experiments could be done to strengthen or refute the argument? This is hard, no doubt, but it is what you should be doing every time you read anything in science or otherwise.

Third, *synthesize* the results and interpretations of a given experiment in the context of the field. How does this study inform other studies? Even though practicing scientists are hesitant to do this in print, everyone does it informally in journal clubs held usually on a weekly basis in every lab all over the world.

—BRUCE WIGHTMAN, PROFESSOR OF BIOLOGY

Using Sources Analytically: An Example

In a recent article on thinking entitled "The Other You" that appeared in the journal *New Scientist*, the writer introduces sources in sequence, wherein each source offers a different researcher's angle on the same central question: how is the subconscious related to the conscious activities of the mind? The writer, Kate Douglas, discusses the implications of each source without choosing any one as "the answer":

- "Shadlin sees the subconscious and conscious as two parts of the same system, rather than two separate thought processors working in the same machine."

- "Others want to further subdivide conscious and subconscious thought and have come up with alternative descriptions to replace the old two-part model."

- "Peter Dayan [and colleagues] see the mind as comprising four systems."

- "Dayan says that our behavior is often driven by more than one of the four controllers."

At the end of this phase of the article, Douglas then states, "Importantly, the subconscious isn't the dumb cousin of the conscious, but rather a cousin with different skills" (Kate Douglas, "The Subconscious Mind: Your Unsung Hero," *New Scientist*, December 1–7, 2007. vol. 196, no. 2632, p. 45.).

As this example demonstrates, often in conversing with sources a writer is not staging conflicts or debates, but bringing together multiple points of view and offering a final synthesis. Those familiar with the popular journalist

Malcolm Gladwell may recognize that he is fond of this method. In books such as *Blink*, Gladwell presents one piece of research, and in making inferences about it leads us to the next and often unexpectedly related piece of research. Part of the appeal of Gladwell's method is how he quilts together a range of disparate voices into one unfolding narrative. The thinking in a Gladwell piece is presented in the way he connects the parts, not in the way that he is critiquing them, finding shortcomings, or emphasizing the differences.

Integrating Quotations Into Your Paper

An enormous number of writers lose authority and readability because they have never learned how to correctly integrate quotations into their own writing. The following guidelines should help. (For more detail on different citation styles, see Chapter 8.) The primary rules of thumb here are that you should:

- Tell your readers in the text of your paper, not just in citations, when you are using someone else's words, ideas, or information; rewording someone else's idea doesn't make it your idea.

- Always attach a quotation to some of your own language; never let it stand as its own sentence in your text.

1. **Acknowledge sources in your text, not just in citations.** *When you incorporate material from a source, attribute it to the source explicitly in your text—not just in a citation.* In other words, when you introduce the material, *frame* it with a phrase such as "according to Marsh" or "as Gruen argues."

   Although it is not required, you are usually much better off making the attribution overtly, even if you have also cited the source within parentheses or with a footnote at the end of the last sentence quoted, paraphrased, or summarized. If a passage does not contain an attribution, your readers will not know that it comes from a source until they reach the citation at the end. Attributing up front clearly distinguishes what one source says from what another says and, perhaps more importantly, what your sources say from what you say. Useful verbs for introducing attributions include the following: notes, observes, argues, comments, writes, says, reports, suggests, and claims. Generally speaking, by the way, you should cite the author by last name only—as "Gruen," not as "William Gruen" or "Mr. Gruen." (In some cases, the first appearance includes both first and last name.)

2. **Splice quotations onto your own words.** *Always attach some of your own language to quotations; don't let them sit in your text as independent sentences with quotation marks around them.* You can normally satisfy this rule with an attributive phrase—commonly known as a tag phrase—that introduces the quotation.

> According to Paul McCartney, "All you need is love."

Note that the tag phrase takes a comma before the quote. Alternatively you can splice quotations into your text with a setup: a statement followed by a colon.

> Patrick Henry's famous phrase is one of the first that American schoolchildren memorize: "Give me liberty, or give me death."

The colon, you should notice, usually comes at the end of an independent clause (that is, a subject plus verb that can stand alone), at the spot where a period normally goes. It would be incorrect to write "Patrick Henry is known for: 'Give me liberty, or give me death.'"

The rationale for this guideline on splicing in quotations is essentially the same as that for the previous one: if you are going to move to quotation, you first need to identify its author so that your readers will be able to put it in context quickly.

Spliced quotations frequently create problems in grammar or punctuation for writers. Whether you include an entire sentence (or passage) of quotation or just a few phrases, you need to take care to integrate them into the grammar of your own sentence.

One of the most common mistaken assumptions is that a comma should always precede a quotation, as in "A spokesperson for the public defender's office demanded, 'an immediate response from the mayor.'" The sentence structure does not call for any punctuation after "demanded."

3. **Cite sources after quotations.** *Locate citations in parentheses after the quotation and before the final period.* The information about the source appears at the end of the sentence, with the final period following the closing parenthesis.

> A recent article on the best-selling albums in America claimed that "Ever since Elvis, it has been pop music's job to challenge the mores of the older generation" (Hornby 168).

Note that there is normally *no punctuation* at the end of the quotation itself, either before or after the closing quotation mark. A quotation that ends either in a question mark or an exclamation mark is an exception to this rule because the sign is an integral part of the quotation's meaning.

> As Hamlet says to Rosencrantz and Guildenstern, "And yet to me what is this quintessence of dust?" (2.2.304–05).

See the section entitled "How to Cite Sources" in Chapter 8 for the appropriate formats for in-text citations.

4. **Use ellipses to shorten quotations.** *Add an ellipsis to indicate that you have omitted some of the language from within the quotation.* Form an ellipses by entering three dots (periods) with spaces in between them, or use four

dots to indicate that the deletion continues to the end of the sentence (the last dot becomes the period). Suppose you wanted to shorten the following quotation from a recent article about Radiohead by Alex Ross:

> The album "OK Computer," with titles like "Paranoid Android," "Karma Police," and "Climbing Up the Walls," pictured the onslaught of the information age and a young person's panicky embrace of it (Ross 85).

Using an ellipsis, you could emphasize the source's claim by omitting the song titles from the middle of the sentence:

> The album "OK Computer"... pictured the onslaught of the information age and a young person's panicky embrace of it (Ross 85).

In most cases, the gap between quoted passages should be short, and in any case, you should be careful to preserve the sense of the original. The standard joke about ellipses is pertinent here: A reviewer writes that a film "will delight no one and appeal to the intelligence of invertebrates only, but not average viewers." An unethical advertiser cobbles together pieces of the review to say that the film "will delight... and appeal to the intelligence of... viewers."

5. **Use square brackets to alter or add information within a quotation.** Sometimes it is necessary to change the wording slightly inside a quotation to maintain fluency. Square brackets indicate that you are altering the original quotation. Brackets are also used when you insert explanatory information, such as a definition or example, within a quotation. Here are a few examples that alter the original quotations previously cited.

> According to one music critic, the cultural relevance of Radiohead is evident in "the album 'OK Computer'...[which] pictured the onslaught of the information age and a young person's panicky embrace of it" (Ross 85).

> Popular music has always "[challenged] the mores of the older generation," according to Nick Hornby (168).

Note that both examples respect the original sense of the quotation; they have changed the wording only to integrate the quotations gracefully within the writer's own sentence structure.

Preparing an Abstract

There is one more skill essential to research-based writing that we need to discuss: how to prepare an abstract. The aim of the nonevaluative summary of a source known as an abstract is to represent a source's arguments as fairly and accurately as possible, not to critique them. Learning how to compose an abstract according to the conventions of a given discipline is a necessary skill for academic researched writing. Because abstracts differ in format and length among disciplines, you should sample some in the reference section of your library or via the Internet to provide you with models to imitate. Some abstracts, such as those in *Dissertation Abstracts*, are very brief—less than 250 words. Others may run as long as two pages.

Despite disciplinary differences, abstracts by and large follow a generalizable format. The abstract should begin with a clear and specific explanation of the work's governing thesis (or argument). In this opening paragraph, you should also define the work's purpose, and possibly include established positions that it tries to refine, qualify, or argue against. What kind of critical approach does it adopt? What are its aims? On what assumptions does it rest? Why did the author feel it necessary to write the work—that is, what does he or she believe the work offers that other sources don't? What shortcomings or misrepresentations in other criticism does the work seek to correct? (For specifics on writing abstracts in the Natural Sciences, see Chapter 9, From Paragraphs to Papers: Forms and Formats Across the Curriculum.)

You won't be able to produce detailed answers to all of these questions in your opening paragraph, but in trying to answer some of them in your note taking and drafting, you should find it easier to arrive at the kind of concise, substantive, and focused overview that the first paragraph of your abstract should provide. Also, be careful not to settle for bland, all-purpose generalities in this opening paragraph. And if you quote there, keep the selections short, and remember that quotations don't speak for themselves.

In summary, your aim in the first paragraph of an abstract is to define the source's particular angle of vision and articulate its main point or points, including the definition of key terms used in its title or elsewhere in its argument.

Once you've set up this overview of the source's central position(s), you should devote a paragraph or so to the source's *organization* (how it divides its subject into parts) and its *method* (how it goes about substantiating its argument). What kind of secondary material does the source use? That is, how do its own bibliographic citations cue you to its school of thought, its point of view, its research traditions?

Your concluding paragraph should briefly recount some of the source's conclusions (as related to, but not necessarily the same as, its thesis). In what way does it go about culminating its argument? What kind of significance does it claim for its position? What final qualifications does it raise? The following model is a good example of an abstract:

Abstract of "William Carlos Williams," an essay

By Christopher MacGowan in *The Columbia History of American Poetry* 1993: 395–418. Print.

MacGowan's is a chronologically organized account of Williams' poetic career and of his relation to both modernism as an international movement and modernism as it affected the development of poetry in America. MacGowan is at some pains both to differentiate Williams from some features of modernism (such as the tendency of American writers to write as well as live away from their own cultural roots) and to link

Williams to modernism. MacGowan argues, for example, that an essential feature of Williams's commitment as a poet was to "the local—to the clear presentation of what was under his nose and in front of his eyes" (385).

But he also takes care to remind us that Williams was in no way narrowly provincial, having studied in Europe as a young man (at Leipzig), having had a Spanish mother and an English father, having become friendly with the poets Ezra Pound and H. D. while getting his medical degree at the University of Pennsylvania, and having continued to meet important figures in the literary and art worlds by making frequent visits to New York and by traveling on more than one occasion to Europe (where Pound introduced him to W. B. Yeats, among others). Williams corresponded with Marianne Moore, he continued to write to Pound and to show Pound some of his work, and he wrote critical essays on the works of other modernists. MacGowan reminds us that Williams also translated Spanish works (ballads) and so was not out of contact with European influences.

Williams had a long publishing career—beginning in 1909 with a self-published volume called *Poems* and ending more than fifty years later with *Pictures from Brueghel* in 1962. What MacGowan emphasizes about this career is not only the consistently high quality of work, but also its great influence on other artists (he names those who actually corresponded with Williams and visited with him, including Charles Olson, Robert Creeley, Robert Lowell, Allen Ginsberg, and Denise Levertov). MacGowan observes that Williams defined himself "against" T. S. Eliot—the more rewarded and internationally recognized of the two poets, especially during their lifetimes—searching for "alternatives to the prevailing mode of a complex, highly allusive poetics," which Williams saw as Eliot's legacy (395). MacGowan depicts Williams as setting himself "against the international school of Eliot and Pound—Americans he felt wrote about rootlessness and searched an alien past because of their failure to write about and live within their own culture" (397).

What Does Plagiarism Do to the Conversation?

A recent survey indicated that 53 percent of Who's Who High Schoolers thought that plagiarism was no big deal (Sally Cole and Elizabeth Kiss, "What Can We Do About Student Cheating?" *About Campus*, May–June 2000, p. 6). So why should institutions of higher learning care about it? Here are two great reasons:

- Plagiarism poisons the environment. Students who don't cheat are alienated by students who do and get away with it, and faculty can become distrustful of students and even disillusioned about teaching when constantly driven to track down students' sources. It's a lot easier, by the way, than most students think for faculty to recognize language and ideas that are not the student's own. And now there are all those search engines provided by firms like Turnitin.com that have been generated in response to the Internet paper-mill boom. Who wants another cold war?

- Plagiarism defeats the purpose of going to college, which is learning how to think. You can't learn to think by just copying others' ideas; you need to learn to trust your own intelligence. Students' panic about deadlines and their misunderstandings about assignments sometimes spur plagiarism. It's a good bet that your professors would much rather take requests for help and give extra time on assignments than have to go through the anguish of confronting students about plagiarized work.

So, plagiarism gets in the way of trust, fairness, intellectual development, and, ultimately, the attitude toward learning that sets the tone for a college or university community.

Frequently Asked Questions (FAQS) about Plagiarism

Is it still plagiarism if I didn't intentionally copy someone else's work and present it as my own; as in, if I plagiarized it by accident?
Yes, it is still plagiarism. Colleges and universities put the burden of responsibility on students for knowing what plagiarism is and then making the effort necessary to avoid it. Leaving out the quotation marks around someone else's words or omitting the attribution after a summary of someone else's theory may be just a mistake—a matter of inadequate documentation—but faculty can only judge what you turn in to them, not what you intended.

If I include a list of works consulted at the end of my paper, doesn't that cover it?
No. A works-cited list (bibliography) tells your readers what you read but leaves them in the dark about how and where this material has been used in your paper. Putting one or more references at the end of a paragraph containing source material is a version of the same problem. The solution is to cite the source at the point that you quote or paraphrase or summarize it. To be even clearer about what comes from where, also use what are called in-text attributions. See the next FAQ on these.

What is the best way to help my readers distinguish between what my sources are saying and what I'm saying?
Be overt. Tell your readers in the text of your paper, not just in citations, when you are drawing on someone else's words, ideas, or information. Do this with phrases like "According to X" or "As noted in X"—called in-text attributions.

Are there some kinds of information that I do not need to document?
Yes. Common knowledge and facts you can find in almost any encyclopedia or basic reference text generally don't need to be documented (that is, John F. Kennedy became president of the United States in 1960). This distinction can get a little tricky because it isn't always obvious what is and is not common knowledge. Often, you need to spend some

time in a discipline before you discover what others take to be known to all. When in doubt, cite the source.

If I put the information from my sources into my own words, do I still need to include citations?
Yes. Sorry, but rewording someone else's idea doesn't make it your idea. Paraphrasing is a useful activity because it helps you to better understand what you are reading, but paraphrases and summaries have to be documented and carefully distinguished from ideas and information you are representing as your own.

If I don't actually know anything about the subject, is it okay to hand in a paper that is taken entirely from various sources?
It's okay if (1) you document the borrowings and (2) the assignment called for summary. Properly documented summarizing is better than plagiarizing, but most assignments call for something more. Often comparing and contrasting your sources begins to give you ideas so that you can have something to contribute. If you're really stumped, go see the professor.

You also reduce the risk of plagiarism if you consult sources after—not before—you have done some preliminary thinking on the subject. If you have become somewhat invested in your own thoughts on the matter, you will be able to use the sources in a more active way, in effect, making them part of a dialogue.

Is it plagiarism if I include things in my paper that I thought of with another student or a member of my family?
Most academic behavior codes, under the category called "collusion," allow for students' cooperative efforts only with the explicit consent of the instructor. The same general rule goes for plagiarizing yourself—that is, for submitting the same paper in more than one class. If you have questions about what constitutes collusion in a particular class, be sure to ask your professor.

What about looking at secondary sources when my professor hasn't asked me to? Is this a form of cheating?
It can be a form of cheating if the intent of the assignment was to get you to develop a particular kind of thinking skill. In this case, looking at others' ideas may actually retard your learning process and leave you feeling that you couldn't possibly learn to arrive at ideas on your own.

Professors usually look favorably on students who are willing to take the time to do extra reading on a subject, but it is essential that, even in class discussion, you make it clear that you have consulted outside sources. To conceal that fact is to present others' ideas as your own. Even in class discussion, if you bring up an idea you picked up on the Internet or somewhere else, be sure to say so explicitly.

Assignments: Conversing with Sources: Writing the Researched Paper

1. **Make One Source Speak to Another**. Choose two articles or book chapters by different authors or by the same author at different points in his or her career. The overriding aim of the assignment is to give you practice in getting beyond merely reacting and generalizing, and, instead, participating in your sources' thinking.

   Keep in mind that your aim is not to arrive at your opinion of the sources, but to construct the conversation that you think the author of one of your sources might have with the author of another. How might they recast each other's ideas, as opposed to merely agreeing or disagreeing with those ideas? It's useful to confine yourself to thinking as impartially as you can about the ideas found in your two sources.

2. **Use PASSAGE-BASED FOCUSED FREEWRITING to Converse with Sources.** Select a passage from a secondary source that appears important to your evolving thinking about a subject you are studying, and do a PASSAGE-BASED FOCUSED FREEWRITE on it. You might choose the passage in answer to the question "What is the one passage in the source that I need to discuss, that poses a question or a problem or that seems in some way difficult to pin down, anomalous or even just unclear?" Copy the passage at the top of the page, and write without stopping for 20 minutes or more. As noted in the discussion of freewriting in Chapter 2, paraphrase key terms as you relentlessly ask "SO WHAT?" about the details.

3. **Use a Source as a Lens on Another Source.** Apply a brief passage from a secondary source to a brief passage from a primary source, using the passage from the secondary source as a lens. Choose the secondary source passage first—one that you find particularly interesting, revealing, or problematic. Then locate a corresponding passage from the primary source to which the sentence from the first passage can be connected in some way. Copy both passages at the top of the page, and then write for 20 minutes. You should probably include paraphrases of key phrases in both—not just the primary text—but your primary goal is to think about the two together, to allow them to interact.

4. **Compose a Research Sequence.** The traditional sequence of steps for building a research paper—or for any writing that relies on secondary materials—is *summary, comparative analysis, and synthesis.* The following sequence of four exercises addresses the first two steps as discrete activities. (You might, of course, choose to do only some of these exercises.)

A. **Compose an Informal Prospectus.** Formulate your initial thinking on a subject before you do more research. Include what you already know about the topic, especially what you find interesting, particularly significant, or strange. This exercise helps deter you from being overwhelmed by and absorbed into the sources you later encounter.

B. **Conduct a "What's Going on in the Field" Search, and Create a Preliminary List of Sources**. This exercise is ideal for helping you to find a topic or, if you already have one, to narrow it. The kinds of bibliographic materials you consult for this portion of the research project depend on the discipline within which you are writing. Whatever the discipline, start in the reference room of your library with specialized indexes (such as the *Social Sciences Index* or the *New York Times Index*), book review indexes, specialized encyclopedias and dictionaries, and bibliographies (print version or CD-ROM) that give you an overview of your subject or topic. If you have access to databases through your school or library, you should also search them. (See the section in Chapter 8 entitled Finding Quality on the Web.)

The "what's going on in the field" search has two aims:

- To survey materials in order to identify trends—the kinds of issues and questions that others in the field are talking about (and, thus, find important)

- To compile a bibliography that includes a range of titles that interest you, that could be relevant to your prospective topic, and that seem to you representative of research trends associated with your subject (or topic)

You are not committed at this point to pursuing all of these sources but rather to reporting what is being talked about. You might also compose a list of keywords (such as Library of Congress headings) that you have used in conducting your search. If you try this exercise, you will be surprised how much value there is in exploring indexes *just for titles*, to see the kinds of topics people are currently conversing about. And you will almost surely discover how *narrowly* focused most research is (which will get you away from global questions).

Append to your list of sources (a very preliminary bibliography) a few paragraphs of informal discussion of how the information you have encountered (the titles, summaries, abstracts, etc.) has affected your thinking and plans for your paper. These paragraphs might respond to the following questions:

i. In what ways has your "what's going on in the field" search led you to narrow or shift direction in or focus your thinking about your subject?

ii. How might you use one or more of these sources in your paper?

iii. What has this phase of your research suggested you might need to look for next?

C. **Write an Abstract of an Article (or Book Chapter).** Use the procedure offered in the preceding section, "How to Prepare an Abstract." Aim for two pages in length. If other members of your class are working on the same or similar subjects, it is often extremely useful for everyone to share copies of their abstracts. Remember that your primary concern should lie with representing the argument and point of view of the source as fairly and accurately as possible.

Append to the end of the abstract a paragraph or two that addresses the question "How has this exercise affected your thinking about your topic?" Objectifying your own research process in this way helps move you away from the cut-and-paste–provide-only-the-transitions mode of writing research papers.

D. **Write a Comparative Summary of Two Reviews.** Most writers, before they invest the significant time and energy required to study a book-length source, take the much smaller amount of time and energy required to find out more about the book. Although you should always include in your final paper your own analytical summary of books you consult on your topic, it's extremely useful also to find out what experts in the field have to say about the source.

Select from your "what's going on" list one book-length source that you've discovered is vital to your subject or topic. As a general rule, if a number of your indexes, bibliographies, and so forth, refer you to the same book, it's a good bet that this source merits consultation.

Locate two book reviews on the book, and write a summary that compares the two reviews. Ideally, you should locate two reviews that diverge in their points of view or in what they choose to emphasize. Depending on the length and complexity of the reviews, your comparative summary should require two or three pages.

In most cases, you will find that reviews are less neutral in their points of view than are abstracts, but they always do more than simply judge. A good review, like a good abstract, should communicate the essential ideas contained in the source. It is the reviewer's aim also to locate the source in some larger context, by, for example, comparing it to other works on the same subject and to the research tradition the book seeks to extend, modify, and so forth. Thus, your summary should try to encompass how the book contributes to the ongoing conversation on a given topic in the field.

Append to your comparative summary a paragraph or two answering the question: How has this exercise affected your thinking about your topic?

Obviously, you could choose to do a comparative summary of two articles, two book chapters, and so forth, rather than of two book reviews. But in any event, if you use books in your research, you should always find a means of determining how these books are received in the relevant discourse community.

The next step, if you were writing a research paper, would involve the task known as *synthesis*, in which you essentially write a comparative discussion that includes more than two sources. Many research papers start with an opening paragraph that synthesizes prevailing, perhaps competing, interpretations of the topic being addressed. Few good research papers consist only of such synthesis, however. Instead, writers use synthesis to frame their ideas and to provide perspective on their own arguments; the synthesis provides a platform or foundation for their own subsequent analysis.

It is probably worth adding that bad research papers fail to use synthesis as a point of departure. Instead, they line up their sources and agree or disagree with them. To inoculate you against this unfortunate reflex, review the section entitled Six Strategies for Analyzing Sources, especially Strategy 6: Find Your Own Role in the Conversation.

CHAPTER 8

Finding, Evaluating, and Citing Sources

Overview This chapter offers a discussion of research methods written by a reference librarian at our college, **Kelly Cannon**. It offers a wealth of insider's tips for making more productive use of your research time. The final section of the chapter explains the four documentation styles that are most common in academic writing: APA (American Psychological Association), CSE (Council of Science Editors), Chicago (University Press of Chicago), and MLA (Modern Language Association).

Three Rules of Thumb for Getting Started with Research

- *A half hour spent with a reference librarian can save you half a day wandering randomly though the stacks selecting sources.*

- *Start your research in the present and work backward.* Usually the most current materials include bibliographical citations that can help you identify the most important sources in the past. Along the same lines, you are usually better off starting with journal articles rather than books because articles are more current.

- *Consistently evaluate the reliability of the source you select in order to detect its potential bias or agenda.* Evidence is always qualified by how it is framed. For example, *Newsweek* can be a useful source if you want evidence about popular understanding of a subject or issue. In this case, the fact that the material comes from *Newsweek* and thus represents a position aimed at a mainstream, nonacademic audience provides the central reason for citing it.

The challenge of doing research in the Information Age is that there is so much information available. How do you know which information is considered authoritative in a particular discipline and which isn't? How can you avoid wasting time with source materials that have been effectively refuted and replaced by subsequent thinking? A short answer to these questions is that you should start in the reference room of your library or with its electronic equivalent. Many if not all of the resources listed below are now available online through your college library website. Your reference librarian can advise you on availability.

Start with Indexes, Specialized Dictionaries, Abstracts, and Bibliographies

These reference sources can rapidly provide you with both a broad perspective on your subject and a summary of what particular sources contain. An **index** offers a list of titles directing you to scholarly journals; often this list is sufficient to give you a clearer idea of the kinds of topics about which writers in the field are conversing. **Compilations of abstracts** and **annotated bibliographies** provide more information—anywhere from a few sentences to a few pages that summarize each source.

Here are a few of the most commonly used indexes, bibliographies, and abstracts:

Art Full Text

Business Source Elite/Premier

ERIC (Education Resource Information Center)

MLA (Modern Language Association)

PubMed

CSA (Cambridge Scientific Abstracts) Sociological Abstracts

Specialized dictionaries and encyclopedias are sometimes extraordinarily useful in sketching the general terrain for a subject, and they often include bibliographical leads as well. Here are some titles, ranging from the expected to the eccentric:

Dictionary of the History of Ideas	*The New Encyclopedia of Unbelief*
Dictionary of Literary Biography	*Encyclopedia of World Art*
Encyclopedia of American History	*Encyclopedic Dictionary of Mathematics*
Encyclopedia of Bioethics	*Macmillan Encyclopedia of Computers*
Encyclopedia of Crime and Justice	*Encyclopedia of Medical History*
Concise Encyclopedia of Economics	*McGraw-Hill Encyclopedia of Science and Technology*
Encyclopedia of Native American Religions	*New Grove Dictionary of Music and Musicians*
Encyclopedia of Philosophy	*Oxford English Dictionary*
Encyclopedia of Psychology	

Most of the resources just listed also include book reviews. Book reviews across all disciplines can be found in multidisciplinary databases like *Academic Search Premier*, *Project Muse*, and *JSTOR*.

Indexes of Scholarly Journals

Nearly every discipline has its own major index, one most consulted by scholars. Here are just a few: *MLA* (literary criticism), *ERIC* (education), *PsycInfo* (psychology), *Historical Abstracts* (non-U.S. history), *Sociological Abstracts* (sociology), and *PubMed* (medicine).

When professors refer to bibliographic research, they probably mean research done with indexes. Again, these indexes are specific to particular subject areas. Their coverage is not broad, but deep and scholarly. These are the indexes to consult when seeking the most scholarly information in your area of study. Although the full text is often not included, the indexing provides information sufficient to track down the complete article.

These indexes are a great aid in evaluating the scholarly merit of a publication, as they usually eliminate any reference that isn't considered scholarly by the academy. For example, *MLA* only indexes literary criticism that appears in peer-reviewed journals and academically affiliated books. So, consider the publications that appear in these indexes to have the academic "seal of approval."

For more information on this crucial aspect of research see the headings later in this chapter entitled "Subscriber-Only Databases" and "Four Steps Toward Productive Research Across the Disciplines."

Finding Your Sources: Articles and Books

The resources above will not only provide you with an excellent overview of your topic, but will also direct you to authoritative books and journal articles. The next step is to find out how to access the full text of those books and articles online or in print form. Your library's online catalog will direct you to books in your local library. You may wish to take advantage of this time in the catalog to run a keyword search on your topic. Watch the subject headings that appear at the bottom of catalog records. You can click on these subject headings to guide you to more books highly relevant to your topic.

Don't be concerned if many of the books that have been recommended in specialized dictionaries, encyclopedias, and indexes don't appear in your library's online catalog. The reference librarian can direct you to *WorldCat*, where you can request, on interlibrary loan, any book to be sent to you from another library for your perusal. This is a valuable service, as it makes available to you the research collections of large universities, all with the stroke of a key.

Journal articles are likely to be the next step in your research. You will need to find which articles are available in-house online or in print, and which you will need to submit an interlibrary loan request for (in this case, unlike with books, you will receive a photocopy of the interlibrary loaned article to keep—no need to return it to the lending library). Your library's online catalog will generally—though not always—provide you with a complete list of journals available electronically or in print. Just title search on the journal name, not the article title, in order to locate the journal. Ask a reference librarian for assistance in locating journals. He or she can also assist you in requesting on interlibrary loan any articles from journals your library does not have.

In the following Voices from Across the Curriculum, a business professor and a psychology professor offer useful tips for searching under more than one heading in order to find more information.

VOICES FROM ACROSS THE CURRICULUM

Finding Quality Sources: Two Professors Speak

A critical part of the bibliographic effort is to find a topic on which there are materials. Most topics can be researched. The key is to choose a flexible keyword/phrase and then try out different versions of it. For example, a bibliography on "women in management" might lead you to look up *women, females, business* (women in), business (females in), *gender in the workplace, sexism and the workplace, careers* (of men, of women, in business), *women and CEOs, women in management, affirmative action and women, women in corporations, female accountants*, and so forth. Be imaginative and flexible. A little bit of time with some of the indexes will provide you with a wealth of sources.

Here is a sampling of indexes heavily used in the social sciences, for instance: *Sociological Abstracts, Wall Street Journal Search Resources Center* (for *Wall Street Journal* stories), *New York Times Article Archive* (for *NYT* stories), *Business Source Elite*, and the *Public Affairs Information Service (PAIS)*.

—FREDERICK NORLING, PROFESSOR OF BUSINESS

Use quality psychological references. That is, use references that professional psychologists use and regard highly. *Psychology Today* is not a good reference; *Newsweek* and *Reader's Digest* are worse. APA journals, such as the *Journal of Abnormal Psychology*, on the other hand, are excellent.

In looking for reference material, be sure to search under several headings. For example, look under *depression, affective disorders,* and *mood disorders*. Books (e.g., *The Handbook of Affective Disorders*) are often very helpful, especially for giving a general overview of a topic. Books addressing a professional audience are generally preferable to those addressing a general, popular audience.

Finally, references should be reasonably current. In general, the newer, the better. For example, with rare exceptions (classic articles), articles from before 1980 are outdated and so should not be used.

—ALAN TJELTVEIT, PROFESSOR OF PSYCHOLOGY

Finding Quality on the Web

Imagine a mega-library to which anyone has access any time of day or night, and to which anyone can contribute material, to inform, but perhaps more so to sell and to promote, no matter how questionable the cause or idea. So it is with the web. A general caveat to this "library of the Internet" might well be User Beware.

Take as an example the website *Martin Luther King Jr.: A True Historical Examination* (www.martinlutherking.org). This site appears prominently in any web search for information about Martin Luther King, Jr. The site is visually appealing, claiming to include "essays, speeches, sermons, and more." But who created the site? As it turns out, after a little digging (see Tips #1 and #2 later in the chapter), the site is sponsored by Stormfront, Inc. (stormfront.org), an organization out of West Palm Beach, Florida, serving "those courageous men and women fighting to preserve their White Western culture, ideals and freedom of speech." This author is concealed behind the work, a ghostwriter of sorts. While the site is at one's fingertips, identifying the author is a challenge, more so than in the world of print publishing, where protocols are followed such as author and publisher appearing on the same pages as the title. For those websites with no visible author, no publishing house, no recognized journal title, no peer-review process, and no library selection process (the touchstones of scholarship in the print world), seemingly easy Internet research is now more problematic: the user must discern for him- or herself what is and is not authoritative information.

Understanding Domain Names

But how is the user to begin evaluating a web document? Fortunately, there are several clues to assist you through the Internet labyrinth. One clue is in the web address itself. For example, the *Internet Movie Database* has www.imdb.com as its web address (also known as URL, or uniform resource locator). One clue lies at the very end of the URL, in what is known as the domain name, in this case the abbreviation ".com." Websites ending in .com are commercial, often with the purpose of marketing a product. Sites ending in .org generally signal nonprofits, but many have a veiled agenda, whether it is marketing or politics. Like the .coms, .org addresses are sold on a first-come, first-served basis. (The organization that oversees the many vendors of .com and .org domain names is The Internet Corporation for Assigned Names and Numbers, or ICANN [www.icann.org/].)

On the other hand, .edu and .gov sites may indicate less bias, as they are ostensibly limited exclusively to educational and government institutions, and they are often the producers of bona fide research. In particular, .gov sites contain some of the best information on the Internet. This is in part because the U.S. government is required by an act of Congress to disseminate to the general public a large portion of its research. The U.S. government, floated as it is by tax dollars, provides the high-quality, free websites reminiscent of the precommercial Internet era. This means that government sites offer high-quality data, particularly of a statistical nature. Scholars in the areas of business, law, and the social sciences can benefit tremendously, without subscription fees, from a variety of government databases. Prime examples are the legislative site known as *Thomas* (thomas.loc.gov) and data gathered at the website of the Census Bureau (www.census.gov).

Print Corollaries

But a domain name can be misleading; it is simply one clue in the process of evaluation. Another clue is the correlation between a website and the print world. Many websites correlate with a print edition, such as the web version of the *Economist* (economist.com), offering some unique information, some identical to that offered in the print subscription. (Access to some web articles may be limited to subscribers.) Moreover, some websites are the equivalents of their print editions. For example, Johns Hopkins University Press now publishes its journals, known and respected for years by scholars, in both print and electronic formats. Many college and university libraries subscribe to these Johns Hopkins journals electronically, collectively known as *Project Muse* (muse.jhu.edu). In both cases—the *Economist* and *Project Muse*, the scholar can expect the electronic form of the publication to have undergone the same editorial rigor as the print publication.

Web-Published Gems

Building a reputation of high quality takes time. But the Internet has been around long enough now that some publications with no pre-web history have caught the attention of scholars who turn to these sites regularly for reliable commentary on a variety of subject areas.

These high-quality sites can best be found by tapping into scholarly web directories such as the *ipl2* (www.ipl.org) that work like mini search engines but are managed by humans who sift through the chaff, including in these directories only what they deem to be gems.

The student looking specifically for free, peer-reviewed journals original to the web can visit a highly specific directory called the *Directory of Open Access Journals* (www.doaj.org), listing several hundred journals in a variety of subject areas. Many libraries have begun to link to these journals to promote their use by students and faculty.

Then there are the web treasures that compare to highbrow newspapers or magazines such as *The New Yorker*. Two celebrated examples are *Salon.com* (salon.com), and *Slate* (slate.com), both online journals. Once tapped into, these sites do a good job of recommending other high-quality websites. Scholars are beginning to cite from these web-based publications just as they would from any print publication of long-standing reputation.

An excellent site for links to all kinds of interesting articles from journals and high-level general interest magazine is *Arts and Letters Daily* (aldaily.com), sponsored by *The Chronicle of Higher Education*. You should also be aware of websites run by special interest organizations, such as *The Academy of American Poets* (poets.org), which offers bibliographic resources, interviews, reviews, and the like.

Wikipedia, Google, and Blogs

Three tools have in recent years dramatically altered the nature of web-based research. First and foremost, the search engine *Google*, through a proprietary search algorithm, has increased the relevance and value of search results. Relevance in *Google* is determined by text-matching techniques, while value is determined by a unique "PageRank" technology that places highest on the list those results that are most often linked to from other websites.

However, the determination of value is by no means foolproof. *Google*'s ranking of value assesses less a website's authoritativeness than its popular appeal. For example, a recent search on "marijuana" yielded as its second result (*Wikipedia*'s entry on marijuana is first) a private website promoting the use of marijuana and selling marijuana paraphernalia. This site could be useful in any number of ways in a research paper (i.e., as a primary resource reflecting public perceptions and use of marijuana in the United States). That it appears first suggests *Google*'s algorithm of popularity over authoritativeness. This is not necessarily a bad thing, just something to be aware of. It is a little like picking a pebble off the ground. Its value is not inherent: responsibility rests with the user to discover its value. Finding information in *Google* is never the challenge. Discerning appropriateness and authoritativeness is the bigger task.

High on the list of most search results in *Google*—if not first—is *Wikipedia*. Is this an authoritative source? Certainly *Wikipedia* has revolutionized the way web pages are authored. The world is the author of every entry. That is the beauty and the hazard, and the secret to its broad scope and thus to its popularity. Anyone can write and edit in *Wikipedia*. In this way, *Wikipedia* is infinitely democratic. All opinions count equally, for better or worse—while authority languishes. Consequently, *Wikipedia* is likely to contribute little to a scholarly research project. In fact, it could detract from an assertion of authority. In short, use *Wikipedia* entries judiciously. Like any encyclopedia, *Wikipedia* will be viewed by the informed reader as introductory, not as the hallmark of thorough research.

Just as *Wikipedia* invites all of us to be writers, so too do blogs. But unlike *Wikipedia*, blogs typically reveal the identity or at least the assumed identity of the author, and are written by a closed group of people, often one individual. As such, over time the identity and politics of the author(s) show through. In the best tradition of the World Wide Web, blogs have extended the sphere of publication, inviting everyone to be published authors, possibly achieving popularity and authority on a topic—no matter how narrow—by being at the right place at the right time, with access to the right information written in a voice of confidence. Blogs invite outside comment, but lack the formal structure of a peer review. As such, use blogs sparingly in academic research, being attentive to the credentials of the author(s), and to the wider acceptance of a particular blog in the scholarly community.

Asking the Right Questions

In the end, it is up to the individual user to evaluate each website independently. Here are some critical questions to consider:

Question: Who is the author?
Response: Check the website's home page, probably near the bottom of the page.

Question: Is the author affiliated with any institution?
Response: Check the URL to see who sponsors the page.

Question: What are the author's credentials?
Response: Check *Google Schola*r (scholar.google.com) to see if this person is published in scholarly journals or books.

Question: Has the information been reviewed or peer-edited before posting?
Response: Probably not, unless the posting is part of a larger scholarly project; if so, the submission process for publication can be verified at the publication home page.

Question: Is the page part of a larger publication that may help to assess authoritativeness?
Response: Try the various links on the page to see if there is an access point to the home page of the publication. Or try the backspacing technique mentioned later in the chapter.

Question: Is the information documented properly?
Response: Check for footnotes or methodology.

Question: Is the information current?
Response: Check the "last update," usually printed at the bottom of the page.

Question: What is the purpose of the page?
Response: Examine content and marginalia.

Question: Does the website suit your purposes?
Response: Review what the purpose of your project is. Review your information needs: primary vs. secondary, academic vs. popular. And always consult with your instructor.

Subscriber-Only Databases

An organized and indexed collection of discrete pieces of information is called a *database*. Two examples of databases are a library's card catalogue and online catalogue. The World Wide Web is full of databases, though they are often restricted to subscribers. Subscription fees can be prohibitive, but fortunately for the average researcher, most college and university libraries foot the bill. The names of these databases are now well known, and arguably contain the most thoroughly reviewed (i.e., scholarly) full texts available on the web. Inquire at your library to see if you have access to these databases:

Academic Search Premier from EBSCO (www.ebscohost.com)

Academic ASAP/Onefile from Gale Cengage (www.gale.cengage.com)

JSTOR from ITHAKA (www.jstor.org)

Project Muse from Johns Hopkins (muse.jhu.edu/)

ProQuest Central from ProQuest (www.proquest.com)

Each of these databases contains its own proprietary search engine, allowing refinement of searches to a degree unmatched by search engines on the Internet at large. How does this refinement occur? For one, these databases are exclusive rather than inclusive, as the Internet is. More is not better in an information age. The fact that information is at your fingertips, and sometimes "in your face," can be a problem. Well-organized databases are shaped and limited by human hands and minds, covering only certain media types or subject areas.

Second, databases allow searching by subject heading, in addition to keyword searching. This means that a human has defined the main subject areas of each entry, consequently allowing the user much greater manipulation of the search. For example, if I enter the words "New York City" in a simple keyword search, I will retrieve everything that simply mentions New York City even once; the relevance will vary tremendously. On the other hand, if subject headings have been assigned, I can do a subject search on New York City and find only records that are devoted to my subject. This may sound trivial, but in the age of information overload, precision searching is a precious commodity.

The most specialized databases are those whose primary purpose is not to provide full text but to index all of the major journals, along with books and/or book chapters, in a discipline, regardless of where the full text to that journal can be found. These electronic indexes provide basic bibliographic information and sometimes an abstract (summary) of the article or book chapter. (See Scholarly Indexes earlier in the chapter.)

TRY THIS 7.1: Tuning in to Your Research Environment: Four Exercises

Every university and college is different, each with its own points of access to information. Following are some exercises to help you familiarize yourself with your own scholarly environment.

Exercise #1: Go to your library's reference desk and get a list of all the scholarly journal indexes that are available electronically at your school. Then get a list of all online, full-text databases that are available to you.

Exercise #2: Contact your reference librarian to get a list of all the journals that the library subscribes to electronically. Then get a list of all journals that are available at your library either in print or electronically in your major area of study.

Exercise #3: Ask the reference librarian about web access in general for your major area of study. What tips can the library give you about doing electronic research at your academic institution? Are there any special databases, web search engines/directories, or indexes that you should consult in your research?

Exercise #4: Try out some or all of the full-text databases available on your campus. Now try the same searches in a scholarly index. What differences do you see in the quality/scope of the information?

Eight Tips for Locating and Evaluating Electronic Sources

Tip #1: Backspacing
"Backspacing" a URL can be an effective way to evaluate a website. It may reveal authorship or institutional affiliation. To do this, place the cursor at the end of the URL and then backspace to the last slash and press Enter. Continue backspacing to each preceding slash, examining each level as you go.

Tip #2: Using WHOIS
WHOIS (www.networksolutions.com/whois/index.jsp) is an Internet service that allows anyone to find out who's behind a website.

Tip #3: Beware of the ~ in a Web Address
Many educational institutions allow the creation of personal home pages by students and faculty. While the domain name remains .edu in these cases, the fact that they are personal means that pretty much anything can be posted and so cannot assure academic quality.

Tip #4: Phrase Searching
Not finding relevant information? Trying using quotation marks around key phrases in your search string. For example, search in *Google* for this phrase, enclosed in quotation marks: "whose woods these are I think I know."

Tip #5: Title Searching
Still finding irrelevant information? Limit your search to the titles of web documents. A title search is an option in *Google* (advanced search) (www .google.com/advanced_search).

Tip #6: *Wikipedia* Discussion Tab
Use *Wikipedia* to full advantage by clicking on the discussion tab located at the top of *Wikipedia* entries. The discussion tabs expose the often intense debates that rage behind the scenes on topics like marijuana, genocide, and Islam. The discussion tab is an excellent source for locating paper topics because it highlights ongoing sources of controversy—those areas worthy of additional writing and research. To find the most controversial topics at any given moment, visit *Wikipedia*'s Controversial Issues page (en.wikipedia.org /wiki/Wikipedia:List_of_controversial_issues).

Tip #7: Full Text

The widest selection of previously published full texts (newspapers, magazines, journals, book chapters) is available in subscription databases via the web. Inquire at your library to see if you have access to *Academic Search Premier* from EBSCO (www.ebscohost.com), *Expanded Academic ASAP with Ingenta (Onefile)* from Gale Cengage (www.gale.cengage.com.), *JSTOR* (www.jstor.org), *Project Muse* from Johns Hopkins (muse.jhu.edu/), *ProQuest Central* from ProQuest (www.proquest.com), or other full-text databases.

For the full text of books, try the *Internet Archive Text Archive* (www.archive.org/details/texts), pointing to the major digital text archives.

Tip #8: Archives of Older Published Periodicals

Full text for newspapers, magazines, and journals published prior to 1990 is difficult to find on the Internet. One subscription site that your library may offer is JSTOR (www.jstor.org), an archive of scholarly full-text journal articles dating back in some cases into the late 1800s. *LexisNexis Academic* (academic.lexisnexis.com), also a subscription service, includes the full text of popular periodicals such as the *New York Times* as far back as 1980.

Two free sites offer the full text of eighteenth- and nineteenth-century periodicals from Great Britain and the U.S. respectively: *Internet Library of Early Journals* (*www.bodley.ox.ac.uk/ilej*) and *Nineteenth Century in Print* (memory.loc.gov/ammem/ndlpcoop/moahtml/snchome.html).

Use your library's interlibrary loan service to acquire articles from periodicals not freely available on the web. Electronic indexing (no full text) for older materials is readily available, back to as early as 1900, sometimes earlier. Inquire at your library.

Four Steps Toward Productive Research Across the Disciplines

The steps below include a few of the sites most relied upon by academic librarians. For the subscription databases, you will need to inquire at your library for local availability.

Step 1: search at least one of these multidisciplinary subscription databases; check your library's website for availability.

- *Academic Search Premier* (EBSCOhost) for journals

- *Academic ASAP/Onefile* (Gale Cengage) for journals

- *JSTOR* for journals

- *Project Muse* for journals

- *ProQuest Central* for journals

- *WorldCat* (OCLC FirstSearch) for books

Step 2: search subject-specific databases. These too are mostly subscription databases; check your library's website for availability.

- Anthropology: *Anthropology Plus*
- Art: *Art Full Text*
- Biology: *ScienceDirect*
- Business: *ABI Inform, Business Source Elite/Premier, Business & Company Resource Center, Dow Jones Factiva, LexisNexis*
- Chemistry: *SciFinder Scholar, ScienceDirect*
- Communication: *Communication and Mass Media Complete*
- Computer Science: *ACM Portal, MathSciNet, ScienceDirect*
- Economics: *EconLit*
- Education: ERIC (free)
- Film Studies: *Communication & Mass Media Complete, Film & Television Literature Index, MLA*
- Geography/Geology: *GeoBase*
- History: *America: History and Life, Historical Abstracts*
- Language, Literature: *MLA, Literature Criticism Online*
- Law: *LexisNexis, Westlaw*
- Mathematics: *MathSciNet*
- Medicine: *PubMed* (free), *ScienceDirect*
- Music: *RILM Abstracts of Music Literature*
- Philosophy: *Philosopher's Index*
- Physics: *arXiv.org* (free), *Physical Review Online Archive (PROLA), ScienceDirect*
- Political Science: *Columbia International Affairs Online (CIAO), ProQuest PAIS International, Worldwide Political Science Abstracts*
- Psychology: *PsycINFO*
- Religion: *ATLA Religion*
- Sociology: *CSA Sociological Abstracts*

Step 3: visit these not-to-be-missed free websites and metasites, that lead to a variety of materials relevant to a discipline:

- All subjects: *Google Scholar* scholar.google.com (books and journals)
- Anthropology: *Anthropological Index Online* aio.anthropology.org.uk/ (journals), *Anthropology Resources on the Internet* www.aaanet.org /resources/

- Art: *Artcyclopedia* www.artcyclopedia.com (images and critical bibliographies)

- Biology: *BiologyBrowser* www.biologybrowser.org (gateway to digital archives of colleges and universities), *Agricola* agricola.nal.usda.gov (journals)

- Business: *EDGAR* www.sec.gov/edgar.shtml (company annual reports)

- Chemistry: *Chemdex* www.chemdex.org (chemical compounds), *Eric Weisstein's World of Chemistry* scienceworld.wolfram.com/chemistry (encyclopedia)

- Communication: *Television News Archive: Vanderbilt University* tvnews. vanderbilt.edu (index to television news)

- Computer Science: *CompInfo* www.compinfo-center.com (magazines and downloads)

- Economics: *Intute: Economics* www.intute.ac.uk/economics/ (reviewed websites associated with economics)

- Education: *Gateway to 21st Century Skills* www.thegateway.org/ (resource guides and lesson plans)

- Film Studies: *Film Studies Resources* www.lib.berkeley.edu/MRC/filmstudies /index.html (index to reviews and criticism)

- Geography/Geology: *U.S. Geological Survey* www.usgs.gov/pubprod/ (array of maps and other resources)

- History: *American Memory* memory.loc.gov/ammem/index.html (primary documents)

- Language, Literature: *Online Literary Criticism Collection* www.ipl.org/div /litcrit (biography and criticism)

- Law: *FindLaw* www.findlaw.com (free legal information)

- Mathematics: *arXiv.org* arxiv.org/ (non-peer-reviewed but moderated scholarly e-print submissions), *Wolfram MathWorld* mathworld .wolfram.com/ (encyclopedia)

- Medicine: *BioMed Central* www.biomedcentral.com (journals)

- Music: *Online Resources for Music Scholars* hcl.harvard.edu /research/guides/onmusic/ (gateway to music resources on the web)

- Philosophy: *Stanford Encyclopedia of Philosophy* plato.stanford.edu

- Physics: *arXiv.org* arxiv.org/ (non-peer-reviewed but moderated scholarly e-print submissions), *Eric Weisstein's World of Physics* scienceworld.wolfram.com/physics

- Political Science: Political Resources on the Net www.politicalresources.net/ *THOMAS* thomas.loc.gov (U.S. government documents)

- Psychology: Psych Web www.psywww.com/

- Religion: *Religion Online* www.religion-online.org/ (articles and book chapters), *Hartford Institute for Religion Research* hirr.hartfordinstitute.org (surveys and statistics)

- Sociology: *Intute: Sociology* www.intute.ac.uk/sociology (web resources)

    Step 4: search the web using the following selective search engine:

- *ipl2 www.ipl.org/*

Use with discretion. Contains a moderate percentage of academic websites. Favors nonprofit over commercial sites.

The Four Documentation Styles: Similarities and Differences

The four most common styles of documentation are those established by:

- the American Psychological Association (APA),

- the Council of Science Editors (CSE),

- the University Press of Chicago, and

- the Modern Language Association (MLA).

Note: The University of North Carolina at Chapel Hill Libraries offers authoritative examples of basic citations of electronic and print resources in all four styles at www.lib.unc.edu/instruct/citations/.

For citation examples not given at the University of North Carolina at Chapel Hill Libraries website, it is advisable to consult the various organizations' printed manuals—*Publication Manual of the American Psychological Association* (6th edition), the *Chicago Manual of Style* (16th edition), *Scientific Style and Format: The CSE Manual for Authors, Editors, and Publishers*, and the *MLA Handbook for Writers of Research Papers* (7th edition). It is important to use the most recent edition available of each of these manuals.

You have probably already discovered that some professors are more concerned than others that students obey the particulars of a given documentation style. Virtually all faculty across the curriculum agree, however, that *the most important rule for writers to follow in documenting sources is formal consistency*. That is, all of your in-text citations, or footnotes/endnotes, should follow the same format, and all of your end-of-text citations should follow the same format.

Once you begin doing most of your writing in a particular discipline, you may want to purchase or access on the Internet the more detailed style guide adhered to by that discipline. Because documentation styles differ not only from discipline to discipline but also even from journal to journal within a discipline, you should consult your professor about which documentation format he or she wishes you to use in a given course.

The various styles differ in the specific ways that they organize the bibliographical information, but they also share some common characteristics.

1. They place an extended citation for each source, including the author, the title, the date, and the place of publication, at the end of the paper (though in Chicago this end-of-text list is optional when employing footnotes/endnotes: consult with your professor). These end-of-text citations are organized in a list, usually alphabetically.

2. All four styles distinguish among different kinds of sources—providing slightly differing formulas for citing books, articles, encyclopedias, government documents, interviews, and so forth.

3. They all ask for these basic pieces of information to be provided whenever they are known: author, title of larger work along with title of article or chapter as appropriate, date of publication, and publisher or institutional affiliation.

To briefly distinguish the styles:

- the APA style employs the author-date format of parenthetical in-text citation and predominates in the social sciences,

- the Chicago style, best known for its use of footnotes or endnotes, is employed in history, the fine arts, and some other humanities disciplines,

- the CSE (aka CBE) style, which employs alternately the citation-sequence system and the name-year system, is commonly used throughout the sciences, especially the natural sciences, and

- the MLA style, which uses the author-page format of parenthetical in-text citation, prevails in the humanities disciplines of language, literature, film, and cultural studies.

Here are a few basic examples of in-text and end-of-text citations in the four most commonly used styles, followed by a brief discussion of the rules that apply.

APA Style

In-text citation: Studies of students' changing attitudes towards the small colleges that they attend suggest that their loyalty to the institution declines steadily over a four-year period, whereas their loyalty to individual professors or departments increases "markedly, by as much as twenty-five percent over the last two years" (Brown, 1994, p. 41).

For both books and articles, include the author's last name, followed by a comma, and then the date of publication. If you are quoting or referring to a specific passage, include the page number as well, separated from the date by a comma and the abbreviation "p." (or "pp.") followed by a space. If the author's name has been mentioned in the sentence, include only the date in the parentheses immediately following the author's name.

In-text citation: Brown (1992) documents the decline in students' institutional loyalty.

End-of-text book citation:

Tannen, D. (1991). *You just don't understand: Women and men in conversation.* New York, NY: Ballantine Books.

End-of-text journal article citation:

Baumeister, R. (1987). How the self became a problem: A psychological review of historical research. *Journal of Personality and Psychology, 52,* 163–176.

End-of-text website citation:

Hershey Foods Corporation. (2001, March 15). *2001 Annual Report.* Retrieved from www.thehersheycompany.com/investors/financial-reports /annual-and-quarterly-reports.aspx

End-of-text citation of a journal article retrieved from a website or database:

Paivio, A. (1975). Perceptual comparisons through the mind's eye. *Memory & Cognition, 3,* 635–647. doi:10.1037/0278-6133.24.2.225

Note that citations of journal articles retrieved on the web include a DOI, a unique code that allows easy retrieval of the article. The DOI is typically located on the first page of the electronic journal article near the copyright notice. When a DOI is used in your citation, no other retrieval information is needed. Use this format for the DOI in references: doi:xxxxxxx

If no DOI has been assigned to the content, provide the home page URL of the journal or report publisher. If you retrieve an article from a library (subscription) database, in general it is not necessary to include the database information in the citation. Do not include retrieval dates unless the source material has changed over time.

APA style requires an alphabetical list of references (by author's last name, which keys the reference to the in-text citation). This list is located at the end of the paper on a separate page and entitled "References." Regarding manuscript form, the first line of each reference is not indented, but all subsequent lines are indented three spaces.

In alphabetizing the references list, place entries for a single author before entries that he or she has coauthored, and arrange multiple entries by a single author by beginning with the earliest work. If there are two or more works by the same author in the same year, designate the second with an "a," the third a "b," and so forth, directly after the year. For all subsequent entries by an author after the first, substitute three hyphens followed by a period [---.] for his or her name. For articles by two or more authors, use commas to connect the authors, and precede the last one with a comma and an ampersand (&).

The APA style divides individual entries into the following parts: author (using initials only for first and middle names), year of publication (in parentheses), title, and publication data. Each part is separated by a period from the others. Note that only the first letter of the title and subtitle of books is capitalized (although proper nouns would be capitalized as necessary).

Journal citations differ from those for books in a number of small ways. The title of a journal article is neither italicized (nor underlined) nor enclosed in quotation marks, and only the first word in the title and subtitle is capitalized. The name of the journal is italicized (or underlined), however, and the first word and all significant words are capitalized. Also, notice that the volume number (which is separated by a comma from the title of the journal) is italicized (or underlined) to distinguish it from the page reference. Page numbers for the entire article are included, with no "p." or "pp.," and are separated by a comma from the preceding volume number. If the journal does not use volume numbers, then p. or pp. is included.

Chicago Style

Footnote or endnote citation: The earliest groups to explore that part of the country spent much of their time finding out of the way places to "hide their families and cache their grain."[1]

The raised numeral indicates a footnote at the bottom of the page or an endnote at the conclusion of a chapter. Following is an example of what that note would look like, assuming this is the first note to have appeared in the paper, thus listed as note number one:

Footnote/endnote book citation:

1. Juanita Brooks, *The Mountain Meadows Massacre* (Norman: University of Oklahoma Press, 1991), 154.

Here are some examples of other types of notes, numbered consecutively as if each were appearing in the same paper, in this order:

Footnote/endnote journal article citation:

2. Richard Jackson, "Running Down the Up-Escalator: Regional Inequality in Papua New Guinea," *Australian Geographer* 14 (May 1979): 180.

Footnote/endnote website citation:

3. Baha'i International Community. "The Baha'i Faith," *The Baha'i World*, accessed September 20, 2013, info.bahai.org.

Footnote/endnote citation of a journal article retrieved from a website:

4. Linda Belau, "Trauma and the Material Signifier," *Postmodern Culture* 11, no. 2 (2001): par. 6, www.iath.virginia.edu/pmc/text-only/issue.101/11.2 belau.txt.

Footnote/endnote library (subscription) database journal article citation:

5. Ilan Rachum, "The Meaning of 'Revolution' in the English Revolution (1648–1660)," *Journal of the History of Ideas* 56, no. 2 (1995): 196. www.jstor .org/stable/2709835.

In addition to footnotes/endnotes, the Chicago style recommends but does not require an alphabetical list of references (by author's last name). This list is located at the end of the paper on a separate page and is entitled "Bibliography." Listed below are the same references employed above, formatted for the bibliography:

End-of-text book citation:

Brooks, Juanita. *The Mountain Meadows Massacre*. Norman: University of Oklahoma Press, 1991.

End-of-text journal article citation:

Jackson, Richard. "Running Down the Up-Escalator: Regional Inequality in Papua New Guinea." Australian Geographer 14 (May 1979): 175–84.

End-of-text website citation:

Baha'i International Community. "The Baha'i Faith." The Baha'i World. Accessed September 20, 2013. info.bahai.org.

End-of-text citation of a journal article retrieved from a website:

Belau, Linda. "Trauma and the Material Signifier." Postmodern Culture 11, no. 2 (2001), www.iath.virginia.edu/pmc/text-only/issue.101/11.2belau.txt.

End-of-text library (subscription) database journal article citation:

Rachum, Ilan. "The Meaning of 'Revolution' in the English Revolution (1648–1660)." Journal of the History of Ideas 56, no. 2 (1995): 195–215. www.jstor.org /stable/2709835.

Each entry in the bibliography is divided into three parts: author, title, and publication data. Each of these parts is separated by a period from the others. Titles of book-length works are italicized. Journal citations differ slightly: article names go inside quotations, no punctuation follows the titles of journals, and a colon precedes the page numbers when pagination is known.

CSE Style Employing Name-Year (Author-Date) System

In-text citation: Soap works as a cleaning agent because of the distinctiveness of each end of the soap molecule, their "opposing tendencies," that is (McMurry and others 2010, p 768).

For both books and articles, include the author's last name followed by the date of publication. For two authors, include the two last names (Smith and Jones 2013). For more than two authors, as in the case above, employ the phrase "and others." If you are quoting or referring to a specific passage, include the page number as well, separated from the date by a comma and the abbreviation "p" (or "pp") followed by a space. If the author's name has been mentioned in the sentence, include only the date in the parentheses immediately following the author's name wherever it appears in the sentence.

In-text citation: Romero (2008) reviews the transformation of scientific knowledge about the polymer.

End-of-text book citation: McMurry J, Castellion ME, Ballantine DS. 2010. Fundamentals of general, organic, and biological chemistry. New York: Prentice Hall.

End-of-text journal article citation: Healy R, Cerio R, Hollingsworth A, Bewley A. 2010. Acquired perforating dermatosis associated with pregnancy. Clin Exp Dermatol. 35(6): 621–623.

End-of-text website citation: International Union for Conservation of Nature and Natural Resources. 2013. IUCN red list of threatened species [Internet]. Gland, Switzerland and Cambridge, UK: IUCN. [cited 2013 Aug 12]. Available from: www. iucnredlist.org/

End-of-text citation of journal article retrieved from a website: Philippi TE, Dixon PM, Taylor BE. 1998. Detecting trends in species composition. Ecol Appl [Internet]. [cited 2013 Aug 12]; 8(2): 300–308. Available from: dx.doi .org/10.1890/1051-0761(1998)008[0300:DTISC]2.0.CO;2

End-of-text library (subscription) database journal article citation: Kenny G, Yardley J, Brown C, Sigal R, Jay O. 2010. Heat stress in older individuals and patients with common chronic diseases. Can Med Assoc J [Internet]. [cited 2010 June 12]; 182(10): 1053–1060. Available from Health Source: Academic/Nursing Edition: 0-search.ebscohost.com.library .muhlenberg.edu/login.aspx?direct=true&db=hch&AN=52226611&site=e host-live&scope=site.

CSE style requires an alphabetical list of references (by author's last name, which keys the reference to the in-text citation). This list is located at the end of the paper on a separate page and is titled "Cited References." Regarding manuscript form, the first line of each reference is not indented, but all subsequent lines are indented three spaces.

In alphabetizing the references list, place entries for a single author before entries that he or she has coauthored, and arrange multiple entries by a single author by beginning with the earliest work.

The CSE style divides individual entries into the following parts: author (using initials only for first and middle names), year of publication, title, and publication data. Each part is separated by a period from the others. Note that only the first letter of the title and subtitle of books is capitalized (although proper nouns would be capitalized as necessary).

Journal citations differ from those for books in a number of small ways. The title of a journal article is neither italicized (nor underlined) nor enclosed in quotation marks, and only the first word in the title and subtitle is capitalized. CSE style requires that journal titles be abbreviated in the standard manner used by science researchers, found at ISI Journal Title Abbreviations www.efm.leeds.ac.uk/~mark/ISIabbr/. This is followed by a volume number and an issue number if available. Page numbers for the entire article are included, with no "p." or "pp.," and are separated by a colon from the preceding volume or issue number.

CSE Style Employing Citation Sequence System

In-text citation: Soap works as a cleaning agent because of the distinctiveness of each end of the soap molecule, their "opposing tendencies," that is[1].

Page numbers are generally not included in this system of CSE, but point to the source generally.

End-of-text book citation:

1. McMurry J, Castellion ME, Ballantine DS. Fundamentals of general, organic, and biological chemistry. New York: Prentice Hall; 2010.

End-of-text journal article citation:

2. Healy R, Cerio R, Hollingsworth A, Bewley A. Acquired perforating dermatosis associated with pregnancy. Clin Exp Dermatol. 2010;35(6):621–623.

End-of-text website citation:

3. International Union for Conservation of Nature and Natural Resources. IUCN red list of threatened species [Internet]. Gland, Switzerland and Cambridge, UK: IUCN; 2013 [cited 2013 Aug 12]. Available from: www.iucnredlist.org

End-of-text citation of journal article retrieved from a website:

4. Philippi TE, Dixon PM, Taylor BE. Detecting trends in species composition. Ecol Appl [Internet]. 1998 [cited 2013 Aug 12];8(2):300–308. Available from: dx.doi.org/10.1890/1051-0761(1998)008[0300:DTISC]2.0.CO;2

End-of-text library (subscription) database journal article citation:

5. Kenny G, Yardley J, Brown C, Sigal R, Jay O. Heat stress in older individuals and patients with common chronic diseases. Can Med Assoc J [Internet]. 2010 [cited 2013 Jun 12];182(10):1053–1060. Available from Health Source: Academic/Nursing Edition: 0-search.ebscohost.com.library.muhlenberg.edu/login .aspx?direct=true&db=hch&AN=52226611&site=ehost-live&scope=site. System requirements: Adobe Acrobat. Subscription required for access.

In the CSE style, end-of-text citations appear in a list titled "Cited References," and correspond to the superscript numeral appearing in the text, in the order of their introduction in the text.

In CSE style, individual entries into the following parts: author (using initials only for first and middle names), title, and publication data. Each part is separated by a period from the others. Note that only the first letter of the title and subtitle of books is capitalized (although proper nouns would be capitalized as necessary).

Journal citations differ from those for books in a number of small ways. The title of a journal article is neither italicized (nor underlined) nor enclosed in quotation marks, and only the first word in the title and subtitle is capitalized. CSE style requires that journal titles be abbreviated in the standard manner used by science researchers, found at ISI Journal Title Abbreviations www.efm.leeds.ac.uk/~mark /ISIabbr/. This is followed by a volume number and an issue number if available. Page numbers for the entire article are included, with no "p." or "pp.," and are separated by a colon from the preceding volume or issue number.

MLA Style

In-text citation: The influence of Seamus Heaney on younger poets in Northern Ireland has been widely acknowledged, but Patrick Kavanagh's "plain-speaking, pastoral" influence on him is "less recognized" (Smith 74).

"(Smith 74)" indicates the author's last name and the page number on which the cited passage appears. If the author's name had been mentioned in the sentence—had the sentence begun "According to Smith"—you would include only the page number in the citation. Note that there is no abbreviation for "page," that there is no intervening punctuation between name and page, and that the parentheses precede the period or other punctuation. If the sentence ends with a direct quotation, the parentheses come after the quotation marks but before the closing period. Also note that no punctuation occurs between the last word of the quotation ("recognized") and the closing quotation mark.

End-of-text book citation:

Douglas, Ann. *Terrible Honesty: Mongrel Manhattan in the 1920s.* New York: Farrar, 1995. Print.

End-of-text journal article citation:

Cressy, David. "Foucault, Stone, Shakespeare and Social History." *English Literary Renaissance* 21 (1991): 121–33. Print.

End-of-text website citation:

Landow, George, ed. *Contemporary Postcolonial and Postimperial Literature in English.* Brown U, 2002. Web. 25 June 2013.

End-of-text citation of a journal article retrieved from a website:

Nater, Miguel. "El beso de la Esfinge: La poética de lo sublime en *La amada inmóvil* de Amado Nervo y en los *Nocturnos* de José Asunción Silva." *Romanitas* 1.1 (2006): n. pag. Web. 25 June 2013.

End-of-text library (subscription) database journal article citation:

Arias, Judith H. "The Devil at Heaven's Door." *Hispanic Review* 61.1 (1993): n. pag. *Academic Search Premier.* Web. 25 June 2013.

Note that the above citations all indicate a format type (print or web) and the web citations end with the date the researcher accessed the website or database.

MLA style stipulates an alphabetical list of references (by author's last name, which keys the reference to the in-text citation). This list is located at the end of the paper on a separate page and entitled "Works Cited."

Each entry in the Works Cited list is divided into three parts: author, title, and publication data. Each of these parts is separated by a period from the others. Titles of book-length works are italicized, unless your instructor prefers underlining. (Underlining is a means of indicating italics.) Journal citations differ slightly: article names go inside quotations, no punctuation follows the titles of journals, and a colon precedes the page numbers when pagination is known.

Guidelines for Finding, Evaluating, and Citing Sources

1. Examine bibliographies at the end of the articles and books you've already found. Remember that one quality source can, in its bibliography, point to many other resources.

2. Citing sources isn't just about acknowledging intellectual or informational debts; it's also a courtesy to your readers, directing them how to find out more about the subject cited.

3. Before you settle in with one author's book-length argument, use indexes and bibliographies and other resources to achieve a broader view.

4. URLs with domain names ending in .edu and .gov usually offer more reliable choices than the standard .com.

5. When professors direct you to do bibliographic research, they usually are referring to research done with indexes; these are available in print, online, and CD-ROM formats.

6. In evaluating a website about which you don't know much, try "backspacing" a URL to trace back to its authorship or institutional affiliation.

CHAPTER 9

From Paragraphs to Papers: Forms and Formats Across the Curriculum

Overview This is a chapter about organization, about the various formats writers use to structure their ideas. You will learn the *why* as well as the *how* of the formats prescribed by particular academic disciplines in the humanities and in the natural and social sciences, such as English, political science, psychology, biology, and chemistry. The chapter argues that these formats are actually much more similar than their stylistic differences may lead you to believe. The chapter also includes discussion of transitions and of typical paragraph shapes, including introductions and conclusions—the building blocks of writing in any discipline.

Overall, the chapter seeks to increase your **rhetorical awareness**, that is, your awareness of how an audience's attitudes and needs can affect the shape of your writing.

The Two Functions of Formats

We began this book by saying that learning to write well means learning to use writing in order to think well. Writing is not just a way of organizing thoughts; it is a way of making thoughts happen. This chapter asks you to consider the relationship between the forms of certain kinds of academic writing, such as the lab report, and the way these forms shape thinking. Once you train yourself to see the kind of thinking a format asks you to do, you will be able to adapt your writing process accordingly.

It's important to recognize that all organizational schemes are conventional—which is to say, they are agreed-upon protocols with social functions. They show you how to write in a way that will allow you to be heard by others in a particular discourse community—a group of people connected by shared ways of talking and thus of thinking. But it's also important to recognize that these protocols are not just containers for information; they are tools of invention.

Most of the writing (and thinking) people do is generated by some kind of format, even if they are not aware of it. Accordingly, you should not regard the formats that you encounter simply as *prescriptive* sets of artificial rules. Rather, try to think of them as *descriptive* accounts of the various heuristics—sets of questions and categories—that humans typically use to guide and stimulate their thinking.

TWO FUNCTIONS OF FORMATS: RHETORICAL AND HEURISTIC

- Rhetorical: formats make communication among members of a discipline easier and more efficient.

- Heuristic: formats offer writers a means of finding and exploring ideas.

Because formats offer a means not only of displaying thinking in a discipline, but also of shaping it, the format that a discipline requires (whether tacitly or overtly) conditions its members to think in particular ways. Learning to use the format that scientists use predisposes you to think like a scientist. Although knowing the required steps of a discipline's writing format won't write your papers for you, not knowing how writers in that discipline characteristically proceed can keep you from being read.

Academic disciplines differ in the extent to which they adhere to prescribed organizational schemes. In biology and psychology, for example, formal papers and reports generally follow an explicitly prescribed pattern of presentation. Some other disciplines are less uniform and less explicit about their reliance on formats, but writers in these fields—economics, for example, or history or English or religion—usually operate within fairly established forms as well.

The writing strategies and heuristics in this book are formats in the sense that most prescribe a series of steps. The emphasis of *Writing Analytically* rests more on the process of invention than it does on the organization of the finished paper, but, as we have been suggesting, the two are not really separate. The book's heuristics can be used as organizational models; they can also be adapted for use in the various disciplinary formats that college writing requires.

Using Formats Heuristically: An Example

To lose sight of the heuristic value of formats is to become preoccupied with formats merely as disciplinary etiquette. The solution to this problem is to find the spaces in a format that will allow it to work as a heuristic. Consider how you might go about using even a highly specified organizational scheme like the following.

1. State the problem.

2. Develop criteria of adequacy for a solution.

3. Explore at least two inadequate solutions.

4. Explicate the proposed solution.

5. Evaluate the proposed solution.

6. Reply to anticipated criticisms.

The best reason not to ignore any of the six steps in this problem/solution format is that the format does have a logic, although it leaves that logic unstated. The purpose of including at least two inadequate solutions (step 3), for example, is to protect the writer against moving to a conclusion too quickly on the basis of too little evidence. The requirements that the writer evaluate the solution and reply to criticisms (steps 5 and 6) press the writer toward complexity, preventing a one-sided and uncritical answer. In short, heuristic value in the format is there for a writer to use if he or she doesn't allow a premature concern with matters of form to take precedence over thinking. It would be a mistake, in other words, to assume that one must move through the six steps consecutively; the writer would only need to arrange his or her thinking in that order when putting together the final product.

The Common Structure of Most Academic Writing

Differences in surface features—sentence style, word choice—tend to obscure the fact that a common underlying structure and set of aims unites most kinds of academic writing across the curriculum.

You can train yourself to start seeing this underlying structure by first recognizing that academic writing in all disciplines is **problem-oriented**, which is to say that academic writing typically starts by noting something that is missing from previous writing and research. As you will see, disciplines differ in how overtly writers may single out problems in other writers' thinking. And yet, in one way or another, most academic writing begins by locating something that needs to be done—something that calls for more research, for example—and saying why this new work might matter.

Science Format Compared with Other Kinds of Writing

Here is a quick overview of the organizational scheme prescribed in the natural sciences and for some kinds of papers in the social sciences, such as reports on research in psychology and political science. Although not all writing in these disciplines follows this format, most does—especially lab reports and articles based on the experimental method and quantitative research. The structure is commonly referred to as IMRAD:

I   introduction

M   methods

R   results

A   and

D   discussion

You can think of this format as two descriptions of the research (methods and results) framed by two sections (introduction and discussion) that locate it in the context of existing knowledge in the field. The introduction locates the new work in terms of what has already been done (which points to what still needs to be done). The discussion section considers how knowledge in the field might be changed by the addition of the new results. (See LabWrite Program sponsored by NSF at www.ncsu.edu/labwrite. Also see advice from the Council of Science Editors—CSE.)

The following Voice from Across the Curriculum offers a fuller definition of the parts of the report format used in the sciences, a format we will then restate in a way that makes the common denominators of this and other formats easier to recognize.

VOICES FROM ACROSS THE CURRICULUM

Writing in the Sciences: A Biochemistry Professor Speaks

The lab report as taught in college science courses teaches students to mimic the process of thinking required to write a scientific paper. The governing question of the lab report is, "To what extent is my data consistent with what I was supposed to get?"

The lab report, like most scientific writing, has four parts (five if you include the abstract):

Abstract
—The short synoptic version of essentially the entire paper: What you did, what you found, and how you did it.

Introduction/Purpose/Objective
—What you are trying to accomplish and why it is important

Methods/Experimental Procedures
—The details of how you performed the experiments

Results/Data
—Reporting of the data without commentary, often done with tables, graphs, and figures rather than text.

—Primarily summative and descriptive

Discussion/Conclusions
—This is where the analysis happens. Cite the data, then make qualified, evidence-based claims from the data; draw implications.

In the written accounts of scientific experiments, some information is repeated across sections. This repetition is deliberate. No scientist reads a paper in order, and so every section has to stand by itself.

—KERI COLABROY, PROFESSOR OF BIOCHEMISTRY

Here is a restatement of the IMRAD format demonstrating how similar it is in its aims and methods to other kinds of academic writing.

THE COMMON FORMAT OF ACADEMIC WRITING

1. Begin with some kind of problem or question or uncertainty. Say why the new study might matter, why it needs doing. Offer a theory to be tested (working thesis/hypothesis).

2. Test the adequacy of the theory by conducting some kind of experimental procedure or other way of analyzing evidence.

3. Report resulting data—what was revealed by the experiment or other analytical method such as close reading of textual evidence or statistical analysis.

4. Interpret the results and draw conclusions about their significance. How might the results change current thinking and/or open the way to new questions and further study?

If you are just learning to write and think in an academic discipline, you cannot be expected to say in the opening paragraph the state of knowledge in the field on a particular question. Nor can you be expected to arrive at something that will alter thinking in a discipline—although sometimes this does, in fact, happen. Nevertheless, college writers and their teachers across the curriculum write with similar goals: *ask and answer a new question, offer alternatives to existing ideas or evidence, or provide a new perspective or better evidence on something already known.*

The observations in the following Voices from Across the Curriculum apply to much, but certainly not all, of the writing that goes on in the sciences. Writing in physics, for example, in which research is more theoretical, often takes a different form. There are other exceptions. Writing in psychology can appear in the form of the case study, rather than in reports on experiments.

VOICES FROM ACROSS THE CURRICULUM

How to Write—and Read—Scientific Formats: Two Professors Speak

Experimental Psychology uses a very rigid format. I explain to the students the functions of the different sections for the reader. Once students start to read journal articles themselves, the functions of the sections become clear. Readers do not always want to read or reread the whole article. If I want to replicate someone's research, I may read just the "Methods" section to get the technical details I need. I may read just the "Results" section to get a sense of the numerical results I might expect. On the other hand, I may not care about the details of how the experiment was run. I might just want to know if it worked, in which case I would read the first few sentences of the "Discussion" section. The format lets me know exactly where to find whatever I might be looking for, without having to read through the whole article.

—LAURA EDELMAN, PROFESSOR OF PSYCHOLOGY

In writing in the social sciences, there is a standard plot with three alternative endings. The "Introduction" (a standard section of APA style) sets forth the problem, which the "Methods" section promises to address. The "Results" section "factually" reports the outcome of the study, with the "Discussion" section interpreting the results. "The data" are given the starring role in determining which ending is discussed in the "Discussion" section: hypothesis confirmed, hypothesis rejected, or hard to say. (I would say "which ending the author chooses" versus "which ending is discussed," but the data are supposed to be determinative, and the role of the author/investigator neutral.) Analytical thinking comes in setting up the problem and making sense of the results in conjunction with existing literature on the subject.

—ALAN TJELTVEIT, PROFESSOR OF PSYCHOLOGY

Three Organizing Strategies

Here are three organizational patterns that are useful in many kinds of writing. They have both rhetorical and idea-generating (heuristic) value.

Climactic Order: Saving the Best for Last

Climactic order arranges elements from least to most important. The idea is to build to your best points, rather than leading with them and thereby allowing the paper to trail off from your more minor and less interesting observations.

But what are your best points? A frequent mistake that writers commit in arranging their points climactically—and one that has much to do with the rhetoric of form—is to assume that the best point is the most obvious, the one with the most data attached to it and the one least likely to produce disagreement with readers. Such writers end up giving more space than they should to ideas that really don't need much development because they are already evident to most readers.

If you follow the principle of climactic order, you would begin with the most obvious and predictable points—and ones that, psychologically speaking, would get readers assenting—and then build to the more revealing and less obvious ones. So, for example, if the comparisons between film A and film B are fairly mundane but the contrasts are really provocative, you'd get the comparisons out of the way first and build to the contrasts, exploiting DIFFERENCE WITHIN SIMILARITY (see Chapter 3).

If, for example, there are four important reasons for labeling genetically modified foods, you might choose to place the most compelling one last. If you were to put it first, you might draw your readers in quickly (a principle used by news stories) but then lose them as your argument seemed to trail off into less interesting rationales.

Comparison/Contrast: Two Formats

In Chapter 3, we discuss comparison as an invention strategy. We now want to address this subject from the perspective of organizing a paper. The first decision a writer has to make when arranging comparisons and contrasts is whether to address the two items being compared and contrasted in sequential blocks (A and then B) or point by point.

- Organize by subjects being compared (subject A and then subject B), or
- Organize the comparison under a series of topics (Topic 1: A and B, Topic 2: A and B, etc.)

If you are comparing subject A with subject B, you might first make all the points you wish to make about A and then make points about B by explicitly referring back to A as you go. The advantage of this format is that it will allow you to use comparing and contrasting to figure out what you wish to say as you are drafting.

The disadvantage of this "subject-A-then-subject-B" format is that it can easily lose focus. If you don't manage to keep the points you raise about each side of your comparison parallel, you may end up with a paper comprised of two loosely connected halves. The solution is to make your comparisons and contrasts in the second half of the paper connect explicitly with what you said in the first half. What you say about subject A, in other words, should set the subtopics and terms for discussion of subject B.

The alternative pattern of organization for comparisons and contrasts is to organize by topic—not A and then B, but A1 and B1, A2 and B2, A3 and B3, and so forth. That is, you talk about both A and B under a series of subtopics. If, for example, you were comparing two films, you might organize your work under such headings as directing, script, acting, special effects, and so forth.

The advantage of this format is that it better focuses the comparisons, pressing you to use them to think with. The disadvantage is that organizing in this way is sometimes difficult to manage until you've already done quite a bit of thinking about the two items you're comparing. The solution, particularly in longer papers, is sometimes to use both formats. You begin by looking at each of your subjects separately to make the big links and distinctions apparent and then focus what you've said by further pursuing selected comparisons one topic at a time.

Concessions and Refutations: Giving and Taking Away

In the language of argument, you *concede* whenever you acknowledge that a position at odds with your own does indeed have merit, even though you continue to believe that your position overall is the more reasonable one. When making a concession, a writer needs to represent this competing point of view as genuinely creditable—rather than only seemingly creditable until he or she lays out a means of opposing it. Another option is to argue against these views so as to *refute* their reasonableness. (*For a misuse of concessions and refutations, see Straw Man under A Brief Glossary of Common Logical Fallacies in Chapter 5, Interpretation.*)

As a rule of thumb, avoid making your readers wait too long before you either concede or refute a view that you can assume will already have occurred to them. If you delay too long, you may inadvertently suggest either that you are unaware of the competing view or that you are afraid to bring it up.

In the case of short and easily managed concessions and refutations, you can often house these within the first several paragraphs and, in this way, clear a space for the position you wish to promote. In the case of more complicated and potentially more threatening alternative arguments, you may need to express your own position clearly and convincingly first. But to avoid the rhetorical problem of appearing to ignore the threat, you will probably need to give it a nod, telling readers that you will return to a full discussion of it later, once you have laid out your own position in some detail.

The placement of arguments has much to do with their relative complexity. Reasonably straightforward and easily explained concessions and refutations can often all be grouped in one place, perhaps as early as the second or third paragraph of a paper. The approach to concession and refutation in more complex arguments does not allow for such grouping. For each part of your argument, you will probably need to concede and refute as necessary, before moving to the next part of your argument and repeating the procedure.

TRY THIS 9.1: Locating Concessions and Refutations

Study the paragraph on gender inequality and language to answer the following questions: (1) What language functions as concession? (2) What language functions as refutation? (3) What part of the competing argument does the refutation still appear willing to concede? (4) How is the refutation that the writer offers different from the position to which he concedes?

Gender Inequality and Linguistic Bias

The more conservative side on this issue questions whether the elimination of generic pronouns can, in fact, change attitudes, and whether intentionally changing language is even possible. The reformist side believes that the elimination of generic pronouns is necessary for women's liberation from oppression and that reshaping the use of male pronouns as generic is both possible and effective. Although the answer to the debate over the direct link between a change in language and a change in society is not certain, it is certain that the attitudes and behaviors of societies are inseparable from language. Language conditions what we feel and think. The act of using "they" to refer to all people rather than the generic "he" will not automatically change collective attitudes toward women. These generic pronouns should be changed, however, because 1) the struggle itself increases awareness and discussion of the sexual inequalities in society, and subsequently, this awareness will transform attitudes and language, and 2) the power of linguistic usage has been mainly controlled by and reserved for men. Solely by participating in linguistic reform, women have begun to appropriate some of the power for themselves.

What Introductions Do: "Why What I'm Saying Matters"

As we have said, introductions in all disciplines have some underlying commonalities. Most kinds of academic writing begin by telling readers what the writer found interesting, worth pursuing, and why. The Latin roots of the word suggest that introductions bring the reader into a subject (*intro*, meaning "within," and *ducere*, meaning "to lead or bring"). Its length varies, depending on the scope of the writing project. An introduction may take a paragraph, a few paragraphs, a few pages, a chapter, or even a book. In most academic writing, one or two paragraphs is a standard length.

The primary challenge in writing introductions lies in occupying the middle ground between saying too much too soon (overassertive prejudgment) and saying too little up front (avoidance of taking a position). The most important thing to do in the introductory paragraph of an analytical paper is to lay out a *genuine issue*, something that seems to be *at stake* in whatever it is you are studying.

Set up this issue as quickly and concretely as you can. The introduction should give your reader a quick sampling of some feature or features in your evidence that initially aroused your curiosity. As a general rule, you should assume that readers of your essay will need to know on page one—preferably by the end of your first paragraph—what your paper is attempting to resolve or negotiate. Your introduction is saying: "Look at this, reader; it is worth thinking about, and here's why."

As we said in Chapter 6, Finding and Evolving a Thesis, in most academic disciplines (with some significant exceptions, such as philosophy) the first paragraph of a paper usually does not need to—and most often can't—offer your conclusion; it will take the body of your paper to accomplish that. The introduction should, however, provide a quick look at particular details that set up the issue. You can then use these details to generate a *theory*, a *working hypothesis*, about whatever it is you think is at stake in the material. The rest of the paper then tests and develops this theory. (See "Introductions, Conclusions, and the Thesis" in Chapter 6.)

In the sciences, the standard instructions for composing an introduction are worded somewhat differently, but with similar intent: create a context by citing all previous work relevant to your study, show the need for new information by pointing to an uncertainty or problem in existing knowledge, say what you are trying to accomplish and why it is important.

We here repeat from Chapter 6 a list of kinds of questions that introductory paragraphs usually answer:

What is potentially interesting about what I have noticed, and why?
What am I seeing that other people perhaps have not seen or have not sufficiently acknowledged?
Why might what I have noticed matter in relation to the usual ways of thinking about my subject?
How might what I have noticed require a new way of thinking about my subject, or at least a revision, however slight, of the usual ways of thinking?

How Much to Introduce Up Front: Typical Problems

The danger is trying to turn the introduction into a miniature essay. Consider the three problems discussed next as symptoms of overcompression, telltale signs that you need to reconceive, and probably reduce, your introduction.

Digression: Digression results when you try to include too much background. If, for example, you plan to write about a recent innovation in video technology, you'll need to monitor the amount and kind of technical information you include in your opening paragraphs. You'll also want to avoid starting at a point that is too far away from your immediate concerns, as in "From the beginning of time humans have needed to communicate."

As a general rule in academic writing, don't assume that your readers know little or nothing about the subject. Instead, use the social potential of the introduction to negotiate with your audience, setting up your relationship with your readers and making clear what you are assuming they do and do not know.

Incoherence: Incoherence results when you try to preview too much of your paper's conclusion in the introduction. Such introductions move in too many directions at once, usually because the writer is trying to conclude before going through the discussion that will make the conclusion comprehensible. The language you are compelled to use in such cases tends to be too dense, and the connections between the sentences tend to get left out, because there isn't enough room to include them. After having read the entire paper, your readers may be able to make sense of the introduction, but in that case, the introduction has not done its job.

The following introductory paragraph is incoherent, primarily because it tries to include too much. It neither adequately connects its ideas nor defines its terms.

> Twinship is a symbol in many religious traditions. The significance of twinship will be discussed and explored in the Native American, Japanese Shinto, and Christian religions. Twinship can be either in opposing or common forces in the form of deities or mortals. There are several forms of twinship that show duality of order versus chaos, good versus evil, and creation versus destruction. The significance of twinship is to set moral codes for society and to explain the inexplicable.

Prejudgment: Prejudgment results when you appear to have already settled the question to be pursued in the rest of the paper. The problem here is logical. In the effort to preview your paper's conclusion at the outset, you risk appearing to assume something as true that your paper will, in fact, need to test. In most papers in the humanities and social sciences, where the thesis evolves in specificity and complexity between the introduction and conclusion, writers and readers can find such assumptions prejudicial. Opening in this way, in any event, can make the rest of the paper seem redundant. Even in the sciences, in which a concise statement of objectives, plan of attack, and hypothesis are usually required up front, separate "Results" and "Discussion" sections are reserved for the conclusion.

VOICES FROM ACROSS THE CURRICULUM

Avoiding Strong Claims in the Introduction: An Economics Professor Speaks

I advise students to be careful about how they set up tentative conclusions in the opening paragraph, because these can easily slide into a prejudging of the question at hand. I would be more comfortable with a clear statement of the prevailing views held by others. For example, a student could write on the question, "Was Franklin Delano Roosevelt a Keynesian?" What purpose would it serve in an opening paragraph to reveal without any supporting discussion that FDR was or was not a Keynesian?

What might be better would be to say that in the public mind FDR is regarded as the original big spender, that some people commonly associate New Deal policies with general conceptions of Keynesianism, but that there may be some surprises in store as that common notion is examined.

In sum, I would discourage students from making strong claims at or near the beginning of a paper. Let's see the evidence first. We should all have respect for the evidence. Strong assertions, bordering on conclusions, too early on are inappropriate.

—JAMES MARSHALL, PROFESSOR OF ECONOMICS

Some Good Ways to Begin a Paper

All of the following ways to begin a paper enable you to play an ace, establishing your authority with your readers, without having to play your whole hand. They offer a starting position, rather than a miniaturized version of the entire paper. Remember that the aim of the introduction is to answer the question, Why does what I'm about to say matter? What makes it especially interesting or revealing, and in what context? Here are a few methods of accomplishing this aim.

CHALLENGE A COMMONLY HELD VIEW This move provides you with a framework against which to develop your ideas; it allows you to begin with some back pressure, which will help you to define your position. Because you are responding to a known point of view, you have a ready way of integrating context into your paper. As the economics professor notes of the FDR example, until we understand what the prevailing view is on FDR, it is pointless to start considering whether or not he was a Keynesian.

BEGIN WITH A DEFINITION Beginning with a definition is a reliable way to introduce a topic, so long as that definition has some significance for the discussion to follow. If the definition doesn't do any conceptual work in the introduction, the definition gambit becomes a pointless cliché.

You are most likely to avoid cliché if you cite a source other than a standard dictionary for your definition. The reference collection of any academic library contains a range of discipline-specific lexicons that provide more precise and authoritative definitions than Webster ever could. A useful alternative is to quote a particular author's definition of a key term because you want to make a point about his or her particular definition: for example, "Although the *Dictionary of Economics* defines Keynesianism as XYZ, Smith treats only X and Y (or substitutes A for Z, and so forth)."

LEAD WITH YOUR SECOND-BEST EXAMPLE Another versatile opening gambit, where disciplinary conventions allow, is to use your *second-best example* to set up the issue or question that you later develop in-depth with your best example. This gambit is especially useful in papers that proceed inductively on the strength of representative examples, an organizational pattern common in the humanities. As you are assembling evidence in the outlining and pre-writing stage, in many cases you will accumulate a number of examples that illustrate the same basic point. For example, several battles might illustrate a particular general's military strategy; several primaries might exemplify how a particular candidate tailors his or her speeches to appeal to the religious right; several scenes might show how a particular playwright romanticizes the working class; and so on.

Save the best example to receive the most analytical attention in your paper. If you were to present this example in the introduction, you would risk making the rest of the essay vaguely repetitive. A quick close-up of another example will strengthen your argument or interpretation. By using a different example to raise the issues, you suggest that the phenomenon exemplified is not an isolated case and that the major example you will eventually concentrate upon is, indeed, representative.

EXEMPLIFY THE TOPIC WITH A NARRATIVE The narrative opening, an occasional gambit in the humanities and social sciences, introduces a short, pertinent, and vivid story or anecdote that exemplifies a key aspect of a topic. Although generally not permissible in the formal reports assigned in the natural and social sciences, narrative openings turn up in virtually all other kinds of writing across the curriculum.

As the introduction funnels to its thesis, the readers receive a graphic sense of the issue that the writer will now develop nonnarratively. Nonnarrative treatment is necessary because by itself anecdotal evidence can be seen as merely personal. Storytelling is suggestive but usually does not constitute sufficient proof; it needs to be corroborated.

What Conclusions Do: The Final "SO WHAT?"

Like the introduction, the conclusion has a key social function: it escorts the readers out of the paper, just as the introduction has escorted them in. The concluding paragraph presents the paper's final "SO WHAT?"

Conclusions always state the thesis in its most fully evolved form (See "The Conclusion: Returning the Thesis to the Larger Conversation" in Chapter 6.) In addition, the conclusion usually makes all of the following moves:

- *It comes full circle*. That is, it creates a sense of closure by revisiting the way the paper began. Often it returns to some key phrase from the context established in the introduction and updates it.

- *It pursues implications*. That is, it reasons from the particular focus of the essay to broader issues, such as the study's practical consequences or applications, or future-oriented issues, such as avenues for further research. To unfold implications in this way is to broaden the view from the here and now of the paper by looking outward to the wider world and forward to the future.

- *It identifies limitations*. That is, it acknowledges restrictions of method or focus in the analysis, and qualifies the conclusion (and its implications) accordingly.

These moves are quite literally movements—they take the thinking in the essay, and the readers with it, both backward and forward. The backward thrust we call *culmination*; the forward thrust we call *send-off*.

When you culminate a paper, you bring together things that you have already said, establishing their connection and ascending to one final statement of your thinking. The word "culminate" is derived from the Latin "*columen*," meaning "top or summit." To culminate is to reach the highest point, and it implies a mountain (in this case, of information and analysis) that you have scaled.

The climactic effects of culmination provide the basis for the send-off. The send-off is both social and conceptual, a final opening outward of the topic that leads the reader out of the paper with something further to think about. Here the thinking moves beyond the close analysis of data that has occupied the body of the paper into a kind of speculation that the writer has earned the right to formulate.

Simply put, you culminate with the best statement of your big idea, and your send-off gets you and the reader out of the paper. The professors in the following Voices from Across the Curriculum suggest ways of ending on a note of expanded implication, bringing the paper's more focused analysis to a larger perspective.

VOICES FROM ACROSS THE CURRICULUM

Beyond Restatement: A Business and a Political Science Professor Speak

I tell my students that too many papers "just end," as if the last page or so were missing. I tell them the importance of ending a work. One could summarize main points, but I tell them this is not heavy lifting.

I believe the ending should be an expansion of possibilities, sort of like an introduction to some much larger "mental" paper out there. I sometimes encourage students to see the concluding section as an option to introduce ideas that can't be dealt with now. Sort of a "Having done this, I would want to explore boom, boom, boom if I were to continue further." Here the students can critique and recommend ("Having seen 'this,' one wonders 'that'").

—FREDERICK NORLING, PROFESSOR OF BUSINESS

The conclusion does not appear simply as a restatement of a thesis, but rather as an attempt to draw out its implications and significance (the "SO WHAT?"). This is what I usually try to impress upon students. For instance, if a student is writing on a particular proposal for party reform, I would expect the concluding paragraph to consider both the significance of the reform and its practicality.

I should note that professional papers often indicate the tentativeness of their conclusions by stressing the need for future research and indicating what these research needs might be. Although I haven't tried this, maybe it would be useful to have students conclude papers with a section entitled "For Further Consideration" in which they would indicate those things that they would have liked to have known but couldn't, given their time constraints, the availability of information, and lack of methodological sophistication. This would serve as a reminder of the tentativeness of conclusions and the need to revisit and revise arguments in the future (which, after all, is a good scholarly habit).

—JACK GAMBINO, PROFESSOR OF POLITICAL SCIENCE

Solving Typical Problems in Conclusions

The primary challenge in writing conclusions lies in finding a way to culminate your analysis without claiming either too little or too much. There are a number of fairly common problems to guard against if you are to avoid either of these two extremes.

Redundancy: In Chapter 4 we lampooned an exaggerated example of the five-paragraph form for constructing its conclusion by stating "Thus, we see" and then repeating the introduction verbatim. The result is redundancy. It's a good idea to refer back to the opening, but it's a bad idea just to reinsert it mechanically. Instead, reevaluate what you said there in light of where you've ended up, repeating only key words or phrases from the introduction. This kind of selective repetition is a desirable way of achieving unity and will keep you from making one of two opposite mistakes—either repeating too much or bringing up a totally new point in the conclusion.

Raising a Totally New Point: Raising a totally new point can distract or bewilder a reader. This problem often arises out of a writer's praiseworthy desire to avoid repetition. As a rule, you can guard against the problem by making sure that you have clearly expressed the conceptual link between your central conclusion and any implications you may draw. An implication is not a totally new point but rather one that follows from the position you have been analyzing.

Similarly, although a capping judgment or send-off may appear for the first time in your concluding paragraph, it should have been anticipated by the body of your paper. Conclusions often indicate where you think you (or an interested reader) may need to go next, but you don't actually go there. In a paper on the economist Milton Friedman, for example, if you think that another economist offers a useful way of critiquing him, you probably should not introduce this person for the first time in your conclusion.

Overstatement: Many writers are confused over how much they should claim in the conclusion. Out of the understandable (but mistaken) desire for a grand (rather than a modest and qualified) culmination, writers sometimes overstate the case. They assert more than their evidence has proven or even suggested. Must a conclusion arrive at some comprehensive and final answer to the question that your paper has analyzed?

Depending on the question and the disciplinary conventions, you may need to come down exclusively on one side or another. In a great many cases, however, the answers with which you conclude can be more moderate. Especially in the humanities, good analytical writing seeks to unfold successive layers of implication, so it's not even reasonable for you to expect neat closure. In such cases, you are usually better off qualifying your final judgments, drawing the line at points of relative stability.

Anticlimax: The end of the conclusion is a "charged" site, because it gives the reader a last impression of your paper. If you end with a concession—an acknowledgment of a rival position at odds with your thesis—you risk leaving the reader unsettled and possibly confused. The term for this kind of letdown is "anticlimax." In most cases, you will flub the send-off if you depart the paper on an anticlimax.

There are many forms of anticlimax besides ending with a concession. If your conclusion peters out in a random list or an apparent afterthought or a last-minute qualification of your claims, the effect is anticlimactic. And for many readers, if your final answer comes from quoting an authority in place of establishing your own, that, too, is an anticlimax.

A useful rule for the introduction is to play an ace but not your whole hand. In the context of this card-game analogy, it is similarly effective to save an ace for the conclusion. In most cases, this high card will provide an answer to some culminating "SO WHAT?" question—a last view of the implications or consequences of your analysis.

Introductions and Conclusions Across the Curriculum

Throughout the following discussion of disciplinary practices in introductions and conclusions, we quote first-hand advice from faculty colleagues at our college. You will notice differences in the guidelines that the various disciplines offer, but you will also see that the jobs introductions and conclusions do are actually quite similar across the curriculum.

Introductory Paragraphs in the Humanities

Here is a typical set of guidelines for writing introductory paragraphs in a humanities paper—in this case, a poetry analysis in an English course. Introductions are not the same across all disciplines in the humanities, but much in the following guidelines is representative.

An introduction is not a conclusion. You do not need to announce, in short form, your whole argument. In English papers, the introductory paragraph is an opening gambit. The thesis you state at the end of paragraph one should be an idea, not a statement of fact. For example, you might offer an idea about what you think is the most important difference and/or similarity between the poem you have chosen to analyze and another poem. This statement will get qualified and expanded and tested in the paper. You should not simply march the statement through the paper and prove that you are right.

The intro offers readers some piece of your evidence—some data from your poem: perhaps a binary that you see in both poems or some other tendency of the language in both that you found interesting and that you think is worth exploring. The reader should come away from your opening paragraph knowing what you found interesting and worth pursuing and why.

Resist dumping a great lump of background into the intro. You should do some contextualizing in the opening but don't overdo it. Stay focused on the poem and what you notice about the kind of thinking it is inviting us to do.

Resist what is known as "freshman omniscience"—recognizable by sweeping claims and a grandiose tone…"Since the beginning of time poets have been…"

The last sentence of the paragraph should make some kind of claim—probably a comparative claim about the relation between your two poems. This claim should not take the form of the standard tripartite thesis typical of the 5-paragraph form essay. Rather than offering three points, each of which would then get a paragraph or two, you want to set up a sequence of thought in which you try on various ways of understanding your subject.

Here are a couple of differences between science and humanities papers that are worth noting. In the sciences it is considered inappropriate to name and especially to criticize particular pieces of research or their authors. Writers in the humanities, however, are much more likely to name names, to quote other studies, and to be explicit on where these studies seem to fall short. Papers in the humanities often begin with a compressed account of who said what, why they may have said it, and what in it needs revising.

Writers in the humanities quote and then paraphrase key statements, rather than summarizing and paraphrasing without the original language, as is the rule in psychology and other science and social science writing. Because most writing in the humanities is grounded in textual analysis, humanities writers think it important to attend to the actual language of other people's writing. Words and their meanings are data to humanities writers. It is a habit of mind in the humanities to always share the actual evidence with readers—the language being paraphrased and cited—rather than asking readers to take the writer's word for it.

Using Procedural Openings

In the interests of clear organization, some academic disciplines require students to include in the introduction an explanation of how the paper will proceed. Such a general statement of method and/or intention is known as a *procedural opening*. Among the disciplines in which you are most likely to find this format are philosophy, political science, and sociology. The danger of procedural openings is that the writer will avoid making a claim at all.

The statement of a paper's plan is not and cannot take the place of a thesis (an idea about the topic that the paper will explore and defend). Consider the deficiencies of the following procedural opening.

> In this paper I will first discuss the strong points and weak points in America's treatment of the elderly. Then I will compare this treatment with that in other industrial nations in the West. Finally, I will evaluate the various proposals for reform that have been advanced here and abroad.

This paragraph identifies the subject, but it neither addresses why the subject matters nor suggests the writer's approach. Nor does it provide background to the topic or suggest a hypothesis that the paper will pursue. In some kinds of essays, especially those that move (inductively) from specific observations to more general claims, there is little need for procedural openings, with their declaration of intention and method at the outset. As the following Voice from Across the Curriculum reveals, however, the introductory "road map" is a common strategy in some disciplines.

VOICES FROM ACROSS THE CURRICULUM

Using Procedural Openings: A Political Science Professor Speaks

I encourage students to provide a "road map" paragraph early in the paper, perhaps the second or third paragraph. (This is a common practice in professional journals.) The "road map" tells the reader the basic outline of the argument. Something like the following: "In the first part of my paper I will present a brief history of the issue. . . . This will be followed by an account of the current controversy. . . . Part III will spell out my alternative account and evidence. . . . I then conclude. . . ." I think such a paragraph becomes more necessary with longer papers.

—JACK GAMBINO, PROFESSOR OF POLITICAL SCIENCE

Putting an Issue or Question in Context

Rather than leaping immediately to the paper's issue, question, or problem, most effective introductions provide some broader context to indicate why the issue matters. Things don't just "mean" in the abstract; they mean in particular contexts.

In the following Voice from Across the Curriculum, Political Science Professor, Jack Gambino, notes the usefulness of anomalies for contextualizing papers in his discipline. The discovery of an anomaly, something that does not fit with conventional ways of thinking, can serve as a useful point of departure in a paper that goes on to revise an existing theory or opinion.

VOICES FROM ACROSS THE CURRICULUM

Providing an Introductory Context: A Political Science Professor Speaks

An introduction is not simply the statement of a thesis but also the place where the student needs to set a context, a framework that makes such a thesis statement interesting, timely, or in some other way important. It is common to see papers in political science begin by pointing out a discrepancy between conventional wisdom (what the pundits say) and recent political developments, between popular opinion and empirical evidence, or between theoretical frameworks and particular test cases. Papers, in other words, often begin by presenting *anomalies*.

I encourage students to write opening paragraphs that attempt to elucidate such anomalies by:

1. Stating the specific point of departure: are they taking issue with a bit of conventional wisdom? Popular opinions? A theoretical perspective? This provides the context in which a student is able to "frame" a particular problem, issue, and so forth.

2. Explaining why the wisdom/opinion/theory has become problematic or controversial by focusing on a particular issue, event, test case, or empirical evidence.

3. Formulating a brief statement of the tentative thesis/position to be pursued in the paper. This can take several forms, including the revising of conventional wisdom/theory/opinion, discarding it in favor of alternative conceptions, or calling for redefinition of an issue and question.

—JACK GAMBINO, PROFESSOR OF POLITICAL SCIENCE

In the following Voice from Across the Curriculum, Political Science Professor, Chris Borick, explains effective and less effective ways of stating research questions and hypotheses in the introduction.

VOICES FROM ACROSS THE CURRICULUM

Framing Research Questions and Hypotheses: A Political Science Professor Speaks

Different fields within Political Science—legal writing, political theory, political policy, and behavior—prescribe different forms of writing. Political policy and political behavior papers adhere to a version of the format used in science writing. This format has six parts: statement of the research question, literature review (context), statement of hypothesis, measurement of variables, description of tests, and analysis of findings. The literature review describes the conversation that is going on in the field on the paper's topic. It explains what others know. The research question tells readers what the writer is trying to do. The hypothesis states a claim that is specific enough to test.

The research question sets up the hypothesis; it is the point from which everything flows. Consider the following two versions of a research question on capital punishment. 1) In this study I seek to examine the capital punishment laws used at the state level. 2) In this study I seek to explain why some states adopt capital punishment and others do not. The second version is clearly better. It gives much better direction.

The hypothesis needs to indicate some direction for the research. Although general in scope, it must be specific enough to test. Here again are two examples. Which do you think would make the better hypothesis? 1) The greater the percentage of college educated individuals in a state, the more likely that state will be to allow same sex marriage. 2) The more educated a society, the more liberal it will be.

—CHRIS BORICK, PROFESSOR OF POLITICAL SCIENCE

Writing Introductions in the Sciences

In the following Voices from Across the Curriculum, Biochemistry Professor, Keri Colabroy, and Psychology Professors, Laura Edelman and Mark Sciutto, address the challenges of introducing and contextualizing research in science writing.

VOICES FROM ACROSS THE CURRICULUM

Introductions in the Sciences: Three Professors Speak

In scientific papers, introductions serve two purposes:

1. to orient your readers to the scientific context of your work while showing them the inherent need for new (your) information to solve an *uncertainty* or *problem*, something you or the community doesn't quite understand. (In *Writing Analytically*, the prompts "interesting, significant, or strange" focus writers on problems and areas of uncertainty.)

2. to state succinctly what the paper/study has accomplished and what that means for the big picture you outlined in point #1 .

The introduction of a scientific paper is full of references to primary literature (other scientific papers). In most undergraduate science courses, students are not asked to write the introduction section. Instead, the professor provides a paraphrase of the question/problem that the experiment is meant to solve.

—KERI COLABROY, PROFESSOR OF BIOCHEMISTRY

The introduction is one of the hardest sections to write. In the introduction, students must summarize, analyze, and integrate the work of numerous other authors and use that to build their own argument.

The task is to read each article and *summarize* it in their own words. The key is to analyze rather than just repeat material from the articles so as to make clear the connections among them. (It is important to note that experimental psychologists almost never use direct quotes in their writing. Many of my students have been trained to use direct quotation for their other classes, and so I have to spend time explaining how to summarize without directly quoting or plagiarizing the work that they have read.)

Finally, in the introduction the students must show explicitly how the articles they have summarized lead to the hypothesis they have devised. Many times the students see the connection as implicitly obvious, but I require that they explicitly state the relationships between what they read and what they plan to do.

—LAURA EDELMAN, PROFESSOR OF PSYCHOLOGY

The format of the empirical paper in Psychology resembles an hour glass. It starts reasonably broad, narrows, and then broadens again to the larger perspective: "Now that we know this, where can we go with it? What are the implications?" The introduction is especially difficult to write because it must contextualize the new research by pulling together a lot of reading from a variety of sources. This part of the introduction, the literature review, answers the question, "What do we know?"

In order to efficiently locate the new study in the context of others' work on the subject, writers must **integrate** citations. Rather than summarize what Johnson found and then what Smith found and then what Moore found, the writer needs to bring these together into a more concise summary. All three studies might be summarized and cited in one paragraph or even a single sentence. As a rule of thumb, citations should include more than one source. Single citations don't allow enough integration.

—MARK SCIUTTO, PROFESSOR OF PSYCHOLOGY

Integration of Citations in a Literature Review: A Brief Example

Note that in the following paragraph from a 1999 article in *Personality and Social Psychology Bulletin* the citations (in parentheses) include more than one study:

Self-presentational motives play a role in a variety of potentially dangerous health-related behaviors, including behaviors that lead to risk of HIV infection; accidental death and injury; and alcohol, tobacco, and drug use (Leary, Tchividjian, & Kraxberger, 1994; Martin, Leary, & Rejeski, in press). The desire to be perceived as a risk-taker, brave, or one of the crowd (or conversely, concerns about being viewed as overly cautious or neurotic) may lead people to take chances with their health to create the desired image. (Denscombe, 1993; Finney, 1978)

Introductions in Scientific Papers: A Brief Example

The following example comes from a set of excerpted introductions that Biochemistry Professor, Keri Colabroy, uses to teach her students how to write concise, focused sentences of two types: Type #1: sentences that orient readers to the scientific context of a new study while also showing the need for it, and Type #2: sentences that succinctly state what the paper/study has accomplished. The sentences come from a paper published in *Nature Chemical Biology* 2006.

> #1 Although the antitumor activity of these two compounds has been shown to involve binding to microtubules, the targets and modes of actions for many other bioactive cyanobacterial metabolites remain elusive.

Dr. Colabroy comments: *This is a great sentence. You can see the tension. Some activity has been shown, but there is still something we don't understand . . .and that is the problem this paper will solve.*

> #2 Here we examine the mode of action of apratoxin A using a number of approaches based on functional genomics, including mRNA expression analysis and genome-wise, arrayed cDNA overexpression. These and other studies suggest that apratoxin A acts in part by blocking the FGFR signaling pathway.

Dr. Colabroy comments: *The use of "here" focuses your attention on the action that immediately follows—"we examine." That is different from "we found" or "we propose," and it implies that the authors didn't really have a hypothesis going in. They were just trying to learn some stuff, and in the process, they came up with some "implications" from the data.*

Writing Conclusions in the Sciences: The Discussion Section

As is the case with introductions, the conclusions of reports written in the natural sciences and psychology are regulated by formalized disciplinary formats. Conclusions, for example, occur in a section entitled "Discussion." There the writer analyzes conclusions and qualifies them in relation to some larger experimental context, "the big picture."

First specific results are interpreted (but not restated), and then their implications and limitations are discussed. At the end, the writer should rephrase the original research question and discuss it in light of the results presented. It is at this point that alternative explanations may be considered and new questions may be posed.

In the following Voices from Across the Curriculum, a Psychology Professor and a Biochemistry Professor explain how the Discussion section of a scientific paper locates its conclusions in the context of other research—that which came before and that which will follow.

VOICES FROM ACROSS THE CURRICULUM

Writing Conclusions in the Sciences: Two Professors Speak

The conclusion occurs in a section labeled "Discussion" and, as specified by the *Publication Manual of the American Psychological Association*, is guided by the following questions:

> What have I contributed here?
> How has my study helped to resolve the original problem?
> What conclusions and theoretical implications can I draw from my study?

In a broad sense, a particular research report should be seen as but one moment in a broader research tradition that *preceded* the particular study being written about and that will *continue after* this study is published. And so the conclusion should tie this particular study into both previous research considering implications for the theory guiding this study and (when applicable) practical implications of this study. One of the great challenges of writing a research report is thus to place this particular study within that broader research tradition. That's an analytical task.

—ALAN TJELTVEIT, PROFESSOR OF PSYCHOLOGY

The Discussion section is where the scientist finally gets to analyze the data. The previous two sections of a science paper—Methods and Results—report rather than analyze. The discussion section is not a summary; rather, the writer makes qualified claims and backs them up with evidence (data). Analysis of the data tells readers what the study found in the context of current knowledge in the field and the researcher's expectations. The discussion section completes the frame set up by the introduction by arguing for the significance of the study within its scientific context.

The paper's conclusions, which usually appear in the last paragraph of the Discussion, always look back and then forward—first back to previous research and then forward to remaining questions. The conclusion explains how questions have been answered and how knowledge in the field might be changed because of the new information.

—KERI COLABROY, PROFESSOR OF BIOCHEMISTRY

Conclusions in Scientific Papers: A Brief Example

The following example is part of the discussion/conclusion section of a scientific paper.

As you read this sample Discussion/Conclusion section of a scientific paper, refer back to Dr. Colabroy's preceding comments.

The rapid and sustained elevations in 2-AG induced by JZL 184 were accompanied by an array of CB1-dependent behavioral effects, including analgesia, hypomotility, and hypothermia. This collection of phenotypes qualitatively resembles those induced by direct CB1 agonists. Overall these data suggest that MAGL-regulated 2-AG pathways endogenously modulate several behavioral processes classically associated with the pharmacology of cannabinoids . . .

In summary, we believe that the properties of JZL184 warrant inclusion of this compound among the growing arsenal of efficacious and selective pharmacological probes used to examine the endocannabinoid system. JZL184 could itself serve as a lead scaffold for the development of such dual inhibitors, given that at high concentrations this compound inhibited both MAGL and FAAH without affecting other brain serine hydrolases.

Ethos and Style in Scientific Writing: A Biochemistry Professor Speaks

Word choice in scientific papers—especially the choice of verbs—is important. Scientific writing never "proves," for example. It "implies" and "indicates." The science writer chooses verbs to make carefully qualified claims based on an accumulation of evidence.

Scientific writing is corporate, by which I mean that scientific writers speak to and about the community of other science writers. To name a particular scientist is considered pretentious. It is appropriate to point out inconsistencies in thinking as in, "a lot of work has been done here, but we still don't understand X." It is not considered appropriate to locate shortcomings in the work of particular scientists.

—KERI COLABROY, PROFESSOR OF BIOCHEMISTRY

The Idea of the Paragraph

Throughout this section of the chapter, we will focus on what are sometimes called "body" paragraphs, as opposed to the more special-function paragraphs that serve as the beginnings and ends of papers.

It is useful to think of any piece of writing as consisting of parts or blocks. The paragraph is a fundamental building block, bigger than the sentence, smaller than the section or paper. Paragraphs can be thought of by analogy with the paper. Like papers, paragraphs have parts: they make opening gambits, they put forward evidence and analyze it, and they arrive at some kind of summarizing or culminating closure. They have, in short, a beginning, a middle, and an end. But unlike the paper, the paragraph does not stand alone as an independent entity. For a paragraph to be effective, readers need to be able to understand its role in unfolding the thinking of the paper as a whole.

The two primary characteristics of virtually all strong paragraphs are unity and development.

- **unity:** all the sentences in the paragraph should be related to some central idea or focus. Normally, the sentence that serves this function in the paragraph is the topic sentence.

- **development:** the sentences in a paragraph need to connect to each other in some way; a paragraph needs to go somewhere, to build. Normally, the sentences in a paragraph either offer a series of observations about the main idea or build one upon the next to offer a more sustained analysis of one element of the main idea.

Notice that we don't say here that a paragraph offers a claim plus examples and reasons. This model of the paragraph is true in some cases, but paragraphs typically do more than make simple claims and then back them up with one or more examples.

Once you begin paying attention to paragraphs, you will see that they are far less uniform in their shapes and procedures than you may have been taught to believe. The paragraph police will not haul you away for producing a paragraph that lacks a topic sentence, or places it at the end of the paragraph instead of the front, or contains several claims instead of one, or delays the substantiating evidence till later. Nonetheless, most of the paragraphs you encounter—and most that you should write—have unity and development. They are about one thing, and they tell you why it is important.

How Long?: Paragraphs, Readers, and Writers

Paragraphing is a kindness to your reader, since it divides your thinking into manageable bites. If you find a paragraph growing longer than half a page—particularly if it is your opening or second paragraph—find a place to make a paragraph break. More frequent paragraphing provides readers with convenient resting points from which to relaunch themselves into your thinking. In addition, paragraph indentations allow readers to scan essays, searching for connecting words and important ideas.

Long paragraphs are daunting for both readers and writers. When writers try to do too much in a single paragraph, they often lose the focus and lose contact with the larger purpose or point that got them into the paragraph in the first place. Remember that old rule about one idea to a paragraph? Well, it's not a bad rule, though it isn't exactly right because sometimes you need more space than a single paragraph can provide to lay out a complicated phase of your overall argument. In that case, just break wherever it seems reasonable to do so in order to keep your paragraphs from becoming ungainly. Two paragraphs can be about the same thing, the first half and then the second half. This paragraph, for example, might have been easier to process if we had broken it right before the question about that old rule.

A short paragraph will always provide emphasis, for which most readers will thank you.

Paragraphs are a relief not just for your readers: they also give the writer a break. When you draft, start a new paragraph whenever you feel yourself getting stuck: it's the promise of a fresh start. Paragraph breaks are like turning a corner to a new view, even when the thinking is continuous. They also force the writer to make transitions, overt connections among the parts of his or her thinking, and to state or restate key ideas.

It can be extraordinarily useful to draft a paper in phases, as a series of paragraphs:

- Break up the larger interpretation or argument into more manageable pieces.

- Give yourself space to think in short sections that you can then sequence.

- Clean up your thinking in revision by dividing its sections or phases into paragraphs.

Paragraphs need to justify their existence. A paragraph break should remind you to check that you have suggested to the readers why they need to know this information. Ask yourself why you are telling them what you are telling them. How does the thinking in the paragraph relate to the overall idea that your paper is developing? A good way to check if your paragraph is really advancing your claims is to ASK and answer "SO WHAT?" at the end of the paragraph.

Paragraphs Across the Curriculum: Some Common Patterns

The simplest way of thinking about paragraph organization draws on a slightly extended version of what are known as the traditional rhetorical modes: Exemplification, Narration, Description, Process, Comparison/Contrast, Classification/Division, Definition, Cause/Effect, Problem/Solution, and, of course, Analysis.

You have been studying the characteristic shape of analytical thinking throughout this book. It consists of seeing the parts of something in relation to the whole. In practice, this means finding a significant pattern of detail and explaining what this pattern reveals about the nature and purpose of whatever it is you are studying. The practice we call 10 ON 1 (see Chapter 4) is typical of analytical paragraphs. It consists of close scrutiny of a single representative example wherein the writer notices as much as possible about the example and then interprets his or her observations by ASKING and answering the question "SO WHAT?"

Because analysis typically focuses on relationships among the parts and between those parts and the whole, classification and division are well-suited to analytical writing. In the organizational pattern called division, the writer breaks a subject into its component parts. Classification explains how the parts relate to each other by putting them into categories. In practice, classification and division tend to occur together, often in conjunction with definition. When we define something, we locate its defining traits, the features that make it what it is.

Although most paragraphs employ a mix of these modes of organization, the patterns are usually easy to see. For purposes of illustration, we will focus on narrative organization. A surprising amount of writing in the disciplines is **narrative**, which is to say that writers often find themselves needing to explain sequences of action (as in the methods and results sections of a scientific paper or lab report) or events or behaviors or ideas. Notice, for example, how profoundly narrative the writing is in the following excerpt from a lab report.

A set of electrophilic aromatic substitution reactions was performed using two monosubstituted benzenes so as to describe substitution patterns as a function of substrate. Samples of toluene and ethylbenzene each underwent a nitration via a 1:1 mixture of sulfuric and nitric acid. The acid mixture formed a strongly electrophilic nitronium ion which attacked the monosubstituted benzene ring and replaced a proton. Upon mixing the reagents, both nitration reactions turned yellow. The toluene reaction darkened somewhat over the reaction period, while the ethylbenzene reaction turned brown. The color change is evidence of a reaction occurring. The products of each reaction were isolated via a liquid extraction with MTBE and dried. The isolated products were analyzed via GC–MS (gas chromatography – mass spectroscopy), which separates compounds based on their volatility. This was used to both identify the products and determine their respective ratios.

A good piece of writing—at the level of the paragraph as well as at the level of the paper as a whole—tells a story. It explains how and why the writer came to focus on an issue or question or problem. It also narrates for readers how the writer came to understand the meaning and significance of his or her evidence.

Linking the Sentences in Paragraphs: Minding the Gaps

It helps to think of the space between the period at the end of a sentence and the beginning of the next sentence as a gap that the reader has to cross. Start thinking in this way as you follow the train of thought in this paragraph and those that follow it. Keep asking yourself: what is the connection between each sentence and the one that follows it? What keeps the reader from falling out of the paper at the gaps between sentences, losing sight of the thought connections that make a paragraph more than just a collection of sentences?

In many paragraphs, the connections between and among sentences are made apparent by the repetition of **key words**. This idea of key words brings us back to a core principle of this book: that both writers and readers make meaning by locating significant patterns of repetition and contrast. What is the pattern of repeated words in the paragraph above this one, for example? Notice the repetition of the key word "gap," which goes with the idea of falling and which is in opposition to such words as "connection" and "train of thought." The other connecting feature of the paragraph comes with its repeated use of questions. The paragraph you are now reading gets its sense of purpose from the previous paragraph's questions. Here we start answering them.

Sometimes (but not always) the connecting logic that helps readers negotiate the gaps between sentences must be made explicit. So, for example, some sentences begin with the words, "So, for example." The function of this type of connection is illustration. Some other words that operate in this gap-bridging way are "thus," "furthermore," "in addition," "similarly," "in other words," and "on the contrary."

When the organizing principle of a paragraph is sufficiently evident, explicit transitional words are often not needed. If parallelism is the paragraph's organizing principle, for example, readers will be able to see the relationship among the paragraph's sentences without a lot of repetition of connecting words.

What a Paragraph Does: The Paragraph as Movement of Mind

The key to understanding how to write paragraphs, as well as how to analyze what you read in them, is to focus on what the various sentences in a paragraph *do*. To follow what a paragraph does is to follow its succession of sentences as a movement of mind, an unfolding of consciousness on the page that conveys to readers the relationships among its various pieces of information.

The sentences in a paragraph have different jobs; there is a distribution of labor. To see this element of paragraphing, it is essential that you "look beyond content": that is, that you focus on what the sentences are doing, not just on what they are saying. In Chapter 4, Reasoning from Evidence to Claims, we asked you to distinguish which sentences in a paragraph were evidence and which were claims, and to mark these with an E or a C. Those are two functions of sentences in paragraphs—two tasks that sentences in a paragraph can perform.

Paragraph Structure #1: Topic Sentence, Restriction, Illustration   One model for thinking about paragraph structure comes from the rhetorician Alton Becker: Topic sentence (T), Restriction (R), and Illustration (I). The topic sentence states some kind of claim—an idea that the paragraph will develop in some way. This may or may not appear as the first sentence of the paragraph, and there may be more than one claim in the paragraph, although one of these is usually primary. Restriction limits the claim in some way. Illustration supplies examples in support of the claim.

The TRI model does not cover everything that goes on in various kinds of paragraphs, but it is a good way to start looking at paragraphs in order to begin thinking about what the sentences do. Here is a somewhat expanded list of jobs that sentences may do inside paragraphs.

WHAT SENTENCES DO INSIDE PARAGRAPHS

T = topic sentence -> announces the main idea of the paragraph

R = restriction -> qualifies, further defines, limits claims; happens at various points in the paragraph

P = paraphrasing -> restates claims and evidence to analyze them

I = illustration -> provides substantiating evidence

EXP = explains the illustrations -> draws out meaning of evidence

Th = thesis restatement -> offers versions of an evolving thesis

Tr = transitional wording -> links sentences, connects ideas inside paragraph but also connects paragraph to what precedes and follows it

SW= answers "so what?" -> tells readers the purpose of the paragraph, why the writer bothered to tell them this

Let's look at a paragraph to see what some of the sentences are doing. We have labeled some of the sentences (in square brackets) according to our expanded version of Becker's marking scheme.

[T:] Armin Schnider, a neurologist from the Cantonal University Hospital in Geneva, Switzerland, says that the vast majority of confabulations he has heard from his patients over the years relate directly to their earlier lives. **[I:]** One of his patients, a retired dentist, worried while in hospital that he was keeping his patients waiting. **[I:]** Another, an elderly woman, talked regularly about her baby in the present tense. **[EXP:]** Most of these patients had damage to the temporal lobes of the brain, particularly the memory regions of the hippocampus, so it seemed likely that they had somehow lost the ability to make new memories and were retrieving old ones instead. **[EXP:]** The intriguing thing was that they didn't realise these memories were old—they seemed convinced by their stories, and sometimes even acted on them. **[SW:]** So Schnider decided to study their memory in more detail. (Helen Phillips, "Everyday Fairytales," *New Scientist*, 7 October 2006)

TRY THIS 9.2: Label the Function of the Sentences in a Paragraph

One of the best ways to understand how paragraphs work—to apprehend them as tools of thought and to be able to deploy them to work for you—is to assign the abbreviations from page 255 to any paragraph in anything you have written or read, including this book.

Paragraph Structure #2: Observation -> Implication -> Conclusion One of the models described in this book for the analytical movement of mind is as follows: *Observation ->* SO WHAT? *-> implication ->* SO WHAT? *-> tentative conclusions.* This sequence goes beyond the simplest kind of paragraph development— idea + illustration—because it contains more of the writer's thinking on how he or she reasons to the claim from evidence. Explicitly drawing out the implications of evidence complicates, but also more accurately represents the process of thinking, than does simply attaching examples to the idea they support. Not all paragraphs in an analytical paper move in this way, but a significant number of them do. We reprint the following paragraph from Chapter One, adding annotations about what the paragraph does.

[Paragraph opens with empirical observation:] If you look closely at Camilo Vergara's photo of Fern Street, Camden, 1988, you'll notice a sign on the side of a dilapidated building that reads "Danger: Men Working - W. Hargrove Demolition."

[Implication:] Perhaps that warning captures the ominous atmosphere of these very different kinds of photographic documents by Camilo Vergara and Edward Burtynsky: "Danger: Men Working." Watch out—human beings are at work! **[Topic sentence:]** But the work that is presented is not so much a building-up as it is a tearing-down— the work of demolition. **[Qualification of claim:]** Of course, demolition is often necessary in order to construct anew: old buildings are leveled for new projects, whether you are building a highway or bridge in an American city or a dam in the Chinese countryside.

[Paraphrasing—interpretive restatement:] You might call modernity itself, as so many have, a process of creative destruction, a term used variously to describe modern art, capitalism, and technological innovation. **[Topic sentence:]** The photographs in this exhibit, however, force us to pay attention to the "destructive" side of this modern equation. **[Writer asks so what? and concludes:]** What both Burtynsky and Vergara do in their respective ways is to put up a warning sign—they question whether the reworking of our natural and social environment leads to a sustainable human future. **[Restatement]:** And they wonder whether the process of creative destruction may not have spun recklessly out of control, producing places that are neither habitable nor sustainable. **[Supporting observation:]** In fact, a common element connecting the two photographic versions is the near absence of people in the landscape. **[Observation:]** While we see the evidence of the transforming power of human production on the physical and social environment, neither Vergara's urban ruins nor Burtynsky's industrial sites actually show us "men working." **[Observation:]** Isolated figures peer suspiciously out back doors or pick through the rubble, but they appear out of place. **[Writer asks so what? and concludes in reference to the paragraph's opening observation]:** It is this sense of displacement—of human beings alienated from the environments they themselves have created—that provides the most haunting aspect of the work of these two photographers. (Jack Gambino, "Demolition Zones: Contemporary Photography by Edward Burtynsky and Camilo Jose Vergara")

Paragraph Structure #3: Coordinate and Subordinate Paragraphs Here is a third way of thinking about how paragraphs develop. In his influential essay, "A Generative Rhetoric of the Paragraph," Francis Christensen defines the topic sentence as "the one the other sentences depend from, the one they develop or amplify, the one they are a comment on" (*Notes Toward a New Rhetoric*, 1967, page 80). Christensen posits two kinds of paragraphs, coordinate and subordinate. In coordinate structures, all of the sentences following the topic sentence are equal in weight, or as he puts it, "all children of the same mother" (61).

Consider the following example of a (primarily) coordinate paragraph, taken from earlier in this chapter. Most of the sentences relate back to the topic sentence in some way. A number 1 indicates that the sentence is coordinate with the topic sentence, operating on the same level of importance and repeatedly clarifying the topic sentence. The number 2 indicates that the sentence is a subordinate structure, which will be explained below.

[T:] Paragraphs are a relief not just for your readers: they also give the writer a break.

1 When you draft, start a new paragraph whenever you feel yourself getting stuck: it's the promise of a fresh start.
1 Paragraph breaks are like turning a corner to a new view, even when the thinking is continuous.

1 They also force the writer to make transitions, overt connections among the parts of his or her thinking, and to state or restate key ideas.
1 Paragraph indentations allow readers to scan essays, searching for connecting words and important ideas.

The paragraph above best fits the pattern that Christensen calls coordinate because all of the sentences that come after the topic sentence "develop or amplify" it. Each offers reasons for thinking that paragraphs are a relief not just for readers but also for writers.

In what Christensen identifies as subordinate structures, each sentence clarifies or comments on the one before it, as for example in this short sequence that he cites:

1 The process of learning is essential to our lives.
  2 All higher animals seek it deliberately.
    3 They are inquisitive and they experiment.
      4 An experiment is a sort of harmless trial run... (60).

Note how each sentence generates the one that follows it, rather than primarily relating back to the topic sentence.

Here is another example of a subordinate paragraph to contemplate:

1 Another startling conclusion from the science of consciousness is that the intuitive feeling we have that there's another executive "I" that sits in a control room of our brain, scanning the screens of the senses and pushing the buttons of the muscles, is an illusion.
  2 Consciousness turns out to consist of a maelstrom of events distributed across the brain.
    3 These events compete for attention, and as one process outshouts the others, the brain rationalizes the outcome after the fact and concocts the impression that a single self was in charge all along. (Steven Pinker, "The Mystery of Consciousness," *Time*, January 19, 2007)

It is less important to be able to accurately and precisely locate each sentence in a paragraph as coordinate or subordinate than it is to begin to recognize that most paragraphs are some kind of mix of these two thought patterns. In practice, as Christensen observes, most paragraphs combine coordinate and subordinate sequences, although one of the two structures often predominates.

You do not need to ponder these relationships each time you write a new sentence in a paragraph, but, when you find yourself getting stuck in your writing, you can help yourself move forward by thinking about which sentence in the paragraph is the actual generator (or jumping off point) for the next one.

TRY THIS 9.3: Identify the Structure of a Paragraph

Take the paragraph below and apply the terms offered in this chapter (especially from page 255) to describe what various sentences do. Look for coordinate versus subordinate structures, but more specifically, label the mental moves performed by individual sentences. We have numbered the sentences to make the paragraph easier to work with.

1. White might not have succeeded in completely ridding his life of modern civilization, but Strunk's manual in White's hands became a successful *primitivist* tract.

2. Perhaps that seems like an overstatement, but in fact what counts as primitivist is flexible, Marianna Torgovnick reminded us, entirely dependent on what bugs one about the modern.

3. The key feature of primitivism, Torgovnick offered, is defining the primitive in reaction to the present: "Is the present too majestic? Primitive life is not—it is a precapitalist utopia in which only use value, never exchange value, prevails. Is the present sexually repressed? Not primitive life—primitives live life whole, without fear of the body" (8).

4. For Strunk and White, modern life was verbose and obscure, so primitive life must be brief, direct, and clear.

5. New things are bad things, new words the worst of all.

6. The words *offputting* and *ongoing* appear in the third and subsequent editions of *The Elements of Style* as "newfound adjectives, to be avoided because they are inexact and clumsy" (*Third Edition* 54).

7. The suffix *oriented* is lambasted as "a clumsy, pretentious device, much in vogue" (*Third Edition* 55).

8. *The Elements of Style* thus had become, over a period of nearly unprecedented technological progress, the perfect complement to the manual typewriter—a deliberate rejection of "books with permissive steering and automatic transitions" that made our lives easier but rendered our prose impotent and our character lax (xvi).

9. For impotence and laxity, *The Elements of Style* offers a program of stylistic and moral restitution, word by word.

(Catherine Prendergast, "The Fighting Style: Reading the Unabomber's Strunk and White," *College English*, Volume 72, No 1, September 2009)

The Shaping Force of Transitions

The linkage between where you've been and where you're going is usually a point in your writing at which thinking is taking place. This is especially the case in the evolving rather than the static model of thesis development, in which the writer continually *updates* the thesis as it moves through evidence.

- Thinking tends to occur at points of transition.

- A good transition articulates a paper's logical links—how each phase of the paper leads to the next.

- Too many additive transitions ("also," "another example of") produce papers that list, an overly loose form of organization

It is useful to think of transitions as *directional indicators*, especially at the beginnings of paragraphs but also within them. "And," for example, is a plus sign. It indicates that the writer will add something, continuing in the same direction. The words "but," "yet," "nevertheless," and "however" are among the many transitional words that alert readers to changes in the direction of the writer's thinking. They might indicate the introduction of a qualification, or a potentially contradictory piece of evidence, or an alternative point of view.

Some additive transitions do more work than "also" or "another." The word "moreover" is an additive transition, but it adds emphasis to the added point. The transitional sequence "not only . . . but also" restates and then adds information in a way that clarifies what has gone before.

Too many additive transitions can pose a problem for your writing. A list is a slack form of organization, one that fails to identify how this is related to that. Although transitional wording such as "another example of" or "also" at the beginning of paragraphs does tell readers that a related point or example will follow, it does not specify that relationship beyond piling on another "and." Essentially, these words just list.

If you find yourself relying on "another" and "also" at points of transition, force yourself to substitute other transitional wording that indicates more precisely the nature of the relationship with what has gone before in the paper. Language such as "similarly" and "by contrast" can sometimes serve this purpose. Often some restatement is called for to keep your reader on track—brief repetition is not necessarily redundant. A good transition reaches backward, telling where you've been, as the grounds for making a subsequent move forward.

The first step toward improving your use of transitions (and thereby, the organization of your writing) is to become conscious of them. If you notice that you are beginning successive paragraphs with "Another reason," for example, you can probably conclude that you are listing rather than developing your ideas. If you notice a number of sentences that start with the vague referent "This," you probably need to name the thing "This" refers to.

Think of transitions as echoes in the service of continuity. If you study the transitions in a piece, you will usually find that they echo either the language or the ideas of something that precedes them as they point to what is ahead.

TRY THIS 9.4: Tracking Transitions

Track the transitions in a piece of writing. Take a few pages of something you are reading (such as a short article) and circle or underline all of the directional indicators (transitions). Remember to check not only the beginnings of paragraphs but within them. Then, survey your markings. What do you notice now about the shape of the piece? This exercise is also useful for expanding your repertoire of transitional words to use in your own writing.

Assignments: From Paragraphs to Papers: Forms and Formats Across the Curriculum

1. **Infer the Format of a Published Article.** Often the format governing the organization of a published piece is not immediately evident. That is, it is not subdivided according to conventional disciplinary categories that are obeyed by all members of a given discourse community. Especially if you are studying a discipline in which the writing does not follow an explicitly prescribed format, such as history, literature, or economics, you may find it illuminating to examine representative articles or essays in that discipline, looking for an implicit format. You can usually discern some underlying pattern of organization: the formal conventions, the rules that are being followed, even when these are not highlighted.

   The following assignment works well whether you tackle it individually or in a group. It can lead to a paper, an oral report, or both. First, you need to assemble several articles from the same or a similar kind of journal or magazine. "Journal" is the name given to publications aimed at specialized, usually scholarly, audiences, as opposed to general or popular audiences. *Time, Newsweek,* and *The New Yorker* are called "magazines" rather than "journals" because they are aimed at a broader general audience. *Shakespeare Quarterly* is a journal; *Psychology Today* is a magazine.

   Having found at least three journal or magazine articles, study them in order to focus on the following question: *Insofar as there appears to be a format that articles in this journal adhere to, what are its parts?*

   How, for example, does an article in this journal or magazine typically begin and end? Does there seem to be a relatively uniform place in which these articles include opposing arguments? You will, in other words, be analyzing the articles inductively (reasoning from particular details to general principles). Begin with the product and reason backward to the skeleton beneath the skin.

   If you choose to work with a magazine rather than single articles, you should narrow your focus. You might focus on *Time* cover stories, on *The New Yorker*'s "Talk of the Town" or another such recurring feature. Even gossip columns and letters of advice to the lovelorn in teen magazines adhere to certain visible, though not explicitly marked, formats.

Write up your results. Cite particular language from at least two articles in support of your claims about the implicit format.

2. **Analyzing Introductions.** One of the best ways to learn about introductions is to gather some sample introductory paragraphs and, working on your own or in a small group, figure out how each one works, what it accomplishes.

Here are some particular questions you might pose:

- Why does the writer start in this way—what is accomplished?
- What kind of relationship does this opening establish with the audience and to what ends?
- How does the writer let readers know why the writing they are about to read is called for, useful, and necessary?
- Where and by what logic does the introduction funnel?

3. **Introductions and Audience.** Compare and contrast introductory paragraphs from a popular magazine with those from an academic journal aimed at a more specialized audience. Select one of each and analyze them to determine what each author assumes the audience knows. Where in each paragraph are these assumptions most evident? If you write out your analysis, it should probably take about a page, but this exercise can also be done productively with others in a small group.

4. **Analyzing Conclusions.** Find some examples of concluding paragraphs from published writing. First, compare the conclusion with the introduction, looking for the way the conclusion comes full circle. Which elements of the introduction are repeated to accomplish this? Then look for the statement of the essay's thesis in its final, culminating form. Finally, locate the send-off by finding implications and limitations that the writer has noted as part of his or her final "So what?" On the basis of your findings, write a few paragraphs in which you describe the writer's approach to conclusions.

At this point you will be ready to repeat this exercise with some of your own work. Only this time, rather than describing the writer's approach, write an improved version of one of your conclusions based on what you learned from your analysis.

CHAPTER 10

Style: Choosing Words, Shaping Sentences

Overview This chapter on style seeks to make you more conscious of the kinds of words and sentences you use and to expand your range of options. In the book's final chapter we will move from stylistic questions—a matter of choice—to common grammatical errors—a matter of correct versus incorrect forms. In this chapter, we'll be asking you to think rhetorically, that is, in terms of appropriate choices for particular contexts rather than right versus wrong.

A writer who is practiced at different ways of putting sentences together is a writer in touch with the key concept of sentence style, that there is a powerful link between the shape of a sentence and the shape of a thought. A sentence is the shape that thought takes. In order to enhance your awareness of sentence shapes, start analyzing sentences as you read. Keep an eye out for sentences you think are good rather than looking for things that are wrong, as school grammar exercises too often ask us to do. The chapter will provide you with the vocabulary and observation skills you need in order to figure out what makes a sentence good and what causes it to create the effects that it does.

Seeing Style as Inseparable From Meaning

Broadly defined, **style** refers to all of a writer's decisions in selecting, arranging, and expressing what he or she has to say. Getting the style right is not as simple as proofreading your paper in the late stages of drafting, looking for errors in grammar and punctuation. Whereas proofreading occupies the relatively comfortable linguistic world of simple right and wrong, stylistic considerations take place in the more exploratory terrain of making choices among more and less effective ways of formulating and communicating your meaning.

Many people mistakenly assume that style is separate from meaning. From this perspective, paying close attention to style seems finicky, or worse, cynical—a way of dressing up the content to sell it to readers or listeners. The problem with this view is that it subscribes to what we have earlier referred to as *the transparent theory of language.* This theory tries to locate meaning outside of language. It suggests that we somehow see *through* words to meaning and can then address that meaning without addressing the words that embody it. In the transparent theory of language, words are merely pointers to get past to meanings that exist somewhere underneath or beyond them.

Yet style is not a mask you don or a way of icing the cake. Attending to style is more like sculpting. As a sculptor uses a chisel to "bring out" a shape from a block of walnut or marble, a writer uses style to bring out the shape of the conceptual connections in a draft of an essay. This bringing out demands a certain detachment from your own language. It requires that you become aware of your words as words and of your sentences as sentences. You have to look *at* them—as opposed to through them.

If stylistic considerations are not merely cosmetic, then it follows that rethinking the way you have said something can lead you to rethink the substance of what you have said. The decisions you make about how to phrase your meaning inevitably exert a powerful influence on the meaning you make.

Is style a function of character and personality? Is it, in short, personal, and thus something to be preserved in the face of would-be meddlers carrying style manuals and grammar guides? Well, as you might guess at this point in the book, the answer is yes and no. We all need to find our own ways of using words so that they don't succumb to the mind-numbing environment of verbal cliché in which we dwell. Through becoming more self-conscious about style we more easily recognize that it is not inborn. Staying locked into one way of writing because that is "your style" is as limiting as remaining locked into only one way of thinking. Studying and imitating other people's sentences will not, by the way, erase your style. It will instead extend its range.

About Prescriptive Style Manuals: A Word of Warning

The key idea of this chapter is that there are not necessarily right and wrong choices when it comes to sentence style but better and best choices for particular situations. The from-the-hip plain style of a memo or a set of operating instructions for your lawn mower are very likely not the best style choices for a good-bye letter to a best friend, a diplomatic talk on a sensitive political situation, or an analysis of guitar styles in contemporary jazz. Rather than relying on a single set of rules for distinguishing good style from bad, a writer needs to be thinking about how his or her words and arrangement of words are suited to his or her subject matter and audience.

You may have been taught some or all of the following: that you should always avoid the first-person "I" in academic writing, steer clear of jargon, and never start a sentence with *and* or *but*. There are occasions when these rules apply, but there are also many occasions when they don't. Such rules are matters of usage—socially determined conventions—rather than hard-and-fast rules of grammar. All writing is *contextual*. The primary rule is that you should adapt your style to the demands of different rhetorical situations.

Although style manuals and handbooks can be very useful when they illuminate the range of choices a writer has and the implications of those choices, most style manuals value one style and tone over others and tend to present this style as self-evidently good and right. Despite Strunk & White's rule (in their famous book, *Elements of Style*), three words are not better than six in every rhetorical situation. And, their edict against it notwithstanding, passive voice has its place, its own special advantages; active voice is not always better. The key to growing as a stylist is learning to see the choices.

In his essay, "Style and Good Style," philosophy professor Monroe Beardsley takes this point one step further. He writes: "Many charming, clever, and memorable things have been said about style—most of which turn out to be highly misleading when subjected to analysis"(4). Changes in style, says Beardsley, always produce changes in meaning: "If the teacher advises a change of words, or of word order, he is recommending a different meaning" (13). ["Style and Good Style" from *Reflections on High School English: NDEA Institute Lectures 1965*, ed. Gary Tate, University of Tulsa 1966 as reprinted in *Contemporary Essays on Style* by Glen A. Love and Michael Payne, Scott, Foresman and Company 1969]

Here is one of the examples Beardsley offers in response to the common stylistic advice that writers should replace forms of "to be" with active verbs. He cites as an example from Strunk and White the suggestion that the sentence "There were a great number of dead leaves lying on the ground" be replaced with the sentence "Dead leaves covered the ground." Of this suggested change Beardsley observes, "But isn't that a difference in meaning? For one thing, there are more leaves in the second sentence. The second one says that the ground was covered; the first one only speaks of a great number. Stylistic advice is a rather odd sort of thing if it consists in telling students to pile up the leaves in their descriptions" (6).

Sentence Logic: Seeing How the Parts of a Sentence Are Related

Every sentence is composed of moveable parts. To understand your stylistic options fully, you will want to become an adept arranger and rearranger of those parts. You need to learn to see these parts and understand the different relationships they can have to each other. Initially this takes conscious effort—a fair bit of effort. Eventually you will assimilate this knowledge so that it starts to kick in whenever you sit down to write.

There is actually a rather small amount of specialized vocabulary to master in order to see and talk about sentence shapes. You will need this vocabulary in order to better define what you see, but, even before you are in control of the necessary language, you can begin to evolve your understanding of sentences by just trying to describe what you see. Teach yourself to look at sentences and say, "What do I notice?" How are the parts of the sentence laid out? How does the sentence begin and end? What, if anything, repeats in it—what words and what patterns of language?

Finding the Spine of a Sentence: Subjects and Predicates

It is helpful to think of sentences as having spines to which various limbs (modifiers—additional information) can be attached. We will talk first about the spine and then about the ways that writers can build things onto it in various places.

> —The spine of a sentence is its main subject/verb combination.
> —The primary subject/verb combination of a sentence is called the **main clause.**
> —A **clause** is a group of words containing both a subject and a predicate.

Finding the main clause is the first step in understanding how a writer has put a particular sentence together. Look for the key words of the sentence's subject (a noun or noun phrase) and the key words of its predicate (a verb or verb phrase). The **subject** is a noun, noun phrase, or pronoun that serves as the actor of the sentence, the doer of the action that the sentence describes or the thing that has been affected by it. In the following sentence, the subject is "Congress":

> **Congress** passed the bill.

"Congress" does the action that the second part of the sentence, the predicate, names. In the sentence "Bob was hurt," Bob is the subject. Bob has been affected.

You should always start your analysis of sentences by finding what is called the "simple subject," the noun, noun phrase, or pronoun that serves as the sentence subject. In the following examples, we have boldfaced the nouns that are the subjects of the sentences' main clauses.

> Despite objections from local preservationists, the **building** was destroyed.
> A **statue** stands at the center of town. **It** pulled the town together.

In both of these sentences there is more than one noun, but in each case only one of these nouns is the thing that acts (**statue** stands) or is acted upon (**building** was destroyed). "At the center of town" is a prepositional phrase naming where the statue stands. The nouns "objections" and "preservationists" are part of a phrase that modifies the action in the main clause, and so neither of those nouns acts as the sentence's subject.

The **predicate** is the action part of the sentence. It contains a verb or verb phrase that describes some kind of action or that links the subject to a word or words that characterize it. In the sample sentences above, "was destroyed" and "stands at the center of town" are the predicates. To keep your sense of the sentence's spine as clear as possible, look for the predicate's verb or verb phrase. Here are three examples. We have boldfaced the verbs or verb phrases that are the key terms of each sentence's predicate.

> I **have seen** a ship into haven fall.
> The book **was** full of highly detailed drawings.

By the way, if this matter of finding subjects and predicates sounds too simple to require discussion, we can only remark that even our best students sometimes have a hard time finding the main clause of a sentence. As you read further in this chapter, you will come to understand why this is so. More complicated sentence structures have multiple clauses and often a number of separate pieces of modifying information. In order to really see these structures, your ability to see a sentence's primary subject/verb combinations is critical. Your skill with sentences (and with punctuating them accurately) will grow rapidly if you make it a habit to always locate the main clause before going on to other considerations. If you think it is easy and obvious in every case to spot the predicate and its primary verb or verb phrase, consider the following sentence. Which of the sentence's two verbs (both boldfaced) serves as the predicate?

These **are** the times that **try** men's souls.

"These" in the sentence is a demonstrative pronoun. It functions as the subject of the sentence, so the primary verb in the main clause is "are." The word "that" is a relative pronoun that attaches a restrictive dependent clause—"that try men's souls"— to the main clause. The dependent clause is restrictive because it specifies a particular kind of time. This second clause in the sentence functions as an adjective because it modifies the noun, *times*. Soon you will start making a habit of noting the different kinds of connecting words that link the parts of a sentence together. But first you have to become adept at seeing the primary subject/verb combination or combinations that serve as the sentence's spine.

Kinds of Verbs: Transitive, Intransitive, and Linking

When you focus on the spine of a sentence, its main clause, you will notice that there are different kinds of predicates. Sentences often take the form commonly abbreviated as S V O (subject-verb-object). The predicate of such sentences consists of a verb or verb phrase describing an action and a noun that names the thing receiving the action. In the sentence, "The boy kicked the ball," for example, "boy" is the subject, "kicked" is the verb, and "ball" is the **direct object.** The shape of such sentences is usually easy to discern. In a slightly more complicated construction, a writer may include both an **indirect object** and a direct object, as in the sentence: "The teacher gave the student a book." "Teacher" is the subject, "gave" is the verb, "student" is the indirect object, and "book" is the direct object.

A verb that takes an object is called **transitive** from the word "trans," meaning across. Transitive verbs carry action across the sentence from the subject to the recipient of that action. When a verb in a sentence has no object—as in the sentences "He laughed out loud" or "He spoke quickly"—it is called **intransitive**. We recognize whether verbs are transitive or intransitive according to how they are used in a sentence and not because the verb itself is transitive or intransitive. If I were to rewrite the sentences above to "He laughed at Jim" "Or he spoke to himself," the verbs would be transitive. This distinction proves important when you are distinguishing between active and passive voice. (See *Active and Passive Voice: Emphasizing the Doer or the Action* later in this chapter.)

A third type of verb is called a **linking verb** because it links the sentence subject to a word after the verb that in some way describes the subject. The most common linking verbs are forms of "to be": *is, are, was, were*, etc. In the sentence, "My Great Pyrenees dog is white," the verb links the subject to what is called a **complement** or, in this case, a **predicate adjective**—an adjective describing the color of my dog. In the sentence, "The ambassador was gracious," the simple subject (primary noun) of the sentence is "ambassador," the verb is "was," and the predicate adjective is "gracious." A lot of what can go wrong in sentences owes to a writer locating modifiers (words that qualify other words in the sentence) in places that create confusion for the reader, as in, for example, the sentence "The boy threw a ball with a broken arm." (In Chapter 11 see *BWE 6: Misplaced Modifiers and Dangling Participles*.)

Verbals: Verb Forms that Function as Other Parts of Speech

The task of finding a sentence's main clause can be made more difficult by the presence of words that look like—but don't actually function as—verbs. These words, called **verbals**, come in three different forms: present participles (-ing), past participles (-ed), and infinitives (to). A verbal (verb-like word) ending in –ing that acts as a noun is called a **gerund**. In the sentence "Dancing is easy," dancing is a gerund that serves as the sentence subject. In the sentence "To judge is easy; suspending judgment is the more difficult task," the infinitive "to judge" acts as a noun as does the gerund phrase "suspending judgment." Verbals can appear as the object of a preposition, as in "The dog could always find time for fetching the ball" or as the object of a verb: "The committee wanted to understand their responsibilities." Verbals can function as adjectives: "Worried that I had somehow hurt her feelings, I stayed away from my friend." "Referring angrily to the school dress code, the principal asked him to leave." The point of recognizing verbals is to avoid confusing them with verbs. The subject and verb of the main clause in the previous sentence are "The point is." The other verb-like words in the sentence are verbals.

Sentence Combining: Coordination

We have been looking at sentences containing only one main clause. Such sentences are called **simple sentences**, not because their ideas are simple, but because all of the sentence's information is added onto a single subject/verb combination. A writer may add a large number of words to a sentence and have it remain simple, provided that he or she does not add any more clauses. In the following sentence, a significant amount of modifying information has been added, but, because the sentence includes only one independent clause, it is still a simple sentence. In the following example, we have boldfaced the main clause. Everything else in the sentence modifies one of the words in that clause. There are no other clauses in the sentence.

Just before midnight, **Lesley**, one of the party guests, **gulped down her champagne** with a flourish, having promised herself to never again be unprepared when the clock struck.

The spine of a sentence may, however, include more than one clause. When two or more clauses (each containing a subject plus a predicate) are linked in the same sentence by what is called a **coordinating conjunction** or by a **semicolon** (which is the equivalent of a coordinating conjunction or of a period), the resulting sentence is referred to as a **compound sentence**. We have italicized each of the clauses in the following compound sentences. We have boldfaced the coordinating conjunctions that connect the clauses.

The *house of representatives favored the bill,* **and** *the governor did not.*

The *house of representatives passed the bill,* **but** *the governor refused to sign it.*

Notice that a **comma** comes before the coordinating conjunction in each case. The comma tells the reader that a **new** clause is coming. *The primary rule of comma placement is that commas are there to help the reader easily find the sentence's main clause or clauses.* (We will have to say more about this a little further on in the chapter when we discuss what the different punctuation marks do, which we will ask you to think of in terms of the signals they send to readers.)

These two compound sentences are not, of course, identical in structure. In the first sentence, the word **"and"** indicates that another clause is simply being added to the sentence. The word "and" functions like a plus sign. It is, therefore, a rather imprecise kind of conjunction (joining element). The word **"but"** in the second sentence indicates the relationship between the two clauses more precisely. It indicates that the two clauses stand in opposition to each other. The word "but" says that the relation between the two clauses is one of contrast.

The fastest way to see the shape of coordinate structures—compound sentences—is to look for the conjunctions that serve as the glue, the connectors between the clauses. Coordinating conjunctions connect grammatically equal elements in a sentence. "*The professor called on the first-year students* **but** not the sophomores." "*Speak up,* **and** *you will be heard.*" In the first example the conjunction connects two noun phrases. In the second, it connects two independent clauses.

Coordinating conjunctions: *and, for, nor, but, or, yet, so*

Style fact about coordinate structures: Ideas located in coordinate clauses tend to be seen by readers as equal in importance since the coordinate clauses are equal grammatically, although, as we will soon discuss, the order of clauses has an impact on which one is perceived by the reader as having the most weight.

Two other types of connecting words, **conjunctive adverbs** and **correlative conjunctions**, link grammatically equal clauses in a sentence. Conjunctive adverbs, like coordinating conjunctions, connect independent clauses and indicate the relation between them. Correlative conjunctions do the same job; they come in pairs.

Common Conjunctive adverbs: *however, therefore, thus, moreover, then, furthermore, finally, nevertheless, similarly, accordingly, consequently, subsequently, otherwise, still, hence, also, besides, now, specifically, conversely*

Correlative conjunctions: either/or, neither/nor, not only/but also, whether/or, both/and

Conjunctive adverbs serving to connect independent clauses in a sentence should be preceded by a semicolon, the purpose of which is to make it clear which of the two clauses the conjunctive adverb describes. "Scientists observe things very closely; however, they still can make mistakes." "Boys will be boys; nevertheless, they can choose behaviors not described by this too-popular cliché."

Correlative conjunctions are especially useful for defining terms. They tend to play one phrase or clause against another: "She was neither angry nor sad." "The cause of the recession was not only greed, but also lack of effective legislation."

There used to be a rule, by the way, that writers should not start sentences with coordinating conjunctions or conjunctive adverbs. This rule most likely owed to the fact that these conjunctions typically operate inside sentences. This did not need to mean, however, that these handy words couldn't be used at the beginning of sentences, where they would also indicate a relationship between clauses. In conservative writing environments, you may still be expected to avoid starting sentences with the various kinds of coordinating conjunctions. A quick look, however, at a reputable magazine or newspaper—or a grammar handbook for that matter—will reveal that writers commonly start sentences with words like "and," "but," and "however." Because these words so efficiently indicate certain kinds of relationships among clauses, they have proved too handy to be ruled out as sentence openers.

Compound Predicates: A common problem in seeing the shape of compound sentences (and thus in punctuating them in a way that sends the right signals to readers) is to confuse compound sentences with sentences containing **compound predicates**. Both of the following sentences contain compound predicates. Notice that in each case there is only one sentence subject, while the predicate contains two verbs. We have boldfaced the verbs in each predicate, and we have italicized the conjoining word, "and."

> The governor **criticized** the bill *and* **refused** to sign it.
> The house of representatives **resented** the governor's resistance *and **said*** so.

If you learned sentence diagramming in school, you will have discovered how useful this practice can be for revealing the relationship among the various parts of a sentence. There are not many rules to sentence diagramming. It is just a way to help you visualize the shape of sentences. Here is what sentence diagramming reveals about the shape of a sentence with a compound predicate:

> The governor **criticized the bill**
> and
> **refused to sign it**.

Both verbs in the sentence refer back to the same sentence subject. So, rather than being a compound sentence—one that has two or more independent clauses—the sentence has a compound predicate.

Notice that it would send readers the wrong message if a writer were to put a comma in front of the word "and." A comma in that position would lead readers to expect another clause (subject/verb combination) rather than just another verb that refers back to the same subject. The comma would make the sentence illogical by, in effect, separating the second verb from its subject. If, however, you were to add the word "he" to the compound predicate above, you would convert the simple sentence with a compound predicate into a compound sentence—a sentence with two independent clauses: The governor criticized the bill, and he refused to sign it.

Sentence Combining: Subordination

When children learn to speak , they tend to put each piece of information into a separate sentence: "I fell down. My mother was there. She made me feel better." As the child grows older, she starts to combine related thoughts into more complex syntactical units, such as compound sentences: "I fell down, and my mother was there, and she made me feel better." These sentences read rather like a leaky faucet. Drip, drip, drip. Each thought unit gets equal weight. There is not much happening to cause one idea to stand out as more important or more interesting than another. Eventually, as the child becomes more proficient with language, she will write sentences that better indicate the relationship among her ideas and that allow some ideas to stand out as more important—more emphatic—than others: "After I fell down, my mother appeared and made me feel better." This sentence contains one independent clause preceded by a dependent clause indicating the time, roughly, when mother appeared. This first idea has been subordinated—in a dependent clause—to the one that follows in the independent clause, which has a compound predicate (two verbs that both have the same subject: mother).

A **dependent clause** cannot stand alone as a sentence, while an **independent clause** can. It is from this sense of elements of a sentence depending on other elements that we derive our analogy for sentence shapes—spine plus limbs (or scaffold plus words and phrases that hang on the scaffold). An **independent clause** is a group of words that contains both a subject and a predicate and that can stand alone as a sentence. This definition becomes clearer if you consider the literal meaning of the words independent and dependent.

The word "depend" means literally "to hang from." A dependent clause hangs from and thus relies on an independent clause. This kind of sentence, containing both independent and dependent clauses, is called a **complex sentence**. Such sentences are called complex, not because they are more difficult to read or to write, but because they contain different kinds of clauses and because the relationship among these clauses is explicitly specified.

At this point in our discussion, it is worth saying that sentences become complicated not because the writer doesn't know how to say things more simply (though this is sometimes true) but because complex sentences are one of the shapes that complex thinking takes. The governing idea of this chapter is that a sentence is the shape that thought takes. A piece of thinking that provides careful specification of the way that ideas relate to each other will require a sentence structure that states these relationships explicitly.

In a complex sentence, clauses are not equally important grammatically. This inequality is marked by the use of **subordinating conjunctions**, which specify the subordinate status of some clauses in relation to others. The word "subordinate" means literally "arranged under" or "ordered under." Another useful word for describing sentences with subordinate elements is **hypotactic**, which means "arranged under." If you have had a hypodermic injection (under the skin), you are familiar with the prefix "hypo" for *under*. Coordinate structures are sometimes called **paratactic**, a word meaning "arranged next to each other."

The strength of complex sentences is that they specifically name the kind of relationship among clauses, and they present the information in some clauses (the main or independent clause or clauses) as more central, more important than the information in others. Below are two examples of complex sentences. In each case we have boldfaced the subordinating conjunction and we have italicized the independent clause upon which the dependent clause depends. Notice in these sentences that if you were to delete the subordinating conjunction, and add a comma plus a coordinating conjunction between the clauses, you would convert the complex to a compound sentence.

> **Although** the vote was unanimous, *people continued to complain.*
> **Because** the poverty level of the country had risen, *its citizens began to emigrate.*

In the dependent clause that opens the second sentence, the subject is "poverty level," and the predicate is "had risen." If you were to delete the subordinating conjunction at the beginning of either sentence, but leave the comma in between the two clauses, you would have created what is known as a **comma splice**—two independent clauses spliced together with a comma when another form of punctuation, such as a period or a semicolon, is called for. If you were to remove instead the second clause in each sentence— the independent clause upon which the subordinate clause depends—you would be left with what is known as a **sentence fragment**: a group of words that can't stand alone as a sentence but which is punctuated as a sentence. (For more on comma splices and sentence fragments, see Chapter 11, *Nine Basic Writing Errors (BWEs) and How to Fix Them*).

In sum, writers create complex (subordinated, hypotactic) sentences when it is important to specify the type of relationship and the relative importance of one idea to the main idea to which it is attached. Here is a list of some common subordinating conjunctions. The list allows you to see the kinds of relationships that these words assert between the dependent (subordinate) clause and the independent clause it modifies.

Some subordinate conjunctions: *Although, if, after, before, because, since, until, when, while, where, unless, even though, whether, though, as, in order that, whereas, provided that, just as*

Style fact about subordinate structures: Ideas located in subordinate clauses tend to be seen by readers as less important than ideas located in independent clauses. As we shall see, however, in the section below called "Emphasis and the Order of Clauses," the perceived importance of an idea in a subordinate clause also depends on where it is located in a sentence.

TRY THIS 10.1: Identify Clauses and Conjunctions

Examine a piece of writing for the way it constructs and connects clauses. Start by finding the sentences' independent clause or clauses. Do this by underlining the main subject/verb combinations. Next, circle all of the conjunctions—coordinate, subordinate, conjunctive adverbs, and correlatives. What do you notice about the way that the writer puts sentences together? How is the writer's style related to the kind of thinking he or she is doing in the piece?

Seeing the Shape of Sentences: Why Commas Matter

Consider the following sentence in which a needed comma has been left out.

> After eating the couple left the restaurant.

From this example you can infer the primary role commas play in a sentence. *Commas cause readers to distinguish the main clause or clauses of a sentence from various kinds of modifiers.* Once a comma is in place after the introductory prepositional phrase at the beginning of the sentence above, readers can easily see the shape of the sentence because the comma makes the sentence spine (main clause) stand out. No one has eaten the couple. They have gone home from the restaurant unharmed.

Commas allow writers to add modifying information at various places in a sentence without causing readers to lose track of the thinking in the main clause. Consider, for example, how information might be added to the following rather silly clause—and where commas would have to be located in order for readers to keep this clause in sight.

> The cat was happy.

Let's say we wish to add some modifying information to this sentence, such as "despite not having enough for breakfast." There are three places (slots) in sentences where this modifying phrase might be added. In each sample sentence below we have underlined the main clause and italicized the modifying information.

> **beginning:** *Despite not having enough for breakfast,* <u>the cat was happy</u>.
> **middle:** <u>The cat</u>, *despite not having enough for breakfast,* <u>was happy</u>.
> **end:** <u>The cat was happy</u>, *despite not having enough for breakfast.*

These "slots" for adding information at the beginning, middle, and end are generally separated from the main clause by commas. *The commas are there to help the reader easily find and recognize the main clause.*

The first example, with the modifying phrase at the end, doesn't absolutely need a comma; we won't misread the sentence without it, though the comma does help clarify matters. And what if we raise the level of complexity by adding more modifiers to a more complicated idea?

> **modifying phrase at beginning:** *Although both candidates claimed to be running clean races and blamed the other for the mudslinging,* <u>the campaign was ugly</u>.
> **modifying phrase at middle:** <u>The campaign</u>, *although both candidates claimed to be running clean races and blamed the other for the mudslinging,* <u>was ugly</u>.
> **modifying phrase at end:** <u>The campaign was ugly</u>, *although both candidates claimed to be running clean races and blamed the other for the mudslinging.*

TRY THIS 10.2: Find and Explain Commas in a Piece of Writing
Circle all of the commas in a page of an essay. Figure out why each one is there. What modifying elements do the commas allow us to see as separate from the main clause or clauses?

Commas With Restrictive and Nonrestrictive Modifiers: That vs. Which
Because commas cause readers to distinguish a sentence's main clause or clauses from modifying information, it is important that commas not be placed in ways that send the wrong message about what are and aren't essential parts of the main clause. Consider the following sentences.

> People who live in glass houses should not throw stones.
> My sister, who lives in a glass house, has a stone collection.
>
> The tower that stands in the center of campus fell down.
> The tower, which had been slowly crumbling, fell down.

Why does the second sentence in each of these pairs require a pair of commas, while the first sentences do not? To answer this question, find the main clause in each sentence. Notice that in the second sentence of each pair you could take out the information enclosed in commas and the sentence would still make sense. The commas act, in effect, like **parentheses**. They close off a qualifying idea (something that can be referred to as a parenthetical element) that adds information to the sentence, but which is not essential to the meaning of the main clause.

> My sister has a stone collection.
> The tower fell down.

The sentence "People who live in glass houses should not throw stones" refers not just to people in general but to particular people, those who live in glass houses. So "who live in glass houses" is part of the sentence subject—part of the main clause. Putting commas around this information would cause readers to misunderstand the main clause. Similarly, in the sentence "The tower that stands in the center of campus fell down," the sentence refers not just to any tower, but to a particular tower, the one in the center of campus.

Modifying information that is essential to a clause's meaning is called **restrictive** because it restricts the meaning of the sentence subject. Information that is not essential to the meaning of the main clause—does not limit it—is called **nonrestrictive**. If you can take out words without changing the meaning of the sentence, those words are nonrestrictive. If you can't take out the words without changing the meaning of the sentence, the words are restrictive.

Nonrestrictive elements in a sentence require commas to close them off from the main clause, thus making the main clause easier to see. Restrictive elements do not get commas because they are part of the main clause. As we will discuss further in our discussion of **relative clauses** and **relative pronouns**, restrictive information in a sentence calls for the pronoun **that** and no commas. Nonrestrictive information is identified as such through the use of commas plus the relative pronoun **which**.

> The lights **that** shine in my window keep me awake at night.
> The lights, **which** are rarely turned off, keep me awake.

What Punctuation Marks Say: A Quick-Hit Guide

The **period** [.] marks the end of a sentence. Make sure what precedes it is an independent clause, that is, a subject plus verb that can stand alone. The period says to a reader, "This is the end of this particular statement. I'm a mark of closure."

> Lennon rules.

As noted in the section above on why commas matter, the **comma** [,] separates the main (independent) clause from dependent elements that modify the main clause. It also separates two main clauses joined by a conjunction—known as a compound sentence. Information that is not central to the main clause is set off in a pair of commas, a comma sandwich. The comma does *not* signify a pause. The comma says to the reader, "Here is where the main clause begins (or ends)," or "Here is a break in the main clause."

In the case of compound sentences (containing two or more independent clauses), the comma says, "Here is where one main clause ends, and after the conjunction that follows me, another main clause begins."

Lennon rules, and McCartney is cute.
Lennon rules, although McCartney is arguably more tuneful.

The **semicolon** [;] separates two independent clauses not joined by a conjunction. Secondarily, the semicolon can separate two independent clauses joined by a conjunction if either of the clauses already contains commas. In either case, the semicolon both shows a close relationship between the two independent clauses that it connects and distinguishes where one ends and the other begins. It is also the easiest way to fix comma splices (see Chapter 11).

The semicolon says to the reader, "What precedes and what follows me are conceptually close but grammatically independent and thus equal statements."

> Lennon's lyrics show deep sympathy for the legions of "Nowhere Men" who inhabit the "Strawberry Fields" of their imaginations; McCartney's lyrics, on the other hand, are more upbeat, forever bidding "Good Day, Sunshine" to the world at large and "Michelle" in particular.

The **colon** [:] marks the end of a setup for something coming next. It provides a frame, pointing beyond itself, like a spotlight. The colon is quite dramatic, and unlike the semicolon, it links what precedes and follows it formally and tightly rather than loosely and associatively. It usually operates with dramatic force. It can frame a list to follow, separate cause and effect, or divide a brief claim from a more expanded version of the claim. The language on at least one side of the colon must be an independent clause, though both sides can be.

The colon says to the reader, "Concentrate on what follows me for a more detailed explanation of what preceded me" or "What follows me is logically bound with what preceded me."

> *Rubber Soul* marked a change in The Beatles' songwriting: the sentimentality of earlier efforts gave way to a new complexity, both in the range of their subjects and the sophistication of their poetic devices.
> Nowhere is this change more evident than in a sequence of songs near the album's end: "I'm Looking Through You," "In My Life," "Wait," and "If I Needed Someone."

The **dash** [—] provides an informal alternative to the colon for adding information to a sentence. Its effect is sudden, of the moment—what springs up impulsively to disrupt and extend in some new way the ongoing train of thought. A **pair of dashes** provides an invaluable resource to writers for inserting information within a sentence. In this usage, the rule is that the sentence must read coherently if the inserted information is left out. (To type a dash, type two hyphens with no space between, before, or after. This distinguishes the dash from a hyphen [-], which is the mark used for connecting two words into one.)

The dash says to the reader, "This too!" or, in the case of a pair of them, "Remember the thought in the beginning of this sentence because we're jumping to something else before we come back to finish that thought."

> For all their loveliness, the songs on *Rubber Soul* are not without menace—"I'd rather see you dead little girl than to see you with another man."
>
> In addition to the usual lead, rhythm, and bass guitar ensemble, *Rubber Soul* introduced new instruments—notably, the harpsichord interlude in "In My Life," the sitar spiraling through "Norwegian Wood"—that had not previously been heard in rock 'n roll.

Emphasis and the Order of Clauses: The Importance of What Comes Last

Here are two ways of arranging the same sentence. Notice what happens to emphasis when we change the order of the clauses.

> Turkey has battled the party for more than 30 years, though peace talks are now underway.
>
> Although peace talks are now underway, Turkey has battled the party for more than 30 years.

Which sentence holds out the most hope for the success of the peace talks? Climactic order is a fact of sentence style. Sentences will seem to build up to and emphasize whatever comes last. This fact takes precedence over another fact of sentence style—that ideas placed in independent as opposed to dependent (subordinate) clauses tend to get more emphasis. In the first sentence above, the idea in the subordinate clause gets more emphasis than the one in the main clause simply because it comes last. Here is another example.

> The history of Indochina is marked by colonial exploitation as well as international cooperation.
>
> The history of Indochina, although marked by colonial exploitation, testifies to the possibility of international cooperation.

In the second sentence the emphasis at the end of the sentence is made even more pronounced because the information about colonial exploitation is located in a subordinate clause that interrupts the main clause. As we will demonstrate soon in our discussion of **periodic vs. cumulative sentences**, creating **grammatical tension** by delaying closure—in this case, by putting information between the subject and the verb of the main clause—adds powerfully to emphasis.

Experiment with these stylistic principles. See what happens if you try moving the information you wish to emphasize to the end of your sentences. You will find that this tactic also improves the coherence of your writing because the placement of key ideas at the ends of sentences will press you to bridge from those ideas to whatever happens in the subsequent sentence. Also experiment with what you put into dependent as opposed to independent clauses. Try locating information in between the subject and verb of your main clause so as to exaggerate the emphasis naturally bestowed by climactic order.

TRY THIS 10.3: Order Clauses in a Sentence for Emphasis
Try some sentence combining in which you experiment with the effect of locating key information at the end of the sentence. Here are three ideas stated in separate sentences. Combine these into a single sentence. What happens to emphasis—to the meaning of the sentence—if you put the information about the time of year or the location of the proposal at the end of the sentence? Under what circumstances might a writer want to do this?

> I asked her to marry me.
> It was October.
> We were in a shop on Tremont Street.

Embedding Modifiers: Relative Clauses, Words, and Phrases

Other than coordination and subordination, there are a number of other ways that a writer can go about connecting information to the spine of a sentence. In order to understand these easily, you need to think about the different roles that modifiers can play in a sentence. A **modifier** is a word or a phrase or a clause that elaborates on an element in the sentence by describing it, limiting it somehow, or just by adding additional information. Consider the modifiers that we have boldfaced in each of the following sentences:

> My **white** dog is huge.
> My house, **which is painted yellow**, is cheerful.
> The sun rose **slowly**.
> I took the job **in 1987**.

> The college chose students **who appreciated diversity**.
> The things **[that]** we come to miss the most are things **[that]** we once took for granted.

Adjectives modify nouns or pronouns. **Adverbs**, usually recognizable by their –ly ending, modify verbs, adjectives, or other adverbs.

In the first two examples above, the boldfaced modifiers—a single word in the first sentence, and a relative clause in the second—operate as adjectives. This relationship among sentence parts is easy to see in these simple sentences because the modifiers and the words they modify are so close together. The modifier in the third sentence functions as an adverb, because it modifies an action ("rose"). The prepositional phrase "in 1987" also operates as an adverb because it modifies the verb "took." It answers the question, "when did you take the job?" Prepositional phrases are the most common modifiers. When we aren't careful, prepositional phrases can proliferate and overrun a sentence.

The last pair of sentences above are examples of modifiers taking the form of relative clauses—because they relate to other words in the sentence. The **relative clause** "who appreciated diversity" modifies the word "students," and so it is an **adjective clause**. The word "who" is a **relative pronoun**; "who appreciated diversity" is a clause because it has a subject (the pronoun "who") and a predicate ("appreciated diversity"). The clause is dependent because it cannot stand alone; it relates to and depends on the word in the main clause that it modifies. The sentence with the two longer relative clauses contains the relative pronoun "that," which you encountered earlier in our discussion of punctuating restrictive and nonrestrictive clauses. Both of these clauses also function as adjectives because they both modify nouns—"students" and "things." When the noun referred to is a person, use the relative pronoun "who" or "whom." When the noun is not a person, use "that" or "which."

Modifiers enhance a writer's stylistic choices. Writers have a lot of choices about where to place them in a sentence. Modifiers also present writers with choices about emphasis—whether, for example, an idea should be embedded in a sentence as a modifying word, clause, or phrase or whether it should stand alone as a sentence.

We have already looked at clauses functioning as adverbs, since this is what subordinate clauses do. **Adverb clauses** modify some action in the sentence. If you look back at our list of subordinating conjunctions, you will see that they tell when, why, where, or how an action took place.

When the lights came on, the skating rink filled up.
Now that the waiting was over, the team came onto the field.

Relative pronouns: *who, whom, which, that,* (and sometimes *where* or *when*)

Demonstrative pronouns: *this, that, these, those*

Demonstrative pronouns function as adjectives because they point to nouns, as in "This is my favorite time of the year." They can also substitute for nouns ("This is my house").

Academic writing and, in fact, most forms of writing beyond elemental description, require writers to load various kinds of information into one sentence, a process known as **embedding**. At its worst, embedding produces overloaded, unwieldy sentences wherein readers and emphasis get lost. The opposite extreme—one idea to a sentence—produces disjointed writing in which sentences start to sound, as we said earlier, like the drip, drip of a leaky faucet, each drop equal in importance and nothing standing out as what the writer especially wants the reader to pay attention to. In most good writing, each individual sentence does a fair bit of work. *The trick is to learn how to embed information in sentences in a way that doesn't drag the sentence to the ground like an overloaded branch.*

Appositives and **absolutes** offer another way of embedding information in a sentence and thus keeping your emphasis where you want it. An appositive comes immediately after a noun or noun phrase and renames it. The following two sentences can be combined into one by using an appositive.

Sean was a key member of the cast.

He is an able musician.

Revision: Sean, **an able musician**, was a key member of the cast.

Absolutes act like appositives, but, rather than echoing a single noun or noun phrase, the absolute phrase modifies the sentence as a whole.

> He found the beach especially beautiful, **its blowing sand and broken shells always evocative, occasionally haunting.**

Periodic and Cumulative Styles: Two Ways of Locating Closure

The shape of a sentence governs the way it delivers information. The order of clauses, especially the placement of the main clause, affects what the sentence means. There are two common sentence shapes defined by the location of their main clauses; these are known as *periodic* and *cumulative* sentences. The periodic sentence is built on suspense and delay: it puts maximum emphasis on the way the sentence ends. The cumulative sentence aims for upfront impact; there is no suspense, but rather, the rolling momentum of an extended follow-through.

The Periodic Sentence: Delay Closure to Achieve Emphasis

The main clause in a periodic sentence builds to a climax that is not completed until the end. Often, a piece of the main clause (such as the subject) is located early in the sentence, as in the following example:

> The **way** that beverage companies market health—"No Preservatives," "No Artificial Colors," "All Natural," "Real Brewed"—**is** often, because the product also contains a high percentage of sugar or fructose, **misleading**.

We have boldfaced parts of the main clause to clarify how various modifiers interrupt it. The effect is suspenseful: not until the final word does the sentence consummate its fundamental idea. Pieces of the main clause are spread out across the sentence.

Another version of the periodic sentence locates the entire main clause at the end, after introductory modifiers.

> Using labels that market health—such as "No Preservatives," "No Artificial Colors," "All Natural," and "Real Brewed"—while producing drinks that contain a high percentage of sugar or fructose, **beverage companies are misleading.**

As previously discussed, the end of a sentence normally receives emphasis. When you use a periodic construction, the pressure on the end intensifies because the sentence waits until the end to complete its grammatical sense. In both of the preceding examples, the sentences "snap shut." They string readers along, delaying *grammatical closure*—the point at which the sentences can stand alone independently—until they arrive at climactic ends. Periodic sentences are also known as *climactic sentences*. Periodic sentences can be arranged so as to produce different levels of grammatical tension—high, middle, and low. The longer the reader has to wait in order to arrive at sentence closure, the higher the grammatical tension.

Of the periodic sentence, Richard Lanham writes (in his book *Analyzing Prose*): "Some tangible ingredients for a "periodic" style [are]: (1) suspension, ...; (2) parallelism of phrases and clauses...; (3) balance, the antiphonal chorus; (4) climax, the final thrust that nails Seneca to the wall. And to these we must add a last quality that exudes from periodic structure, *virtuoso display*." (57)

You should be aware of one risk that accompanies periodic constructions. If the delay lasts too long because there are too many "interrupters" before the main clause gets completed, your readers may forget the subject being predicated. To illustrate, let's add more subordinated material to one of the preceding examples.

> The way that beverage companies market health—"No Preservatives," "No Artificial Colors," "All Natural," "Real Brewed"—is often, because the product also contains a high percentage of sugar or fructose, not just what New Agers would probably term "immoral" and "misleading" but what a government agency such as the Food and Drug Administration should find illegal.

Arguably, the additions (the "not just" and "but" clauses after "fructose") push the sentence into incoherence. The main clause has been stretched past the breaking point. If readers don't get lost in such a sentence, they are at least likely to get irritated and wish the writer would finally get to the point.

Nonetheless, with a little care, periodic sentences can be extraordinarily useful in locating emphasis. If you are revising and want to underscore some point, try letting the sentence snap shut upon it. Often the periodic potential will already be present in the draft, and stylistic editing can bring it out more forcefully. Note how minor the revisions are in the following example:

Draft: The novelist Virginia Woolf suffered from acute anxieties for most of her life. She had several breakdowns and finally committed suicide on the eve of World War II.

Revision: Suffering from acute anxieties for most of her life, the novelist Virginia **Woolf** not only **had** several **breakdowns but**, finally, on the eve of World War II, **committed suicide** as well.

This revision has made two primary changes. It has combined two short sentences into a longer sentence, and it has made the sentence periodic by stringing out the main clause. What is the effect of this revision? Stylistically speaking, the revision radiates a greater sense of its writer's authority. The information has been arranged for us. After the opening dependent clause ("Suffering..."), the subject of the main clause ("Woolf") is introduced, and the predicate is protracted in a *not only/but also* parallelism. The interrupters that follow "had several breakdowns" ("finally, on the eve of World War II") increase the suspense, before the sentence snaps shut with "committed suicide."

In general, when you construct a periodic sentence with care, you can give readers the sense that you are in control of your material. You do not seem to be writing off the top of your head, but rather from a position of greater detachment, rationally composing your meaning.

The Cumulative Sentence: Start Fast to Build Momentum

The cumulative sentence is in many respects the opposite of the periodic. Rather than delaying the main clause or its final piece, the cumulative sentence begins by presenting the independent clause as a foundation and then *accumulates* a number of modifications and qualifications. As the following examples illustrate, the independent clause provides quick grammatical closure, freeing the rest of the sentence to amplify and develop the main idea:

> **Robert F. Kennedy was assassinated** by Sirhan B. Sirhan, a twenty-four-year-old Palestinian immigrant, prone to occultism and unsophisticated left-wing politics and sociopathically devoted to leaving his mark in history, even if as a notorious figure.
>
> **There are two piano concerti** composed solely for the left hand, one by Serge Prokofiev and one by Maurice Ravel, and both commissioned by Paul Wittgenstein, a concert pianist (and the brother of the famous philosopher Ludwig Wittgenstein) who had lost his right hand in combat during World War I.

Anchored by the main clause, a cumulative sentence moves serially through one thing and another thing and the next thing, close to the associative manner in which people think. To an extent, then, cumulative sentences can convey more immediacy and a more conversational tone than can other sentence shapes. Look at the following example:

> **The film version of Lady Chatterley's Lover changed D. H. Lawrence's famous novel** a lot, omitting the heroine's adolescent experience in Germany, making her husband much older than she, leaving out her father and sister, including a lot more lovemaking, and virtually eliminating all of the philosophizing about sex and marriage.

Here, we get the impression of a mind in the act of thinking. Using the generalization of changes in the film as a base, the sentence then appends a series of parallel participial phrases ("omitting," "making," "leaving," "including," "eliminating") that moves forward associatively, gathering a range of information and laying out possibilities. Cumulative sentences perform this outlining and prospecting function very effectively. On the other hand, if we were to add four or five more changes to the sentence, readers would likely find it tedious, or worse, directionless. As with periodic sentences, overloading the shape can short-circuit its desired effect.

If you consciously practice using periodic and cumulative constructions, you will be surprised how quickly you can learn to produce their respective effects in your own writing. You will also discover that both of these sentence shapes are already present in your prose in some undiscovered and thus unrefined way. It is often simply a case of bringing out what is already there. Try including at least one of each in the next paper you write.

TRY THIS 10.4: Write Periodic and Cumulative Sentences
Compose a simple sentence on any subject—a sentence with one main clause. Then construct two variations expanding it, one periodic and one cumulative. Here, as a model, is an example using the core sentence "James Joyce was a gifted singer."

Periodic: Although known primarily as one of the greatest novelists of the twentieth century, James Joyce, the son of a local political functionary who loved to tip a few too many at the pub, was also a gifted—and prizewinning—singer.

Cumulative: James Joyce was a gifted singer, having listened at his father's knee to the ballads sung in pubs, having won an all-Ireland prize in his early teens, and having possessed a miraculous ear for the inflections of common speech that was to serve him throughout the career for which he is justly famous, that of a novelist.

Can't think of a core sentence? Okay, here are two:

> Why do airlines show such mediocre films?
> Every senator is a millionaire.

Symmetry and Sense: Balance, Antithesis, and Parallelism

Long and grammatically complicated sentences achieve clarity and emphasis primarily through various kinds of repetition. A writer can repeat similar words and phrases at the beginning of sentences (a device called **anaphora**,) and he or she can accumulate a series of parallel clauses or phrases of the same or similar length (**isocolon**). Symmetry makes sentences easier to follow, whether the sentence shape is one that balances similar ideas or one that sets them up in contrast to each other (**antithesis**).

Parallel Structure: Put Parallel Information into Parallel Form

One of the most important and useful devices for shaping sentences is **parallel structure** or, as it is also known, **parallelism**. Parallelism is a form of symmetry: it involves placing sentence elements that correspond in some way into the same (that is, parallel) grammatical form. Consider the following examples, in which the parallel items are boldfaced or italicized:

> The three kinds of partners in a law firm who receive money from a case are popularly known as **finders**, **binders**, and **grinders**.

> The Beatles acknowledged their musical debts **to** American rhythm and blues, **to** English music hall ballads and ditties, and later **to** classical Indian ragas.
>
> There was **no way that** the President **could gain** the support of party regulars *without alienating* the Congress, and **no way that** he **could appeal** to the electorate at large *without alienating* both of these groups.
>
> In the entertainment industry, the money that **goes out** to hire *film stars* or *sports stars* **comes back** in increased ticket sales and video or television rights.

As all of these examples illustrate, at the core of parallelism lies repetition—of a word, a phrase, or a grammatical structure. Parallelism uses repetition to organize and emphasize certain elements in a sentence, so that readers can perceive more clearly the shape of your thought. In the Beatles example, each of the prepositional phrases beginning with to contains a musical debt. In the President example, the repetition of the phrase **no way that** emphasizes his entrapment.

Parallelism has the added advantage of economy: each of the musical debts or presidential problems might have had its own sentence, but in that case the prose would have been wordier and the relationships among the parallel items more obscure. Along with this economy come balance and emphasis. The trio of rhyming words (finders, binders, and grinders) that concludes the law-firm example gives each item equal weight; in the entertainment-industry example, "comes back" answers "goes out" in a way that accentuates their symmetry.

It is important to avoid what is known as *faulty parallelism*, which occurs when the items that are parallel in content are not placed in the same grammatical form.

> **Faulty: To study** hard for four years and then **getting** ignored once they enter the job market is a hard thing for many recent college graduates to accept.
>
> **Revised: To study** hard for four years and then **to get** ignored once they enter the job market is a hard thing for many recent college graduates to accept.

TRY THIS 10.5: Correct Errors in Parallelism

Rewrite the following examples of faulty parallelism using correct parallel structure:

1. The problems with fast food restaurants include the way workers are exploited, eating transfatty acids, and that the food can damage your liver.

2. Venus Williams likes to play tennis and also designing clothes.

3. In the 1960s the use of drugs and being a hippie were ways for some people to let society know their political views and that they were alienated from the mainstream.

Two Powerful Forms of Parallelism: Antithesis and Chiasmus

One particularly useful form of balance that parallel structure accommodates is known as **antithesis** (from the Greek word for "opposition"), a conjoining of contrasting ideas. Here, the pattern sets one thing against another thing, as in the following example:

> Where bravura failed to settle the negotiations, tact and patience succeeded.

"Failed" is balanced antithetically against "succeeded," as "bravura" against "tact and patience." Antithesis commonly takes the form of "if not x, at least y" or "not x, but y."

Another specialized form of parallelism known as **chiasmus** is a rhetorical pattern that organizes elements in an ABBA structure. The most famous chiasmus known to most Americans comes from a speech by John F. Kennedy: "Ask not what your country can do for you; ask what you can do for your country."

Note how this form also uses antithesis—the JFK example moves from "ask not" to "ask"—which is why it is known as a form of inverted parallelism, the second half of the expression balanced against the first, with the parts reversed. You can more easily remember the term chiasmus once you realize that it derives from the Greek letter *chi*, meaning X, as that is the shape of the AB -> BA structure. Here is another example of chiasmus from Matthew 19:30: "But many that are **first** shall be **last**; and the **last** shall be **first**." The effect is memorable.

As you write, and especially as you revise for style, search for opportunities to place sentence elements in parallel structure. Remember that parallelism can occur with clauses and phrases, especially prepositional phrases. Often, the parallels will be hidden in the sentences of your draft, but they can be brought out with a minimum of labor. After you've acquired the habit of casting your thinking in parallel structures, they will rapidly become a staple of your stylistic repertoire, making your prose more graceful, clear, and logically connected.

Noun Styles, Verb Styles, "Official Style"

Richard Lanham, in his influential style guide, *Revising Prose*, coined the term "Official Style" for the kinds of sentences he thought were steadily draining the life out of English prose style. For such sentences—the product of bureaucrats—Lanham prescribed his paramedic method, which calls for finding the action in sentences rather than allowing them to sink under the weight of nouns and strings of prepositions. For Lanham, perhaps the primary characteristic of Official Style is its reliance on forms of "to be," with the resulting conversion of verbs into nouns. In his paramedic method, Lanham instructs writers to mark all of the prepositions, identify the forms of *to be*, and find the action buried in the sentence and make it into an active verb. As you will see, avoiding Official Style is a matter not only of syntax, but also of concise and effective word choice.

Finding the Action in a Sentence: "To Be" Or Not "To Be"

Verbs energize a sentence. They actively connect the parts of the sentence with each other, as opposed to less active forms of connection such as relative pronouns (clauses beginning with "that" or "which") and prepositions. In a sentence of the subject–verb–direct object pattern, the verb—known as a *transitive verb*—functions as a kind of engine, driving the subject into the predicate, as in the following examples.

> John F. Kennedy effectively **manipulated** his image in the media.
> Thomas Jefferson **embraced** the idea of America as a country of yeoman farmers.

By contrast, "is" and other forms of the verb "to be" provide an equals sign between the subject and the predicate but otherwise tell us nothing about the relationship between them. "To be" is an *intransitive verb*; it cannot take a direct object. Compare the two preceding transitive examples with the following versions of the same sentences using forms of the verb "to be."

> John F. Kennedy **was** effective at the manipulation of his image in the media.
> Thomas Jefferson's idea **was** for America to be a country of yeoman farmers.

Rather than making things happen through an active transitive verb, these sentences let everything just hang around in a state of being. In the first version, Kennedy did something—*manipulated* his image—but in the second he just *is* (or *was*), and the energy of the original verb has been siphoned into an abstract noun, "manipulation." The revised Jefferson example suffers from a similar lack of momentum compared with the original version: the syntax doesn't help the sentence get anywhere.

Certain situations, however, dictate the use of forms of "to be." For definitions in particular, the equals sign that an "is" provides works well. For instance, "Organic gardening is a method of growing crops without using synthetic fertilizers or pesticides." As with choosing between active and passive voices, the decision to use "to be" should be just that—a conscious decision on your part.

If you can train yourself to eliminate every unnecessary use of "to be" in a draft, you will make your prose more lively and direct. In most cases, you will find the verb that you need to substitute for "is" lurking somewhere in the sentence in some other grammatical form. In the preceding sentence about Kennedy, "manipulate" is implicit in "manipulation." In Table 10.1, each of the examples in the left-hand column uses a form of "to be" for its verb (italicized) and contains a potentially strong active verb lurking in the sentence in some other form (boldfaced). These "lurkers" have been converted into active verbs (italicized) in the revisions in the right-hand column.

Clearly, the examples in the left-hand column have problems in addition to their reliance on forms of "to be"—notably circumlocution and verbosity.

TABLE 10.1

Static and Active Verbs

Action Hidden in Nouns and "To Be" Verbs	Action Emphasized in Verbs
The **cost** of the book *is* ten dollars.	The book *costs* ten dollars.
The **acknowledgment** of the fact *is* increasingly widespread that television *is* a **replacement** for reading in American culture.	People increasingly *acknowledge* that television *has replaced* reading in American culture.
A computer *is* ostensibly a **labor-saving** device— until the hard drive *is* the victim of a **crash**.	A computer ostensibly *saves* labor— until the hard drive *crashes*.
In the **laying** of a flagstone patio, the important preliminary steps to remember *are* the **excavating** and the **leveling** of the area and then the **filling** of it with a fine grade of gravel.	To *lay* a flagstone patio, first *excavate* and *level* the area and then *fill* it with a fine grade of gravel.

TRY THIS 10.6: Find Active Verbs in Your Sentences

Take a paper you've written and circle the sentences that rely on forms of "to be." Then, examine the other words in these sentences, looking for "lurkers." Rewrite the sentences, converting the lurkers into vigorous verbs. You will probably discover many lurkers, and your revisions will acquire more energy and directness.

Active and Passive Voice: Emphasizing the Doer or the Action

In the **active voice**, the grammatical subject acts; in the **passive voice**, the subject is acted upon. Here are two examples.

> **Active:** Adam Smith wrote *The Wealth of Nations* in 1776.
> **Passive:** *The Wealth of Nations* was written by Adam Smith in 1776.

The two sentences convey identical information, but the emphasis differs—the first focuses on the author, the second on the book.

As the examples illustrate, using the passive normally results in a longer sentence than using the active. If we consider how to convert the passive into the active, you can see why. In the passive, the verb requires a form of "to be" plus a past participle. (For more on participles, see the Glossary of Grammatical Terms in Chapter 11.) In this case, the active verb "wrote" becomes the passive verb "was written," the grammatical subject ("Smith") becomes the object of the preposition "by," and the direct object (*The Wealth of Nations*) becomes the grammatical subject.

Now consider the activity described in the two versions of this example: a man wrote a book. That's what happened in life. The grammar of the active version captures that action most clearly: the grammatical subject ("Smith") performs the action, and the direct object (*The Wealth of Nations*) receives it, just as in life. By contrast, the passive version alters the close link between the syntax and the event: the object of the action in life (*The Wealth of Nations*) has become the grammatical subject, whereas the doer in life ("Smith") has become the grammatical object of a prepositional phrase.

Note, too, that the passive would allow us to omit "Smith" altogether: "*The Wealth of Nations* was written in 1776." A reader who desired to know more and was not aware of the author would not appreciate this sentence. More troubling, the passive can also be used to conceal the doer of an action—not "I made a mistake" (active) but rather "A mistake has been made" (passive).

In sum, there are three reasons for avoiding the passive voice when you can: (1) it's longer, (2) its grammatical relationships are (or seem to be) the reverse of what happened in life, and (3) it can omit the performer responsible for the action.

On the other hand, sometimes there are good reasons for using the passive. If you want to emphasize the object or recipient of the action rather than the performer, the passive will do that for you: "*The Wealth of Nations* was written in 1776 by Adam Smith" places initial stress on the book. The passive is also preferable when the doer remains unknown: "The president has been shot!" is probably a better sentence than "Some unknown assailant has shot the president!"

Especially in the natural sciences, the use of the passive voice is a standard practice. There are sound reasons for this disciplinary convention: science tends to focus on what happens to something in a given experiment, rather than on the person performing the experiment. Compare the following sentences:

> **Passive:** Separation of the protein was achieved by using an electrophoretic gel.

> **Active:** The researcher used an electrophoretic gel to separate the protein.

If you opted for the active version, the emphasis would rest, illogically, on the agent of the action (the researcher) rather than on what happened and how (electrophoretic separation of the protein).

On balance, "consider" is the operative term when you choose between passive and active as you revise the syntax of your drafts. Recognize that you do have choices—in emphasis, in relative directness, and in economy. All things being equal and disciplinary conventions permitting, the active is usually the better choice.

TRY THIS 10.7: Analyze the Effect of Passive Voice in a Speech
In the speech below, the Declaration of Independence, please do the following:
  —Circle the verb in each clause. Identify which clauses exhibit passive construction.

  —Convert each sentence in passive voice to active voice.

  —Explain how the meaning of the passive voice sentences change when rewritten in active voice.

"We hold these truths to be self-evident, that all men are created equal, that they   1
are endowed by their Creator with certain unalienable Rights, that among these are   2
Life, Liberty and the pursuit of Happiness. That to secure these rights, Governments   3
are instituted among Men, deriving their just powers from the consent of the governed,   4
That whenever any Form of Government becomes destructive of these ends, it is the   5
Right of the People to alter or to abolish it, and to institute new Government, laying its   6
foundation on such principles and organizing its powers in such form, as to them shall   7
seem most likely to effect their Safety and Happiness."   8

Passive Voice: construction in which the subject of the sentence is the recipient of the action

Transitive Verb: action verbs that have an object to receive that action

Intransitive Verb: action verbs that do not have an object receiving the action

TRY THIS 10.8: Write Passive and Active Voice Sentences
Identify all of the sentences that use the passive voice in one of your papers. Then, rewrite these sentences, converting passive into active wherever appropriate. Finally, count the total number of words, the total number of prepositions, and the average sentence length (words per sentence) in each version. What do you discover?

For more practice, here's another exercise. Compose a paragraph of at least half a page in which you use only the passive voice and verbs of being, followed by a paragraph in which you use only the active voice. Then, rewrite the first paragraph using only active voice, if possible, and rewrite the second paragraph using only passive voice and verbs of being as much as possible. How do the paragraphs differ in shape, length, and coherence?

Expletives: Beginning with "It Is" or "There Is"

Sentences that begin with openers like "It is" or "There is" are known as *expletive* constructions. The term *expletive* comes from a Latin word that means "serving to fill out." Most of the time, you can streamline your prose by getting rid of expletive constructions. Consider how the expletives function in the following examples:

> **There are** several prototypes for the artificial heart.
> **It is** obvious that the American West exerted a profound influence on the photography of Ansel Adams.

Compare these with versions that simply eliminate the expletives.

> The artificial heart has several prototypes.
> The American West exerted a profound influence on the photography of Ansel Adams.

Expletives, such as the "It is obvious that" opening, cause the grammar of the sentence to subordinate its real emphasis.

In some cases, though, an expletive can provide useful emphasis, as in the following example: "There are three primary reasons that you should avoid litigation." Although this sentence grammatically subordinates its primary content (avoiding litigation), the expletive provides a useful frame for what is to follow.

In an excellent book entitled *Rhetorical Grammar* (Longman, 2009), Martha Kolln and Loretta Gray make the case for using what they term "the there-transformation" as a strategy for adding emphasis. They do so by focusing on what they call "the rhythm pattern" of the sentence. Compare "There's a stranger standing on the porch," where the accent falls on "stranger," with "The stranger stands on the porch," where the accent—and thus the emphasis—falls on "porch."

Concrete vs. Evaluative Adjectives and Intensifiers: What's Bad About "Good" and "Bad"

Good. Pretty. Boring. Negative. Positive. All of these words are **evaluative adjectives**. They offer judgments without any supporting data. *Green* and *small* and *bright* are examples of **concrete (descriptive) adjectives**. They give us something specific to think with. Broad evaluative terms such as *good* and *bad* can seduce you into stopping your thinking while it is still too general and ill-defined—a matter discussed at length in. "The Judgment Reflex" section of Chapter 1. If you train yourself to select more precise words whenever you encounter *good* and *bad* in your drafts, not only will your prose become clearer, but also the search for new words will start you thinking again, sharpening your ideas.

If, for example, you find yourself writing a sentence such as "The subcommittee made a bad decision," ask yourself why you called it a bad decision. A revision to "The subcommittee made a shortsighted decision" indicates what in fact is bad about the decision and sets you up to discuss why the decision was myopic, further developing the idea.

Be aware that often evaluative terms are disguised as neutrally descriptive ones—*natural*, for instance, and *realistic*. Realistic according to whom, and defined by what criteria? Something is natural according to a given idea about nature—an assumption—and the same goes for *moral*. These are not terms that mean separately from a particular context or ideology, that is, an assumed hierarchy of value. Similarly, in a sentence such as "Society disapproves of interracial marriage," the broad and apparently neutral term *society* can blind you to a host of important distinctions about social class, about a particular culture, and so on.

Many words fall somewhere between being evaluative and concrete. The word "complicated," for example, is concrete in that it means "having more than one side (complex)," but complicated or complex can be evaluative depending on context. In some circles, a complicated idea is thought to be insufficiently straightforward. In academic circles, wherein accuracy is valued more highly than ease of expression, complicated ideas are good.

Another type of word prone to adding evaluation without data is the kind of adverb called an **intensifier**—really, truly, actually, very, entirely, etc. These words add little—except an overstated tone—to writing. It is usually (though not always) best to eliminate them.

Concrete and Abstract Diction

At its best, effective analytical prose uses both concrete and abstract words. Simply defined, concrete diction brings things to life by offering readers words that play on their senses. *Telephone, eggshell, crystalline, azure, striped, kneel, flare,* and *burp* are examples of concrete diction. You need concrete language whenever you are describing what happens or what something looks like—in a laboratory experiment, in a military action, in a painting or film sequence. The language of evidence consists of concrete diction. It allows us to see for ourselves the basis of a person's convictions in the stuff of lived experience.

By contrast, abstract diction refers to words that designate concepts and categories. *Virility, ideology, love, definitive, desultory, conscientious, classify,* and *ameliorate* are examples of abstract diction. So are *democracy, fascism, benevolence,* and *sentimentality.* Abstract words give us the language of ideas. We cannot do without abstract terms, and yet writing made up only of such words loses contact with experience, with the world that we can apprehend through our senses.

The line between abstract and concrete is not always as clear as these examples may suggest. You may recall the ladder of abstraction that we discuss in the section entitled Generalizing in Chapter 1. There, we propose that abstract and concrete are not hard-and-fast categories so much as a continuum, a sliding scale. Word A (for example, machine) may be more abstract than word B (computer) but more concrete than word C (technology).

Concrete and abstract diction need each other. Concrete diction illustrates and anchors the generalizations that abstract diction expresses. Notice the concrete language used to define the abstraction *provinciality* in this example:

> There is no cure for **provinciality** like traveling abroad. In America, the waiter who fails to bring the check promptly at the end of the meal we rightly convict for not being watchful. But in England, after waiting interminably for the check and becoming increasingly irate, we learn that only an ill-mannered waiter would bring it without being asked. We have been rude, not he.

In the following example, the abstract terms *causality, fiction,* and *conjunction* are integrated with concrete diction in the second sentence:

> According to the philosopher David Hume, **causality** is a kind of **fiction** that we ascribe to what he called "the constant **conjunction**

of observed events." If a person gets hit in the eye and a black semi-circle develops underneath it, that does not necessarily mean the blow caused the black eye.

A style that omits concrete language can leave readers lost in a fog of abstraction that only tangible details can illuminate. The concrete language helps readers see what you mean, much in the way that examples help them understand your ideas. Without the shaping power of abstract diction, however, concrete evocation can leave you with a list of graphic but ultimately pointless facts. The best writing integrates concrete and abstract diction, the language of showing and the language of telling.

Latinate Diction

One of the best ways to sensitize yourself to the difference between abstract and concrete diction is to understand that many abstract words are examples of what is known as Latinate diction. This term describes words in English that derive from Latin roots, words with such endings as –tion, –ive, –ity, –ate, and –ent. (Such words are designated by an L in the etymological section of dictionary definitions.) Taken to an extreme, Latinate diction can leave your meaning vague and your readers confused. This is not because there is something dubious about words that come into English from Latin. A large percentage of English words have Latin or Greek roots, words like *pentagon* (Greek for five sides), *anarchy* (Latin for without order), and *automobile* (Latin for self-moving).

The problem with Latinate diction lies in the way it is sometimes used. Latin endings such as –tion make it too easy for writers to construct sentences made up of a high percentage of vague nouns, as in the following example:

> The examination of different perspectives on the representations of socio-political anarchy in media coverage of revolutions can be revelatory of the invisible biases that afflict television news.

This sentence actually makes sense, but the demands it makes on readers will surely drive off most of them before they have gotten through it. Reducing the amount of Latinate diction can make it more readable:

> Because we tend to believe what we see, the political biases that afflict television news coverage of revolutions are largely invisible. We can begin to see these biases when we focus on how the medium reports events, studying the kinds of footage used, for example, or finding facts from other sources that the news has left out.

Although the preceding revision retains a lot of Latinate words, it provides a ballast of concrete, sensory details that allows readers to follow the idea. It's fine to use Latinate diction; just don't make it the sole staple of your verbal diet.

Etymology: Finding a Word's Physical History

In choosing the right shade of meaning, you will get a sharper sense for the word by knowing its etymological history—the word or words from which it evolved. In the preceding example, *aggressive* derives from the Latin *aggressus*, meaning "to go to or approach"; and *aggressus* is itself a combination of *ad*, a prefix expressing motion, and *gradus*, meaning "a step." An aggressive person, then, is "coming at you." *Assertive*, on the other hand, comes from the Latin *asserere*, combining *ad*, meaning "to or toward," with *serere*, meaning "join or bind together." An assertive person is "coming to build or put things together"—certainly not to threaten.

The best dictionary for pursuing word histories, by the way, is the *Oxford English Dictionary*, which commonly goes by its initials, *OED*. Available in every library reference collection and usually online at colleges and universities as well, it provides examples of how words have been used over time.

TRY THIS 10.9: Tracing Word Histories

Look up one of the following pairs of words in the *OED* (*Oxford English Dictionary*). Write down the etymology of each word in the pair, and then, in a paragraph for each, summarize the words' linguistic histories—how their meanings have evolved across time. (The *OED*'s examples of how the word has been used over time will be helpful here.)

ordinal/ordinary
explicate/implicate
tenacious/stubborn
induce/conducive
enthusiasm/ecstasy
adhere/inhere
monarchy/oligarchy
overt/covert

"Right" and "Wrong" Words: Shades of Meaning

The nineteenth-century English statesman Benjamin Disraeli once differentiated between *misfortune* and *calamity* by using these words in a sentence describing his political rival William Gladstone: "If Mr. Gladstone fell into the Thames, it would be a misfortune; but if someone dragged him out, it would be a calamity." Misfortune and calamity might mean the same thing to some people, but in fact the two words allow a careful writer to discriminate fine shades of meaning.

One of the best ways to pay attention to words as words is to practice making subtle distinctions among related words. The "right" word contributes accuracy and precision to your meaning. The "wrong" word, it follows, is inaccurate or imprecise. The most reliable guide to choosing the right word and avoiding the wrong word is a dictionary that includes not only concise definitions but also the origin of words (their *etymology*). A dicey alternative is a thesaurus (a dictionary of synonyms, now included in most word processing software). A thesaurus can offer you a host of choices, but you run a fairly high risk of choosing an inappropriate word because the thesaurus lists words as synonyms that really have different shades of meaning and connotation.

Many of the most common diction errors happen because the writer has not learned the difference between similar terms that actually have different meanings. A common error of this kind is use of the word "notorious" when what the writer means to say is "famous." A *notorious* figure is widely but unfavorably known, whereas a *famous* person is usually recognized for accomplishments that are praiseworthy. Referring to a famous person as notorious—a rather comic error—could be an embarrassing mistake.

A slightly less severe version of getting the wrong word occurs when a writer uses a word with a shade of meaning that is inappropriate or inaccurate in a particular context. Take, for example, the words *assertive* and *aggressive*. Often used interchangeably, they don't really mean the same thing—and the difference matters. Loosely defined, both terms mean forceful. But assertive suggests being bold and self-confident, whereas aggressive suggests being eager to attack. In most cases, you compliment the person you call assertive but raise doubts about the person you call aggressive.

One particularly charged context in which shades of meaning matter involves the potentially sexist implications of using one term for women and another for men. If, for example, in describing a woman and a man up for the same job, the employer were to refer to the woman as *aggressive* but the man as *assertive*, his diction would deservedly be considered sexist. It would reveal that what is perceived as poised and a sign of leadership potential in a man is construed as unseemly belligerence in a woman. The sexism enters when word choice suggests that what is assertive in a man is aggressive in a woman.

Tone

Tone is the *implied attitude* of a piece of language toward its subject and audience. Whenever you revise for style, your choices in syntax and diction affect the tone. There are no hard-and-fast rules to govern matters of tone, and your control of it depends on your sensitivity to the particular context—your understanding of your own intentions and your readers' expectations.

Let's consider, for example, the tonal implications of the warning signs in the subways of London as compared with New York.

> **London:** Leaning out of the window may cause harm.
> **New York:** Do not lean out of the window.

Initially, you may find the English injunction laughably indirect and verbose in comparison with the shoot-from-the-hip clarity of the American sign. But that is to ignore the very thing we are calling *style*. The American version appeals to authority, commanding readers what not to do without telling them why. The English version, by contrast, appeals to logic; it is more collegial toward its readers and assumes they are rational beings rather than children prone to misbehave.

In revising for tone, you need to ask yourself if the attitude suggested by your language is appropriate to the aim of your message and to your audience. Your goal is to keep the tone *consistent* with your rhetorical intentions. The following paragraph, from a college catalogue, offers a classic mismatch between the overtly stated aim and the tonal implications:

> The student affairs staff believes that the college years provide a growth and development process for students. Students need to learn about themselves and others and to learn how to relate to individuals and groups of individuals with vastly different backgrounds, interests, attitudes and values. Not only is the tolerance of differences expected, but also an appreciation and a celebration of these differences must be an outcome of the student's experience. In addition, the student must progress toward self-reliance and independence tempered by a concern for the social order.

The explicit content of this passage—*what* it says—concerns tolerance. The professed point of view is student-friendly, asserting that the college exists to allow students "to learn about themselves and others" and to support the individual in accord with the "appreciation… of… differences." But note that the implicit tone—*how* the passage goes about saying *what* it says—is condescending and intolerant. Look at the verbs. An imperious authority lectures students about what they "*need* to learn," that tolerance is "*expected*," that "celebration… *must* be an outcome," and that "the student *must* progress" along these lines. Presumably, the paragraph does not intend to adopt this high-handed manner, but its deafness to tone subverts its desired meaning.

TRY THIS 10.10: Analyze Tone-Deaf Prose

Using the example from the college catalogue as a model, locate and bring to class examples of tonal inconsistency or inappropriateness that you encounter in your daily life. If you have difficulty finding examples, try memos from those in authority at your school or workplace, which often contain excruciating examples of officialese. Type one of your passages, and underneath it compose a paragraph of analysis in which you single out particular words and phrases and explain how the tone is inappropriate. Then, rewrite the passage to remedy the problem.

TRY THIS 10.11: Analyze Effective Tone

Find an example of tone that you think is just about perfect for the message and audience. Type it, and underneath discuss why it succeeds. Be as specific as you can about how the passage functions stylistically. Talk about particular phrasings and the match between what is being said and how it is said. Factor into your discussion the relationship between levels of style in the example and its presumed audience.

The Politics of Language

Style has political and ethical implications. A little over a half century ago, in his famous essay "Politics and the English Language," George Orwell warns of the "invasion of one's mind by ready-made phrases… [which] can only be prevented if one is constantly on guard against them." The worst modern writing, he declares, "consists in gumming together long strips of words which have already been set in order by someone else, making the results presentable by sheer humbug." It was Orwell who characterized what has come to be called the "Official Style" in terms of euphemism—calling a spade a certain garden implement. Orwell was also concerned with the substitution of abstract for concrete language for the purpose of what he called "the defense of the indefensible." His example was referring to attacks on a country's people as relocation of unreliable elements.

Insofar as style is an expression of the writer's self, Orwell implies, (1) we are under attack from broad cultural clichés and sentimental nostrums that do our thinking for us, and (2) it is thus a matter of personal integrity and civic responsibility to ask ourselves a series of questions about the sentences that we write. As Orwell says, What am I trying to say? What words will express it? What image or idiom will make it clearer? Is this image fresh enough to have an effect? Could I put it more shortly? Have I said anything that is avoidably ugly?

Words matter. They matter in how we name things, in how we phrase meanings—and also in how we are shaped by the words we read and hear in the media. Words don't simply reflect a neutral world that is out there in some objective way that offers self-evident meanings we can universally agree upon. Words don't reflect—they constitute; they call the world into being. They call us into being when we write them.

In a previous example we noted, for example, that the decision to call a woman "aggressive" as opposed to "assertive" matters. There are examples all around you of language creating rather than merely reflecting reality. Start looking for these on the front page of your newspaper, in political speeches, in advertising, even in everyday conversation. Does it matter, for instance, that there are no equivalents to the words "spinster" or "whore" for men? Does it change things to refer to a bombing mission as a "containment effort" or, by way of contrast, to call an enthusiastic person "a fanatic"?

Ethos, Audience, and Levels of Style

Style can be thought of as occupying various levels depending on whether it is formal or informal, personal or impersonal, though most styles blend these extremes. It is best to think of levels of style in terms of **ethos**, the character of the speaker that your style creates, and the kind of relationship with and attitude toward your audience that your style suggests. Some rhetoricians classify levels of style in terms of a writer positioning himself or herself *above*, *below*, or *at the same level* as the reader. When analyzing a writer's style, try looking for sentences that reveal the writer's rhetorical choices—those that reveal the kind of relationship he or she wishes to establish with readers in order to engage their support: expert and authoritative (above), companionable (at the same level as readers—at least some of the time), or below (aware that readers may have some advantage in terms of knowledge or attitude).

Transparent vs. Opaque Styles: Knowing When to Be Visible

In his insightful book on style, *Analyzing Prose*, Richard Lanham speaks of two kinds of style—transparent and opaque. Usually, "opaque" is a negative word for describing a writer's style, suggesting that it is unduly dense and hard to understand, something through which light cannot pass. Lanham, however, uses the word in a different sense. He observes that some styles try to come off as transparent, by which he means that the style does its best not to be noticed. Opaque styles, on the other hand, like opaque rather than transparent surfaces, call attention to themselves. They are meant to be seen. Opaque styles, unlike transparent ones, do not create the illusion that the writer has disappeared into the fabric of his or her prose. Instead, opaque styles make the writer and his or her stylistic choices visible and relatively prominent. Style is an explicit component of whatever it is the writer has come to say.

These terms are especially useful for understanding how a writer is meant to position himself or herself in the style prescriptions of different academic disciplines. Nowhere are misunderstandings across the disciplines more pronounced. Writers in the humanities and in some social sciences are allowed, in fact even expected, to be present in their prose. Readers are meant to know that a human being is writing to them. In the natural and some of the social sciences, writers are expected to pull the strings but remain more or less invisible. In these disciplines, style is not meant to call attention to itself—though for outsiders the style of science writing is anything but transparent. When a science writer criticizes the writing of a student from the humanities as "flowery" (decorative), he or she is saying that the student's style is calling too much attention to itself. It is opaque.

The Person Question: When and When Not to Use "I"

The matter of transparent vs. opaque styles is especially evident in a writer's choice of writing in first rather than third person. Most analytical prose is more precise and straightforward for the reader in the third person. When you cut "I am convinced that" or "In my opinion" from the beginning of a claim, what you lose in personal conviction you gain in concision and directness by keeping the focus on the main idea in a main clause. Most academic analysis focuses on the subject matter rather than on you as you respond to it. If you use the third person, you keep the attention where it belongs.

First person: I believe Heraclitus is an underrated philosopher.

Third person: Heraclitus is an underrated philosopher.

Although using the first-person "I" can throw the emphasis on the wrong place in a sentence, you might consider using the first person in the drafting stage if you are having trouble bringing your own point of view to the forefront. In this situation, the "I" becomes a strategy for loosening up and saying what you really think about a subject rather than adopting conventional and faceless positions.

The argument for using the first and second person ("you") is that "I" and "you" are personal and engage readers. Finding opportunities to do some kind of personal writing is important because it can help inexperienced writers to find the voice and kind of engagement they need in order to energize whatever kind of writing they are asked to do. And, contrary to the general rule, some professors actually prefer the first-person pronoun in particular contexts, as noted in the following Voices from Across the Curriculum. As a general rule, however, in the formal products of most academic writing, especially in the sciences and social sciences, you should avoid personal pronouns.

It is not necessarily the case that the third person is therefore impersonal. Just as film directors put their stamps on films by the way they organize the images, move among camera viewpoints, and orchestrate the sound tracks, so writers, even when writing in the third person, have a wide variety of resources at their disposal for making the writing more personal and accessible for their audiences.

Proceed with caution with the second person, direct address. Using "you" is a fairly assertive gesture. Readers could easily be annoyed, for example, by a paper about advertising that states, "When you read about a sale at the mall, you know it's hard to resist." Most readers resent a writer airily making assumptions about them or telling them what to do. Some rhetorical situations, however, call for the use of "you." Textbooks, for example, use "you" frequently because it creates a more direct relationship between authors and readers. Yet, even in appropriate situations, directly addressing readers as "you" may alienate them by ascribing to them attitudes and needs they may not have.

VOICES FROM ACROSS THE CURRICULUM

Using the First-Person "I": Two Professors Speak

The biggest stylistic problem is that students tend to be too personal or colloquial in their writing, using phrases such as the following: "Scientists all agree," "I find it amazing that," "The thing that I find most interesting." Students are urged to present data and existing information in their own words, but in an objective way. My preference in writing is to use the active voice in the past tense. I feel this is the most direct and least wordy approach: "I asked this," "I found out that," "These data show."

—RICHARD NIESENBAUM, PROFESSOR OF BIOLOGY

Avoid phrases like "The author believes (or will discuss)." Except in the paper's abstract, "*I* believe (or will discuss)" is okay, and often best.

—ALAN TJELTVEIT, PROFESSOR OF PSYCHOLOGY

In the following Voice from Across the Curriculum, biochemistry professor Keri Colabroy shares the basic style guidelines that she provides to her science majors.

VOICES FROM ACROSS THE CURRICULUM

Sentence Style in Science Writing: A Biochemistry Professor Speaks

The voice, ethos, and tone of science writing is typically quite muted. Active verbs appear, but the style goes out of its way to not call attention to itself, and especially not to the writer. This muted quality is, in fact, true of most academic writing, but it is markedly so in the sciences.

Subjects (the "actor" is absent)

- Passive voice

  Correct: The gel was run. (*Not*: I ran the gel.)

  Better: The protein migrated at a molecular weight of… (data first, not procedure)

- Pronouns—it's safer to avoid them

Verbs (qualify, qualify, qualify…)

- Do: demonstrate, indicate, suggest, construct, deliver, observe
- Don't: show, prove, make

Sentences

- Don't say in two sentences what you can say with one (embedding).
- Subordinate and coordinate.

Words

- Data are plural.
- When making observations, use academic, not conversational, language.
- Choose words for precision and tone (qualify your verbs, not your adjectives).

—KERI COLABROY, PROFESSOR OF BIOCHEMISTRY

Formal vs. Colloquial Styles

Imagine that you call your friend on the phone, and a voice you don't recognize answers. You ask to speak with your friend, and the voice responds, "With whom have I the pleasure of speaking?" By contrast, what if the voice instead responds, "Who's this?" What information do these two versions of the question convey, beyond the obvious request for your name?

The first response—"With whom have I the pleasure of speaking?"—tells you that the speaker is formal and polite. He is also probably fastidiously well educated: he not only knows the difference between "who" and "whom" but also obeys the etiquette that outlaws ending a sentence with a preposition ("Whom have I the pleasure of speaking *with*?"). The very formality of the utterance, however, might lead you to label the speaker pretentious. His assumption that conversing with you is a "pleasure" suggests empty flattery.

On the other hand, the second version—"Who's this?"—while also grammatically correct, is less formal. It is more direct and also terse to a fault; the speaker does not seem particularly interested in treating you politely.

The two hypothetical responses represent two different levels of style. Formal English obeys the basic conventions of standard written prose, and most academic writing is fairly formal. An informal style—one that is more conversational—can have severe limitations in an academic setting. The syntax and vocabulary of written prose aren't the same as those of speech, and so attempts to import the language of speech into academic writing can result in your communicating less meaning with less precision. Let's look at one brief example:

> Internecine quarrels within the corporation destroyed morale and sent
>   the value of the stock plummeting.

The phrase "internecine quarrels" may strike some readers as a pretentious display of formal language, but consider how difficult it is to communicate this concept economically in more colloquial (talk-like, conversational) terms. "Fights that go on between people related to each other" is awkward; "brother against brother" is sexist and a cliché; and "mutually destructive disputes" is acceptable but long-winded and less precise.

It is arguably a part of our national culture to value the simple and the direct as more genuine and democratic than the sophisticated, which is supposedly more aristocratic and pretentious. This "plain-speaking" style, however, can hinder your ability to develop and communicate your ideas. In the case of *internecine*, the more formal diction choice actually communicates more, and more effectively, than the less formal equivalents.

The Problem of Inflated Diction

The flip side of overly colloquial (informal and conversational) word choice is the problem of writers choosing words that are several steps further up the abstraction scale than they need to be, such as using the phrase "linguistic option" when you mean "word choice." Inflated diction usually results from one of two related causes. The first of these comes from the laudable goal of college students trying to acclimate to all of the new vocabulary they need to learn in order to speak the languages of the various academic disciplines. Academic disciplines are discourse communities—groups of people connected by a shared way of speaking. While trying to learn these new language sets, students understandably have trouble knowing when to choose a familiar word and when to reach for a more rarified term. Probably it is better to make some mistakes trying to gain control of the new vocabularies than to not try them at all.

The other cause of inflated diction is insecurity, which causes the writer to cloak ideas in words larger and more abstract than called for by the writing situation in order to assuage their fear of sounding stupid. This is understandable, but also avoidable. When in doubt, choose the more familiar and less polysyllabic word except in cases where a specialized vocabulary or an unusually high level of formality are called for.

Jargon: When to Use Insider Language

Many people assume that all jargon—the specialized vocabulary of a particular group—is bad: pretentious language designed to make most readers feel inferior. Many writing textbooks attack jargon in similar terms, calling it either polysyllabic balderdash or a specialized, gatekeeping language designed by an in-group to keep others out.

Yet, in many academic contexts, jargon is downright essential. It is conceptual shorthand, a technical vocabulary that allows the members of a group (or a discipline) to converse with one another more clearly and efficiently. Certain words that may seem odd to outsiders in fact function as connective tissue for a way of thought shared by insiders.

The following sentence, for example, although full of botanical jargon, is also admirably cogent:

> In angiosperm reproduction, if the number of pollen grains deposited on the stigma exceeds the number of ovules in the ovary, then pollen tubes may compete for access to ovules, which results in fertilization by the fastest growing pollen tubes.

We would label this use of jargon acceptable because it is written, clearly, by insiders *for* fellow insiders. It might not be acceptable language for an article intended for readers who are not botanists, or at least not scientists.

The problem with jargon comes when this insiders' language is directed at outsiders as well. The language of contracts offers a prime example of such jargon at work:

> The Author hereby indemnifies and agrees to hold the Publisher, its licensees, and any seller of the Work harmless from any liability, damage, cost, and expense, including reasonable attorney's fees and costs of settlement, for or in connection with any claim, action, or proceeding inconsistent with the Author's warranties or representations herein, or based upon or arising out of any contribution of the Author to the Work.

Run for the lawyer! What does it mean to "hold the Publisher . . . harmless"? To what do "the Author's warranties or representations" refer? What exactly is the author being asked to do here—release the publisher from all possible lawsuits that the author might bring? A lawyer might reasonably argue that contract language, designed to communicate clearly and concisely to other lawyers, is not meant to be understood by the layperson. Such documents are written by lawyers for other lawyers—although non-lawyers are asked to sign them.

At what point do insiders need to aim at language that the outsiders affected by it might understand? A lawyer's translation for the layperson would not, necessarily, mean the same thing as the language of the contract, but it is the language of the contract by which the layperson will be bound.

As the botanical and legal examples suggest, the line between acceptable and obfuscating jargon is complicated. Because most academic writing is addressed to insiders, students studying a particular area need to learn its jargon. By demonstrating that you can "talk the talk," you will validate your authority to pronounce an opinion on matters in the discipline. But it is also important for writers to recognize when insider-language needs to be defined or replaced with more generally known terms.

Style Analysis: A Summary of Things to Look For

This chapter has presented terms and techniques for experimenting with sentence styles and word choice. Equipped with these, you might profitably begin to read and listen for style more self-consciously. Find models. When a style appeals to you, figure out what makes it work. Copy sentences you like. Try imitating them.

Most people simply don't pay attention to words. They use words as if their sounds were inaudible, their shapes were invisible, and their meanings were single and self-evident. One goal of this chapter is to interest you in words themselves—as things with particular qualities, complex histories, and varied shades of meaning.

Start your practice by finding a piece of writing that you think is interesting for style. Or you could find two pieces to analyze so that you can use comparison and contrast to help you notice things. Mark up your chosen passages. Put a single line under sentence subjects and two lines under the verb in independent clauses. Start by finding the main clause or clauses in each sentence. Then circle all of the conjunctions—coordinating, conjunctive, correlative, subordinating, relative. You might want to use different colors in order to better see the balance of coordinate to subordinate structures in the piece. Also circle all of the commas and dashes and semicolons and colons.

Your goal is to be able to see the shapes of sentences: where the main clauses are in each sentence, how often a clause is interrupted or predication is in some way delayed, where modifying information has been added onto the main clause or clauses and in what form. Are the sentences primarily compound or complex?

How does the writer like to start his or her sentences? How do they typically end? Does the writer use a mostly periodic or a cumulative style or some combination of the two? Is there a lot of parallelism in the piece? Where is this most noticeable? Does the writer tend toward short or long sentences and clauses? How much variety of sentence types do you find? Where do short sentences occur? Why might the writer have used short sentences where he or she did?

Try to find the writer's **"go-to" sentence shapes**—the ones he or she seems fond of. When you have done all of this observation, try to explain why, given the subject matter, the writer might have been attracted to certain kinds of sentence shapes. What, in other words, seems to you to be the relation between form and content—*what* the sentences say and *how* they go about saying it?

Assignments: Style: Choosing Words, Shaping Sentences

1. **Compare the Style of Two Writers.** Analyze the style—the syntax and also the diction—of two writers doing a similar kind of writing; for example, two sportswriters, two rock music reviewers, or two presidents. Study first the similarities. What style characteristics does this type of writing seem to invite? Then study the differences. How is one writer recognizable through his or her style? The American Rhetoric website is a wonderful place to go hunting.

2. **Analyze Your Own Style.** Assemble some pieces you have written, preferably of a similar type, and study them for style. Do you have some favorite stylistic moves? What sentence shapes (simple, compound, complex, highly parallel, periodic, or cumulative) dominate in your writing? What verbs? Do you use forms of "to be" a lot? What is the balance of abstract to concrete words?

3. **Find Go-To Sentences.** Whether we recognize it or not, most of us have a "go-to" sentence—the sentence shape we repeatedly go to as we write and talk. If a person's "go-to" sentence takes the form "Although _____, the fact is that _____," we might see that person as inclined to qualify his or her thoughts ("Although") and disinclined to immediately impose his or her ideas on others ("the fact that" comes in the second half of the sentence, where it gets a lot of emphasis but is also delayed and qualified by the sentence's opening observation).

   First, select one sentence in something you've been reading that you think is typical of that writer's way of putting sentences together. Describe that sentence shape and speculate about what it accomplishes and how it reveals the writer's characteristic mode of thinking in some way.

   Then, find a "go-to" sentence of your own in something that you've written. What does this structure reveal to you about how you think? Look for repeated conjunctions or subordinators, such as "x; however, y" or "although x, nevertheless, y," or "not only x, but also y."

4. **Analyze the Gettysburg Address.** For many people, Lincoln's Gettysburg Address is one of the best examples of the careful matching of style to situation. Delivered after a long talk by a previous speaker at the dedication of a Civil War battlefield on a rainy day, the speech composed by Abraham Lincoln (some say on the back of an envelope) is a masterpiece

of style. Analyze its sentence structure, such as its use of parallelism, antithesis, and other kinds of repetition. Which features of Lincoln's style seem most important in creating the overall effect of the piece? Or do this with any popular journalist you read regularly and who you think has an especially effective style. Or look for another inspirational speech and see if such occasional writing has anything in common. (You can download and print the Gettysburg Address from many sites on the web.)

5. **Do a Full-fledged Stylistic Revision of a Paper.** As you revise, try to accomplish each of the following:

   a. Sharpen the diction.

   b. Blend concrete and abstract diction.

   c. Experiment with the order of and relation among subordinate and coordinate clauses. Locate things that you wish to emphasize at the end of sentences.

   d. Choose more knowingly between active and passive voice.

   e. Cut the fat, especially by eliminating unnecessary "to be" constructions.

   f. Vary sentence length and shape.

   g. Use parallelism.

   h. Experiment with periodic and cumulative sentences.

   i. Fine-tune the tone.

CHAPTER 11

Nine Basic Writing Errors (BWEs) and How to Fix Them

Overview The chapter shows writers how to recognize and correct the nine basic writing errors most likely to disrupt reader understanding. The chapter also includes discussion of the difference between grammatical errors and matters of usage. The chapter argues that, in many cases, errors are not just the product of carelessness but of the writer's ways of thinking about sentences. Until writers can uncover the logic of some of the errors they regularly make, they have a hard time fixing these errors or even finding them in their drafts.

The Concept of Basic Writing Errors (BWEs)

Error correction can be overwhelming. You get a paper back, and it's a sea of red ink. Fortunately, if you look more closely, you'll often find that you haven't made hundreds of mistakes—you've made only a few, but over and over in various forms. This phenomenon is what the rhetorician Mina Shaughnessy addressed in a book called *Errors & Expectations* by creating the category she called "basic writing errors," or BWEs. Shaughnessy argues that, in order to improve your writing for style and correctness, you need to do two things:

- Look for a *pattern of error,* which will require you to understand your own logic in the mistakes you typically make.

- Recognize that not all errors are created equal, which means that you need to *address errors in some order of importance*—beginning with those most likely to interfere with your readers' understanding.

This chapter reflects Shaughnessy's view. It does not cover *all* of the rules of grammar, punctuation, diction, and usage—such as where to place the comma or period when you close a quotation or whether or not to write out numerals. Instead, it emphasizes the errors that are potentially the most damaging to the clarity of your writing and to your credibility with readers. We have arranged the error types in a hierarchy, moving in descending order of severity (from most to least problematic).

As in our discussion of style in Chapter 10, the key premises of this chapter are that a sentence is made up of moveable parts and that sentences disclose the relationships among those parts. Keep these premises in mind, and you will see what the errors have in common.

Nine Basic Writing Errors

For each basic writing error listed below, the chapter offers a definition with examples and then talks you through how to fix it—with a "Test Yourself" section to help you apply what you have learned. At the end of the chapter, a brief Glossary of Grammatical Terms defines and illustrates many of the key terms used in this chapter and the previous one (on style). Use the Glossary to look up any terms mentioned in our explanations that you don't understand, such as independent clause, subordinating conjunction, participle, etc. For more comprehensive explanation of such terms as these, in the context of sentence types, see Chapter 10. There is also an appendix that provides solutions to the chapter's various "Test Yourself" exercises.

- Sentence fragments
- Comma splices and fused (run-on) sentences
- Errors in subject–verb agreement
- Shifts in sentence structure (faulty predication)
- Errors in pronoun reference
- Misplaced modifiers and dangling participles
- Errors in using possessive apostrophes
- Comma errors
- Spelling/diction errors that interfere with meaning

Some Advice on Proofreading

- Have a separate proofreading phase at the end of your composing process in which you attend only to grammar and punctuation.
- Look at each sentence as a discrete unit. If you have trouble doing this—if you get caught up in the flow of your thinking—try proofreading the paper backward. Start with the last sentence, then the next-to-last, and move all the way from back to front.
- Circle each punctuation mark, and ask yourself why it is there. In this way, you will be more likely to find commas where there should be periods.
- Read your paper out loud with a pencil in hand. Writers are much more likely to notice errors when they hear them. (Many of the BWEs typically make sentences difficult to follow and difficult to read out loud.)

BWE 1: Sentence Fragments

The most basic of writing errors, a **sentence fragment**, is a group of words punctuated like a complete sentence but lacking the necessary structure: it is only part of a sentence. Typically, a sentence fragment occurs when the group of words in question (1) lacks a subject, (2) lacks a predicate, or (3) is a subordinate (or dependent) clause.

To fix a sentence fragment, either turn it into an independent clause by providing whatever is missing—a subject or a predicate—or attach it to an independent clause on which it can depend.

Noun Clause (No Predicate) as a Fragment

A world where imagination takes over and sorrow is left behind.

This fragment is not a sentence but rather a noun clause—a sentence subject with no predicate. The fragment lacks a verb that would assert something about the subject. (The verbs *takes over* and is *left* are in a dependent clause created by the subordinating conjunction *where*.)

Corrections

A world **arose** where imagination takes over and sorrow is left behind.
    [new verb matched to "a world"]
She entered a world where imagination takes over and sorrow is left
    behind. *[new subject and verb added]*

The first correction adds a new verb ("arose"). The second introduces a new subject and verb, converting the fragment into the direct object of "she entered."

Verbal as a Fragment

Falling into debt for the fourth consecutive year.

"Falling" in the preceding fragment is not a verb. Depending on the correction, "falling" is either a verbal or part of a verb phrase.

Corrections

The company was falling into debt for the fourth consecutive year.
    [subject and helping verb added]
Falling into debt for the fourth consecutive year **led the company
    to consider relocating**. *[new predicate added]*
Falling into debt for the fourth consecutive year, **the company
    considered relocating**. *[new subject and verb added]*

In the first correction, the addition of a subject and the helping verb "was" converts the fragment into a sentence. The second correction turns the fragment into a gerund phrase functioning as the subject of a new sentence. The third correction converts the fragment into a participial phrase attached to a new independent clause. (See the section entitled Glossary of Grammatical Terms and look under "verbal" for definitions of "gerund" and "participle.")

Subordinate Clause as a Fragment

> I had an appointment for 11:00 and was still waiting at 11:30. Although I did get to see the dean before lunch.

"Although" is a subordinating conjunction that calls for some kind of completion. Like "if," "when," "because," "whereas," and other subordinating conjunctions (see the Glossary of Grammatical Terms), "although" *always* makes the clause that it introduces dependent.

Correction

> I had an appointment for 11:00 and was still waiting at 11:30, **although** I did get to see the dean before lunch. [*fragment attached to preceding sentence*]

As the correction demonstrates, the remedy lies in attaching the fragment to an independent clause on which it can depend (or, alternatively, making the fragment into a sentence by dropping the conjunction).

Sometimes writers use sentence fragments deliberately, usually for rhythm and emphasis or to create a conversational tone. In less formal contexts, they are generally permissible, but you run the risk that the fragment will not be perceived as intentional. In formal writing assignments, it is safer to avoid intentional fragments.

Test Yourself 11.1: Fragments

There are fragments in each of the following three examples, probably the result of their proximity to legitimate sentences. What's the problem in each case, and how would you fix it?

1. Like many other anthropologists, Margaret Mead studied non-Western cultures in such works as *Coming of Age in Samoa*. And influenced theories of childhood development in America.

2. The catastrophe resulted from an engineering flaw. Because the bridge lacked sufficient support.

3. In the 1840s the potato famine decimated Ireland. It being a country with poor soil and antiquated methods of agriculture.

Using Dashes and Colons to Correct Fragments

Beyond what the punctuation guide in Chapter 10 has offered, the particular virtues of the dash and colon as ways to correct sentence fragments deserve brief mention. One way to correct a fragment is to replace the period with a dash: "The campaign required commitment. Not just money." becomes "The campaign required commitment—not just money." The dash offers you one way of attaching a phrase or dependent clause to a sentence without having to construct another independent clause. In short, it's succinct.

(Compare the correction that uses the dash with another possible correction: "The campaign required commitment. It also required money.") Moreover, with the air of sudden interruption that the dash conveys, it can capture the informality and immediacy that the intentional fragment offers a writer.

You should be wary of overusing the dash as the slightly more presentable cousin of the intentional fragment. The energy it carries can clash with the decorum of formal writing contexts; for some readers, its staccato effect quickly becomes too much of a good thing.

One alternative to this usage of the dash is the colon. It can substitute because it also can be followed by a phrase, a list, or a clause. It must be preceded by an independent clause. And like the dash, it carries dramatic force because it abruptly halts the flow of the sentence.

The colon, however, does not convey informality. In place of a slapdash effect, it trains a light on what is to follow it. Hence, as in this sentence you are reading, it is especially appropriate for setting up certain kinds of information: explanations, lists, or results. In the case of results, the cause or action precedes the colon; the effect or reaction follows it.

BWE 2: Comma Splices and Fused (or Run-On) Sentences

A comma splice consists of two independent clauses connected ("spliced") with a comma; a fused (or run-on) sentence combines two such clauses with no conjunction or punctuation. The solutions for both comma splices and fused sentences are the same.

1. Place a conjunction (such as "and" or "because") between the clauses.

2. Place a semicolon between the clauses.

3. Make the clauses into separate sentences.

All of these solutions solve the same logical problem: they clarify the boundaries of the independent clauses for your readers.

Comma Splice

He disliked discipline, he avoided anything demanding.

Correction

Because he disliked discipline, he avoided anything demanding.
   [subordinating conjunction added]

Comma Splice

Today most TV programs are violent, almost every program is about cops and detectives.

Correction

> Today most TV programs are violent; almost every program is about cops and detectives. [*semicolon replaces comma*]

Because the two independent clauses in the first example contain ideas that are closely connected logically, the most effective of the three comma-splice solutions is to add a subordinating conjunction ("because") to the first of the two clauses, making it depend on the second. For the same reason—close conceptual connection—the best solution for the next comma splice is to substitute a semicolon for the comma. The semicolon signals that the two independent clauses are closely linked in meaning. In general, you can use a semicolon where you could also use a period.

Cures for the Perpetual Comma Splicer

The comma splice is remarkably common, even among fairly sophisticated writers. It indicates two things: (1) the writer is not distinguishing between independent and dependent clauses and (2) he or she is operating on the so-called "pause theory" of punctuation. All of the clauses in our two preceding examples are independent. As written, each of these should be punctuated not with a comma but rather with a period or a semicolon. Instead, the perpetual comma splicer, as usual, acts on the "pause theory": because the ideas in the independent clauses are closely connected, the writer hesitates to separate them with a period. And so the writer inserts what he or she takes to be a shorter pause—the comma.

But a comma is not a "breath" mark; it provides readers with specific grammatical information, in each of these cases mistakenly suggesting there is only one independent clause separated by the comma from modifying information. In the corrections, by contrast, the semicolon sends the appropriate signal to the reader: the message that it is joining two associated but independent statements. Adding a coordinating conjunction such as "and" would also be grammatically correct, though possibly awkward. (*See the discussion of independent clauses and comma rules in Chapter 10.*)

Fused Sentence

> The Indo-European language family includes many groups most languages in Europe belong to it.

Correction

> The Indo-European language family includes many groups. Most languages in Europe belong to it. [*period inserted after first independent clause*]

You could also fix this fused sentence with a comma plus the coordinating conjunction "and." Alternatively, you might condense the whole into a single independent clause.

> Most languages in Europe belong to the Indo-European language family.

Comma Splices with Conjunctive Adverbs

> Quantitative methods of data collection show broad trends, however, they ignore specific cases.

Sociobiology poses a threat to traditional ethics, for example, it asserts that human behavior is genetically motivated by the "selfish gene" to perpetuate itself.

Corrections

> Quantitative methods of data collection show broad trends; however, they ignore specific cases. [*semicolon replaces comma before "however"*]

> Sociobiology poses a threat to traditional ethics; for example, it asserts that human behavior is genetically motivated by the "selfish gene" to perpetuate itself. [*semicolon replaces comma before "for example"*]

Both of these examples contain one of the most common forms of comma splices. Both of them are compound sentences, that is, they contain two independent clauses. Normally, connecting the clauses with a comma and a conjunction would be correct: for example, "Most hawks hunt alone, but osprey hunt in pairs." In the preceding two comma splices, however, the independent clauses are joined by transitional expressions known as conjunctive adverbs. *(See the Glossary of Grammatical Terms and the discussion of conjunctive adverbs in Chapter 10.)* When a conjunctive adverb is used to link two independent clauses, it *always* requires a semicolon. By contrast, when a coordinating conjunction links the two clauses of a compound sentence, it is *always* preceded by a comma.

In most cases, depending on the sense of the sentence, the semicolon precedes the conjunctive adverb and clarifies the division between the two clauses. There are exceptions to this general rule, though, as in the following sentence:

> The lazy boy did finally read a **book, however;** it was the least he could do.

Here, "however" is a part of the first independent clause and qualifies its claim. The sentence thus suggests the boy was not totally lazy because he did get around to reading a book. Note how the meaning changes when "however" becomes the introductory word for the second independent clause.

> The lazy boy did finally read a **book; however**, it was the least he could do.

Here, the restricting force of "however" suggests that reading the book was not much of an accomplishment.

Test Yourself 11.2: Comma Splices

What makes each of the following sentences a comma splice? Determine the best way to fix each one and why, and then make the correction.

1. "Virtual reality" is a buzzword, so is "hyperspace."

2. Many popular cures for cancer have been discredited, nevertheless, many people continue to buy them.

3. Elvis Presley's home, Graceland, attracts many musicians as a kind of shrine, even Paul Simon has been there.

4. She didn't play well with others, she sat on the bench and watched.

BWE 3: Errors in Subject–Verb Agreement

The subject and the verb must agree in number, a singular subject taking a singular verb and a plural subject taking a plural verb. Errors in subject–verb agreement usually occur when a writer misidentifies the subject or verb of a clause.

Agreement Problem: Plural Subject, Singular Verb

> Various kinds of vandalism has been rapidly increasing.

Correction

> Various kinds of vandalism **have** been rapidly increasing. [*verb made plural to match "kinds"*]

When you isolate the grammatical subject ("kinds") and the verb ("has") of the original sentence, you can tell that they do not agree. Although "vandalism" might seem to be the subject because it is closest to the verb, it is actually the object of the preposition "of." The majority of agreement problems arise from mistaking the object of a preposition for the actual subject of a sentence. If you habitually make this mistake, you can begin to remedy it by familiarizing yourself with the most common prepositions. (*See the Glossary of Grammatical Terms, which contains a list of these terms.*)

Agreement Problem: Singular Subject, Plural Verb

> Another aspect of territoriality that differentiates humans from animals are their possession of ideas and objects.

Correction

> Another aspect of territoriality that differentiates humans from animals **is** their possession of ideas and objects. [*verb made singular to match subject "aspect"*]

The subject of the sentence is "aspect." The two plural nouns ("humans" and "animals") probably encourage the mistake of using a plural verb ("are"), but "humans" is part of the "that" clause modifying "aspect," and "animals" is the object of the preposition "from."

Agreement Problem: "Each" Must Take Singular Verb

> The Republican and the Democrat both believe in doing what's best for America, but each believe that the other doesn't understand what's best.

Correction

> The Republican and the Democrat both believe in doing what's best for America, but each **believes** that the other doesn't understand what's best. [*verb made singular to agree with subject "each"*]

The word "each" is *always* singular, so the verb ("believes") must be singular as well. The presence of a plural subject and verb in the sentence's first independent clause ("the Republican and the Democrat both believe") has probably encouraged the error.

Test Yourself 11.3: Subject–Verb Agreement

Diagnose and correct the error in the following example:

The controversies surrounding the placement of Arthur Ashe's statue in Richmond was difficult for the various factions to resolve.

A Note on Dialects and Standard Written English

Some people have trouble recognizing and fixing certain errors because they are not errors in their discourse communities. Different cultures inside the larger culture of English-language speakers use different syntactical forms. This fact has given rise to the phrase "Standard Written English," which names one particular version of English as the norm. People whose language practices constitute a dialect, for example, are told they have to acquire the other dialect—Standard Written English.

The concept of Standard Written English has been controversial. Critics argue that the concept enforces the language practices of privileged groups and discriminates against the practices of less powerful groups in the culture. The best-known instance of this discrimination appears in the matter of subject–verb agreement among some African-Americans who leave off the verb ending -s in the third person singular present tense.

Standard Written English: He walks to town. (singular)
They walk to town. (plural)
Dialect: He walk to town. (singular)
They walk to town. (plural)

Speakers of the dialect do not differentiate singular from plural verb forms with a terminal "–s" in the present tense (only), as in Standard Written English.

If you look up the term "Ebonics", you can study the debate about whether or not this particular "error" is descended from syntactical patterns in African languages. Like all ethical debates, this one is not easily resolved. In practical terms, however, you should be aware that these two ways of handling subject–verb agreement are recognized by linguists not in terms of right versus wrong but rather in terms of dialect difference.

A *dialect* is a version of a language characteristic of a region or culture and is sometimes unintelligible to outsiders. The problem for speakers of a dialect that differs from the norm is that they can't always rely on the ear—on what sounds right—when they are editing according to the rules of Standard Written English. Such speakers need, in effect, to learn to speak more than one dialect so that they can edit according to the rules of Standard Written English in situations in which this would be expected. This adaptation often requires adding a separate proofreading stage for particular errors, like subject–verb agreement, rather than relying on what sounds right.

BWE 4: Shifts in Sentence Structure (Faulty Predication)

This error involves an illogical mismatch between subject and predicate. If you continually run afoul of faulty predication, you might use the exercises in a handbook to drill you on isolating the grammatical subjects and verbs of sentences because that is the first move you need to make in fixing the problem.

Faulty Predication

> In 1887, the release of more information became available.

Correction

> In 1887, more **information** became available **for release**. *[new subject]*

It was the "information," not the "release," that "became available." The correction relocates "information" from its position as object of the preposition "of" to the subject position in the sentence; it also moves "release" into a prepositional phrase.

Faulty Predication

> The busing controversy was intended to rectify the inequality of educational opportunities.

Correction

> Busing was intended to rectify the inequality of educational opportunities. *[new subject formulated to match verb]*

The *controversy* wasn't intended to rectify, but busing was.

Test Yourself 11.4: Faulty Predication

Identify and correct the faulty predication in this example:

The subject of learning disabilities are difficult to identify accurately.

BWE 5: Errors in Pronoun Reference

There are at least three forms of this problem. All of them involve a lack of clarity about whom or what a pronoun (a word that substitutes for a noun) refers to. The surest way to avoid difficulties is to make certain the pronoun relates back unambiguously to a specific word to which it refers, known as the antecedent. In the sentence "Nowadays appliances don't last as long as they once did," the noun "appliances" is the antecedent of the pronoun "they."

Pronoun–Antecedent Agreement

> A pronoun must agree in number (and gender) with the noun or noun phrase that it refers to.

Pronoun Error: Plural Pronoun With Singular Antecedent

> It can be dangerous if a child, after watching TV, decides to practice what they saw.

Corrections

> It can be dangerous if **children,** after watching TV, **decide** to practice what **they** saw. *[antecedent (and verb) made plural to agree with plural pronoun.*

> It can be dangerous if a child, after watching TV, decides to practice what **he or she** saw. *[singular pronouns substituted to match singular antecedent "child"]*

The error occurs because "child" is singular, but the pronoun referring to it, "they," is plural. The first correction makes both singular; the second makes both plural. You might also observe in the first word of the example—the impersonal "it"—an exception to the rule that pronouns must have antecedents.

Test Yourself 11.5: Pronoun–Antecedent Agreement

What is wrong with the following sentence, and how would you fix it?

> Every dog has its day, but all too often when that day happens, they can be found barking up the wrong tree.

Ambiguous Reference A pronoun should have only one possible antecedent. The possibility of two or more confuses relationships within the sentence.

Pronoun Error: More Than One Possible Referent for "They"

> Children like comedians because they have a sense of humor.

Corrections

> Because children have a sense of humor, **they** like comedians. *[subordinate "because" clause placed first, and relationship between noun "children" and pronoun "they" tightened]*

> Children like comedians because **comedians** have a sense of humor. *[pronoun eliminated and replaced by repetition of noun]*

Does "they" in the original example refer to "children" or "comedians"? The rule in such cases of ambiguity is that the pronoun refers to the nearest possible antecedent, so here "comedians" possess the sense of humor, regardless of what the writer may intend. As the corrections demonstrate, either reordering the sentence or repeating the noun can remove the ambiguity.

Test Yourself 11.6: Ambiguous Reference

As you proofread, it's a good idea to target your pronouns to make sure they cannot conceivably refer to more than one noun. What's wrong with the following sentences?

1. Alexander the Great's father, Philip of Macedon, died when he was twenty-six.

2. The committee could not look into the problem because it was too involved.

Broad Reference Broad reference occurs when a pronoun refers loosely to a number of ideas expressed in preceding clauses or sentences. It causes confusion because the reader cannot be sure which of the ideas the pronoun refers to.

Pronoun Error: Use of "This" Makes Referent Unclear

> As a number of scholars have noted, Sigmund Freud and Karl Marx offered competing but also at times complementary critiques of the dehumanizing tendencies of Western capitalist society. We see this in Christopher Lasch's analysis of conspicuous consumption in *The Culture of Narcissism*.

Correction

> As a number of scholars have noted, Sigmund Freud and Karl Marx offered competing but also at times complementary critiques of the dehumanizing tendencies of Western capitalist society. We see **this complementary view** in Christopher Lasch's analysis of conspicuous consumption in *The Culture of Narcissism*. [broad "this" clarified by addition of noun phrase]

The word "this" in the second sentence of the uncorrected example could refer to the fact that "a number of scholars have noted" the relationship between Freud and Marx, to the competition between Freud's and Marx's critiques of capitalism, or to the complementary nature of the two men's critiques.

Beware "this" as a pronoun: it's the most common source of broad reference. The remedy is generally to avoid using the word as a pronoun. Instead, convert "this" into an adjective and let it modify some noun that more clearly specifies the referent: "this complementary view," as in the correction or, alternatively, "this competition" or "this scholarly perspective."

Test Yourself 11.7: Broad Reference

Locate the errors in the following examples and provide a remedy for each.

1. Regardless of whether the film is foreign or domestic, they can be found in your neighborhood video store.

2. Many experts now claim that dogs and other higher mammals dream; for those who don't own such pets, this is often difficult to believe.

A Note on Sexism and Pronoun Usage

Errors in pronoun reference sometimes occur because of a writer's praiseworthy desire to avoid sexism. In most circles, the following correction of a previous example would be considered sexist.

> It can be dangerous if a child, after watching TV, decides to practice what **he** saw.

Though the writer of such a sentence may intend "he" to function as a gender-neutral impersonal pronoun, it in fact excludes girls on the basis of gender. Implicitly, it also conveys sexual stereotypes (for example, that only boys are violent, or perhaps stupid enough to confuse TV with reality).

The easiest way to avoid the problem of sexism in pronoun usage usually lies in putting things into the plural form because plural pronouns ("we," "you," "they") have no gender. (See the use of "children" in the first correction of the pronoun–antecedent agreement example.) Alternatively, you can use the phrase "he or she." Many readers, however, find this phrase and its variant, "s/he," to be awkward constructions. Another remedy lies in rewriting the sentence to avoid pronouns altogether, as in the following revision.

It can be dangerous if a child, after watching TV, decides to practice **some violent activity portrayed on the screen**.

BWE 6: Misplaced Modifiers and Dangling Participles

Modifiers are words or groups of words used to qualify, limit, intensify, or explain some other element in a sentence. A misplaced modifier is a word or phrase that appears to modify the wrong word or words.

Misplaced Modifier: Modifier Appears to Modify Wrong Word

At the age of three he caught a fish with a broken arm.

Correction

At the age of three **the boy with a broken arm** caught a fish.
[noun replaces pronoun; prepositional phrase revised and relocated]

The original sentence mistakenly implies that the fish had a broken arm. Modification errors often occur in sentences with one or more prepositional phrases, as in this case.

Misplaced Modifier: Modifier Appears to Modify Wrong Word

According to legend, General George Washington crossed the Delaware and celebrated Christmas in a small boat.

Correction

According to legend, General George Washington crossed the Delaware **in a small boat** and **then** celebrated Christmas **on shore**. *[prepositional phrase relocated; modifiers added to second verb]*

As a general rule, you can avoid misplacing a modifier by keeping it as close as possible to what it modifies. Thus, the second correction removes the implication that Washington celebrated Christmas in a small boat. When you cannot relocate the modifier, separate it from the rest of the sentence with a comma to prevent readers from connecting it to the nearest noun.

A dangling participle creates a particular kind of problem in modification: the noun or pronoun that the writer intends the participial phrase to modify is not actually present in the sentence. Thus, we have the name dangling participle: the participle has been left dangling because the word or phrase it is meant to modify is not there.

Dangling Participle: Subject That Participle Modifies Does Not Appear in the Sentence

> After debating the issue of tax credits for the elderly, the bill passed in a close vote.

Correction

> After debating the issue of tax credits for the elderly, **the Senate passed the bill** in a close vote. *[appropriate noun added for participle to modify]*

The bill did not debate the issue, as the original example implies. As the correction demonstrates, fixing a dangling participle involves tightening the link between the activity implied by the participle ("debating") and the entity performing that activity ("the Senate").

Test Yourself 11.8: Modification Errors

Find the modification errors in the following examples and correct them.

1. After eating their sandwiches, the steamboat left the dock.

2. The social workers saw an elderly woman on a bus with a cane standing up.

3. Crossing the street, a car hit the pedestrian.

BWE 7: Errors in Using Possessive Apostrophes

Adding 's to most singular nouns will make them show possession, for example, the plant's roots, the accountant's ledger. You can add the apostrophe alone, without the "s," for example, to make plural nouns that already end with "s" show possession: the flowers' fragrances or the ships' berths (although you may also add an additional "s").

Apostrophe Error

> The loyal opposition scorned the committees decisions.

Corrections

> The loyal opposition scorned the committee's decisions.

> The loyal opposition scorned the committees' decisions. *[possessive apostrophe added]*

The first correction assumes there was one committee; the second assumes there were two or more.

Apostrophe Error

> The advisory board swiftly transacted it's business.

Correction

> The advisory board swiftly transacted **its** business. *[apostrophe dropped]*

Unlike possessive nouns, possessive pronouns ("my," "your," "yours," "her," "hers," "his," "its," "our," "ours," "their," "theirs") *never* take an apostrophe.

Test Yourself 11.9: Possessive Apostrophes

Find and correct any errors in the following sentence:

The womens movement has been misunderstood by many of its detractors.

BWE 8: Comma Errors

As with other rules of punctuation and grammar, the many that pertain to comma usage share an underlying aim: to clarify the relationships among the parts of a sentence. Commas separate the parts of a sentence grammatically. One of their primary uses, then, is to help your readers distinguish the main clause from dependent elements such as subordinate clauses and long prepositional phrases. (See also "Why Commas Matter" in Chapter 10.) They do not signify a pause, as was discussed in BWE 2.

Comma Error: Comma Missing After Introductory Phrase

> After eating the couple went home.

Correction

> After eating, the couple went home. *[comma added before independent clause]*

The comma after "eating" is needed to keep the main clause "visible" or separate; it marks the point at which the prepositional phrase ends and the independent clause begins. Without this separation, readers would be invited to contemplate cannibalism as they move across the sentence.

Comma Error: Comma Missing After Introductory Phrase

> In the absence of rhetoric study teachers and students lack a vocabulary for talking about their prose.

Correction

> In the absence of rhetoric study, teachers and students lack a vocabulary for talking about their prose. *[comma added to separate prepositional phrase from main clause]*

Without the comma, readers would have to read the sentence twice to find out where the prepositional phrase ends—with "study"—to figure out where the main clause begins.

Comma Error: Two Commas Needed Around Parenthetical Element

> Dog owners, despite their many objections will have to obey the new law.

Correction

> Dog owners, despite their many objections, will have to obey the new law.
> *[single comma converted to a pair of commas]*

A comma is needed after "objections" to isolate the phrase in the middle of the sentence ("despite their many objections") from the main clause. The phrase needs to be set off with commas because it contains additional information not essential to the meaning of what it modifies. (Dog owners must obey the law whether they object or not.) Phrases and clauses that function in this way are called *nonrestrictive*.

A Note on Restrictive versus Nonrestrictive Elements

As we noted in Chapter 10, the test of nonrestrictive phrases and clauses is to see if they can be omitted without substantially changing the message that a sentence conveys ("Dog owners will have to obey the new law," for example). Nonrestrictive elements always take two commas—a comma "sandwich"—to set them off. Using only one comma illogically separates the sentence's subject ("dog owners") from its predicate ("will have to obey"). This problem is easier to see in a shorter sentence. You wouldn't, for example, write "I, fell down." As a rule, commas virtually never separate the subject from the verb of a sentence. (Here's an exception: "Ms. Smith, a high fashion model, watches her diet scrupulously.")

Comma Error: Two Commas Needed Around Parenthetical Element

> Most people regardless of age like to spend money.

Correction

> Most people, regardless of age, like to spend money. *[comma sandwich added]*

Here, commas enclose the nonrestrictive elements; you could omit this information without significantly affecting the sense. Such is not the case in the following two examples.

Comma Error: Restrictive Elements Should Not Be Enclosed Within Commas

> People, who live in glass houses, should not throw stones.

Correction

> People who live in glass houses should not throw stones. *[commas omitted]*

Comma Error: No Comma Setting Off Restrictive Clause

Please return the library book, that I left on the table.

Correction

Please return the library book that I left on the table. *[comma omitted]*

As we noted with the same example in Chapter 10, it is incorrect to place commas around "who live in glass houses." It is also incorrect to place a comma before "that I left on the table." Each of these is a *restrictive clause,* that is, each contains information that is an essential part of what it modifies. In the first sentence, for example, if "who live in glass houses" is left out, the fundamental meaning of the sentence is lost: "People should not throw stones." The word "who" is defined by restricting it to "people" in the category of glass-house dwellers. Similarly, in the second example the "that" clause contributes an essential meaning to "book"; the sentence is referring to not just any book but to a particular one, the one "on the table."

So, remember the general rule: if the information in a phrase or clause can be omitted—if it is nonessential and therefore nonrestrictive—it needs to be separated by commas from the rest of the sentence. Moreover, note that nonrestrictive clauses are generally introduced by the word "which," so a "which" clause interpolated into a sentence takes a comma sandwich. ("The dinner, which I bought for $20, made me sick.") By contrast, a restrictive clause is introduced by the word "that" and takes no commas.

Test Yourself 11.10: Comma Errors

Consider the following examples as a pair. Punctuate them as necessary, and then briefly articulate how the meanings of the two sentences differ.

1. The book which I had read a few years ago contained a lot of outdated data.

2. The book that I had read a few years ago contained a lot of outdated data.

BWE 9: Spelling/Diction Errors That Interfere with Meaning

Misspellings are always a problem in a final draft, insofar as they undermine your authority by inviting readers to perceive you as careless (at best). If you make a habit of using the spellchecker of a word processor, you will take care of most misspellings; however, the problems a spellchecker won't catch are the ones that can often hurt you most. These are actually diction errors—incorrect word choices in which you have confused one word with another that it closely resembles. In such cases, you have spelled the word correctly, but it's the wrong word. Because it means something other than what you've intended, you end up misleading your readers.

The best way to avoid this problem is to memorize the differences between pairs of words commonly confused with each other but that have distinct meanings. The following examples illustrate a few of the most common and serious of these errors. Most handbooks contain a glossary of usage that *cites* more of these *sites* of confusion.

Spelling/Diction Error: "It's" versus "Its"

> Although you can't tell a book by its' cover, its fairly easy to get the general idea from the introduction.

Correction

> Although you can't tell a book by **its** cover, **it's** fairly easy to get the general idea from the introduction. *[apostrophe dropped from possessive and added to contraction]*

"It's" is a contraction for "it is." "Its" is a possessive pronoun meaning "belonging to it." If you confuse the two, it's likely that your sentence will mislead its readers.

Spelling/Diction Error: "Their" versus "There" versus "They're"

> Their are ways of learning about the cuisine of northern India besides going their to watch the master chefs and learn there secrets— assuming their willing to share them.

Correction

> **There** are ways of learning about the cuisine of northern India besides going **there** to watch the master chefs and learn **their** secrets— assuming **they're** willing to share them. *[expletive "there," adverb "there," possessive pronoun "their," and contraction "they're" inserted appropriately]*

"There" as an adverb normally refers to a place; "there" can also be used as an expletive to introduce a clause, as in the first usage of the correction. "Their" is a possessive pronoun meaning "belonging to them." "They're" is a contraction for "they are."

Spelling/Diction Error: "Then" versus "Than"

> If a person would rather break a law then obey it, than he or she must be willing to face the consequences.

Correction

> If a person would rather break a law **than** obey it, **then** he or she must be willing to face the consequences. *[comparative "than" distinguished from temporal "then"]*

"Than" is a conjunction used with a comparison, for example, "rather X than Y." "Then" is an adverb used to indicate what comes next in relation to time, for example, "first X, then Y."

Spelling/Diction Error: "Effect" versus "Affect"

> It is simply the case that BWEs adversely effect the way that readers judge what a writer has to say. It follows that writers who include lots of BWEs in their prose may not have calculated the disastrous affects of these mistakes.

Correction

> It is simply the case that BWEs adversely **affect** the way that readers judge what a writer has to say. It follows that writers who include lots of BWEs in their prose may not have calculated the disastrous **effects** of these mistakes. *[verb "affect" and noun "effects" inserted appropriately]*

In their most common usages, "affect" is a verb meaning "to influence," and "effect" is a noun meaning "the result of an action or cause." The confusion of "affect" and "effect" is enlarged by the fact that both of these words have secondary meanings: the verb "to effect" means "to cause or bring about"; the noun "affect" is used in psychology to mean "emotion or feeling." Thus, if you confuse these two words, you will inadvertently make a meaning radically different from the one you intend.

Test Yourself 11.11: Spelling/Diction Errors

Make corrections as necessary in the following paragraph.

Its not sufficiently acknowledged that the behavior of public officials is not just an ethical issue but one that effects the sale of newspapers and commercial bytes in television news. When public officials don't do what their supposed to do, than their sure to face the affects of public opinion—if they get caught—because there are dollars to be made. Its that simple: money more then morality is calling the tune in the way that the press treats it's superstars.

Correctness vs. Usage: Grammar Rules and Social Convention

Grammar is a volatile subject. Grammatical errors evoke not just disapproval but anger in some people. Why? Well, clearly correct grammar matters. Readers should not have to struggle to figure out where your sentences begin and end or what goes with what. But the fact that correctness matters—that correctness is necessary to being taken seriously as a writer—does not account for the sheer venom that goes into spotting other people's grammatical errors.

Language use is social and conventional. Conforming to the rules is, in a sense, a sign that you agree to be governed by the same conventions that others conform to. Perhaps this is why the intentional sentence fragment has the impact that it does. Really. The gesture makes the writer's style seem daring. It says, "You and I both recognize that I control the standard conventions with sufficient assurance to break them on purpose, not by accident."

Usage: How Language Customs Change

Errors of grammar are relatively stable and locked down. "The eggs was tasty" is wrong; so is "Obama are President" and "Obama is Presidents." But usage, a kind of troublesome and embarrassing cousin to grammar, is a more vexed subject. According to the *Oxford English Dictionary*, usage has to do with "established or customary use or employment of language, words, expressions, etc." Established by whom? Customary within what group? Usage, in short, tends to be less clear cut than grammar.

That is why some dictionaries offer brief paragraphs of discussion from a "usage panel"—a group of experts who weigh in on what is proper and improper in language use. Most of the usage guides you will find at the back of grammar handbooks offer a range of examples of usage. At one end of the range, there are examples in which one form is clearly preferred and another disapproved.

Usage: Some Examples of Right & Wrong versus Etiquette

Here is a set of examples, organized on a sliding scale, from clearly distinguished right and wrong to less defensible distinctions.

- **fewer vs. less**: Countable things are fewer: fewer pencils; amounts that can't be counted are less: less support. This is a helpful distinction, one the language needs.

- **good vs. well**: *Good* is an adjective, a part of speech that modifies (describes) nouns and other adjectives. *It was a good movie. Well* is an adverb, a part of speech that modifies a verb or another adverb. *She does not feel well. Good* modifies *movie; well* modifies *feel*. This is another helpful distinction; therefore, most people consider this word choice a matter of right and wrong.

- **can vs. may**: *Can* refers to what one is able to do; *may* refers to what one is permitted to do. *He can spit across the classroom, but according to the teacher, he may not.* Again, this distinction conveys a meaningful difference, although in actual practice, the word *may* is starting to lose its clout—it sounds fussy to many contemporary ears.

- **between vs. among**: *Between* refers to two items, *among* to more than two. *The difference between sushi and sashimi is more easily understood than the differences among sushi, sashimi, and maki.* In this case, we can clearly see that if you used *between* in both cases, a reader would still be able to make sense of the sentence, but the use of *among* is helpful—it lets us know that more than two items are coming. Still, as you can see, this example of usage is less significant, more a matter of good manners, than *can* vs. *may*. Nonetheless, it is arguably a useful distinction.

- **different from vs. different than**: Some say a writer should not use *different than*, because *than* is comparative, but different already signifies that a comparison is coming, so you should always say *different from*. Let's use this example—and there are others like it—as an emblem of a preference for which there is not really much of a reason.

- **ending a sentence with a preposition**: The prescription that one should not end a sentence with a preposition or—if you will—that a preposition is a part of speech you should not end a sentence with, is a case of rather arbitrary usage. In this same category goes the split infinitive—the practice of locating a word inside a *to* + verb construction, such as *to boldly go where no one has gone before*. In a formal setting—an application to law school, say—you would want to be careful to avoid these usages, even though they are not actually wrong.

Why then do some guardians of the language insist that we not end sentences with prepositions? Is it snobbery? Etiquette? First of all, let's admit that etiquette serves a definite purpose, as anyone who has gone out to dinner and had the misfortune to sit next to a food fight will attest. To be understanding, let's assume that the person who enforces usage distinctions as hard-and-fast rules, even when they are not, is a person who wishes to maintain standards in the face of change. And that, too, is a position one may (and can!) respect.

But the fact is that the language is always changing, not just with the addition of new words to the standard dictionaries, but also with the circumstances of usage—"the established or customary use or employment of language, words, expressions, etc." Ultimately, a panel of experts cannot control usage, and that is a healthy thing, allowing a language to evolve over time.

When Usage Begins to Change Grammar

Which brings us back to the issue of grammatical correctness, a subject that impelled this digression into usage in the first place (yes, we know it's a fragment). Usage and, more particularly, changes in usage affect grammar because, although relatively fixed, grammar does not stand still. Some grammatical rules do change when people begin using words differently.

Here are three common examples of how changing usage appears to be inspiring a change in the grammatical conventions of right and wrong. These changes have not yet occurred, but arguably, they are in the process of occurring.

- **possessive apostrophes:** An increasing number of writers simply leave these out. If one writes, *The cars fender was dented* (not car's) or *Max Scherzers slider is the best in the American League* (not Scherzer's), virtually every reader will understand the meaning, though not as quickly as the apostrophe would allow.

- **I vs. me:** especially in prepositional phrases: This one has to do with what grammarians call the case of pronouns. We use one form of a pronoun when it is in the subject and another when it is the object of a verb or a preposition. For example,

  - *My mother and I argue about grammar*—not *My mother and me*. We would not say *"Me argues about grammar." I* is in the subjective case; *me* is in the objective case.

  - *According to my mother and me, grammar matters a lot*—not *According to my mother and I*. We would not say *According to I*. "According to" is a preposition, so you have to use the objective case, as the pronoun in question is the object of the preposition.

But increasingly, we hear native speakers saying things such as *Joe and me are going to get a beer* or *For Jill and I, voting is an undeniable civic duty, virtually an ethical imperative.* In the first example, a speaker might say *Joe and me* because it sounds "natural," that is, unpretentious, as unpretentious as having a beer. In the second example, a speaker might say *For Jill and I* because (and we're not sure why this is!), the use of "and I" sometimes sounds classier, more high style, and in a sentence where lofty concepts such as civic duty and ethical imperatives occur, you might wish to sound classy. But "I" in "For Jill and I" must be changed to "me," the objective case because it is the object of the preposition "For."

- **who versus whom:** This is another version of the pronoun problem. *Who* is subjective case; *whom* is objective case. For example: *I want to know who ate the last slice of pie I left in the refrigerator.* Compare that with *Ask not for whom the bell tolls*—where *whom* is the object of the preposition *for*. Yet increasingly, speakers seem to fear working out the grammar necessary to figure out if the who/whom in question is a subject or an object, so they tend either to eliminate *whom* altogether and just use *who* for every case, or they assume that *whom* is classier, as they do with "and I," and they end up misusing *whom*. Here are examples:

  - *Who is Derek Jeter going to sign with, now that he has become a free agent?* This sentence is grammatically incorrect: we need a *Whom* to be the object of the preposition *with*—*With whom will Jeter sign?*

  - *I read a book by the cognitive therapist whom is most famous for formulating rational emotive therapy.* The loftiness of the topic misleads the writer into using the supposedly classier *whom* even though grammar tells us the pronoun *who* is in the subjective case.

Usage as Cultural Marker

You can think of usage in terms of markers—indicators of something. So, for example:

- usage as marker for informal, conversational versus formal style:

    And then she _goes_, _"that's the silliest thing I've ever heard"_ versus _And then she _says_, . . ._

    And some people disallow contractions as too informal.

- usage as marker for social class:

    Where is he at? versus _Where is he?_

    I ain't going versus _I am not going._

- usage as gender marker:

    Poetess versus _poet_, _actress_ versus _actor_, _waitress_ versus _waiter_ or _waitperson_

    Most people have not heard the word _poetess_—how long before the same will be said of _actress_? (The _–ess_ suffix indicating female is now considered sexist by many people because it relegates women to a separate category.)

TRY THIS 11.1: Discover the Rationale for Usage Choices

Research the following pairs of terms. Locate the usage "rules" that govern them, and if you can, uncover the rationale that informs these rules.

> Try and / try to
> Shall / will
> Disinterested / uninterested
> Raise / rise

Glossary of Grammatical Terms

adjective   An adjective is a part of speech that usually modifies a noun or pronoun—for example, _blue, boring, boisterous._

adverb   An adverb is a part of speech that modifies an adjective, adverb, or verb—for example, _heavily, habitually, very._ The adverbial form generally differs from the adjectival form via the addition of the ending "–ly"; for example, _happy_ is an adjective, and _happily_ is an adverb.

clause (independent and dependent)   A clause is any group of words that contains both a **subject** and a **predicate**. An **independent clause** (also known as a **main clause**) can stand alone as a sentence. For example,

> The most famous revolutionaries of this century have all, in one way or another, offered a vision of a classless society.

The subject of this independent clause is "revolutionaries," the verb is "have offered," and the direct object is "vision." By contrast, a **dependent** (or **subordinate**) **clause** is any group of words containing a subject and verb that cannot stand alone as a separate sentence because it depends on an independent clause to complete its meaning. The following sentence adds two dependent clauses to our previous example:

> The most famous revolutionaries of this century have all, in one way or another, offered a vision of a classless society, **although** most historians would agree **that** this ideal has never been achieved.

The origin of the word "depend" is "to hang": a dependent clause literally hangs on the independent clause. In the preceding example, neither "although most historians would agree" nor "that this ideal has never been achieved" can stand independently. The "that" clause relies on the "although" clause, which in turn relies on the main clause. "That" and "although" function as **subordinating conjunctions**; by eliminating them, we could rewrite the sentence to contain three independent clauses:

> The most famous revolutionaries of this century have all, in one way or another, offered a vision of a classless society. Most historians would agree on one judgment about this vision: it has never been achieved.

comma splice A comma splice consists of two independent clauses incorrectly connected (spliced) with a comma. See BWE 2.

conjunction (coordinating and subordinating) A conjunction is a part of speech that connects words, phrases, or clauses—for example, *and, but, although*. The conjunction in some way defines that connection: for example, *and* links; *but* separates. All conjunctions define connections in one of two basic ways. Coordinating conjunctions connect words or groups of words that have equal grammatical importance. The coordinating conjunctions are *and, but, or, nor, for, so,* and *yet*. Subordinating conjunctions introduce a dependent clause and connect it to a main clause. Here is a partial list of the most common subordinating conjunctions: *after, although, as, as if, as long as, because, before, if, rather than, since, than, that, though, unless, until, when, where, whether,* and *while*.

conjunctive adverb A conjunctive adverb is a word that links two independent clauses (as a conjunction) but that also modifies the clause it introduces (as an adverb). Some of the most common conjunctive adverbs are *consequently, furthermore, however, moreover, nevertheless, similarly, therefore,* and *thus*. Phrases can also serve this function, such as *for example* and *on the other hand*. When conjunctive adverbs are used to link two independent clauses, they always require a semicolon:

> Many pharmaceutical chains now offer their own generic versions of common drugs; however, many consumers continue to spend more for name brands that contain the same active ingredients as the generics.

When conjunctive adverbs occur within an independent clause, however, they are enclosed in a pair of commas, as is the case with the use of *however* earlier in this sentence.

coordination Coordination refers to grammatically equal words, phrases, or clauses. Coordinate constructions are used to give elements in a sentence equal weight or importance. In the sentence "The tall, thin lawyer badgered the witness, but the judge interceded," the clauses "The tall, thin lawyer badgered the witness" and "but the judge interceded" are coordinate clauses; "tall" and "thin" are coordinate adjectives.

dependent clause (see clause)

direct object The direct object is a noun or pronoun that receives the action carried by the verb and performed by the subject. In the sentence, "Certain mushrooms can kill you," "you" is the direct object.

gerund (see verbals)

fused (or run-on) sentence A fused sentence incorrectly combines two independent clauses with no conjunction or punctuation. See BWE 2.

independent clause (see clause)

infinitive (see verbals)

main clause (see clause)

noun A noun is a part of speech that names a person (*woman*), place (*town*), thing (*book*), idea (*justice*), quality (*irony*), or action (*betrayal*).

object of the preposition (see preposition)

participle and participial phrase (see verbals)

phrase A phrase is a group of words occurring in a meaningful sequence that lacks either a subject or a predicate. This absence distinguishes it from a clause, which contains both a subject and a predicate. Phrases function in sentences as adjectives, adverbs, nouns, or verbs. They are customarily classified according to the part of speech of their keyword: "over the mountain" is a **prepositional phrase**; "running for office" is a **participial phrase**; "had been disciplined" is a **verb phrase**; "desktop graphics" is a **noun phrase**; and so forth.

predicate The predicate contains the verb of a sentence or clause, making some kind of statement about the subject. The predicate of the preceding sentence is "contains the verb, making some kind of statement about the subject." The simple predicate—the verb to which the other words in the sentence are attached—is "contains."

preposition, prepositional phrase A preposition is a part of speech that links a noun or pronoun to some other word in the sentence. Prepositions usually express a relationship of time (*after*) or space (*above*) or direction (*toward*). The noun to which the preposition is attached is known as the object of the preposition. A preposition, its object, and any modifiers comprise a prepositional phrase. "With love *from* me *to* you" strings together three prepositional phrases. Here is a partial list of the most common prepositions: *about, above, across, after, among, at, before, behind, between, by, during, for, from, in, into, like, of, on, out, over, since, through, to, toward, under, until, up, upon, with, within,* and *without.*

pronoun   A pronoun is a part of speech that substitutes for a noun, such as *I*, *you*, *he*, *she*, *it*, *we*, and *they*.

run-on (or fused) sentence   A run-on sentence incorrectly combines two independent clauses with no conjunction or punctuation. See BWE 2.

sentence   A sentence is a unit of expression that can stand independently. It contains two parts, a **subject** and a **predicate**. The shortest sentence in the Bible, for example, is "Jesus wept." "Jesus" is the subject; "wept" is the predicate.

sentence fragment   A sentence fragment is a group of words incorrectly punctuated like a complete sentence but lacking the necessary structure; it is only a part of a sentence. "Walking down the road" and "the origin of the problem" are both fragments because neither contains a **predicate**. See BWE 1.

subject   The subject, in most cases a noun or pronoun, names the doer of the action in a sentence or identifies what the predicate is about. The subject of the previous sentence, for example, is "the subject, in most cases a noun or pronoun." The simple subject of that sentence—the noun to which the other words in the sentence are attached—is "subject."

subordination, subordinating conjunctions   "Subordination" refers to the placement of certain grammatical units, particularly phrases and clauses, at a lower, less important structural level than other elements. As with coordination, the grammatical ranking carries conceptual significance as well: whatever is grammatically subordinated appears less important than the information carried in the main clause. In the following example, Microsoft is subordinated both grammatically and conceptually to Apple:

> Although Microsoft continues to upgrade the operating system and special features on its computers, the more stylish and virus-free Apple Macintosh computers continue to outclass them.

Here, "although" is a **subordinating conjunction** that introduces a subordinate clause, also known as a **dependent clause**.

verb   A verb is a part of speech that describes an action (*goes*), states how something was affected by an action (*became angered*), or expresses a state of being (*is*).

verbals   Verbals are words derived from verbs. They are verb forms that look like verbs but, as determined by the structure of the sentence they appear in, they function as nouns, adjectives, or adverbs. There are three forms of verbals.

An **infinitive**—composed of the root form of a verb plus *to* (*to be, to vote*)—becomes a verbal when it is used as a noun ("*To eat* is essential"), an adjective ("These are the books *to read*"), or an adverb ("He was too sick *to walk*").

Similarly, a **participle**—usually composed of the root form of a verb plus "–ing" (present participle) or "–ed" (past participle)—becomes a verbal when used as an adjective. It can occur as a single word, modifying a noun, as in *faltering negotiations* or *finished business*. But it also can occur in a participial phrase, consisting of the participle, its object, and any modifiers. Here are two examples:

> **Having been tried and convicted**, the criminal was sentenced to life imprisonment.

> **Following the path of most resistance**, the masochist took deep pleasure in his frustration.

"Having been tried and convicted" is a participial phrase that modifies "criminal"; "Following the path of most resistance" is a participial phrase that modifies "masochist." In each case, the participial phrase functions as an adjective.

The third form of verbal, the **gerund**, resembles the participle. Like the participle, it is formed by adding "–ing" to the root form of the verb, but unlike the participle, it is used as a noun. In the sentence "Swimming is extraordinarily aerobic," the gerund "swimming" functions as the subject. Again like participles, gerunds can occur in phrases. The gerund phrases are italicized in the following example: "*Watching a film adaptation* takes less effort than *reading the book* from which it was made."

When using a verbal, remember that although it resembles a verb, it cannot function alone as the verb in a sentence: "Being a military genius" is a fragment, not a sentence. (Also see the discussion of verbals in Chapter 10.)

Assignments: Nine Basic Writing Errors (BWEs) and How to Fix Them

1. **Chart the BWEs**. Write an example for each of the BWEs, along with a corrected version.

2. **Compose a Grammar and Style Quiz**. Write a paragraph that contains all of the basic writing errors. Not every sentence should contain an error, and you may contain multiple examples of the errors, but make sure you include all nine. Then, append an answer key in which you identify the errors and provide corrections.

3. **Research Online Resources**. Go online to different universities and colleges in search of their writing centers, and then look for the ways these websites handle the problem of grammatical correctness. See as an example OWL at Purdue University. Write a brief summary of what you find there.

4. **Circle Every Punctuation Mark**. Take a short piece of writing, your own or someone else's, published or unpublished. Circle every punctuation mark and explain why it is there. This is a useful exercise to do in pairs or in small groups. As a follow-up exercise, you might underline every independent clause and double-underline every dependent clause, circling the subordinating conjunctions.

Appendix
Basic Writing Errors (BWEs) Test Yourself Section Answer Key (With Discussion)

Test Yourself 11.1: Fragments (Page 308)

1. **EXAMPLE:** Like many other anthropologists, Margaret Mead studied non-Western cultures in such works as *Coming of Age in Samoa*. And influenced theories of childhood development in America.

   PROBLEM: The second sentence is actually a fragment, a predicate in need of a subject.

   POSSIBLE CORRECTION: Like many other anthropologists, Margaret Mead studied non-Western cultures (in such works as *Coming of Age in Samoa*) in ways that influenced theories of childhood development in America.

   COMMENT: There are many ways to fix this example, but its original form leaves ambiguous whether the fragment refers only to *Mead*, or to *many other anthropologists* as well. The correction offered includes the other anthropologists in the referent and diminishes the emphasis on Mead's book by placing it within parentheses. Although the correction uses a subordinating *that* to incorporate the fragment into the first sentence, it keeps this information in an emphatic position at the end of the sentence.

2. **EXAMPLE:** The catastrophe resulted from an engineering flaw. Because the bridge lacked sufficient support.

   PROBLEM: The second sentence is actually a dependent clause; *because* always subordinates.

   POSSIBLE CORRECTION: The catastrophe resulted from an engineering flaw: the bridge lacked sufficient support.

   COMMENT: Because the colon has causal force, this is an ideal spot to use one, identifying the "flaw."

3. **EXAMPLE:** In the 1840s the potato famine decimated Ireland. It being a country with poor soil and antiquated methods of agriculture.

   PROBLEM: The second sentence is actually a fragment, a subject plus a long participial phrase.

   POSSIBLE CORRECTION: In the 1840s the potato famine decimated Ireland, a country with poor and antiquated methods of agriculture.

COMMENT: The cause of this kind of fragment is usually that the writer mistakenly believes that *being* is a verb rather than a participle that introduces a long phrase (modifying "Ireland" in this case). It would also be correct simply to change the period to a comma in the original sentence.

Test Yourself 11.2: Comma Splices (Page 311)

1. **EXAMPLE:** "Virtual reality" is a new buzzword, so is "hyperspace."

   PROBLEM: This is a comma splice—both clauses are independent, yet they are joined with a comma.

   POSSIBLE CORRECTION: "Virtual reality" is a new buzzword; so is "hyperspace."

   COMMENT: Because the clauses are linked by association—both naming buzzwords—a semicolon would show that association. A writer could also condense the clauses into a simple sentence with a compound subject, for example, "Both 'virtual reality' and 'hyperspace' are new buzzwords."

2. **EXAMPLE:** Many popular cures for cancer have been discredited, nevertheless, many people continue to buy them.

   PROBLEM: A comma splice results from the incorrectly punctuated conjunctive adverb *nevertheless*.

   POSSIBLE CORRECTION: Many popular cures for cancer have been discredited; nevertheless, many people continue to buy them.

   COMMENT: Without the semicolon to separate the independent clauses, the conjunctive adverb could conceivably modify either the preceding or the following clause. This problem is usually worse with *however*.

3. **EXAMPLE:** Elvis Presley's home, Graceland, attracts many musicians as a kind of shrine, even Paul Simon has been there.

   PROBLEM: This is a comma splice—the two independent clauses are linked by a comma without a conjunction. The problem is exacerbated by the number of commas in the sentence; the reader cannot easily tell which one is used to separate the clauses.

   POSSIBLE CORRECTION: Elvis Presley's home, Graceland, attracts many musicians as a kind of shrine—even Paul Simon has been there.

   COMMENT: Although one could justly use a semicolon here, the dash conveys the impromptu effect of an afterthought.

4. **EXAMPLE:** She didn't play well with others, she sat on the bench and watched.

PROBLEM: Because the second clause develops the first one, a writer might think that it is dependent on the first; conceptually, yes, but grammatically, no.

POSSIBLE CORRECTION: She didn't play well with others; she sat on the bench and watched.

COMMENT: If the writer wanted to link the two clauses more tightly, a colon would be appropriate instead of the semicolon.

Test Yourself 11.3: Subject–Verb Agreement (Page 312)

EXAMPLE: The controversies surrounding the placement of Arthur Ashe's statue in Richmond was difficult for the various factions to resolve.

PROBLEM: The grammatical subject of the main clause (controversies) is plural; the verb (was) is singular.

POSSIBLE CORRECTIONS: The controversies surrounding the placement of Arthur Ashe's statue in Richmond were difficult for the various factions to resolve (or, The controversy... was).

COMMENT: An error of this kind is encouraged by two factors: the distance of the verb from the subject and the presence of intervening prepositional phrases that use singular objects, either of which a writer might mistake for the grammatical subject of the main clause.

Test Yourself 11.4: Faulty Predication (Page 314)

EXAMPLE: The subject of learning disabilities are difficult to identify accurately.

PROBLEM: The predicate matches the object of the preposition (learning disabilities) rather than the subject of the main clause (subject).

POSSIBLE CORRECTIONS: Learning disabilities are difficult to identify accurately.

COMMENT: Omitting the abstract opening (The subject of) enables the predicate (are) to fit the new grammatical subject (disabilities).

Test Yourself 11.5: Pronoun–Antecedent Agreement (Page 314)

EXAMPLE: Every dog has its day, but all too often when that day happens, they can be found barking up the wrong tree.

PROBLEM: The plural pronoun *they* that is the grammatical subject of the second clause does not have a plural antecedent in the sentence.

POSSIBLE CORRECTION: Every dog has its day, but all too often when that day happens, the dog can be found barking up the wrong tree.

COMMENT: If a writer vigilantly checks all pronouns, he or she will identify the intended antecedent of the pronoun *they* to be the singular *dog,* and will revise accordingly. The sentence would still be incorrect if the pronoun *it* were used instead of the repeated *dog* because *it* could refer to the nearest preceding noun, *day.*

Test Yourself 11.6: Ambiguous Reference (Page 315)

1. **EXAMPLE:** Alexander the Great's father, Philip of Macedon, died when he was twenty-six.

    PROBLEM: A reader can't be sure whether *he* refers to Alexander or to Philip.

    POSSIBLE CORRECTION: Alexander the Great's father, Philip of Macedon, died at the age of twenty-six.

    COMMENT: The correction rewords to remove the ambiguous pronoun. This solution is less awkward than repeating *Philip* in place of *he,* though that would also be correct.

2. **EXAMPLE:** The committee could not look into the problem because it was too involved.

    PROBLEM: A reader can't be sure whether *it* refers to *the committee* or to *the problem.*

    POSSIBLE CORRECTION: The committee was too involved with other matters to look into the problem.

    COMMENT: As with the previous example, rewording to eliminate the ambiguous pronoun is usually the best solution.

Test Yourself 11.7: Broad Reference (Page 316)

1. **EXAMPLE:** Regardless of whether the film is foreign or domestic, they can be found in your neighborhood video store.

    PROBLEM: The plural pronoun *they* does not have a plural antecedent in the sentence.

    POSSIBLE CORRECTION: Regardless of whether the film is foreign or domestic, it can be found in your neighborhood video store.

    COMMENT: Although the sentence offers two options for films, the word *film* is singular and so, as antecedent, requires a singular pronoun (it). It is probably worth noting here that it would still be correct even if the original sentence began, "Regardless of whether the film is a foreign film or a domestic film." The rule for compound subjects that use an either/or construction is as follows: the number (singular or plural) of the noun or pronoun that follows *or* determines the number of the verb. Compare the following two examples: "Either several of his aides *or* the *candidate* is going to speak" and "Either the candidate *or* several of his *aides are* going to speak."

2. **EXAMPLE:** Many experts now claim that dogs and other higher mammals dream; for those who don't own such pets, this is often difficult to believe.

PROBLEM: The referent of the pronoun *this* is unclear. Precisely what is difficult to believe—that mammals dream or that experts would make such a claim?

POSSIBLE CORRECTION: Many experts now claim that dogs and other higher mammals dream; for those who don't own such pets, this claim is often difficult to believe.

COMMENT: Often the best way to fix a problem with broad reference produced by use of *this* as a pronoun is to attach *this* to the noun to which it refers, as in "this book." As a rule, when you find an isolated *this* in your draft, ask and answer the question "This what?"

Test Yourself 11.8: Modification Errors (Page 317)

1. **EXAMPLE:** After eating their sandwiches, the steamboat left the dock.

PROBLEM: This is a dangling participle—the grammar of the sentence conveys that the steamboat ate their sandwiches.

POSSIBLE CORRECTIONS: After the girls ate their sandwiches, the steamboat left the dock. Or, After eating their sandwiches, the girls boarded the steamboat, and it left the dock.

COMMENT: The two corrections model the two ways of remedying most dangling participles. Both provide an antecedent (the girls) for the pronoun *their.* The first correction eliminates the participial phrase and substitutes a subordinate clause. The second correction adds to the existing main clause (steamboat left) another one (girls boarded) for the participial phrase to modify appropriately.

2. **EXAMPLE:** The social workers saw an elderly woman on a bus with a cane standing up.

PROBLEM: Misplaced modifiers create the problems in this sentence, which implies that the bus possessed a cane that was standing up. The problem exemplified here is produced by the series of prepositional phrases—"on a bus *with* a cane"—followed by the participial phrase *standing up,* which is used as an adjective and intended to modify *woman.*

POSSIBLE CORRECTION: The social workers saw an elderly woman on a bus. She was standing up with the help of a cane.

COMMENT: Writers often try to cram too much into sentences, piling on the prepositions. The best remedy is sometimes to break up the sentence, a move that usually involves eliminating prepositions, which possess a sludgy kind of movement, and adding verbs, which possess more distinct movement.

3. **EXAMPLE:** Crossing the street, a car hit the pedestrian.

PROBLEM: The dangling participle (Crossing the street) does not have a word to modify in the sentence. The sentence conveys that the car crossed the street.

POSSIBLE CORRECTIONS: Crossing the street, the pedestrian was hit by a car. Or: As the pedestrian crossed the street, a car hit him.

COMMENT: The first solution brings the participial phrase closest to the noun it modifies (pedestrian). The second converts the participle into the verb (crossed) of a dependent *as* clause and moves *pedestrian* into the clause as the subject for that verb. As in the *steamboat* example, one correction provides an appropriate noun for the participial phrase to modify, and the other eliminates the participle.

Test Yourself 11.9: Possessive Apostrophes (Page 318)

EXAMPLE: The womens movement has been misunderstood by many of its detractors.

PROBLEM: The possessive apostrophe for *womens* is missing. The trickiness here in inserting the apostrophe is that this word is already plural.

POSSIBLE CORRECTION: The women's movement has been misunderstood by many of its detractors.

COMMENT: Because the word is already plural, it takes a simple "–'s" to indicate a movement belonging to women—not "–s'" (womens').

Test Yourself 11.10: Comma Errors (Page 320)

PAIRED EXAMPLES: The book which I had read a few years ago contained a lot of outdated data.

The book that I had read a few years ago contained a lot of outdated data.

PROBLEM: In the first example, the modifying clause "which I had read a few years ago" is nonrestrictive: it could be omitted without changing the essential meaning of the sentence. Therefore, it needs to be enclosed in commas—as the *which* signals.

POSSIBLE CORRECTION: The book, which I had read a few years ago, contained a lot of outdated data.

COMMENT: The second example in the pair is correct as it stands. The restrictive clause, "that I had read a few years ago," does not take commas around it because the information it gives readers is an essential part of the meaning of *book*. That is, it refers to not just any book read a few years ago, as in the first example in the pair, but rather specifies the one containing outdated data. "The book that I had read a few years ago" thus functions as what is known as a *noun phrase*.

Test Yourself 11.11: Spelling/Diction Errors (Page 322)

EXAMPLE: Its not sufficiently acknowledged that the behavior of public officials is not just an ethical issue but one that effects the sale of newspapers and commercial bytes in television news. When public officials don't do what their supposed to do, than their sure to face the affects of public opinion—if they get caught—because there are dollars to be made. Its that simple: money more then morality is calling the tune in the way that the press treats it's superstars.

PROBLEMS: The paragraph confuses the paired terms discussed under BWE 9. It mistakes

its for *it's* before *not sufficiently.*

effects for *affects* before *the sale.*

their for *they're* before *supposed.*

than for *then* before *their sure.*

their for *they're* before *sure.*

affects for *effects* before *of public opinion.*

its for *it's* before *that simple.*

then for *than* before *morality.*

it's for *its* before *superstars.*

POSSIBLE CORRECTION: It's not sufficiently acknowledged that the behavior of public officials is not just an ethical issue but one that affects the sale of newspapers and commercial bytes in television news. When public officials don't do what they're supposed to do, then they're sure to face the effects of public opinion—if they get caught—because there are dollars to be made. It's that simple: money more than morality is calling the tune in the way that the press treats its superstars.

COMMENT: If you confuse similar words, the only solution is to memorize the differences and consciously check your drafts for any problems until habit takes hold.

PART 2

The Readings

CHAPTER 12

Manners, Communication, and Technology

One of our preliminary titles for this chapter was "How We Live Now." All of the readings in this chapter focus on the relationships between the public and the private, with particular focus on how those relationships are affected by the technologies of the information age—technologies that have brought us closer together in some ways, and further estranged us from each other in other ways.

The writers in this chapter come from disparate backgrounds, but they share a conviction that manners are anything but trivial—not simply a sign of your upbringing, the product of a parent's scolding about which fork to use or how to answer the phone. Rather, manners have to do with the fundamental ways that people in the public sphere interact with one another; they have to do with the boundaries of civility. And so to understand manners is to understand how we live as social beings.

ABOUT THE READINGS IN THIS UNIT

The readings in this unit explore the links among manners, communication, and technology. Christine Rosen starts things off with a historical piece (and position paper) on the cultural impact of cell phones: "They encourage talk, not conversation." This focus leads her to voice the need for us to reclaim what she calls "social space." Paul Goldberger adopts a complementary view in his short piece on the tendency of cell phones to transport us "out of real space into a virtual realm."

Next, Jeffrey Rosen broadens the focus to consider how individuals today "brand" themselves as part of what he calls "America's culture of self-revelation." The proliferation of weblogs, for example, he interprets as a sign of how the Internet complicates "our ability to negotiate the boundary between public and private." Geoffrey Nunberg does a variation on this theme in his short radio piece on the style of weblogs and the audiences they target and exclude.

The chapter then turns toward the personal essay in the novelist Jonathan Franzen's witty discussion of the mismatch between the outcry against the loss of privacy and the fact that we are "drowning" in it. He demonstrates how the concern with our private lives and those of public figures threatens to overwhelm the public sphere.

At the end of the chapter, we encounter Sam Anderson's rambunctious discussion of multitasking, ADHD, lifehacking, and the perpetual battle between staying focused and pursuing the pleasures of (mostly electronic) distraction.

Christine Rosen

Our Cell Phones, Our Selves

A historian by training, Rosen is a senior editor of *The New Atlantis: A Journal of Technology and Society*, where this piece first appeared in 2004. Rosen here offers a brief history of the cell phone and begins to chart the implications of its conquest of contemporary culture. The author of three books and many articles, she writes about the cultural impact of technology, as well as bioethics. Her forthcoming book is called *The Extinction of Experience*.

"Hell is other people," Sartre observed, but you need not be a misanthrope or   1
a diminutive French existentialist to have experienced similar feelings during the course of a day. No matter where you live or what you do, in all likelihood you will eventually find yourself participating in that most familiar and exasperating of modern rituals: unwillingly listening to someone else's cell phone conversation. Like the switchboard operators of times past, we are now all privy to calls being put through, to the details of loved ones contacted, appointments made, arguments aired, and gossip exchanged.

Today, more people have cell phones than fixed telephone lines, both in the United States and internationally. There are more than one billion cell phone users worldwide, and as one wireless industry analyst recently told *Slate*, "some time between 2010 and 2020, everyone who wants and can afford a cell phone will have one." Americans spend, on average, about seven hours a month talking on their cell phones. Wireless phones have become such an important part of our everyday lives that in July, the country's major wireless industry organization featured the following "quick poll" on its website: "If you were stranded on a desert island and could have one thing with you, what would it be?" The choices: "Matches/Lighter," "Food/Water," "Another Person," "Wireless Phone." The World Health Organization has even launched an "International EMF Project" to study the possible health effects of the electromagnetic fields created by wireless technologies.

But if this ubiquitous technology is now a normal part of life, our adjustment to it has not been without consequences. Especially in the United States, where cell phone use still remains low compared to other countries, we are rapidly approaching a tipping point with this technology. How has it changed our behavior, and how might it continue to do so? What new rules ought we to impose on its use? Most importantly, how has the wireless telephone encouraged us to connect individually but disconnect socially,

Christine Rosen, "Our Cell Phones, Our Selves," *The New Atlantis: A Journal of Technology and Society.* Copyright © 2001. Reprinted by permission.

ceding, in the process, much that was civil and civilized about the use of public space?

Untethered

Connection has long served as a potent sign of power. In the era before cell phones, popular culture served up presidents, tin-pot dictators, and crime bosses who were never far from a prominently placed row of phones, demonstrating their importance at the hub of a vast nexus. Similarly, superheroes always owned special communications devices: Batman had the Batphone, Dick Tracy his wrist-phone, Maxwell Smart his shoe spy phone. (In the Flash comics of the 1940s, the hero simply outraces phone calls as they are made, avoiding altogether the need for special communication devices.) To be able to talk to anyone, at any time, without the mediator of the human messenger and without the messenger's attendant delays, is a thoroughly modern triumph of human engineering.

5   In 1983, Motorola introduced DynaTAC, now considered the first truly mobile telephone, and by the end of that year, the first commercial cellular phone systems were being used in Chicago and in the Baltimore/Washington, D.C. area. Nokia launched its own mobile phone, the cumbersome Cityman, in 1987. Americans were introduced to the glamour of mobile telephone communication that same year in a scene from the movie *Wall Street*. In it, the ruthless Gordon Gekko (played by Michael Douglas) self-importantly conducts his business on the beach using a large portable phone. These first-generation cell phones were hardly elegant—many people called them "luggables" rather than "portables," and as one reporter noted in *The Guardian*, "mobiles of that era are often compared to bricks, but this is unfair. Bricks are quite attractive and relatively light." But they made up in symbolic importance what they lacked in style; only the most powerful and wealthiest people owned them. Indeed, in the 1980s, the only other people besides the elite and medical professionals who had mobile technologies at all (such as pagers) were presumed to be using them for nefarious reasons. Who else but a roving drug dealer or prostitute would need to be accessible at all times?

This changed in the 1990s, when cell phones became cheaper, smaller, and more readily available. The technology spread rapidly, as did the various names given to it: in Japan it is *keitai*, in China it's *sho ji*, Germans call their cell phones *handy*, in France it is *le portable* or *le G*, and in Arabic, *el mobile*, *telephone makhmul*, or *telephone gowal*. In countries where cell phone use is still limited to the elite—such as Bulgaria, where only 2.5 percent of the population can afford a cell phone—its power as a symbol of wealth and prestige remains high. But in the rest of the world, it has become a technology for the masses. There were approximately 340,000 wireless subscribers in the United States in 1985, according to the Cellular Telecommunications and Internet Associate (CTIA); by 1995, that number had increased to more than 33 million, and by 2003, more than 158 million people in the country had gone wireless.

Why do people use cell phones? The most frequently cited reason is convenience, which can cover a rather wide range of behaviors. Writing in the Wall Street Journal this spring, an executive for a wireless company noted that "in Slovakia, people are using mobile phones to remotely switch on the heat before they return home," and in Norway, "1.5 million people can confirm their tax returns" using cell phone short text messaging services. Paramedics use camera phones to send ahead to hospitals pictures of the incoming injuries; "in Britain, it is now commonplace for wireless technology to allow companies to remotely access meters or gather diagnostic information." Construction workers on-site can use cell phones to send pictures to contractors off-site. Combined with the individual use of cell phones—to make appointments, locate a friend, check voicemail messages, or simply to check in at work—cell phones offer people a heretofore unknown level of convenience.

More than ninety percent of cell phone users also report that owning a cell phone makes them feel safer. The CTIA noted that in 2001, nearly 156,000 wireless emergency service calls were made every day—about 108 calls per minute. Technological Good Samaritans place calls to emergency personnel when they see traffic accidents or crimes-in-progress; individuals use their cell phones to call for assistance when a car breaks down or plans go awry. The safety rationale carries a particular poignancy after the terrorist attacks of September 11, 2001. On that day, many men and women used cell phones to speak their final words to family and loved ones. Passengers on hijacked airplanes called wives and husbands; rescue workers on the ground phoned in to report their whereabouts. As land lines in New York and Washington, D.C., became clogged, many of us made or received frantic phone calls on cell phones—to reassure others that we were safe or to make sure that our friends and family were accounted for. Many people who had never considered owning a cell phone bought one after September 11th. If the cultural image we had of the earliest cell phones was of a technology glamorously deployed by the elite, then the image of cell phones today has to include people using them for this final act of communication, as well as terrorists who used cell phones as detonators in the bombing of trains in Madrid.

Of course, the perceived need for a technological safety device can encourage distinctly irrational behavior and create new anxieties. Recently, when a professor at Rutgers University asked his students to experiment with turning off their cell phones for 48 hours, one young woman told University Wire, "I felt like I was going to get raped if I didn't have my cell phone in my hand. I carry it in case I need to call someone for help." Popular culture endorses this image of cell-phone-as-lifeline. The trailer for a new suspense movie, Cellular, is currently making the rounds in theaters nationwide. In it, an attractive young man is shown doing what young men apparently do with their camera-enabled cell phones: taking pictures of women in bikinis and emailing the images to himself. When he receives a random but desperate phone call from a woman who claims to be the victim of a kidnapping, he finds himself drawn into a race to find and save her, all the while trying to maintain that tenuous cell phone connection. It is indicative of our near-fetishistic attachment to our cell phones that we can relate (and treat as a serious moment of suspense) a scene in the movie where the protagonist, desperately trying to locate a cell phone charger before his battery runs out, holds the patrons of an electronics store at gunpoint until the battery is rejuvenated. After scenes of high-speed car chases and large explosions, the trailer closes with a disembodied voice asking the hero, "How did you get involved?" His response? "I just answered my phone."

10   Many parents have responded to this perceived need for personal security by purchasing cell phones for their children, but this, too, has had some unintended consequences. One sociologist has noted that parents who do this are implicitly commenting on their own sense of security or insecurity in society. "Claiming to care about their children's safety," Chantal de Gournay writes, "parents develop a 'paranoiac' vision of the community, reflecting a lack of trust in social institutions and in any environment other than the family." As a result, they choose surveillance technologies, such as cell phones, to monitor their children, rather than teaching them (and trusting them) to behave appropriately. James E. Katz, a communications professor at Rutgers who has written extensively about wireless communication, argues that parents who give children cell phones are actually weakening the traditional bonds of authority; "parents think they can reach kids any time they want, and thus are more indulgent of their children's wanderings," Katz notes. Not surprisingly, "my cell phone battery died" has become a popular excuse among teenagers for failure to check in with their parents. And I suspect nearly everyone, at some point, has suffered hours of panic when a loved one who was supposed to be "reachable" failed to answer the cell phone.

Although cell phones are a technology with broad appeal, we do not all use our cell phones in the same way. In June 2004, Cingular announced that "for the fourth year in a row, men prove to be the more talkative sex in the wireless world," talking 16 percent more on their phones than women. Women, however, are more likely to use a cell phone "to talk to friends and family" while men use theirs for business—including, evidently, the business of mating. Researchers found that "men are using their mobile phones as peacocks use their immobilizing feathers and male bullfrogs use their immoderate croaks: To advertise to females their worth, status, and desirability," reported the New York Times. The researchers also discovered that many of the men they observed in pubs and nightclubs carried fake cell phones, likely one of the reasons they titled their paper "Mobile Phones as Lekking Devices

Among Human Males," a lek being a "communal mating area where males gather to engage in flamboyant courtship displays." Or, as another observer of cell phone behavior succinctly put it: "the mobile is widely used for psychosexual purposes of performance and display."

The increasingly sophisticated accessories available on cell phones encourage such displays. One new phone hitting the market boasts video capture and playback, a 1.2 megapixel camera, a 256 color screen, speakerphone, removable memory, mp3 player, Internet access, and a global positioning system. The *Wall Street Journal* recently reported on cell phones that will feature radios, calculators, alarm clocks, flashlights, and mirrored compacts. Phones are "becoming your Swiss army knife," one product developer enthused. Hyperactive peacocking will also be abetted by the new walkie-talkie function available on many phones, which draws further attention to the user by broadcasting to anyone within hearing distance the conversation of the person on the other end of the phone.

With all these accoutrements, it is not surprising that one contributor to a discussion list about wireless technology recently compared cell phones and BlackBerrys to "electronic pets." Speaking to a group of business people, he reported, "you constantly see people taking their little pets out and stroking the scroll wheel, coddling them, basically "petting' them." When confined to a basement conference room, he found that participants "were compelled to "walk' their electronic pets on breaks" to check their messages. In parts of Asia, young women carry their phones in decorated pouches, worn like necklaces, or in pants with specially designed pockets that keep the phone within easy reach. We have become thigmophilic with our technology—touch-loving—a trait we share with rats, as it happens. We are constantly taking them out, fiddling with them, putting them away, taking them out again, reprogramming their directories, text messaging. And cell phone makers are always searching for new ways to exploit our attachments. Nokia offers "expression" phones that allow customization of faceplates and ring tones. Many companies, such as Modtones, sell song samples for cell phone ringers. In Asia, where cell phone use among the young is especially high, companies offer popular anime and manga cartoons as downloadable "wallpaper" for cell phones.

Cell phone technology is also creating new forms of social and political networking. "Moblogging," or mobile web logging, allows cell phone users to publish and update content to the World Wide Web. An increasing number of companies are offering cell phones with WiFi capability, and as Sadie Plant noted recently in a report she prepared for Motorola, "On the Mobile," "today, the smallest Motorola phone has as much computing power in it as the largest, most expensive computer did less than a generation ago." In his *Forbes* "Wireless Outlook" newsletter, Andrew Seybold predicted, "in twenty-five years there aren't going to be any wired phones left and I think it might happen even much sooner than that—ten to fifteen years." As well, "the phone will be tied much more closely to the person. Since the phone is the person, the person will be the number." It isn't surprising that one of Seybold's favorite movies is the James Coburn paranoid comedy, *The Presidents' Analyst* (1967), whose premise "centered on attempts by the phone company to capture the president's psychoanalyst in order to further a plot to have phone devices implanted in people's brains at birth." Ma Bell meets *The Manchurian Candidate*.

15   Dodgeball.com, a new social-networking service, applies the principles of websites such as Friendster to cell phones. "Tell us where you are and we'll tell you who and what is around you," Dodgeball promises. "We'll ping your friends with your whereabouts, let you know when friends-of-friends are within ten blocks, allow you to broadcast content to anyone within ten blocks of you or blast messages to your groups of friends." The service is now available in fifteen cities in the U.S., enabling a form of friendly pseudo-stalking. "I was at 'Welcome to the Johnson's' and a girl came up behind me and gave a tap on the shoulder," one recent testimonial noted. 'Are you this guy?' she inquired while holding up her cell phone to show my Dodgeball photo. I was indeed."

Political organizers have also found cell phone technology to be a valuable tool. Throughout 2000 in the Philippines, the country's many cell phone users were text-messaging derogatory slogans and commentary about then-President Joseph Estrada. With pressure on the Estrada administration mounting, activists organized large demonstrations against the president by activating cell phone "trees" to summon protesters to particular locations and to outmaneuver riot police. Estrada was forced from office in January 2001. Anti-globalization protesters in Seattle and elsewhere (using only non-corporate cell phones, surely) have employed the technology to stage and control movements during demonstrations.

Communication Delinquents

The ease of mobile communication does not guarantee positive results for all those who use it, of course, and the list of unintended negative consequences from cell phone use continues to grow. The BBC world service reported in 2001, "senior Islamic figures in Singapore have ruled that Muslim men cannot divorce their wives by sending text messages over their mobile phones." (Muslims can divorce their wives by saying the word "talaq," which means "I divorce you," three times).

Concerns about the dangers of cell phone use while driving have dominated public discussion of cell phone risks. A 2001 study by the National Highway Traffic Safety Administration estimated that "54 percent of drivers 'usually' have some type of wireless phone in their vehicle with them" and that this translates into approximately 600,000 drivers "actively using cell phones at any one time" on the road. Women and drivers in the suburbs were found to talk and drive more often, and "the highest national use rates were observed for drivers of vans and sport utility vehicles." New York, New Jersey, and Washington, D.C. all require drivers to use hands-free technology (headsets or speakerphones) when talking on the cell.

Cell phones can also play host to viruses, real and virtual. A 2003 study presented at the American Society for Microbiology's conference on infectious disease found that twelve percent of the cell phones used by medical personnel in an Israeli hospital were contaminated with bacteria. (Another recent cell phone-related health research result, purporting a link between cell phone use and decreased sperm counts, has been deemed inconclusive.) The first computer virus specifically targeting cell phones was found in late June. As *The Guardian* reported recently, anti-virus manufacturers believe that "the mobile phone now mirrors how the Net has developed over the past two or three years—blighted with viruses as people got faster connections and downloaded more information."

With technology comes addiction, and applicable neologisms have entered 20 the lexicon—such as "crackberry," which describes the dependence exhibited by some BlackBerry wireless users. In a 2001 article in *New York* magazine about feuding couples, one dueling duo, Dave and Brooke, traded barbs about her wireless addictions. "I use it when I'm walking down the street," Brooke said proudly. "She was checking her voice mail in the middle of a seder!" was Dave's exasperated response. "Under the table!" Brooke clarified. A recent survey conducted by the Hospital of Seoul National University found that "3 out of 10 Korean high school students who carry mobile phones are reported to be addicted" to them. Many reported feeling anxious without their phones and many displayed symptoms of repetitive stress injury from obsessive text messaging.

The cell phone has also proven effective as a facilitator and alibi for adulterous behavior. "I heard someone (honest) talking about their 'shag phone' the other day," a visitor to a wireless technology blog recently noted. "He was a married man having an affair with a lady who was also married. It seems that one of the first heady rituals of the affair was to purchase a 'his and her' pair of prepay shag phones." A recent story in the *New York Times* documented the use of cell phone "alibi and excuse clubs" that function as an ethically challenged form of networking—Dodgeball for the delinquent. "Cell phone-based alibi clubs, which have sprung up in the United States, Europe, and Asia, allow people to send out mass text messages to thousands of potential collaborators asking for help. When a willing helper responds, the sender and the helper devise a lie, and the helper then calls the victim with the excuse," the report noted. One woman who started her own alibi club, which has helped spouses cheat on each other and workers mislead their bosses, "said she was not terribly concerned about lying," although she did concede: "You wouldn't really want your friends to know you're sparing people's feelings with these white lies." Websites such as Kargo offer features like "Soundster," which allows users to "insert sounds into your call and control your environment." Car horns, sirens, the coughs and sniffles of the sick room—all can be simulated in order to fool the listener on the other end of the call. Technology, it seems, is allowing people to make instrumental use of anonymous strangers while maintaining the appearance of trustworthiness within their own social group.

Technology has also led to further incursions on personal privacy. Several websites now offer "candid pornography," peeping-Tom pictures taken in locker rooms, bathrooms, and dressing rooms by unscrupulous owners of cell phone cameras. Camera phones pose a potentially daunting challenge to privacy and security; unlike old-fashioned cameras, which could be confiscated and the film destroyed, digital cameras, including those on cell phones, allow users to send images instantaneously to any email address. The images can be stored indefinitely, and the evidence that a picture was ever taken can be destroyed.

Will You Please Be Quiet, Please?

Certain public interactions carry with them certain unspoken rules of behavior. When approaching a grocery store checkout line, you queue behind the last person in line and wait your turn. On the subway, you make way for passengers entering and exiting the cars. Riding on the train, you expect the interruptions of the ticket taker and the periodic crackling blare of station announcements. What you never used to expect, but must now endure, is the auditory abrasion of a stranger arguing about how much he does, indeed, owe to his landlord. I've heard business deals, lovers' quarrels, and the most unsavory gossip. I've listened to strangers discuss in excruciating detail their own and others' embarrassing medical conditions; I've heard the details of recent real estate purchases, job triumphs, and awful dates. (The only thing I haven't heard is phone sex, but perhaps it is only a matter of time.) We are no longer *overhearing*, which implies accidentally stumbling upon a situation where two people are talking in presumed privacy. Now we are all simply *hearing*. The result is a world where social space is overtaken by anonymous, unavoidable background noise—a quotidian narration that even in its more interesting moments rarely rises above the tone of a penny dreadful. It seems almost cruel, in this context, that Motorola's trademarked slogan for its wireless products is "Intelligence Everywhere."

Why do these cell phone conversations bother us more than listening to two strangers chatter in person about their evening plans or listening to a parent scold a recalcitrant child? Those conversations are quantitatively greater, since we hear both sides of the discussion—so why are they nevertheless experienced as qualitatively different? Perhaps it is because cell phone users harbor illusions about being alone or assume a degree of privacy that the circumstances don't actually allow. Because cell phone talkers are not interacting with the world around them, they come to believe that the world around them isn't really there and surely shouldn't intrude. And when the cell phone user commandeers the space by talking, he or she sends a very clear message to others that they are powerless to insist on their own use of the space. It is a passive-aggressive but extremely effective tactic.

Such encounters can sometimes escalate into rude intransigence or even 25 violence. In the past few years alone, men and women have been stabbed, escorted off of airplanes by federal marshals, pepper-sprayed in movie theaters, ejected from concert halls, and deliberately rammed with cars as a result of their bad behavior on their cell phones. The *Zagat* restaurant guide reports that cell phone rudeness is now the number one complaint of diners, and *USA Today* notes that "fifty-nine percent of people would rather visit the dentist than sit next to someone using a cell phone."

The etiquette challenges posed by cell phones are universal, although different countries have responded in slightly different ways. Writing about the impact of cell phone technology in *The Guardian* in 2002, James Meek noted, with moderate horror, that cell phones now encourage British people to do what "British people aren't supposed to do: invite strangers, spontaneously, into our personal worlds. We let everyone know what our accent is, what we do for a living, what kind of stuff we do in our nonworking hours." In France, cell phone companies were pressured by the public to censor the last four digits of phone numbers appearing on monthly statements, because so many French men and women were using them to confirm that their significant other was having an affair.

In Israel, where the average person is on a cell phone four times as much as the average American, and where cell phone technology boasts an impressive 76 percent penetration rate (the United States isn't projected to reach that level until 2009), the incursion of cell phones into daily life is even more dramatic. As sociologists Amit Schejter and Akiba Cohen found, there were no less than ten cell phone interruptions during a recent staging of *One Flew Over the Cuckoos' Nest* at Israel's National Theater, and "there has even been an anecdote reported of an undertaker's phone ringing inside a grave as the deceased was being put to rest." The authors explain this state of affairs with reference to the Israeli personality, which they judge to be more enthusiastic about technology and more forceful in exerting itself in public; the subtitle of their article is "chutzpah and chatter in the Holy Land."

In the U.S., mild regional differences in the use of cell phones are evident. Reporting on a survey by Cingular wireless, CNN noted that cell phone users in the South "are more likely to silence their phones in church," while Westerners "are most likely to turn a phone off in libraries, theaters, restaurants, and schools." But nationwide, cell phones still frequently interrupt movie screenings, theater performances, and concerts. Audience members are not the sole offenders, either. My sister, a professional musician, told me that during one performance, in the midst of a slow and quiet passage of Verdi's *Requiem,* the cell phone of one of the string players in the orchestra began ringing, much to the horror of his fellow musicians.

We cannot simply banish to Tartarus—the section of Hades reserved for punishment of the worst offenders—all those who violate the rules of social space. And the noise pollution generated by rude cell phone users is hardly the worst violation of social order; it is not the same as defacing a statue, for example. Other countries offer some reason for optimism: In societies that maintain more formality, such as Japan, loud public conversation is considered rude, and Japanese people will often cover their mouths and hide their phones from view when speaking into them.

30   Not surprisingly, Americans have turned to that most hallowed but least effective solution to social problems: public education. Cingular Wireless, for example, has launched a public awareness campaign whose slogan is "Be Sensible." The program includes an advertisement shown in movie theaters about "Inconsiderate Cell Phone Guy," a parody of bad behavior that shows a man talking loudly into his cell phone at inappropriate times: during a date, in a movie, at a wedding, in the middle of a group therapy session. It is a miniature manners nickelodeon for the wireless age. July is now officially National Cell Phone Courtesy Month, and etiquette experts such as Jacqueline Whitmore of the Protocol School of Palm Beach advise companies such as Sprint about how to encourage better behavior in their subscribers. Whitmore is relentlessly positive: "Wireless technology is booming so quickly and wireless phones have become so popular, the rules on wireless etiquette are still evolving," she notes on her website. She cites hopeful statistics culled from public opinion surveys that say "98 percent of Americans say they move away from others when talking on a wireless phone in public" and "the vast majority (86 percent) say they 'never' or 'rarely' speak on wireless phones while conducting an entire public transaction with someone else such as a sales clerk or bank teller." If you are wondering where these examples of wireless rectitude reside, you might find them in the land of wishful thinking. There appears to be a rather large disconnect between people's actual behavior and their reports of their behavior.

Whitmore is correct to suggest that we are in the midst of a period of adjustment. We still have the memory of the old social rules, which remind us to be courteous towards others, especially in confined environments such as trains and elevators. But it is becoming increasingly clear that cell phone technology itself has disrupted our ability to insist on the enforcement of social rules. Etiquette experts urge us to adjust—be polite, don't return boorish behavior with boorish behavior, set a standard of probity in your own use of cell phones. But in doing so these experts tacitly concede that every conversation is important, and that we need only learn how and when to have them. This elides an older rule: when a conversation takes place in public, its merit must be judged in part by the standards of the other participants in the social situation. By relying solely on self-discipline and public education (or that ubiquitous modern state of "awareness"), the etiquette experts have given us a doomed manual. Human nature being what it is, individuals will spend more time rationalizing their own need to make cell phone calls than thinking about how that need might affect others. Worse, the etiquette experts offer diversions rather than standards, encouraging alternatives to calling that nevertheless still succeed in removing people from the social space. "Use text messaging," is number 7 on Whitmore's Ten Tips for the Cell Phone Savvy.

These attempts at etiquette training also evade another reality: the decline of accepted standards for social behavior. In each of us lurks the possibility of a Jekyll-and-Hyde-like transformation, its trigger the imposition of some arbitrary rule. The problem is that, in the twenty-first century, with the breakdown of hierarchies and manners, all social rules are arbitrary. "I don't think we have to worry about people being rude intentionally," Whitmore told *Wireless Week*. "Most of us simply haven't come to grips with the new responsibilities wireless technologies demand." But this seems foolishly optimistic. A psychologist quoted in a story by UPI recently noted the "baffling sense of entitlement" demonstrated by citizens in the wireless world. "They don't get sheepish when shushed," he marveled. "You're the rude one." And *contra* Ms. Whitmore, there is intention at work in this behavior, even if it is not intentional rudeness. It is the intentional removal of oneself from the social situation in public space. This removal, as sociologists have long shown, is something more serious than a mere manners lapse. It amounts to a radical disengagement from the public sphere.

Spectator Sport

We know that the reasons people give for owning cell phones are largely practical—convenience and safety. But the reason we answer them whenever they ring is a question better left to sociology and psychology. In works such as *Behavior in Public Spaces*, *Relations in Public*, and *Interaction Ritual*, the great sociologist Erving Goffman mapped the myriad possibilities of human interaction in social space, and his observations take on a new relevance in our cell phone world. Crucial to Goffman's analysis was the notion that in social situations where strangers must interact, "the individual is obliged to 'come into play' upon entering the situation and to stay 'in play' while in the situation." Failure to demonstrate this presence sends a clear message to others of one's hostility or disrespect for the social gathering. It effectively turns them into "non-persons." Like the piqued lover who rebuffs her partner's attempt to caress her, the person who removes himself from the social situation is sending a clear message to those around him: I don't need you.

Although Goffman wrote in the era before cell phones, he might have judged their use as a "subordinate activity," a way to pass the time such as reading or doodling that could and should be set aside when the dominant activity resumes. Within social space, we are allowed to perform a range of these secondary activities, but they must not impose upon the social group as a whole or require so much attention that they remove us from the social situation altogether. The opposite appears to be true today. The group is expected never to impinge upon—indeed, it is expected to tacitly endorse by enduring—the individual's right to withdraw from social space by whatever means he or she chooses: cell phones, BlackBerrys, iPods, DVDs screened on laptop computers. These devices are all used as a means to refuse to be "in" the social space; they are technological cold shoulders that are worse than older forms of subordinate activity in that they impose visually and auditorily on others. Cell phones are not the only culprits here. A member of my family, traveling recently on the Amtrak train from New York, was shocked to realize that the man sitting in front of her was watching a pornographic movie on his laptop computer—a movie whose raunchy scenes were reflected in the train window and thus clearly visible to her. We have allowed what should be subordinate activities in social space to become dominant.

35   One of the groups Goffman studied keenly were mental patients, many of them residents at St. Elizabeth's Hospital in Washington, D.C., and his comparisons often draw on the remarkable disconnect between the behavior of people in normal society and those who had been institutionalized for mental illness. It is striking in revisiting Goffman's work how often people who use cell phones seem to be acting more like the people in the asylum than the ones in respectable society. Goffman describes "occult involvements," for example, as any activity that undermines others' ability to feel engaged in social space. "When an individual is perceived in an occult involvement, observers may not only sense that they are not able to claim him at the moment," Goffman notes, "but also feel that the offender's complete activity up till then has been falsely taken as a sign of participation with them, that all along he has been alienated from their world." Who hasn't observed someone sitting quietly, apparently observing the rules of social space, only to launch into loud conversation as soon as the cell phone rings? This is the pretense of social participation Goffman observed in patients at St. Elizabeth's.

Goffman called those who declined to respond to social overtures as being "out of contact," and said "this state is often felt to be full evidence that he is very sick indeed, that he is, in fact, cut off from all contact with the world around him." To be accessible meant to be available in the particular social setting and to act appropriately. Today, of course, being accessible means answering your cell phone, which brings you in contact with your caller, but "out of contact" in the physical social situation, be it a crosstown bus, a train, an airplane, or simply walking down the street.

In terms of the rules of social space, cell phone use is a form of communications panhandling—forcing our conversations on others without first gaining their tacit approval. "The force that keeps people in their communication place in our middle-class society," Goffman observed, "seems to be the fear of being thought forward and pushy, or odd, the fear of forcing a relationship where none is desired." But middle class society itself has decided to upend such conventions in the service of greater accessibility and convenience. This is a dramatic shift that took place in a very short span of time, and it is worth at least considering the long-term implications of this subversion of norms. The behavioral rules Goffman so effectively mapped exist to protect everyone, even if we don't, individually, always need them. They are the social equivalent of fire extinguishers placed throughout public buildings. You hope not to have to use them too often, but they can ensure that a mere spark does not become an embarrassing conflagration. In a world that eschews such norms, we find ourselves plagued by the behavior that Goffman used to witness only among the denizens of the asylum: disembodied talk that renders all of us unwilling listeners.

We also use our cell phones to exert our status in social space, like the remnants of the entourage or train, which "led a worthy to demonstrate his status by the cluster of dependent supporters that accompanied him through a town or a house of parliament." Modern celebrities still have such escorts (a new cable television series, *Entourage,* tracks a fictional celebrity posse). But cell phones give all of us the unusual ability to simulate an entourage. My mother-in-law recently found herself sharing an elevator (in the apartment building she's lived in for forty years) with a man who was speaking very loudly into his cell phone. When she asked him to keep his voice down, he became enraged and began yelling at her; he was, he said, in the midst of an "important" conversation with his secretary. He acted, in other words, as if she'd trounced on the hem of his royal train. She might have had a secretary too, of course—for all he knew she might have a fleet of assistants at her disposal—but because she wasn't communicating with someone *at that moment* and he, thanks to his cell phone, was, her status in the social space was, in effect, demoted.

The language of wireless technology itself suggests its selfishness as a medium. One of the latest advances is the "Personal Area Network," a Bluetooth technology used in Palm Pilots and other personal digital assistants. The network is individualized, closed to unwelcome intruders, and totally dependent on the choices of the user. We now have our own technological assistants and networks, quite an impressive kingdom for ordinary mortals. In this kingdom, our cell phones reassure us by providing constant contact, and we become much like a child with a security blanket or Dumbo with his feather. Like a security blanket, which is also visible to observers, cell phones provide the "'publicization' of emotional fulfillment," as French sociologist Chantal de Gournay has argued. "At work, in town, while traveling—every call on the mobile phone secretly expresses a message to the public: 'Look how much I'm in demand, how full my life is.'" Unlike those transitional objects of childhood, however, few of us are eager to shed our cell phones.

Absent Without Leave

40 Our daily interactions with cell phone users often prompt heated exchanges and promises of furious retribution. When *New York Times* columnist Joe Sharkey asked readers to send in their cell phone horror stories, he was deluged with responses: "There is not enough time in the day to relay the daily torment I must endure from these cell-yellers," one woman said. "There's always some self-important jerk who must holler his business all the way into Manhattan," another commuter wearily noted. Rarely does one find a positive story about cell phone users who behaved politely, observing the common social space.

Then again, we all apparently have a cell phone *alter idem*, a second self that we endlessly excuse for making just such annoying cell phone calls. As a society, we are endlessly forgiving of our own personal "emergencies" that require cell phone conversation and easily apoplectic about having to listen to others'. At my local grocery store around 6:30 in the evening, it is not an uncommon sight to see a man in business attire, wandering the frozen food aisle, phone in hand, shouting, "Bird's Eye or Jolly Green Giant? What? Yes, I got the coffee filters already!" How rude, you think, until you remember that you left your own grocery list on the kitchen counter; in a split second you are fishing for your phone so that you can call home and get its particulars. This is the quintessential actor-observer paradox: as actors, we are always politely exercising our right to be connected, but as observers we are perpetually victimized by the boorish bad manners of other cell phone users.

A new generation of sociologists has begun to apply Goffman's insights to our use of cell phones in public. Kenneth J. Gergen, for example, has argued that one reason cell phones allow a peculiar form of diversion in public spaces is that they encourage "absent presence," a state where "one is physically present but is absorbed by a technologically mediated world of elsewhere." You can witness examples of absent presence everywhere: people in line at the bank or a retail store, phones to ear and deep into their own conversations— so unavailable they do not offer the most basic pleasantries to the salesperson or cashier. At my local playground, women deep in cell phone conversations are scattered on benches or distractedly pushing a child on a swing— physically present, to be sure, but "away" in their conversations, not fully engaged with those around them.

The first time you saw a person walking down the street having a conversation using a hands-free cell phone device you intuitively grasped this state. Wildly gesticulating, laughing, mumbling—to the person on the other end of the telephone, their street-walking conversation partner is engaged in normal conversation. To the outside observer, however, he looks like a deranged or slightly addled escapee from a psychiatric ward. Engaged with the ether, hooked up to an earpiece and dangling microphone, his animated voice and gestures are an anomaly in the social space. They violate our everyday sense of normal behavior.

The difficulty of harmonizing real and virtual presence isn't new. As Mark Caldwell noted in *A Short History of Rudeness* about the first telephones, "many early phone stories involved a bumpkin who nods silently in reply to a caller's increasingly agitated, 'Are you there?' " Even young children know Goffman's rules. When a parent is in front of a child but on the telephone (physically present but mentally "away"), a child will frequently protest—grabbing for the phone or vocalizing loudly to retrieve the parent's attention. They are expressing a need for recognition that, in a less direct and individualized way, we all require from strangers in public space. But the challenge is greater given the sheer number of wireless users, a reality that is prompting a new form of social criticism. As a "commentary on the potential of the mobile phone for disrupting and disturbing social interactions," the Interaction Design Institute Ivrea recently sponsored a project called "Mass Distraction." The project featured jackets and cell phones that only allowed participants to talk on their phones if the large hood of the jacket was closed completely over their head or if they continued to insert coins into the pocket of the jacket like an old fashioned pay phone. "In order to remain connected," the project notes, "the mobile phone user multitasks between the two communication channels. Whether disguised or not, this practice degrades the quality of the interaction with the people in his immediate presence."

Cocooned within our "Personal Area Networks" and wirelessly trans- 45 ported to other spaces, we are becoming increasingly immune to the boundaries and realities of physical space. As one reporter for the *Los Angeles Times* said, in exasperation, "Go ahead, floss in the elevator. You're busy; you can't be expected to wait until you can find a bathroom.... [T]he world out there? It's just a backdrop, as movable and transient as a fake skyline on a studio lot." No one is an outsider with a cell phone—that is why foreign cab drivers in places like New York and Washington are openly willing to ignore laws against driving-and-talking. Beyond the psychic benefits cell phone calls provide (cab driving is a lonely occupation), their use signals the cab driver's membership in a community apart from the ever-changing society that frequents his taxi. Our cell phones become our talismans against being perceived as (or feeling ourselves to be) outsiders.

Talk and Conversation

Recently, on a trip to China, I found myself standing on the Great Wall. One of the members of our small group had hiked ahead, and since the rest of us had decided it was time to get back down the mountain, we realized we would need to find him. Despite being in a remote location at high altitude, and having completely lost sight of him in the hazy late morning air, this proved to be the easiest of logistical tasks. One man pulled out his cell phone, called his wife back in the

United States, and had her send an email to the man who had walked ahead. Knowing that our lost companion religiously checked his BlackBerry wireless, we reasoned that he would surely notice an incoming message. Soon enough he reappeared, our wireless plea for his return having successfully traveled from China to Washington and back again to the Wall in mere minutes.

At the time, we were all caught up in the James Bond-like excitement of our mission. Would the cell phone work? (It did.) Would the wife's email get through to our companion's BlackBerry? (No problem.) Only later, as we drove back to Beijing, did I experience a pang of doubt about our small communications triumph. There, at one of the Great Wonders of the World, a centuries-old example of human triumph over nature, we didn't hesitate to do something as mundane as make a cell phone call. It is surely true that wireless communication is its own wondrous triumph over nature. But cell phone conversation somehow inspires less awe than standing atop the Great Wall, perhaps because atop the Great Wall we are still rooted in the natural world that we have conquered. Or perhaps it is simply because cell phones have become everyday wonders—as unremarkable to us as the Great Wall is to those who see it everyday.

Christian Licoppe and Jean-Philippe Heurtin have argued that cell phone use must be understood in a broader context; they note that the central feature of the modern experience is the "deinstitutionalization of personal bonds." Deinstitutionalization spawns anxiety, and as a result we find ourselves working harder to build trust relationships. Cell phone calls "create a web of short, content-poor interactions through which bonds can be built and strengthened in an ongoing process."

But as trust is being built and bolstered moment by moment between individuals, public trust among strangers in social settings is eroding. We are strengthening and increasing our interactions with the people we already know at the expense of those who we do not. The result, according to Kenneth Gergen, is "the erosion of face-to-face community, a coherent and centered sense of self, moral bearings, depth of relationship, and the uprooting of meaning from material context: such are the dangers of absent presence."

50   No term captures this paradoxical state more ably than the word "roam," which appears on your phone when you leave an area bristling with wireless towers and go into the wilds of the less well connected. The word appears when your cell phone is looking for a way to connect you, but the real definition of roam is "to go from place to place without purpose or direction," which has more suggestive implications. It suggests that we have allowed our phones to become the link to our purpose and the symbol of our status— without its signal we lack direction. Roaming was a word whose previous use was largely confined to describing the activities of herds of cattle. In her report on the use of mobile phones throughout the world, Sadie Plant noted, "according to the *Oxford English Dictionary*, one of the earliest uses of the word

'mobile' was in association with the Latin phrase *mobile vulgus*, the excitable crowd," whence comes our word "mob."

Convenience and safety—the two reasons people give for why they have (or "need") cell phones—are legitimate reasons for using wireless technology; but they are not neutral. Convenience is the major justification for fast food, but its overzealous consumption has something to do with our national obesity "epidemic." Safety spawned a bewildering range of antibacterial products and the overzealous prescription of antibiotics—which in turn led to disease-resistant bacteria.

One possible solution would be to treat cell phone use the way we now treat tobacco use. Public spaces in America were once littered with spittoons and the residue of the chewing tobacco that filled them, despite the disgust the practice fostered. Social norms eventually rendered public spitting déclassé. Similarly, it was not so long ago that cigarette smoking was something people did everywhere—in movie theaters, restaurants, trains, and airplanes. Nonsmokers often had a hard time finding refuge from the clouds of nicotine. Today, we ban smoking in all but designated areas. Currently, cell phone users enjoy the same privileges smokers once enjoyed, but there is no reason we cannot reverse the trend. Yale University bans cell phones in some of its libraries, and Amtrak's introduction of "quiet cars" on some of its routes has been eagerly embraced by commuters. Perhaps one day we will exchange quiet cars for wireless cars, and the majority of public space will revert to the quietly disconnected. In doing so, we might partially reclaim something higher even than healthy lungs: civility.

This reclaiming of social space could have considerable consequences. As sociologist de Gournay has noted, "the telephone is a device ill suited to listening...it is more appropriate for exchanging information." Considering Americans' obsession with information—we are, after all, the "information society"—it is useful to draw the distinction. Just as there is a distinction between information and knowledge, there is a vast difference between conversation and talk.

Conversation (as opposed to "talk") is to genuine sociability what courtship (as opposed to "hooking up") is to romance. And the technologies that mediate these distinctions are important: the cell phone exchange of information is a distant relative of formal conversation, just as the Internet chat room is a far less compelling place to become intimate with another person than a formal date. In both cases, however, we have convinced ourselves as a culture that these alternatives are just as good as the formalities—that they are, in fact, improvements upon them.

"A conversation has a life of its own and makes demands on its own 55 behalf," Goffman wrote. "It is a little social system with its own boundary-making tendencies; it is a little patch of commitment and loyalty with its own heroes and its own villains." According to census data, the percentage of Americans who live alone is the highest it has ever been in our country's history, making a return to genuine sociability and conversation more important than ever. Cell phones provide us with a new, but not necessarily superior means of communicating with each other. They encourage talk, not conversation. They link us to those we know, but remove us from the strangers who surround us in public space. Our constant accessibility and frequent exchange of information is undeniably useful. But it would be a terrible irony if "being connected" required or encouraged a disconnection from community life—an erosion of the spontaneous encounters and everyday decencies that make society both civilized and tolerable.

Things to Do with the Reading

1. Talk and conversation offer an organizing contrast (binary) in Rosen's essay. Track the strands attached to each of these key terms and write a paragraph or two about how they suggest what is at stake in this piece. What other binaries figure prominently?

2. What is this piece assuming about the function of manners in a culture? In other words, reason back to premises in regard to Rosen's point of view. Rosen refers, for example, to something she calls "social space." What are some of Rosen's stated—and unstated—assumptions about this space? (See Chapter 2 on UNCOVERING ASSUMPTIONS.)

3. Rosen's essay is a piece of research writing that makes use of a number of other writers and theorists, most notably the sociologist Erving Goffman. What use does Rosen make of this research?

4. Write an essay in which you extend Rosen's observations to include the impact of texting and the smart phone.

5. Application: Near the end of the section "Will You Please Be Quiet, Please?", in the paragraph beginning "Not surprisingly," Rosen cites an etiquette expert, Jacqueline Whitmore, who observes, "Wireless technology is booming so quickly and wireless phones are becoming so popular, the rules on wireless etiquette are still evolving." This idea is worth investigating. Spend a few days observing cell phone behavior; take careful notes. Your goal is to look for trends in cell phone etiquette. What is that etiquette? Where and how do you see it evolving? Write up your results.

   You might extend this project by exploring further the disagreement between Rosen and Whitmore on what Rosen calls "wireless rectitude." Rosen claims at the end of the paragraph that there is a mismatch between people's reports of their behavior and their actual behavior. Develop a few questions about cell phone use and ask them of your friends or peers. Compare the results with your actual observations.

Paul Goldberger

Disconnected Urbanism

Paul Goldberger is a contributing editor at *Vanity Fair*. From 1997 through 2011 he served as the architecture critic for *The New Yorker*. Formerly Dean of the Parsons school of design, Goldberger currently holds the Joseph Urban Chair in Design and Architecture at The New School in New York City. He began his career at *The New York Times,* where in 1984 his architecture criticism was awarded a Pulitzer Prize. His most recent book is entitled *Why Architecture Matters* (2009). In this short piece, taken from Metropolismag.com (November 2003), Goldberger considers the impact of the cell phone on our sense of place.

There is a connection between the idea of place and the reality of cellular tele- 1
phones. It is not encouraging. Places are unique—or at least we like to believe they are—and we strive to experience them as a kind of engagement with particulars. Cell phones are precisely the opposite. When a piece of geography is doing what it is supposed to do, it encourages you to feel a connection to it that, as in marriage, forsakes all others. When you are in Paris you expect to wallow in its Parisness, to feel that everyone walking up the Boulevard Montparnasse is as totally and completely there as the lampposts, the kiosks, the façade of the Brasserie Lipp—and that they could be no place else. So we want it to be in every city, in every kind of place. When you are in a forest, you want to experience its woodsiness; when you are on the beach, you want to feel connected to sand and surf.

This is getting harder to do, not because these special places don't exist or because urban places have come to look increasingly alike. They have, but this is not another rant about the monoculture and sameness of cities and the suburban landscape. Even when you are in a place that retains its intensity, its specialness, and its ability to confer a defining context on your life, it doesn't have the all-consuming effect these places used to. You no longer feel that being in one place cuts you off from other places. Technology has been doing this for a long time, of course—remember when people communicated with Europe by letter and it took a couple of weeks to get a reply? Now we're upset if we have to send a fax because it takes so much longer than email.

But the cell phone has changed our sense of place more than faxes and computers and email because of its ability to intrude into every moment in every possible place. When you walk along the street and talk on a cell phone, you are not on the street sharing the communal experience of urban life. You are in some other place—someplace at the other end of your phone

Disconnected Urbanism, Paul Goldberger. Reprinted with permission of the author.

conversation. You are there, but you are not there. It reminds me of the title of Lillian Ross's memoir of her life with William Shawn, *Here But Not Here*. Now that is increasingly true of almost every person on almost every street in almost every city. You are either on the phone or carrying one, and the moment it rings you will be transported out of real space into a virtual realm.

This matters because the street is the ultimate public space and walking along it is the defining urban experience. It is all of us—different people who lead different lives—coming together in the urban mixing chamber. But what if half of them are elsewhere, there in body but not in any other way? You are not on Madison Avenue if you are holding a little object to your ear that pulls you toward a person in Omaha.

5   The great offense of the cell phone in public is not the intrusion of its ring, although that can be infuriating when it interrupts a tranquil moment. It is the fact that even when the phone does not ring at all, and is being used quietly and discreetly, it renders a public place less public. It turns the boulevardier into a sequestered individual, the flaneur into a figure of privacy. And suddenly the meaning of the street as a public place has been hugely diminished.

I don't know which is worse—the loss of the sense that walking along a great urban street is a glorious shared experience or the blurring of distinctions between different kinds of places. But these cultural losses are related, and the cell phone has played a major role in both. The other day I returned a phone call from a friend who lives in Hartford. He had left a voicemail message saying he was visiting his son in New Orleans, and when I called him back on his cell phone—area code 860, Hartford—he picked up the call in Tallahassee. Once the area code actually meant something in terms of geography: it outlined a clearly defined piece of the earth; it became a form of identity. Your telephone number was a badge of place. Now the area code is really not much more than three digits; and if it has any connection to a place, it's just the telephone's home base. An area code today is more like a car's license plate. The downward spiral that began with the end of the old telephone exchanges that truly did connect to a place—RHinelander 4 and BUtterfield 8 for the Upper East Side, or CHelsea 3 downtown, or UNiversity 4 in Morningside Heights—surely culminates in the placeless area codes such as 917 and 347 that could be anywhere in New York—or anywhere at all.

It's increasingly common for cell-phone conversations to begin with the question, "Where are you?" and for the answer to be anything from "out by the pool" to "Madagascar." I don't miss the age when phone charges were based on distance, but that did have the beneficial effect of reinforcing a sense that places were distinguishable from one another. Now calling across the street and calling from New York to California or even Europe are precisely the same thing. They cost the same because to the phone they are the same. Every place is exactly the same as every other place. They are all just nodes on a network—and so, increasingly, are we.

Things to Do with the Reading

1. In "Our Cell Phones, Our Selves," Christina Rosen writes of the use of cell phones in public, "It is the intentional removal of oneself from the social situation in public. This removal, as sociologists have long shown, is something more serious than a mere manners lapse. It amounts to a radical disengagement from the public sphere." Locate any statement in Goldberger's essay that connects in some interesting way with Rosen's remark. Then do a focused freewriting (see Chapter 2) on the two together, getting them to interact.

2. How is Goldberger using the term "public space"? The idea of a public sphere and of public space is one that connects not only the readings in this chapter but those in several other chapters as well. You might compare Goldberger's sense of the term with the way public space is valued in the essays by Adam Gopnik, Jane Jacobs, or Mike Davis in Chapter 13.

Jeffrey Rosen

The Naked Crowd

"Why is it that American anxiety about identity has led us to value exposure over privacy? Why, in short, are we so eager to become members of the Naked Crowd, in which we have the illusion of belonging only when we are exposed?" This essay by a professor of law at George Washington University and legal affairs editor of the *New Republic* is excerpted from his book, *The Naked Crowd: Reclaiming Security and Freedom in an Anxious Age* (2004). Jeffrey Rosen's most recent book, *The Supreme Court: The Personalities and Rivalries that Defined America*, was published in 2007. Since 2013, he has served as the President and CEO of the National Constitution Center in Philadelphia.

1   After 9/11, the most celebrated ritual of mourning was the *New York Times'* Portraits of Grief. For months after the attack, the *New York Times* published more than 1,800 sketches of those who died in the collapse of the World Trade Centre. Not designed as obituaries in the traditional sense—at 200 words, there was no space for a full accounting of the lives that had been cut short—the Portraits were offered up as "brief, informal, and impressionistic, often centred on a single story or idiosyncratic detail," intended not "to recount a person's résumé, but rather to give a snapshot of each victim's personality, of a life lived."

   The Portraits were intended to be democratic—showing the personal lives of janitors as well as chief executives. Above all, they attempted to recognise the victims as distinctive individuals, each distinguished from the crowd. "One felt, looking at those pages every day, that real lives were jumping out at you," said Paul Auster, the novelist, when interviewed by the *New York Times* about the profiles. "We weren't mourning an anonymous mass of people, we were mourning thousands of individuals. And the more we knew about them, the more we could wrestle with our own grief."[1]

   Although public criticism of the Portraits of Grief was hard to detect during the months of their publication, a few dissident voices emerged after the series came to an end. More than 80 percent of the victims' families agreed to talk to the *New York Times*, but a handful of them later complained that the Portraits had failed to capture the people they had known. In an eloquent essay in the *American Scholar*, the literary critic Thomas Mallon echoed this criticism, arguing that in the process of trying to individualise their subjects, the Portraits of Grief had managed to homogenise them instead. "To read the Portraits one would believe that work counted for next to nothing, that every

The Naked Crowd, Jeffrey Rosen. © Jeffrey Rosen. This essay, which appeared in Spiked.com, is an excerpt from *The Naked Crowd: Reclaiming Security and Freedom in an Anxious Age*, (Random House, 2004), and is reprinted by permission of the author.

hard charging bond trader and daredevil fireman preferred—and managed—to spend more time with his family than at the office," Mallon wrote.

American obituaries, to a certain extent, tend to obey the convention of speaking well of the dead (British obituaries are far nastier), but the Portraits of Grief were not successful on their own terms: instead of recognising the public achievements of lives that had reached some kind of fulfillment, the Portraits instead trivialised their subjects by emphasising one or two private hobbies or quirks. As a result, any genuine achievements or complexity of personality were airbrushed away in the narrative effort to reduce each person to a single, memorable, and democratically accessible detail. "If Mayor Rudolph Giuliani had perished in the attacks, as he nearly did," Mallon concluded, "he would be remembered in the Portraits as a rabid Yankee fan who sometimes liked to put on lipstick."[2]

The homogenising effects of the Portraits of Grief were inherent in the 5 project itself. The *New York Times* instructed its reporters to convey a sense of the victims as distinct individuals by extracting from conversations with their families a single representative detail about their lives that would give readers the illusion of having known them. In each case, complexity and accuracy had to be sacrificed to the narrative imperative of finding a memorable quirk of personality with which the audience could quickly identify.

But the Portraits of Grief were not designed to do justice to the victims in all of their complexity. They were designed as a form of therapy for the families of the victims and as a source of emotional connection for the readers of the *New York Times*. They aspired to give all Americans the illusion of identifying with the victims, and therefore allowing them to feel that they themselves had somehow been touched by the horrific event. What was flattened out in this juggernaut of democratic connection was the individuality of the victims themselves.

This flattening resulted from a broader demand: the crowd's insistence on emotionally memorable images at the expense of genuine human individuality. The crowd, which thinks in terms of images rather than arguments, demands a sense of emotional connection with everyone who catches its fleeting attention. This means that everyone who is subject to the scrutiny of the crowd—from celebrities to political candidates to the families of terrorists' victims—will feel pressure to parcel out bits of personal information in order to allow unseen strangers to experience a sense of vicarious identification.

But revealing one or two personal details to strangers is inevitably a trivialising experience that leads us to be judged out of context. It's impossible to know someone on the basis of snippets of information; genuine knowledge is something that can only be achieved slowly, over time, behind a shield of privacy, with the handful of people to whom we've chosen to reveal ourselves whole.

The sociologist Thomas Mathiesen has contrasted Michel Foucault's Panopticon—a surveillance house in which the few watched the many—with what he called the "Synopticon" created by modern television, in which the many watch the few. But in the age of the Internet, we are experiencing something that might be called the "Omnipticon" in which the many are watching the many, even though no one knows precisely who is watching or being watched at any given time. The homogenisation wrought by the Portraits of Grief is a symptom of the identity crisis that Americans are experiencing as they attempt to negotiate the challenges of the Omnipticon—a world in which more and more citizens are subject to the scrutiny of strangers. The challenges of interacting with strangers have increased the pressures on Americans to trade privacy for an illusory sense of security and connection, turning many of us into virtual portraits of grief.

Exposing Ourselves

10 The British sociologist Anthony Giddens has described the ways that citizens in a risk society can no longer rely on tradition or fixed hierarchies to establish their identity or to give them reliable guidance about whom to trust in a society of strangers. Confused and anxious about status in a world where status is constantly shifting, we feel increasing pressure to expose details of our personal lives to strangers in order to win their trust, and we demand that they expose themselves in order to win our trust in return. "Trust—in a person or in a system, such as a banking system—can be a means of coping with risk, while acceptance of risk can be a means of generating trust," Giddens writes.[3]

In the past, intimate relationships of trust—such as marriage, friendship, and business associations—were based on rigidly controlled status hierarchies, which brought with them codes of expected behaviours: you could behave one way with your wife and another with your servant and another with your boss, because you had no doubt where you stood in relationship to each of them, and where they stood in relation to you. Today, by contrast, intimacy and trust are increasingly obtained not by shared experiences or fixed social status but by self-revelation: people try to prove their trustworthiness by revealing details of their personal lives to prove that they have nothing to hide before a crowd whose gaze is turned increasingly on all the individuals that compose it.

A world where individuals have to prove their trustworthiness and value every day before the crowd, choosing among an infinite range of lifestyles, behaviours, clothes, and values, is inevitably a world that creates great anxiety about identity. Rather than conforming to preexisting social roles, individuals are expected to find their true selves and constantly to market themselves to a sceptical world. In the 1950s, Eric Fromm wrote about the "marketing orientation" of the American self, in which "man experiences himself as a thing to be employed successfully on the market.... His sense of value depends on his success: on whether he can sell himself favourably.... If the individual fails in a profitable investment of himself, he feels that he is a failure; if he succeeds, *he* is a success."[4] Fromm worried that the marketed personality, whose precarious sense of self-worth was entirely dependent on the fickle judgements of the market, would be wracked by alienation and anxiety.

The Internet has vastly increased the opportunities for individuals to subject themselves to the demands of the personality market, resulting in ever increasing confusion and anxiety about how much of ourselves to reveal to strangers. The logic of Fromm's marketed self as being extended into a virtual world where the easiest way to attract the attention and winning the trust of strangers is to establish an emotional connection with them by projecting a consistent, memorable, and trustworthy image. In an ideal relationship of trust, self-revelation should be reciprocal. In the age of the Internet, however, we are increasingly forced to interact with strangers whom we will never meet face-to-face. As a result, individuals find themselves in more and more situations where they feel pressure to reveal details of their personal lives without being able to gauge the audience's reaction. But the quest for attention from and emotional connection with strangers is fraught with peril.[5]

In 2000, for example, Laurence Tribe, the constitutional scholar from Harvard Law School, posted a personal statement on his family's website. "I'm Larry," Tribe wrote. "I love brilliant magenta sunsets, unagi, Martin Amis' *Time's Arrow*, the fish tank at MGH, T.S. Eliot's 'Love Song of J Alfred Prufrock,' eating, my stairmaster, looking at the ocean, dreaming about impossible things, *New Yorker* cartoons, the twist in a short story, *The Hotel New Hampshire*, good (and even not-so-good) movies, rereading *The Great Gatsby* and *Ethan Frome*, and Monet and Vermeer." Several websites devoted to media gossip posted links mocking Tribe's statement for displaying the overly intimate tones of a personal ad. Embarrassed by the public reaction, Tribe tried to remove the statement, but one of the media gossip sites resurrected it from the archives of Google, the popular Internet search engine. Tribe was then ridiculed more for his attempt to cover his tracks than for his initial act of self exposure.

"The website itself was a thing our son helped Carolyn and me put 15 together one Christmas," Tribe emailed me later, reflecting on his experience. "I was having fun letting my hair down, as it were, in just chatting about myself as unselfconsciously as I could, not giving much of a thought to who might read it but probably assuming, naively it now seems, that it wouldn't really be of interest to anybody. When I learned that people were finding it a source of public amusement, I do admit to being nonplussed and unsure of what to do." Tribe's understandable error shows how hard it is to strike a decent balance between personal disclosure and the projection of a consistent image, especially on the Internet.

Many citizens, of course, don't care if they embarrass themselves before strangers on the Internet, as the proliferation of personal websites shows. It is now commonplace on a website to reveal hobbies, favourite foods and music, and pictures of children, in an effort to create an illusion of intimacy. Even the most intimate moments of life, such as a wedding, are now being posted on the web for public consumption. The private moments offered up for public consumption tend to be generic tropes of informality which, like the Portraits of Grief, have a homogenising effect. Instead of the beginning of a romantic partnership, one often has the impression of watching a particularly excruciating episode of *The Dating Game*. And then there are the reality TV shows, which represent the most absurd examples of the application of the values of the public opinion society to the most intimate activities of life.

One way of understanding privacy is not whether we choose to expose personal information in public—we all do at different times and places—but the ease with which we can return to being private. The Internet, however, is complicating our ability to negotiate the boundary between public and private, making it hard to recover a private self that has been voluntarily exposed. Consider the proliferation of weblogs—personal Internet journals that often combine political musings with intimate disclosures about daily life. There are more than half a million, according to a recent estimate.[6] Some are devoted exclusively to public affairs, while others are nothing more than published diaries. A website called Diarist.net collects more than 5,000 journals from self-styled "online exhibitionists."[7] Often, these diaries are virtually unreadable examples of self display, dreary accounts of daily navel gazing whose primary function seems to be therapeutic. But they reflect a common but treacherous error: that thoughts appropriate to reveal to friends and intimates are also appropriate to reveal to the world.

In a pluralistic society, people are and should be free to have different instincts about the proper balance between reticence and self-revelation. If exercises in personal exhibitionism give pleasure to the exhibitionists and an illusory sense of emotional connection for the virtual audience, there's no harm done except to the dignity of the individuals concerned, and that's nobody's business but their own. But the growing pressure to expose ourselves in front of strangers has obvious and important consequences for a democracy's ability to strike a reasonable balance between liberty and security. The ease with which we reveal ourselves suggests that in the face of widespread anxiety about identity, people are more concerned with the feeling of connection than with the personal and social costs of exposure. Why is it that American anxiety about identity has led us to value exposure over privacy? Why, in short, are we so eager to become members of the Naked Crowd, in which we have the illusion of belonging only when we are exposed?

From Sincerity to Authenticity

Anxiety about how much of ourselves to reveal to strangers has always been a defining trait of the American character. But the form of the anxiety changed over the course of the nineteenth and twentieth centuries, reflecting changes in society and technology. In the late nineteenth century, conceptions of personal truthfulness changed in a way that the critic Lionel Trilling has described as a change from sincerity to authenticity.[8]

By sincerity, Trilling meant the expectation that individuals should avoid 20 duplicity in their dealings with each other: there should be an honest correlation between what is exposed in public and what is felt in private; but not everything that is felt has to be exposed. By authenticity, Trilling meant the expectation that instead of being honest with each other, individuals should be honest with themselves, and should have no compunction about directly exposing strangers to their most intimate emotions. Sincerity requires that whatever is exposed must be true; authenticity requires that everything must be exposed as long as it is deeply felt.

In an age of sincerity, the fine clothes and family crest of an aristocrat were the markers of the self; in an age of authenticity, as the sociologist Peter Berger has noted, "the escutcheons hide the true self. It is precisely the naked man, and even more specifically the naked man expressing his sexuality, who represents himself more truthfully."[9] The motto for the age of sincerity came from the Delphic Oracle: Know Thyself. The motto for the age of authenticity comes from the therapist: Be Thyself.

As self-disclosure became the yardstick of trustworthiness, individuals began to relate to strangers in psychological terms. Politicians, like actors on the stage, came to be judged as trustworthy only if they could convincingly dramatise their own emotions and motivations. "The content of political belief recedes as in public, people become more interested in the content of the politician's life," Richard Sennett writes. "The modern charismatic leader destroys any distance between his own sentiments and impulses and those of his audience, and so, focusing his followers on his motivations, deflects them from measuring him in terms of his acts."[10] The earnest nod, the brow furrowed by concern, and the well-timed tear are now more important for politicians than traditional skills of oratory.

In *The Image*, Daniel Boorstin explored the way the growth of movies, radio, print, and television had transformed the nature of political authority, which came to be exercised not by distant and remote heroes but instead by celebrities, whom Boorstin defined as "a person who is known for his well-knownness." "Neither good nor bad," a celebrity is "morally neutral," "the human pseudo-event," who has been "fabricated on purpose to satisfy our exaggerated expectations of human greatness."[11] While the heroes of old exercised authority by being remote and mysterious, modern celebrities exercise authority by being familiar and intelligible, creating the impression—but not the reality—of emotional accessibility. Heroes were distinguished by their achievement, celebrities by their images or trademarks or "name brands."

In an age when images were becoming more important than reality, Boorstin lamented the fact that politicians were trying to hold the attention of the crowd by recasting themselves in the mould of celebrities, projecting an image of emotional authenticity through selective self-disclosure. He feared that as synthesised images took the place of complicated human reality, the result would be a proliferation of conformity: politicians would have to alter their personalities to fit with the images that the crowd expected them to present; and the believability of the image would become more important than the underlying human truth.

25   Boorstin wrote before the development of the Internet. But as life increasingly takes place in cyberspace, private citizens are now facing some of the same social pressures and technological opportunities as politicians to expose and market themselves to strangers, with similarly homogenising results. As the Internet has increased the circumstances in which ordinary citizens are forced to present a coherent image to strangers, the methodology of public relations is increasingly being applied to the presentation of the self. Ordinary citizens are now being forced to market themselves like pseudo-events, using techniques that used to be reserved for politicians, corporations, and celebrities. In an eerie fulfillment of Boorstin's fears, business gurus today are urging individuals to project a consistent image to the crowd by creating a personal brand.

Personal Branding

The idea of selling people as products began to appear in magazines like *Ad Age* as early as the 1970s; but the idea of personal branding didn't proliferate until the 1990s, when a series of business books emerged with names like *Brand You*, *The Personal Branding Phenomenon*, and *Be Your Own Brand: A Breakthrough Formula for Standing Out from the Crowd*. To invent a successful brand you have to establish trust with strangers, argues the personal branding guru, Tom Peters. A brand is a "trust mark" that "reaches out with a powerful connecting experience." To connect with colleagues and customers, you have to decide the one thing you want them to know about you and create an "emotional context" by telling stories about yourself. Peters's nostrums are an example of the banalisation of Gustave Le Bon; and *Be Your Own Brand* is in the same vein. It defines a personal brand as "a perception or emotion, maintained by somebody other than you, that describes the total experience of having a relationship with you."

Like the brand of a corporation or product, personal brands are defined by whether people trust, like, remember, and value you: "your brand, just like the brand of a product, exists on the basis of a set of perceptions and emotions stored in someone else's head." To create a strong personal brand that makes and maintains an emotional connection with strangers, individuals are advised to be "distinctive, relevant, and consistent."

To achieve the goals of distinctiveness, relevance, and consistency, branded individuals are urged to simplify the complex characteristics that make up a genuine individual. Following the model of the Portraits of Grief, personal branders urge their clients to write down a list of the adjectives that best describe their personal style and values, and to incorporate three of them in a "personal brand promise" that can easily be remembered. For example, a surgeon who says he is "humble, collaborative, and friendly" promises "the discipline to achieve world-class results"; a writer who claims to be "enthusiastic, energetic, and professional" promises "enthusiasm that will make your day." These brand attributes are so abstract and banal that they are impossible to remember, which is why the entire enterprise seems dubious, even on its own terms; but they neatly achieve the goal of turning individuals into stereotypes, for the purpose of making them intelligible to strangers with short attention spans.

In *The Lonely Crowd*, his classic study of the American self in the 1950s, the sociologist David Riesman distinguished between the inner-directed individual, who derives his identity from an internal moral gyroscope, and the outer-directed individual, who derives his identity from the expectations of the crowd. By measuring individuals in terms of their success on the personality market, the personal branding strategy seems at first to be an apotheosis of outer-directedness. But the personal branding books deny this, emphasising that successfully branded individuals must first look inward, to discover their authentic selves, and then turn outward, attempting to market that self to the world.

"Trust is built faster and maintained longer when people believe you are 30 being real, not putting on a false front to cover up what's really going on inside of you," the branding manual counsels. "When it comes to relationships, authenticity is what others say they want most from us. We make the most lasting and vivid impressions when people witness us being true to our beliefs, staying in alignment with who and what we really are."[12] The self constructed by the personal branders, then, is an anxious hybrid of Riesman's two types: a form of marketed authenticity in which the self is turned inside out, and then sold to the world.

Although the phenomenon of personal brand management is in its infancy, it represents the logical application of marketing technologies to the most intimate aspects of the self. But its hazards are already becoming evident; and they have to do with the substitution of image-making for genuine individuality. As early as 1997, the *New York Times* reported that an unhappy bachelor had convened a focus group of the single women who had rejected him. As he watched from behind a one-way mirror, they evaluated his dating performance, and offered advice for improvement. Meeting in the studios of a market research company called Focus Suites, where consumers usually gather to criticise soap or cereal, the women urged him to bolster his confidence and change his wardrobe. "I think it's really alarming that we let a market economy dictate our human relationships," the head of the company told the *New York Times*. "I think it's much more healthy for the human model to dictate to the business world than for the business model to inform human life."[13]

Allowing public opinion to expand into the recesses of the soul, the entrepreneurs of the self insist that personal branding is a spiritual as well as an economic imperative. Nick Shore, the head of a New York advertising agency called the Way Group, is writing a book called *Who Are You: The Search for Your Authentic Self in Business*. Over the phone, Shore told me that his personal "brand DNA" was "a punk rocker in a pinstripe suit—that's how I understand myself." But when I met him at his stylish loft office in the Chelsea Market, he turned out to be a young British man in khakis and a sweater. "The classical distinctions between personal life, professional life, what I do in my family, how I set up my business, how I plan my career" are breaking down, Shore said. "It's this whole postmodern idea of the script to life just basically being thrown away and no one quite knows exactly what they're supposed to do in any given situation.... If I can't find true worth by looking to the corporation that I work for or by looking to the government or the queen, then ultimately you end up with yourself, you have to find your own truth."

In the 1950s, the organisation man was told to find what the marketplace wants and supply it. But in a talent economy, Shore says, "it's the other way around: find out what you are then go look for the space in the market place that needs that." Successful brands must be authentic because "the marketplace smells a rat," and consumers, in deciding whom to trust, are suspicious of any gaps between the image of the person or product being marked and the underlying reality. "In the old days somebody would look at a business card and say, 'oh, this guy's a vice president; I'll put him on a hierarchy.' Now they look at your haircut and your shirt and a box of other stuff, and they say, 'this is the box this guy fits in.' And if what he's doing is not real, if he's only trying to protect an image, they notice."

This leads to the phenomenon of marketed authenticity. "Because consumers are sensitive to inauthenticity, you have to look inside out, not outside in: you have to start from the core and then move outward," Shore said. Only those whose public and private reality are aligned can sustain the attention of the marketplace. Far from trying to capture the authentic self in all of its complexities, however, branding is a technology for the simplification of identity, a response to the short attention spans of the audience. "In marketing terms, it's always been about, strip away, strip away," Shore emphasised. "People are troubled about thinking about more than one thing at once. If you're trying to project something and you try to be penetrative into people's consciousness you have to be absolutely simple and to the point about it all—otherwise people can't hold it." In trying to excavate a person's "brand DNA," Shore says that he is suspicious of long lists of abstract characteristics. "It's too complicated, it's too generic. If I said, you are an 'Individualistic Maverick,' that can describe all people. But if I tell you that someone's a 'Modern-Day Robin Hood,' that's pointed. You'll remember 'Modern-Day Robin Hood' for 10 years." (A few hours later, when I tried to repeat this slogan to my wife, I had already managed to forget it.)

35   Although presented in the therapeutic language of self-actualisation, personal branding is ultimately a technology for the rigid control of personal identity. Personal branding claims to help individuals be distinctive, so that they can differentiate themselves from the crowd and become more successful competitors in the marketplace of the self. But in the process of seeking

distinctiveness, personal branding is ultimately a recipe for a smothering conformity. Branding confuses distinctiveness and individuality.

Products can be differentiated from each other, with the techniques of advertising and public relations. But the application of branding technologies to the self is based on a category error: individuals can't distinguish themselves from the crowd by measuring their value to the crowd. All of the private attributes of human individuality change shape when they are turned outward and presented to the public: Eros becomes sex; sin becomes crime; guilt becomes shame.

When everything is exposed to the crowd, as John Stuart Mill recognised, individuality is impossible. "As the various social eminences which enabled persons entrenched on them to disregard the opinion of the multitude, gradually become levelled; as the very idea of resisting the will of the public, when it is positively known that they have a will disappears more and more from the minds of practical politicians; there ceases to be any social support for nonconformity," Mill lamented. "It is individuality we war against," he concluded, because of the "ascendancy of public opinion in the State."[14]

We can now appreciate with special force the distinction between the individuality praised by Mill and the individualism lamented by Alexis de Tocqueville, which he defined as the tendency of citizens in a democracy to isolate themselves from each other and to focus obsessively on their own self-interest. Even more than the Victorian era, ours is an age of individualism rather than individuality. The growth of media technologies such as the Internet and television have increased the overwhelming authority of public opinion, as citizens in the Omnipticon find more and more aspects of their personal and public lives observed and evaluated by strangers. These technologies tend to encourage citizens to be self-absorbed, as terrifying images from across the country or across the globe give them an exaggerated sense of personal vulnerability.

At the same time, by decreasing the distance between central authorities and individual citizens, these technologies lead people to expect personal protection from national leaders, rather than taking responsibility for their own freedom and security at a local level. The related feelings of personal anxiety and personal helplessness feed on themselves, and the technology now exists to bring about the conformity that Mill most feared.

The Comfort of Strangers?

The personal branding movement is based on the same fantasy that underlay 40 the Portraits of Grief, which is the fantasy that people can achieve emotional intimacy with strangers. But there is no such thing as public intimacy. Intimacy can be achieved only with those who know us; and strangers cannot know us; they can only have information about us or impressions of us. To offer up personal information that has been taken out of context, in an effort to create the illusion of emotional connection with strangers, requires us to homogenise and standardise the very qualities that made the information personal in the first place. The family members of the 9/11 victims who offered up details of their mourning to the *New York Times* are not so different from the family members of the victim of a car crash who, moments after the accident, weep on cue for the local news. What is most alarming about these scenes is not the tears but the fact that, even at moments of tragedy, we instinctively look at the camera and talk into the microphone.

The personal branding phenomenon is a crude attempt to provide regulated forms of self-exposure, to maintain some kind of boundary between public and private in a world where self-revelation has become a social imperative. And of course most citizens will never resort to expert assistance in their efforts to present a coherent face to the world. But living in the Omnipticon, where we are increasingly unsure about who is observing us, individuals will have to worry more about acting consistently in public and private, in precisely the way the branding advisors prescribe.

In the 1980s, before the proliferation of the web, the sociologist Joshua Meyrowitz discussed the way the electronic media were changing what he called the "situational geography" of social life.[15] As television made us one large audience to performances that occurred in other places, the old walls that separated backstage areas, where people could let down their hair and rehearse for public performances, from the frontstage areas, where the formal performances occurred, began to collapse. Television made viewers aware of the discrepancy between front- and backstage behaviour (such as the woman who plays hard to get, or the fearful man who acts confident in a reality TV dating show), and it became increasingly hard for people to project different images in public and in private without appearing artificial or inauthentic.

Now that the Internet is allowing strangers to observe us even as we observe them, ordinary citizens have to worry more about being caught off guard, like actors with their wigs off. As a form of self-defence, all citizens face the same pressures that confused Laurence Tribe: we will increasingly adopt what Meyrowitz called "middle region" behaviour in public: a blend of the formal frontstage and informal backstage, with a bias toward self-conscious informality. As private concerns like sexual behaviour and depression, anxieties and doubts become harder to conceal, they have to be integrated into the public performance. The result can create an illusion of familiarity—the crazy heavy metal rock star Ozzy Osborne looked cuddlier (though still scatological) as MTV cameras recorded every moment of his domestic life for a reality TV show. But the cuddly domesticated Osborne was far less eccentric, and far less distinctive, than his onstage persona had led audiences to expect.

Like Boorstin, Meyrowitz worried that conformity and homogeneity would result as the electronic media expanded the middle region at the expense of front- and backstage behaviour. In addition to blurring the boundaries between political leaders and followers, Meyrowitz predicted that the electronic technologies of exposure would blur the boundaries between the behaviour of men and women, as well as children and adults. All of these groups speak and act differently when they are segregated from each other; and once the boundaries that separate the groups began to collapse, each of these groups would begin to act more like the others. Now the democratising technology of the Internet is fulfilling Meyrowitz's fears: as more personal information about ourselves is available on the web, private figures are feeling the same pressure that public figures have long experienced to expose details of their personal lives as a form of self-defence; and men, women, and children are blurring into a indistinguishable cacophony of intimate exposure.

To the degree that self-revelation to strangers is a bid for relief from anxiety about identity, however, it may not succeed. Social psychologists who have studied the therapeutic effects of emotional disclosure have discovered a consistent pattern: people who receive positive social support for their emotional disclosures tend to feel better as a result, while those who receive negative responses—from indifference to hostility—feel worse.

For example, a nationwide study of psychological responses to 9/11 found that those who sought social support and vented their anxieties without receiving positive reinforcement were more likely to feel greater distress during the six months after the attack than those who engaged in more social coping activities such as giving blood or attending memorial services.[16] This is consistent with studies of Vietnam veterans and survivors of the California firestorms, who actually felt worse after sharing their feelings with strangers who made clear they didn't want to listen. ("Thank you for not sharing your earthquake story," read an especially wounding T-shirt.) Those who shared their pain with unreceptive audiences felt worse than those who didn't talk at all, although not as good as those who shared their pain with a receptive audience.

Studies of the benefits of writing as well as talking about emotional experiences confirm the same insight: emotional disclosure can have therapeutic effects when it helps people to become less isolated and more integrated with social networks, but it can have negative effects when it leads people to vent their feelings in a void, without the support of a receptive audience.[17] This suggests that therapeutic venting on the Internet to a faceless audience in an unreciprocated bid for attention and emotional support is unlikely to help, and may well make things worse.

In *The Book of Laughter and Forgetting*, Milan Kundera examines the phenomenon of graphomania—the pathological desire to express yourself in writing before a public of unknown readers. "General isolation breeds graphomania, and generalised graphomania in turn intensifies and worsens isolation," Kundera writes. "Everyone [is] surrounded by his own words as by a wall of mirrors, which allows no voice to filter through from outside." Kundera contrasts the reticence of his heroine, who is mortified by the idea that anyone except for her beloved might read her love letters, with the graphomania of a writer like Johann Wolfgang von Goethe, who is convinced that his worth as a human being will be called into question if a single human being fails to read his words. The difference between the lover and Goethe, he says, "is the difference between a human being and a writer."

In an indifferent and socially atomised universe, "everyone is pained by the thought of disappearing, unheard and unseen" as a result, everyone is tempted to become a writer, turning himself "into a universe of words." But "when everyone wakes up as a writer," Kundera warns, "the age of universal deafness and incomprehension will have arrived."[18] Now, we are living in an age of graphomania; we are experiencing the constant din of intimate typing—in email, in chatrooms, on the web and in the workplace. The clacking noise we hear in the air is the noise of endless personal disclosure. But as Kundera recognised, instead of forging emotional connections with strangers, personal exposure in a vacuum may increase social isolation, rather than alleviate it.

50   Many factors put tremendous pressure on individuals in the Naked Crowd, to expose personal details of their lives and strip themselves bare. The crowd demands exposure out of a combination of voyeurism, desire for emotional connection, fear of strangers, democratic suspicion of reticence as sign of elitism, demand for markers of trustworthiness, and an unwillingness to conceive of public events or to relate to public figures except in personal terms. From the perspective of the individual who is pursuing the attention of the crowd, there is, as Charles Derber has suggested, the hope of gaining a mass audience by self-exposure; the demands of a therapeutic culture, which rewards people who talk about intimate problems in public by casting them as victims and survivors; the narcissism that leads people obsessively to call attention to their own fears and insecurities about their identity, in a world where identity is always up for grabs; and the expansion of democratic technologies, which create so many new opportunities for individuals to expose themselves before the crowd.[19] Above all, there is the desire to establish oneself as trustworthy in a risk society by proving—through exposure—that we have nothing to hide.

All this suggests little cause for optimism that, in the face of future terrorist threats, the crowd will strike the balance between personal security and personal exposure in a reasonable way. Individuals, as we've seen, don't care much about privacy in the aggregate at all: faced with a choice between privacy and exposure, many people would rather be exposed than be private, because the crowd demands no less. Concerned mainly about controlling the conditions of their own exposure, many people are only too happy to reveal themselves promiscuously if they have the illusion of control.

Anxious exhibitionists, trained from the cradle to believe that there is no more valuable currency than personal exposure, are not likely to object when their neighbors demand that they strip themselves bare. But just as public intimacy is a kind of delusion, so is the hope of distinguishing ourselves from the crowd by catering to the crowd's insatiable demands for exposure. It is impossible to achieve genuine distinction without a certain heedlessness of public opinion. We can turn ourselves into Portraits of Grief only at the cost of looking more like each other. As both spectators and actors in the Naked Crowd, we are too willing to surrender privacy for an illusory sense of emotional connection and security. Perhaps we will realise what a poor bargain we have struck only after it is too late.

Notes

[1] "Closing a Scrapbook Full of Life and Sorrow," Janny Scott, *New York Times*, 31 December 2001.

[2] "The Mourning Paper," Thomas Mallon, *The American Scholar*, Spring 2002, p 6–7.

[3] *Conversations with Anthony Giddens: Making Sense of Modernity*, Anthony Giddens and Christopher Pierson, Stanford University Press, 1998, p 101.

[4] *The Sane Society*, Erich Fromm, Reinhart, 1955, p141–42.

[5] *The Pursuit of Attention: Power and Ego in Everyday Life*, Charles Derber, Oxford University Press, 2000, p 81.

[6] See "Online Diary: Blog Nation," *New York Times*, 22 August 2002.

[7] See the Diarist.net website.

[8] *Sincerity and Authenticity*, Lionel Trilling, Harvard University Press, 1972.

[9] *The Homeless Mind: Modernisation and Consciousness*, Peter L Berger, Brigitte Berger and Hansfried Kellner, Random House, 1973, p 90

[10] *The Fall of Public Man*, Richard Sennett, WW Norton & Co, 1974, p 196, 265.

[11] *The Image: A Guide to Pseudo-Events in America*, Daniel J. Boorstin, Atheneum, 1977, p 57–58.

[12] *Be Your Own Brand: A Breakthrough Formula for Standing Out from the Crowd*, David McNally and Karl D Speak, Berrett-Koehler, 2002, p 4, 7, 11, 13, 47.

[13] "Hold Me! Squeeze Me! Buy a Six-Pack!," Alex Kuczynski, *New York Times*, 16 November 1997.

[14] *On Liberty*, in *On Liberty and Other Essays*, John Stuart Mill, Oxford University Press, 1998, p 82, 79.

[15] *No Sense of Place: The Impact of Electronic Media on Social Behaviour*, Joshua Meyrowitz, Oxford University Press, 1985, p 6.

[16] "Nationwide Longitudinal Study of Psychological Responses to September 11," Roxane Cohen Silver, E Alison Holman, Daniel N McIntosh, Michael Poulin, and Virginia Gil-Rivas, 288 *Journal of the American Medical Association* 1235, p 1241–1242, 2002.

[17]"Patterns of Natural Language Use: Disclosure, Personality, and Social Integration," JW Pennebaker and A Graybeal, 10 *Current Directions In Psychological Science* 92, 2001.

[18]*The Book of Laughter and Forgetting*, Milan Kundera, Perennial Classics, 1999, p 127–28, 146, 147.

[19]*The Pursuit of Attention: Power and Ego in Everyday Life*, Charles Derber, Oxford University Press, 2000, p xv–xviii.

Things to Do with the Reading

1. Binaries are usually a sign of what is at stake in a piece of writing. They are also the place where key terms and often subtle distinctions tend to congregate. Consider the distinction that Rosen makes between "the individuality praised by Mill and the individualism lamented by Alexis de Tocqueville." Define the difference, and then track the ways the concept of individuality is used in the piece. What other key terms get aligned with it? And what are the various terms that are opposed to it? Make two lists.

2. Make a list of other significant binaries in the piece and write about the one that you think is most interesting or revealing. (See THE METHOD in Chapter 1 and REFORMULATING BINARIES in Chapter 2.) You might consider, for example, sincerity versus authenticity or "heroes of old" versus modern celebrities.

3. It is often productive to think about a piece of writing in terms of its hopes and its fears. In this piece, the fears are fairly clear. For example, the essay ends with a warning. Why does Rosen think that we have struck "a poor bargain" in exchanging "privacy" for "an illusory sense of emotional connection"? To answer this question is to get at what this piece is worried about. Less immediately accessible are its hopes. What are its hopes? Is there a better bargain Rosen would have us strike?

4. Consider *to what extent* Jeffrey Rosen and Christina Rosen might agree on the place of private experience in public life. Imagine the conversation they might have on locating the line between public and private. What would be the primary thing they'd agree on? If it's fair to say that Jeffrey Rosen is concerned with the loss of what he calls "genuine individuality," what is Christina Rosen's primary concern?

5. Application—Using the Reading as a Lens: Look at either the self-representation of a current politician (national or local) or a modern hero. In light of Rosen's claims (taken from Boorstin in paragraph 23), what do you notice?

Geoffrey Nunberg

Blogging in the Global Lunchroom

Geoffrey Nunberg is the emeritus chair of the usage panel of the *American Heritage Dictionary*. He is a linguist and an adjunct full professor at U.C. Berkeley School of Information. The author of a number of books and articles on the nature of contemporary language practices, Nunberg frequently contributes to the National Public Radio show "Fresh Air," where this piece originally appeared in 2004.

Over the last couple of months, I've been posting on a group blog called 1 languagelog.org, which was launched by a couple of linguists as a place where we could vent our comments on the passing linguistic scene.

Still, I don't quite have the hang of the form. The style that sounds perfectly normal in a public radio feature or an op-ed piece comes off as distant and pontifical when I use it in a blog entry. Reading over my own postings, I recall what Queen Victoria once said about Gladstone: "He speaks to me as if I were a public meeting."

I'm not the only one with this problem. A lot of newspapers have been encouraging or even requiring their writers to start blogs. But with some notable exceptions, most journalists have the same problems that I do. They do all the things you should do in a newspaper feature. They fashion engaging leads, they develop their arguments methodically, they give context and background, and tack helpful ID's onto the names they introduce—"New York Senator Charles E. Schumer (D)."

That makes for solid journalism, but it's not really blogging. Granted, that word can cover a lot of territory. A recent Pew Foundation study found that around three million Americans have tried their hands at blogging, and sometimes there seem to be almost that many variants of the form. Blogs can be news summaries, opinion columns, or collections of press releases, like the official blogs of the presidential candidates. But the vast majority are journals posted by college students, office workers, or stay-at-home moms, whose average readership is smaller than a family Christmas letter. (The blog hosting site livejournal.com reports that two-thirds of bloggers are women— I'm not sure what to make of that proportion.)

But when people puzzle over the significance of blogs nowadays, they 5 usually have in mind a small number of A-List sites that traffic in commentary about politics, culture, or technology—blogs like Altercation, Instapundit, Matthew Yglesias, Talking Points, or Doc Searls. It's true that bloggers like

Blogging in the Global Lunchroom, Geoffrey Nunberg, Center for the Study of Language and Information. Reprinted with permission of the author.

these have occasionally come up with news scoops, but in the end they're less about breaking stories than bending them. And their language is a kind of anti-journalese. It's informal, impertinent, and digressive, casting links in all directions. In fact one archetypal blog entry consists entirely of a cryptic comment that's linked to another blog or a news item—"Oh, please," or "He's married to her?"

That interconnectedness is what leads enthusiasts to talk about the blogosphere, as if this were all a single vast conversation—at some point in these discussions, somebody's likely to trot out the phrase "collective mind." But if there's a new public sphere assembling itself out there, you couldn't tell from the way bloggers address their readers—not as anonymous citizens, the way print columnists do, but as co-conspirators who are in on the joke.

Taken as a whole, in fact, the blogging world sounds a lot less like a public meeting than the lunchtime chatter in a high-school cafeteria, complete with snarky comments about the kids at the tables across the room. (Bloggers didn't invent the word snarky, but they've had a lot to do with turning it into the metrosexual equivalent of bitchy. On the Web, blogs account for more than three times as large a share of the total occurrences of snarky as of the occurrences of irony.)[1]

Some people say this all started with Mickey Kaus's column in *Slate,* though Kaus himself cites the old *San Francisco Chronicle* columns of Herb Caen. And Camille Paglia not surprisingly claims that her column in *Salon.com* was the first true blog, and adds that the genre has been going downhill ever since.

But blogs were around on the web well before Kaus or Paglia first logged in.[2] And if you're of a mind to, you can trace their print antecedents a lot further back than Caen or Hunter S. Thompson. That informal style recalls the colloquial voice that Addison and Steele devised when they invented the periodical essay in the early 18th century, even if few blogs come close to that in artfulness. Then too, those essays were written in the guise of fictive personae like Isaac Bickerstaff and Sir Roger de Coverly, who could be the predecessors of pseudonymous bloggers like Wonkette, Atrios, or Skippy the Bush Kangaroo, not to mention the mysterious conservative blogger who goes by the name of Edward Boyd.[3]

10   For that matter, my languagelog co-contributor Mark Liberman recalls that Plato always had Socrates open his philosophical disquisitions with a little diary entry, the way bloggers like to do: "I went down yesterday to see the festival at the Peiraeus with Glaucon, the son of Ariston, and I ran into my old buddy Cephalus and we got to talking about old age…"

Of course whenever a successful new genre emerges, it seems to have been implicit in everything that preceded it. But in the end, this is a mug's game, like asking whether the first SUV was a minivan, a station wagon, or an off-road vehicle.

The fact is that this is a genuinely new language of public discourse—and a paradoxical one. On the one hand, blogs are clearly a more democratic form of expression than anything the world of print has produced. But in some ways they're also more exclusionary, and not just because they only reach about a tenth of the people who use the web.[4] The high, formal style of the newspaper op-ed page may be nobody's native language, but at least it's a neutral voice that doesn't privilege the speech of any particular group or class. Whereas blogspeak is basically an adaptation of the table talk of the urban middle class—it isn't a language that everybody in the cafeteria is equally adept at speaking. Not that there's anything wrong with chewing over the events of the day with the other folks at the lunch table, but you hope that everybody in the room is at least reading the same newspapers at breakfast.[5]

Notes

[1]This is a rough estimate, arrived at by taking the proportion of total Google hits for a word that occurs in a document that also contains the word blog:

> snarky: 87,700
> snarky + blog: 32,600 (37%)
> irony: 1,600,000
> irony + blog: 168,000 (10.5%)

Of course, the fact that the word blog appears in a page doesn't necessarily mean that it is a blog, but it turns out that more than 90 percent of the pages containing the word are blog pages, and in any case, the effect would be the same for both terms. And while some part of this variation no doubt reflects the status of snarky as a colloquial word that is less likely to show up in serious literary discussions and the like, the effect is nowhere near so marked when we look at the word bitchy:

> bitchy: 250,000
> bitchy + blog: 43,700 (17.5%)

> That is, the specialization to blogs is more than twice as high for snarky as for bitchy, even though both are colloquial items.

[2]Many have given credit for inventing the genre to Dave Winer, whose Scripting News was one of the earliest weblogs, though Winer himself says that the first weblog was Tim Berners-Lee's page at CERN. But you could argue that blog has moved out from under the derivational shadow of its etymon—the word isn't just a truncation of weblog anymore. In which case, the identity of the first "real blog" is anybody's guess—and it almost certainly will be.

[3]James Wolcott makes a similar comparison in the current *Vanity Fair*, and goes so far as to suggest that "If Addison and Steele, the editors of *The Spectator* and *The Tatler*, were alive and holding court at Starbucks, they'd be WiFi-ing into a joint blog." That's cute, but I think it gets Addison and Steele wrong—the studied effusions of

Isaac Bickertaff and Sir Roger de Coverly may have sounded like blogs, but they were fashioned with an eye toward a more enduring literary fame. Which is not to say that blogs couldn't become the basis for a genuine literary form. As I noted in a "Fresh Air" piece a few years ago that dealt more with blogs as personal journals:

> There's something very familiar about that accretion of diurnal detail. It's what the novel was trying to achieve when eighteenth-century writers cobbled it together out of subliterary genres like personal letters, journals, and newspapers, with the idea of reproducing the inner and outer experience that makes up daily life. You wonder whether anything as interesting could grow up in the intimate anonymity of cyberspace. (See "I Have Seen the Future, and It Blogs," in Going Nucular, PublicAffairs, May, 2004.)
>
> So it's not surprising that a number of fictional blogs ("flogs"? "blictions"?) have begun to emerge, adapting the tradition of the fictional diary that runs from Robinson Crusoe to Bridget Jones' Diary. As to whether that will ultimately amount to "anything as interesting" as the novel, the jury is likely to be out for a while.

[4]The Pew study found that 11 percent of Internet users have read the blogs or diaries of other Internet users.

[5]For a diverting picture of the blogosphere-as-lunchroom, see Whitney Pastorek's recent piece in the Village Voice, "Blogging Off."

Things to Do with the Reading

1. Given that this is a short radio piece, Nunberg doesn't have the time to develop the implications of his observations at much length. So, this piece would be useful for practicing skills described in Chapter 7: especially ways to use a source as a point of departure.

   First, determine what Nunberg's primary claims are in this piece. Locate sentences that you think best capture his main ideas about blogs. (One of these has to do with his analogy between blogs and high school lunchrooms, about which he says, "blogspeak is basically an adaptation of the table talk of the urban middle class: it isn't a language that everybody in the cafeteria is equally adept at speaking.")

   Then go after assumptions and implications. What are some of the implications of the thinking that Nunberg lays out in his final paragraph? And what assumption underlies his final sentence?

2. Put Nunberg's piece into conversation with one or more of the other essays in this unit using the strategy called "SIMILARITY WITHIN DIFFERENCE" (Chapter 3). Goldberger's piece "Disconnected Urbanism" might be a good choice, and—like Nunberg's essay—it's short. First, develop the

difference. Then look past the difference to locate a point of contact, or similarity. Or, if you think the similarity between the two is more obvious than the difference, start with the similarity and then look past the similarity to what you take to be a significant difference.

3. Application: Clearly, this piece could launch a more extended project in which you follow up some of Nunberg's leads and look for trends in blog-speak. With the definition of style from Chapter 10 in mind, you might explore to what extent there is a discernible blog style. You might check out the range of blogs listed on aldaily.com, or alternatively, those listed on Nunberg's own website, http://www-csli.stanford.edu/~nunberg/.

Imperial Bedroom

Jonathan Franzen is the author of four novels, including the recent *Freedom* (2010), as well as *The Corrections*, which won the National Book Award in 2001. In this essay, taken from his collection *How to Be Alone* (2002), Franzen meditates on the invasion of public space by the private and mourns the eroding of the distinction between the two. He is a gifted stylist and an agile thinker, full of surprising reversals. For example: "The real reason that Americans are apathetic about privacy is so big as to be almost invisible: we're flat-out *drowning* in privacy. What's threatened isn't the private sphere. It's the public sphere." Franzen's second collection of essays, *Farther Away*, was published in 2012.

1   Privacy, privacy, the new American obsession: espoused as the most fundamental of rights, marketed as the most desirable of commodities, and pronounced dead twice a week.

Even before Linda Tripp pressed the "Record" button on her answering machine, commentators were warning us that "privacy is under siege," that "privacy is in a dreadful state," that "privacy as we now know it may not exist in the year 2000." They say that both Big Brother and his little brother, John Q. Public, are shadowing me through networks of computers. They tell me that security cameras no bigger than spiders are watching from every shaded corner, that dour feminists are monitoring bedroom behavior and watercooler conversations, that genetic sleuths can decoct my entire being from a droplet of saliva, that voyeurs can retrofit ordinary camcorders with a filter that lets them *see through people's clothing.* Then comes the flood of dirty suds from the Office of the Independent Counsel, oozing forth through official and commercial channels to saturate the national consciousness. The Monica Lewinsky scandal marks, in the words of the philosopher Thomas Nagel, "the culmination of a disastrous erosion" of privacy; it represents, in the words of the author Wendy Kaminer, "the utter disregard for privacy and individual autonomy that exists in totalitarian regimes." In the person of Kenneth Starr, the "public sphere" has finally overwhelmed—shredded, gored, trampled, invaded, run roughshod over—"the private."

The panic about privacy has all the finger-pointing and paranoia of a good old American scare, but it's missing one vital ingredient: a genuinely alarmed public. Americans care about privacy mainly in the abstract. Sometimes a well-informed community unites to defend itself, as when Net users bombarded the White House with emails against the "clipper chip," and

"Imperial Bedroom" from HOW TO BE ALONE by Jonathan Franzen. Copyright © 2002, 2003 by Jonathan Franzen. Reprinted by permission of Farrar, Straus and Giroux, LLC. All rights reserved.

sometimes an especially outrageous piece of news provokes a national out-cry, as when the Lotus Development Corporation tried to market a CD-ROM containing financial profiles of nearly half the people in the country. By and large, though, even in the face of wholesale infringements like the war on drugs, Americans remain curiously passive. I'm no exception. I read the edi-torials and try to get excited, but I can't. More often than not, I find myself feeling the opposite of what the privacy mavens want me to. It's happened twice in the last month alone.

On the Saturday morning when the *Times* came carrying the complete text of the Starr report, what I felt as I sat alone in my apartment and tried to eat my breakfast was that my own privacy—not Clinton's, not Lewinsky's—was being violated. I love the distant pageant of public life. I love both the pageantry and the distance. Now a President was facing impeachment, and as a good citizen I had a duty to stay informed about the evidence, but the evidence here con-sisted of two people's groping, sucking, and mutual self-deception. What I felt, when this evidence landed beside my toast and coffee, wasn't a pretend revul-sion to camouflage a secret interest in the dirt; I wasn't offended by the sex qua sex; I wasn't worrying about a potential future erosion of my own rights; I didn't feel the President's pain in the empathic way he'd once claimed to feel mine; I wasn't repelled by the revelation that public officials do bad things; and, although I'm a registered Democrat, my disgust was of a different order from my partisan disgust at the news that the Giants have blown a fourth-quarter lead. What I felt I felt personally. I was being intruded on.

A couple of days later, I got a call from one of my credit-card provid- 5 ers, asking me to confirm two recent charges at a gas station and one at a hardware store. Queries like this are common nowadays, but this one was my first, and for a moment I felt eerily exposed. At the same time, I was perversely flattered that someone, somewhere, had taken an interest in me and had bothered to phone. Not that the young male operator seemed to care about me personally. He sounded like he was reading his lines from a laminated booklet. The strain of working hard at a job he almost certainly didn't enjoy seemed to thicken his tongue. He tried to rush his words out, to speed through them as if in embarrassment or vexation at how nearly worthless they were, but they kept bunching up in his teeth, and he had to stop and extract them with his lips, one by one. It was the computer, he said, the computer that routinely, ah, scans the, you know, the pattern of charges… and was there something else he could help me with tonight? I decided that if this young person wanted to scroll through my charges and ponder the significance of my two fill-ups and my gallon of latex paint, I was fine with it.

So here's the problem. On the Saturday morning the Starr Report came out, my privacy was, in the classic liberal view, absolute. I was alone in my home and unobserved, unbothered by neighbors, unmentioned in the news, and perfectly free, if I chose, to ignore the report and do the pleasantly *al dente*

Saturday crossword; yet the report's mere existence so offended my sense of privacy that I could hardly bring myself to touch the thing. Two days later, I was disturbed in my home by a ringing phone, asked to cough up my mother's maiden name, and made aware that the digitized minutiae of my daily life were being scrutinized by strangers; and within five minutes I'd put the entire episode out of my mind. I felt encroached on when I was ostensibly safe, and I felt safe when I was ostensibly encroached on. And I didn't know why.

The right to privacy—defined by Louis Brandeis and Samuel Warren, in 1890, as "the right to be let alone"—seems at first glance to be an elemental principle in American life. It's the rallying cry of activists fighting for reproductive rights, against stalkers, for the right to die, against a national health-care database, for stronger data-encryption standards, against paparazzi, for the sanctity of employee email, and against employee drug testing. On closer examination, though, privacy proves to be the Cheshire cat of values: not much substance, but a very winning smile.

Legally, the concept is a mess. Privacy violation is the emotional core of many crimes, from stalking and rape to Peeping Tommery and trespass, but no criminal statute forbids it in the abstract. Civil law varies from state to state but generally follows a forty-year-old analysis by the legal scholar Dean William Prosser, who dissected the invasion of privacy into four torts: *intrusion* on my solitude, the publishing of *private facts* about me which are not of legitimate public concern, publicity that puts my character in a *false light*, and *appropriation* of my name or likeness without my consent. This is a crumbly set of torts. Intrusion looks a lot like criminal trespass, false light like defamation, and appropriation like theft; and the harm that remains when these extraneous offenses are subtracted is so admirably captured by the phrase "infliction of emotional distress" as to render the tort of privacy invasion all but superfluous. What really undergirds privacy is the classical liberal conception of personal autonomy or liberty. In the last few decades, many judges and scholars have chosen to speak of a "zone of privacy," rather than a "sphere of liberty," but this is a shift in emphasis, not in substance: not the making of a new doctrine but the repackaging and remarketing of an old one.

Whatever you're trying to sell, whether it's luxury real estate or Esperanto lessons, it helps to have the smiling word "private" on your side. Last winter, as the owner of a Bank One Platinum Visa Card, I was offered enrollment in a program called PrivacyGuard®, which, according to the literature promoting it, "*puts you in the know* about the very personal records available to your employer, insurers, credit card companies, and government agencies." The first three months of PrivacyGuard® were free, so I signed up. What came in the mail then was paperwork: envelopes and request forms for a Credit Record Search and other searches, also a disappointingly undeluxe logbook in which to jot down the search results. I realized immediately that I didn't care enough about, say, my driving records to wait a month to get them; it was only when I called PrivacyGuard® to cancel my membership, and was all but begged not to, that I realized that the whole point of this "service" was to harness my time and energy to the task of reducing Bank One Visa's fraud losses.

Even issues that legitimately touch on privacy are rarely concerned with the actual emotional harm of unwanted exposure or intrusion. A proposed national Genetic Privacy Act, for example, is premised on the idea that my DNA reveals more about my identity and future health than other medical data do. In fact, DNA is as yet no more intimately revealing than a heart murmur, a family history of diabetes, or an inordinate fondness for Buffalo chicken wings. As with any medical records, the potential for abuse of genetic information by employers and insurers is chilling, but this is only tangentially a privacy issue; the primary harm consists of things like job discrimination and higher insurance premiums.

In a similar way, the problem of online security is mainly about nuts and bolts. What American activists call "electronic privacy" their European counterparts call "data protection." Our term is exciting; theirs is accurate. If someone is out to steal your Amex number and expiration date, or if an evil ex-boyfriend is looking for your new address, you need the kind of hard-core secrecy that encryption seeks to guarantee. If you're talking to a friend on the phone, however, you need only a *feeling* of privacy.

The social drama of data protection goes something like this: a hacker or an insurance company or a telemarketer gains access to a sensitive database, public-interest watchdogs bark loudly, and new firewalls go up. Just as most people are moderately afraid of germs but leave virology to the Centers for Disease Control, most Americans take a reasonable interest in privacy issues but leave the serious custodial work to experts. Our problem now is that the custodians have started speaking a language of panic and treating privacy not as one of many competing values but as the one value that trumps all others.

The novelist Richard Powers recently declared in a *Times* op-ed piece that privacy is a "vanishing illusion" and that the struggle over the encryption of digital communications is therefore as "great with consequence" as the Cold War. Powers defines "the private" as "that part of life that goes unregistered," and he sees in the digital footprints we leave whenever we charge things the approach of "that moment when each person's every living day will become a Bloomsday, recorded in complete detail and reproducible with a few deft keystrokes." It is scary, of course, to think that the mystery of our identities might be reducible to finite data sequences. That Powers can seriously compare credit-card fraud and intercepted cell-phone calls to thermonuclear incineration, however, speaks mainly to the infectiousness of privacy panic. Where, after all, is it "registered" what Powers or anybody else is thinking, seeing, saying, wishing, planning, dreaming, and feeling ashamed of? A digital *Ulysses* consisting of nothing but a list of its hero's purchases and other recordable transactions might run, at most, to four pages: was there really nothing more to Bloom's day?

When Americans do genuinely sacrifice privacy, moreover, they do so for tangible gains in health or safety or efficiency. Most legalized infringements—HIV notification, airport X-rays, Megan's Law, Breathalyzer roadblocks, the drug-testing of student athletes, laws protecting fetuses, laws protecting the vegetative, remote monitoring of automobile emissions, county-jail strip searches, even Ken Starr's exposure of presidential corruption—are essentially public health measures. I resent the security cameras in Washington Square, but I appreciate the ones on a subway platform. The risk that someone is abusing my E-ZPass toll records seems to me comfortably low in comparison with my gain in convenience. Ditto the risk that some gossip rag will make me a victim of the First Amendment; with two hundred and seventy million people in the country, any individual's chances of being nationally exposed are next to nil.

15   The legal scholar Lawrence Lessig has characterized Americans as "bovine" for making calculations like this and for thereby acquiescing in what he calls the "Sovietization" of personal life. The curious thing about privacy, though, is that simply by expecting it we can usually achieve it. One of my neighbors in the apartment building across the street spends a lot of time at her mirror examining her pores, and I can see her doing it, just as she can undoubtedly see me sometimes. But our respective privacies remain intact as long as neither of us *feels* seen. When I send a postcard through the U.S. mail, I'm aware in the abstract that mail handlers may be reading it, may be reading it aloud, may even be laughing at it, but I'm safe from all harm unless, by sheer bad luck, the one handler in the country whom I actually know sees the postcard and slaps his forehead and says, "Oh, jeez, I know this guy."

OUR PRIVACY panic isn't merely exaggerated. It's founded on a fallacy. Ellen Alderman and Caroline Kennedy, in *The Right to Privacy*, sum up the conventional wisdom of privacy advocates like this: "There is less privacy than there used to be." The claim has been made or implied so often, in so many books and editorials and talk-show dens, that Americans, no matter how passive they are in their behavior, now dutifully tell pollsters that they're very much worried about privacy. From almost any historical perspective, however, the claim seems bizarre.

In 1890, an American typically lived in a small town under conditions of near-panoptical surveillance. Not only did his every purchase "register," but it registered in the eyes and the memory of shopkeepers who knew him, his parents, his wife, and his children. He couldn't so much as walk to the post office without having his movements tracked and analyzed by neighbors. Probably he grew up sleeping in the same bed with his siblings and possibly with his parents, too. Unless he was well off, his transportation—a train, a horse, his own two feet—either was communal or exposed him to the public eye.

In the suburbs and exurbs where the typical American lives today, tiny nuclear families inhabit enormous houses, in which each person has his or her own bedroom and, sometimes, bathroom. Compared even with suburbs in the sixties and seventies, when I was growing up, the contemporary condominium development or gated community offers a striking degree of anonymity. It's no longer the rule that you know your neighbors. Communities increasingly tend to be virtual, the participants either faceless or firmly in control of the face they present. Transportation is largely private: the latest SUVs are the size of living rooms and come with onboard telephones, CD players, and TV screens; behind the tinted windows of one of these high-riding I-see-you-but-you-can't-see-me mobile PrivacyGuard® units, a person can be wearing pajamas or a licorice bikini, for all anybody knows or cares. Maybe the government intrudes on the family a little more than it did a hundred years ago (social workers look in on the old and the poor, health officials require inoculations, the police inquire about spousal battery), but these intrusions don't begin to make up for the small-town snooping they've replaced.

The "right to be left alone"? Far from disappearing, it's exploding. It's the *essence* of modern American architecture, landscape, transportation, communication, and mainstream political philosophy. The real reason that Americans are apathetic about privacy is so big as to be almost invisible: we're flat-out *drowning* in privacy.

What's threatened, then, isn't the private sphere. It's the public sphere. 20 Much has been made of the discouraging effect that the Starr investigation may have on future aspirants to public office (only zealots and zeros need apply), but that's just half of it. The public world of Washington, because it's public, belongs to everyone. We're all invited to participate with our votes, our patriotism, our campaigning, and our opinions. The collective weight of a population makes possible our faith in the public world as something larger and more enduring and more dignified than any messy individual can be in private. But, just as one sniper in a church tower can keep the streets of an entire town empty, one real gross-out scandal can undermine that faith.

If privacy depends upon an expectation of invisibility, the expectation of *visibility* is what defines a public space. My "sense of privacy" functions to keep the public out of the private *and* to keep the private out of the public. A kind of mental Border collie yelps in distress when I feel that the line between the two has been breached. This is why the violation of a public space is so similar, as an experience, to the violation of privacy. I walk past a man taking a leak on a sidewalk in broad daylight (delivery-truck drivers can be especially self-righteous in their "Ya gotta go, ya gotta go" philosophy of bladder management), and although the man with the yawning fly is ostensibly the one whose privacy is compromised by the leak, I'm the one who feels the impingement. Flashers and sexual harassers and fellators on the pier and self-explainers on the crosstown bus all similarly assault our sense of the "public" by exposing themselves.

Since really serious exposure in public today is assumed to be synony-mous with being seen on television, it would seem to follow that televised space is the premier public space. Many things that people say to me on television, however, would never be tolerated in a genuine public space—in a jury box, for example, or even on a city sidewalk. TV is an enormous, ramified extension of the billion living rooms and bedrooms in which it's consumed. You rarely hear a person on the subway talking loudly about, say, incontinence, but on television it's been happening for years. TV is devoid of shame, and without shame there can be no distinction between public and private. Last winter, an anchorwoman looked me in the eye and, in the tone of a close female relative, referred to a litter of babies in Iowa as "America's seven little darlin's." It was strange enough, twenty-five years ago, to get Dan Rather's reports on Watergate between spots for Geritol and Bayer aspirin, as if Nixon's impending resignation were somehow located in my medicine chest. Now, shelved between ads for Promise margarine and Celebrity Cruises, the news itself is a soiled cocktail dress—TV the bedroom floor and nothing but.

Reticence, meanwhile, has become an obsolete virtue. People now readily name their diseases, rents, antidepressants. Sexual histories get spilled on first dates, Birkenstocks and cutoffs infiltrate the office on casual Fridays, telecommuting puts the boardroom in the bedroom, "softer" modern office design puts the bedroom in the boardroom, sales-people unilaterally address customers by their first name, waiters won't bring me food until I've established a personal relationship with them, voice-mail machinery stresses the "I" in "I'm sorry, but I don't understand what you dialed," and cyberenthusiasts, in a particularly grotesque misnomer, designate as "public forums" pieces of etched silicon with which a forum's unshaved "participant" may communicate while sitting crosslegged in tangled sheets. The networked world as a threat to privacy? It's the ugly spectacle of a privacy triumphant.

A genuine public space is a place where every citizen is welcome to be present and where the purely private is excluded or restricted. One reason that attendance at art museums has soared in recent years is that museums still feel public in this way. After those tangled sheets, how delicious the enforced decorum and the hush, the absence of in-your-face consumerism. How sweet the promenading, the seeing and being seen. Everybody needs a promenade sometimes—a place to go when you want to announce to the world (not the little world of friends and family but the big world, the real world) that you have a new suit, or that you're in love, or that you suddenly realize you stand a full inch taller when you don't hunch your shoulders.

25   Unfortunately, the fully public place is a nearly extinct category. We still have courtrooms and the jury pool, commuter trains and bus stations, here and there a small-town Main Street that really is a main street rather than a strip mall, certain coffee bars, and certain city sidewalks. Otherwise, for American adults, the only halfway public space is the world of work. Here, especially in the upper echelons of business, codes of dress and behavior are routinely enforced, personal disclosures are penalized, and formality is still

the rule. But these rituals extend only to the employees of the firm, and even they, when they become old, disabled, obsolete, or outsourceable, are liable to be expelled and thereby relegated to the tangled sheets.

The last big, steep-walled bastion of public life in America is Washington, D.C. Hence the particular violation I felt when the Starr Report crashed in. Hence the feeling of being intruded on. It was privacy invasion, all right: private life brutally invading the most public of public spaces. I don't want to see sex on the news from Washington. There's sex everywhere else I look—on sitcoms, on the Web, on dust jackets, in car ads, on the billboards at Times Square. Can't there be one thing in the national landscape that isn't about the bedroom? We all know there's sex in the cloakrooms of power, sex behind the pomp and circumstance, sex beneath the robes of justice; but can't we act like grownups and pretend otherwise? Pretend not that "no one is looking" but that *everyone* is looking?

For two decades now, business leaders and politicians across much of the political spectrum, both Gingrich Republicans and Clinton Democrats, have extolled the virtues of privatizing public institutions. But what better word can there be for Lewinskygate and the ensuing irruption of disclosures (the infidelities of Helen Chenoweth, of Dan Burton, of Henry Hyde) than "privatization"? Anyone who wondered what a privatized presidency might look like may now, courtesy of Mr. Starr, behold one.

In Denis Johnson's short story "Beverly Home," the young narrator spends his days working at a nursing home for the hopelessly disabled, where there is a particularly unfortunate patient whom no one visits:

> A perpetual spasm forced him to perch sideways on his wheelchair and peer down along his nose at his knotted fingers. This condition had descended on him suddenly. He got no visitors. His wife was divorcing him. He was only thirty-three, I believe he said, but it was hard to guess what he told about himself because he really couldn't talk anymore, beyond clamping his lips repeatedly around his protruding tongue while groaning.
>
> No more pretending for him! He was completely and openly a mess. Meanwhile the rest of us go on trying to fool each other.

In a coast-to-coast, shag-carpeted imperial bedroom, we could all just be messes and save ourselves the trouble of pretending. But who wants to live in a pajama-party world? Privacy loses its value unless there's something it can be defined against. "Meanwhile the rest of us go on trying to fool each other"—and a good thing, too. The need to put on a public face is as basic as the need for the privacy in which to take it off. We need both a home that's not like a public space and a public space that's not like home.

Walking up Third Avenue on a Saturday night, I feel bereft. All around 30 me, attractive young people are hunched over their StarTacs and Nokias with preoccupied expressions, as if probing a sore tooth, or adjusting a hearing aid, or squeezing a pulled muscle; personal technology has begun to look like a personal handicap. All I really want from a sidewalk is that people see me and let themselves be seen, but even this modest ideal is thwarted by cell-phone users and their unwelcome privacy. They say things like "Should we have couscous with that?" and "I'm on my way to Blockbuster." They aren't breaking any law by broadcasting these breakfast-nook conversations. There's no PublicityGuard that I can buy, no expensive preserve of public life to which I can flee. Seclusion, whether in a suite at the Plaza or in a cabin in the Catskills, is comparatively effortless to achieve. Privacy is protected as both commodity and right; public forums are protected as neither. Like old-growth forests, they're few and irreplaceable and should be held in trust by everyone. The work of maintaining them gets only harder as the private sector grows ever more demanding, distracting, and disheartening. Who has the time and energy to stand up for the public sphere? What rhetoric can possibly compete with the American love of "privacy"?

When I return to my apartment after dark, I don't immediately turn my lights on. Over the years, it's become a reflexive precaution on my part not to risk spooking exposed neighbors by flooding my living room with light, although the only activity I ever seem to catch them at is watching TV.

My skin-conscious neighbor is home with her husband tonight, and they seem to be dressing for a party. The woman, a vertical strip of whom is visible between the Levelors and the window frame, is wearing a bathrobe and a barrette and sitting in front of a mirror. The man, slick-haired, wearing suit pants and a white T-shirt, stands by the sofa in the other room and watches television in a posture that I recognize as uncommitted. Finally the woman disappears into the bedroom. The man puts on a white shirt and a necktie and perches sidesaddle on the arm of the sofa, still watching television, more involved with it now. The woman returns wearing a strapless yellow dress and looking like a whole different species of being. Happy the transformation! Happy the distance between private and public! I see a rapid back-and-forth involving jewelry, jackets, and a clutch purse, and then the couple, dressed to the nines, ventures out into the world.

[1998]

Things to Do with the Reading

1. Much of the effect of Franzen's piece has to do with its style, and one element of the style is the repetition of certain metaphors. These metaphors are themselves complex nodes of meaning—usually an image that has been introduced and laden with feeling and point of view. In music and in some literary study as well, the use of a repeated image that accumulates meaning as it recurs is known as a *leitmotif*. There are

numerous examples of this technique in the essay, but two prominent ones are "tangled sheets" and the "skin-conscious neighbor." Take notes on where and how any of these repeated terms are used in the essay. How does the meaning of the leitmotif grow?

2. The sinuous turns of thought in Franzen's essay—which is clearly inductive and does not start with a thesis—make it a rich candidate for analyzing how the thesis evolves in a piece of writing. Familiarize yourself with the discussion of the evolving thesis in Chapter 6 and then locate the various evolutions of Franzen's thesis. See "Practice Tracking Thesis Statements in Finished Drafts" in Chapter 6. List all of the different versions of his primary claims to compose a chart of how the thinking in the piece moves.

3. A primary point made in *Writing Analytically* about conclusions is to culminate, not simply summarize. (See What Conclusions Do: the Final "So WHAT?" in Chapter 9.) Study the way that Franzen culminates his essay. What do you notice about his final paragraph? How does it proceed? What key terms from the essay does it include? How does it provide judgment, culmination, and send-off?

4. Think about the connection between Franzen's favored sentence shapes and his way of thinking. See Chapter 10, the section entitled Style Analysis: A Summary of Things to Look For on "go to" sentence shapes. A striking and thus emphatic "go to" sentence shape of Franzen's is called chiasmus, which is described under parallelism in Chapter 10. Here are some examples of chiasmus from his essay:

> "I felt encroached on when I was ostensibly safe, and I felt safe when I was ostensibly encroached on."
>
> "My 'sense of privacy' functions to keep the public out of the private and to keep the private out of the public."
>
> "Telecommunicating puts the boardroom in the bedroom, 'softer' modern office design puts the bedroom in the boardroom (…)"

And here is a variant, not quite chiasmus:

> "If privacy depends upon an expectation of invisibility, the expectation of visibility is what defines a public space."

Ponder the relationship between this chiasmic sentence shape and the way that Franzen's thinking proceeds in general in the essay. What do you notice about the structure of thinking in Franzen's essay that might prompt him to shape his sentences in this way?

5. Style creates what rhetoricians call *persona*—a version of the writer that he or she creates for the purpose at hand. Describe Franzen's persona in this piece, the sort of person he comes off as being on the page and the kind of relationship he seeks to establish with the reader. Determine what features of Franzen's style (word choice, tone, sentence shape) are most significant in creating this persona. Once you have gotten to this point, ask yourself: Why this persona for this piece?

6. Links: In their essays, Christina Rosen and Paul Goldberger mourn the loss of public space, as does Franzen. How does Franzen's thinking about public vs. private compare with the viewpoints of the other two writers in this regard? Find sentences about public space from each of the three essays and put these into conversation with each other. What similarities and differences do you find? Here, for example, is a relevant passage from Rosen: "As trust is being built and bolstered moment by moment between individuals, public trust among strangers in social settings is eroding. We are strengthening and increasing our interactions with the people we already know at the expense of those who we do not."

7. Link Across Chapters: Compare and contrast with other writers in this volume Franzen's thinking on the ways that public space is threatened. Consider, for example, James Howard Kunstler's and Jane Jacobs' pieces in Chapter 13, as well as the discussions of public versus private in Chapter 14 (such as Ishmael Reed's "My Neighborhood"). See Comparison/Contrast in Chapter 3.

8. Application: Use the essay as a lens to locate interesting instances of what Franzen calls "the panic about privacy." Alternatively, locate examples from your experience of public spaces as Franzen defines the term. Or apply the following remark as a lens to any show on the airwaves: "TV is devoid of shame, and without shame there can be no distinction between public and private." Use analysis of your examples in order to explore the meaning of the quotation.

Sam Anderson

In Defense of Distraction

Sam Anderson is the critic at large for *The New York Times Magazine*; before that he reviewed books and occasionally wrote longer pieces for *New York* magazine, such as "In Defense of Distraction," which was the cover story of the May 2009 issue. He has become increasingly interested in broader cultural criticism, for example, the way our reading habits as a culture have continued to change with technology.

I. The Poverty of Attention

I'm going to pause here, right at the beginning of my riveting article about atten- 1
tion, and ask you to please get all of your precious 21st-century distractions out of your system now. Check the score of the Mets game; text your sister that pun you just thought of about her roommate's new pet lizard ("iguana hold yr hand LOL get it like Beatles"); refresh your work email, your home email, your school email; upload pictures of yourself reading this paragraph to your "me reading magazine articles" Flickr photostream; and alert the fellow citizens of whatever Twittertopia you happen to frequent that you will be suspending your digital presence for the next twenty minutes or so (I know that seems drastic: Tell them you're having an appendectomy or something and are about to lose consciousness). Good. Now: Count your breaths. Close your eyes. Do whatever it takes to get all of your neurons lined up in one direction. Above all, resist the urge to fixate on the picture, right over there, of that weird scrambled guy typing. Do not speculate on his ethnicity (German-Venezuelan?) or his back-story (Witness Protection Program?) or the size of his monitor. Go ahead and cover him with your hand if you need to. There. Doesn't that feel better? Now it's just you and me, tucked like fourteenth-century Zen masters into this sweet little nook of pure mental focus. (Seriously, stop looking at him. I'm over here.)

Over the last several years, the problem of attention has migrated right into the center of our cultural attention. We hunt it in neurology labs, lament its decline on op-ed pages, fetishize it in grassroots quality-of-life movements, diagnose its absence in more and more of our children every year, cultivate it in yoga class twice a week, harness it as the engine of self-help empires, and pump it up to superhuman levels with drugs originally intended to treat Alzheimer's and narcolepsy. Everyone still pays some form of attention all of the time, of course—it's basically impossible for humans not to—but the currency in which we pay it, and the goods we get in exchange, have changed dramatically.

Sam Anderson/New York Magazine. Reprinted by permission.

Back in 1971, when the web was still twenty years off and the smallest computers were the size of delivery vans, before the founders of Google had even managed to get themselves born, the polymath economist Herbert A. Simon wrote maybe the most concise possible description of our modern struggle: "What information consumes is rather obvious: It consumes the attention of its recipients. Hence a wealth of information creates a poverty of attention, and a need to allocate that attention efficiently among the over-abundance of information sources that might consume it." As beneficiaries of the greatest information boom in the history of the world, we are suffering, by Simon's logic, a correspondingly serious poverty of attention.

If the pundits clogging my RSS reader can be trusted (the ones I check up on occasionally when I don't have any new email), our attention crisis is already chewing its hyperactive way through the very foundations of Western civilization. Google is making us stupid, multitasking is draining our souls, and the "dumbest generation" is leading us into a "dark age" of bookless "power browsing." Adopting the Internet as the hub of our work, play, and commerce has been the intellectual equivalent of adopting corn syrup as the center of our national diet, and we've all become mentally obese. Formerly well-rounded adults are forced to MacGyver worldviews out of telegraphic blog posts, bits of YouTube videos, and the first nine words of *Times* editorials. Schoolkids spread their attention across 30 different programs at once and interact with each other mainly as sweatless avatars. (One recent study found that American teenagers spend an average of 6.5 hours a day focused on the electronic world, which strikes me as a little low; in South Korea, the most wired nation on earth, young adults have actually died from exhaustion after multiday, online gaming marathons.) We are, in short, terminally distracted. And *distracted*, the alarmists will remind you, was once a synonym for *insane*. (Shakespeare: "poverty hath distracted her.")

5   This doomsaying strikes me as silly for two reasons. First, conservative social critics have been blowing the apocalyptic bugle at every large-scale tech-driven social change since Socrates' famous complaint about the mem-ory-destroying properties of that newfangled technology called "writing." (A complaint we remember, not incidentally, because it was written down.) And, more practically, the virtual horse has already left the digital barn. It's too late to just retreat to a quieter time. Our jobs depend on connectivity. Our pleasure-cycles—no trivial matter—are increasingly tied to it. Information rains down faster and thicker every day, and there are plenty of non-moronic reasons for it to do so. The question, now, is how successfully we can adapt.

Although attention is often described as an organ system, it's not the sort of thing you can pull out and study like a spleen. It's a complex process that shows up all over the brain, mingling inextricably with other quasi-mystical processes like emotion, memory, identity, will, motivation, and mood. Psychologists have always had to track attention secondhand. Before the sixties, they measured it through easy-to-monitor senses like vision and hearing (if you listen to one voice in your right ear and another in your left, how much information can you absorb from either side?), then eventually graduated to PET scans and EEGs and electrodes and monkey brains. Only in the last ten years—thanks to neuroscientists and their functional MRIs—have we been able to watch the attending human brain in action, with its coordinated storms of neural firing, rapid blood surges, and oxygen flows. This has yielded all kinds of fascinating insights—for instance, that when forced to multitask, the overloaded brain shifts its processing from the hippocampus (responsible for memory) to the striatum (responsible for rote tasks), making it hard to learn a task or even recall what you've been doing once you're done.

When I reach David Meyer, one of the world's reigning experts on multitasking, he is feeling alert against all reasonable odds. He has just returned from India, where he was discussing the nature of attention at a conference with the Dalai Lama (Meyer gave a keynote speech arguing that Buddhist monks multitask during meditation), and his trip home was hellish: a canceled flight, an overnight taxi on roads so rough it took thirteen hours to go 200 miles. This is his first full day back in his office at the University of Michigan, where he directs the Brain, Cognition, and Action Laboratory—a basement space in which finger-tapping, card-memorizing, tone-identifying subjects help Meyer pinpoint exactly how much information the human brain can handle at once. He's been up since 3 a.m. and has by now goosed his attention several times with liquid stimulants: a couple of cups of coffee, some tea. "It does wonders," he says.

My interaction with Meyer takes place entirely via the technology of distraction. We scheduled and rescheduled our appointment, several times, by email. His voice is now projecting, tinnily, out of my cell phone's speaker and into the microphone of my digital recorder, from which I will download it, as soon as we're done, onto my laptop, which I currently have open on my desk in front of me, with several windows spread across the screen, each bearing nested tabs, on one of which I've been reading, before Meyer even had a chance to tell me about it, a blog all about his conference with the Dalai Lama, complete with RSS feed and audio commentary and embedded YouTube videos and pictures of His Holiness. As Meyer and I talk, the universe tests us with a small battery of distractions. A maximum-volume fleet of emergency vehicles passes just outside my window; my phone chirps to tell us that my mother is calling on the other line, then beeps again to let us know she's left a message. There is, occasionally, a slight delay in the connection. Meyer ignores it all, speaking deliberately and at length, managing to coordinate tricky subject-verb agreements over the course of multi-clause sentences. I begin, a little sheepishly, with a question that strikes me as sensationalistic, nonscientific, and probably unanswerable by someone who's been professionally trained in the discipline of cautious objectivity: Are we living through a crisis of attention?

Before I even have a chance to apologize, Meyer responds with the air of an Old Testament prophet. "Yes," he says. "And I think it's going to get a lot worse than people expect." He sees our distraction as a full-blown epidemic—a cognitive plague that has the potential to wipe out an entire generation of focused and productive thought. He compares it, in fact, to smoking. "People aren't aware what's happening to their mental processes," he says, "in the same way that people years ago couldn't look into their lungs and see the residual deposits."

10   I ask him if, as the world's foremost expert on multitasking and distraction, he has found his own life negatively affected by the new world order of multitasking and distraction.

"Yep," he says immediately, then adds, with admirable (although slightly hurtful) bluntness: "I get calls all the time from people like you. Because of the way the Internet works, once you become visible, you're approached from left and right by people wanting to have interactions in ways that are extremely time-consuming. I could spend my whole day, my whole night, just answering emails. I just can't deal with it all. None of this happened even ten years ago. It was a lot calmer. There was a lot of opportunity for getting steady work done."

Over the last twenty years, Meyer and a host of other researchers have proved again and again that multitasking, at least as our culture has come to know and love and institutionalize it, is a myth. When you think you're doing two things at once, you're almost always just switching rapidly between them, leaking a little mental efficiency with every switch. Meyer says that this is because, to put it simply, the brain processes different kinds of information on a variety of separate "channels"—a language channel, a visual channel, an auditory channel, and so on—each of which can process only one stream of information at a time. If you overburden a channel, the brain becomes inefficient and mistake-prone. The classic example is driving while talking on a cell phone, two tasks that conflict across a range of obvious channels: Steering and dialing are both manual tasks, looking out the windshield and reading a phone screen are both visual, etc. Even talking on a hands-free phone can be dangerous, Meyer says. If the person on the other end of the phone is describing a visual scene—say, the layout of a room full of furniture—that conversation can actually occupy your visual channel enough to impair your ability to see what's around you on the road.

The only time multitasking does work efficiently, Meyer says, is when multiple simple tasks operate on entirely separate channels—for example, folding laundry (a visual-manual task) while listening to a stock report (a verbal task). But real-world scenarios that fit those specifications are very rare.

This is troubling news, obviously, for a culture of BlackBerrys and news crawls and Firefox tabs—tools that, critics argue, force us all into a kind of elective ADHD. The tech theorist Linda Stone famously coined the phrase "continuous partial attention" to describe our newly frazzled state of mind. American office workers don't stick with any single task for more than a few minutes at a time; if left uninterrupted, they will most likely interrupt themselves. Since every interruption costs around 25 minutes of productivity, we spend nearly a third of our day recovering from them. We keep an average of eight windows open on our computer screens at one time and skip between them every twenty seconds. When we read online, we hardly even read at all—our eyes run down the page in an F pattern, scanning for keywords. When you add up all the leaks from these constant little switches, soon you're hemorrhaging a dangerous amount of mental power. People who frequently check their email have tested as less intelligent than people who are actually high on marijuana. Meyer guesses that the damage will take decades to understand, let alone fix. If Einstein were alive today, he says, he'd probably be forced to multitask so relentlessly in the Swiss patent office that he'd never get a chance to work out the theory of relativity.

II. The War on the Poverty of Attention

For Winifred Gallagher, the author of *Rapt*, a new book about the power of attention, it all comes down to the problem of jackhammers. A few minutes before I called, she tells me, a construction crew started jackhammering outside her apartment window. The noise immediately captured what's called her bottom-up attention—the broad involuntary awareness that roams the world constantly looking for danger and rewards: shiny objects, sudden movements, pungent smells. Instead of letting this distract her, however, she made a conscious choice to go into the next room and summon her top-down attention—the narrow, voluntary focus that allows us to isolate and enhance some little slice of the world while ruthlessly suppressing everything else.

This attentional self-control, which psychologists call executive function, is at the very center of our struggle with attention. It's what allows us to invest our focus wisely or poorly. Some of us, of course, have an easier time with it than others.

Gallagher admits that she's been blessed with a naturally strong executive function. "It sounds funny," she tells me, "but I've always thought of paying attention as a kind of sexy, visceral activity. Even as a kid, I enjoyed focusing. I could feel it in almost a mentally muscular way. I took a lot of pleasure in concentrating on things. I'm the sort of irritating person who can sit down to work at nine o'clock and look up at two o'clock and say, 'Oh, I thought it was around 10:30.'"

Gallagher became obsessed with the problem of attention five years ago, when she was diagnosed with advanced and aggressive breast cancer. She was devastated, naturally, but then realized, on her way out of the hospital, that even the cancer could be seen largely as a problem of focus—a terrifying, deadly, internal jackhammer. It made her realize, she says, that attention was "not just a latent ability, it was something you could marshal and use as a tool." By the time she reached her subway station, Gallagher had come up with a strategy: She would make all the big pressing cancer-related decisions as quickly as possible, then, in order to maximize whatever time she had left, consciously shift her attention to more positive, productive things.

One of the projects Gallagher worked on during her recovery (she is now cancer free) was *Rapt*, which is both a survey of recent attention research and a testimonial to the power of top-down focus. The ability to positively wield your attention comes off, in the book, as something of a panacea; Gallagher describes it as "the sine qua non of the quality of life and the key to improving virtually every aspect of your experience." It is, in other words, the Holy Grail of self-help: the key to relationships and parenting and mood disorders and weight problems. (You can apparently lose seven pounds in a year through the sheer force of paying attention to your food.)

20   "You can't be happy all the time," Gallagher tells me, "but you can pretty much focus all the time. That's about as good as it gets."

The most promising solution to our attention problem, in Gallagher's mind, is also the most ancient: meditation. Neuroscientists have become obsessed, in recent years, with Buddhists, whose attentional discipline can apparently confer all kinds of benefits, even on non-Buddhists. (Some psychologists predict that, in the same way we go out for a jog now, in the future we'll all do daily 20- to 30-minute "secular attentional workouts.") Meditation can make your attention less "sticky," able to notice images flashing by in such quick succession that regular brains would miss them. It has also been shown to elevate your mood, which can then recursively stoke your attention: Research shows that positive emotions cause your visual field to expand. The brains of Buddhist monks asked to meditate on "unconditional loving-kindness and compassion" show instant and remarkable changes: Their left prefrontal cortices (responsible for positive emotions) go into overdrive, they produce gamma waves 30 times more powerful than novice meditators, and their wave activity is coordinated in a way often seen in patients under anesthesia.

Gallagher stresses that because attention is a limited resource—one psychologist has calculated that we can attend to only 110 bits of information per second, or 173 billion bits in an average lifetime—our moment-by-moment choice of attentional targets determines, in a very real sense, the shape of our lives. *Rapt*'s epigraph comes from the psychologist and philosopher William James: "My experience is what I agree to attend to." For Gallagher, everything comes down to that one big choice: investing your attention wisely or not. The jackhammers are everywhere—iPhones, email, cancer—and Western culture's attentional crisis is mainly a widespread failure to ignore them.

"Once you understand how attention works and how you can make the most productive use of it," she says, "if you continue to just jump in the air every time your phone rings or pounce on those buttons every time you get an instant message, that's not the machine's fault. That's your fault."

Making the responsible attention choice, however, is not always easy. Here is a partial list, because a complete one would fill the entire magazine, of the things I've been distracted by in the course of writing this article: my texting wife, a very loud seagull, my mother calling from Mexico to leave voice mails in terrible Spanish, a man shouting "Your weed-whacker fell off! Your weed-whacker fell off!" at a truck full of lawn equipment, my Lost-watching wife, another man singing some kind of Spanish ballad on the sidewalk under my window, streaming video of the NBA playoffs, dissertation-length blog breakdowns of the NBA playoffs, my toenail spontaneously detaching, my ice-cream-eating wife, the subtly shifting landscapes of my three different email in-boxes, my Facebooking wife, infinite YouTube videos (a puffin attacking someone wearing a rubber boot, Paul McCartney talking about the death of John Lennon, a chimpanzee playing Pac-Man), and even more infinite, if that is possible, Wikipedia entries: puffins, MacGyver, Taylorism, the phrase "bleeding edge," the Boston Molasses Disaster. (If I were going to excuse you from reading this article for any single distraction, which I am not, it would be to read about the Boston Molasses Disaster.)

When the jackhammers fire up outside my window, in other words, I rarely ignore them—I throw the window open, watch for a while, bring the crew sandwiches on their lunch break, talk with them about the ins and outs of jackhammering, and then spend an hour or two trying to break up a little of the sidewalk myself. Some of my distractions were unavoidable. Some were necessary work-related evils that got out of hand. Others were pretty clearly inexcusable. (I consider it a victory for the integrity of pre-Web human consciousness that I was able to successfully resist clicking on the first "related video" after the chimp, the evocatively titled "Guy shits himself in a judo exhibition.") In today's attentional landscape, it's hard to draw neat borders.

I'm not ready to blame my restless attention entirely on a faulty willpower. Some of it is pure impersonal behaviorism. The Internet is basically a Skinner box engineered to tap right into our deepest mechanisms of addiction. As B. F. Skinner's army of lever-pressing rats and pigeons taught us, the most irresistible reward schedule is not, counterintuitively, the one in which we're rewarded constantly but something called "variable ratio schedule," in which the rewards arrive at random. And that randomness is practically the Internet's defining feature: It dispenses its never-ending little shots of positivity—a life-changing email here, a funny YouTube video there—in gloriously unpredictable cycles. It seems unrealistic to expect people to spend all day clicking reward bars—searching the Web, scanning the relevant blogs, checking email to see if a co-worker has updated a project—and then just leave those distractions behind, as soon as they're not strictly required, to engage in "healthy" things like books and ab crunches and undistracted deep conversations with neighbors. It would be like requiring employees to take a few hits of opium throughout the day, then being surprised when it becomes a problem. Last year, an editorial in the *American Journal of Psychiatry* raised the prospect of adding "Internet addiction" to the DSM, which would make it a disorder to be taken as seriously as schizophrenia.

A quintessentially Western solution to the attention problem—one that neatly circumvents the issue of willpower—is to simply dope our brains into focus. We've done so, over the centuries, with substances ranging from tea to tobacco to NoDoz to Benzedrine, and these days the tradition seems to be approaching some kind of zenith with the rise of neuroenhancers: drugs designed to treat ADHD (Ritalin, Adderall), Alzheimer's (Aricept), and narcolepsy (Provigil) that can produce, in healthy people, superhuman states of attention. A grad-school friend tells me that Adderall allowed him to squeeze his mind "like a muscle." Joshua Foer, writing in Slate after a weeklong experiment with Adderall, said the drug made him feel like he'd "been bitten by a radioactive spider"—he beat his unbeatable brother at Ping-Pong, solved anagrams, devoured dense books. "The part of my brain that makes me curious about whether I have new emails in my in-box apparently shut down," he wrote.

Although neuroenhancers are currently illegal to use without a prescription, they're popular among college students (on some campuses, up to 25 percent of students admitted to taking them) and—if endless anecdotes can be believed—among a wide spectrum of other professional focusers: journalists on deadlines, doctors performing high-stakes surgeries, competitors in poker tournaments, researchers suffering through the grind of grant-writing. There has been controversy in the chess world recently about drug testing at tournaments.

In December, a group of scientists published a paper in *Nature* that argued for the legalization and mainstream acceptance of neuroenhancers, suggesting that the drugs are really no different from more traditional "cognitive enhancers" such as laptops, exercise, nutrition, private tutoring, reading, and sleep. It's not quite that simple, of course. Adderall users frequently complain that the drug stifles their creativity—that it's best for doing ultrarational, structured tasks. (As Foer put it, "I had a nagging suspicion that I was thinking with blinders on.") One risk the scientists do acknowledge is the fascinating, horrifying prospect of "raising cognitive abilities beyond their species-typical upper bound." Ultimately, one might argue, neuroenhancers spring from the same source as the problem they're designed to correct: our lust for achievement in defiance of natural constraints. It's easy to imagine an endless attentional arms race in which new technologies colonize ever-bigger zones of our attention, new drugs expand the limits of that attention, and so on.

30   One of the most exciting—and confounding—solutions to the problem of attention lies right at the intersection of our willpower and our willpower-sapping technologies: the grassroots Internet movement known as "lifehacking." It began in 2003 when the British tech writer Danny O'Brien, frustrated by his own lack of focus, polled 70 of his most productive friends to see how

they managed to get so much done; he found that they'd invented all kinds of clever little tricks—some high-tech, some very low-tech—to help shepherd their attention from moment to moment: ingenious script codes for to-do lists, software hacks for managing email, rituals to avoid sinister time-wasting traps such as "yak shaving," the tendency to lose yourself in endless trivial tasks tangentially related to the one you really need to do. (O'Brien wrote a program that prompts him every ten minutes, when he's online, to ask if he's procrastinating.) Since then, lifehacking has snowballed into a massive self-help program, written and revised constantly by the online global hive mind, that seeks to help you allocate your attention efficiently. Tips range from time-management habits (the 90-second shower) to note-taking techniques (mind mapping) to software shortcuts (how to turn your Gmail into a to-do list) to delightfully retro tech solutions (turning an index card into a portable dry-erase board by covering it with packing tape).

When I call Merlin Mann, one of lifehacking's early adopters and breakout stars, he is running late, rushing back to his office, and yet he seems somehow to have attention to spare. He is by far the fastest-talking human I've ever interviewed, and it crosses my mind that this too might be a question of productivity—that maybe he's adopted a time-saving verbal lifehack from auctioneers. He talks in the snappy aphorisms of a professional speaker ("Priorities are like arms: If you have more than two of them, they're probably make-believe") and is always breaking ideas down into their atomic parts and reassessing the way they fit together: "What does it come down to?" "Here's the thing." "So why am I telling you this, and what does it have to do with lifehacks?"

Mann says he got into lifehacking at a moment of crisis, when he was "feeling really overwhelmed by the number of inputs in my life and managing it very badly." He founded one of the original lifehacking websites, 43folders.com (the name is a reference to David Allen's Getting Things Done, the legendarily complex productivity program in which Allen describes, among other things, how to build a kind of "three-dimensional calendar" out of 43 folders) and went on to invent such illustrious hacks as "in-box zero" (an email-management technique) and the "hipster PDA" (a stack of three-by-five cards filled with jotted phone numbers and to-do lists, clipped together and tucked into your back pocket). Mann now makes a living speaking to companies as a kind of productivity guru. He Twitters, podcasts, and runs more than half a dozen websites.

Despite his robust Web presence, Mann is skeptical about technology's impact on our lives. "Is it clear to you that the last fifteen years represent an enormous improvement in how everything operates?" he asks. "Picasso was somehow able to finish the *Demoiselles of Avignon* even though he didn't have an application that let him tag his to-dos. If John Lennon had a BlackBerry, do you think he would have done everything he did with the Beatles in less than ten years?"

One of the weaknesses of lifehacking as a weapon in the war against distraction, Mann admits, is that it tends to become extremely distracting. You can spend solid days reading reviews of filing techniques and organizational software. "On the web, there's a certain kind of encouragement to never ask yourself how much information you really need," he says. "But when I get to the point where I'm seeking advice twelve hours a day on how to take a nap, or what kind of notebook to buy, I'm so far off the idea of lifehacks that it's indistinguishable from where we started. There are a lot of people out there that find this a very sticky idea, and there's very little advice right now to tell them that the only thing to do is action, and everything else is horseshit. My wife reminds me sometimes: 'You have all the information you need to do *something* right now.'"

35   For Mann, many of our attention problems are symptoms of larger existential issues: motivation, happiness, neurochemistry. "I'm not a physician or a psychiatrist, but I'll tell you, I think a lot of it is some form of untreated ADHD or depression," he says. "Your mind is not getting the dopamine or the hugs that it needs to keep you focused on what you're doing. And any time your work gets a little bit too hard or a little bit too boring, you allow it to catch on to something that's more interesting to you." (Mann himself started getting treated for ADD a year ago; he says it's helped his focus quite a lot.)

Mann's advice can shade, occasionally, into Buddhist territory. "There's no shell script, there's no fancy pen, there's no notebook or nap or Firefox extension or hack that's gonna help you figure out why the fuck you're here," he tells me. "That's on you. This makes me sound like one of those people who swindled the Beatles, but if you are having attention problems, the best way to deal with it is by admitting it and then saying, 'From now on, I'm gonna be in the moment and more cognizant.' I said not long ago, I think on Twitter—God, I quote myself a lot, what an asshole—that really all self-help is Buddhism with a service mark."

"Where you allow your attention to go ultimately says more about you as a human being than anything that you put in your mission statement," he continues. "It's an indisputable receipt for your existence. And if you allow that to be squandered by other people who are as bored as you are, it's gonna say a lot about who you are as a person."

III. Embracing the Poverty of Attention

Sometimes I wonder if the time I'm wasting is actually being wasted. Isn't blowing a couple of hours on the Internet, in the end, just another way of following your attention? My life would be immeasurably poorer if I hadn't stumbled a few weeks ago across the Boston Molasses Disaster. (Okay, seriously, forget it: I hereby release you to go look up the Boston Molasses Disaster. A giant wave of molasses destroyed an entire Boston neighborhood 90 years ago, swallowing horses and throwing an elevated train off its track. It took months to scrub all the molasses out of the cobblestones! The harbor was brown until summer! The world is a stranger place than we will ever know.)

The prophets of total attentional meltdown sometimes invoke, as an example of the great culture we're going to lose as we succumb to e-thinking, the canonical French juggernaut Marcel Proust. And indeed, at seven volumes, several thousand pages, and 1.5 million words, À la Recherche du Temps Perdu is in many ways the anti-Twitter. (It would take, by the way, exactly 68,636 tweets to reproduce.) It's important to remember, however, that the most famous moment in all of Proust, the moment that launches the entire monumental project, is a moment of pure distraction: when the narrator, Marcel, eats a spoonful of tea-soaked madeleine and finds himself instantly transported back to the world of his childhood. Proust makes it clear that conscious focus could never have yielded such profound magic: Marcel has to abandon the constraints of what he calls "voluntary memory"—the kind of narrow, purpose-driven attention that Adderall, say, might have allowed him to harness—in order to get to the deeper truths available only by distraction. That famous cookie is a kind of hyperlink: a little blip that launches an associative cascade of a million other subjects. This sort of free-associative wandering is essential to the creative process; one moment of judicious unmindfulness can inspire thousands of hours of mindfulness.

My favorite focusing exercise comes from William James: Draw a dot on 40 a piece of paper, then pay attention to it for as long as you can. (Sitting in my office one afternoon, with my monkey mind swinging busily across the lush rain forest of online distractions, I tried this with the closest dot in the vicinity: the bright-red mouse-nipple at the center of my laptop's keyboard. I managed to stare at it for 30 minutes, with mixed results.) James argued that the human mind can't actually focus on the dot, or any unchanging object, for more than a few seconds at a time: It's too hungry for variety, surprise, the adventure of the unknown. It has to refresh its attention by continually finding new aspects of the dot to focus on: subtleties of its shape, its relationship to the edges of the paper, metaphorical associations (a fly, an eye, a hole). The exercise becomes a question less of pure unwavering focus than of your ability to organize distractions around a central point. The dot, in other words, becomes only the hub of your total dot-related distraction.

This is what the web-threatened punditry often fails to recognize: Focus is a paradox—it has distraction built into it. The two are symbiotic; they're the systole and diastole of consciousness. Attention comes from the Latin "to stretch out" or "reach toward," distraction from "to pull apart." We need both. In their extreme forms, focus and attention may even circle back around and bleed into one other. Meyer says there's a subset of Buddhists who believe that the most advanced monks become essentially "world-class multitaskers"—that all those years of meditation might actually speed up their mental processes enough to handle the kind of information overload the rest of us find crippling.

The truly wise mind will harness, rather than abandon, the power of distraction. Unwavering focus—the inability to be distracted—can actually be just as problematic as ADHD. Trouble with "attentional shift" is a feature common to a handful of mental illnesses, including schizophrenia and OCD. It's been hypothesized that ADHD might even be an advantage in certain change-rich environments. Researchers have discovered, for instance, that a brain receptor associated with ADHD is unusually common among certain nomads in Kenya, and that members who have the receptor are the best nourished in the group. It's possible that we're all evolving toward a new techno-cognitive nomadism, a rapidly shifting environment in which restlessness will be an advantage again. The deep focusers might even be hampered by having too much attention: Attention Surfeit Hypoactivity Disorder.

I keep returning to the parable of Einstein and Lennon—the great historical geniuses hypothetically ruined by modern distraction. What made both men's achievements so groundbreaking, though, was that they did something modern technology is getting increasingly better at allowing us to do: They very powerfully linked and synthesized things that had previously been unlinked—Newtonian gravity and particle physics, rock and blues and folk and doo-wop and bubblegum pop and psychedelia. If Einstein and Lennon were growing up today, their natural genius might be so pumped up on the possibilities of the new technology they'd be doing even more dazzling things. Surely Lennon would find a way to manipulate his BlackBerry to his own ends, just like he did with all the new technology of the sixties—he'd harvest spam and text messages and Web snippets and build them into a new kind of absurd poetry. The Beatles would make the best viral videos of all time, simultaneously addictive and artful, disposable and forever. All of those canonical songs, let's remember, were created entirely within a newfangled mass genre that was widely considered to be an assault on civilization and the sanctity of deep human thought. Standards change. They change because of great creations in formerly suspect media.

Which brings me, finally, to the next generation of attenders, the so-called "net-gen" or "digital natives," kids who've grown up with the Internet and other time-slicing technologies. There's been lots of hand-wringing about all the skills they might lack, mainly the ability to concentrate on a complex task from beginning to end, but surely they can already do things their elders can't—like conduct 34 conversations simultaneously across six different media, or pay attention to switching between attentional targets in a way that's been considered impossible. More than any other organ, the brain is designed to change based on experience, a feature called neuroplasticity. London taxi drivers, for instance, have enlarged hippocampi (the brain region for memory and spatial processing)—a neural reward for paying attention to the tangle of the city's streets. As we become more skilled at the 21st-century task Meyer calls "flitting," the wiring of the brain will inevitably change to deal more efficiently with more information. The neuroscientist Gary Small speculates that the human brain might be changing faster today than it has since the prehistoric discovery of tools. Research suggests we're already picking up new skills: better peripheral vision, the ability to sift information rapidly. We recently elected the first-ever BlackBerry president, able to flit between sixteen national crises while focusing at a world-class level. Kids growing up now might have an associative genius we don't—a sense of the way ten projects all dovetail into something totally new. They might be able to engage in seeming contradictions: mindful web-surfing, mindful Twittering. Maybe, in flights of irresponsible responsibility, they'll even manage to attain the paradoxical, Zen-like state of focused distraction.

Things to Do with the Reading

1. What rhetorical choices has Anderson made in his essay? How does the ethos (the kind of persona a writer creates) of the piece reveal Anderson's attitude toward both his subject and his audience(s)? Anchor your answer to a few sample passages in the essay that you think typify these rhetorical choices. Anderson is known, by the way, for his "imitative reviews," which copy the style of their subjects.

2. Insofar as the essay has a single governing claim—a thesis—what is it? What are the primary claims of Anderson's essay (list these or mark them in the margins)? By what logic does one claim evolve into the next? How, for example, does the piece function as a "defense" of distraction suggested by its title?

3. The Boston Molasses Disaster is mentioned several times in the essay. How does Anderson put it to use rhetorically? What, that is, are the various functions this example serves in helping Anderson to achieve his ends?

4. Links: "In Defense of Distraction" is one of a number of recent pieces worrying aloud about the effects of an increasingly electronic environment, especially given our increasing awareness of neuroplasticity—of the effects such technology might have on the way our brains function. Use Anderson's essay as a lens for reconsidering the discussions of technology in the other readings in this chapter. Alternatively, look for points of contact with an essay by Nicholas Carr in The Atlantic (2008), "Is Google Making Us Stupid?: What the Internet Is Doing to Our Brains" [http://www.theatlantic.com/magazine/archive/2008/07/is-google-making-us-stupid/6868/], which grew into his book The Shallows (2010).

FOR FURTHER RESEARCH: MANNERS, COMMUNICATION, AND TECHNOLOGY

By Kelly Cannon, Reference Librarian

The readings and activities below invite you to further explore the theme of Manners, Communication, and Technology. URLs are provided for those readings that you can access freely online. For proprietary resources, ask your librarian about print or online access.

Open access

Blumberg, Andrew J. and Peter Eckersley. "On Locational Privacy, and How to Avoid Losing it Forever." Electronic Frontier Foundation. August 2009. 14 May 2014. http://www.eff.org/wp/locational-privacy
Your comings and goings are being monitored whether you know it or not.

> Explore: What is EFF? What do you find most interesting or troubling with the foundation's stance on civil liberties and technology? What makes the foundation trustworthy or not?

Cowen, Tyler. "Three Tweets for the Web." *Wilson Quarterly* (2009): 54–58. 19 May 2014. http://www.wilsonquarterly.com/article.cfm?aid=1481
Multitasking engendered by the Internet is not a distraction at all, but rather a series of "long strands of continued involvement," the result of voluntary choices a person has made, creating a highly "personalized mix of stimuli."

> Explore: Cowen offers direct counterpoint to other articles referenced in this chapter of the reader. Note the rhetorical moves Cowen makes, such as comparing Internet multitasking to an intimate marriage. Would you consider this to be "evidence"? To what extent are you persuaded?

Emily Post Institute Etipedia. Emily Post Institute, 2013. 11 May 2014. http://www.emilypost.com/etipedia
Your online etiquette encyclopedia.

> Explore: Navigate the section titled "Communication and Technology" or search the site for the keyword: "cell phones." How does your online behavior rate with Ms. Post?

Gitlin, Todd. "Uses of Half True Alarms." *New Republic*, 7 June 2010. 11 May 2014. http://www.newrepublic.com/book/review/the-uses-half-true-alarms
Gitlin gives mixed reviews to the endless technological interruptions typifying the Google era.

> Explore: Consider your own experience. To what extent do you have difficulty paying attention in a long face-to-face discussion? Can you turn off

your cell phone easily or set it aside when needed? Viewed another way, do you find you can attend to many conversations at once, all adequately?

Hampton, Keith N., et al. "Social Isolation and New Technology." *Pew Internet and American Life Project*. Pew Research Center, November 2009. 14 May 2014. http://www.pewinternet.org/~/media//Files/Reports/2009/PIP_Tech_and _Social_Isolation.pdf
This respected think tank on Internet use found that "when we examine people's full personal network— their strong ties and weak ties—Internet use in general, and use of social networking services such as Facebook in particular, are associated with having a more diverse social network.... This flies against the notion that technology pulls people away from social engagement."

> Explore: Compare the findings of this report with the conclusions drawn by Christine Rosen and Paul Goldberger in their essays, printed above, and another Christine Rosen essay, with reference following, on virtual friendship. What do you find most convincing about the Hampton report? What is not as strong or is missing as evidence altogether?

"LISTEN: 5 Ideas That May Change How You Think About Privacy." *Huffington Post*. 2 April 2014. 14 May 2014. http://www.huffingtonpost.com/tedtalks /ted-npr-huffpost-the-end-of-privacy_b_4696444.html
Five different perspectives from influential thinkers of our day on the subject of privacy.

> Explore: Consider these short talks in light of Jonathan Franzen's and Jeffrey Rosen's essays on technology's effects on the public vs. private spheres. Is privacy all that important? Why or why not? To what extent should we be more concerned about the public good and less about individual privacy?

Madden, Mary, et al. "Digital Footprints: Online Identity Management and Search in the Age of Transparency." *Pew Internet and American Life Project*. Pew Research Center, 16 December 2007. 14 May 2014. http://www.pewinternet .org/~/media//Files/Reports/2007/PIP_Digital_Footprints.pdf.pdf
The more we contribute information voluntarily to the public or semi-public corners of the Web, the more we are not only findable, but also knowable.

> Explore: Perform a Google Search on your name, adding details like city or high school to distinguish you from others with the same name. What digital footprints have you left for others to find?

Nextdoor. 2014. 13 May 2014. https://nextdoor.com/
Free app that helps you meet your neighbors.

> Explore: Goldberger makes the claim that we are disconnected from our locale because of technology. Here is technology that purports to draw

us closer to our physical neighbors. Test the application for yourself. How well does it work? How does this application address Goldberger's concern?

Rosen, Christine. "Virtual Friendship and the New Narcissism." *The New Atlantis: A Journal of Technology and Society* (Summer 2007). 19 May 2014. http://www.thenewatlantis.com/publications/virtual-friendship-and-the-new-narcissism

Rosen argues that virtual connections may not be all they are cracked up to be; something gets lost in the translation from face-to-face to remote.

> Explore: Compare this Rosen essay with the essays printed in the reader by Christine Rosen and by Paul Goldberger. What stylistic features do the two Christine Rosen essays share? What kind of evidence and rhetoric does Rosen bring to bear in this essay on narcissism and technology? What's the most important similarity between the two essays? Given that similarity, what's the biggest difference, and so what?

Shea, Virginia. *Netiquette*. Albion, 2004. 11 May 2014. http://www.albion.com/netiquette/book/index.html

An online classic, this textbook for proper online behavior espouses ten core rules.

> Explore: Compare with Emily Post's *Etipedia*, mentioned above. What does Shea name as the first of her ten rules? Why?

Trott, Mena. *Meet the Founder of the Blog Revolution*. TED, February 2006. 14 May 2014. http://www.ted.com/talks/mena_trott_tours_her_blog_world

Mena Trott, one of the first and most influential bloggers, reminisces about the early days.

> Explore: Trott first blogged in 2001. To what extent does her vision of blogging coordinate with Geoffrey Nunberg's assessment of blogging (2004) as communication with a style distinct from earlier forms of journalism? Consider particularly the public vs. private spheres.

Proprietary

Hosking, Simon G., Kristie L. Young, and Michael A. Regan. "The Effects of Text Messaging on Young Drivers." *Human Factors: The Journal of the Human Factors and Ergonomics Society* 51.4 (2009): 582–592.

This research article confirms earlier studies about the effects of text messaging on driving abilities and advances some new findings.

> Explore: Sam Anderson references scientific research articles much like this one—though not this one precisely—throughout his essay printed above. What advantages does an article like Anderson's have over this

research article in the ways it persuades a lay audience of claims concerning multitasking? What audience is the Hosking article written for? How do these two types of articles—primary research and popular—work symbiotically to reach and convince a broad audience—even if in the end they reach different conclusions? More importantly, how do you explain that difference in conclusions?

Humphreys, Lee. "Social Topography in a Wireless Era: the Negotiation of Public and Private Space." *Journal of Technical Writing and Communication* **35.4 (2005): 367–84.**
In this study, the author explores how callers and bystanders negotiate privacy.

> Explore: This study typifies "empirical research." What is empirical about it? In what section can the results of the research be found? What other elements make this article typical of research performed in the social sciences?

Pauwels, Luc. "A Private Visual Practice Going Public? Social Functions and Sociological Research Opportunities of Web-Based Family Photography." *Visual Studies* **23.1 (2008): 34–49.**
The sharing of family photos on the Internet showcases the blending of public and private spheres engendered by Web 2.0 technology.

> Explore: Look closely at the family websites depicted in this article. Are there hints that these were meant for a wider audience than just family members? What would be the motive of placing these sometimes awkward pictures on the web for all to see? What does the presentational form of this article suggest about the nature of privacy today? To what extent do the conclusions of Pauwels' research corroborate Jeffrey Rosen's essay above on "America's culture of self-revelation"?

CHAPTER 13

Places and Spaces: Cities and Suburbs

The readings in this section call to mind a provocative definition of nostalgia offered by a character in Don DeLillo's 1985 novel *White Noise*: "Nostalgia is a product of dissatisfaction and rage; a settling of grievances between the present and the past" (258). All of the essays in this unit cast a skeptical eye on the future of urban and suburban life in America, and, explicitly or implicitly, they look back with a certain degree of nostalgia to a lost past when life appeared more genuinely democratic—and livable.

The writers all converse in one way or another with what is known as the New Urbanism, a movement seeking to rethink the ways our cities have declined and our suburbs have expanded in the past half-century. The interest in public versus private life treated in Manners, Communication, and Technology returns here in the concern with impersonal living spaces—barren suburbs fueled by the car culture and fortressed cities fraught with risk.

ABOUT THE READINGS IN THIS UNIT

"The United States is the wealthiest nation in the history of the world," begins the first essay in this unit, by James Howard Kunstler, "yet its inhabitants are strikingly unhappy." Kunstler's is an ethical call to attention, a plea for us to become citizens rather than simply consumers by rebuilding the material culture that surrounds us in the public realm, starting at the level of the neighborhood. Jack Gambino's discussion of the landscapes of two contemporary photographers provides graphic illustration of Kunstler's vision. Although the two photographers' work differs widely in focus and tone, it shares a fascination with "creative destruction" that Gambino sees as distinctively modern, and it functions, in both cases, as a kind of visual cultural memory against a past too easily forgotten.

Next, Adam Gopnik offers a wry history of the redevelopment of Times Square in New York City, providing a lens for viewing redevelopment anywhere. Gopnik's piece provides insight into the actual jostlings for power that accompany redevelopment, in this case, wherein "a question of virtue had to be disguised as a necessity of commerce." We move next from New York City to the Long Island suburbs, a chapter from Rosalyn Baxandall and Elizabeth Ewen's history of how the suburbs happened. Focusing on Robert Moses, their work casts a revealing eye on the vexed politics of urban planning and the way it reinscribes longstanding class privileges as the nation moves from the city to the suburbs.

The chapter concludes with two classic essays on civic space that might be fruitfully compared. A selection from Jane Jacobs' pioneering study of city life analyzes safe versus unsafe neighborhoods. One conclusion she draws about her late 1950s' New York City neighborhood is that "thinning out a city does not insure safety from crime and fear of crime." This line rings ominously against Mike Davis's chilling account of the spatial imperatives militating against the urban poor and the homeless in 1990s' Los Angeles.

James Howard Kunstler

The Public Realm and the Common Good

The author and journalist James Howard Kunstler is an eloquent advocate of what is known as the "New Urbanism"—an urban design movement that arose in the late 1980s. The New Urbanism supports walkable neighborhoods, mixed use and mixed income housing, and a restored sense of community feeling, and it vigorously opposes urban sprawl. The following piece is excerpted from his book *Home from Nowhere: Remaking Our Everyday World for the Twenty-first Century* (1996). In it, Kunstler argues that the development of American towns and cities since World War II has been marked by an absence of respect for what he terms the "public realm," defined as "the physical manifestation of the common good."

The United States is the wealthiest nation in the history of the world, yet its 1 inhabitants are strikingly unhappy. Unhappiness is manifest at every level of the national scene. From big city to the remotest rural trailer court, our civic life is tattered and frayed. Unspeakable crimes occur in the most ordinary places. Government can't fulfill its most basic role in guaranteeing the public safety. Our schools, in many cases, barely function. The consensus of what constitutes decent behavior fractured with the social revolutions of the 1960s and has not been restored. Anything goes.

Community, as it once existed in the form of places worth caring about, supported by local economies, has been extirpated by an insidious corporate colonialism that doesn't care about the places from which it extracts its profits or the people subject to its operations.

The Public Realm and the Common Good

American cities are dismal. The majority of American small towns have become dismal. Of course, those two types of places represent America as it developed before World War Two, and their current state must be understood as one of abandonment and dereliction. The newer suburban subdivisions are dismal, too, in their own unique way, as are the commercial highway strips, the malls, the office parks, and the rest of the autocentric equipment of the human habitat. Their architectural shortcomings aside, these places are dismal because the public realm that binds them together is degraded, incoherent, ugly and meaningless. In case the term *public realm* seems vague or mystifying, I shall attempt to define it with some precision.

The public realm is the connective tissue of our everyday world. It is made of those pieces of terrain left between the private holdings. It exists

Reprinted with the permission of Simon & Schuster Publishing Group, from HOME FROM NOWHERE: REMAKING OUR EVERYDAY WORLD FOR THE TWENTY-FIRST CENTURY by James Howard Kunstler. Copyright © 1996 by James Howard Kunstler. All rights reserved.

in the form of streets, highways, town squares, parks, and even parking lots. It includes rural or wilderness landscape: stretches of the seacoast, national forests, most lakes and rivers, and even the sky (though "air rights" are sometimes bought and sold in the cities). The public realm exists mainly outdoors because most buildings belong to private individuals or corporations. Exceptions to this are public institutions such as libraries, museums, and town halls, which are closed some hours of the day, and airports and train stations, which may be open around the clock. Some places, while technically private, function as quasi-public realm—for instance, college campuses, ballparks, restaurants, theaters, nightclubs, and, yes, shopping malls, at least the corridors between the private shops. Their owners retain the right to regulate behavior within, particularly the terms of access, and so the distinction must be made that they are only nominally public. The true public realm then, for the sake of this argument, is that portion of our everyday world which belongs to everybody and to which everybody ought to have access most of the time. The public realm is therefore a set of real places possessing physical form.

5   The public realm in America became so atrocious in the postwar decades that the Disney Corporation was able to create an artificial substitute for it and successfully sell it as a commodity. That's what Disney World is really about. In France, where the public realm possesses a pretty high standard of design quality and is carefully maintained as well, there is much less need for artificial substitutes, so few people feel compelled to go to EuroDisney (it lost over $1 billion in its first two years of operation). The design quality of everything at EuroDisney is about five notches *beneath* that of the most mediocre French street corner. The quality of the park benches and street lamps in EuroDisney is recognizably inferior to the quality of the park benches and street lamps in ordinary French towns. Even the flower beds lack finesse. They look like berms designed for corporate parking lots. There are more interesting things to eat along nine linear yards of the Rue Buci on the Left Bank than in all the magic kingdoms of EuroDisney.

The design quality of Disney World in Orlando, on the other hand, is about 1.5 notches better than the average American suburban shopping mall or housing subdivision—so Americans love it. Forget about how cheap-looking the benches and lampposts might be —we don't even have sidewalks in most of suburbia (and besides, nobody walks there anyway)—so *any* benches and lampposts seem swell. Americans love Disney World, above all, because it is uncontaminated by cars, except for a few antique vehicles kept around as stage props. By and large, they do not know that this is the reason they love Disney World. Americans are amazingly unconscious of how destructive the automobile has been to their everyday world.

Main Street USA is America's obsolete model for development—we stopped assembling towns this way after 1945. The pattern of Main Street is pretty simple: mixed use, mixed income, apartments and offices over the stores, moderate density, scaled to pedestrians, vehicles permitted but not allowed to dominate, buildings detailed with care, all built to last (though we still trashed it). Altogether it was a pretty good development pattern. It produced places that people loved deeply. That is the reason Main Street persists in our cultural memory. Many people still alive remember the years before World War Two and what it felt like to live in integral towns modeled on this pattern. Physical remnants of the pattern still stand in parts of the country for people to see, though the majority of Americans have moved into the new model habitat called suburban sprawl.

For all its apparent success, Suburban Sprawl sorely lacks many things that make life worth living, particularly civic amenities, which Main Street offered in spades. Deep down, many Americans are dissatisfied with suburbia—though they have trouble understanding what's missing—which explains their nostalgia for the earlier model. Their dissatisfaction is literally a *dis-ease*. They feel vaguely and generally unwell where they are. Nostalgia in its original sense means homesickness. Americans essay to cure their homesickness with costly visits to Disney World. The crude, ineffective palliatives they get there in the form of brass bands and choo-choo train rides leave them more homesick and more baffled as to the nature of their disease than when they arrived—like selling chocolate bars to someone suffering from scurvy—and pathetically, of course, they must return afterward to the very places that induce the disease of homesickness.

Historically Americans have a low regard for the public realm, and this is very unfortunate because the public realm is the physical manifestation of the common good. When you degrade the public realm, as we have, you degrade the common good.

Civic life is what goes on in the public realm. Civic life refers to our relations with our fellow human beings—in short, our roles as citizens. Sometime in the past forty years we ceased to speak of ourselves as citizens and labeled ourselves consumers. That's what we are today in the language of the evening news—*consumers*—in the language of the Sunday panel discussion shows—*consumers*—in the blizzard of statistics that blows out of the U.S. Department of Commerce every month. Consumers, unlike citizens, have no responsibilities, obligations, or duties to anything larger than their own needs and desires, certainly not to anything like the common good. How can this be construed as anything other than an infantile state of existence? In degrading the language of our public discussion this way—labeling ourselves consumers—have we not degraded our sense of who we are? And is it any wonder that we cannot solve any of our social problems, which are problems of the public realm and the common good?

Charm, Sanity, and Grace

During America's financially richest period, we put up almost nothing but the cheapest possible buildings, particularly civic buildings. Look at any richly embellished 1904 firehouse or post office and look at its dreary concrete box counterpart today. Compare the home of a small-town bank president dating from the 1890s, with its masonry walls and complex roof articulation, to the flimsy house of a 1990s business leader, made of two-by-fours, sheetrock, and fake fanlight windows. When we were a far less wealthy nation, we built things with the expectation that they would endure. To throw away money (painfully expended) on something guaranteed to fall apart in thirty years would have seemed immoral, if not insane, in our great-grandfathers' day.

The buildings they constructed paid homage to history in their design—including elegant solutions to age-old problems posed by the cycles of light and weather—and they paid respect to the future through the expectation that they would endure through the lifetimes of the people who built them. They there-fore evinced a sense of chronological connectivity—one of the fundamental patterns of the universe—an understanding that time is a defining dimension of existence, particularly the existence of living things, such as human beings, who miraculously pass into life and then tragically pass out of it, perhaps forever—we do not know—our self-awareness of this fate making it tragic.

Chronological connectivity lends meaning and dignity to our little lives. It charges the present with a more vividly conscious validation of our own aliveness. It puts us in touch with the ages and the eternities, suggesting that we are part of a larger and more significant organism. It even suggests that the larger organism we are part of *cares* about us, and that, in turn, we should respect ourselves, our fellow creatures, and all those who will follow us in time, as those preceding us respected us who followed them. In short, chron-ological connectivity puts us in touch with the holy. It is at once humbling and exhilarating. I say this as someone who has never followed any formal religious practice. Connection with the past and the future is a pathway that literally charms us in the direction of sanity and grace.

The antithesis to this can be seen in the way we have built since 1945. We reject the past and the future, and it shows in our graceless constructions. Our houses, commercial, and civic buildings are constructed with the fully conscious certainty that they will disintegrate in a few decades. There is even a name for this condition: the *design life*. Strip malls and elementary schools have short design lives. They are not expected to endure through the span of a human life. In fact, they fall apart in under fifty years. Since there is not expectation that these things will last, nor that they will speak to any era but their own, we seem to believe that there is no point in putting any money or effort into their embellishment—except for the sort of cartoon decoration that serves to advertise whatever product is sold on the premises. Nor do we care about age-old solutions to the problems of weather and light, because we have technical artifacts to mitigate these problems, namely electricity and central heating. In especially bad buildings, like the average WalMart, there may be no windows. Yet this process of disconnection from the past and future, and from the organic patterns of weather and light, all done for the sake of expedience, ends up diminishing us spiritually, impoverishing us socially, and degrading the aggregate set of cultural patterns that we call civilization. We register these discontinuities as *ugliness,* or the absence of beauty.

Our streets used to be charming and beautiful. The public realm of the street was understood to function as an outdoor room. Like any room, it required walls to define the essential *void* of the room itself. Where I live, Saratoga Springs, New York, there once existed a magnificent building called the Grand Union Hotel. It was enormous—the largest hotel in the world in the late nineteenth century—occupying a six-acre site in the heart of town. The hotel consisted of a set of rather narrow buildings which lined the outside of an unusually large superblock. Inside the block was a semipublic parklike courtyard. Any reasonably attired person could walk in off the street, pass through the hotel lobby, and enjoy the interior park. The sides of the hotel that faced the street incorporated a gigantic veranda twenty feet deep, with a roof three stories high supported by columns. This facade functioned as a marvelous street-wall. Its size—a central cupola reached seven stories— was appropriate to the scale of the town's main street, called Broadway. The facade, or street-wall, was active and permeable. The veranda that lined it was filled with people sitting perhaps eight feet above the sidewalk grade, talking to each other while they watched the pageant life of the street. These veranda sitters were protected from the weather by the roof, and protected from the sun by elm trees along the sidewalk. The orderly rows of elm trees performed an additional architectural function. Their trunks were straight and round, like columns, reiterating and reinforcing the pattern of the hotel facade, while the crowns formed a vaulted canopy over the sidewalk, pleasantly filtering the sunlight for pedestrians as well as the hotel patrons. Notice that the integral soundness of all these patterns worked to enhance the lives of everybody in town, a common laborer on his way home as well as a railroad millionaire rocking on the hotel veranda. In doing so, they supported civic life as a general proposition. They nourished our civilization.

While nothing lasts forever, it was tragic that this magnificent building was destroyed less than a hundred years after it was built. In 1953 America stood at the brink of the greatest building spree in history, and the very qualities that made the Grand Union Hotel so wonderful were antithetical to all the new stuff that America was about to build. The town demolished it with a kind of mad glee. What replaced the hotel was a strip mall anchored by, of all things, a *Grand Union* supermarket. This Grand Union shopping plaza was prototypical of its time. Tens of thousands of strip malls like it have been built all over America since then. It is in absolutely all its details a perfect piece of junk. It is the anti-place.

What had been the heart and soul of the town was now converted into a kind of mini-Outer Mongolia. The strip mall buildings were set back from

Broadway one hundred and fifty feet, the setback now comprising a parking lot. The street and the buildings commenced a non-relationship. Since the new buildings were one story high, their scale bore no relation to the scale of the town's most important street. They failed to create a street-wall. The perception of the street functioning as an outdoor room was lost. The space between the buildings and the street now had one function: automobile storage. The street, and consequently, the public realm in general, was degraded by the design of the new strip mall. As the street's importance as a public space declined, people ceased to care what happened in it. If it became jammed with cars, so much the better, because individual cars were understood not merely as "personal transportation" but as *personal home delivery vehicles,* enabling people to physically haul home enormous volumes of merchandise very efficiently, at no cost to the merchandizer—a great boon for business. That is why the citizens of Saratoga in 1953 were willing to sacrifice the town's most magnificent building. It was okay to simply throw away the past. The owners of the supermarket chain that anchored the strip mall didn't live in town. They didn't care what effect their style of doing business would have on the town. They certainly didn't care about the town's past, and their interest in the town's future was limited only to technicalities of selling dog food and soap flakes.

What has happened to the interrelation of healthy, living patterns of human ecology in the town where I live has happened all over the country. Almost everywhere, the larger patterns are in such a sorry state that the details seem almost irrelevant. When my town invested tens of thousands of dollars in Victorian-style street lamps in an effort to create instant charm, the gesture seemed pathetic, because there was no awareness of the larger design failures. It is hard to overstate how ridiculous these lampposts look in the context of our desolate streets and the cheap, inappropriate new buildings amid their parking lots in what remains of our downtown. The lamppost scheme was like putting Band-Aids on someone who had tripped and fallen on his chainsaw.

Burn Your Zoning Laws

It is literally against the law almost everywhere in the United States to build the kind of places that Americans themselves consider authentic and traditional. It's against the law to build places that human beings can feel good in, or afford to live in. It's against the law to build places that are worth caring about.

20   Is Main Street your idea of a nice business district? Sorry, your zoning laws won't let you build it, or even extend it where it already exists. Is Elm Street your idea of a nice place to live—you know, the houses with the front porches on a tree-lined street? Sorry, that's against the law, too. All you can build where I live, in upstate New York, is another version of Los Angeles. The zoning laws say so.

This is not a gag. Our zoning laws comprise the basic manual of instruction for how we create the stuff of our communities. Most of these laws have only been in place since World War Two. For the previous 300-odd years of American history we didn't have zoning laws. We had a popular *consensus* about the right way to assemble a town, or a city. Our best Main Streets and Elm Streets were not created by municipal ordinances, but by cultural agreement. Everybody agreed that buildings on Main Street ought to be more than one story tall, that corner groceries were good to have in residential neighborhoods, that streets ought to intersect with other streets to facilitate movements, that sidewalks were necessary, and that orderly rows of trees planted along them made the sidewalks much more pleasant, that rooftops should be pitched to shed rain and snow, that doors should be conspicuous so you could easily find the entrance to a building, that windows should be vertical to dignify a house. Everybody agreed that communities needed different kinds of housing to meet the needs of different families and individuals, and the market was allowed to supply it. Our great-grandfathers didn't have to argue endlessly over these matters of civic design. Nor did they have to reinvent civic design every fifty years because everybody forgot what they agreed about.

Zoning began as a political response to the obnoxious effect of industry on human settlements. Originally, its intent was to keep factories away from houses, to create separate zones for industry to carry on its noisy and dirty activities. Over the twentieth century, the imposition of motor vehicles brought the obnoxious noise and danger of industry to virtually every doorstep, and so zoning became preoccupied with problems posed by the movement and storage of cars. The problem became so pervasive that zoning completely replaced civic art as the ordering principle of human settlement, especially in the years since 1945.

The place that results from zoning is suburban sprawl. It must be understood as the product of a particular set of institutions. Its chief characteristics are the strict separation of human activities (or *uses*), mandatory driving to get from one use to the other, and huge supplies of free parking. After all, it's called *zoning* because the basic idea is that every activity demands a separate zone of its own. You can't allow people to live around shopping. That would be harmful and indecent. Better not even allow them within walking distance of it. They'll need their cars to haul all that stuff home, anyway—in case you haven't noticed, most supermarkets don't deliver these days. While you're at it, let's separate the homes, too, by income gradients. Don't let the $75,000-a-year families live near the $200,000-a-year families—they'll bring down your *property values*—and, for Godsake don't let some $25,000-a-year recent college graduate live near any of them, or a $19,000-a-year widowed grandmother on Social Security. There goes the neighborhood! Now, put all the workplaces in a separate office "park" or industrial "park," and make sure nobody can walk to them either. As for nice public squares, parks, and the like—forget it, we can't afford them because we spent all our public funds paving the four-lane highways and collector roads and the parking lots, and laying sewer and water lines out to the housing subdivisions, and hiring traffic cops to regulate the movement of people in their cars going back and forth to these segregated areas.

It soon becomes obvious that the model of the human habitat dictated by zoning is a formless, soulless, centerless, demoralizing mess. It bankrupts families and townships. It causes mental illness. It disables whole classes of decent, normal citizens. It ruins the air we breathe. It corrupts and deadens our spirits.

25   In the absence of a new widespread consensus about how to build a better everyday environment, we'll have to replace the old set of rules with an explicit new set of rules. Or, to put it a slightly different way, replace zoning laws with principles of civic art.

A Short Course in the General Principles of Civic Art

The pattern under discussion here has been called variously *neo-traditional planning, traditional neighborhood development* (or the *TND*), *low-density urbanism, Transit-Oriented Development* (or the *TOD*), *the New Urbanism,* or just plain civic art. Its principles produce a setting that resembles the American town prior to World War Two.[1]

The Neighborhood

The basic unit of planning is the neighborhood. A neighborhood standing alone can be a village or a town. A cluster of neighborhoods becomes a bigger town. Clusters of a great many neighborhoods become a city. The population of a neighborhood can vary, depending on local conditions.

The neighborhood is limited in physical size, with a well-defined edge and a focused center. Human scale is the standard for proportion in buildings and their accessories. Automobiles and other wheeled vehicles are permitted, but do not take precedence over human needs, including aesthetic needs. The neighborhood contains a public transit stop.

The size of a neighborhood is defined as a five-minute walking distance (or a quarter-mile) from the edge to the center, thus a ten-minute walk edge to edge, or one-half a square mile. Chores that may require many separate, tedious car trips in sprawl can be accomplished in a single outing on foot (shop owners may offer home delivery of bulky merchandise). Walking allows a person to visit many different types of shops—thereby promoting small-scale, locally owned businesses, which, in turn, promote manifold civic benefits from the support of local institutions to the physical caretaking of the street. Walking down the street permits casual socializing. Pedestrians make streets safer by their mere presence in numbers. Finally, walking down the street is spiritually elevating. When neighborhoods are used by pedestrians, a much finer detailing inevitably occurs. Building facades become more richly ornamented and interesting. Little gardens and window boxes appear. Shop windows create a continuity of public spectacle, as do outdoor cafes, both for walkers and the sitters. There is much to engage the eye and heart. In such a setting, we feel more completely human. This is not trivial.

The boundaries between neighborhoods are formed by corridors, which 30 both connect and define them. Corridors can incorporate natural features like streams or canyons. They can take the form of parks, natural preserves, travel corridors, railroad lines, or some integral combination of all these things. In towns and cities, a neighborhood or parts of neighborhoods can comprise a district. Districts are composed of streets or ensembles of streets where special activities get preferential treatment. The French Quarter of New Orleans is an example of a district. It is a whole neighborhood dedicated to entertainment in which housing, shops, and offices are also integral. A corridor can also be a district—for instance, a major shopping avenue between adjoining neighborhoods.

The neighborhood is emphatically mixed-use and provides housing for people with different incomes. Commerce is integrated with residential, business, and even industrial use, though not necessarily on the same street in a given neighborhood. Apartments are permitted over stores. There is a mixture of housing types.

The Street

The street is understood to be the preeminent form of public space and buildings that define it are expected to honor and embellish it. In the absence of a consensus about the appropriate decoration of buildings, an architectural code may be devised to establish some fundamental unities of massing, fenestration, materials, and roof pitch, within which many variations may function harmoniously. Buildings also define parks and squares, which are distributed throughout the neighborhood and appropriately designated for recreation, repose, periodic commercial uses (e.g., farmers' markets), or special events such as political meetings, concerts, theatricals, exhibitions, and fairs.

The street pattern is conceived as a network in order to create the greatest number of alternative routes from one part of the neighborhood to another. This has the beneficial effect of relieving vehicular congestion. This network can be a grid. Networks based on a grid must be modified by parks, squares, diagonals, T-intersections, roundabouts, and other devices that relieve the grid's tendency to monotonous regularity. The streets exist in a hierarchy from broad boulevards to narrow lanes and alleys. In a town or city, limited access highways may exist only in a corridor, preferably in the form of parkways. Cul-de-sacs (dead ends) are strongly discouraged except under extraordinary circumstances—e.g., where rugged topography requires them. In the New Urbanism, the meaning of the street as the essential fabric of public life is restored.

Under the regime of Zoning, all streets were made as wide as possible because the specialist in charge—the zoning engineer—was concerned solely with the movement of cars and trucks. In the process, much of the traditional decor that made streets pleasant for people was gotten rid of. For instance, street trees were eliminated. It is hard to overstate how much orderly rows of mature trees can improve even the most dismal street by softening its hard edges and sun-blasted bleakness. Under zoning, street trees were deemed a hazard to motorists and chopped down in many American towns after World War Two.

35   The practice of maximizing car movement, at the expense of all other concerns, was applied with particular zeal to housing subdivisions. Suburban streets were given the speed characteristics of country highways, though children played in them. Suburbs notoriously lack parks. The spacious private lots were supposed to make up for the lack of parks, but children have an uncanny tendency to play in the street anyway—bicycles don't work too well on the lawn. In the suburbs, where street trees were expressly forbidden, we see those asinine exercises in romantic landscaping that attempt to recapitulate the North Woods in clumps of ornamental juniper. Sidewalks, in a setting so inimical to walking, were deemed a waste of money.

Parallel parking is emphatically permitted along the curbs of all streets, except under the most extraordinary conditions. Parallel parking is desirable for two reasons: (1) Parked cars create a physical barrier, and a psychological buffer, that protects pedestrians on the sidewalk from moving vehicles; and (2) a rich supply of parallel parking can eliminate the need for parking lots, which are extremely destructive of civic fabric. Anyone who thinks that parallel parking "ruins" a residential street should take a look at some of the most desirable real estate in America (as reflected by house prices): Georgetown, Beacon Hill, Nob Hill, Alexandria, Charleston, Savannah, Annapolis, Princeton, Greenwich Village, Marblehead, et cetera. All permit parallel parking.

Civic buildings (town halls, churches, schools, libraries, museums) are placed on preferential building sites such as the frontage of squares, neighborhood centers, and where street vistas terminate, in order to serve as landmarks and to reinforce their symbolic importance.

Can America Become Civilized?

I don't know if we will be able to reinstate a social contract that recognizes both rights and responsibilities in a civic context. It will certainly not be possible unless we restore that context, and I mean in bricks and mortar. There is a vital relationship between the character of our surroundings and the common good. Rights and responsibilities need a civic setting in which to dwell. Such a setting is identical with the physical setting of our lives, an actual place that must be worth caring about.

It is easy to be discouraged. The general political attitude among the sub-urban well-off is that they have been willing to try almost any expensive social experiment *except* returning to live in towns and cities. In the face of this shunning, the will to behave constructively has been rather conspicuously absent among the urban poor themselves. But the poor nevertheless have responsibilities and obligations too, beginning with civil behavior and extending to useful work. One of the unfortunate side effects of the psychology of entitlement is the notion both among the poor and government officials that jobs must be *given* to idle people, and that they must be *good* jobs—which I take to mean something like professional careers. Nothing could be further from the way the world really operates.

It may strike some readers as an unbelievable effrontery to state that 40 the poor ought to work in menial jobs. I am not arguing that they ought to live in violence and squalor—just the opposite. Before World War Two this was a nation full of menial employments, and many people so employed lived more decently than today's poor do, particularly in the cities where, for all the cities' historic shortcomings, the poor at least had easy access to a great deal of cultural and civic equipment. Poor people may have lived in cramped tenements in 1911, but they had access to well-maintained parks, low-cost public transit, safe streets, free public schools, excellent public libraries, museums, baths, and infirmaries. Most important, this civic equipment was shared by everybody. People of all stations in life went to parks, museums, and libraries. The poor *saw* the middle class and the wealthy every day in the public realm of the streets. They observed their behavior, and were constrained in their own behavior by seeing them. The poor saw where the rich lived. A boy from Hell's Kitchen could walk ten minutes across town and stand within a few yards of William H. Vanderbilt's front door on Fifty-ninth Street and Fifth Avenue with no fear of being hassled by private security guards. In short, the poor lived in a civic context that included the entire range of social classes, so that many of the problems of the poor in the cities were also the problems of the middle class and the rich.

Today the poor in most American cities live only in the context of the poor. The only place they see the other America is on television, and then through a wildly distorting lens that stimulates the most narcissistic, nihilistic consumer fantasies. Since the poor, by definition, can't participate fully in consumer culture, the predictable result is rage at what appears to be a cruel tease, and this rage is commonly expressed in crime. What may be equally damaging is that the poor see very little in the way of ordinary polite conduct, very little civil behavior. They do not see people routinely going about honorable occupations. What they do see all around is mayhem, squalor, and disorder, and almost no evidence that it is possible to live a happy life without being a sports hero, a gangster, or a television star.

The problems of the cities are not going to be relieved unless the middle class and the wealthy return to live there. For the moment these classes are off in suburbia. All the evidence demonstrates that suburbia is becoming unaffordable and unsustainable. The economy makes them nervous. Companies are shedding employees. They feel anxious, trapped. For the first time in American history, there is nowhere else left to go, no place to escape to. What will they do?

I'm afraid they may misunderstand the crisis of the suburbs, particularly as it manifests itself in the personal catastrophes of lost jobs, declining incomes, falling property values, family breakups, and misbehavior. Poor people are not the only Americans afflicted by the psychology of entitlement. Middle-class suburbanites really believe that they are owed a package of goodies called the American Dream, and when they are suddenly deprived of it, they may get very angry and vote for political maniacs.

The Republicans are now in charge of things at many levels of government, and though they have been shouting the loudest about the crisis of "family values," they are also the chief boosters of suburbia, which is to say, a profoundly uncivil living arrangement. Their chosen way of life is therefore at odds with their most cherished wishes for a civil society, and so it is unlikely that they are going to be able to solve any of the social problems they deplore—even the problems of their own children's behavior.

45   Suburban Moms and Dads wonder why their fifteen-year-old children seem so alienated. These kids are physically disconnected from the civic life of their towns. They have no access to the civic equipment. They have to be chauffeured absolutely everywhere, to football practice, to piano lessons, to their friends' houses, to the library, and, of course, to the mall. All they live for is the day that they can obtain a driver's license and use their environment. Except then, of course, another slight problem arises: they need several thousand dollars to buy a used car and pay for insurance, which is usually exorbitant for teens, often more than the price of their cars. Is it really any wonder that these kids view their situation as some kind of swindle?

Americans are convinced that suburbia is great for kids. The truth is, kids older than seven need more from their environment than a safe place to ride their bikes. They need at least the same things adults need. Dignified places to hang out. Shops. Eating establishments. Libraries, museums, and theaters. They need a public realm worthy of respect. All of which they need access to on their own, without our assistance—which only keeps them in an infantile state of dependency. In suburbia, as things presently stand, children have access only to television. That's their public realm. It's really a wonder that more American children are not completely psychotic.

In order to make American towns and cities habitable again, we will have to take the greater portion of public money now spent on subsidizing car use and redirect it into replacing the civic equipment of the cities that was allowed to be trashed over the past several decades. The cost of doing these things is, fortunately, apt to be less than the cost of continuing to subsidize the suburban automobile infrastructure. For instance, a single new freeway exchange can cost $600,000,000, which is the same cost as building and equipping an entire twenty-mile-long electric trolley line.[2]

Making our cities habitable again will take a rededication to forms of buildings that were largely abandoned in America after World War Two. It will call for devices of civic art that *never* really caught on here, but have always existed in older parts of the world—for instance, waterfronts that are integral with the rest of the city. The human scale will have to prevail over the needs of motor vehicles. There will have to be ample provision for green space of different kinds—neighborhood squares, wildlife corridors, parks—because people truly crave regular contact with nature, especially pockets of repose and tranquillity, and having many well-cared-for parcels of it distributed equitably around town improves civic life tremendously.

The transformation I propose will not be possible unless Americans recognize the benefits of a well-designed public realm, and the civic life that comes with it, over the uncivil, politically toxic, socially impoverished, hyper-privatized realm of suburbia, however magnificent the kitchens and bathrooms may be there. I don't believe that we can be an advanced society without cities. Tragically, American cities have become unworthy of the American republic. Our task is to make them worthy, to reconstruct them in a physical form that is worth caring about, and to reinhabit them.

The common good demands a public realm in which to dwell. It can't 50 sustain itself merely in our hearts or memories. This is, finally, the sentimental fallacy of the suburban patriot: that hanging a cast-iron eagle over your garage door proves you care about your country.

Notes

[1] The principles outlined here are derived from a consensus among members of the Congress for the New Urbanism. Other lists of principles exist and have been articulated in various formats by Elizabeth Plater-Zyberk and Andrés Duany, Peter Calthorpe, Daniel Solomon, Peter Katz, and Anthony Nelessen. A complementary list, called the Ahwahnee Principles, was drawn up in a 1991 conference at the Ahwahnee Lodge in Yosemite Park. Among the participants were Duany and Plater-Zyberk, Katz, Stefanos Polyzoides, and Elizabeth Moule, architects and planners, and Michael Corbett, a former mayor of Davis, California. The book *Town Planning in Practice*, by Raymond Unwin (1863–1940) republished in 1994 by the Princeton Architectural Press, is also a classic source.

[2] Author's interview with Milwaukee Mayor John O. Norquist, June 1995.

Things to Do with the Reading

1. Apply THE METHOD (aka Looking for Patterns of Repetition and Contrast—see Chapter 1) to Kunstler's piece. Make a list in the margins of the key terms repeated, the strands in which they participate, and the binary oppositions into which they are aligned. Then choose what you consider to be the two most important repetitions, the two most interesting strands, and the two most significant binaries. Finally, choose any ONE of these and write for a paragraph or two about what it means and why it matters to Kunstler's vision.

2. In Chapter 2, we offer as a frame for reading critically the notion of understanding a piece of writing in terms of THE PITCH, THE COMPLAINT, AND THE MOMENT. Locate Kunstler's piece in this context: find language that you think reveals THE PITCH, THE COMPLAINT AND THE MOMENT. Explain your reasoning for selecting these passages.

3. Kunstler argues that "in the past forty years we ceased to speak of ourselves as citizens and labeled ourselves consumers" (paragraph 10). He then builds an argument on the different implications of these two key terms, citizen and consumer. What are these implications?

   Note: the words citizen, civic (as in civic center), and civilized play a key role in Kunstler's piece. Look up the etymology (word history) of these terms: how might they enrich your understanding of his point of view?

4. Application: Kunstler asserts that "the basic unit of planning is the neighborhood" (paragraph 27). Apply his perceptions to your neighborhood or to one close to you. How is it constructed? How does it locate parking? Public transportation? How does it set up housing—and in what relation to income levels? Where, if at all, does it attend to what Kunstler terms "human needs" and "aesthetic needs"? What ultimately does Kunstler's lens allow you to discover about your neighborhood?

5. Link Across Chapters: Kunstler makes an argument for the importance of people from different socioeconomic classes encountering each other in public spaces and neighborhoods. First, explain his argument and the means he suggests for accomplishing this goal. Then put Kunstler's thinking into conversation with Ishmael Reed's in Chapter 14. What observations might Reed offer to Kunstler on Kunstler's argument that the poor and the middle class need to be brought closer together in cities?

Jack Gambino

Demolition Zones: Contemporary Photography by Edward Burtynsky and Camilo José Vergara

Political scientist Jack Gambino looks at two contemporary photographers' representations of urban and industrial landscapes as sites of "creative destruction," commenting, "It is this sense of displacement—of human beings alienated from the environments they have created—that provides the common theme that haunts these two very different photographers."

If you look closely at Camilo José Vergara's "Fern Street, Camden" (1988), you'll 1 notice a sign on the side of a dilapidated building:

> *"Danger: Men Working*
>
> *W. Hargrove Demolition"*

Perhaps that warning captures the ominous atmosphere evoked in the human and natural landscapes of two very different kinds of photographers, Camilo José Vergara and Edward Burtynsky. "Danger: Men Working." Watch out—human beings are at work! But the work they present is not so much a building-up as it is a tearing-down—the work of demolition. Of course, demolition is often necessary in order to construct anew: old buildings are leveled for new projects, whether they are the highways and high rises that dominate the contemporary American city or the massive dams now transforming portions of the Chinese countryside. To destroy in order to create: that is a modern formula. Modernity is, after all, a process of "creative destruction," a term used variously to describe the dynamics of modern art, capitalism, and technological innovation. The photographs in this exhibit, however, force us to pay attention to the destructiveness, both deliberate and unintentional, at the very heart of modern creation. What both Burtynsky and Vergara do in their respective ways is to point to the warning signs already posted on the modern landscape. They compel us to wonder whether the process of creative-destruction may not have spun recklessly out of control, producing places that are not just unsustainable in the future, but uninhabitable in the present. Indeed, a common element connecting their photographic visions is the near absence of people in the landscape. While we see the evidence of the transforming power of human production on the physical and social environment, neither Vergara's urban ruins nor Burtynsky's industrial sites actually show us "men working." Isolated figures peer suspiciously out back doors or pick through the rubble, but they appear out-of-place. It is this sense

Demolition Zones, Jack Gambino. Reprinted with permission of the author.

of displacement—of human beings alienated from the environments they themselves have created—that provides the common theme that haunts the work of these two very different photographers.

The dominant theme in Burtynsky's work, as he puts it, is "nature transformed through industry." His photos are large industrial landscapes—quarries, oil refineries, mines, dams—mostly dedicated to the extraction and production of energy resources. Burtynsky's landscapes vividly portray what landscape historian J.B. Jackson called the "engineered landscape"—a landscape developed for "the production, conservation, and use of energy." The Three Gorges Dam is, of course, one of the latest and largest of the modern engineer's remaking of the social and physical environment. Highways are another, more familiar example, with their horizontal forms and parallel lines, similar to the shiny, sleek pipeline cutting its way through the forest in Burtynsky ("Oil Fields #22. Cold Lake, Alberta, Canada, 2001"). [See Figure 13.1.] What better image of the triumph of precision, linearity, efficiency, and clarity? Even the forest appears as a controlled environment, an ecological monoculture made available for easy exploitation. "To the engineer (and the engineer-minded society)," Jackson wrote, "a landscape is beautiful when the energy-flow system is functioning with unimpeded efficiency." A

San Francisco – Nicholas Metivier

FIGURE 13.1

"Oil Fields #22. Cold Lake, Alberta, Canada, 2001" by Edward Burtynsky well-engineered highway or pipeline aims for this kind of efficiency. So will Three Gorges Dam, which, when completed, is expected to generate 8.4 billion kilowatts-per-hour of unimpeded energy for China's exploding industrial cities (one ninth of its electricity needs, according to some estimates). This massive attempt at state enforced modernization will not only meet practical energy needs; it will fulfill China's socialist destiny, as proclaimed by former President Jiang Zemin in a 1997 celebration of the Three Gorges Dam. Yet that destiny—"the great feat of conquering, developing and exploiting nature," to quote President Zemin—is hardly an exclusively socialist dream: it's what modernization is all about in capitalist societies as well.

The fact that the process of energy extraction and transfer, once initiated, could be maintained with little direct human presence suggests all the more that the engineer's quest for efficiency culminates in a kind of robotic automatism portrayed in "Oil Fields #13. Taft, California, USA, 2002." [See Figure 13.2.] Earthmoving machines, cranes, and oil derricks largely occupy the industrial landscape Burtynsky portrays. But the engineer's ingenious instruments are not his real subject, as much as their unintentional and unexpected effects. Burtynsky is attracted to the awesome (awful) beauty of the industrial

San Francisco – Nicholas Metivier

FIGURE 13.2
"Oil Fields #13. Taft, California, USA, 2002" by Edward Burtynsky

landscapes (something, one suspects, that the engineers may not have noticed), most notably in the chiseled shapes of the quarries of Utah and Vermont.[1] Yet whether they produce the effect of gigantic, abstract sculptures, as in the Vermont quarry, or the semblance of a classical amphitheatre, as in the Utah copper mine, Burtynsky's photos remind us that the beauty of these landscapes cannot be separated from the industrial power that *forcefully cuts* them from the earth. Like all sculptures, they are creative works of violence—a form hammered and chiseled out of rock ("Rock of Ages," 1991). Here Burtynsky suggests a fascination with something deeper than the engineer's desire for efficiency—a fascination with the violence at the heart of the modern creative process. For the remnants of the violence are evident in the denuded forests, the pulverized concrete, the piles of rubble, the incisions in the earth, the jagged debris of partially demolished buildings. The sites of production are necessarily demolition zones.

To many modern architects, urban planners, and engineers, demolition is merely the prelude to a new construction, which, once completed, will cover over (and make us forget) both the physical scars to the land and the emotional scars of displaced people who found themselves in the way. We may join with the modern builders in justifying the violence of means—the sculptor's hammer and chisel—by applauding the greater goods these violent means serve. Sometimes the beauty of the end result does in fact conceal the violent incisions: we may still enjoy Paris' famed boulevard even after acknowledging that its designer, Baron Haussmann, under Louis Napoleon's authoritarian rule, had to *cut* through medieval streets of old Paris, uprooting tens of thousands of urban poor in the mid 19th century. Yet too often modern planners and engineers would justify the creative destruction of habitat as necessary for doubtful utopias: think of Le Corbusier who would have demolished those same 19th-century boulevards to create "a blank piece of paper" for an even more modern city of highways and skyscrapers! Stalin—whose displacement of Russian peasants through forced collectivization reached a level of unprecedented and perhaps unsurpassed brutality—bluntly insisted that "you can't make an omelet without breaking eggs." This was a maxim that Robert Moses, the master planner who ruthlessly leveled New York City neighborhoods to make way for expressways, loved to quote, adding his own: "When you operate in an overbuilt metropolis, you have to hack your way with a meat axe." Here the butcher's axe replaces the sculpture's chisel, but the point is the same—big modern projects require the demolition of existing structures and the displacement of people. The Three Gorges Dam also is a monument to modern ambition—a work in progress, which when completed, will literally *cut* the flow of the Yangtze River, causing it to form a 400 mile long reservoir that will eventually hide, it is hoped, the physical and human scars caused by the demolition of 11 cities and displacement of 1.2 million people.

5   Perhaps Burtynsky's monumental prints remind us that the scars created by such modernization projects cannot be made over by the engineers' sense

of beauty in efficiency. He insists on keeping those scars exposed, even finding a seductive beauty in the jagged edges of demolished buildings and the raw incisions into the surface of the earth.[2] It seems to me, however, that it is a beauty we can only contemplate at a distance, by subtracting ourselves from the scene. We can be struck by the eerie surrealism of "Uranium Tailings" (2002), but we can't imagine human beings walking about in such a landscape. At the same time, he tells us that these inhuman places are part of the industrial infrastructure of a world dependent on energy extraction and consumption. We are made accomplices to those industrial processes and its byproducts: mountains of used tires, rusted hulks of ships, piles of rubble, demolished buildings. His landscapes are thus, as he understands them, a "metaphor for the dilemma of our modern existence: they search for a dialogue between attraction and repulsion, seduction and fear. We are drawn by desire—a chance at good living, yet we are consciously or unconsciously aware that the world is suffering for our success."[3] His images—especially the series on the Three Gorges Dam—not only bid us to gaze at the human and ecological costs of modernity's creative destructive process, but also warn us that these sites of demolition are never very far from our own safe places. [See Figure 13.3.]

San Francisco – Nicholas Metivier

FIGURE 13.3
"Wan Zhou #4, Three Gorges Dam Project, Yangtze River, 2002" by Edward Burtynsky

If Burtynsky provokes questions about the seductive beauty of "nature transformed through industry," Camilo Vergara insists that we directly confront urban landscapes transformed by deindustrialization. Vergara's series on the hard luck city of Camden—which is part of a larger project documenting the "process of decline" of the American industrial city—invites us to move closer to inspect the details of places that few of us would call beautiful and most of us would like to avoid. Although we don't see them, the men working in Camden nowadays are doing the work of demolition. This is a bleak, harsh view with little to offer of the awesome industrial monuments found in Burtynsky's work. It is the view most suburbanites (now the majority of Americans) only catch glimpse of as they speed by on the highways and bridges to and from Philadelphia. Yet by placing us "among dereliction and destruction," Vergara calls on us to search for signs of resurgent life—what he calls "the energies of the outmoded."

The Camden he documents is a site marked by a series of displacements. Once upon a time, the city was home to Walt Whitman and, later, Campbell Soups, and it could boast (despite W.C. Fields' joke that Camden is "the pimple on Philadelphia's ass") that it was "the biggest little city in the nation" making "everything from fountain pens to battleships." With over 105,000 people in the 1920s, it was home to thirteen downtown theatres, an opera company, a major shipbuilding port, an airport with flights to Europe, and a railroad terminus. The factories along the waterfront provided employment to large numbers of European immigrants and African-Americans. On Independence Day, 1926, when President Coolidge participated in the dedication ceremony for the Ben Franklin Bridge (called the Delaware River Bridge back then), the city notables could look forward to what they foresaw as an era of urban growth, with the new bridge making possible the city's "venture in progress."[4]

By now the story of urban decline of old industrial powerhouses like Camden, St. Louis, Detroit, and my hometown, Newark, is a familiar one. Factories moved to more spacious accommodations in the suburbs.[5] The Federal Housing Administration, which underwrote mortgages for families seeking to relocate in the suburbs, virtually wrote off loans to urban dwellers by "redlining" whole neighborhoods as too risky. Moreover, its misguided urban renewal projects during the 1950s and 1960s condemned and demolished entire neighborhoods, displacing thousands of urban families (one out of every 15 families in Camden). Low-income, high-rise apartments were built (the "projects" as they were called), which separated the poor both from the middle class and from places of employment. Many poor but settled neighborhoods were demolished only to be paved into parking lots. Along with the loss of jobs and the increasingly dilapidated housing, the exodus of the white middle class, the deterioration of the downtown commercial district, and mounting racial tensions and riots appeared to doom Camden by the early 1970s.

The irony is that the very structure that would lead to Camden's "venture in progress"—the Ben Franklin Bridge—helped facilitate its undoing. The construction of the bridge itself required the displacement of an entire neighborhood in the city. On and off ramps not only required the bulldozing of established neighborhoods in order to widen access roads, the roads themselves acted as a barrier effectively cutting the city into segments. Like Three Gorges Dam, the bridge was supposed to serve a larger public need by re-engineering the landscape for efficiency and ease of mobility. Such large-scale projects, which embodied the muscular industrial modernity of urban planners and engineers like Moses and Le Corbusier, actually replaced one icon of modernity, the bourgeois city, with another, the automobile. In the new city cars would displace pedestrians, and highways displace the street (Le Corbusier famously declared the "death of the street") as primary urban space. More than anything else, the car and highway transformed the American landscape. As urban problems became more intractable, more Americans fled to the suburbs fulfilling an early prophesy of no less a modernist than Henry Ford: "The ultimate solution [to urban problems everywhere] will be the abandonment of the city, its abandonment as a blunder."[6]

The process of urban decay was well underway when Vergara began his documentary project in the 1970s. What his time-series photos help us to see is the "process of decline" unfolding over many years, even decades.[7] The Fern Street series, for instance, shows the decay and eventual demolition of most of the houses on an urban residential street and their replacement by rubble strewn empty lots. [See Figure 13.4.] Abandoned buildings and vacant lots have become dead spaces, gaps in the urban fabric and depositories for all kinds of junk. It used to be that the city street was the scene of diversity and vitality—think of Jacob Riis' famous shot of Mulberry St. Bend in NY—life may have been tough, but it was teeming with energy. In a more optimistic vein, Jane Jacobs pointed out that the vitality of great American cities was always on the sidewalks where "a constant succession of eyes" of those passing by made the street both vitally interesting and safe.[8] In contrast, Vergara shows us urban scenes largely devoid of people; the isolated figures which emerge here and there only reinforce the sense of loneliness and exhaustion. In contrast, automobiles are present in virtually all of the photos, occupying not only the street, but empty lots and sidewalks as well. Vergara is haunted by the disappearance of a once vibrant "street life," so much so that he can't resist poking about the physical and psychic rubble for ghosts.

Anyone who has visited cities like Camden sees this strange process of the city "emptying out," becoming less densely populated (my hometown went from around 420,000 when I was born, to about 250,000). Abandoned buildings decay, are demolished, and eventually paved into parking lots to accommodate suburban commuters. Many downtowns are nothing more than anonymous office buildings, surrounded by parking lots and a ring of run

FIGURE 13.4
Collage of four color photographs, "Fern Street"—photographed by Camilo José Vergara "clockwise from top left," in 1979, 1988, 1997, 2004

FIGURE 13.4
Continued

down houses. The parking lots erase the history of the place; the junk is gone, the buildings cleared, but so are the memories of the people who once lived there. But these empty spaces are for Vergara's lens not Le Corbusier's blank piece of paper; they are haunted places filled with fragmentary evidence of a former human presence. The exteriors of such places—which Vergara usually photographs directly from the street—go mostly unnoticed, both by those who live among them (notice the pedestrian in front of the dilapidated public library) and the suburban commuters. With his camera, he becomes the eyes on the empty streets that most of us overlook. More poignant are the images in which Vergara enters the interiors of dangerous buildings, an intruder who insists on exposing what is hidden inside those demolition zones, as in his eerie portrait of the Camden Public Library. [See Figure 13.5.]

Such photographic intrusion into unoccupied spaces (both physical and mental)—while often appearing merely as objective documentation—is in fact driven by his own sense of the "terrible loss" of urban decline, as he puts it.[9] His abandoned spaces are not only physical "gaps" in the urban fabric (representing the physical displacement of individuals and families), but interruptions in our collective memory and history. This points to an important feature of Vergara's work, and that which makes it more than a sociological record of the process of urban decline: he wants to meditate on

Camilo José Vergara

FIGURE 13.5

"Camden Library" by Camilo José Vergara

the violent contradictions in modernity itself. Vergara, who grew up in a poor agricultural town in Chile and dreamed of a modern life of "Flash Gordon," came to America to study electrical engineering at Notre Dame: "I wanted to believe that science and technology would keep me from being poor."[10] What he discovered in America was not just the landscape of technical innovation and creativity but the contradictory underworld of decay and exhaustion. Modernity is not just about transforming nature and building an industrial civilization; it's about the violence that leaves the human habitat in fragments and a state of disrepair: "I became so attached to derelict buildings that sadness came not from seeing them overgrown and deteriorating—this often rendered them more picturesque—but from the violent destruction, which often left a big gap in the urban fabric."[11]

Like Burtynsky, Vergara is intent on showing us demolition sites that contradict the more sanguine representations of the modern landscape. Both remind us that continuous innovation ("development," "modernization") of industrial civilization comes at a price: continuous demolition and displacement. But whereas Burtynsky bids us to keep a distant gaze on the monuments of creative-destruction in order to coolly resist the seduction of industrial power, Vergara wants us to join him as intruders into abandoned libraries and boarded-up houses, not just to expose the violent destruction in our midst, but, more importantly, to fill in the "gaps" in our collective memory. By photographing urban "ruins," Vergara hopes to search out and preserve traces of the "soul" "among the dereliction and destruction." What kind of soul might we find? Certainly not the "soul" in the machines that earlier modernists like Le Corbusier and Henry Ford celebrated. The automobile, of course, dominates the urban landscape, along with utility poles, garbage pails, barred windows and doors. But in Vergara's photos the presence of automobiles (often they, too, are left abandoned among the weeds) reminds us that the assumptions of the modern American dream—mobility based on cheap energy, prosperity defined as unlimited consumption, technology as the ever-expanding control over nature—have exacted a terrible price on the landscape.

But even among the ruins there remain signs of hope and redemption, evidenced by the many churches and religious symbols that fill Vergara's photos. Pentecostal churches have reoccupied numerous structures originally built for other purposes. (In my old Newark neighborhood, Hispanic Pentecostal churches have occupied what were once a delicatessen, a candy store, a firehouse, and a former go-go bar.) But unlike the stone-built churches—built to symbolize stability and permanence, not just of the church itself, but of the whole neighborhood in which it was located—these makeshift churches, whatever personal sense of salvation they provide their members, seem to be as temporary as the buildings surrounding them. They offer an enclave of survival in the urban landscape, but they are inward looking, often windowless structures seeking to defend themselves against the hostile world outside, just like the barred-pink fortress-house Vergara shows us on Fern Street.

Other signs of transcendence are scattered throughout Vergara's urbanscapes—"Jesus" graffitied on a boarded-up house; a billboard advertising "detoxification" treatments ("Procedure Confidential"); a middle school sign proclaiming that "Everybody is Somebody and We Are Rising" (with several of its letters having already dropped to the ground). Christians might read spiritual significance in the mundane storefront sign of the "Penn Fish Co.," the fish as symbol of Christ, the fisher of men. Yet, I don't see Vergara searching for a form of religious redemption in the urban wilderness he documents. His photographs fill in the "gaps" of historical memory by memorializing the fragmentary remains of a past. Abandoned buildings and empty lots become haunted ruins. "Penn Fish Co." thus evokes an era when the urban street formed the backdrop of a contemporary life—a scene of diversity, vitality, and permanence. Vergara knows he's playing with nostalgia in his photos: "I imagine Gary and Detroit as the noisy, dramatic cities they once were and I see myself photographing the ghosts left behind."[12] Like Burtynsky's, there is nothing in Vergara's vision to suggest what we might do to control the creative-destructive processes of modernity; rather, his stark images call upon us to stop, look around us and think what we are doing. In a world that is obsessed with erasing the past, he would have us regain a sense of history by reflecting on the remnants of what we have lost.

Notes

[1] The unintended sculptured forms appear in other of Burtynsky's work, for example, in the series on ship breakers in Bangladesh.

[2] While demolition is shown to be the underside of energy production in his Three Gorges Dam series, Burtynsky also points to another paradigmatic site of industrial modernization: the landfill. Mountains of used tires transform the landscape by "building it up," whereas energy extraction appears as a digging out (mines, quarries). The depletion of resources (abandoned mines) is thus coupled with the accumulation of waste. In his novel, *Underworld*, Don DeLillo also proposed the landfill—where the "waste stream ended"—as a paradigmatic site of industrial America.

[3] "Artist Statement." (http://www.edwardburtynsky.com/)

[4] Quotations from David L. Kirp, John P. Dwyer, Larry A. Rosenthal, *Our Town: Race, Housing, and the Soul of Suburbia*, (New Brunswick, NJ: Rutgers University Press, 1997), pp. 15, 20.

[5] While manufacturing boomed in the outlying suburbs of Camden County during 1950–1970, the city of Camden lost half of its manufacturing jobs. Ibid.

[6] Ibid, 23.

[7] Vergara, *American Ruins* (New York: The Monacelli Press, 1999), p. 12.

[8] Jane Jacobs, *The Death and Life of Great American Cities.*

[9] *American Ruins*, 23.

[10] *American Ruins*, 22.

[11] *American Ruins*, 23.

[12] Op. cit. 24.

Things to Do with the Reading

1. **Link:** Locate a point of contact between Kunstler's essay and Gambino's— find a significant passage from each. Decide what Kunstler might say about one or more of the images that Gambino discusses and that are included with his essay. Consider, for example, Gambino's treatment of the Ben Franklin Bridge. See "Put Your Sources into Conversation with Another" in Chapter 7.

2. Gambino notes how often human figures are conspicuously absent in Burtynsky's and Vergara's photographs. But there are in fact some people in Burtynsky's "Three Gorges" and in Vergara's "Fern Street." Write about the role that human figures play in terms of how each photograph communicates—perhaps in relation to the absence of human figures in other of their photographs.

3. In much analytical writing the writer does not simply set out to prove a thesis but instead formulates a thesis in order to create a workable space in which a range of related claims might be made about the subject. Gambino's essay is a good place to observe this aspect of essay construction/ organization—the evolving thesis in action.

   First, find a sentence that serves as a thesis—the claim that causes the piece to cohere, to possess a sense of direction. (Note: you will find more than one version of this primary claim in an essay.) Then locate interesting claims in the piece that the thesis seems to allow Gambino the space to produce. You'll notice these are connected to the thesis but are not necessarily just another version of the same thing. Write down three or four of these, noting where you find them.

4. Look at how Gambino uses the formula that *Writing Analytically* calls "SEEMS TO BE ABOUT X" (see Chapter 5) in paragraph 3. Here he says that the engineers' "ingenious instruments are not [Burtynsky's] real subject." As the paragraph progresses, Gambino complicates the essay's thinking, noting "Burtynsky's photos remind us that the beauty of these landscapes cannot be separated from the industrial power that *forcefully cuts* them from the earth." This is a symptom of the essay's fondness for paradox, also evident in the title of the photo, "Rock of Ages" (an

old religious hymn about how some things can be relied on to last forever), and elsewhere in the piece. What do you make of these paradoxes? How do they function to organize the piece? What are the terms of the ambivalence that Gambino is investigating in this essay, and what point of view is he ultimately inviting us to take toward it?

5. Application: Imagine that Vergara and Burtynsky planned to spend a week taking photographs in the area around which you live. Where would each of them go to shoot, and why? Be as specific as you can. (Maybe you could take some photographs in one or more of these places yourself.)

Note: You may wish to look ahead to the discussion of contemporary photography in the interview with Joseph Elliott, which opens Chapter 16, "Seeing." It will give you a crash course in thinking about photographs, and in it Elliott discusses Vergara and Burtynsky overtly.

Adam Gopnik

Times Regained: How the Old Times Square Was Made New

Nominally a book review about two recent histories of the revitalization of Times Square in New York City, this essay also offers a resonant analysis of the patterns and politics of urban redevelopment. Adam Gopnik is an essayist, cultural commentator, and an award-winning journalist for *The New Yorker*. Most recent of his eight books is *The Table Comes First: France, Family, and the Meaning of Food* (2011).

This year marks the hundredth anniversary of the decision to take an hourglass-shaped traffic funnel between Forty-second Street and Forty-seventh Street on Broadway, which had been called Longacre Square, and rename it after *The New York Times*, which had just built its office there. This was less an honor than a consolation prize. The other, then bigger and brighter newspaper, the *New York Herald*, had claimed the other, then brighter and better square, eight blocks south, which still bears its ghostly name. Nine years later, in 1913, the *Times* scurried off to a prim side street and a Gothic Revival bishop's palace, where it has been lifting its skirts and shyly peeking around the corner at its old home ever since.

No other part of New York has had such a melodramatic, mood-ring sensitivity to the changes in the city's history, with an image for every decade. There was the turn-of-the-century Times Square, with its roof gardens and showgirls; the raffish twenties Times Square of Ziegfeld and Youmans' tunes; the thirties Times Square of "42nd Street," all chorus lines and moxie; the forties, V-J "On the Town" Times Square, full of sailors kissing girls; the wizened black-and-white fifties Times Square of "Sweet Smell of Success," steaming hot dogs, and grungy beats; and then the sixties and the seventies Times Square of "Midnight Cowboy" and "Taxi Driver," where everything fell apart and Hell wafted up through the manhole covers. No other place in town has been quite so high and quite so low. Within a single half decade, it had Harpo Marx in the Marx Brothers' valedictory movie, "Love Happy," leaping ecstatically from sign to sign and riding away on the flying Mobilgas Pegasus, and, down below, the unforgettable image of James Dean, hunched in his black overcoat, bearing the weight of a generation on his shoulders.

Now, of course, we have the new Times Square, as fresh as a neon daisy, with a giant Gap and a Niketown and an Applebee's and an ESPN Zone and television announcers visible through tinted windows, all family retailing and

Times Regained: First published in The New Yorker, March 2004. Copyright © 2004 by Adam Gopnik, by permission of the author.

national brands. In some ways, the Square has never looked better, with the diagonal sloping lines of the Reuters Building, the curving Deco zipper, even the giant mock dinosaur in the Toys R Us. There are, of course, people who miss the old Times Square, its picturesque squalor and violence and misery and exploitation. Those who pointed at the old Times Square as an instance of everything that capitalism can do wrong now point to the new Times Square as an instance of everything that capitalism can do worse. Where once Times Square was hot, it is now cold, where once varied, now uniform, where once alive, now dead. Which just proves, as with the old maxim about belief, that people who refuse to be sentimental about the normal things don't end up being sentimental about nothing; they end up being sentimental about anything, shedding tears about muggings and the shards of crack vials glittering like diamonds in the gutter.

And yet, whatever has been gained, something really is missing in the new Times Square. The forces that created it, and the mixed emotions that most of us have in its presence, are the subject of James Traub's *The Devil's Playground* (Random House; $25.95), which is both an engaged civics lesson and a work of social history. The book begins with an ironic moment—Traub takes his eleven-year-old son to the new Forty-second Street to see the old "42nd Street"—and then spirals back into history, moving decade by decade over the past century.

5   Traub, a writer for the *Times,* hates city myth but loves city history: on every page you learn something about how the city really happened, and how it really happens now. He is particularly good at wrestling complicated history into a few tight pages. He gives the best account we have of the original sin of New York: the birth, in 1811, of the iron street grid almost before there were any streets. The decision to lay a crisscross of numbers over the city without any breaks for public squares, plazas, or parks—a deliberately brutal nod to the governing principle of commerce—is why we still, sadly, call any awkward and accidental space created by the diagonal of Broadway intersecting an avenue a "square."

Traub also has a gift for filtering social history through a previously invisible individual agent. As always, the vast forces of mass culture turn out to be the idiosyncratic choices of a few key, mostly hidden players. The character of the signs in Times Square, for instance, was mostly the invention of O. J. Gude, the Sign King of Times Square. Gude, a true aesthete with a significant art collection, was the first to sense that the peculiar shape of Times Square—a triangle with sign-friendly "flats" at the base and the apex—made it the perfect place for big electric national-brand signs, or "spectaculars," as they were called, even before the First World War. In 1917, when Gude put up a two-hundred-foot-long spectacular, on the west side of Broadway between Forty-third and Forty-fourth, featuring twelve gleaming "spearmen" who went through spasmodic calisthenics, it was as big an event in American pop culture, in its way, as the opening of "The Jazz Singer," ten years later. Gude also had the bright idea of joining the Municipal Art Society, the leading opponent of big signs, and later helped shape the zoning ordinances that essentially eliminated big electric signs anywhere in midtown *except* in Times Square.

Times Square is famous for what used to be called its "denizens"—Damon Runyon, George S. Kaufman, Clifford Odets, A. J. Liebling—and Traub writes brief lives of a lot of them. But the history of the place isn't really a history of its illuminati; it's a history of its illuminations. Though social forces and neon signs flow out of individuals, they don't flow back into individuals so transparently. George S. Kaufman, to take one instance, was exclusively a creature of the theatre; if, like the galleries in SoHo in the nineteen-nineties, the Broadway theatre had in the thirties picked up and moved to Chelsea, Kaufman would have followed it blindly and would never have been seen on Forty-second Street again. Even Runyon has about as much to do with the history of Times Square as P. G. Wodehouse does with the history of Mayfair: his subject is language, not place, and in all of Runyon's stories it would be hard to find a single set-piece description of Times Square, a single bulb on a single sign. Individual artists help make cities, but cities don't make their artists in quite so neatly reciprocal a way. Dr. Johnson's "London" is a poem; "The London of Dr. Johnson" is a tour-bus ride.

Traub gives no false gloss to the decay of Times Square; it was really bad. The neighborhood declined to a point where, by the mid-seventies, the Times Square precincts placed first and second in New York in total felonies. (Harlem had a third as many.) These were crimes of violence, too: a rape or an armed robbery or a murder took place nearly every day and every night. Stevie Wonder's great 1973 song "Living for the City" has a spoken-word interlude in which the poor black kid from the South arrives on West Forty-second Street and in about five minutes is lured into the drug business. This was a song, but it was not a lie.

Traub's account of the area's transformation is lit from behind by another, still longer and larger one—Lynne B. Sagalyn's masterly *Times Square Roulette: Remaking the City Icon*, just issued in paperback (M.I.T.; $29.95). Sagalyn teaches real estate at the University of Pennsylvania, and her book, the fruit of more than a decade of scholarly labor, is as mind-bendingly detailed an account of the relations of property and culture as one can find outside Galsworthy or Trollope.

It's full of eye-opening material, if one can keep one's eyes open long 10 enough to find it. Sagalyn's book is written, perhaps of necessity, in a prose so dense with city acronyms and cross-referential footnotes that it can defeat even the most earnest attention. Nonetheless, its material is the material of the city's existence. Reading it is like reading an advanced-biology textbook and then discovering that its sole subject is your own body.

Traub and Sagalyn agree in dispelling a myth and moving toward a history, and the myth irritates them both—Traub's usual tone of intelligent skepticism sometimes boils over here into exasperation. The myth they want to dispel is that the cleanup of Times Square in the nineties was an expression of Mayor Giuliani's campaign against crime and vice, and of his companion tendency to accept a sterilized environment if they could be removed, and that his key corporate partner in this was the mighty Disney, which led the remaking of West Forty-second Street as a theme park instead of an authentic urban street. As Traub and Sagalyn show, this is nearly the reverse of the truth. It was Mayor Koch who shaped the new Times Square, if anyone did, while the important private profit-makers and players were almost all purely local: the Old Oligarchs, the handful of rich, and mostly Jewish, real-estate families—the Rudins, Dursts, Roses, Resnicks, Fishers, Speyers, and Tishmans, as Sagalyn crisply enumerates them. Mayor Giuliani, basically, was there to cut the ribbon, and Disney to briefly lend its name.

The story follows, on a larger scale than usual, the familiar form of New York development, whose stages are as predictable as those of a professional wrestling match: first, the Sacrificial Plan; next, the Semi-Ridiculous Rhetorical Statement; then the Staged Intervention of the Professionals; and, at last, the Sorry Thing Itself. The Sacrificial Plan is the architectural plan or model put forward upon the announcement of the project, usually featuring some staggeringly obvious and controversial device—a jagged roof or a startling pediment—which even the architect knows will never be built, and whose purpose is not to attract investors so much as to get people used to the general idea that something is going to be built there. (Sometimes the Sacrificial Plan is known by all to be sacrificial, and sometimes, as in "The Lottery," known to everyone but the sacrifice.) The Semi-Ridiculous Rhetorical Statement usually accompanies, though it can precede, the Sacrificial Plan, and is intended to show that the plan is not as brutal and cynical as it looks but has been designed in accordance with the architectural mode of the moment. ("The three brass lambs that stand on the spires of Sheep's Meadow Tower reflect the historical context of the site…" was the way it was done a decade ago; now it's more likely to be "In its hybrid façade, half mirror, half wool, Sheep's Meadow Tower captures the contradictions and deconstructs the flow of…") The Staged Intervention marks the moment when common sense and common purpose, in the form of the Old Oligarchs and their architects—who were going to be in charge in the first place—return to rescue the project from itself. The Sorry Thing itself you've seen. (At Ground Zero, Daniel Libeskind supplied the sacrificial plan, and now he is pursuing all of the semi-ridiculous rhetoric, in the forlorn hope that, when the professionals stage their intervention, he will be the professional called on.)

The only difference in the Times Square project was that, because of its size, it all happened twice. (Actually, there were two dimensions to the remaking of Times Square—the West Forty-second Street projects, and the reclaiming of the Square itself—but each depended on the other, and, though administratively distinct, they were practically joined.) The first Sacrificial

Plan appeared in the late seventies, and was called "the City at Forty-second Street." Presented by the developer Fred Papert, with the support of the Ford Foundation and with proposed backing from Paul Reichmann, of Olympia & York, it envisioned a climate-controlled indoor-mall Forty-second Street, with a five-hundred-thousand-square-foot "educational, entertainment, and exhibit center," and a 2.1-million-square-foot merchandise mart for the garment trade, all strung together with aerial walkways and, lovely period touch, equipped with a monorail. Mayor Koch wasn't happy about the plan; "We've got to make sure that they have seltzer"—that it's echt New York—"instead of orange juice," he said. But mostly he worried because someone else would be squeezing the oranges.

Still, the plan did what such plans are meant to do: establish the principle, civic-minded rather than commercial, that something had to be done here, and the larger principle that whatever was done should be done on a large scale—the old, outdoor theatre-and-arcade Forty-second Street could be turned into "a consumer-oriented exposition center with people moving across 42nd Street by means of pedestrian bridges," as one early draft of the rhetoric put it. As the initiative passed from the developers to the Koch administration, a further principle was established. The transformation could be made only by large-scale condemnation of what was already there, and the city and state together proposed a new way to link up private and public: the developers would get the right to build on condition that they paid directly for public improvements. The price of your tower on top was a cleaner subway station below.

Still more significant, and what should have been seen as a portent in the 15 first Sacrificial Plan, was the felt need to pull away from the street completely. This was not simply snobbery but self-preservation; Forty-second Street wasn't dying but raving. The porno shops on West Forty-second Street weren't there because the middle class had fled. They were there because the middle class was there. The people who bought from the porn industry were the office workers who walked by the stores on the way to and from work, and the tourists who wanted to take back a little something not for the kids. The XXX video rooms and bookstores and grind-house theatres were going concerns, paying an average of thirty-two thousand dollars a year in rent; peep shows could gross five million a year. Though the retailers were obviously entangled with the Mafia, the buildings were owned by respectable real-estate families—for the most part, the same families who had owned the theatres since the thirties, the Brandts and the Shuberts. Times Square was Brechtville: a perfect demonstration of the principle that the market, left to itself, will produce an economy of crime as happily as an economy of virtue.

This—the crucial underlying reality in the Forty-second Street redevelopment—meant that the city, if it was to get the legal right to claim and condemn property in order to pass it over, had to be pointing toward some enormous, unquestioned commercial goal, larger or at least more concrete than the real goal, which was essentially ethical and "cultural." For once, the usual New York formula had to be turned right around: a question of virtue had to be disguised as a necessity of commerce. On Forty-second Street, a group of perfectly successful private businessmen in the movie-theatre business were being pushed aside in favor of a set of private businessmen in the tall-building business, and the legal argument for favoring the businessmen in the tall-building business was that they had promised that if you let them build a really tall building they would fix up the subway station.

This produced the Second Sacrificial Plan, of 1983: Philip Johnson and John Burgee's immense four towers straddling either side of Times Square on Forty-second, each with a slightly different pedimented top. The Semi-Ridiculous Rhetorical Statement invoked for this plan was that the pedimented tops "contextualized" the big buildings because they recalled the roofline of the old Astor Hotel, a victim of development twenty years before. They were by far the biggest and bulkiest buildings that had ever been proposed for midtown; Sagalyn gasps at the sheer zoning outrage of it. They had to be that big to establish their right to be at all. The Brandt family, which owned many of the theatres, sued and lost. "The Durst family interests put their name on five lawsuits," Sagalyn reports, "but the rumors of their financial backing of many more are legion." (The Dursts owned various individual lots along the street, which they intended to put together for their own giant building.) After ten years, they lost, too. Forty-seven suits were launched, and the plan withstood them all. The Johnson models, fortresses designed to withstand a siege of litigation, had triumphed. But nobody really wanted to build the buildings.

In the interim between the First Sacrificial Plan and the Second, however, something had changed in the ideology of architecture. A new orthodoxy had come into power, with an unapologetic emphasis on formal "delirium" and the chaotic surface of the city. In Rem Koolhaas's epoch-marking manifesto "Delirious New York" (1978), the buzz, confusion, danger, and weirdness of New York were no longer things to worry about. In fact, they were pretty much all we had to boast of. To an increasing bias in favor of small-scale streetscapes and "organic" growth was added a neon zip of pop glamour. The new ideology was Jane Jacobs dressed in latex and leather.

By what turned out to be a happy accident, this previously academic, pop-perverse set of ideas had influenced minds at the Municipal Art Society—the very group that had fought against the idea of signs and signage in Times Square at the turn of the century. In 1985, after the appearance of the Johnson plan, the Municipal Art Society, under the impeccable direction of the white-shoed Hugh Hardy, took on as its cause the preservation of the "bowl of light" in Times Square and "the glitz of its commercial billboards and electronic signs." After being digested in various acronymic gullets, this campaign produced not only new zoning text (sections ZR81-832 and ZR81-85, as Sagalyn duly notes) but, as an enforcement mechanism, an entirely new unit of measurement: the LUTS, or "Light Unit Times Square." (Each sign had to produce a minimum LUTS reading; the lighting designer Paul Marantz gave it its name.)

And so the Municipal Art Society became the major apostle of a con- 20 tinuing chaotic commercial environment in Times Square, while the big developers had to make the old Beaux-Arts case for classical order, lucidity, and space—for "trees and clean streets…museums and sidewalk cafés," in the plaintive words of the developer David Solomon. Eventually, in the early-nineties decline, Prudential, which had been holding on to the development on West Forty-second Street, was forced to sell its rights at a discount—to the Durst family, which had been leading the litigation against the plan all along but which, as everyone could have predicted, was there at the finale to develop and build, including 4 Times Square, the big building in which these words are being written.

None of this, however, could have created the new Times Square had it not been for other, unforeseeable changes. The first, and most important, was the still poorly explained decline in violent crime. (Traub tours the Eighth Avenue end of Forty-second with one of the district's privately financed security officers, who points out that there is still plenty of prostitution and drug-trafficking but very few muggings or assaults; even chain-snatching and petty theft are now rare.) This decline allowed for the emergence of the real hyperdrive of the new Square, the arrival of what every parent knows is the engine of American commerce: branded, television-based merchandise directed at "families" (that is, directed at getting children to torture their parents until they buy it). The critical demographic fact, as a few have pointed out, is the late onset of childbearing, delayed here until the habit of New York is set and the disposable income to spend on children is larger. When Damon Runyon was writing, the presence of Little Miss Marker in the Square was the material for a story. Now Little Miss Marker runs the place.

Of all the ironies of the Times Square redevelopment, the biggest is this: that the political right is, on the whole, happy with what has happened, and points to Times Square as an instance of how private enterprise can cure things that social engineering had previously destroyed, while the left points to Times Square as an instance of how market forces sterilize and drive out social forces of community and authenticity. But surely the ghosts of the old progressives in Union Square should be proudest of what has happened. It was, after all, the free market that produced the old Times Square: the porno stores were there because they made money, as part of a thriving market system. Times Square, and Forty-second Street, was saved by government decisions, made largely on civic grounds. Nothing would have caused more merriment on the conservative talk shows than the LUTS regulations—imagine some bureaucrat telling you how bright your sign should be—but it is those lights which light the desks of the guys at the offices of Clear Channel on Forty-second Street, and bring the crowds that make them safe. Civic-mindedness, once again, saved capitalism from itself.

And yet you don't have to have nostalgia for squalor and cruelty to feel that some vital chunk of New York experience has been replaced by something different, and less. Traub ends with the deconstructionist Mark Taylor, who trots out various depressions about the Society of Spectacle to explain the transformation, all of which are marvellously unilluminating. Times Square may be spectacular—that is what its signmakers have called their own signs for a century—but in the theoretical sense it's not a spectacle at all. It's not filled by media images that supplant the experience of real things. It's a tangible, physical, fully realized public square in which real people stare at things made by other people. The absence of spectacle, in that sense—the escape from the domination of isolated television viewing—is what still draws people on New Year's Eve, in the face of their own government's attempts to scare them away. (Dick Clark, of course, is a simulacrum, but he was born that way.)

Traub toys with the idea that the real problem lies in the replacement of an authentic "popular" culture, of arcades and Runyonesque song-pluggers, with a "mass" culture, of national brands and eager shoppers. But it's hard to see any principled way in which the twenty-foot-tall animatronic dinosaur at the new Toys R Us howls at the orders of mass culture, while O. J. Gude's dancing spearmen were purely Pop. The distinction between popular culture and mass culture is to our time what the distinction between true folk art and false folk art was to the age of Ruskin and Morris; we want passionately to define the difference because we know in our hearts that it doesn't exist. Even fairy tales turn out to be half manufactured by a commercial enterprise, half risen from the folkish ground. The idea that there is a good folkish culture that comes up from the streets and revivifies the arts and a bad mass culture imposed from above is an illusion, and anyone who has studied any piece of the history knows it.

25   All the same, there is something spooky about the contemporary Times Square. It wanders through you; you don't wander through it. One of the things that make for vitality in any city, and above all in New York, is the trinity of big buildings, bright lights, and weird stores. The big buildings and bright lights are there in the new Times Square, but the weird stores are not. By weird stores one means not simply small stores, mom-and-pop operations, but stores in which a peculiar and even obsessive entrepreneur caters to a peculiar and even an obsessive taste. (Art galleries and modestly ambitious restaurants are weird stores by definition. It's why they still feel very New York.) If the big buildings and the bright signs reflect the city's vitality and density, weird stores refract it; they imply that the city is so varied that someone can make a mundane living from one tiny obsessive thing. Poolrooms and boxing clubs were visible instances of weird stores in the old

Times Square; another, slightly less visible, was the thriving world of the independent film business, negative cutters, and camera-rental firms.

There is hardly a single weird store left on Broadway from Forty-second Street to Forty-sixth Street—hardly a single place in which a peculiar passion seems to have committed itself to a peculiar product. You have now, one more irony, to bend east, toward respectable Fifth Avenue, toward the diamond merchants and the Brazilian restaurants and the kosher cafeterias that still fill the side streets, to recreate something that feels a little like the old Times Square. (Wonderful Forty-fifth Street! With the Judaica candlesticks and the Japanese-film rental and the two-story shops selling cheap clothes and stereos, lit up bright.) Social historians like to talk about the Tragedy of the Commons, meaning the way that everybody loses when everybody overgrazes the village green, though it is in no individual's interest to stop. In New York, we suffer from a Tragedy of the Uncommons: weird things make the city worth living in, but though each individual wants them, no one individual wants to pay to keep them going. Times Square, as so often in the past, is responding, in typically heightened form, to the general state of the city: the loss of retail variety troubles us everywhere, as a new trinity of monotony—Starbucks, Duane Reade, and the Washington Mutual Bank—appears to dominate every block. We just feel it more on Broadway.

Do we overdraw Times Square history, make it more epic than it ought to be? Piccadilly and Soho, in London, and Place de Clichy, in Paris, are similar places, have known similar kinds of decline and similar kinds of pickup—but without gathering quite the same emotion. We make Times Square do more work than it ought to. Other great cities have public spaces and pleasure spaces, clearly marked, and with less confusion between them. When Diana died, it was Kensington Palace, not Piccadilly, that got the flowers, and in Paris it is the Champs-Élysées, not Place de Clichy, that gets the military parade on the fourteenth of July. Which returns us, with a certain sense of awe, to the spell still cast by the original sin of the 1811 grid plan. We make our accidental pleasure plazas do the work of the public squares we don't have. This is asking a lot of a sign, or even a bunch of bright ones lighting up the night.

Things to Do with the Reading

1. This essay offers a number of models for how to analyze that are worthy of imitating. One is its use of the APPEARS TO BE ABOUT X, BUT IS REALLY ABOUT Y gambit (see Chapter 5) to distinguish the "myths" about rebuilding from the "history." Make note of all the too-easy answers—the misconceptions—that Gopnik points out.

2. Link: The reversals in this essay (mentioned above) also call to mind the fondness for paradox we pointed to in Gambino's piece. How

does Gambino's treatment of such complicated notions as "creative destruction" resemble and differ from Gopnik's treatment of the tangled history of Times Square's redevelopment? You might note, by the way, (and analyze) Gopnik's own fondness for verbal paradox, as in his discussion of the responses of the political left and right (see paragraph 22). A sentence in Gopnik that invites linkage to Gambino's perspective is "the transformation [of Times Square] could be made only by large-scale condemnation of what was already there" (paragraph 14).

3. **Link:** In his essay, "The Public Realm and the Common Good," Kunstler has much to say about "civic" matters and about the commercial pressures that have shaped Americans' use of space. Use Kunstler as a lens for looking at Gopnik's essay. What, for example, might Kunstler say about the various plans for Times Square? Also consider how Gopnik's perspective might alter (complicate, qualify) Kunstler's. Useful sentences in Gopnik for this purpose are: "Civic-mindedness, once again, saved capitalism from itself" and "Times Square, and Forty-second Street, were saved by government decisions, made largely on civic grounds" (paragraph 22).

4. This essay is full of proper names. See, for example, paragraph 7: Damon Runyan (whose name coined the adjective "Runyonesque," which appears throughout the piece), P.G. Wodehouse, and [Samuel] Johnson, among others. Make a list of names mentioned in Gopnik's piece and then Google them. How are these "allusions" functioning in this essay— what do they provide? Why does Gopnik do this? And what does this way of proceeding suggest about his assumptions about his audience— readers of The New Yorker? (See the discussion of ethos in Chapter 1.)

5. **Application:** Don't let the witty way that Gopnik names the stages of redevelopment lead you to dismiss them as merely comic. The "familiar form" that he educes in four parts—the Sacrificial Plan, the Semi-Ridiculous Rhetorical Statement, the Staged Intervention of the Professionals, and the Sorry Thing Itself—offers a potent lens for examining redevelopment elsewhere. An obvious case in point is New Orleans. How might we apply the four steps to the rebuilding efforts going on there? Do some research in the popular press (and/or Google) on the way that this (or any) major project of urban rebuilding is being talked about and planned. Identify one or more Sacrificial Plans, Semi-Ridiculous Rhetorical Statements, and so forth. Then use your answers to fuel a few pages (or more) of analysis.

You could also use Gopnik as a lens for examining something more local. Gopnik, like Kunstler, addresses the issue of zoning. Locate a zoning issue where you live and analyze it from Gopnik's and/or Kunstler's point of view.

Rosalyn Baxandall and Elizabeth Ewen

Suburban Birth Pangs

This piece, taken from the authors' book entitled *Picture Windows: How the Suburbs Happened*, documents the rise of Long Island as an example of suburban expansion. The discussion focuses on the role that urban planner Robert Moses played in the conversion of Long Island from an unregulated and sparsely populated enclave for the rich to a diverse network of communities. The story of the development of Long Island reveals how deeply embedded our national assumptions are about social class, race, and land ownership.

When New York City folk decided to take advantage of their new free 1 weekends by packing a picnic, hopping into a car, and heading to the country for sunshine and space, Long Island seemed a logical destination. Around the turn of the century New York City had built many bridges linking the city to the island by automobile; Long Island therefore was accessible as well as close.[1] Although the landed gentry did everything in their power to keep city people out of their private playgrounds, urban interlopers in their new, affordable Model Ts began to acquire a taste for space, sun, and sea—and some even dared to dream of owning a home on Long Island.

In 1925, for instance, Brooklyn-bred Seth and Peggy Mills inherited a dry goods store, bought a Model T, and began taking day trips to Long Island. As Peggy put it, "In those days it took a long time; the roads were so bad, the car often broke down. But still it was worth it. The sight of those rolling hills, something you'd only see in the pictures, I'll never forget it. Coming from Brooklyn, the countryside seemed endless and you could finally be alone. Even on weekends when we couldn't make the trip, we'd sit around and dream of what it would be like to live there."[2]

Clearly these dreams could not be realized on the elite North Shore, which estate owners considered their personal domain. They went to great lengths to keep it so, building huge walls around their estates and posting armed guards at the borders to prevent errant day-trippers from meandering onto the grounds.

Wealthy Long Islanders also made sure the North Shore was difficult to circumnavigate. At their behest, officials in Nassau County allowed all public roads to fall into disrepair. Moreover, private estate roads were built like mazes—winding and deliberately confusing. Most of the North and South Shore beaches were marked CLOSED with large private property signs, and were guarded as well. The only beaches open to the public were rocky, unappealing, and pitifully narrow, and city residents had to pay exorbitant rates to the local towns to use them.

Copyright © 2000 Elizabeth Ewen, *Picture Windows*. Reprinted by permission of Perseus Books Group.

5   Opulent estate owners also made sure that the journey itself to Long Island was arduous. Northern Boulevard, a main access road through Queens to the North Shore, was the widest highway, 160 feet of macadam (a pavement of small layers of stone, bound with tar). At the city line, it shrank to 18 feet of deteriorating pavement, eventually becoming dirt and dust. Cars had to go single file and watch for gaping holes and unpaved stretches. Desperate families often tried to picnic at the side of the road, but the ever vigilant guards made their stops brief. The average Sunday journey of thirty-two miles in 1923, from the Queensborough Bridge to Huntington, took four hours. As Robert Caro noted, "when the families of New York City reached Long Island, they found the milk and honey sour indeed."[3]

The robber barons also insured that railroad travel to Long Island was difficult. A wealthy group led by Charles Pratt, a partner of John D. Rockefeller, bought enough stock in the Long Island Railroad to control the North Shore lines.[4] Following the dictum of a Long Island Railroad vice-president that "population follows transportation," Pratt made sure that the North Shore branches were never electrified, because it would make for faster, more comfortable, and cheaper travel.[5]

As more city residents bought Model Ts, an increasing number of people became frustrated by the inaccessibility of Long Island's vast stretches of pristine beach lands. Mounting pressure for access to Long Island's sun and sand and the relentless intransigence of the rich combined to create an impasse.

The influential urban planner Robert Moses was one of the few men with enough power, guts, know-how, and vision to confront the estate owners and insist that they open up Long Island. Moses had worked in progressive reform organizations, such as the Good Government Commission, and had the ear and respect of powerful politicians, such as Al Smith, then governor of New York State. In his capacity, first as the president of the Long Island Park Commission (1924–1936) and later as park commissioner for the metropolitan area and surroundings (1936–1964), Moses wielded the political power to float special bond issues to finance and appropriate land for highways, water crossings, beaches, and parks.[6] He believed that the public had as much right to recreation and leisure activity as the wealthy.

In 1922, Moses rented a summer bungalow in Babylon with his wife and small children and fell in love "with the town, with the bay, with the whole South Shore."[7] As he commuted on the Long Island Railroad and looked out the window, he saw "thick leafy bands of wood and through the trees the blue waters of ponds and streams." Moses began to explore, looking up the property rights in local libraries and trekking by foot through vast forests and streams. His eyes burned with ideas, and he soon discovered that the South Shore contained 3,500 acres of empty, unused land close to the city line not owned by the robber barons or local Long Island governments. It was owned by the government of New York City, which meant that "land could be opened to the cities' people merely by turning a key." Moreover, beyond lay another vast reserve of unused land, reachable only by boat: Jones Beach and Fire Island. Jones Beach seemed remote, but Moses realized that it was a mere twenty-five miles from Times Square.[8]

Moses proposed building two connecting highways to link the city to the beach, and making the beach a public park. The idea was revolutionary. Up to that point, most country parks were originally conceived as habitats to be hiked and canoed through and kept in their natural wild state—they could not be reached by automobile and so remained unused. Yet Moses' proposal to make Jones Beach into a park transformed and domesticated the concept of the pristine nature preserve. His plan incorporated baseball diamonds, tennis courts, golf courses, and swimming pools—not exclusively for the rich but for less affluent city people.

Even though Moses wanted to see Long Island more accessible, his desire for democratization was limited. Like most mainstream progressives of the time, Moses made a distinction between the public and the common people. As Frances Perkins, later the secretary of labor under Franklin D. Roosevelt and a longtime associate of Moses, observed:

> He'd denounce the common people terribly. To him they were lousy, dirty people, throwing bottles all over Jones Beach.... He loves the public, but not as people. The public is just the public. It's a great amorphous mass to him; it needs to be bathed, it needs to be aired, it needs recreation, but not for personal reasons—just to make it a better public.[9]

As parks commissioner, Moses had the clout to put his convictions into practice. Although he opened the beach to automobile traffic, making sure there was sufficient parking for huge numbers of cars, he vetoed any plans for making the parks accessible by rapid public transit; Moses wouldn't even extend a Long Island Railroad line to Jones Beach. He made park access to those without cars even more difficult by building bridges across the new parkways so low that chartered buses had to take slow, indirect local roads. Later on, during the Depression, Moses charged 50 cents for entry to Jones Beach, in violation of the American tradition of free public parks.

Moses considered African-Americans inherently "dirty" and took specific measures to deny them access to the parks. Permits required for buses to enter public parks often were denied to black groups, especially permits for Jones Beach. Most chartered trips were shunted to parks many miles away from the entrance to Jones Beach, and even in those parks buses carrying black passengers were directed to the farthest reaches of the parking areas. Blacks were discouraged by park officials from using the best "white" beaches; and the handful of black lifeguards were stationed at the most distant and least developed beaches. Moses believed that African-Americans did not like cold water and had the temperature at the Jones Beach swimming pool deliberately kept ice cold in an effort to keep blacks out.[10]

Despite his undemocratic definition of the people, these actions taken by Moses were still far too democratic for the Long Island elite. While wealthy Long Islanders did not contest the construction of the Southern State Parkway, which provided access to Jones Beach but did not trespass on their vast holdings, the construction of the Northern State Parkway was another story. When the plans of the Long Island State Park Commission called for a parkway to be built in the northern part of Nassau and Suffolk counties—cutting east through their estates—the ruling class issued a clarion call to halt the highway's invasion of their territory.

15 Declaring that the parkway would allow the Gold Coast to be "overrun with rabble from the city,"[11] estate owners used their powerful connections in Long Island and Albany to pass legislation abolishing the Long Island State Park Commission and its authority to allocate money for construction. Moses, however, had the ear of the Governor, Al Smith, who considered himself one of the rabble and their chief defender. The war was on. The state legislature favored Long Island's elite and passed bill after bill, only to be thwarted by the governor's veto.

After many years of skirmishes, a compromise was struck. The Northern State Parkway was built in spite of the estate owners' opposition, but the highway was routed far from the estates of the most powerful group of landowners. This compromise was costly for both drivers, who now had to go miles out of their way, and taxpayers, who had to finance a land purchase for the 2.3 miles of additional road. This might seem minute, but it illustrates the power of the estate owners: Drivers now had to go 839.5 miles out of their way each year.

The North Shore elite may have won the battle to preserve their dominion, but they lost the war. After the completion of the highways and beaches, an infrastructure that supported the development of housing, industry, leisure, and recreation on the South Shore sprang up seemingly overnight. In 1920 there were no highways on Long Island; but 12 years later there was a modern interconnected parkway system linking the various Long Island communities and allowing easy access to New York City. When Moses became president of Long Island State Park Commission, there was only one underutilized state park. In 1928, only four years later, there were fourteen state parks totaling 9,700 acres—parks that were automobile-accessible and outfitted with modern recreational facilities.[12]

Many people who flocked to Long Island for recreation and a temporary respite from city life decided to settle permanently, especially on the flatter, less well-landscaped South Shore, which was not dominated by powerful elites. At the turn of the century the South Shore of Long Island—which eventually would house the quintessential suburb of Levittown—was still predominantly rural, inhabited by fishermen, farmers, artisans, and trades-people. Freeport, the second-largest village in Nassau County, was a major South Shore fishing port; oystering, clamming, and whaling were the predominant industries. In 1892, Freeport became an incorporated village, which attested to its economic importance.

By the early 1920s, Freeport had emerged as an open, public resort and summer haven. Located near Astoria, Queens, then the moviemaking capital of the East Coast, Freeport became a vacation center for the aristocracy of the burgeoning entertainment industry. Freeport developed its own entertainment, too, with summer theaters and a giant amusement park that opened in 1923 on the waterfront. Playland had numerous rides, vaudeville shows, dance halls, and a saltwater swimming pool.[13] Mimicking the industrial elite, the entertainers built large and luxurious mansions and hotels, albeit on a smaller scale. This in turn attracted actors, movie stars, comedians, singers, and stagehands.

By the mid-1920s, Freeport's original working population of artisans 20 and farmers swelled to include European immigrants and a small colony of African-Americans who migrated from South Carolina and Georgia to work as domestic servants for rich entertainers and a newly arrived middle class. Recruited or brought to Long Island by relatives or agencies, they settled in small, segregated enclaves, many near the railroad tracks and some in Bennington Park in the center of Freeport. These South Shore communities originally were built through family, church, and kinship ties.

Local resident Louise Simpson, who worked on voter registration forms that included information on where people were born, observed this distinct pattern:

> I realized that they were all from the same area in South Carolina, a lot from Charleston.... Freeport was a hub, it had good transportation for people migrating to do domestic work. For domestics, it was okay, you had one day off and every other Sunday. Freeport got to be a meeting place for people who did domestic work and they were able to find work in the large homes; there were rooming houses, so when they quit a job they could find a room. This is how friendships developed: if you're from my hometown, I'm going to seek you out. You felt comfortable, you knew each other. If you didn't go that route of family and friends, there was this particular family who was sort of like a personnel person for employment. She would go to where she came from in Carolina and bring people up, or tell them to get in touch and their transportation would be paid. Freeport blossomed like that.[14]

Harve Sinklar-Herring, who came from South Carolina, ran such an employment agency. Her first contact with Freeport was in 1927, when she came up with her cousin to work as a domestic servant for the summer. She also found work as a chauffeur and a caterer. Using these skills, she opened a domestic service agency, first in her home and then in a large house that encompassed an office, a dormitory, and a staff of twenty. She recruited and trained women from South Carolina in domestic work. She claims to have had "the only agency like this. I advertised in local papers. I charged employers who hired the women. I charged the domestics room and board while I trained them."[15]

Like other railroad depot towns of the South Shore, Freeport had significant real estate activity. Large tracts of land were bought by speculators, builders, and developers. Freeport participated in a nationwide suburban housing boom. Indeed, Nassau County, including Freeport, was the fastest growing county in the United States in the 1920s.[16] Planned communities and large subdivisions promoted by developers like the Freeport Land Company were aimed at upper-middle-class families, some of whom had vacationed in and around Freeport and were drawn to town life within easy access of the city.

Seth and Peggy Mills could not find a house on the North Shore, so they bought a lot and built a Tudor house in Freeport. "We couldn't move to the North Shore, our original dream, but we did find a house within reach of the city with beautiful beaches, quiet streets, and flowers and trees," said Peggy. "We felt like we were living rich in miniature."[17] The Mills were part of a trend of new upper-middle-class suburban home owners.

25   Between 1922 and 1929, six million new homes went up across the nation—twice as many as in any previous seven-year period. Well over half were single-family homes. Rising wages and falling housing prices propelled the construction industry. The suburbs grew twice as rapidly as the center cities in the 1920s; nearly one out of six Americans lived in the suburbs by 1930.[18] The increased availability of mortgages made it easier to borrow money. This growth, however, benefited only the upper and upper-middle classes. Three quarters of the new housing continued to be marketed to the top third of the household income spectrum, and there was no production at all for the bottom third, categorized as living below "any decent standard."[19] The 1920 census indicated that 46 percent of all American families were home owners, although in metropolitan areas—where the poor lived—fewer families owned homes. New York City had the lowest rate of home ownership with only 12 percent. Residential patterns remained segregated along economic and racial lines.

This segregation reflected deep prejudices that were manifested in Freeport. Freeport's expansion was welcomed by many of its summer visitors and new residents, but many older local Anglo-Saxon residents felt threatened by the flamboyant entertainers and the new immigrants who had come to settle there. The Ku Klux Klan flourished in the 1920s, reflecting and inflaming local fears of immigrants, Catholics, Jews, African-Americans, and ethnic entertainers. During the early 1920s, one out of every eight white residents in Nassau and Suffolk counties was a member of the Klan. On July 4, 1924, 30,000 spectators looked on as 2,000 robed Klansmen marched with their floats down Main Street. In Freeport, the Klan's membership included several local ministers, the chief of police, county workers, and a wide array of other townspeople—a list that would have made a civic club or organization proud; but the Klan was no Kiwanis club. It held cross burnings at Christmastime, Lincoln's birthday, and the Fourth of July. It actively tried to keep black people confined to Bennington Park and out of Roosevelt, a neighboring white community.[20]

In her 1993 book *Having Our Say*, Elizabeth (Bessie) Delany provides a rare firsthand account of a confrontation between the Ku Klux Klan and African Americans on Long Island. In the 1920s the Delany sisters had moved to New York City in search of further education and greater opportunities. Bessie was solidly middle class and one of the few female black dentists in Harlem. One Sunday she and her boyfriend were returning from the beach, heading back toward Sag Harbor, a predominantly black seaside resort town:

> We came around the corner of this two-lane road, and there are about twenty men dressed in white robes, hoods and all, stopping cars and searching. You could see that they were making colored people get out of their cars! Well, my eyes popped out of my head, I said, "Aren't you going to stop?" But my friend never answered me. He stepped on the gas and drove around them, up an embankment and everything, and next thing I knew we had just zoomed around them.... I believe we simply outran them. Here, all those long years in the South they [our parents] had managed to keep us Delany children out of the hands of the KKK and they'd almost got their hands on me—on Long Island.[21]

Racism did not only manifest itself through the organizational activities of the Klan. It was deeply inscribed into all the codes that governed who could live where. During the 1920s, restrictive covenants prevented the sale of property to Mexicans, Asians, blacks, and Jews. Although the U.S. Supreme Court struck down municipal and residential segregation laws in 1917, real estate boards and property owner associations concocted contractual "gentlemen's" agreements to prevent class, religious, and racial integration. Economic restrictions such as house prices, codes that prevented the construction of two-family houses and apartments, loan and mortgage policies, and minimum lot sizes all kept the suburbs closed to anyone who wasn't white, Protestant, wealthy, or upper middle class.[22] Zoning regulations also determined whether towns would be industrial and working class or residential and suburban.

Even the select segment of the population *not* excluded from the new suburbs by restrictive covenants or zoning encountered problems. The housing industry at the time was small, makeshift, local, and unregulated. At best it was a patchwork that included genuine growth in real estate sales and housing subdivisions, as well as unscrupulous promoters and developers creating speculative profit-making schemes. By the mid-1920s, large auctions of land tracts were opening, promoted for investment speculation. Developers used newly conceived advertising techniques to sell both property and whole communities not yet built.

30   Lavish brochures and advertising folders, for example, claimed the Biltmore Shores in Massapequa had "paved streets, fine homes, a vast park, modern shops, churches, schools, golf, tennis, yachting and riding clubs, and a splendid fire department and complete administrative system."[23] This was all fiction. When people bought land sight unseen from speculators, they risked getting burned. One group of investors from Dayton, Ohio, tried to sell their Long Island property only to learn it was nothing but worthless land. The unscrupulous activities of the "land sharks" caused one reader of the *New York Times* to write to the editor, "My advice is to leave all Long Island property alone."[24]

According to *Architectural Forum*, much of this fly-by-night development was shoddy. Suburban home construction in Long Island was considered the worst in the nation. Bradley Randall, chief underwriter for New York, did a study of Long Island building and found that "examples of faulty construction most prevalent were two plaster coats instead of three, no fire stopping, insufficient thickness of foundation walls, poor quality timber and flooring ... no collar beams between rafters and other minor sins of commission and omission."[25] One writer in *Architectural Forum* observed that "no phrase more aptly conveys the thought of miserable home development practice than the brand, 'cheap Long Island.'"[26]

Although there was a housing boom in the 1920s—albeit mainly shoddy and speculative—by 1925 it had peaked, followed by a rapid downturn in construction. By 1929, residential housing had dropped 46 percent to 509,000 units. In dollars this meant a decline from $4.5 billion in 1925 to $2.45 billion in 1929.[27] The breakdown of the housing market was the bellwether of the Great Depression.

Suburban housing had accelerated in the early 1920s, but its financing had become precarious. Single-family dwellings typically were purchased through an unsound web of first, second, and even third mortgages generally of short terms and without any built-in orderly system for repayment.[28] As the depression deepened and people lost their jobs, they were sitting ducks for defaults and foreclosures.

With the onset of the Great Depression, credit was frozen and no capital was available for speculation in housing. Upscale 1920s housing based on speculation by unscrupulous promoters failed. The widespread failure of real estate and bond scandals resulted in the loss of new high-priced city apartments and suburban developments. By 1932 the housing decline reached epic proportions. As one scholar noted, "In 1930 total housing production receded to a point 60 percent below the 1922–28 average; by 1931 the rate had descended 69 percent below that average. ... In 1932 foreclosures reached the disastrous level of 250,000 homes."[29]

Unlike European countries, the United Stated had never developed strat- 35
egies to deal with the issue of housing on a national level. It had no federal
housing programs or policies, no public housing for low-income and working-
class families, and no financial guarantees to aid the middle class in case
of bank credit or mortgage failures. The federal government's lack of federal housing policies reflected the American belief in individualism, private
enterprise, and individual home ownership, an ideology eloquently expressed
by President Herbert Hoover, who claimed with confidence, "The sentiment
for home ownership is so embedded in the American heart that millions of
people who dwell in tenements, apartments, and rental rows of solid brick
have the aspirations for wider opportunity in ownership of their own home."[30]
The sentiment might have been there, but sentiment alone could not build
houses—especially when the fledging housing industry had already collapsed.

Notes

[1] Robert A. Caro, *The Power Broker: Robert Moses and the Rise and Fall of New York* (New York: Vintage, 1975), 144–47. Westchester barred its parks to anyone not a resident of the county, and New Jersey was accessible only by privately operated ferries that took a long time. Long Island was accessible by the Brooklyn Bridge (1883), the Williamsburg Bridge (1903), the Queensborough Bridge (1909), and the Manhattan Bridge (1909).

[2] Peggy and Seth Mills, interview by authors, March 1993.

[3] Caro, *Power Broker*, 153.

[4] Ibid, 151.

[5] Dennis P. Sorbin, *The Dynamics of Community Control*, Empire State Historical Publication Series 59 (Port Washington: Ira Friedman Inc., 1968), 113.

[6] On Long Island Moses built the Van Wyck, Long Island, Willowbrook, Northern State, and Seaford-Oyster Bay Expressways, the Wantaugh, Bethpage, Grand Central, Southern State, Meadowbrook, and Cross Island Parkways, and the Cross Bay, Queensborough, Bronx Whitestone, and Triborough Bridges, and the Robert Moses Causeway, as well as twenty-one parks. See http://www.boone.calstatela .edu/g476winter98KirbyMoses.html.

[7] Caro, *Power Broker*, 157.

[8] Ibid., 157–59.

[9] Ibid., 318.

[10] Ibid., 318–19.

[11] Bernie Bookbinder, *Long Island People and Places Past and Present* (New York: Newsday Books/Harry Abrams, 1983), 202.

[12] Caro, *Power Broker*, 238.

[13] Bookbinder, *Long Island People*, 139.

[14] Louise Simpson, interview by authors, April 1991.

[15] Harve Sinklar-Herring, interview by authors, September 1991.

[16] Jon C. Teaford, *Post-Suburbia, Government and Politics in the Edge Cities* (Baltimore, MD: Johns Hopkins University Press, 1997), 33.

[17] Peggy Mills, interview by authors, March 1993.

[18] Kenneth Jackson, *Crabgrass Frontier: The Suburbanisation of the United States* (New York: Oxford University Press, 1985), 174–75; *Who Built America: From the Gilded Age to the Present*, vol. 11. American Social History Project, ed. (New York: Pantheon Books, 1992), 274–75.

[19] Nathaniel Schneider Keith, *Politics and the Housing Crisis Since 1930* (New York: Universe Books, 1973), 17; Gwendolyn Wright, *Building the Dream: A Social History of Housing in America* (Boston: MIT Press, 1983), 195.

[20] *The New York Times*, 19 January 1923, 13 February 1923, 19 March 1923, 29 August 1923, 16 August 1924, 15 December 1924, 11 August 1992, *Newsday*, 7 November 1982. See Jane Gombieski, "Klokards, Kleagles, Kludds, and Kluxers: The Ku Klux Klan in Suffolk County, 1915–1928." *Long Island Historical Journal* 6 (Fall 1993): 41–62, for an informative analysis of the growth of the KKK and its activities on Long Island.

[21] Sarah Delany and Elizabeth Delany, *Having Our Say: The Delany Sisters' First Hundred Years* (New York: Kodansha International, 1993), 139.

[22] Wright, *Building the Dream*, 212.

[23] Edward Smits, *Nassau Suburbia USA* (Garden City, NY: Doubleday, 1974; rev. ed., 1990), 184.

[24] Marilyn E. Weingold, *American Mediterranean: An Environmental, Economic, and Social History of the Long Island Sound* (Port Washington, NY: Kennikat Press, 1974), 91.

[25] *Architectural Forum*, "Sub Divisions and the FHA," May 1935, 487.

[26] Ibid., "Nassau Shores," 465.

[27] Keith, *Politics and the Housing Crisis*, 17.

[28] Ibid., 18.

[29] Ibid., 19.

[30] Richard O. Davies, *Housing Reform During the Truman Administration* (Columbia: University of Missouri Press, 1966), 11.

Things to Do with the Reading

1. Look over the essay, focusing on how the authors use numbers and dates. What is the relation between these kinds of facts and the various firsthand accounts the authors include from ordinary people and from famous ones? Examine how the essay uses different kinds of evidence. (See More Than Just "the Facts": What Counts as Evidence? in Chapter 4.) To what ends does it marshal evidence—to support and advance what

claims? How does the piece ultimately wish us to regard the rise of Long Island and—more generally— the rise of the suburbs? To what extent can you determine its point of view?

2. Link: Among the most notorious remarks about Robert Moses is Francis Perkins' comment that "He'd denounce the common people terribly. To him they were lousy, dirty people, throwing bottles all over Jones Beach. … He loves the public, but not as people" (paragraph 11). How does Moses' notion of the public compare with other writers' notions included in this book? How does it compare with the point of view toward the public in Kunstler's essay at the beginning of this chapter, or of Gopnik's? How does the way Jonathan Franzen thinks about the public and the private (in Chapter 12) compare with the way Baxandall and Ewen conceive of them? Locate specific sentences from both "Suburban Birth Pangs" and the essay of your choice and use them to anchor your comparison.

3. Application: The essay concludes by distinguishing the United States from Europe, in that it "never developed strategies to deal with the issue of housing on a national level," and the authors assert that "the federal government's lack of housing policies reflected the American belief in individualism, private enterprise, and individual home owner- ship" (paragraph 35). They follow this assertion with a quotation from President Hoover identifying home ownership with the American dream. How might we use these concluding remarks as a lens for interpret- ing the state of the housing market in America today? Look up recent commentaries on housing. Check the records on the numbers of fore- closures. How has the credit crisis affected those trying to refinance? How are the banks, which lost millions on poor-risk mortgages, playing a role, making it difficult for some categories of people to get mortgages?

Jane Jacobs

The Uses of Sidewalks: Safety

This piece is excerpted from Jane Jacobs' *The Death and Life of Great American Cities* (1961), a work commonly ranked among the most influential American books on urban planning. A journalist, activist, and author, Jacobs fought to protect neighborhoods from projects, such as Robert Moses' plans for a lower Manhattan expressway through Washington Square Park. In a style of simple eloquence, Jacobs argues against the prevailing approach toward urban renewal in the 1950s, offering a point of view that remains pertinent today:"that the sight of people attracts still other people, is something that city planners and city architectural designers seem to find incomprehensible. They operate on the premise that city people seek the sight of emptiness, obvious order, and quiet. Nothing could be less true."Jacobs is credited with being one of the inspirations for the New Urbanist movement. In 2004, two years before her death, she published her last book, *Dark Age Ahead*.

1 Streets in cities serve many purposes besides carrying vehicles, and city side-walks—the pedestrian parts of the streets—serve many purposes besides carrying pedestrians. These uses are bound up with circulation but are not identical with it and in their own right they are at least as basic as circulation to the proper workings of cities.

A city sidewalk by itself is nothing. It is an abstraction. It means something only in conjunction with the buildings and other uses that border it, or border other sidewalks very near it. The same might be said of streets, in the sense that they serve other purposes besides carrying wheeled traffic in their middles. Streets and their sidewalks, the main public places of a city, are its most vital organs. Think of a city and what comes to mind? Its streets. If a city's streets look interesting, the city looks interesting; if they look dull, the city looks dull.

More than that, and here we get down to the first problem, if a city's streets are safe from barbarism and fear, the city is thereby tolerably safe from barbarism and fear. When people say that a city, or a part of it, is dangerous or is a jungle what they mean primarily is that they do not feel safe on the sidewalks.

But sidewalks and those who use them are not passive beneficiaries of safety or helpless victims of danger. Sidewalks, their bordering uses, and their users, are active participants in the drama of civilization versus barbarism in cities. To keep the city safe is a fundamental task of a city's streets and its sidewalks.

5 This task is totally unlike any service that sidewalks and streets in little towns or true suburbs are called upon to do. Great cities are not like towns,

From THE DEATH AND LIFE OF GREAT AMERICAN CITIES by Jane Jacobs, copyright © 1961, 1989 by Jane Jacobs. Used by permission of Random House, Inc.

only larger. They are not like suburbs, only denser. They differ from towns and suburbs in basic ways, and one of these is that cities are, by definition, full of strangers. To any one person, strangers are far more common in big cities than acquaintances. More common not just in places of public assembly, but more common at a man's own doorstep. Even residents who live near each other are strangers, and must be, because of the sheer number of people in small geographical compass.

The bedrock attribute of a successful city district is that a person must feel personally safe and secure on the street among all these strangers. He must not feel automatically menaced by them. A city district that fails in this respect also does badly in other ways and lays up for itself, and for its city at large, mountain on mountain of trouble.

Today barbarism has taken over many city streets, or people fear it has, which comes to much the same thing in the end. "I live in a lovely, quiet residential area," says a friend of mine who is hunting another place to live. "The only disturbing sound at night is the occasional scream of someone being mugged." It does not take many incidents of violence on a city street, or in a city district, to make people fear the streets. And as they fear them, they use them less, which makes the streets still more unsafe.

To be sure, there are people with hobgoblins in their heads, and such people will never feel safe no matter what the objective circumstances are. But this is a different matter from the fear that besets normally prudent, tolerant and cheerful people who show nothing more than common sense in refusing to venture after dark—or in a few places, by day—into streets where they may well be assaulted, unseen or unrescued until too late.

The barbarism and the real, not imagined, insecurity that gives rise to such fears cannot be tagged a problem of the slums. The problem is most serious, in fact, in genteel-looking "quiet residential areas" like that my friend was leaving.

It cannot be tagged as a problem of older parts of cities. The problem 10 reaches its most baffling dimensions in some examples of rebuilt parts of cities, including supposedly the best examples of rebuilding, such as middle-income projects. The police precinct captain of a nationally admired project of this kind (admired by planners and lenders) has recently admonished residents not only about hanging around outdoors after dark but has urged them never to answer their doors without knowing the caller. Life here has much in common with life for the three little pigs or the seven little kids of the nursery thrillers. The problem of sidewalk and doorstep insecurity is as serious in cities which have made conscientious efforts at rebuilding as it is in those cities that have lagged. Nor is it illuminating to tag minority groups, or the poor, or the outcast with responsibility for city danger. There are immense variations in the degree of civilization and safety found among such groups and among the city areas where they live. Some of the safest sidewalks in New York City, for example, at any time of day or night, are those along which poor people or minority groups live. And some of the most dangerous are in streets occupied by the same kinds of people. All this can also be said of other cities.

Deep and complicated social ills must lie behind delinquency and crime, in suburbs and towns as well as in great cities. This book will not go into speculation on the deeper reasons. It is sufficient, at this point, to say that if we are to maintain a city society that can diagnose and keep abreast of deeper social problems, the starting point must be, in any case, to strengthen whatever workable forces for maintaining safety and civilization do exist—in the cities we do have. To build city districts that are custom made for easy crime is idiotic. Yet that is what we do.

The first thing to understand is that the public peace—the sidewalk and street peace—of cities is not kept primarily by the police, necessary as police are. It is kept primarily by an intricate, almost unconscious, network of voluntary controls and standards among the people themselves, and enforced by the people themselves. In some city areas—older public housing projects and streets with very high population turnover are often conspicuous examples—the keeping of public sidewalk law and order is left almost entirely to the police and special guards. Such places are jungles. No amount of police can enforce civilization where the normal, casual enforcement of it has broken down.

The second thing to understand is that the problem of insecurity cannot be solved by spreading people out more thinly, trading the characteristics of cities for the characteristics of suburbs. If this could solve danger on the city streets, then Los Angeles should be a safe city because superficially Los Angeles is almost all suburban. It has virtually no districts compact enough to qualify as dense city areas. Yet Los Angeles cannot, any more than any other great city, evade the truth that, being a city, it is composed of strangers not all of whom are nice. Los Angeles' crime figures are flabbergasting. Among the seventeen standard metropolitan areas with populations over a million, Los Angeles stands so pre-eminent in crime that it is in a category by itself. And this is markedly true of crimes associated with personal attack, the crimes that make people fear the streets.

Los Angeles, for example, has a forcible rape rate (1958 figures) of 31.9 per 100,000 population, more than twice as high as either of the next two cities, which happen to be St. Louis and Philadelphia; three times as high as the rate of 10.1 for Chicago, and more than four times as high as the rate of 7.4 for New York.

15   In aggravated assault, Los Angeles has a rate of 185, compared with 149.5 for Baltimore and 139.2 for St. Louis (the two next highest), and with 90.9 for New York and 79 for Chicago.

The overall Los Angeles rate for major crimes is 2,507.6 per 100,000 people, far ahead of St. Louis and Houston, which come next with 1,634.5 and 1,541.1, and of New York and Chicago, which have rates of 1,145.3 and 943.5.

The reasons for Los Angeles' high crime rates are undoubtedly complex, and at least in part obscure. But of this we can be sure: thinning out a city does not insure safety from crime and fear of crime. This is one of the conclusions that can be drawn within individual cities too, where pseudosuburbs or superannuated suburbs are ideally suited to rape, muggings, beatings, hold-ups and the like.

Here we come up against an all-important question about any city street: How much easy opportunity does it offer to crime? It may be that there is some absolute amount of crime in a given city, which will find an outlet somehow (I do not believe this). Whether this is so or not, different kinds of city streets garner radically different shares of barbarism and fear of barbarism.

Some city streets afford no opportunity to street barbarism. The streets of the North End of Boston are outstanding examples. They are probably as safe as any place on earth in this respect. Although most of the North End's residents are Italian or of Italian descent, the district's streets are also heavily and constantly used by people of every race and background. Some of the strangers from outside work in or close to the district; some come to shop and stroll; many, including members of minority groups who have inherited dangerous districts previously abandoned by others, make a point of cashing their paychecks in North End stores and immediately making their big weekly purchases in streets where they know they will not be parted from their money between the getting and the spending.

Frank Havey, director of the North End Union, the local settlement house, 20 says, "I have been here in the North End twenty-eight years, and in all that time I have never heard of a single case of rape, mugging, molestation of a child or other street crime of that sort in the district. And if there had been any, I would have heard of it even if it did not reach the papers." Half a dozen times or so in the past three decades, says Havey, would-be molesters have made an attempt at luring a child or, late at night, attacking a woman. In every such case the try was thwarted by passers-by, by kibitzers from windows, or shopkeepers.

Meantime, in the Elm Hill Avenue section of Roxbury, a part of inner Boston that is suburban in superficial character, street assaults and the ever present possibility of more street assaults with no kibitzers to protect the victims, induce prudent people to stay off the sidewalks at night. Not surprisingly, for this and other reasons that are related (dispiritedness and dullness), most of Roxbury has run down. It has become a place to leave.

I do not wish to single out Roxbury or its once fine Elm Hill Avenue section especially as a vulnerable area; its disabilities, and especially its Great Blight of Dullness, are all too common in other cities too. But differences like these in public safety within the same city are worth noting. The Elm Hill Avenue section's basic troubles are not owing to a criminal or a discriminated against or a poverty-stricken population. Its troubles stem from the fact that it is physically quite unable to function safely and with related vitality as a city district.

Even within supposedly similar parts of supposedly similar places, drastic differences in public safety exist. An incident at Washington Houses, a public housing project in New York, illustrates this point. A tenants' group at this project, struggling to establish itself, held some outdoor ceremonies in mid-December 1958, and put up three Christmas trees. The chief tree, so cumbersome it was a problem to transport, erect, and trim, went into the project's inner "street," a landscaped central mall and promenade. The other two trees, each less than six feet tall and easy to carry, went on two small fringe plots at the outer corners of the project where it abuts a busy avenue and lively cross streets of the old city. The first night, the large tree and all its trimmings were stolen. The two smaller trees remained intact, lights, ornaments and all, until they were taken down at New Year's. "The place where the tree was stolen, which is *theoretically* the most safe and sheltered place in the project, is the same place that is unsafe for people too, especially children," says a social worker who had been helping the tenants' group. "People are no safer in that mall than the Christmas tree. On the other hand, the place where the other trees were safe, where the project is just one corner out of four, happens to be safe for people."

This is something everyone already knows: A well-used city street is apt to be a safe street. A deserted city street is apt to be unsafe. But how does this work, really? And what makes a city street well used or shunned? Why is the sidewalk mall in Washington Houses, which is supposed to be an attraction, shunned? Why are the sidewalks of the old city just to its west not shunned? What about streets that are busy part of the time and then empty abruptly?

25   A city street equipped to handle strangers, and to make a safety asset, in itself, out of the presence of strangers, as the streets of successful city neighborhoods always do, must have three main qualities:

First, there must be a clear demarcation between what is public space and what is private space. Public and private spaces cannot ooze into each other as they do typically in suburban settings or in projects.

Second, there must be eyes upon the street, eyes belonging to those we might call the natural proprietors of the street. The buildings on a street equipped to handle strangers and to insure the safety of both residents and strangers, must be oriented to the street. They cannot turn their backs or blank sides on it and leave it blind.

And third, the sidewalk must have users on it fairly continuously, both to add to the number of effective eyes on the street and to induce the people in buildings along the street to watch the sidewalks in sufficient numbers. Nobody enjoys sitting on a stoop or looking out a window at an empty street. Almost nobody does such a thing. Large numbers of people entertain themselves, off and on, by watching street activity.

In settlements that are smaller and simpler than big cities, controls on acceptable public behavior, if not on crime, seem to operate with greater or lesser success through a web of reputation, gossip, approval, disapproval and sanctions, all of which are powerful if people know each other and word travels. But a city's streets, which must control not only the behavior of the people of the city but also of visitors from suburbs and towns who want to have a big time away from the gossip and sanctions at home, have to operate by more direct, straightforward methods. It is a wonder cities have solved such an inherently difficult problem at all. And yet in many streets they do it magnificently.

It is futile to try to evade the issue of unsafe city streets by attempting to 30 make some other features of a locality, say interior courtyards, or sheltered play spaces, safe instead. By definition again, the streets of a city must do most of the job of handling strangers for this is where strangers come and go. The streets must not only defend the city against predatory strangers, they must protect the many, many peaceable and well-meaning strangers who use them, insuring their safety too as they pass through. Moreover, no normal person can spend his life in some artificial haven, and this includes children. Everyone must use the streets.

On the surface, we seem to have here some simple aims: To try to secure streets where the public space is unequivocally public, physically unmixed with private or with nothing-at-all space, so that the area needing surveillance has clear and practicable limits; and to see that these public street spaces have eyes on them as continuously as possible.

But it is not so simple to achieve these objects, especially the latter. You can't make people use streets they have no reason to use. You can't make people watch streets they do not want to watch. Safety on the streets by surveillance and mutual policing of one another sounds grim, but in real life it is not grim. The safety of the street works best, most casually, and with least frequent taint of hostility or suspicion precisely where people are using and most enjoying the city streets voluntarily and are least conscious, normally, that they are policing.

The basic requisite for such surveillance is a substantial quantity of stores and other public places sprinkled along the sidewalks of a district; enterprises and public places that are used by evening and night must be among them especially. Stores, bars and restaurants, as the chief examples, work in several different and complex ways to abet sidewalk safety.

First, they give people—both residents and strangers—concrete reasons for using the sidewalks on which these enterprises face.

Second, they draw people along the sidewalks past places which have 35 no attractions to public use in themselves but which become traveled and peopled as routes to somewhere else; this influence does not carry very far geographically, so enterprises must be frequent in a city district if they are to populate with walkers those other stretches of street that lack public places along the sidewalk. Moreover, there should be many different kinds of enterprises, to give people reasons for crisscrossing paths.

Third, storekeepers and other small businessmen are typically strong proponents of peace and order themselves; they hate broken windows and holdups; they hate having customers made nervous about safety. They are great street watchers and sidewalk guardians if present in sufficient numbers.

Fourth, the activity generated by people on errands, or people aiming for food or drink, is itself an attraction to still other people.

This last point, that the sight of people attracts still other people, is something that city planners and city architectural designers seem to find incomprehensible. They operate on the premise that city people seek the sight of emptiness, obvious order and quiet. Nothing could be less true. People's love of watching activity and other people is constantly evident in cities everywhere. This trait reaches an almost ludicrous extreme on upper Broadway in New York, where the street is divided by a narrow central mall, right in the middle of traffic. At the cross-street intersections of this long north-south mall, benches have been placed behind big concrete buffers and on any day when the weather is even barely tolerable these benches are filled with people at block after block after block, watching the pedestrians who cross the mall in front of them, watching the traffic, watching the people on the busy sidewalks, watching each other. Eventually Broadway reaches Columbia University and Barnard College, one to the right, the other to the left. Here all is obvious order and quiet. No more stores, no more activity generated by the stores, almost no more pedestrians crossing—and no more watchers. The benches are there but they go empty in even the finest weather. I have tried them and can see why. No place could be more boring. Even the students of these institutions shun the solitude. They are doing their outdoor loitering, outdoor homework and general street watching on the steps overlooking the busiest campus crossing.

It is just so on city streets elsewhere. A lively street always has both its users and pure watchers. Last year I was on such a street in the Lower East Side of Manhattan, waiting for a bus. I had not been there longer than a minute, barely long enough to begin taking in the street's activity of errand goers, children playing, and loiterers on the stoops, when my attention was attracted by a woman who opened a window on the third floor of a tenement across the street and vigorously yoo-hooed at me. When I caught on that she wanted my attention and responded, she shouted down, "The bus doesn't run here on Saturdays!" Then by a combination of shouts and pantomime she directed me around the corner. This woman was one of thousands upon thousands of people in New York who casually take care of the streets. They notice strangers. They observe everything going on. If they need to take action, whether to direct a stranger waiting in the wrong place or to call the police, they do so. Action usually requires, to be sure, a certain self-assurance about the actor's proprietorship of the street and the support he will get if necessary, matters which will be gone into later in this book. But even more fundamental than the action and necessary to the action, is the watching itself.

Not everyone in cities helps to take care of the streets, and many a city 40 resident or city worker is unaware of why his neighborhood is safe. The other day an incident occurred on the street where I live, and it interested me because of this point.

My block of the street, I must explain, is a small one, but it contains a remarkable range of buildings, varying from several vintages of tenements to three- and four-story houses that have been converted into low-rent flats with stores on the ground floor, or returned to single-family use like ours. Across the street there used to be mostly four-story brick tenements with stores below. But twelve years ago several buildings, from the corner to the middle of the block, were converted into one building with elevator apartments of small size and high rents.

The incident that attracted my attention was a suppressed struggle going on between a man and a little girl of eight or nine years old. The man seemed to be trying to get the girl to go with him. By turns he was directing a cajoling attention to her, and then assuming an air of nonchalance. The girl was making herself rigid, as children do when they resist, against the wall of one of the tenements across the street.

As I watched from our second-floor window, making up my mind how to intervene if it seemed advisable, I saw it was not going to be necessary. From the butcher shop beneath the tenement had emerged the woman who, with her husband, runs the shop; she was standing within earshot of the man, her arms folded and a look of determination on her face. Joe Cornacchia, who with his sons-in-law keeps the delicatessen, emerged about the same moment and stood solidly to the other side. Several heads poked out of the tenement windows above, one was withdrawn quickly and its owner reappeared a moment later in the doorway behind the man. Two men from the bar next to the butcher shop came to the doorway and waited. On my side of the street, I saw that the locksmith, the fruit man and the laundry proprietor had all come out of their shops and that the scene was also being surveyed from a number of windows besides ours. That man did not know it, but he was surrounded. Nobody was going to allow a little girl to be dragged off, even if nobody knew who she was.

I am sorry—sorry purely for dramatic purposes—to have to report that the little girl turned out to be the man's daughter.

Throughout the duration of the little drama, perhaps five minutes in all, 45 no eyes appeared in the windows of the high-rent, small-apartment building. It was the only building of which this was true. When we first moved to our block, I used to anticipate happily that perhaps soon all the buildings would be rehabilitated like that one. I know better now, and can only anticipate with gloom and foreboding the recent news that exactly this transformation is scheduled for the rest of the block frontage adjoining the high-rent building. The high-rent tenants, most of whom are so transient we cannot even keep track of their faces,[1] have not the remotest idea of who takes care of their street, or how. A city neighborhood can absorb and protect a substantial number of these birds of passage, as our neighborhood does. But if and when the neighborhood finally *becomes* them, they will gradually find the streets less secure, they will be vaguely mystified about it, and if things get bad enough they will drift away to another neighborhood which is mysteriously safer.

In some rich city neighborhoods, where there is little do-it-yourself surveillance, such as residential Park Avenue or upper Fifth Avenue in New York, street watchers are hired. The monotonous sidewalks of residential Park Avenue, for example, are surprisingly little used; their putative users are populating, instead, the interesting store-, bar- and restaurant-filled sidewalks of Lexington Avenue and Madison Avenue to east and west, and the cross streets leading to these. A network of doormen and superintendents, of delivery boys and nursemaids, a form of hired neighborhood, keeps residential Park Avenue supplied with eyes. At night, with the security of the doormen as a bulwark, dog walkers safely venture forth and supplement the doormen. But this street is so blank of built-in eyes, so devoid of concrete reasons for using or watching it instead of turning the first corner off of it, that if its rents were to slip below the point where they could support a plentiful hired neighborhood of doormen and elevator men, it would undoubtedly become a woefully dangerous street.

Once a street is well equipped to handle strangers, once it has both a good, effective demarcation between private and public spaces and has a basic supply of activity and eyes, the more strangers the merrier.

Strangers become an enormous asset on the street on which I live, and the spurs off it, particularly at night when safety assets are most needed. We are fortunate enough, on the street, to be gifted not only with a locally supported bar and another around the corner, but also with a famous bar that draws continuous troops of strangers from adjoining neighborhoods and even from out of town. It is famous because the poet Dylan Thomas used to go there, and mentioned it in his writing. This bar, indeed, works two distinct shifts. In the morning and early afternoon it is a social gathering place for the old community of Irish longshoremen and other craftsmen in the area, as it always was. But beginning in mid-afternoon it takes on a different life, more like a college bull session with beer, combined with a literary cocktail party, and this continues until the early hours of the morning. On a cold winter's night, as you pass the White Horse, and the doors open, a solid wave of conversation and animation surges out and hits you; very warming. The comings and goings from this bar do much to keep our street reasonably populated until three in the morning, and it is a street always safe to come home to. The only instance I know of a beating in our street occurred in the dead hours between the closing of the bar and dawn. The beating was halted by one of our neighbors who saw it from his window and, unconsciously certain that even at night he was part of a web of strong street law and order, intervened.

A friend of mine lives on a street uptown where a church youth and community center, with many night dances and other activities, performs the same service for his street that the White Horse bar does for ours. Orthodox planning is much imbued with puritanical and Utopian conceptions of how people should spend their free time, and in planning, these moralisms on people's private lives are deeply confused with concepts about the workings of cities. In maintaining city street civilization, the White Horse bar and the church-sponsored youth center, different as they undoubtedly are, perform much the same public street civilizing service. There is not only room in cities for such differences and many more in taste, purpose and interest of occupation; cities also have a need for people with all these differences in taste and proclivity. The preferences of Utopians, and of other compulsive managers of other people's leisure, for one kind of legal enterprise over others is worse than irrelevant for cities. It is harmful. The greater and more plentiful the range of all legitimate interests (in the strictly legal sense) that city streets and their enterprises can satisfy, the better for the streets and for the safety and civilization of the city.

Bars, and indeed all commerce, have a bad name in many city districts 50 precisely because they do draw strangers, and the strangers do not work out as an asset at all.

This sad circumstance is especially true in the dispirited gray belts of great cities and in once fashionable or at least once solid inner residential areas gone into decline. Because these neighborhoods are so dangerous, and the streets typically so dark, it is commonly believed that their trouble may be insufficient street lighting. Good lighting is important, but darkness alone does not account for the gray areas' deep, functional sickness, the Great Blight of Dullness.

Under the seeming disorder of the old city, wherever the old city is working successfully, is a marvelous order for maintaining the safety of the streets and the freedom of the city. It is a complex order. Its essence is intricacy of sidewalk use, bringing with it a constant succession of eyes. This order is all composed of movement and change, and although it is life, not art, we may fancifully call it the art form of the city and liken it to the dance—not to a simple-minded precision dance with everyone kicking up at the same time, twirling in unison and bowing off en masse, but to an intricate ballet in which the individual dancers and ensembles all have distinctive parts which miraculously reinforce each other and compose an orderly whole. The ballet of the good city sidewalk never repeats itself from place to place, and in any one place is always replete with new improvisations.

The stretch of Hudson Street where I live is each day the scene of an intricate sidewalk ballet. I make my own first entrance into it a little after eight when I put out the garbage can, surely a prosaic occupation, but I enjoy my part, my little clang, as the droves of junior high school students walk by the center of the stage dropping candy wrappers. (How do they eat so much candy so early in the morning?)

While I sweep up the wrappers I watch the other rituals of morning: Mr. Halpert unlocking the laundry's handcart from its mooring to a cellar door, Joe Cornacchia's son-in-law stacking out the empty crates from the delicatessen, the barber bringing out his sidewalk folding chair, Mr. Goldstein arranging the coils of wire which proclaim the hardware store is open, the wife of the tenement's superintendent depositing her chunky three-year-old with a toy mandolin on the stoop, the vantage point from which he is learning the English his mother cannot speak. Now the primary children, heading for St. Luke's, dribble through to the south; the children for St. Veronica's cross, heading to the west, and the children for P.S. 41, heading toward the east. Two new entrances are being made from the wings: well-dressed and even elegant women and men with briefcases emerge from doorways and side streets. Most of these are heading for the taxis are part of a wider morning ritual: having dropped passengers from midtown in the downtown financial district, they are now bringing downtowners up to midtown. Simultaneously, numbers of women in housedresses have emerged and as they crisscross with one another they pause for quick conversations that sound with either laughter or joint indignation, never, it seems, anything between. It is time for me to hurry to work too, and I exchange my ritual farewell with Mr. Lofaro, the short, thick-bodied, white-aproned fruit man who stands outside his doorway a little up the street, his arms folded, his feet planted, looking solid as earth itself. We nod; we each glance quickly up and down the street, then look back to each other and smile. We have done this many a morning for more than ten years, and we both know what it means: All is well.

55   The heart-of-the-day ballet I seldom see, because part of the nature of it is that working people who live there, like me, are mostly gone, filling the roles of strangers on other sidewalks. But from days off, I know enough of it to know that it becomes more and more intricate. Longshoremen who are not working that day gather at the White Horse or the Ideal or the International for beer and conversation. The executives and business lunchers from the industries just to the west throng the Dorgene restaurant and the Lion's Head Coffeehouse; meat-market workers and communications scientists fill the bakery lunchroom. Character dancers come on, a strange old man with strings of old shoes over his shoulders, motor-scooter riders with big beards and girl friends who bounce on the back of the scooters and

wear their hair long in front of their faces as well as behind, drunks who follow the advice of the Hat Council and are always turned out in hats, but not hats the Council would approve. Mr. Lacey, the locksmith, shuts up his shop for a while and goes to exchange the time of day with Mr. Slube at the cigar store. Mr. Koochagian, the tailor, waters the luxuriant jungle of plants in his window, gives them a critical look from the outside, accepts a compliment on them from two passers-by, fingers the leaves on the plane tree in front of our house with a thoughtful gardener's appraisal, and crosses the street for a bite at the Ideal where he can keep an eye on customers and wigwag across the message that he is coming. The baby carriages come out, and clusters of everyone from toddlers with dolls to teenagers with homework gather at the stoops.

When I get home after work, the ballet is reaching its crescendo. This is the time of roller skates and stilts and tricycles, and games in the lee of the stoop with bottletops and plastic cowboys; this is the time of bundles and packages, zigzagging from the drug store to the fruit stand and back over to the butcher's; this is the time when teenagers, all dressed up, are pausing to ask if their slips show or their collars look right; this is the time when beautiful girls get out of MGs; this is the time when the fire engines go through; this is the time when anybody you know around Hudson Street will go by.

As darkness thickens and Mr. Halpert moors the laundry cart to the cellar door again, the ballet goes on under lights, eddying back and forth but intensifying at the bright spotlight pools of Joe's sidewalk pizza dispensary, the bars, the delicatessen, the restaurant and the drug store. The night workers stop now at the delicatessen, to pick up salami and a container of milk. Things have settled down for the evening but the street and its ballet have not come to a stop.

I know the deep night ballet and its seasons best from waking long after midnight to tend a baby and, sitting in the dark, seeing the shadows and hearing the sounds of the sidewalk. Mostly it is a sound like infinitely pattering snatches of party conversation and, about three in the morning, singing, very good singing. Sometimes there is sharpness and anger or sad, sad weeping, or a flurry of search for a string of beads broken. One night a young man came roaring along, bellowing terrible language at two girls whom he had apparently picked up and who were disappointing him. Doors opened, a wary semicircle formed around him, not too close, until the police came. Out came the heads, too, along Hudson Street, offering opinion, "Drunk ... Crazy ... A wild kid from the suburbs."[2]

Deep in the night, I am almost unaware how many people are on the street unless something calls them together, like the bagpipe. Who the piper was and why he favored our street I have no idea. The bagpipe just skirled out in the February night, and as if it were a signal the random, dwindled movements of the sidewalk took on direction. Swiftly, quietly, almost magically a little crowd was there, a crowd that evolved into a circle with a Highland fling inside it. The crowd could be seen on the shadowy sidewalk, the dancers could be seen, but the bagpiper himself was almost invisible because his bravura was all in his music. He was a very little man in a plain brown overcoat. When he finished and vanished, the dancers and watchers applauded, and applause came from the galleries too, half a dozen of the hundred windows on Hudson Street. Then the windows closed, and the little crowd dissolved into the random movements of the night street.

60 The strangers on Hudson Street, the allies whose eyes help us natives keep the peace of the street, are so many that they always seem to be different people from one day to the next. That does not matter. Whether they are so many always-different people as they seem to be, I do not know. Likely they are. When Jimmy Rogan fell through a plate-glass window (he was separating some scuffling friends) and almost lost his arm, a stranger in an old T shirt emerged from the Ideal bar, swiftly applied an expert tourniquet and, according to the hospital's emergency staff, saved Jimmy's life. Nobody remembered seeing the man before and no one has seen him since. The hospital was called in this way: a woman sitting on the steps next to the accident ran over to the bus stop, wordlessly snatched the dime from the hand of a stranger who was waiting with his fifteen-cent fare ready, and raced into the Ideal's phone booth. The stranger raced after her to offer the nickel too. Nobody remembered seeing him before, and no one has seen him since. When you see the same stranger three or four times on Hudson Street, you begin to nod. This is almost getting to be an acquaintance, a public acquaintance, of course.

I have made the daily ballet of Hudson Street sound more frenetic than it is, because writing it telescopes it. In real life, it is not that way. In real life, to be sure, something is always going on, the ballet is never at a halt, but the general effect is peaceful and the general tenor even leisurely. People who know well such animated city streets will know how it is. I am afraid people who do not will always have it a little wrong in their heads—like the old prints of rhinoceroses made from travelers' descriptions of rhinoceroses.

On Hudson Street, the same as in the North End of Boston or in any other animated neighborhoods of great cities, we are not innately more competent at keeping the sidewalks safe than are the people who try to live off the hostile truce of Turf in a blind-eyed city. We are the lucky possessors of a city order that makes it relatively simple to keep the peace because there are plenty of eyes on the street. But there is nothing simple about that order itself, or the bewildering number of components that go into it. Most of those components are specialized in one way or another. They unite in their joint effect upon the sidewalk, which is not specialized in the least. That is its strength.

Notes

[1] Some, according to the storekeepers, live on beans and bread and spend their sojourn looking for a place to live where all their money will not go for rent.

[2] He turned out to be a wild kid from the suburbs. Sometimes, on Hudson Street, we are tempted to believe the suburbs must be a difficult place to bring up children.

Things to Do with the Reading

1. Summarize Jacobs' argument, using the technique that *Writing Analytically* calls ranking (see NOTICE AND FOCUS in Chapter 1). Do this by locating all of the characteristics that Jacobs says a neighborhood has to have to remain safe. Concentrate on the one or two characteristics that Jacobs would say are most important.

2. Write a summary in which you focus on the mistakes that Jacobs says housing authorities and city planners make. Also focus on what Jacobs claims are mistaken assumptions about the causes of unsafe neighborhoods. How, for example, does she dispute the charge that the presence of poor people and minorities makes neighborhoods unsafe?

3. Link: Look at Kunstler's attack on the kind of segregation that zoning causes, and locate the common ground between Kunstler and Jacobs in this regard. It is interesting that Jacobs makes little mention of the impact of cars, except perhaps in her discussion of what she calls "pseudo-suburbs." Theoretically, both Kunstler and Jacobs would welcome the arrival of a restaurant in a residential area. How does the car culture complicate both writers' advocacy of mixed use (commercial and residential) areas?

4. Link: Now that you have read this essay, go back to the reference to Jane Jacobs in Gopnik's essay and explain it. Speaking of a change in architectural orthodoxy in New York, Gopnik writes, "The new ideology was Jane Jacobs dressed in latex and leather" (paragraph 18).

5. Application: Use Jacobs' essay as a lens for observing and analyzing a neighborhood that you know. You might, for example, station yourself some place in this neighborhood as Jacobs did: on the benches, on the median strip, on upper Broadway, or in front of the White Horse in the Village. What do you notice about the way people behave in this area? Gopnik notes that there is always a close relationship between property and culture. Consider how the neighborhood's architecture and the uses its buildings serve influence the absence or presence of what Jacobs calls "eyes on the street." You might also consider to what extent there is a "clear demarcation between what is public space and what is private space" (paragraph 26).

Mike Davis

Fortress Los Angeles

In the following excerpt from his most famous book, an urban study of contemporary Los Angeles entitled *City of Quartz* (1992), Mike Davis examines how cultural attitudes and social class provide the actual material shape of urban design. Now a Distinguished Professor in the Department of Creative Writing at the University of California, Riverside, Davis has also taught urban theory at the Southern California Institute of Architecture and at Stony Brook University. Davis is the author of more than 20 books and the 1998 winner of a MacArthur Foundation grant, the so-called "genius" award given to the nation's most gifted creative minds. In addition to urban studies, he has written on economic history and social movements.

1   In Los Angeles—once a paradise of free beaches, luxurious parks, and "cruising strips"—genuinely democratic space is virtually extinct. The pleasure domes of the elite Westside rely upon the social imprisonment of a third-world service proletariat in increasingly repressive ghettos and barrios. In a city of several million aspiring immigrants (where Spanish-surname children are now almost two-thirds of the school-age population), public amenities are shrinking radically, libraries and playgrounds are closing, parks are falling derelict, and streets are growing ever more desolate and dangerous.

Here, as in other American cities, municipal policy has taken its lead from the security offensive and the middle-class demand for increased spatial and social insulation. Taxes previously targeted for traditional public spaces and recreational facilities have been redirected to support corporate redevelopment projects. A pliant city government—in the case of Los Angeles, one ironically professing to represent a liberal biracial coalition—has collaborated in privatizing public space and subsidizing new exclusive enclaves (benignly called "urban villages"). The celebratory language used to describe contemporary Los Angeles—"urban renaissance," "city of the future," and so on—is only a triumphal gloss laid over the brutalization of its inner-city neighborhoods and the stark divisions of class and race represented in its built environment. Urban form obediently follows repressive function. Los Angeles, as always in the vanguard, offers an especially disturbing guide to the emerging liaisons between urban architecture and the police state.

Forbidden City

Los Angeles's first spatial militarist was the legendary General Harrison Gray Otis, proprietor of the *Times* and implacable foe of organized labor. In the 1890s,

From *City of Quartz*, Verso Books, 1990. Reprinted by permission.

after locking out his union printers and announcing a crusade for "industrial freedom," Otis retreated into a new *Times* building designed as a fortress with grim turrets and battlements crowned by a bellicose bronze eagle. To emphasize his truculence, he later had a small, functional cannon installed on the hood of his Packard touring car. Not surprisingly, this display of aggression produced a response in kind. On October 1, 1910, the heavily fortified *Times* headquarters— the command-post of the open shop on the West Coast—was destroyed in a catastrophic explosion, blamed on union saboteurs.

Eighty years later, the martial spirit of General Otis pervades the design of Los Angeles's new Downtown, whose skyscrapers march from Bunker Hill down the Figueroa corridor. Two billion dollars of public tax subsidies have enticed big banks and corporate headquarters back to a central city they almost abandoned in the 1960s. Into a waiting grid, cleared of tenement housing by the city's powerful and largely unaccountable redevelopment agency, local developers and offshore investors (increasingly Japanese) have planted a series of block-square complexes: Crocker Center, the Bonaventure Hotel and Shopping Mall, the World Trade Center, California Plaza, Arco Center, and so on. With an increasingly dense and self-contained circulation system linking these superblocks, the new financial district is best conceived as a single, self-referential hyperstructure, a Miesian skyscape of fantastic proportions.

5   Like similar megalomaniacal complexes tethered to fragmented and desolate downtowns—such as the Renaissance Center in Detroit and the Peachtree and Omni centers in Atlanta—Bunker Hill and the Figueroa corridor have provoked a storm of objections to their abuse of scale and composition, their denigration of street life, and their confiscation of the vital energy of the center, now sequestered within their subterranean concourses or privatized plazas. Sam Hall Kaplan, the former design critic of the *Times*, has vociferously denounced the antistreet bias of redevelopment; in his view, the superimposition of "hermetically sealed fortresses" and random "pieces of suburbia" onto Downtown has "killed the street" and "dammed the rivers of life."[1]

Yet Kaplan's vigorous defense of pedestrian democracy remains grounded in liberal complaints about "bland design" and "elitist planning practices." Like most architectural critics, he rails against the oversights of urban design without conceding a dimension of foresight, and even of deliberate repressive intent. For when Downtown's new "Gold Coast" is seen in relation to other social landscapes in the central city, the "fortress effect" emerges, not as an inadvertent failure of design, but as an explicit—and, in its own terms, successful—socio-spatial strategy.

The goals of this strategy may be summarized as a double repression: to obliterate all connection with Downtown's past and to prevent any dynamic association with the non-Anglo urbanism of its future. Los Angeles is unusual among major urban centers in having preserved, however negligently, most of its Beaux Arts commercial core. Yet the city chose to transplant—at immense public cost—the entire corporate and financial district from around Broadway and Spring Street to Bunker Hill, a half-dozen blocks further west.

Photographs of the old Downtown in its 1940s prime show crowds of Anglo, black, and Mexican shoppers of all ages and classes. The contemporary Downtown "renaissance" renders such heterogeneity virtually impossible. It is intended not just to "kill the street" as Kaplan feared, but to "kill the crowd," to eliminate that democratic mixture that Olmsted believed was America's antidote to European class polarization. The new Downtown is designed to ensure a seamless continuum of middle-class work, consumption, and recreation, insulated from the city's "unsavory" streets. Ramparts and battlements, reflective glass and elevated pedways, are tropes in an architectural language warning off the underclass Other. Although architectural critics are usually blind to this militarized syntax, urban pariah groups—whether young black men, poor Latino immigrants, or elderly homeless white females—read the signs immediately.

Finding the Analytical Lens

This strategic armoring of the city against the poor is especially obvious at street level. In his famous study of the "social life of small urban spaces," William Whyte points out that the quality of any urban environment can be measured, first of all, by whether there are convenient, comfortable places for pedestrians to sit. This maxim has been warmly taken to heart by designers of the high corporate precincts of Bunker Hill and its adjacent "urban villages." As part of the city's policy of subsidizing the white-collar residential colonization of Downtown, tens of millions of dollars of tax revenue have been invested in the creation of attractive, "soft" environments in favored areas. Planners envision a succession of opulent piazzas, fountains, public art, exotic shrubbery, and comfortable street furniture along a ten-block pedestrian corridor from Bunker Hill to South Park. Brochures sell Downtown's "livability" with idyllic representations of office workers and affluent tourists sipping cappuccino and listening to free jazz concerts in the terraced gardens of California Plaza and Grand Hope Park.

10   In stark contrast, a few blocks away, the city is engaged in a relentless struggle to make the streets as unlivable as possible for the homeless and the poor. The persistence of thousands of street people on the fringes of Bunker Hill and the Civic Center tarnishes the image of designer living Downtown and betrays the laboriously constructed illusion of an urban "renaissance." City Hall has retaliated with its own version of low-intensity warfare.

Although city leaders periodically propose schemes for removing indigents *en masse*—deporting them to a poor farm on the edge of the desert, confining them in camps in the mountains, or interning them on derelict ferries in the harbor—such "final solutions" have been blocked by council members' fears of the displacement of the homeless into their districts.

Instead the city, self-consciously adopting the idiom of cold war, has promoted the "containment" (the official term) of the homeless in Skid Row, along Fifth Street, systematically transforming the neighborhood into an outdoor poorhouse. But this containment strategy breeds its own vicious cycle of contradiction. By condensing the mass of the desperate and helpless together in such a small space, and denying adequate housing, official policy has transformed Skid Row into probably the most dangerous ten square blocks in the world. Every night on Skid Row is Friday the 13th, and, unsurprisingly, many of the homeless seek to escape the area during the night at all costs, searching safer niches in other parts of Downtown. The city in turn tightens the noose with increased police harassment and ingenious design deterrents.

One of the simplest but most mean-spirited of these deterrents is the Rapid Transit District's new barrel-shaped bus bench, which offers a minimal surface for uncomfortable sitting while making sleeping impossible. Such "bumproof" benches are being widely introduced on the periphery of Skid Row. Another invention is the aggressive deployment of outdoor sprinklers. Several years ago the city opened a Skid Row Park; to ensure that the park could not be used for overnight camping, overhead sprinklers were programmed to drench unsuspecting sleepers at random times during the night. The system was immediately copied by local merchants to drive the homeless away from (public) storefront sidewalks. Meanwhile Downtown restaurants and markets have built baroque enclosures to protect their refuse from the homeless. Although no one in Los Angeles has yet proposed adding cyanide to the garbage, as was suggested in Phoenix a few years back, one popular seafood restaurant has spent $12,000 to build the ultimate bag-lady-proof trash cage: three-quarter-inch steel rod with alloy locks and vicious out-turned spikes to safeguard moldering fishheads and stale french fries.

Public toilets, however, have become the real frontline of the city's war on the homeless. Los Angeles, as a matter of deliberate policy, has fewer public lavatories than any other major North American city. On the advice of the Los Angeles police, who now sit on the "design board" of at least one major Downtown project, the redevelopment agency bulldozed the few remaining public toilets on Skid Row. Agency planners then considered whether to include a "free-standing public toilet" in their design for the upscale South Park residential development; agency chairman Jim Wood later admitted that the decision not to build the toilet was a "policy decision and not a design decision." The agency preferred the alternative of "quasi-public restrooms"—toilets in restaurants, art galleries, and office buildings—which can be made available selectively to tourists and white-collar workers while being denied to vagrants and other unsuitables. The same logic has inspired the city's transportation planners to exclude toilets from their designs for Los Angeles's new subway system.[2]

Bereft of toilets, the Downtown badlands east of Hill Street also lack outside water sources for drinking or washing. A common and troubling sight these days is the homeless men—many of them young refugees from El Salvador—washing, swimming, even drinking from the sewer effluent that flows down the concrete channel of the Los Angeles River on the eastern edge of Downtown. The city's public health department has made no effort to post warning signs in Spanish or to mobilize alternative clean-water sources.

15   In those areas where Downtown professionals must cross paths with the homeless or the working poor—such as the zone of gentrification along Broadway just south of the Civic Center—extraordinary precautions have been taken to ensure the physical separation of the different classes. The redevelopment agency, for example, again brought in the police to help design "twenty-four-hour, state-of-the-art security" for the two new parking structures that serve the *Los Angeles Times* headquarters and the Ronald Reagan State Office Building. In contrast to the mean streets outside, both parking structures incorporate beautifully landscaped microparks, and one even boasts a food court, picnic area, and historical exhibit. Both structures are intended to function as "confidence-building" circulation systems that allow white-collar workers to walk from car to office, or from car to boutique, with minimum exposure to the public street. The Broadway-Spring Center, in particular, which links the two local hubs of gentrification (the Reagan Building and the proposed Grand Central Square) has been warmly praised by architectural critics for adding greenery and art to parking. It also adds a considerable dose of menace—armed guards, locked gates, and ubiquitous security cameras—to scare away the homeless and the poor.

The cold war on the streets of Downtown is ever escalating. The police, lobbied by Downtown merchants and developers, have broken up every attempt by the homeless and their allies to create safe havens or self-governed encampments. "Justiceville," founded by homeless activist Ted Hayes, was roughly dispersed; when its inhabitants attempted to find refuge at Venice Beach, they were arrested at the behest of the local council member (a renowned environmentalist) and sent back to Skid Row. The city's own brief experiment with legalized camping—a grudging response to a series of deaths from exposure during the cold winter of 1987—was abruptly terminated after only four months to make way for the construction of a transit maintenance yard. Current policy seems to involve perverse play upon the famous irony about the equal rights of the rich and poor to sleep in the rough. As the former head of the city planning commission explained, in the City of the Angels it is not against the law to sleep on the street per se—"only to erect any sort of protective shelter."[3] To enforce this proscription against "cardboard condos," the police periodically sweep the Nickel, tearing down shelters, confiscating possessions, and arresting resisters. Such cynical repression has turned the majority of the homeless into urban bedouins. They are visible all over Downtown, pushing their few pathetic possessions in stolen shopping carts, always fugitive, always in motion, pressed between the official policy of containment and the inhumanity of Downtown streets.

Sequestering the Poor

An insidious spatial logic also regulates the lives of Los Angeles's working poor. Just across the moat of the Harbor Freeway, west of Bunker Hill, lies the MacArthur Park district—once upon a time the city's wealthiest neighborhood. Although frequently characterized as a no-man's-land awaiting resurrection by developers, the district is, in fact, home to the largest Central American community in the United States. In the congested streets bordering the park, a hundred thousand Salvadorans and Guatemalans, including a large community of Mayan-speakers, crowd into tenements and boarding houses barely adequate for a fourth as many people. Every morning at 6 A.M. this Latino Bantustan dispatches armies of sewing *operadoras*, dishwashers, and janitors to turn the wheels of the Downtown economy. But because MacArthur Park is midway between Downtown and the famous Miracle Mile, it too will soon fall to redevelopment's bulldozers.

Hungry to exploit the lower land prices in the district, a powerful coterie of developers, represented by a famous ex-councilman and the former president of the planning commission, has won official approval for their vision of "Central City West": literally, a second Downtown comprising 25 million square feet of new office and retail space. Although local politicians have insisted upon a significant quota of low-income replacement housing, such a palliative will hardly compensate for the large-scale population displacement sure to follow the construction of the new skyscrapers and yuppified "urban villages." In the meantime, Korean capital, seeking *lebensraum* for Los Angeles's burgeoning Koreatown, is also pushing into the MacArthur Park area, uprooting tenements to construct heavily fortified condominiums and office complexes. Other Asian and European speculators are counting on the new Metrorail station, across from the park, to become a magnet for new investment in the district.

The recent intrusion of so many powerful interests into the area has put increasing pressure upon the police to "take back the streets" from what is usually represented as an occupying army of drug-dealers, illegal immigrants, and homicidal homeboys. Thus in the summer of 1990 the LAPD announced a massive operation to "retake crime-plagued MacArthur Park" and surrounding neighborhoods "street by street, alley by alley." While the area is undoubtedly a major drug market, principally for drive-in Anglo commuters, the police have focused not only on addict-dealers and gang members, but also on the industrious sidewalk vendors who have made the circumference of the park an exuberant swap meet. Thus Mayan women selling such local staples as tropical fruit, baby clothes, and roach spray have been rounded up in the same sweeps as alleged "narcoterrorists."[4] (Similar dragnets in other Southern California communities have focused on Latino day-laborers congregated at streetcorner "slave markets.")

20   By criminalizing every attempt by the poor—whether the Skid Row homeless or MacArthur Park venders—to use public space for survival purposes, law-enforcement agencies have abolished the last informal safety-net separating misery from catastrophe. (Few third-world cities are so pitiless.) At the same time, the police, encouraged by local businessmen and property owners, are taking the first, tentative steps toward criminalizing entire inner-city communities. The "war" on drugs and gangs again has been the pretext for the LAPD's novel, and disturbing, experiments with community blockades. A large section of the Pico-Union neighborhood, just south of MacArthur Park, has been quarantined since the summer of 1989; "Narcotics Enforcement Area" barriers restrict entry to residents "on legitimate business only." Inspired by the positive response of older residents and local politicians, the police have subsequently franchised "Operation Cul-de-Sac" to other low-income Latino and black neighborhoods.

Thus in November 1989 (as the Berlin Wall was being demolished), the Devonshire Division of the LAPD closed off a "drug-ridden" twelve-block section of the northern San Fernando Valley. To control circulation within this largely Latino neighborhood, the police convinced apartment owners to finance the construction of a permanent guard station. Twenty miles to the south, a square mile of the mixed black and Latino Central-Avalon community has also been converted into Narcotic Enforcement turf with concrete roadblocks. Given the popularity of these quarantines—save amongst the ghetto youth against whom they are directed—it is possible that a majority of the inner city may eventually be partitioned into police-regulated "no-go" areas.

The official rhetoric of the contemporary war against the urban underclasses resounds with comparisons to the War in Vietnam a generation ago. The LAPD's community blockades evoke the infamous policy of quarantining suspect populations in "strategic hamlets." But an even more ominous emulation is the reconstruction of Los Angeles's public housing projects as "defensible spaces." Deep in the Mekong Delta of the Watts-Willowbrook ghetto, for example, the Imperial Courts Housing Project has been fortified with chain-link fencing, restricted entry signs, obligatory identity passes— and a substation of the LAPD. Visitors are stopped and frisked, the police routinely order residents back into their apartments at night, and domestic life is subjected to constant police scrutiny. For public-housing tenants and inhabitants of narcotic-enforcement zones, the loss of freedom is the price of "security."

Notes

[1] *Los Angeles Times*, Nov. 4, 1978.

[2] Tom Chorneau, "Quandary Over a Park Restroom," *Downtown News*, Aug. 25, 1986.

[3] See "Cold Snap's Toll at 5 as Its Iciest Night Arrives," *Los Angeles Times*, Dec. 29, 1988.

[4] *Los Angeles Times*, June 17, 1990.

Things to Do with the Reading

1. Apply THE METHOD AND PARAPHRASE × 3 to the reading (see Chapters 1 and 2). What significant words repeat? What strands do you find? What is opposed to what? And so WHAT? How would you paraphrase the first sentence of paragraph 6?

2. UNCOVER ASSUMPTIONS in the piece; that is, reason back to its premises, the unstated givens upon which Davis' argument rests (see Chapter 2). First, list a few of the unstated assumptions. What, for example, are some of his unstated assumptions about the homeless and the poor in cities? Try reasoning back to premises with the first two sentences of the piece: if Davis believes this, what must he also already believe?

3. Link: Bring Davis and Jacobs together by locating DIFFERENCE WITHIN SIMILARITY (see Chapter 3). Find the most significant point of contact between Davis' and Jacobs' ways of thinking about public spaces in cities. Given that similarity, what is the most revealing difference between the two arguments? Which of Davis' key words does Jacobs' piece usefully illuminate? Consider, for example, the way that the two writers use the word "street."

4. Application: Describe Davis' analytical method. List the key words that reveal his way of seeing a city. Then experiment with using his method as a lens for looking at a part of your campus or town. Is there, for example, a place where town or campus authorities have arranged things physically so as to encourage or discourage certain kinds of use and/or certain kinds of people? Note: you don't have to focus on homelessness or poverty. Make your priority thinking about public spaces and how they are managed.

FOR FURTHER RESEARCH: PLACES AND SPACES: CITIES AND SUBURBS

By Kelly Cannon, Reference Librarian

The readings and activities below invite you to explore further the theme of Places and Spaces: Cities and Suburbs. URLs are provided for those readings that you can access freely online. For proprietary resources, ask your librarian about print or online access.

Open access

"Charter of the New Urbanism." *New Urbanism*. NewUrbanism.org, 2011. 9 May 2014. http://www.newurbanism.org/newurbanism/principles.html
Lists the basic tenets of New Urbanism, as viewed by New Urbanism.org, a major not-for-profit concerned with remedies to urban blight and sprawl.

> Explore: How does the website move beyond providing information to promoting action? See, for example, the "Principles" subsection: "Obstacles to Overcome." Compare the values espoused by New Urbanism with those represented in the claims of Jack Gambino and James Howard Kunstler.

Hetzler, Olivia, et al. "Gentrification, Displacement, and the New Urbanism." *Sociation Today* 4.2 (2006). 11 May 2014. http://www.ncsociology.org/sociationtoday/v42/gent.htm
This article, published in a peer-reviewed journal, contends that New Urbanism is seriously flawed.

> Explore: What about the presentation of this article strikes you as academic (scholarly) as opposed to popular? What is the argument presented here? What types of evidence are used to support that argument? How do the conclusions of this essay compare with those drawn by Mike Davis in his essay on Los Angeles?

Lubell, Sam. "Welcome to Smallville." *New York Times Magazine* (2010): 38. 11 May 2014. http://www.nytimes.com/2010/10/03/t-magazine/03remix-lubell-t.html
Lately the American dream has been looking smaller—much smaller. The fabled McMansion is becoming a thing of the past.

> Explore: If large size is no longer a virtue in homes, what is? How does this shift away from the McMansion resonate with James Howard Kunstler's plea in "The Public Realm and the Common Good" to begin to alter our material culture at the neighborhood level?

McMahon, Edward T. "The Place Making Dividend." *PlannersWeb* 20 October 2010. 9 May 2014. http://plannersweb.com/2010/10/the-place -making-dividend/

Technology giant Apple had to rethink its architectural design before the Georgetown area of Washington, DC, would let it build a store there.

> Explore: This article quotes novelist Wallace Stegner as saying, "If you don't know where you are, you don't know who you are." What about your own community or neighboring communities instills a distinctive sense of identity in the people who live there through its architecture and use of space? How do the community values of this correspond with or differ from the values espoused by Adam Gopnik in his essay earlier in the chapter on redevelopment in New York City?

Neighborhood Scout. 2011. 9 May 2014. http://www.neighborhoodscout.com/

Developed by Location Inc., a Massachusetts-based company, this website helps people who wish to relocate find the neighborhood that's right for them.

> Explore: What qualities does this website think are important to someone who is relocating? Can you find your neighborhood? To what extent do you agree with the assessment of your neighborhood?

Taylor, Jerry, and Peter Van Doren. "Sprawl for Me, But Not for Thee." *Cato Institute.* 1 January 2000. 6 May 2014. http://www.cato.org/publications /commentary/sprawl-me-not-thee

Contends that urban sprawl is loathed by the very people who cause it.

> Explore: In further examination of the website, how does this one article on sprawl reflect Cato Institute's larger views on the public sphere?

"The U.S. Cities Where College Grads Are Most Segregated From Everyone Else." *The Atlantic Cities.* 14 April 2014. 9 May 2014. http://www.theatlanticcities .com/neighborhoods/2014/04/us-cities-where-college-grads-are-most -segregated-everyone-else/8803/

Analyzes census data to reveal some of the most segregated communities in the United States.

> Explore: Considering Mike Davis' essay on Los Angeles, how and why are some of the most elite, walkable neighborhoods in the United States (college neighborhoods) also the most segregated from the neighborhoods that surround them? Consider your own college experience. What are the barriers that separate your campus from the neighborhoods that surround them? SO WHAT?

Walk Score. 2014. 11 May 2014. http://www.walkscore.com/

This website allows you to assess your own neighborhood and then explore neighborhoods you are thinking of moving to for college or work.

Explore: How does your neighborhood rate? Consider this website in light of Jane Jacobs' essay on sidewalks. How does walkability coordinate with desirability of a neighborhood? What are the components of that desirability? What changes in neighborhoods where destinations can only be reached by car? Visit the Walk Score Blog http://blog.walkscore.com/.

Proprietary

Birch, Dr. Eugenie L., and Susan Wachter. *The Shape of the New American City.* Sage Publications, Inc., 2009.

Leading scholars conclude that America will see a resurgence of growth in urban areas and a slowdown of sprawl.

> Explore: What chief factor, based on the studies contained in this book, is luring people back to cities from the suburbs? To what extent do you see this happening in the cities near you? To what extent does this realignment of values provide hope for the visions of James Howard Kunstler and Jack Gambino?

Cuff, Dana. "The Figure of the Neighbor: Los Angeles Past and Future." *American Quarterly* 56.3(2004): 559–582.

Los Angeles is the perfect site for the study of people as neighbors, since its modern residential environment is peppered with housing experiments, each one unique. The continuous population booms, the absence of a historic building fabric (as compared to Boston's Back Bay, for example), and the uniquely strong home-building industry set L.A. up as a neighborhood laboratory. This article examines four neighborhoods across the city that offer physical evidence of the space between house and city, and the zone between domestic privacy and the public realm.

> Explore: Of the four neighborhoods studied in this article, which ones function most effectively for their residents and why? Are Dana Cuff and Mike Davis in his essay on L.A. writing about the same city? How so?

Ruff, Joshua. "For Sale: The American Dream." *American History* 42.5(2007): 42–49.

This article from a history magazine with broad readership takes the reader back in time to post-war suburbia of the 1940s and 1950s. The American dream was not without its thorns.

> Explore: What were the people of Levittown searching for? To what extent does this version of the American dream hold true for you and your peers? How does this essay confirm or contradict the notes of nostalgia in the essays by Jack Gambino and James Howard Kunstler?

CHAPTER 14

Race, Ethnicity, and the Melting Pot

At the heart of this chapter is the contested concept of the "melting pot"—a phrase that belongs inside quotations as a mark of its uncertain status. To what extent does it actually exist, some merging of diverse peoples into an undifferentiated national whole? To what extent is it a utopian dream? More troublingly, might it be a sham that serves entrenched interests and oppresses others—those to be "melted"? Lurking in many of the selections in this unit is an alternative term to melting pot: rainbow (itself a Biblical sign of promise). The image here is one of separate bands of color harmoniously aligned.

It is probably accurate to say that matters of race and ethnicity in U.S. history have been powder kegs. They have often found homes in the vitriol of diatribes and jeremiads rather than in more dispassionate and subtle reflection. The writers assembled here offer a kind of tonic response to the usual clamoring. They comprise a community of voices who occupy very different positions but all, in one way or another, see the questions raised by the prospect of assimilation as anything but easy and clear.

ABOUT THE READINGS IN THIS CHAPTER

Over half of the selections in the unit are first-person narratives: stories by people who chronicle their own divided allegiance to the expectations of their more local ethnic neighborhood on the one hand, and to the lures of a denatured—but really "whiter"?—American dream of assimilation on the other. These narratives are framed by a range of essays that treat matters of race and assimilation from a broader social scientific perspective.

The chapter opens with three of these framing lenses. First, comes a trenchant analysis by Benjamin DeMott of interracial buddy films in which, as he says, "the long-running struggle between disenfranchised blacks and the majority white culture" is presented as easily reparable by one-on-one acts of friendship and good will. DeMott indicts the attempts of modern America to forget about white guilt and thus also to deny the need for affirmative action. Next, Peter Salins offers a brief history of the "melting pot," seen in the context of the tension between assimilation and multiculturalism. Then Peggy McIntosh considers the long-term historical effects of institutionalized racial oppression as she catalogues the nearly invisible privileges that accrue to white folks on the basis of race.

These three rather theoretical pieces contextualize the first-person memoirs that follow—analyses that spring from personal experience but do not remain there. Richard Rodriguez invites us to imagine a nation transformed by the marriage of Latin culture with the Protestant individualism that has been our country's past. The British-born novelist and essayist Zadie Smith considers the fear of losing a culture in the context of voice, of ways of speaking. She posits a space, for her a dream space, in which people may be double-voiced and where the unified single self is an illusion. Amy Tan offers a complementary view of differently voiced cultures in a daughter's attempt to inhabit two different verbal worlds, her own and that of her Chinese mother's "fractured" English. Then Henry Louis Gates, Jr. recalls his childhood experience with African-American hairstyles: a platform for thinking about identity and difference.

Next, there are two narratives about neighborhoods. Ishmael Reed focuses on the implications of moving into the kind of African-American neighborhood in Oakland, California, that his parents had "spent about a third of their lives trying to escape." By contrast, in Marianna Torgovnick's homecoming to her Italian-American neighborhood in Brooklyn, the comforts of the neighborhood and the past are undercut by the claustrophobia and potential for violence in the present.

The chapter ends with two pieces, one theoretical and one narrative, that seek to test the limits of the category. Michael Jonas reviews a study by Harvard political scientist Robert Putnam that complicates the orthodoxy that our differences make us stronger. Finally, the Northern Irish novelist Robert McLiam Wilson brings matters to a close by challenging many of the assumptions the other writers share. To what extent, he wonders, are national and even some racial identities inevitably fabrications?

Benjamin DeMott

Put on a Happy Face: Masking the Differences between Blacks and Whites

Focusing on the "romance" of black-white friendship represented in popular American films, this piece argues, with angry irony, that "the cleansing social force" of friendship has been embraced by mainstream white culture as an easy out from the responsibility for historically produced and institutionalized racism. "People forget the theoretically unforgettable—the caste history of American blacks, the connection between no schools for longer than a century and bad school performance now," declares Benjamin DeMott, and this essay, which first appeared in *Harper's Magazine* in 1995, seeks to make us remember. A scholar and cultural critic who taught at Amherst College for more than forty years, DeMott wrote a popular trilogy of books on Americans' difficulties thinking about class, race, and gender. *The Imperial Middle: Why Americans Can't Think Straight about Class* (1990), *The Trouble with Friendship: Why Americans Can't Think Straight about Race* (1995), and *Killer Woman Blues: Why Americans Can't Think Straight about Gender* (2000).

At the movies these days, questions about racial injustice have been amicably resolved. Watch *Pulp Fiction* or *Congo* or *A Little Princess* or any other recent film in which both blacks and whites are primary characters and you can, if you want, forget about race. Whites and blacks greet one another on the screen with loving candor, revealing their common humanity. In *Pulp Fiction*, an armed black mobster (played by Samuel L. Jackson) looks deep into the eyes of an armed white thief in the middle of a holdup (played by Tim Roth) and shares his version of God's word in Ezekiel, whereupon the two men lay aside their weapons, both more or less redeemed. The moment inverts an earlier scene in which a white boxer (played by Bruce Willis) risks his life to save another black mobster (played by Ving Rhames), who is being sexually tortured as a prelude to his execution.

Pulp Fiction (gross through July [1995]: $107 million) is one of a series of films suggesting that the beast of American racism is tamed and harmless. Close to the start of *Die Hard with a Vengeance* (gross through July [1995]: $95 million), the camera finds a white man wearing sandwich boards on the corner of Amsterdam Avenue and 138th Street in Harlem. The boards carry a horrific legend: I HATE NIGGERS. A group of young blacks approach the man with murderous intent, bearing guns and knives. They are figures straight out of a national nightmare—ugly, enraged, terrifying. No problem. A black man, again played by Jackson, appears and rescues the white man, played by

Copyright © 1995 by Harper's Magazine. All rights reserved. Reproduced from the September issue by special permission.

Willis. The black man and white man come to know each other well. In time the white man declares flatly to the black, "I need you more than you need me." A moment later he charges the black with being a racist—with not liking whites as much as the white man likes blacks—and the two talk frankly about their racial prejudices. Near the end of the film, the men have grown so close that each volunteers to die for the other.

Pulp Fiction and *Die Hard with a Vengeance* follow the pattern of *Lethal Weapon* 1, 2, and 3, the Danny Glover/Mel Gibson buddy vehicles that collectively grossed $357 million, and *White Men Can't Jump*, which, in the year of the L.A. riots, grossed $76 million. In *White Men Can't Jump*, a white dropout, played by Woody Harrelson, ekes out a living on black-dominated basketball courts in Los Angeles. He's arrogant and aggressive but never in danger because he has a black protector and friend, played by Wesley Snipes. At the movie's end, the white, flying above the hoop like a stereotypical black player, scores the winning basket in a two-on-two pickup game on an alley-oop pass from his black chum, whereupon the two men fall into each other's arms in joy. Later, the black friend agrees to find work for the white at the store he manages.

WHITE (helpless): I gotta get a job. Can you get me a job?

BLACK (affectionately teasing): Got any references?

WHITE (shy grin): You.

Such dialogue is the stuff of romance. What's dreamed of and gained is a place where whites are unafraid of blacks, where blacks ask for and need nothing from whites, and where the sameness of the races creates a common fund of sweet content.[1] The details of the dream matter less than the force that makes it come true for both races, eliminating the constraints of objective reality and redistributing resources, status, and capabilities. That cleansing social force supersedes political and economic fact or policy; that force, improbably enough, is friendship.

5   Watching the beaming white men who know how to jump, we do well to remind ourselves of what the camera shot leaves out. Black infants die in America at twice the rate of white infants. (Despite the increased numbers of middle-class blacks, the rates are diverging, with black rates actually rising.) One out of every two black children lives below the poverty line (as compared with one out of seven white children). Nearly four times as many black families exist below the poverty line as white families. More than 50 percent of African-American families have incomes below $25,000. Among black youths under age twenty, death by murder occurs nearly ten times as often as among whites. Over 60 percent of births to black mothers occur out of wedlock, more than four times the rate for white mothers. The net worth of the typical white household is ten times that of the typical black household. In many states, five to ten times as many blacks as whites age eighteen to thirty are in prison.

The good news at the movies obscures the bad news in the streets and confirms the Supreme Court's recent decisions on busing, affirmative action, and redistricting. Like the plot of *White Men Can't Jump*, the Court postulates the existence of a society no longer troubled by racism. Because black-white friendship is now understood to be the rule, there is no need for integrated schools or a congressional Black Caucus or affirmative action. The Congress and state governors can guiltlessly cut welfare, food assistance, fuel assistance, Head Start, housing money, fellowship money, vaccine money. Justice Anthony Kennedy can declare, speaking for the Supreme Court majority last June, that creating a world of genuine equality and sameness requires only that "our political system and our society cleanse themselves . . . of discrimination."

The deep logic runs as follows: *Yesterday white people didn't like black people, and accordingly suffered guilt, knowing that the dislike was racist and knowing also that as moral persons they would have to atone for the guilt. They would have to ante up for welfare and Head Start and halfway houses and free vaccine and midnight basketball and summer jobs for schoolkids and graduate fellowships for promising scholars and craft-union apprenticeships and so on, endlessly. A considerable and wasteful expense. But at length came the realization that by ending dislike or hatred it would be possible to end guilt, which in turn would mean an end to redress: no more wasteful ransom money. There would be but one requirement: the regular production and continuous showing forth of evidence indisputably proving that hatred has totally vanished from the land.*

I cannot tell the reader how much I would like to believe in this sunshine world. After the theater lights brighten and I've found coins for a black beggar on the way to my car and am driving home through downtown Springfield, Massachusetts, the world invented by *Die Hard with a Vengeance* and America's highest court gives way only slowly to the familiar urban vision in my windshield—homeless blacks on trash-strewn streets, black prostitutes staked out on a corner, and signs of a not very furtive drug trade. I know perfectly well that most African-Americans don't commit crimes or live in alleys. I also know that for somebody like myself, downtown Springfield in the late evening is not a good place to be.

The movies reflect the larger dynamic of wish and dream. Day after day the nation's corporate ministries of culture churn out images of racial harmony. Millions awaken each morning to the friendly sight of Katie Couric nudging a perky elbow into good buddy Bryant Gumbel's side. My mailbox and millions of demographically similar others are choked with flyers from companies (Wal-Mart, Victoria's Secret) bent on publicizing both their wares and their social bona fides by displaying black and white models at cordial ease with one another. A torrent of goodwill messages about race arrives daily—revelations of corporate largesse, commercials, news features, TV specials, all proclaiming that whites like me feel strongly positive impulses of friendship for blacks and that those same admirable impulses are effectively eradicating racial differences, rendering blacks and whites the same. BellSouth TV commercials present children singing "I am the keeper of the world"—first a white child, then a black child, then a white child, then a black child. Because Dow Chemical likes black America, it recruits young black college grads for its research division and dramatizes, in TV commercials, their tearful-joyful partings from home. ("Son, show 'em what you got," says a black lad's father.) American Express shows an elegant black couple and an elegant white couple sitting together in a theater, happy in one another's company. (The couples share the box with an oversized Gold Card.) During the evening news I watch a black mom offer Robitussin to a miserably coughing white mom. Here's *People* magazine promoting itself under a photo of John Lee Hooker, the black bluesman. "We're these kinds of people, too," *People* claims in the caption. In [a recent] production of *Hamlet* on Broadway, Horatio [was] played by a black actor. On *The 700 Club*, Pat Robertson joshes Ben Kinchlow, his black sidekick, about Ben's far-out ties.

10   What counts here is not the saccharine clumsiness of the interchanges but the bulk of them—the ceaseless, self-validating gestures of friendship, the humming, buzzing background theme: *All decent Americans extend the hand of friendship to African-Americans; nothing but nothing is more auspicious for the African-American future than this extended hand.* Faith in the miracle cure of racism by change-of-heart turns out to be so familiar as to have become unnoticeable. And yes, the faith has its benign aspect. Even as they nudge me and others toward belief in magic (instant pals and no-money-down equality), the images and messages of devoted relationships between blacks and whites do exert a humanizing influence.

Nonetheless, through these same images and messages the comfortable majority tells itself a fatuous untruth. Promoting the fantasy of painless answers, inspiring groundless self-approval among whites, joining the Supreme Court in treating "cleansing" as *inevitable*, the new orthodoxy of friendship incites culture-wide evasion, justifies one political step backward after another, and greases the skids along which, tomorrow, welfare block grants will slide into state highway-resurfacing budgets. Whites are part of the solution, says this orthodoxy, if we break out of the prison of our skin color, say hello, as equals, one-on-one, to a black stranger, and make a black friend. We're part of the problem if we have an aversion to black people or are frightened of them, or if we feel that the more distance we put between them and us the better, or if we're in the habit of asserting our superiority rather than acknowledging our common humanity. Thus we shift the problem away from politics—from black experience and the history of slavery—and perceive it as a matter of the suspicion and fear found within the white heart; solving the problem asks no more of us than that we work on ourselves, scrubbing off the dirt of ill will.

The approach miniaturizes, personalizes, and moralizes; it removes the large and complex dilemmas of race from the public sphere. It tempts audiences to see history as irrelevant and to regard feelings as decisive—to believe that the fate of black Americans is shaped mainly by events occurring in the hearts and minds of the privileged. And let's be frank: the orthodoxy of friendship feels *nice*. It practically *consecrates* self-flattery. The "good" Bill Clinton who attends black churches and talks with likable ease to fellow worshipers was campaigning when Los Angeles rioted in '92. "White Americans," he said, "are gripped by the isolation of their own experience. Too many still simply have no friends of other races and do not know any differently." Few black youths of working age in South-Central L.A. had been near enough to the idea of a job even to think of looking for work before the Rodney King verdict, but the problem, according to Clinton, was that whites need black friends.

Most of the country's leading voices of journalistic conscience (editorial writers, television anchorpersons, syndicated columnists) roundly endorse the doctrine of black-white friendship as a means of redressing the inequalities between the races. Roger Rosenblatt, editor of the *Columbia Journalism Review* and an especially deft supplier of warm and fuzzy sentiment, published an essay in *Family Circle* arguing that white friendship and sympathy for blacks simultaneously make power differentials vanish and create interracial identity between us, one by one. The author finds his *exemplum* in an episode revealing the personal sensitivity, to injured blacks, of one of his children.

"When our oldest child, Carl, was in high school," he writes, "he and two black friends were standing on a street corner in New York City one spring evening, trying to hail a taxi. The three boys were dressed decently and were doing nothing wild or threatening. Still, no taxi would pick them up. If a driver spotted Carl first, he might slow down, but he would take off again when he saw the others. Carl's two companions were familiar with this sort of abuse. Carl, who had never observed it firsthand before, burned with anger and embarrassment that he was the color of a world that would so mistreat his friends."

Rosenblatt notes that when his son "was applying to colleges, he wrote 15 his essay on that taxi incident with his two black friends. . . . He was able to articulate what he could not say at the time—how ashamed and impotent he felt. He also wrote of the power of their friendship, which has lasted to this day and has carried all three young men into the country that belongs to them. To all of us."

In this homily white sympathy begets interracial sameness in several ways. The three classmates are said to react identically to the cabdrivers' snub; i.e., they feel humiliated. "[Carl] could not find the words to express his humiliation and his friends *would* not express theirs."

The anger that inspires the younger Rosenblatt's college-admission essay on racism is seen as identical with black anger. Friendship brings the classmates together as joint, equal owners of the land of their birth ("the country that belongs to [all of] them"). And Rosenblatt supplies a still larger vision of essential black-white sameness near the end of his essay: "Our proper hearts tell the truth," he declares, "which is that we are all in the same boat, rich and poor, black and white. We are helpless, wicked, heroic, terrified, and we need one another. We need to give rides to one another."

Thus do acts of private piety substitute for public policy while the possibility of urgent political action disappears into a sentimental haze. "If we're looking for a formula to ease the tensions between the races," Rosenblatt observes, then we should "attack the disintegration of the black community" and "the desperation of the poor." Without overtly mocking civil rights activists who look toward the political arena "to erase the tensions," Rosenblatt alludes to them in a throwaway manner, implying that properly adjusted whites look elsewhere, that there was a time for politicking for "equal rights" but we've passed through it. Now is a time in which we should listen to our hearts at moments of epiphany and allow sympathy to work its wizardry, cleansing and floating us, blacks and whites "all in the same boat," on a mystical undercurrent of the New Age.

Blacks themselves aren't necessarily proof against this theme, as witness a recent essay by James Alan McPherson in the Harvard journal *Reconstruction*. McPherson, who received the 1977 Pulitzer Prize for fiction for his collection of stories *Elbow Room*, says that "the only possible steps, the safest steps . . . small ones" in the movement "toward a universal culture" will be those built not on "ideologies and formulas and programs" but on experiences of personal connectedness.

20   "Just this past spring," he writes, "when I was leaving a restaurant after taking a [white] former student to dinner, a black [woman on the sidewalk] said to my friend, in a rasping voice, 'Hello, girlfriend. Have you got anything to spare?'" The person speaking was a female crack addict with a child who was also addicted. "But," writes McPherson, when the addict made her pitch to his dinner companion, "I saw in my friend's face an understanding and sympathy and a shining which transcended race and class. Her face reflected one human soul's connection with another. The magnetic field between the two women was charged with spiritual energy."

The writer points the path to progress through interpersonal gestures by people who "insist on remaining human, and having human responses. . . . Perhaps the best that can be done, now, is the offering of understanding and support to the few out of many who are capable of such gestures, rather than devising another plan to engineer the many into one."

The elevated vocabulary ("soul," "spiritual") beatifies the impulse to turn away from the real-life agenda of actions capable of reducing racial injustice.

Wherever that impulse dominates, the rhetoric of racial sameness thrives, diminishing historical catastrophes affecting millions over centuries and inflating the significance of tremors of tenderness briefly troubling the heart or conscience of a single individual—the boy waiting for a cab, the woman leaving the restaurant. People forget the theoretically unforgettable—the caste history of American blacks, the connection between no schools for longer than a century and bad school performance now, between hateful social attitudes and zero employment opportunities, between minority anguish and majority fear.

How could this way of seeing have become conventional so swiftly? How did the dogmas of instant equality insinuate themselves so effortlessly into courts and mass audiences alike? How can a white man like myself, who taught Southern blacks in the 1960s, find himself seduced—as I have been more than once—by the orthodoxy of friendship? In the civil rights era, the experience for many millions of Americans was one of discovery. A hitherto unimagined continent of human reality and history came into view, inducing genuine concern and at least a temporary setting aside of self-importance. I remember with utter clarity what I felt at Mary Holmes College in West Point, Mississippi, when a black student of mine was killed by tailgating rednecks; my fellow tutors and I were overwhelmed with how shamefully wrong a wrong could be. For a time, we were released from the prisons of moral weakness and ambiguity. In the year or two that followed—the mid-sixties— the notion that some humans are more human than others, whites more human than blacks, appeared to have been overturned. The next step seemed obvious: society would have to admit that when one race deprives another of its humanity for centuries, those who have done the depriving are obligated to do what they can to restore the humanity of the deprived. The obligation clearly entailed the mounting of comprehensive long-term programs of developmental assistance—not guilt-money handouts—for nearly the entire black population. The path forward was unavoidable.

It was avoided. Shortly after the award of civil rights and the institution, in 1966, of limited preferential treatment to remedy employment and educational discrimination against African-Americans, a measure of economic progress for blacks did appear in census reports. Not much, but enough to stimulate glowing tales of universal black advance and to launch the good-news barrage that continues to this day (headline in the New York Times, June 18, 1995: "Moving On Up: The Greening of America's Black Middle Class").

After Ronald Reagan was elected to his first term, the new dogma of black-white sameness found ideological support in the form of criticism of so-called coddling. Liberal activists of both races were berated by critics of both races for fostering an allegedly enfeebling psychology of dependency that discouraged African-Americans from committing themselves to individual self-development. In 1988, the charge was passionately voiced in an essay in these pages, "I'm Black, You're White, Who's Innocent?" by Shelby Steele, who attributed the difference between black rates of advance and those of other minority groups to white folks' pampering. Most blacks, Steele claimed, could make it on their own—as voluntary immigrants have done—were they not held back by devitalizing programs that presented them, to themselves and others, as somehow dissimilar to and weaker than other Americans. This argument was all-in-the-same-boatism in a different key; the claim remained that progress depends upon recognition of black-white sameness. Let us see through superficial differences to the underlying, equally distributed gift for success. Let us teach ourselves—in the words of the Garth Brooks tune—to ignore "the color of skin" and "look for . . . the beauty within."

Still further support for the policy once known as "do-nothingism" came from points-of-light barkers, who held that a little something might perhaps be done *if* accompanied by enough publicity. Nearly every broadcaster and publisher in America moves a bale of reportage on pro bono efforts by white Americans to speed the advance of black Americans. Example: McDonald's and the National Basketball Association distribute balloons when they announce they are addressing the dropout problem with an annual "Stay in School" scheme that gives schoolkids who don't miss a January school day a ticket to an all-star exhibition. The publicity strengthens the idea that these initiatives will nullify the social context—the city I see through my windshield. Reports of white philanthropy suggest that the troubles of this block and the next should be understood as phenomena in transition. The condition of American blacks need not be read as the fixed, unchanging consequence of generations of bottom-caste existence. Edging discreetly past a beggar posted near the entrance to Zabar's or H&H Bagels, or, while walking the dog, stepping politely around black men asleep on the sidewalk, we need not see ourselves and our fellows as uncaring accomplices in the acts of social injustice.

Yet more powerful has been the ceaseless assault, over the past generation, on our knowledge of the historical situation of black Americans. On the face of things it seems improbable that the cumulative weight of documented historical injury to African-Americans could ever be lightly assessed. Gifted black writers continue to show, in scene after scene—in their studies of middle-class blacks interacting with whites—how historical realities shape the lives of their black characters. In *Killer of Sheep*, the brilliant black filmmaker Charles Burnett dramatizes the daily encounters that suck poor blacks into will-lessness and contempt for white fairy tales of interracial harmony; he quickens his historical themes with images of faceless black meat processors gutting undifferentiated, unchoosing animal life. Here, say these images, as though talking back to Clarence Thomas, here is a basic level of black life unchanged over generations. Where there's work, it's miserably paid and ugly.

Space allotments at home and at work cramp body and mind. Positive expectation withers in infancy. People fall into the habit of jeering at aspiration as though at the bidding of physical law. Obstacles at every hand prevent people from loving and being loved in decent ways, prevent children from believing their parents, prevent parents from believing they themselves know anything worth knowing. The only true self, now as in the long past, is the one mocked by one's own race. "Shit on you, nigger," says a voice in *Killer of Sheep.* "Nothing you say matters a good goddamn."

For whites, these words produce guilt, and for blacks, I can only assume, pain and despair. The audience for tragedy remains small, while at the multiplex the popular enthusiasm for historical romance remains constant and vast. During the last two decades, the entertainment industry has conducted a siege on the pertinent past, systematically excising knowledge of the consequences of the historical exploitation of African-Americans. Factitious renderings of the American past blur the outlines of black-white conflict, redefine the ground of black grievances for the purpose of diminishing the grievances, restage black life in accordance with the illusory conventions of American success mythology, and present the operative influences on race history as the same as those implied to be pivotal in *White Men Can't Jump* or a BellSouth advertisement.

Although there was scant popular awareness of it at the time (1977), the television miniseries *Roots* introduced the figure of the Unscathed Slave. To an enthralled audience of more than 80 million the series intimated that the damage resulting from generations of birth-ascribed, semi-animal status was largely temporary, that slavery was a product of motiveless malignity on the social margins rather than of respectable rationality, and that the ultimate significance of the institution lay in the demonstration, by freed slaves, that no force on earth can best the energies of American Individualism. ("Much like the Waltons confronting the Depression," writes historian Eric Foner, a widely respected authority on American slavery, "the family in 'Roots' neither seeks nor requires outside help; individual or family effort is always sufficient.") Ken Burns's much applauded PBS documentary *The Civil War* (1990) went even further than *Roots* in downscaling black injury; the series treated slavery, birth-ascribed inferiority, and the centuries-old denial of dignity as matters of slight consequence. (By "implicitly denying the brutal reality of slavery," writes historian Jeanie Attie, Burns's programs crossed "a dangerous moral threshold." To a group of historians who asked him why slavery had been so slighted, Burns said that any discussion of slavery "would have been lengthy and boring.")

Mass media treatments of the civil rights protest years carried forward 30 the process, contributing to the "positive" erasure of difference. Big-budget films like *Mississippi Burning,* together with an array of TV biographical specials on Dr. Martin Luther King and others, presented the long-running struggle between disenfranchised blacks and the majority white culture as a heartwarming episode of interracial unity; the speed and caringness of white response to the oppression of blacks demonstrated that broadscale race conflict or race difference was inconceivable.

A consciousness that ingests either a part or the whole of this revisionism loses touch with the two fundamental truths of race in America; namely, that because of what happened in the past, blacks and whites cannot yet be the same; and that because what happened in the past was no mere matter of ill will or insult but the outcome of an established caste structure that has only very recently begun to be dismantled, it is not reparable by one-on-one goodwill. The word "slavery" comes to induce stock responses with no vital sense of a grinding devastation of mind visited upon generation after generation. Hoodwinked by the orthodoxy of friendship, the nation either ignores the past, summons for it a detached, correct "compassion," or gazes at it as though it were a set of aesthetic conventions, like twisted trees and fragmented rocks in nineteenth-century picturesque painting—lifeless phenomena without bearing on the present. The chance of striking through the mask of corporate-underwritten, feel-good, ahistorical racism grows daily more remote. The trade-off—whites promise friendship, blacks accept the status quo—begins to seem like a good deal.

Cosseted by Hollywood's magic lantern and soothed by press releases from Washington and the American Enterprise Institute, we should never forget what we see and hear for ourselves. Broken out by race, the results of every social tabulation from unemployment to life expectancy add up to a chronicle of atrocity. The history of black America fully explains—to anyone who approaches it honestly—how the disaster happened and why neither guilt money nor lectures on personal responsibility can, in and of themselves, repair the damage. The vision of friendship and sympathy placing blacks and whites "all in the same boat," rendering them equally able to do each other favors, "to give rides to one another," is a smiling but monstrous lie.

Notes

[1] I could go on with examples of movies that deliver the good news of friendship: *Regarding Henry, Driving Miss Daisy, Forrest Gump, The Shawshank Redemption, Philadelphia, The Last Boy Scout, 48 Hours I–II, Rising Sun, Iron Eagle I–II, Rudy, Sister Act, Hearts of Dixie, Betrayed, The Power of One, White Nights, Clara's Heart, Doc Hollywood, Cool Runnings, Places in the Heart, Trading Places, Fried Green Tomatoes, Q & A, Platoon, A Mother's Courage: The Mary Thomas Story, The Unforgiven, The Air Up There, The Pelican Brief, Losing Isaiah, Smoke, Searching for Bobby Fischer, An Officer and a Gentleman, Speed,* etc.

Things to Do with the Reading

1. How does this essay use references to time? Look for mention of dates, of terms such as "history" and "long-term" and "centuries-old," as well as various aspects of the present, the contemporary scene. Write a short essay in which you analyze DeMott's argument about historical consciousness in America.

2. What is DeMott's answer to the idea that blacks in America don't need government aid because they should be able to harness "the energies of American individualism" to improve their condition? Write a short essay in answer to this question.

   The following question may help you to focus. So WHAT that DeMott holds both blacks and whites responsible for projecting these "'positive' erasures of difference" (paragraph 30)? Consider, for example, the message that DeMott says the African-American-made miniseries *Roots* sent about the situation of blacks in America and what they should rely on as their best hope for the future.

3. **Link:** Write a short essay in which you use DeMott as a lens for analyzing the representation of black-white relationships and black-black relationships in Ishmael Reed's essay "My Neighborhood," which appears later in this chapter. What are the chances DeMott would find Reed unduly "rosy" about black-black relationships?

4. **Links Across Chapters:** Notice how, in Chapter 15, James Peck defines melodrama against tragedy in his analysis, "September 11—A National Tragedy." In what ways do Peck's anxieties about representations of 9/11 occupy the same ground (sharing assumptions) with DeMott? Find sentences in each essay to put into conversation with each other. Write a short essay in which you consider the extent to which DeMott's term *romance* means the same thing as Peck does by *melodrama*.

   Alternatively, study Kera Bolonik's analysis of *Will & Grace* in her review entitled "Oy Gay!" in Chapter 16. Write an essay in which you ponder the extent to which the deception Bolonik sees in the television show resembles the one DeMott observes in his list of films.

5. **Application:** DeMott cites at least two dozen films that he says present "the long-running struggle between disenfranchised blacks and the majority white culture as a heartwarming episode of interracial unity" (see note at the end of the essay). Using the black-white buddy film *White Men Can't Jump* as a primary example of what he calls the "good will messages about race," DeMott argues that the effect of this cultural trend is to create the illusion that blacks and whites are "all in the same boat," so that all that is needed to solve centuries of disaster for blacks are displays of warmhearted sympathy.

DeMott's essay was published in 1995. Your task is to write an essay in which you update it in one of the following ways:

- Consider the extent to which the trend he describes in movies and other media is still alive and well today. Locate one or more current films or other media that seem to you to send the message of black-white friendship as an indication of sameness and as evidence that one-on-one compassion can solve the problems of race in America.

- Locate one or more films or other media that seem to be representative of a different trend in the way that black-white relationships are being represented now. Determine what you think this new trend offers as a message about the state of black-white relations in America, the situation of blacks in America, and what does or does not need to be done about it.

- Use DeMott's analysis as a model for looking at representational trends depicting marginalized groups besides blacks in contemporary films or other media. Does the trend that you locate seem to fall into DeMott's category of "deceptive romances"? Or, does the trend represent the group in a way that DeMott might be more optimistic about? In either case, what does this representation "say" about the situation of this group in America?

Peter Salins

Assimilation, American Style

This essay offers a brief history of that influential American myth, "the melting pot." It locates the melting pot in relation to such key terms in thinking about race as "assimilation" and "multiculturalism." The piece was written in 1997 by the urban planning scholar Peter Salins, a professor of political science at SUNY at Stony Brook and a former Provost and Vice Chancellor for Academic Affairs of the State University of New York system. Salins is also a senior fellow of the Manhattan Institute's Center for State and Local Leadership. Along with his many academic books and articles, he has also published a number of articles in the popular press on the housing crisis in urban areas. His most recent book is *The Smart Society: Strengthening America's Greatest Resource, Its People* (2014).

> California Chinese, Boston Irish, Wisconsin Germans, yes, and Alabama Negroes, have more in common than they have apart. . . . It is a fact that Americans from all sections and of all racial extractions are more alike than the Welsh are like the English, the Lancashireman like the Cockney, or for that matter the Lowland Scot like the Highlander.
>
> —John Steinbeck, 1962

Most Americans, both those who favor and those who oppose assimilation, believe   1
that for immigrants to assimilate, they must abandon their original cultural attributes and conform entirely to the behaviors and customs of the majority of the native-born population. In the terminology of the armed forces, this represents a model of "up or out": Either immigrants bring themselves "up" to native cultural standards or they are doomed to live "out" of the charmed circle of the national culture.

The notion is not entirely far-fetched because this is exactly what assimilation demands in other societies. North African immigrants to France are, for example, expected to assimilate by abandoning their native folkways with alacrity. Official French policy has been zealous in making North African and other Muslim women give up wearing their *chador*[1] and, in the schools, instilling a disdain for North African and Muslim culture in their children. To varying degrees, most European countries that have had to absorb large numbers of immigrants since World War II interpret assimilation this way—an interpretation that has promoted national and ethnic disunity.

In America, however, assimilation has not meant repudiating immigrant culture. Assimilation, American style has always been much more flexible and accommodating and, consequently, much more effective in achieving its

Assimilation, American Style, Peter Salins. REASON MAGAZINE. Reprinted with permission.

purpose—to allow the United States to preserve its "national unity in the face of the influx of hordes of persons of scores of different nationalities," in the words of the sociologist Henry Fairchild.

A popular way of getting hold of the assimilation idea has been to use a metaphor, and by far the most popular metaphor has been that of the "melting pot," a term introduced in Israel Zangwill's 1908 play of that name: "There she lies, the great Melting-Pot—Listen! Can't you hear the roaring and the bubbling? . . .Ah, what a stirring and a seething! Celt and Latin, Slav and Teuton, Greek and Syrian, black and yellow . . . Jew and Gentile. . . . East and West, and North and South, the palm and the pine, the pole and the equator, the crescent and the cross—how the great Alchemist melts and fuses them with his purifying flame! Here shall they all unite to build the Republic of Man and the Kingdom of God."

5   For all its somewhat ahistorical idealism, the melting-pot metaphor still represents the standard around which fervent proponents of assimilation have rallied over the years. According to the melting-pot metaphor, assimilation involved the fine-grained intermingling of diverse ethnicities and cultures into a single national "alloy." If taken literally, this metaphor implied two things. The point most commonly taken is that the new human products of the melting pot would, of necessity, be culturally indistinguishable. Presumably every piece of metal taken from a melting pot should have the same chemical composition. Less frequently understood is the metaphor's implication that natives and their indigenous cultural characteristics would also be irreversibly changed—blended beyond recognition—because they constituted the base material of the melting pot.

These two corollaries of the melting-pot metaphor have long invited criticism by those who thought they were inconsistent with the ethnic realities of American society. Critics of the metaphor have spanned the ideological spectrum and mounted several different lines of attack on it. Empiricists submitted evidence that the melting pot wasn't working as predicted and concluded, as did Nathan Glazer and Daniel Patrick Moynihan in *Beyond the Melting Pot* (1963), "The point about the melting pot—is that it did not happen." Other critics rejected the second corollary of the metaphor—that natives were changed by it, too—and saw no reason that native Americans should give up any part of their cultural attributes to "melt" into the alloy. If true assimilation were to occur, the criticism went, immigrants would have to abandon all their cultural baggage and conform to American ways. It is the immigrant, said Fairchild, representing the views of many Americans, "who must undergo the entire transformation; the true member of the American nationality is not called upon to change in the least."

A third strain of criticism was first voiced by sociologist Horace Kallen in the early part of this century. Among the most prolific American scholars of ethnicity, Kallen argued that it was not only unrealistic but cruel and harmful to force new immigrants to shed their familiar, lifelong cultural attributes as the price of admission to American society. In place of the melting pot, he called for "cultural pluralism." In Kallen's words, national policy should "seek to provide conditions under which each [group] might attain the cultural perfection that is proper to its kind."

Kallen introduced the concept in 1916, only eight years after publication of Zangwill's *The Melting Pot*, determined to challenge that work's premises. Cultural pluralism rejects melting-pot assimilationism not on empirical grounds but on ideological ones. Kallen and his followers believed that immigrants to the United States should not "melt" into a common national ethnic alloy but, rather, should steadfastly hang on to their cultural ethnicity and band together for social and political purposes even after generations of residence in the United States. As such, cultural pluralism is not an alternative theory of assimilation; it is a theory opposed to assimilation.

Cultural pluralism is, in fact, the philosophical antecedent of modern multiculturalism—what I call "ethnic federalism": official recognition of distinct, essentially fixed ethnic groups and the doling out of resources based on membership in an ethnic group. Ethnic federalism explicitly rejects the notion of a transcendent American identity, the old idea that out of ethnic diversity there would emerge a single, culturally unified people. Instead, the United States is to be viewed as a vast ethnic federation—Canada's Anglo-French arrangement, raised to the nth power. Viewing ethnic Americans as members of a federation rather than a union, ethnic federalism, a.k.a. multiculturalism, asserts that ethnic Americans have the right to proportional representation in matters of power and privilege, the right to demand that their "native" culture and putative ethnic ancestors be accorded recognition and respect, and the right to function in their "native" language (even if it is not the language of their birth or they never learned to speak it), not just at home but in the public realm.

Ethnic federalism is at all times an ideology of ethnic grievance and 10 inevitably leads to and justifies ethnic conflict. All the nations that have ever embraced it, from Yugoslavia to Lebanon, from Belgium to Canada, have had to live with perpetual ethnic discord.

Kallen's views, however, stop significantly short of contemporary multiculturalism in their demands on the larger "native" American society. For Kallen, cultural pluralism was a defensive strategy for "unassimilable" immigrant ethnic groups that required no accommodation by the larger society. Contemporary multiculturalists, on the other hand, by making cultural pluralism the basis of ethnic federalism, demand certain ethnic rights and concessions. By emphasizing the failure of assimilation, multiculturalists hope to provide intellectual and political support for their policies.

The multiculturalists' rejection of the melting-pot idea is seen in the metaphors they propose in its place. Civil rights activist Jesse Jackson suggested that Americans are members of a "rainbow coalition." Former New York Mayor

David Dinkins saw his constituents constituting a "gorgeous mosaic." Former Congresswoman Shirley Chisholm characterized America's ethnic groups as being like ingredients in a "salad bowl." Barbara Jordan, recent chairperson of the U.S. Commission on Immigration Reform, said: "We are more than a melting-pot; we are a kaleidoscope."

These counter-metaphors all share a common premise: that ethnic groups in the United States may live side by side harmoniously, but on two conditions that overturn both assumptions of the melting-pot metaphor. First, immigrants (and black Americans) should never have to (or maybe should not even want to) give up any of their original cultural attributes. And second, there never can or will be a single unified national identity that all Americans can relate to. These two principles are the foundations of cultural pluralism, the antithesis of assimilationism.

While all these metaphors—including the melting pot—are colorful ways of representing assimilation, they don't go far in giving one an accurate understanding of what assimilation is really about. For example, across the ideological spectrum, they all invoke some external, impersonal assimilating agent. Who, exactly, is the "great alchemist" of the melting pot? What force tosses the salad or pieces together the mosaic? By picturing assimilation as an impersonal, automatic process and thus placing it beyond analysis, the metaphors fail to illuminate its most important secrets. Assimilation, if it is to succeed, must be a voluntary process, by both the assimilating immigrants and the assimilated-to natives. Assimilation is a human accommodation, not a mechanical production.

15 The metaphors also mislead as to the purposes of assimilation. The melting pot is supposed to turn out an undifferentiated alloy—a uniform, ethnically neutral, American protoperson. Critics have long pointed out that this idea is far-fetched. But is it even desirable? And if it is desirable, does it really foster a shared national identity? The greatest failing of the melting-pot metaphor is that it overreaches. It exaggerates the degree to which immigrants' ethnicity is likely to be extinguished by exposure to American society and it exaggerates the need to extinguish ethnicity. By being too compelling, too idealistic, the melting-pot idea has inadvertently helped to discredit the very assimilation paradigm it was meant to celebrate.

On the other hand, behind their unexceptionable blandness, the antithetical cultural pluralist metaphors are profoundly insidious. By suggesting that the product of assimilation is mere ethnic coexistence without integration, they undermine the objectives of assimilation, even if they appear more realistic. Is assimilation only about diverse ethnic groups sharing the same national space? That much can be said for any multiethnic society. If the ethnic greens of the salad or the fragments of the mosaic do not interact and identify with each other, no meaningful assimilation is taking place.

Perhaps a new assimilation metaphor should be introduced—one that depends not on a mechanical process like the melting pot but on human dynamics. Assimilation might be viewed as more akin to religious conversion than anything else. In the terms of this metaphor, the immigrant is the convert, American society is the religious order being joined, and assimilation is the process by which the conversion takes place. Just as there are many motives for people to immigrate, so are there many motives for them to change their religion: spiritual, practical (marrying a person of another faith), and materialistic (joining some churches can lead to jobs or subsidized housing). But whatever the motivation, conversion usually involves the consistent application of certain principles. Conversion is a mutual decision requiring affirmation by both the convert and the religious order he or she wishes to join. Converts are expected in most (but not all) cases to renounce their old religions. But converts do not have to change their behavior in any respects other than those that relate to the new religion. They are expected only to believe in its theological principles, observe its rituals and holidays, and live by its moral precepts. Beyond that, they can be rich or poor, practice any trade, pursue any avocational interests, and have any racial or other personal attributes. Once they undergo conversion, they are eagerly welcomed into the fellowship of believers. They have become part of "us" rather than "them." This is undoubtedly what writer G. K. Chesterton had in mind when he said: "America is a nation with the soul of a church."

Notes

[1]*Chadors* are the long black veils worn by Muslim women.

Things to Do with the Reading

1. Salins's essay is good at making the implicit explicit and at UNCOVERING ASSUMPTIONS (reasoning back to premises—see Chapter 2). He is especially interested in the implications of the metaphors that have been used to talk about cultural identity and assimilation in America, such as the melting pot. Using Salins's method as a model, write an essay in which you draw out the implications of Jesse Jackson's metaphor—the rainbow coalition. (See Chapter 5 on figurative logic.)

   Here are some supporting questions. How is the rainbow metaphor like and unlike the melting pot metaphor? Next, draw out the implications of Salins's proposed religious conversion metaphor as defined in the last paragraph of the essay. How is this metaphor like and unlike the rainbow and the melting pot?

2. A metaphor is a comparison, a way of thinking by analogy (see Chapter 5 on metaphor). In order to be persuasive and fair, the two things being

compared need to have enough in common to justify the comparison. What is compared to what in Salins's conversion metaphor? Write a short essay on what this analogy suggests about Salins's way of thinking about being (and becoming) American?

3. Though Salins's piece is a historical analysis, it also is a problem/solution piece with a point of view. This point of view emerges gradually, but it becomes evident when you notice that the critique offered of each idea on assimilation, starting with the melting pot, is essentially the same critique. Write a few paragraphs in which you compare paragraphs 6 and 11, locating and exploring the significance of the common element.

4. Write a rhetorical analysis of the Salins essay (for discussion of rhetorical analyses, see especially Chapter 1). Locate word choice that seems to you to reveal something about Salins's target audience and the kind of relationship he wishes to establish with these readers. What, for example, does the phrase "native folkways" (in the essay's second paragraph) reveal in this regard?

5. **Links Across Chapters:** First visit the website for the Manhattan Institute for Policy Research, of which Salins is a fellow. Then write an essay in which you apply the lexicon contained in Chris Borick's "On Political Labels" (in Chapter 15) to the key words in the website's articulation of its mission.

   Here are some ways to prompt your analysis. Where does the website fit in terms of the political categories discussed in Borick's essay? Find language in Borick's essay that would make Salins's point of view identifiable among the categories discussed in "On Political Labels."

6. **Application:** The issues and questions raised in Salins's essay are far from dead. On the basis of the historical definitions Salins provides, spend some time (perhaps a week) observing and making note of the language used in the media (newspapers, websites, television) for talking about issues of assimilation and cultural identity. What metaphors do you find and what do these reveal about contemporary thinking on this issue? Write a short essay in which you present your results.

Peggy McIntosh

White Privilege and Male Privilege: [...Unpacking the Invisible Knapsack]

In this classic analysis, Peggy McIntosh takes a look at her own "overprivilege" by virtue of her skin color and asks the question, what do I take for granted as a white person in ways that I am blind to? To answer, she inventories herself, arriving at a list of "unacknowledged privileges" that express "unconscious oppressiveness" as she imagines it can be perceived by persons of color. For many years the associate director of the Wellesley College Center for Research on Women, McIntosh is the founder and co-director of the National S.E.E.D (Seeking Educational Equity and Diversity) Project on Inclusive Curriculum.

Through work to bring materials and perspectives from Women's Studies 1 into the rest of the curriculum, I have often noticed men's unwillingness to grant that they are overprivileged in the curriculum, even though they may grant that women are disadvantaged. Denials that amount to taboos surround the subject of advantages that men gain from women's disadvantages. These denials protect male privilege from being fully recognized, acknowledged, lessened, or ended.

Thinking through unacknowledged male privilege as a phenomenon with a life of its own, I realized that since hierarchies in our society are interlocking, there was most likely a phenomenon of white privilege that was similarly denied and protected, but alive and real in its effects. As a white person, I realized I had been taught about racism as something that puts others at a disadvantage, but had been taught not to see one of its corollary aspects, white privilege, which puts me at an advantage.

I think whites are carefully taught not to recognize white privilege, as males are taught not to recognize male privilege. So I have begun in an untutored way to ask what it is like to have white privilege. This paper is a partial record of my personal observations and not a scholarly analysis. It is based on my daily experiences within my particular circumstances.

I have come to see white privilege as an invisible package of unearned assets that I can count on cashing in each day, but about which I was "meant" to remain oblivious. White privilege is like an invisible weightless knapsack of special provisions, assurances, tools, maps, guides, codebooks, passports, visas, clothes, compass, emergency gear, and blank checks.

Since I have had trouble facing white privilege, and describing its results 5 in my life, I saw parallels here with men's reluctance to acknowledge male

White Privilege and Male Privilege: A Personal Account of Coming to See Correspondences Through Work in Women's Studies (1988) Working Paper 189, Wellesley Centers for Women, Wellesley, MA. This work may not be reproduced without permission of the author, Peggy McIntosh, mmcintosh@wellesley.edu: 781-283-2520.

privilege. Only rarely will a man go beyond acknowledging that women are disadvantaged to acknowledging that men have unearned advantage, or that unearned privilege has not been good for men's development as human beings, or for society's development, or that privilege systems might ever be challenged and *changed*.

I will review here several types or layers of denial that I see at work protecting, and preventing awareness about, entrenched male privilege. Then I will draw parallels, from my own experience, with the denials that veil the facts of white privilege. Finally, I will list forty-six ordinary and daily ways in which I experience having white privilege, by contrast with my African-American colleagues in the same building. This list is not intended to be generalizable. Others can make their own lists from within their own life circumstances.

Writing this paper has been difficult, despite warm receptions for the talks on which it is based.[1] For describing white privilege makes one newly accountable. As we in Women's Studies work reveal male privilege and ask men to give up some of their power, so one who writes about having white privilege must ask, "Having described it, what will I do to lessen or end it?"

The denial of men's overprivileged state takes many forms in discussions of curriculum change work. Some claim that men must be central in the curriculum because they have done most of what is important or distinctive in life or in civilization. Some recognize sexism in the curriculum but deny that it makes male students seem unduly important in life. Others agree that certain *individual* thinkers are male oriented but deny that there is any *systemic* tendency in disciplinary frameworks or epistemology to overempower men as a group. Those men who do grant that male privilege takes institutionalized and embedded forms are still likely to deny that male hegemony has opened doors for them personally. Virtually all men deny that male overreward alone can explain men's centrality in all the inner sanctums of our most powerful institutions. Moreover, those few who will acknowledge that male privilege systems have overempowered them usually end up doubting that we could dismantle these privilege systems. They may say they will work to improve women's status, in the society or in the university, but they can't or won't support the idea of lessening men's. In curricular terms, this is the point at which they say that they regret they cannot use any of the interesting new scholarship on women because the syllabus is full. When the talk turns to giving men less cultural room, even the most thoughtful and fair-minded of the men I know will tend to reflect, or fall back on, conservative assumptions about the inevitability of present gender relations and distributions of power, calling on precedent or sociobiology and psychobiology to demonstrate that male domination is natural and follows inevitably from evolutionary pressures. Others resort to arguments from "experience" or religion or social responsibility or wishing and dreaming.

After I realized, through faculty development work in Women's Studies, the extent to which men work from a base of unacknowledged privilege, I understood that much of their oppressiveness was unconscious. Then I remembered the frequent charges from women of color that white women whom they encounter are oppressive. I began to understand why we are justly seen as oppressive, even when we don't see ourselves that way. At the very least, obliviousness of one's privileged state can make a person or group irritating to be with. I began to count the ways in which I enjoy unearned skin privilege and have been conditioned into oblivion about its existence, unable to see that it put me "ahead" in any way, or put my people ahead, overrewarding us and yet also paradoxically damaging us, or that it could or should be changed.

My schooling gave me no training in seeing myself as an oppressor, as   10
an unfairly advantaged person, or as a participant in a damaged culture. I was taught to see myself as an individual whose moral state depended on her individual moral will. At school, we are not taught about slavery in any depth; we are not taught to see slaveholders as damaged people. Slaves were seen as the only group at risk of being dehumanized. My schooling followed the pattern which Elizabeth Minnich has pointed out: whites are taught to think of their lives as morally neutral, normative, and average, and also ideal, so that when we work to benefit others, this is seen as work that will allow "them" to be more like "us." I think many of us know how obnoxious this attitude can be in men.

After frustration with men who would not recognize male privilege, I decided to try to work on myself at least by identifying some of the daily effects of white privilege in my life. It is crude work, at this stage, but I will give here a list of special circumstances and conditions I experience that I did not earn but that I have been made to feel are mine by birth, by citizenship, and by virtue of being a conscientious law-abiding "normal" person of goodwill. I have chosen those conditions that I think in my case *attach somewhat more to skin-color privilege* than to class, religion, ethnic status, or geographical location, though these other privileging factors are intricately intertwined. As far as I can see, my Afro-American co-workers, friends, and acquaintances with whom I come into daily or frequent contact in this particular time, place, and line of work cannot count on most of these conditions.

1. I can, if I wish, arrange to be in the company of people of my race most of the time.

2. I can avoid spending time with people whom I was trained to mistrust and who have learned to mistrust my kind or me.

3. If I should need to move, I can be pretty sure of renting or purchasing housing in an area which I can afford and in which I would want to live.

4. I can be reasonably sure that my neighbors in such a location will be neutral or pleasant to me.

5. I can go shopping alone most of the time, fairly well assured that I will not be followed or harassed by store detectives.

6. I can turn on the television or open to the front page of the paper and see people of my race widely and positively represented.

7. When I am told about our national heritage or about "civilization," I am shown that people of my color made it what it is.

8. I can be sure that my children will be given curricular materials that testify to the existence of their race.

9. If I want to, I can be pretty sure of finding a publisher for this piece on white privilege.

10. I can be fairly sure of having my voice heard in a group in which I am the only member of my race.

11. I can be casual about whether or not to listen to another woman's voice in a group in which she is the only member of her race.

12. I can go into a book shop and count on finding the writing of my race represented, into a supermarket and find the staple foods that fit with my cultural traditions, into a hairdresser's shop and find someone who can deal with my hair.

13. Whether I use checks, credit cards, or cash, I can count on my skin color not to work against the appearance that I am financially reliable.

14. I could arrange to protect our young children most of the time from people who might not like them.

15. I did not have to educate our children to be aware of systemic racism for their own daily physical protection.

16. I can be pretty sure that my children's teachers and employers will tolerate them if they fit school and workplace norms; my chief worries about them do not concern others' attitudes toward their race.

17. I can talk with my mouth full and not have people put this down to my color.

18. I can swear, or dress in secondhand clothes, or not answer letters, without having people attribute these choices to the bad morals, the poverty, or the illiteracy of my race.

19. I can speak in public to a powerful male group without putting my race on trial.

20. I can do well in a challenging situation without being called a credit to my race.

21. I am never asked to speak for all the people of my racial group.

22. I can remain oblivious to the language and customs of persons of color who constitute the world's majority without feeling in my culture any penalty for such oblivion.

23. I can criticize our government and talk about how much I fear its policies and behavior without being seen as a cultural outsider.

24. I can be reasonably sure that if I ask to talk to "the person in charge," I will be facing a person of my race.

25. If a traffic cop pulls me over or if the IRS audits my tax return, I can be sure I haven't been singled out because of my race.

26. I can easily buy posters, postcards, picture books, greeting cards, dolls, toys, and children's magazines featuring people of my race.

27. I can go home from most meetings of organizations I belong to feeling somewhat tied in, rather than isolated, out of place, outnumbered, unheard, held at a distance, or feared.

28. I can be pretty sure that an argument with a colleague of another race is more likely to jeopardize her chances for advancement than to jeopardize mine.

29. I can be fairly sure that if I argue for the promotion of a person of another race, or a program centering on race, this is not likely to cost me heavily within my present setting, even if my colleagues disagree with me.

30. If I declare there is a racial issue at hand, or there isn't a racial issue at hand, my race will lend me more credibility for either position than a person of color will have.

31. I can choose to ignore developments in minority writing and minority activist programs, or disparage them, or learn from them, but in any case, I can find ways to be more or less protected from negative consequences of any of these choices.

32. My culture gives me little fear about ignoring the perspectives and powers of people of other races.

33. I am not made acutely aware that my shape, bearing, or body odor will be taken as a reflection on my race.

34. I can worry about racism without being seen as self-interested or self-seeking.

35. I can take a job with an affirmative action employer without having my co-workers on the job suspect that I got it because of my race.

36. If my day, week, or year is going badly, I need not ask of each negative episode or situation whether it has racial overtones.

37. I can be pretty sure of finding people who would be willing to talk with me and advise me about my next steps, professionally.

38. I can think over many options, social, political, imaginative, or professional, without asking whether a person of my race would be accepted or allowed to do what I want to do.

39. I can be late to a meeting without having the lateness reflect on my race.

40. I can choose public accommodation without fearing that people of my race cannot get in or will be mistreated in the places I have chosen.

41. I can be sure that if I need legal or medical help, my race will not work against me.

42. I can arrange my activities so that I will never have to experience feelings of rejection owing to my race.

43. If I have low credibility as a leader, I can be sure that my race is not the problem.

44. I can easily find academic courses and institutions that give attention only to people of my race.

45. I can expect figurative language and imagery in all of the arts to testify to experiences of my race.

46. I can choose blemish cover or bandages in "flesh" color and have them more or less match my skin.

I repeatedly forgot each of the realizations on this list until I wrote it down. For me, white privilege has turned out to be an elusive and fugitive subject. The pressure to avoid it is great, for in facing it I must give up the myth of meritocracy. If these things are true, this is not such a free country; one's life is not what one makes it; many doors open for certain people through no virtues of their own. These perceptions mean also that my moral condition is not what I had been led to believe. The appearance of being a good citizen rather than a troublemaker comes in large part from having all sorts of doors open automatically because of my color.

A further paralysis of nerve comes from literary silence protecting privilege. My clearest memories of finding such analysis are in Lillian Smith's unparalleled *Killers of the Dream* and Margaret Andersen's review of Karen and Mamie Field's *Lemon Swamp*. Smith, for example, wrote about walking toward black children on the street and knowing they would step into the gutter; Andersen contrasted the pleasure that she, as a white child, took on summer driving trips to the south with Karen Fields' memories of driving in a closed car stocked with all necessities lest, in stopping, her black family should suffer "insult, or worse." Adrienne Rich also recognizes and writes about daily experiences of privilege, but in my observation, white women's writing in this area is far more often on systemic racism than on our daily lives as light-skinned women.[2]

In unpacking this invisible knapsack of white privilege, I have listed conditions of daily experience that I once took for granted, as neutral, normal, and universally available to everybody, just as I once thought of a male-focused curriculum as the neutral or accurate account that can speak for all. Nor did I think of any of these perquisites as bad for the holder. I now think that we need a more finely differentiated taxonomy of privilege, for some of these varieties are only what one would want for everyone in a just society, and others give license to be ignorant, oblivious, arrogant, and destructive. Before proposing some more finely tuned categorization, I will make some observations about the general effects of these conditions on my life and expectations.

In this potpourri of examples, some privileges make me feel at home in 15 the world. Others allow me to escape penalties or dangers that others suffer. Through some, I escape fear, anxiety, insult, injury, or a sense of not being welcome, not being real. Some keep me from having to hide, to be in disguise, to feel sick or crazy, to negotiate each transaction from the position of being an outsider or, within my group, a person who is suspected of having too close links with a dominant culture. Most keep me from having to be angry.

I see a pattern running through the matrix of white privilege, a pattern of assumptions that were passed on to me as a white person. There was one main piece of cultural turf; it was my own turf, and I was among those who could control the turf. I could measure up to the cultural standards and take advantage of the many options I saw around me to make what the culture would call a success of my life. *My skin color was an asset for any move I was educated to want to make.* I could think of myself as "belonging" in major ways and of making social systems work for me. I could freely disparage, fear, neglect, or be oblivious to anything outside of the dominant cultural forms. Being of the main culture, I could also criticize it fairly freely. My life was reflected back to me frequently enough so that I felt, with regard to my race, if not to my sex, like one of the real people.

Whether through the curriculum or in the newspaper, the television, the economic system, or the general look of people in the streets, I received daily signals and indications that my people counted and that others *either didn't exist or must be trying, not very successfully, to be like people of my race.* I was given cultural permission not to hear voices of people of other races or a tepid cultural tolerance for hearing or acting on such voices. I was also raised not to suffer seriously from anything that darker-skinned people might say about my group, "protected," though perhaps I should more accurately say *prohibited*, through the habits of my economic class and social group, from living in racially mixed groups or being reflective about interactions between people or differing races.

In proportion as my racial group was being made confident, comfortable, and oblivious, other groups were likely being made unconfident, uncomfortable, and alienated. Whiteness protected me from many kinds of hostility, distress, and violence, which I was being subtly trained to visit in turn upon people of color.

For this reason, the word "privilege" now seems to me misleading. Its connotations are too positive to fit the conditions and behaviors which "privilege systems" produce. We usually think of privilege as being a favored state, whether earned, or conferred by birth or luck. School graduates are reminded they are privileged and urged to use their (enviable) assets well. The word "privilege" carries the connotation of being something everyone must want. Yet some of the conditions I have described here work to systematically overempower certain groups. Such privilege simply *confers dominance*, gives permission to control, because of one's race or sex. The kind of privilege that gives license to some people to be, at best, thoughtless and, at worst, murderous should not continue to be referred to as a desirable attribute. Such "privilege" may be widely desired without being in any way beneficial to the whole society.

20   Moreover, though "privilege" may confer power, it does not confer moral strength. Those who do not depend on conferred dominance have traits and qualities that may never develop in those who do. Just as Women's Studies courses indicate that women survive their political circumstances to lead lives that hold the human race together, so "underprivileged" people of color who are the world's majority have survived their oppression and lived survivors' lives from which the white global minority can and must learn. In some groups, those dominated have actually become strong through *not* having all of these unearned advantages, and this gives them a great deal to teach the others. Members of so-called privileged groups can seem foolish, ridiculous, infantile, or dangerous by contrast.

I want, then, to distinguish between earned strength and unearned power conferred systemically. Power from unearned privilege can look like strength when it is, in fact, permission to escape or to dominate. But not all of the privileges on my list are inevitably damaging. Some, like the expectation that neighbors will be decent to you, or that your race will not count against you in court, should be the norm in a just society and should be considered as the entitlement of everyone. Others, like the privilege not to listen to less powerful people, distort the humanity of the holders as well as the ignored groups. Still others, like finding one's staple foods everywhere, may be a function of being a member of a numerical majority in the population. Others have to do with not having to labor under pervasive negative stereotyping and mythology.

We might at least start by distinguishing between positive advantages that we can work to spread, to the point where they are not advantages at all but simply part of the normal civic and social fabric, and negative types of advantage that unless rejected will always reinforce our present hierarchies. For example, the positive "privilege" of belonging, the feeling that one belongs within the human circle, as Native Americans say, fosters development and should not be seen as privilege for a few. It is, let us say, an entitlement that none of us should have to earn; ideally it is an *unearned entitlement*. At present, since only a few have it, it is an *unearned advantage* for them. The negative "privilege" that gave me cultural permission not to take darker-skinned Others seriously can be seen as arbitrarily conferred dominance and should not be desirable for anyone. This paper results from a process of coming to see that some of the power that I originally saw as attendant on being a human being in the United States consisted in *unearned advantage* and *conferred dominance*, as well as other kinds of special circumstance not universally taken for granted.

In writing this paper I have also realized that white identity and status (as well as class identity and status) give me considerable power to choose whether to broach this subject and its trouble. I can pretty well decide whether to disappear and avoid and not listen and escape the dislike I may engender in other people through this essay, or interrupt, answer, interpret, preach, correct, criticize, and control to some extent what goes on in reaction to it. Being white, I am given considerable power to escape many kinds of danger or penalty as well as to choose which risks I want to take.

There is an analogy here, once again with Women's Studies. Our male colleagues do not have a great deal to lose in supporting Women's Studies, but they do not have a great deal to lose if they oppose it either. They simply have the power to decide whether to commit themselves to more equitable distributions of power. They will probably feel few penalties whatever choice they make; they do not seem, in any obvious short-term sense, the ones at risk, though they are, we are all at risk because of the behaviors that have been rewarded in them.

Through Women's Studies work I have met very few men who are truly 25
distressed about systemic, unearned male advantage and conferred dominance. And so one question for me and others like me is whether we will be like them, or whether we will get truly distressed, even outraged, about unearned race advantage and conferred dominance and if so, what we will do to lessen them. In any case, we need to do more work in identifying how they actually affect our daily lives. We need more down-to-earth writing by people about these taboo subjects. We need more understanding of the ways in which white "privilege" damages white people, for these are not the same ways in which it damages the victimized. Skewed white psyches are an inseparable part of the picture, though I do not want to confuse the kinds of damage done to the holders of special assets and to those who suffer the deficits. Many, perhaps most, of our white students in the United States think that racism doesn't affect them because they are not people of color; they do not see "whiteness" as a racial identity. Many men likewise think that Women's Studies does not bear on their own existences because they are not female; they do not see themselves as having gendered identities. Insisting on the universal "effects" of "privilege" systems, then, becomes one of our chief tasks, and being more explicit about the *particular* effects in particular contexts is another. Men need to join us in this work.

In addition, since race and sex are not the only advantaging systems at work, we need to similarly examine the daily experience of having age advantage, or ethnic advantage, or physical ability, or advantage related to nationality, religion, or sexual orientation. Professor Marnie Evans suggested to me that in many ways the list I made also applies directly to heterosexual privilege. This is a still more taboo subject than race privilege: the daily ways in which heterosexual privilege makes some persons comfortable or powerful, providing supports, assets, approvals, and rewards to those who live or expect to live in heterosexual pairs. Unpacking that content is still more difficult, owing to the deeper imbeddedness of heterosexual advantage and dominance and stricter taboos surrounding these.

But to start such an analysis I would put this observation from my own experience: The fact that I live under the same roof with a man triggers all kinds of societal assumptions about my worth, politics, life, and value and triggers a host of unearned advantages and powers. After recasting many elements from the original list I would add further observations like these:

1. My children do not have to answer questions about why I live with my partner (my husband).
2. I have no difficulty finding neighborhoods where people approve of our household.
3. Our children are given texts and classes that implicitly support our kind of family unit and do not turn them against my choice of domestic partnership.
4. I can travel alone or with my husband without expecting embarrassment or hostility in those who deal with us.
5. Most people I meet will see my marital arrangements as an asset to my life or as a favorable comment on my likability, my competence, or my mental health.
6. I can talk about the social events of a weekend without fearing most listeners' reactions.
7. I will feel welcomed and "normal" in the usual walks of public life, institutional and social.
8. In many contexts, I am seen as "all right" in daily work on women because I do not live chiefly with women.

Difficulties and dangers surrounding the tasks of finding parallels are many. Since racism, sexism, and heterosexism are not the same, the advantages associated with them should not be seen as the same. In addition, it is hard to isolate aspects of unearned advantage that derive chiefly from social class, economic class, race, religion, region, sex, or ethnic identity. The oppressions are both distinct and interlocking, as the Combahee River Collective statement of 1977 continues to remind us eloquently.[3]

One factor seems clear about all of the interlocking oppressions. They take both active forms that we can see and embedded forms that members of the dominant group are taught not to see. In my class and place, I did not see myself as racist because I was taught to recognize racism only in individual acts of meanness by members of my group, never in invisible systems conferring racial dominance on my group from birth. Likewise, we are taught to think that sexism or heterosexism is carried on only through intentional, individual acts of discrimination, meanness, or cruelty, rather than in invisible systems conferring unsought dominance on certain groups. Disapproving of the systems won't be enough to change them. I was taught to think that racism could end if white individuals changed their attitudes; many men think sexism can be ended by individual changes in daily behavior toward women. But a man's sex provides advantage for him whether or not he approves of the way in which dominance has been conferred on his group. A "white" skin in the United States opens many doors for whites whether or not we approve of the way dominance has been conferred on us. Individual acts can palliate, but cannot end, these problems. To redesign social systems, we need first to acknowledge their colossal unseen dimensions. The silences and denials surrounding privilege are the key political tool here. They keep the thinking about equality or equity incomplete, protecting unearned advantage and conferred dominance by making these taboo subjects. Most talk by whites about equal opportunity seems to me now to be about equal opportunity to try to get into a position of dominance while denying that *systems* of dominance exist.

Obliviousness about white advantage, like obliviousness about male advantage, is kept strongly inculturated in the United States so as to maintain the myth of meritocracy, the myth that democratic choice is equally available to all. Keeping most people unaware that freedom of confident action is there for just a small number of people props up those in power and serves to keep power in the hands of the same groups that have most of it already. Though systemic change takes many decades, there are pressing questions for me and I imagine for some others like me if we raise our daily consciousness on the perquisites of being light-skinned. What will we do with such knowledge? As we know from watching men, it is an open question whether we will choose to use unearned advantage to weaken invisible privilege systems and whether we will use any of our arbitrarily awarded power to try to reconstruct power-systems on a broader base.

Notes

[1] This paper was presented at the Virginia Women's Studies Association conference in Richmond in April 1986, and the American Educational Research Association conference in Boston in October 1986, and discussed with two groups of participants in the Dodge seminars for Secondary School Teachers in New York and Boston in the spring of 1987.

[2] Andersen, Margaret, "Race and the Social Science Curriculum: A Teaching and Learning Discussion." *Radical Teacher*, November, 1984, pp. 17–20. Smith, Lillian, *Killers of the Dream*, New York: W. W. Norton, 1949.

[3] "A Black Feminist Statement," The Combahee River Collective, pp. 13–22 in G. Hull, P. Scott, B. Smith, Eds., *All the Women Are White, All the Blacks Are Men, But Some of Us Are Brave: Black Women's Studies*, Old Westbury, NY: The Feminist Press, 1982.

Things to Do with the Reading

1. McIntosh organizes her essay around a single simile (comparison) in the fourth paragraph: "White privilege is like an invisible weightless knapsack of special provisions, assurances, tools, maps, guides, codebooks, passports, visas, clothes, compass, emergency gear, and blank checks." Find and discuss single sentences and short passages in the essay that explain some of the word choice in this simile—"invisible," for example, and "weightless." Also paraphrase both the sentence we've quoted and the ones you find. Then write a short interpretive essay on the items in the backpack as listed in the quoted sentence and other similar ones. To what does the figurative language in these sentences correspond?

2. McIntosh presents this essay (originally given as a paper at a Women's Studies conference) as a personal reflection: "This paper is a partial record of my personal observations and not a scholarly analysis. It is based on my daily experiences within my particular circumstances." Even though the piece is written in the first person and includes the author's personal experience, it also employs language characteristic of academic discourse in the social sciences. The more specialized, more academic language allows McIntosh to give her argument greater specificity.

   Do PARAPHRASE × 3 (see Chapter 2) with the following sentences from the essay and then write a short essay in which you explain what these add to the essay's way of defining white privilege.

   - "Others agree that certain individual thinkers are male oriented but deny that there is any systemic tendency in disciplinary frameworks or epistemology to overempower men as a group" (paragraph 8).

   - "The negative 'privilege' that gave me cultural permission not to take darker-skinned Others seriously can be seen as arbitrarily conferred dominance and should not be desirable for anyone" (paragraph 22).

3. Write a short essay in which you explore McIntosh's analogy between male privilege and white privilege. What features of her experience—as a white woman—does McIntosh posit as analogous to those of white males?

4. Link: Write an essay in which you use the following two sentences, one from McIntosh's essay and one from DeMott's, to put these two writers' thinking into conversation. Which key words in each quote are the best indications of common ground between McIntosh and DeMott? (See Chapter 7 on putting sources into conversation with each other.)

   - McIntosh: "Obliviousness about white advantage, like obliviousness about male advantage, is kept strongly inculturated in the United

States so as to maintain the myth of meritocracy, the myth that democratic choice is equally available to all" (paragraph 30).

- DeMott: "Factitious renderings of the American past blur the outlines of black-white conflict, redefine the ground of black grievances for the purpose of diminishing those grievances, [and] restage black life in accordance with the illusory conventions of American success mythology" (paragraph 28).

5. Application: Before she offers her list of privileges, McIntosh offers a somewhat disingenuous disclaimer—"This list is not intended to be generalizable"—and then proceeds to invite her readers to undergo the same self-scrutiny she has undertaken: "Others can make their own lists from within their own life circumstances."

This challenge brings to mind two obvious applications: to expand McIntosh's list and/or to corroborate it (that is, find confirming evidence) with your own experience.

Give yourself at least a week. Carry around a special notebook for the purpose. Keep the idea of unacknowledged privilege alive in the back of your mind, as you visit sites where people congregate—a square, a shopping district, a lunchroom—with the conscious project of conducting observation.

At the end of the week, write up your results. Start with a list, but then take the most vivid instances and expand them into brief narratives.

Richard Rodriguez

The Fear of Losing a Culture

Richard Rodriguez provides a distinctively Latin American spin on the concept of the melting pot. He argues that Latin America was "formed by a rape that became a marriage" and goes on to tell his North American audience, "Expect marriage." A teacher, journalist (formerly on PBS), and award-winning essayist, Rodriguez is the child of Mexican American immigrants. He earned degrees at Stanford and Columbia and also did graduate work at UC-Berkeley, before deciding to become a freelance essayist. In addition to his famous 1982 memoir, *Hunger of Memory*, from which this piece is taken, Rodriguez has written four other books, including *Brown* and in 2013, *Darling: A Spiritual Autobiography*, a collection of essays about spirituality that focus on the failure of our sense of place in the world.

1   What is culture?

The immigrant shrugs. Latin American immigrants come to the United States with only the things they need in mind—not abstractions like culture. Money. They need dollars. They need food. Maybe they need to get out of the way of bullets.

Most of us who concern ourselves with Hispanic-American culture, as painters, musicians, writers—or as sons and daughters—are the children of immigrants. We have grown up on this side of the border, in the land of Elvis Presley and Thomas Edison; our lives are prescribed by the mall, by the DMV and the Chinese restaurant. Our imaginations yet vacillate between an Edenic Latin America (the blue door)—which nevertheless betrayed our parents—and the repellent plate glass of a real American city—which has been good to us.

Hispanic-American culture is where the past meets the future. Hispanic-American culture is not a Hispanic milestone only, not simply a celebration at the crossroads. America transforms into pleasure what America cannot avoid. Is it any coincidence that at a time when Americans are troubled by the encroachment of the Mexican desert, Americans discover a chic in cactus, in the decorator colors of the Southwest? In sand?

5   Hispanic-American culture of the sort that is now showing (the teen movie, the rock songs) may exist in an hourglass; may in fact be irrelevant to the epic. The U.S. Border Patrol works through the night to arrest the flow of illegal immigrants over the border, even as Americans wait in line to get into "La Bamba." Even as Americans vote to declare, once and for all, that English shall be the official language of the United States, Madonna starts recording in Spanish.

©1988 Time Inc. All rights reserved. Reprinted from TIME Magazine and published with permission of Time Inc. Reproduction in any manner in any language in whole or in part without written permission is prohibited.

But then so is Bill Cosby's show irrelevant to the 10 o'clock news, where families huddle together in fear on porches, pointing at the body of the slain boy bagged in tarpaulin. Which is not to say that Bill Cosby or Michael Jackson are irrelevant to the future or without neo-Platonic influence. Like players within the play, they prefigure, they resolve. They make black and white audiences aware of a bond that may not yet exist.

Before a national TV audience, Rita Moreno tells Geraldo Rivera that her dream as an actress is to play a character rather like herself: "I speak English perfectly well . . . I'm not dying from poverty . . . I want to play *that* kind of Hispanic woman, which is to say, an American citizen." This is an actress talking, these are showbiz pieties. But Moreno expresses as well the general Hispanic-American predicament. Hispanics want to belong to America without betraying the past.

Hispanics fear losing ground in any negotiation with the American city. We come from an expansive, an intimate culture that has been judged second-rate by the United States of America. For reasons of pride, therefore, as much as of affection, we are reluctant to give up our past. Hispanics often express a fear of "losing" culture. Our fame in the United States has been our resistance to assimilation.

The symbol of Hispanic culture has been the tongue of flame—Spanish. But the remarkable legacy Hispanics carry from Latin America is not language—an inflatable skin—but breath itself, capacity of soul, an inclination to live. The genius of Latin America is the habit of synthesis.

We assimilate. Just over the border there is the example of Mexico, the 10 country from which the majority of U.S. Hispanics come. Mexico is *mestizo*—Indian and Spanish. Within a single family, Mexicans are light-skinned and dark. It is impossible for the Mexican to say, in the scheme of things, where the Indian begins and the Spaniard surrenders.

In culture as in blood, Latin America was formed by a rape that became a marriage. Due to the absorbing generosity of the Indian, European culture took on new soil. What Latin America knows is that people create one another as they marry. In the music of Latin America you will hear the litany of bloodlines—the African drum, the German accordion, the cry from the minaret.

The United States stands as the opposing New World experiment. In North America the Indian and the European stood apace. Whereas Latin America was formed by a medieval Catholic dream of one world—of meltdown conversion—the United States was built up from Protestant individualism. The American melting pot washes away only embarrassment; it is the necessary initiation into public life. The American faith is that our national strength derives from separateness, from "diversity." The glamour of the United States is a carnival promise: You can lose weight, get rich as Rockefeller, tough up your roots, get a divorce.

Immigrants still come for the promise. But the United States wavers in its faith. As long as there was space enough, sky enough, as long as economic success validated individualism, loneliness was not too high a price to pay. (The cabin on the prairie or the Sony Walkman.)

As we near the end of the American century, two alternative cultures beckon the American imagination—both highly communal cultures—the Asian and the Latin American. The United States is a literal culture. Americans devour what we might otherwise fear to become. Sushi will make us corporate warriors. Combination Plate #3, smothered in *mestizo* gravy, will burn a hole in our hearts.

15   Latin America offers passion. Latin America has a life—I mean *life*—big clouds, unambiguous themes, death, birth, faith, that the United States, for all its quality of life, seems without now. Latin America offers communal riches: an undistressed leisure, a kitchen table, even a full sorrow. Such is the solitude of America, such is the urgency of American need, Americans reach right past a fledgling, homegrown Hispanic-American culture for the real thing—the darker bottle of Mexican beer; the denser novel of a Latin American master.

For a long time, Hispanics in the United States withheld from the United States our Latin American gift. We denied the value of assimilation. But as our presence is judged less foreign in America, we will produce a more generous art, less timid, less parochial. Carlos Santana, Luis Valdez, Linda Ronstadt—Hispanic Americans do not have a "pure" Latin American art to offer. Expect bastard themes, expect ironies, comic conclusions. For we live on this side of the border, where Kraft manufactures bricks of "Mexican style" Velveeta, and where Jack in the Box serves "Fajita Pita."

The flame-red Chevy floats a song down the Pan American Highway: From a rolled-down window, the grizzled voice of Willie Nelson rises in disembodied harmony with the voice of Julio Iglesias. Gabby Hayes and Cisco are thus resolved.

Expect marriage. We will change America even as we will be changed. We will disappear with you into a new miscegenation.

Along the border, real conflicts remain. But the ancient tear separating Europe from itself—the Catholic Mediterranean from the Protestant north—may yet heal itself in the New World. For generations, Latin America has been the place—the bed—of a confluence of so many races and cultures that Protestant North America shuddered to imagine it.

20   Imagine it.

Things to Do with the Reading

1. Rodriguez has an interesting fix on the way that Americans react to other cultures. He says that "America transforms into pleasure what America cannot avoid" (paragraph 4) and that "Americans devour what we might otherwise fear to become" (paragraph 14). Try paraphrasing these remarks in their given context, as a way of uncovering their implications. Be alert to figurative language—why, for example, "devour"? Write a short essay on the rhetoric the essay employs to talk about

(crossing) cultural boundaries. You might find it useful to focus on the use of figurative language in particular (see Chapter 5).

2. Paraphrase the following assertions from Rodriguez's essay: "Expect bastard themes" and "We will disappear with you into a new miscegenation." Be sure to look up the word "miscegenation" and the history of anti-miscegenation laws in America. Then use your paraphrases to write a paragraph or so on where you think Rodriguez stands on a sliding scale in which the melting pot, standing for assimilation, is at one end and Jesse Jackson's metaphor of the rainbow coalition, standing for coexistence and respect for diversity, is on the other.

3. One of your ongoing projects in this unit should be to work out the logic and implications of these two governing metaphors: rainbow and melting pot. Rodriquez says, for example, that "The genius of Latin America is the habit of synthesis." To what extent do "synthesis" and "assimilation" have subtly but significantly different meanings?

4. Link: What is the source of hope in Rodriguez's argument? What objections, if any, do you think DeMott would have to Rodriguez's position on the issue of diversity vs. assimilation, and how might Rodriguez respond?

5. Link: In an interview conducted 15 years after the publication of *Hunger of Memory*, Rodriguez said, "I am no more in favor of assimilation than I am in favor of the Pacific Ocean. Assimilation is not something to oppose or favor—it just happens." Write an essay in which you explore how Rodriguez's point of view conflicts with the view of assimilation offered by Peter Salins in "Assimilation, American Style." How might we account for the difference in the two writers' perspectives? What are the assumptions that underlie each of their essays? (For UNCOVERING ASSUMPTIONS, see Chapter 2.)

6. Take the passage at the end of paragraph 16, which reads, "Expect bastard themes, expect ironies, comic conclusions. For we live on this side of the border where Kraft manufactures bricks of 'Mexican style' Velveeta, and where Jack in the Box serves 'Fajita Pita.'" How does the essay condition us to respond to this passage? In what verbal strands (see THE METHOD, Chapter 1) does this language participate? This passage occurs shortly before the conclusion. Write a short essay on the way Rodriguez chooses to bring his ruminations to a close in the final five paragraphs.

Zadie Smith

Speaking in Tongues

Whereas DeMott's "Put On a Happy Face" suggests that diversity is more real, more terrible, and more intractable than feel-good assimilationist films want us to think, Zadie Smith argues in "Speaking in Tongues" that assimilation is also real—and that difference can be easy to lose and impossible to reclaim. Originally a lecture given at the New York Public Library in 2008, this essay begins as a memoir but then expands to include Eliza Doolittle (from *Pygmalion* and *My Fair Lady*), Shakespeare, and most notably, Barack Obama—all speakers with "double voices." One of the most important younger novelists writing in English, Zadie Smith was born and raised in a London suburb as a member of a mixed race family. She is the author of three novels (most famously, *White Teeth*) and a collection of essays.

1.

1 Hello. This voice I speak with these days, this English voice with its rounded vowels and consonants in more or less the right place—this is not the voice of my childhood. I picked it up in college, along with the unabridged *Clarissa* and a taste for port. Maybe this fact is only what it seems to be—a case of bald social climbing—but at the time I genuinely thought *this* was the voice of lettered people, and that if I didn't have the voice of lettered people I would never truly be lettered. A braver person, perhaps, would have stood firm, teaching her peers a useful lesson by example: not all lettered people need be of the same class, nor speak identically. I went the other way. Partly out of cowardice and a constitutional eagerness to please, but also because I didn't quite see it as a straight swap, of this voice for that.

My own childhood had been the story of this and that combined, of the synthesis of disparate things. It never occurred to me that I was leaving the London district of Willesden for Cambridge. I thought I was *adding* Cambridge to Willesden, this new way of talking to that old way. Adding a new kind of knowledge to a different kind I already had. And for a while, that's how it was: at home, during the holidays, I spoke with my old voice, and in the old voice seemed to feel and speak things that I couldn't express in college, and vice versa. I felt a sort of wonder at the flexibility of the thing. Like being alive twice.

But flexibility is something that requires work if it is to be maintained. Recently my double voice has deserted me for a single one, reflecting the smaller world into which my work has led me. Willesden was a big, colorful, working-class sea; Cambridge was a smaller, posher pond, and almost univocal; the literary world is a puddle. This voice I picked up along the way is no

"Speaking in Tongues" by Zadie Smith, The New York Review of Books, February 26, 2009. Used by permission.

longer an exotic garment I put on like a college gown whenever I choose—now it is my only voice, whether I want it or not. I regret it; I should have kept both voices alive in my mouth. They were both a part of me. But how the culture warns against it! As George Bernard Shaw delicately put it in his preface to the play *Pygmalion*, "many thousands of [British] men and women . . . have sloughed off their native dialects and acquired a new tongue."

Few, though, will admit to it. Voice adaptation is still the original British sin. Monitoring and exposing such citizens is a national pastime, as popular as sex scandals and libel cases. If you lean toward the Atlantic with your high-rising terminals you're a sell-out; if you pronounce borrowed European words in their original style—even if you try something as innocent as *parmigiano* for "parmesan"—you're a fraud. If you go (metaphorically speaking) down the British class scale, you've gone from Cockney to "mockney," and can expect a public tar and feathering; to go the other way is to perform an unforgivable act of class betrayal. Voices are meant to be unchanging and singular. There's no quicker way to insult an ex-pat Scotsman in London than to tell him he's lost his accent. We feel that our voices are who we are, and that to have more than one, or to use different versions of a voice for different occasions, represents, at best, a Janus-faced duplicity, and at worst, the loss of our very souls.

Whoever changes their voice takes on, in Britain, a queerly tragic dimension. They have betrayed that puzzling dictum "To thine own self be true," so often quoted approvingly as if it represented the wisdom of Shakespeare rather than the hot air of Polonius. "*What's to become of me? What's to become of me?*" wails Eliza Doolittle, realizing her middling dilemma. With a voice too posh for the flower girls and yet too redolent of the gutter for the ladies in Mrs. Higgins's drawing room.

But Eliza—patron saint of the tragically double-voiced—is worthy of closer inspection. The first thing to note is that both Eliza and *Pygmalion* are entirely didactic, as Shaw meant them to be. "I delight," he wrote:

> in throwing [*Pygmalion*] at the heads of the wiseacres who repeat the parrot cry that art should never be didactic. It goes to prove my contention that art should never be anything else.

He was determined to tell the unambiguous tale of a girl who changes her voice and loses herself. And so she arrives like this:

> Don't you be so saucy. You ain't heard what I come for yet. Did you tell him I come in a taxi? . . . Oh, we are proud! He ain't above giving lessons, not him: I heard him say so. Well, I ain't come here to ask for any compliment; and if my money's not good enough I can go elsewhere. . . . Now you know, don't you? I'm come to have lessons, I am. And to pay for em too: make no mistake. . . . I want to be a lady in a flower shop stead of selling at the corner of Tottenham Court Road. But they won't take me unless I can talk more genteel.

And she leaves like this:

I can't. I could have done it once; but now I can't go back to it. Last night, when I was wandering about, a girl spoke to me; and I tried to get back into the old way with her; but it was no use. You told me, you know, that when a child is brought to a foreign country, it picks up the language in a few weeks, and forgets its own. Well, I am a child in your country. I have forgotten my own language, and can speak nothing but yours.

By the end of his experiment, Professor Higgins has made his Eliza an awkward, in-between thing, neither flower girl nor lady, with one voice lost and another gained, at the steep price of everything she was, and everything she knows. Almost as afterthought, he sends Eliza's father, Alfred Doolittle, to his doom, too, securing a three-thousand-a-year living for the man on the condition that Doolittle lecture for the Wannafeller Moral Reform World League up to six times a year. This burden brings the philosophical dustman into the close, unwanted embrace of what he disdainfully calls "middle class morality." By the time the curtain goes down, both Doolittles find themselves stuck in the middle, which is, to Shaw, a comi-tragic place to be, with the emphasis on the tragic. What are they fit for? What will become of them?

10   How persistent this horror of the middling spot is, this dread of the interim place! It extends through the specter of the tragic mulatto, to the plight of the transsexual, to our present anxiety—disguised as genteel concern—for the contemporary immigrant, tragically split, we are sure, between worlds, ideas, cultures, voices—whatever will become of them? Something's got to give—one voice must be sacrificed for the other. What is double must be made singular.

But this, the apparent didactic moral of Eliza's story, is undercut by the fact of the play itself, which is an orchestra of many voices, simultaneously and perfectly rendered, with no shade of color or tone sacrificed. Higgins's Harley Street high-handedness is the equal of Mrs. Pierce's lower-middle-class gentility, Pickering's kindhearted aristocratic imprecision every bit as convincing as Arthur Doolittle's Nietzschean Cockney-by-way-of-Wales. Shaw had a wonderful ear, able to reproduce almost as many quirks of the English language as Shakespeare's. Shaw was in possession of a gift he wouldn't, or couldn't, give Eliza: he spoke in tongues.

It gives me a strange sensation to turn from Shaw's melancholy Pygmalion story to another, infinitely more hopeful version, written by the new president of the United States of America. Of course, his ear isn't half bad either. In *Dreams from My Father*, the new president displays an enviable facility for dialogue, and puts it to good use, animating a cast every bit as various as the one James Baldwin—an obvious influence—conjured for his own many-voiced novel *Another Country*. Obama can do young Jewish male, black old lady from the South Side, white woman from Kansas, Kenyan elders, white Harvard nerds, black Columbia nerds, activist women, churchmen, security guards, bank tellers, and even a British man called Mr. Wilkerson, who on a starry night on safari says credibly British things like: "I believe that's the Milky Way." This new president doesn't just speak *for* his people. He can *speak* them. It is a disorienting talent in a president; we're so unused to it. I have to pinch myself to remember who wrote the following well-observed scene, seemingly plucked from a comic novel:

> "Man, I'm not going to any more of these bullshit Punahou parties."

> "Yeah, that's what you said the last time . . . ."

> "I mean it this time . . . . These girls are A-1, USDA-certified racists. All of 'em. White girls. Asian girls—shoot, these Asians worse than the whites. Think we got a disease or something."

> "Maybe they're looking at that big butt of yours. Man, I thought you were in training."

> "Get your hands out of my fries. You ain't my bitch, nigger . . . buy your own damn fries. Now what was I talking about?"

> "Just 'cause a girl don't go out with you doesn't make her a racist."

This is the voice of Obama at seventeen, as remembered by Obama. He's still recognizably Obama; he already seeks to unpack and complicate apparently obvious things ("Just 'cause a girl don't go out with you doesn't make her a racist"); he's already gently cynical about the impassioned dogma of other people ("Yeah, that's what you said the last time"). And he has a sense of humor ("Maybe they're looking at that big butt of yours"). Only the voice is different: he has made almost as large a leap as Eliza Doolittle. The conclusions Obama draws from his own Pygmalion experience, however, are subtler than Shaw's. The tale he tells is not the old tragedy of gaining a new, false voice at the expense of a true one. The tale he tells is all about addition. His is the story of a genuinely many-voiced man. If it has a moral it is that each man must be true to his selves, plural.

For Obama, having more than one voice in your ear is not a burden, or not solely a burden—it is also a gift. And the gift is of an interesting kind, not well served by that dull publishing-house title *Dreams from My Father: A Story of Race and Inheritance* with its suggestion of a simple linear inheritance, of paternal dreams and aspirations passed down to a son, and fulfilled. *Dreams from My Father* would have been a fine title for John McCain's book *Faith of My Fathers*, which concerns exactly this kind of linear masculine inheritance, in his case from soldier to soldier. For Obama's book, though, it's wrong, lopsided. He corrects its misperception early on, in the first chapter, while discussing the failure of his parents' relationship, characterized by their only son as the end of a dream. "Even as that spell was broken," he writes, "and the worlds that they thought they'd left behind reclaimed each of them, I *occupied the place* where their dreams had been."

15   To *occupy* a dream, to exist in a dreamed space (conjured by both father and mother), is surely a quite different thing from simply *inheriting* a dream. It's more interesting. What did Pauline Kael call Cary Grant? "*The Man from Dream City.*" When Bristolian Archibald Leach became suave Cary Grant, the transformation happened in his voice, which he subjected to a strange, indefinable manipulation, resulting in that heavenly sui generis accent, neither west country nor posh, American nor English. It came from nowhere, *he* came from nowhere. Grant seemed the product of a collective dream, dreamed up by moviegoers in hard times, as it sometimes feels voters have dreamed up Obama in hard times. Both men have a strange reflective quality, typical of the self-created man—we see in them whatever we want to see. "*Everyone wants to be Cary Grant,*" said Cary Grant. "*Even I want to be Cary Grant.*" It's not hard to imagine Obama having that same thought, backstage at Grant Park, hearing his own name chanted by the hopeful multitude. *Everyone wants to be Barack Obama. Even I want to be Barack Obama.*

2.

But I haven't described Dream City. I'll try to. It is a place of many voices, where the unified singular self is an illusion. Naturally, Obama was born there. So was I. When your personal multiplicity is printed on your face, in an almost too obviously thematic manner, in your DNA, in your hair and in the neither this nor that beige of your skin—well, anyone can see you come from Dream City. In Dream City everything is doubled, everything is various. You have no choice but to cross borders and speak in tongues. That's how you get from your mother to your father, from talking to one set of folks who think you're not black enough to another who figure you insufficiently white. It's the kind of town where the wise man says "I" cautiously, because "I" feels like too straight and singular a phoneme to represent the true multiplicity of his experience. Instead, citizens of Dream City prefer to use the collective pronoun "we."

Throughout his campaign Obama was careful always to say we. He was noticeably wary of "I." By speaking so, he wasn't simply avoiding a singularity he didn't feel, he was also drawing us in with him. He had the audacity to suggest that, even if you can't see it stamped on their faces, most people come from Dream City, too. Most of us have complicated back stories, messy histories, multiple narratives.

It was a high-wire strategy, for Obama, this invocation of our collective human messiness. His enemies latched on to its imprecision, emphasizing the exotic, un-American nature of Dream City, this ill-defined place where you could be from Hawaii and Kenya, Kansas and Indonesia all at the same time, where you could jive talk like a street hustler and orate like a senator. What kind of a crazy place is that? But they underestimated how many people come from Dream City, how many Americans, in their daily lives, conjure contrasting voices and seek a synthesis between disparate things. Turns out, Dream City wasn't so strange to them.

Or did they never actually see it? We now know that Obama spoke of *Main Street* in Iowa and of *sweet potato pie* in Northwest Philly, and it could be argued that he succeeded because he so rarely misspoke, carefully tailoring his intonations to suit the sensibility of his listeners. Sometimes he did this within one speech, within one line: "We worship an *awesome* God in the blue states, and we don't like federal agents poking around our libraries in the red states." *Awesome God* comes to you straight from the pews of a Georgia church; *poking around* feels more at home at a kitchen table in South Bend, Indiana. The balance was perfect, cunningly counterpoised and never accidental. It's only now that it's over that we see him let his guard down a little, on *60 Minutes*, say, dropping in that culturally, casually black construction "Hey, I'm not stupid, *man*, that's why I'm president," something it's hard to imagine him doing even three weeks earlier. To a certain kind of mind, it must have looked like the mask had slipped for a moment.

Which brings us to the single-voiced Obamanation crowd. They rage on 20 in the blogs and on the radio, waiting obsessively for the mask to slip. They have a great fear of what they see as Obama's doubling ways. "He says one thing but he means another"—this is the essence of the fear campaign. He says he's a capitalist, but he'll spread your wealth. He says he's a Christian, but really he's going to empower the Muslims. And so on and so forth. These are fears that have their roots in an anxiety about voice. *Who is he?* people kept asking. *I mean, who is this guy, really?* He says *sweet potato pie* in Philly and *Main Street* in Iowa! When he talks to us, he sure *sounds* like us—but behind our backs he says we're clinging to our religion, to our guns. And when Jesse Jackson heard that Obama had lectured a black church congregation about the epidemic of absent black fathers, he experienced this, too, as a tonal betrayal; Obama was "talking down to black people." In both cases, there was the sense of a double-dealer, of someone who tailors his speech to fit the audience, who is not *of* the people (because he is able to look at them objectively) but always above them.

The Jackson gaffe, with its Oedipal violence ("I want to cut his nuts out"), is especially poignant because it goes to the heart of a generational conflict in the black community, concerning what we will say in public and what we say in private. For it has been a point of honor, among the civil rights generation, that any criticism or negative analysis of our community, expressed, as they often are by white politicians, without context, without real empathy or understanding, should not be repeated by a black politician when the white community is listening, even if (*especially if*) the criticism happens to be true (more than half of all black American children live in single-parent households). Our business is our business. Keep it in the family; don't wash your dirty linen in public; stay unified. (Of course, with his overheard gaffe, Jackson unwittingly broke his own rule.)

Until Obama, black politicians had always adhered to these unwritten rules. In this way, they defended themselves against those two bogeymen of black political life: the Uncle Tom and the House Nigger. The black politician who played up to, or even simply echoed, white fears, desires, and hopes for the black community was in danger of earning these epithets—even Martin Luther King was not free from such suspicions. Then came Obama, and the new world he had supposedly ushered in, the postracial world, in which what mattered most was not blind racial allegiance but factual truth. It was felt that Jesse Jackson was sadly out of step with this new postracial world: even his own son felt moved to publicly repudiate his "ugly rhetoric." But Jackson's anger was not incomprehensible nor his distrust unreasonable. Jackson lived through a bitter struggle, and bitter struggles deform their participants in subtle, complicated ways. The idea that one should speak one's cultural allegiance first and the truth second (and that this is a sign of authenticity) is precisely such a deformation.

Right up to the wire, Obama made many black men and women of Jackson's generation suspicious. How can the man who passes between culturally black and white voices with such flexibility, with such ease, be an honest man? How *will* the man from Dream City keep it real? Why won't he speak with a clear and unified voice? These were genuine questions for people born in real cities at a time when those cities were implacably divided, when the black movement had to yell with a clear and unified voice, or risk not being heard at all. And then he won. Watching Jesse Jackson in tears in Grant Park, pressed up against the varicolored American public, it seemed like he, at least, had received the answer he needed: only a many-voiced man could have spoken to that many people.

A *clear and unified voice*. In that context, this business of being biracial, of being half black and half white, is awkward. In his memoir, Obama takes care to ridicule a certain black girl called Joyce—a composite figure from his college days who happens also to be part Italian and part French and part Native American and is inordinately fond of mentioning these facts, and who likes to say:

25
I'm not black. . . . I'm *multiracial*. . . . Why should I have to choose between them? . . . It's not white people who are making me choose. . . . No—it's *black people* who always have to make everything racial. *They're* the ones making me choose. *They're* the ones who are telling me I can't be who I am. . . .

He has her voice down pat and so condemns her out of her own mouth. For she's the third bogeyman of black life, the tragic mulatto, who secretly wishes she "passed," always keen to let you know about her white heritage. It's the fear of being mistaken for Joyce that has always ensured that I ignore the box marked "biracial" and tick the box marked "black" on any questionnaire I fill out, and call myself unequivocally a black writer and roll my eyes at anyone who insists that Obama is not the first black president but the first biracial one. But I also know in my heart that it's an equivocation; I know that Obama has a double consciousness, is black and, at the same time, white, as I am, unless we are suggesting that one side of a person's genetics and cultural heritage cancels out or trumps the other.

But to mention the double is to suggest shame at the singular. Joyce insists on her varied heritage because she fears and is ashamed of the singular black. I suppose it's possible that subconsciously I am also a tragic mulatto, torn between pride and shame. In my conscious life, though, I cannot honestly say I feel proud to be white and ashamed to be black or proud to be black and ashamed to be white. I find it impossible to experience either pride or shame over accidents of genetics in which I had no active part. I understand how those words got into the racial discourse, but I can't sign up to them. I'm not proud to be female either. I am not even proud to be human—I only love to be so. As I love to be female and I love to be black, and I love that I had a white father.

It's telling that Joyce is one of the few voices in *Dreams from My Father* that is truly left out in the cold, outside of the expansive sympathy of Obama's narrative. She is an entirely didactic being, a demon Obama has to raise up, if only for a page, so everyone can watch him slay her. I know the feeling. When I was in college I felt I'd rather run away with the Black Panthers than be associated with the Joyces I occasionally met. It's the Joyces of this world who "talk down to black folks." And so to avoid being Joyce, or being seen to be Joyce, you unify, you speak with one voice.

And the concept of a unified black voice is a potent one. It has filtered down, these past forty years, into the black community at all levels, settling itself in that impossible injunction "keep it real," the original intention of which was unification. We were going to unify the concept of Blackness in order to strengthen it. Instead we confined and restricted it. To me, the instruction "keep it real" is a sort of prison cell, two feet by five. The fact is, it's too narrow. I just can't live comfortably in there. "*Keep it real*" replaced the blessed and solid genetic fact of Blackness with a flimsy imperative. It made Blackness a quality each individual black person was constantly in danger of losing. And almost anything could trigger the loss of one's Blackness: attending certain universities, an impressive variety of jobs, a fondness for opera, a white girlfriend, an interest in golf. And of course, any change in the voice. There was a popular school of thought that maintained the voice was at the very heart of the thing; fail to keep it real there and you'd never see your Blackness again.

How absurd that all seems now. And not because we live in a postracial 30 world—we don't—but because the reality of race has diversified. Black reality has diversified. It's black people who talk like me, and black people who talk like L'il Wayne. It's black conservatives and black liberals, black sportsmen and black lawyers, black computer technicians and black ballet dancers and black truck drivers and black presidents. We're all black, and we all love to be black, and we all sing from our own hymn sheet. We're all surely black people, but we may be finally approaching a point of human history where you can't talk up or down to us anymore, but only to us. *He's talking down to white people* — how curious it sounds the other way round! In order to say such a thing one would have to think collectively of white people, as a people of one mind who speak with one voice—a thought experiment in which we have no practice. But it's worth trying. It's only when you play the record backward that you hear the secret message.

3.

For reasons that are obscure to me, those qualities we cherish in our artists we condemn in our politicians. In our artists we look for the many-colored voice, the multiple sensibility. The apogee of this is, of course, Shakespeare: even more than for his wordplay we cherish him for his lack of allegiance. *Our* Shakespeare sees always both sides of a thing, he is black and white, male and female—he is everyman. The giant lacunae in his biography are merely a convenience; if any new facts of religious or political affiliation were ever to arise we would dismiss them in our hearts anyway. Was he, for example, a man of Rome or not? He has appeared, to generations of readers, not of one religion but of both, in truth, beyond both. Born into the middle of Britain's fierce Catholic–Protestant culture war, how could the bloody absurdity of those years not impress upon him a strong sense of cultural contingency?

It was a war of ideas that began for Will—as it began for Barack—in the dreams of his father. For we know that John Shakespeare, a civic officer in Protestant times, oversaw the repainting of medieval frescoes and the destruction of the rood loft and altar in Stratford's own fine Guild Chapel, but we also know that in the rafters of the Shakespeare home John hid a secret Catholic "Spiritual Testament," a signed profession of allegiance to the old faith. A strange experience, to watch one's own father thus divided, professing one thing in public while practicing another in private. John Shakespeare was a kind of equivocator: it's what you do when you're in a corner, when you can't be a Catholic and a loyal Englishman at the same time. When you can't be both black and white. Sometimes in a country ripped apart by dogma, those who wish to keep their heads—in both senses—must learn to split themselves in two.

And this we *still* know, here, at a four-hundred-year distance. No one can hope to be president of these United States without professing a committed and straightforward belief in two things: the existence of God and the principle of American exceptionalism. But how many of them equivocated, and who, in their shoes, would not equivocate, too?

Fortunately, Shakespeare was an artist and so had an outlet his father didn't have—the many-voiced theater. Shakespeare's art, the very medium of it, allowed him to do what civic officers and politicians can't seem to: speak simultaneous truths. (Is it not, for example, experientially true that one can both believe and *not* believe in God?) In his plays he is woman, man, black, white, believer, heretic, Catholic, Protestant, Jew, Muslim. He grew up in an atmosphere of equivocation, but he lived in freedom. And he offers us freedom: to pin him down to a single identity would be an obvious diminishment, both for Shakespeare and for us. Generations of critics have insisted on this irreducible multiplicity, though they have each expressed it different ways, through the glass of their times. Here is Keats's famous attempt, in 1817, to give this quality a name:

> At once it struck me, what quality went to form a Man of Achievement especially in Literature and which Shakespeare possessed so enormously—I mean *Negative Capability*, that is when man is capable of being in uncertainties, Mysteries, doubts, without any irritable reaching after fact and reason.

And here is Stephen Greenblatt doing the same, in 2004:   35

> There are many forms of heroism in Shakespeare, but ideological heroism—the fierce, self-immolating embrace of an idea or institution—is not one of them.

For Keats, Shakespeare's many voices are quasi-mystical as suited the Romantic thrust of Keats's age. For Greenblatt, Shakespeare's negative capability is sociopolitical at root. Will had seen too many wild-eyed martyrs, too many executed terrorists, too many wars on the Catholic terror. He had watched men rage absurdly at rood screens and write treatises in praise of tables. He had seen men disemboweled while still alive, their entrails burned before their eyes, and all for the preference of a Latin Mass over a common prayer or vice versa. He understood what fierce, singular certainty creates and what it destroys. In response, he made himself a diffuse, uncertain thing, a mass of contradictory, irresolvable voices that speak truth plurally. Through the glass of 2009, "negative capability" looks like the perfect antidote to "ideological heroism."

From our politicians, though, we still look for ideological heroism, despite everything. We consider pragmatists to be weak. We call men of balance naive fools. In England, we once had an insulting name for such people: trimmers. In the mid-1600s, a trimmer was any politician who attempted to straddle the reviled middle ground between Cavalier and Roundhead, Parliament and the Crown; to call a man a trimmer was to accuse him of being insufficiently committed to an ideology. But in telling us of these times, the nineteenth-century English historian Thomas Macaulay draws our attention to Halifax, great statesman of the Privy Council, set up to mediate between Parliament and Crown as London burned. Halifax proudly called himself a trimmer, assuming it, Macaulay explains, as

> a title of honour, and vindicat[ing], with great vivacity, the dignity of the appellation. Everything good, he said, trims between extremes. The temperate zone trims between the climate in which men are roasted and the climate in which they are frozen. The English Church trims between the Anabaptist madness and the Papist lethargy. The English constitution trims between the Turkish despotism and Polish anarchy. Virtue is nothing but a just temper between propensities any one of which, if indulged to excess, becomes vice.

Which all sounds eminently reasonable and Aristotelian. And Macaulay's description of Halifax's character is equally attractive:

> His intellect was fertile, subtle, and capacious. His polished, luminous, and animated eloquence . . . was the delight of the House of Lords. . . . His political tracts well deserve to be studied for their literary merit.

In fact, Halifax is familiar—he sounds like the man from Dream City. This makes Macaulay's caveat the more striking:

> Yet he was less successful in politics than many who enjoyed smaller advantages. Indeed, those intellectual *peculiarities which make his writings valuable* frequently impeded him in the contests of active life. For he always saw passing events, not in the point of view in which they commonly appear to one who bears a part in them, but in the point of view in which, after the lapse of many years, they appear to the philosophic historian.

40   To me, this is a doleful conclusion. It is exactly men with such intellectual peculiarities that I have always hoped to see in politics. But maybe Macaulay is correct: maybe the Halifaxes of this world make, in the end, better writers than politicians. A lot rests on how this president turns out—but that's a debate for the future. Here I want instead to hazard a little theory, concerning the evolution of a certain type of voice, typified by Halifax, by Shakespeare, and very possibly the President. For the voice of what Macaulay called "the philosophic historian" is, to my mind, a valuable and particular one, and I think someone should make a proper study of it. It's a voice that develops in a man over time; my little theory sketches four developmental stages.

The first stage in the evolution is contingent and cannot be contrived. In this first stage, the voice, by no fault of its own, finds itself trapped between two poles, two competing belief systems. And so this first stage necessitates the second: the voice learns to be flexible between these two fixed points, even to the point of equivocation. Then the third stage: this native flexibility leads to a sense of being able to "see a thing from both sides." And then the final stage, which I think of as the mark of a certain kind of genius: the voice relinquishes ownership of itself, develops a creative sense of disassociation in which the claims that are particular to it seem no stronger than anyone else's. There it is, my little theory—I'd rather call it a story. It is a story about a wonderful voice, occasionally used by citizens, rarely by men of power. Amidst the din of the 2008 culture wars it proved especially hard to hear.

In this lecture I have been seeking to tentatively suggest that the voice that speaks with such freedom, thus unburdened by dogma and personal bias, thus flooded with empathy, might make a good president. It's only now that I realize that in all this utilitarianism I've left joyfulness out of the account, and thus neglected a key constituency of my own people, the poets! Being many-voiced may be a complicated gift for a president, but in poets it is a pure delight in need of neither defense nor explanation. Plato banished them from his uptight and annoying republic so long ago that they have lost all their anxiety. They are fancy-free.

"I am a Hittite in love with a horse," writes Frank O'Hara.

I don't know what blood's
in me I feel like an African prince I am a girl walking downstairs
in a red pleated dress with heels I am a champion taking a fall
I am a jockey with a sprained ass-hole I am the light mist
in which a face appears
and it is another face of blonde I am a baboon eating a banana
I am a dictator looking at his wife I am a doctor eating a child
and the child's mother smiling I am a Chinaman climbing a mountain
I am a child smelling his father's underwear I am an Indian
sleeping on a scalp
and my pony is stamping in
the birches,
and I've just caught sight of the
Niña, the Pinta and the Santa Maria.
What land is this, so free?

Frank O'Hara's republic is of the imagination, of course. It is the only land of perfect freedom. Presidents, as a breed, tend to dismiss this land, thinking it has nothing to teach them. If this new president turns out to be different, then writers will count their blessings, but with or without a president on board, writers should always count their blessings. A line of O'Hara's reminds us of this. It's carved on his gravestone. It reads: "Grace to be born and live as variously as possible."

But to live variously cannot simply be a gift, endowed by an accident of birth; it has to be a continual effort, continually renewed. I felt this with force the night of the election. I was at a lovely New York party, full of lovely people, almost all of whom were white, liberal, highly educated, and celebrating with one happy voice as the states turned blue. Just as they called Iowa my phone rang and a strident German voice said: "Zadie! Come to Harlem! It's vild here. I'm in za middle of a crazy Reggae bar—it's so vonderful! Vy not come now!"

I mention he was German only so we don't run away with the idea that flexibility comes only to the beige, or gay, or otherwise marginalized. Flexibility is a choice, always open to all of us. (He was a writer, however. Make of that what you will.)

But wait: all the way uptown? A crazy reggae bar? For a minute I hesitated, because I was at a lovely party having a lovely time. Or was that it? There was something else. In truth I thought: but I'll be ludicrous, in my silly dress, with this silly posh English voice, in a crowded bar of black New Yorkers celebrating. It's amazing how many of our cross-cultural and cross-class encounters are limited not by hate or pride or shame, but by another equally insidious, less-discussed, emotion: embarrassment. A few minutes later, I was in a taxi and heading uptown with my Northern Irish husband and our half-Indian, half-English friend, but that initial hesitation was ominous; the first step on a typical British journey. A hesitation in the face of difference, which leads to caution before difference and ends in fear of it. Before long, the only voice you recognize, the only life you can empathize with, is your own. You will think that a novelist's screwy leap of logic. Well, it's my novelist credo and I believe it. I believe that flexibility of voice leads to a flexibility in all things. My audacious hope in Obama is based, I'm afraid, on precisely such flimsy premises.

It's my audacious hope that a man born and raised between opposing dogmas, between cultures, between voices, could not help but be aware of the extreme contingency of culture. I further audaciously hope that such a man will not mistake the happy accident of his own cultural sensibilities for a set of natural laws, suitable for general application. I even hope that he will find himself in agreement with George Bernard Shaw when he declared, "Patriotism is, fundamentally, a conviction that a particular country is the best in the world because you were born in it." But that may be an audacious hope too far. We'll see if Obama's lifelong vocal flexibility will enable him to say proudly with one voice "I love my country" while saying with another voice "It is a country, like other countries." I hope so. He seems just the man to demonstrate that between those two voices there exists no contradiction and no equivocation but rather a proper and decent human harmony.

Things to Do with the Reading

1. In the early part of the essay, in reference to her own life, Zadie Smith argues that assimilation is real, and potentially a threat: you can lose your multilingualism, and be left stranded, like Eliza Doolittle, between two identity groups. On the other hand, the essay also discloses a lot of anxiety about what Smith calls "the concept of a unified black voice." As she remarks, the "impossible injunction 'keep it real'"—which was

intended to produce "unification," a single black voice—"is a sort of prison cell." How, ultimately, does the essay work out this dilemma?

2. The word "dream" is a key repetition in this essay. Apply THE METHOD (see Chapter 1) and REFORMULATING BINARIES (see Chapter 2) to the essay. Most immediately, the piece is a meditation on race in response to Obama's memoir, *Dreams from My Father*. The term resurfaces with the idea of "Dream City," which initially refers to the self-created persona of the actor Cary Grant, "The Man from Dream City." And later Smith attaches the term to the statesman of the Privy Council, Halifax ("he sounds like the man from Dream City"). Study the sentences in which the dream language occurs. What are the values (ideological values) attached to it? You should be able to discover the contexts in which the dream is a source of anxiety for Smith, as well as the contexts in which it is associated with a kind of admirable middle ground. The essay is full of binary oppositions: what are the key terms against which "dream" is paired? What ultimately is the status of dream in this essay, and how is it related, if at all, to the central organizing binary between separation/singlevoicedness versus integration/multivoicedness?

3. Link: Discuss the differences between Smith's and Rodriguez's visions for the future. How might Zadie Smith respond to the following short paragraph from Richard Rodriguez's essay: "Expect marriage. We will change America even as we will be changed. We will disappear with you into a new miscegenation"? (paragraph 18). Also consider his remark that "The genius of Latin America is the habit of synthesis" (paragraph 9) and that we should all "expect bastard themes" (paragraph 16). To what extent do these notions conflict with Smith's concept of double voicing and of the unified self as an illusion? See Chapter 3, Difference within Similarity.

4. Near the end of the essay, just as she introduces the poem by Frank O'Hara, Smith remarks, "being many-voiced may be a complicated gift for a president, but in poets it is a pure delight in need of neither defense nor explanation." Implicit here are a range of interesting binaries. List them. Why does Smith distinguish the "land" of the imagination from the usual presidential terrain? At the very end of the essay, Smith refers to two voices, the one that utters "I love my country" and the one that says "It is a country, like other countries." Are these the voices, respectively, of the statesman and the artist? Why, in any case, is uniting them so important for Smith in this essay?

Amy Tan

Mother Tongue

In this provocative essay about her mother's "broken" English, the novelist Amy Tan distinguishes at least four different "Englishes" that she learned to speak as a Chinese American daughter called upon to succeed in U.S. schools, to communicate with her mother, and to become a writer. Along the way she provides glimpses into the quandaries that face children for whom standard English is not the language spoken at home: we see how the particular language she learns there does not equip her to navigate standardized tests in which, for example, she must discern whether "a sunset precedes nightfall" is analogous to "a chill precedes a fever." The author of seven novels and a number of nonfiction works, Tan's most recent novel is *The Valley of Amazement* (2013).

1   I am not a scholar of English or literature. I cannot give you much more than personal opinions on the English language and its variations in this country or others.

I am a writer. And by that definition, I am someone who has always loved language. I am fascinated by language in daily life. I spend a great deal of my time thinking about the power of language—the way it can evoke an emotion, a visual image, a complex idea, or a simple truth. Language is the tool of my trade. And I use them all—all the Englishes I grew up with.

Recently, I was made keenly aware of the different Englishes I do use. I was giving a talk to a large group of people, the same talk I had already given to half a dozen other groups. The nature of the talk was about my writing, my life, and my book, *The Joy Luck Club*. The talk was going along well enough, until I remembered one major difference that made the whole talk sound wrong. My mother was in the room. And it was perhaps the first time she had heard me give a lengthy speech, using the kind of English I have never used with her. I was saying things like, "The intersection of memory upon imagination" and "There is an aspect of my fiction that relates to thus-and-thus"—a speech filled with carefully wrought grammatical phrases, burdened, it suddenly seemed to me, with nominalized forms, past perfect tenses, conditional phrases, all the forms of standard English that I had learned in school and through books, the forms of English I did not use at home with my mother.

Just last week, I was walking down the street with my mother, and I again found myself conscious of the English I was using, the English I do use with her. We were talking about the price of new and used furniture and I heard myself saying this: "Not waste money that way." My husband was with us as

Copyright © 1989. First appeared in Threepenny Review. Reprinted by permission of the author and the Sandra Dijkstra Literary Agency.

well, and he didn't notice any switch in my English. And then I realized why. It's because over the twenty years we've been together I've often used that same kind of English with him, and sometimes he even uses it with me. It has become our language of intimacy, a different sort of English that relates to family talk, the language I grew up with.

So you'll have some idea of what this family talk I heard sounds like, I'll 5 quote what my mother said during a recent conversation, which I videotaped and then transcribed. During this conversation, my mother was talking about a political gangster in Shanghai who had the same last name as her family's, Du, and how the gangster in his early years wanted to be adopted by her family, which was rich by comparison. Later, the gangster became more powerful, far richer than my mother's family, and one day showed up at my mother's wedding to pay his respects. Here's what she said in part: "Du Yusong having business like fruit stand. Like off the street kind. He is Du like Du Zong—but not Tsung-ming Island people. The local people call putong, the river east side, he belong to that side local people. That man want to ask Du Zong father take him in like become own family. Du Zong father wasn't look down on him, but didn't take seriously, until that man big like become a mafia. Now important person, very hard to inviting him. Chinese way, came only to show respect, don't stay for dinner. Respect for making big celebration, he shows up. Mean gives lots of respect. Chinese custom. Chinese social life that way. If too important won't have to stay too long. He come to my wedding. I didn't see, I heard it. I gone to boy's side, they have YMCA dinner. Chinese age I was nineteen."

You should know that my mother's expressive command of English belies how much she actually understands. She reads the *Forbes* report, listens to *Wall Street Week*, converses daily with her stockbroker, reads all of Shirley MacLaine's books with ease—all kinds of things I can't begin to understand. Yet some of my friends tell me they understand 50 percent of what my mother says. Some say they understand 80 to 90 percent. Some say they understand none of it, as if she were speaking pure Chinese. But to me, my mother's English is perfectly clear, perfectly natural. It's my mother tongue. Her language, as I hear it, is vivid, direct, full of observation and imagery. That was the language that helped shape the way I saw things, expressed things, made sense of the world.

Lately, I've been giving more thought to the kind of English my mother speaks. Like others, I have described it to people as "broken" or "fractured" English. But I wince when I say that. It has always bothered me that I can think of no way to describe it other than "broken," as if it were damaged and needed to be fixed, as if it lacked a certain wholeness and soundness. I've heard other terms used, "limited English," for example. But they seem just as bad, as if everything is limited, including people's perceptions of the limited English speaker.

I know this for a fact, because when I was growing up, my mother's "limited" English limited *my* perception of her. I was ashamed of her English. I believed that her English reflected the quality of what she had to say. That is, because she expressed them imperfectly her thoughts were imperfect. And I had plenty of empirical evidence to support me: the fact that people in department stores, at banks, and at restaurants did not take her seriously, did not give her good service, pretended not to understand her, or even acted as if they did not hear her.

My mother has long realized the limitations of her English as well. When I was fifteen, she used to have me call people on the phone to pretend I was she. In this guise, I was forced to ask for information or even to complain and yell at people who had been rude to her. One time it was a call to her stockbroker in New York. She had cashed out her small portfolio and it just so happened we were going to go to New York the next week, our very first trip outside California. I had to get on the phone and say in an adolescent voice that was not very convincing, "This is Mrs. Tan." And my mother was standing in the back whispering loudly, "Why he don't send me check, already two weeks late. So mad he lie to me, losing me money. And then I said in perfect English, 'Yes, I'm getting rather concerned. You had agreed to send the check two weeks ago, but it hasn't arrived.'"

10 Then she began to talk more loudly. "What he want, I come to New York tell him front of his boss, you cheating me?" And I was trying to calm her down, make her be quiet, while telling the stockbroker, "I can't tolerate any more excuses. If I don't receive the check immediately, I am going to have to speak to your manager when I'm in New York next week." And sure enough, the following week there we were in front of this astonished stockbroker, and I was sitting there red-faced and quiet, and my mother, the real Mrs. Tan, was shouting at his boss in her impeccable broken English.

We used a similar routine just five days ago, for a situation that was far less humorous. My mother had gone to the hospital for an appointment, to find out about a benign brain tumor a CAT scan had revealed a month ago. She said she had spoken very good English, her best English, no mistakes. Still, she said, the hospital did not apologize when they said they had lost the CAT scan and she had come for nothing. She said they did not seem to have any sympathy when she told them she was anxious to know the exact diagnosis, since her husband and son had both died of brain tumors. She said they would not give her any more information until the next time and she would have to make another appointment for that. So she said she would not leave until the doctor called her daughter. She wouldn't budge. And when the doctor finally called her daughter, me, who spoke in perfect English—lo and behold—we had assurances the CAT scan would be found, promises that a conference call on Monday would be held, and apologies for any suffering my mother had gone through for a most regrettable mistake.

I think my mother's English almost had an effect on limiting my possibilities in life as well. Sociologists and linguists probably will tell you that a person's developing language skills are more influenced by peers. But I do think that the language spoken in the family, especially in immigrant families which are more insular, plays a large role in shaping the language of the child. And I believe that it affected my results on achievement tests, I.Q. tests, and the SAT. While my English skills were never judged as poor, compared to math, English could not be considered my strong suit. In grade school I did moderately well, getting perhaps B's, sometimes B-pluses, in English and scoring perhaps in the sixtieth or seventieth percentile on achievement tests. But those scores were not good enough to override the opinion that my true abilities lay in math and science, because in those areas I achieved A's and scored in the ninetieth percentile or higher.

This was understandable. Math is precise; there is only one correct answer. Whereas, for me at least, the answers on English tests were always a judgment call, a matter of opinion and personal experience. Those tests were constructed around items like fill-in-the-blank sentence completion, such as, "Even thought Tom was _____, Mary thought he was _____." And the correct answer always seemed to be the most bland combinations of thoughts, for example, "Even though Tom was shy, Mary thought he was charming" with the grammatical structure "even though" limiting the correct answer to some sort of semantic opposites, so you wouldn't get answers like, "Even though Tom was foolish, Mary thought he was ridiculous." Well, according to my mother, there were very few limitations as to what Tom could have been and what Mary might have thought of him. So I never did well on tests like that.

The same was true with word analogies, pairs of words in which you were supposed to find some sort of logical, semantic relationship—for example, "*Sunset* is to *nightfall* as _____ is to _____. " And here you would be presented with a list of four possible pairs, one of which showed the same kind of relationship: red is to stoplight, bus is to arrival, chills is to fever, yawn is to boring. Well, I could never think that way. I knew what the tests were asking, but I could not block out of my mind the images already created by the first pair, "sunset is to nightfall"—and I would see a burst of colors against a darkening sky, the moon rising, the lowering of a curtain of stars. And all the other pairs of words—red, bus, stoplight, boring—just threw up a mass of confusing images, making it impossible for me to sort out something as logical as saying: "A sunset precedes nightfall" is the same as "a chill precedes a fever." The only way I would have gotten that answer right would have been to imagine an associative situation, for example, my being disobedient and staying out past sunset, catching a chill at night, which turns into feverish pneumonia as punishment, which indeed did happen to me.

I have been thinking about all this lately, about my mother's English, about achievement tests. Because lately I've been asked, as a writer, why there are not more Asian-Americans represented in American literature. Why are there few Asian-Americans enrolled in creative writing programs? 15

Why do so many Chinese students go into engineering? Well, these are broad sociological questions I can't begin to answer.

But I have noticed in surveys—in fact, just last week—that Asian students, as a whole, always do significantly better on math achievement tests than in English. And this makes me think that there are other Asian-American students whose English spoken in the home might also be described as "broken" or "limited." And perhaps they also have teachers who are steering them away from writing and into math and science, which is what happened to me.

Fortunately, I happen to be rebellious in nature and enjoy the challenge of disproving assumptions made about me. I became an English major my first year in college, after being enrolled as pre-med. I started writing nonfiction as a freelancer the week after I was told by my former boss that writing was my worst skill and I should hone my talents toward account management.

But it wasn't until 1985 that I finally began to write fiction. And at first I wrote using what I thought to be wittily crafted sentences, sentences that would finally prove I had mastery over the English language. Here's an example from the first draft of a story that later made its way into *The Joy Luck Club*, but without this line: "That was my mental quandary in its nascent state." A terrible line, which I can barely pronounce.

Fortunately, for reasons I won't get into today, I later decided I should envision a reader for the stories I would write. And the reader I decided upon was my mother, because these were stories about mothers. So with this reader in mind—and in fact she did read my early drafts—I began to write stories using all the Englishes I grew up with: the English I spoke to my mother, which for lack of a better term might be described as "simple"; the English she used with me, which for lack of a better term might be described as "broken"; my translation of her Chinese, which could certainly be described as "watered down"; and what I imagined to be her translation of her Chinese if she could speak in perfect English, her internal language, and for that I sought to preserve the essence, but neither an English nor a Chinese structure. I wanted to capture what language ability tests can never reveal: her intent, her passion, her imagery, the rhythms of her speech and the nature of her thoughts. Apart from what any critic had to say about my writing, I knew I had succeeded where it counted when my mother finished reading my book and gave me her verdict: "So easy to read."

Things to Do with the Reading

1. Link: Imagine that Peggy McIntosh, the author of "White Privilege and Male Privilege," read Tan's essay. Write an essay in which you first identify and discuss passages from both essays that illustrate some common ground. Then determine the biggest difference between these two

women writers' points of view, and ASK SO WHAT? (see Chapter 1 on the SO WHAT? question.) Then answer it. You might use the heuristic in Chapter 3 that we call LOOKING FOR DIFFERENCE WITHIN SIMILARITY.

2. One organizing binary in the essay is between standard English and Tan's mother's English. (See THE METHOD in Chapter 1 and REFORMULATING BINARIES in Chapter 2.) What claims does Tan make for the advantages of her mother's English? Why does she speak it with her non-Chinese husband? Use these questions to develop an essay on the extent to which Tan implicitly critiques standard English, even as she uses it. What is it that Tan seems to believe standard English cannot so easily say?

3. Link: Write an essay in which you compare and contrast Tan's complex point of view on assimilation with that of Richard Rodriguez in "The Fear of Losing a Culture." To what extent do both writers complicate the melting pot model of assimilation? If you wish, consider the role that style plays in establishing each author's point of view. (See the beginning of Chapter 10 on style.)

4. Link: To whose experience and point of view do Tan's seem closest— Richard Rodriguez or Zadie Smith? Cite and reflect on specific sentences from the three readings in support of your answer. Pay particular attention to the way that Tan's essay ends. What does Tan hope to accomplish in her writing—and why?

Henry Louis Gates, Jr.

In the Kitchen

In this carefully crafted and subtly inflected memoir, Henry Louis Gates, Jr. uses his own memories of African-American hairstyling figuratively—as a way of thinking about more than just hair. Neither an apology nor a diatribe, the piece offers a complex and affectionate parable of assimilation. Henry Louis "Skip" Gates, Jr., is the Alphonse Fletcher University Professor at Harvard University, and director of the W.E.B. Du Bois Institute for African and African-American Research at the university. He is the author or editor of over twenty-five books, and he has been involved in a series of films. Most recently, in 2014 "The African-Americans: Many Rivers to Cross with Henry Louis Gates, Jr." won a Peabody Award for this PBS miniseries in which he served as producer, writer, and host. Like a number of authors included in this book, he, too, won a MacArthur "genius" Fellowship.

1   We always had a gas stove in the kitchen, in our house in Piedmont, West Virginia, where I grew up. Never electric, though using electric became fashionable in Piedmont in the sixties, like using Crest toothpaste rather than Colgate, or watching Huntley and Brinkley rather than Walter Cronkite. But not us: gas, Colgate, and good ole Walter Cronkite, come what may. We used gas partly out of loyalty to Big Mom, Mama's Mama, because she was mostly blind and still loved to cook, and could feel her way more easily with gas than with electric. But the most important thing about our gas-equipped kitchen was that Mama used to do hair there. The "hot comb" was a fine-toothed iron instrument with a long wooden handle and a pair of iron curlers that opened and closed like scissors. Mama would put it in the gas fire until it glowed. You could smell those prongs heating up.

I liked that smell. Not the smell so much, I guess, as what the smell meant for the shape of my day. There was an intimate warmth in the women's tones as they talked with my Mama, doing their hair. I knew what the women had been through to get their hair ready to be "done," because I would watch Mama do it to herself. How that kink could be transformed through grease and fire into that magnificent head of wavy hair was a miracle to me, and still is.

Mama would wash her hair over the sink, a towel wrapped around her shoulders, wearing just her slip and her white bra. (We had no shower—just a galvanized tub that we stored in the kitchen—until we moved down Rat Tail Road into Doc Wolverton's house, in 1954.) After she dried it, she would grease her scalp thoroughly with blue Bergamot hair grease, which came in a short, fat jar with a picture of a beautiful colored lady on it. It's important

"In the Kitchen" from COLORED PEOPLE: A MEMOIR by Henry Louis Gates, Jr., copyright © 1994 by Henry Louis Gates, Jr. Used by permission of Alfred A. Knopf, an imprint of the Knopf Doubleday Publishing Group, a division of Random House LLC. All rights reserved.

to grease your scalp real good, my Mama would explain, to keep from burning yourself. Of course, her hair would return to its natural kink almost as soon as the hot water and shampoo hit it. To me, it was another miracle how hair so "straight" would so quickly become kinky again the second it even approached some water.

My Mama had only a few "clients" whose heads she "did"—did, I think, because she enjoyed it, rather than for the few pennies it brought in. They would sit on one of our red plastic kitchen chairs, the kind with the shiny metal legs, and brace themselves for the process. Mama would stroke that red-hot iron—which by this time had been in the gas fire for half an hour or more—slowly but firmly through their hair, from scalp to strand's end. It made a scorching, crinkly sound, the hot iron did, as it burned its way through kink, leaving in its wake straight strands of hair, standing long and tall but drooping over at the ends, their shape like the top of a heavy willow tree. Slowly, steadily, Mama's hands would transform a round mound of Odetta kink into a darkened swamp of everglades. The Bergamot made the hair shiny; the heat of the hot iron gave it a brownish-red cast. Once all the hair was as straight as God allows kink to get, Mama would take the well-heated curling iron and twirl the straightened strands into more or less loosely wrapped curls. She claimed that she owed her skill as a hairdresser to the strength in her wrists, and as she worked her little finger would poke out, the way it did when she sipped tea. Mama was a southpaw, and wrote upside down and backward to produce the cleanest, roundest letters you've ever seen.

The "kitchen" she would all but remove from sight with a handheld pair 5 of shears, bought just for this purpose. Now, the kitchen was the room in which we were sitting—the room where Mama did hair and washed clothes, and where we all took a bath in that galvanized tub. But the word has another meaning, and the kitchen that I'm speaking of is the very kinky bit of hair at the back of your head, where your neck meets your shirt collar. If there was ever a part of our African past that resisted assimilation, it was the kitchen. No matter how hot the iron, no matter how powerful the chemical, no matter how stringent the mashed-potatoes-and-lye formula of a man's "process," neither God nor woman nor Sammy Davis, Jr., could straighten the kitchen. The kitchen was permanent, irredeemable; irresistible kink. Unassimilably African. No matter what you did, no matter how hard you tried, you couldn't de-kink a person's kitchen. So you trimmed it off as best you could.

When hair had begun to "turn," as they'd say—to return to its natural kinky glory—it was the kitchen that turned first (the kitchen around the back, and nappy edges at the temples). When the kitchen started creeping up the back of the neck, it was time to get your hair done again.

Sometimes, after dark, a man would come to have his hair done. It was Mr. Charlie Carroll. He was very light-complected and had a ruddy nose—it made me think of Edmund Gwenn, who played Kris Kringle in "Miracle on

34th Street." At first, Mama did him after my brother, Rocky, and I had gone to sleep. It was only later that we found out that he had come to our house so Mama could iron his hair—not with a hot comb or a curling iron but with our very own Proctor-Silex steam iron. For some reason I never understood, Mr. Charlie would conceal his Frederick Douglass-like mane under a big white Stetson hat. I never saw him take it off except when he came to our house, at night, to have his hair pressed. (Later, Daddy would tell us about Mr. Charlie's most prized piece of knowledge, something that the man would only confide after his hair had been pressed, as a token of intimacy. "Not many people know this," he'd say, in a tone of circumspection, "but George Washington was Abraham Lincoln's daddy." Nodding solemnly, he'd add the clincher: "A white man told me." Though he was in dead earnest, this became a humorous refrain around our house—"a white man told me"—which we used to punctuate especially preposterous assertions.)

My mother examined my daughters' kitchens whenever we went home to visit, in the early eighties. It became a game between us. I had told her not to do it, because I didn't like the politics it suggested—the notion of "good" and "bad" hair. "Good" hair was "straight," "bad" hair kinky. Even in the late sixties, at the height of Black Power, almost nobody could bring themselves to say "bad" for good and "good" for bad. People still said that hair like white people's hair was "good," even if they encapsulated it in a disclaimer, like "what we used to call 'good.'"

Maggie would be seated in her high chair, throwing food this way and that, and Mama would be cooing about how cute it all was, how I used to do just like Maggie was doing, and wondering whether her flinging her food with her left hand meant that she was going to be left-handed like Mama. When my daughter was just about covered with Chef Boyardee Spaghetti-O's, Mama would seize the opportunity: wiping her clean, she would tilt Maggie's head to one side and reach down the back of her neck. Sometimes Mama would even rub a curl between her fingers, just to make sure that her bifocals had not deceived her. Then she'd sigh with satisfaction and relief: No kink . . . yet. Mama! I'd shout, pretending to be angry. Every once in a while, if no one was looking, I'd peek, too.

10   I say "yet" because most black babies are born with soft, silken hair. But after a few months it begins to turn, as inevitably as do the seasons or the leaves on a tree. People once thought baby oil would stop it. They were wrong.

Everybody I knew as a child wanted to have good hair. You could be as ugly as homemade sin dipped in misery and still be thought attractive if you had good hair. "Jesus moss," the girls at Camp Lee, Virginia, had called Daddy's naturally "good" hair during the war. I know that he played that thick head of hair for all it was worth, too.

My own hair was "not a bad grade," as barbers would tell me when they cut it for the first time. It was like a doctor reporting the results of the first full physical he has given you. Like "You're in good shape" or "Blood pressure's kind of high—better cut down on salt."

I spent most of my childhood and adolescence messing with my hair. I definitely wanted straight hair. Like Pop's. When I was about three, I tried to stick a wad of Bazooka bubble gum to that straight hair of his. I suppose what fixed that memory for me is the spanking I got for doing so: he turned me upside down, holding me by my feet, the better to paddle my behind. Little *nigger*, he had shouted, walloping away. I started to laugh about it two days later, when my behind stopped hurting.

When black people say "straight," of course, they don't usually mean literally straight—they're not describing hair like, say, Peggy Lipton's (she was the white girl on "The Mod Squad"), or like Mary's of Peter, Paul & Mary fame; black people call that "stringy" hair. No, "straight" just means not kinky, no matter what contours the curl may take. I would have done *anything* to have straight hair—and I used to try everything, short of getting a process.

Of the wide variety of techniques and methods I came to master in the challenging prestidigitation of the follicle, almost all had two things in common: a heavy grease and the application of pressure. It's not an accident that some of the biggest black-owned companies in the fifties and sixties made hair products. And I tried them all, in search of that certain silken touch, the one that would leave neither the hand nor the pillow sullied by grease.

I always wondered what Frederick Douglass put on *his* hair, or what Phillis Wheatley put on hers. Or why Wheatley has that rag on her head in the little engraving in the frontispiece of her book. One thing is for sure: you can bet that when Phillis Wheatley went to England and saw the Countess of Huntingdon she did not stop by the Queen's coiffeur on her way there. So many black people still get their hair straightened that it's a wonder we don't have a national holiday for Madame C. J. Walker, the woman who invented the process of straightening kinky hair. Call it Jheri-Kurled or call it "relaxed," it's still fried hair.

I used all the greases, from sea-blue Bergamot and creamy vanilla Duke (in its clear jar with the orange-white-and-green label) to the godfather of grease, the formidable Murray's. Now, Murray's was some *serious* grease. Whereas Bergamot was like oily Jell-O, and Duke was viscous and sickly sweet, Murray's was light brown and *hard*. Hard as lard and twice as greasy, Daddy used to say. Murray's came in an orange can with a press-on top. It was so hard that some people would put a match to the can, just to soften the stuff and make it more manageable. Then, in the late sixties, when Afros came into style, I used Afro Sheen. From Murray's to Duke to Afro Sheen: that was my progression in black consciousness.

We used to put hot towels or wash-rags over our Murray-coated heads, in order to melt the wax into the scalp and the follicles. Unfortunately, the wax also had the habit of running down your neck, ears, and forehead. Not to

15

mention your pillowcase. Another problem was that if you put two palmfuls of Murray's on your head your hair turned white. (Duke did the same thing.) The challenge was to get rid of that white color. Because if you got rid of the white stuff you had a magnificent head of wavy hair. That was the beauty of it: Murray's was so hard that it froze your hair into the wavy style you brushed it into. It looked really good if you wore a part. A lot of guys had parts *cut* into their hair by a barber, either with the clippers or with a straightedged razor. Especially if you had kinky hair—then you'd generally wear a short razorcut, or what we called a Quo Vadis.

We tried to be as innovative as possible. Everyone knew about using a stocking cap, because your father or your uncle wore one whenever something really big was about to happen, whether sacred or secular: a funeral or a dance, a wedding or a trip in which you confronted official white people. Any time you were trying to look really sharp, you wore a stocking cap in preparation. And if the event was really a big one, you made a new cap. You asked your mother for a pair of her hose, and cut it with scissors about six inches or so from the open end—the end with the elastic that goes up to the top of the thigh. Then you knotted the cut end, and it became a beehive-shaped hat, with an elastic band that you pulled down low on your forehead and down around your neck in the back. To work well, the cap had to fit tightly and snugly, like a press. And it had to fit that tightly because it *was* a press: it pressed your hair with the force of the hose's elastic. If you greased your hair down real good, and left the stocking cap on long enough, voila: you got a head of pressed-against-the-scalp waves. (You also got a ring around your forehead when you woke up, but it went away.) And then you could enjoy your concrete do. Swore we were bad, too, with all that grease and those flat heads. My brother and I would brush it out a bit in the mornings, so that it looked—well, "natural." Grown men still wear stocking caps—especially older men, who generally keep their stocking caps in their top drawers, along with their cufflinks and their see-through silk socks, their "Maverick" ties, their silk handkerchiefs, and whatever else they prize the most.

20   A Murrayed-down stocking cap was the respectable version of the process, which, by contrast, was most definitely not a cool thing to have unless you were an entertainer by trade. Zeke and Keith and Poochie and a few other stars of the high-school basketball team all used to get a process once or twice a year. It was expensive, and you had to go somewhere like Pittsburgh or D.C. or Union-town—somewhere where there were enough colored people to support a trade. The guys would disappear, then reappear a day or two later, strutting like peacocks, their hair burned slightly red from the lye base. They'd also wear "rags"—cloths or handkerchiefs—around their heads when they slept or played basketball. Do-rags, they were called. But the result was straight hair, with just a hint of wave. No curl. Do-it-yourselfers took their chances at home with a concoction of mashed potatoes and lye.

The most famous process of all, however, outside of the process Malcolm X describes in his "Autobiography," and maybe the process of Sammy Davis, Jr., was Nat King Cole's process. Nat King Cole had patent-leather hair. That man's got the finest process money can buy, or so Daddy said the night we saw Cole's TV show on NBC. It was November 5, 1956. I remember the date because everyone came to our house to watch it and to celebrate one of Daddy's buddies' birthdays. Yeah, Uncle Joe chimed in, they can do shit to his hair that the average Negro can't even *think* about—secret shit.

Nat King Cole was *clean*. I've had an ongoing argument with a Nigerian friend about Nat King Cole for twenty years now. Not about whether he could sing—any fool knows that he could—but about whether or not he was a handkerchief head for wearing that patent-leather process.

Sammy Davis, Jr.'s process was the one I detested. It didn't look good on him. Worse still, he liked to have a fried strand dangling down the middle of his forehead, so he could shake it out from the crown when he sang. But Nat King Cole's hair was a thing unto itself, a beautifully sculpted work of art that he and he alone had the right to wear. The only difference between a process and a stocking cap, really, was taste; but Nat King Cole, unlike, say, Michael Jackson, looked *good* in his. His head looked like Valentino's head in the twenties, and some say it was Valentino the process was imitating. But Nat King Cole wore a process because it suited his face, his demeanor, his name, his style. He was as clean as he wanted to be.

I had forgotten all about that patent-leather look until one day in 1971, when I was sitting in an Arab restaurant on the island of Zanzibar surrounded by men in fezzes and white caftans, trying to learn how to eat curried goat and rice with the fingers of my right hand and feeling two million miles from home. All of a sudden, an old transistor radio sitting on top of a china cupboard stopped blaring out its Swahili music and started playing "Fly Me to the Moon," by Nat King Cole. The restaurant's din was not affected at all, but in my mind's eye I saw it: the King's magnificent sleek black tiara. I managed, barely, to blink back the tears.

Things to Do with the Reading

1. Write a short essay in which you identify the attitude in this piece towards the way that the America in which the author grew up dealt with the "problem" of kinky hair. What sentences in the piece seem most revealing of the point of view that Gates wishes us to take? How in particular does the piece make use of the various meanings of the word "kitchen"?

2. Endings of essays are sites where some resolution of an issue or problem usually occurs. So WHAT that Gates is in an Arab restaurant on the island

of Zanzibar trying to eat curried goat with his right hand when he hears Nat King Cole's "Fly Me to the Moon" and sees in his mind's eye "King's magnificent sleek black tiara"? What makes this a fitting end to the essay? What complex attitude does it invite us to have on assimilation vs. diversity? How would the ending of the essay have been different if Gates had tried to picture Nat King Cole with naturally curly hair rather than with his "process"?

3. **Link:** The subject of assimilation is a primary thread of this chapter. Write an essay in which you determine how this piece compares with Salins's and Rodriguez's outlooks on assimilation. Consider especially the impact of the essay's final paragraph in this regard.

Ishmael Reed

My Neighborhood

In this piece, Ishmael Reed takes the reader on a meditative tour through the various neighborhoods in which he has dwelled as an adult, using these places as sites for thinking about race and matters of assimilation. Reed has been nominated for the Pulitzer Prize and twice shortlisted for the National Book Award. He has published novels, essays, poems, and stories. The musician Max Roach has called him the Charlie Parker of American fiction, and in the biographical sketch of him in the *Dictionary of Literary Biography*, Henry Louis Gates, Jr. (author of the previous selection) argued that he has "no true predecessor or counterpart" in American letters. His most recent publication is *Going Too Far: Essays About America's Nervous Breakdown* (2012).

My stepfather is an evolutionist. He worked for many years at the Chevrolet 1 division of General Motors in Buffalo, a working-class auto and steel town in upstate New York, and was able to rise from relative poverty to the middle class. He believes that each succeeding generation of Afro-Americans will have it better than its predecessor. In 1979 I moved into the kind of neighborhood that he and my mother spent about a third of their lives trying to escape. According to the evolutionist integrationist ethic, this was surely a step backward, since "success" was seen as being able to live in a neighborhood in which you were the only black and joined your neighbors in trying to keep out "them."

My neighborhood, bordered by Genoa, Market Street, and 48th and 55th streets in North Oakland, is what the media refer to as a "predominantly black neighborhood." It's the kind of neighborhood I grew up in before leaving for New York City in 1962. My last New York residence was an apartment in a brownstone, next door to the building in which poet W. H. Auden lived. There were trees in the backyard, and I thought it was a swell neighborhood until I read in Robert Craft's biography of [the composer] Stravinsky that "when Stravinsky sent his chauffeur to pick up his friend Auden, the chauffeur would ask, 'Are you sure Mr. Auden lives in this neighborhood?'" By 1968 my wife and I were able to live six months of the year in New York and the other six in California. This came to an end when one of the people I sublet the apartment to abandoned it. He had fled to England to pursue a romance. He didn't pay the rent, and so we were evicted long distance.

My first residence in California was an apartment on Santa Ynez Street, near Echo Park Lake in Los Angeles, where I lived for about six months in 1967. I was working on my second novel, and Carla Blank, my wife, a dancer, was

Excerpted from the book, Writin' is Fightin' by Ishmael Reed. Copyright © 2004 by Houghton Mifflin Company. Permission granted by Lowenstein Associates, Inc.

teaching physical education at one of Eddie Rickenbacker's camps, located on an old movie set in the San Bernardino Mountains. Carla's employers were always offering me a cabin where they promised I could write without interruption. I never took them up on the offer, but for years I've wondered about what kind of reception I would have received had they discovered that I am black.

During my breaks from writing I would walk through the shopping areas near Santa Ynez, strolling by vending machines holding newspapers whose headlines screamed about riots in Detroit. On some weekends we'd visit novelist Robert Gover (*The One Hundred Dollar Misunderstanding*) and his friends in Malibu. I remember one of Gover's friends, a scriptwriter for the *Donna Reed Show*, looking me in the eye and telling me that if he were black he'd be "on a Detroit rooftop, sniping at cops," as he reclined, glass of scotch in hand, in a comfortable chair whose position gave him a good view of the rolling Pacific.

5   My Santa Ynez neighbors were whites from Alabama and Mississippi, and we got along fine. Most of them were elderly, left behind by white flight to the suburbs, and on weekends the street would be lined with cars belonging to relatives who were visiting. While living here I observed a uniquely Californian phenomenon. Retired men would leave their houses in the morning, enter their cars, and remain there for a good part of the day, snoozing, reading newspapers, or listening to the radio.

I didn't experience a single racial incident during my stay in this Los Angeles neighborhood of ex-southerners. Once, however, I had a strange encounter with the police. I was walking through a black working-class neighborhood on my way to the downtown Los Angeles library. Some cops drove up and rushed me. A crowd gathered. The cops snatched my briefcase and removed its contents: books and notebooks having to do with my research of voodoo. The crowd laughed when the cops said they thought I was carrying a purse.

In 1968 my wife and I moved to Berkeley, where we lived in one Bauhaus box after another until about 1971, when I received a three-book contract from Doubleday. Then we moved into the Berkeley Hills, where we lived in the downstairs apartment of a very grand-looking house on Bret Harte Way. There was a Zen garden with streams, waterfalls, and bridges outside, along with many varieties of flowers and plants. I didn't drive, and Carla was away at Mills College each day, earning a master's degree in dance. I stayed holed up in that apartment for two years, during which time I completed my third novel, *Mumbo Jumbo*.

During this period I became exposed to some of the racism I hadn't detected on Santa Ynez or in the Berkeley flats. As a black male working at home, I was regarded with suspicion. Neighbors would come over and warn me about a heroin salesman they said was burglarizing the neighborhood, all the while looking over my shoulder in an attempt to pry into what I was up to. Once, while I was eating breakfast, a policeman entered through the garden door, gun drawn. "What on earth is the problem, officer?" I asked. He said they got word that a homicide had been committed in my apartment, which I recognized as an old police tactic used to gain entry into somebody's house. Walking through the Berkeley Hills on Sundays, I was greeted by unfriendly stares and growling, snarling dogs. I remember one pest who always poked her head out of her window whenever I'd walk down Bret Harte Way. She was always hassling me about parking my car in front of her house. She resembled Miss Piggy. I came to think of this section of Berkeley as "Whitetown."

Around 1974 the landlord raised the rent on the house in the hills, and we found ourselves again in the Berkeley flats. We spent a couple of peaceful years on Edith Street, and then moved to Jayne Street, where we encountered another next-door family of nosy, middle-class progressives. I understand that much time at North Berkeley white neighborhood association meetings is taken up with discussion of and fascination with blacks who move through the neighborhoods, with special concern given those who tarry, or who wear dreadlocks. Since before the Civil War, vagrancy laws have been used as political weapons against blacks. Appropriately, there has been talk of making Havana—where I understand a woman can get turned in by her neighbors for having too many boyfriends over—Berkeley's sister city.

In 1976 our landlady announced that she was going to reoccupy the   10 Jayne Street house. I facetiously told a friend that I wanted to move to the most right-wing neighborhood he could think of. He mentioned El Cerrito. There, he said, your next-door neighbor might even be a cop. We moved to El Cerrito. Instead of the patronizing nosiness blacks complain about in Berkeley, I found the opposite on Terrace Drive in El Cerrito. The people were cold, impersonal, remote. But the neighborhood was quiet, serene even—the view was Olympian, and our rented house was secluded by eucalyptus trees. The annoyances were minor. Occasionally a car would careen down Terrace Drive full of white teenagers, and one or two would shout, "Hey, nigger!" Sometimes as I walked down The Arlington toward Kensington Market, the curious would stare at me from their cars, and women I encountered would give me nervous, frightened looks. Once, as I was walking to the market to buy magazines, a white child was sitting directly in my path. We were the only two people on the street. Two or three cars actually stopped, and their drivers observed the scene through their rearview mirrors until they were assured I wasn't going to abduct the child.

At night the Kensington Market area was lit with a yellow light, especially eerie during a fog. I always thought that this section of Kensington would be a swell place to make a horror movie—the residents would make great extras—but whatever discomfort I felt about traveling through this area at 2 A.M. was mixed with the relief that I had just navigated safely through Albany, where the police seemed always to be lurking in the shadows, prepared to ensnare blacks, hippies, and others they didn't deem suitable for such a neighborhood.

In 1979 our landlord, a decent enough fellow in comparison to some of the others we had (who made you understand why the communists shoot the landlords first when they take over a country), announced he was going to sell the house on Terrace Drive. This was the third rented house to be sold out from under us. The asking price was way beyond our means, and so we started to search for another home, only to find that the ones within our price range were located in North Oakland, in a "predominantly black neighborhood." We finally found a huge Queen Anne Victorian, which seemed to be about a month away from the wrecker's ball if the termites and the precarious foundation didn't do it in first, but I decided that I had to have it. The oldest house on the block, it was built in 1906, the year the big earthquake hit Northern California, but left Oakland unscathed because, according to Bret Harte, "there are some things even the earth can't swallow." If I was apprehensive about moving into this neighborhood—on television all black neighborhoods resemble the commotion of the station house on *Hill Street Blues*—I was later to learn that our neighbors were just as apprehensive about us. Were we hippies? Did I have a job? Were we going to pay as much attention to maintaining our property as they did to theirs? Neglected, the dilapidated monstrosity I'd got myself into would blight the entire block.

While I was going to college I worked as an orderly in a psychiatric hospital, and I remember a case in which a man was signed into the institution, after complaints from his neighbors that he mowed the lawn at four in the morning. My neighbors aren't that finicky, but they keep very busy pruning, gardening, and mowing their laws. Novelist Toni Cade Bambara wrote of the spirit women in Atlanta who plant by moonlight and use conjure to reap gorgeous vegetables and flowers. A woman on this block grows roses the size of cantaloupes.

On New Year's Eve, famed landscape architect John Roberts accompanied me on my nightly walk, which takes me from 53rd Street to Aileen, Shattuck, and back to 53rd Street. He was able to identify plants and trees that had been imported from Asia, the Middle East, and Australia. On Aileen Street he discovered a banana tree! And Arthur Monroe, a painter and art historian, traces the "Tabby" garden design—in which seashells and plates are mixed with lime, sand, and water to form decorative borders, found in this Oakland neighborhood, and others—to the influence of Islamic slaves brought to the Gulf Coast.

15   I won over my neighbors, I think, after I triumphed over a dozen generations of pigeons that had been roosting in the crevices of this house for many years. It was a long and angry war, and my five year old constantly complained to her mother about Daddy's bad words about the birds. I used everything I could get my hands on, including chicken wire and mothballs, and I would have tried the clay owls if the only manufacturer hadn't gone out of business. I also learned never to underestimate the intelligence of

pigeons; just when you think you've got them whipped, you'll notice that they've regrouped on some strategic rooftop to prepare for another invasion. When the house was free of pigeons and their droppings, which had spread to the adjoining properties, the lady next door said, "Thank you."

Every New Year's Day since then our neighbors have invited us to join them and their fellow Louisianans for the traditional Afro-American good luck meal called Hoppin' John. This year the menu included black-eyed peas, ham, corn bread, potato salad, chitterlings, greens, fried chicken, yams, head cheese, macaroni, rolls, sweet potato pie, and fruitcake. I got up that morning weighing 214 pounds and came home from the party weighing 220.

We've lived on 53rd Street for three years now. Carla's dance and theater school, which she operates with her partner, Jody Roberts—Roberts and Blank Dance/Drama—is already five years old. I am working on my seventh novel and a television production of my play *Mother Hubbard*. The house has yet to be restored to its 1906 glory, but we're working on it.

I've grown accustomed to the common sights here—teenagers moving through the neighborhood carrying radios blasting music by Grandmaster Flash and Prince, men hovering over cars with tools and rags in hand, decked-out female church delegations visiting the sick. Unemployment up, one sees more men drinking from sacks as they walk through Market Street or gather in Helen McGregor Plaza, on Shattuck and 52nd Street, near a bench where mothers sit with their children, waiting for buses. It may be because the bus stop is across the street from Children's Hospital (exhibiting a brand-new antihuman, postmodern wing), but there seem to be a lot of sick black children these days. The criminal courts and emergency rooms of Oakland hospitals, both medical and psychiatric, are also filled with blacks.

White men go from door to door trying to unload spoiled meat. Incredibly sleazy white contractors and hustlers try to entangle people into shady deals that sometimes lead to the loss of a home. Everybody knows of someone, usually a widow, who has been gypped into paying thousands of dollars more than the standard cost for, say, adding a room to a house. It sure ain't El Cerrito. In El Cerrito the representatives from the utilities were very courteous. If they realize they're speaking to someone in a black neighborhood, however, they become curt and sarcastic. I was trying to arrange for the gas company to come out to fix a stove when the woman from Pacific Gas and Electric gave me some snide lip. I told her, "Lady, if you think what you're going through is an inconvenience, you can imagine my inconvenience paying the bills every month." Even she had to laugh.

The clerks in the stores are also curt, regarding blacks the way the media 20 regard them, as criminal suspects. Over in El Cerrito the cops were professional, respectful—in Oakland they swagger about like candidates for a rodeo. In El Cerrito and the Berkeley Hills you could take your time paying some bills, but in this black neighborhood if you miss paying a bill by one day, "reminders" printed in glaring and violent typefaces are sent to you, or you're threatened with discontinuance of this or that service. Los Angeles police victim Eulia Love, who was shot in the aftermath of an argument over an overdue gas bill, would still be alive if she had lived in El Cerrito or the Berkeley Hills.

I went to a bank a few weeks ago that advertised easy loans on television, only to be told that I would have to wait six months after opening an account to be eligible for a loan. I went home and called the same bank, this time putting on my Clark Kent voice, and was informed that I could come in and get the loan the same day. Other credit unions and banks, too, have different lending practices for black and white neighborhoods, but when I try to tell white intellectuals that blacks are prevented from developing industries because the banks find it easier to lend money to communist countries than to American citizens, they call me paranoid. Sometimes when I know I am going to be inconvenienced by merchants or creditors because of my 53rd Street address, I give the address of my Berkeley studio instead. Others are not so fortunate.

Despite the inconveniences and antagonism from the outside world one has to endure for having a 53rd Street address, life in this neighborhood is more pleasant than grim. Casually dressed, well-groomed elderly men gather at the intersections to look after the small children as they walk to and from school, or just to keep an eye on the neighborhood. My next-door neighbor keeps me in stitches with his informed commentary on any number of political comedies emanating from Washington and Sacramento. Once we were discussing pesticides, and the man who was repairing his porch told us that he had a great garden and didn't have to pay all that much attention to it. As for pesticides, he said, the bugs have to eat, too.

There are people on this block who still know the subsistence skills many Americans have forgotten. They can hunt and fish (and if you don't fish, there is a man who covers the neighborhood selling fresh fish and yelling, "Fishman," recalling a period of ancient American commerce when you didn't have to pay the middleman). They are also loyal Americans—they vote, they pay taxes—but you don't find the extreme patriots here that you find in white neighborhoods. Although Christmas, Thanksgiving, New Year's, and Easter are celebrated with all get-out, I've never seen a flag flying on Memorial Day, or on any holiday that calls for the showing of the flag. Blacks express their loyalty in concrete ways. For example, you rarely see a foreign car in this neighborhood. And this 53rd Street neighborhood, as well as black neighborhoods like it from coast to coast, will supply the male children who will bear the brunt of future jungle wars, just as they did in Vietnam.

We do our shopping on a strip called Temescal, which stretches from 46th to 51st streets. Temescal, according to Oakland librarian William Sturm, is an Aztec word for "hothouse," or "bathhouse." The word was borrowed from the Mexicans by the Spanish to describe similar hothouses, early saunas, built by the California Indians in what is now North Oakland. Some say the hot-houses were used to sweat out demons; others claim the Indians used them for medicinal purposes. Most agree that after a period of time in the steam, the Indians would rush en masse into the streams that flowed through the area. One still runs underneath my backyard—I have to mow the grass there almost every other day.

Within these five blocks are the famous Italian restaurant Bertola's, "Since 1932"; Siam restaurant; La Belle Creole, a French-Caribbean restaurant; Asmara, an Ethiopian restaurant; and Ben's Hof Brau, where white and black senior citizens, dressed in the elegance of a former time, congregate to talk or to have an inexpensive though quality breakfast provided by Ben's hardworking and courteous staff. 25

The Hof Brau shares its space with Vern's market, where you can shop to the music of DeBarge. To the front of Vern's is the Temescal Delicatessen, where a young Korean man makes the best po' boy sandwiches north of Louisiana, and near the side entrance is Ed Fraga's Automotive. The owner is always advising his customers to avoid stress, and he says goodbye with a "God bless you." The rest of the strip is taken up by the Temescal Pharmacy, which has a resident health advisor and a small library of health literature; the Aikido Institute; an African bookstore; and the internationally known Genova deli, to which people from the surrounding cities travel to shop. The strip also includes the Clausen House thrift shop, which sells used clothes and furniture. Here you can buy novels by J.D. Salinger and John O'Hara for ten cents each.

Space that was recently occupied by the Buon Gusto Bakery is now for rent. Before the bakery left, an Italian lady who worked there introduced me to a crunchy, cookie-like treat called "bones," which she said went well with Italian wine. The Buon Gusto had been a landmark since the 1940s, when, according to a guest at the New Year's Day Hoppin' John supper, North Oakland was populated by Italians and Portuguese. In those days a five-room house could be rented for $45 a month, she said.

The neighborhood is still in transition. The East Bay Negro Historical Society, which was located around the corner on Grove Street, included in its collection letters written by nineteenth-century macho man Jack London to his black nurse. They were signed, "Your little white pickaninny." It's been replaced by the New Israelite Delight restaurant, part of the Israelite Church, which also operates a day care center. The restaurant offers homemade Louisiana gumbo and a breakfast that includes grits.

Unlike the other California neighborhoods I've lived in, I know most of the people on this block by name. They are friendly and cooperative, always offering to watch your house while you're away. The day after one of the few whites who lives on the block—a brilliant muckraking journalist and former student of mine—was robbed, neighbors gathered in front of his house to offer assistance.

30   In El Cerrito my neighbor was indeed a cop. He used pomade on his curly hair, sported a mustache, and there was a grayish tint in his brown eyes. He was a handsome man, with a smile like a movie star's. His was the only house on the block I entered during my three-year stay in that neighborhood, and that was one afternoon when we shared some brandy. I wanted to get to know him better. I didn't know he was dead until I saw people in black gathered on his doorstep.

I can't imagine that happening on 53rd Street. In a time when dour thinkers view alienation and insensitivity toward the plight of others as characteristics of the modern condition, I think I'm lucky to live in a neighborhood where people look out for one another.

A human neighborhood.

Things to Do with the Reading

1. How does Reed's account of his battle to remove pigeons from his house in the "predominantly black neighborhood" (paragraph 15) function in the essay's tonally complex account of integrated vs. segregated neighborhoods? What is ironic about Reed's battle to evict the pigeons, especially in the context of his essay's opening paragraph?

2. At one point in the essay (paragraph 14), Reed goes on a New Year's Eve walk with a landscape architect who identifies plants imported from "Asia, the Middle East, and Australia. On Aileen Street he discovered a banana tree!" Reed tells us in the same paragraph that a painter and art historian had traced the "Tabby" garden design in Oakland gardens to the "influence of Islamic slaves brought to the Gulf Coast." Like the paragraph in which Reed recounts his battle with the pigeons, this seemingly trivial account of an evening's walk is richly suggestive of the kind of thinking Reed is inviting us to do in response to the piece. Write a paragraph in which you make the implicit explicit in this paragraph. So What that the walkers discover a banana tree? So What that the garden design owes to the influence of Islamic slaves? See Chapter 1, Move 3: Make the Implicit Explicit.

3. Reed's essay is whimsical in tone and often comic. How does Reed manage to get us to understand and feel the harmful effects of racism while still maintaining the essay's relatively light tone? How, for example, does the use of the word "inconvenienced" (paragraph 21) function in this regard? What is the effect of Reed's use of the word "swell" in paragraphs 2 and 11? What does Reed accomplish in his brief recounting of the incident when a scriptwriter friend of one of his friends said "looking me in the eye [. . .] that if he were black he'd be 'on a Detroit rooftop, sniping

at cops,' as he reclined, glass of scotch in hand, in a comfortable chair whose position gave him a good view of the rolling Pacific" (paragraph 4)?

4. Track and analyze the ways that the police function as a strand (see Chapter 2 on THE METHOD) in the essay. See especially paragraphs 6, 8, and 20, as well as the essay's last four paragraphs. Write up your results in a short essay.

5. **Link:** Consider paragraphs 25–28 wherein Reed catalogues the names and ethnic origins of shops—mostly shops selling food in his neighborhood. Use Rodriguez's essay as a lens for thinking about Reed's essay, starting with this point of contact between the two essays: food. Write an essay on how Reed's thinking about assimilation fits and does not fit with Rodriguez's. Would Salins see Reed as an "ethnic federalist"?

6. **Link Across Chapters:** Put Reed's discussion of the various neighborhoods he has lived in into conversation with Jane Jacobs's essay "The Uses of Sidewalks" in Chapter 13. How would Jacobs respond to the different neighborhoods Reed describes? What perspective might Reed offer on the New York City neighborhood Jacobs lived in (the West Village of Manhattan) and loved?

Marianna Torgovnick

On Being White, Female, and Born in Bensonhurst

A visit to her old neighborhood in Brooklyn shortly after a racially motivated killing provides the occasion for Marianna Torgovnick to reevaluate her conflicted attitudes toward her own past. Wandering the neighborhood, she reflects on the legacy of ethnic and gender prejudice in her own family, on the desire it bore in her not only to escape her upbringing but to obscure it, and ultimately, on the cost of doing so. Torgovnick is a professor of English at Duke University with a special interest in cultural studies. A version of this essay appeared in her 1994 book, *Crossing Ocean Parkway: Readings by an Italian-American Daughter*, which won the American Book Award.

1   The mafia protects the neighborhood, our fathers say, with that peculiar satisfied pride with which law-abiding Italian-Americans refer to the Mafia: the Mafia protects the neighborhood from "the coloreds." In the fifties and sixties, I heard that information repeated, in whispers, in neighborhood parks and in the yard at school in Bensonhurst. The same information probably passes today in the parks (the word now "blacks," not "coloreds") but perhaps no longer in the schoolyards. From buses each morning, from neighborhoods outside Bensonhurst, spill children of all colors and backgrounds—American black, West Indian black, Hispanic, and Asian. But the blacks are the only ones especially marked for notice. Bensonhurst is no longer entirely protected from "the coloreds." But in a deeper sense, at least for Italian-Americans, Bensonhurst never changes.

Italian-American life continues pretty much as I remember it. Families with young children live side by side with older couples whose children are long gone to the suburbs. Many of those families live "down the block" from the last generation or, sometimes still, live together with parents or grandparents. When a young family leaves, as sometimes happens, for Long Island or New Jersey or (very common now) for Staten Island, another arrives, without any special effort being required, from Italy or a poorer neighborhood in New York. They fill the neat but anonymous houses that make up the mostly tree-lined streets: two-, three-, or four-family houses for the most part (this is a working, lower to middle-middle class area, and people need rents to pay mortgages), with a few single family or small apartment houses tossed in at random. Tomato plants, fig trees, and plaster madonnas often decorate small but well-tended yards which face out onto the street; the grassy front lawn, like the grassy back yard, is relatively uncommon.

Reprinted with permission. "On Being White, Female, and Born in Bensonhurst," from Crossing Ocean Parkway, by Marianna De Marco Torgovnick. The University of Chicago Press.

Crisscrossing the neighborhood and making out ethnic zones—Italian, Irish, and Jewish, for the most part, though there are some Asian Americans and some people (usually Protestants) called simply Americans—are the great shopping streets: Eighty-sixth Street, Kings Highway, Bay Parkway, Eighteenth Avenue, each with its own distinctive character. On Eighty-sixth Street, crowds bustle along sidewalks lined with ample, packed fruit stands. Women wheeling shopping carts or baby strollers check the fruit carefully, piece by piece, and often bargain with the dealer, cajoling for a better price or letting him know that the vegetables, this time, aren't up to snuff. A few blocks down, the fruit stands are gone and the streets are lined with clothing and record shops, mobbed by teenagers. Occasionally, the el rumbles overhead, a few stops out of Coney Island on its way to the city, a trip of around one hour.

On summer nights, neighbors congregate on stoops which during the day serve as play yards for children. Air conditioning exists everywhere in Bensonhurst, but people still sit outside in the summer—to supervise children, to gossip, to stare at strangers. "*Buona sera*," I say, or "*Buona notte*," as I am ritually presented to Sal and Lily and Louie, the neighbors sitting on the stoop. "*Grazie*," I say when they praise my children or my appearance. It's the only time I use Italian, which I learned at high school, although my parents (both second-generation Italian-Americans, my father Sicilian, my mother Calabrian) speak it at home to each other but never to me or my brother. My accent is the Tuscan accent taught at school, not the southern Italian accents of my parents and the neighbors.

It's important to greet and please the neighbors, any break in this deco- 5
rum would seriously offend and aggrieve my parents. For the neighbors are the stern arbiters of conduct in Bensonhurst. Does Mary keep a clean house? Did Gina wear black long enough after her mother's death? Was the food good at Tony's wedding? The neighbors know and pass judgment. Any news of family scandal (my brother's divorce, for example) provokes from my mother the agonized words: "But what will I tell people?" I sometimes collaborate in devising a plausible script.

A large sign on the church I attended as a child sums up for me the ethos of Bensonhurst. The sign urges contributions to the church building fund with the message, in huge letters: "Each year St. Simon and Jude saves this neighborhood one million dollars in taxes." Passing the church on the way from largely Jewish and middle-class Sheepshead Bay (where my in-laws live) to Bensonhurst, year after year, my husband and I look for the sign and laugh at the crass level of its pitch, its utter lack of attention to things spiritual. But we also understand exactly the values it represents.

In the summer of 1989, my parents were visiting me at my house in Durham, North Carolina, from the apartment in Bensonhurst where they have lived since 1942: three small rooms, rent-controlled, floor clean enough to eat off, every corner and crevice known and organized. My parents' longevity in a single apartment is unusual even for Bensonhurst, but not that unusual; many people live for decades in the same place or move within a ten-block radius. When I lived in this apartment, there were four rooms; one has since been ceded to a demanding landlord, one of the various landlords who have haunted my parents' life and must always be appeased lest the ultimate threat—removal from the rent-controlled apartment—be brought into play. That summer, during their visit, on August 23 (my younger daughter's birthday) a shocking, disturbing, news report issued from the neighborhood: it had become another Howard Beach.

Three black men, walking casually through the streets at night, were attacked by a group of whites. One was shot dead, mistaken, as it turned out, for another black youth who was dating a white, although part-Hispanic, girl in the neighborhood. It all made sense: the crudely protective men, expecting to see a black arriving at the girl's house and overreacting; the rebellious girl dating the outsider boy; the black dead as a sacrifice to the feelings of the neighborhood.

I might have felt outrage, I might have felt guilt or shame, I might have despised the people among whom I grew up. In a way I felt all four emotions when I heard the news. I expect that there were many people in Bensonhurst who felt the same rush of emotions. But mostly I felt that, given the setup, this was the only way things could have happened. I detested the racial killing, but I also understood it. Those streets, which should be public property available to all, belong to the neighborhood. All the people sitting on the stoops on August 23 knew that as well as they knew their own names. The black men walking through probably knew it too—though their casual walk sought to deny the fact that, for the neighbors, even the simple act of blacks walking through the neighborhood would be seen as invasion.

10   Italian-Americans in Bensonhurst are notable for their cohesiveness and provinciality; the slightest pressure turns those qualities into prejudice and racism. Their cohesiveness is based on the stable economic and ethical level that links generation to generation, keeping Italian-Americans in Bensonhurst and the Italian American community alive as the Jewish-American community of my youth is no longer alive. (Its young people routinely moved to the suburbs or beyond and were never replaced, so that Jews in Bensonhurst today are almost all very old people.) Their provinciality results from the Italian-Americans' devotion to jealous distinctions and discriminations. Jews are suspect, but (the old Italian women admit) "they make good husbands." The Irish are okay, fellow Catholics, but not really "like us"; they make bad husbands because they drink and gamble. Even Italians come in varieties, by region (Sicilian, Calabrian, Neapolitan, very rarely any region further north) and by history in this country (the newly arrived and ridiculed "gaffoon" versus the second or third generation).

Bensonhurst is a neighborhood dedicated to believing that its values are the only values; it tends toward certain forms of inertia. When my parents visit me in Durham, they routinely take chairs from the kitchen and sit out on the lawn in front of the house, not on the chairs on the back deck; then they complain that the streets are too quiet. When they walk around my neighborhood (these De Marcos who have friends named Travaglianti and Occhipinti), they look at the mailboxes and report that my neighbors have strange names. Prices at my local supermarket are compared, in unbelievable detail, with prices on Eighty-sixth Street. Any rearrangement of my kitchen since their last visit is registered and criticized. Difference is not only unwelcome, it is unacceptable. One of the most characteristic things my mother ever said was in response to my plans for renovating my house in Durham. When she heard my plans, she looked around, crossed her arms, and said, "If it was me, I wouldn't change nothing." My father once asked me to level with him about a Jewish boyfriend who lived in a different part of the neighborhood, reacting to his Jewishness, but even more to the fact that he often wore Bermuda shorts: "Tell me something, Marianna. Is he a Communist?" Such are the standards of normality and political thinking in Bensonhurst.

I often think that one important difference between Italian-Americans in New York neighborhoods like Bensonhurst and Italian-Americans elsewhere is that the others moved on—to upstate New York, to Pennsylvania, to the Midwest. Though they frequently settled in communities of fellow Italians, they did move on. Bensonhurst Italian-Americans seem to have felt that one large move, over the ocean, was enough. Future moves could be only local: from the Lower East Side, for example, to Brooklyn, or from one part of Brooklyn to another. Bensonhurst was for many of these people the summa of expectations. If their America were to be drawn as a *New Yorker* cover, Manhattan itself would be tiny in proportion to Bensonhurst and to its satellites, Staten Island, New Jersey, and Long Island.

"Oh, no," my father says when he hears the news about the shooting. Though he still refers to blacks as "coloreds," he's not really a racist and is upset that this innocent youth was shot in his neighborhood. He has no trouble acknowledging the wrongness of the death. But then, like all the news accounts, he turns to the fact, repeated over and over, that the blacks had been on their way to look at a used car when they encountered the hostile mob of whites. The explanation is right before him but, "Yeah," he says, still shaking his head, "yeah, but what were they *doing* there? They didn't belong."

Over the next few days, the television news is even more disturbing. Rows of screaming Italians lining the streets, most of them looking like my relatives. I focus especially on one woman who resembles almost completely my mother: stocky but not fat, mid-seventies but well preserved, full face showing only minimal wrinkles, ample steel-gray hair neatly if rigidly coiffed in a modified beehive hairdo left over from the sixties. She shakes her fist at the camera, protesting the arrest of the Italian American youths in the neighborhood and the incursion of more blacks into the neighborhood, protesting the shooting. I look a little nervously at my mother (the parent I resemble), but she has not even noticed the woman and stares impassively at the television.

15   What has Bensonhurst to do with what I teach today and write? Why did I need to write about this killing in Bensonhurst, but not in the manner of a news account or a statistical sociological analysis? Within days of hearing the news, I began to plan this essay, to tell the world what I knew, even though I was aware that I could publish the piece only someplace my parents or their neighbors would never see or hear about it. I sometimes think that I looked around from my baby carriage and decided that someday, the sooner the better, I would get out of Bensonhurst. Now, much to my surprise, Bensonhurst—the antipode of the intellectual life I sought, the least interesting of places—had become a respectable intellectual topic. People would be willing to hear about Bensonhurst—and all by the dubious virtue of a racial killing in the streets.

The story as I would have to tell it would be to some extent a class narrative: about the difference between working class and upper middle class, dependence and a profession, Bensonhurst and a posh suburb. But I need to make it clear that I do not imagine myself as writing from a position of enormous self-satisfaction, or even enormous distance. You can take the girl out of Bensonhurst (that much is clear), but you may not be able to take Bensonhurst out of the girl. And upward mobility is not the essence of the story, though it is an important marker and symbol.

In Durham today, I live in a twelve-room house surrounded by an acre of trees. When I sit on my back deck on summer evenings, no houses are visible through the trees. I have a guaranteed income, teaching English at an excellent university, removed by my years of education from the fundamental economic and social conditions of Bensonhurst. The one time my mother ever expressed pleasure at my work was when I got tenure, what my father still calls, with no irony intended, "ten years." "What does that mean?" my mother asked when she heard the news. Then she reached back into her experience as a garment worker, subject to periodic layoffs. "Does it mean they can't fire you just for nothing and can't lay you off?" When I said that was exactly what it means, she said, "Very good. Congratulations. That's *wonderful*." I was free from the *padrones*, from the network of petty anxieties that had formed, in large part, her very existence. Of course, I wasn't really free of petty anxieties: would my salary increase keep pace with my colleagues', how would my office compare, would this essay be accepted for publication, am I happy? The line between these worries and my mother's is the line between the working class and the upper middle class.

But getting out of Bensonhurst never meant to me a big house, or nice clothes, or a large income. And it never meant feeling good about looking down on what I left behind or hiding my background. Getting out of Bensonhurst meant freedom—to experiment, to grow, to change. It also meant knowledge in some grand, abstract way. All the material possessions I have acquired, I acquired simply along the way—and for the first twelve years after I left Bensonhurst, I chose to acquire almost nothing at all. Now, as I write about the neighborhood, I recognize that although I've come far in physical and material distance, the emotional distance is harder to gauge. Bensonhurst has everything to do with who I am and even with what I write. Occasionally I get reminded of my roots, of their simultaneously choking and nutritive power.

Scene one: It's after a lecture at Duke, given by a visiting professor from Princeton. The lecture was long and a little dull and—bad luck—I had agreed to be one of the people having dinner with the lecturer afterward. We settle into our table at the restaurant: this man, me, the head of the comparative literature program (also a professor of German), and a couple I like who teach French, the husband at my university, the wife at one nearby. The conversation is sluggish, as it often is when a stranger, like the visiting professor, has to be assimilated into a group, so I ask the visitor from Princeton a question to personalize things a bit. "How did you get interested in what you do? What made you become a professor of German?" The man gets going and begins talking about how it was really unlikely that he, a nice Jewish boy from Bensonhurst, would have chosen, in the mid-fifties, to study German. Unlikely indeed.

I remember seeing *Judgment at Nuremberg* in a local movie theater and having a woman in the row in back of me get hysterical when some clips of a concentration camp were shown. "My God," she screamed in a European accent, "look at what they did. Murderers, MURDERERS!"—and she had to be supported out by her family. I couldn't see, in the dark, whether her arm bore the neatly tattooed numbers that the arms of some of my classmates' parents did—and that always affected me with a thrill of horror. Ten years older than me, this man had lived more directly through those feelings, lived with and *among* those feelings. The first chance he got, he raced to study in Germany. I myself have twice chosen not to visit Germany, but I understand his impulse to identify with the Other as a way of getting out of the neighborhood. 20

At the dinner, the memory about the movie pops into my mind but I pick up instead on the Bensonhurst—I'm also from there, but Italian-American. Like a flash, he asks something I haven't been asked in years: Where did I go to high school and (a more common question) what was my maiden name? I went to Lafayette High School, I say, and my name was De Marco. Everything changes: his facial expression, his posture, his accent, his voice. "Soo, Dee Maw-ko," he says, "dun anything wrong at school today—got enny pink slips? Wanna meet me later at the park on maybe bye the Baye?" When I laugh, recognizing the stereotype that Italians get pink slips for misconduct at school and the notorious chemistry between Italian women and Jewish men, he says, back in his Princetonian voice: "My God, for a minute I felt like I was turning into a werewolf."

It's odd that although I can remember almost nothing else about this man—his face, his body type, even his name—I remember this lapse into his "real self" with enormous vividness. I am especially struck by how easily he was able to slip into the old, generic Brooklyn accent. I myself have no memory of ever speaking in that accent, though I also have no memory of trying not to speak it, except for teaching myself, carefully, to say "oil" rather than "earl."

But the surprises aren't over. The female French professor, whom I have known for at least five years, reveals for the first time that she is also from the neighborhood, though she lived across the other side of Kings Highway, went to a different, more elite high school, and was Irish American. Three of six professors, sitting at an eclectic vegetarian restaurant in Durham, all from Bensonhurst—a neighborhood where (I swear) you couldn't get *The New York Times* at any of the local stores.

Scene two: I still live in Bensonhurst. I'm waiting for my parents to return from a conference at my school, where they've been summoned to discuss my transition from elementary to junior high school. I am already a full year younger than any of my classmates, having skipped a grade, a not uncommon occurrence for "gifted" youngsters. Now the school is worried about putting me in an accelerated track through junior high, since that would make me two years younger. A compromise was reached: I would be put in a special program for gifted children, but one that took three, not two, years. It sounds okay.

25   Three years later, another wait. My parents have gone to school this time to make another decision. Lafayette High School has three tracks: academic, for potentially college-bound kids; secretarial, mostly for Italian American girls or girls with low aptitude-test scores (the high school is de facto segregated, so none of the tracks is as yet racially coded, though they are coded by ethnic group and gender); and vocational, mostly for boys with the same attributes, ethnic or intellectual. Although my scores are superb, the guidance counselor has recommended the secretarial track; when I protested, the conference with my parents was arranged. My mother's preference is clear: the secretarial track—college is for boys; I will need to make a "good living" until I marry and have children. My father also prefers the secretarial track, but he wavers, half proud of my aberrantly high scores, half worried. I press the attack, saying that if I were Jewish I would have been placed, without question, in the academic track. I tell him I have sneaked a peek at my files and know that my IQ is at genius level. I am allowed to insist on the change into the academic track.

What I did, and I was ashamed of it even then, was to play upon my father's competitive feelings with Jews: his daughter could and should be as good as theirs. In the bank where he was a messenger, and at the insurance company where he worked in the mailroom, my father worked with

Jews, who were almost always his immediate supervisors. Several times, my father was offered the supervisory job but turned it down after long conversations with my mother about the dangers of making a change, the difficulty of giving orders to friends. After her work in a local garment shop, after cooking dinner and washing the floor each night, my mother often did piecework making bows; sometimes I would help her for fun, but it *wasn't* fun, and I was free to stop while she continued for long, tedious hours to increase the family income. Once a week, her part-time boss, Dave, would come by to pick up the boxes of bows. Short, round, with his shirttails sloppily tucked into his pants and a cigar almost always dangling from his lips, Dave was a stereotyped Jew but also, my parents always said, a nice guy, a decent man.

Years after, similar choices come up, and I show the same assertiveness I showed with my father, the same ability to deal for survival, but tinged with Bensonhurst caution. Where will I go to college? Not to Brooklyn College, the flagship of the city system—I know that, but don't press the invitations I have received to apply to prestigious schools outside of New York. The choice comes down to two: Barnard, which gives me a full scholarship, minus five hundred dollars a year that all scholarship students are expected to contribute from summer earnings, or New York University, which offers me one thousand dollars above tuition as a bribe. I waver. My parents stand firm: they are already losing money by letting me go to college; I owe it to the family to contribute the extra thousand dollars plus my summer earnings. Besides, my mother adds, harping on a favorite theme, there are no boys at Barnard; at NYU I'm more likely to meet someone to marry. I go to NYU and do marry in my senior year, but he is someone I didn't meet at college. I was secretly relieved, I now think (though at the time I thought I was just placating my parents' conventionality), to be out of the marriage sweepstakes.

The first boy who ever asked me for a date was Robert Lubitz, in eighth grade: tall and skinny to my average height and teenage chubbiness. I turned him down, thinking we would make a ridiculous couple. Day after day, I cast my eyes at stylish Juliano, the class cutup; day after day, I captivated Robert Lubitz. Occasionally, one of my brother's Italian American friends would ask me out, and I would go, often to ROTC dances. My specialty was making political remarks so shocking that the guys rarely asked me again. After a while I recognized destiny: the Jewish man was a passport out of Bensonhurst. I of course did marry a Jewish man, who gave me my freedom and, very important, helped remove me from the expectations of Bensonhurst. Though raised in a largely Jewish section of Brooklyn, he had gone to college in Ohio and knew how important it was, as he put it, "to get past the Brooklyn Bridge." We met on neutral ground, in Central Park, at a performance of Shakespeare. The Jewish-Italian marriage is a common enough catastrophe in Bensonhurst for my parents to have accepted, even welcomed, mine—though my parents continued to treat my husband like an outsider for the first twenty years ("Now Marianna. Here's what's going on with you brother. But don't tell-a you husband").

Along the way I make other choices, more fully marked by Bensonhurst cautiousness. I am attracted to journalism or the arts as careers, but the prospects for income seem iffy. I choose instead to imagine myself as a teacher. Only the availability of NDEA fellowships when I graduate, with their generous terms, propels me from high school teaching (a thought I never much relished) to college teaching (which seems like a brave new world). Within the college teaching profession, I choose offbeat specializations: the novel, interdisciplinary approaches (not something clear and clubby like Milton or the eighteenth century). Eventually I write the book I like best about primitive others as they figure within Western obsessions: my identification with "the Other," my sense of being "Other," surfaces at last. I avoid all mentoring structures for a long time but accept aid when it comes to me on the basis of what I perceive to be merit. I'm still, deep down, Italian-American Bensonhurst, though by this time I'm a lot of other things as well.

30 Scene three: In the summer of 1988, a little more than a year before the shooting in Bensonhurst, my father woke up trembling and in what appeared to be a fit. Hospitalization revealed that he had a pocket of blood on his brain, a frequent consequence of falls for older people. About a year earlier, I had stayed home, using my children as an excuse, when my aunt, my father's much loved sister, died, missing her funeral; only now does my mother tell me how much my father resented my taking his suggestion that I stay home. Now, confronted with what is described as brain surgery but turns out to be less dramatic than it sounds, I fly home immediately.

My brother drives three hours back and forth from New Jersey every day to chauffeur me and my mother to the hospital: he is being a fine Italian-American son. For the first time in years, we have long conversations alone. He is two years older than I am, a chemical engineer who has also left the neighborhood but has remained closer to its values, with a suburban, Republican inflection. He talks a lot about New York, saying that (except for neighborhoods like Bensonhurst) it's a "third-world city now." It's the summer of the Tawana Brawley incident, when Brawley accused white men of abducting her and smearing racial slurs on her body with her own excrement. My brother is filled with dislike for Al Sharpton and Brawley's other vocal supporters in the black community—not because they're black, he says, but because they're troublemakers, stirring things up. The city is drenched in racial hatred that makes itself felt in the halls of the hospital: Italians and Jews in the beds and as doctors; blacks as nurses and orderlies.

This is the first time since I left New York in 1975 that I have visited Brooklyn without once getting into Manhattan. It's the first time I have spent several days alone with my mother, living in her apartment in Bensonhurst. My every move is scrutinized and commented on. I feel like I am going to go crazy.

Finally, it's clear that my father is going to be fine, and I can go home. She insists on accompanying me to the travel agent to get my ticket for home, even though I really want to be alone. The agency (a mafia front?) has no one who knows how to ticket me for the exotic destination of North Carolina and no computer for doing so. The one person who can perform this feat by hand is out. I have to kill time for an hour and suggest to my mother that she go home, to be there for my brother when he arrives from Jersey. We stop in a Pork Store, where I buy a stash of cheeses, sausages, and other delicacies unavailable in Durham. My mother walks home with the shopping bags, and I'm on my own.

More than anything I want a kind of *sorbetto* or ice I remember from my childhood, a *cremolata*, almond-vanilla-flavored with large chunks of nuts. I pop into the local bakery (at the unlikely hour of 11 A.M.) and ask for a *cremolata*, usually eaten after dinner. The woman—a younger version of my mother—refuses: they haven't made a fresh ice yet, and what's left from the day before is too icy, no good. I explain that I'm about to get on a plane for North Carolina and want that ice, good or not. But she has her standards and holds her ground, even though North Carolina has about the same status in her mind as Timbuktoo and she knows I will be banished, perhaps forever, from the land of *cremolata*.

Then, while I'm taking a walk, enjoying my solitude, I have another idea. 35 On the block behind my parents' house, there's a club for men, for men from a particular town or region in Italy: six or seven tables, some on the sidewalk beneath a garish red, green, and white sign; no women allowed or welcome unless they're with men, and no women at all during the day when the real business of the club—a game of cards for old men—is in progress. Still, I know that inside the club would be coffee and a *cremolata* ice. I'm thirty-eight, well-dressed, very respectable looking; I know what I want. I also know I'm not supposed to enter that club. I enter anyway, asking the teenage boy behind the counter firmly, in my most professional tones, for a *cremolata* ice. Dazzled, he complies immediately. The old men at the card table have been staring at this scene, unable to place me exactly, though my facial type is familiar. Finally, a few old men's hisses pierce the air. "Strega," I hear as I leave, "*mala strega*"—"witch," or "brazen whore." I have been in Bensonhurst less than a week, but I have managed to reproduce, on my final day there for this visit, the conditions of my youth. Knowing the rules, I have broken them. I shake hands with my discreetly rebellious past, still an outsider walking through the neighborhood, marked and insulted—though unlikely to be shot.

Things to Do with the Reading

1. It's a paradox of effective reading that sometimes you can see more out of the corner of your eye than by staring straight ahead. That is, looking at issues aslant, from one side, rather than directly, can be especially revealing. Write an essay on the functions that Torgovnick's brother, husband, high school boyfriends, and the female French professor who has been her friend for five years serve in her larger discussion of ethnicity and the melting pot.

2. A key word in this essay is the often-capitalized "Other." It is used in reference to the visiting lecturer at the end of paragraph 20, for example: "I myself have twice chosen not to visit Germany, but I understand his impulse to identify with the Other as a way of getting out of the neighborhood." Find other references in the essay to the Other, or situations of Otherness, and write an essay on how this concept operates in Torgovnick's struggle to understand Assimilation American Style.

3. Torgovnick explicitly names social class as a barrier between, for example, herself and her parents. In paragraph 16, Torgovnick asserts, "The story as I would have to tell it would be *to some extent* a class narrative" (our italics). To what extent? As you write in response to this question, take care to look for ways that her thinking about class—and about her parents—changes as the essay progresses.

4. Link: Write an essay on how Torgovnick's Bensonhurst compares and contrasts with Reed's El Cerrito. What features of El Cerrito might Reed point to as preventing it from having the kind of provinciality that Torgovnick shows us leads to racism and violence in Bensonhurst? To what extent do Reed and Torgovnick find similar things to celebrate in their largely unassimilated neighborhoods?

5. Link: Write an essay analyzing the brief scene in which Torgovnick is treated as an outsider by a group of Italian-American men. In this case, they have verbally insulted her primarily for her gender. Where else does gender discrimination appear in the essay? How does it compare as a lens—seeing as a woman—with the lens of race adopted by Reed and Gates in their essays? What are the biggest similarities? And given those similarities, what's the biggest difference? (See Chapter 3 on DIFFERENCE WITHIN SIMILARITY.)

6. Link Across Chapters: Torgovnick's essay begins with the issue of neighborhood safety as seen by her Italian-American parents and neighbors, wherein safety and racism are directly connected. Write an essay in which you put Torgovnick's piece into conversation with Jacobs' essay, "Uses of Sidewalks: Safety" in Chapter 13. What might Jacobs find to

praise about Bensonhurst, and why? What's different about the neighborhoods that Jacobs describes that apparently make them safer for strangers and outsiders? How is Bensonhurst different from the neighborhood around the White Horse Tavern that Jacobs describes, and So What?

7. **Application:** Equipped with a notebook or laptop, spend an afternoon wandering around your old neighborhood. Make a point of stopping every half hour or so to freewrite on the question, "How has my neighborhood shaped me?" Obviously, the readings in this chapter should have enriched the implications of that question for you, to include such matters as:

- the marks of social class

- the elements in yourself you have wished to conceal or make over

- your tastes to this day, but also your "local" prejudices

- your own ambivalence to your past, that strange mix of reverence and dread that neighborhoods specialize in inspiring

Make at least three entries of 20 minutes or more. (If you are currently living away from your neighborhood, you can write from memory.) Then return to these—type them if you have handwritten them—and revise and expand them. If you carried this project through to some sort of completion, one or more of them might open out into your own personal essay about the complex hold that a neighborhood can claim on who and what we become. See Chapter 2 on freewriting.

Michael Jonas

The Downside of Diversity

With this analysis of a controversial survey by Harvard political scientist Robert Putnam, the chapter opens back out to a wider theoretical frame, providing a new context for reconsidering the series of first-person memoirs by Rodriguez, Smith, Tan, Gates, Reed, and Torgovnick. It is the first of two concluding readings to this chapter, both aimed at challenging conventional assumptions about the melting pot. The article, which first appeared in the *Boston Globe*, discusses Putnam's findings—suggesting racial and ethnic diversity diminishes rather than increases civic strength. The article also surveys the responses Putnam's findings evoked from both the right and the left, as well as the rhetorical challenges Putnam faced in finding a way to contextualize results that challenged his own vision of the melting pot. The author of the piece, Michael Jonas, is executive editor of *CommonWealth*, a journal published by MassINC, an independent think tank using nonpartisan research, civic journalism, and public forums to stimulate debate and shape public policy.

1   It has become increasingly popular to speak of racial and ethnic diversity as a civic strength. From multicultural festivals to pronouncements from political leaders, the message is the same: our differences make us stronger.

But a massive new study, based on detailed interviews of nearly 30,000 people across America, has concluded just the opposite. Harvard political scientist Robert Putnam—famous for *Bowling Alone*, his 2000 book on declining civic engagement—has found that the greater the diversity in a community, the fewer people vote and the less they volunteer, the less they give to charity and work on community projects. In the most diverse communities, neighbors trust one another about half as much as they do in the most homogenous settings. The study, the largest ever on civic engagement in America, found that virtually all measures of civic health are lower in more diverse settings.

"The extent of the effect is shocking," says Scott Page, a University of Michigan political scientist.

The study comes at a time when the future of the American melting pot is the focus of intense political debate, from immigration to race-based admissions to schools, and it poses challenges to advocates on all sides of the issues. The study is already being cited by some conservatives as proof of the

From The New York Times, August 5, 2007. Reprinted by permission of the author.

harm large-scale immigration causes to the nation's social fabric. But with demographic trends already pushing the nation inexorably toward greater diversity, the real question may yet lie ahead: how to handle the unsettling social changes that Putnam's research predicts.

"We can't ignore the findings," says Ali Noorani, executive director of 5 the Massachusetts Immigrant and Refugee Advocacy Coalition. "The big question we have to ask ourselves is, what do we do about it; what are the next steps?"

The study is part of a fascinating new portrait of diversity emerging from recent scholarship. Diversity, it shows, makes us uncomfortable—but discomfort, it turns out, isn't always a bad thing. Unease with differences helps explain why teams of engineers from different cultures may be ideally suited to solve a vexing problem. Culture clashes can produce a dynamic give-and-take, generating a solution that may have eluded a group of people with more similar backgrounds and approaches. At the same time, though, Putnam's work adds to a growing body of research indicating that more diverse populations seem to extend themselves less on behalf of collective needs and goals.

His findings on the downsides of diversity have also posed a challenge for Putnam, a liberal academic whose own values put him squarely in the pro-diversity camp. Suddenly finding himself the bearer of bad news, Putnam has struggled with how to present his work. He gathered the initial raw data in 2000 and issued a press release the following year outlining the results. He then spent several years testing other possible explanations.

When he finally published a detailed scholarly analysis in June in the journal *Scandinavian Political Studies*, he faced criticism for straying from data into advocacy. His paper argues strongly that the negative effects of diversity can be remedied, and says history suggests that ethnic diversity may eventually fade as a sharp line of social demarcation.

"Having aligned himself with the central planners intent on sustaining such social engineering, Putnam concludes the facts with a stern pep talk," wrote conservative commentator Ilana Mercer, in a recent *Orange County Register* op-ed titled "Greater diversity equals more misery."

Putnam has long staked out ground as both a researcher and a civic 10 player, someone willing to describe social problems and then have a hand in addressing them. He says social science should be "simultaneously rigorous and relevant," meeting high research standards while also "speaking to concerns of our fellow citizens." But on a topic as charged as ethnicity and race, Putnam worries that many people hear only what they want to.

"It would be unfortunate if a politically correct progressivism were to deny the reality of the challenge to social solidarity posed by diversity," he writes in the new report. "It would be equally unfortunate if a historical and ethnocentric conservatism were to deny that addressing that challenge is both feasible and desirable."

Putnam is the nation's premier guru of civic engagement. After studying civic life in Italy in the 1970s and 1980s, Putnam turned his attention to the United States, publishing an influential journal article on civic engagement in 1995 that he expanded five years later into the best-selling *Bowling Alone*. The book sounded a national wake-up call on what Putnam called a sharp drop in civic connections among Americans. It won him audiences with presidents Bill Clinton and George W. Bush, and made him one of the country's best known social scientists.

Putnam claims the United States has experienced a pronounced decline in "social capital," a term he helped popularize. Social capital refers to the social networks—whether friendships or religious congregations or neighborhood associations—that he says are key indicators of civic well-being. When social capital is high, says Putnam, communities are better places to live. Neighborhoods are safer; people are healthier; and more citizens vote.

The results of his new study come from a survey Putnam directed among residents in 41 U.S. communities, including Boston. Residents were sorted into the four principal categories used by the U.S. Census: black, white, Hispanic, and Asian. They were asked how much they trusted their neighbors and those of each racial category, and questioned about a long list of civic attitudes and practices, including their views on local government, their involvement in community projects, and their friendships. What emerged in more diverse communities was a bleak picture of civic desolation, affecting everything from political engagement to the state of social ties.

15   Putnam knew he had provocative findings on his hands. He worried about coming under some of the same liberal attacks that greeted Daniel Patrick Moynihan's landmark 1965 report on the social costs associated with the breakdown of the black family. There is always the risk of being pilloried as the bearer of "an inconvenient truth," says Putnam.

After releasing the initial results in 2001, Putnam says he spent time "kicking the tires really hard" to be sure the study had it right. Putnam realized, for instance, that more diverse communities tended to be larger, have greater income ranges, higher crime rates, and more mobility among their residents—all factors that could depress social capital independent of any impact ethnic diversity might have.

"People would say, 'I bet you forgot about X,'" Putnam says of the string of suggestions from colleagues. "There were 20 or 30 X's."

But even after statistically taking them all into account, the connection remained strong: Higher diversity meant lower social capital. In his findings, Putnam writes that those in more diverse communities tend to "distrust their neighbors, regardless of the color of their skin, to withdraw even from close friends, to expect the worst from their community and its leaders, to volunteer less, give less to charity and work on community projects less often, to register to vote less, to agitate for social reform more but have less faith that they can actually make a difference, and to huddle unhappily in front of the television."

"People living in ethnically diverse settings appear to 'hunker down'— that is, to pull in like a turtle," Putnam writes.

In documenting that hunkering down, Putnam challenged the two domi- 20 nant schools of thought on ethnic and racial diversity, the "contact" theory and the "conflict" theory. Under the contact theory, more time spent with those of other backgrounds leads to greater understanding and harmony between groups. Under the conflict theory, that proximity produces tension and discord.

Putnam's findings reject both theories. In more diverse communities, he says, there were neither great bonds formed across group lines nor heightened ethnic tensions, but a general civic malaise. And in perhaps the most surprising result of all, levels of trust were not only lower between groups in more diverse settings, but even among members of the same group.

"Diversity, at least in the short run," he writes, "seems to bring out the turtle in all of us."

The overall findings may be jarring during a time when it's become commonplace to sing the praises of diverse communities, but researchers in the field say they shouldn't be.

"It's an important addition to a growing body of evidence on the challenges created by diversity," says Harvard economist Edward Glaeser.

In a recent study, Glaeser and colleague Alberto Alesina demonstrated 25 that roughly half the difference in social welfare spending between the United States and Europe—Europe spends far more—can be attributed to the greater ethnic diversity of the U.S. population. Glaeser says lower national social welfare spending in the United States is a "macro" version of the decreased civic engagement Putnam found in more diverse communities within the country.

Economists Matthew Kahn of UCLA and Dora Costa of MIT reviewed 15 recent studies in a 2003 paper, all of which linked diversity with lower levels of social capital. Greater ethnic diversity was linked, for example, to lower school funding, census response rates, and trust in others. Kahn and Costa's own research documented higher desertion rates in the Civil War among Union Army soldiers serving in companies whose soldiers varied more by age, occupation, and birthplace.

Birds of different feathers may sometimes flock together, but they are also less likely to look out for one another. "Everyone is a little self-conscious that this is not politically correct stuff," says Kahn.

So how to explain New York, London, Rio de Janeiro, Los Angeles—the great melting-pot cities that drive the world's creative and financial economies?

30 The image of civic lassitude dragging down more diverse communities is at odds with the vigor often associated with urban centers, where ethnic diversity is greatest. It turns out there is a flip side to the discomfort diversity can cause. If ethnic diversity, at least in the short run, is a liability for social connectedness, a parallel line of emerging research suggests it can be a big asset when it comes to driving productivity and innovation. In high-skill workplace settings, says Scott Page, the University of Michigan political scientist, the different ways of thinking among people from different cultures can be a boon.

"Because they see the world and think about the world differently than you, that's challenging," says Page, author of *The Difference: How the Power of Diversity Creates Better Groups, Firms, Schools, and Societies*. "But by hanging out with people different than you, you're likely to get more insights. Diverse teams tend to be more productive."

In other words, those in more diverse communities may do more bowling alone, but the creative tensions unleashed by those differences in the workplace may vault those same places to the cutting edge of the economy and of creative culture.

Page calls it the "diversity paradox." He thinks the contrasting positive and negative effects of diversity can coexist in communities, but "there's got to be a limit." If civic engagement falls off too far, he says, it's easy to imagine the positive effects of diversity beginning to wane as well. "That's what's unsettling about his findings," Page says of Putnam's new work.

Meanwhile, by drawing a portrait of civic engagement in which more homogeneous communities seem much healthier, some of Putnam's worst fears about how his results could be used have been realized. A stream of conservative commentary has begun—from places like the Manhattan Institute and "The American Conservative"—highlighting the harm the study suggests will come from large-scale immigration. But Putnam says he's also received hundreds of complimentary emails laced with bigoted language. "It certainly is not pleasant when David Duke's website hails me as the guy who found out racism is good," he says.

In the final quarter of his paper, Putnam puts the diversity challenge in 35 a broader context by describing how social identity can change over time. Experience shows that social divisions can eventually give way to "more encompassing identities" that create a "new, more capacious sense of 'we,'" he writes.

Growing up in the 1950s in a small Midwestern town, Putnam knew the religion of virtually every member of his high school graduating class because, he says, such information was crucial to the question of "who was a possible mate or date." The importance of marrying within one's faith, he says, has largely faded since then, at least among many mainline Protestants, Catholics, and Jews.

While acknowledging that racial and ethnic divisions may prove more stubborn, Putnam argues that such examples bode well for the long-term prospects for social capital in a multiethnic America.

In his paper, Putnam cites the work done by Page and others, and uses it to help frame his conclusion that increasing diversity in America is not only inevitable, but ultimately valuable and enriching. As for smoothing over the divisions that hinder civic engagement, Putnam argues that Americans can help that process along through targeted efforts. He suggests expanding support for English-language instruction and investing in community centers and other places that allow for "meaningful interaction across ethnic lines."

Some critics have found his prescriptions underwhelming. And in offering ideas for mitigating his findings, Putnam has drawn scorn for stepping out of the role of dispassionate researcher. "You're just supposed to tell your peers what you found," says John Leo, senior fellow at the Manhattan Institute, a conservative think tank. "I don't expect academics to fret about these matters."

But fretting about the state of American civic health is exactly what 40 Putnam has spent more than a decade doing. While continuing to research questions involving social capital, he has directed the Saguaro Seminar, a project he started at Harvard's Kennedy School of Government that promotes efforts throughout the country to increase civic connections in communities.

"Social scientists are both scientists and citizens," says Alan Wolfe, director of the Boisi Center for Religion and American Public Life at Boston College, who sees nothing wrong in Putnam's efforts to affect some of the phenomena he studies.

Wolfe says what is unusual is that Putnam has published findings as a social scientist that are not the ones he would have wished for as a civic leader. There are plenty of social scientists, says Wolfe, who never produced research results at odds with their own worldview.

"The problem too often," says Wolfe, "is people are never uncomfortable about their findings."

Things to Do with the Reading

1. There are at least two primary foci to this piece: Putnam's findings and his subsequent struggles with how to present these findings. What, according to Jonas, are the issues at stake in the second focus—the question of presentation? Find the various places where Jonas treats this question, both from Putnam's point of view and that of his detractors. What are the larger issues here—issues involving the ethics of presentation, the partisan nature of all research projects, and the like? Once you have drafted some answers to these questions, write an essay on how, finally, Jonas invites us to regard Putnam and his work.

2. **Link:** Imagine that Ishmael Reed had read "The Downside of Diversity" and sent Putnam "My Neighborhood," and then they arranged to meet. Write an essay in which you discuss what each would find most interesting in the other's work. The following questions might help to guide you.

   How does Reed reflect on what Putnam terms "social capital"? Find sentences in Reed that shed light on how he might respond to Putnam's challenges to the "contact" theory and the "conflict" theory of ethnic and racial diversity. Ultimately, what common ground do the two figures share, and where do they appear to diverge most significantly? (See Chapter 7 on conversing with sources.)

3. **Link:** Imagine that Peter Salins read the article by Michael Jonas, and the two met for conversation. Both writers are affiliated with think tanks—Jonas with MassINC and Salins with the Manhattan Institute (which Jonas references near the end of his piece). Write an essay in which you imagine what Salins and Jonas might have to say to each other. Locate sentences from both pieces that might justify your answer.

4. **Application:** According to Jonas, "Putnam claims the US has experienced a pronounced decline in 'social capital,'" defined as "social networks—whether friendships or religious congregations or neighborhood associations—that are key indicators of civic well-being." Write an essay in which you assess the status of the social capital of some social network on your campus or in your neighborhood. How would you begin to make a case for the civic health of some particular aspect of your local community? Your report will of necessity be largely anecdotal, comprised mainly of what you can observe.

Robert McLiam Wilson

Sticks and Stones: The Irish Identity

In this salty, iconoclastic piece, the Northern Irish novelist Robert McLiam Wilson offers a broadly subversive response to many of the assumptions about both national identity and racial identity shared by the other contributors to this chapter. "Our racial authenticity," Wilson says of the Irish, "is an extremely negotiable commodity"—a flabby myth, prone to marketing and mistruth.

I am five foot eleven. I weigh around 170 pounds. I have brown hair, green eyes, and 1 no real distinguishing marks. I'm heterosexual, atheist, liberal, and white. I don't shave as often as I should and I have pale, Irish skin. I smoke and I always wear a suit. I drive a small black car and I don't drink much alcohol. I prefer cats to dogs.

I don't know what that makes me, but I suspect that it makes me what I am.

When I was seventeen, I decided that I wanted to be Jewish. Like most Roman Catholics, I had only the vaguest notion of what this might entail. I stopped being good at sports and frequented the only kosher butcher in the city. (How he blushed for me, the poor man). I could never understand why no one took me seriously. I could never understand why I should not simply decide such questions for myself. Why was I such a goy? Who had decided that this should be so?

Like that of most citizens of Belfast, my identity is the subject of some local dispute. Some say I'm British, some say I'm Irish, some even say that there's no way I'm five foot eleven and that I'm five ten at best. In many ways I'm not permitted to contribute to this debate. If the controversy is ever satisfactorily concluded, I will be whatever the majority of people tell me I am.

As a quotidian absolute, nationality is almost meaningless. For an Italian 5 living in Italy, Italianness is patently not much of a distinction. What really gives nationality its chiaroscuro, its flavor, is a little dash of hatred and fear. Nobody really knows or cares what they are until they meet what they don't want to be. Then it's time for the flags and guns to come out.

So when the airport cops ask me what I am, how do I explain that I live in the northeastern segment of an island sliced like a cheap pizza and with as many titles as a bar full of yuppie cocktails—Ireland, Northern Ireland, Britain, Eire, Ulster, etc. How do I explain how little that would tell them?

I suppose I could tell them that I live in a place where people have killed and died in an interminable fight over the names they should call themselves and each other. (In Belfast, sticks and stones may break your bones but names will blow you to pieces on a regular basis.) I could tell them about the

"Sticks and Stones: The Irish Identity" by Robert McLiam Wilson. Reprinted with permission of Antony Harwood, Ltd., Agent for Robert McLiam Wilson.

self-defeating eugenic templates of racial purity by which no human being still living on the island can be properly deemed Irish. That the English and the Scottish have been here a long time and that we're all smudged by now—café au lait, mulattoes, half-breeds, spics, wops, and dagos. I could tell them that I don't really understand the question.

Irishness is unique amongst the self-conscious nationalisms. A self-conscious Frenchman bores everyone. A self-conscious American is a nightmare. And a self-conscious Englishman makes you want to lie down in a darkened room. But a self-conscious Irishman is a friend to the world and the world listens attentively. The reviews are always good. There's a global appetite for Irishness that is almost without parallel.

Nationalistic self-obsession is corrupt, corrosive, and bogus enough without this extra angle. When well-received, this fake concoction of myth and bullshit is reflected in the mirror of imprecise good will and sentimental foolishness. This in itself produces further distortions which are then seamlessly incorporated into the "genuine" article. Over the years I've watched the fundamental concepts of what it is to be Irish being altered by common-currency American errors. Here in the "old country," when we hear that New Yorkers are marching in green-kilted bagpipe bands (an entirely Scottish phenomenon) on St. Patrick's Day, we immediately look around for somewhere to buy green kilts and bagpipes. Our racial authenticity is an extremely negotiable commodity.

10   Yet I've always believed that such Americans have it just about right. Their ideas of Irishness are as fake as a hooker's tit, but then so are ours.

To understand all things Irish, you must understand something fundamental. Everyone knows that Ireland is the land of myth. And myth is a beautiful and resonant word. It sounds so profound, so spiritual. There is something visceral in it. Our mythmaking is vital to the self-imposed standardized norms of nationality that are current here at home. Catholics are Irish, so Irish, and Protestants are British, poor things. The common assumption that the Irish language, Irish music, and Irish history are pure Catholic monoliths, and the oft-suppressed expression of the indigenous culture, ignores the truth that the Irish linguistic, musical, and cultural revivals were the product of nineteenth-century Protestant historicism. Everything we say is myth. The lies are old and dusty. The waters are muddy and the truth long gone.

Even our understanding of our own history—you know the kind of thing, perfidious Albion, eight hundred years of oppression, etc.—teems with bullshit. King William of Orange waged war in seventeenth-century Ireland and is still a Catholic-baiting Protestant icon who causes trouble here. No one remembers that he was blessed by the Pope. Wolfe Tone is a much-loved historical rebel leader who sailed with a French army to liberate Catholic Ireland. No one mentions that he was defeated by a Catholic militia. The President of

Ireland called on a German minister to express his official condolences after Hitler's suicide at the end of World War II. Nobody wrote any songs about that.

In some ways, the Irish tendency for romancing can be seen as harmless, almost charming. It is, after all, what produces our leprechauns, our fairy rings, all our beguiling fakery. But it also produces people who will murder for lies they only half-believe and certainly never understand—for the Irish have always armed their ideas. We don't have any white lies here anymore. We only have the deadly barbaric type.

Given the wildest differences in latitude and climate, it is remarkable how countries can remind you of one another. In cold March Manhattan, the air is as thick, dark, and injurious as any Berlin winter. In Paris, the rain falls and stains the pale stone with the same dispiriting grace you find in Cambridge on most days of the year. London can look and feel like everywhere.

If true of the places, how much truer of the people. *Quod erat demonstran-* 15 *dum* and then some.

We are a pretty poor species. Even the most gifted of us, the wisest and most studious of us, are weak-minded. We toss aside our Pushkin and read Judith Krantz. We watch goofy TV shows and asinine movies. We can't help liking big noises, colored lights, and pictures of naked people.

Our beliefs are often fantastic alloys of fear, self-interest, prejudice, and ignorance. As Tolstoy gloriously demonstrates, our finest moments of hero-ism, selflessness, and grandeur are usually founded on the meanest egotisms and vanities. Our notion of the sublime is laughable. In acts of worship, many of us pay homage to some form of invisible man who mimics us in the pet-tiest detail. Apart from our uncharacteristic capacity for love (a mistake, a design flaw), we're a shambles.

It is the things we say that most prove what monkeys we still are. We are driven to generalize, to sweep on through, to prognosticate, to diagnose. Typically male, we say, typically female. That's the problem with rich people, we opine. The poor were ever so. Gentlemen prefer blondes. Fuck right off, I can't help thinking.

Our most outrageous banalities are reserved for questions of race and nationality. This is how the French behave, we say. How do we know? Have we met them all? Have we asked any of them? Millions of people are summoned and dismissed in a few moments of robust fatuousness.

I'm five foot eleven. I weigh around 170 pounds. I have brown hair, green eyes, and so on. Irish or British is very far down on my list—somewhere 20 below my favorite color. Nonetheless, I must concede that nationality is tenacious. People have real stamina when it comes to this business. I must further concede that Irishness is a great arena for disquisitions on national identity. Because the Irish conflict is internecine (it has nothing to do with the English anymore), definitions of Irishness have particular charm. Nationalities primarily define themselves by what they're not. The Swiss are not German, the Scottish are not English, and the Canadians are definitely not American. But the Irish make internal distinctions as well. Some of the Irish aren't properly Irish. Some of the Irish aren't even vaguely Irish. In pursuit of the mantle of absolute Irishness, brother kills brother and sisters look on and applaud.

A few years ago I had an apartment on a leafy South Belfast street called Adelaide Park. A police station was being rebuilt across the street from my building (the original had been flattened by a bomb a few years before). It was a controversial building site, naturally. Apart from their well-known attacks on the policemen, soldiers, prison officers, and almost everyone else, the IRA liked to target construction workers who helped build police stations. Thus, the site was guarded round the clock by the police. For nearly six months there were always a couple of cops standing in my driveway, all peaked caps, submachine guns, and high anxiety. This was okay in the spring. It was fine in the summer, and manageable in the fall. But as winter set in, the position of these guys became more and more unpleasant. It was windy and cold, and it rained for months. As night fell, I would look out my apartment window and watch the damp rozzers. It was obviously not a good gig.

For weeks I debated whether or not I should take them cups of coffee. It was more complicated than it might sound. Policemen and soldiers here are very unlikely to accept such things from the public now. Twenty-five years of ground glass, rat poison, and Drano in friendly cups of tea discouraged them from accepting such largesse. Not long before, a woman had handed some soldiers a bomb in a biscuit tin in a charming incident near Derry. Additionally, of course, there might have been swathes of people willing to do me grief for being nice to the police.

Policemen are usually Protestant and I myself am customarily Catholic. They couldn't have known that I was a Catholic, but they would have been suspicious. (In this country, the big haters can't really tell each other apart. How we envy those who hate black or white people—that obvious difference, that demonstrable objection.)

It was a small thing, a minor transaction, an unimportant detail. The weeks passed, the wind blew, and the rain rained. I didn't hand out any coffee.

—July 1997

Things to Do with the Reading

1. Wilson's essay is the kind of writing that sometimes gets called a *tour de force* (a feat of strength, power or skill, according to the *OED*). In writing of this sort, authors often deliberately overstate their points, using exaggeration and an aggressively assertive tone to jolt people into seeing absurdity in what they might otherwise wish to guard as cherished positions. There is strategy in this. If the writer tries to take a mile, we

might be cajoled by his sheer audacity into giving him an inch, which is perhaps all that he really wanted in the first place.

Write an essay in which you determine what you think Wilson actually hoped to accomplish, given that his piece is unlikely to cause the Irish (or any other group) to completely give up on "Irishness." Start with paragraphs 16 and 17 and analyze the rhetoric of Wilson's piece. What do these two paragraphs reveal about Wilson's aims and his means of achieving those aims through style?

2. Link: Wilson's essay challenges and interestingly undercuts many of the assumptions about cultural identity that inform previous essays in this chapter. For reasons particular to his own circumstances as a citizen of Belfast (Northern Ireland), Wilson is extremely dubious about the concept of national identity. "Nationalistic self-obsession," he writes, "is corrupt, corrosive, and bogus.... When well-received, this fake concoction of myth and bullshit is reflected in the mirror of imprecise good will and sentimental foolishness. This in itself produces further distortions which are then seamlessly incorporated into the 'genuine' article" (paragraph 9). A repeated word in the essay is "bullshit," part of a strand including "fake," "fake concoction," "myth," "beguiling fakery," "bogus," and "lies." The word "genuine" is placed emphatically in quotes.

Write an essay in which you reflect backward from Wilson's piece to one or more other pieces in this chapter that you think it illuminates. What might Wilson say, for example, about Salins's position on the importance of people choosing to "convert" to being American? Alternatively, how might he respond to Jesse Jackson's rainbow metaphor or to what Salins has to say about ethnic federalism or to Torgovnick's mixed emotions about the cohesiveness and tenacity of Italian-American neighborhoods?

3. Link: Because of the long-standing civil war in Northern Ireland between Catholics and Protestants—between proponents of a United Ireland and those supporting Northern Ireland remaining under English rule—Wilson worries about the potential of nationalism and cultural identities to fuel violence. "In pursuit of the mantle of absolute Irishness," he writes, "brother kills brother and sisters look on and applaud." In the second to last paragraph of his essay, however, he writes, "In this country, the big haters can't really tell each other apart. How we envy those who hate black or white people—that obvious difference, that demonstrable objection."

What are we to do about racial identities—whether the product of mythologizing and stereotyping or not—where physical difference and long histories of struggle and oppression come more starkly into play? To what extent can these be willed out of existence? Write a paper in which you bring Wilson's point of view on cultural and racial difference into conversation with one or more of the following writers: Reed, Smith, and Rodriguez. To what extent would Rodriguez agree with Wilson on the phoniness and foolishness and even the potential danger of so valuing distinct national identities? What sort of conversation do you imagine Reed or Smith would have with Wilson on the same issue?

4. Application: It is interesting to consider which of our personal tendencies and traits each of us would choose to include if asked to identify ourselves to others. This is especially interesting to think about in America, which contains so many different racial, national, and ethnic groups, and so many different religions, customs, and regions. Write your own version of Wilson's opening paragraph as a means of generating some thinking about the markers of particular identities in America. The second sentence of Wilson's essay is, "I don't know what that makes me, but I suspect that it makes me what I am." After you have written your paragraph of identifying traits, write a second paragraph in which you try to explain how the information you chose to include in your first paragraph makes you what you are.

FOR FURTHER RESEARCH: RACE, ETHNICITY, AND THE MELTING POT

By Kelly Cannon, Reference Librarian

The readings and activities that follow invite you to explore further the theme of Race, Ethnicity, and the Melting Pot. URLs are provided for those readings that you can access freely online. For proprietary resources, ask your librarian about print or online access.

Open Access

"Almost All Millennials Accept Interracial Dating and Marriage." *Pew Research Center*. 1 February 2010. 11 May 2014. http://pewresearch.org/pubs/1480 /millennials-accept-interracial-dating-marriage-friends-different-race -generations
Perhaps the litmus test of the melting-pot theory, interracial dating and marriage find much greater acceptance among millennials than among preceding generations, in a study conducted by the Pew Research Center.

> Explore: To what extent do the results of this survey ring true to you? Find out more about the Pew Research Center. What is it? What is its agenda? To what extent does this agenda support or detract from the validity of the findings? Can you infer what Peter Salins would think about interracial dating, given his article in this chapter?

"Between Two Worlds: How Young Latinos Come of Age." *Pew Hispanic Center*. Pew Research Center, 1 July 2013. 12 May 2014. http://pewhispanic.org/reports /report.php?ReportID=117
A long report, summarized at this website, looks closely at how young Latinos navigate two worlds, American and Latin American.

> Explore: To what extent does the behavior of Latin American youth in the majority assert or contradict the melting-pot theory? How so? Why did the Pew Research Center launch the Pew Hispanic Center? To what extent do you think the center is well-positioned to fulfill its mission? Why?

"A Conversation about Identity." *Pew Research Hispanic Trends Project*. 2012. 17 May 2014. http://www.pewhispanic.org/2012/05/30/a-conversation -about-identity-tell-us-your-story/
Part of an extensive study on Hispanic populations in the United States.

> Explore: Visit the Facebook page referred to in the article and add your own comments about ethnic identity if you wish. Follow the link to the Pew study *When Labels Don't Fit* to find a wealth of data on this subject of identity. In light of Zadie Smith's and Richard Rodriguez's essays,

contemplate how identity is complicated by individuals and cultures that are fundamentally mixed, *mestizo*. How might that lead one to resist any labels? How and why do the labels persist?

Fortgang, Tal. "Why I'll Never Apologize for My White Privilege." *Time*. **2 May 2014. 13 May 2014. http://time.com/author/tal-fortgang/**
A Princeton University student decries claims that he is where is he is because of white male privilege.

> Explore: In light of this editorial, and the response to it (link accessible via a link at the end of the essay), consider Benjamin DeMott's essay on the persistent challenges of being black in America. How much do the effects of history persist in the present day? And what about Peggy McIntosh's essay on privilege? To what extent is the individual ever truly free of the burdens or privileges of history one finds oneself born into?

Le, C. N. "Assimilation and Ethnic Identity." *Asian-Nation: The Landscape of Asian America*. **2014. 12 May 2014. http://www.asian-nation.org/assimilation .shtml**
Looks succinctly yet eloquently at assimilation and the melting pot through the lens of Asian America.

> Explore: How important is it that an essay on this topic be written by someone from the subject community, in this case Asian American? To what extent do the struggles of representation to the larger culture surface? How do such struggles converse with those outlined in the McLiam Wilson essay on Irishness? How does Amy Tan's thesis correspond with that of Le?

The Loving Story. **2011. 13 May 2014. http://createdequal.neh.gov/films /loving-story**
17 minutes of highlights from the award-winning film documentary of an interracial couple in 1960s Virginia whose case for the right to marry one another went all the way to the Supreme Court.

> Explore: Zadie Smith writes of a multivocal, multiracial America epitomized by Barack Obama. To what extent could the *Loving* case be seen as the legal precursor to race in America today? What most threatened white Virginia in the Sixties in the legal case before them? How has America adjusted, or not, to the dramatic demographic change witnessed in the past few decades? Are their winners or losers? How so? To what extent do the questions underlying the *Loving* case correspond with questions of assimilation described by Ishmael Reed and Henry Louis Gates, Jr.?

Marr, Carolyn J. *Assimilation through Education: Indian Boarding Schools in the Pacific Northwest*. **University of Washington Libraries, n.d. 18 May 2014. https://content.lib.washington.edu/aipnw/marr.html**

Essay and supporting primary documents related to an extensive assimilation effort in the late 19th and early 20th centuries in the United States.

> Explore: How does this essay and supporting documents inform the discussion of the melting pot and assimilation? What is desirable in a culture? What is earnestly sought for in such initiatives, a mosaic or an "undifferentiated alloy"? In light of the essay by Richard Rodriguez, to what extent is assimilation a gentle, natural process or a violent act? Do the subjects of assimilation have anything to fear? How so? Examine some of the supporting documents provided with Carolyn Marr's essay. How do such artifacts help to support her arguments about assimilation?

Noah, Timothy. "Why American Muslims don't join al-Qaida." *Slate Magazine* (4 March 2009). 19 May 2014. http://www.slate.com/id/2211996
Noah conjectures that assimilation à la the melting pot may be what sets American Muslims apart from Muslims in other parts of the world.

> Explore: The author of this conjectural piece refers to a study conducted by the Pew Foundation. Link to this study. Scan the sections of this study and ask yourself, to what extent does it appear to confirm Noah's hypothesis about American Muslims and the melting pot? How does this essay confirm or contradict the ideas of assimilation presented by Henry Louis Gates, Jr. and Ishmael Reed? To what extent does this article confirm Peter Salins's claims about the melting pot vs. multiculturalism in his essay printed in the chapter?

Piper, Greg. "Laughter Is the Best Melanin." *Cultural Imperialist*. 2010. 11 May 2014. http://www.culturalimperialist.com/2010/09/race-bottom-nix-mixed-ethnicities
This essay good naturedly takes issue with anyone who would argue that the dilution of racial distinctiveness is a good thing. Piper's view finds its counterpoint in the companion piece "Genetic Carpool" by Jeremiah Lewis.

> Explore: Scroll to the bottom of the page and click on "About Cultural Imperialist." What rhetorical space has this website carved out for itself? To what extent has it been successful in its enterprise, as illustrated by the two opposing articles named above? Consider the subject of racial or ethnic dilution presented here in light of Marianna Torgovnick's essay on Bensonhurst. What is the substance of attitudes that allow or even encourage "mixing."? What leads others to draw clear racial and ethnic boundaries? Compare these arguments with those espoused in the Peter Salins piece.

Taylor, Paul. *The Next America*. Pew Research Center, 2014. 17 May 2014. http://www.pewresearch.org/next-america/

A landmark study documenting the changing racial and ethnic composition of America.

> Explore: Referencing Zadie Smith's essay that explores the implications of Barack Obama's biracial identity, consider this study of the changing racial composition of the United States. How does biracial or multiracial identity coordinate with changing attitudes about race? To what extent did Obama's election as President promote or discourage a change in racial attitudes?

Thompson, Ginger. "Where Education and Assimilation Collide." *The New York Times*. 15 March 2009. 11 May 2014. http://www.nytimes.com/2009/03/15 /us/15immig.html

On the surface, Cecil D. Hylton High School, just outside of D.C., exemplifies assimilation. And yet those who speak English and those who are learning English as a second language exist in two separate worlds, all under the same roof.

> Explore: Click on the interactive map adjacent to the article. What do you think contributes to the high number of ESL students in the following counties? Fairfax County, VA? Chatham County, NC? Todd County, SD? Where does your home county fall in this respect? To what extent do multilingual areas like Northern Virginia share in what Zadie Smith calls "Dream City"? To what extent might Amy Tan have been representative of students in such a multilingual area? Do the concerns about educating a diverse population echo the concerns voiced in the essay on diversity by Michael Jonas? How so?

Proprietary

Firmat, Gustavo Pérez. "On Bilingualism and Its Discontents." *Daedalus* 134.3 (Summer 2005): 89–92.

A Spanish professor whose native language is Spanish but who teaches in the United States reveals some discontent over his bilingual existence.

> Explore: What is at the heart of Firmat's discontent? If you speak a second language, how does this affect your "language loyalty"? Does some of Firmat's discontent correspond with that felt by McLiam Wilson regarding Irish Americanness? What do both essays say about mixed identities?

Liu, Haiming, and Lianlian Lin. "Food, Culinary Identity, and Transnational Culture: Chinese Restaurant Business in Southern California." *Journal of Asian American Studies* 12.2 (2009): 135–162.

Food serves as the litmus test here of assimilation, with a paradoxical outcome.

> Explore: How does food both permit and restrict assimilation? In your own experience, how does the food you prepare and eat reinforce your sense of who you are?

Slate, Nico. "Race As Freedom: How Cedric Dover And Barack Obama Became Black." *Ethnic & Racial Studies* 37.2 (2014): 222–240.
A comparison between two "cosmopolitan" figures, the late zoologist Cedric Dover, from India, and Barack Obama, both of whom embraced blackness, though each of them was in fact multiracial.

> Explore: How can this essay on Dover and Obama inform Zadie Smith's essay on Barack Obama? What is cosmopolitanism? Does being multiracial insist upon cosmopolitanism? How so? How does language—how one describes oneself and writes and speaks to the larger community—assist or undermine cosmopolitanism?

Utkin, Anatolii. "The Future of the West." *Russian Social Science Review* 45.4 (July/August 2004): 4–27.
A thought-provoking peer-reviewed article forecasting the apocalyptic effect that changing demographics will have on world powers. Europe is losing population rapidly. In the United States, non-European minorities will soon be the majority.

> Explore: What does Utkin think of the melting-pot idea? How important is immigrant assimilation in determining the future? Do you agree with the author's prediction, or does it seem extreme? How so? To what extent does Utkin's essay compare with Peter Salins's?

Wilkes, Rima, and John Iceland. "Hypersegregation in the Twenty-First Century." *Demography* 41.1 (2004): 23–36.
A population study that indicates startling differences in segregation geographically and between different minority groups.

> Explore: Reflect on how your own community is or is not racially segregated. To what extent does it reflect the trends in this article? How have things changed, or not, since the middle and latter twentieth century, as described in the essays by Ishmael Reed and Marianna Torgovnick?

CHAPTER 15

The Language of Politics and the Politics of Language

This is a chapter about a particular kind of rhetoric—political rhetoric. Its aim is to equip you to analyze political language, attuning you to the characteristic vocabularies of different political orientations, and sensitizing you to the politics of spin. The writers sampled here share the assumption that we inhabit a world of competing voices telling us what to believe and whom to support. And they share the conviction that political language is always partisan: it's never just the facts, though that is the position it most often claims to be presenting.

And so as citizens of a democratic society, we are faced with the challenge of figuring out what others who have political designs upon us "really" believe, or at least, what they are "really" saying. This challenge has been rendered more difficult by the rise in the last few decades of increasingly subtle methods of crafting and wording political positions, methods that build upon what political rhetoricians glean from focus groups and public opinion polls. In this context, the selections in this unit offer a primer in decoding the language of politics that surrounds us.

ABOUT THE READINGS IN THIS CHAPTER

The opening selection, Christopher Borick's "On Political Labels," offers the primary lens through which to read subsequent pieces in this unit, and for that matter, to interpret examples of political speeches wherever you find them. Borick provides a brief history of key terms such as liberal, conservative, and libertarian; charts the ways they overlap; and then offers readers a simple test to measure the gap between the labels they embrace and their actual beliefs. Toward the end of the essay, Borick includes a "vocabulary of contemporary ideological positions" that can be used to smoke out the political leanings of articles and speeches one is likely to encounter in the popular press. Following this piece are five editorials that readers can use to test out the tools that Borick has provided. What are the key words and phrases in each piece, we ask, that enable you to identify each piece as primarily liberal or conservative?

Next come two essays that serve as a frame for subsequent pieces, all of which examine the contemporary politics of spin. The first is a classic essay, George Orwell's "Politics and the English Language." Orwell's analysis of the strategies by which political language tends to "defend the indefensible" concludes with a list of prescriptions for writing politically responsible prose. The second is a brief essay by the journalist Drake Bennett, which synthesizes current thinking on metaphors. Like Orwell and the other writers in this chapter, Bennett focuses on the relationship between metaphors and how we think. He demonstrates that the way we are influenced by language, much of it implicitly metaphorical, is far from simple.

Then comes an interview with the conservative pollster and image consultant Frank Luntz conducted on PBS's *Frontline* series about the shaping of public opinion in U.S. politics today. Says Luntz, "We as Americans and as humans have very selective hearing and very selective memory. We only hear what we want to hear and disregard the rest." Such comments invite us to contemplate how Borick and Orwell might interpret Luntz's views on the language of politics.

Next come three short selections, all related to the "Framing Wars," as these played out during the Obama-Romney presidential campaign. These pieces were written before Obama's reelection in 2012. We include them because they illustrate how political commentators analyze rhetoric. We encourage you to apply these as lenses through which to examine the language of politics in the present—legislation now before Congress or elections that are upcoming.

The first "Framing Wars" selection, co-authored by political consultant (and linguist) George Lakoff and political analyst Elisabeth Wehling, explains how and why Obama fared badly in what they call "The Framing Matchup, Round One." The concept of framing, first introduced by Lakoff, involves locating individual issues in the context of broader, usually moral, storylines. In his 1996 book *Moral Politics*, Lakoff explains that metaphorical frames cause people to react to political ideologies on an unconscious level. As a prominent advisor to the Democratic leadership, Lakoff offers an intriguing opportunity for comparison with Luntz, advisor to the Republican leadership.

David Green's blog post, "Four Words That Will Decide the Election," explains how Democrats might reclaim political initiative by redefining the four key words of the Republican campaign. Geoffrey Nunberg, a linguist, author, and NPR contributor, offers "With Ryan's Ascent: A Few Thoughts on 'Entitlement,'" a brief history of the word "entitlement," one of the four words that Green and Lakoff address. Together these three pieces make clear the tight connection between the language of politics and the politics of language.

The chapter then moves to Harvard historian Jill Lepore's essay called "The Lie Factory: How Politics Became a Business," which first appeared in *The New Yorker*. The essay traces the influential careers of Leone Baxter and Clem Whitaker, whom she describes as the founders of political consulting. The fascinating account of their rise to power in the 1930s adds depth and resonance to the contemporary framing wars that the earlier selections analyze.

The final essay of the chapter provides a different slant, designed to get readers to test the limits of the lenses they have been offered. James Peck's "September 11—a National Tragedy?" suggests that while most politicians and members of the press labeled the terrorist attacks as a tragedy, they actually treated the event as a melodrama. He concludes by inviting us to interpret the event as tragedy, but to take that label seriously. Drawing on the history of theater and dramatic theory, Peck argues that tragedy is not only about loss but also about painful self-assessments.

Christopher Borick

On Political Labels

Written specifically for this book, "On Political Labels" is a primer for decoding the spin now employed by both political parties. The author, Christopher P. Borick, is a professor of political science and the director of an institute of public opinion that has conducted over 100 large-scale surveys during the past decade. The findings from these surveys have been published in a wide range of publications, including the *Wall Street Journal, Los Angeles Times, London Guardian,* and *Washington Post.* Borick has also provided analysis for the BBC, National Public Radio's *Morning Edition,* and *CBS* News and NBC *Nightly News.* "On Political Labels" offers a history of the key terms "liberal" and "conservative." Borick charts the ways that each of these terms is connected to a set of assumptions about what government should be and do. Ultimately, this essay, which has been revised for this edition, provides a lens for analyzing the rest of the readings in this chapter.

Note: Respond to the questionnaires in Boxes 15.1 and 15.2 of this essay as you are reading it for the first time. Do so before you get to the interpretation and the statistics that are subsequently provided about them.

1   In the world of politics labels are a currency. Labels allow politicians to set the public's image of themselves and their opponents and help advance and destroy plans and policies. Even though history shows us that labels are as much a part of politics as waving flags or kissing babies, the meaning of labels remains quite elusive. What does it really mean to call oneself a libertarian, a compassionate conservative, a progressive? Is there actually such a thing as a "Massachusetts Liberal" or "Blue Dog Democrat"? While there are no easy answers to those questions, the legendary Humpty Dumpty of Alice in Wonderland fame offers some insight on the matter. When Humpty tells Alice that there is "glory for you" on your birthday, Alice replies, "I don't know what you mean by glory." Humpty answers, "of course you don't until I tell you . . . when I use a word it means what I choose it to mean—neither more or less!" This wisdom, while emanating from a fictional egg-shaped character, is used regularly by today's real world political consultants. Wordsmiths such as the Republican political consultant Frank Luntz have crafted careers out of making words mean just what they want them to. Luntz advises his politician clients to change the name of the "estate tax" to the "death tax" and to switch the word "privatize" to "personalize" in an attempt to sway public perceptions.

"On Political Labels" by Christopher Borick. Reprinted with permission of the author.

There is evidence that Luntz and others have been successful in making the public believe that words mean what they want them to, and that this success is changing the way politics is done in the United States. But just what changes are taking place and what can you do as a citizen to better understand the use of labels in our political discourse?

To answer this question, it is essential to realize that political labels are often more about emotion than reason. Politicians have long made the assumption that the public lacks the interest and attention to critically analyze government affairs. Constitutional architect James Madison went to great measures to try to limit public control over government because he viewed the public as prone to emotional reactions that lacked insight into the complexities of governance. Fearful that public opinion could be shaped through the linguistic trickery of a demagogue, Madison tried to insulate government from direct public pressure through institutions such as the Electoral College and Supreme Court. In the end, Madison simply was not confident enough that the general public had the tools necessary to critically engage the debates pertinent to governing.

In contrast, Madison's counterpart Thomas Jefferson did not share his skepticism about the public's ability to analyze political matters. Instead, Jefferson believed citizens could be educated in a manner that could enhance their ability to make political judgments. In essence, he thought regular citizens, given proper training, could get beyond the emotional trickery of political language and discern broader meaning. While strong arguments can be made for both the Madisonian and Jeffersonian positions, I believe that Jefferson's approach to this matter must be the framework for how we are to think about political labels today. Simply accepting that the public will act on emotion rather than reason, and therefore the government should be insulated from public pressures, is not a very attractive proposition. This approach undermines the central role of the citizen in a democratic system of government, and in some ways creates a self-fulfilling prophecy where citizens have limited need to think analytically about politics. Such an approach to democratic discourse also plays into the hands of political consultants and strategists who want the public to act on emotion rather than reason because emotion is often easier to manipulate.

Thus, I suggest that we take some time to think about political labels in a manner that allows for critical reflection—especially given the threat posed by today's spin doctors. Since in all likelihood you will encounter thousands of political labels over the course of your lifetime as a citizen, it is important to develop a lens that will allow for a productive analysis of a label's use and effects. It is not my purpose to contend that labels have no place in politics or political discourse. Quite the contrary, labels help us organize our thoughts and provide meaningful reference points from which citizens can engage in thoughtful political discussions. But while labels are completely necessary for productive discourse, they can also be used to confuse and control the voting public. Therefore, in the remainder of this article I offer a number of suggestions for you (in your capacity as one of Jefferson's informed citizens) to consider when you are confronted with a label. In particular much of my attention will be directed to the most commonly used political labels in the United States: liberal and conservative. While my suggestions are by no means inclusive, the following list offers some perspective on how you might think about political labels.

1. Think About the Historical Background of the Label

5 One of the first things you should think about when you see or hear a political label is where it came from. Common political labels such as "liberal" or "conservative" have long histories that shed light on their contemporary use. It's important to recognize that a label's meaning differs from place to place and over time. A conservative in Texas may believe much differently from a conservative in New York, just as an American conservative varies in view points from a conservative in Norway. Similarly, someone calling herself a conservative in 2005 would significantly differ from someone calling himself a conservative in 1905 or even 1975. You may wonder, with such variation over time and place, how can we attach meaning to key political terms at all? While not always easy to see, at least part of the answer can be discovered through an examination of the history of the terms.

Let's look at liberalism for a start. The term liberal can be traced at least back to 17th-century England, where it evolved from debates dealing with the voting franchise among English citizens. Proponents of including greater numbers of Englishmen in elections came to be known as liberals, thanks in part to the writings of John Locke, whose ideas about the social contract helped to build the philosophical underpinnings of this political ideology. Over time liberalism has maintained its focus on public control over government actions, but there have been splits that have led to its current manifestation. In the 18th and 19th centuries, liberalism began to stress the importance of individual freedom and broader rights of the citizenry in terms of limits on government. In essence, this type of liberalism focused on "negative rights" or the restrictions on what government could do to its citizens. The First Amendment of the Constitution includes numerous examples of negative rights. The granting of the right to freedom of speech or the press is achieved through the prohibition of government from creating laws that abridge such freedoms. Thus negating an action of government creates rights for the people.

In the 20th century, however, liberalism became synonymous with the view that government had to be much more active in helping citizens get to the point where they would be able to truly live a free life. In this expanding view of liberalism, government intervention in society is necessary to create a more level playing field on which individuals can then use their freedom to achieve desired goals. Such beliefs have been at the roots of government expansion into social welfare policies such as public housing, food stamps and affirmative action, and have formed the core of government agendas such as Franklin Roosevelt's New Deal and Lyndon Johnson's Great Society.

It is also this focus on active government that has helped transform the term liberal into a derogatory term in contemporary political dialogue. For example, let's look at the title of the recent best-selling book *Treason: Liberal Treachery from the Cold War to the War on Terrorism*. As can be seen, author Ann Coulter equates a liberal philosophy with treason against the nation itself. She finds liberalism's focus on protecting individual rights to be detrimental to the security of the United States and a threat to the very survival of the republic. Thus Coulter attaches a scarlet "L" to anyone and anything that places high value on civil rights or civil liberties if those rights and liberties can be seen as undermining national security.

While Coulter uses the term liberal to slam those who believe government is a positive force in society, conservative author Sean Hannity tries to disentangle contemporary liberalism from its historical focus on individual liberty. In his book, *Let Freedom Ring: Winning the War of Liberty Over Liberalism*, Hannity contends that it's conservatism that is really interested in liberty, while it's liberalism that creates an environment where government activity limits individual freedom and autonomy. He sees the regulations and programs that are designed to create level playing fields for citizens as counterproductive to democracy and the vitality of the country. Hannity is reflecting the beliefs of modern conservative thinkers such as Russell Kirk who equate government efforts to achieve equality with severely limiting individualism. Kirk famously stated, "men are created different; and a government which ignores this law becomes an unjust government, for it sacrifices nobility to mediocrity; it pulls down the aspiring natures to gratify the inferior natures." In other words, for conservatives, government is not a force for improving the human condition; rather it's an anchor on the driving force of individual motivation.

While someone identifying herself or himself as a liberal may take great 10 exception to the arguments and reasoning of writers like Coulter and Hannity, the core belief that government can be a force for positive social change is a fundamental element of modern liberalism. Liberalism's interest in the equality of citizens may indeed come at the expense of individual liberties. For example, in trying to create a fair playing field for candidates in elections, contemporary liberalism embraces strong government regulations on campaign contributions and spending. The "liberal" defense of such restrictions rests in the notion that the compelling public interest in having elections that are not controlled by those with the greatest financial resources trumps any individual's claim to spend as one chooses. So aspects of freedom are sometimes reduced in the name of equality—in this case, the freedom to spend as much as one wants on a political campaign. Similarly, liberals tend to believe that government should limit the freedom of businesses when such freedom comes into conflict with the public good—such as the right to clean air and clean water.

Unlike liberalism's evolution to the point where authors like Hannity and Coulter use it as a negative label, the history of the term conservative is one of increasing political value. Like liberalism, conservatism has a long history that can be traced back to the 18th century. The Anglo-Irish philosopher Edmund Burke is generally credited with developing the core ideas associated with conservative thought. In particular, Burke espoused a philosophy that rested on individual control of property and small and limited government. These tenets of conservatism are in large part the cornerstone of contemporary conservatism in the United States. In essence, government is often more of the problem than the answer. Here is an example of these beliefs coming out in a famous quote by Ronald Reagan during his presidency. Reagan claimed that most terrifying words in the English language are: "I'm from the government and I'm here to help." The clear animosity to government intervention in Reagan's words symbolizes the core conservative belief that the best government is the smallest government. As we shall see, this conviction is not always upheld, as in the case of defense spending for national security.

While conservatism has consistently focused on the role of limited government and private property rights, self-identified American conservatives are increasingly interested in using government to limit individual behaviors that are considered counter to the traditional values of the nation. In particular, behaviors such as homosexuality and choosing abortion are seen as direct threats to the order of society and thus require government intervention in the lives of individuals. This tendency to embrace government intervention as a means of protecting values has become an accepted principle for many in the United States, but also a persistent point of tension among individuals identifying themselves as conservative. In particular, many contemporary conservatives who have found a home in the Republican Party are uneasy with the inconsistency of endorsing government intervention in some aspects of an individual's life such as reproductive rights, while excoriating government intervention in other areas such as property rights. For some, these inconsistencies in contemporary American conservatism are too great to accept; thus, many individuals identify themselves more as libertarian rather than conservative.

A libertarian generally agrees with the conservative focus on limited government, but can't accept exceptions where government limits freedoms to preserve traditional values. A libertarian stresses the minimal role of government, with functions such as public safety and defense the only necessary roles of government. A quote from the 2004 United States Libertarian Party platform nicely summarizes this philosophy:

We, the members of the libertarian party challenge the cult of the omnipresent state and defend the rights of the individual. We hold that all individuals have the right to exercise sole dominion over their own lives, and have the right to live in whatever manner they choose, so long as they do not forcibly interfere with the equal right of others to live in whatever manner they choose.

Thus, a libertarian would likely agree with a contemporary conservative on issues like low taxes and fewer government programs, but disagree with policies that might limit individual freedom such as restrictions on marijuana use and abortion. Similarly, libertarians and liberals share a belief in free expression even in controversial areas such as flag burning, yet libertarians would split with their liberal counterparts on topics such as government restrictions on the ownership and use of firearms. In Figure 15.1 below you can see that while the ideologies of liberalism, conservatism, and libertarianism may have distinctive qualities, they also can have areas of commonality.

The shared positions of various ideological positions are often obscured   15 by their differences. Therefore, it is essential to dig deeper beneath broad ideological labels to discern important nuances of thought.

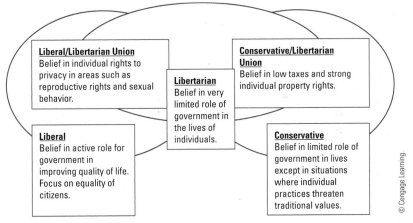

FIGURE 15.1

2. Labels Can Exaggerate Difference

While labels can be used to demonstrate real differences among individuals and political parties, they may mask similarities that cut across ideologies in the United States. It is important to note that American liberals and conservatives have more in common than one might anticipate. For foreign observers of politics in the United States there is often a belief that there is very little difference between Democrats and Republicans and liberals and conservatives. Let's look in particular at the role of government in the area of the economy and taxes. Among conservatives and liberals in the United States there is general agreement that government control of the economy should be limited. While there may be some argument about how government should regulate businesses, there is almost no discussion about government ownership or control of companies. Conversely, in Sweden the government owns 25% of businesses in the country.

Similarly, while it may appear that liberals and conservatives in the United States vehemently disagree on the issue of taxation, the scope of the debate is fairly limited. The highly debated 2003 tax cuts in the United States lowered tax rates in the top bracket from 39.6% to 35%. Compare these tax rates to those in Sweden where the top rate is 47% or France where the richest are taxed at 49% of their income.

Thus while the American liberal and conservative may have real differences, the divide may be exaggerated when labels are being applied in the heat of political debate. It serves the interest of politicians to distinguish differences between themselves and their opponents for voters. It would be a bad political strategy to campaign on the platform that "my opponent and I are in agreement on most issues." Nevertheless, the reality of American politics is that the differences between liberalism and conservatism may not be as great as we are led to believe.

3. The Source of the Label Matters

When a label is applied to something or someone, it's rarely a spontaneous off the cuff remark. In a world where political campaigns are priced in the billions and government budgets are measured in trillions, politics is a high stakes endeavor. Not surprisingly, then, each word used is measured very carefully in an attempt to elicit desired responses from the public. Take for example the term "Massachusetts Liberal" that was used against presidential candidate John Kerry in the 2004 campaign for the White House. During the presidential race the Bush campaign regularly added a Massachusetts qualifier to the time honored liberal label. A good example of the use of this label is a quote by Bush campaign manager Ken Mehlman, who, in regard to John Kerry's nomination, stated, "America doesn't need a Massachusetts liberal today." Why would Mehlman feel the need to use Massachusetts in this context? The answer is found in the desired effect that he seeks to elicit from voters.

20   Massachusetts is home to a number of prominent politicians such as Senator Ted Kennedy and Representative Barney Frank who have been outspoken proponents of policies that are considered both liberal and contentious. Among these policies are equal rights for homosexuals and preferential treatment for minority individuals in the areas of education and employment. Furthermore, in a well-publicized 2003 decision the Massachusetts Supreme Court ruled to allow gay and lesbian couples to legally marry. With a history of controversial officials and legal precedents, the term *Massachusetts* carried with it a degree of political baggage. By applying the term to John Kerry, Mehlman and the rest of the Bush campaign were hoping to attach the polarizing aspects of Massachusetts

politics to their Democratic opponent, even if Kerry himself did not support the positions that were synonymous with his home state. Given the number of times that this label was used, we can be confident that at least the Bush campaign thought the label was scoring political points for the conservatives.

Sometimes a politician gives himself or herself a label as part of a broader goal of shaping public perceptions. Such was the case with George W. Bush's self-identification as a "compassionate conservative." While long referring to himself as a conservative, Bush began adding the term compassionate as he began to pursue the White House in the late 1990s. What was the reason for including this new term with the time honored conservative moniker? It seems to me that Bush is using compassionate as a qualifier for conservative. The term conservative, while generally regarded more positively than liberal, has been associated with a cold-heartedness in the past. Conservatives in their zest to keep government out of the public's business were accused of neglecting the needs of the poor and minorities, and being out of touch with the struggles facing the common person. Thus, in packaging himself as a viable presidential candidate, Bush and his handlers sought to qualify conservative with a term that displayed caring and understanding for all Americans.

But what are we to do with labels that are applied by politicians themselves? Just as you probably would question the validity of someone at your college who gave himself his own nickname, you should always question the names that politicians give themselves. When a guy calls himself "Romeo" or "Stud," you would probably think twice before accepting the accuracy of the tag. So, shouldn't you think twice when you come across the "compassionate conservatives" and "new Democrats" of the world?

4. Does the Label Hold Up to Facts?

Another thing to think about regarding labels is their ability to measure reality. Earlier I discussed some of the general tenets of conservatives and liberals in the United States. For example, liberals are generally considered to favor government activity to level the playing field in society. Therefore such policies as affirmative action and a high minimum wage are often thought of as core liberal beliefs. If one's overall ideological stance guides his or her positions on particular issues, we might reasonably expect an individual who self-identifies as a "liberal" to support government policies that are consistent with an active government approach. These expectations can actually be tested fairly easily by looking at public opinion data from surveys of the American public. By asking individuals to state their opinion on key issues that are indicative of broader political philosophies such as liberalism and conservatism, it's possible to measure how consistent their beliefs may be. For example, let's look at the relationship between what label you use to identify your political beliefs and your views on a number of specific political issues. Start by answering the question in Box 15.1.

BOX 15.1 Which of the Following Best Describes Your Overall Political Beliefs?

Very Liberal

Somewhat Liberal

Moderate

Somewhat Conservative

Very Conservative

© Cengage Learning.

Next, take the survey in Box 15.2 regarding key issues in contemporary American politics. Mark the box that best describes your position on each of the statements that is given.

BOX 15.2 Survey of Political Attitudes

Statement	Agree	Disagree
The practice of abortion should be made illegal.	☐	☐
Prayer should be allowed in public schools.	☐	☐
Burning the American flag should be made illegal.	☐	☐
There should be a national law prohibiting marriage between members of the same sex.	☐	☐
Citizens should be allowed to own assault weapons.	☐	☐
The 10 Commandments should be allowed to be displayed in government buildings.	☐	☐
Affirmative Action policies should be abolished in the United States.	☐	☐
The minimum wage should not be increased.	☐	☐

© Cengage Learning.

25   Now, add up the total number of times that you agreed with the statements given. Each check mark in the "agree" column signifies that you support a position that is generally perceived as conservative in the United States.

Thus, if you identified yourself as very conservative and agreed with 8 out of 8 statements presented, your policy positions appear consistent with your self-identified political ideology. However, if you call yourself very conservative and only agree with a few of the statements presented, there appears to be a disconnect between your perception of your ideological standing and the issue positions that define one as conservative. Similarly, if you agreed with most of the statements presented, and call yourself a liberal, then the label might be misplaced.

While the previous exercise may have demonstrated an inconsistency between the label you used to describe yourself and your beliefs on specific issues, many surveys have found that the American public as a whole demonstrates similar inconsistencies. For example, each year I survey hundreds of students at Muhlenberg College to see if the labels they use to describe themselves are consistent with their positions on particular issues. What I have regularly found is that while our self-identified ideological labels may paint a generally accurate picture of our political views, these labels mask key inconsistencies that are common among individuals. In Box 15.3 the responses of self-identified conservative students to the policy questions are presented.

As can be seen in Box 15.3, there is by no means consensus among self-identified conservatives regarding the array of issues that were presented to them. While all of the positions presented in the table are considered conservative viewpoints, many of those students who view themselves as conservative disagree with the conservative stances. For example, the issue of same sex marriage in the United States has been seen as divisive between liberals and conservatives, with conservative Americans supporting bans on marriages between individuals of the same sex. In our surveys we find that while about 2 out of 3 conservatives support a ban on same sex marriage, 1 out of 3 oppose such action. Similarly, while allowing prayer in public schools is seen as a conservative position, about 4 in 10 self-identified conservatives in our surveys oppose such policies.

Clearly, the conservative and liberal labels that are so commonly used in the United States often mask important details about the individuals that the labels are applied to. Public opinion researchers have recognized the inconsistencies that are associated with broad labels, and have thus tried to come up with labels that capture patterns. Labels such as "Reagan Democrat," "Christian Conservative," "Limousine Liberal," and "Country Club Republican," are used to describe individuals who share some of the characteristics of the core label (e.g., conservative, liberal) but differ on other key factors. For example, the term "Country Club Republican" is commonly used to describe individuals who vote Republican because of the party's pro-business and anti-tax positions, yet oppose the party's increasing emphasis on socially conservative issues such as banning abortion or restricting same-sex marriage. In contrast, the label "Christian Conservative" is used to describe individuals whose major goal is for government to intervene in social matters to preserve traditional values (e.g., marriage between a man and a woman). While both "Country Club Republicans" and "Christian Conservatives" would likely identify themselves as conservative when asked in a survey question such as the example from Box 15.1, they by no means share identical ideological perspectives.

BOX 15.3 Policy Positions of Self-Identified Conservative Students

Statement	Agree	Disagree
The practice of abortion should be made illegal.	43%	57%
Prayer should be allowed in public schools.	63%	37%
Burning the American flag should be made illegal.	77%	23%
There should be a national law prohibiting marriage between members of the same sex.	62%	38%
Citizens should be allowed to own assault weapons.	23%	77%
The 10 Commandments should be allowed to be displayed in government buildings.	60%	40%
Affirmative Action policies should ·be abolished in the United States.	79%	21%
The minimum wage should not be increased.	24%	76%

© Cengage Learning.

Survey results drawn from surveys of Muhlenberg College students conducted between 2002 and 2005. Survey conducted by the Muhlenberg College Institute of Public Opinion. The respondents were drawn randomly from the student body and completed the survey via telephone. Sample sizes ranged from 350 to 400 respondents.

5. An Alternative Vocabulary of Ideology

Finally, while labels such as liberal and conservative can be used by political figures to elicit desired reactions from the public, there are other terms to look for when reading literature related to political affairs. There are times when a commentator, speechwriter, or politician does not want to use labels such as liberal or conservative for fear of losing credibility with the general public. Thus, it becomes useful to adopt a language that captures ideological leanings without sounding partisan. For example, if the term *liberal* has indeed taken on a negative connotation for many Americans, it becomes necessary for advocates of liberal policies to adopt other terms in an attempt to persuade the public. Similarly, while politicians don't run from the term *conservative* like they run from the liberal moniker, there are times when it's better to avoid explicit use of any politically charged label.

Without using terms that are considered too partisan or controversial, how 30
can individuals still make arguments that rest on strong ideological beliefs?
The answer lies in an alternate vocabulary that helps to transmit ideological
beliefs without the partisan baggage. This vocabulary includes terms that capture elements of partisanship without sounding overly divisive, and are thus
attractive forms of language for those engaging in political persuasion.

Political language guru Frank Luntz, whom you will read about later in this
unit of the book, has regularly advised his Republican clients to avoid words
that may sound overtly partisan, and instead embrace language that resonates
as more neutral. By no means are Luntz and other political linguists advocating that political figures should abandon partisan positions, but simply that
they embrace language that most effectively shapes public perceptions in a
way that helps them advance their agenda in a more effective way.

Not only is the choice of words important in shaping public opinion,
but also the number of times the words are used. You may have heard the
expression, "if you say something enough times, people will start to believe
it." For political consultants this adage is a guiding principle that permeates
their communication strategies. Repetition of key words is seen as essential
to conveying a message that people will remember. This repetition is commonly referred to as staying "on message." Political party leaders regularly
encourage their members to uniformly employ language that is considered
effective in shaping public perceptions. One of the most prominent examples
of staying on message is the use of the term "war on terror." When President
Bush was making his case for going to war in Iraq, he framed the military
campaign as part of a broader war on terror. While Saddam Hussein and the
Iraqi regime had clearly committed atrocities during its tenure, there was
no compelling evidence that Iraq had any substantial role in the attacks of
9/11. Nevertheless, in almost every speech where he discussed the invasion
of Iraq, the president included the military endeavor as part of the war on
terror, often mentioning 9/11 and Saddam Hussein in the same sentence.
While never going so far as pinning the attacks directly on the Iraqi dictator,
the linguistic connection of the terrorist threat with Iraq helped reinforce the
impression that the two were linked. It appears from looking at public opinion
polls conducted as the invasion began in 2003 that the White House's framing strategy had paid dividends, with almost half of the American population
indicating a belief that Hussein was "personally involved" in the attacks of
September 11, 2001. Once again, if you say something enough times, people
will believe it.

As with the selection of "war on terror," many other words are regularly
employed to achieve partisan ends through less overtly partisan language. Box
15.4 includes a selection of terms that are commonly used by individuals to
make ideological arguments. These terms are directly related to the underlying roots of liberalism and conservatism, but may be perceived as more

politically neutral. For example, the word *ownership* has become popular in many speeches and articles from self-described conservatives, often in the form of a call to create an "ownership society." The principle of ownership usually resonates among Americans who have come to strive for the day when they can buy that first new car or house. The idea of owning a piece of property can hardly be viewed as a highly ideological or partisan notion when an overwhelming majority of Americans make such action a life goal. The safety of the word helps explain why it has been regularly employed in debates on one of the most controversial topics of the day—Social Security reform. When President Bush advocates allowing Americans to invest part of their Social Security savings in individual retirement accounts, he claims his plan is part of the broader "ownership society" that benefits all Americans. The safety and acceptance of the ownership concept helps him to sell an idea that regularly draws high levels of concern and suspicion from a public that has become very attached to Social Security as a key source of retirement income.

BOX 15.4 Vocabulary of Contemporary Ideological Positions

Conservative	Liberal
Individualism	Community
Ownership	Equality
Traditional	Progressive
Free Market	Social Justice
Property Rights	Human Rights

© Cengage Learning.

A Note on Neo

If the evolving use of political terms such as liberal and conservative were not complex enough, these political labels are often modified with the prefix "neo." If "neo" means "new" or "revived," as the dictionary tells us, then neo versions of conservative or liberal would appear to mean a new or revived version of the original. As I have discussed throughout this essay, political labels such as liberal and conservative have complex and evolving histories that make their use far from simple. Therefore you shouldn't be surprised to hear that the addition of a "neo" prefix does not simply update current forms of liberal and conservative but instead creates new political categories. And just as the base terms liberal and conservative can be understood to mean varying things, the neo-prefixed versions can be interpreted in more than one way.

35   The term neo-conservative or "neo-con" remains one of the most difficult labels to define. When the label first came to prominence in the 1970s, it was used derisively to describe former Democrats who had moved to the Republican Party. In essence, calling someone a neoconservative back in the

1970s was to say that an old liberal had become a "new conservative." Some of those who were labeled neoconservative began to accept the label and to apply their own definition to the term. Irving Kristol, who is one of the most prominent figures to embrace the neocon label, defined neoconservatives as "liberals mugged by reality" who, unlike previous conservatives, went beyond simply criticizing liberal ideas by proposing their own solutions to societal problems.

After the neocon label appeared in the 1970s, it wasn't commonly used until the 1990s, when it became popular as a means of describing Americans who had a specific view on foreign policy. Calling someone a neoconservative today is likely to imply that he or she believes the United States' interest is best served when it has a strong military that is ready to be used, and that diplomacy through multinational organizations such as the United Nations is not as productive as the U.S. acting alone.

The decision by the United States to invade Iraq in 2003 is commonly seen as the key example of a neoconservative approach to foreign policy. Given the ultimately unpopular public reaction to the War in Iraq, it may not surprise you to hear that the label neoconservative is often used in a demeaning fashion to describe someone who maintains a world-view that has produced undesired outcomes. Although their views remain the same, many neocons have abandoned the prefix and slid back inside the label of just plain old conservative.

While you may continue to hear the neocon label, you are less likely to hear "neoliberal." Unlike the term neoconservative, the term neoliberal has been used largely in academic circles. For academics, it refers primarily to economic policy. Given the earlier discussion of the use of the label liberal in American politics, you might expect a neoliberal's views on the economy to stress an active role for government in managing economic affairs. The label neoliberal, however, has been assigned to individuals who prefer the most limited role possible for government in economic matters. American scholar Robert McChesney has defined neoliberalism as "capitalism with the gloves off," nicely capturing the free-market and anti-government intervention views that are central to neoliberal thought.

As with the origin of neoconservative, the neoliberal label was coined by critics of this set of political views. These critics believed that those in favor of free market economic policies wanted to liberalize the government's policies economic policies, limiting intervention. Thus arose the tag of neoliberal. An example that might help clarify the use of liberal in this way is when alcohol policies were said to be liberalized at the end of prohibition when the government ban on alcohol consumption was removed. In both cases liberalization infers that less rather than more government involvement is the preferred option, which is of course quite different from the standard definition of liberal which stresses active government intervention in economic affairs. Thus, contemporary liberals and neoliberals may be considered as occupying opposite sides of a spectrum of economic thought.

40   As with the origin of neoconservative, the neoliberal label was coined by critics of this set of political views. These critics believed that those in favor of free market economic policies wanted to liberalize the government's economic policies, limiting intervention. Thus arose the tag neoliberal. Here is an example to help clarify this use of liberal: at the end of Prohibition, alcohol policies were said to be liberalized when the government ban on alcohol consumption was removed.

In both cases—free market economics and ending Prohibition—liberalization implies that less rather than more government involvement is the preferred option. But this use of liberal stands in opposition to today's commonly accepted definition of liberal, which stresses active government intervention in economic affairs. Thus, contemporary liberals and neoliberals may be considered as occupying opposite sides on a spectrum of economic thought.

It's very possible, in fact quite likely, to find an American who could simultaneously wear both the neoconservative and neoliberal labels comfortably. While the labels liberal and conservative can be considered mutually exclusive (e.g., being one precludes being the other), many contemporary Republicans might very well fit under the labels of both neoliberal and neoconservative. Of course, most contemporary Republicans would not be happy to be called liberal, even if it's the neo variety, so be careful when you break out those neo labels.

Conclusion

As I noted earlier in this article, labels permeate the political discourse in the United States. It has not been my intent to have you believe that labels are necessarily a negative part of politics, but to empower you to better control the effects of labels on your own thoughts about politics and government. I have tried to provide you with a list of things to consider when you are confronted with a political label that can be applied when you are listening to a speech, watching the news or reading an editorial in a newspaper. It is through the process of evaluating political language that you can limit the control that politicians and consultants believe they have over the political discourse in the nation. When Frank Luntz says that most of politics is about emotion he assumes a public that does not reflect upon political language, but instead one that simply responds to feelings. While I don't disagree with his appraisal, I take great offense at the arrogance that it demonstrates. Luntz is practically flaunting the fact that he can consistently trick the public into reacting in ways that he desires by simply changing language to induce emotional rather than reasoned reactions.

Luntz assumes a laziness in the electorate that is indeed all too present. However, the control that he wields is very tenuous. By simply looking more closely at political labels, you and your counterparts can diminish the control that Luntz and other language gurus claim over the public. Remember the fate of another character who claimed that he could make words mean just what he wanted to. The arrogant Humpty Dumpty met his end during a fateful fall, with all the king's horses and all the king's men unable to put him together again. A more careful and thoughtful consideration of political language may crack the control that today's masters of the word believe they have.

Things to Do with the Reading

1. Using Borick's discussion of the questionnaires in as a model, write a short essay in which you interpret the results of your own answers to the questionnaires in Boxes 15.1 and 15.2. Where (if at all) does your self-identification (on the continuum from "Very Liberal" to "Very Conservative" in Box 15.1) diverge from your stance on political attitudes, as ascertained by Box 15.2? How (if at all) do you account for these divergences? How do you "fit" relative to the statistical profile offered in Box 15.3?

2. Borick's essay explains that the political labels "liberal" and "conservative" have long histories and that the meaning of the labels has changed over time. Summarize the steps that Borick lays out in paragraphs 6, 7, and 8 in the evolution of the meaning of the term "liberal" to what it has come to mean today. What is Borick's explanation of how "liberal" came to be a derogatory term? To what extent would it be accurate to say that the label "conservative" today is close in meaning to what the label "liberal" meant prior to the 20th Century? Cite and explain relevant claims in the Borick essay in support of your answer.

3. Both conservatives and liberals claim to defend the rights of the individual. How, according to Borick, do the two orientations differ in this respect and how have these differences evolved historically?

4. The essay points out that broad labels tend to obscure inconsistencies within an ideological orientation as well as positions that the two orientations share. What inconsistencies in conservative thinking do the labels "Christian Conservative" and "Country Club Republican" reveal?

5. "On Political Labels" seeks to sensitize you to the keywords used by different political orientations (conservative, libertarian, and liberal) by seeing them in historical context. Consider the following list of terms. What would a conservative think of each term? What would a liberal think? What would a libertarian think? Why?

    National security
    Negative rights
    Property rights

Write up the results of your thinking in a short essay.

6. Throughout this unit on political language we will be asking you to attend closely to metaphor. A metaphor is a way of thinking by analogy (comparison) in which one side of the comparison is named while the other is un-named but implied. (See Figurative Logic, Reasoning with Metaphors in Chapter 5.) What is the logic of the metaphor, "level playing field"? What is being compared to what and So WHAT? Why should we not be surprised to hear this metaphor in the context of liberal thinking about the role of government and the rights of the individual? (Note: A key method of judging the suitability of a metaphor for making claims about a subject is get literal about the metaphor. What, for example, do you have to do in order to level a playing field? Which particular features of this metaphor seem to apply when using it to justify the liberal view that government should be "more active in helping citizens get to the point where they would be able to truly live a free life"? (Borick paragraph 7))

7. **Link Across Chapters:** Once you have become comfortable with the essay's terminology, use "On Political Labels" as a tool for indexing the political orientation of any other chapter in this book. Compose an essay in which you arrange the writers that you have read in that chapter from most conservative to most liberal, briefly citing the telltale sentences and word choice that allow you to make this kind of discrimination. The chapter on race might be a good place to start. The public versus private language in the chapters on Manners and on Places and Spaces could also yield interesting political analysis.

8. **Application:** Use Borick's essay as a lens for analyzing news articles and editorials on matters such as social security, the winding down of the war in Afghanistan, tax cuts, and healthcare reform. See especially Box 15.4 on the Vocabulary of Contemporary Ideological Positions. *Resist the urge to take a position on any of these issues.* Instead, locate the key terms in your article or editorial that reveal political orientation and explain what they reveal. Once you have "decoded" your chosen piece, write an essay in which you explain what makes it essentially liberal or conservative or libertarian (or some combination of these) in its orientation.

FIVE EDITORIALS

Robert J. Fisher, "In Election, U.S. Should Not Return to 'Rugged Individualism'"

James J. Kirkpatrick, "Justices Amended Constitution on Their Own..."

Richard A. Epstein, "... By Letting Redevelopers Take Little Guy's Property"

John F. Grim, "More than Abortion Is at Stake in Supreme Court Picks"

Paul Krugman, "Losing Our Country"

> What follows are five newspaper editorials to which you can apply Borick's essay on political labels. In effect, you will be trying to decode their politics by using his lexicon.
>
> The first editorial locates competing attitudes to the American ideal of rugged individualism as a way of understanding contemporary political arguments. The next three editorials concern Supreme Court decisions and the makeup of the Court. The final editorial is a *New York Times* opinion piece on the status of the middle class in early twenty first-century America.

Note: The editorials refer to two eras in twentieth-century America—the New Deal, which was President Franklin Roosevelt's response to the Depression of the 1930s, and the Robber Baron era—a reference to the pre-taxation open market years early in the twentieth century when there were few limits on the methods industrial entrepreneurs could use to amass wealth.

Robert J. Fisher

In Election, U.S. Should Not Return to "Rugged Individualism"

In 1890, the Census Bureau declared that any region in the United States could 1 no longer be classified as a frontier—a region where population density was less than one person per square mile. In 1893, noted historian Frederick Jackson Turner theorized that the passing of the frontier was a defining turning point in American history.

The Turner thesis stated, "Individualism struck its frontier when the pioneer struck his." In other words, economic individualism could only exist with an unlimited supply of free land and natural resources. Turner theorized Americans would have to begin to seek collective and cooperative solutions to economic challenges.

In the 25 years after 1893, the United States experienced two significant periods of economic reform. In a rare nonpartisan effort, three Republican

"In Election, US Should Not Return to 'Rugged Individualism'" by Robert J. Fisher, The Morning Call, Oct. 14, 2010. Used by permission.

and two Democratic administrations gradually established regulatory controls over railroads, pipelines, communications, environmentally sensitive areas, banking, and the food and drug industries. Establishment of the Federal Trade Commission gave the government controls over business practices in general and institutionalized the nascent antitrust movement.

The adoption of the 16th Amendment deliberately legalized the concept of "ability to pay" with respect to taxation. In essence, the government recognized the validity of the Turner thesis by establishing a neo-socialistic economic system for the United States.

5   Americans have never been comfortable with the decline of individualism. Romanticism of frontier life, today referred to as the "cowboy mentality," has remained an increasingly elusive ideal in American culture while socialism is regarded as a negative and otherworldly concept.

In the 1920s, three Republican presidents, Harding, Coolidge and Hoover, governed under a masculine mantra of "rugged individualism," which included tax cuts, deregulation and isolationist tariff policies.

After the stock market crash of 1929, President Hoover reduced government spending, rejected welfare relief and balanced the budget. The results were catastrophic as unemployment reached 25 percent and homelessness and malnutrition became commonplace. Historians have estimated that as many as 1 million Americans may have died as a result of the Great Depression.

In the 1932 election, Franklin D. Roosevelt ousted Hoover and established the New Deal, which cemented the neo-socialistic economy in place.

Unions were legalized in a deliberate attempt to redistribute income. Banking and stock market regulations were strengthened. The New Deal created Social Security and unemployment insurance and mandated wage and hours standards. Massive deficit spending and a system of "war socialism" during World War II finally ended the Depression and eroded any lingering support for "rugged individualism."

10   In the post-war era, the U.S. economy experienced generally mild recessions alternating with impressive prosperity, particularly in the 1950s and 1990s. The neo-socialistic system matured with the enactment of Medicare/Medicaid, the Environmental Protection Agency, Occupational Safety and Health Administration, the War on Poverty and, most recently, health insurance reform.

Periodically, however, conservative extremists attempted to resurrect "rugged individualism" and castigate neo-socialism as unworkable and even unpatriotic. They seek a return to laissez-faire capitalism whose limitations and failures inspired neo-socialism in the first place.

In the 1980s, "Reaganomics" included a massive tax cut, mainly for upper-income Americans, and deregulation of banking and Wall Street.

This country now has a declining middle class and the largest wage gap in the developed world. The poverty level has risen from 10 percent to 14 percent; more than 45 million Americans lack basic health insurance.

Finally, in 2008, the second most serious recession/depression in American history resulted in the current economic crisis.

In 2008, voters enthusiastically elected Barack Obama, an obviously progressive president, presumably to undo damages caused, in part, by the latest flirtation with the ongoing fantasy of "rugged individualism."

Now, only two years later, conservative Republicans, pressured by the 15 tea party fringe element, are attempting to convince voters that 125 years of neo-socialism can be reversed.

What exactly is there in the economic record of the last 30 years that suggests this would be desirable or even feasible? One can only imagine what life would be like in the current recession without Social Security, Medicare, unemployment compensation and stimulus spending. America cannot afford another 30 years of naive, wishful thinking about frontier individualism.

The only real choice is to accept the inevitability of the existing economic system and to work constructively to solve problems and make needed improvements.

James J. Kirkpatrick

Justices Amended Constitution on Their Own...

The Supreme Court ended its current term on Monday with more of a whimper 1 than a bang. In the Ten Commandments cases, the justices further muddied the muddy waters of the First Amendment. In a Colorado case, they found no way to compensate a victim of grossly incompetent cops. They refused even to hear the appeal of two reporters who face prison for doing their job. Then they doffed their robes and departed for the summer.

One is reminded of Oliver Cromwell's farewell to the Rump Parliament of 1653: "You have sat too long for any good you have done. Let us have done with you! In the name of God, go!"

The most regrettable decision of a regrettable term came a week ago, in the eminent domain case of *Kelo v. City of New London*. Speaking through Justice John Paul Stevens, the court applied the law according to Humpty Dumpty. To that eminent jurist, words meant only what he chose them to mean, and neither more nor less. Until last week, the words "public use" meant "public use." Now they mean "public purpose or private benefit."

To be sure, this was not the first time the court has effectively amended the Constitution by judicial interpretation. The subtle process dates from

"Justices Amended Constitution on Their Own..." by James J. Kilpatrick, The Morning Call, July 6, 2005. Used by permission.

the days of John Marshall. Only a few weeks ago the court rewrote the 21st Amendment in order to nullify the liquor laws of Michigan and New York. Last week's plastic surgery on the Fifth was surgery at a more critical level.

5   Every sixth-grader can identify a public "use." The indispensable power of eminent domain permits governments to build roads, establish parks, erect public buildings and establish public schools. These are *public uses*.

Nothing of the sort was at the heart of last week's decision. The city now may proceed to seize the unoffending home of Susette Kelo, smash it to bits, haul away the debris, and sell the vacant land to the highest bidder. A few doors away, the redevelopers will evict Wilhelmina Dery from the home she has occupied for more than 80 years.

Will the owners receive "just compensation"? Of course, but for Kelo and other owners, the modifying "just" mocks the noun. Their property will not be put to a "public use." It will pass unjustly to private developers. If all goes well, the developers can go to their banks with a bundle. Ms. Kelo and her neighbors can go to—they can go to some other neighborhood, somewhere else.

In his majority opinion for the court, Justice John Paul Stevens smiled upon the city's rose-petaled justification. The city has been slowly losing jobs and population. What to do? Get rid of the owners! Then land could be cleared for the Pfizer corporation to build a $300 million research facility. The city fathers licked their chops. Their eyes rolled around like Mr. Toad's when he saw the motorcar. They saw classy restaurants, retail stores, a marina! There would be 80 new residences, none of which Susette Kelo could afford. What a deal!

To Stevens and his four colleagues, the "narrow view" that "use" means "use" is a view that has steadily eroded over time. A literal interpretation has proved to be "impractical" and "difficult to administer." Mrs. Kelo's eviction must be viewed "in light of the entire plan." This plan "unquestionably serves a public purpose, and the takings satisfy the public use requirement of the Fifth Amendment."

10   Justice Sandra Day O'Connor filed a powerful dissent: "Today the court abandons a long-held, basic limitation on government power. Under the banner of economic development, all private property is now vulnerable to being taken and transferred to another private owner, so long as it might be upgraded—i.e., given to an owner who will use it in a way that the legislature deems more beneficial to the public."

She asked rhetorically: "Are economic development takings constitutional?" She answered without equivocation: "I would hold that they are not."

In a separate dissenting opinion, Justice Clarence Thomas agreed with O'Connor: "If 'economic development' takings are for a 'public use,' any taking is, and the court has erased the Public Use Clause from our Constitution. . . . Once one permits takings for public *purposes* in addition to public *uses,* no coherent principle limits what could constitute a valid public use . . . "

So ends the court's term. It should have ended when it began nine months ago.

Richard A. Epstein

... By Letting Redevelopers Take Little Guy's Property

The dreadful decision of the U.S. Supreme Court in *Kelo v. City of New London* 1
recently held that New London, Conn., could take the homes of ordinary citizens in the name of urban planning. It didn't seem to matter to the five-member majority that the city's porous redevelopment plan did not evince any intelligible purpose, let alone the public use that the Constitution requires.

The good news in the aftermath of *Kelo* is that it has forced people, especially on the political left, to rethink their views on the place of private property. Ever since the decisive and wrongheaded New Deal decisions in the mid-1930s, the Supreme Court has by and large held that the constitutional protections of private property should be read weakly so as to allow governments to act in ways that advance some notion of the common or public good. The underlying liberal vision was that private property was the instrument of individuals of privilege and power, which had to be cut down to size by an alert legislature that had the interests of the little man at heart. The liberal justices on the Supreme Court have accordingly done everything to give their blessing to local land use condemnation and regulation.

Kelo shows the utter fatuity in that position. There is of course every reason to believe that people with great wealth will use their power and influence to turn legislative decisions in their direction. But it hardly follows that private property is the villain of the piece. In many cases, the system of strong property rights works to protect people of limited wealth from the machinations of others. This defensive use of private property was evident to such philosophers as John Locke and such economists as Adam Smith. It impressed itself on this nation's Founders, who understood the risk that political factions put to the stability of our social order.

Here is one telltale sign of the massive amounts of political favoritism in *Kelo*. One common argument in favor of a broad use of the eminent domain power is that it is necessary to allow developers to assemble large parcels of land for major developments. But in *Kelo* the New London planners were quite happy to slate private homes for destruction while allowing the Italian Dramatic Club (a watering hole for local politicians) to remain untouched, even though it abutted one of the private homes that was taken.

Last year, the Michigan Supreme Court held that its state constitu- 5
tion blocked the use of the eminent domain power for so-called economic

"... by Letting Redevelopers Take Little Guy's Property" by Richard A. Epstein, The Morning Call, July 6, 2005. Reprinted with permission of the author.

development. Other states are now falling into line. With a little bit of hard work, the instinctive revulsion toward the *Kelo* decision could lead to a groundswell of public action. But whatever the future brings, remember that the four dissenters—Rehnquist, O'Connor, Scalia and Thomas—all so-called conservatives, were the defenders of the Constitution and the little man.

John F. Grim

More than Abortion Is at Stake in Supreme Court Picks

Far-right Republicans were incensed that 14 U.S. senators brokered a deal to avoid the "nuclear option" to bar a filibuster on judicial nominations, news reports said. And a Republican activist wrote an op-ed column on June 18 that said 14 "centrist" senators may hold the key to confirming Supreme Court nominees who would overturn *Roe v. Wade*.

1   Again, the foes of a woman's right to choose show tunnel vision, because a court with just one or two more members who share the aggressive and ideologically extreme philosophy of Justices Antonin Scalia and Clarence Thomas could overturn not only *Roe v. Wade* but also more than 100 high court precedents protecting civil rights, privacy and reproductive choice, the environment, worker rights, consumer rights, religious liberty and much more.

"Courting Disaster 2005," a report by the liberal People for the American Way Foundation, documents how President Bush has picked lawyers and judges who favor a pre-New Deal approach to the Constitution: An era when property rights and states' rights were given greater weight than protecting individual rights, and when the courts forbade Congress to address urgent issues of poverty and health care.

Examining the concurring and sometimes angry dissenting opinions of Scalia and Thomas, the report (www.pfaw.org) lists decisions that could be overturned by more justices with the same philosophy. Some of those cases, their dates and what a reversal would do are:

5   *Ferguson v. Charleston* (2001): Hospitals would be allowed to test pregnant women without their knowledge and consent for drug use and give results to police.

Hill v. Colorado (2000): States would be forbidden to pass laws to protect people approaching health care facilities from harassment.

"More Than Abortion Is at Stake in Supreme Court Picks," John F. Grim, The Morning Call, July 27, 2005. Reprinted with permission of the author.

City of Indianapolis v. Edmond (2000): Police would be free to set up road-blocks and randomly stop motorists to look for drugs.

Lawrence v. Texas (2003): Criminal prosecution of private sexual conduct by consenting adults would be allowed.

Grutter v. Bollinger (2003): Affirmative action in higher education would be forbidden.

Jackson v. Birmingham Bd. of Educ. (2005): Retaliation against those who 10 complain about illegal sex discrimination in education under federal law would be allowed.

Johnson v. Transportation Agency (1987): Affirmative action for women under Title VII of the 1964 Civil Rights Act would be eliminated.

J.E.B. v. Alabama (1994): Sex discrimination in jury selection would be allowed.

Olmstead v. L.C. (1999): Improper and unnecessary institutionalization of disabled persons would no longer violate the Americans With Disabilities Act.

Hibbs v. Winn (2004): Federal courts would be forbidden to decide challenges to discriminatory and unconstitutional state tax laws.

Zadvydas v. Davis (2001): The government would be allowed to keep an 15 immigrant who is under a final order of removal in jail indefinitely, even though no other country will accept that person.

Rasul v. Bush (2004): It would be impossible to challenge the indefinite imprisonment of foreign nationals on U.S. territory in Guantanamo, even if they contend they have been tortured or are not combatants.

Chavez v. Martinez (2003) and *Hope v. Pelzer* (2002): The ability to sue law enforcement officials for violating constitutional rights would be severely limited.

Lee v. Weisman (1992) and *Santa Fe Independent School Dist. v. Doe* (2000): True government neutrality toward religion would be eliminated, and government-sponsored prayer at graduation and at other public school events would be allowed.

Kiryas Joel Village School District v. Grumet (1994): School district lines could be drawn to permit one religious sect to predominate.

Rutan v. Republican Party of Illinois (1990): Government employees could be 20 fired for belonging to the wrong political party.

Alaska Department of Conservation v. EPA (2004): EPA would be stripped of the authority to prevent damaging air pollution by industries when state agencies improperly fail to do so.

Americans deserve high court justices who are fair to all sides, who guard against abuses of power by the executive and legislative branches, and who protect our rights and liberties. Returning the nation to the early 20th century and the days of the robber barons is an exorbitant price to pay to satisfy people who were characterized by U.S. Rep. Barney Frank on the House floor as believing life begins at conception and ends at birth.

Paul Krugman

Losing Our Country

1 Baby boomers like me grew up in a relatively equal society. In the 1960s America was a place in which very few people were extremely wealthy, many blue-collar workers earned wages that placed them comfortably in the middle class, and working families could expect steadily rising living standards and a reasonable degree of economic security.

But as *The Times*'s series on class in America reminds us, that was another country. The middle-class society I grew up in no longer exists.

Working families have seen little if any progress over the past 30 years. Adjusted for inflation, the income of the median family doubled between 1947 and 1973. But it rose only 22 percent from 1973 to 2003, and much of that gain was the result of wives' entering the paid labor force or working longer hours, not rising wages.

Meanwhile, economic security is a thing of the past: year-to-year fluctuations in the incomes of working families are far larger than they were a generation ago. All it takes is a bit of bad luck in employment or health to plunge a family that seems solidly middle-class into poverty.

5 But the wealthy have done very well indeed. Since 1973 the average income of the top 1 percent of Americans has doubled, and the income of the top 0.1 percent has tripled.

Why is this happening? I'll have more to say on that another day, but for now let me just point out that middle-class America didn't emerge by accident. It was created by what has been called the Great Compression of incomes that took place during World War II, and sustained for a generation by social norms that favored equality, strong labor unions and progressive taxation. Since the 1970s, all of those sustaining forces have lost their power.

Since 1980 in particular, U.S. government policies have consistently favored the wealthy at the expense of working families—and under the current administration, that favoritism has become extreme and relentless. From tax cuts that favor the rich to bankruptcy "reform" that punishes the unlucky, almost every domestic policy seems intended to accelerate our march back to the robber baron era.

It's not a pretty picture—which is why right-wing partisans try so hard to discredit anyone who tries to explain to the public what's going on.

These partisans rely in part on obfuscation: shaping, slicing and selectively presenting data in an attempt to mislead. For example, it's a plain fact

From The New York Times, June 10, 2005. © 2005 The New York Times. All rights reserved. Used by permission and protected by the Copyright Laws of the United States. The printing, copying, redistribution, or retransmission of this Content without express written permission is prohibited.

that the Bush tax cuts heavily favor the rich, especially those who derive most of their income from inherited wealth. Yet this year's *Economic Report of the President*, in a bravura demonstration of how to lie with statistics, claimed that the cuts "increased the overall progressivity of the federal tax system."

The partisans also rely in part on scare tactics, insisting that any attempt to 10 limit inequality would undermine economic incentives and reduce all of us to shared misery. That claim ignores the fact of U.S. economic success after World War II. It also ignores the lesson we should have learned from recent corporate scandals: Sometimes the prospect of great wealth for those who succeed provides an incentive not for high performance, but for fraud.

Above all, the partisans engage in name-calling. To suggest that sustaining programs like Social Security, which protects working Americans from economic risk, should have priority over tax cuts for the rich is to practice "class warfare." To show concern over the growing inequality is to engage in the "politics of envy."

But the real reasons to worry about the explosion of inequality since the 1970s have nothing to do with envy. The fact is that working families aren't sharing in the economy's growth, and face growing economic insecurity. And there's good reason to believe that a society in which most people can reasonably be considered middle class is a better society—and more likely to be a functioning democracy—than one in which there are great extremes of wealth and poverty.

Reversing the rise in inequality and economic insecurity won't be easy: The middle-class society we have lost emerged only after the country was shaken by depression and war. But we can make a start by calling attention to the politicians who systematically make things worse in catering to their contributors. Never mind that straw man, the politics of envy. Let's try to do something about the politics of greed.

Things to Do with the Reading

1. **Link:** Write a paragraph on each editorial in which you use Borick's "On Political Labels" as a lens to identify the language—the key words and phrases—that most clearly enables readers to identify the given editorial as primarily liberal or conservative or libertarian. You may wish to review the discussion of UNCOVERING ASSUMPTIONS in Chapter 2 to help you unearth the various premises that underlie each editorial.

2. Write a brief essay in which you explain how Fisher uses the word "neo-socialist" in "In Election, U.S. Should Not Return to 'Rugged Individualism.'" This is an interesting word choice, because *socialist* has been used recently by politicians and the press in an almost entirely negative light. What positive spin does Fisher wish to put on the term, based on what historical precedents and rationale?

3. Throughout Fisher's editorial and in the title, the phrase "rugged individualism" is placed inside quotation marks. Why? What spin does the editorial take on the rights of individuals? Write a short essay in which you analyze how Fisher uses the word, in comparison with how Kilpatrick spins individualism in "Justices Amended Constitution on Their Own . . ." Be sure to discuss what individual right the Kilpatrick editorial is defending, and on what grounds.

4. Use the reading strategy in Chapter 2 called finding "THE PITCH, THE COMPLAINT, AND THE MOMENT" to write an analysis of what Epstein is trying to accomplish in ". . . By Letting Redevelopers Take Little Guy's Property." Against which positions (the complaint) is he arguing? One of these is fairly explicit, but another is handled more subtly. What potential attack on conservatives is the writer somewhat worried about, and how does he defend against it?

5. In "More than Abortion Is at Stake in Supreme Court Picks" John F. Grim reveals himself from the beginning as an opponent of what he calls "far-right Republicans." He then offers a list of relatively recent high court decisions that he claims could be reversed by a more decidedly Republican (conservative) Supreme Court. The reader is left to decide why a Republican court would make the decisions the writer says it would make. Do so in a short essay. Choose the three cases that you find most interesting, and using Borick's article as a lens, articulate for each legal decision the political philosophy that might cause conservative Supreme Court judges to rule in the way the writer fears. See UNCOVERING ASSUMPTIONS in Chapter 2.

6. Paul Krugman's "Losing Our Country" is filled not only with the key words of the liberal political orientation but with some dire predictions about the direction in which the country is heading. Write a short essay in which you analyze the attacks the writer makes on the policies of the Bush administration and its Republican predecessors. How do these attacks reveal both the writer's liberal orientation and the conservative orientation of the Bush administration?

7. Krugman's editorial anticipates an issue that will occupy many of the subsequent readings in this chapter: the politics of spin, which Krugman attacks as "name-calling." He cites two phrases: "class warfare" and "the politics of envy." Write a brief essay in which you explore why he finds these labels not only objectionable but essentially inaccurate.

George Orwell

Politics and the English Language

The British writer George Orwell has left so emphatic a mark on modern think-ing about politics and language that the adjective "Orwellian" has arisen to characterize forms of political oppression, especially those involving the manipulation of language. The dystopian vision of the future in his novel *1984* is probably the source of the adjective that bears his name, but in the influential essay "Politics and The English Language" (1946) Orwell first gives voice to the ominous tendency of modern public prose to obscure its aims.

Most people who bother with the matter at all would admit that the English lan- 1
guage is in a bad way, but it is generally assumed that we cannot by conscious action do anything about it. Our civilization is decadent and our language—so the argument runs—must inevitably share in the general collapse. It follows that any struggle against the abuse of language is a sentimental archaism, like preferring candles to electric light or hansom cabs to aeroplanes. Underneath this lies the half-conscious belief that language is a natural growth and not an instrument which we shape for our own purposes.

Now, it is clear that the decline of a language must ultimately have political and economic causes: It is not due simply to the bad influence of this or that individual writer. But an effect can become a cause, reinforcing the original cause and producing the same effect in an intensified form, and so on indefi-nitely. A man may take to drink because he feels himself to be a failure, and then fail all the more completely because he drinks. It is rather the same thing that is happening to the English language. It becomes ugly and inaccurate because our thoughts are foolish, but the slovenliness of our language makes it easier for us to have foolish thoughts. The point is that the process is reversible. Modern English, especially written English, is full of bad habits which spread by imitation and which can be avoided if one is willing to take the necessary trouble. If one gets rid of these habits one can think more clearly, and to think clearly is a necessary first step towards political regeneration: so that the fight against bad English is not frivolous and is not the exclusive concern of profes-sional writers. I will come back to this presently, and I hope that by that time the meaning of what I have said here will have become clearer. Meanwhile, here are five specimens of the English language as it is now habitually written.

These five passages have not been picked out because they are espe-cially bad—I could have quoted far worse if I had chosen—but because they

"Politics and the English Language" from A COLLECTION OF ESSAYS by George Orwell. Copyright 1950 by Sonia Brownell Orwell. Copyright © renewed 1978 by Sonia Pitt-Rivers. Reprinted by permission of Houghton Mifflin Harcourt Publishing Company. All rights reserved. Reprinted by permission of Bill Ham-ilton as the Literary Executor of the Estate of the Late Sonia Brownell Orwell and Secker & Warburg Ltd.

illustrate various of the mental vices from which we now suffer. They are a little below the average, but are fairly representative samples. I number them so that I can refer back to them when necessary:

(1) I am not, indeed, sure whether it is not true to say that the Milton who once seemed not unlike a seventeenth-century Shelley had not become, out of an experience ever more bitter in each year, more alien [sic] to the founder of that Jesuit sect which nothing could induce him to tolerate.

Professor Harold Laski (Essay in Freedom of Expression)

(2) Above all, we cannot play ducks and drakes with a native battery of idioms which prescribes such egregious collocations of vocables as the Basic *put up with* for *tolerate* or *put at a loss* for *bewilder*.

Professor Lancelot Hogben (Interglossa)

(3) On the one side we have the free personality: by definition it is not neurotic, for it has neither conflict nor dream. Its desires, such as they are, are transparent, for they are just what institutional approval keeps in the forefront of consciousness; another institutional pattern would alter their number and intensity; there is little in them that is natural, irreducible, or culturally dangerous. But *on the other* side, the social bond itself is nothing but the mutual reflection of these self-secure integrities. Recall the definition of love. Is not this the very picture of a small academic? Where is there a place in this hall of mirrors for either personality or fraternity?

Essay on psychology in Politics (New York)

(4) All the 'best people' from the gentlemen's clubs, and all the frantic fascist captains, united in common hatred of Socialism and bestial horror of the rising tide of the mass revolutionary movement, have turned to acts of provocation, to foul incendiarism, to medieval legends of poisoned wells, to legalize their own destruction of proletarian organizations, and rouse the agitated petty-bourgeoisie to chauvinistic fervour on behalf of the fight against the revolutionary way out of the crisis.

Communist pamphlet

(5) If a new spirit is to be infused into this old country, there is one thorny and contentious reform which must be tackled, and that is the humanization and galvanization of the B.B.C. Timidity here will be-speak cancer and atrophy of the soul. The heart of Britain may be sound and of strong beat, for instance, but the British lion's roar at present is like that of Bottom in Shakespeare's *Midsummer Night's Dream*—as gentle as any sucking dove. A virile new Britain cannot continue indefinitely to be traduced in the eyes or rather ears, of the

world by the effete languors of Langham Place, brazenly masquerading as 'standard English.' When the Voice of Britain is heard at nine o'clock, better far and infinitely less ludicrous to hear aitches honestly dropped than the present priggish, inflated, inhibited, school-ma'amish arch braying of blameless bashful mewing maidens!

Letter in Tribune

Each of these passages has faults of its own, but, quite apart from avoidable ugliness, two qualities are common to all of them. The first is staleness of imagery: the other is lack of precision. The writer either has a meaning and cannot express it, or he inadvertently says something else, or he is almost indifferent as to whether his words mean anything or not. This mixture of vagueness and sheer incompetence is the most marked characteristic of modern English prose, and especially of any kind of political writing. As soon as certain topics are raised, the concrete melts into the abstract and no one seems able to think of turns of speech that are not hackneyed: prose consists less and less of *words* chosen for the sake of their meaning, and more and more of *phrases* tacked together like the sections of a prefabricated henhouse. I list below, with notes and examples, various of the tricks by means of which the work of prose-construction is habitually dodged:

Dying Metaphors

A newly invented metaphor assists thought by evoking a visual image, while 5 on the other hand a metaphor which is technically "dead" (e.g., *iron resolution*) has in effect reverted to being an ordinary word and can generally be used without loss of vividness. But in between these two classes there is a huge dump of worn-out metaphors which have lost all evocative power and are merely used because they save people the trouble of inventing phrases for themselves. Examples are: "Ring the changes on," "take up the cudgels for," "toe the line," "ride roughshod over," "stand shoulder to shoulder with," "play into the hands of," "no axe to grind," "grist to the mill," "fishing in troubled waters," "on the order of the day," "Achilles' heel," "swan song," "hotbed." Many of these are used without knowledge of their meaning (what is a "rift," for instance?), and incompatible metaphors are frequently mixed, a sure sign that the writer is not interested in what he is saying. Some metaphors now current have been twisted out of their original meaning without those who use them even being aware of the fact. For example, "toe the line" is sometimes written "tow the line." Another example is "the hammer and the anvil," now always used with the implication that the anvil gets the worst of it. In real life it is always the anvil that breaks the hammer, never the other way about: a writer who stopped to think what he was saying would be aware of this, and would avoid perverting the original phrase.

Operators or Verbal False Limbs

These save the trouble of picking out appropriate verbs and nouns, and at the same time pad each sentence with extra syllables which give it an appearance of symmetry. Characteristic phrases are: "render inoperative," "militate against," "make contact with," "be subjected to," "give rise to," "give grounds for," "have the effect of," "play a leading part (role) in," "make itself felt," "take effect," "exhibit a tendency to," "serve the purpose of," etc., etc. The keynote is the elimination of simple verbs. Instead of being a single word, such as "break," "stop," "spoil," "mend," "kill," a verb becomes a "phrase," made up of a noun or adjective tacked on to some general-purposes verb such as "prove," "serve," "form," "play," "render." In addition, the passive voice is wherever possible used in preference to the active, and noun constructions are used instead of gerunds ("by examination of" instead of "by examining"). The range of verbs is further cut down by means of the -ize and de- formation, and the banal statements are given an appearance of profundity by means of the not un- formation. Simple conjunctions and prepositions are replaced by such phrases as "with respect to," "having regard to," "the fact that," "by dint of," "in view of," "in the interests of," "on the hypothesis that"; and the ends of sentences are saved from anticlimax by such resounding commonplaces as "greatly to be desired," "cannot be left out of account," "a development to be expected in the near future," "deserving of serious consideration," "brought to a satisfactory conclusion," and so on and so forth.

Pretentious Diction

Words like "phenomenon," "element," "individual" (as noun), "objective," "categorical," "effective," "virtual," "basic," "primary," "promote," "constitute," "exhibit," "exploit," "utilize," "eliminate," "liquidate," are used to dress up simple statements and give an air of scientific impartiality to biased judgments. Adjectives like "epoch-making," "epic," "historic," "unforgettable," "triumphant," "age-old," "inevitable," "inexorable," "veritable," are used to dignify the sordid processes of international politics, while writing that aims at glorifying war usually takes on an archaic color, its characteristic words being: "realm," "throne," "chariot," "mailed fist," "trident," "sword," "shield," "buckler," "banner," "jackboot," "clarion." Foreign words and expressions such as "cul de sac," "ancien régime," "deus ex machina," "mutatis mutandis," "status quo," "Gleichschaltung," "weltanschauung," are used to give an air of culture and elegance. Except for the useful abbreviations "i.e.," "e.g.," and "etc.," there is no real need for any of the hundreds of foreign phrases now current in English. Bad writers, and especially scientific, political and sociological writers, are nearly always haunted by the notion that Latin or Greek words are grander than Saxon ones, and unnecessary words like "expedite," "ameliorate," "predict," "extraneous," "deracinated," "clandestine," "subaqueous," and hundreds of others constantly gain ground from their Anglo-Saxon opposite numbers.[1]

The jargon peculiar to Marxist writing ("hyena," "hangman," "cannibal," "petty bourgeois," "these gentry," "lackey," "flunky," "mad dog," "White Guard," etc.) consists largely of words and phrases translated from Russian, German, or French; but the normal way of coining a new word is to use a Latin or Greek root with the appropriate affix and, where necessary, the -ize formation. It is often easier to make up words of this kind ("deregionalize," "impermissible," "extramarital," "nonfragmentatory," and so forth) than to think up the English words that will cover one's meaning. The result, in general, is an increase in slovenliness and vagueness.

Meaningless Words

In certain kinds of writing, particularly in art criticism and literary criticism, it is normal to come across long passages which are almost completely lacking in meaning.[2] Words like "romantic," "plastic," "values," "human," "dead," "sentimental," "natural," "vitality," as used in art criticism, are strictly meaningless in the sense that they not only do not point to any discoverable object, but are hardly ever expected to do so by the reader. When one critic writes, "The outstanding feature of Mr. X's work is its living quality," while another writes, "The immediately striking thing about Mr. X's work is its peculiar deadness," the reader accepts this as a simple difference of opinion. If words like "black" and "white" were involved, instead of the jargon words "dead" and "living," he would see at once that language was being used in an improper way. Many political words are similarly abused. The word "Fascism" has now no meaning except in so far as it signifies "something not desirable." The words "democracy," "socialism," "freedom," "patriotic," "realistic," "justice," have each of them several different meanings which cannot be reconciled with one another. In the case of a word like "democracy," not only is there no agreed definition, but the attempt to make one is resisted from all sides. It is almost universally felt that when we call a country democratic we are praising it: consequently the defenders of every kind of régime claim that it is a democracy, and fear that they might have to stop using the word if it were tied down to any one meaning. Words of this kind are often used in a consciously dishonest way. That is, the person who uses them has his own private definition, but allows his hearer to think he means something quite different. Statements like "Marshal Pétain was a true patriot," "The Soviet Press is the freest in the world," "The Catholic Church is opposed to persecution," are almost always made with intent to deceive. Other words used in variable meanings, in most cases more or less dishonestly, are: "class," "totalitarian," "science," "progressive," "reactionary," "bourgeois," "equality."

Now that I have made this catalog of swindles and perversions, let me give another example of the kind of writing that they lead to. This time it must of its nature be an imaginary one. I am going to translate a passage of good English into modern English of the worst sort. Here is a well-known verse from Ecclesiastes:

I returned and saw under the sun, that the race is not to the swift, nor the battle to the strong, neither yet bread to the wise, nor yet riches to men of understanding, nor yet favor to men of skill; but time and chance happeneth to them all.

10   Here it is in modern English:

Objective consideration of contemporary phenomena compels the conclusion that success or failure in competitive activities exhibits no tendency to be commensurate with innate capacity, but that a considerable element of the unpredictable must invariably be taken into account.

This is a parody, but not a very gross one. Exhibit (3), above, for instance, contains several patches of the same kind of English. It will be seen that I have not made a full translation. The beginning and ending of the sentence follow the original meaning fairly closely, but in the middle the concrete illustrations—race, battle, bread—dissolve into the vague phrase "success or failure in competitive activities." This had to be so, because no modern writer of the kind I am discussing—no one capable of using phrases like "objective consideration of contemporary phenomena"—would ever tabulate his thoughts in that precise and detailed way. The whole tendency of modern prose is away from concreteness. Now analyse these two sentences a little more closely. The first contains forty-nine words but only sixty syllables, and all its words are those of everyday life. The second contains thirty-eight words of ninety syllables: eighteen of its words are from Latin roots, and one from Greek. The first sentence contains six vivid images, and only one phrase ("time and chance") that could be called vague. The second contains not a single fresh, arresting phrase, and in spite of its ninety syllables it gives only a shortened version of the meaning contained in the first. Yet without a doubt it is the second kind of sentence that is gaining ground in modern English. I do not want to exaggerate. This kind of writing is not yet universal, and outcrops of simplicity will occur here and there in the worst-written page. Still, if you or I were told to write a few lines on the uncertainty of human fortunes, we should probably come much nearer to my imaginary sentence than to the one from *Ecclesiastes*.

As I have tried to show, modern writing at its worst does not consist in picking out words for the sake of their meaning and inventing images in order to make the meaning clearer. It consists in gumming together long strips of words which have already been set in order by someone else, and making the results presentable by sheer humbug. The attraction of this way of writing is that it is easy. It is easier—even quicker, once you have the habit—to say "In my opinion it is a not unjustifiable assumption that" than to say "I think." If you use ready-made phrases, you not only don't have to hunt about for words; you also don't have to bother with the rhythms of your sentences, since these phrases are generally so arranged as to be more or less euphonious. When you are composing in a hurry—when you are dictating to a stenographer, for instance, or making a public speech—it is natural to fall into a pretentious, Latinized style. Tags like "a consideration which we should do well to bear in mind" or "a conclusion to which all of us would readily assent" will save many a sentence from coming down with a bump. By using stale metaphors, similes and idioms, you save much mental effort, at the cost of leaving your meaning vague, not only for your reader but for yourself. This is the significance of mixed metaphors. The sole aim of a metaphor is to call up a visual image. When these images clash—as in "The Fascist octopus has sung its swan song, the jackboot is thrown into the melting pot"—it can be taken as certain that the writer is not seeing a mental image of the objects he is naming; in other words he is not really thinking. Look again at the examples I gave at the beginning of this essay. Professor Laski (1) uses five negatives in fifty-three words. One of these is superfluous, making nonsense of the whole passage, and in addition there is the slip "alien" for akin, making further nonsense, and several avoidable pieces of clumsiness which increase the general vagueness. Professor Hogben (2) plays ducks and drakes with a battery which is able to write prescriptions, and, while disapproving of the everyday phrase "put up with," is unwilling to look "egregious" up in the dictionary and see what it means. In (3), if one takes an uncharitable attitude towards it, is simply meaningless: probably one could work out its intended meaning by reading the whole of the article in which it occurs. In (4), the writer knows more or less what he wants to say, but an accumulation of stale phrases chokes him like tea leaves blocking a sink. In (5), words and meaning have almost parted company. People who write in this manner usually have a general emotional meaning—they dislike one thing and want to express solidarity with another—but they are not interested in the detail of what they are saying. A scrupulous writer, in every sentence that he writes, will ask himself at least four questions, thus: "What am I trying to say?" "What words will express it?" "What image or idiom will make it clearer?" "Is this image fresh enough to have an effect?" And he will probably ask himself two more: "Could I put it more shortly?" "Have I said anything that is avoidably ugly?" But you are not obliged to go to all this trouble. You can shirk it by simply throwing your mind open and letting the ready-made phrases come crowding in. They will construct your sentences for you—even think your thoughts for you, to a certain extent—and at need they will perform the important service of partially concealing your meaning even from yourself. It is at this point that the special connection between politics and the debasement of language becomes clear.

In our time it is broadly true that political writing is bad writing. Where it is not true, it will generally be found that the writer is some kind of rebel, expressing his private opinions and not a "party line." Orthodoxy, of whatever color, seems to demand a lifeless, imitative style. The political dialects to be found in pamphlets, leading articles, manifestos, White Papers and the speeches of under-secretaries do, of course, vary from party to party, but they are all alike in that one almost never finds in them a fresh, vivid, home-made turn of speech. When one watches some tired hack on the platform mechanically repeating the familiar phrases—"bestial atrocities," "iron heel," "bloodstained tyranny," "free peoples of the world," "stand shoulder to shoulder"—one often has a curious feeling that one is not watching a live human being but some kind of dummy: a feeling which suddenly becomes stronger at moments when the light catches the speaker's spectacles and turns them into blank discs which seem to have no eyes behind them. And this is not altogether fanciful. A speaker who uses that kind of phraseology has gone some distance towards turning himself into a machine. The appropriate noises are coming out of his larynx, but his brain is not involved as it would be if he were choosing his words for himself. If the speech he is making is one that he is accustomed to make over and over again, he may be almost unconscious of what he is saying, as one is when one utters the responses in church. And this reduced state of consciousness, if not indispensable, is at any rate favorable to political conformity.

In our time, political speech and writing are largely the defense of the indefensible. Things like the continuance of British rule in India, the Russian purges and deportations, the dropping of the atom bombs on Japan, can indeed be defended, but only by arguments which are too brutal for most people to face, and which do not square with the professed aims of political parties. Thus political language has to consist largely of euphemism, question-begging and sheer cloudy vagueness. Defenseless villages are bombarded from the air, the inhabitants driven out into the countryside, the cattle machine-gunned, the huts set on fire with incendiary bullets: this is called "pacification." Millions of peasants are robbed of their farms and sent trudging along the roads with no more than they can carry: this is called "transfer of population" or "rectification of frontiers." People are imprisoned for years without trial, or shot in the back of the neck or sent to die of scurvy in Arctic lumber camps: this is called "elimination of unreliable elements." Such phraseology is needed if one wants to name things without calling up mental pictures of them. Consider for instance some comfortable English professor defending Russian totalitarianism. He cannot say outright, "I believe in killing off your opponents when you can get good results by doing so." Probably, therefore, he will say something like this:

15 "While freely conceding that the Soviet régime exhibits certain features which the humanitarian may be inclined to deplore, we must, I think, agree that a certain curtailment of the right to political opposition is an unavoidable concomitant of transitional periods, and that the rigors which the Russian people have been called upon to undergo have been amply justified in the sphere of concrete achievement."

The inflated style is itself a kind of euphemism. A mass of Latin words falls upon the facts like soft snow, blurring the outlines and covering up all the details. The great enemy of clear language is insincerity. When there is a gap between one's real and one's declared aims, one turns as it were instinctively to long words and exhausted idioms, like a cuttlefish squirting out ink. In our age there is no such thing as "keeping out of politics." All issues are political issues, and politics itself is a mass of lies, evasions, folly, hatred and schizophrenia. When the general atmosphere is bad, language must suffer. I should expect to find—this is a guess which I have not sufficient knowledge to verify—that the German, Russian, and Italian languages have all deteriorated in the last ten or fifteen years, as a result of dictatorship.

But if thought corrupts language, language can also corrupt thought. A bad usage can spread by tradition and imitation, even among people who should and do know better. The debased language that I have been discussing is in some ways very convenient. Phrases like "a not unjustifiable assumption," "leaves much to be desired," "would serve no good purpose," "a consideration which we should do well to bear in mind," are a continuous temptation, a packet of aspirins always at one's elbow. Look back through this essay, and for certain you will find that I have again and again committed the very faults I am protesting against. By this morning's post I have received a pamphlet dealing with conditions in Germany. The author tells me that he "felt impelled" to write it. I open it at random, and here is almost the first sentence that I see: "(The Allies) have an opportunity not only of achieving a radical transformation of Germany's social and political structure in such a way as to avoid a nationalistic reaction in Germany itself, but at the same time of laying the foundations of a cooperative and unified Europe." You see, he "feels impelled" to write—feels, presumably, that he has something new to say—and yet his words, like cavalry horses answering the bugle, group themselves automatically into the familiar dreary pattern. This invasion of one's mind by ready-made phrases ("lay the foundations," "achieve a radical transformation") can only be prevented if one is constantly on guard against them, and every such phrase anaesthetizes a portion of one's brain.

I said earlier that the decadence of our language is probably curable. Those who deny this would argue, if they produced an argument at all, that language merely reflects existing social conditions, and that we cannot influence its development by any direct tinkering with words and constructions. So far as the general tone or spirit of a language goes, this may be true, but it is not true in detail. Silly words and expressions have often disappeared, not through any evolutionary process but owing to the conscious action of a minority. Two recent examples were "explore every avenue" and "leave no stone unturned," which were killed by the jeers of a few journalists. There is a long list of flyblown metaphors which could similarly be got rid of if enough people would interest themselves in the job; and it should also be possible to laugh the *not un*-formation out of existence,[3] to reduce the amount of Latin and Greek in the average sentence, to drive out foreign phrases and strayed scientific words, and, in general, to make pretentiousness unfashionable. But all these are minor points. The defense of the English language implies more than this, and perhaps it is best to start by saying what it does *not* imply.

To begin with, it has nothing to do with archaism, with the salvaging of obsolete words and turns of speech, or with the setting up of a "standard English" which must never be departed from. On the contrary, it is especially concerned with the scrapping of every word or idiom which has outworn its usefulness. It has nothing to do with correct grammar and syntax, which are of no importance so long as one makes one's meaning clear, or with the avoidance of Americanisms, or with having what is called a "good prose style." On the other hand it is not concerned with fake simplicity and the attempt to make written English colloquial. Nor does it even imply in every case preferring the Saxon word to the Latin one, though it does imply using the fewest and shortest words that will cover one's meaning. What is above all needed is to let the meaning choose the word, and not the other way about. In prose, the worst thing one can do with words is to surrender to them. When you think of a concrete object, you think wordlessly, and then, if you want to describe the thing you have been visualizing you probably hunt about till you find the exact words that seem to fit. When you think of something abstract, you are more inclined to use words from the start, and unless you make a conscious effort to prevent it, the existing dialect will come rushing in and do the job for you, at the expense of blurring or even changing your meaning. Probably it is better to put off using words as long as possible and get one's meaning as clear as one can through pictures or sensations. Afterwards one can choose—not simply *accept*—the phrases that will best cover the meaning, and then switch round and decide what impression one's words are likely to make on another person. This last effort of the mind cuts out all stale or mixed images, all prefabricated phrases, needless repetitions, and humbug and vagueness generally. But one can often be in doubt about the effect of a word or a phrase, and one needs rules that one can rely on when instinct fails. I think the following rules will cover most cases:

(i) Never use a metaphor, simile or other figure of speech which you are used to seeing in print.

(ii) Never use a long word where a short one will do.

(iii) If it is possible to cut a word out, always cut it out.

(iv) Never use the passive where you can use the active.

(v) Never use a foreign phrase, a scientific word or a jargon word if you can think of an everyday English equivalent.

(vi) Break any of these rules sooner than say anything outright barbarous.

These rules sound elementary, and so they are, but they demand a deep change of attitude in anyone who has grown used to writing in the style now fashionable. One could keep all of them and still write bad English, but one could not write the kind of stuff that I quoted in those five specimens at the beginning of this article.

I have not here been considering the literary use of language, but merely language as an instrument for expressing and not for concealing or preventing thought. Stuart Chase and others have come near to claiming that all abstract words are meaningless, and have used this as a pretext for advocating a kind of political quietism. Since you don't know what Fascism is, how can you struggle against Fascism? One need not swallow such absurdities as this, but one ought to recognize that the present political chaos is connected with the decay of language, and that one can probably bring about some improvement by starting at the verbal end. If you simplify your English, you are freed from the worst follies of orthodoxy. You cannot speak any of the necessary dialects, and when you make a stupid remark its stupidity will be obvious, even to yourself. Political language—and with variations this is true of all political parties, from Conservatives to Anarchists—is designed to make lies sound truthful and murder respectable, and to give an appearance of solidity to pure wind. One cannot change this all in a moment, but one can at least change one's own habits, and from time to time one can even, if one jeers loudly enough, send some wornout and useless phrase—some "jackboot," "Achilles' heel," "hotbed," "melting pot," "acid test," "veritable inferno," or other lump of verbal refuse—into the dustbin where it belongs.

Notes

[1] An interesting illustration of this is the way in which the English flower names that were in use till very recently are being ousted by Greek ones, "snapdragon" becoming "antirrhinum," "forget-me-not" becoming "myosotis," etc. It is hard to see any practical reason for this change of fashion: it is probably due to an instinctive turning-away from the more homely word and a vague feeling that the Greek word is scientific.

[2] Example: "Comfort's catholicity of perception and image, strangely Whitmanesque in range, almost the exact opposite in aesthetic compulsion, continues to evoke that trembling atmospheric accumulative hinting at a cruel, an inexorably serene timelessness . . . Wrey Gardiner scores by aiming at simple bull's-eyes with precision. Only they are not so simple, and through this contented sadness runs more than the surface bittersweet of resignation" (*Poetry Quarterly*).

[3] One can cure oneself of the *not un*-formation by memorizing this sentence: A *not unblack dog was chasing a not unsmall rabbit across a not ungreen field.*

Things to Do with the Reading

1. In the section "Operators or Verbal False Limbs" (paragraph 6) and again in the "rules" offered at the end of the essay (paragraph 19), Orwell articulates (and justifies) his preference for cutting unnecessary words and avoiding the passive voice. With these notions in mind, apply the discussions in Chapter 10 of Noun Styles, Verb Styles, "Official Style," Finding the Action in a Sentence: "To Be" Or Not "To Be," and Active and Passive Voice to produce a revision of anything you have written. To prepare you, first experiment with Try This exercises 10.7 and 10.8 to sharpen your ability to distinguish active voice from passive voice and to refine your understanding of what each of these options offers a writer.

2. Application: In paragraph 14 Orwell delivers one of the most famous sentences in the essay: "In our time political speech and writing are largely the defense of the indefensible." He illustrates this declaration with a series of examples of "euphemism, question-begging, and sheer cloudy vagueness," such as use of the term "pacification" to describe "defenseless villages bombarded from the air, inhabitants driven out into the countryside, the cattle machine-gunned, the huts set on fire with incendiary bullets" (paragraph 14).

   That was a half-century ago. How about now? Visit a wonderful website for its collection of speeches, American Rhetoric, at http://www.americanrhetoric.com/. Find a speech that you think Orwell would condemn for defending the indefensible. Then write an essay in which you produce an Orwellian analysis of its methods of doing so.

3. Application: Orwell's essay also conveys, both explicitly and by implication, a set of traits that characterize politically responsible language. Review the essay to extract a list of those traits Orwell approves of in political speech. Then go to the American Rhetoric website (cited in the previous question) and locate an example of a speech he would like. Write an essay in which you point out specific features Orwell would like about it, explaining the reasoning behind your judgment. You might want to start by looking at speeches by Barbara Jordan, the first African-American woman to be elected to the House of Representatives in Texas. She went on to a high-profile career in Congress where she came to be recognized as one of America's great orators. Try to find the speech she gave in Congress on the occasion of the House Judiciary Committee, of which she was a member, being asked to speak about their deliberations on the question of impeaching a president (Richard Nixon). This speech made Jordan a nationally known and admired speaker. Why?

Drake Bennett

Thinking Literally: The Surprising Ways That Metaphors Shape Your World

In this admirably concise and illuminating synthesis of current thinking among cognitive linguists about metaphor, journalist Drake Bennett demonstrates that "psychologists are upending traditional ideas of how we learn, reason, and make sense of the world around us." Abstract thought, Bennett explains, would be meaningless without bodily experience. This is an idea that Bennett attributes to George Lakoff and Mark Johnson's influential book, *Metaphors We Live By* (1980). (See the piece co-authored by Lakoff later in this chapter.) Bennett cites an experiment, for example, in which subjects using heavy clipboards responded differently from subjects using lighter clipboards.

They gave more careful (weightier) answers to questions on a questionnaire. This piece follows interestingly on the case Orwell makes for the importance of concrete rather than abstract language in enabling readers to discern what's really happening in descriptions of political situations.

When we say someone is a warm person, we do not mean that they are running a fever. When we describe an issue as weighty, we have not actually used a scale to determine this. And when we say a piece of news is hard to swallow, no one assumes we have tried unsuccessfully to eat it.

These phrases are metaphorical—they use concrete objects and qualities to describe abstractions like kindness or importance or difficulty—and we use them and their like so often that we hardly notice them. For most people, metaphor, like simile or synecdoche, is a term inflicted upon them in high school English class: "all the world's a stage," "a house divided against itself cannot stand," Gatsby's fellow dreamers are "boats against the current, borne back ceaselessly into the past." Metaphors are literary creations—good ones help us see the world anew, in fresh and interesting ways, the rest are simply clichés: a test is a piece of cake, a completed task is a load off one's back, a momentary difficulty is a speed bump.

But whether they're being deployed by poets, politicians, football coaches, or realtors, metaphors are primarily thought of as tools for talking and writing—out of inspiration or out of laziness, we distill emotions and thoughts into the language of the tangible world. We use metaphors to make sense to one another.

"Thinking Literally: The Surprising Ways That Metaphors Shape Your World," by Drake Bennett, from The Boston Globe, September 27, 2009. © 2009 Boston Globe. All rights reserved. Used by permission and protected by the Copyright Laws of the United States. The printing, copying, redistribution, or retransmission of this Content without express written permission is prohibited.

Now, however, a new group of people has started to take an intense interest in metaphors: psychologists. Drawing on philosophy and linguistics, cognitive scientists have begun to see the basic metaphors that we use all the time not just as turns of phrase, but as keys to the structure of thought. By taking these everyday metaphors as literally as possible, psychologists are upending traditional ideas of how we learn, reason, and make sense of the world around us. The result has been a torrent of research testing the links between metaphors and their physical roots, with many of the papers reading as if they were commissioned by Amelia Bedelia, the implacably literal-minded children's book hero. Researchers have sought to determine whether the temperature of an object in someone's hands determines how "warm" or "cold" he considers a person he meets, whether the heft of a held object affects how "weighty" people consider topics they are presented with, or whether people think of the powerful as physically more elevated than the less powerful.

5   What they have found is that, in fact, we do. Metaphors aren't just how we talk and write, they're how we think. At some level, we actually do seem to understand temperament as a form of temperature, and we expect people's personalities to behave accordingly. What's more, without our body's instinctive sense for temperature—or position, texture, size, shape, or weight—abstract concepts like kindness and power, difficulty and purpose, and intimacy and importance would simply not make any sense to us. Deep down, we are all Amelia Bedelia.

Metaphors like this "don't invite us to see the world in new and different ways," says Daniel Casasanto, a cognitive scientist and researcher at the Max Planck Institute for Psycholinguistics in the Netherlands. "They enable us to understand the world at all."

Our instinctive, literal-minded metaphorizing can make us vulnerable to what seem like simple tweaks to our physical environment, with ramifications for everything from how we build polling booths to how we sell cereal. And at a broader level it reveals just how much the human body, in all its particularity, shapes the mind, suggesting that much of what we think of as abstract reasoning is in fact a sometimes awkward piggybacking onto the mental tools we have developed to govern our body's interactions with its physical environment. Put another way, metaphors reveal the extent to which we think with our bodies.

"The abstract way we think is really grounded in the concrete, bodily world much more than we thought," says John Bargh, a psychology professor at Yale and leading researcher in this realm.

Philosophers have long wondered about the connection between metaphor and thought, in ways that occasionally presaged current-day research. Friedrich Nietzsche scornfully described human understanding as nothing more than a web of expedient metaphors, stitched together from our shallow impressions of the world. In their ignorance, he charged, people mistake these familiar metaphors, deadened from overuse, for truths. "We believe that we know something about the things themselves when we speak of trees, colors, snow, and flowers," he wrote, "and yet we possess nothing but metaphors for things—metaphors which correspond in no way to the original entities." Like Nietzsche, George Lakoff, a professor of linguistics at the University of California at Berkeley, and Mark Johnson, a philosophy professor at the University of Oregon, see human thought as metaphor-driven. But, in the two greatly influential books they have co-written on the topic, "Metaphors We Live By" in 1980 and "Philosophy in the Flesh" in 1999, Lakoff and Johnson focus on the deadest of dead metaphors, the ones that don't even rise to the level of cliché. They call them "primary metaphors," and they group them into categories like "affection is warmth," "important is big," "difficulties are burdens," "similarity is closeness," "purposes are destinations," and even "categories are containers."

Rather than so much clutter standing in the way of true understanding, to Lakoff and Johnson these metaphors are markers of the roots of thought itself. Lakoff and Johnson's larger argument is that abstract thought would be meaningless without bodily experience. And primary metaphors, in their ubiquity (in English and other languages) and their physicality, are some of their most powerful evidence for this.

"What we've discovered in the last 30 years is—surprise, surprise—people 10 think with their brains," says Lakoff. "And their brains are part of their bodies."

Inspired by this argument, psychologists have begun to make their way, experiment by experiment, through the catalog of primary metaphors, altering one side of the metaphorical equation to see how it changes the other.

Bargh at Yale, along with Lawrence Williams, now at the University of Colorado, did studies in which subjects were casually asked to hold a cup of either iced or hot coffee, not knowing it was part of the study, then a few minutes later asked to rate the personality of a person who was described to them. The hot coffee group, it turned out, consistently described a warmer person—rating them as happier, more generous, more sociable, good-natured, and more caring—than the iced coffee group. The effect seems to run the other way, too: In a paper published last year, Chen-Bo Zhong and Geoffrey J. Leonardelli of the University of Toronto found that people asked to recall a time when they were ostracized gave lower estimates of room temperature than those who recalled a social inclusion experience.

In a paper in the current issue of Psychological Science, researchers in the Netherlands and Portugal describe a series of studies in which subjects were given clipboards on which to fill out questionnaires—in one study subjects were asked to estimate the value of several foreign currencies, in another they were asked to rate the city of Amsterdam and its mayor. The clipboards, however, were two different weights, and the subjects who took the questionnaire on the heavier clipboards tended to ascribe more metaphorical weight to the questions they were asked—they not only judged the foreign currencies to be more valuable, they gave more careful, considered answers to the questions they were asked.

Similar results have proliferated in recent years. One of the authors of the weight paper, Thomas Schubert, has also done work suggesting that the fact that we associate power and elevation ("your highness," "friends in high places") means we actually unconsciously look upward when we think about power. Bargh and Josh Ackerman at MIT's Sloan School of Business, in work that has yet to be published, have done studies in which subjects, after handling sandpaper-covered puzzle pieces, were less likely to describe a social situation as having gone smoothly. Casasanto has done work in which people who were told to move marbles from a lower tray up to a higher one while recounting a story told happier stories than people moving them down.

15   Several studies have explored the metaphorical connection between cleanliness and moral purity. In one, subjects who were asked to recall an unethical act, then given the choice between a pencil and an antiseptic wipe, were far more likely to choose the cleansing wipe than people who had been asked to recall an ethical act. In a follow-up study, subjects who recalled an unethical act acted less guilty after washing their hands. The researchers dubbed it the "Macbeth effect," after the guilt-ridden, compulsive hand washing of Lady Macbeth.

To the extent that metaphors reveal how we think, they also suggest ways that physical manipulation might be used to shape our thought. In essence, that is what much metaphor research entails. And while psychologists have thus far been primarily interested in using such manipulations simply to tease out an observable effect, there's no reason that they couldn't be put to other uses as well, by marketers, architects, teachers, parents, and litigators, among others.

A few psychologists have begun to ponder applications. Ackerman, for example, is looking at the impact of perceptions of hardness on our sense of difficulty. The study is ongoing, but he says he is finding that something as simple as sitting on a hard chair makes people think of a task as harder. If those results hold up, he suggests, it might make sense for future treaty negotiators to take a closer look at everything from the desks to the upholstery of the places where they meet. Nils Jostmann, the lead author of the weight study, suggests that pollsters might want to take his findings to heart: heavier clipboards and heavier pens for issues that they want considered answers for, lighter ones for questions that they want gut reactions on.

How much of an effect these tweaks might have in a real-world setting, researchers emphasize, remains to be seen. Still, it probably couldn't hurt to try a few in your own life. When inviting a new friend over, suggest a cup of hot tea rather than a cold beer. Keep a supply of soft, smooth objects on hand at work—polished pebbles, maybe, or a silk handkerchief—in case things start to feel too daunting. And if you feel a sudden pang of guilt about some long-ago transgression, try taking a shower.

Things to Do with the Reading

1. The basic definition of metaphor, as offered by Bennett, is that metaphorical phrases "use concrete objects and qualities to describe abstractions like kindness or importance or difficulty—and we use them . . . so often that we hardly notice them" (paragraph 2). Rather than being solely the province of literature, metaphors, according to cognitive scientists, structure the way we think. In particular, what George Lakoff and Mark Johnson call "primary metaphors" have implications for how we go about making sense of the world. What are some of the implications? You might wish to consider the implications of the primary metaphor that life is a journey.

2. Link: Prepare to do a pointing exercise (see pointing in Chapter 2) in which you read sentences aloud from Bennett that seem to capture best his essay's ideas about metaphorical language. During the pointing exercise, jot down key words you hear in the sentences that people read aloud. At the end of the pointing exercise, people should read aloud some of the key words that they jotted down. Next, return to the Orwell essay and read aloud sentences that seem to you to be especially interesting in light of Bennett's essay. At the end of the pointing exercise, members of the group might wish to do a 10-minute passage-based focused freewrite, laying out the connections between one sentence from the Orwell essay and one sentence from Bennett's (see Chapter 2). This should fuel a discussion on ways in which current developments in thinking about metaphor, as defined by Bennett, reinforce and extend Orwell's arguments.

3. Find a copy of the children's book *Amelia Bedelia*, which is an entertaining account of a person who takes all metaphors literally. Once you have browsed this book, (from which it is fun to read aloud with other people) write a brief explanation of what Bennett means when he says, "Deep down, we are all Amelia Bedelia." Then go on to explain Bennett's sentence in paragraph 6: "Our instinctive, literal-minded metaphorizing can make us vulnerable to what seem like simple tweaks to our physical environment. . ." Start by PARAPHRASING × 3 (see Chapter 2).

4. Application: Spend a week trying to pay attention to metaphorical language that you hear (or overhear) in casual conversation. Start making a list of metaphors that seem to you to crop up with some frequency. Then try to categorize the metaphors according to concrete things they refer to. "Laying the cards on the table," for example, is a reference to card games. What similarities do you notice, if any, in the kinds of metaphors that people use in conversation? You could also do a more extended version

of this exercise by tracking metaphors in either political speeches or in newspaper editorials or blogs or newspaper articles on political subjects. What metaphors seem to recur? Insofar as the writing you are observing has a fairly clear political orientation (liberal or conservative, as defined in the essay by Christopher Borick at the beginning of this unit), write a short piece on which metaphors seem to appeal to liberals and which to conservatives and why.

Interview with Frank Luntz

This interview with the controversial pollster Frank Luntz first appeared on PBS's *Frontline* on December 15, 2003, as part of a series of interviews entitled *The Persuaders*. The series explored the broader influence that the cultures of marketing and advertising have had on American life. In the interview, Luntz discusses his central role in crafting the Contract with America that the Republican Party presented to voters in 1994, as well as his theories about the construction and presentation of messages in political language. Along with Borick and Orwell, Luntz offers a theoretical lens for thinking about the language of politics. As Luntz explained in a later interview with Terry Gross on *Fresh Air* in 2007, he is a "Johnny Appleseed of language": through the use of focus groups and polling and other means, he discovers "the words that work" with the majority of people and shares these discoveries with his clients. A graduate of the University of Pennsylvania with a PhD from Oxford, Luntz currently heads Luntz Global, LLC, which creates messages and manages images for political and commercial clients. He has instructed Senate Republicans in talking about healthcare, and a leaked 17-page memo he wrote in January 2011 advises the Republican Party about the words to use in the financial regulation debate. He is a frequent commentator and analyst for Fox News as well.

What are you measuring with the dial technology? [A mechanism Luntz uses 1 **whereby people in a focus group register their moment by moment responses to a speech or presentation.]**

It's like an X-ray that gets inside your head, and it picks out every single word, every single phrase [that you hear], and you know what works and what doesn't. And you do it without the bias of a focus group. People are quiet as they're listening, and they're reacting anonymously. The key to dial technology is that it's immediate, it's specific, and it's anonymous.

It's so immediate, it feels instantaneous.

But it is, because politics is instantaneous. Politics is gut; commercials are gut. You're watching a great show on TV, you now come to that middle break, you decide in a matter of three seconds whether or not you're going to a) flip the channel; b) get up; or c) keep watching. It's not intellectual; it is gut.

Is it the same for political decisions about power companies and politicians, 5 **though?**

We decide based on how people look; we decide based on how people sound; we decide based on how people are dressed. We decide based on their passion. If I respond to you quietly, the viewer at home is going to have a different reaction than if I respond to you with emotion and with passion and I wave my arms

From FRONTLINE/WGBH Boston. Copyright © 1995–2011 WGBH Educational Foundation.

around. Somebody like this is an intellectual; somebody like this is a freak. But that's how we make up our minds. Look, this is about the real-life decisions of real-life Americans, who to vote for, what to buy, what to agree with, what to think, how to act. This is the way it is.

You think emotions are more revelatory than the intellect for predicting these decisions?

80 percent of our life is emotion, and only 20 percent is intellect. I am much more interested in how you feel than how you think. I can change how you think, but how you feel is something deeper and stronger, and it's something that's inside you. How you think is on the outside, how you feel is on the inside, so that's what I need to understand.

And this technology can get at that?

10 The great thing about dial technology is you can get a small response on the dial, or you can get a huge jump. You watch with your own eyes: At some points, the lines are way up at the top of the screen or even out beyond. People were practically breaking their dials in agreement at certain points, and at other points, they were flat. It measures intensity. And if you want to understand public opinion, if you want to understand public behavior, if you want to understand the way we operate as Americans and as humans, you've got to understand that one word: intensity.

It can be anything, then, that you're selling.

I'm not going to let you twist the words, because if I say to you that you can sell a politician the way you sell soap—and it may even look that way from the outside—that says to Americans that they shouldn't respect politicians or soap. It really isn't that way. The way you communicate an idea is different than the way you communicate a product. However, the way you measure [the response of the public in both instances] is quite similar. And the principles behind explaining and educating the product or the elected official is similar, even though the actual execution of it is very, very different.

Are there different techniques you use when working with politics versus corporations?

The technique is a little bit different because politics and corporations are a little bit different. But in the end you're still using the same focus groups; you're still using the same dial technology; you're still using the same quantitative data; you're still doing split samples where you ask half a sample one way and the other half a different way. You're still asking and re-asking the questions. You're still showing them visuals to see what they like the best, and you're still showing them or having them listen to audio track to see how they respond. So the actual techniques are the same, but how they are applied is different. And that really is the separation; that's the differentiation between politics and the corporate world.

Was there a eureka moment, watching the responses of these people to the 15
power company's ideas, where you figured out what really worked?

The eureka moment is two reasons why the output-based standard should be adopted: common sense and accountability. Input-based standards don't encourage energy diversity; they don't create any incentives; they don't produce solar, hydro, nuclear. As a result, companies are actually penalized if they use the cleanest fuels, and it doesn't make sense. It's not substance; it's language. And when they heard the language that they wanted to hear and they were able to apply it to an idea that at least they were open to, you watched a marriage of good communication and good policy. That was the eureka moment: I watched people nod their heads; I watched them look to each other, and they were willing at this point to fight for this position. Now I'll be able to walk to this electricity company on Monday and be able to say to them, "Your policy makes sense, and here's the language to explain it."

And the amazing thing was, it explained a very complicated policy. That's the job of language; that's the job of English. This is not about politics; this is not about selling soap. This is taking very traditional, simple, clear-cut words of the English language and figuring out which words, which phrases to apply at which opportunities, which times.

So what will you say at that Monday meeting?

On Monday I will sit down with a Washington representative of Florida Power & Light and I will tell him that what he wants to do, his goal for his company, is the goal of America; that if he uses this language to explain his principles and his policies, not only will the company benefit, but the public will be appreciative of what they're trying to do. This is a good company, this is a clean company, but it's got all the baggage of every other electric company, of every other power company. We as Americans assume that big companies are bad, and big power companies are even worse. This language, what we saw tonight, is a demonstration that a single company can differentiate itself, can improve its public image.

You believe language can change a paradigm. 20

I don't believe it—I know it. I've seen it with my own eyes. I have seen how effective language attached to policies that are mainstream and delivered by people who are passionate and effective can change the course of history. I watched in 1994 when the group of Republicans got together and said: "We're going to do this completely differently than it's ever been done before. We are going to prove to the American people that we are different." And so instead of a platform, instead of a policy, instead of a mass of different issues and policies, they came up with a "contract," because a contract is different. A contract says that it is a legal document. It says that you put your name on it, and it says that there is enforcement if you don't do it. The word "contract" means something different than "platform." Every politician and every political party issues a platform, but only these people signed a contract.

Was that your idea?

The concept of it was hatched in Salisbury, MD, at a Republican retreat. I was fortunate enough to have been invited to do a presentation about how the American people didn't trust politicians in general and, quite frankly, didn't trust Republicans in particular. And Newt Gingrich was there, and he listened to the presentation, and he said: "We have to do it differently in this election. We have to find a way to communicate that takes all of these policies that we believe in, that the Democrats don't, and articulates that difference. How can we do it?" I presented at that presentation a proclamation. I got the idea from a Massachusetts campaign I was involved with. Gingrich saw that, and he came up with the phrase "contract."

I didn't create the "Contract with America;" I was the pollster for it. I said, "If you're going to do a contract, you've got to make it a contract." For example, "Keep this page to hold us accountable"—that did not exist in the original document. I insisted that that be added, because they wanted to know that you could actually hold these guys accountable. One of the things that you have trouble with politicians, particularly in Washington, is when you get mad at them and you can't touch them; you can't punch them; you can't yell at them. This accountability says, "I can really demand that they do what they promise."

25   This sentence was the one that I had the most trouble keeping in this final document: "If we break this contract, throw us out. We mean it." When has a politician ever said, "If I don't come through with what I promise, boot me"? I said: "You need that sentence in there, and you need it at the very bottom of the document. People will read the top, and they read the bottom, and only if they believe in the top and the bottom will they actually read the text, will they read the substance." This is the enforcement clause, and this is what told people that this was for real.

It's not the "Republican Contract with America," because in 1994, as it is today, Americans don't want partisanship. So you will notice that there are mentions of the word "Republican," but I did not want it in red; I did not want it as the lead line that people would see because it was too overtly partisan. Part of my job is to teach subtlety. I may not be a subtle person—I'm pretty loud and outspoken—but so often subtlety, the quiet voice, actually communicates.

"We listen to your concerns, and we hear you loud and clear." [The contract] is responsive. That's what the public was looking for back in 1994: a politician who was responsive and responding to them. And all of this language was all tested to make sure it would be effective. The whole document is filled with listening, with responsiveness, with accountability.

Who hired you?

The Republican National Committee hired me, and they hired me because they wanted someone who could look members straight in the eye and tell them the truth. There's a problem with political polling in that you have so much pressure to do what your client wants you to do and say what your client wants you to say. I've never felt that pressure. I am independent of the political parties. I came up outside that structure so that I could tell these members: "This document is going to work. People are going to believe you." And they would believe me because they knew that I was not making money from it.

You must admit that language can cloud as well as clarify. 30

If it doesn't describe what it's selling, then it is a very poor descriptor. If you've got a bad product, you shouldn't be selling it. And people like me have to have the discipline only to work for clients, corporations, political people, products, services, networks that we believe in and we want to see succeed. I don't believe that good language can obscure a bad product.

What about replacing "global warming" with "climate change"?

What is the difference? It is climate change. Some people call it global warming; some people call it climate change. What is the difference?

Look, for years, political people and lawyers—who, by the way, are the worst communicators—used the phrase "estate tax." And for years they couldn't eliminate it. The public wouldn't support it because the word "estate" sounds wealthy. Someone like me comes around and realizes that it's not an estate tax, it's a death tax, because you're taxed at death. And suddenly something that isn't viable achieves the support of 75 percent of the American people. It's the same tax, but nobody really knows what an estate is. But they certainly know what it means to be taxed when you die. I argue that is a clarification; that's not an obfuscation.

The language of America changed with the election of Bill Clinton, because 35 with all due respect to my friends on the Republican side, Bill Clinton is the best communicator of the last 50 years. He felt your pain. Now, I'd argue that he caused your pain, but at least he felt it while he was causing it. When Bill Clinton spoke, his words were so good, and they were spoken with such passion. And that biting of the lower lip and the squinching of the eyes—you just couldn't turn away. Bill Clinton made Frank Luntz because Bill Clinton discovered the power and the influence of words. Now, I'd like to think that I apply them to clients, to philosophies, to products and services and corporations that I believe in, that are good. I don't argue with you that words can sometimes be used to confuse, but it's up to the practitioners of the study of language to apply them for good and not for evil. It is just like fire; fire can heat your house or burn it down.

There are words that work, that are meant to explain and educate on policies that work, on products that work, on services that work. I'm not going to ever try to sell a lemon. I don't do that. I work for pharmaceutical companies because my dad was kept alive for a long time on medications thanks to companies like Pfizer. I work for a company like Federal Express because it allows me to get my packages there the next morning. It's a wonderful, innovative corporation. I work for a company like Merrill Lynch because I believe in the financial services and the quality of the product.

I believe in the people who work at the corporations that I work for, and the political people. The best example is Rudy Giuliani. What have I done that's wrong if I provide someone like a Rudy Giuliani or a corporation like a Pfizer language that helps them explain or educate? I've simplified the process for them which allows them to explain. What did they say in there [in the focus group]? They kept coming back to it again and again: What they want from their elected officials, from the CEOs, from the elite of America is clarity. They said it again and again: "Be clear with us. Be straight with us. Common sense; clarity; down the road, look us straight in the eye." That's exactly what I do. I help them do that.

Talk to me about the Healthy Forests Initiative of President Bush. Isn't calling it "Healthy Forests" obfuscating the fact that it entails keeping the forests healthy with widespread logging?

Yes, the Bush administration benefited from the phrase "healthy forest." But what do we know as a fact? If you allow this underbrush to subsume the forest, to get so thick that you can't walk through it, you can't get through it, if you don't touch a twig or a tree and you say, "Oh, let Mother Nature deal with it," then you get these catastrophic forest fires that we saw in Arizona, Colorado and in California. The Native Americans, they know how to thin a forest, and yes, they do take trees out, and what happens? A fire burns, and it stops right where that thinning process took place. But thanks to environmentalists who are extreme and radical in their approach, who say that we must not touch anything at any time in any way, we lose thousands, thousands, hundreds of thousands of acres of forests and all the wildlife that was inside it. And they don't come back again. It takes generations for it to regenerate. So don't tell me about language, because "healthy forests" actually is what it means. And you have to understand the policy, and you've got to understand the product if you want to be able to communicate it. You can't just approach it naively.

40 **Is there a line you won't cross in the creative use of language?**

You cannot lie ever, because a lie destroys the credibility of the product, and credibility is more important than anything. Credibility's even more important than clarity. They have to believe you before they will listen to you. So you can't lie. This is an interesting line, because in my own life, in some of the things I've worked for, I get angry. I am a proponent of the pharmaceutical industry. I believe in these heart medications and these anti-cancer drugs. I'm a supporter of a very famous medication right now, OxyContin, because I think that this is a miracle drug which allows people to get through the day. And this is a medication that some people want to see taken off the market. There are all sorts of lawsuits. I believe that there are things worth fighting for. I believe that there are things worth explaining and educating, even if it takes months or years. The only thing I don't believe in is lying. Beyond that, you can use almost anything. You can use emotion. It is acceptable to bring someone to tears if it explains to them in an emotional way why a product, a service, or a candidate is the right person, is the right thing to do.

Do facts matter?

Of course facts matter. And what we do—and you watched it here—is to give them accurate facts and see which facts matter. My point is that when you're talking issues like the environment, a straight recitation of facts is going to fall on deaf ears, and that industry has been very ineffective. Even by using that word "industry," people think of smokestacks. So often corporate America, business America, are the worst communicators because all they understand are facts, and they cannot tell a story. They know how to explain their quarterly results, but they don't know how to explain what they mean.

I don't understand why people whose entire lives or their corporate success depends on communication, and yet they are led on occasion by CEOs who cannot talk their way out of a paper bag and don't care to. I know some CEOs who are outstanding communicators, and those individuals have a much better time with shareholders, have a much better time with the media, and, most importantly, with their consumers and the general public, because they know how to explain the benefits; they know how to put things in context. But there are so many CEOs that only know how to talk about numbers. Numbers don't mean anything. You talk about billions and tax procedures and all sorts of acronyms, and the only people who understand that are government bureaucrats and accountants. Americans don't want to hear the language of accountants; they want to hear the language of teachers and social workers.

Do you think Republicans do this better than Democrats?   45

That is brand new. When I started in this business, everybody said the Democrats were the better communicators because they sounded like social workers, and Republicans were awful because they sounded like morticians. In some cases. they actually dressed like morticians. That has changed over the last 10 years. Bill Clinton brought the change in the Democratic Party, and George W. Bush brought a significant change in the Republican Party: that it was not enough to have a superior policy, or it was not enough to have all the facts at your fingertips; it became essential that you be able to communicate that on a one-to-one basis, as individuals on a personal level rather than a philosophical or ideological level.

There are people still in the Republican Party that I believe practice the communication of anger, of disappointment, of regret, of pain, of sorrow, of suffering. That's not what the American people want to hear. For 20 years, the Democrats were effective at the communication of hope and things that are positive. I asked Republicans at one point to do this little test, to turn down the television set in a debate between Republicans and Democrats, just look at the two individuals—which one would you want to hang out with? Which one would you want to have a beer with? Which one would you want as your uncle, or who would you want to hang out with at Thanksgiving? For years the Democratic candidate was the one that smiled; the Republican candidate was the one that was angry. Now, there are always exceptions to this, and I'm sure you can come up with 10 of them. But basically, Republicans practiced the politics of anger, and Democrats practiced the politics of hope. And all that began to change in 1994, and it finally came to fruition in 2000. And now it's the Democrats who are angry and the Republicans who are hopeful.

Who else were the visionaries?

The change in Republican language began with Newt Gingrich in 1994, and while much of his communication still came across as angry and partisan, when Newt was speaking about policy and not talking about those who opposed him, there was none better, and there has been none better. Newt Gingrich had the ability to explain a very complicated process in very clear-cut, common-sense ways, unlike anyone I've ever seen. He explained the difference between taxing and spending. He explained the difference between investment and savings. He explained the difference between a weak foreign policy and a strong one. This is a guy who knew how to articulate a philosophical point of view in a way that just made sense. And if it wasn't coming from Newt Gingrich, you believed it; you absolutely supported it. The problem with Gingrich was he was too angry in some of his communication.

50   So what we needed was someone with that level of explanatory ability with a gentle heart and a gentle soul, and that's where George W. Bush came in. The Bush that we know now is not the Bush that ran for election in 2000. The one who ran in 2000 talked about education; talked about Social Security; talked about a kinder, gentler conservatism; talked about an inclusive conservatism. And it's exactly what the public wanted.

And you compare that with Al Gore. The Democrats became the party of the cold and the aloof. And in 2004, you look at Howard Dean and John Kerry and to a lesser extent Dick Gephardt; the Democratic Party is now the party of anger. I know that this is what happens when you're an opposition party, but that's not what Republicans did in 1994 or 2000. In '94 they offered a "contract." They offered something positive, and people voted for it. And in 2000 they offered a change, an alternative to Bill Clinton; people voted for it. George Bush attacked Al Gore a lot less than Gore attacked Bush. And now in 2004 the Democrats are making the same mistakes. We don't want our messages screamed at us. We don't want to be yelled at.

How important is keeping the consistency of the message in political language?

The advantage of working for a corporation is that it has only one message, because a product or a service doesn't speak; it's just there, and you can advertise it. The challenge in working in politics, particularly if you're working for a political party, is that everyone's a messenger. I think the best example of this, frankly, is Israel, where you can have 20 members of the Cabinet, and they've got 68 messages between them, because among the 20, all of them think that they're prime minister or will be prime minister or should be prime minister or hate the person who is prime minister. And when you have all these people saying things in a different way, nobody hears anything.

I've got a certain rule that I always teach my staff: It's not what you say; it's what people hear that matters. I may respond to you effectively, but if you edit it in such a way that they only hear the negativity of what I do, then that's all they're going to know. And so they're going to conclude that my profession isn't an honorable profession. And that's why how I say it has as much of an impact on what people think of me as what I say.

[Regarding consistency,] there's a simple rule: You say it again, and you say it again, and you say it again, and you say it again, and you say it again, and then again and again and again and again, and about the time that you're absolutely sick of saying it is about the time that your target audience has heard it for the first time. And it is so hard, but you've just got to keep repeating, because we hear so many different things—the noises from outside, the sounds, all the things that are coming into our head, the 200 cable channels and the satellite versus cable, and what we hear from our friends. We as Americans and as humans have very selective hearing and very selective memory. We only hear what we want to hear and disregard the rest.

Republicans use think tanks to come up with a lot of their messages.

The think tanks are the single worst, most undisciplined example of communication I've ever seen. Cato [Institute] still calls it the "privatization of Social Security." Heritage [Foundation] did so until a couple of years ago. Every time you use the words "privatization" and "Social Security" in the same sentence, you frighten seniors, and more of them turn against you. This is a specific and perfect example of the intellectual goo-goo heads who are more interested in policy than they were in success. Changing the word from "privatize" to "personalize," which is the work that we had done, they wouldn't accept it, because to them it was selling an idea short.

They would rather communicate their way and lose the issue than communicate in a sensible way and win. The fact is, ideology and communication more often than not run into each other rather than complement each other. Principle and communication work together. Ideology and communication often work apart.

Tell me about your work for Rudy Giuliani.

Rudy Giuliani hired me because I was recommended by his political consultant and because I love baseball. I hate to admit this, but I brought my baseball card collection to show him, because I'd heard he was a fanatic Yankee fan, and I figured this would be a way that we could bond. We ended up talking for 22 minutes. My whole interview with Rudy Giuliani in 1993 lasted for 22 minutes, and at least 19 of the 22 minutes was focused on baseball. So I don't know if he got it right or wrong; all I know is that this was a guy who understood the value of words and understood the value of language, but even more than that, it's the power of personality. You know, you have asked me what matters in research and how do you apply different components.

What matters most in politics is personality. It's not issues; it's not image. It's who you are and what you represent. And this guy, from the very beginning of his administration, even if people disagreed with what he was doing, they trusted him to do it, and even if they didn't like him, they respected him.

My job as a pollster is to understand what really matters. Those levers of importance—sometimes they're called levers; sometimes they're called triggers. What causes people to buy a product? What causes someone to pull a lever and get them to vote? I need to know the specifics of that. And in politics, more often than not, it's about the personality and the character of the individual rather than where they stand, and that's exactly the opposite of what your viewers will think.

Did you help him?

Part of the task is using language and using speeches and using photo ops and using the power of campaign to convey a specific message. And my job in '93 and '97 was to explain to the campaign what the public wanted and to help explain to the public that that's exactly what he was offering. A pollster, a marketer, someone who is the explainer of public opinion, has the ability to inform somebody like Rudy Giuliani [of] what really matters to the public, and so that makes Rudy Giuliani an even better candidate.

Can you talk about how you've applied your approach to the use of language to corporate America?

65 I've done reasonably well over the last 10 years because I took the strategy of language and politics and applied it to the corporate world, which has never been done before. Up to this point, the only people who ever communicated were those little 30-second characters, the little Alka-Seltzer guy or the StaPuf, whatever his name is.

And were your ideas well received in corporate America?

Oh, you have no idea. I am amazed at how eager the CEOs of the biggest companies are today to communicate as effectively as possible, to employ the skills and the language of what you saw right here earlier. They want to know that they can talk to a shareholder one-on-one, not just through their head but also through their heart. They want to know that they can reach their consumer not just on an intellectual basis, but on an emotional basis. In fact, I'd argue that CEOs, with all the corporate scandals that have taken place, are more interested in effective communication than even political people, because corporate people are interested in the bottom line, and so for them good words, good phrases, good presentation matter more than anything.

If we're getting information from 200 cable channels, if we're talking to 200 people a day, there are so many different messages that are cluttering our heads. It's the same way in corporate America. If a CEO speaks and no one hears it, it doesn't matter. And so they're looking for people like me to help them cut through the clutter, to help them explain and educate why their product or their service or their company is better. And the challenge for CEOs is that they generally came up through the ranks by being good numbers people. And I have seen 99 out of 100 cases, if you're a good numbers person, you're a bad language person.

What kind of reception do you get from their marketing departments?

There are two people that tend to beat up on me. One are the ideologues, 70 particularly in the far left or the far right, who don't want to communicate to everybody; they don't want to be loved; they don't even want to be respected. They want to say it their own way, and they don't like people like me who challenge the way they communicate their policies, their platforms or their principles. The other people who beat me up are the market research people in some of these big companies, because they don't understand language.

The problem with the job and the service that I provide is that I have to be involved in it. I can't write a memo from somebody else's focus group. I can't do this from traditional polling of 1,000 people on the telephone. I have to be able to hear it. Traditional market researchers are cold and calculating and scientific. In this business of language, you have to have a heart, and you have to have emotion, and you have to be willing to become what you are studying, no matter what it puts you through.

So the main point is emotion.

It's all emotion. But there's nothing wrong with emotion. When we are in love, we are not rational; we are emotional. When we are on vacation, we are not rational; we are emotional. When we are happy, we are not [rational]. In fact, in more cases than not, when we are rational, we're actually unhappy. Emotion is good; passion is good. Being into what we're into, provided that it's a healthy pursuit, it's a good thing.

But if emotion is the main point, why go for the words?

Because the words provide the emotions. 75

Words are keys to the emotions?

Yeah. You call it keys, but my job is to look for the words that trigger the emotion. Words alone can be found in a dictionary or a telephone book, but words with emotion can change destiny, can change life as we know it. We know it has changed history; we know it has changed behavior; we know that it can start a war or stop it. We know that words and emotion together are the most powerful force known to mankind.

What new directions do you see for market research like yours?

Part of what market research and the understanding of language that has not been exploited sufficiently is actually in the courtroom. There are jury consultants and there are message consultants for trials, but not to the degree that it's been applied to politics and the corporate world. This is where people are going next, and frankly, this is where I'm going next. There's a lot of money with a lot of big law firms that have a tremendous amount at stake by getting the right language to convince the right jury that my client is either innocent or that the opposition is guilty.

Things to Do with the Reading

1. Another of "the persuaders" interviewed in the PBS series from which this interview was taken commented that the influx of marketing and advertising into politics has created an environment in which "the principal of democracy yields to the practice of demography." How would you paraphrase that remark? (See PARAPHRASE × 3 in Chapter 2.) And how would Luntz respond to that charge? Write an essay in answer to these two questions. As you do so, review Borick's discussion at the beginning of "On Political Labels" on Madisonian versus Jeffersonian views on democracy. Whose point of view is Luntz closer to and SO WHAT?

2. If you were to do THE METHOD on Luntz's interview (see Chapter 1), you would undoubtedly discover repetitions of such terms as the heart, emotion, and passion, which comprise a strand we might label "Emotion" (including as well enthusiasm, empathy, feeling, etc.) and which constitute half of an organizing contrast opposed to what Luntz names "Intellect." (See paragraph 8: "80 percent of our life is emotion, and only 20 percent is intellect.")

   Write an essay in which you account for the emphasis Luntz places on emotion. How does the language of emotion figure in the way that Luntz thinks about politics, and more, about winning in the political arena? What, in short, is the logic of his argument about emotion?

3. Toward the end of the interview, in response to a question about working for Rudy Giuliani, Luntz says, "What matters most in politics is personality. It's not the issues; it's not image. It's who you are and what you represent" (paragraph 60). Rhetoricians study the role that a speaker's character plays in his or her ability to persuade others under the category "ethos," a word that comes from the Greek for "character, a person's nature or disposition" (OED). (See the section of Chapter 1 entitled "Ethos and Analysis" for a discussion of ethos.)

   Write an essay on what we might call the "ethos strand" in the Luntz interview. Note places where Luntz seems to be supplying language or information (especially biographical information) designed to win readers and listeners through winning their support for his character and personality. Consider, for example, what Luntz says in response to the question "Who hired you?" See also the personal information he offers when explaining why he works for pharmaceutical companies. What kind of ethos is Luntz trying to establish? What possible criticisms of Luntz might this ethos help him to deflect? Given that Luntz has a PhD in political science from Oxford, why do you think he refers to intellectuals as "goo-goo heads" in his response to a question about Republican think tanks?

4. **Link:** Write an essay in which you put Orwell's arguments in "Politics and the English Language" into conversation with Luntz's arguments. Interestingly, in an interview with Terry Gross on NPR's Fresh Air in 2007, Luntz offered an unconventional redefinition of Orwellian:

> Everything I do in terms of language has to be accurate. It's to those who believe in clarity and one of the things I would very much encourage listeners to do is to read George Orwell's essay 'On Language' [sic]. The average American assumes that being Orwellian is a negative. That being Orwellian means that you mislead. If you read, "On Language" "To be 'Orwellian' is to speak with absolute clarity, to be succinct, to explain what the event is, to talk about what triggers something happening, and to do so without any kind of pejorative whatsoever."

Consider, for example, what Orwell might say to Luntz on Luntz's assertion, "I don't believe that good language can obscure a bad product." Luntz does not here define what he means by "good language," but elsewhere in the piece he talks about using "traditional, simple, clear-cut words of the English language" (paragraph 18). He says that what Americans want is clarity: "Be clear with us. Be straight with us" (paragraph 38). He also says that his job is "to look for the words that trigger emotion." Presumably, Orwell would agree with these criteria for good language, since he is opposed to language that hides its real intent and that seeks to soften people's response to what is being talked about—the brutality of war, for example. But Orwell also speaks of language "as an instrument for expressing and not for concealing or preventing thought." Luntz says that changing the phrase "estate tax" to "death tax" is a clarification and does not obscure. Would Orwell agree with Luntz that this change is a clarification and that it does not, in Orwell's terms, conceal and prevent thought? Why or why not?

George Lakoff and Elisabeth Wehling

Obama Versus Romney: The Framing Matchup, Round One

This blog entry by the influential cognitive linguist George Lakoff and Elisabeth Wehling, his associate at the University of California–Berkeley, offers an excellent definition by example of framing, one of the keywords for this chapter. It does so in the context of their assessment of the presidential candidates' performances at their first debate. Lakoff and Wehling also co-author *The Little Blue Book. The Essential Guide to Thinking and Talking Democratic* (2012). Lakoff is most famous for his 1980 book *Metaphors We Live By*, in which he demonstrates the role of metaphors as powerful conceptual tools that shape our thinking. As the blog post makes clear with the concept of framing, Lakoff locates his focus on metaphor in a profoundly moral context.

1 Framing is (or should be) about moral values, deep truths, and the policies that flow from them.

As of their kickoff speeches in Ohio, Romney and Obama have both chosen economics as their major campaign theme. And thus the question of how they frame the economy will be crucial throughout the campaign. Their two speeches could not be more different.

Where Romney talks morality (conservative style), Obama mainly talks policy. Where Romney reframes Obama, Obama does not reframe Romney. In fact, he reinforces Romney's frames in the first part of his speech by repeating Romney's language word for word – without spelling out his own values explicitly.

Where Romney's framing is moral, simple and straightforward, Obama's is policy-oriented, filled with numbers, details, and so many proposals that they challenge ordinary understanding.

5 Where Obama talks mainly about economic fairness, Romney reframes it as economic freedom.

Here's a discussion of Obama's speech.

Obama began his kickoff campaign speech in Cleveland stating that he is "in complete agreement" with Romney: "This election is about our economic future. Yes, foreign policy matters. Social issues matter. But more than anything else, this election presents a choice between two fundamentally different visions" regarding economic policy.

Obama's strategy is to pin the Bush economic disaster on Romney, with good reason, since Romney has essentially the same policies as Bush. Since

"Obama vs. Romney: Framing Matchup, Round One" by George Lakoff and Elisabeth Wehling, The Little Blue Blog, June 18, 2012. Reprinted by permission of the authors.

Obama has not consistently pinned the blame on Bush over the past four years, he comes off as defensive.

Romney's strategy is to pin the disaster on Obama. He uses the Caretaker Metaphor — Obama has been the national caretaker, so the present condition is his responsibility. Since Obama started out assuming a caretaker's responsibility, it is difficult for him to escape the frame now. He should have avoided it from the beginning. Pinning the disaster on Bush is possible, but it will take a lot of repetition, not just by the president, but by Democrats in general. Not just a repetition of economic facts, but of the moral differences that led to both the Bush disaster and the Obama attempt to recoup.

Perhaps the most important omission from the Obama speech was any overt mention of The Public — everything that our citizenry as a whole provides to all, e.g., roads, bridges, infrastructure, education, protection, a health system, and systems for communication, energy development and supply, and so on. The Private — private life and private enterprise — depends on The Public. There is no economic freedom without all of this. So-called "free enterprise" is not free. A free market economy depends on a strong Public. This is a deep truth, easy to recognize. It undercuts Romney's central pitch, that is it private enterprise alone that has made our country great, and that as much as possible of The Public should be eliminated. 10

Romney calls free enterprise "one of the greatest forces of good this world has ever known." In reality, America free enterprise has always required The Public.

Romney attacks The Public, speaking of "the heavy hand of government" and "the invisible boot of government." The contrast is with the putative "invisible hand" of the market — which leads to the good of all if everyone follows their self-interest and the market's natural force is not interfered with. Romney's "invisible boot" evokes the image of a storm trooper's boot on your neck. The government is the storm trooper, your enemy. You are weak and in an impossible position. You can't move — a metaphor for being held back and not being able to freely engage in the economy. Romney uses the frame consistently: "The federal establishment," he says, "has never seemed so hostile." The Public is an "establishment"—an undemocratic institution—which is the enemy of the people. It is implicit in this frame that the government is not the people.

Romney's assumption here is that democracy is based on the "liberty" to seek one's self-interest with minimal regard to the interests or well being of others. People who are good at this will succeed, and they deserve to. People who are not good at this will fail, and they should. In Romney's speech, "The Freedom to Dream," he used the word "freedom" 29 times. This is what he means.

Although Obama intends to argue against this understanding, he unintentionally feeds it. He does so in three ways: First, by accepting and reinforcing many of Romney's central frames (often by negating them); second, by moving to the right in his own argumentation; and third, by not spelling out his own moral principles explicitly right from the start.

15   First, here are three examples of Obama repeating Romney's frames (in bold):

"Governor Romney and his allies in Congress **believe deeply in the theory that the best way to grow the economy is from the top down.**"

"They maintain that **if we eliminate most regulations, if we cut taxes by trillions of dollars, if we strip down government to national security and a few other basic functions, the power of businesses to create jobs and prosperity will be unleashed and that will automatically benefit us all.**"

Republicans "**believe that if you simply take away regulations and cut taxes by trillions of dollars, the market will solve all of our problems on its own.**"

Though Obama's statements are supposed to be taken sarcastically, they actually are positive, straightforward, easy to understand versions of Romney's positions and beliefs.

Second, Obama argues for his willingness to compromise by giving examples of his "bipartisanship," where he did just what conservatives wanted and had argued for as the right thing to do: cutting taxes and eliminating regulations. Here is Obama:

20   "Understand, despite what you hear from my opponent, this has never been a vision about how government creates jobs or has the answers to all our problems. Over the last three years, I've cut taxes for the typical working family by $3,600. I've cut taxes for small businesses 18 times. I have approved fewer regulations in the first three years of my presidency than my Republican predecessor did in his."

Conservatives talk endlessly about "cutting spending." The president uses the same frame: "I've signed a law that cuts spending and reduces our deficit by $2 trillion."

Language is important here, as well as policy. "Spending" is a conservative term; it suggests a needless draining of financial resources, a waste of money. But most of that money was "invested" in our people or used to maintain our infrastructure — not just "spent." Though a tax reduction for working families may very well have been a good idea, the term "cutting taxes" is a conservative term, suggesting that taxes in general are bad and should be "cut."

There is of course a deeper problem here. Anyone this me-too-conservatism might appeal to would most likely vote for a real conservative over Obama.

Third, in his speech, the president gives a long list of perfectly reasonable policies: ending oil subsidies, investing in education, hiring more teachers and pay them better, not deporting young immigrants, investing in clean energy, encouraging energy innovation, supporting R&D tax credits, rebuilding crumbling infrastructure, reforming the tax code, eliminating tax breaks for businesses that ship jobs overseas, strengthening Medicare and Medicaid, and so on.

No such list is going to be remembered by most of those who heard it. 25 Moreover, what is said first matters; it sets the moral frame. In his speech, Obama first repeats the Romney frames, opposes them to numbers and policy lists, and only at the end talks about his own moral vision.

What could Obama have done better?

Frame everything from his own moral perspective, including Romney's positions and assumptions. Avoid the Romney language. Start with his own moral position, which he stated beautifully in his 2008 campaign but has since dropped: That democracy is based on empathy (citizens caring about fellow citizens), responsibility both for oneself and others, and an ethic of excellence (doing one's best not just for oneself, but for one's family, community, and country).

What else?

Repeat the truth that The Private depends on The Public. It is The Public that provides economic freedom. Give a vision of responsible, progressive business. Talk freedom — as well as fairness. Point out that the hoarding of wealth by the 1 percent kills opportunity, as Joseph Stieglitz has discussed at length. Speak of an "Economy for All — not just rich bankers, managers, and job killers like private equity firms." Yes, Romney and those like him are job killers. Say it. Point out that during the economic recovery of 2010, 93 percent of the additional income went to the richest 1 percent of taxpayers. Stop using "top" to mean rich. "Top" suggests high morality, merit, and ability. "Bottom" signifies the opposite.

We are now in a situation where conservatives have framed almost every 30 issue. The least Democrats can do is to refuse to repeat their language and so help them.

Things to Do with the Reading

1. Do THE METHOD (see Chapter 1) on Lakoff and Wehling's blog post, "Obama vs. Romney: The Framing Matchup, Round One." What repeats? What goes with what (strands)? What's opposed to what (binaries)? And SO WHAT? How many times, for example, does the word "moral" repeat in the essay? To what is the word "moral" opposed, and So What? Pay particular attention to binaries in the essay, starting with the ones in the first four paragraphs. Then write a paragraph saying what you think is the most significant binary in the piece and why you think so.

2. Lakoff and Wehling are interested in what they call "reframing." Use examples from the essay to explain what reframing means. Think about reframing in the context of REFORMULATING BINARIES in Chapter 2. How do the essay's suggested reframings accord with the definition of liberal thinking in Borick's essay on political labels with which this chapter began?

3. **Link:** What problems do Lakoff and Wehling find with the use of the word "top" as in "top 1%"? What perspective would Bennett's discussion of primary metaphors add to the matter of using the word "top"?

4. **Link Across Chapters:** The public/private binary features prominently in Lakoff and Wehling's analysis and in other chapters in this book. See, for example, Kunstler's essay "The Public Realm and the Common Good" in Chapter 13, Places and Spaces: Cities and Suburbs. Consider how Kunstler frames the issue of public vs. private space in his essay. Find some sentences in Kunstler's essay to analyze in the terms provided by Lakoff and Wehling and by Borick.

5. **Application:** Lakoff and Wehling's essay and the two that follow it (by Green and Nunberg) address the politics of language in Obama's campaign against Mitt Romney for reelection to the presidency. What, if anything, has changed since that time in the way that liberals and their conservative political opponents are waging framing wars? Find a recent speech of some significance by Obama or another significant Democratic figure and analyze the extent to which he or she is using verbal strategies in the ways that Lakoff and others have proposed. You might also consider the extent to which a conservative politician is continuing to frame key words in the way that Lakoff and Wehling describe.

David Green

Four Words That Will Decide the Election

In this incisive look into the keywords of the last presidential election, the linguist David Green offers us a vision of what, in a recent scholarly article in *The American Interest*, he calls "linguistic gridlock." He defines this condition as one "in which bipartisan dialogue has been replaced by competing efforts to manipulate voters with loaded vocabularies" ("A Call to Linguistic Disobedience"). Focusing on four primary keywords, Green makes the case that "framing is what this election is about," and he is keenly aware of the ironies that result.

If there is anyone out there who still doubts that framing is what this election is   1
about, just look at the vocabularies of the contending parties. It's already down to a non-stop battle of mantras, buzzwords, epithets and self-designations.

For Mitt Romney, it's about "the entitlement society" versus "the opportunity society." For Barack Obama, it's about "a make-or-break moment for the middle class." For Republican surrogates, it's about defeating "big unions" and "Euro-socialists." For their Democratic counterparts, it's about resisting the onslaught of the "radical right."

There is a certain symmetry to it. Each side paints the other as out of touch with the American mainstream. Each accuses the other of wanting to lead the country down an unsustainable path. Each side tries to frame issues so as to ignite emotional responses that will immunize voters against whatever arguments the other side offers.

Yet there is also a profound asymmetry at work. Whether Democrats admit it or not, Republicans have been far more effective at emotional mobilization. Republicans have long since grasped what Democrats are still puzzling over. You choose the words that trigger the emotions. And the four words at the heart of Republican strategy this year are "entitlements," "redistribution," and "job creators." Why those four? Because they load the dice most effectively against the President. To be in favor of "entitlements" is to favor giving people things to which they aren't really entitled, such as other people's money. To favor "redistribution" is to favor taking away what hardworking people have earned and giving it to people who don't truly earn anything. And to tax "job creators" is to kill any hope of economic recovery.

And how have Democrats responded? It's a "war on women," it's a "war   5
on the middle class," it's an attempt to "bring back the policies that got us into this mess." That plays fine with the choir, but it's not bringing a lot of new people into church. Why not? Because however justified as policy arguments,

"Four Words That Will Decide the Election" by David Green, Wordpress.com, July 2012. Reprinted by permission of the author.

the first two mantras come across as insulting and the third asks people to ignore the last three and a half years. This is not the way to trigger emotional responses among the uncommitted.

So what should Democrats be doing? Ah, the irony. While Republicans not only lionize their Dear Departed Leader but mimic his rhetorical strategy to a fault, Democrats exalt the memory of their Greatest Leader and totally ignore *his* rhetorical strategy. All Republicans know that Ronald Reagan's stock in trade was denigrative language. "Government isn't the solution; government is the problem." Yet how many Democrats have any *idea* of Franklin Delano Roosevelt's verbal strategy? From the show they're putting on, I'd say very few to none. A history lesson for Democrats:

Against whom did F.D.R. run in 1932? That's easy. The ultimate conservative, Herbert Hoover. WRONG. Hoover never called himself a conservative in 1932. Hard as it may be for Democrats to believe, throughout his career as both Secretary of Commerce and President, Hoover always called himself a "progressive" and a "liberal." In its review of his book *American Individualism*, the *New York Times* itself stated: "His liberalism, his progressivism, is a thing of the heart no less than of the head." If no less an authority than the *New York Times* validated Hoover's credentials as a progressive and a liberal, WHAT HAPPENED IN 1932, and how does it relate to 2012?

Remember how Reagan took the cherished self-designation of the Democrats and turned it into a bad label, an epithet? "It's time to . . . use the dreaded L-word; to say the policies of our opposition . . . are liberal, liberal, liberal." And a dreaded word it has been ever since. How many Democrats are even running this year as self-styled liberals?

Roosevelt *could have* done the same in 1932. He could have turned Hoover's liberal label into a bad label, an epithet. Hoover was far more vulnerable in 1932 than were the Democrats of the 1980s. It would have been easy for F.D.R. to attack Hoover's "liberal failures" and position himself as a "conservative," as a restorer of traditional American values. Indeed, many historians have since analyzed the New Deal in terms of F.D.R.'s conserving, indeed saving, American capitalism. So why didn't he go that road?

10   Because he knew better. Because he understood that his strongest emotional appeal was to challenge Hoover's right to his own label. This he did *immediately* and *consistently*, starting with his nomination acceptance speech in which he proclaimed the Democratic Party "the bearer of liberalism and of progress" and the "party of liberal thought, of planned action," while attacking Hoover and the Republican leadership as "reactionary." F.D.R. took away Hoover's liberal label, redefined it and made it his own. It worked so brilliantly that Hoover spent the next twelve years of his life in a vain effort to recapture his cherished liberal label. He never succeeded. Finally, after F.D.R.'s death, Hoover gave up and at age 71 started calling himself a conservative.

So what's the lesson for Democrats in 2012? Do what F.D.R. did. Take away Republican vocabulary. Turn it around on them, redefine their own words as F.D.R. did eighty years ago. Entitlements? Who's the *real* entitlement candidate? Who's proposing continued, massive subsidies to big corporations from oil companies to agribusiness, subsidies to which those corporations feel they're *entitled*? Who's proposing indefinite continuation of ridiculously low tax rates for the wealthiest Americans, millionaires and billionaires who also feel *entitled* to them? Who's in favor of continuing to fatten up the industrial-military complex with huge government contracts to which those corporations feel *entitled*? And when you frame it that way, who's the *real* opportunity candidate?

We're not talking semantics here; we're talking framing. We're talking politics. We're talking emotional mobilization. We're talking what F.D.R. did best. He turned the vocabulary of his opponents to his own advantage and their detriment.

The same holds true for word number two: redistribution. Who's the *real* redistribution candidate? The way Republicans are using the word, they're igniting huge emotional reactions against the idea of redistributing wealth *downward*. What Democrats have failed to grasp is both the necessity and the opportunity of turning that very word around on the Republicans. Romney is hugely vulnerable on the issue of redistributing wealth *upward*. That's what his tax break policies are about. That's what his spending cuts are about. That's what his entire economic program is about. All the statistics are already there proving how dramatically the wealth has been redistributed *upward* ever since the Reagan era, and Romney wants to continue that. What hasn't happened is that Democrats haven't framed that data using Romney's own vocabulary. Again, we're not talking semantics; we're talking emotional mobilization. Democrats need to take over the word redistribution, and they need to do it now.

Finally, words three and four: job creators. Tailor-made for Democrats. What have big corporations done most effectively over the last twenty years? Romney's corporate supporters have been creating jobs, all right, in China, India, the Philippines, Mexico, Cambodia, Singapore, Vietnam – everywhere *but* the United States. At the same time, Republicans in Congress have consistently sabotaged the administration's efforts to create jobs at home, and then blamed the President for lack of job creation. Again, the vocabulary is tailor-made for a Democratic counterattack. The Republicans are great at creating jobs *outside* the United States, and every time they create a job *outside* the United States they kill a job *inside* the United States. So who is the *real* job creator?

And the biggest irony of all? Who said, "Don't retreat; reload"? She was 15 right, but what she didn't realize is that it works both ways. Reload indeed, but with the other side's ammunition. Democrats should not only *let* Republicans compete with them over the vocabulary; they should *force* them to. Democrats should get off the defensive and go on the offensive, using the opposition's own weaponry. They should be making Republicans afraid even to use those words. And when Republicans start to run away, Democrats should chase after them with the same weaponry. "Republicans don't want to talk about entitlements any more, now that the American people realize who the real entitlement candidate is. And they don't want to talk about redistribution any more, or about job creators." When Democrats reach that point, they'll know they have won.

And it not only works for the big four words; it works with other words such as "Obamacare" and "class warfare." Again, we're talking emotion here. Republicans have been yelling "Obamacare" since long before the Supreme Court decision, but they don't dare talk about "Romneycare." Well, why not? Now that the Court has rendered its decision, it's the perfect time to turn that vocabulary around. As for "class warfare," Democrats need to turn that around in the same way as they do the word redistribution.

Homework for Democrats: Go through the entire list of Republican buzz-words and turn each and every one of them against the Republicans. It not only *can* be done; it *has* to be done, because if it *isn't* done, the Republicans will win the framing war, and if they win the framing war, they win the election.

But again, it's the big four words that will be front and center for the rest of this campaign. Democrats have only two choices. They can keep running away from the ghost of Ronald Reagan and stay on the defensive, or they can finally learn from their deservedly greatest hero and do what he did so brilliantly and with such telling effect. There is no time to lose. The time to reclaim the offensive, and the vocabulary, is now.

Things to Do with the Reading

1. Like Borick's essay on political labels, Green's essay traces the evolution of the political label "liberal" and, like Lakoff and Wehling, Green offers advice on how liberals might go about redefining the favored words of their conservative opponents. In a spin on Sarah Palin's charge to her fellow Republicans, "Don't retreat; reload," Green argues that Democrats should reload "with the other side's ammunition" (paragraph 15). Explain what this imperative means. And what does Green mean when he says that FDR succeeded by challenging "Hoover's right to his own label" (paragraph 10)?

2. **Link:** What does Green mean when he says "we're talking emotion here" (paragraph 16)? Which examples from Green's essay best illustrate what he means by "emotional mobilization" (paragraph 4)? To what extent would Frank Luntz agree with Green's recommendations?

(What, for example, does Luntz say about emotion?) Then, apply the strategy called looking for DIFFERENCE WITHIN SIMILARITY (in Chapter 3). What remarks of Luntz's in the interview suggest that he might offer different advice?

3. Application: Green and other analysts in this unit are interested in what Green calls "buzzwords." As the Luntz interview reveals, a successful strategy is to pick a set of key terms, define them in the way that best suits your purposes, and then just keep repeating the same message. To what extent have the buzzwords of each party—Democratic and Republican—changed or remained the same since the reelection campaign?

Geoffrey Nunberg

With Ryan's Ascent: A Few Thoughts on "Entitlement"

This is the second brief essay by Geoffrey Nunberg in this volume; both were originally radio pieces for National Public Radio's *Fresh Air*, where Nunberg has been a longtime commentator on language in American culture. He is also the author of many books, both scholarly and popular, on this subject. Most recently, in 2012 he published *Ascent of the A-Word: Assholism, the First Sixty Years*—a fascinating study of the word, its history, what it means now, and how it reveals us. He does the same thing, in miniature, in the paragraphs below, focusing on entitlement, a key word as well for both David Green and Lakoff & Wehling in the previous two readings in this chapter. People have said that Mitt Romney's selection of Wisconsin Rep. Paul Ryan as his running mate created an opportunity to hold what Ryan likes to call an "adult conversation" about entitlement spending. But bear in mind that "entitlement" doesn't put all its cards on the table. Like a lot of effective political language, it enables you to slip from one idea to another without ever letting on that you've changed the subject.

1   "Entitlement" originally had two separate meanings, which entered the language along very different paths. One sense of the word was an obscure political legalism until the advent of the Great Society programs that some economists called "uncontrollables." Technically, entitlements are just programs that provide benefits that aren't subject to budgetary discretion. But the word also implied that the recipients had a moral right to the benefits. As LBJ said in justifying Medicare: "By God, you can't treat Grandma this way. She's entitled to it."

The negative connotations of the word arose in another, very distant corner of the language, when psychologists began to use a different notion of entitlement as a diagnostic for narcissism. Both of those words entered everyday usage in the late 1970s, with a big boost from Christopher Lasch's 1979 best-seller *The Culture of Narcissism*, an indictment of the pathological self-absorption of American life. By the early '80s, you no longer had to preface "sense of entitlement" with "unwarranted" or "bloated." That was implicit in the word "entitlement" itself, which had become the epithet of choice whenever you wanted to scold a group like the baby boomers for their superficiality and selfishness.

"With Ryan's Ascent, a Few Thoughts on 'Entitlement'" by Geoffrey Nunberg, NPR.org, 8/12/12. Reprinted by permission.

True, these polemics belong to an ancient genre. People may not have talked about entitlement as such before the boomers and Generation X. But critics were saying similar things about the generations of the '50s, of the '20s, of the 1890s, and so on back to Generations A and B. It's hard to think of any age when people weren't saying: "Kids today, I'm here to tell you."

Still, "entitled" isn't quite the same as time-honored reproaches like "spoiled." Like "narcissistic," "entitled" adds a tone of clinical authority. If you want to know if someone is spoiled, you ask your grandmother; if you want to know if they've got a sense of entitlement, you ask Dr. Joyce. And while "spoiled" suggests someone at the mercy of infantile needs, a sense of entitlement implies a legal or moral claim. When you give a kid who's spoiled a B minus on his final, he comes to your office hours and throws a tantrum about how he needs an A to get into medical school. When you give the same grade to a kid with a sense of entitlement, you're apt to get a call from the family lawyer.

The two words spread the blame around differently, too. Spoiling begins 5 and ends at home. But while parents get a lot of the blame for creating entitled children, too, critics of the entitlement epidemic find lots of other culprits for it—from the media-fed obsession with celebrity to schools that overpraise their pupils, and so on to feminism, affirmative action, plastic surgery, cheap credit cards and Wikipedia.

But it's only when critics get to the role of government that the two meanings of "entitlement" start to seep into each other. On the one hand, the psychological sense of the word colors its governmental meaning. When people fulminate about the cost of government entitlements these days, there's often the implicit modifier "unearned" lurking in the background. And that in turn makes it easier to think of those programs as the cause of a wider social malaise—that they create what critics call a "culture of dependency" or a class of "takers," which are basically ways of referring to what the Victorians called the undeserving poor.

That isn't a new argument. The early opponents of Social Security charged that it would discourage individual thrift and reduce Americans to the level of Europeans. But now the language itself helps make the argument, by using the same word for the political cause and the cultural effects. You can deplore "the entitlement society" without actually having to say whether you mean the social or political sense of the word, or even acknowledging that there's any difference. It's a strategic rewriting of linguistic history, as if we call the programs entitlements simply because people feel entitled to them.

But to make that linguistic fusion work, you have to bend the meanings of the words to fit. When people rail about the cost of government entitlements, they're thinking of social benefit programs like Medicare, not the price supports or the tax breaks that some economists call hidden entitlements. And what people call the culture of entitlement is elastic enough to include both the high school senior who's been told he has a right to get into Harvard and the out-of-work plumber who isn't bothering to look for a job because he knows his unemployment check is in the mail. But it rarely stretches to include the hedge-fund manager who makes a life model of Ayn Rand's Howard Roark, who is the most conspicuous monster of entitlement in all of modern American literature.

No question, it would be useful to have an adult conversation about entitlement and entitlements. Not that politicians or pundits are about to abandon the words or the semantic sleight of hand that's built into them. But with more people paying close attention, those moves may be a little harder to get away with.

Things to Do with the Reading

1. What are the implications and connotations of Paul Ryan's use of the phrase "adult conversation"?

2. Nunberg begins his essay on the word entitlement with a metaphor: "'entitlement' doesn't put all its cards on the table." Make the logic of this metaphor explicit, and then explain which cards, according to Nunberg, users of the word "entitlement" are hiding.

3. Link: Christopher Borick in his essay "On Political Labels" quotes modern conservative thinker Russell Kirk: "Men are created different; and a government which ignores this law becomes an unjust government, for it sacrifices nobility to mediocrity; it pulls down the aspiring natures to gratify the inferior natures" (paragraph 9). Borick goes on to say, "In other words, for conservatives, government is not a force for improving the human condition; rather it's an anchor on the driving force of individual motivation." Use the language of these quotations to explain which of the meanings of entitlement, as defined by Nunberg, a conservative like Paul Ryan would be likely to favor. Be sure to provide the reasons for the answer you give. Include in your answer some paraphrase of (synonyms for) the words entitlement, spoiled, and narcissism.

Jill Lepore

The Lie Factory: How Politics Became a Business

This essay by Harvard historian Jill Lepore tells the story, as the subtitle suggests, of "how politics became a business." Lepore focuses on the founders of political consulting, Leone Baxter and Clem Whitaker, and their company, Campaigns, Inc. Coming near the end of this unit, the essay offers a rich context for the various "framers"—Luntz, Lakoff and Wehling, Green, and Nunberg—whose work has been included here. Lepore is the author of eight books, most recently a life of Jane Franklin, sister of Benjamin, who was situated, like many of Lepore's subjects, on the margins of official history. (The book was a finalist for the 2013 National Book Award for Nonfiction.) She is also a frequent contributor to *The New Yorker*, where this essay first appeared in 2012.

"I, Governor of California, and How I Ended Poverty," by Upton Sinclair, is prob- 1 ably the most thrilling piece of campaign literature ever written. Instead of the usual flummery, Sinclair, the author of forty-seven books, including, most famously, "The Jungle," wrote a work of fiction. "I, Governor of California," published in 1933, announced Sinclair's gubernatorial bid in the form of a history of the future, in which Sinclair is elected governor in 1934, and by 1938 has eradicated poverty. "So far as I know," the author remarked, "this is the first time an historian has set out to make his history true."

It was only sixty-four pages, but it sold a hundred and fifty thousand copies in four months. Chapter 1: "On an evening in August, 1933, there took place a conference attended by five members of the County Central Committee of the Democratic party, Sixtieth Assembly District of the State of California." That might not sound like a page-turner, unless you remember that at the time California was a one-party state: in 1931, almost all of the hundred and twenty seats in the state legislature were held by Republicans; not a single Democrat held a statewide office. Also useful to recall: the unemployment rate in the state was twenty-nine per cent. Back to that meeting in August, 1933: "The purpose was to consider with Upton Sinclair the possibility of his registering as a Democrat and becoming the candidate of the party for Governor of California." What if Sinclair, a lifelong socialist, ran as a Democrat? That's one nifty plot twist.

The pace really picks up after Sinclair adopts an acronymic campaign slogan, "END POVERTY IN CALIFORNIA" ("It was pointed out that the initials of these words spell 'EPIC'"); picks a campaign emblem, passing over the eagle and the hawk ("I personally can get up no enthusiasm for any kind of bird of

Copyright © 2012 by Jill Lepore. "The Lie Factory: How Politics Became a Business" was first published in The New Yorker (September 24, 2012).

prey," the candidate says) in favor of the busy bee ("she not only works hard but has means to defend herself"); explains a program of coöperative factories and farms that would implement his philosophy of "production for use" rather than for profit; proposes killing the sales tax while levying something like a thirty-per-cent income tax on anyone earning more than fifty thousand dollars a year; and promises not only to raise hell but also, preposterously, to win.

All the same, it was a shock to pretty much everyone that, in August of 1934, Sinclair won the Democratic nomination, with more votes than any primary candidate in California had ever won before. That happens in the novel, too, which is what made reading it so thrilling (or, for many people, so terrifying): watching what Sinclair imagined coming to pass. Chapter 4: "The news that the Democratic voters of California had committed their party to the EPIC plan caused a sensation throughout the country." True! "It resulted in wide discussion of the plan in the magazines, and the formation of an EPIC Committee for the Nation." Sort of! "A statement endorsing Sinclair for Governor was signed by a hundred leading writers, and college groups were formed everywhere throughout the country to recommend the plan for their cities and states. A group of forward-looking economists endorsed the plan, and letters of support were received from a score of United States senators and some fifty congressmen." O.K., that part never happened.

5   In 1934, Sinclair explained what did happen that election year, in a non-fiction sequel called "I, Candidate for Governor, and How I Got Licked." "When I was a boy, the President of Harvard University wrote about 'the scholar in politics,'" Sinclair began. "Here is set forth how a scholar went into politics, and what happened to him." "How I Got Licked" was published in daily installments in fifty newspapers. In it, Sinclair described how, immediately after the Democratic Convention, the Los Angeles Times began running on its front page a box with an Upton Sinclair quotation in it, a practice that the paper continued, every day, for six weeks, until the opening of the polls. "Reading these boxes day after day," Sinclair wrote, "I made up my mind that the election was lost."

Sinclair got licked, he said, because the opposition ran what he called a Lie Factory. "I was told they had a dozen men searching the libraries and reading every word I had ever published." They'd find lines he'd written, speeches of fictional characters in novels, and stick them in the paper, as if Sinclair had said them. "They had a staff of political chemists at work, preparing poisons to be let loose in the California atmosphere on every one of a hundred mornings."

Actually, they had, at the time, a staff of only two, and the company wasn't called the Lie Factory. It was called Campaigns, Inc.

Campaigns, Inc., the first political-consulting firm in the history of the world, was founded, in 1933, by Clem Whitaker and Leone Baxter. Whitaker, thirty-four, had started out as a newspaperman, or, really, a newspaper boy; he was working as a reporter at the age of thirteen. By nineteen, he was city editor for the Sacramento Union and, a couple of years later, a political writer for the San Francisco Examiner. He was friendly and gangly, and had big ears, and smoked, and never stopped talking, and typed with two fingers. He started a newspaper wire service, the Capitol News Bureau, distributing stories to eighty papers. In 1930, he sold that business to the United Press. Three years later, he was, for his political ingenuity, hired by, among others, Sheridan Downey, a prominent Democrat, to help defeat a referendum sponsored by Pacific Gas and Electric.

Downey also hired Baxter, a twenty-six-year-old widow who had been a writer for the Portland Oregonian, and suggested that she and Whitaker join forces.

Baxter was small, fine-featured, red-headed, and elegant. "Oh, he was such a dear," she would say, about someone she liked. Whitaker's suits never looked like they fit him; Baxter's looked like they'd fit Audrey Hepburn. Whitaker and Baxter started doing business as Campaigns, Inc. The referendum was defeated. Whitaker separated from his wife. In 1938, he and Baxter married. They lived in Marin County, in a house with a heated swimming pool. They began every day with a two-hour breakfast to plan the day. She sometimes called him Clem; he only ever called her Baxter.

In 1934, when Sinclair won the Democratic nomination, he chose Downey 10 as his running mate. ("Uppie and Downey," the ticket was called.) Working for Downey had been an aberration for Whitaker and Baxter, people who, it was said, "work the Right side of the street." Campaigns, Inc., specialized in running political campaigns for businesses, especially monopolies like Standard Oil and Pacific Telephone and Telegraph. Pacific Gas and Electric was so impressed that it put Campaigns, Inc., on retainer.

Political consulting is often thought of as an offshoot of the advertising industry, but closer to the truth is that the advertising industry began as a form of political consulting. As the political scientist Stanley Kelley once explained, when modern advertising began, the big clients were just as interested in advancing a political agenda as a commercial one. Monopolies like Standard Oil and DuPont looked bad: they looked greedy and ruthless and, in the case of DuPont, which made munitions, sinister. They therefore hired advertising firms to sell the public on the idea of the large corporation, and, not incidentally, to advance pro-business legislation. It's this kind of thing that Sinclair was talking about when he said that American history was a battle between business and democracy, and, "So far," he wrote, "Big Business has won every skirmish."

Like most California Republicans, Clem Whitaker and Leone Baxter, who were the publicists for the California League Against Sinclairism, were horrified at the prospect of Sinclair in the governor's office.* They had to work fast. They were hired just two months before the election by George Hatfield, the candidate for lieutenant governor on a Republican ticket headed by the incumbent governor, Frank Merriam, but, mostly, they were hired to destroy Sinclair. They began by locking themselves in a room for three days with everything he had ever written. "Upton was beaten," Whitaker later said, "because he had written books." And, so, those boxes in the L.A. Times:

Sinclair on marriage:

The sanctity of marriage. . . . I have had such a belief . . . I have it no longer.

The excerpt, as Sinclair explained in "How I Got Licked," was taken from a passage in his 1911 novel, "Love's Pilgrimage," in which one character writes a heartbroken letter to a man having an affair with his wife. (The novel, which Sinclair later found greatly embarrassing, is an autobiographical account of his disastrous first marriage, which ended in 1912 when, citing his wife's adultery, he divorced her; he married his second wife in 1913; their marriage lasted until her death, in 1961.) "Sure, those quotations were irrelevant," Baxter later said. "But we had one objective: to keep him from becoming Governor."

15   Sinclair lost. He probably would have been a terrible governor. That, though, wasn't really what was at stake.

No single development has altered the workings of American democracy in the last century so much as political consulting, an industry unknown before Campaigns, Inc. In the middle decades of the twentieth century, political consultants replaced party bosses as the wielders of political power gained not by votes but by money. Whitaker and Baxter were the first people to make politics a business. "Every voter, a consumer" was the mantra of a latter-day consulting firm, but that idea came from Campaigns, Inc. Political management is now a diversified, multibillion-dollar industry of managers, speechwriters, pollsters, and advertisers who play a role in everything from this year's Presidential race to the campaigns of the candidates for your local school committee. (Campaigns, now, never end. And consultants not only run campaigns; they govern. Mitt Romney, asked by the Wall Street Journal's editorial board how he would choose his Cabinet, said that he'd probably bring in McKinsey to sort that out.) But for years Whitaker and Baxter had no competition, which is one reason that, between 1933 and 1955, they won seventy out of seventy-five campaigns. The campaigns they chose to run, and the way they decided to run them, shaped the history of California, and of the country. Campaigns, Inc., is shaping American politics still.

In 1934, Upton Sinclair got licked, but a great many End Poverty in California candidates got elected, as Democrats. California became a two-party state. Twenty-four EPIC candidates, among them a Los Angeles lawyer named Culbert Olson, took their seats in the state legislature, and, four years later, Olson, the leader of the state's EPIC caucus, was elected governor. Olson named Carey McWilliams, a Los Angeles attorney, writer, and reporter, as his chief of the California State Division of Immigration and Housing.

In 1938, McWilliams, a friend of Sinclair's, had campaigned for Olson while writing "Factories in the Field: The Story of Migratory Farm Labor in California." It reads like a nonfiction version of "The Grapes of Wrath." Both books were published in 1939. Steinbeck's was banned, and Republicans in the state legislature attempted to abolish the Division of Immigration and Housing, just to get McWilliams fired.

In 1942, Republicans backing the state's attorney general, Earl Warren, in a bid to replace Olson in the governor's office urged him to hire Whitaker and Baxter to run his campaign. Warren agreed, somewhat reluctantly. In the years since defeating Sinclairism, Whitaker and Baxter had put a few more items in their campaign tool kit. In 1939, with pamphlets like "Hoaxing the Hungry," Campaigns, Inc., had led the effort to defeat California's Proposition 1, the "Ham and Eggs" referendum, which would have instituted a three-per-cent income tax to provide a thirty-dollar-a-week pension to every citizen over fifty: ham and eggs every Thursday. (Harper's later reported, "In a typical campaign they employed ten million pamphlets and leaf-lets; 50,000 letters to 'key individuals and officers of organizations'; 70,000 inches of advertising in 700 newspapers; 3,000 spot announcements on 109 radio stations; theater slides and trailers in 160 theaters; 1,000 large billboards and 18,000 or 20,000 smaller posters.") In 1940, they produced materials for the Republican Wendell Willkie's Presidential campaign, including a speaker's manual that offered advice about how to handle Democrats in the audience: "rather than refer to the opponent as the 'Democratic Party' or 'New Deal Administration' refer to the Candidate by name only."

Whitaker and Baxter worked together flawlessly. They answered the telephone together. They read each other's mail. They swapped jobs every year: one year, Whitaker was president and Baxter vice-president; the next year, the reverse. They made heaps of money. For, say, a referendum campaign, they charged between twenty-five thousand and seventy-five thousand dollars. They required complete control of the budget for campaign expenses. (One of their rules: save seventy-five per cent of your budget for the month before Election Day.) The firm grossed about two hundred and fifty thousand dollars a year. Campaigns, Inc., was only one part of the empire. Whitaker and Baxter also ran the Clem Whitaker Advertising Agency, which charged a fifteen-per-cent commission from clients for every ad. They ran a newspaper wire service, the California Feature Service, which sent a political clipsheet every week, to fifteen hundred "thought leaders," and cartoons, editorials, and articles to three hundred newspapers. Rural newspapers were so desperate for copy that many printed whatever the California Feature Service sent them, including documents that were basically press releases disguised as editorials endorsing whatever political position Campaigns, Inc., was being paid to advocate. The trick was to send out clippings so sly that a tired editor might not notice that they were written by an advertising outfit. One California newspaper editor used to play a game with his staff, while reading the stuff. It was called "Where's the Plug?"

Whitaker and Baxter weren't just inventing new techniques; they were writing a rule book. Never lobby; woo voters instead. "Our conception of practical politics is that if you have a sound enough case to convince the folks back home, you don't have to buttonhole the Senator," Baxter explained. Make it personal: candidates are easier to sell than issues. If your position doesn't have an opposition, or if your candidate doesn't have an opponent, invent one. Once, when fighting an attempt to recall the mayor of San Francisco, Whitaker and Baxter waged a campaign against the Faceless Man—the idea was Baxter's—who might end up replacing him. Baxter drew a picture, on a tablecloth, of a fat man with a cigar poking out from beneath a face hidden by a hat, and then had him plastered on billboards all over the city, with the question "Who's Behind the Recall?" Pretend that you are the Voice of the People. Whitaker and Baxter bought radio ads, sponsored by "the Citizens Committee Against the Recall," in which an ominous voice said, "The real issue is whether the City Hall is to be turned over, lock, stock, and barrel, to an unholy alliance fronting for a faceless man." (The recall was defeated.) Attack, attack, attack. Whitaker said, "You can't wage a defensive campaign and win!"

Never underestimate the opposition. The first thing Whitaker and Baxter always did, when they took on a campaign, was to "hibernate" for a week, to write a Plan of Campaign. Then they wrote an Opposition Plan of Campaign, to anticipate the moves made against them. Every campaign needs a theme. Keep it simple. Rhyming's good. ("For Jimmy and me, vote 'yes' on 3.") Never explain anything. "The more you have to explain," Whitaker said, "the more difficult it is to win support." Say the same thing over and over again. "We assume we have to get a voter's attention seven times to make a sale," Whitaker said. Subtlety is your enemy. "Words that lean on the mind are no good," according to Baxter. "They must dent it." Simplify, simplify, simplify. "A wall goes up," Whitaker warned, "when you try to make Mr. and Mrs. Average American Citizen work or think."

Fan flames. "We need more partisanship in this country," Whitaker said. Never shy from controversy; instead, win the controversy. "The average American doesn't want to be educated; he doesn't want to improve his mind; he doesn't even want to work, consciously, at being a good citizen," Whitaker advised. "But there are two ways you can interest him in a campaign, and only two that we have ever found successful." You can put on a fight ("he likes a good hot battle, with no punches pulled"), or you can put on a show ("he likes the movies; he likes mysteries; he likes fireworks and parades"): "So if you can't fight, PUT ON A SHOW! And if you put on a good show, Mr. and Mrs. America will turn out to see it."

Winner takes all. "If you launch a campaign for a new car, your client doesn't expect you to lead the field necessarily in the first year, or even the tenth year," Whitaker once said. "But in politics, they don't pay off for PLACE OR SHOW! You have to win, if you want to stay in business."

In 1942, the problem with Earl Warren was that he was grim. Baxter said 25 that, to get women to vote for him, he and his wife had to agree to have a picture of their family taken, and publicized. Warren's wife, Nina, objected. "She didn't want to exploit her family," Baxter said. "But we knew that he had to get that family." They took a picture—Earl, Nina, and their six children. They look like the Von Trapp Family Singers. Campaigns, Inc., distributed three million copies.

Still, there was no denying that Warren was solemn, and unsmiling. Turn your liabilities into assets! Baxter said that a grave, resolute man was just the kind of man California needed, in time of war. "War-time voters live at an emotional pitch that is anything but normal," Whitaker wrote. "This must be a campaign that makes people hear the beat of drums and the thunder of bombs. . . . This must be A CALL TO ARMS IN DEFENSE OF CALIFORNIA!"

Warren looked strong on defense partly because, as attorney general, he had advocated for the internment of Japanese-Americans. "If the Japs are released," he warned, "no one will be able to tell a saboteur from any other Jap." (Warren later publicly expressed great remorse about this policy and, in a 1972 interview, wept over it.) Carey McWilliams was one of the few people in public office to oppose internment. Warren vowed that his first public act as governor would be to fire McWilliams.

In the last thirty days before the election, Whitaker and Baxter advertised in four hundred newspapers and on five hundred billboards. They flooded the airwaves. They sent out sound trucks, to drive around and honk and blast. They attacked Olson's economic policies. They wrote a speakers' manual, for anyone giving a speech in support of Warren; it included drafts of a "Six-Minute Talk" and a "Fifteen-Minute Talk." (Their stock advice: Try not to speak for more than fifteen minutes—people get bored—and never for more than half an hour.)

Warren won, but he didn't like the way he had won. Just before the election, after Whitaker and Baxter issued a press release without his approval, he fired them. They never forgave him.

In the fall of 1944, Warren got a serious kidney infection. This set him 30 thinking about the rising costs of medical care, and the catastrophic effects that sudden illness could have on a family less well provided for than his own. "I came to the conclusion that the only way to remedy this situation was to spread the cost through insurance," he wrote in his memoirs. He asked his staff to develop a proposal. "We concluded that health insurance should be collected through the Social Security System. After some studies, it was determined that the employers and employees in that system should each contribute one and one half per cent of wages paid by or to them." After conferring with the California Medical Association, he anticipated no objections from doctors. And so, in January of 1945, during his State of the State address, he announced his proposal for comprehensive, compulsory health insurance for the state of California.

Earl Warren began his political career as a conservative and ended it as one of the most hated liberals in American history. What happened to him? One answer is: Whitaker and Baxter.

Retained by the California Medical Association for an annual fee of twenty-five thousand dollars to campaign against the Governor's plan, Whitaker and Baxter took a piece of legislation that most people liked and taught them to hate it. "You can't beat something with nothing," they liked to say. They launched a drive for Californians to buy their own insurance, privately. Voluntary Health Insurance Week, driven by forty thousand inches of advertising in more than four hundred newspapers, was observed in fifty-three of the state's fifty-eight counties. Whitaker and Baxter sent more than nine thousand doctors out with prepared speeches. They coined a slogan: "Political medicine is bad medicine."

They lobbied newspaper editors. Whitaker boasted that "our people have personally called at more than 500 newspaper offices," to persuade editors to change their positions. Many of these newspapers did a vast amount of advertising business with Campaigns, Inc., and received hundreds of words of free copy, each week, from the California Feature Service. "In three years," Whitaker reported, "the number of newspapers supporting socialized medicine has dwindled from fifty to about twenty. The number of papers opposing compulsory health insurance has jumped from about 100 to 432."

They invented an enemy. They sent out twenty-seven thousand copies of a pamphlet called "The Health Question," which featured a picture of a man, a woman, and a child in the woods—"a forest of fear"—menaced by skeletons who have in their mouths, instead of teeth, the word "BILL." Whitaker and Baxter sent out two and a half million copies of another pamphlet, called "Politically-Controlled Medicine." They printed postcards, for voters to stick in the mail:

Dear Senator:

Please vote against all Compulsory Health Insurance Bills pending before the Legislature. We have enough regimentation in this country now. Certainly we don't want to be forced to go to "A State doctor," or to pay for such a doctor whether we use him or not. That system was born in Germany—and is part and parcel of what our boys are fighting overseas. Let's not adopt it here.

35   In 1945, Warren's bill failed to pass by just one vote. As Warren's biographer G. Edward White remarked, "The scuttling of his health insurance plan was a confirmation for Warren of the nature of the political process, in which advocates of programs based on humanity and common sense were pitted

against selfish, vindictive special interests." Warren reintroduced the bill. And again Whitaker and Baxter defeated it. "They stormed the Legislature with their invective," Warren later wrote, "and my bill was not even accorded a decent burial." It was the greatest legislative victory at the hands of admen the country had ever seen. It was not, of course, the last.

In 1945, months after Earl Warren proposed compulsory health insurance in California, Harry Truman proposed a national program. "The health of American children, like their education, should be recognized as a definite public responsibility," the President said. When Republicans took control of Congress in 1946, Truman's proposed federal health-insurance program, which, like Warren's, was funded by a payroll tax, stalled. In his State of the Union address in 1948, an election year, Truman urged passage of his plan, which enjoyed widespread popular support. In November, Truman won the election. Days afterward, the American Medical Association called up the San Francisco offices of Campaigns, Inc. The A.M.A. retained Whitaker and Baxter at a fee of a hundred thousand dollars a year, and with an annual budget of more than a million dollars, to thwart Truman's plan. The A.M.A. raised the money by assessing twenty-five dollars a year from every one of its members.

At the beginning of 1949, Whitaker and Baxter, the directors of the A.M.A.'s National Education Campaign, entered national politics, setting up headquarters in Chicago, with a staff of thirty-seven. "This must be a campaign to arouse and alert the American people in every walk of life, until it generates a great public crusade and a fundamental fight for freedom," their Plan of Campaign began. "Any other plan of action, in view of the drift toward socialization and despotism all over the world, would invite disaster." But when Whitaker told the Washington press corps, at a luncheon, that the F.B.I. was terrorizing the A.M.A., the Washington Post offered that maybe the A.M.A., at the hands of Whitaker and Baxter, ought to stop "whipping itself into a neurosis and attempting to terrorize the whole American public every time the Administration proposes a Welfare Department or a health program."

Whitaker and Baxter went to Washington and persuaded a hundred congressmen to let them read their constituent mail. At the start of the campaign, Whitaker reported, mail from voters "was running four and half to one in favor" of Truman's plan. Whitaker and Baxter went to work. "Nine months later it was running four to one against."

By then, Campaigns, Inc., had come to seem, at least to a handful of critics, nefarious and mysterious. "There isn't any mystery about it," Whitaker insisted. In a brilliant maneuver, Whitaker had "A Simplified Blueprint of the Campaign Against Compulsory Health Insurance" distributed, by the hundreds of thousands, to reporters and editors, among others, and to every member of Congress.

Meanwhile, inside Campaigns, Inc., a much more detailed Plan of Campaign circulated, in typescript, marked "CONFIDENTIAL:— NOT FOR

PUBLICATION." (It can be found with the firm's papers, which are housed at the California State Archives, in Sacramento.) It reads, in part:

1. The immediate objective is the defeat of the compulsory health insurance program pending in Congress. 2. The long-term objective is to put a permanent stop to the agitation for socialized medicine in this country by (a) awakening the people to the danger of a politically-controlled, government-regulated health system; (b) convincing the people, through a nationwide campaign of education, of the superior advantages of private medicine, as practiced in America, over the State-dominated medical systems of other countries; (c) stimulating the growth of voluntary health insurance systems to take the economic shock out of illness and increase the availability of medical care to the American people.

As Whitaker and Baxter put it, in an earlier version of the plan, "Basically, the issue is whether we are to remain a free Nation, in which the individual can work out his own destiny, or whether we are to take one of the final steps toward becoming a Socialist or Communist State. We have to paint the picture, in vivid verbiage that no one can misunderstand, of Germany, Russia—and finally, England." They settled on a slogan: "KEEP POLITICS OUT OF MEDICINE." And they settled on a smear, one that they had used against Warren's plan: they called Truman's plan "socialized medicine."

In an attempt to educate every doctor, nurse, and druggist in the United States about the dangers of socialized medicine, they went on the road. Whitaker, speaking to two hundred doctors at a meeting of the Council of the New England Medical Societies, said:

Hitler and Stalin and the socialist government of Great Britain all have used the opiate of socialized medicine to deaden the pain of lost liberty and lull the people into non-resistance. Old World contagion of compulsory health insurance, if allowed to spread to our New World, will mark the beginning of the end of free institutions in America. It will only be a question of time until the railroads, the steel mills, the power industry, the banks and the farming industry are nationalized.

45 Political advertising, he said, was the last best hope of democracy: "We're going to put the foes of American medicine on trial before the bar of public opinion, and let the people decide."

To that end, the National Education Campaign sent out millions of pieces of mail. It wasn't always well met. "RECEIVED YOUR SCARE LETTER. AND HOW PITYFUL," an angry pharmacist wrote from Stamford, New York. "I DO HOPE PRESIDENT TRUMAN HAS HIS WAY. GOOD LUCK TO HIM."

Whitaker and Baxter liked to talk about their work as "grass roots" campaigning. The fight against socialized medicine was a case in point: "The A.M.A. in its campaign is carrying its case to the people of America in a grass roots crusade which we hope, with your help, and the help of tens of thousands of others, will reach every corner of this country." Not everyone was convinced that a lavishly paid advertising agency distributing 7.5 million copies of a pamphlet called "The Voluntary Way Is the American Way" to doctors' offices constituted a "grass roots" movement. "Dear Sirs," one doctor wrote them. "Is it 2 ½ or 3 ½ million dollars you have allotted for your 'grass roots lobby'?"

Whitaker and Baxter's campaign against Harry Truman's national-health-insurance proposal cost the A.M.A. nearly five million dollars, and it took more than three years. But they turned the President's sensible, popular, and urgently needed legislative reform into a bogeyman so scary that, even today, millions of Americans are still scared.

Truman was furious. As to what in his plan could possibly be construed as "socialized medicine," he told the press in 1952, he didn't know what in the Sam Hill that could be. He had one more thing to say: there was "nothing in this bill that came any closer to socialism than the payments the American Medical Association makes to the advertising firm of Whitaker and Baxter to misrepresent my health program."

Carey McWilliams had kept an eye on Whitaker and Baxter since Uppie 50 and Downey, since Ham and Eggs, since Earl Warren and the C.M.A. He pitched to The Nation a story about Whitaker and Baxter. His editor, Harold Field, wanted it straightaway, but McWilliams put him off. He said that he needed to go to San Francisco and "dig out the facts."

He wrote Whitaker and Baxter, requesting an interview. "The questions are serious and they are neither barbed nor loaded," he promised. "I really am not captious: I'm simply curious." He met them. He liked them. He just happened to disagree with their political agenda, and, more, he thought that their business was bad for democracy. He wrote the piece and, in May of 1950, sent Whitaker and Baxter a draft. They read it and sent changes, correcting a few small matters of fact. But they were disappointed by a revised draft.

"We are not quite the diabolical characters you have portrayed," Whitaker wrote McWilliams. "I am disappointed that you were disappointed," McWilliams replied. "Don't you agree that about the best we can hope for or expect on this score is the maximum good will, factual accuracy, and the observance of some fundamentals of fair play?"

"Government by Whitaker and Baxter" appeared in The Nation in three parts, in April and May of 1951. Whitaker and Baxter wrote McWilliams, "It seems to both of us that while you have not spared the spurs where you feel they will do the most good, you certainly have not done anything to injure Whitaker and Baxter personally. Everything considered, that may have been quite a strain. We are deeply grateful, Carey."

McWilliams, as Whitaker and Baxter must have very well understood, had played by different rules from theirs. He hadn't been simple. He hadn't attacked them. He had taken time to explain. He hadn't invented an enemy. He hadn't taken remarks out of context. He hadn't made anything up. He hadn't lied.

55   "In labor and liberal circles in California people hiss when Whitaker and Baxter are mentioned," he reported in The Nation, "but it must be acknowledged that they know how to reach the people. True, they have had lots of money to spend; but their opponents have not always been broke, either." He talked about how much money unions had, for instance. McWilliams did, however, believe that Whitaker and Baxter had too much power. For the A.M.A., they had written, he said, "a political script in which doctors, originally cast as special-interest heavies, emerge as crusaders for the people's health." It was incredible. And it was dangerous. "This is expert political management; this is government by Whitaker and Baxter." This is how we live now.

    The piece was not without effect. By 1952, a number of doctors had resigned from the A.M.A. James H. Means, Jackson professor of Medicine at Harvard and the chief of medicine at the Massachusetts General Hospital, explained that he was no longer willing to pay dues that had been used to support an activity that he considered "contrary to public welfare and unworthy of a learned profession."

    That fall, the A.M.A. let Whitaker and Baxter go, explaining that it had decided that keeping the agency on retainer would compromise its nonpartisan status. Whitaker and Baxter were untroubled. They went to work for Eisenhower-Nixon.

    In 1952, television was used, for the first time, in a Presidential campaign. In 1948, less than three per cent of American homes had a television; by 1952, that figure was fast approaching fifty per cent. That year, Republicans spent $1.5 million on television advertising; Democrats spent seventy-seven thousand dollars. On television, spots for Eisenhower—"I Like Ike" and "The Man from Abilene"—whose themes were based on George Gallup's polling, masqueraded as documentaries; they looked like the March of Time newsreels.

    Eisenhower was so unfamiliar with recording equipment that once, in front of a microphone, which was on, he grumbled, "How the hell does this thing work?" But, like everyone running for office after him, he was coached, and groomed, and buffed, and polished. And made up. In a TV spot called "Eisenhower Answers America," a young black man says, "General, the Democrats are telling me I never had it so good." Eisenhower replies, "Can that be true, when America is billions in debt, when prices have doubled, when taxes break our backs, and we are still fighting in Korea? It's tragic." Then he looks, sternly, straight into the camera. "It's time for a change."

60   In 1953, Earl Warren became Chief Justice of the United States. The "Impeach Earl Warren" campaign began not long after Warren wrote the Court's opinion in Brown v. Board of Education, in 1954, declaring school segregation unconstitutional. In 1955, Carey McWilliams became the editor of The Nation. In 1956, Whitaker and Baxter did P.R. for the G.O.P. Nominating Convention, in San Francisco. Meanwhile, they were interviewed by a Special Senate Committee to Investigate Political Activities, Lobbying, and Campaign

Contributions. Whitaker told the committee he opposed government funding of campaigns and favored lifting restrictions on corporate campaign donations. The committee's investigators puzzled over campaign consultants. Should they be classed as lobbyists? As political-action committees? Shouldn't they be regulated? Whitaker insisted that the work his firm did constituted grassroots organizing, and should not to be subject to any regulation.

Later that year, Whitaker and Baxter, working with the California firm of Baus and Ross, campaigned on behalf of Proposition 4, a ballot measure favoring the oil industry and giving it more license to drill. The measure was written by attorneys for Standard Oil. Whitaker and Baxter prevailed, mainly by getting the referendum's name changed to the Oil and Gas Conservation Act.

In 1958, Whitaker's oldest son by his first marriage, Clem Whitaker, Jr., bought Campaigns, Inc., with two partners. In 1960, when Nixon ran for President, Campaigns, Inc., organized his campaign in California. "The great need is to go on the offensive—and to attack," one of Whitaker's partners advised. Best to forget "the liberal Democrats who wouldn't vote for Nixon if he received the joint personal endorsement of Jesus Christ and Karl Marx via a séance with Eleanor Roosevelt." Nixon won California but lost the election. He was terrible on television. "It was TV more than anything else that turned the tide," Kennedy said. By now, Democrats were beginning to hire political-consulting firms, too.

Everyone did. It was an arms race.

Clem Whitaker, Sr., died of emphysema in 1961. Four years later, when Ronald Reagan ran for governor of California, he hired the California firm of Spencer-Roberts. Spencer-Roberts used the Whitaker and Baxter rule book. "You know something, Stu?" Reagan said to Stuart Spencer in 1966. "Politics is just like show business. . . . You begin with a hell of an opening, you coast for a while, and you end with a hell of a closing."

Upton Sinclair died in a nursing home in New Jersey in 1968. That year, H. R. Haldeman left his job as manager of the Los Angeles office of the J. Walter Thompson advertising agency to run Nixon's Presidential campaign. Haldeman had offered his services to Eisenhower-Nixon in 1952, and worked for the Vice-President's campaign in 1956. He had learned the tools of the trade from the best of them. "Whitaker and Baxter was the great old campaign," he once said, remembering the old days, "the granddaddy."

"Voters are basically lazy, basically uninterested in making an effort to understand what we're talking about," the Nixon adviser William Gavin wrote in a memo. "Reason requires a higher degree of discipline, of concentration; impression is easier," he wrote in another memo. "Reason pushes the viewer back, it assaults him, it demands that he agree or disagree; impression can envelop him, invite him in, without making an intellectual demand. . . . When we argue with him we demand that he make the effort of replying. We seek to engage his intellect, and for most people this is the most difficult work of all. The emotions are more easily roused, closer to the surface, more malleable."

The Nixon campaign studied the tapes of its candidate on television. Insufficient emotion. "He still uses his arms a little too 'predictably' and a little too often," Roger Ailes, Richard Nixon's chief television adviser, said in 1968. "But at this point it is better not to inhibit him." Ailes is now the president of Fox News.

After Clem Whitaker died, Leone Baxter continued to run a firm of her own, Whitaker and Baxter International. She lived in a penthouse apartment at the Fairmont Hotel in San Francisco. She liked to work behind the scenes. In all her long life—she died in 2001, at the age of ninety-five—she rarely gave interviews. She made an exception in the nineteen-sixties. She was asked, "Do the procedures you designed early in the game and utilized so successfully over the years, Leone, still work today, or have you found it necessary to change them?"

"The basic rules I would say are wholly unchanged," she said. "The strategies are unchanged." There was television, of course. "But I would say that the philosophy of political campaigning hasn't changed a whit. The tools have changed, the philosophy has not."

70 She was also asked, "Does political public relations actually transfer political power into the hands of those who exercise it?"

"It certainly could and has in some instances," she said, carefully. "In this profession of leading men's minds, this is the reason I feel it must be in the hands of the most ethical, principled people—people with real concern for the world around them, for people around them—or else it will erode into the hands of people who have no regard for the world around them. It could be a very, very destructive thing."

Things to Do with the Reading

1. In one of her essays, Lepore distinguishes between biography and what she terms "Microhistory," which is a subset of biography. A self-styled microhistorian, she assumes that the value of an individual's life story "lies in how it serves as an allegory for the culture as a whole" ("Historians Who Love Too Much: Reflections on Microhistory and Biography"). This tension between event and larger meaning is also evident in a 2009 handout for one of her history classes at Harvard entitled "How to Write a Paper for This Class." There Lepore writes, "Good questions come in all shapes and sizes. [. . .] One kind is more empirical (what happened?) [. . .] The other is historiographical (what's at stake in the debate among historians about what happened?)."

With these two quotations in mind, write an analysis of how "The Lie Factory" uses the empirical facts attached to Campaigns, Inc. to explore what's at stake in larger (more allegorical) terms for the language of politics and the politics of language in America. Locate key passages where Lepore examines what's at stake. How might this piece shed light, for example, on the current debate over healthcare?

2. How might the impact of Campaign, Inc. be different now, in the era of the Internet?

3. Link: We have delayed this historical account of the rise of political consultants until late in the unit so that you may read it through the lens of the earlier pieces, which analyze more recent political strategizing. What are the most striking similarities between the practices of Campaign, Inc. and the practices of these more recent accounts? Also locate what you take to be some interesting differences.

For example, at one point in the essay, Lepore discusses how Whitaker and Baxter composed "a Plan of Campaign." She summarizes their philosophy in the following combination of quotation and paraphrase:

> "Never explain anything. 'The more you have to explain,' Whitaker said, 'the more difficult it is to win support.' Say the same thing over and over again. 'We assume we have to get a voter's attention seven times to make a sale,' Whitaker said. Subtlety is your enemy. 'Words that lean on the mind are no good.' According to Baxter. 'They must dent it.' Simplify, simplify, simplify. 'A wall goes up,' Whitaker warned, 'when you try to make Mr. and Mrs. Average American Citizen *work or think*.'"

Reflect on this passage. What are its implications for the ways Whitaker and Baxter think about their audience, the American voting public? With these results in mind, consider the vast difference in the way that Luntz deals with his audiences—exploring the effects of different words on focus groups and other sample audiences. What does Luntz think people are most likely to be affected by and why, compared with Whitaker and Baxter?

James Peck

September 11th—a National Tragedy?

A director and professor of theater, James Peck feels troubled by the label so casually attached by the press, politicians, and the rest of us to the September 11th attacks: "a national tragedy." In applying tragic theory to American response to the attack, Peck calls us to distinguish tragic events from just bad stuff happening and reminds us that "we have our own hubris to face." This piece helps us to see how much the label can matter when we talk about what things mean.

> It is not the grave we mourn, but the dead.
> Clytemnestra, in Euripides' *Iphigenia at Aulis*

1   Since the events of September 11th, I've been pursued by thoughts and images of tragedy. Frequently, I hear the terrorist attacks called "tragic" or "a national tragedy." The lead article in The *New York Times Magazine* the following Sunday, for example, was a collection of short pieces by prominent writers called "Elements of Tragedy." The title alludes to a key passage of Aristotle's *Poetics*, the canonical treatment of Greek tragedy and the most influential book of dramatic theory in the Western world. Subsequently, I've heard the tragic evoked by Sunday morning pundits, politicians of the left, right, and center, rock stars, talk-show hosts, the mayor of New York, professional athletes, my friends and colleagues, preachers, and members of my family. Probably others, too. As a lifelong theater person, this use of the language always triggers specific associations in me. Tragedy, of course is a theatrical genre dating in its origins from the fifth-century B.C. in Athens. The idea of the tragic recalls a long, vexed history in my art form. For many centuries, tragedy was the gold standard of drama, and debates about the definition and meaning of tragedy constitute some of the most vital episodes in the history of the theater. People in my field still make their reputations arguing the grounds or even the possibility of tragedy. Given my intellectual context, I confess to a certain proprietary interest in the way the concept of tragedy is deployed. Usually when I hear current events called tragic, I privately roll my eyes and lament the abuse of a term that is, if not exacting, at least rich, complicated, and possessed of a distinctive critical lineage. A voluminous literature theorizes the limits of tragic form, and I admit it rankles me to hear the word "tragic" used as a generic modifier for anything really bad that happens.

"September 11th: A National Tragedy?" by James Peck, from Aftermath: Thinking After September 11th: Occasional Papers of the Center for Ethics and Leadership. Reprinted with permission of the author.

With the events of September 11th, however, I have found myself using the language of tragedy pretty indiscriminately. My immediate reaction to the attacks was precise and striking. Right after learning that the Twin Towers had collapsed, I wanted to read Euripides. I had an urge to go get *Iphigenia at Aulis* from the library and read it. Like scripture—for metaphors, sustenance, moral compass. I had not read this play in several years and still don't know it especially well, but it seemed at the time like my best hope for some kind of framework to apprehend what I was experiencing. I shuffled numbly around my office for a while feeling like this was kind of a silly notion till something else took over and I went about trying to make it through the day. But the impulse persisted, and eventually I found my way to the bottom floor of Trexler to browse the Greeks. I can't say and won't boast that reading a few tragedies has clarified much about the socio-political, ethical, and spiritual crisis in which we find ourselves. But I am coming to the conviction that tragedy offers a demanding, stark paradigm that at least accounts for some of the emotional force of these events and may even suggest some generative ways to think about them. Beyond simply capturing a bit of the devastation wrought by the attacks, can the form of tragedy help us narrate, image, or otherwise represent these horrors?

I acknowledge that it may seem frivolous, even blasphemous, to discuss these overwhelming and all too real events in a matrix borrowed from the relatively rarified topic of dramatic form. I do know that life is life and theater is theater. And though I have faith that theater is enormously important, I recognize that it is not quite life. The suffering of the thousands of people who died, lost their loved ones, or lost their livelihoods is quite real. Retaliatory air strikes and civilian casualties in Afghanistan are quite real. It's essential to mark the distance between aesthetic forms and world events. At the same time, it is also the case that we have no choice but to narrate September 11th. In fact, the story is being told all the time— on news reports, in snappily edited video clips, in press conferences, in office conversations while the xeroxing goes on. A truism of contemporary narrative theory states that humans order their world by telling stories about it. We innately turn people into characters and assemble incidents into narratives. We are hardwired to do this. But an array of incidents can be strung together in an endless variety of ways. Who's in our cast of characters? What's the plot? Whose point of view predominates? The choices we make matter because they articulate our perspective on how the world works. They matter, too, because narratives often function as guides for action. Stories are, among many other things, templates of behavior. They propose options and suggest outcomes; they mediate relations between people. What kind of a person can I be? Given the sort of person I am, how might I act? With what likely consequences? What should I expect from people seemingly unlike myself? In the end, the stories we experience collapse back onto the material world because they shape our deeds. If we are to assimilate the events of September 11th into a meaningful context (or allow them to alter our sense of what a meaningful context might be), we have no choice but to hear them as stories.

I'm suggesting that the form of tragedy might accommodate some of the affective power of September 11th, and even point towards some of its moral claims. It seems fitting to me that the rhetoric of the tragic is so frequently invoked of late. Tragedy is above all a genre of suffering and witness. A form of lamentation, it facilitates mourning and generates memory. In its classical form, tragedy oscillates between a protagonist caught in an unlivable situation and a chorus who collectively responds to his or her anguish. While it does not celebrate or fetishize pain, it places hope in the belief that pain can catalyze insight. Above all, tragedy investigates contradiction. Tragedy stages moments when the systems people live by fall apart and fail them. It examines the inadequacy of familiar categories to provide meaningful accounts of catastrophic experiences. It resists easy resolution, preferring a difficult, even agonizing process of self-recognition to the reassuring comforts of self-deception. It is both analytic and empathetic. It defers closure in quest of revelation. Tragedy recognizes tensions between individual ambitions and group solidarity, and it often turns its self-scrutinizing impulse to the struggles of civic life. In fact, tragedy has flourished in epochs (Classical Athens, Renaissance England, Absolutist France, Romantic Germany) endeavoring to remake the social order or authorize a social order recently remade. It speaks to adversities faced on the cusp of history; considered historically, it often gives testament to the death of one era as another labors to be born. Tragedy admits the seemingly arbitrary nature of so much human suffering, even as it finds the will to go on living through communal rites that grieve the persistence of this condition.

5   I think this ought to be the tenor of our discourse in the wake of September 11th. As a nation, I believe we would benefit from seeking out the tragic potential in the destruction of the Twin Towers, the attack on the Pentagon, and the crash of a plane in southwestern Pennsylvania destined for an undetermined Washington landmark. A tragic response to September 11th, a tragic witnessing of it, would try to hold at least three contradictory impulses together. First, we need to mourn, and stories of loss seem fundamental. Many people died and many more have seen their lives irrevocably altered. The ripples are endless, from the unremitting absence of dead friends and family members to the slow burn of a faltering economy to the muscle tension that arises at the sight of camouflaged military personnel patrolling the airport with M-16s, to the permanent gap in the Manhattan skyline. I suspect most Americans feel a level of anxiety for their personal safety that they did not experience prior to September 11th. I admit that I do. Degrees of

loss differ widely and are by no means commensurate. But loss is widespread and deserves to be marked.

A tragic witnessing of September 11th must also preserve outrage at these callous acts. "Terror is theater," said the leader of the terrorists who kidnapped and murdered Israeli athletes at the Munich Olympics. Human carnage for the sake of good video is indisputably evil. It may turn out to be the greatest, most characteristically postmodern of evils. The attackers need to be (as they have been) resoundingly and unequivocally condemned. A tragic perspective particularly rejects the murder of innocents in the service of signification. Deeply invested in a politics of empathy, tragedy asserts that insight into the order of things arises only through compassion. It demands the imaginative leap of trying to see the world from someone else's position in it, and insists that we act based on these imaginative identifications. Tragedy deals harshly with those who inflict suffering, in order to hold to or advance an idea. It names this unfeeling form of arrogance *hubris*, and punishes it.

Finally, a tragic witnessing of these events should squarely face some awful truths, dwell in the full weight of those truths, and try to see ourselves anew as a result of doing so. The terrorists staged September 11th for maximum semiotic impact. Their message was clear. In their rhetoric, the World Trade Center figures America's global economic power and a certain modernist insouciance; the Pentagon figures America's military power. The attacks construct America as the wealthy superpower it is, and dramatize its destruction. Clearly, these attacks were a despicable criminal act. The perpetrators must be brought to justice through appropriate processes of national and international law. However, they do articulate some partial truths about the United States. We are the principal agents and beneficiaries of globalization. We have the most powerful military in the world and often deploy it in bellicose ways. I think we need to hear that much of the world perceives us in this manner and accept that this perception, while not the whole story, has its basis in US actions. Since becoming the world's lone superpower in 1989, we have moved toward a dangerous and arrogant isolationism in foreign affairs. We have tended toward self-congratulatory smugness, representing ourselves as the victors of history, the champions of an economic system that will inevitably bring peace and prosperity to the entire planet. We have not adequately appreciated other peoples' fears for their material and cultural autonomy, nor have we done enough to temper the material and cultural inequities that have thus far accompanied globalization. We have our own hubris to face.

The cornerstone of Aristotle's theory of tragedy is the dual principle of *peripety* and *recognition*. A peripety is a reversal, a moment when the plot shifts powerfully for better or worse. In tragedies, peripeties are catastrophic, often unbearable. But terrible events do not alone make for tragedy. For Aristotle, the defining feature of tragedy is that peripety leads to recognition. As a result of their bad fortune, tragic characters see themselves in a new light. They recognize some unfortunate, painful, even devastating truth about themselves. From suffering comes insight. Nationally, we have endured peripety but are refusing recognition. We ought to take seriously the view of the United States that generated these evil acts. How did it arise? How is it justified? What can we do to change it? I do not stand with those who believe that if we change, "the terrorists will have won." We have already changed, and inevitably so given the magnitude of events and the levels of loss endured. But how will we change? Will we take up the moral rigor of tragedy and examine ourselves anew? Will we question and alter those policies and practices that inhibit reciprocity in our material and cultural relations with other nations? It is a sad truth that the rest of the world knows much more of us than we know of it. Let us consider the discomfiting possibility that it may also know something of us that we do not yet know of ourselves.

I worry that my discussion may seem tasteless, or worse, coy. Who cares whether we witness September 11th in the spirit of tragedy? I actually think the stakes of the genre are concrete, the consequences of it utterly material. In point of fact, since September 11th, our national policy has been determined by a narrative borrowed from a dramatic form. That form is melodrama. Melodrama is a genre of moral absolutes. It traffics in heroes and villains, white hats and black hats. It dates from the early nineteenth-century and dominated American theater into the early twentieth-century. It remains powerfully with us in film, television, and to some lesser degree theater. Luke Skywalker and Darth Vader are its progeny, as are Buffy and Angel, Rambo, professional wrestling, and soap opera. To its credit, melodrama cares about questions of morality and takes seriously the evil that men do. But it also divides the world into stark, simplistic categories. It thrives on a politics of us and them. Since September 11th, I believe we've been living out a national melodrama. The defining moment of this melodrama came when President Bush cast Osama bin Laden as the villain in a movie Western: "Wanted: Dead or Alive," he announced. I've since seen bin Laden's visage in a mock Old West poster many times in many places. I am not so much concerned with the representation of bin Laden here as I am with the implicit representation of the United States. In this scenario, the US is a hero without blemish crusading for a rugged, frontier justice. I share the President's view that the people involved in planning these attacks should be pursued, captured, and prosecuted. All signs point to al Qaeda. However, our intervention into Afghanistan has come perilously close to state-sponsored vigilantism. We have not acted within the most relevant and authoritative legal framework, seeking an international tribunal under the authority of the United Nations to apprehend these criminals and to prosecute their crimes. We have opted instead to proclaim the post-September 11th world a new place, the rule of law obsolete, and invent new rules of engagement to fight "a new kind of war." To me, this seems more like the plot of a John Ford film than a considered, far-seeing approach to international leadership.

I don't want to live in a melodrama. Melodrama is pleasing like a 10 Twinkie is pleasing, but like a Twinkie it's a lie. Melodrama makes for dissatisfying theater. More gravely, it makes for disastrous foreign policy. I do not believe that in the long term the "war on terrorism" as we are currently waging it will make us safer. If anything, it will harden the resolve of people sufficiently desperate to kill themselves and murder massive numbers of innocent civilians to voice their opinions. Even more pragmatically, most of the foreign policy analysis I've read since September 11th suggests that a bombing campaign is a grossly ineffective way to combat terrorism. Human intelligence (spying), combined with cross-national cooperation between domestic law enforcement agencies (states the consensus), is far more effective. To defeat terrorism, we need to cultivate friends, not make more enemies. We need to place ourselves within the norms and constraints of international law to demonstrate our genuine desire to be a leader within the community of nations rather than the boss country that unilaterally determines its agenda. Nor do I believe that the war on terrorism as we are currently waging it will lead to a lasting peace. Everything I've ever read on the subject of terrorism suggests that terrorist violence correlates most consistently and most strongly with poverty. The experience of abjection powerfully nurtures feelings of resentment that easily grow into hatred. People turn to terrorism when they believe they have no other means of influencing public affairs. Ultimately, the solution is economic. The best assurance that the US will not again be the object of a comparably horrific terrorist attack is an equitable distribution of global capital that moves wealth more evenly throughout the world and generates genuinely reciprocal forms of cultural encounter. In the wake of September 11th, we should be as powerfully concerned to work toward this goal as we are urgently resolved to bring to justice the perpetrators of these terrible crimes.

It deeply worries me that the dominant national discourse in the aftermath of September 11th is melodramatic. As I write this, it looks like the Northern Alliance, aided by the US bombing campaign, will win the war in Afghanistan and preside over a broad-based coalition government. I hope this brings some stability to the people of Afghanistan and relieves the poverty and repression that, by all reports, they have endured under the Taliban. When this happens, the melodramatic narrative put in motion by the Bush administration will reach at least a temporary denouement. However, I fear that by donning the white hat we are refusing to hear some necessary lessons of September 11th. I fear we are failing to recognize our role in creating the circumstances that led to such intense hatred of the United States. I fear that by acting above the community of nations we are confirming our enemies' worst view of us. I fear that in turning tragedy into melodrama, we are inviting more terror onto our shores.

I'd like to close by evoking the function of tragedy in Athenian democracy. Throughout the fifth-century B.C. tragedies were performed every spring at the City Dionysia, an annual theater festival sponsored by the state. The City Dionysia was a competition—five comic writers competed for one prize, three tragedians for the other. The tragic writers each staged a tragic cycle comprised of three tragedies and a satyr play. The festival lasted several days (between five and eight, depending upon how you read the evidence), with prizes awarded at the end. Most recent work on Greek theater emphasizes the civic character of theater-going in classical Athens. Theater-going was a privilege of citizenship and the theater a significant institution of political life. Approximately half the voting population of Athens attended the City Dionysia each year. Audience members sat with their tribes, a distribution of spectators that echoed the city's political structure. The judges were similarly appointed, one from each tribe. Wealthy citizens could pay their taxes by sponsoring a production. The performers were not professionals, but were themselves citizens. Rituals performed on the first day framed the festival within Athenian civic discourse. These rituals particularly emphasized Athens' military prowess: generals from each tribe poured libations; the children of those who had died in war were brought on stage; tribute from subject nations was paraded in the arena; names of men who had greatly benefited the city were read aloud.

Given this avowedly patriotic context, the most remarkable thing about the City Dionysia was its frank criticism of Athenian public life. The City Dionysia consistently and ferociously scrutinized the *polis*. Comedy specialized in scurrilous mockery of leading public figures. Tragedy placed local questions into contexts of ultimate concern. Tragedies especially investigated the fissures of civic ideology—the relationships, impulses, and desires that the dominant discourse could not accommodate. I don't want to totally romanticize Athenians; they were, in many ways, a belligerent, exclusionary society. However, I do find it inspiring that they gathered on a yearly basis to collectively consider the contradictions, failures, and inadequacies of their political system. Doing so was in fact an expression of their loyalty to and love of their homeland. It quite literally constituted them as democratic subjects. In this moment of national crisis, I think we would benefit from bringing the same questioning, restless, self-critical spirit to our own national conversation.

I hope we take seriously our casual language, and witness September 11th as a tragedy. Remember the dead. Pursue their killers. Interrogate ourselves.

Things to Do with the Reading

1. Chapter 5 discusses at some length the idea of interpretive context. Peck's essay is a good example of arguing carefully for the appropriateness and usefulness of an interpretive context. Peck invites us to view the events of September 11th in two contexts: tragedy and melodrama. Locate the places in the essay where Peck defends his choice of these interpretive contexts. Then write a brief essay in which you discuss the grounds on which he defends his choice of tragedy as a productive lens.

2. The essay reveals its anxiety about seeming to trivialize a very real event by locating it in the context of dramatic and narrative theory. Look at the shape of Peck's argument to see where it locates its concessions and what these are. Also determine where and how it introduces its more challenging points. How, for example, would the essay differ if Peck rearranged the order of the "three contradictory impulses" announced in paragraph 5? Then write up the results of this analysis in a brief essay. (See Chapter 9 on Concessions and Refutations.)

3. Link: Find the keywords in Peck's piece that locate him politically, as defined by Borick. Write a short essay on how the thinking and value system in his piece fit in the categories that Borick lays out.

4. Application: Where do you see evidence of melodrama in the national or international news? And what would a rescripting of melodrama into tragedy for this particular event entail? For example, what would the melodramatic and then the tragic readings of Hurricane Katrina be? Write an essay in which you interpret a current event, offering both melodramatic and tragic versions.

FOR FURTHER RESEARCH: THE LANGUAGE
OF POLITICS AND THE POLITICS OF LANGUAGE

By Kelly Cannon, Reference Librarian

The readings and activities below invite you to explore further the theme of The Language of Politics and the Politics of Language. URLs are provided for those readings that you can access freely online. For proprietary resources, ask your librarian about print or online access.

Open Access

American Rhetoric Online Speech Bank. Ed. Michael E. Eidenmuller. 2014. 31 May 2014. http://www.americanrhetoric.com
A searchable collection of thousands of public speeches, with a preponderance of political voices. Speech categories include "Rhetoric of 9/11," "Christian Rhetoric," and "Iraq War Speeches."

> Explore: Can you find a speech with a tendency to "defend the indefensible," as described by George Orwell? (Don't forget to try out the "Cool Exercises" to test your rhetorical savvy.)

capitolwords. Sunlight Foundation, 2014. 31 May 2014. http://capitolwords.org
"Capitol Words lets you see what are the most popular words spoken by lawmakers on the House and Senate floor."

> Explore: George Lakoff and Elizabeth Wehling in their essay on Obama vs. Romney employ certain words and phrases that highlight the distinction between these two then-presidential candidates. Plug terms like "free enterprise" and "undemocratic" into the database. Are these terms used predominantly by one party over another? Is there a spike in the use of a term in a particular Congress? What was happening at that time that might have prompted the increase? Try the same activity using words highlighted in the David Green essay.

FactCheck.org. Annenberg Public Policy Center, University of Pennsylvania, 2014. 11 May 2014. http://factcheck.org
"A nonpartisan, nonprofit, 'consumer advocate' for voters that aims to reduce the level of deception and confusion in U.S. politics."

> Explore: Examine the "About Us" portion of the website. Then look at a number of entries. To what extent does this website live up to its claim of nonpartisanship? How so? How would George Orwell respond to this site? Cite a passage from his essay to anchor your answers. Consider this website in light of Jill Lepore's essay on the political "lie factory." How has modern technology—specifically the Internet—made it both easier and

more difficult to disseminate political lies? Compare this website with features like the "Truth-o-meter" found in *Politifact*. **Tampa Bay Times, 2014. 18 May 2014. http://politifact.com**

Geary, James. *Metaphorically Speaking.* 2009. 13 May 2014. https://www.ted.com /talks/james_geary_metaphorically_speaking
Geary discusses the considerable power of metaphor in the hands of skilled rhetoricians.

> Explore: What does Geary add to Drake Bennett's argument about the subtle powers of metaphor to persuade? What precisely, according to each author, is the source of metaphor's power?

Hardisty, Jean, and Deepak Bhargava. "Wrong About the Right." *Political Research Associates*. 2005. 11 May 2014. http://www.publiceye.org/hardisty /wrong_about_right.html
Originally published in *The Nation* magazine, this article contends that the conservative rise to power is not just about rhetoric and framing, but about such things as ideas and organization.

> Explore: Is the political orientation of these authors evident? What are the clues? How well do the labels used here correspond with political labels as defined by Christopher Borick?

Harris-Lacewell, Melissa. "Katrina Is Not A Metaphor." *Nation* 291.5/6 (2010): 10. 18 May 2014. http://www.thenation.com/article/37476/katrina-not-metaphor#
The author inveighs against an inappropriate use of metaphor.

> Explore: How does this essay inform Drake Bennett's essay on metaphor as fundamental to our understanding of the world? How might the use of Katrina as a metaphor prove irresistible in describing later events? How would you respond to Harris-Lacewell? What do the essays say together about the power of metaphor?

House, Patrick. "Schizophrenic Is the New Retarded: The Word Doesn't Mean What You Think It Means, and That Matters." *Slate.* 22 January 2013. 18 May 2013. http://www.slate.com/articles/health_and_science/science/2013/01 /schizophrenia_definition_and_metaphor_schizophrenic_does_not_mean _multiple.html
An essay that examines the slipperiness of a word's definition when it is borrowed from one context for use in another, and the consequences of that shift.

> Explore: To what extent is this type of shift in meaning occurring in the events discussed in Geoffrey Nunberg's essay on Paul Ryan? And how does this essay on the uses of the word "schizophrenic" correlate with Drake Bennett's comments on metaphor?

"Knowing Best Is Not Enough." Economist 407.8830 (2013): 42. 11 May 2014. http://www.economist.com/news/united-states/21575777-voter-unhappiness -not-invitation-rational-bustle-and-take

The *Economist*, a respected source for national and international news, takes on the notion promoted by the "No Labels" bipartisan group that centrist politics (and a removal of partisanship labeling) is what Americans want.

> Explore: Considering David Green's essay on the use (and rhetorical value) of political labels, to what extent do you think a "no labels" movement would/could succeed in America? Regardless of success or failure, is a negation of labeling something you think would be valuable? How so?

Kolbert, Elizabeth. "Firebrand: Phyllis Schlafly and the Conservative Revolution." *New Yorker* (7 November 2005): 134–38. 11 May 2014. http://www .newyorker.com/archive/2005/11/07/051107crbo_books

"Schlafly's denunciatory tone, more than any of her actual campaigns, probably represents her most lasting contribution to American life. While Ann Coulter and Laura Ingraham were still playing tea party, she recognized that deliberation was no match for diatribe, and logic no equal to contempt. She was, in this way, a woman ahead of her time."

> Explore: What is the tone of this essay (its attitude toward Schlafly)? Condemnatory? Admiring? What does the rhetoric of this essay reveal about its author, in light of Christopher Borick's definitions?

The Living Room Candidate. Museum of the Moving Image, 2012. 18 May 2014. http://www.livingroomcandidate.org/

An archive of television advertisements used in presidential campaigns.

> Explore: George Lakoff and Elizabeth Wehling write of the rhetorical frames created by and for Mitt Romney and Barack Obama in their respective presidential campaigns. How do television ads contribute powerfully to those frames? Consider the ads too in light of the interview with Frank Luntz, himself one of the campaign "persuaders." As for David Green's essay on important campaign words, do the words Green references, or related terms, appear with any frequency in the advertisements?

Martin, Jonathan, et al. "Violence and Politics Merge." *Politico.com.* 9 January 2011. 18 May 2014. http://www.politico.com/news/stories/0111/47294.html

Asks to what extent political rhetoric is to blame for the shooting of Congresswoman Gifford and others in Tucson, Arizona, in January of 2011.

> Explore: The Tucson shootings brought rhetoric into the foreground. President Barack Obama responded with a certain type of rhetoric, Sarah Palin with another. And then there was the shooter himself. What rhetoric, as reported in any news stories you can find, did the shooter employ in his

online and handwritten notes? To what extent can rhetoric really lead people to violence? Consider this "tragedy" in light of the tragedy analyzed rhetorically in James Peck's essay. Are there similarities in the way the media and politicians chose to describe each of these events?

The Persuaders. PBS, 2004. 19 May 2014. http://www.pbs.org/wgbh/pages /frontline/shows/persuaders/
The PBS program that includes the interview with Frank Luntz printed in this reader.

> Explore: Watch other interviews and compare with the comments by Luntz. Look at some of the value-added material such as the discussion forum. How would you reply to one of the discussion questions?: "Is there something distinctive in the American character that makes us susceptible to this world of advertising and messages?"

"Rhetoric of 9-11." *American Rhetoric.* 2014. 18 May 2014. http://www .americanrhetoric. com/rhetoricofterrorism.htm
Access to over 150 files of key speeches and rhetorical artifacts relating to the September 11, 2001, terrorist attacks against the Pentagon and World Trade Center. These include speeches and addresses to the nation by American President George W. Bush, British Prime Minister Tony Blair, and other key politicians. Also accessible is a tape of Osama Bin Laden.

> Explore: Examine the list of "most accessed 9/11 rhetoric." What tops the list? Why? How do the "sides" begin to take shape in these most accessed speeches? What would you identify as the most powerful rhetorical moves on either side, those that would most affect the intended audience? Listen to some of the speeches archived by figures renowned as conservative or liberal. What rhetorical aspects do they share with the editorials by Kilpatrick and others printed above that would make them stand out as politically right or left?

Sherwood, Jeff. "Henry James Is Cited More Than 1,000 Times in the OED. Here's Why." *Slate Magazine* (22 April 2014). 14 May 2014. http://www.slate .com/blogs/lexicon_valley/2014/04/22/oed_henry_james_is_cited_more _than_one_thousand_times_in_the_oxford_english.html
A tribute to the nineteenth-century American novelist and essayist Henry James whose inventive use of English forever changed the language.

> Explore: James Peck, in his essay about 9/11, questions the use of labels to adequately capture a thing. How does Henry James get around this problem? What does it mean to be "euphemistically elliptical"? How does Henry James' use of English compare with the political labeling discussed by Christopher Borick?

"Top 10 Examples of Liberal Hate." *Human Events Online.* 11 January 2011. 18 May 2014. http://www.humanevents.com/article.php?id=41108
A leading conservative news source responds to liberals' allegations of hate-filled rhetoric coming from the right.

> Explore: How well do the labels employed here correspond to the definitions provided by Christopher Borick?

Zukin, Cliff. "Sources of Variation in Published Election Polling: A Primer." *American Association for Public Opinion Research.* October 2004. 17 May 2014. http://aapor.org/uploads/zukin_election_primer.pdf
Zukin, a Rutgers University professor of public policy, outlines the major liabilities in polling.

> Explore: According to Zukin, how much does the wording of questions in polls play a role in poll results? What factor, according to Zukin, most heavily affects the outcome of a poll? Interestingly, Zukin only deals with one type of election polling. What type does Zukin expressly exclude from his article? What strikes you as important about naming this distinction up front? To what extent can polling questions themselves be "liberal" or "conservative"?

Proprietary

Chavkin, Sasha. "Snow Job?." *Columbia Journalism Review* 51.5 (2013): 34–36.
Looks at the financial pressures on local news media to run lucrative political ads, countered by the pressure to fact check these ads or risk lawsuits.

> Explore: How does this article speak to Jill Lepore's essay on lies in political campaigning? How has electronic media "upped the ante"? Who should be responsible for fact checking?

Conniff, Ruth. "George Lakoff." *Progressive* 78.5 (2014): 31–36.
Ruth Conniff interviews George Lakoff about, among other things, linguistic framing.

> Explore: Compare the interview format with the essay format. How is Lakoff able to get at his ideas differently when speaking to an interviewer rather than writing them down? What are the advantages of each format? To what extent does Lakoff seem to have changed his ideas about framing and about politics in general since he wrote his essay on Obama and Romney in 2012? Does this interview itself have a frame? Does Lakoff or the interviewer ever depart from this frame, if such a one exists?

Crook, Clive. "Mine, Thine, And Robert Nozick's Unfinished Business." *National Journal* 34.7 (2002): 450.

Recalls the highly influential ideas and rhetoric of philosopher Robert Nozick on poverty and societal aid.

> Explore: How does this essay illuminate Geoffrey Nunberg's essay on the word "entitlement"? What is at the core of contemporary society's resistance to entitlement programs? Where is the power in Nozick's thesis, and how might it have informed the rhetoric against entitlement programs?

Rubin, Lillian B. "Why Don't They Listen to Us?" *Dissent* 52.1 (Winter 2005): 86–91.

This article from the liberal press explains why liberals have lost out to conservatives. Conclusion: It's all about rhetoric.

> Explore: What aspect of liberal rhetoric does Rubin find most counterproductive? How does this essay stand up to Christopher Borick's definitions of political labels?

CHAPTER 16

Seeing

An article entitled "The Image Culture" by Christine Rosen (whose essay on cell phones is the first of the readings in this book) begins by reflecting on the deluge of apocalyptic images that washed over us on the television and Internet in the wake of Hurricane Katrina. Rosen goes on to consider the footage of the 9/11 attacks, citing our "saturation" by images. She quotes novelist Don DeLillo: "In our world we sleep and eat the image and pray to it and wear it too" (*The New Atlantis: A Journal of Technology and Society*, Fall 2005).

It has become a virtual cliché that in America the image has come to displace the word, and accordingly, in the schools and in the media, verbal literacy has lost ground to visual literacy. The aim of this chapter is not, however, to defend one side against the other. Rather, our overarching goal is to provide you with a vocabulary for seeing more acutely. This is a cultural as well as a perceptual matter. Inevitably, it involves attention to both the producing and the consuming ends of the so-called Image Culture: how images are created and for what ends, and how we have been conditioned to value and resist them.

We have made "Seeing" the final chapter by design, for it raises topics relating back to the previous four chapters of readings. The readings in these earlier chapters are united by their concern with matters of rhetoric and representation: how issues get phrased and framed, to whom, and for what purposes. In this final chapter, the readings focus on the visual element of this rhetorical framing. The writers encourage us to ponder not only how we see, but how the surrounding culture and the images it offers us affect how we see. You can expect to revisit the issues that drive the earlier chapters—issues of technology, place, race, and power—but this time, with special attention to their life in the Image Culture.

ABOUT THE READINGS IN THIS CHAPTER

The interview that we conducted with photographer Joseph Elliott offers the primary lens for the selections in "Seeing." Elliott distinguishes two primary ways of producing images—staging them and recording them. Attached to each of these approaches are assumptions that Elliott uncovers about how images communicate. Eventually, he elaborates a series of qualified positions within the recorder/stager binary to arrive at a system for classifying a wide range of photographic approaches. Additionally, he offers specific technical advice for apprehending the formal elements of an image—what he refers to as "seeing the hand" of the photographer.

Next comes a classic piece entitled "In Plato's Cave" by the philosopher and cultural critic Susan Sontag. Whereas Elliott values the photographer's role as a recorder of events, Sontag is concerned that the desire to record will supplant the desire to experience and become involved. She worries that photography tends to appropriate (that is, "leach out") real life in a predatory fashion. And because photos tend to look recorded even when they are staged, she argues, those in power exploit this fact to deceive us. Seeing, after all, tends to be believing.

Barry Lopez's "Learning to See" relocates the ethical discussion to the terrain of nature photography. He also returns the focus to some of the concerns with form discussed by Elliott. Lopez concentrates on the elusive photographic pursuit of light and spatial volume—of "the deep pattern of turbulence" and "indigenous time." The backbone of his essay is a narrative of how he came to give up his career as a photojournalist to concentrate on words rather than images. In the process of telling this story, he offers a striking comparison of the mindsets that go into capturing an event in words versus in pictures—and what each medium inevitably leaves out or keeps us from seeing.

Next, the chapter moves to John Berger's famous analysis of nudes in classical art, taken from his book *Ways of Seeing*. Like the other writers, he is interested in issues of spectatorship and power. His focus rests on the representation of the female form, and in particular, on how the nude functions as a category within which "women have been seen and judged as sights" and so, as Berger comments, "They do to themselves what men do to them. They survey, like men, their own femininity" (paragraph 63).

Susan Bordo's "Beauty (Re)discovers the Male Body" offers a rich comparison with Berger's essay, as it focuses on images of men rather than women. The essay also marks a shift in the chapter's orientation, as Bordo focuses not on high art but on images from advertising. Her goal, shared with the other writers in this chapter, is to invite us to question our assumptions about the way we see and about how our seeing is shaped by the culture. She takes issue with the conventional idea of the sex object, for example, arguing that "the most compelling images are suffused with 'subjectivity'—they speak to us, they seduce us. Unlike other kinds of 'objects' (chairs and tables, for example) they don't let us use them in any way we like."

Next, Malcolm Gladwell's "Listening to Khakis" extends Berger's and Bordo's focus on gender through his journalistic study of ad campaigns aimed at men, especially the highly successful Dockers campaign, with its key phrase, "Nice pants." Gladwell's interviewing style gives voice to a range of resonant cultural commentators about how we live now. Some of these voices address how men as opposed to women see—an issue that takes us back to Berger and Bordo. What Gladwell discovers about how those who make ads theorize gender and perception provides rich matter for both analysis and application.

"Seeing" concludes, as most of the book's reading chapters have, with something a little different—in this case, two short pieces that test the flexibility of the chapter's analytical project. In "Oy Gay!" Kera Bolonik provides a revelatory way of thinking about the television sitcom *Will & Grace*, less as a show about gays (as it is usually seen) than about Jews and Gentiles.

The chapter's final essay, X. J. Kennedy's "Who Killed King Kong?" is a mid-twentieth-century review, which, like other readings in the chapter, takes a cultural studies approach to how we see. Written in the era of the Civil Rights movement, Kennedy's review of the original 1933 film *King Kong* invites us to see the volatile issues of race, class, and gender that burble just below the surface of the film. Ultimately, we can use Kennedy not only to contemplate how our own moment has reenvisioned *King Kong* (in Peter Jackson's 2005 remake), but how revisiting any image of the past may open up the way we see now.

Finally, mention should be made of an essay included elsewhere in this anthology that easily could be incorporated here: Jack Gambino's "Demolition Zones: Contemporary Photography by Edward Burtynsky and Camilo José Vergara" (Chapter 12). Vergara is frequently mentioned in Elliott's interview as a representative recorder.

Joseph Elliott, David Rosenwasser, and Jill Stephen

Looking at Photographs: Stagers and Recorders—an Interview with Joseph Elliott

Composed specifically for this book, this interview features Joseph Elliott, a noted photographer and a professor of art, on the subject of how photographers see. Elliott offers here a kind of short course on visual literacy from a photographer's point of view as he offers a guided tour through the two primary traditions of thinking about images: as recorded and as staged. In addition, he offers ways of analyzing the work of reigning art photographers in both traditions and suggests how we can expand our powers of observing the world that surrounds us. Since graduating with an M.F.A. from Pratt Institute, Elliott has had his photographs featured in 10 solo exhibits, 12 group exhibits, and many publications. He has also received 15 commissions from the Historic American Buildings Survey as well as numerous grants. In 2013, his book *The Steel: Photographs of the Bethlehem Steel Plant, 1989–1996* was published by Columbia College Chicago Press.

Note: The interviews that follow were conducted over a period of several months and are divided into seven meetings, each with its own title.

The First Meeting: 8/29/05 "The Two Camps"

1 **David:** Our book uses the metaphor of the lens to think about analyzing. Are there primary lenses that you use when you think about photographers?

Joe: I see two camps: staging versus recording. Edward S. Curtis, the photographer of the American West, is a stager. He's not observing but staging. He's a romantic who fabricates a vision of the West. An interesting photographer to compare him to is Timothy H. O'Sullivan. If you Google-image O'Sullivan, you'll see that he's a more dispassionate, severe recorder of the West.

David: So these approaches—staging and recording—are still present today?

Joe: Yes. Gregory Crewdson is a stager you might look at. His work has a cinematic feel. His point of view goes against the purist-observers, the ones who want to approach matters solely in the context of "Let's see what seeing is …"

5   Another stager you might check out is Cindy Sherman, who has photographed herself for years in all manner of costumes and disguises (such as 1970s period dress). You might compare her with Diane Arbus, but with this difference: Arbus *found* the grotesque, but Sherman seems to say, "Let's just

"Looking at Photographs: Stagers and Recorders-An Interview with Joseph Elliott." Interviewed by David Rosenwasser and Jill Stephen. Reprinted with permission.

invent it." Sherman doesn't derive from Arbus; she draws on 1950s–60s popular culture, advertising images, movies, and movie stills. In the current scene it seems as if films are getting more and more "still," and still photographers are getting more and more staged.

Jill: And contemporary recorders?

Joe: Andreas Gursky is an interesting recorder. His work seems to say, "Let's look at something clearly and make a giant print of it." Although he's a recorder most of the time, sometimes he digitally alters his images in subtle ways, perhaps in search of a more perfect banality. (For other straightforward types like Gursky, see Eggleston, Struth, Shore, and Sternfeld, who are replaying O'Sullivan. You could also think about my work and Vergara's.)

Jill: So you see yourself as a recorder, then?

Joe: I'm interested in a quality of seeing, with the aim to see things well and make a strong image. Then it is a matter of how to construct a frame and where to position the vantage point. I like to control frame and vantage point, as do all straight photographers, but not the object, so I'm not a fabricator. But like the fabricators, any photographer is clearly implicated by the process of taking photos. You are making an object, a photograph; you're creating, not just recording.

The Second Meeting: 10/21/05 "Burning Down the House"

The session begins with brief discussion of Alice in Wonderland *and the notion that that text is not simply words but a hybrid work of words and pictures—in which the pictures are integral—with a long history of illustration, starting with Lewis Carroll's own sketches (circa 1860) and famously followed by John Tenniel, whose illustrations are featured in the first edition.*

Joe: Carroll was also a well-known photographer of young girls in the early days 10 of photography as an art. Have you ever heard of Jock Sturges? Google-image him. He's a kind of modern-day Carroll who photographs children and adolescents, and who has been hounded by the authorities as morally suspicious.

Henry Peach Robinson and Oscar Rejlander were Carroll contemporaries, who we might term "Victorian fabricators."

Most photographers at this time were referred to as camera operators—recorders of images, trying to capture the real in some unmediated, unadulterated way, insofar as that is ever possible for a person with a camera. A photographer is inevitably selecting what to shoot and thus what not to shoot, and he or she is always framing the shot in various ways.

The Victorian fabricators saw themselves as artists. They embraced a belief in photography as an art form. The thought was, if you were going to produce a work of art, you had to make it entirely. You had to be seen as not just taking a picture of something out there and using factory-made materials to make the

Digital Image © The Museum of Modern Art/Licensed by SCALA/Art Resource, NY

FIGURE 16.1

"Poling the Marsh Hay, England," 1886 by Peter Henry Emerson and Thomas Frederick Goodall

print. The audience had to be sure that the artist made the whole thing. From the 1870s–1890s the artist-photographer was a pictorialist—a person who had applied the emulsion and had made each photograph as its own object. The finished photos were often fabricated from many separate images, or were impressionistic, soft focused, subtly toned, resembling paintings and drawings.

Queen Victoria purchased a huge photo of the Last Supper done by Rejlander. A third key member of early Victorian photographic circles was Julia Margaret Cameron, who was well known in artistic and literary circles and was a friend of Tennyson. [See Figure 16.1.]

The discussion moves to contemporary stagers and recorders in the world of art photography.

15 **David:** I saw in an interview with Gregory Crewdson, the stager you told me to Google, that he had traveled to various rust belt cities in the Northeast, and that Pittsfield, Massachusetts, was eager to woo him, once he selected it as a possible site for his next project, Beneath the Roses. In a meeting with town officials, including the mayor and fire chief, he mentioned that he would like to burn down a house for one of his photographs, and, Crewdson reports, "a few

hours later they showed us up to 40 possible houses we were welcome to burn down. They were all owned by the city, on schedule for demolition."

What's the difference between the photo that resulted and one of a house burning down here in Allentown? If he waited awhile listening to a police channel, he could have found many burning Rust Belt houses to photograph without employing 7 best boys and a huge production crew.

Joe: First of all, look at the context. Crewdson is a sophisticated Yale professor, top end. He sells in the most fashionable galleries in Chelsea. These factors in combination affect what he decides to shoot and how he decides to shoot it, the kind of art he decides to make. The image is designed in advance of the actual shooting, as it would be in filmmaking or advertising. Control is more complete that way. Racing to a real fire leaves too much to chance. Too much room for error. With such a huge production crew, Crewdson cannot afford to waste time. Crewdson isn't interested in making art using the real; his art isn't about the real.

David: Why burn a house down to make a picture?

Joe: It involves decadence, a level of decadence, the end of some period of American art. Decadence implies something that is over-ripe. It implies money, an affluence that is without striving. You see it in how carefully the water is spread on the ground to simulate recent rain in the photograph of the burning house, and in how big the image is, how lush the image is.

You can understand this better by comparing Crewdson to somebody like 20 Vergara. Vergara offers a counterpoint to this more fashionable art world. He actually photographs burnt out houses in Camden, New Jersey. [*See the Vergara photos in Jack Gambino's essay, "Demolition Zones: Contemporary Photography by Edward Burtynsky and Camilo Jose Vergara" in Chapter 13.*]

Crewdson is also attracted to burnt out Rust Belt cities, with a decayed past. But we need to focus on what he's looking at, and what world will receive his art. [See Figures 16.2, 16.3, 16.4.]

The postmodern art world would say that Vergara, the more honest observer, doesn't get it. There is no irony in his work. He thinks real information matters. A gallery owner once told me, "You can't show documentary photographs (like Vergara's). It's not cool."

David: What is the "it" that Vergara doesn't get?

Joe: The idea that it's hopelessly romantic to think you can capture an image in real life, and bring it to people. But there's a step missing here. In the past there was a belief that you could shoot a picture of Omaha Beach as Robert Capa did, and the image would become vitally important to almost everyone. Spielberg's *Saving Private Ryan* fashions a long sequence of the D-Day invasion of Omaha beach based on this single Capa image.

FIGURE 16.2
Untitled (house fire) 1999 by Gregory Crewdson

FIGURE 16.3
Untitled (pregnant woman) 2001 by Gregory Crewdson

© Gregory Crewdson. Courtesy Gagosian Gallery

FIGURE 16.4
Untitled (ray of light) 2001 by Gregory Crewdson

Along these lines, Steichen's 1950s MOMA (Museum of Modern Art) 25 exhibit, *The Family of Man,* tried to show the universal commonalities of all world cultures in an effort to bring people together and promote world peace. Also see Lewis Hine, and the effect of his photos to motivate Congress to pass child labor protection laws. [See Figure 16.5.]

Now that position gets discounted. It's seen as pretentious and as denying that the photographer is part of a world that oppresses anyway. So the thought is, if you cannot deny your complicity, maybe you just have to accept the construct, and make the biggest staged image you can and sell it to the wealthiest buyer you can find.

Vergara, to return to our previous contrast, occupies a middle ground. His work won't tug at your heartstrings or show you the distended belly of a starving African child, but he'll show you picture after picture of Camden, and want you to *see* the setting as it is.

Another kind of straight photographer, less the anthropologist than Vergara, and more of what we might call a sensationalist, is the legendary Weegee, the 1940s photojournalist who listened to his police scanner in New York City and raced to position himself next to the guy who had jumped out of the window and splattered on the street. You might check out his famous book called *The Naked City.* Weegee anticipates Diane Arbus in some sense, and in another, Crewdson, who *aestheticizes* the crime scene. Arbus makes an art form out of the blunt, unflinching encounter. After we've seen Crewdson, Weegee's photos also seem staged. [See Figure 16.6.]

Lewis W. Hine/George Eastman House/Getty Images

FIGURE 16.5
Portrait of a girl in mill (child labor) by Lewis Hine

Weegee (Arthur Fellig)/International Center of Photography/Getty Images

FIGURE 16.6
Brooklyn school children see gambler murdered in street, 1941 aka "Their First Murder" by Arthur Fellig (Weegee)

David: You were speaking a few moments ago about the ethical position of the photographer, how he or she can get seen as contributing to some kind of oppression. Could you say more about that?

Joe: I have a friend, Bill Burke, who does what he calls "Docu-art": it looks like 30
documentary investigation but is really an investigation of his own life choices and the resulting situations he finds himself in. In this case, Bill went to Vietnam and Cambodia to take photographs (he had skipped the actual war with a college deferment), and when he returned, he was attacked for "imaging the Other" (people of cultures and ethnicities unlike his own), using the "Other" as fodder for his work; he was accused of parasitism.

Burke's work fits the category of personal documentation, occupying a middle ground between the stagers and the recorders. His images are not staged, but are more consciously self-involved than the documentarians we have been discussing. Other members of this school are Larry Clark, *Tulsa* (teenage heroin addicts, his high school classmates), Sally Mann (her children), and Nan Goldin (street life in New York City in the 80s).

David: How do you categorize your own recent work in Costa Rica on the legacy of gold mining? Do your photos differ from the kind of documentary work that you've been talking about as more consciously self-involved?

Joe: The documentary, in the simplified sense of the word, means making the photographs that will become part of the history of a people or culture; you're trying to have as little influence as possible on the photographed subject. Of course, you do make decisions about what to shoot. You want it to last. You are "recording the site," which goes along with other methods of surveying, mapping, oral history, research, etc.—and otherwise, without the documenting, it could be lost. So you want to preserve it simply and cleanly, to be of use for the future. And the document itself also becomes part of the history.

We could apply this to Vergara's work. He'll have the map of Camden and drive up and down every street in his area of concentration to get total coverage. And he is not after some representative or iconic or symbolic images, but rather a density of images, a collecting.

Jill: Why does he record that space? 35

Joe: Vergara wants to record change over time. He is interested in what happens to a place, the effects of politics, weather, crime, economic decline, etc. Only now, parts of Camden have become gentrified. What happens to the people? He doesn't follow them. (See the four Fern Street photos in Gambino's essay.)

Along these lines, you might look up Milton Rogovin, who returned to the same neighborhood in Buffalo over 20–30 years at regular intervals.

He would find the same people and re-photograph them. Also you could look up Mark Klett's re-photographic surveys. He goes to sites that Timothy O'Sullivan, a documenter of the American West, had photographed and sets up his camera to see the site again but also to reveal how O'Sullivan had shaped the shot.

The Third Meeting: 10/28/05 "The Photographer's Hand"

David: At your direction, we've been spending a lot of time looking at books by John Szarkowski, the longtime director of photography at MOMA. How would you categorize him according to your Recorder/Stager categories?

Joe: Szarkowski was an advocate of the straight approach for many years. He seemed to ignore the fabricators. And so he essentially bypassed in his curatorship of MOMA's photographic collection the rise of the postmoderns (like Sherman and Wegman) who say all photographic representations are constructions, are contextualizations, are whatever the photographer makes of it, so let's make up the whole thing!

40   Szarkowski thus missed the boat when it came to including the fabricators in the MOMA collection. And of course, this tradition had been producing work all along—e.g., Ray Metzger, Ralph Eugene Meatyard. In the 1970s Cindy Sherman would have given photos to MOMA for the asking. By the time MOMA came on board, five years ago, they paid a million dollars to catch up.

David: Szarkowski isn't still at MOMA, is he?

Joe: He has retired. Peter Galassi is now curator at MOMA. There is no one curator as influential as Szarkowski had been. But there are now many galleries in Chelsea that show photographers, whereas there were really only two in the mid 1970s, Witkin and Light galleries.

    Szarkowski's choices are back in vogue, extolling the straightforward value of the big camera, showing meticulous details, as evident in certain photographers of the 1970s who are again becoming prominent. These include Stephen Shore, Joe Sternfeld, and William Eggleston, all color photographers. [See Figure 16.7.]

    Another change in the photography curatorial scene is that it has become more academy-oriented. Szarkowski was himself a photographer, as Stieglitz and Steichen before him had been. They were not trained in art programs or art history. Now the curators all have that training.

45 **David:** I've been meaning to ask you, how do the recorders view the stagers? And how do the stagers, or, as you sometimes call them, the fabricators tend to view themselves?

Joe: The photo-art world is so diverse that there is a "live and let live" mentality now. The fabricators see themselves as being in some sense more honest,

William Eggleston

FIGURE 16.7
Untitled (two men standing by car, Sumner, MS, ca. 1970) by William Eggleston

for admitting that they're making it up. This is the implicit argument in Crewdson's work. In his photo of the house on fire, the people on the train track on the other side of the frame are a competing focal point by design. Nothing is an accident in the photo. He wants it to be carefully observed, to invite a close reading. We may think of a photograph having an initial impact, but there's also something else going on, a counterpoint, a set of messages. A lot of this kind of work resembles film-making; the photograph is only a piece of it. The photograph is like a performance piece recorded by a camera that is being used in a straightforward way. Is it a photograph or an installation (or performance piece?) recorded in a photograph?

On the other hand, some of the recorders probably resent the success of the fashionable stagers for being driven by trend rather than the search for truth.

Jill: This reminds me of a remark that Szarkowski makes in *The Photographer's Eye*—that we tend to have faith in what we see in a photograph as real, but in fact the photographer is always "hiding his hand."

Joe: The question to ask beginning students is not, How does the photographer hide his hand? but Where is the photographer's hand? They assume there is no hand! In that famous Alfred Stieglitz photograph "Georgia

Engelhard"–it's on the cover of Szarkowski's *Looking at Photographs*—we need to ask why Stieglitz included the edge, with the part of an urn and a rubber tree. *Where is the hand? is the question they need to lead with.* In Crewdson, by contrast, the hand is much easier to see. In the straightshooters it is less obvious. [See Figure 16.8.]

50   The tradition of fabricators is full of other rich examples where we can easily see the hand. Check out the work of Les Krims. His work was part of a 1970s phase in which photographers made little books. One is called "Making

Digital Image © The Museum of Modern Art/Licensed by SCALA / Art Resource, NY

FIGURE 16.8
"Georgia Engelhard," 1921 by Alfred Stieglitz

Chicken Soup," and features his mother doing exactly that in the kitchen—only she's naked. Another is called "The Incredible Case of the Stack'O'Wheat Murders" and features shots of murder scenes, but in each one there is a stack of pancakes. These are precedents for Crewdson.

O. Winston Link's photos of 1950s' steam trains lit by hundreds of flash bulbs are another great precedent for Crewdson. Link in turn reminds us of the train motif in the surreal paintings of De Chirico and Magritte. In their paintings, though, the train, along with clocks, represents Modernism's rebellion against notions of Progress and clock time. But in Link's case the train represents the nostalgic past. The symbol has taken on a different meaning.

David: So in the kinds of photographs you've been talking about, the photographer tries to show his hand . . . ?

Joe: At the root of so much of the history of photography as a tradition is the question of where the art lies. Is the art in the making, the fabricating of the image? Is the art in the recording as cleanly and accurately as possible? Is the art an intellectual activity such as Duchamp's urinal, where naming it as art, framing it as art, makes it art? Szarkowski is most faithful to the second item in this list: if you take the machine and use it precisely and consciously, it will produce art. So, for example, he includes anonymous aerial shots taken from bombers in World War II in his book *Looking at Photographs*.

Photography became widely marketable in galleries when the whole process became detached from the hand of the photographer. Some prefer to be called "an artist who works with a camera" rather than "photographer." Photographers who make their own prints in the darkroom are now seen as hopelessly craftsy.

Jill: This whole discussion is making me think about the effects of digital technology. How does the rise of the computerized image affect the way you think about "the hand"? 55

Joe: Students who take beginning photography with me love to work in the dark room; it's all about the difference from producing digital images. Traditional photography is simpler, more tangible, more hands-on.

I also teach a course in digital photography. I can teach it coming out of the way I teach black and white—that there are certain roadblocks and limitations. But people don't normally think of it that way. The lens, the ability to capture light, too much or too little, these things are usually taken care of in automatic mode, but the digital camera can be taken back to a manual mode.

Manipulation of the image using Photoshop is not without precedent. Collage and montage, which the Modernists were famous for, anticipate the way a computer cuts and pastes. It's just easier now to amend the image, and it can be done so mindlessly.

Jill: So at least to some people, digitalization has to do with interfering somehow with the original recorded image?

60 **Joe:** For Vergara the photograph is evidence, with minimal "interference." It's straight photography. This raises the question, how is evidence affected by "the hand" of the photographer? Photographs are of course all evidence, but evidence of what? And they are all inevitably constructs.

Vergara is coming from the surveyors, the Western survey photographers, a tradition of imperialist mapping. He is standing that tradition on its head by mapping the results of cultural and economic imperialism within American cities.

David: Can you tell us more about the tradition of survey photography? What made it imperialist?

Joe: The photographers—people like Carleton Watkins, O'Sullivan, and A.J. Russell—were hired by the U.S. Geological Survey and by the railroads in order to photograph all of the resources along new routes. Photographers were mapping the stuff that was ready to be taken by new investors. This was part of the exercise of Manifest Destiny in the opening of the West to commerce. So people argued that these new surveys of the West were needed to map our country, but one motivation was to discover the country's resources and know where they were. It's imperialist because you push the Native Americans out of the way.

Vergara comes at the other end of this tradition. His photographs say, well, this is what happened as a result of political and economic decisions that have shaped land use, property values, and people's lives.

65 Other documentarians were more sensationalist. In the tradition of newspaper photography, for example, the photographs of Weegee convey the circumstances in which they were taken. This is unlike Vergara, whose work is much more distanced. Weegee is more of a raw sensationalist, an inverted Crewdson, almost a sentimentalist. When I look at Weegee's images, it's as if he's saying, "If you can't smell your subject, you're not close enough." They're taken with a big flash to produce that gritty light. There's a coarse tonal range, it's stark: the technology of the newspaper. The gritty light seems to fall off around the edges.

The Fourth Meeting: 11/10/05 "Photographs and Paintings"

Jill: Last time you were talking about the photographer's hand and the charge from some quarters that darkroom work has become quaint and nostalgic. Could you say more about that?

Joe: Fabricators tend to view the need for the dark room and the artist's hand as quaint—as too "craftsy," too absorbed in the making of "the thing itself."

If you are Cindy Sherman and don't make it yourself, your art has moved to the realm of idea. For the postmodern photographer, the dark room is a waste of time. In this context, we might consider Crewdson as an impresario and director, who looks through the lens to make sure the shot is framed the right way but doesn't click the shutter. What the darkroom ace knows is just not that important. Crewdson hires darkroom aces (technicians) to work for him.

Jill: You've been telling us that there are different kinds of recorders and different schools of thought on fabrication. What at base is fabrication?

Joe: It is anything beyond point-and-shoot, whether the artist is building an elaborate set, like Crewdson, or cutting up and reassembling collages, like Metzger. You might also check out the work of Ralph Meatyard (an optometrist in Louisville). This collage process is also absorbed into painting, as in the "stuttering" Cubistic painting of *Nude Descending a Staircase* by Marcel Duchamp. Some people think that photography imitated Modernist painting, but the fact is that Modernist painters were influenced by photography. Cubism sees things from a lot of different angles at virtually the same time. [See Figure 16.9.]

Jill: So the Cubists were influenced by photography?   70

Joe: At least by their knowledge of what the camera could do—how it sees.

Jill: Szarkowski points out that Edgar Degas, the French impressionist painter, was also an amateur photographer whose paintings were influenced by the structure of photographs.

Joe: Fabricators come from more than one tradition. One of these is the tradition of late 19th-century photographers like Henry Peach Robinson and Oscar Rejlander and Lewis Carroll, who dressed young girls in costumes. The other tradition comes out of European Modernism, and includes Bauhaus figures such as Moholy-Nagy, Hannah Hoch, and John Heartfield. This latter tradition features a combination of photography and print and drawing, in some cases reframing images from the popular press, as in Dada. You might want to check out Hans Belmer, who did grotesque, reconstructed dolls. His work is interesting in the context of the contemporary photographer Loretta Lux, a subtle fabricator who makes doll-like images of children. At the (Chicago) Institute of Design, Moholy-Nagy reinvents Bauhaus aesthetic, where Metzger is his student.

In the 1930s Bauhaus, there was the conviction that the machine should be used to make art—that intelligent art for the masses could be the product of the machine. But it is not art if no hand is involved (versus Szarkowski's assumption that you can make art without pretense, as in the aerial photographs). Multiple exposures like Metzger's make the constructedness of the image overt; they render the photographic process more self-conscious. If you have a machine and use it thoughtfully, it makes art.

Philadelphia Museum of Art/Fine Art/Corbis

FIGURE 16.9
Nude Descending a Staircase #2 by Marcel Duchamp

The Fifth Meeting: 11/18/05 "On Portraiture"

David: I spent some time Googling the photographers you mentioned last 75 week. In particular I was intrigued by Loretta Lux [*takes out copies—starting with a portrait of a girl in pigtails*]. What's the difference between this photograph and a snapshot? What do you notice about it?

Joe: First of all, the color. It's so flat; we could call it desaturated. Look at the tonal difference between the complexion of the face and the sky behind her. The difference is very slight. So the effect is to flatten the space. And the sky is straight out of Photoshop. This photograph is constructed in a computer.

It's interesting to compare Lux's work with Crewdson's. Hers is not like Crewdson's work, which operates in real space. He's limited to what the camera can record. But her work, with that spatial flattening, is comparatively unreal. Crewdson thinks of his art more as a film-maker would. You build a set; you control the lighting. If you went there and looked into the lens, it would look the way the photograph does.

But Lux, if you look at the heads in those portraits of the young boy set against the clouds, they're ever so slightly stretched ... it creates a kind of surrealist effect. The viewer says, "Oh, okay, wait a minute. The space is a little weird in this photograph, isn't it? Why are the colors this way? Why are the heads this way? Am I awake? Or am I dreaming?" [See Figure 16.10.]

Lorette Lux/Artist Rights Society

FIGURE 16.10
Boy in a Blue Raincoat #2 by Loretta Lux

David: So what is Lux getting at?

80 **Joe:** Well, maybe it's something like this: we all like to have our kids have their portraits taken at a studio. She's playing with and calling attention to our sense of what a portrait is. It's fabricated. And it's cheesey. "Why do we go to Wal-Mart and get these portraits made?," her work might be asking.

Her work is getting us to see that the typical child's portrait is staged. It's projecting an idealized image, a serene and perfect vision, not the messy room and screaming kid. The portrait represents what we think things should be like, not what they're really like.

And she's interested in this—our interest in portraits. Portraits and snap-shots make up the vast majority of all photos made. People want to look at other people. In Lux, the children are idealized in a surreal way. The image is perfect in its own self-containment, but disorienting, off in ways that are hard to put your finger on.

David: Okay, so you're saying that these photos are satiric; they're sending up the conventions of portraiture. If you look at satire in literary terms, however, it's not only directed at certain targets; it's also coming from some relatively stable point of view. Where is Lux standing for her critique?

Joe: I think that the visual artist does not usually want to go that far. She's satis-fied to point it out. What else is it? What is the surrealists' goal? Must it be an avant garde position, something never seen before? Or can her artist's role be that of a barometer, reflecting back to the culture what we are?

85 This can lead us to wonder, are artists really at the forefront of the cul-ture, as a lot of people like to think, or are they rather a barometer bringing out for the rest of us what is already happening, but which we may not be seeing? Maybe they're barometers rather than initiators.

I took a field trip with the senior art majors last Monday to the studio of a working sculptor. He made a powerful impression on them. The guy was a kind of living caricature of the self-involved, arrogant artist. He claimed that to make an impact you needed to create stuff that had never been seen before, and if he decided any of his own work was derivative, he'd throw it out. He was saying that the artist's role is to be the inventor of culture, not just a cultural analyst using the culture as material to work over.

This reminds me of another book by Szarkowski called *Mirrors and Windows*. The mirrors part suggests that photographs cause the viewer to see himself or herself. The windows help us to see what's out there more carefully, by framing it. In this context, Lux's portraits bounce us back to the conventions normally used to set up a portrait. But her work is twisting this and making us self-conscious of the conventions. But it's subtle, and things we think are natural—children's portraits—are really not natural; they're fabricated.

David: Could you say more about the frame?

Joe: A frame requires a different kind of seeing, entirely different from the way we normally see. It makes us see and construct in a formal sense that has its own reasons for being; it's about conveying space, about balance, about traditional beauty in the relationship among the parts. Another way to look at it is that it forces us to examine everything inside the frame. Burtynski and the straightforward photographers induce us to look at what's inside the frame in some dispassionate way—all is equal inside the frame; things included are carefully chosen.

An illuminating comparison in this context might be between Lux and 90 the work of Eugene Smith. [*Joe turns to the portrait of the country doctor, which first appeared in the 1950s in* Life Magazine, *on page 150 of Szarkowski's* Looking at Photographs.] Smith's work has classical form—note how the figure of the doctor is centered, and thrust forward into the frame. He wants us to see a more heroic figure than the rest of us are. But framing gets us to examine carefully what's inside. [See Figure 16.11.]

Jill: This reminds me of what the contemporary American poet Robert Pinsky has said about artistic truth: that it is not insistent but poised. Poise is a key word for him.

Joe: I would connect the word poise with the work of Walker Evans, Helen Levitt, and Roy DeCarava as well as with Eugene Smith. Smith's work is so sculpturesque. It's like Michelangelo. He's a good example of romantic intensification. He's got a journalistic code to obey. But there is fabrication of a sort. "This is why people want to become doctors," his photograph is saying. Smith is interesting to contemplate, because he's so different from Crewdson or Lux.

Jill: Some fabricators overdo romantic intensification on purpose, don't they?

Joe: Yes, like Lux, though I'm not sure that romantic is the correct word for Lux. Lux calls attention to this. Try to compare Lux to another photographer named Rineke Dijkstra, who compares with Gursky and Burtynsky—she's very straight.

[*Joe looks at the famous Andreas Gursky photograph of the candy and other food* 95 *items, "99 Cent" (1999).*] This photograph is huge—10' × 8'—and you can read the label on every Snickers bar, and all the things inside the frame are equal. He's showing us how we're surrounded with unending crappy stuff. The photograph is making a huge critique in a dispassionate way.

David: Well, who is doing romantic portraiture?

Joe: We have the clearly fabricated portraiture of Edward Curtis; he puts Native Americans up against a sylvan background in all their tribal gear and feathers.

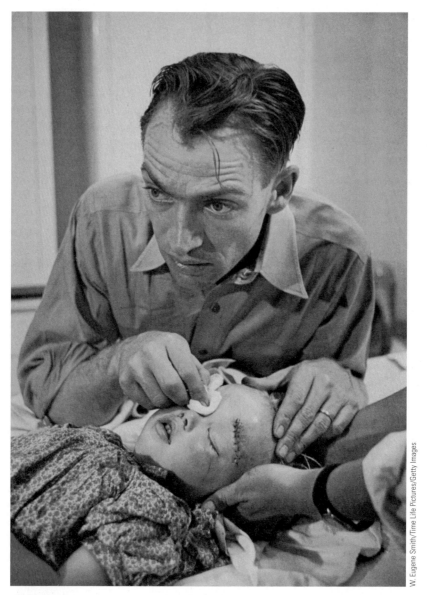

FIGURE 16.11
Untitled (Dr. Ceriani with Injured Child, 1948)—black and white photo by
W. Eugene Smith

And while W. Eugene Smith has been out of fashion for all his romanticizing, at least he is doing it in a real context.

In thinking about portraits, it is interesting to think about the relationship between photographers and their subjects. In the famous Walker Evans' portraits of sharecroppers, the figure of the woman is tight-lipped. She does not want to be photographed, but she is allowing it. The husband is more accommodating, but he is still resisting. But Smith's figures do not resist the camera. They go along with it. They are part of the project.

The Sixth Meeting: 12/2/05 "Varieties of Documentarians" (Recorders)

Note: The photographers discussed in this interview later appear in a list of categories that Elliott has composed, which is included at the end of these interviews. The boldfaced labels in this interview are taken from that list.

Joe: In contemporary photography we want to be aware of the distance, that a photo is not just a piece of life; it's detached. One of the earlier assumptions was that a little camera could take you *into* life (for example: Brassai, Capa, Weegee).

From 1925 until recently, there was the assumption that the small, porta- 100 ble, fast camera could bring us a slice of life, the essence of an event, a decisive moment. That slice of life, Salgado, Cartier-Bresson tradition has come to an end in art photography. And that may be because, why try to catch life in still form? Because it's superseded by video, by the videographers. But when things are moving, you can't meditate on them. We need the camera to stop time.

Jill: So is the small camera/slice of life approach always in the service of what you call recording?

Joe: In the documentary tradition, such as the photographs of W. Eugene Smith, *you are there.* As a photographer you bring the world to people with all the sweat attached. But Smith has also fabricated; he has framed the shot, controlling where we look, and so forth. And he has taken a lot of pictures of this guy. All in all, he has intensified the tools for making us see.

If you wanted to look at other comparable heroic photographs of this sort by Smith, check out the Albert Schweitzer picture, the white doctor in the jungle, bringing hope to these unfortunate lepers. Or there's a similar one of a Pittsburgh steel worker.

Or if you wanted to move to more contemporary documentarians, try Sebastião Salgado's *Workers* or Eugene Richards, who is grittier. These people are documentarians, but I call them **idea-driven documentarians** because they have a position that shapes the way they execute their photographs. [See Figure 16.12.]

There is another interesting photographer in this category, Lauren 105 Greenfield, who is making a big splash. She focuses on girl culture. She's look-ing at suburban culture, not at Africa like Salgado or the ghetto, like Richards, who looks at crack addicts in Philly (and gets flak for exploiting their dire situation for his own benefit). She critiques young women's obsession with beauty in the culture. Is she saying this consumption is a bad thing? I don't

Sebastião Salgado/Contact Press Images

FIGURE 16.12

A community above Chimborazo, Ecuador, 1982 by Sebastião Salgado

know. See her image of teenagers in a convertible in California on the way to the beach, in swimsuits. [See Figure 16.13.]

Jill: You also have a category that you call personal documentarians. How do they differ from the ones you call idea-driven?

Joe: Let's consider Nan Goldin. Her work is a cross between self-portraiture and the totally fabricated world of Cindy Sherman. But Goldin is a participant observer, as in anthropology. Whereas Eugene Smith is supposed to be a fly on the wall, Goldin turns the camera on herself as much as she does on the subcultures she documents. That's why I would call her a **personal documentarian**. The same goes for Sally Mann, who documents her own family. Her kids become actors in their own documentation, so she produces a documentary with the explicit cooperation of the subject.

Or consider Larry Sultan. He is a photographer of identity issues. He does "Pictures from Home," a series of his parents. He is a documentarian *and* a stager, doing photo essays about life in California. His colors and style anticipate Crewdson.

Jill: There are, then, documentarians who cross the line between the two camps, stagers and recorders?

Joe: Yes. And there are fabricators whose work comes out of the documentary 110 tradition of recorders, but in a clearly staged way. Consider Lorna Simpson, an African American who photographs staged re-enactments of black women dressed in colonial costumes as slaves in the house. She is examining identity though these re-enactments—her work offers *pictures of representations: it's a framing of the representation.*

There is another interesting photographer in this context, An-My Le. She teaches at Bard, went to Yale. She photographs re-enactments of battles in Vietnam; this is a search for identity (she is Vietnamese). She does not use her own family history but someone else's fabrication of that history.

David: This leads to a problem common in post-modernism. Once you get rid of authenticity as a viable concept (since everything is a representation or role), it is extremely difficult to distinguish between kinds or degrees of fabrication in photographs, between Smith and Crewdson.

Joe: Do people no longer care where truth is located?

Jill: Your post-modernist would say it's all images on TV.

Joe: These images really are beautiful, technologically speaking—spectacular, 115 if you choose to look at them.

Jill: How do we deal with those who are captivated by the televised image?

Lauren Greenfield/INSTITUTE

FIGURE 16.13
Lauren Greenfield, "Ashleigh, 13, with her friends and parents, Santa Monica"

Joe: I pretend the TV world is not out there. The students have the camera, and within that context they'll explore and appreciate the world of black and white, learning to distinguish a good image from a bad one. It's simpler, quieter, bucolic, and they can claim ownership.

Jill: One of my students who is also taking your photography course mentioned that he was told to go shoot, and he started with guys in the middle of the frame and nothing else going on. But soon he learned how much more there was to think about in taking a good photograph.

Joe: Yeah, for example, I do not allow beginning students to crop their images. The frame of the image must be thought through by the artist. It would violate the art to crop; a photograph, they learn, is meticulously put together.

One of my models here is Eugene Smith, who was an anomaly in the 120 world of *Life Magazine* photographers. In the old days, the magazine would develop and select images from among all those submitted on film by its photographers. But Smith refused. He wanted to select and print the image himself. So he quit *Life*. He wanted the control to exhibit the maximum romantic values, as in the "Country Doctor" series.

David: On that note, what about photographers who are primarily interested in the medium itself?

Joe: I know this is a category we haven't discussed—the **Formalists**. It exists between the documentarians and the post-modern stagers. Formalists are mostly interested in how the image is framed and how photographic controls are used to form the image—its design. This category includes small camera explorers like André Kertész and Lee Friedlander, but also artists who work on a more monumental scale, like Edward Weston, Aaron Siskind, and Hiroshi Sugimoto.

David: I've been looking at the photos in the *Blind Spot* magazines you gave me, especially from John Divola's "As Far As I Can Get" series. How would you locate his work?

Joe: His work is a form of fabrication. He is doing a kind of conceptual art move. You set up a lot of parameters with instructions in order to accomplish your art, and then you apply them. Sol LeWitt is an example. Divola does this. So does Ed Ruscha in his "26 Gasoline Stations" series. There is also his small fires series—it includes pictures of the flame on a glass ring, a cigarette, some pieces of paper burning. Another conceptual person is William Wegman, who established a basic collaboration with his dog, and he was determined to operate within that framework. My category for these artists is **Prescribed Process** (more commonly called Conceptual Art).

Jill: Oh, so the artist makes some rules to follow, and then the photographing 125 becomes a kind of controlled experiment?

Joe: Yes, it's not like Ruscha picked only certain gas stations to photograph because they were beautiful, or whatever, he had decided to photograph them all within a certain space—that was his rule.

The Seventh Meeting: 12/13/05 "Writing about Photographs"

David: One photographer you've said very little about is … you. We're sitting in this room across from one of the photographs that is part of your Bethlehem Steel series. [See Figure 16.14. A second photograph from this series is shown in Figure 16.15.]

Joseph Elliott

FIGURE 16.14
Blast furnace rest area, Bethlehem, PA, 1992. 20" × 24" gelatin silver print by Joseph Elliott

Joseph Elliott

FIGURE 16.15
Attic, Founders Hall, Girard College, Philadelphia, PA, 2000. 20" × 24"
gelatin silver print by Joseph Elliott

Joe: I began making photos at Bethlehem Steel in 1989 and continued until the plant closed in 1999. The motive was fascination with this gargantuan relic of the Machine Age. If I had to categorize the work, I would have to call myself a structural documentarian.

Jill: It's an interesting photograph. There's the protective clothing hanging on the wall. Is that a hat? Did you light the picture?

Joe: No, the light came in from the window. I got that picture in less than minute. 130 The subject did not know he was being photographed. I just looked over and saw it, and I set up really quickly and took the shot. The foot of another man sneaks into the frame on the lower left. I only noticed this when I printed the photograph. The foot reminds us that there is a world going on outside the frame.

Jill: When I teach poetry-writing, we spend time thinking about how the details in most descriptive writing are implicitly metaphorical—that is, they are both literal and figurative.

David: What do you see as metaphorical in Joe's photograph?

Jill: Well, the man is slightly out of focus, as if in motion; the image reminds us of the passage of time. He is in a box surrounded by his protective clothing, the hat, the gas mask. So the picture is all about containment and safety, but we also know it's a picture about something—the soon to be closed Bethlehem Steel—about to pass into oblivion.

Joe: Yes, I can see the containment, but if you look at it another way, it is hard to tell where the man is in relation to the space. We could be seeing a mirror reflection of him, or he could be inside the box.

Jill: As we talk I am thinking about how some people are inclined to look for "messages" in photographs, which isn't exactly right. Others decide that they can make of the photograph whatever they wish, which isn't right either.

Joe: I have been reading a small book called A *Primer for Visual Literacy* by Donis A. Dondis. She says there are three levels on which we can look at a visual image: the representational, the formal, and the symbolic. People often want to jump to the symbolic. But we also need to deal with the other two levels whenever we discuss an image. The levels are not always equally important. As a practitioner I usually stay in the realms of the first two. When I teach beginning students we spend most of our time talking about the second.

Jill: In closing, could you talk to us a little bit about how you look at photographs, and how you teach your students to look at them?

David: How do you begin?

Joe: Well, first, I try to see everything that is in the frame. Too often we engage in unconscious cropping—we look at a piece of the photo instead of taking it all in. In a good photograph, you can't take a piece of it for the whole. It's all important.
One way to get inexperienced viewers to see more is to take a piece of paper and slide it around, cutting off one side or another. Then you re-describe the work: what do you see now that you didn't see before? What does it feel like?

As for other moves, I sometimes give students a cardboard frame, and have them use it to frame the world—to think of the world in terms of framing shots.

Or a viewer can sometimes see more freshly by squinting at the image or turning it upside down. That has the effect of denaturalizing it, so you can see it freshly. Too often inexperienced viewers *get so stuck on the information that they can't see how it is put together.*

The more you look, the finer the distinctions you can learn to see.

Second, there is a kind of memory bank of images that I have access to in my brain when I look at photographs. This comes from a knowledge of the history of photography. I see photographs in the context of other photographs that I have seen.

Third, I try to fit the image roughly into one or more of the categories we have been discussing. What is the cultural, conceptual, political basis for the image? What mode did the photographer choose to express the work? 145

Jill: Any favorite questions?

Joe: One question I really encourage asking is "Why is this art?" Note that the question is *not* "Is this art?" The implication is that these images are all art. We are looking for what makes them art. It is not our job to judge.

Try asking this question with Ed Ruscha's work, who in "26 Gasoline Stations" does 1950s Americana in canvases 7' × 30' long, featuring smoking rabbits, dogs' heads, phone poles, and other iconic images.

David: Thanks so much for talking to us, Joe.

Jill: Yes, and we'll be sure to call you before we burn down any houses.

Joseph Elliott's Photo-Categories

Note: Some artists fall into more than one category.
Stagers (Fabricators)
> Prescribed Process
>> Edward Muybridge
>> Sol LeWitt
>> Bernd and Hilla Becher
>> Ed Ruscha
>> John Divola
>> William Wegman

> Tableaux, Constructed in front of the camera or in the computer
>> Julia Cameron
>> Peter Henry Emerson
>> Edward Curtis
>> Gregory Crewdson
>> Cindy Sherman
>> Loretta Lux

Philip-Lorca diCorcia

Jeff Wall

Almost all advertising images (GAP and Apple have used existing images of famous personalities, re-contextualizing them)

John Heartfield

An-My Le

Lorna Simpson (records other people's tableaux)

Larry Fink

David LaChapelle

Recorders (Observers)

Detached Documentarians

Timothy O'Sullivan

Eugène Atget

August Sander

Walker Evans

Alfred Stieglitz

Joel Sternfeld

Edward Burtynsky

Camilo Jose Vergara

William Eggleston

Joseph Elliott

An-My Le

Idea-driven Documentarians, lead with ideological frame

Eugene Smith

Dorothea Lange

Weegee

Larry Fink

Sebastião Salgado

Diane Arbus

Lauren Greenfield (Girl Culture)

Arlene Gottfried

Eugene Richards

Personal Documentarians

Nan Goldin

Larry Sultan

Robin Schwartz

Bill Burke

Sally Mann

Formalists
>   Walker Evans
>   Edward Weston
>   Ray Metzger
>   Hiroshi Sugimoto
>   Lee Friedlander

Works Cited or Recommended

Robert Adams, *On Beauty in Photography*

Roland Barthes, *Camera Lucida: Reflections on Photography*

Vicki Goldberg, *Photographers on Photography*

Lincoln Kirsten, *American Photographs: The 1939 Walker Evans MOMA Exhibition Catalogue*

Janet Malcolm, *Diana & Nikon: Essays on the Aesthetic of Photography*

October Magazine, "The Judgment Seat of Photography" (on Szarkowski's influence)

Aaron Scharf, *Art and Photography*

John Szarkowski, *American Landscapes: Photographs from the Collection of the Museum of Modern Art*

John Szarkowski, *Looking at Photographs*

John Szarkowski, *Mirrors and Windows*

John Szarkowski *The Photographer's Eye*

Alan Trachtenberg, *Reading American Photographs: Images as History: Mathew Brady to Walker Evans*

Things to Do with the Reading

1. In the Seventh Meeting Elliott refers to a book entitled *A Primer for Visual Literacy* by Donis A. Dondis in which the author claims that there are three levels on which we can look at a visual image: the representational, the formal, and the symbolic. Elliott asserts that people too often leap to the symbolic before considering the other two levels. In other words, they leap to some larger (symbolic) meaning that they ascribe to the photo before they have dwelled with the representational details (what it is a picture of) or the formal way that shapes and perspectives are arranged inside the frame.

   Use description as an analytical tool for thinking about and writing a short essay on the William Eggleston photograph of two men by a car (see Figure 16.7). First describe the photograph as a representation. What is it a picture of? You might wish to use the method of sliding a piece of paper around the photograph to make sure you don't leave important details out of your description.

Next, write a second description in which you attend to the formal level—the arrangement of elements in the frame, including various kinds of shapes and patterns of light and dark (this will require you to "see past the content").

Finally, use these descriptions to prompt some interpretive leaps about the way the photograph operates beyond the literal. Which details of the photograph seem to invite a more figurative reading, one concerned with meaning, with what the photographer might be trying to "say"? Why? It would probably be useful at this stage to consider as well what elements of the photograph seem staged. You might also try this exercise with Lauren Greenfield's photograph, "Ashleigh, 13, with her friend and parents, Santa Monica" (Figure 16.13).

2. Write an essay comparing Gregory Crewdson and Loretta Lux. Like all good thinkers and writers, Elliott not only creates categories but qualifies them and doesn't allow the categorizing process to cause him to gloss over photographers who don't neatly fit. So, for example, in one of his two primary categories, fabricators (aka stagers), he notes that the works of Gregory Crewdson and Loretta Lux are staged but with interesting differences. Locate this section of the interview (in the Fifth Meeting), choose relevant quotations, and paraphrase them in order to articulate and develop this difference. Apply your conclusions to photographs by Crewdson and Lux.

3. In the Third Meeting, "The Photographer's Hand," Elliott comments,

> In [Crewdson's] photo of the house on fire, the people on the train track on the other side of the frame are a competing focal point by design. Nothing is an accident in the photo. He wants it to be carefully observed, to invite a close reading. We may think of a photograph having an initial impact, but there's also something else going on, a counterpoint, a set of messages (paragraph 46).

Use these observations as a lens for writing an analysis of the photograph. Here are some questions you might consider. If the photo has competing focal points by design, what is achieved in this way? If the photo has an initial impact but also a counterpoint—more than one, potentially opposed "message"—what would you say these are? Make sure to share your reasoning about the evidence: why you think particular details mean what you claim they mean. (See Chapter 4, the section called "Giving Evidence a Point: Making Details Speak.") You might also try this with another Crewdson photograph—either another one in this book or one that you locate online.

4. Write a short essay based on Elliott's observations in the Third Meeting, "The Photographer's Hand," about looking for the photographer's

hand in the Alfred Stieglitz photograph of "Georgia Engelhard" (see Figure 16.8). He asks, for example, why Stieglitz included the edge with the part of an urn and a rubber tree. Where is there evidence of the presence of the photographer's shaping influence—his "hand"—in the photograph?

At the end of the Seventh Meeting, Elliott describes an exercise that can help a viewer see the photographer's hand. He has viewers take a piece of paper and slide it around on a photograph, blocking one side or another. He then asks them to re-describe the work each time: "What do you see now that you didn't see before?" Apply this procedure to the Stieglitz photograph.

5. In his famous book *Camera Lucida: Reflections on Photography*, Roland Barthes speaks of the Punctum, which he defines as the single detail in a photograph that "arouses greatest sympathy" and is primarily responsible for the impact of the image on a viewer. In the previous exercise, you were asked to notice as much as you could about the details Stieglitz chooses to frame in his photograph. Barthes' approach is like the technique we call ranking, choosing and arguing for the importance of a single element as a means of prompting an interpretive leap about the whole photograph (see Chapter 1, "NOTICE AND FOCUS (Ranking)"). Select a Punctum for Stieglitz's "Georgia Englehard" and use it to anchor a short interpretive essay.

6. Application: Write a paper about some trend you notice in advertising photography. Here are some questions to help. To what extent do you find evidence of documentary style photography in the world of print advertising? How is it being used, and for what purposes? You might also look for at least one clearly staged advertising photo that you think is representative of staging among advertising photos. And can you find an example of a hybrid, an image that seems to combine staging and recording in the service of advertising some product?

7. Application: Elliott discusses the work of Loretta Lux as a commentary on the conventions of portraiture, inviting us to think about what portraits are and why all of us (not just professional photographers) take portraits of people. Elliott refers to these conventions as "idealizing." Apply Elliott's discussion to other portraits—of your own (or family photographs), or of other photographers mentioned in the interview. As you study the portraits you've assembled, try to make a list of what you think the conventions of portraiture actually *are*. Then work out their implications, the meanings attached to them. Your goal will be to write an essay in which you make some claims about what the photographer of your choice seems to be saying about portraiture. Keep in mind that in Elliott's terms, portraits can be to varying degrees both recorded and staged.

8. **Application:** Near the end of the Sixth Meeting, Elliott discusses those photographers he labels Prescribed Processors—that is, those who "set up a lot of parameters, with instructions to accomplish [their] art" (paragraph 124). John Divola (not included here) photographs a lone runner against a variety of settings in his "As Far as I Can Get" series; Ed Ruscha trains his camera on "26 Gasoline Stations." Try the following experiment with prescribed processing as the basis for a paper: get a camera and then select an object (or subject) and shoot the first 26 that you see. Use the photographs as a subject for analysis. What did you learn about your subject by repeatedly photographing it? How do you see this subject differently now? What did you learn about seeing—and about taking pictures—by doing this project?

9. **Link Across Chapters:** In Chapter 13, James Howard Kunstler writes (in "The Public Realm and the Common Good") that public space has been seriously eroded by contemporary zoning and construction practices. Be a documentarian and try to record in both writing and images what you take to be evidence for the degeneration of what he terms the "public realm," defined as "the physical manifestation of the common good."

   Go to places on your campus or in a neighborhood nearby and record (in writing and in photographs) examples of what you take to be good and less good examples of the preservation of public spaces. Use both images and verbal depictions to compose a photo-essay in which you capture what you think to be the essence of one or more of these places.

Susan Sontag

In Plato's Cave

This essay from the influential cultural critic Susan Sontag first appeared as a chapter in her 1977 essay collection *On Photography*, which won the National Book Critics' Circle Award for Criticism in 1977. The art establishment regarded the book with horror, though over time many have come around to acknowledge its stimulating and disturbing discussion of the role of photography in contemporary culture. In an article commemorating the twentieth anniversary of its publication, Michael Starenko claimed that "Perhaps no photography book [...] has been analyzed and discussed with more intensity, from so many different and competing perspectives. [...] Sontag's claims about photography as well as her mode of argument have become part of the rhetorical 'tool kit' that photography theorists and critics carry around in their heads ("Sontag's On Photography at 20," *Afterimage*, March–April 1998)." One of America's most influential public intellectuals, Sontag authored *Against Interpretation*, *The Way We Live Now*, *Illness as Metaphor*, and the essay "Notes on Camp." She died in 2004.

Humankind lingers unregenerately in Plato's cave, still revelling, its age-old 1 habit, in mere images of the truth. But being educated by photographs is not like being educated by older, more artisanal images. For one thing, there are a great many more images around, claiming our attention. The inventory started in 1839 and since then just about everything has been photographed, or so it seems. This very insatiability of the photographing eye changes the terms of confinement in the cave, our world. In teaching us a new visual code, photographs alter and enlarge our notions of what is worth looking at and what we have a right to observe. They are a grammar and, even more importantly, an ethics of seeing. Finally, the most grandiose result of the photographic enterprise is to give us the sense that we can hold the whole world in our heads—as an anthology of images.

To collect photographs is to collect the world. Movies and television programmes light up walls, flicker, and go out; but with still photographs the image is also an object, lightweight, cheap to produce, easy to carry about, accumulate, store. In Godard's *Les Carabiniers* (1963), two sluggish lumpen-peasants are lured into joining the King's Army by the promise that they will be able to loot, rape, kill, or do whatever else they please to the enemy, and get rich. But the suitcase of booty that Michel-Ange and Ulysse triumphantly bring home, years later, to their wives turns out to contain only picture postcards, hundreds of them, of Monuments, Department Stores, Mammals,

"In Plato's Cave" from ON PHOTOGRAPHY by Susan Sontag. Copyright © 1977 by Susan Sontag. Reprinted by permission of Farrar, Straus and Giroux, LLC.

Wonders of Nature, Methods of Transport, Works of Art, and other classified treasures from around the globe. Godard's gag vividly parodies the equivocal magic of the photographic image. Photographs are perhaps the most mysterious of all the objects that make up, and thicken, the environment we recognise as modern. Photographs really are experience captured, and the camera is the ideal arm of consciousness in its acquisitive mood.

To photograph is to appropriate the thing photographed. It means putting oneself into a certain relation to the world that feels like knowledge—and, therefore, like power. A now notorious first fall into alienation, habituating people to abstract the world into printed words, is supposed to have engendered that surplus of Faustian energy and psychic damage needed to build modern, inorganic societies. But print seems a less treacherous form of leaching out the world, of turning it into a mental object, than photographic images, which now provide most of the knowledge people have about the look of the past and the reach of the present. What is written about a person or an event is frankly an interpretation, as are handmade visual statements, like paintings and drawings. Photographed images do not seem to be statements about the world so much as pieces of it, miniatures of reality that anyone can make or acquire.

Photographs, which fiddle with the scale of the world, themselves get reduced, blown up, cropped, retouched, doctored, tricked out. They age, plagued by the usual ills of paper objects; they disappear; they become valuable, and get bought and sold; they are reproduced. Photographs, which package the world, seem to invite packaging. They are stuck in albums, framed and set on tables, tacked on walls, projected as slides. Newspapers and magazines feature them; cops alphabetise them; museums exhibit them; publishers compile them.

5   For many decades the book has been the most influential way of arranging (and usually miniaturising) photographs, thereby guaranteeing them longevity, if not immortality—photographs are fragile objects, easily torn or mislaid—and a wider public. The photograph in a book is, obviously, the image of an image. But since it is, to begin with, a printed, smooth object, a photograph loses much less of its essential quality when reproduced in a book than a painting does. Still, the book is not a wholly satisfactory scheme for putting groups of photographs into general circulation. The sequence in which the photographs are to be looked at is proposed by the order of pages, but nothing holds readers to the recommended order or indicates the amount of time to be spent on each photograph. Chris Marker's film, *Si j'avais quatre dromadaires* (1966), a brilliantly orchestrated meditation on photographs of all sorts and themes, suggests a subtler and more rigorous way of packaging (and enlarging) still photographs. Both the order and the exact time for looking at each photograph are imposed; and there is a gain in visual legibility and emotional impact. But photographs transcribed in a film cease to be collectable objects, as they still are when served up in books.

Photographs furnish evidence. Something we hear about, but doubt, seems proven when we're shown a photograph of it. In one version of its utility, the camera record incriminates. Starting with their use by the Paris police in the murderous roundup of Communards in June 1871, photographs became a useful tool of modern states in the surveillance and control of their increasingly mobile populations. In another version of its utility, the camera record justifies. A photograph passes for incontrovertible proof that a given thing happened. The picture may distort; but there is always a presumption that something exists, or did exist, which is like what's in the picture. Whatever the limitations (through amateurism) or pretensions (through artistry) of the individual photographer, a photograph—any photograph—seems to have a more innocent, and therefore more accurate, relation to visible reality than do other mimetic objects. Virtuosi of the noble image like Alfred Stieglitz and Paul Strand, composing mighty, unforgettable photographs decade after decade, still want, first of all, to show something "out there," just like the Polaroid owner for whom photographs are a handy, fast form of note-taking, or the shutterbug with a Brownie who takes snapshots as souvenirs of daily life.

While a painting or a prose description can never be other than a narrowly selective interpretation, a photograph can be treated as a narrowly selective transparency. But despite the presumption of veracity that gives all photographs authority, interest, seductiveness, the work that photographers do is no generic exception to the usually shady commerce between art and truth. Even when photographers are most concerned with mirroring reality, they are still haunted by tacit imperatives of taste and conscience. The immensely gifted members of the Farm Security Administration photographic project of the late 1930s (among them Walker Evans, Dorothea Lange, Ben Shahn, Russell Lee) would take dozens of frontal pictures of one of their sharecropper subjects until satisfied that they had gotten just the right look on film—the precise expression on the subject's face that supported their own notions about poverty, light, dignity, texture, exploitation, and geometry. In deciding how a picture should look, in preferring one exposure to another, photographers are always imposing standards on their subjects. Although there is a sense in which the camera does indeed capture reality, not just interpret it, photographs are as much an interpretation of the world as paintings and drawings are. Those occasions when the taking of photographs is relatively undiscriminating, promiscuous, or self-effacing do not lessen the didacticism of the whole enterprise. This very passivity—and ubiquity—of the photographic record is photography's "message," its aggression.

Images which idealise (like most fashion and animal photography) are no less aggressive than work which makes a virtue of plainness (like class pictures, still lifes of the bleaker sort, and mug shots). There is an aggression implicit in every use of the camera. This is as evident in the 1840s and 1850s, photography's glorious first two decades, as in all the succeeding decades, during which technology made possible an ever increasing spread of that mentality which looks at the world as a set of potential photographs. Even for such early masters as David Octavius Hill and Julia Margaret Cameron who used the camera as a means of getting painterly images, the point of taking photographs was a vast departure from the aims of painters. From its start, photography implied the capture of the largest possible number of subjects. Painting never had so imperial a scope. The subsequent industrialisation of camera technology only carried out a promise inherent in photography from its very beginning: to democratise all experiences by translating them into images.

That age when taking photographs required a cumbersome and expensive contraption—the toy of the clever, the wealthy, and the obsessed—seems remote indeed from the era of sleek pocket cameras that invite anyone to take pictures. The first cameras, made in France and England in the early 1840s, had only inventors and buffs to operate them. Since there were then no professional photographers, there could not be amateurs either, and taking photographs had no clear social use; it was a gratuitous, that is, an artistic activity, though with few pretensions to being an art. It was only with its industrialisation that photography came into its own as art. As industrialisation provided social uses for the operations of the photographer, so the reaction against these uses reinforced the self-consciousness of photography-as-art.

10   Recently, photography has become almost as widely practised an amusement as sex and dancing—which means that, like every mass art form, photography is not practised by most people as an art. It is mainly a social rite, a defence against anxiety, and a tool of power.

Memorialising the achievements of individuals considered as members of families (as well as of other groups) is the earliest popular use of photography. For at least a century, the wedding photograph has been as much a part of the ceremony as the prescribed verbal formulae. Cameras go with family life. According to a sociological study done in France, most households have a camera, but a household with children is twice as likely to have at least one camera as a household in which there are no children. Not to take pictures of one's children, particularly when they are small, is a sign of parental indifference, just as not turning up for one's graduation picture is a gesture of adolescent rebellion.

Through photographs, each family constructs a portrait-chronicle of itself—a portable kit of images that bears witness to its connectedness. It hardly matters what activities are photographed so long as photographs get taken and are cherished. Photography becomes a rite of family life just when, in the industrialising countries of Europe and America, the very institution of the family starts undergoing radical surgery. As that claustrophobic unit, the nuclear family, was being carved out of a much larger family aggregate, photography came along to memorialise, to restate symbolically, the imperilled continuity and vanishing extendedness of family life. Those ghostly traces, photographs, supply the token presence of the dispersed relatives. A family's photograph album is generally about the extended family—and, often, is all that remains of it.

As photographs give people an imaginary possession of a past that is unreal, they also help people to take possession of space in which they are insecure. Thus, photography develops in tandem with one of the most characteristic of modern activities: tourism. For the first time in history, large numbers of people regularly travel out of their habitual environments for short periods of time. It seems positively unnatural to travel for pleasure without taking a camera along. Photographs will offer indisputable evidence that the trip was made, that the programme was carried out, that fun was had. Photographs document sequences of consumption carried on outside the view of family, friends, neighbours. But dependence on the camera, as the device that makes real what one is experiencing, doesn't fade when people travel more. Taking photographs fills the same need for the cosmopolitans accumulating photograph-trophies of their boat trip up the Albert Nile or their fourteen days in China as it does for lower-middle-class vacationers taking snapshots of the Eiffel Tower or Niagara Falls.

A way of certifying experience, taking photographs is also a way of refusing it —by limiting experience to a search for the photogenic, by converting experience into an image, a souvenir. Travel becomes a strategy for accumulating photographs. The very activity of taking pictures is soothing, and assuages general feelings of disorientation that are likely to be exacerbated by travel. Most tourists feel compelled to put the camera between themselves and whatever is remarkable that they encounter. Unsure of other responses, they take a picture. This gives shape to experience: stop, take a photograph, and move on. The method especially appeals to people handicapped by a ruthless work ethic—Germans, Japanese, and Americans. Using a camera appeases the anxiety which the work-driven feel about not working when they are on vacation and supposed to be having fun. They have something to do that is like a friendly imitation of work: they can take pictures.

People robbed of their past seem to make the most fervent picture takers, 15 at home and abroad. Everyone who lives in an industrialised society is obliged gradually to give up the past, but in certain countries, such as the United States and Japan, the break with the past has been particularly traumatic. In the early 1970s, the fable of the brash American tourist of the 1950s and 1960s, rich with dollars and Babbittry, was replaced by the mystery of the group-minded Japanese tourist, newly released from his island prison by the miracle of overvalued yen, who is generally armed with two cameras, one on each hip.

Photography has become one of the principal devices for experiencing something, for giving an appearance of participation. One full-page ad shows a small group of people standing pressed together, peering out of the photograph, all but one looking stunned, excited, upset. The one who wears a different expression holds a camera to his eye; he seems self-possessed, is almost smiling. While the others are passive, clearly alarmed spectators, having a camera has transformed one person into something active, a voyeur: only he has mastered the situation. What do these people see? We don't know. And it doesn't matter. It is an Event: something worth seeing—and therefore worth photographing. The ad copy, white letters across the dark lower third of the photograph like news coming over a teletype machine, consists of just six words: " . . . Prague . . . Woodstock . . . Vietnam . . . Sapporo . . . Londonderry . . . LEICA." Crushed hopes, youth antics, colonial wars, and winter sports are alike—are equalised by the camera. Taking photographs has set up a chronic voyeuristic relation to the world which levels the meaning of all events.

A photograph is not just the result of an encounter between an event and a photographer; picture-taking is an event in itself, and one with ever more peremptory rights—to interfere with, to invade, or to ignore whatever is going on. Our very sense of situation is now articulated by the camera's interventions. The omnipresence of cameras persuasively suggests that time consists of interesting events, events worth photographing. This, in turn, makes it easy to feel that any event, once underway, and whatever its moral character, should be allowed to complete itself—so that something else can be brought into the world, the photograph. After the event has ended, the picture will still exist, conferring on the event a kind of immortality (and importance) it would never otherwise have enjoyed. While real people are out there killing themselves or other real people, the photographer stays behind his or her camera, creating a tiny element of another world: the imagine-world that bids to outlast us all.

Photographing is essentially an act of non-intervention. Part of the horror of such memorable coups of contemporary photojournalism as the pictures of a Vietnamese bonze reaching for the gasoline can, of a Bengali guerrilla in the act of bayoneting a trussed-up collaborator, comes from the awareness of how plausible it has become, in situations where the photographer has the choice between a photograph and a life, to choose the photograph. The person who intervenes cannot record; the person who is recording cannot intervene. Dziga Vertov's great film, *Man with a Movie Camera* (1929), gives the ideal image of the photographer as someone in perpetual movement, someone moving through a panorama of disparate events with such agility and speed that any intervention is out of the question. Hitchcock's *Rear Window* (1954) gives the complementary image: The photographer played by James Stewart has an intensified relation to one event, through his camera, precisely because he has a broken leg and is confined to a wheelchair; being temporarily immobilised prevents him from acting on what he sees, and makes it even more important to take pictures. Even if incompatible with intervention in a physical sense, using a camera is still a form of participation. Although the camera is an observation station, the act of photographing is more than passive observing. Like sexual voyeurism, it is a way of at least tacitly, often explicitly, encouraging whatever is going on to keep on happening. To take a picture is to have an interest in things as they are, in the status quo remaining unchanged (at least for as long as it takes to get a "good" picture), to be in complicity with whatever makes a subject interesting, worth photographing— including, when that is the interest, another person's pain or misfortune.

"I always thought of photography as a naughty thing to do—that was one of my favourite things about it," Diane Arbus wrote, "and when I first did it I felt very perverse." Being a professional photographer can be thought of as naughty, to use Arbus's pop word, if the photographer seeks out subjects considered to be disreputable, taboo, marginal. But naughty subjects are harder to find these days. And what exactly is the perverse aspect of picture-taking? If professional photographers often have sexual fantasies when they are behind the camera, perhaps the perversion lies in the fact that these fantasies are both plausible and so inappropriate. In *Blowup* (1966), Antonioni has the fashion photographer hovering convulsively over Veruschka's body with his camera clicking. Naughtiness, indeed! In fact, using a camera is not a very good way of getting at someone sexually. Between photographer and subject, there has to be distance. The camera doesn't rape, or even possess, though it may presume, intrude, trespass, distort, exploit, and, at the farthest reach of metaphor, assassinate—all activities that, unlike the sexual push and shove, can be conducted from a distance, and with some detachment.

There is a much stronger sexual fantasy in Michael Powell's extraordinary movie *Peeping Tom* (1960), which is not about a Peeping Tom but about a psychopath who kills women with a weapon concealed in his camera, while photographing them. Not once does he touch his subjects. He doesn't desire their bodies; he wants their presence in the form of filmed images—those showing them experiencing their own death—which he screens at home for his solitary pleasure. The movie assumes connections between impotence and aggression, professionalised looking and cruelty, which point to the central fantasy connected with the camera. The camera as phallus is, at most, a flimsy variant of the inescapable metaphor that everyone unselfconsciously employs. However hazy our awareness of this fantasy, it is named without subtlety whenever we talk about "loading" and "aiming" a camera, about "shooting" a film.

The old-fashioned camera was clumsier and harder to reload than a brown Bess musket. The modern camera is trying to be a ray gun. One ad reads:

> The Yashica Electro-35 GT is the spaceage camera your family will love. Take beautiful pictures day or night. Automatically. Without any nonsense. Just aim, focus and shoot. The GT's computer brain and electronic shutter will do the rest.

Like a car, a camera is sold as a predatory weapon—one that's as automated as possible, ready to spring. Popular taste expects an easy, an invisible technology. Manufacturers reassure their customers that taking pictures demands no skill or expert knowledge, that the machine is all-knowing, and responds to the slightest pressure of the will. It's as simple as turning the ignition key or pulling the trigger.

Like guns and cars, cameras are fantasy-machines whose use is addictive. However, despite the extravagances of ordinary language and advertising, they are not lethal. In the hyperbole that markets cars like guns, there is at least this much truth: except in wartime, cars kill more people than guns do. The camera/gun does not kill, so the ominous metaphor seems to be all bluff—like a man's fantasy of having a gun, knife, or tool between his legs. Still, there is something predatory in the act of taking a picture. To photograph people is to violate them, by seeing them as they never see themselves, by having knowledge of them they can never have; it turns people into objects that can be symbolically possessed. Just as the camera is a sublimation of the gun, to photograph someone is a sublimated murder—a soft murder, appropriate to a sad, frightened time.

Eventually, people might learn to act out more of their aggressions with cameras and fewer with guns, with the price being an even more image-choked world. One situation where people are switching from bullets to film is the photographic safari that is replacing the gun safari in East Africa. The hunters have Hasselblads instead of Winchesters; instead of looking through a telescopic sight to aim a rifle, they look through a viewfinder to frame a picture. In end-of-the-century London, Samuel Butler complained that "there is a photographer in every bush, going about like a roaring lion seeking whom he may devour." The photographer is now charging real beasts, beleaguered and too rare to kill. Guns have metamorphosed into cameras in this earnest comedy, the ecology safari, because nature has ceased to be what it always had been—what people needed protection from. Now nature—tamed, endangered, mortal—needs to be protected from people. When we are afraid, we shoot. But when we are nostalgic, we take pictures.

It is a nostalgic time right now, and photographs actively promote nostalgia. Photography is an elegiac art, a twilight art. Most subjects photographed are, just by virtue of being photographed, touched with pathos. An ugly or grotesque subject may be moving because it has been dignified by the attention of the photographer. A beautiful subject can be the object of rueful feelings, because it has aged or decayed or no longer exists. All photographs are *memento mori*. To take a photograph is to participate in another person's (or thing's) mortality, vulnerability, mutability. Precisely by slicing out this moment and freezing it, all photographs testify to time's relentless melt.

Cameras began duplicating the world at that moment when the human 25 landscape started to undergo a vertiginous rate of change: while an untold number of forms of biological and social life are being destroyed in a brief span of time, a device is available to record what is disappearing. The moody, intricately textured Paris of Atget and Brassaï is mostly gone. Like the dead relatives and friends preserved in the family album, whose presence in photographs exorcises some of the anxiety and remorse prompted by their disappearance, so the photographs of neighbourhoods now torn down, rural places disfigured and made barren, supply our pocket relation to the past.

A photograph is both a pseudo-presence and a token of absence. Like a wood fire in a room, photographs—especially those of people, of distant landscapes and faraway cities, of the vanished past—are incitements to reverie. The sense of the unattainable that can be evoked by photographs feeds directly into the erotic feelings of those for whom desirability is enhanced by distance. The lover's photograph hidden in a married woman's wallet, the poster photograph of a rock star tacked up over an adolescent's bed, the campaign-button image of a politician's face pinned on a voter's coat, the snapshots of a cabdriver's children clipped to the visor—all such talismanic uses of photographs express a feeling both sentimental and implicitly magical: they are attempts to contact or lay claim to another reality.

Photographs can abet desire in the most direct, utilitarian way—as when someone collects photographs of anonymous examples of the desirable as an aid to masturbation. The matter is more complex when photographs are used to stimulate the moral impulse. Desire has no history—at least, it is experienced in each instance as all foreground, immediacy. It is aroused by archetypes and is, in that sense, abstract. But moral feelings are embedded in history, whose personae are concrete, whose situations are always specific. Thus, almost opposite rules hold true for the use of the photograph to awaken desire and to awaken conscience. The images that mobilise conscience are always linked to a given historical situation. The more general they are, the less likely they are to be effective.

A photograph that brings news of some unsuspected zone of misery cannot make a dent in public opinion unless there is an appropriate context of feeling and attitude. The photographs Mathew Brady and his colleagues took of the horrors of the battlefields did not make people any less keen to go on with the Civil War. The photographs of ill-clad, skeletal prisoners held at Andersonville inflamed Northern public opinion—against the South. (The effect of the Andersonville photographs must have been partly due to the very novelty, at that time, of seeing photographs.) The political understanding that many Americans came to in the 1960s would allow them, looking at the photographs Dorothea Lange took of Nisei on the West Coast being transported to internment camps in 1942, to recognise their subject for what it was—a crime committed by the government against a large group of American citizens. Few people who saw those photographs in the 1940s could have had so unequivocal a reaction; the grounds for such a judgment were covered over by the pro-war consensus. Photographs cannot create a moral position, but they can reinforce one—and can help build a nascent one.

Photographs may be more memorable than moving images, because they are a neat slice of time, not a flow. Television is a stream of underselected images, each of which cancels its predecessor. Each still photograph is a privileged moment, turned into a slim object that one can keep and look at again. Photographs like the one that made the front page of most newspapers in the world in 1972—a naked South Vietnamese child just sprayed by American napalm, running down a highway toward the camera, her arms open, screaming with pain—probably did more to increase the public revulsion against the war than a hundred hours of televised barbarities.

30 One would like to imagine that the American public would not have been so unanimous in its acquiescence to the Korean War if it had been confronted with photographic evidence of the devastation of Korea, an ecocide and genocide in some respects even more thorough than those inflicted on Vietnam a decade later. But the supposition is trivial. The public did not see such photographs because there was, ideologically, no space for them. No one brought back photographs of daily life in Pyongyang, to show that the enemy had a human face, as Felix Greene and Marc Riboud brought back photographs of Hanoi. Americans did have access to photographs of the suffering of the Vietnamese (many of which came from military sources and were taken with quite a different use in mind) because journalists felt backed in their efforts to obtain those photographs, the event having been defined by a significant number of people as a savage colonialist war. The Korean War was understood differently—as part of the just struggle of the Free World against the Soviet Union and China—and, given that characterisation, photographs of the cruelty of unlimited American firepower would have been irrelevant.

Though an event has come to mean, precisely, something worth photographing, it is still ideology (in the broadest sense) that determines what constitutes an event. There can be no evidence, photographic or otherwise, of an event until the event itself has been named and characterised. And it is never photographic evidence which can construct—more properly, identify—events; the contribution of photography always follows the naming of the event. What determines the possibility of being affected morally by photographs is the existence of a relevant political consciousness. Without a politics, photographs of the slaughter-bench of history will most likely be experienced as, simply, unreal or as a demoralising emotional blow.

The quality of feeling, including moral outrage, that people can muster in response to photographs of the oppressed, the exploited, the starving, and the massacred also depends on the degree of their familiarity with these images. Don McCullin's photographs of emaciated Biafrans in the early 1970s had less impact for some people than Werner Bischof's photographs of Indian famine victims in the early 1950s because those images had become banal, and the photographs of Tuareg families dying of starvation in the sub-Sahara that appeared in magazines everywhere in 1973 must have seemed to many like an unbearable replay of a now familiar atrocity exhibition.

Photographs shock insofar as they show something novel. Unfortunately, the ante keeps getting raised—partly through the very proliferation of such images of horror. One's first encounter with the photographic inventory of ultimate horror is a kind of revelation, the prototypically modern revelation, a negative epiphany. For me, it was photographs of Bergen-Belsen and Dachau which I came across by chance in a bookstore in Santa Monica in July 1945. Nothing I have seen—in photographs or in real life—ever cut me as sharply, deeply, instantaneously. Indeed, it seems plausible to me to divide my life into two parts, before I saw those photographs (I was twelve) and after, though it was several years before I understood fully what they were about. What good was served by seeing them? They were only photographs—of an event I had scarcely heard of and could do nothing to affect, of suffering I could hardly imagine and could do nothing to relieve. When I looked at those photographs, something broke. Some limit had been reached, and not only that of horror; I felt irrevocably grieved, wounded, but a part of my feelings started to tighten; something went dead; something is still crying.

To suffer is one thing; another thing is living with the photographed images of suffering, which does not necessarily strengthen conscience and the ability to be compassionate. It can also corrupt them. Once one has seen such images, one has started down the road of seeing more—and more. Images transfix. Images anaesthetise. An event known through photographs certainly becomes more real than it would have been if one had never seen the photographs—think of the Vietnam War. (For a counter-example, think of the Gulag Archipelago, of which we have no photographs.) But after repeated exposure to images it also becomes less real.

The same law holds for evil as for pornography. The shock of photographed atrocities wears off with repeated viewings, just as the surprise and bemusement felt the first time one sees a pornographic movie wear off after one sees a few more. The sense of taboo which makes us indignant and sorrowful is not much sturdier than the sense of taboo that regulates the definition of what is obscene. And both have been sorely tried in recent years. The vast photographic catalogue of misery and injustice throughout the world has given everyone a certain familiarity with atrocity, making the horrible seem more ordinary—making it appear familiar, remote ("it's only a photograph"), inevitable. At the time of the first photographs of the Nazi camps, there was nothing banal about these images. After thirty years, a saturation point may have been reached. In these last decades, "concerned" photography has done at least as much to deaden conscience as to arouse it.

The ethical content of photographs is fragile. With the possible exception of photographs of those horrors, like the Nazi camps, that have gained the status of ethical reference points, most photographs do not keep their emotional charge. A photograph of 1900 that was affecting then because of its subject would, today, be more likely to move us because it is a photograph taken in 1900. The particular qualities and intentions of photographs tend to be swallowed up in the generalised pathos of time past. Aesthetic distance seems built into the very experience of looking at photographs, if not right away, then certainly with the passage of time. Time eventually positions most photographs, even the most amateurish, at the level of art.

The industrialisation of photography permitted its rapid absorption into rational—that is, bureaucratic—ways of running society. No longer toy images, photographs became part of the general furniture of the environment—touchstones and confirmations of that reductive approach to reality which is considered realistic. Photographs were enrolled in the service of important institutions of control, notably the family and the police, as symbolic objects and as pieces of information. Thus, in the bureaucratic cataloguing of the world, many important documents are not valid unless they have, affixed to them, a photograph-token of the citizen's face.

The "realistic" view of the world compatible with bureaucracy redefines knowledge—as techniques and information. Photographs are valued because they give information. They tell one what there is; they make an inventory. To spies, meteorologists, coroners, archaeologists, and other information professionals, their value is inestimable. But in the situations in which most people use photographs, their value as information is of the same order as fiction. The information that photographs can give starts to seem very important at that moment in cultural history when everyone is thought to have a right to something called news. Photographs were seen as a way of giving information to people who do not take easily to reading. The *Daily News* still calls itself "New York's Picture Newspaper," its bid for populist identity. At the opposite end of the scale, *Le Monde,* a newspaper designed for skilled, well-informed readers, runs no photographs at all. The presumption is that, for such readers, a photograph could only illustrate the analysis contained in an article.

A new sense of the notion of information has been constructed around the photographic image. The photograph is a thin slice of space as well as time. In a world ruled by photographic images, all borders ("framing") seem arbitrary. Anything can be separated, can be made discontinuous, from anything else. All that is necessary is to frame the subject differently. (Conversely, anything can be made adjacent to anything else.) Photography reinforces a nominalist view of social reality as consisting of small units of an apparently infinite number— as the number of photographs that could be taken of anything is unlimited. Through photographs, the world becomes a series of unrelated, freestanding particles; and history, past and present, a set of anecdotes and *faits divers*. The camera makes reality atomic, manageable, and opaque. It is a view of the world which denies interconnectedness, continuity, but which confers on each moment the character of a mystery. Any photograph has multiple meanings; indeed, to see something in the form of a photograph is to encounter a potential object of fascination. The ultimate wisdom of the photographic image is to say: "There is the surface. Now think—or rather feel, intuit—what is beyond it, what the reality must be like if it looks this way." Photographs, which cannot themselves explain anything, are inexhaustible invitations to deduction, speculation, and fantasy.

Photography implies that we know about the world if we accept it as the 40 camera records it. But this is the opposite of understanding, which starts from *not* accepting the world as it looks. All possibility of understanding is rooted in the ability to say no. Strictly speaking, one never understands anything from a photograph. Of course, photographs fill in blanks in our mental pictures of the present and the past: for example, Jacob Riis's images of New York squalor in the 1880s are sharply instructive to those unaware that urban poverty in late-nineteenth-century America was really that Dickensian. Nevertheless, the camera's rendering of reality must always hide more than it discloses. As Brecht points out, a photograph of the Krupp works reveals virtually nothing about that organisation. In contrast to the amorous relation, which is based on how something looks, understanding is based on how it functions. And functioning takes place in time, and must be explained in time. Only that which narrates can make us understand.

The limit of photographic knowledge of the world is that, while it can goad conscience, it can, finally, never be ethical or political knowledge. The knowledge gained through still photographs will always be some kind of sentimentalism, whether cynical or humanist. It will be a knowledge at bargain prices—a semblance of knowledge, a semblance of wisdom; as the act of taking pictures is a semblance of appropriation, a semblance of rape. The very muteness of what is, hypothetically, comprehensible in photographs is what constitutes their attraction and provocativeness. The omnipresence of photographs has an incalculable effect on our ethical sensibility. By furnishing this already crowded world with a duplicate one of images, photography makes us feel that the world is more available than it really is.

Needing to have reality confirmed and experience enhanced by photographs is an aesthetic consumerism to which everyone is now addicted. Industrial societies turn their citizens into image-junkies; it is the most irresistible form of mental pollution. Poignant longings for beauty, for an end to probing below the surface, for a redemption and celebration of the body of the world—all these elements of erotic feeling are affirmed in the pleasure we take in photographs. But other, less liberating feelings are expressed as well. It would not be wrong to speak of people having a *compulsion* to photograph: to turn experience itself into a way of seeing. Ultimately, having an experience becomes identical with taking a photograph of it, and participating in a public event comes more and more to be equivalent to looking at it in photographed form. That most logical of nineteenth-century aesthetes, Mallarmé, said that everything in the world exists in order to end in a book. Today everything exists to end in a photograph.

Things to Do with the Reading

1. The word "power" repeats frequently in Sontag's essay. Write a three- to four-page paper in which you quote, paraphrase, and more fully explain the relationship between photography and power that Sontag is concerned about.

2. The novelist and critic William Gass wrote of *On Photography* that

> No simple summary of the views contained in Susan Sontag's brief but brilliant work on photography is possible, first because there are too many, and second because the book is a thoughtful meditation, not a treatise, and its ideas are grouped more nearly like a gang of keys upon a ring than a run of onions on a string.

   The same might be said of the essay "In Plato's Cave"—that it is too conceptually rich and meditative to allow simple summary. And yet, we can probably improve our ability to understand this densely idea-laden essay if we make a list of the most important statements or claims that Sontag makes. Copy out the five sentences you find most arresting in the piece, each from a different paragraph. Then use these to generate a focused freewrite—an opportunity for your own meditation.

   Here are three possible ways of proceeding. (1) You might write about the single sentence you find most compelling, beginning by paraphrasing it. (2) You might look for some repeated element or contrast that figures in several of your sentences. (3) You might pair any of the sentences with one of the images included in the book in the essays by Elliott, Berger, or Gambino. (See Chapter 2 on Passage-BASED FOCUSED FREEWRITING.)

3. Write an essay in which you reflect on Sontag's claims about the moral, ethical, and psychological effects of photography. In these contexts Sontag talks both about photography as an activity and photographs as objects that have some supposed impact on the world. Study paragraphs 29–36 of Sontag's essay, which deal with the impact and ethics of photographs that record atrocities—"the vast catalogue of misery and injustice throughout the world."

   In what terms does Sontag reject the often-made defense of photographs of atrocities and exploitation—that they call people's attention to problems and thus inspire people to address them? You might wish to include in your thinking the brief autobiographical account that Sontag provides in paragraph 33 of her first experience at age 12 with photographs of the Holocaust. (It is worth noting in this context that Sontag was a noted human rights activist for more than two decades, serving for several years as president of the American Center of PEN, the international writers' organization dedicated to freedom of expression and the advancement of literature.)

4. **Application:** Sontag in her role of provocateur loves to make bold claims—for example, that people take photos to opt out of life and to construct a family album of the ever-vanishing extended family. Use your own experience to engage these volatile notions.

   Locate either some family photographs or photographs that you have taken as a tourist, select five or six, and then write a short essay on what you think the photographer (possibly you) was trying to accomplish in taking them. Be sure to include your reasoning. Next, consider a few single sentences you've selected from Sontag's commentary on family photographs and vacation photographs (see paragraphs 10–18) and use these as a springboard for some sustained reflection on photography as an activity.

   Alternatively, write an essay in which you reflect on and analyze the role of photographs and photo-taking in your life. Notice photos that are prominent in your environment—in your room, in your wallet, on your computer or phone, on your Facebook page. What do you notice about these pictures and your use and placement of them? Be sure to use Sontag's essay as a lens to prompt your own thinking.

   Warning: Don't turn this into an agree–disagree exercise. Use Sontag's thinking to provide starting points for your thinking about the topic, not *primarily* as the impetus to support or refute her position.

5. **Application:** On the matter of the ethics of photography and its potential to effect social change, do some research on the life and work of one of the photographers that Joseph Elliot describes at the end of the interview as an Opinionated Documentarian or a Personal Documentarian. Try Nan Goldin, Lauren Greenfield, Sally Mann, or Sebastião Salgado. Find claims in the Sontag essay that you think are interesting and illuminating in the context of your chosen photographer. Try to find not only a range of images by the photographer of your choice but perhaps artistic statements by him or her, as well as short biographies. Write up your results in an essay. Here are some questions to help: What might Sontag praise about this photographer's work? What might make her anxious about it? How might the photographer respond?

Barry Lopez

Learning to See

Barry Lopez is an award-winning writer of both nonfiction and fiction. In this essay he gives an account of his decision to stop pursuing his "other" career, as a landscape photographer. In the process of telling this story, Lopez focuses astutely on an area of photography that neither Joseph Elliott nor Susan Sontag directly addresses: nature photography. His photographic career (which he decided to end in 1981) focused on subjects that included only the land—no people and, for the most part, no animals. But as you will see, the land for Lopez is no inert entity, but the home of small miracles of physics. Lopez is the author of many works of fiction and nonfiction, including *Arctic Dreams*, for which he received the National Book Award for Nonfiction in 1986 and most recently, *Outside* (2014), a collection of stories.

1   In June 1989, I received a puzzling letter from the Amon Carter Museum in Fort Worth, Texas, an invitation to speak at the opening of a retrospective of the work of Robert Adams. The show, "To Make It Home: Photographs of the American West, 1965–1985," had been organized by the Philadelphia Museum of Art and would travel to the Los Angeles County Museum and the Corcoran Gallery of Art in Washington, D.C., before being installed at the Amon Carter, an institution renowned for its photographic collections, in the spring of 1990.

Robert Adams, an un-self-promoting man who has published no commercially prominent book of photographs, is routinely referred to as one of the most important landscape photographers in America, by both art critics and his colleagues. His black-and-white images are intelligently composed and morally engaged. They're also hopeful, despite their sometimes depressing subject matter—brutalized landscapes and the venality of the American Dream as revealed in suburban life. Adams doesn't hold himself apart from what he indicts. He photographs with compassion and he doesn't scold. His pictures are also accessible, to such a degree that many of them seem casual. In 1981 he published *Beauty in Photography: Essays in Defense of Traditional Values*, one of the clearest statements of artistic responsibility ever written by a photographer.

If there is such a thing as an ideal of stance, technique, vision, and social contribution toward which young photographers might aspire, it's embodied in this man.

I suspected the Amon Carter had inadvertently invited the wrong person to speak. I'd no knowledge of the history of American photography sufficient to situate Robert Adams in it. I couldn't speak to the technical perfection of

"Learning to See" from ABOUT THIS LIFE: JOURNEYS ON THE THRESHOLD OF MEMORY by Barry Lopez, copyright © 1998 by Barry Holstun Lopez. Used by permission of Alfred A. Knopf, an imprint of the Knopf Doubleday Publishing Group, a division of Random House LLC. All rights reserved.

his prints. I'd no credentials as an art critic. As an admirer of the work, of course, I'd have something to say, but it could only be that, the words of an amateur who admired Adams's accomplishment.

I wondered for days what prompted the invitation. For about fifteen years, before putting my cameras down on September 13, 1981, never to pick them up again, I'd worked as a landscape photographer, but it was unlikely anyone at the Amon Carter knew this. I'd visited the museum in the fall of 1986 to see some of their luminist paintings and had met several of the curators, but our conversations could not have left anyone with the impression that I had the background to speak about Adams's work.

I finally decided to say yes. I wrote and told the person coordinating the program, Mary Lampe, that though I didn't feel qualified to speak I admired Mr. Adams's work, and further, I presumed an affinity with his pursuits and ideals as set forth in *Beauty in Photography*. And I told her I intended to go back and study the work of Paul Strand, Wynn Bullock, Minor White, Harry Callahan, and others who'd been an influence on my own work and thought, in order to prepare my lecture.

Months later, when I arrived at the museum, I asked Ms. Lampe how they had come to invite me and not someone more qualified. She said Mr. Adams had asked them to do so. I sensed she believed Robert Adams and I were good friends and I had to tell her I didn't know him at all. We'd never met, never corresponded, had not spoken on the phone. I was unaware, even, that it was "Bob" Adams, as Ms. Lampe called him.

"But why did you agree to come?" she asked.

"Out of respect for the work," I said. "Out of enthusiasm for the work." I also explained that I was intimidated by the prospect, and that sometimes I felt it was good to act on things like that.

Ms. Lampe subsequently sent Robert Adams a tape of my talk. He and I later met and we now correspond and speak on the phone regularly. He set the course of our friendship in the first sentence of a letter he wrote me after hearing my presentation. "Your willingness to speak in my behalf," he wrote, "confirms my belief in the community of artists."

He believed from work of mine that he'd read that we shared a sensibility, that we asked similar questions about the relationship between culture and landscape, and that our ethical leanings and our sense of an artist's social responsibility were similar. He later told me that for these reasons he'd given my name, hopefully but somewhat facetiously, to Ms. Lampe, not knowing the curators and I were acquainted and that they would write me.

I've long been attracted to the way visual artists like Robert Adams imagine the world. The emotional impact of their composition of space and light is as clarifying for me as immersion in a beautifully made story. As with the work of a small group of poets I read regularly—Robert Hass, Pattiann Rogers, Garrett Hongo—I find healing in their expressions. I find reasons not to give up.

Though I no longer photograph, I have maintained since 1981 a connection with photographers and I keep up a sort of running conversation with several of them. We talk about the fate of photography in the United States, where of course art is increasingly more commodified and where, with the advent of computer manipulation, photography is the art most likely to mislead. Its history as a purveyor of objective reality, the idea that "the camera never lies," is specious, certainly; but with some artistic endeavors, say those of Cartier-Bresson, Aaron Siskind, or W. Eugene Smith, and in the fields of documentary photography, which would include some news photography, and nature photography, one can assert that the authority of the image lies with the subject. With the modern emphasis on the genius of the individual artist, however, and with the arrival of computer imaging, authority in these areas now more often lies with the photographer. This has become true to such an extent that the reversal that's occurred—the photographer, not the subject, is in charge—has caused the rules of evidence to be changed in courts of law; and it has foisted upon an unwitting public a steady stream, for example, of fabricated images of wildlife.

As a beginning photographer I was most attracted to color and form, to the emotional consequence of line. It is no wonder, looking back now, that I pored over the images of someone like Edward Weston, or that I felt isolated in some of my pursuits because at the time few serious photographers outside Ernst Haas and Eliot Porter worked as I did in color. I wanted to photograph the streaming of light. For a long while it made no difference whether that light was falling down the stone walls of a building in New York or lambent on the corrugations of a wheat field. Ansel Adams was suggested to me early on as a model, but he seemed to my eye inclined to overstate. I wanted the sort of subtlety I would later come to admire in Bob Adams's work and in the aerial photographs of Emmet Gowin.

15   The more I gravitated as a writer toward landscape as a context in which to work out what I was thinking as a young man about issues like justice, tolerance, ambiguity, and compassion, the more I came to concentrate on landforms as a photographer. I valued in particular the work of one or two wildlife photographers shooting *in situ*, in the bush. (I remember enthusiastically contacting friends about John Dominis's groundbreaking portfolio of African cat photographs, which appeared in three successive issues of *Life* in January 1967.) But I was not inclined toward mastering the kind of technical skill it took to make such photographs. More fundamentally, I had misgivings about what I regarded as invasions of the privacy of wild animals. The latter notion I thought so personal an idea I kept it mostly to myself; today, of course, it's a central concern of wildlife photographers, especially for a contingent that includes Frans Lanting, the late Michio Hoshino, Gary Braasch, Tui De Roy, and the team of Susan Middleton and David Liittschwager.

I began photographing in a conscientious way in the summer of 1965. I was soon concentrating on landscapes, and in the mid-1970s, with a small list of publication credits behind me, I made an appointment to see Joe Scherschel, an assistant director of the photographic staff at *National Geographic*. He told me frankly that though my landscape portfolio was up to the standards of the magazine, the paucity of wildlife images and human subjects made it unlikely that he could offer me any assignments. In response I remember thinking this was unlikely to change, for either of us. Discouraged, I started to scale back the effort to market my photographs and to make part of my living that way. I continued to make pictures, and I was glad that much of this work was still effectively represented by a stock agency in New York; but by 1978 I knew photography for me was becoming more a conscious exercise in awareness, a technique for paying attention. It would finally turn into a sequestered exploration of light and spatial volume.

Three events in the late 1970s changed the way I understood myself as a photographer. One summer afternoon I left the house for an appointment with an art director in a nearby city. Strapped to the seat of my motorcycle was a box of photographs, perhaps three hundred images representative of the best work I had done. The two-lane road I traveled winds gently through steep mountainous country. When I got to town, the photographs were gone. I never found a trace of them, though I searched every foot of the road for two days. The loss dismantled my enthusiasm for photography so thoroughly that I took it for a message to do something else.

In the summer of 1976 my mother was dying of cancer. To ease her burden, and to brighten the sterile room in Lenox Hill Hospital in New York where she lay dying, I made a set of large Cibachrome prints from some of my 35-mm Kodachrome images—a white horse standing in a field of tall wild grasses bounded by a white post-and-plank fence; a faded pink boat trailer from the 1940s, abandoned in the woods; a small copse of quaking aspen, their leaves turning bright yellow on the far side of a remote mountain swamp. It was the only set of prints I would ever make. As good as they were, the change in color balance and the loss of transparency and contrast when compared with the originals, the reduction in sharpness, created a deep doubt about ever wanting to do such a thing again. I hung the images in a few shows, then put them away. I knew if I didn't start developing and printing my own images, I wouldn't be entering any more shows.

I winced whenever I saw my photographs reproduced in magazines and books, but I made my peace with that. Time-Life Books was publishing a series then called *American Wilderness*, each volume of which was devoted to a different landscape—the Maine woods, the Cascade Mountains, the Grand Canyon. I was pleased to see my work included in these volumes, but I realized that just as the distance between what I saw and what I was able to record was huge, so was that between what I recorded and what people saw. Seeing the printed images on the page was like finding one's haiku published as nineteen-syllable poems.

20   The third event occurred around the first serious choice I made as a photographer to concentrate on a limited subject. The subject was always light, but I wanted to explore a single form, which turned out to be the flow of water in creeks and rivers near my home. I photographed in every season, when the water was high in February and March, when it was low in August, when it was transparent in July, when it was an opaque jade in December. In 1980 I began to photograph moving water in moonlight, exposures of twenty-five or thirty minutes. These images suffered from reciprocity failure—the color balance in them collapsed—but they also recorded something extraordinary, a pattern of flow we cannot actually see. They revealed the organizing principle logicians would one day call a strange attractor.

The streaming of water around a rock is one of the most complex motions of which human beings are aware. The change from a laminar, more or less uniform flow to turbulent flow around a single rock is so abstruse a transition mathematically that even the most sophisticated Cray computer cannot make it through to a satisfactory description.

Aesthetically, of course, no such difficulty exists. The eye dotes on the shift, delights in the scintillating sheeting, the roll-off of light around a rock, like hair responding to the stroke of a brush. Sometimes I photographed the flow of water in sunshine at 1/2000 of a second and then later I'd photograph the same rock in moonlight. Putting the photos side by side, I could see something hidden beneath the dazzle of the high-speed image that compared with our renderings of the Milky Way from space: the random pin-dot infernos of our own and every other sun form a spiraling, geometrical shape motionless to our eyes. In the moonlit photographs, the stray streaks from errant water splashes were eliminated (in light that weak, they occur too quickly to be recorded); what was etched on the film instead were orderly, fundamental lines of flow, created by particle after illuminated particle of gleaming water, as if each were a tracer bullet. (Years later, reading *Chaos*, James Gleick's lucid report on chaos theory, I would sit bolt upright in my chair. What I'd photographed was the deep pattern in turbulence, the clothing, as it were, of the strange attractor.)

In the months I worked at making these photographs, I came to realize I actually had two subjects as a photographer. First, these still images of a moving thing, a living thing—as close as I would probably ever come to fully photographing an animal. Second, natural light falling on orchards, images of a subject routinely understood as a still life. The orchards near me were mostly filbert orchards. In their change of color and form through the seasons, in the rain and snow that fell through them, in crows that sat on their winter branches, in leaves accumulated under them on bare dark ground, in the wind that coursed them, in the labyrinths of their limbs, ramulose within the imposed order of the orchard plot, I saw the same profundity of life I found in literature.

This was all work I was eager to do, but I would never get to it.

In September 1981 I was working in the Beaufort Sea off the north coast of Alaska with several marine biologists. We were conducting a food-chain survey intended to provide baseline data to guide offshore oil drilling, an impulsive and politically motivated development program funded by the Bureau of Land Management and pushed hard at the time by the Reagan government. On September 12, three of us rendezvoused at Point Barrow with a National Oceanic and Atmospheric Administration research vessel, the *Oceanographer.* They hoisted us, our gear, and our twenty-foot Boston Whaler aboard and we sailed west into pack ice in the northern Chukchi Sea.

Scientific field research is sometimes a literally bloody business. In our study we were trying to determine the flow of energy through various "levels" (artificially determined) of the marine food web. To gather data we retrieved plankton and caught fish with different sorts of traps and trawls, and we examined the contents of bearded seal, ringed seal, and spotted seal stomachs. To accomplish the latter, we shot and killed the animals. Shooting seals located us squarely in the moral dilemma of our work, and it occasioned talk aboard the *Oceanographer* about the barbarousness of science. The irony here was that without these data creatures like the ringed seal could not be afforded legal protection against oil development. The killings were a manifestation of the perversions in our age, our Kafkaesque predicaments.

I was disturbed by the fatal aspects of our work, as were my companions, but I willingly participated. I would later write an essay about the killing, but something else happened during that trip, less dramatic and more profound in its consequences for me.

Late one afternoon, working our way back to the *Oceanographer* through a snow squall, the three of us came upon a polar bear. We decided to follow him for a few minutes and I got out my cameras. The bear, swimming through loose pack ice, was clearly annoyed by our presence, though in our view we were maintaining a reasonable distance. He very soon climbed out on an ice floe, crossed it, and dropped into open water on the far side. We had to go the long way around in the workboat, but we caught up. He hissed at us and otherwise conveyed his irritation, but we continued idling along beside him.

Eventually we backed off. The bear disappeared in gauze curtains of blowing snow. We returned to the *Oceanographer,* to a warm meal and dry clothes.

Once the boat was secure and our scientific samples squared away in the lab, I went to my cabin. I dropped my pack on the floor, stripped off my heavy clothes, showered, and lay down in my bunk. I tried to recall every detail of the encounter with the bear. What had he been doing when we first saw him? Did he change direction then? How had he proceeded? Exactly how did he climb out of the water onto the ice floe? What were the mechanics of it? When he shook off seawater, how was it different from a dog shucking water? When he hissed, what color was the inside of his mouth?

I don't know how long I lay there, a half hour perhaps, but when I was through, when I'd answered these questions and was satisfied that I'd recalled the sequence of events precisely and in sufficient detail, I got up, dressed, and went to dinner. Remembering what happened in an encounter was crucial to my work as a writer, and attending to my cameras during our time with the bear had altered and shrunk my memory of it. While the polar bear was doing something, I was checking f-stops and attempting to frame and focus from a moving boat.

I regarded the meeting as a warning to me as a writer. Having successfully recovered details from each minute, I believed, of that encounter, having disciplined myself to do that, I sensed I wouldn't pick up a camera ever again.

It was not solely contact with this lone bear a hundred miles off the northwest coast of Alaska, of course, that ended my active involvement with photography. The change had been coming for a while. The power of the polar bear's presence, his emergence from the snow squall and his subsequent disappearance, had created an atmosphere in which I could grasp more easily a complex misgiving that had been building in me. I view any encounter with a wild animal in its own territory as a gift, an opportunity to sense the real animal, not the zoo creature, the TV creature, the advertising creature. But this gift had been more overwhelming. In some way the bear had grabbed me by the shirtfront and said, Think about this. Think about what these cameras in your hands are doing.

Years later, I'm still thinking about it. Some of what culminated for me that day is easy to understand. As a writer, I had begun to feel I was missing critical details in situations such as this one because I was distracted. I was also starting to feel uncomfortable about the way photographs tend to collapse events into a single moment, about how much they leave out. (Archeologists face a similar problem when they save only what they recognize from a dig. Years afterward, the context long having been destroyed, the archeologist might wonder what was present that he or she didn't recognize at the time. So begins a reevaluation of the meaning of the entire site.)

35   I was also disturbed about how nature and landscape photographs, my own and others', were coming to be used, not in advertising where you took your chances (some photographers at that time began labeling their images explicitly: NO TOBACCO, NO ALCOHOL), but in the editorial pages of national magazines. It is a polite fiction of our era that the average person, including the average art director, is more informed about natural history than an educated person was in Columbus's age. Because this is not true, the majority of nature photographers who work out in the field have felt a peculiar burden to record accurately the great range of habitat and animal behavior they see, including nature's "dark" side. (Photographers accepted the fact back then that magazines in the United States, generally speaking, were not interested in photographs of mating animals—unless they were chaste or cute—or in predatory encounters if they were bloody or harrowing, as many were.)

What happened as a result of this convention was that people looking at magazines in the 1970s increasingly came to think of wild animals as vivacious and decorative in the natural world. Promoted as elegant, brave, graceful, sinister, wise, etc., according to their species, animals were deprived of personality and the capacity to be innovative. Every wildlife photographer I know can recount a story of confrontation with an art director in which he or she argued unsuccessfully for an image that told a fuller or a truer story about a particular species of animal in a layout. It was the noble lion, the thieving hyena, and the mischievous monkey, however, who routinely triumphed. A female wolf killing one of her pups, or a male bonobo approaching a female with a prominent erection, was not anything magazine editors were comfortable with.

In the late seventies, I asked around among several publishers to see whether they might have any interest in a series of disturbing photographs made in a zoo by a woman named Ilya. She'd taken them on assignment for *Life*, but very few of them were ever published because she'd concentrated on depicting animals apparently driven insane by their incarceration. I remember as particularly unsettling the look of psychosis in the face of a male lion, its mane twisted into knots. I could develop no interest in publishing her work. An eccentric view, people felt. Too distressing.

So, along with a growing political awareness of endangered landscapes and their indigenous animals in the 1970s came, ironically, a more and more dazzling presentation of those creatures in incomplete and prejudicial ways. Photo editors made them look not like what they were but the way editors wanted them to appear—well-groomed, appropriate to stereotype, and living safely apart from the machinations of human enterprise. To my mind there was little difference then between a *Playboy* calendar and a wildlife calendar. Both celebrated the conventionally gorgeous, the overly endowed, the seductive. I and many other photographers at the time were apprehensive about the implications of this trend.

Another concern I had that September afternoon, a more complicated one, was what was happening to memory in my generation. The advertising injunction to preserve family memories by taking photographs had become so shrill a demand, and the practice had become so compulsive, that recording the event was more important for some than participating in it. The inculcated rationale which grew up around this practice was that to take and preserve family photos was to act in a socially responsible way. The assumption seemed specious to me. My generation was the first to have ready access to inexpensive tape recorders and cameras. Far from recording memories of these talks and events, what we seemed to be doing was storing memories that would never be retrieved, that would never form a coherent narrative. In the same way that our desk drawers and cabinet shelves slowly filled with these "personal" sounds and images, we were beginning, it seemed to me, to live our lives in dissociated bits and places. The narrative spine of an individual life was disappearing. The order of events was becoming increasingly meaningless.

40   This worry, together with the increasingly commercial use to which the work of photographers like myself was being put and the preference for an entertaining but not necessarily coherent landscape of wild animals (images that essentially lied to children), made me more and more reluctant to stay involved. Some of the contemporary photographers I most respect—Lanting, Hoshino, Braasch, De Roy, Jim Brandenburg, Flip Nicklin, Sam Abell, Nick Nichols, Galen Rowell—have managed through the strength of their work and their personal integrity to overcome some of these problems, which are part and parcel of working in a world dominated more and more by commercial interests pursuing business strategies. But I knew I had no gift here to persevere. That realization, and my reluctance to photograph animals in the first place, may have precipitated my decision that day in the Chukchi.

As a writer, I had yet other concerns, peculiar to that discipline. I had begun to wonder whether my searching for the telling photographic image in a situation was beginning to interfere with my writing about what happened. I was someone who took a long time to let a story settle. I'd began to suspect that the photographs made while I was in a note-taking stage were starting to lock my words into a pattern, and that the pattern was being determined too early. Photographs, in some way, were introducing preconceptions into a process I wanted to keep fluid. I often have no clear idea of what I'm doing. I just act. I pitch in, I try to stay alert to everything around me. I don't want to stop and focus on a finished image, which I'm inclined to do as a photographer. I want, instead, to see a sentence fragment scrawled in my notebook, smeared by rain. I don't want the clean, fixed image right away.

An attentive mind, I'm sure, can see the flaws in my reasoning. Some photographers are doing no more than taking notes when they click the shutter. It's only after a shoot that they discover what the story is. But by trying to both photograph and write, I'd begun to feel I was attempting to create two parallel but independent stories. The effort had become confusing and draining. I let go of photography partly because its defining process, to my mind, was less congruent with the way I wanted to work.

On June 16, 1979, forty-one sperm whales beached themselves at the mouth of the Siuslaw River on the Oregon coast, about one hundred miles from my home. I wrote a long essay about the stranding but didn't start work on it until after I'd spent two days photographing the eclipse of these beasts' lives and the aftermath of their deaths. That was the last time I attempted to do both things.

Perhaps the most rarefied of my concerns about photography that day in the Chukchi was one that lay for me at the heart of photography: recording a fleeting pattern of light in a defined volume of space. Light always attracted me. Indeed, twenty-five years after the fact, I can still vividly recall the light falling at dusk on a windbreak of trees in Mitchell, Oregon. It rendered me speechless when I saw it, and by some magic I managed to get it down on film. The problem of rendering volume in photography, however, was one I never solved beyond employing the conventional solutions of perspective and depth of field. I could recognize spatial volume successfully addressed in the work of other photographers—in Adams's work, for example, partly because so many of his photographs do not have an object as a subject. Finding some way myself to render volume successfully in a photograph would mean, I believed, walking too far away from my work as a writer. And, ultimately, it was as a writer that I felt more comfortable.

I miss making photographs. A short while ago I received a call from a 45 curator at the Whitney Museum in New York named May Castleberry. She had just mounted a show called "Perpetual Mirage: Photographic Narratives of the Desert West" and I had been able to provide some minor assistance with it. She was calling now to pursue a conversation we'd begun at the time about Rockwell Kent, an illustrator, painter, and socialist widely known in the thirties, forties, and fifties. She wanted to hang a selection of his "nocturnes," prints and drawings Kent had made of people under starlit night skies. She was calling to see what I could suggest about his motivation.

Given Kent's leanings toward Nordic myth and legend and his espousal of Teddy Roosevelt's "strenuous life," it seemed obvious to me that he would want to portray his heroic (mostly male) figures against the vault of the heavens. But there were at least two other things at work here, I believed. First, Kent was strongly drawn to high latitudes, like Greenland, where in winter one can view the deep night sky for weeks on end. It was not really the "night" sky, however, he was drawing; it was the sunless sky of a winter day. Quotidian life assumes mythic proportions here not because it's heroic, but because it's carried out beneath the stars.

Secondly, I conjectured, because Kent was an artist working on flat surfaces, he sought, like every such artist, ways to suggest volume, to make the third dimension apparent. Beyond what clouds provide, the daytime sky has no depth; it's the night sky that gives an artist volume. While it takes an extraordinary person—the light and space artist James Turrell, say—to make the celestial vault visible in sunshine, many artists have successfully conveyed a sense of the sky's volume by painting it at night.

The conceit can easily grow up in a photographer that he or she has pretty much seen all the large things—the range of possible emotion to be evoked with light, the contrasts to be made by arranging objects in different scales, problems in the third and fourth dimension. But every serious photographer, I believe, has encountered at some point ideas unanticipated and dumbfounding. The shock causes you to reexamine all you've assumed about your own work and the work of others, especially the work of people you've never particularly understood. This happened most recently for me in seeing the photography of Linda Connor. While working on a story about international air freight, I became so disoriented, flying every day from one spot on the globe to another thousands of miles away, I did not know what time I was living in. Whatever time it was, it was out of phase with the sun, a time not to be dialed up on a watch, mine or anyone else's.

At a pause in this international hurtling, during a six-hour layover in Cape Town, I went for a ride with an acquaintance. He drove us out to Clifton Bay on the west side of Table Mountain. I was so dazed by my abuse of time that I was open to thoughts I might otherwise never have had. One of those thoughts was that I could recognize the physicality of time. We can discern the physical nature of space in a picture, grasp the way, for example, Robert Adams is able to photograph the air itself, making it visible like a plein air painter. In Cape Town that day I saw what I came to call indigenous time. It clung to the flanks of Table Mountain. It resisted being absorbed into my helter-skelter time. It seemed not yet to have been subjugated by Dutch and British colonial expansion, as the physical landscape so clearly had been. It was time apparent to the senses, palpable. What made me believe I was correct in this perception was that, only a month before, I'd examined a collection of Linda Connor's work, a book called *Luminance*. I realized there at Table Mountain that she'd photographed what I was looking at. She'd photographed indigenous time.

50   I'd grasped Ms. Connor's photographs in some fashion after an initial pass, but I hadn't sensed their depth, their power, what Gerard Manley Hopkins called "the achieve of the thing." With this new insight I wrote her an excited note, an attempt to thank her for work that opened the door to a room I'd never explored.

One of the great blessings of our modern age, a kind of redemption for its cruelties and unmitigated greed, is that one can walk down to a corner book-store and find a copy of Ms. Connor's book. Or of Robert Adams's *What We Brought: The New World,* or Frans Lanting's *Bonobo: The Forgotten Ape,* or, say, Mary Peck's *Chaco Canyon: A Center and Its World,* and then be knocked across the room by a truth one had not, until that moment, clearly discerned.

It is more than illumination, though, more than a confirmation of one's intuition, aesthetics, or beliefs that comes out of the perusal of such a photographer's images. It's regaining the feeling that one is not cut off from the wellsprings of intelligence and goodwill, of sympathy for human plight.

I do not know, of course, why the photographers I admire, even the ones I know, photograph, but I am acutely aware that without the infusion of their images hope would wither in me. I feel an allegiance to their work more as a writer than as someone who once tried to see in this way, perhaps because I presume we share certain principles related to the effort to imagine or explain.

It is correct, I think, as Robert Adams wrote me that day, to believe in a community of artists stimulated by and respectful of one another's work. But it's also true that without an audience (of which we're all a part) the work remains unfinished, unfulfilled. A photographer seeks intimacy with the world and then endeavors to share it. Inherent in that desire to share is a love of humanity. In different media, and from time to time, we have succeeded, I believe, in helping one another understand what is going on. We have come to see that, in some way, this is our purpose with each other.

Things to Do with the Reading

1. Link: so WHAT that Lopez repeatedly uses the phrase "making photographs" rather than "taking photographs," which is the more common phrase and the one upon which Sontag offers a powerful critique? Write an essay in which you locate Lopez's word choice in terms of Sontag's observations about cameras as guns and Eliott's commentary on fabrication versus recording.

2. Like Sontag, Lopez has his anxieties about the artistic, psychological, and ethical impact of photography—both as product and as activity. But he also testifies to the importance of photography in his life in strong terms: "I do not know, of course, why the photographers I admire, even the ones I know, photograph, but I am acutely aware that without the infusion of their images hope would wither in me" (paragraph 53). Write and reflect on Lopez's anxieties about photography, especially in relation to his work as a writer. Then try to negotiate the gap between this anxiety and Lopez's powerful praise for photography as a source of hope.

   You might want to Google images from the photographers Lopez feels most strongly about, Linda Connors and Robert Adams, and make your analysis of these part of your essay. On the relationship between photography and writing, see paragraphs 31–34, Lopez's account of the aftermath of his encounter with the polar bear; also see the thinking in paragraph 34 about the way that "photographs tend to collapse events into a single moment."

3. Link: It is interesting to consider what Lopez thinks a photograph—at least his idea of photographs—is. Summarize and reflect on Lopez's various accounts of what he was trying to photograph, and then write a short essay in which you locate him in the context of the Elliott interview. What, for example, does Lopez mean when he says "The subject was always light" (paragraph 20)?

4. Link: The moral and psychological dimension that was central in the Sontag essay is central in Lopez's essay as well. Although Lopez finds things to worry about in landscape and nature photography, he also offers powerful praise of its recuperative and moral value, as is evident in the following statement: "The more I gravitated as a writer toward

landscape as a context in which to work out what I was thinking as a young man about issues like justice, tolerance, ambiguity, and compassion, the more I came to concentrate on landforms as a photographer" (see paragraph 15).

Find points of contact among Sontag, Elliott, and Lopez, and synthesize these into a short paper on photography—what it is, what it can and cannot do, and what it perhaps should and should not do.

5. Application: In his essay Lopez relives his arrival at an awareness of tension, in fact, competition, between his two art forms—writing and taking photographs. The result of this awareness is that he stops taking photographs. Why? The essay keeps returning to the day in Chukchi when Lopez saw the polar bear. Using Lopez's essay as a model, write a reflective essay on a moment when you came to recognize some kind of incompatibility between two ways you approach the world—two things you like to do, wherein one was starting to interfere with the other. Choose something fairly serious, but not necessarily life-shaking.

6. Application: There is an interesting moment in paragraph 23 in which Lopez offers the verbal equivalent of something that he repeatedly tried to photograph (the natural light falling on orchards). This is a form of writing called *ekphrasis*. An ekphrastic piece of writing tries to be the verbal equivalent of a photograph. It strives to create the same mental images and the same emotional/psychological effect as a photograph or painting of the same thing might produce. Much ekphrastic writing takes the form of verbal reenactments of paintings or photographs. Ekphrasis offers an illuminating exercise for thinking about visual images. Experiment with ekphrasis in one or both of the following ways:

—Go somewhere that you might feel inspired to take a picture. Write a verbal equivalent of the picture that you would like to take. Take a photograph of the same subject. Write a short essay on what you learned by comparing and contrasting the two. Note: Avoid talking about which was better; concentrate instead on describing and reflecting on the differences.

—Start with a photograph, preferably one of the type that you think Lopez would want to take. This can be a photograph of your own or one that you find by Googling some of the photographers that Lopez cites in his essay. Write a verbal equivalent of the photograph and then reflect (in writing) on what you learned in the process.

John Berger

Images of Women in European Art

Originally produced for television in England, John Berger's book *Ways of Seeing* (1972), from which this essay is taken, focuses on the relationship between the implied spectator or viewer and a work of art. Interested especially in the history of the nude in European painting, Berger demonstrates the ways that these paintings were designed to flatter and enhance the power of male viewers, while inducing the women to see themselves as males would see them. Berger's discussion of nudes is part of a larger cultural and aesthetic discourse on what is called "the gaze." This concept originates with French theorists Jean-Paul Sartre, Simone de Beauvoir, Jacques Lacan, and Michel Foucault and has been extended and applied by other writers, such as the film theorist Teresa de Lauretis. Besides being an art critic, Berger is also a painter, essayist, novelist (his novel *G.* won the coveted 1972 Booker Prize), poet, and translator. He has published nearly fifty works, most recently *Understanding a Photograph* (Geoff Dyer, ed.) in 2013 at the age of 87.

According to usage and conventions which are at last being questioned but 1
have by no means been overcome, the social presence of a woman is different
in kind from that of a man. A man's presence is dependent upon the promise
of power which he embodies. If the promise is large and credible, his presence
is striking. If it is small or incredible, he is found to have little presence. The
promised power may be moral, physical, temperamental, economic, social,
sexual—but its object is always exterior to the man. A man's presence suggests
what he is capable of doing to you or for you. His presence may be fabricated,
in the sense that he pretends to be capable of what he is not. But the pretense
is always toward a power which he exercises on others.

By contrast, a woman's presence expresses her own attitude to herself,
and defines what can and cannot be done to her. Her presence is manifest
in her gestures, voice, opinions, expressions, clothes, chosen surroundings,
taste—indeed there is nothing she can do which does not contribute to her
presence. Presence, for a woman, is so intrinsic to her person that men tend
to think of it as an almost physical emanation, a kind of heat or smell or aura.

To be born a woman has been to be born, within an allotted and confined
space, into the keeping of men. The social presence of women has developed as a result of their ingenuity in living under such tutelage within such
a limited space. But this has been at the cost of a woman's self being split
into two. A woman must continually watch herself. She is almost continually

From WAYS OF SEEING by John Berger, copyright © 1972 by Penguin Books Limited. Used by permission of Viking Penguin, a division of Penguin Group (USA) LLC.

accompanied by her own image of herself. Whilst she is walking across a room or whilst she is weeping at the death of her father, she can scarcely avoid envisaging herself walking or weeping. From earliest childhood she has been taught and persuaded to survey herself continually.

And so she comes to consider the *surveyor* and the *surveyed* within her as the two constituent yet always distinct elements of her identity as a woman.

5   She has to survey everything she is and everything she does because how she appears to others, and ultimately how she appears to men, is of crucial importance for what is normally thought of as the success of her life. Her own sense of being in herself is supplanted by a sense of being appreciated as herself by another.

Men survey women before treating them. Consequently, how a woman appears to a man can determine how she will be treated. To acquire some control over this process, women must contain it and interiorize it. That part of a woman's self which is the surveyor treats the part which is the surveyed so as to demonstrate to others how her whole self would like to be treated. And this exemplary treatment of herself by herself constitutes her presence. Every woman's presence regulates what is and is not "permissible" within her presence. Every one of her actions—whatever its direct purpose or motivation—is also read as an indication of how she would like to be treated. If a woman throws a glass on the floor, this is an example of how she treats her own emotion of anger and so of how she would wish it to be treated by others. If a man does the same, his action is only read as an expression of his anger. If a woman makes a good joke, this is an example of how she treats the joker in herself and accordingly of how she as a joker-woman would like to be treated by others. Only a man can make a good joke for its own sake.

One might simplify this by saying: *Men act* and *women appear.* Men look at women. Women watch themselves being looked at. This determines not only most relations between men and women but also the relation of women to themselves. The surveyor of woman in herself is male: the surveyed female. Thus, she turns herself into an object—and most particularly an object of vision: a sight.

In one category of European oil painting women were the principal, ever-recurring subject. That category is the nude. In the nudes of European painting we can discover some of the criteria and conventions by which women have been seen and judged as sights.

The first nudes in the tradition depicted Adam and Eve. It is worth referring to the story as told in Genesis:

And when the woman saw that the tree was good for food, and that it was a delight to the eyes, and that the tree was to be desired to make one wise, she took of the fruit thereof and did eat; and she gave also unto her husband with her, and he did eat.

And the eyes of them both were opened, and they knew that they were naked; and they sewed fig-leaves together and made themselves aprons. And the Lord God called unto the man and said unto him, "Where are thou?" And he said, "I heard thy voice in the garden, and I was afraid, because I was naked; and I hid myself."

Unto the woman God said, "I will greatly multiply thy sorrow and thy conception; in sorrow thou shalt bring forth children; and thy desire shall be to thy husband and he shall rule over thee."

What is striking about this story? They became aware of being naked 10 because, as a result of eating the apple, each saw the other differently. Nakedness was created in the mind of the beholder.

The second striking fact is that the woman is blamed and is punished by being made subservient to the man. In relation to the woman, the man becomes the agent of God.

In the medieval tradition the story was often illustrated, scene following scene, as in a strip cartoon. [See Figure 16.16.]

During the Renaissance the narrative sequence disappeared, and the single moment depicted became the moment of shame. The couple wear fig leaves or make a modest gesture with their hands. But now their shame is not so much in relation to one another as to the spectator. [See Figure 16.17.]

Later the shame becomes a kind of display.

When the tradition of painting became more secular, other themes also 15 offered the opportunity of painting nudes. But in them all there remains the implication that the subject (a woman) is aware of being seen by a spectator.

She is not naked as she is.

She is naked as the spectator sees her.

Often—as with the favourite subject of Susannah and the Elders—this is the actual theme of the picture. We join the Elders to spy on Susannah taking her bath. She looks back at us looking at her. [See Figure 16.18.]

In another version of the subject by Tintoretto, Susannah is looking at herself in a mirror. Thus, she joins the spectators of herself. [See Figure 16.19.]

The mirror was often used as a symbol of the vanity of woman. The mor- 20 alizing, however, was mostly hypocritical.

You painted a naked woman because you enjoyed looking at her, you put a mirror in her hand and you called the painting *Vanity*, thus morally condemning the woman whose nakedness you had depicted for your own pleasure.

The real function of the mirror was otherwise. It was to make the woman connive in treating herself as, first and foremost, a sight.

The judgment of Paris was another theme with the same inwritten idea of a man or men looking at naked women.

But a further element is now added. The element of judgment. Paris awards the apple to the woman he finds most beautiful. Thus Beauty becomes

Ms 65/1284 f.25v Adam and Eve in the Garden of Eden, from the 'Tres Riches Heures du Duc de Berry' (vellum), Limbourg, Pol de (d.c.1416)/Musee Conde, Chantilly, France/Giraudon/The Bridgeman Art Library International

FIGURE 16.16

Adam and Eve in the Garden of Eden; Fall and Expulsion miniature from Les Tres Riches Heures du Duc de Berry by Pol de Limbourg

FIGURE 16.17
Fall of Man, ca. 1525 by Jan Gossaert called Mabuse. Oil on oak, 170 × 114 cm

Bildarchiv Preussischer Kulturbesitz/Art Resource, NY

FIGURE 16.18
Susannah in Her Bath. Canvas, 167 × 238 cm by Jacopo Robusti Tintoretto

FIGURE 16.19
Susannah Bathing. Oil on canvas (after 1560) by Jacopo Robusti Tintoretto

FIGURE 16.20
The Judgement of Paris, 1639 (oil on canvas) by Peter Paul Rubens

competitive. (Today The Judgment of Paris has become the Beauty Contest.) Those who are not judged beautiful are *not beautiful*. Those who are, are given the prize. [See Figure 16.20.]

The prize is to be owned by a judge—that is to say to be available for 25 him. Charles the Second commissioned a secret painting from Lely. It is a highly typical image of the tradition. Nominally it might be a *Venus and Cupid*. In fact it is a portrait of one of the King's mistresses, Nell Gwynne. It shows her passively looking at the spectator staring at her naked. [See Figure 16.21.]

This nakedness is not, however, an expression of her own feelings; it is a sign of her submission to the owner's feelings or demands. (The owner of both woman and painting.) The painting, when the King showed it to others, demonstrated this submission and his guests envied him.

It is worth noticing that in other non-European traditions—in Indian art, Persian art, African art, Pre-Columbian art—nakedness is never supine in this way. And if, in these traditions, the theme of a work is sexual attraction, it is likely to show active sexual love as between two people, the woman as active as the man, the actions of each absorbing the other.

We can now begin to see the difference between nakedness and nudity in the European tradition. In his book *The Nude*, Kenneth Clark maintains that to be naked is simply to be without clothes, whereas the nude is a form of art. According to him, a nude is not the starting point of a painting but a way of seeing which the painting achieves. To some degree, this is true—although the way of seeing "a nude" is not necessarily confined to art. There are also

FIGURE 16.21
Portrait of Nell Gwynne as Venus with her son as Cupid by Sir Peter Lely

Portrait of Nell Gwynne (1650–87) as Venus, with her son, Charles Beauclerk (1670–1726), as Cupid (oil on canvas), Lely, Sir Peter (1618–80) (follower of)/© Army and Navy Club, London, UK/The Bridgeman Art Library International

nude photographs, nude poses, nude gestures. What is true is that the nude is always conventionalized—and the authority for its conventions derives from a certain tradition of art.

What do these conventions mean? What does a nude signify? It is not sufficient to answer these questions merely in terms of the art form, for it is quite clear that the nude also relates to lived sexuality.

30   To be naked is to be oneself.

To be nude is to be seen naked by others and yet not recognized for one-self. A naked body has to be seen as an object in order to become a nude. (The sight of it as an object stimulates the use of it as an object.) Nakedness reveals itself. Nudity is placed on display.

To be naked is to be without disguise.

To be on display is to have the surface of one's own skin, the hairs of one's own body, turned into a disguise which, in that situation, can never be discarded. The nude is condemned to never being naked. Nudity is a form of dress.

In the average European oil painting of the nude, the principal protagonist is never painted. He is the spectator in front of the picture, and he is presumed to be a man. Everything is addressed to him. Everything must appear to be the result of his being there. It is for him that the figures have assumed their nudity. But he, by definition, is a stranger—with his clothes still on.

Consider the *Allegory of Time and Love* by Bronzino. The complicated sym- 35 bolism which lies behind this painting need not concern us now, because it does not affect its sexual appeal—at the first degree. Before it is anything else, this is a painting of sexual provocation.

The painting was sent as a present from the Grand Duke of Florence to the King of France. The boy kneeling on the cushion and kissing the woman is Cupid. She is Venus. But the way her body is arranged has nothing to do with their kissing. Her body is arranged in the way it is, to display it to the man looking at the picture. This picture is made to appeal to *his* sexuality. It has nothing to do with her sexuality. (Here and in the European tradition generally, the convention of not painting the hair on a woman's body helps towards the same end. Hair is associated with sexual power, with passion. The woman's sexual passion needs to be minimized so that the spectator may feel that he has the monopoly of such passion.) Women are there to feed an appetite, not to have any of their own. [. . .]

It is true that sometimes a painting includes a male lover.

But the woman's attention is very rarely directed towards him. Often she looks away from him, or she looks out of the picture toward the one who considers himself her true lover—the spectator-owner.

There was a special category of private pornographic paintings (especially in the eighteenth century) in which couples making love make an appearance. But even in front of these it is clear that the spectator-owner will in fantasy oust the other man, or else identify with him. By contrast the image of the couple in non-European traditions provokes the notion of many couples making love. "We all have a thousand hands, a thousand feet and will never go alone."

Almost all post-Renaissance European sexual imagery is frontal—either 40 literally or metaphorically—because the sexual protagonist is the spectator-owner looking at it.

The absurdity of this male flattery reached its peak in the public academic art of the nineteenth century.

Men of state, of business, discussed under paintings like this. When one of them felt he had been outwitted, he looked up for consolation. What he saw reminded him that he was a man. [See Figure 16.22.]

There are a few exceptional nudes in the European tradition of oil painting to which very little of what has been said above applies. Indeed, they are no longer nudes—they break the norms of the art form; they are paintings of loved women, more or less naked. Among the hundreds of thousands of nudes which make up the tradition, there are perhaps a hundred of these exceptions. In each case, the painter's personal vision of the particular woman he is

FIGURE 16.22
Bacchus, Ceres and Amor. Canvas by Hans von Aachen

Erich Lessing/Art Resource, NY

painting is so strong that it makes no allowance for the spectator. The painter's vision binds the woman to him so that they become as inseparable as couples in stone. The spectator can witness their relationship—but he can do no more: He is forced to recognize himself as the outsider he is. He cannot deceive himself into believing that she is naked for him. He cannot turn her into a nude. The way the painter has painted her includes her will and her intentions in the very structure of the image, in the very expression of her body and her face.

The typical and the exceptional in the tradition can be defined by the simple naked/nude antinomy, but the problem of painting nakedness is not as simple as it might at first appear.

What is the sexual function of nakedness in reality? Clothes encumber 45 contact and movement. But it would seem that nakedness has a positive visual value in its own right: we want to *see* the other naked: The other delivers to us the sight of themselves, and we seize upon it—sometimes quite regardless of whether it is for the first time or the hundredth. What does this sight of the other mean to us, how does it, at that instant of total disclosure, affect our desire?

Their nakedness acts as a confirmation and provokes a very strong sense of relief. She is a woman like any other: or he is a man like any other: we are overwhelmed by the marvelous simplicity of the familiar sexual mechanism.

We did not, of course, consciously expect this to be otherwise: Unconscious homosexual desires (or unconscious heterosexual desires if the couple concerned are homosexual) may have led each to half expect something different. But the "relief" can be explained without recourse to the unconscious.

We did not expect them to be otherwise, but the urgency and complexity of our feelings bred a sense of uniqueness which the sight of the other, as she is or as he is, now dispels. They are more like the rest of their sex than they are different. In this revelation lies the warm and friendly—as opposed to cold and impersonal—anonymity of nakedness.

One could express this differently: At the moment of nakedness first perceived, an element of banality enters: an element that exists only because we need it.

Up to that instant the other was more or less mysterious. Etiquettes of 50 modesty are not merely puritan or sentimental: It is reasonable to recognize a loss of mystery. And the explanation of this loss of mystery may be largely visual. The focus of perception shifts from eyes, mouth, shoulders, hands—all of which are capable of such subtleties of expression that the personality expressed by them is manifold—it shifts from these to the sexual parts, whose formation suggests an utterly compelling but single process. The other is reduced or elevated—whichever you prefer—to their primary sexual category: male or female. Our relief is the relief of finding an unquestionable reality to whose direct demands our earlier, highly complex awareness must now yield.

We need the banality which we find in the first instant of disclosure because it grounds us in reality. But it does more than that. This reality, by promising the familiar, proverbial mechanism of sex, offers, at the same time, the possibility of the shared subjectivity of sex.

The loss of mystery occurs simultaneously with the offering of the means for creating a shared mystery. The sequence is: subjective—objective—subjective to the power of two.

We can now understand the difficulty of creating a static image of sexual nakedness. In lived sexual experience nakedness is a process rather than a state. If one moment of that process is isolated, its image will seem banal, and its banality, instead of serving as a bridge between two intense imaginative states, will be chilling. This is one reason why expressive photographs of the naked are even rarer than paintings. The easy solution for the photographer is to turn the figure into a nude, which, by generalizing both sight and viewer and making sexuality unspecific, turns desire into fantasy.

Let us examine an exceptional painted image of nakedness. It is a painting by Rubens of his young second wife, whom he married when he himself was relatively old. [See Figure 16.23.]

55   We see her in the act of turning, her fur about to slip off her shoulders. Clearly she will not remain as she is for more than a second. In a superficial sense her image is as instantaneous as a photograph's. But, in a more profound sense, the painting "contains" time and its experience. It is easy to imagine that a moment ago, before she pulled the fur round her shoulders, she was entirely naked. The consecutive stages up to and away from the moment of total disclosure have been transcended. She can belong to any or all of them simultaneously.

Her body confronts us, not as an immediate sight but as experience—the painter's experience. Why? There are superficial anecdotal reasons: her dishevelled hair, the expression of her eyes directed toward him, the tenderness with which the exaggerated susceptibility of her skin has been painted. But the profound reason is a formal one. Her appearance has been literally recast by the painter's subjectivity. Beneath the fur that she holds across herself, the upper part of her body and her legs can never meet. There is a displacement sideways of about nine inches: her thighs, in order to join onto her hips, are at least nine inches too far to the left.

Rubens probably did not plan this: The spectator may not consciously notice it. In itself it is unimportant. What matters is what it permits. It permits the body to become impossibly dynamic. Its coherence is no longer within itself but within the experience of the painter. More precisely, it permits the upper and lower halves of the body to rotate separately, and in opposite directions, round the sexual center which is hidden: the torso turning to the right, the legs to the left. At the same time this hidden sexual center is connected by means of the dark fur coat to all the surrounding darkness in the picture, so that she is turning both around and within the dark, which has been made a metaphor for her sex.

Helena Fourment in a Fur Wrap, 1636–38. Rubens, Peter Paul (1577–1640)/Kunsthistorisches Museum, Vienna, Austria/The Bridgeman Art Library

FIGURE 16.23
Peter Paul Rubens, Helene Fourment in a Fur Coat

Apart from the necessity of transcending the single instant and of admitting subjectivity, there is, as we have seen, one further element which is essential for any great sexual image of the naked. This is the element of banality which must be undisguised but not chilling. It is this which distinguishes between voyeur and lover. Here such banality is to be found in Rubens's compulsive painting of the fat softness of Hélène Fourment's flesh, which continually breaks every ideal convention of form and (to him) continually offers the promise of her extraordinary particularity.

The nude in European oil painting is usually presented as an admirable expression of the European humanist spirit. This spirit was inseparable from individualism. And without the development of a highly conscious individualism, the exceptions to the tradition (extremely personal images of the naked), would never have been painted. Yet the tradition contained a contradiction which it could not itself resolve. A few individual artists intuitively recognized this and resolved the contradiction in their own terms, but their solutions could never enter the tradition's *cultural* terms.

60   The contradiction can be stated simply. On the one hand the individualism of the artist, the thinker, the patron, the owner: on the other hand, the person who is the object of their activities—the woman—treated as a thing or an abstraction.

Dürer believed that the ideal nude ought to be constructed by taking the face of one body, the breasts of another, the legs of a third, the shoulders of a fourth, the hands of a fifth—and so on. [See Figure 16.24.]

The result would glorify Man. But the exercise presumed a remarkable indifference to who any one person really was.

In the art form of the European nude, the painters and spectator-owners were usually men and the persons treated as objects, usually women. This unequal relationship is so deeply embedded in our culture that it still

FIGURE 16.24

Artist drawing a model in foreshortening through a frame using a grid system. Woodcut from Unterweysung der Messung Nuremberg, 1527 by Albrecht Dürer

Foto Marburg/Art Resource, NY

FIGURE 16.25
The Venus of Urbino by Titian

Alinari Archives/Fratelli Alinari/Corbis

structures the consciousness of many women. They do to themselves what men do to them. They survey, like men, their own femininity.

In modern art the category of the nude has become less important. Artists themselves began to question it. In this, as in many other respects, Manet represented a turning point. If one compares his *Olympia* with Titian's original, one sees a woman, cast in the traditional role, beginning to question that role, somewhat defiantly. [See Figures 16.25 and 16.26.]

The ideal was broken. But there was little to replace it except the "realism" of the prostitute—who became the quintessential woman of early avant-garde twentieth-century painting (Toulouse-Lautrec, Picasso, Rouault, German Expressionism, etc.). In academic painting the tradition continued. 65

Today the attitudes and values which informed that tradition are expressed through other, more widely diffused media—advertising, journalism, television.

But the essential way of seeing women, the essential use to which their images are put, has not changed. Women are depicted in a quite different way from men—not because the feminine is different from the masculine—but because the "ideal" spectator is always assumed to be male, and the image of the woman is designed to flatter him. If you have any doubt that this is so, make the following experiment. Choose an image of a traditional nude. Transform the woman into a man, either in your mind's eye or by drawing on the reproduction. Then notice the violence which that transformation does—not to the image, but to the assumptions of a likely viewer.

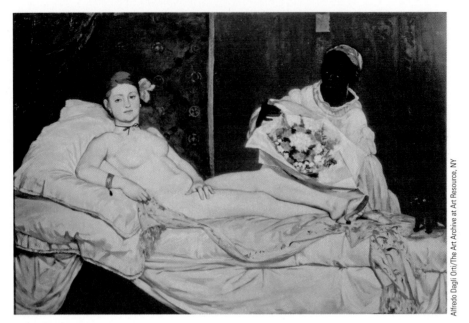

FIGURE 16.26
Olympia by Edouard Manet

Things to Do with the Reading

1. Write a paper in which you use Berger's essay as a lens for thinking about representations of women in, for example, fashion photography or on magazine covers aimed at either male or female audiences. Select particular sentences from Berger's essay as starting points. Consider, for example, the sentence, "And so she comes to consider the surveyor and the surveyed within her as the two constituent yet always distinct elements of her identity as a woman" (paragraph 4). Whatever sentence you choose as your starting point, do *not* write about whether you agree or disagree with Berger. Write so as to deepen your understanding of Berger's ideas and to make them your own.

2. Link: Several of the photographers discussed in the interview with Joseph Elliott have made a project of photographing women—Lauren Greenfield's "Girl Culture," for example. What might Berger notice about the Greenfield photograph we have included in this book, the one of the girl on the scale (Figure 16.13)? How might we see the gender of the photographer (female) having a shaping effect in this photograph? Write an essay in which you explore this question as well as analyze the photograph in light of insights you have gained from the Berger essay. There

778 Chapter 16 Seeing

is a mirror in the Greenfield photograph, for example. SO WHAT? For that matter, how do the female figures captured by Greenfield and/or Sally Mann compare with the photograph of the young woman on the porch by Alfred Stieglitz (Figure 16.8)?

3. Application: Berger's essay offers not just an interpretation of selected paintings but a rhetorical analysis of a set of conventions in European art. As in all rhetorical analyses, Berger focuses on how the paintings are designed to appeal to an assumed audience, in this case, an audience of male viewers. This kind of rhetorical analysis has come to be housed under the concept of the "gaze"—a word taken from French (Lacanian) psychology and developed by cultural analysts such as Teresa de Lauretis, who writes about women in film. In this mode of analysis attention is focused on the ways in which assumptions about the values and interests of particular viewers have shaped the painting or photograph or advertisement or building (etc.) under consideration. One of the reasons writing teachers so often ask students to write about the visual images in advertising is that the makers of such images can be assumed to be more conscious about their selection of a particular target audience and about the desire to win over that audience.

   Write a paper in which you experiment with this analytical approach by studying something for what it seems to assume about its audience. You might study commercials for products typically aimed at men—beer, for example. It would be interesting to see what is different if you could find a beer commercial (or commercial for some other product typically associated with men) that seems aimed at women.

4. Application: Using the Berger essay as a lens, write an essay about photographs of women in a high-end fashion magazine such as *Vogue*. To what extent do the photographs reveal themselves as shaped by or appealing to the male gaze, even if the assumed audience of the magazine is female? You might wish to apply the thinking in paragraph 7 of Berger's essay. There, for example, he states, "Men look at women. Women watch themselves being looked at. This determines not only most relations between men and women, but also the relation of women to themselves. The surveyor of woman in herself is male: the surveyed female." Alternatively, you might study a range of photographs of women by women photographers (such as Annie Liebovitz) in the context of the conventions governing the representation of women in European art. Try to find examples of photographs that seek deliberately to critique or undermine these conventions.

5. Application: Using the Berger essay as a lens, write an essay about one or both of the paintings by Alice Neel—the self-portrait and the painting of her son, Hartley (see Figures 16.27 and 16.28). How might we interpret Neel's self-portrait in the context of the conventions governing the

representation of women as nudes in European art? How does the painting speak to some of the conventions noted by Berger in his essay? What features of Neel's painting of her son Hartley read interestingly in the context of portraits of female nudes in European art? Hartley is neither naked nor nude, and yet he is clearly being put on display. What does the painting arguably reveal about Neel's assumptions about her audience? Which features of the painting might be designed to negotiate the possible anxiety among male viewers being invited to gaze at another male? Which features of the painting might reveal that it is the product of the gaze of a female viewer (the painter herself)?

National Portrait Gallery, Smithsonian Institution/Art Resource, NY

FIGURE 16.27
Self-Portrait, 1980 by Alice Neel. Oil on canvas, 54" × 40"

FIGURE 16.28
Hartley, 1965 by Alice Neel. Oil on canvas, 50" × 36"

National Gallery of Art, Washington, DC

Susan Bordo

Beauty (Re)discovers the Male Body

With this essay, the chapter makes a turn from high art in the direction of popular culture. In this excerpt from her book *The Male Body* (1999), Susan Bordo offers a compelling history of how advertising has rediscovered the male body. She examines how the pressures of commercial culture have expanded the range of acceptable images of masculinity, at once shaping and satisfying an expanding audience of women and men, straight and gay. Bordo's interpretations take us beyond cultural stereotypes, deftly challenging common cultural assumptions about masculinity, femininity, sexuality, and beauty itself. Susan Bordo is Professor of Gender and Women's Studies and holds the Otis A. Singletary Chair in the Humanities at the University of Kentucky. Her most recent book is *The Creation of Anne Boleyn: A New Look at England's Most Notorious Queen* (2013).

Men on Display

1 Putting classical art to the side for the moment, the naked and near-naked female body became an object of mainstream consumption first in *Playboy* and its imitators, then in movies, and only then in fashion photographs. With the male body, the trajectory has been different. Fashion has taken the lead, the movies have followed. Hollywood may have been a chest-fest in the fifties, but it was male clothing designers who went south and violated the really powerful taboos—not just against the explicit depiction of penises and male bottoms but against the admission of all sorts of forbidden "feminine" qualities into mainstream conceptions of manliness.

It was the spring of 1995, and I was sipping my first cup of morning coffee, not yet fully awake, flipping through *The New York Times Magazine*, when I had my first real taste of what it's like to inhabit this visual culture as a man. It was both thrilling and disconcerting. It was the first time in my experience that I had encountered a commercial representation of a male body that seemed to deliberately invite me to linger over it. Let me make that stronger—that seemed to reach out to me, interrupting my mundane but peaceful Sunday morning, and provoke me into erotic consciousness, whether or not I wanted it. Women—both straight and gay—have always gazed covertly, of course, squeezing our illicit little titillations out of representations designed for— or pretending to—other purposes than to turn us on. *This* ad made no such pretense. It caused me to knock over my coffee cup, ruining the more cerebral

"Beauty (Re)discovers the Male Body," from THE MALE BODY: A NEW LOOK AT MEN IN PUBLIC AND IN PRIVATE by Susan Bordo. Copyright © 1999 by Susan Bordo. Used by permission of Farrar, Straus and Giroux, LLC.

pleasures of the *Book Review*. Later, when I had regained my equilibrium, I made a screen-saver out of him, so I could gaze at my leisure.

I'm sure that many gay men were as taken as I was, and perhaps some gay women too. The erotic charge of various sexual styles is not neatly mapped onto sexual orientation (let alone biological sex). Brad Pitt's baby-butch looks are a turn-on to many lesbians, while I—regarded by most of my gay friends as a pretty hard-core heterosexual—have always found Anne Heche irresistible (even before Ellen did). A lesbian friend of mine, reading a draft of my section on biblical S&M, said the same movies influenced her later attraction to butch *women*. Despite such complications, until recently only heterosexual men have continually been inundated by popular cultural images *designed* with their sexual responses (or, at least, what those sexual responses are imagined to be) in mind. It's not entirely a gift. On the minus side is having one's composure continually challenged by what Timothy Beneke has aptly described as a culture of "intrusive images," eliciting fantasies, emotions, and erections at times and in places where they might not be appropriate. On the plus side is the cultural permission to be a voyeur.

Some psychologists say that the circuit from eyes to brain to genitals is a quicker trip for men than for women. "There's some strong evidence," popular science writer Deborah Blum reports, citing studies of men's responses to pictures of naked women, "that testosterone is wired for visual response." Maybe. But who is the electrician here? God? Mother Nature? Or Hugh Hefner? Practice makes perfect. And women have had little practice. The Calvin Klein ad made me feel like an adolescent again, brought me back to that day when I saw Barry Resnick on the basketball court of Weequahic High and realized that men's legs could make me weak in the knees. Men's legs? I knew that *women's* legs were supposed to be sexy. I had learned that from all those hose-straightening scenes in the movies. But men's legs? Who had ever seen a woman gaga over some guy's legs in the movies? Or even read about it in a book? Yet the muscular grace of Barry's legs took my breath away. Maybe something was wrong with me. Maybe my sex drive was too strong, too much like a man's. By the time I came across that Calvin Klein ad, several decades of feminism and life experience had left me a little less worried about my sex drive. Still, the sight of that model's body made me feel that my sexual education was still far from complete.

I brought the ad to classes and lectures, asking women what they thought 5 of him. Most began to sweat the moment I unfolded the picture, then got their bearings and tried to explore the bewitching stew of sexual elements the picture has to offer. The model—a young Jackson Browne look-alike—stands there in his form-fitting and rip-speckled Calvin Klein briefs, head lowered, dark hair loosely falling over his eyes. His body projects strength, solidity; he's no male waif. But his finely muscled chest is not so overdeveloped as to suggest a sexuality immobilized by the thick matter of the body. Gay theorist Ron Long, describing contemporary gay sexual aesthetics—lean, taut, sinuous muscles rather than Schwarzenegger bulk—points to a "dynamic tension" that the incredible hulks lack. Stiff, engorged Schwarzenegger bodies, he says, seem to *be* surrogate penises—with nowhere to go and nothing to do but stand there looking massive—whereas muscles like this young man's seem designed for movement, for sex. His body isn't a stand-in phallus; rather, he *has* a penis—the real thing, not a symbol, and a fairly breathtaking one, clearly outlined through the soft jersey fabric of the briefs. It seems slightly erect, or perhaps that's his non-erect size; either way, there's a substantial presence there that's palpable (it looks so touchable, you want to cup your hand over it) and very, very male.

At the same time, however, my gaze is invited by something "feminine" about the young man. His underwear may be ripped, but ever so slightly, subtly; unlike the original ripped-underwear poster boy Kowalski, he's hardly a thug. He doesn't stare at the viewer challengingly, belligerently, as do so many models in other ads for male underwear, facing off like a street tough passing a member of the rival gang on the street. ("Yeah, this is an underwear ad and I'm half naked. But I'm still the one in charge here. Who's gonna look away first?") No, this model's languid body posture, his averted look are classic signals, both in the "natural" and the "cultural" world, of willing subordination. He offers himself nonaggressively to the gaze of another. Hip cocked in the snaky S-curve usually reserved for depictions of women's bodies, eyes downcast but not closed, he gives off a sultry, moody, subtle but undeniably seductive consciousness of his erotic allure. Feast on me, I'm here to be looked at, my body is for your eyes. Oh my.

Such an attitude of male sexual supplication, although it has (as we'll see) classical antecedents, is very new to contemporary mainstream representations. Homophobia is at work in this taboo, but so are attitudes about gender that cut across sexual orientation. For many men, both gay and straight, to be so passively dependent on the gaze of another person for one's sense of self-worth is incompatible with being a real man. As we'll see, such notions about manliness are embedded in Greek culture, in contemporary visual representation, and even (in disguised form) in existentialist philosophy. "For the woman," as philosopher Simone de Beauvoir writes, ". . . the absence of her lover is always torture; he is an eye, a judge . . . away from him, she is dispossessed, at once of herself and of the world." For Beauvoir's sometime lover and lifelong soul mate Jean-Paul Sartre, on the other hand, the gaze (or the Look, as he called it) of another person—including the gaze of one's lover—is the "hell" that other people represent. If we were alone in the world, he argues, we would be utterly free—within physical constraints—to be whomever we wanted to be, to be the creatures of our own self-fantasies, to define our behavior however we like. Other people intrude on this solipsism, and have the audacity to see us from their own perspective rather than ours. The result is what Sartre calls primordial Shame under the eyes of the Other, and a fierce desire to reassert one's freedom. The other person has stolen "the secret" of who I am. I must fight back, resist their attempts to define me.

I understand, of course, what Sartre is talking about here. We've all, male and female alike, felt the shame that another pair of eyes can bring. Sartre's own classic example is of being caught peeking through a keyhole by another person. It isn't until those other eyes are upon you that you truly feel not just the "wrongness" of what you are doing, but—Sartre would argue—the very fact that you are doing it. Until the eyes of another are upon us, "catching us" in the act, we can deceive ourselves, pretend. Getting caught in moments of fantasy or vanity may be especially shameful. When I was an adolescent, I loved to pretend I was a radio personality, and talking into an empty coffee can created just the right sound. One day, my mother caught me speaking in the smooth and slightly sultry tones that radio personalities had even in those days. The way I felt is what Sartre means when he describes the Look of another person as the fulcrum of shame-making. My face got hot, and suddenly I saw how ridiculous I must have seemed, my head in the Chock Full O' Nuts, my narcissistic fantasies on full display. I was caught, I wanted to run.

The disjunction between self-conception and external judgment can be especially harsh when the external definitions carry racial and gender stereotypes with them. Sartre doesn't present such examples—he's interested in capturing the contours of an existential situation shared by all rather than in analyzing the cultural differences that affect that situation—but they are surely relevant to understanding the meaning of the Look of the Other. A black man jogs down the street in sweat clothes, thinking of the class he is going to teach later that day; a white woman passes him, clutches her handbag more tightly, quickens her step; in her eyes, the teacher is a potentially dangerous animal. A Latin American student arrives early the first day of college; an administrator, seeing him in the still-deserted hall, asks him if he is the new janitor. The aspiring student has had his emerging identity erased, a stereotype put in its place by another pair of eyes. When women are transformed from professionals to "pussies" by the comments of men on the street, it's humiliating, not so much because we're puritans as because we sense the hostility in the hoots, the desire to bring an uppity woman down to size by reminding her that she's just "the sex" (as Beauvoir put it).

We may all have felt shame, but—as the different attitudes of Beauvoir 10 and Sartre suggest—men and women are socially sanctioned to deal with the gaze of the Other in different ways. Women learn to anticipate, even play to the sexualizing gaze, trying to become what will please, captivate, turn shame into pride. (In the process, we also learn how sexy being gazed at can feel— perhaps precisely because it walks the fine edge of shame.) Many of us, truth be told, get somewhat addicted to the experience. I'm renting a video, feeling a bit low, a bit tired. The young man at the counter, unsolicited, tells me I'm "looking good." It alters everything, I feel fine, alive; it seems to go right down to my cells. I leave the store feeling younger, stronger, more awake. When women sense that they are not being assessed sexually—for example, as we age, or if we are disabled—it may feel like we no longer exist.

Women may dread being surveyed harshly—being seen as too old, too fat, too flat-chested—but men are not supposed to enjoy being surveyed *period*. It's feminine to be on display. Men are thus taught—as my uncle Leon used to say—to be a moving target. Get out of range of those eyes, don't let them catch you—even as the object of their fantasies (or, as Sartre would put it, don't let them "possess," "steal" your freedom). This phobia has even distorted scientific research, as mentioned earlier. Evolutionary theorists have long acknowledged display as an important feature of courting behavior among primates—except when it comes to *our* closest ancestors. With descriptions of hominid behavior, male display behavior "suddenly drops out of the primate evolutionary picture" (Sheets-Johnstone) and is replaced by the concept of year-round female sexual receptivity. It seems that it has been intolerable, unthinkable for male evolutionary theorists to imagine the bodies of their male ancestors being on display, sized up, dependent on selection (or rejection) by female hominids.

Scientists and "ordinary guys" are totally in synch here, as is humorously illustrated in Peter Cattaneo's popular 1997 British film *The Full Monty*. In the film, a group of unemployed metalworkers in Sheffield, England, watch a Chippendale's show and hatch the money-making scheme of presenting their own male strip show in which they will go right down to the "full Monty." At the start of the film, the heroes are hardly pillars of successful manliness (Gaz, their leader, refers to them as "scrap"). Yet even they have been sheltered by their guy-hood, as they learn while putting the show together. One gets a penis pump. Another borrows his wife's face cream. They run, they wrap their bellies in plastic, they do jumping jacks, they get artificial tans. The most overweight one among them (temporarily) pulls out of the show. Before, these guys hadn't lived their lives under physical scrutiny, but in male action mode, in which men are judged by their accomplishments. Now, anticipating being on display to a roomful of spectators, they suddenly realize how it feels to be judged as women routinely are, sized up by another pair of eyes. "I pray that they'll be a bit more understanding about us" than they've been with women, David (the fat one) murmurs.

They get past their discomfort, in the end, and their show is greeted with wild enthusiasm by the audience. The movie leaves us with this feel-good ending, not raising the question obvious to every woman watching the film: would a troupe of out-of-shape women be received as warmly, as affectionately? The climactic moment when the men throw off their little pouches is demurely shot from the rear, moreover, so we—the audience—don't get "the full Monty." Nonetheless, the film gently and humorously makes an important point: for a heterosexual man to offer himself up to a sexually evaluating gaze is for him to make a large, scary leap—and not just because of the anxieties about size discussed earlier in this book (the guy who drops out of the show, remember, is embarrassed by his fat, not his penis). The "full Monty"—the naked penis—is not merely a body part in the movie (hence it doesn't really matter that the film doesn't show it). It's a symbol for male exposure, vulnerability to an evaluation and judgment that women—clothed or naked—experience all the time.

I had to laugh out loud at a 1997 *New York Times Magazine* "Style" column, entitled "Overexposure," which complained of the "contagion" of nudity spreading through celebrity culture. "Stars no longer have private parts," the author observed, and fretted that civilians would soon also be measured by the beauty of their buns. I share this author's concern about our body-obsessed culture. But, pardon me, he's just noticing this now??? Actresses have been baring their breasts, their butts, even their bushes, for some time, and ordinary women have been tromping off to the gym in pursuit of comparably perfect bodies. What's got the author suddenly crying "overkill," it turns out, is Sly Stallone's "surreally fat-free" appearance on the cover of *Vanity Fair*, and Rupert Everett's "dimpled behind" in a Karl Lagerfeld fashion spread. Now that *men* are taking off their clothes, the culture is suddenly going too far. Could it be that the author doesn't even "read" all those naked female bodies as "overexposed"? Does he protest a bit too much when he declares in the first sentence of the piece that he found it "a yawn" when Dirk Diggler unsheathed his "prosthetic shillelagh" ("penis" is still a word to be avoided whenever possible) at the end of *Boogie Nights*? A yawn? My friend's palms were sweating profusely, and I was not about to drop off to sleep either.

As for dimpled behinds, my second choice for male pinup of the decade 15 is the Gucci series of two ads in which a beautiful young man, shot from the rear, puts on a pair of briefs. In the first ad, he's holding them in his hands, contemplating them. Is he checking out the correct washing-machine temp? It's odd, surely, to stand there looking at your underwear, but never mind. The point is: his underwear is in his hands, not on his butt. It—his bottom, that is—is gorgeously, completely naked—a motif so new to mainstream advertising (but since then catching on rapidly) that several of my friends, knowing I was writing about the male body, E-mailed me immediately when they saw the ad. In the second ad, he's put the underwear on, and is adjusting it to fit. Luckily for us, he hasn't succeeded yet, so his buns are peeking out the bottom of the underwear, looking biteable. For the *Times* writer, those buns may be an indecent exposure of parts that should be kept private (or they're a boring yawn, I'm afraid he can't have it both ways), but for me—and for thousands of gay men across the country—this was a moment of political magnitude, and a delicious one. The body parts that *we* love to squeeze (those plastic breasts, they're the real yawn for me) had come out of the closet and into mainstream culture, where *we* can enjoy them without a trip to a specialty store.

But all this is very new. Women aren't used to seeing naked men frankly portrayed as "objects" of a sexual gaze (and neither are heterosexual men, as that *Times* writer makes clear). So pardon me if I'm skeptical when I read arguments about men's greater "biological" responsiveness to visual stimuli. These "findings," besides being ethnocentric (no one thinks to poll Trobriand Islanders), display little awareness of the impact of changes in cultural representations on our capacities for sexual response. Popular science writer Deborah Blum, for example, cites a study from the Kinsey Institute which showed a group of men and women a series of photos and drawings of nudes, both male and female:

> Fifty-four percent of the men were erotically aroused versus 12 percent of the women—in other words, more than four times as many men. The same gap exists, on a much larger scale, in the business of pornography, a $500-million-plus industry in the U.S. which caters almost exclusively to men. In the first flush of 1970s feminism, two magazines—Playgirl and Viva—began publishing male centerfolds. *Viva* dropped the nude photos after surveys showed their readers didn't care for them; the editor herself admitted to finding them slightly disgusting.

Blum presents these findings as suggestive of a hard-wired difference between men and women. I'd be cautious about accepting that conclusion. First of all, there's the question of which physiological responses count as "erotic arousal" and whether they couldn't be evidence of other states. Clearly, too, we can *learn* to have certain physiological responses—and to suppress them—so nothing biologically definitive is proved by the presence or absence of physical arousal.

Studies that rely on viewers' *own* reports need to be carefully interpreted too. I know, from talking to women students, that they sometimes aren't all that clear about *what* they feel in the presence of erotic stimuli, and even when they are, they may not be all that comfortable admitting what they feel. Hell, not just my students! Once, a lover asked me, as we were about to part for the evening, if there was anything that we hadn't done that I'd really like to do. I knew immediately what that was: I wanted him to undress, very slowly, while I sat on the floor and just watched. But I couldn't tell him. I was too embarrassed. Later, alone in my compartment on the train, I sorely regretted my cowardice. The fact is that I love to watch a man getting undressed, and I especially like it if he is conscious of being looked at. But there is a long legacy of shame to be overcome here, for both sexes, and the cultural models are only now just emerging which might help us move beyond it.

Perhaps, then, we should wait a bit longer, do a few more studies, before we come to any biological conclusions about women's failure to get aroused by naked pictures. A newer (1994) University of Chicago study found that 30 percent of women ages eighteen to forty-four and 19 percent of women ages forty-five to fifty-nine said they found "watching a partner undress" to be "very appealing." ("Not a bad percentage," Nancy Friday comments, "given that Nice Girls didn't look.") There's still a gender gap—the respective figures for men of the same age groups were 50 percent and 40 percent. We're just learning, after all, to be voyeuses. Perhaps, too, heterosexual men could learn to be less uncomfortable offering themselves as "sexual objects" if they realized the pleasure women get from it. Getting what you have been most deprived of is the best gift, the most healing gift, the most potentially transforming gift—because it has the capacity to make one more whole. Women have been deprived not so much of the *sight* of beautiful male bodies as the experience of having the male body *offered* to us, handed to us on a silver platter, the way female bodies—in the ads, in the movies—are handed to men. Getting this from her partner is the erotic equivalent of a woman's coming home from work to find a meal prepared and ready for her. Delicious—even if it's just franks and beans.

Thanks, Calvin!

Despite their bisexual appeal, the cultural genealogy of the ads I've been discussing and others like them is to be traced largely through gay male aesthetics, rather than a sudden blossoming of appreciation for the fact that women might enjoy looking at sexy, well-hung young men who don't appear to be about to rape them. Feminists might like to imagine that Madison Avenue heard our pleas for sexual equality and finally gave us "men as sex objects." But what's really happened is that women have been the beneficiaries of what might be described as a triumph of pure consumerism—and with it, a burgeoning male fitness and beauty culture—over homophobia and the taboos against male vanity, male "femininity," and erotic display of the male body that have gone along with it.

    Throughout this century, gay photographers have created a rich, sensuous, and dramatic tradition which is unabashed in eroticizing the male body, male sensuousness, and male potency, including penises. But until recently, such representations have been kept largely in the closet. Mainstream responses to several important exhibits which opened in the seventies—featuring the groundbreaking early work of Wilhelm von Gloeden, George Dureau, and George Platt Lynes as well as then-contemporary artists such as Robert Mapplethorpe, Peter Hujar, and Arthur Tress—would today probably embarrass the critics who wrote about them when they opened. John Ashbery, in *New York* magazine, dismissed the entire genre of male nude photography with the same sexist tautology that covertly underlies that *Times* piece on cultural "overexposure": "Nude women seem to be in their natural state; men, for some reason, merely look undressed . . . When is a nude not a nude? When it is male." (Substitute "blacks" and "whites" for "women" and "men" and you'll see how offensive the statement is.)

For other reviewers, the naked male, far from seeming "merely undressed," was unnervingly sexual. *New York Times* critic Gene Thompson wrote that "there is something disconcerting about the sight of a man's naked body being presented as a sexual object"; he went on to describe the world of homoerotic photography as one "closed to most of us, fortunately." Vicki Goldberg, writing for the *Saturday Review*, was more appreciative of the "beauty and dignity" of the nude male body, but concluded that so long as its depiction was erotic in emphasis, it will "remain half-private, slightly awkward, an art form cast from its traditions and in search of some niche to call its home."

Goldberg needed a course in art history. It's true that in classical art, the naked human body was often presented as a messenger of spiritual themes, and received as such. But the male bodies sculpted by the Greeks and Michelangelo were not exactly nonerotic. It might be more accurate to say that in modernity, with the spiritual interpretation of the nude body no longer a convention, the contemporary homophobic psyche is not screened from the sexual charge of the nude male body. Goldberg was dead wrong about something else too. Whatever its historical lineage, the frankly sexual representation of the male body was to find, in the next twenty years, a far from private "niche to call its home": consumer culture discovered its commercial potency.

Calvin Klein had his epiphany, according to one biography, one night in 1974 in New York's gay Flamingo bar:

> As Calvin wandered through the crowd at the Flamingo, the body heat rushed through him like a revelation; this was the cutting edge. . . . [The] men! The men at the Flamingo had less to do about sex for him than the notion of portraying men as gods. He realized that what he was watching was the freedom of a new generation, unashamed, in-the-flesh embodiments of Calvin's ideals: straight-looking, masculine men, with chiseled bodies, young Greek gods come to life. The vision of shirtless young men with hardened torsos, all in blue jeans, top button opened, a whisper of hair from the belly button disappearing into the denim pants, would inspire and inform the next ten years of Calvin Klein's print and television advertisements.

25   Klein's genius was that of a cultural Geiger counter; his own bisexuality enabled him to see that the phallic body, as much as any female figure, is an enduring sex object within Western culture. In America in 1974, however, that ideal was still largely closeted. Only gay culture unashamedly sexualized the lean, fit body that virtually everyone, gay and straight, now aspires to. Sex, as Calvin Klein knew, sells. He also knew that gay sex wouldn't sell to straight men. But the rock-hard, athletic gay male bodies that Klein admired at the

Flamingo did not advertise their sexual preference through the feminine codes—limp wrists, raised pinkie finger, swishy walk—which the straight world then identified with homosexuality. Rather, they embodied a highly masculine aesthetic that—although definitely exciting for gay men—would scream "heterosexual" to (clueless) straights. Klein knew just the kind of clothing to show that body off in too. As Steven Gaines and Sharon Churcher tell it:

> He had watched enough attractive young people with good bodies in tight jeans dancing at the Flamingo and Studio 54 to know that the "basket" and the behind was what gave jeans sex appeal. Calvin sent his assistants out for several pairs of jeans, including the classic five-button Levi's, and cut them apart to see how they were made. Then he cut the "rise," or area from the waistband to under the groin, much shorter to accentuate the crotch and pull the seam up between the buttocks, giving the behind more shape and prominence. The result was instant sex appeal—and a look that somehow Calvin just knew was going to sell.

So we come to the mainstream commercialization of the aesthetic legacy of Stanley Kowalski and those inspired innovations of Brando's costumer in *A Streetcar Named Desire*. When I was growing up, jeans were "dungarees"—suitable for little kids, hayseeds, and juvenile delinquents, but not for anyone to wear on a date. Klein transformed jeans from utilitarian garments to erotic second skins. Next, Klein went for underwear. He wasn't the first, but he was the most daring. In 1981, Jockey International had broken ground by photographing Baltimore Oriole pitcher Jim Palmer in a pair of briefs (airbrushed) in one of its ads—selling $100 million worth of underwear by year's end. Inspired by Jockey's success, in 1983 Calvin Klein put a forty-by-fifty-foot Bruce Weber photograph of Olympic pole vaulter Tom Hintnaus in Times Square, Hintnaus's large penis clearly discernible through his briefs. The Hintnaus ad, unlike the Palmer ad, did not employ any of the usual fictional rationales for a man's being in his underwear—for example, the pretense that the man is in the process of getting dressed—but blatantly put Hintnaus's body on display, sunbathing on a rooftop, his skin glistening. The line of shorts "flew off the shelves" at Bloomingdale's and when Klein papered bus shelters in Manhattan with poster versions of the ad, they were all stolen overnight. [See Figure 16.29.]

Images of masculinity that will do double (or triple or quadruple) duty with a variety of consumers, straight and gay, male and female, are not difficult to create in a culture like ours, in which the muscular male body has a long and glorious aesthetic history. That's precisely what Calvin Klein was the first to recognize and exploit—the possibility and profitability of what is known in the trade as a "dual marketing" approach.

FIGURE 16.29
Bronzed and beautiful Tom Hintnaus: a breakthrough ad for Calvin Klein—
and the beginning of a new era for the unabashed erotic display of the
male body

Image Courtesy of The Advertising Archives

Since then, many advertisers have taken advantage of Klein's insight. A recent Abercrombie & Fitch ad, for example, depicts a locker room full of young, half-clothed football players getting a postmortem from their coach after a game. Beautiful, undressed male bodies doing what real men are "supposed to do." Dirty uniforms and smudged faces, wounded players, helmets. What could be more straight? But as iconography depicting a culture of exclusively male bodies, young, gorgeous, and well-hung, what could be more "gay"?

It required a Calvin Klein to give the new vision cultural form. But the fact is that if we've entered a brave, new world of male bodies it is largely because of a more "material" kind of epiphany—a dawning recognition among advertisers of the buying power of gay men. For a long time prejudice had triumphed over the profit motive, blinding marketers to just how sizable—and well-heeled—a consumer group gay men represent. (This has been the case with other "minorities" too. Hollywood producers, never bothering to do any demographics on middle-class and professional African-American women—or the issues that they share with women of other races and classes in this culture—were shocked at the tremendous box office success of *Waiting to Exhale*. They won't make that particular mistake again.) It took a survey conducted by *The Advocate* to jolt corporate America awake about gay consumers. The survey, done between 1977 and 1980, showed that 70 percent of its readers aged twenty to forty earned incomes well above the national median. Soon, articles were appearing on the business pages of newspapers, like one in 1982 in *The New York Times Magazine,* which described advertisers as newly interested in "wooing ... the white, single, well-educated, well-paid man who happens to be homosexual."

"Happens to be homosexual": the phrasing—suggesting that sexual identity is peripheral, even accidental—is telling. Because of homophobia, dual marketing used to require a delicate balancing act, as advertisers tried to speak to gays "in a way that the straight consumer will not notice." Often, that's been accomplished through the use of play and parody, as in Versace's droll portraits of men being groomed and tended by male servants, and Diesel's overtly narcissistic gay posers. "Thanks, Diesel, for making us so very beautiful," they gush. Or take the ad [. . .] with its gorgeous, mechanically inept model admitting that he's "known more for my superb bone construction and soft, supple hair than my keen intellect." The playful tone reassures heterosexual consumers that the vanity (and mechanical incompetence) of the man selling the product is "just a joke." For gay consumers, on the other hand, this reassurance is *itself* the "joke"; they read the humor in the ad as an insider wink, which says, "This is for *you*, guys." The joke is further layered by the fact that they know the model in the ad is very likely to be gay.

30   Contrast this ad to the ostentatious heterosexual protest of a Perry Ellis ad which appeared in the early 1990s (and no, it's not a parody):

> I hate this job. I'm not just an empty suit who stands in front of a camera, collects the money and flies off to St. Maarten for the weekend.
>
> I may model for a living, but I hate being treated like a piece of meat. I once had a loud-mouthed art director say "Stand there and pretend you're a human." I wanted to punch him, but I needed the job.
>
> What am I all about? Well, I know I'm very good-looking, and there are days when that is enough. Some nights, when I'm alone, it's not.
>
> I like women—all kinds.
>
> I like music—all kinds.
>
> I like myself so I don't do drugs.
>
> Oh yeah, about this fragrance. It's good. Very good.
>
> When I posed for this picture, the art director insisted that I wear it while the pictures were being taken. I thought it was silly, but I said "What the hell? It's their money."
>
> After a while, I realized I like this fragrance a lot. When the photo shoot was over, I walked right over, picked up the bottle, put it in my pocket and said "If you don't mind, I'd like to take this as a souvenir." Then I smiled my best f— you smile and walked out.
>
> Next time, I'll pay for it.
>
> It's that good.

Today, good-looking straight guys are flocking to the modeling agencies, much less concerned about any homosexual taint that will cleave to them. It's no longer necessary for an ad to plant its tongue firmly in cheek when lavishing erotic attention on the male body—or to pepper the ad with proofs of heterosexuality. It used to be, if an advertisement aimed at straight men dared to show a man fussing over his looks with seemingly romantic plans in mind, there had better be a woman in the picture, making it clear just *whom* the boy was getting pretty for. To sell a muscle-building product to heterosexuals, of course, you had to link it to virility and the ability to attract women on the beach. Today, muscles are openly sold for their looks; Chroma Lean nutritional supplement unabashedly compares the well-sculpted male body to a work of art (and a gay male icon, to boot)—Michelangelo's "David." Many ads display the naked male body without shame or plot excuse, and often exploit rather than resolve the sexual ambiguity that is generated.

Today, too, the athletic, muscular male body that Calvin plastered all over buildings, magazines, and subway stops has become an aesthetic norm, for straights as well as gays. "No pecs, no sex," is how the trendy David Barton gym sells itself: "My motto is not 'Be healthy'; it's 'Look better naked,'" Barton says. The notion has even made its way into that most determinedly heterosexual of contexts, a Rob Reiner film. In *Sleepless in Seattle*, Tom Hanks's character, who hasn't been on a date in fifteen years, asks his friend (played by Rob) what women are looking for nowadays. "Pecs and a cute butt," his friend replied without hesitation. "You can't even turn on the news nowadays without hearing about how some babe thought some guy's butt was cute. Who the first woman to say this was I don't know, but somehow it caught on." Should we tell Rob that it wasn't a woman who started the craze for men's butts?

Rocks and Leaners

We "nouvelles voyeuses" thus owe a big measure of thanks to gay male designers and consumers, and to the aesthetic and erotic overlap—not uniform or total, but significant—in what makes our hearts go thump. But although I've been using the term for convenience, I don't think it's correct to say that these ads depict men as "sex objects." Actually, I find that whole notion misleading, whether applied to men or women, because it seems to suggest that what these representations offer is a body that is inert, depersonalized, flat, a mere thing. In fact, advertisers put a huge amount of time, money, and creativity into figuring out how to create images of beautiful bodies that are heavy on attitude, style, associations with pleasure, success, happiness. The most compelling images are suffused with "subjectivity"—they *speak* to us, they seduce us. Unlike other kinds of "objects" (chairs and tables, for example), they don't let us use them in any way we like. In fact, they exert considerable power over us—over our psyches, our desires, our self-image.

How do male bodies in the ads speak to us nowadays? In a variety of ways. Sometimes the message is challenging, aggressive. Many models stare coldly at the viewer, defying the observer to view them in any way other than how they have chosen to present themselves: as powerful, armored, emotionally impenetrable. "I am a rock," their bodies (and sometimes their genitals) seem to proclaim. Often, as in the Jackson Browne look-alike ad, the penis is prominent, but *unlike* the penis in that ad, its presence is martial rather than sensual. Overall, these ads depict what I would describe as "face-off masculinity," in which victory goes to the dominant contestant in a game of will against will. Who can stare the other man down? Who will avert his eyes first? Whose gaze will be triumphant? Such moments—"facing up," "facing off," "staring down"—as anthropologist David Gilmore has documented, are a test of macho in many cultures, including our own.

"Don't eyeball me!" barks the sergeant to his cadets in training in *An Officer and a Gentleman*; the authority of the stare is a prize to be won only with full manhood. Before then, it is a mark of insolence—or stupidity, failure to understand the codes of masculine rank. In *Get Shorty*, an unsuspecting film director challenges a mob boss to look him in the eye; in return, he is hurled across the room and has his fingers broken.

"Face-off" ads, except for their innovations in the amount of skin exposed, are pretty traditional—one might even say primal—in their conception of masculinity. Many other species use staring to establish dominance, and not only our close primate relatives. It's how my Jack Russell terrier intimidates my male collie, who weighs over four times as much as the little guy but cowers under the authority of the terrier's macho stare. In the doggie world, size doesn't matter; it's the power of the gaze—which indicates the power to stand one's ground—that counts. My little terrier's dominance, in other words, is based on a convincing acting job—and it's one that is very similar, according to William Pollack, to the kind of performance that young boys in our culture must learn to master. Pollack's studies of boys suggest that a set of rules—which he calls "The Boy Code"—govern their behavior with each other. The first imperative of the code—"Be a sturdy oak"—represents the emotional equivalent of "face-off masculinity": Never reveal weakness. Pretend to be confident even though you may be scared. Act like a rock even when you feel shaky. Dare others to challenge your position. [See Figure 16.30.]

The face-off is not the only available posture for male bodies in ads today. Another possibility is what I call "the lean"—because these bodies are almost always reclining, leaning against, or propped up against something in the fashion typical of women's bodies. James Dean was probably our first pop-culture "leaner"; he made it stylish for teenagers to slouch. Dean, however, never posed as languidly or was as openly seductive as some of the high-fashion leaners are today. A recent Calvin Klein "Escape" ad depicts a young, sensuous-looking man leaning against a wall, arm raised, dark underarm hair exposed. His eyes seek out the imagined viewer, soberly but flirtatiously. "*Take Me,*" the copy reads. [See Figure 16.31]

Languid leaners have actually been around for a long time. Statues of sleeping fauns, their bodies draped languorously, exist in classical art alongside more heroic models of male beauty. I find it interesting, though, that Klein has chosen Mr. Take Me to advertise a perfume called "Escape." Klein's "Eternity" ads usually depict happy, heterosexual couples, often with a child. "Obsession" has always been cutting-edge, sexually ambiguous erotica. This ad, featuring a man offering himself up seductively, invitingly to the observer, promises "escape." From what? *To what?* Men have complained, justly, about the burden of always having to be the sexual initiator, the pursuer, the one of whom sexual "performance" is expected. Perhaps the escape is from these burdens, and toward the freedom to indulge in some of the more receptive pleasures traditionally reserved for women. The pleasures, not of staring someone down but of feeling one's body caressed by another's eyes, of being the one who receives the awaited call rather than the one who must build up the nerve to make the call, the one who doesn't have to hump and pump, but is permitted to lie quietly, engrossed in reverie and sensation.

FIGURE 16.30
Face-off masculinity

Calvin Klein Jeans

Image Courtesy of The Advertising Archives

FIGURE 16.31
A languid leaner

Some people describe these receptive pleasures as "passive"—which gives them a bad press with men, and is just plain inaccurate too. "Passive" hardly describes what's going on when one person offers himself or herself to another. Inviting, receiving, responding—these are active behaviors too, and rather thrilling ones. It's a macho bias to view the only *real* activity as that which takes, invades, aggresses. It's a bias, however, that's been with us for a long time, in both straight and gay cultures. In many Latin cultures, it's not a disgrace to sleep with other men, so long as one is *activo* (or *machista*)—the penetrator rather than the penetratee. To be a *pasivo*, on the other hand, is to be socially stigmatized. It's that way in prison cultures, too—a good indication of the power hierarchies involved. These hierarchies date back to the ancient Greeks, who believed that passivity, receptivity, penetrability were marks of inferior feminine being. The qualities were inherent in women; it was our nature to be passively controlled by our sexual needs. (Unlike us, the Greeks viewed women—not men—as the animalistic ones.) Real Men, who unlike women had the necessary rationality and will, were expected to be judicious in the exercise of their desires. But being judicious and being "active"—deciding when to pursue, whom to pursue, making advances, pleading one's case—went hand in hand.

40   Allowing oneself to be pursued, flirting, accepting the advances of another, offering one's body—these behaviors were permitted also (but

798   Chapter 16   Seeing

only on a temporary basis) to still-developing, younger men. These young men—not little boys, as is sometimes incorrectly believed—were the true "sex objects" of elite Greek culture. Full-fledged male citizens, on the other hand, were expected to be "active," initiators, the penetrators not the penetratees, masters of their own desires rather than the objects of another's. Plato's *Symposium* is full of speeches on the different sexual behaviors appropriate to adult men with full beards and established professions and glamorous young men still revered more for their beauty than their minds. But even youth could not make it okay for a man to behave *too much* like a woman. The admirable youth was the one who—unlike a woman—was able to remain sexually "cool" and remote, to keep his wits about him. "Letting go" was not seemly.

Where does our culture stand today with respect to these ideas about men's sexuality? Well, to begin with, consider how rarely male actors are shown—on their faces, in their utterances, and not merely in the movements of their bodies—having orgasms. In sex scenes, the moanings and writhings of the female partner have become the conventional cinematic code for heterosexual ecstasy and climax. The male's participation is largely represented by caressing hands, humping buttocks, and—on rare occasions—a facial expression of intense concentration. She's transported to another world; he's the pilot of the ship that takes her there. When men are shown being transported themselves, it's usually been played for comedy (as in Al Pacino's shrieks in *Frankie and Johnny*, Eddie Murphy's moanings in *Boomerang*, Kevin Kline's contortions in *A Fish Called Wanda*), or it's coded to suggest that something is not quite normal about the man—he's sexually enslaved, for example (as with Jeremy Irons in *Damage*). Mostly, men's bodies are presented like action-hero toys—wind them up and watch them perform.

Hollywood—still an overwhelmingly straight-male-dominated industry—is clearly not yet ready to show us a man "passively" giving himself over to another, at least not when the actors in question are our cultural icons. Too feminine. Too suggestive, metaphorically speaking, of penetration by another. But perhaps fashion ads are less uptight? I decided to perform an experiment. I grouped ads that I had collected over recent years into a pile of "rocks" and a pile of "leaners" and found, not surprisingly, that both race and age played a role. African-American models, whether in *Esquire* or *Vibe*, are almost always posed facing-off. And leaners tend to be younger than rocks. Both in gay publications and straight ones, the more languid, come-hither poses in advertisements are of boys and very young men. Once a certain maturity line is crossed, the challenging stares, the "face-off" postures are the norm. What does one learn from these ads? Well, I wouldn't want to claim too much. It used to be that one could tell a lot about gender and race from looking at ads. Racial stereotypes were transparent, the established formulas for representing men and women were pretty clear (sociologist Erving Goffman even called ads "gender advertisements"), and when the conventions were defied it was usually because advertisers sensed (or discovered in their polls) that social shifts had made consumers ready to receive new images. In this "post-modern" age, it's more of a free-for-all, and images are often more reactive to each other than to social change. It's the viewers' jaded eye, not their social prejudices, that is the prime consideration of every ad campaign, and advertisers are quick to tap into taboos, to defy expectations, simply in order to produce new and arresting images. So it wouldn't surprise me if we soon find languid black men and hairy-chested leaners in the pages of *Gentlemen's Quarterly*.

But I haven't seen any yet. At the very least, the current scene suggests that even in this era of postmodern pastiche racial clichés and gender taboos persist; among them, we don't want grown men to appear too much the "passive" objects of another's sexual gaze, another's desires. We appear, still, to have somewhat different rules for boys and men. As in ancient Greece, boys are permitted to be seductive, playful, to flirt with being "taken." *Men* must still be in command. Leonardo DiCaprio, watch out. Your days may be numbered.

Things to Do with the Reading

1. This essay exemplifies what Chapter 6 calls "the evolving thesis"—in which a broad opening claim leads the writer to engage evidence that continually reshapes that claim, often in surprising ways. Track the evolving thesis in "Beauty (Re)discovers the Male Body" to help you control the overarching argument, but also to grasp a model of how an evolving thesis can enable a writer to develop her ideas across a range of associations. See if you can make a list of perhaps five sentences that offer the essay's essential claims. Then connect these into a summary of the essay's argument. This exercise could be very helpful as a prelude to more analytical uses of the essay, because writing the summary of claims will enable you to understand and respect the complexity of its argument. Also see Chapter 3 on summary.

2. Link: Write an essay in which you apply Berger's categories *naked* and *nude* to the photos of men in Bordo's article and then consider how and to what extent Bordo is interested in the same binary. Pick any two images in Bordo's article and explain what Berger might see in these images. The treatment of the naked-nude binary is arguably an essential element of similarity and difference between the two writers. See Chapter 3 on Difference within Similarity.

3. Application: Look for some kind of depiction of men that is apparently aimed at female viewers, such as pictures of men in women's fashion magazines or in magazines aimed at (mostly female) teenagers. Write

an essay in which you examine the assumptions about this female audience suggested by the visual language of your chosen images. How, conceivably, have these assumptions shaped the image?

4. **Link & Application:** John Berger's "Images of Women in European Art" concludes in the final paragraph that

> Women are depicted in a quite different way from men—not because the feminine is different from the masculine—but because the "ideal" spectator is always assumed to be male, and the image of the woman is designed to flatter him.

Berger then invites readers to conduct an "experiment"—to transform the image of traditional female nude into a man and take note of the violence this "transformation does—not to the image, but to the assumptions of a likely viewer." Obviously, Bordo's essay revels in examining just such assumptions. As she notes, "men and women are socially sanctioned to deal with the gaze of the Other in different ways" (paragraph 10).

Write an essay in which you apply Berger's experiment *in reverse* to Bordo's essay. What is revealed when you take an example of any of the images of men that Bordo examines (or image types, such as the Leaner or the Rock), and you replace it with an image of a woman?

5. **Application:** To what extent does Bordo argue that gender taboos about men appearing as "'passive' objects of another's sexual gaze" have really changed (paragraph 43)? Locate images of men (not nudes) in print materials that are local—at your own campus or workplace, for example, or on billboards near where you live. Use these as the basis for a short analytical essay on changing attitudes towards representations of men and masculinity.

Alternatively, do some primary research to see if images of men, clothed or not, in advertising for other kinds of products such as Wall Street, banking, alcohol, cars, etc., display some of the same characteristics that Bordo notices. Your aim here is to write a paper in which you try to extend or refine Bordo's analysis, not simply reject it.

6. **Application:** The essay concludes by returning to a subject raised at the beginning: taboos. In the next to last paragraph Bordo suggests that "advertisers are quick to tap into taboos," and she predicts that ads representing the male body are likely to move increasingly in this direction. Test that prediction by locating a recent ad that taps into a taboo. Write a paper in which you carefully describe and analyze it, keeping its evident audience in mind.

Malcolm Gladwell

Listening to Khakis: What America's Most Popular Pants Tell Us About the Way Guys Think

Named one of the "100 most influential people" by *Time* magazine in 2005, Malcolm Gladwell is the author of five best-selling books on trends or patterns: *The Tipping Point: How Little Things Can Make a Big Difference* (2000), *Blink: The Power of Thinking Without Thinking* (2006), *Outliers: The Story of Success* (2008), *What the Dog Saw: And Other Adventures* (2009), and *David and Goliath: Underdogs, Misfits, and the Art of Battling Giants* (2013). Originally trained as a historian, Gladwell entered journalism as a science writer (for the *Washington Post*) but has become, to use one of the terms that *The Tipping Point* made famous, "a connector"—one who bridges different fields of knowledge. In "Listening to Khakis," which was first published in 1997 in *The New Yorker*, Gladwell explores the success of the ad campaign for Dockers pants, talking with ad designers and social psychologists on the challenges of producing successful fashion advertising for men.

1   In the fall of 1987, Levi Strauss & Co. began running a series of national television commercials to promote Dockers, its new brand of men's khakis. All the spots—and there were twenty-eight—had the same basic structure. A handheld camera would follow a group of men as they sat around a living room or office or bar. The men were in their late thirties, but it was hard to tell, because the camera caught faces only fleetingly. It was trained instead on the men from the waist down—on the seats of their pants, on the pleats of their khakis, on their hands going in and out of their pockets. As the camera jumped in quick cuts from Docker to Docker, the men chatted in loose, overlapping non sequiturs—guy-talk fragments that, when they are rendered on the page, achieve a certain Dadaist poetry. Here is the entire transcript of "Poolman," one of the first—and, perhaps, best—ads in the series:

> "She was a redhead about five foot six inches tall."

> "And all of a sudden this thing starts spinning, and it's going round and round."

> "Is that Nelson?"

> "And that makes me safe, because with my wife, I'll never be that way."

> "It's like your career, and you're frustrated. I mean that—that's—what you want."

"Listening to Khakis: What America's Most Popular Pants Tell Us About the Way Guys Think," by Malcolm Gladwell. Copyright © 1997 by Malcolm Gladwell. Originally Published in THE NEW YORKER. Reprinted with permission of the author.

"Of course, that's just my opinion."

"So money's no object."

"Yeah, money's no object."

"What are we going to do with our lives, now?"

"Well . . ."

"Best of all . . ."

[Voice-over] *"Levi's one-hundred-percent-cotton Dockers. If you're not wearing Dockers, you're just wearing pants."*

"And I'm still paying the loans off."

"You've got all the money in the world."

"I'd like to at least be your poolman."

By the time the campaign was over, at the beginning of the nineties, Dockers had grown into a six-hundred-million-dollar business—a brand that if it had spun off from Levi's would have been (and would still be) the fourth-largest clothing brand in the world. Today, seventy percent of American men between the ages of twenty-five and forty-five own a pair of Dockers, and khakis are expected to be as popular as blue jeans by the beginning of the next century. It is no exaggeration to call the original Dockers ads one of the most successful fashion-advertising campaigns in history.

This is a remarkable fact for a number of reasons, not the least of which is that the Dockers campaign was aimed at men, and no one had ever thought you could hit a home run like that by trying to sell fashion to the American male. Not long ago, two psychologists at York University, in Toronto—Irwin Silverman and Marion Eals—conducted an experiment in which they had men and women sit in an office for two minutes, without any reading material or distraction, while they ostensibly waited to take part in some kind of academic study. Then they were taken from the office and given the real reason for the experiment: to find out how many of the objects in the office they could remember. This was not a test of memory so much as it was a test of awareness—of the kind and quality of unconscious attention that people pay to the particulars of their environment. If you think about it, it was really a test of fashion sense, because, at its root, this is what fashion sense really is—the ability to register and appreciate and *remember* the details of the way those around you look and dress, and then reinterpret those details and memories yourself.

When the results of the experiment were tabulated, it was found that the women were able to recall the name and the placement of seventy percent more objects than the men, which makes perfect sense. Women's fashion, after all, consists of an endless number of subtle combinations and variations—of skirt, dress, pants, blouse, T-shirt, hose, pumps, flats, heels, necklace, bracelet, cleavage, collar, curl, and on and on—all driven by the fact that when a woman walks down the street she knows that other women, consciously or otherwise, will notice the name and the placement of what she is wearing. Fashion works for women because women can appreciate its complexity. But when it comes to men what's the point? How on earth do you sell fashion to someone who has no appreciation for detail whatsoever?

5   The Dockers campaign, however, proved that you could sell fashion to men. But that was only the first of its remarkable implications. The second—which remains as weird and mysterious and relevant to the fashion business today as it was ten years ago—was that you could do this by training a camera on a man's butt and having him talk in yuppie gibberish.

* * *

I watched "Poolman" with three members of the new team handling the Dockers account at Foote, Cone & Belding (F.C.B.), Levi's ad agency. We were in a conference room at Levi's Plaza, in downtown San Francisco, a redbrick building decorated (appropriately enough) in khaki-like earth tones, with the team members—Chris Shipman, Iwan Thomis, and Tanyia Kandohla—forming an impromptu critical panel. Shipman, who had thick black glasses and spoke in an almost inaudible laid-back drawl, put a videocassette of the first campaign into a VCR—stopping, starting, and rewinding—as the group analyzed what made the spots so special.

"Remember, this is from 1987," he said, pointing to the screen, as the camera began its jerky dance. "Although this style of filmmaking looks everyday now, that kind of handheld stuff was very fresh when these were made."

"They taped real conversations," Kandohla chimed in. "Then the footage was cut together afterward. They were thrown areas to talk about. It was very natural, not at all scripted. People were encouraged to go off on tangents."

After "Poolman," we watched several of the other spots in the original group—"Scorekeeper" and "Dad's Chair," "Flag Football," and "The Meaning of Life"—and I asked about the headlessness of the commercials, because if you watch too many in a row all those anonymous body parts begin to get annoying. But Thomis maintained that the headlessness was crucial, because it was the absence of faces that gave the dialogue its freedom. "They didn't show anyone's head because if they did the message would have too much weight," he said. "It would be too pretentious. You know, people talking about their hopes and dreams. It seems more genuine, as opposed to something stylized."

10   The most striking aspect of the spots is how different they are from typical fashion advertising. If you look at men's fashion magazines, for example, at the advertisements for the suits of Ralph Lauren or Valentino or Hugo Boss, they almost always consist of a beautiful man, with something interesting done to his hair, wearing a gorgeous outfit. At the most, the man may be gesturing discreetly, or smiling in the demure way that a man like that might

smile after, say, telling the supermodel at the next table no thanks he has to catch an early-morning flight to Milan. But that's all. The beautiful face and the clothes tell the whole story. The Dockers ads, though, are almost exactly the opposite. There's no face. The camera is jumping around so much that it's tough to concentrate on the clothes. And instead of stark simplicity, the fashion image is overlaid with a constant, confusing patter. It's almost as if the Dockers ads weren't primarily concerned with clothes at all—and in fact that's exactly what Levi's intended. What the company had discovered, in its research, was that baby-boomer men felt that the chief thing missing from their lives was male friendship. Caught between the demands of the families that many of them had started in the eighties and career considerations that had grown more onerous, they felt they had lost touch with other men. The purpose of the ads—the chatter, the lounging around, the quick cuts—was simply to conjure up a place where men could put on one-hundred-percent-cotton khakis and reconnect with one another. In the original advertising brief, that imaginary place was dubbed Dockers World.

This may seem like an awfully roundabout way to sell a man a pair of pants. But that was the genius of the campaign. One of the truisms of advertising is that it's always easier to sell at the extremes than in the middle, which is why the advertisements for Valentino and Hugo Boss are so simple. The man in the market for a thousand-dollar suit doesn't need to be convinced of the value of nice clothes. The man in the middle, though—the man in the market for a forty-dollar pair of khakis—does. In fact, he probably isn't comfortable buying clothes at all. To sell him a pair of pants you have to take him somewhere he is comfortable, and that was the point of Dockers World. Even the apparent gibberish of lines like "She was a redhead about five foot six inches tall." / "And all of a sudden this thing starts spinning, and it's going round and round."/"Is that Nelson?" have, if you listen closely enough, a certain quintessentially guy-friendly feel. It's the narrative equivalent of the sports-highlight reel—the sequence of five-second film clips of the best plays from the day's basketball or football or baseball games, which millions of American men watch every night on television. This nifty couplet from "Score-keeper," for instance—"'Who remembers their actual first girlfriend?'/ 'I would have done better, but I was bald then, too'"—is not nonsense but a twenty-minute conversation edited down to two lines. A man schooled in the highlight reel no more needs the other nineteen minutes and fifty-eight seconds of that exchange than he needs to see the intervening catch and throw to make sense of a sinking liner to left and a close play at the plate.

"Men connected to the underpinnings of what was being said," Robert Hanson, the vice-president of marketing for Dockers, told me. "These guys were really being honest and genuine and real with each other, and talking about their lives. It may not have been the truth, but it was the fantasy of what a lot of customers wanted, which was not just to be work-focused but to have the opportunity to express how you feel about your family and friends and lives. The content was very important. The thing that built this brand was that we absolutely nailed the emotional underpinnings of what motivates baby boomers."

Hanson is a tall, striking man in his early thirties. He's what Jeff Bridges would look like if he had gone to finishing school. Hanson said that when he goes out on research trips to the focus groups that Dockers holds around the country he often deliberately stays in the background, because if the men in the group see him "they won't necessarily respond as positively or as openly." When he said this, he was wearing a pair of stone-white Dockers, a deep-blue shirt, a navy blazer, and a brilliant-orange patterned tie, and these worked so well together that it was obvious what he meant. When someone like Hanson dresses up that fabulously in Dockers, he makes it clear just how many variations and combinations are possible with a pair of khakis—but that, of course, defeats the purpose of the carefully crafted Dockers World message, which is to appeal to the man who wants nothing to do with fashion's variations and combinations. It's no coincidence that every man in every one of the group settings profiled in each commercial is wearing—albeit in different shades— *exactly the same kind of pants.* Most fashion advertising sells distinctiveness. (Can you imagine, say, an Ann Taylor commercial where a bunch of thirtyish girlfriends are lounging around chatting, all decked out in matching sweater sets?) Dockers was selling conformity.

"We would never do anything with our pants that would frighten anyone away," Gareth Morris, a senior designer for the brand, told me. "We'd never do too many belt loops, or an unusual base cloth. Our customers like one-hundred-percent-cotton fabrics. We would never do a synthetic. That's definitely in the market, but it's not where we need to be. Styling-wise, we would never do a wide, wide leg. We would never do a peg-legged style. Our customers seem to have a definite idea of what they want. They don't like tricky openings or zips or a lot of pocket flaps and details on the back. We've done button-through flaps, to push it a little bit. But we usually do a welt pocket—that's a pocket with a button-through. It's funny. We have focus groups in New York, Chicago, and San Francisco, and whenever we show them a pocket with a flap—it's a simple thing—they hate it. They won't buy the pants. They complain' "How do I get my wallet?' So we compromise and do a welt. That's as far as they'll go. And there's another thing. They go, 'My butt's big enough. I don't want flaps hanging off of it, too.' They like inseam pockets. They like to know where they put their hands." He gestured to the pair of experimental prototype Dockers he was wearing, which had pockets that ran almost parallel to the waistband of the pants. "This is a stretch for us," he said. "If you start putting more stuff on than we have on our product, you're asking for trouble."

15   The apotheosis of the notion of khakis as nonfashion-guy fashion came several years after the original Dockers campaign, when Haggar Clothing

Co. hired the Goodby, Silverstein & Partners ad agency, in San Francisco, to challenge Dockers' khaki dominance. In retrospect, it was an inspired choice since Goodby, Silverstein is Guy Central. It does Porsche ("Kills Bugs Fast") and Isuzu and the recent "Got Milk?" campaign and a big chunk of the Nike business, and it operates out of a gutted turn-of-the-century building downtown, refurbished in what is best described as neo-Erector set. The campaign that it came up with featured voice-overs by Roseanne's television husband, John Goodman. In the best of the ads, entitled "I Am," a thirtyish man wakes up, his hair all mussed, pulls on a pair of white khakis, and half sleepwalks outside to get the paper. "*I am not what I wear. I'm not a pair of pants, or a shirt.*" Goodman intones. The man walks by his wife, handing her the front sections of the paper. "*I'm not in touch with my inner child. I don't read poetry, and I'm not politically correct.*" He heads away from the kitchen, down a hallway, and his kid grabs the comics from him. "*I'm just a guy, and I don't have time to think about what I wear, because I've got a lot of important guy things to do.*" All he has left now is the sports section and, gripping it purposefully, he heads for the bathroom. "*One-hundred-percent-cotton wrinkle-free khaki pants that don't require a lot of thought. Haggar. Stuff you can wear.*"

"We softened it," Richard Silverstein told me as we chatted in his office, perched on chairs in the midst of—among other things—a lacrosse stick, a bike stand, a gym bag full of yesterday's clothing, three toy Porsches, and a giant model of a Second World War Spitfire hanging from the ceiling. "We didn't say 'Haggar Apparel' or 'Haggar Clothing.' We said, 'Hey, listen, guys, don't worry. It's just *stuff.* Don't worry about it.' The concept was 'Make it approachable.'" The difference between this and the Dockers ad is humor. F.C.B. assiduously documented men's inner lives. Goodby, Silverstein made fun of them. But it's essentially the same message. It's instructive, in this light, to think about the Casual Friday phenomenon of the past decade, the loosening of corporate dress codes that was spawned by the rise of khakis. Casual Fridays are commonly thought to be about men rejecting the uniform of the suit. But surely that's backward. Men started wearing khakis to work because Dockers and Haggar made it sound as if khakis were going to be even easier than a suit. The khaki-makers realized that men didn't want to get rid of uniforms; they just wanted a better uniform.

The irony, of course, is that this idea of nonfashion—of khakis as the choice that diminishes, rather than enhances, the demands of fashion— turned out to be a white lie. Once you buy even the plainest pair of khakis, you invariably also buy a sports jacket and a belt and a whole series of shirts to go with it—maybe a polo knit for the weekends, something in plaid for casual, and a button-down for a dressier look—and before long your closet is thick with just the kinds of details and options that you thought you were avoiding. You may not add these details as brilliantly or as consciously as say, Hanson does, but you end up doing it nonetheless. In the past seven years, sales of men's clothing in the United States have risen an astonishing twenty-one percent, in large part because of this very fact—that khakis, even as they have simplified the bottom half of the male wardrobe, have forced a steady revision of the top. At the same time, even khakis themselves—within the narrow constraints of khakidom—have quietly expanded their range. When Dockers were launched, in the fall of 1986, there were just three basic styles: the double-pleated Docker in khaki, olive, navy, and black; the Steamer, in cotton canvas; and the more casual flat-fronted Docker. Now there are twenty-four Dockers and Haggar and everyone else has been playing a game of bait and switch: lure men in with the promise of a uniform and then slip them, bit by bit, fashion. Put them in an empty room and then, ever so slowly, so as not to scare them, fill the room with objects.

* * *

There is a puzzle in psychology known as the canned-laughter problem, which has a deeper and more complex set of implications about men and women and fashion and why the Dockers ads were so successful. Over the years, several studies have been devoted to this problem, but perhaps the most instructive was done by two psychologists at the University of Wisconsin, Gerald Cupchik and Howard Leventhal. Cupchik and Leventhal took a stack of cartoons (including many from *The New Yorker*), half of which an independent panel had rated as very funny and half of which it had rated as mediocre. They put the cartoons on slides, had a voice-over read the captions, and presented the slide show to groups of men and women. As you might expect, both sexes reacted pretty much the same way. Then Cupchik and Leventhal added a laugh track to the voice-over—the subjects were told that it was actual laughter from people who were in the room during the taping—and repeated the experiment. This time, however, things got strange. The canned laughter made the women laugh a little harder and rate the cartoons as a little funnier than they had before. But not the men. They laughed a bit more at the good cartoons but much more at the bad cartoons. The canned laughter also made them rate the bad cartoons as much funnier than they had rated them before, but it had little or no effect on their ratings of the good cartoons. In fact, the men found a bad cartoon with a laugh track to be almost as funny as a good cartoon without one. What was going on?

The guru of male-female differences in the ad world is Joan Meyers-Levy, a professor at the University of Chicago business school. In a groundbreaking series of articles written over the past decade, Meyers-Levy has explained the canned-laughter problem and other gender anomalies by arguing that men and women use fundamentally different methods of processing information. Given two pieces of evidence about how funny something is—their own opinion and the opinion of others (the laugh track)—the women came up with a higher score than before because they added the two clues together: they integrated the information before them. The men, on the other hand, picked one piece of evidence and ignored the other. For the bad cartoons, they got carried away by the laugh track and gave out hugely generous scores for funniness. For the good cartoons, however, they were so wedded to their own opinion that suddenly the laugh track didn't matter at all.

This idea—that men eliminate and women integrate—is called by Meyers-Levy the "selectivity hypothesis." Men are looking for a way to simplify the route to a conclusion, so they seize on the most obvious evidence and ignore the rest, while women, by contrast, try to process information comprehensively. So-called bandwidth research, for example, has consistently shown that if you ask a group of people to sort a series of objects or ideas into categories, the men will create fewer and larger categories than the women will. They use bigger mental bandwidths. Why? Because the bigger the bandwidth the less time and attention you have to pay to each individual object. Or consider what is called the invisibility question. If a woman is being asked a series of personal questions by another woman, she'll say more if she's facing the woman she's talking to than she will if her listener is invisible. With men, it's the opposite. When they can't see the person who's asking them questions, they suddenly and substantially open up. This, of course, is a condition of male communication which has been remarked on by women for millennia. But the selectivity hypothesis suggests that the cause of it has been misdiagnosed. It's not that men necessarily have trouble expressing their feelings; it's that in a face-to-face conversation they experience emotional overload. A man can't process nonverbal information (the expression and body language of the person asking him questions) and verbal information (the personal question being asked) at the same time any better than he can process other people's laughter and his own laughter at the same time. He has to select, and it is Meyers-Levy's contention that this pattern of behavior suggests significant differences in the way men and women respond to advertising.

Joan Meyers-Levy is a petite woman in her late thirties, with a dark pageboy haircut and a soft voice. She met me in the downtown office of the University of Chicago with three large folders full of magazine advertisements under one arm, and after chatting about the origins and the implications of her research she handed me an ad from several years ago for Evian bottled water. It has a beautiful picture of the French Alps and, below that, in large type, "Our factory." The text ran for several paragraphs, beginning:

> You're not just looking at the French Alps. You're looking at one of the most pristine places on earth. And the origin of Evian Natural Spring Water.
>
> Here, it takes no less than 15 years for nature to purify every drop of Evian as it flows through mineral-rich glacial formations deep within the mountains. And it is here that Evian acquires its unique balance of minerals.

"Now, is that a male or a female ad?" she asked. I looked at it again. The picture baffled me. But the word "factory" seemed masculine, so I guessed male.

She shook her head. "It's female. Look at the picture. It's just the Alps, and then they label it 'Our factory.' They're using a metaphor. To understand this, you're going to have to engage in a fair amount of processing. And look at all the imagery they're encouraging you to build up. You're not just looking at the French Alps. It's 'one of the most pristine places on earth' and it will take nature 'no less than fifteen years' to purify." Her point was that this is an ad that works only if the viewer appreciates all its elements—if the viewer integrates, not selects. A man, for example, glancing at the ad for a fraction of a second, might focus only on the words "Our factory" and screen out the picture of the Alps entirely, the same way he might have screened out the canned laughter. Then he wouldn't get the visual metaphor. In fact, he might end up equating Evian with a factory, and that would be a disaster. Anyway, why bother going into such detail about the glaciers if it's just going to get lost in the big male bandwidth?

Meyers-Levy handed me another Evian advertisement. It showed a man—the Olympic Gold Medal swimmer Matt Biondi—by a pool drinking Evian, with the caption "Revival of the fittest." The women's ad had a hundred and nineteen words of text. This ad had just twenty-nine words: "No other water has the unique, natural balance of minerals that Evian achieves during its 15-year journey deep within the French Alps. To be the best takes time." Needless to say, it came from a men's magazine. "With men, you don't want the fluff," she said. "Women, though, participate a lot more in whatever they are processing. By giving them more cues, you give them something to work with. You don't have to be so literal. With women you can be more allusive, so you can draw them in. They will engage in elaboration, and the more associations they make the easier it is to remember and retrieve later on."

25   Meyers-Levy took a third ad from her pile, this one for the 1997 Mercury Mountaineer four-wheel-drive sport-utility vehicle. It covers two pages, has the heading "Take the Rough with the Smooth," and shows four pictures—one of the vehicle itself, one of a mother and her child, one of a city skyline, and a large one of the interior of the car, over which the ad's text is superimposed. Around the border of the ad are forty-four separate, tiny photographs of roadways and buildings and construction sites and manhole covers. *Female.* Next to it on the table she put another ad—this one a single page, with a picture of the Mountaineer's interior, fifteen lines of text, a picture of the car's exterior, and, at the top, the heading: "When the Going Gets Tough, the Tough Get Comfortable." *Male.* "It's details, details. They're saying lots of different stuff," she said, pointing to the female version. "With men, instead of trying to cover everything in a single execution, you'd probably want to have a whole series of ads, each making a different point."

After a while, the game got very easy—if a bit humiliating. Meyers-Levy said that her observations were not anti-male—that both the male and the female strategies have their strengths and their weaknesses—and, of course, she's right. On the other hand, reading the gender of ads makes it painfully obvious how much the advertising world—consciously or not—talks down to men. Before I met Meyers-Levy, I thought that the genius of the famous first set of Dockers ads was their psychological complexity, their ability to capture the many layers of eighties guyness. But when I thought about them again after meeting Meyers-Levy, I began to think that their real genius lay in their heroic simplicity—in the fact that F.C.B. had the self-discipline to fill the allotted thirty seconds with as little as possible. Why no heads? The invisibility rule. Guys would never listen to that Dadaist extemporizing if they had to process nonverbal cues, too. Why were the ads set in people's living rooms *and* at the office? Bandwidth. The message was that khakis were wide-bandwidth pants. And why were all the ads shot in almost exactly the same way, and why did all the dialogue run together in one genial, faux-philosophical stretch of highlight reel? Because of canned laughter. Because if there were more than one message to be extracted men would get confused.

* * *

In the early nineties, Dockers began to falter. In 1992, the company sold sixty-six million pairs of khakis, but in 1993, as competition from Haggar and the Gap and other brands grew fiercer, that number slipped to fifty-nine million six hundred thousand, and by 1994 it had fallen to forty-seven million. In marketing-speak, user reality was encroaching on brand personality; that is, Dockers were being defined by the kind of middle-aged men who wore them, and not by the hipper, younger men in the original advertisements. The brand needed a fresh image, and the result was the "Nice Pants" campaign currently being shown on national television—a campaign widely credited with the resurgence of Dockers' fortunes.

In one of the spots, "Vive la France," a scruffy young man in his early twenties, wearing Dockers, is sitting in a café in Paris. He's obviously a tourist. He glances up and sees a beautiful woman (actually, the supermodel Tatjana Patitz) looking right at him. He's in heaven. She starts walking directly toward him, and as she passes by she says, "*Beau pantalon.*" As he looks frantically through his French phrase book for a translation, the waiter comes by and cuffs him on the head: "Hey, she says, 'Nice pants.'" Another spot in the series, "Subway Love," takes place on a subway car in Chicago. He (a nice young man wearing Dockers) spots her (a total babe), and their eyes lock. Romantic music swells. He moves toward her, but somehow, in a sudden burst of pushing and shoving, they get separated. Last shot: she's inside the car, her face pushed up against the glass. He's outside the car, his face pushed up against the glass. As the train slowly pulls away, she mouths two words: "Nice pants."

It may not seem like it, but "Nice Pants" is as radical a campaign as the original Dockers series. If you look back at the way that Sansabelt pants, say, were sold in the sixties, each ad was what advertisers would call a pure "head" message: the pants were comfortable, durable, good value. The genius of the first Dockers campaign was the way it combined head and heart: these were all-purpose, no-nonsense pants that connected to the emotional needs of baby boomers. What happened to Dockers in the nineties, though, was that everyone started to do head and heart for khakis. Haggar pants were wrinkle-free (head) and John Goodman-guy (heart). The Gap, with its brilliant billboard campaign of the early nineties—"James Dean wore khakis," "Frank Lloyd Wright wore khakis"—perfected the heart message by forging an emotional connection between khakis and a particular nostalgic, glamorous all-Americanness. To reassert itself, Dockers needed to go an extra step. Hence "Nice Pants," a campaign that for the first time in Dockers history raises the subject of sex.

30   "It's always been acceptable for a man to be a success in business," Hanson said, explaining the rationale behind "Nice Pants." "It's always been expected of a man to be a good provider. The new thing that men are dealing with is that it's O.K. for men to have a sense of personal style, and that it's O.K. to be seen as sexy. It's less about the head than about the combination of the head, the heart, and the groin. It's those three things. That's the complete man."

The radical part about this, about adding the groin to the list, is that almost no other subject for men is as perilous as the issue of sexuality and fashion. What "Nice Pants" had to do was talk about sex the same way that "Poolman" talked about fashion, which was to talk about it by not talking about it—or, at least, to talk about it in such a coded, cautious way that no man would ever think Dockers was suggesting that he wear khakis in order to look *pretty*. When I took a videotape of the "Nice Pants" campaign to several of the top agencies in New York and Los Angeles, virtually everyone agreed that the spots were superb, meaning that somehow F.C.B. had managed to pull off this balancing act.

What David Altschiller, at Hill, Holiday/Altschiller, in Manhattan, liked about the spots, for example, was that the hero was naïve: in neither case did he know that he had on nice pants until a gorgeous woman told him so. Naïveté, Altschiller stressed, is critical. Several years ago, he did a spot for Claiborne for Men cologne in which a great-looking guy in a bar, wearing a gorgeous suit, was obsessing neurotically about a beautiful woman at the other end of the room: "*I see this woman. She's perfect. She's looking at me. She's smiling. But wait. Is she smiling at me? Or laughing at me? . . . Or looking at someone else?*" You'd never do this in an ad for women's cologne. Can you imagine? "I see this guy. He's perfect. Ohmigod. Is he looking at me?" In women's advertising, self-confidence is sexy. But if a man is self-confident—if he knows he is attractive and is beautifully dressed—then he's not a man anymore. He's a fop. He's effeminate. The cologne guy had to be neurotic or the ad wouldn't work. "Men are still abashed about acknowledging that clothing is important," Altschiller said. "Fashion can't be important to me as a man. Even when, in the first commercial, the waiter says 'Nice pants,' it doesn't compute to the guy wearing the nice pants. He's thinking. What do you mean, 'Nice pants'?" Altschiller was looking at a videotape of the Dockers ad as he talked—standing at a forty-five-degree angle to the screen, with one hand on the top of the monitor, one hand on his hip, and a small, bemused smile on his lips. "The world may think they are nice, but so long as he doesn't think so he doesn't have to be self-conscious about it, and the lack of self-consciousness is very important to men. Because '*I don't care.*' Or 'Maybe I care, but I can't be *seen to care.*'" For the same reason, Altschiller liked the relative understatement of the phrase "nice pants," as opposed to something like "great pants," since somewhere between "nice" and "great" a guy goes from just happening to look good to the unacceptable position of actually trying to look good. "In focus groups, men said that to be told you had 'nice pants' was one of the highest compliments a man could wish for, Tanyia Kandohla told me later, when I asked about the slogan. They wouldn't want more attention drawn to them than that."

In many ways, the "Nice Pants" campaign is a direct descendant of the hugely successful campaign that Rubin-Postaer & Associates, in Santa Monica, did for Bugle Boy Jeans in the early nineties. In the most famous of those spots, the camera opens on an attractive but slightly goofy-looking man in a pair of jeans who is hitchhiking by the side of a desert highway. Then a black Ferrari with a fabulous babe at the wheel drives by, stops, and backs up. The babe rolls down the window and says, "Excuse me. Are those Bugle Boy Jeans that you're wearing?" The goofy guy leans over and pokes his head in the window, a surprised half smile on his face: "Why, yes, they *are* Bugle Boy Jeans."

"Thank you," the babe says, and she rolls up the window and drives away.

This is really the same ad as "Nice Pants"—the babe, the naïve hero, the 35 punch line. The two ads have something else in common. In the Bugle Boy spot, the hero wasn't some stunning male model. "I think he was actually a boxboy at Vons in Huntington Beach," Larry Postaer, the creative director of Rubin-Postaer & Associates, told me. "I guess someone"—at Bugle Boy—"liked him." He's O.K.-looking, but not nearly in the same class as the babe in the Ferrari. In "Subway Love," by the same token, the Dockers man is medium-sized, almost small, and gets pushed around by much tougher people in the tussle on the train. He's cute, but he's a little bit of a wimp. Kandohla says that F.C.B. tried very hard to find someone with that look—someone who was, in her words, "aspirational real," not some "buff, muscle-bound jock." In a fashion ad for women, you can use Claudia Schiffer to sell a cheap pair of pants. But not in a fashion ad for men. The guy has to be *believable*. "A woman cannot be too gorgeous," Postaer explained. "A man, however, can be too gorgeous, because then he's not a man anymore. It's pretty rudimentary. Yet there are people who don't buy that, and have gorgeous men in their ads. I don't get it. Talk to Barneys about how well that's working. It couldn't stay in business trying to sell that high-end swagger to a mass market. The general public wouldn't accept it. Look at beer commercials. They always have these gorgeous girls—even now, after all the heat—and the guys are always just guys. That's the way it is. We only reflect what's happening out there, we're not creating it. Those guys who run the real high-end fashion ads—they don't understand that. They're trying to remold how people think about gender. I can't explain it, though I have my theories. It's like a Grecian ideal. But you can't be successful at advertising by trying to re-create the human condition. You can't alter men's minds, particularly on subjects like sexuality. It'll never happen."

Postaer is a gruff, rangy guy, with a Midwestern accent and a gravelly voice, who did Budweiser commercials in Chicago before moving West fifteen years ago. When he wasn't making fun of the pretentious style of East Coast fashion advertising, he was making fun of the pretentious questions of East Coast writers. When, for example, I earnestly asked him to explain the logic behind having the goofy guy screw up his face in such a—well, goofy—way when he says, "Why, yes, they *are* Bugle Boy Jeans," Postaer took his tennis shoes off his desk, leaned forward bemusedly in his chair, and looked at me as if my head came to a small point. "Because that's the only way he could say it," he said. "I suppose we might have had him say it a little differently if he could actually *act*.

Incredibly, Postaer said, the people at Bugle Boy wanted the babe to invite the goofy guy into the car, despite the fact that this would have violated the most important rule that governs this new style of groin messages in men's-fashion advertising, which is that the guy absolutely cannot ever get the girl. It's not just that if he got the girl the joke wouldn't work anymore; it's that if he got the girl it might look as if he had deliberately dressed to get the girl, and although at the back of every man's mind as he's dressing in the morning there is the thought of getting the girl, any open admission that that's what he's actually trying to do would undermine the whole unself-conscious, antifashion statement that men's advertising is about. If Tatjana Patitz were to say "*Beau garçon*" to the guy in "Vive la France," or the babe on the subway were to give the wimp her number, Dockers would suddenly become terrifyingly conspicuous—the long-pants equivalent of wearing a tight little Speedo to the beach. And if the Vons boxboy should actually get a ride from the Ferrari babe, the ad would suddenly become believable only to that thin stratum of manhood which thinks that women in Ferraris find twenty-four-dollar jeans irresistible. "We fought that tooth and nail," Postaer said. "And it more or less cost us the account, even though the ad was wildly successful." He put his tennis shoes back up on the desk. "But that's what makes this business fun—trying to prove to clients how wrong they are."

* * *

The one ad in the "Nice Pants" campaign which isn't like the Bugle Boy spots is called "Motorcycle." In it a nice young man happens upon a gleaming Harley on a dark back street of what looks like downtown Manhattan. He strokes the seat and then, unable to contain himself, climbs aboard the bike and bounces up and down, showing off his Dockers (the "product shot") but accidentally breaking a mirror on the handlebar. He looks up. The Harley's owner—a huge, leather-clad biker—is looking down at him. The biker glowers, looking him up and down, and says, "Nice pants." Last shot: the biker rides away, leaving the guy standing on the sidewalk in just his underwear.

What's surprising about this ad is that, unlike "Vive la France" and "Subway Love," it *does* seem to cross the boundaries of acceptable sex talk. The rules of guy advertising so carefully observed in those spots—the fact that the hero has to be naïve, that he can't be too good-looking, that he can't get the girl, and that he can't be told anything stronger than. "Nice pants"—are all, in some sense, reactions to the male fear of appearing too concerned with fashion, of being too pretty, of not being masculine. But what is "Motorcycle"? It's an ad about a sweet-looking guy down in the Village somewhere who loses his pants to a butch-looking biker in leather. "I got so much feedback at the time of 'Well, God, that's kind of *gay*, don't you think?'" Robert Hanson said. "People were saying, 'This buff guy comes along and he rides off with the guy's pants. I mean, what the hell were they doing?' It came from so many different people within the industry. It came from some of our most conservative retailers. But do you know what? If you put these three spots up—'Vive La France,' 'Subway Love,' and 'Motorcycle'—which one do you think men will talk about ad nauseam? 'Motorcycle.' It's No. 1. It's because he's really cool. He's in a really cool environment, and it's every guy's fantasy to have a really cool, tricked-out fancy motorcycle."

Hanson paused, as if he recognized that what he was saying was quite 40 sensitive. He didn't want to say that men failed to pick up the gay implications of the ad because they're stupid, because they aren't stupid. And he didn't want to sound condescending, because Dockers didn't build a six-hundred-million-dollar business in five years by sounding condescending. All he was trying to do was point out the fundamental exegetical error in calling this a gay ad, because the only way for a Dockers man to be offended by "Motorcycle" would be if he thought about it with a little imagination, if he picked up on some fairly subtle cues, if he integrated an awful lot of detail. In other words, a Dockers man could only be offended if he did precisely what, according to Meyers-Levy, men don't do. It's not a gay ad because it's a guy ad. "The fact is," Hanson said, "that most men's interpretation of that spot is:

You know what? Those pants must be really cool, because they prevented him from getting the shit kicked out of him."

Things to Do with the Reading

1. **Link:** This essay is interesting in the context of Bordo's essay because it analyzes the ways Docker ads seek to negotiate taboos among men about how they are represented. Write an essay in which you first look for common ground between Bordo's essay and Gladwell's. Where, in the analysis of which images, are Bordo's and Gladwell's perspectives on the representation of men most similar? Where do they differ most? How might you account for the differences? (See Chapter 3, "LOOKING FOR DIFFERENCE WITHIN SIMILARITY.")

2. What reasons does the essay offer for the differences between men and women in the two experiments it describes—one testing men's and women's ability to remember detail and the other testing the response of men versus women to canned laughter when assessing the humor of cartoons? Write an essay in which you first explain the use Gladwell makes of these experiments in his analysis of men's versus women's response to advertising. Then locate some print ads in magazines, and answer the question that Joan Meyers-Levy repeatedly poses to Gladwell: "Is that a male or a female ad?"

   Gladwell concludes his analysis of male-oriented fashion advertising campaigns not with summary but with a final and culminating example. Inclusion of the word "integrating" makes the link with a binary (selective versus integrating) that advertisers consider when designing ads for either gender (see paragraphs 19–20). Begin an essay by explaining how Gladwell's final paragraph (about response to the "Motorcycle" commercial) ties together and culminates the essay's main ideas. According to the essay, why was the ad successful with male viewers?

   Then further develop your essay by comparing and contrasting two current commercials of your choice—one that you think operates in the way Gladwell defines, and another like the motorcycle ad that you think crosses the boundaries of "guy-ad" acceptability.

3. **Link:** Throughout this book we have argued that interpretation always takes place inside particular interpretive contexts and that more than one plausible interpretive context may apply to the same data (see Chapter 5.) Compare the conclusions Gladwell arrives at about headlessness in the early Dockers ad campaign with the conclusions that Berger might arrive at about the same feature. Berger, in his essay on the nude in European art, theorizes that the image of the female nude in

European paintings was designed to flatter a presumed male viewer. He argues that as a result of this tradition women come to see themselves in a divided way—as both spectacle and spectator. Use this interpretive context to write an essay in which you offer an alternative explanation of headlessness in the early Docker ads and of the importance of guy fashion being represented as "nonfashion." What might Berger say to the claim from Gladwell's essay that "A woman cannot be too gorgeous. A man, however, can be too gorgeous, because then he's not a man anymore" (paragraph 35)?

4. **Application:** Gladwell's analysis offers interesting ideas about ad design—about how ad makers act on theories about gender and perception ("processing") in order to target male or female audiences. Do your own primary research with advertisements in order to illustrate, test, and possibly extend Gladwell's analysis. Look for ads for the same product or kind of product in magazines (mainstream) aimed primarily at women and in magazines aimed primarily at men. Write an essay in which you locate what seem to you to be significant differences and then determine the extent to which the "selectivity" and "integration" hypotheses presented in Gladwell's essay could account for the differences (see paragraph 20).

Alternatively, write an essay in which you test one of the following assertions by surveying current fashion ads aimed at men: (1) "Most fashion advertising sells distinctness. . . . Dockers was selling conformity" (paragraph 13). (2) "What 'Nice Pants' had to do was talk about sex the same way that 'Poolman' talked about fashion, which was to talk about it by not talking about it . . . " (paragraph 31).

Kera Bolonik

Oy Gay!

In this piece Kera Bolonik, a culture writer and formerly the arts editor of *Salon*, uses a review of the TV sitcom *Will & Grace* to anchor a cultural analysis of the representation of Jews and gays on television. Along the way she manages to survey the formulaic "neurotic Levites and their sane-to-a-fault bemused Protestant spouses"—a formula she praises *Will & Grace* for challenging. Bolonik has also written for other magazines, such as *New York*, *Glamour*, the *Village Voice*, and *Bookforum*. Currently, she curates "The T.V. Age" collection for Medium, the blog-publishing platform.

1   Without baring flesh, exchanging fluids or even shedding blood, *Will & Grace* has become the craftiest, if not the most radical, show in the history of network television—though not merely for its unabashed depiction of gay existence, or the risqué, multi-entendre-filled dialogue its writers slyly sneak under the censors' radar.

    Will & Grace is revolutionary for something so utterly conventional it would warm the hearts of *bubbes* and *zeydes* across America's urban landscapes: sliding a portrait of a twenty-first-century Jewish American's life into a sitcom about a gay man and his best gal pal. Who in America would want to watch a show explicitly about a Jewish woman living in New York? Sounds like *Rhoda Redux*. But pair a single woman with a gay man and suddenly, you've got a winning formula.

    Actually, it's downright brilliant. There hasn't been a program this overtly Jewish since *The Goldbergs*, a popular show from 1949 to 1955 that depicted the travails of a hard-working Jewish family of Bronx tenement-dwellers. For starters, the show's name is taken from the "I-Thou" treatise by twentieth-century Jewish philosopher Martin Buber, which described the ongoing dialogue between man and God. And *Will & Grace* is the first prime-time sitcom *ever* to feature a wedding between a Jewish woman and a Jewish man. When American viewers watched the nuptials between interior decorator Grace Adler (Debra Messing) and Southern Jewish doctor Marvin "Leo" Markus (Harry Connick, Jr.) last year, they were bearing witness to more than just a sweeps ploy. Those "I do's" doubled as "I don'ts" to decades' worth of assimilationist portrayals of Jews. Two simple words in that context spoke volumes: More than upholding an age-old tradition that would make parents *kvell*, they communicated to Middle America that a Jewish main character does not need a gentile foil to validate his or her presence on television.

Reprinted with permission from the November 17, 2003 issue of The Nation. For subscription information, call 1-800-333-8536. Portions of each week's Nation magazine can be accessed at http://www.thenation.com.

It could've been so easy for the redheaded Manhattan transplant from Schenectady to live out her boob-tube destiny in sexless wedded bliss with her *goyishe* gay best friend, Will Truman (Eric McCormack). They're symbiotic, they love and respect each other, they share man problems and they even considered having a baby together. But co-creators Max Mutchnick and David Kohan decided to thumb their collective nose at television's love affair with interfaith marriage—which, by the way, is *so* 1990s—and delivered Grace a Hebraic knight on a white horse in Central Park just as she was en route to the obstetrician's office to be inseminated with Will's sperm. A few short months later, there stood bride and groom under a *chuppah* amid a sea of white *kippot* for the entire nation to behold.

Until Leo galloped into Grace's life that fateful afternoon, couch potatoes 5 had been barraged with neurotic Levites and their sane-to-a-fault, bemused Protestant spouses for more than ten years. There was nice Jewish boy Paul Buchman and his wispy WASP wife, Jamie Stemple, on *Mad About You;* nasal nanny Fran Fine, the Barbra Streisand-loving borough girl, and her haughty English boss, Maxwell Sheffield, on *The Nanny;* and hippie-dippy Dharma Finkelstein and her buttoned-up blue-blooded hubby, Greg Montgomery, in *Dharma & Greg.* On *Friends,* Ross and Monica Geller are the children of a couple who married outside the faith, and both brother and sister follow suit (Ross does so again and again.). Jerry never married on *Seinfeld,* but neither did he date Jewish women in a city that boasts a surplus of eligible *madelach.* And to think, back in 1972 Jews and Catholics protested the Meredith Baxter and David Birney comic vehicle *Bridget Loves Bernie* for its depiction of a marriage between an Irish Catholic woman and a Jewish man (it was subsequently canceled). This is what you call progress?

Apparently, it *was* a step up. Before the 1990s, the Jew was relegated to a secondary character, at best—Juan Epstein (*Welcome Back, Kotter*), Natalie Green (*The Facts of Life*), Abner and Gladys Kravitz (*Bewitched*), Alex Rieger (*Taxi*)—if their Jewishness was even explicitly articulated. They were the nosy neighbors, the class clowns, the voice of reason and the best friends, and were frequently asexual or spectacular failures in the love department. Rhoda Morgenstern was a rare case, her popularity as a sidekick allowing her to spin off from *The Mary Tyler Moore Show* in 1974 to have her very own sitcom.

Still, a Jew cast as a sitcom lead was usually stuck playing the quirky partner of a straitlaced gentile, the fact of a character's Judaism almost always serving as shorthand for "neurotic," "funny" or "eccentric." (Perhaps the sole, and remarkable, exception is the case of *Seinfeld,* where the show's namesake was both the Jew and the straight man, while his "non-Jewish" friends were the oddballs.) Yet even as Jews vacated the minor-character role, another group was waiting to be typecast. Gays and lesbians (and the occasional transgendered person) turned up all over the tube: Roseanne's gay boss Leon in *Roseanne;* bed-and-breakfast owners Ron and Erick in *Northern Exposure;*

Paul's lesbian sister Debbie in *Mad About You;* Ross's lesbian ex-wife Carol on *Friends,* to name just a few.

Will & *Grace* is the antidote to this long legacy of marginalizing and stereotyping of Jews and gays. Grace Adler and Will Truman are *both* nutty—the two are as competitive as they are insecure and self-deprecating—and enjoy their vanity as much as they do their geeky qualities (Will has a penchant for puns, Grace loves to sing badly). Yet neither Will nor Grace has anything on secondary characters like Jack McFarland (Sean Hayes), a manic Himbo with huge theatrical aspirations, pop-celebrity obsessions and delusions of grandeur, who recognizes little outside his microcosmic world of bad cabaret and gym bunnies; and Grace's gin-soaked assistant, Karen Walker (Megan Mullally), a rich bitch who knows the boldfaced names in all the New York society pages, but most days can barely remember her own. These two, along with Karen's devoted, acid-tongued maid, Rosario Salazar (Shelley Morrison), set the comedy in motion with their outrageous dysfunctions and interactions as Karen and Jack affectionately grope each other, "charge themselves some happy" at Barney's and Hermes, prank-call Marlo Thomas and torture Karen's fleet of servants.

All four friends, plus the deadpan Rosario, are fluent in queerspeak, trading bawdy quips, wicked in-jokes and pop-cultural references. But only the Upper West Side-dwelling Will understands Grace's self-referential humor, which is largely shaped by her Jewish experience. She dubs Will "Uncle Hachel" when he's being a jerk, drops casual mentions of her summers at Camp Ramah and has been known to intone a self-pitying prayer "*Borchu et adonai,* I'm gonna die alone." Jack and Karen would seem to have encountered only one Jew in their life—Grace—so they are often puzzled by her comical asides. But Grace does not become the butt of the joke; rather, we laugh at Karen and Jack for their ignorance about things Jewish. These two *über*-gentiles are the eccentrics for a change.

10   It would be so simple for Mutchnick and Kohan to posit the "straight" pair against the wacky duo. But there is one crucial difference between Will and Grace—one steeped in cultural mores—that threatens to propel one forward in life and leave the other behind. Will cleaves to his WASP reserve out of fear, preferring denial and decorum to confrontation, which can prove paralytic for him. He is out to his parents, for example, but can't bring himself to acknowledge his father's infidelities, even as he meets the mistress. Grace is the product of a theatrical Jewish mother who knows no bounds (or boundaries), and if it isn't confidence that allows it, she at least has the chutzpah to take leaps of faith.

Last year's season finale of Will & *Grace* intimated that the honeymoon between the newlywed Markuses might have been drawing to a close, though the new season shows the couple negotiating their new life together. But the survival of Grace's marriage hardly even matters. The fact that she did it at all demonstrated to her gang that she was ready to reconfigure her friendship with Will so that she could pursue sexual and emotional fulfillment through a marriage built on romance. More so, it conveyed to millions of viewers that, as *Will & Grace* blazes trails by offering fully realized, nonstereotypical gay characters, it is simultaneously an extremely entertaining sitcom about a Jewish gal from Schenectady who is as American as (the Big) Apple Pie.

Things to Do with the Reading

1. Write an essay in which you explain Bolonik's analysis of how the television show *Will & Grace* presses viewers to revise—to re-see—stereotypes about Jews and gays. Because Will and Grace seem often to behave in ways that confirm gay and Jewish stereotypes, what, according to Bolonik, did the show do in order to invite viewers to see these characters differently?

2. Application: Bolonik's review makes repeated reference to the language of stereotypes—both "queerspeak" and the occasional Hebrew phrase and summer camp allusion—and locates these astutely in the context of audience reception for a network sitcom. Indeed, references to other sitcoms that situate ethnic and gendered stereotypes are scattered throughout the piece. We get very little, however, about how *Will & Grace* offers *visual representation* of these groups. Write an essay in which you track the imaging of members of both mainstream and outlier groups in any other television sitcom, with the aim of analyzing how the show predisposes us to see. What are the primary elements of its visual vocabulary? SO WHAT that it invites us to see as it does?

X. J. Kennedy

Who Killed King Kong?

This essay, originally published in *Dissent* in Spring 1960, offers an analysis of the causes for the continued popularity of the original 1933 film of *King Kong* with various audiences, including African-Americans. Other readings in this chapter have focused on ways that cultural forces shape the way we see. In this final reading of the chapter, we end with Kennedy's lively evocation of some of the most famous visual moments in American film history—King Kong tossing subway cars filled with commuters, King Kong carrying a small screaming blonde woman across the tops of buildings, King Kong swatting the small airplanes seeking to knock him off his refuge at the top of the Empire State building. In a final twist on this chapter's scrutiny of "Seeing," Kennedy's review invites readers to consider how images connect with and shape the self-image of their viewers.

1   The ordeal and spectacular death of King Kong, the giant ape, undoubtedly have been witnessed by more Americans than have ever seen a performance of *Hamlet*, *Iphigenia at Aulis*, or even *Tobacco Road*. Since RKO-Radio Pictures first released *King Kong*, a quarter-century has gone by; yet year after year, from prints that grow more rain-beaten, from sound tracks that grow more tinny ticket-buyers by thousands still pursue Kong's luckless fight against the forces of technology, tabloid journalism, and the DAR. They see him chloroformed to sleep, see him whisked from his jungle isle to New York and placed on show, see him burst his chains to roam the city (lugging a frightened blonde), at last to plunge from the spire of the Empire State Building, machine-gunned by model airplanes.

Though Kong may die, one begins to think his legend unkillable. No clearer proof of his hold upon the popular imagination may be seen than what emerged one catastrophic week in March 1955, when New York WOR-TV programmed *Kong* for seven evenings in a row (a total of sixteen showings). Many a rival network vice-president must have scowled when surveys showed that *Kong*—the 1933 B-picture—had lured away fat segments of the viewing populace from such powerful competitors as Ed Sullivan, Groucho Marx and Bishop Sheen.

But even television has failed to run *King Kong* into oblivion. Coffee-in-the-lobby cinemas still show the old hunk of hokum, with the apology that in its use of composite shots and animated models the film remains technically interesting. And no other monster in movie history has won so devoted a popular audience. None of the plodding mummies, the stultified draculas, the white-coated Lugosis[1] with their shiny pinball-machine laboratories, none

"Who Killed King Kong?" by X. J. Kennedy. Originally published in Dissent Magazine in 1961. Reprinted with permission of the author.

of the invisible stranglers, berserk robots, or menaces from Mars has ever enjoyed so many resurrections.

Why does the American public refuse to let King Kong rest in peace? It is true, I'll admit, that *Kong* outdid every monster movie before or since in sheer carnage. Producers Cooper and Schoedsack crammed into it dinosaurs, headhunters, riots, aerial battles, bullets, bombs, bloodletting. Heroine Fay Wray, whose function is mainly to scream, shuts her mouth for hardly one uninterrupted minute from first reel to last. It is also true that *Kong* is larded with good healthy sadism, for those whose joy it is to see the frantic girl dangled from cliffs and harried by pterodactyls. But it seems to me that the abiding appeal of the giant ape rests on other foundations.

Kong has, first of all, the attraction of being manlike. His simian nature 5 gives him one huge advantage over giant ants and walking vegetables in that an audience may conceivably identify with him. Kong's appeal has the quality that established the Tarzan series as American myth—for what man doesn't secretly image himself a huge hairy howler against whom no other monster has a chance? If Tarzan recalls the ape in us, then Kong may well appeal to that great-granddaddy primordial brute from whose tribe we have all deteriorated.

Intentionally or not, the producers of *King Kong* encourage this identification by etching the character of Kong with keen sympathy. For the ape is a figure in a tradition familiar to moviegoers: the tradition of the pitiable monster. We think of Lon Chaney in the role of Quasimodo, of Karloff in the original *Frankenstein*. As we watch the Frankenstein monster's fumbling and disastrous attempts to befriend a flower-picking child, our sympathies are enlisted with the monster in his impenetrable loneliness. And so with Kong. As he roars in his chains, while barkers sell tickets to boobs who gape at him, we perhaps feel something more deep than pathos. We begin to sense something of the problem that engaged Eugene O'Neill in *The Hairy Ape*: the dilemma of a displaced animal spirit forced to live in a jungle built by machines.

King Kong, it is true, had special relevance in 1933. Landscapes of the depression are glimpsed early in the film when an impresario, seeking some desperate pretty girl to play the lead in a jungle movie, visits souplines and a Woman's Home Mission. In Fay Wray—who's been caught snitching an apple from a fruitstand—his search is ended. When he gives her a big feed and a movie contract, the girl is magic-carpeted out of the world of the National Recovery Act. And when, in the film's climax, Kong smashes that very Third Avenue landscape in which Fay had wandered hungry, audiences of 1933 may well have felt a personal satisfaction.

What is curious is that audiences of 1960 remain hooked. For in the heart of urban man, one suspects, lurks the impulse to fling a bomb. Though machines speed him to the scene of his daily grind, though IBM comptometers ("freeing the human mind from drudgery") enable him to drudge more efficiently once he arrives, there comes a moment when he wishes to turn upon his machines and kick hell out of them. He wants to hurl his combination radio-alarmclock out the bedroom window and listen to its smash. What subway commuter wouldn't love—just for once—to see the downtown express smack head-on into the uptown local? Such a wish is gratified in that memorable scene in *Kong* that opens with a wide-angle shot: interior of a railway car on the Third Avenue El. Straphangers are nodding, the literate refold their newspapers. Unknown to them, Kong has torn away a section of trestle toward which the train now speeds. The motorman spies Kong up ahead, jams on the brakes. Passengers hurtle together like so many peas in a pail. In a window of the car appear Kong's bloodshot eyes. Women shriek. Kong picks up the railway car as if it were a rat, flips it to the street and ties knots in it, or something. To any commuter the scene must appear one of the most satisfactory pieces of celluloid ever exposed.

Yet however violent his acts, Kong remains a gentleman. Remarkable is his sense of chivalry. Whenever a fresh boa constrictor threatens Fay, Kong first sees that the lady is safely parked, then manfully thrashes her attacker. (And she, the ingrate, runs away every time his back is turned.) Atop the Empire State Building, ignoring his pursuers, Kong places Fay on a ledge as tenderly as it she were a dozen eggs. He fondles her, then turns to face the Army Air Force. And Kong is perhaps the most disinterested lover since Cyrano: his attentions to the lady are utterly without hope of reward. After all, between a five-foot blonde and a fifty-foot ape, love can hardly be more than an intellectual flirtation. In his simian way King Kong is the hopelessly yearning lover of Petrarchan convention. His forced exit from his jungle, in chains, results directly from his single-minded pursuit of Fay. He smashes a Broadway theater when the notion enters his dull brain that the flashbulbs of photographers somehow endanger the lady. His perilous shinnying up a skyscraper to pluck Fay from her boudoir is an act of the kindliest of hearts. He's impossible to discourage even though the love of his life can't lay eyes on him without shrieking murder.

10 The tragedy of King Kong then, is to be the beast who at the end of the fable fails to turn into the handsome prince. This is the conviction that the scriptwriters would leave with us in the film's closing line. As Kong's corpse lies blocking traffic in the street, the entrepreneur who brought Kong to New York turns to the assembled reporters and proclaims: "That's your story, boys—it was Beauty killed the Beast!" But greater forces than those of the screaming Lady have combined to lay Kong low, if you ask me. Kong lives for a time as one of those persecuted near-animal souls bewildered in the middle of an industrial order, whose simple desires are thwarted at every turn. He climbs the Empire State Building because in all New York it's the closest thing he can find to the clifftop of his jungle isle. He dies, a pitiful dolt, and the army brass and publicity-men cackle over him. His death is the only possible outcome to as neat a tragic dilemma as you can ask for. The machine-guns

do him in, while the manicured human hero (a nice clean Dartmouth boy) carries away Kong's sweetheart to the altar, O, the misery of it all. There's far more truth about upper-middle-class American life in *King Kong* than in the last seven dozen novels of John P. Marquand.

A Negro friend from Atlanta tells me that in movie houses in colored neighborhoods throughout the South, *Kong* does a constant business. They show the thing in Atlanta at least every year, presumably to the same audiences. Perhaps this popularity may simply be due to the fact that Kong is one of the most watchable movies ever constructed, but I wonder whether Negro audiences may not find some archetypical appeal in this serio-comic tale of a huge black powerful free spirit whom all the hardworking white policemen are out to kill.

Every day in the week on a screen somewhere in the world, King Kong relives his agony. Again and again he expires on the Empire State Building, as audiences of the devout assist his sacrifice. We watch him die, and by extension kill the ape within our bones, but these little deaths of ours occur in prosaic surroundings. We do not die on a tower, New York before our feet, nor do we give our lives to smash a few flying machines. It is not for us to bring to a momentary standstill the civilization in which we move. King Kong does this for us. And so we kill him again and again, in much-spliced celluloid; while the ape in us expires from day to day, obscure, in desperation.

Notes

[1] Bela Lugosi, an actor in many horror movies.

Things to Do with the Reading

1. Get a copy of the 1933 version of *King Kong* and watch it. From the perspective of today, which of the claims that Kennedy makes from his own contemporary perspective—one that is now nearly fifty years old—seem least credible, and why? And which arguably are still pertinent interpretations of the original *Kong*? In short, which features of the cultural climate now would require a writer to update and adjust the 1960 lens?

2. The Kennedy essay offers the opportunity to think about how all research needs to be conditioned by a sense of history. In other words, to some extent, "Who Killed King Kong?" is a piece that tells us at least as much about 1960, when it was written, as it does about 1933, when the film was produced. What does the review tell us about 1960—or at least about political attitudes on the left in 1960? (See Chapter 2, the section titled "THE PITCH, THE COMPLAINT, AND THE MOMENT.")

3. **Application:** One interesting analytical project is to study several versions of a film—the original and its remake(s). The fact that the film gets remade speaks to something enduring in its vision of things, something that might be called mythic or transhistorical. But the remake also suggests the desire to update that vision, or at least, it suggests that a new version of the vision might prove newly marketable.

   There are at least three full-fledged versions of *King Kong*: Merian C. Cooper's 1933 original, John Guillerman's 1976 version, and Peter Jackson's 2005 remake. For more data on these see http://www.kongisking .net/index.shtml.

   Write an essay in which you analyze how the remake reshapes the earlier version. What, at the level of representation, remains essentially the same in the way the remake sees the essential story? What has changed most dramatically, and how do you interpret the way that the film is attempting to induce viewers to see themselves differently? Alternatively, you might treat a film and its sequel.

4. "Monster" movies, for lack of a better term, have been with us for a long time—Dracula, the Mummy, Frankenstein, Godzilla. And new "monsters," along with quasi-monstrous superheroes continue to appear—Buffy the vampire slayer, lots of vampires in all walks of life and death, Spiderman, Batman, zombies in all sorts of settings, and so forth. Images of Godzilla flattening buildings in Japanese cities and Spiderman scaling glass-walled high rises in New York are part of our collective visual imaginations. Pick some fairly current monster or supernatural superhero and write an essay in which you analyze it as a reflection of how we see ourselves or would like to see ourselves or are afraid to see ourselves at this moment in time.

5. **Application:** Select a film that has enjoyed significant popularity, and using Kennedy's essay as a model, write an essay in which you analyze the reasons for the film's popularity with a particular audience. Kennedy is particularly effective at describing key scenes in evocative ways, which bring out the affective power of striking cinematic images. As you analyze your chosen film, target its most powerful images and interpret them in ways that bring out their shaping power.

FOR FURTHER RESEARCH: SEEING

By Kelly Cannon, Reference Librarian

The readings and activities below invite you to explore further the theme of "Seeing." URLs are provided for those readings that you can access freely online. For proprietary resources, ask your librarian about print or online access.

Open Access

Advertising Collections. Duke University Libraries, n.d. 30 May 2014. http://library.duke.edu/digitalcollections/advertising/.
A wealth of advertisements, digitally archived, from 19th- and 20th-century America.

> Explore: In light of Malcolm Gladwell's essay on the success of the Dockers ad campaign, consider some of the famous brands represented in this extensive collection. Many—if not all—of the advertisements were created before your lifetime, but the fame of the brands remains, thanks in large part to the success of these advertisements. What visual elements contribute to the most successful campaigns? How do words also play a role? What else makes some ads seem to take on a life of their own, and a lasting place in our national consciousness? Consider this website in relation to Kera Bolonik's essay on the power of visual media to reinforce or undermine stereotypes. How do advertisements operate with considerable force when it comes to deeply embedded cultural stereotypes?

"Documenting America: Photographic Series." *American Memory.* Library of Congress, 1998. 30 May 2014. http://memory.loc.gov/ammem/fsowhome.html.
Includes some of the more renowned photographs and photographers from the Depression-era documentary project associated with the Farm Security Administration.

> Explore: Find out more about the Farm Security Administration. What prompted the taking of these photographs? To what extent do these images appear "staged" or "recorded" according to Joseph Elliott's and Susan Sontag's analyses of photography?

Johnston, Mike. "Evidence, Not Proof." *The Luminous Landscape.* 7 March 2004. 3 May 2014. http://www.luminous-landscape.com/columns/sm-04-03-07.shtml.
Discusses the practical and much-debated matter of how photographers enlist cooperation from their subjects.

Explore: Click on the "discussion" link embedded in the essay. What question is at the center of this discussion? Consider this essay in light of Sontag's thought that all photography is to some extent staged.

"Edward S. Curtis's The North American Indian." *American Memory.* **Northwestern University Library and Library of Congress, 2007. 30 May 2014. http:// memory.loc.gov/ammem/award98/ienhtml/curthome.html.**
A renowned collection of photographs of North American Indians taken in the early 1900s, these striking images have collectively exerted tremendous influence on pop culture's perception of American Indians.

Explore: To what extent do you think Curtis accomplished his goal to accurately document "the old time Indian, his dress, his ceremonies, his life and manners"? How so? To what extent do these images appear "staged" or "recorded" according to Joseph Elliott's and Susan Sontag's analyses of photography in the essays printed earlier in the chapter?

Kipnis, Laura. "The Eloquence of Pornography." *Frontline.* **PBS, 2002. 1 January 2014. http://www.pbs.org/wgbh/pages/frontline/shows/porn/special /eloquence.html.**
Eloquent essay proposing that pornography "insists on a sanctioned space for fantasy."

Explore: According to this essay, what does pornography enable us to see that society would prefer to keep invisible? Compare this essay with the John Berger essay on the female nude. What comprises the pornographic gaze? Considering Susan Bordo's essay, how does pornography look at gender? What does it assume about gender?

Rosen, Christine. "The Image Culture." *The New Atlantis: A Journal of Technology and Society* **10 (Fall 2005): 27–46. 19 May 2014. http://www.thenewatlantis.com /publications/the-image-culture.**
Historical survey of the technology of the image, beginning with the daguerreotype, and then chronicling the rise of photography and film, up to "the MTV effect" (the discontinuous barrage). Along the way, dispassionate history begins to give way to jeremiad.

Explore: How does Rosen's point of view resemble but also differ from that of Susan Sontag in the essay included in this chapter?

SandLotScience.com. **n.d. 30 May 2014. http://www.sandlotscience.com.**
Click on any of the links to the "Optical Illusion Tours." Contains over 100 optical illusions.

Explore: Go to the website's "reading room" to find some of the most recent scientific research on what constitutes an optical illusion.

["Search: King Kong."] *Lantern*. University of Wisconsin-Madison, 2014. 30 May 2014.

Carefully preserved film reviews from the time of *King Kong*'s making have been released in digital form to be viewed by the world at large.

> Explore: Reflecting on X. J. Kennedy's essay on *King Kong*, consider how preservation of artifacts from the time of a historical event helps to keep that event alive in our consciousness.

Proprietary

Barthes, Roland. ["Chapters 25–29."] *Camera Lucida: Reflections on Photography*. New York: Hill and Wang, 1981. 63–72.

In this challenging but stimulating piece, the author sorts through old photographs, trying to find one that captures the essence of his memory of his mother.

> Explore: Look through Barthes' entire book *Camera Lucida*. Find the image that most appeals to you. What is it specifically about the image that draws you in, what Barthes calls its Punctum?

Colbert, Charles. *Seeing What I Like & Liking What I See*. Pendaya Publications, 1991.

Contains 120 "mind-eye" photographs, mostly landscapes, taken by the author, representing a stunning visual feast.

> Explore: What patterns run through some or all of the images that make them visually interesting? How much do these images confirm Barry Lopez's claims regarding the photographer's quest for light and spatial volume?

Elkins, James. "How to Look at a Postage Stamp." *How to Use Your Eyes*. New York: Routledge, 2000. 2–11.

Looks back to old postage stamps designed by people who "knew that there is no reason to make everything easy to see." These old stamps are "tiny worlds" in themselves.

> Explore: Visit the online stamp collection *Arago: People, Postage and the Post* (http://arago.si.edu) created by the National Postal Museum. In what ways do these postage stamps support Elkins' contention that stamps are "tiny worlds"?

Frisby, John P. "Pictures in Our Heads." *Seeing: Illusion, Brain and Mind*. New York: Oxford, 1980. 8–25.

A psychologist scientifically examines what goes on inside our heads when we see.

Explore: In a sentence or two, what would you say is the author's main conclusion? (In other words, what does the author think of the "inner screen" theory?)

Hartnell, Anna. "Katrina Tourism and a Tale of Two Cities: Visualizing Race and Class in New Orleans." *American Quarterly* **61.3 (2009): 723–747.**
Discusses how the site of hurricane Katrina has become a tourist attraction. The difference between the tourist gaze and that of the residents could hardly be more striking, highlighting racial and economic differences.

Explore: How do the ethical concerns raised in this essay about seeing resonate with those discussed in the essays by Sontag and Lopez?

INDEX

Abell, Sam, 758
Abercrombie & Fitch, 793
Abortion, Supreme Court
  picks and, 620, 621
Absolutes, 279–280
Abstract diction, 291–292
Abstraction ladder, 13, 291
Abstract(s)
  compilations of, 208
  preparing, 198–200, 205
  science, 232
Abstract words, 13
Academic ASAP/Onefile,
  215, 217
Academic Search Premier,
  209, 215, 217
Academic writing
  conclusions, 240–251
  introductions, 236–240,
    243–251
  organizing strategies,
    234–236
  paragraphs, 251–259
  structure of, 231–234
  transitions, 259–261
*The Academy of American
  Poets,* 213
Ackerman, Josh, 640
Active reading, 41
Active verbs, 286–287
  thesis statements and,
    152, 154–155
Active voice, 287–289, 634
Ad Age, 372
Adam and Eve, 764–765,
  766–767
Adams, Ansel, 752
Adams, Robert, 750–751,
  752, 760
Adderall, 404
Additive transitions, 260
ADHD, 404, 408
ADHD drugs, 404
Ad hominem argument, 141
Adjective clause, 279
Adjectives, 267, 278
  concrete *vs.* evaluative,
    290–291
  defined, 327
  predicate, 268
Ad populum argument, 141
Adverb clauses, 279

Adverbs, 278
  conjunctive, 269–270,
    311, 328
  defined, 327
Advertising, 827
  aimed at men, 700
  Dockers campaigns,
    802–817
  male body and, 700,
    782–801
The Advocate, 793
"affect" *vs.* "effect," 323
African Americans. *See
  also* Race
  Bensonhurst and, 564,
    566, 568
  development of Long
    Island and, 457–
    458, 459–461
  downscaling black
    injury and, 501–502
  generational conflict
    among, 533–534
  hair care and
    hairstyles, 492,
    548–554
  interracial buddy films,
    493–504
  King Kong and, 822, 825
  male model poses, 799
  neighborhoods, 492,
    555–563
  Robert Moses and,
    457–458
After this, therefore
  because of this
  fallacy, 142–143
Agency, 113
Agenda, of source, 207
Agree/disagree, 80–81
Ailes, Roger, 682
*Alaska Department of
  Conservation v. EPA,*
  621
Alderman, Ellen, 390
Alesina, Alberto, 579
Alibi clubs, 351
Alice in Wonderland
  (Carroll), 703
Allegory of Time and Love
  (Bronzino), 771
Allen, David, 405

Altschiller, David, 812–813
Ambiguous reference, 315
American Dream, 428, 490
*American Journal of
  Psychiatry,* 404
American Muslims, 591
American Psychological
  Association. *See*
  APA (American
  Psychological
  Association) style
American Scholar, 366
American Society for
  Microbiology, 351
Among *vs.* between,
  324–325
Amtrak, 361
Analogy, 127
  false, 141–142
Analysis
  analytical frame of
    mind, 1
  of audience, 55–56
  defining, 2–3
  distinguishing
    argument from,
    4–5, 8–10
  distinguishing
    from summary,
    expressive writing,
    and argument, 4–10
  ethos and, 9–10
  five analytical moves,
    16–33
  as form of detective
    work, 36
  personal associations
    and, 35–36
  process of, 3–4
  reasons faculty want, 2
Analytical writing, 4
Analyzing Prose (Lanham),
  281, 297
Anaphora, 283
"and," 269
Andersen, Margaret, 516
Anderson, Sam, 61, 336,
  389
Annotated
  bibliographies, 208
Anomalies, 134
  locating, 26–32

Housing (continued)
  on Long Island, 461–462
  subdivisions, 426
"however," 311
Hughes, Langston, 50–51
Hujar, Peter, 789
Humanities
  evidence in, 95
  interpretation in, 137
  introductions in, 244–245
  opaque style and, 297
  paraphrasing in, 46, 188
  quoting in, 188
  thesis statements and, 151
  writing format, 230
Hume, David, 143
Hurricane Katrina, 699, 830
Hussein, Saddam, 609
Hyde, Henry, 393
Hypersegregation, 593
Hypotactic, 272
Hypothesis
  evolving thesis as, 160–161
  framing, 246–247
  working, 151, 237

"I"
  use of, 264, 297–299
  vs. "me," 334
ICANN (Internet Corporation for Assigned Names and Numbers), 211
Idea-driven documentarians, 721–723, 729
Ideas
  generating, 28–29
  sources as stimulus for, 185–186
  thesis statements and, 148–149
Identity
  anxiety over, 368–370
  Irish, 583–588
  personal branding and, 372–375, 376
Ideology, alternative vocabulary of, 608–612
Illocutionary force, 53
Illustration

in paragraph, 255
via image, 703
The Image (Boorstin), 371
Image Culture, 699, 828
Image production, 699–700. See also Photography
  recording, 699–700
  staging, 699–700
Images of women, in European art, 763–781
"implication," 21–22
Implications, 256–257
  hidden meaning vs., 125–131
  inferred from observations, 25
  paraphrasing and, 48
  passage-based freewriting and, 49
  pursuing, in conclusion, 241
IMRAD format, 158, 231, 232–233
In Bruges (film), 172–175
Incoherence, in introduction, 238
Income inequality, 622–623
"The Incredible Case of the Stack'O'Wheat Murders" (Krims), 713
"In Defense of Distraction" (Anderson), 61
Independent clause, 271, 327
Indexes, 208, 209, 228
Indian boarding schools, 590–591
Indirect object, 267
Individualism, 615–617
  individuality vs., 375
  Latin culture and, 492
  nude and, 776
Induction, 101–103
  thesis and, 157–159
Industrial landscapes, 432
Inequality, income, 622–623
"inference," 21–22
Infinitive, 330
Inflated diction, 300–301
Information
  attention and, 398
  photography and, 746–747

Information processing, gender and, 808–811
Ingraham, Laura, 694
Institutional racism, 492
Intensifiers, 290–291
Intention, as interpretive context, 122–123
Interaction Design Institute Ivrea, 351
Interaction Ritual (Goffman), 347
"interesting," 18
Internet
  addiction to, 404
  as distraction, 403–404
  exposure of self via, 368, 369, 370
  multitasking and, 398
  self-exposure and, 375–379, 376–377
Interpretation
  Anything Goes School of, 125
  avoiding extremes, 124–125
  common logical fallacies, 140–144
  context and, 119, 120–124
  Fortune Cookie School of, 125
  implications vs. hidden meanings, 125–131
  making, 131–137
  metaphors and, 126–129
  passage-based freewriting and, 49
  plausibility of, 119–120, 136–137
    across the curriculum, 137–140
  plausible vs. implausible, 120
  seems to be about X, but could also be about Y, 129–131
  of statistical data, 137–140
  what is and what isn't meant to be analyzed, 123–124
The Interpretation of Dreams (Freud), 82
Interpretive community, 121
Interpretive conclusion, 120

Rutan v. Republican Party of Illinois, 621
Ryan, Paul, 666, 668

Safety
    cell phones and, 347–348, 361
    pedestrian use of city streets and, 466–479
Sagalyn, Lynne B., 447, 450–451
Saguaro Seminar, 573
Salgado, Sebastião, 721, 722
Salinger, J. D., 561
Salins, Peter, 494, 505
Salon.com, 212
Santa Fe Independent School Dist. v. Doe, 621
Santana, Carlos, 526
Sartre, Jean-Paul, 337, 784–785, 786
Saving Private Ryan (film), 705
Scalia, Antonin, 620
Scandinavian Political Studies (journal), 577
Schafly, Phyllis, 694
Schejter, Amit, 353
Scherschel, Joe, 753
Scholarly journals, indexes of, 209
Scholes, Robert, 44–45
Schubert, Thomas, 640
Schweitzer, Albert, 721
Sciences. See Natural sciences; Social sciences
Scientific method
    induction and deduction and, 103
    thesis and, 160–161
Scientific Style and Format: The CSE Manual for Authors, Editors, and Publishers, 220
Sciutto, Mark
    on habits of mind in psychology, 14
    on introductions in sciences, 248
Scope, reducing writing assignment, 72–73
Scripting News, 383
Search engines, 213, 215, 220
Secondary sources, 181, 182

Second person, 298
Seeing
    process of, 829
    ways of, 700
Segregation, racial, 489, 593
Seinfeld (television program), 819
Selectivity hypothesis, 809
Self-deprecation, 64–68
Self-exposure, Internet and, 375–379
Self-Portrait (Neel), 780
Semicolon, 269, 270, 276, 319
    conjunctive adverbs and, 328
Send-off, 241
Sennett, Richard, 371
Sentence fragments, 272, 306, 307–309, 330
Sentence(s)
    beginning with expletives, 289–290
    climactic, 281
    complex, 271–273
    compound, 269
    coordination, 268–271
    cumulative, 282–283
    defined, 330
    ending with preposition, 325
    finding action in, 286–287
    fused (run-on), 306, 309–312, 329, 330
    logic of, 265–280
    in natural sciences, 299
    ordering for emphasis, 277–278
    in paragraphs, 254, 255–256
    periodic, 280–282
        vs. cumulative, 277
    predicates, 266–267
    reading and focusing on individual, 44–53
    in scientific papers, 248–249
    shape of, 273–275
    shifts in structure (faulty predication), 306, 314
    simple, 268
    subjects, 266–267
    subordination, 271–273
    topic, 255, 257

September 11, 2001
    terrorist attacks, 347, 699
    Portraits of Grief, 366–368
    psychological responses to, 377
    rhetorical artifacts of, 695
    as tragedy vs. melodrama, 597, 684–691
Sexism, 316–317
Seybold, Andrew, 349–350
Shahn, Ben, 737
Shakespeare, John, 536
Shakespeare, William, 26, 129, 179, 536–537, 538
Sharkey, Joe, 358
Sharpton, Al, 572
Shaughnessy, Mina, 305
Shaw, George Bernard, 529–530, 540
Shawn, William, 364
Sherman, Cindy, 702–703, 710, 715, 723
Shipman, Chris, 804
Shklovksy, Victor, 16
Shore, Nick, 373–374
Shore, Stephen, 710
A Short History of Rudeness (Caldwell), 359
Sidewalks, 458–471
Si j'avais quatre dromadaires (film), 736
Silverman, Irwin, 803
Silverstein, Richard, 807
Similarity
    despite difference, 83–84
    difference within, 82–84
Simile, 514, 634
Simon, Herbert A., 399
Simple cause/complex effect, 142
Simple sentences, 268
Simple subject, 266
Simpson, Lorna, 723
Simpson, Louise, 459
Sincerity, 370–372
Sinclair, Upton, 669–670, 671–672, 681
Sinklar-Herring, Harve, 459–460
Siskind, Aaron, 725, 752
Skid Row, 483
Skinner, B. F., 403